AutoCAD® 2022 for Interior Design and Space Planning

The Design Approach

Beverly L. Kirkpatrick

James M. Kirkpatrick

Hossein Assadipour

David Byrnes

AutoCAD 2022® for Interior Design and Space Planning

For information about buying this title in bulk quantities, or for special sales opportunities (which may include electronic versions; custom cover designs; and content particular to your business, training goals, marketing focus, or branding interests), please contact our corporate sales department at corpsales@pearsoned.com or (800) 382-3419.

For government sales inquiries, please contact governmentsales@pearsoned.com.

For questions about sales outside the U.S., please contact intlcs@pearson.com.

Visit us on the Web: informit.com

Library of Congress Control Number: 2021940292

ISBN-13: 978-0-13-678788-4
ISBN-10: 0-13-678788-6

1 2021

Editor-in-Chief: Mark Taub
Acquisitions Editor: Malobika Chakraborty
Development Editor: Chris Zahn
Managing Editor: Sandra Schroeder
Senior Production Editor: Lori Lyons
Cover Designer: Chuti Prasertsith
Copy Editor: Kitty Wilson
Full-Service Project Manager: Vaishnavi Venkatesan
Composition: codeMantra
Indexer: Cheryl Ann Lenser
Proofreader: Abigail Manheim

Features of *AutoCAD® 2022 for Interior Design and Space Planning*

This text uses the features of AutoCAD® 2022 in a variety of exercises specifically for interior design and architecture. Features include:

Chapter Objectives with a bulleted list of learning objectives at the beginning of each chapter provide users with a roadmap to the commands, concepts, and practices to be introduced.

CHAPTER OBJECTIVES

- Describe the AutoCAD user interface and begin using parts of the screen.
- Modify and

TUTORIAL 2-1

Part 1, Beginning an AutoCAD Drawing: Saving Your Work; Setting Units, Limits, Grid, and Snap; Creating Layers

Beginning an AutoCAD Drawing

When you click **New...** from the **Quick Access Toolbar** or **New** from the application menu button, or the **New** down arrow at the left side of the **Start tab**, AutoCAD allows you to select a template file from the **Template** folder or use the default template file. A template file has settings already established. These settings can include units, limits, grid, snap, and a

Because users need a lot of practice, Chapter 2, Quick-Start Tutorials, challenges the user to make 2D drawings. These tutorials are designed with special step-by-step instructions that will walk the reader through the entire development process while raising interest in mastering the content to come in the rest of the chapters.

The first appearance of each key term is bold and italic within the running text and accompanied by a brief definition in the margin. The glossary at the end of the book contains a complete list of the key terms and more detailed definitions to help students understand and use the language of the computer-aided drafting (CAD) world.

Drawing Window and Graphics

user interface: All the elements such as the AutoCAD screen that make up the interface between the user and the AutoCAD program.

The AutoCAD ***user interface*** (Figure 1-4) contains access to commands. The drawing window is wher played. The graphics cursor (or crosshairs) follows mouse when points of a drawing are entered or a c box at the center of the crosshairs is called a *pickb*

OPTIONS	
Ribbon/ Panel	View/ Interface/ Dialog Box Launcher
Menu Bar:	Tools/ Options
Type a Command:	OPTIONS
Command Alias:	OP

Other components of the user interface,

- Application Menu Button
- Quick Access Toolbar
- Share Drawing Button
- Infocenter
- Ribbon and its Tabs and Panels
- ViewCube
- Navigation Bar

Command Grids appear in the margin alongside the discussion of the command or the particular exercise in which it is demonstrated. These grids provide specific information about the ways of invoking each command, including any of the following:

- Ribbon panel
- Toolbar icon
- Pull-down menu
- Command line
- Command alias

Tip, Note, and **For More Details** boxes highlight additional helpful information for the student. Such information may contain dos and don'ts, facts, warnings, and alternative ways of proceeding, as well as cross-references to other chapters and topics.

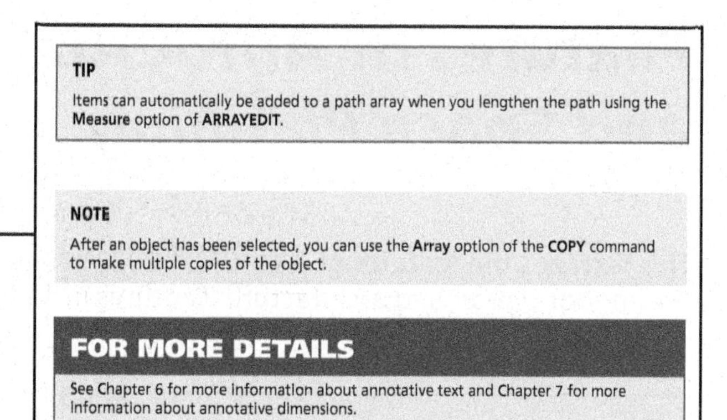

TIP

Items can automatically be added to a path array when you lengthen the path using the **Measure** option of **ARRAYEDIT**.

NOTE

After an object has been selected, you can use the **Array** option of the **COPY** command to make multiple copies of the object.

FOR MORE DETAILS

See Chapter 6 for more information about annotative text and Chapter 7 for more information about annotative dimensions.

EXERCISE 1-1
Examine the AutoCAD User and Save a Workspace

Launching AutoCAD 2022 displays the interface shown the **Start tab** and a drawing tab labeled **Drawing1**. The **Start tab** is controlled by the **STARTMODE** system vari the **Start tab** is visible and remains open as drawing file revised **Start tab** contains three areas.

On the left side area you can **Open** an existing draw drawing. The display in the center and right areas chang

New to AutoCAD® 2022 icons indicate the commands and tools that are new to this specific release of the program. This feature allows instructors and other users to quickly identify topics that are completely new, saving them a good amount of research time. It also demonstrates to students the recent improvements to the AutoCAD software, as well as the valuable updated information contained in this textbook. This book uses many of the features new to the software since the previous release of this book for AutoCAD 2015.

End-of-Chapter material can easily be located by the shading on the page edges. This material will help students evaluate and practice the knowledge they've acquired about the most important concepts explained in the chapter. This material's content includes:

- Chapter Summary
- Chapter Test Questions
  - Multiple Choice
  - Matching
  - True or False
  - List (Five different ways of executing commands in AutoCAD 2022)

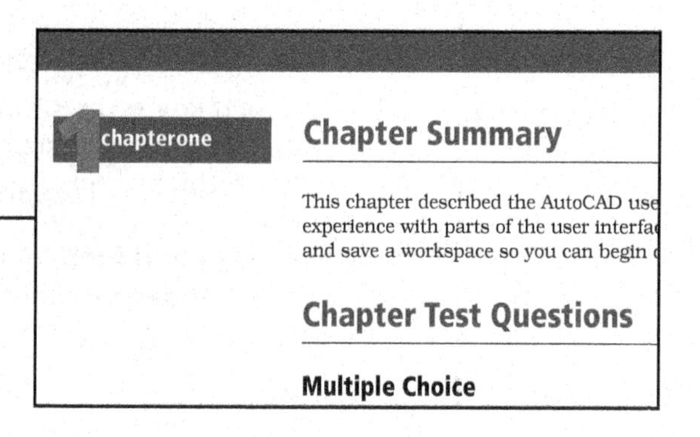

chapterone

Chapter Summary

This chapter described the AutoCAD us experience with parts of the user interfa and save a workspace so you can begin

Chapter Test Questions

Multiple Choice

chapterthree

Chapter Projects

Project 3-1: *Rectangular Including Furniture* **[BASIC]**

1. Draw the floor plan of the lecture room the dimensions shown in Figure 3-58, measure the floor plan and draw it full

Chapter Projects are additional assignments located at the end of each chapter in which students are directed to solve particular tasks on their own. The projects are labeled as basic, intermediate, and advanced according to the degree of complexity. Students will use the knowledge acquired throughout the chapter as well as in previous chapters in completing these assignments.

Preface

AutoCAD has become the industry-standard graphics program for interior design and space planning. This program is used to complete the many contract documents (CDs) that make up a design project. Many design firms have adopted AutoCAD as their standard because:

- It saves time.
- Affiliated professions have chosen it so that they can exchange files and work on the same drawing.
- Their competitors use it.
- Their clients expect it.

To be successful in design today, students must be proficient in the use of AutoCAD as it relates to interior design and space planning. The need for an AutoCAD textbook geared specifically to this field is what led us to write *AutoCAD® 2022 for Interior Design and Space Planning.*

This text, newly updated for AutoCAD® 2022, is divided into three parts:

- Part I: Preparing to Draw with AutoCAD (Chapter 1).
- Part II: Two-Dimensional AutoCAD (Chapters 2–13).
- Part III: Three-Dimensional AutoCAD (Chapters 14–15).

This new edition includes many features designed to help you master AutoCAD® 2022:

- The prompt-response format is clearly defined with numbered steps. This step-by-step approach is used in the beginning exercises of all chapters and then moves to an outline form in projects at the end of most chapters. This allows students to learn commands in a drawing situation and then practice applying them on their own.
- Lineweights have been carefully assigned to provide line contrast in all drawing exercises.
- Plotting is used in Chapter 2 to allow students to plot their first drawings.
- Chapter 7 covers updated ways to change dimension variables, as well as the recently introduced **DIM** command.
- Chapter 9 updates the process of finding and inserting blocks using the **BLOCKS** palette.
- Chapter 15 updates the sections on adding lights and rendering models.
- Exercises are geared to architects, interior designers, and space planners, allowing students to work with real-world situations.
- More than 600 illustrations (many printed to scale) support the text and reinforce the material.
- Screen shots and command grids help the user locate AutoCAD commands within the AutoCAD menus and ribbon.

- "Tip," "Note," and "For More Details" boxes give students additional support and information.
- Practice projects at the end of every chapter review the commands learned.
- Learning objectives and review questions in every chapter reinforce the learning process.
- An online Instructor's Manual is available to support the text.

Organized around architectural and interior design–related projects, *AutoCAD® 2022 for Interior Design and Space Planning* gives students an understanding of the commands and features of AutoCAD® 2022 and demonstrates how to use the program to complete interior design and space planning projects. The book is appropriate for self-paced and lecture classes and covers both two-dimensional and three-dimensional drawings.

Throughout the exercises in this book, steps numbered in color provide instructions. **Prompt** and **Response** columns in the numbered steps provide step-by-step instructions for starting and completing a command. The **Prompt** column text repeats the AutoCAD prompt that appears in the command area of the AutoCAD screen. The **Response** column text shows how you should respond to the AutoCAD prompt. Screen shots of menus and command grids show you how to locate the command you are using.

Using numerous illustrations, the text captures the essence of this powerful program and the importance it plays in the interior design, architecture, and space planning professions.

Most importantly, this text was written to help you, the reader, master the AutoCAD program, which will be a valuable tool in your professional career.

Hallmark Features

Progresses from Basic Commands to Complex Drawing Exercises

- Builds confidence and basic skills before moving on to more complex assignments.
- Ensures students have mastered the fundamental features and commands of the AutoCAD program before they apply it to more complex problems.
- Guides readers step-by-step through each new AutoCAD command.
- Encourages students to learn commands and features on their own.

Provides More Than 100 Exercises and Projects

- Gives students the opportunity to work with a variety of real-world situations, including both commercial and residential projects.

Highlights Projects Appropriate for Interior Design, Space Planning, and Architecture Students

- Projects are a tenant space, hotel room, and wheelchair-accessible commercial restroom.
- Includes project floor plans, dimension plans, elevations, furniture plans, reflected ceiling plans, and voice/data/power plans, as well as isometric drawings, a presentation sheet, and the sheet set command that combines multiple plans.

Includes More Than 600 Figures

- Helps students by allowing them to compare their work and progress with the many figures available.
- Shows many drawings to scale so students can assess and check their understanding of chapter material.

The AutoCAD DesignCenter

- The **DesignCenter** is used to import blocks, layers, and dimension styles from other drawings into existing drawings.

Covers Solid Modeling in Two Chapters

- Splits solid modeling material into two chapters: Chapter 14, Solid Modeling; and Chapter 15, Advanced Modeling.
- Uses the **3DWALK** and **Animation Motion** commands to create walk-through presentations.

New to This 2022 Edition

- **Revised Start Tab**
- **Floating drawing tabs**
- **Commands introduced in all areas of the program since the previous edition**
- **Enhanced Help (to locate tools in AutoCAD)**
- **(View) Ribbon Enhancements**

Instructor Resources

The **Online Instructor's Manual** provides answers to unit exercises and tests, solutions to end-of-chapter questions, and lecture-supporting PowerPoint® slides.

Instructor materials are available from Pearson's Instructor Resource Center. Go to **https://www.pearson.com/us/higher-education/subjectcatalog/download-instructor-resources.html** to register, or to sign in if you already have an account.

Style Conventions in *AutoCAD® 2022 for Interior Design and Space Planning*

Text Element	Example
Key Terms—Boldface and italic on first mention (first letter lowercase, as it appears in the body of the text). Brief definition in margin alongside first mention. Full definition in Glossary at back of book.	Views are created by placing ***viewport*** objects in the paper space layout.
AutoCAD commands—Bold and uppercase.	Start the **LINE** command.
Ribbon and panel names, palette names, toolbar names, menu items, and dialog box names—Bold and follow capitalization convention in AutoCAD toolbar or pull-down menu (generally first letter cap).	The **Layer Properties Manager** palette The **File** menu
Panel tools, toolbar buttons, and dialog box controls/buttons/input items—Bold and follow the name of the item or the name shown in the AutoCAD tooltip.	Choose the **Line** tool from the **Draw** panel. Choose the **Symbols and Arrows** tab in the **Modify Dimension Style** dialog box. Choose the **New Layer** button in the **Layer Properties Manager** palette. In the **Lines and Arrows** tab, set the **Arrow size**: to **.125**.
AutoCAD prompts—Dynamic input prompts are set in a different font to distinguish them from the text. Command window prompts are set to look like the text in the command window, including capitalization, brackets, and punctuation. Text following the colon of the prompts specifies user input in bold.	AutoCAD prompts you to *Specify first point: Specify center point for circle or [3P 2P Ttr (tan radius)]:* 3.5
Keyboard Input—Bold with special keys in brackets.	Type **3.5 <Enter>**

Register Your Book

Register your copy of *AutoCAD 2022 for Interior Design and Space Planning* on the InformIT site for convenient access to updates and/or corrections as they become available. To start the registration process, go to informit.com/register and log in or create an account. Enter the product ISBN (9780136787884) and click Submit. Look on the Registered Products tab for an Access Bonus Content link next to this product, and follow that link to access any available bonus materials. If you would like to be notified of exclusive offers on new editions and updates, please check the box to receive email from us.

Contents at a Glance

Preface v

PART I Preparing to Draw with AutoCAD

Chapter 1 Introducing the AutoCAD User Interface 1

PART II Two-Dimensional AutoCAD

Chapter 2 Quick-Start Tutorials: Basic Settings and Commands 29

Chapter 3 Drawing with AutoCAD: Conference and Lecture Rooms 103

Chapter 4 Adding Text and Tables to the Drawing 183

Chapter 5 Advanced Plotting: Using Plot Styles, Paper Space, Multiple Viewports, and PDF Files 223

Chapter 6 Drawing the Floor Plan: Walls, Doors, and Windows 255

Chapter 7 Dimensioning and Area Calculations 297

Chapter 8 Drawing Elevations, Sections, and Details 337

Chapter 9 Drawing the Furniture Installation Plan, Adding Specifications, and Extracting Data 401

Chapter 10 DesignCenter, Dynamic Blocks, and External References 435

Chapter 11 Drawing the Reflected Ceiling Plan and Voice/Data/Power Plan 471

Chapter 12 Presentations with Layouts and Making a Sheet Set 485

Chapter 13 Isometric Drawing and Gradient Hatch Rendering 509

PART III Three-Dimensional AutoCAD

Chapter 14 Solid Modeling 547

Chapter 15 Advanced Modeling 593

PART IV Appendixes

A Keyboard Shortcuts 633

B Shortcut and Temporary Override Keys 641

Glossary 643

Index 647

Contents

Part I Preparing to Draw with AutoCAD

Chapter 1 Introducing the AutoCAD User Interface 1

Chapter Objectives 1
Introduction 1
Exercise 1-1 Examine the AutoCAD User Interface and Save a Workspace 2
Drawing Window and Graphics Cursor 4
Application Menu Button 7
Inputting or Selecting a Command 8
Ribbon 8
- Expanded Panels 9
- Dialog Boxes and Palettes 9
- Tooltips 10
- Flyouts 10

Command Line Window (<Ctrl>+9) 11
Quick Access Toolbar 11
Customizing the Quick Access Toolbar Down Arrow and Showing the Menu Bar 12
Using AutoCAD Toolbars 13
User Coordinate System Icon 14
- Advantage of Using the UCS 14

Viewport Label Menus 14
ViewCube 16
Navigation Bar 17
Infocenter 18
Status Bar 18
- Drawing Coordinates Values (<Ctrl>+I) 18
- Model or Paper Space 21
- Quick View Tools 21
- Annotation Scaling Tools 21
- Workspace Switching 22
- Lock/Unlock Toolbar and Window Positions 22
- On/Off Hardware Acceleration 22
- Clean Screen (<Ctrl>+0 [Zero]) 22

Modifying and Saving a Workspace 22
Getting Help in AutoCAD 2022 24
Closing AutoCAD 25
- Chapter Summary 26
- Chapter Test Questions 26

Part II Two-Dimensional AutoCAD

Chapter 2 Quick-Start Tutorials: Basic Settings and Commands 29

Chapter Objectives 29
Introduction 29
Following the Tutorials in This Book 30
Tutorial 2-1 Part 1, Beginning an AutoCAD Drawing: Saving Your Work; Setting Units, Limits, Grid, and Snap; Creating Layers 31
Beginning an AutoCAD Drawing 31
Saving the Drawing 32
- Save 32
- Save As 32
- DWT 34
- DWS 34
- DXF 34
- Drawing Name and File Name Extension 35

Units 36
Controlling Your Drawing 36
- Drawing Scale 37
- Drawing Limits and the Cartesian Coordinate System 37

Grid 38
- GRIDDISPLAY 38

Snap 40
Zoom 41
Drafting Settings Dialog Box 41
Layers 42
- Layer Lists 44

Linetypes 46
Lineweights 46
- Lineweight Settings Dialog Box 46
- Lineweight Display 48

Setting the Annotation Scale 50
Saving the Drawing 50
Using the Mouse and Right-Click Customization 51
Tutorial 2-1 Part 2, Drawing Lines, Circles, Arcs, Ellipses, and Donuts 52
Ortho 52
Drawing Lines Using the Grid Marks and Snap Increments 53
Erase and Undo 54

Drawing Lines Using Absolute Coordinates **56**
Drawing Lines Using Relative Coordinates **57**
Drawing Lines Using Polar Coordinates **58**
Drawing Lines Using Direct Distance Entry **59**
DYNMODE 59
Circle **60**
Center, Radius 61
Center, Diameter 62
2 Points 62
3 Points 63
TTR 63
LTSCALE **63**
ZOOM **64**
Zoom-Window 64
Zoom-All 65
Zoom-Previous 65
Zoom-Extents 66
Zoom-Object 66
Zoom-Realtime 66
PAN REALTIME **66**
Transparent Commands **66**
REDRAW **67**
REGEN **67**
HIGHLIGHT **67**
Move and Editing Commands Selection Set **67**
Options for Selecting Objects to Modify 70
Window (W) and Crossing Window (C) 71
All (ALL) 71
Fence (F) 71
Remove (R) and Add (A) 71
Last (L) and Previous (P) 71
Undo (U) 72
Grips **72**
UNDO and REDO **73**
ARC **74**
3-Point 74
Start, Center, End 76
Start, Center, Angle 76
Start, Center, Length 76
Start, End, Angle 77
Start, End, Direction 77
Start, End, Radius 77
Continue 77
ELLIPSE **77**
Axis, End 77
Center 79
DONUT **79**
SCALE **80**
Reference 80
Adding Text **82**
Command History **82**
Tutorial 2-2 Plot Responses for CH2-TUTORIAL1, Using the Model Tab **83**
Plot - Name **84**
Page Setup **84**
Printer/Plotter **84**
Plot to File **85**
Browse for Plot File... **85**
Plot Style Table (Pen Assignments) **85**
Paper Size **86**
Plot Area **87**
Plot Scale **87**
Annotative Property and Annotation Scale **88**
Plot Offset (Origin Set to Printable Area) **89**
Shaded Viewport Options **89**
Plot Options **89**
Drawing Orientation **90**
Preview... **90**
Chapter Summary 92
Chapter Test Questions 92
Chapter Projects 95

Chapter 3 Drawing with AutoCAD: Conference and Lecture Rooms **103**
Chapter Objectives **103**
Exercise 3-1 Drawing a Rectangular Conference Room, Including Furniture **103**
Making a Drawing Template **105**
Polyline **107**
Undo 108
OFFSET **108**
Through 109
Erase 109
Layer 109
EXPLODE **109**
ID Point **109**
TRIM **111**
Rectangle **111**
CHAMFER **114**
Polyline 114
Undo 114
Angle 115
Trim 115
mEthod 115

Multiple 115
FILLET **116**
COPY and Osnap-Midpoint **117**
ROTATE **118**
Reference 119
POINT **119**
DIVIDE **120**
MEASURE **121**
OSNAP **122**
Activating Osnap 122
Copy, Osnap-Midpoint, Osnap-Node 123
MIRROR **124**
Osnap Modes That Snap to Specific Drawing Features **127**
Exercise 3-2 Drawing a Rectangular Lecture Room, Including Furniture **130**
Running Osnap Modes **129**
Osnap Settings: Marker, Aperture, Magnet, Tooltip **130**
Making Solid Walls Using Polyline and Solid Hatch **132**
From **133**
BREAK **133**
First 134
@ 134
Polyline Edit **134**
HATCH **136**
ARRAY **138**
Rectangular 140
Path 141
ARRAYEDIT **141**
Distance **141**
Exercise 3-3 Drawing a Curved Conference Room, Including Furniture **144**
Polyline **145**
Width 146
Half Width 146
Length 147
Close 147
POLYGON **148**
Edge 149
Grips—Add Vertex **149**
Grips—Convert to Arc **151**
ARRAY **152**
Polar 152
Exercise 3-4 Drawing a Conference Room Using Polar Tracking **155**
Polar Tracking **157**
Polyline Edit **159**
Specifying Points with Tracking **160**
Drawing the Chairs around the Conference Table **162**
Completing the Conference Room **164**
Using Command Preview **165**
Choosing Selection Options **166**
Chapter Summary 167
Chapter Test Questions 167
Chapter Projects 170

Chapter 4 **Adding Text and Tables to the Drawing** **183**
Chapter Objectives **183**
Exercise 4-1 Placing Text on Drawings **183**
Making Settings for Text Style **185**
Style Name 185
Font Name 185
Making a New Text Style **186**
Using the Single Line Text Command to Draw Text **189**
Setting the Justify Option **191**
Using Standard Codes to Draw Special Characters **192**
Using the Multiline Text Command to Draw Text Paragraphs in Columns **195**
Changing Text Properties **198**
Checking the Spelling **202**
Exercise 4-2 Using the TABLE Command to Create a Door Schedule **203**
Exercise 4-3 Using the TABLE Command to Create a Window Schedule **214**
Chapter Summary 215
Chapter Test Questions 215
Chapter Projects 218

Chapter 5 **Advanced Plotting: Using Plot Styles, Paper Space, Multiple Viewports, and PDF Files** **223**
Chapter Objectives **223**
Understanding Layer Names, Colors, and Lineweights **223**
Choosing a Plot Style **224**
Named Plot Style (STB) 225
Color-Dependent Plot Style (CTB) 226
Exercise 5-1 Make a Color-Dependent Plot Style to Change Colors to Plot Black **226**
Exercise 5-2 Plot a Layout with One Viewport **228**
Model, Layout1, and Layout2 Tabs **229**
Page Setup Manager **229**

Center and Scale the Plan 230
Complete the Layout 232
Exercise 5-3 Plot a Layout with Two Viewports 233
Insert an Entire Drawing into a Current Drawing 233
Page Setup Manager 236
Copy a Viewport 237
Center and Scale the Plans 237
Complete the Layout 239
Exercise 5-4 Plot a Layout with Four Viewports 241
Viewports (VPORTS) 242
Use MVIEW to Restore the Viewport VP4 into Layout1 244
Page Setup Manager 245
Center and Scale the Plans 246
Complete the Layout 246
Exercise 5-5 Make PDF Files That Can Be Attached to E-mails and Opened without the AutoCAD Program 247
Chapter Summary 250
Chapter Test Questions 250
Chapter Projects 253

Chapter 6 Drawing the Floor Plan: Walls, Doors, and Windows 255

Chapter Objectives 255
The Tenant Space Project 255
Exercise 6-1 Tenant Space Floor Plan 256
RECTANGLE 257
HATCH 258
ARRAY 258
Multiline Style 260
Multiline Command 262
Edit Multiline Command 268
EXTEND 269
PROPERTIES 269
LIST 270
COLOR 270
Linetype 272
Lineweight 272
Make Object's Layer Current 272
Match Properties 272
Block 273
Wblock 276
Insert 278
Insertion Point 281
X Scale Factor, Y Scale Factor 281
Using Annotative Text 282
Inserting Entire Drawings as Blocks 284
Advantages of Using Blocks 284
Exercise 6-2 Hotel Room 1 Floor Plan 285
AutoCAD DesignCenter 287
Chapter Summary 291
Chapter Test Questions 291
Chapter Projects 294

Chapter 7 Dimensioning and Area Calculations 297

Chapter Objectives 297
Eight Basic Types of Dimensions 297
Using Dimension Variables 298
Exercise 7-1 Dimensioning the Tenant Space Floor Plan Using Linear Dimensions 301
Setting the Dimension Variables Using the Command Prompt 303
Setting the Dimension Variables Using the Dimension Style Manager Dialog Box 304
Using the Fit Tab to Scale for Dimension Features 309
Annotative 309
Scale Dimensions to Layout 310
Use Overall Scale of: (DIMSCALE) 310
Linear and Continue Dimensioning 311
Aligned Dimensioning 315
Baseline Dimensioning 315
Adding a Dimension Break 318
Using Adjust Space 318
Exercise 7-2 Revisions and Modifying Dimensions 319
Setting the DIMASSOC Dimension Variable 319
Understanding Associative Dimension Commands 321
Oblique 321
Align Text (Home-Angle-Left-Center-Right) 322
Override 322
Update 322
Defpoints Layer 322
Using the PROPERTIES Palette 323
Accessing Match Properties 323
Using Grips 323

Drawing a Revision Cloud 324
Exercise 7-3 Tenant Space Total Square Footage 326
Defining the Area for Square Footage 326
Using the Cal Calculator 329
Chapter Summary 331
Chapter Test Questions 331
Chapter Projects 334

Chapter 8 Drawing Elevations, Sections, and Details 337
Chapter Objectives 337
Introduction 337
Exercise 8-1 Tenant Space: Elevation of Conference Room Cabinets 337
UCS 339
UCS Icon 340
Draw the Upper Cabinets 341
Mirror 342
Draw the Lower Cabinets 344
Stretch 345
Complete the Drawing 354
Circles to Be Used with Multileaders 357
Exercise 8-2 The Multileader Command 357
Multileader Standard Style 357
Multileader 360
Multileader Align 362
Change Multileader Style 362
Multileader Collect 366
Multileader Add 367
Exercise 8-3 Tenant Space: Section of Conference Room Cabinets with Hatching 368
Prepare to Use the Hatch Command with the Add: Select Objects Boundary Option 371
Use the Hatch Command with the Add: Select Objects Boundary Option 372
Use the Hatch Command with the Add: Pick Points Boundary Option 373
Hatch; Hatch and Gradient Dialog Box; Hatch Tab 376
Type and Pattern 376
Angle and Scale 377
Hatch Origin 378
Boundaries 378
Options 378
More Options 379
Islands 380
Boundary Retention 380
Boundary Set 380
Gap Tolerance 380
Inherit Options 380
Edit Hatch 381
Exercise 8-4 Detail of Door Jamb with Hatching 385
Exercise 8-5 Use Point Filters and Object Snap Tracking to Make an Orthographic Drawing of a Conference Table 386
Point Filters 388
Object Snap Tracking 389
Chapter Summary 393
Chapter Test Questions 393
Chapter Projects 396

Chapter 9 Drawing the Furniture Installation Plan, Adding Specifications, and Extracting Data 401
Chapter Objectives 401
Introduction 401
Exercise 9-1 Tenant Space Furniture Installation Plan with Furniture Specifications 402
Draw the Furniture Symbols 403
Define Attributes… (ATTDEF) 403
Constant Attribute 408
Variable Attribute 410
Verify Attribute 412
Edit Text (TEXTEDIT) 413
QP (Quick Properties) 414
Properties Palette 414
WBLOCK the Furniture with Attributes Symbol 414
Insert the Furniture Symbols with Attributes into the Drawing 416
Complete the Tenant Space Furniture Installation Plan 418
Edit Attribute, Single… 418
Edit Attribute, Global 420
Attribute Display (ATTDISP) 422
Redefining an Inserted Block with Attributes Using the BLOCK Command 422
Block Attribute Manager (BATTMAN) 423
Synchronize Attributes (ATTSYNC) 423
Exercise 9-2 Extracting Attributes from the Tenant Space Furniture Installation Plan 424
Data Extraction… 425
Chapter Summary 430
Chapter Test Questions 430
Chapter Projects 432

Chapter 10 DesignCenter, Dynamic Blocks, and External References 435
Chapter Objectives 435
Introduction 435
Exercise 10-1 Reception Area Furniture Installation Plan Using the DesignCenter 435
The DesignCenter 436
DesignCenter Tabs 436
DesignCenter Buttons 437
Exercise 10-2 Training Room Furniture Installation Plan Using DesignCenter and Dynamic Blocks 440
Use Block Editor to Make Dynamic Blocks 445
Exercise 10-3 Attach an External Reference to an Office Plan 456
XATTACH (Attach External Reference) 456
External Reference (XREF) 457
XBIND 457
Features of External References 457
Chapter Summary 463
Chapter Test Questions 463
Chapter Projects 465

Chapter 11 Drawing the Reflected Ceiling Plan and Voice/Data/Power Plan 471
Chapter Objectives 471
Introduction 471
Exercise 11-1 Part 1, Tenant Space Lighting Legend and Reflected Ceiling Plan 471
Tenant Space Lighting Legend Symbols 473
Tenant Space Reflected Ceiling Plan 473
Exercise 11-1 Part 2, Tenant Space Voice/Data/Power Legend and Plan 474
Tenant Space Voice/Data/Power Legend Symbols 474
Tenant Space Voice/Data/Power Plan 476
Chapter Summary 478
Chapter Test Questions 478
Chapter Projects 480

Chapter 12 Creating Presentations with Layouts and Making a Sheet Set 485
Chapter Objectives 485
Exercise 12-1 Make a Printed Presentation of the Tenant Space Project by Combining Multiple Plans on One Sheet of Paper 485
Use Create Layout Wizard to Set Up Four Viewports on a Single Sheet 486
Complete the Title Block 487
Use Layer Properties Manager to Freeze Viewport Layers 490
Scale and Center the Plans 492
Using MVSETUP to Align the Plans 492
Complete the Presentation 494
Exercise 12-2 Making a Four-Sheet Presentation of the Tenant Space Project Using a Sheet Set 495
Make New Layout Tabs and Rename the New Layout Tabs 496
Prepare the Layout Tabs for Plotting Drawings 496
Use MVSETUP to Insert a Title Block 498
Quick View Tools 500
New Sheet Set and Sheet Set Manager 501
Chapter Summary 504
Chapter Test Questions 504
Chapter Project 507

Chapter 13 Isometric Drawing and Gradient Hatch Rendering 509
Chapter Objectives 509
Axonometric Drawing 509
Isometric Drawing 509
Exercise 13-1 Fundamentals of Isometric Drawing 510
Drafting Settings Dialog Box 512
Shape 1: Drawing the Isometric Rectangle 512
Shape 2: Drawing Isometric Ellipses 513
Shape 3: Drawing a Chair with Ellipses That Show the Thickness of a Material 515
Shape 4: Drawing a Shape That Has a Series of Isometric Ellipses Located on the Same Centerline 518
Shape 5: Isometric Detail with Rounded Corners 520
Shape 6: A TV Shape with an Angled Back 521
Shape 7: Isometric Detail: A Hexagonal-Shaped Vase 524
Exercise 13-2 Tenant Space Reception Desk in Isometric 525
Dimensioning in Isometric 532
Gradient Hatch 532
Exercise 13-3 Using Gradient Patterns to Render the Shapes of Exercise 13-1 533
Chapter Summary 540
Chapter Test Questions 540
Chapter Projects 543

Part III Three-Dimensional AutoCAD

Chapter 14 Solid Modeling 547

Chapter Objectives 547

Introduction 547

Creating Primitive Shapes with Solid Commands 548

Creating Composite Solids with Solid Commands 548

Editing Solids with Solid Commands 548

Controlling UCS in Three Dimensions 549

Dynamic UCS 549

Viewing Solids 549

3D Views Menu Options 549

SteeringWheels 551

ViewCube 552

Editing Solids with Other Commands 552

Controlling Solids Display 552

Exercise 14-1 Part 1, Drawing Primitive Solids 553

Box 555

Sphere 555

Wedge 556

Cone 556

Cylinder 557

Torus 557

Exercise 14-1 Part 2, Using Extrude to Draw Extruded Solids 558

Drawing an Extruded Circle 558

Drawing an Extruded Polygon 558

Drawing an Extruded Rectangle 559

Drawing an Extruded Structural Angle 560

Drawing an Extruded Shape 561

Exercise 14-1 Part 3, Using REVOLVE to Draw Revolved Solids; Using 3DROTATE to Rotate Solids about the X-, Y-, and Z-Axes 562

Drawing Revolved Shape 1 562

Drawing a Revolved Rectangle 564

Drawing a Revolved Paper Clip Holder 565

Using 3DROTATE 565

Exercise 14-1 Part 4, Using CHAMFER and FILLET to Form Chamfers and Fillets on Solid Edges 566

Chamfering and Filleting the Top Four Edges of Two Separate Boxes 566

Chamfering and Filleting the Top Edge of Two Separate Cylinders 567

Exercise 14-1 Part 5, Using UNION to Join Two Solids; Using SUBTRACT to Subtract Solids from Other Solids 568

Drawing Solid Shape 1 568

Drawing Solid Shape 2 569

Joining with Union 570

Using Subtract 570

Performing a Hide 571

Exercise 14-1 Part 6, Using Sweep, Helix, Subtract, Loft, Planar Surface, Thicken, and Polysolid to Draw Solid Shapes 571

Sweeping an Object 571

Using Loft 574

Creating a Bowl-Shaped Object 575

Using Planar Surface 575

Using POLYSOLID 576

Exercise 14-1 Part 7, Using Intersection to Form a Solid Model from the Common Volume of Two Intersecting Solids 577

Drawing Two Extruded Shapes at Right Angles to Each Other 578

Using Intersect 579

Wblocking the Intersected Model 580

Completing Exercise 14-1 581

Chapter Summary 583

Chapter Test Questions 583

Chapter Projects 586

Chapter 15 Advanced Modeling 593

Chapter Objectives 593

Introduction 593

Exercise 15-1 Creating a Solid Model of Chair 2 594

Exercise 15-2 Creating a Solid Model of a Patio 597

RENDER 608

Render Quality 608

Destinations 608

Lights 608

Materials 609

Other Commands Available to Render, Animate, Attach Scanned Files, and Shade 3D Models 609

Exercise 15-3 Use Render Commands to Make a Photo-Realistic Rendering of the Solid Model in Exercise 15-2 610
Exercise 15-4 Create a Walk-Through AVI File for the Rendered 3D Patio 621
Chapter Summary 627
Chapter Test Questions 627
Chapter Projects 630

Part IV Appendixes

Appendix A
Keyboard Shortcuts 633

Appendix B
Shortcut and Temporary Override Keys 641

Glossary 643

Index 647

chapter one

Introducing the AutoCAD User Interface

CHAPTER OBJECTIVES

- Describe the AutoCAD user interface and begin using parts of the screen.
- Modify and save a workspace.

Introduction

Before you start using the exercises in this book, you need to understand their structure and purpose. Throughout the exercises in this book:

- Numbered steps provide instructions.
- **Prompt** and **Response** columns within the numbered steps provide step-by-step instructions for starting and completing a command.
- The **Prompt** column text repeats the AutoCAD prompt that appears in the command line area of the AutoCAD screen.
- The **Response** column text shows your response to the AutoCAD prompt.
- Command grids in the margins and menu screens show you how to locate the command you are using.

EXERCISE 1-1
Examine the AutoCAD User Interface and Save a Workspace

Launching AutoCAD 2022 displays the interface shown in Figure 1-1, with the **Start tab** and a drawing tab labeled **Drawing1**. The presence of the **Start tab** is controlled by the **STARTMODE** system variable. By default, the **Start tab** is visible and remains open as drawing files are opened. The revised **Start tab** contains three areas.

On the left side area you can **Open** an existing drawing or create a **New** drawing. The display in the center and right areas changes depending on your choice of **Recent**, **Autodesk Docs**, or **Learning**. Below those three options are six links to different options and applications:

- **What's new:** Displays links to new features in AutoCAD 2022 in a new browser window
- **Online help:** Opens AutoCAD 2022 Help in a browser window
- **Community forum:** Opens the main page for all AutoCAD forums of the Autodesk Knowledge Network in a browser window
- **Customer support:** Opens the Support & Learning page of the Autodesk Knowledge Network in a browser window
- **AutoCAD mobile app:** The AutoCAD mobile app is a paid subscription available from Google Play and Apple's App Store
- **AutoCAD web app:** If you have an Autodesk account, you can run all tools and commands in a web browser.

By default, **Recent** in the left side of the **Start tab** is selected. The center area of the tab displays a list of recently open drawings, and the right side shows Announcements from Autodesk. Clicking a filename or icon in the center area opens the drawing on its own file tab.

The area on the right is visible only when the **Recent** option on the left is selected. In it, you see **Announcements** and "Have you tried..." items.

Autodesk Docs is a file management system that requires a subscription to AutoCAD. It links to a system of virtual drives connected through the cloud. Autodesk Docs is primarily intended as a way for teams remote from one another to connect remotely. This option is not covered in this book.

Clicking **Learning** on the left side of the **Start tab** displays links to specific tips to learning and using AutoCAD, to a series of videos showing program operation, and to a series of free online learning resources (see Figure 1-2).

Clicking **New** at the left side of the **Start tab** prompts you to select from a series of drawing template files to begin your new drawing. Figure 1-3 shows the list of available drawing templates. The last template used becomes the default template.

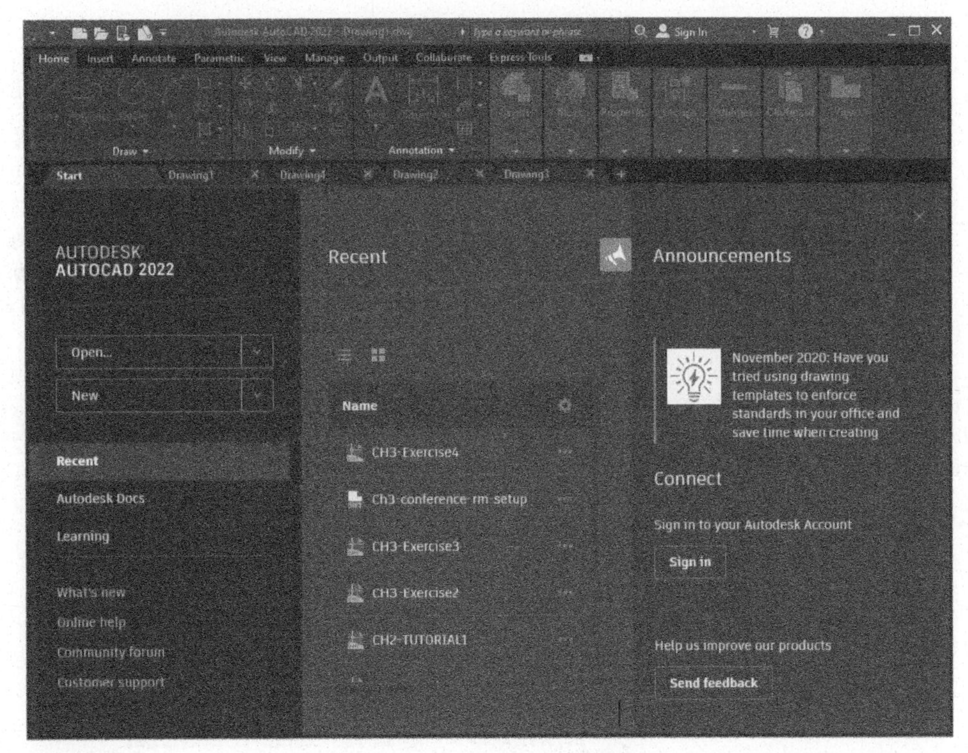

Figure 1-1
The **Start tab** of AutoCAD 2022 showing recently opened files in the center area

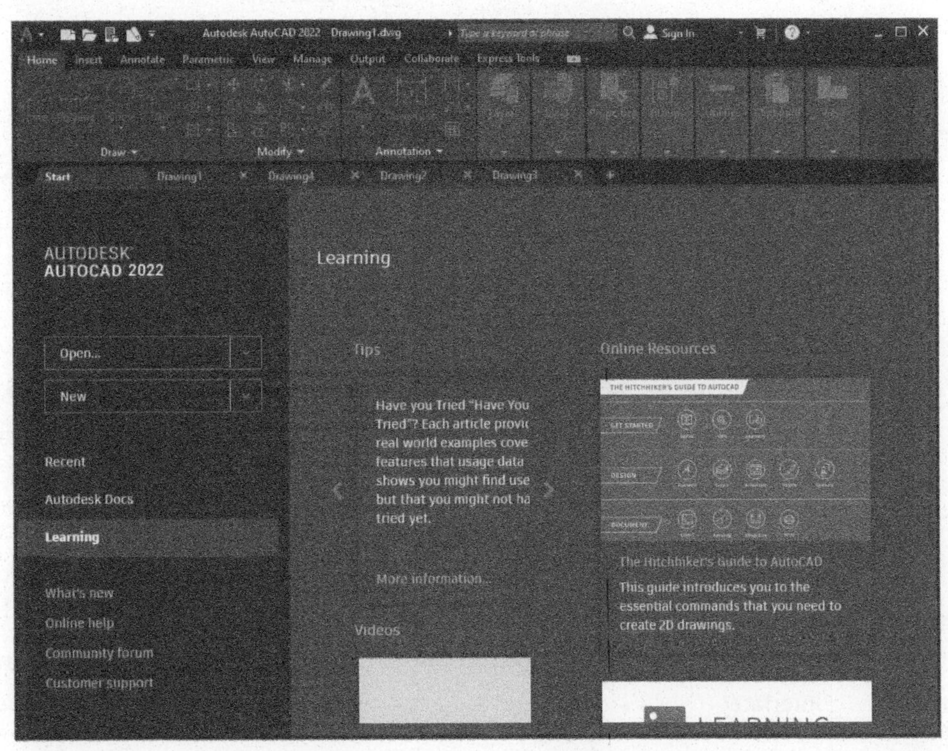

Figure 1-2
Click **Learning** on the **Start tab** to display aids to learning AutoCAD

The real advantage is that each drawing that you open, whether from a tab or by using the **Open** command, has its own tab. Now switching among drawings is easy to do.

AutoCAD 2022 introduces **Floating Drawing tabs**. You can now drag a tab to an area outside AutoCAD's application window and view two drawings at the same time, without having to switch tabs and see them one at a time. The command line window and all other interface features are active in the floated window. To return a **Floating Drawing tab** to the application window, simply drag it next to another tab in the main window.

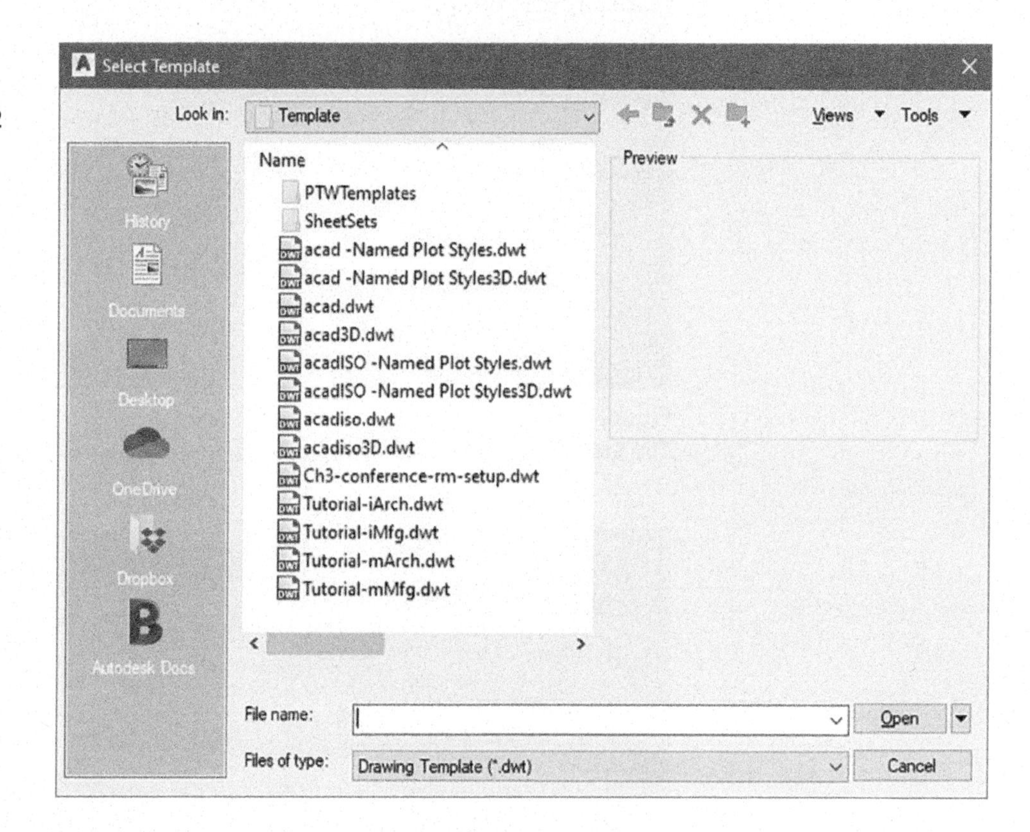

Figure 1-3
List of available drawing templates in AutoCAD 2022

Drawing Window and Graphics Cursor

user interface: All the elements such as the AutoCAD screen that make up the interface between the user and the AutoCAD program.

The AutoCAD ***user interface*** (Figure 1-4) contains the drawing window and access to commands. The drawing window is where your drawing is displayed. The graphics cursor (or crosshairs) follows the movement of a mouse when points of a drawing are entered or a command is selected. The box at the center of the crosshairs is called a *pickbox*.

Other components of the user interface, as shown in Figure 1-4, are

- Application Menu Button
- Quick Access Toolbar
- Share Drawing Button
- Infocenter
- Ribbon and its Tabs and Panels
- ViewCube
- Navigation Bar

OPTIONS	
Ribbon/ Panel	View/ Interface/ Dialog Box Launcher
Menu Bar:	Tools/ Options
Type a Command:	OPTIONS
Command Alias:	OP

- User Coordinate System Icon
- Status Bar
- Command Line

The size of the graphics cursor and pickbox can be changed to accommodate individual preferences. The colors of the elements in the drawing window also can be changed.

Information regarding commands is attached to the cursor. This can be turned on or off using the **DYNMODE** toggle in the status bar, as described later in this chapter.

Step 1. Locate the **Options** dialog box, where you can change the size of the graphics cursor, the colors of the elements in the drawing window, and the pickbox, as described next.

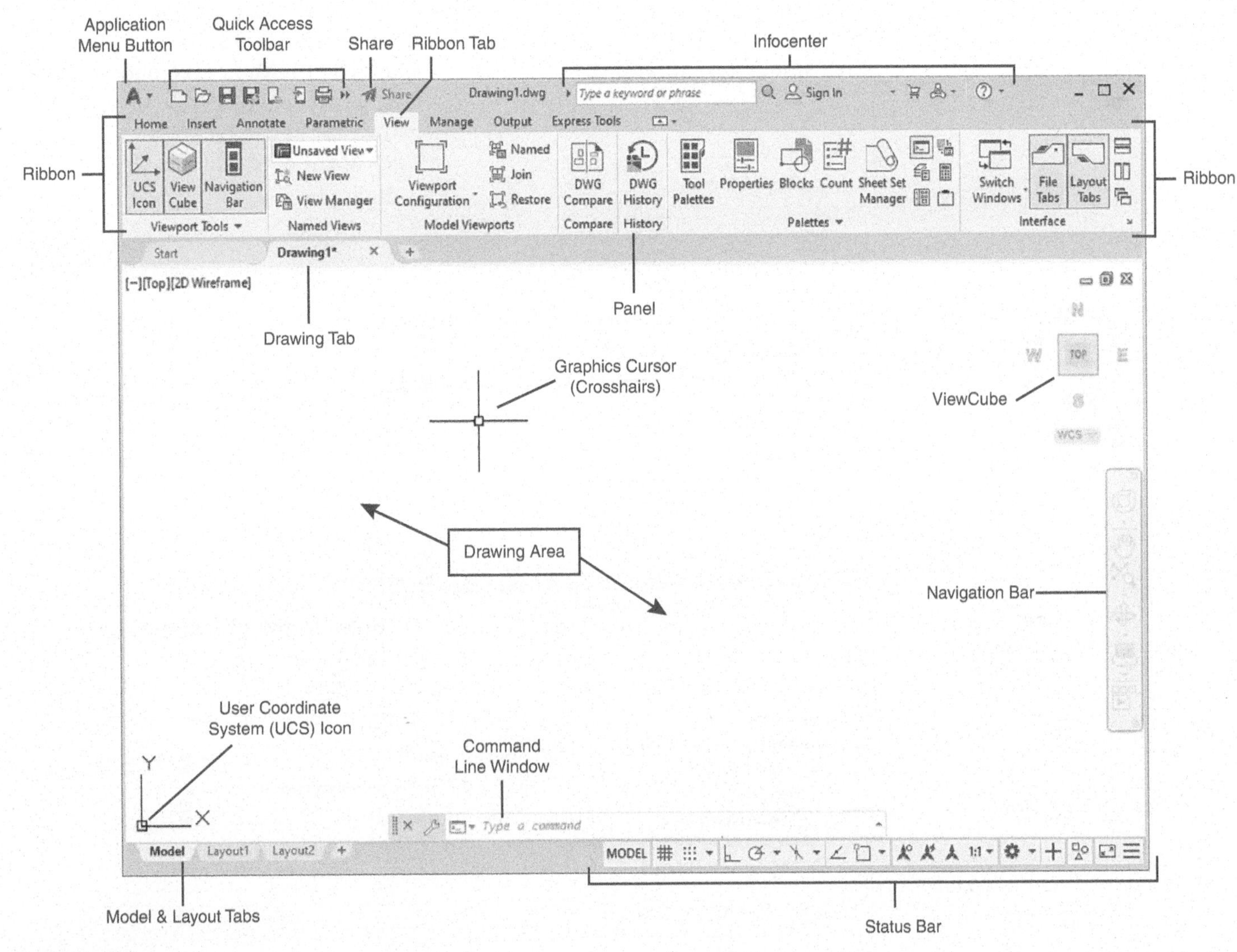

Figure 1-4
The AutoCAD user interface

Prompt	**Response**
Type a command:	Type **OP <Enter>** (in this book, **<Enter>** means to press the **<Enter>** key or press the right mouse button to enter a command)
The **Options** dialog box appears	Click the **Display** tab
The **Display** tab appears (Figure 1-5):	Click the **Crosshair size** slider in the lower right to decrease or increase the size of the crosshairs
	Click the **Colors...** button on the left
The **Drawing Window Colors** dialog box (Figure 1-6) appears:	This is where you can change colors of the elements in the drawing window
	Click **Cancel** to exit the **Drawing Window Colors** dialog box
	Click the **Selection** tab
The **Selection** tab appears:	Click the **Pickbox size** slider in the upper left to decrease or increase the size of the pickbox
	Click **Cancel** to exit the **Options** dialog box

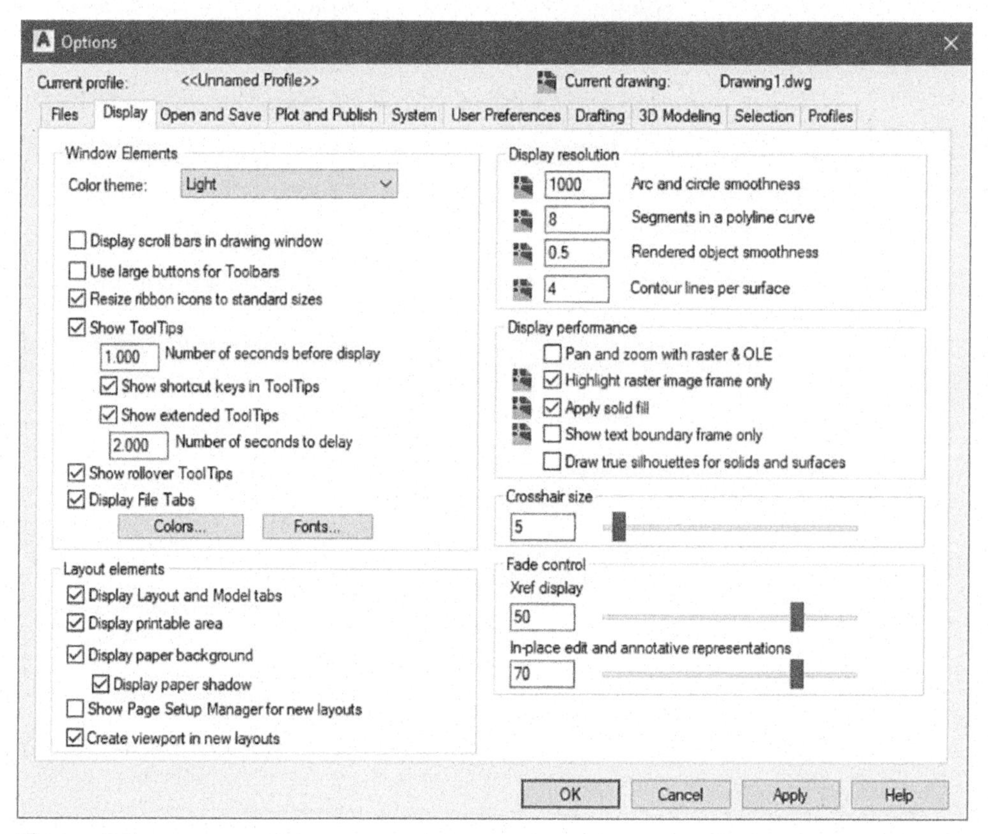

Figure 1-5
Options dialog box—**Display** tab

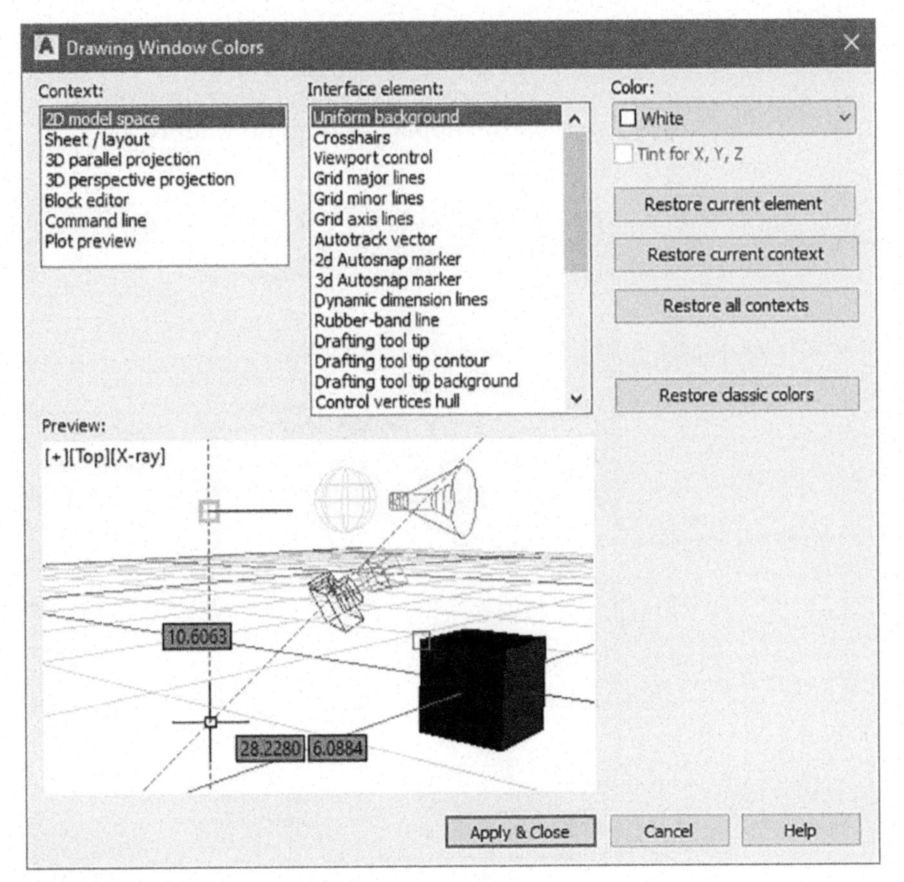

Figure 1-6
Drawing Window Colors dialog box

Application Menu Button

When you click (quickly press and release the left mouse button) on the **Application** menu button, the application menu opens. The application menu commands (Figure 1-7) can be used to

- Create a new drawing
- Open an existing drawing
- Save a drawing
- Save a drawing as another format
- Import a PDF, Microstation DGN drawing, or numerous other file formats
- Export your drawing to a different format
- Publish or share a drawing
- Print or plot a drawing
- Access tools to maintain your drawing
- Close a drawing

At the top of the application menu, you can enter key words in the text box to search for additional menu items.

Step 2. Click the application menu button with your left mouse button to open it. Hold your cursor over each command to see the brief descriptions of the command options. Press the **<Esc>** key to exit the application menu (Figure 1-7).

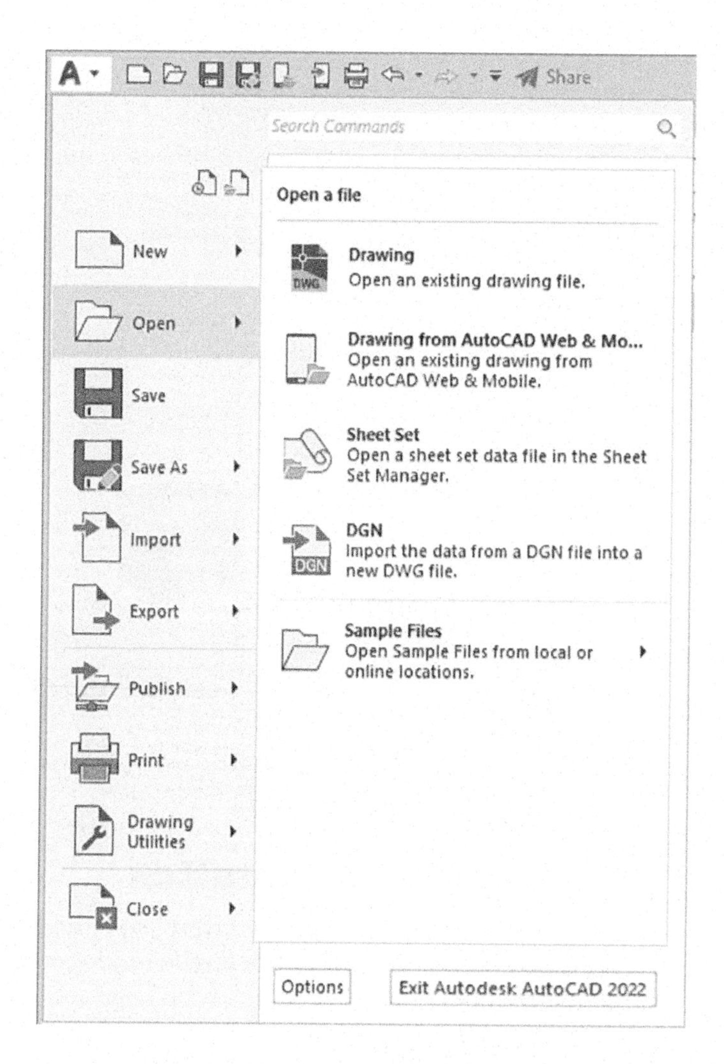

Figure 1-7
Application menu

Inputting or Selecting a Command

AutoCAD provides four major ways to input or select a command:

1. Select a command icon from the ***ribbon***.
2. Type a full command name or command alias (for example, **L** for **line**) at the ***command line window***.
3. Use the **Quick Access** toolbar customization button to show the menu bar. You can then select an icon/command from the ***menu bar***.
4. Use the **Tools** menu on the menu bar to access the AutoCAD toolbars. You can then select a command icon from a ***toolbar***.

ribbon: The user interface below the **Quick Access** toolbar that comprises tabs and panels with flyouts used to access the commands for both 2D drawing and annotation and 3D modeling, viewing, and rendering.

command line window: The text area above the status bar used for keyboard input and prompts, and where AutoCAD displays messages.

menu bar: The bar containing menus displayed using the **Quick Access** toolbar customization button; contains commonly used commands.

toolbar: A graphical interface containing icons that represent commands.

Ribbon

The ribbon displays the commands used to make a drawing. If you right-click (quickly press and release the right mouse button) on any menu tab, you will get a right-click menu (Figure 1-8) that has commands to hide or show tabs, panels, and panel titles. This right-click menu also has commands to close the ribbon or undock it. If you close the ribbon, type **RIBBON <Enter>** at the command prompt to reopen it.

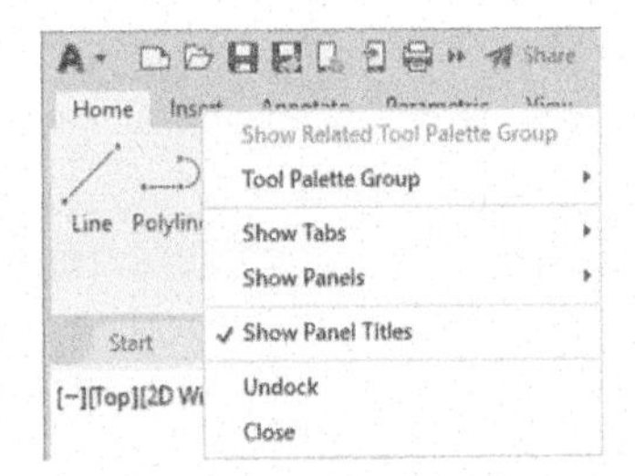

Figure 1-8
Display the right-click menu by right-clicking on a ribbon tab

When you undock the ribbon, you can drag it to display as horizontal, vertical, or floating.

You can also drag individual panels of the ribbon into your drawing window and float them. You can drag them back into the ribbon, or you can click on **Return Panels to Ribbon** in the upper-right corner grab bar (Figure 1-9) to return the panel to the ribbon.

Step 3. Click each menu tab—**Home**, **Insert**, **Annotate**, **Parametric**, **View**, **Manage**, **Output**, and **Express Tools**—in the ribbon to view the commands available.

Expanded Panels

Panels with an arrow to the immediate right of the panel title can be expanded to display additional commands. When you left-click on the arrow, the panel will expand. When the panel is expanded, you can use the pushpin icon to the left of the panel title to keep the panel expanded (Figure 1-10). A few panels also display a down-to-the-right arrow at the far-right end of the panel label. This arrow is called the **Dialog Box Launcher**. Click the arrow to display the appropriate dialog box.

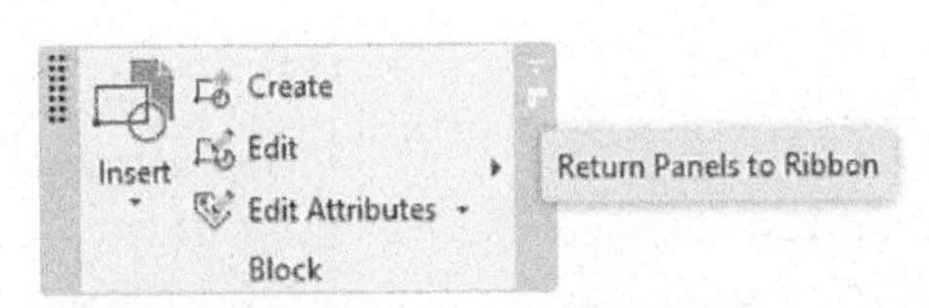

Figure 1-9
Return Panels to Ribbon option in the upper right corner of a floating panel

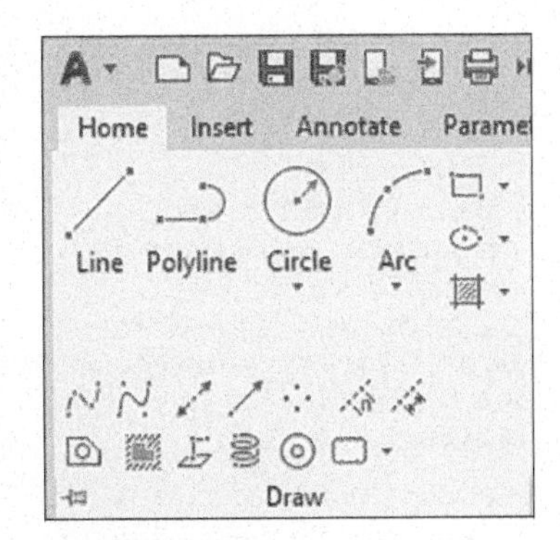

Figure 1-10
Expanded panel

Dialog Boxes and Palettes

Panels with a diagonal arrow in the lower-right corner of the panel title can open dialog boxes or palettes. When you left-click on the diagonal arrow, a dialog box or palette appears, as shown in Figure 1-11.

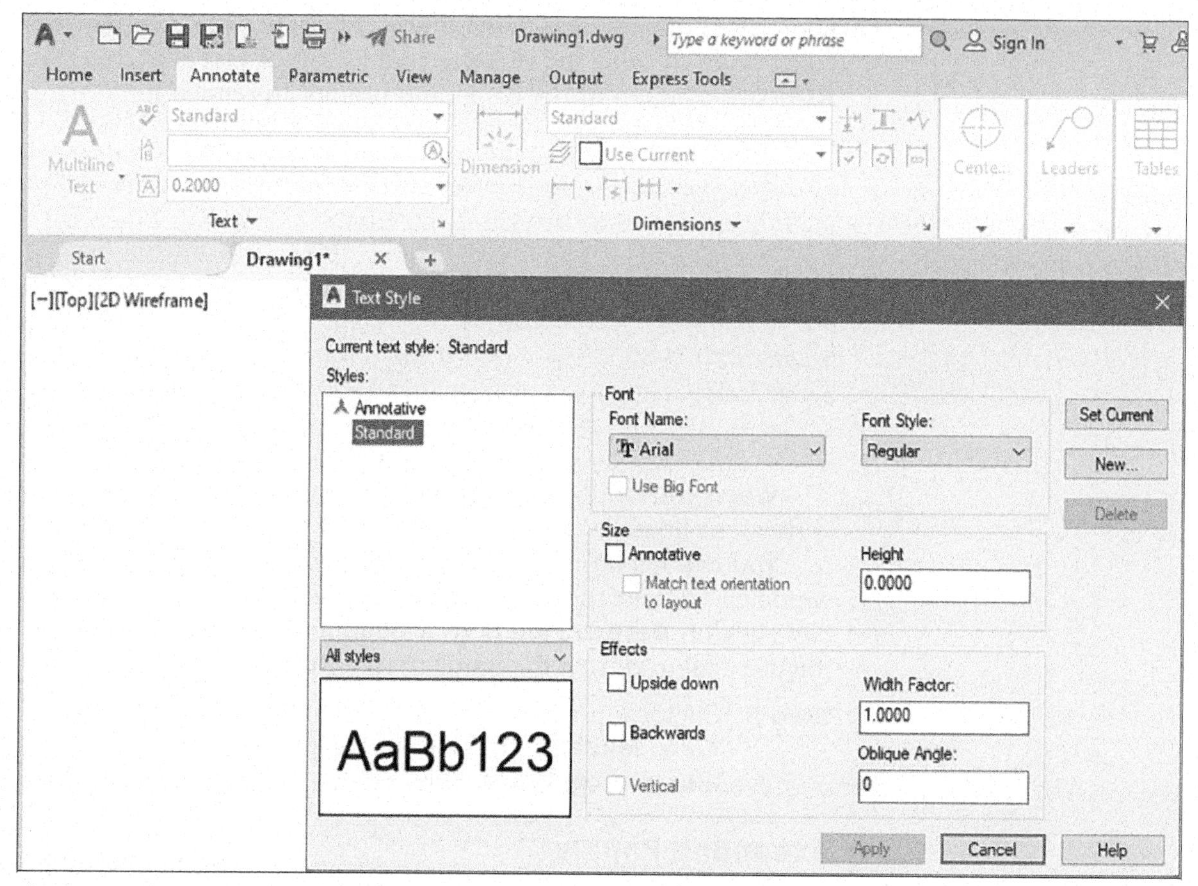

Figure 1-11
Clicking the diagonal arrow in the lower-right corner of a panel displays a dialog box or palette

Tooltips

When you hold the mouse pointer steady (do not click) on any command in the ribbon, a tooltip displays the name of the command, and a text string gives a brief description of the command (Figure 1-12).

Flyouts

Tool buttons with a small arrow have flyouts. When you left-click on the arrow, the flyout appears, as shown in Figure 1-13. When you click on a command in the flyout, a command is activated.

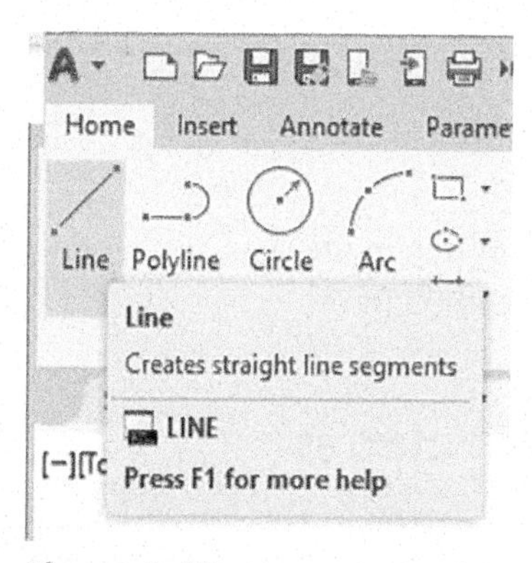

Figure 1-12
Tooltips

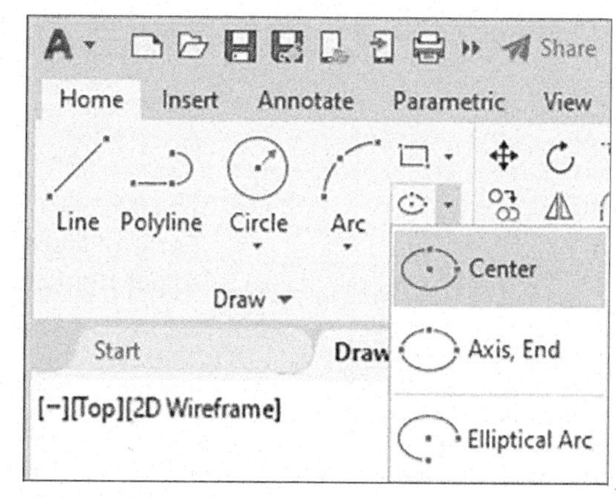

Figure 1-13
Flyouts

Command Line Window (<Ctrl>+9)

You can move, resize, or turn off the command line window shown at the bottom of the screen. The command line window is where you can see AutoCAD respond to a command you have started. After a command is started, AutoCAD prompts you to enter specific information. Always watch the command line to make sure you and AutoCAD are communicating.

AutoComplete command entry: When you start to type a command (for example, **L** for **Line**) at the *command line window*, AutoCAD provides a list of commands that start with L, command aliases, and system variables (Figure 1-14). You can scroll through the list and select the command you want. When you right-click on the command line, the right-click menu shown in Figure 1-14 appears. You can turn off **AutoComplete** (delete the check mark beside the suggestion list) and also change the amount of time it takes for the list to appear.

Quick Access Toolbar

This toolbar contains the **New**, **Open**, **Save**, **Save As...**, **Open from Web & Mobile**, **Save to Web & Mobile**, **Plot**, **Undo**, and **Redo** commands.

When you right-click on the **Quick Access** toolbar, the right-click menu shown in Figure 1-15 appears:

Remove from Quick Access Toolbar: Allows you to remove commands from the **Quick Access** toolbar

Add Separator: Allows you to add a separator line between command icons in the **Quick Access** toolbar

Customize Quick Access Toolbar: Allows you to add frequently used commands to the **Quick Access** toolbar

Show Quick Access Toolbar below the Ribbon: Allows you to move the **Quick Access** toolbar from above to below the ribbon

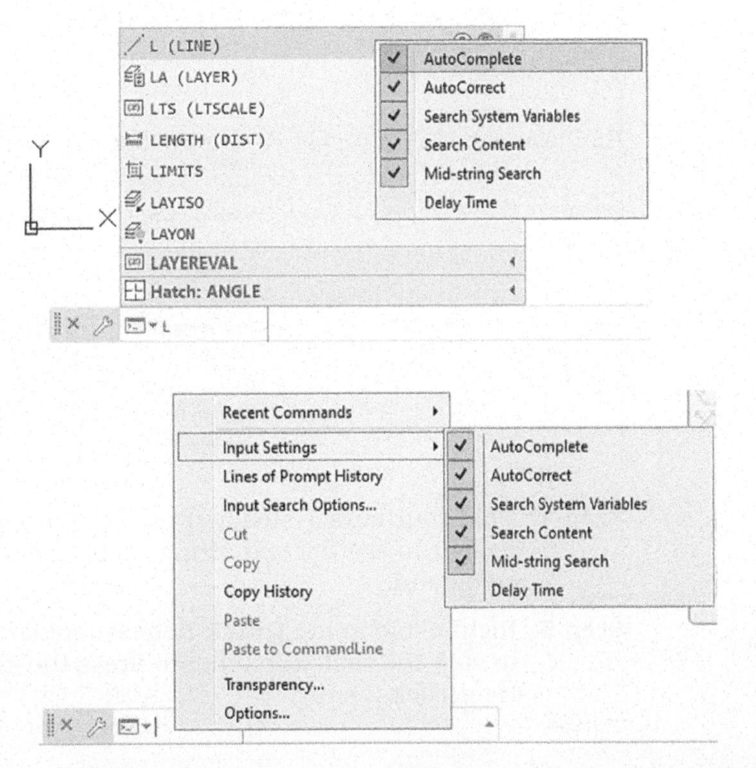

Figure 1-14 **AutoComplete** command entry list and right-click menu

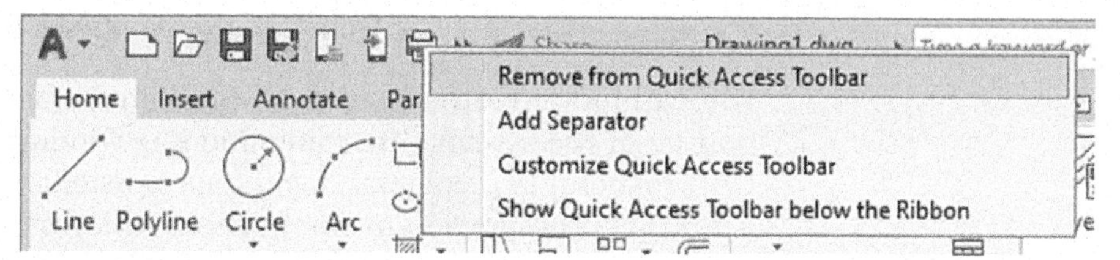

Figure 1-15
Right-click on the **Quick Access** toolbar

Customizing the Quick Access Toolbar Down Arrow and Showing the Menu Bar

When you click the **Customize Quick Access Toolbar** down arrow to the right of the **Quick Access** toolbar, the menu shown in Figure 1-16 appears:

Commands: Clicking a command to display the check mark adds the command icon to the **Quick Access** toolbar.

More Commands...: Takes you to the **Customize User Interface Editor** and allows you to add frequently used commands to the **Quick Access** toolbar.

Show Menu Bar: Allows you to display the menu bar shown in Figure 1-17.

Show Below the Ribbon: Allows you to move the **Quick Access** toolbar below the ribbon.

Figure 1-16
Customize Quick Access Toolbar

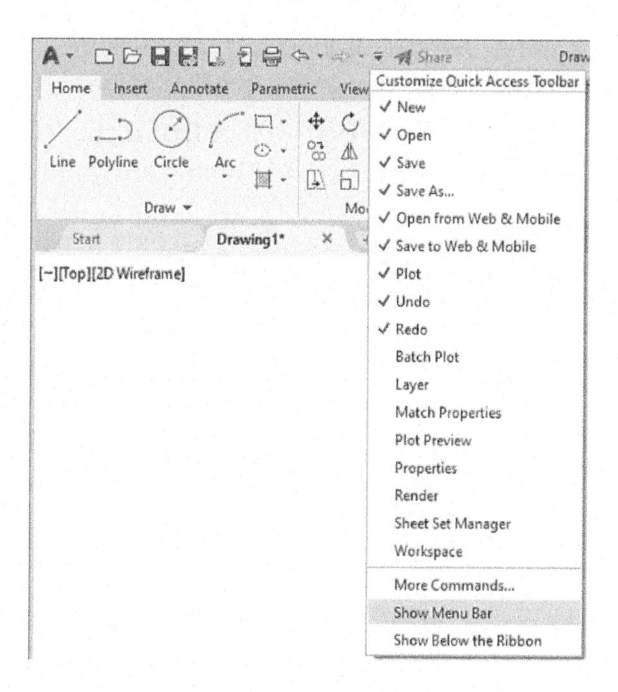

Step 4. Hold your cursor steady over each icon in the **Quick Access** toolbar to see the text string that gives a brief description of each command.

Step 5. Right-click on the **Quick Access** toolbar (refer to Figure 1-15) to view the right-click menu. Press the **<Esc>** key to exit the right-click menu.

Step 6. Click on the **Customize Quick Access Toolbar** down arrow to view the menu shown in Figure 1-16. Select **Show Menu Bar** to add the menu bar and the commands you can use to make a drawing (Figure 1-17). Press the **<Esc>** key to exit the menu.

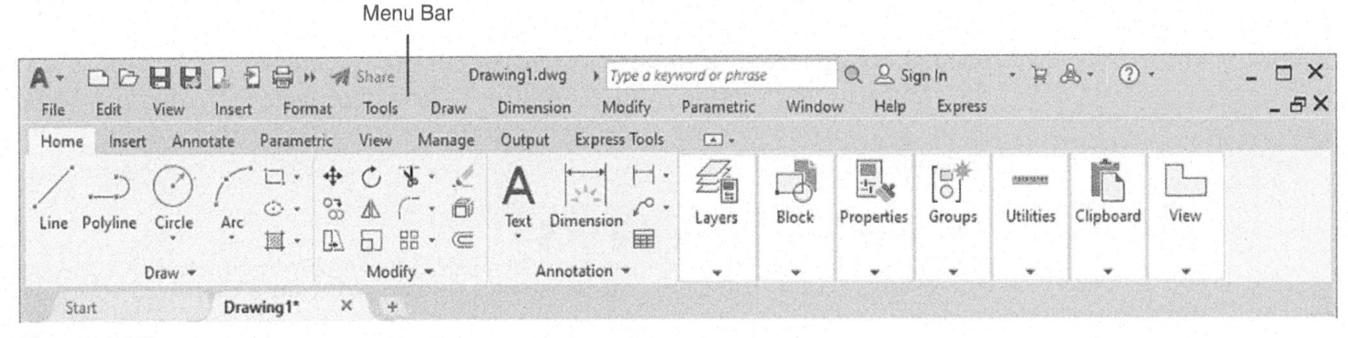

Figure 1-17
Display the menu bar

Using AutoCAD Toolbars

The AutoCAD toolbars have buttons that start commands you can use to make a drawing. You can display, hide, dock, and resize toolbars. You can create your own toolbars and turn a toolbar into a ribbon panel.

Step 7. Click the **View** pull-down menu from the menu bar, and then select **Toolbars** (Figure 1-18) to view the list of toolbars you can add to the Quick Access toolbar or to available toolbars.

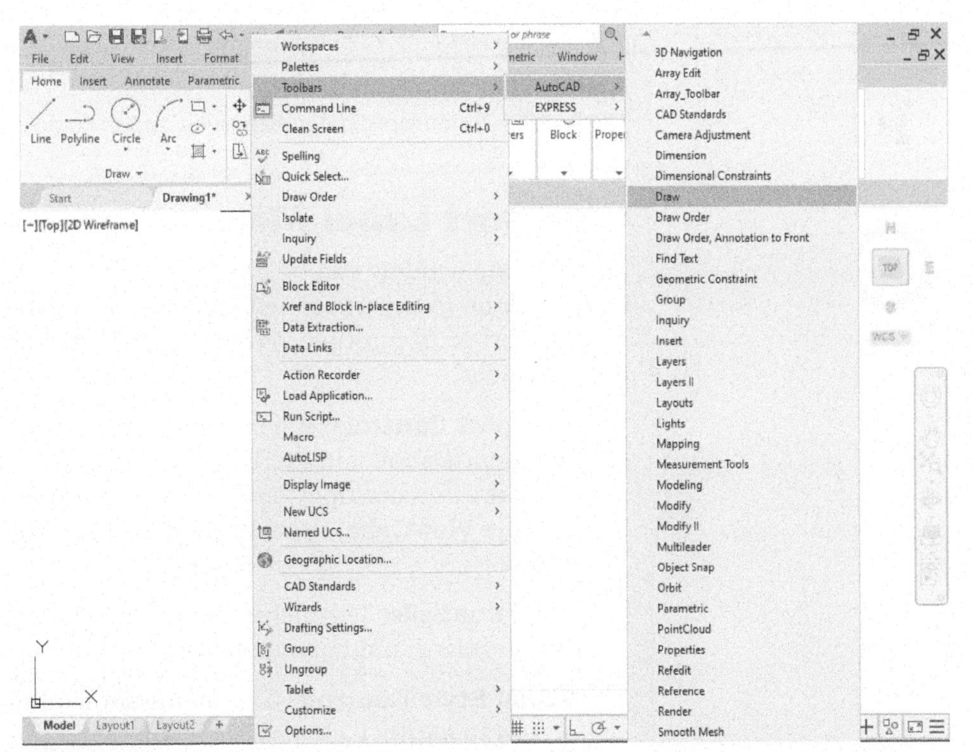

Figure 1-18
Available toolbars

User Coordinate System Icon

user coordinate system icon: An icon showing the orientation of the x-, y-, and z-axes of the current coordinate system. In two-dimensional drawings, only the x- and y-axes are used. The UCS icon is located at the origin of the current UCS (0,0).

All AutoCAD drawings are made on a coordinate system (Figure 1-19). The ***user coordinate system (UCS) icon*** in the lower-left corner of the drawing window shows the orientation of the x-, y-, and z-axes of the current coordinate system. In 2D drawings, only the x- and y-axes are used. The UCS icon is located at the origin of the UCS (0,0). In this figure, the lines (grid marks) are spaced 1/2″ apart. The crosshairs of the cursor are located 3″ to the right (the X direction) and 2″ up (the Y direction) from 0,0. The numbers in the gray area show the cursor coordinate values (the location of the crosshairs).

Advantage of Using the UCS

The origin (0,0) of the UCS can be moved to any point on a drawing; when the origin is relocated, you can easily draw from that point. When a drawing contains dimension information from a specific location, relocating the origin to that specific location makes drawing much easier.

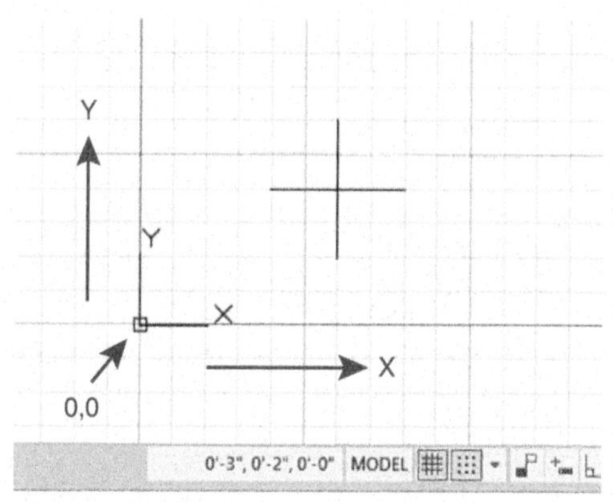

Figure 1-19
The AutoCAD user coordinate system—Cartesian coordinates

Viewport Label Menus

The drawing window can be divided into multiple viewports. The **Viewport Label Menus** in the upper-left drawing area can be used in the current single viewport or in multiple viewports. The **Viewport Label Menus** consist of the following:

Viewport Controls: When you click on the **Viewport Controls** icon, the menus shown in Figure 1-20 open. You can change from a single viewport to a multiple viewport configuration and use the display options **ViewCube**, **SteeringWheels**, and the navigation bar for each viewport.

View Controls: The menu shown in Figure 1-21 provides a list of all the standard and custom views available to use in each viewport.

Visual Style Controls: The menu shown in Figure 1-22 provides access to all the visual styles available to use in each viewport.

These menus can be turned OFF. Type and enter **VPCONTROL** at the command line; type **OFF** to respond to the prompt *Enter new value for VPCONTROL <ON>.*

Figure 1-20
Viewport controls

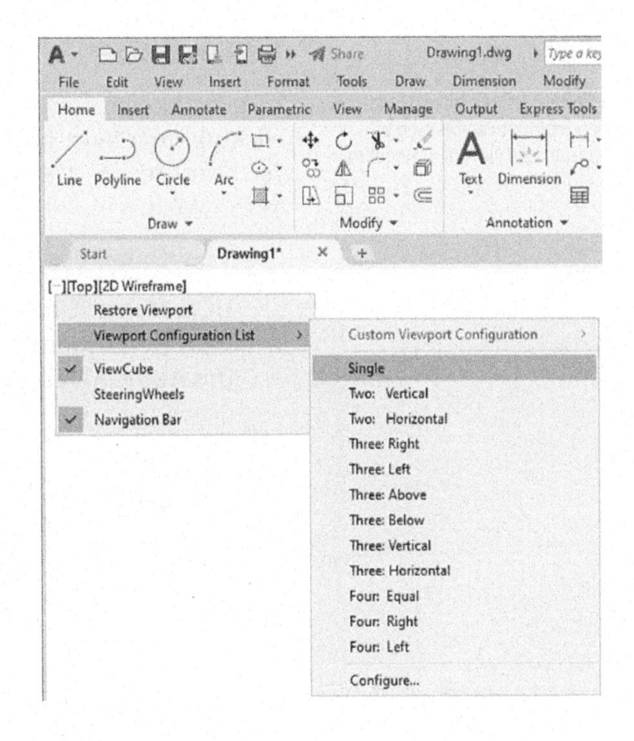

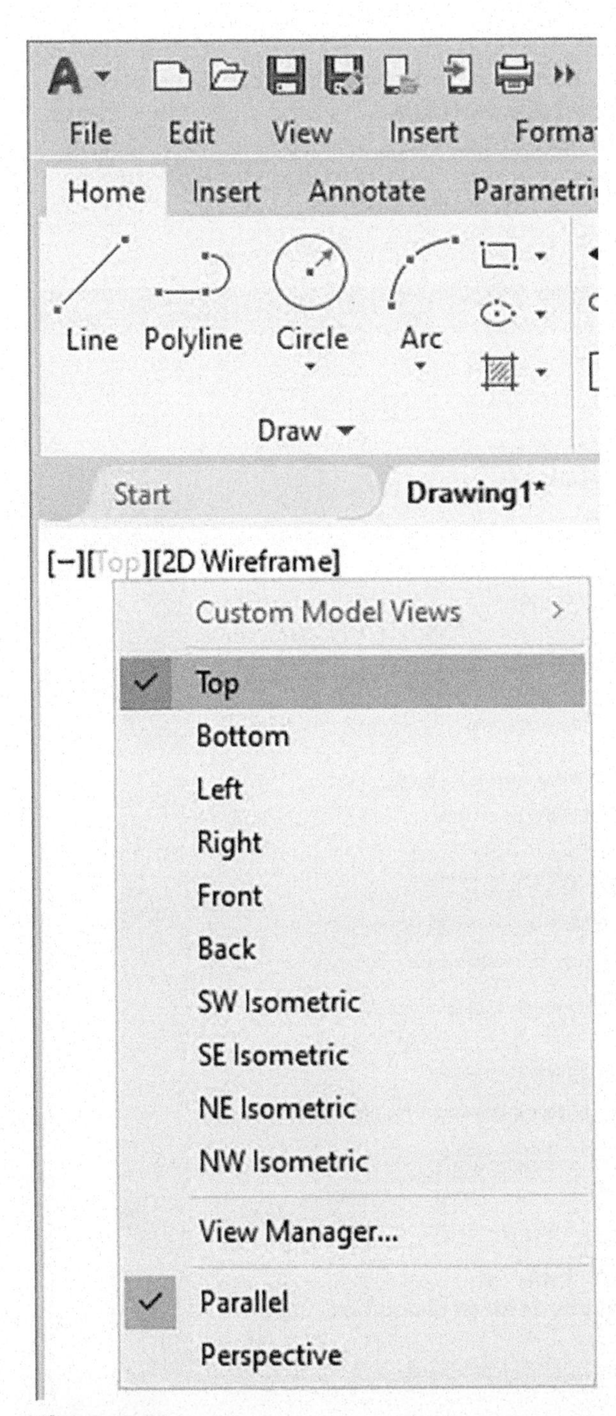

Figure 1-21
View controls

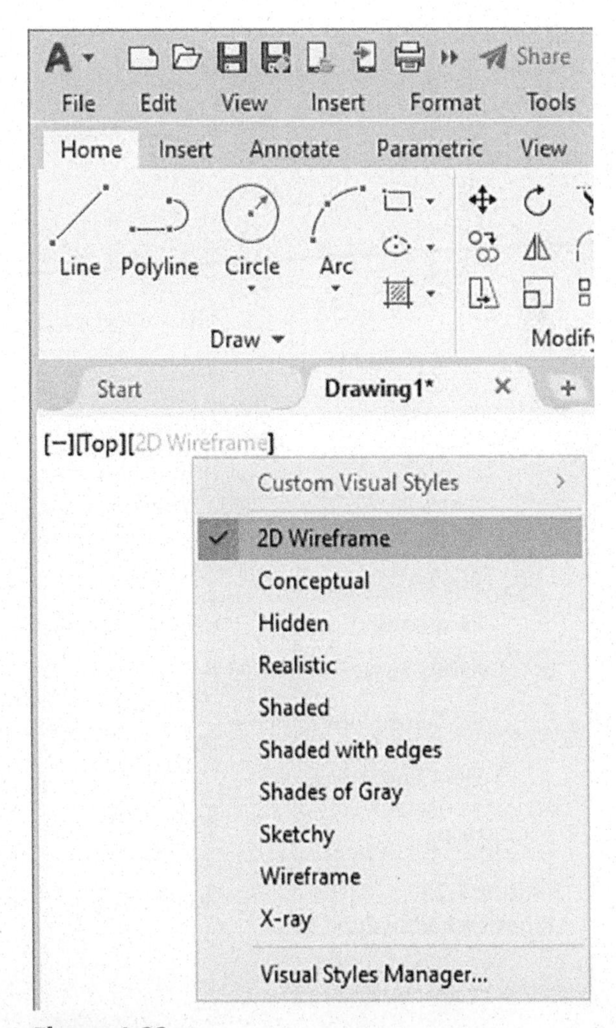

Figure 1-22
Visual style controls

ViewCube

ViewCube: A three-dimensional viewing tool that can be used to switch from one view of a model to another.

You can use AutoCAD's ***ViewCube*** to navigate in the 3D drawing by left-clicking on a face, an edge, or a corner and dragging the mouse to the view you want to see. Use the WCS button to restore an existing UCS or return to the WCS.

ViewCube: Used to navigate the 3D drawing.

UCS Menu: Used in 2D and 3D drawing to change the origin of the UCS (user coordinate system). WCS stands for *world coordinate system*, the AutoCAD fixed-coordinate system, which is common to all AutoCAD drawings.

Step 8. Right-click in the ViewCube area to display the right-click menu (Figure 1-23). Click **ViewCube Settings...** on the right-click menu to access the **ViewCube Settings** dialog box (Figure 1-24), where you can change the display of the ViewCube and the **UCS** menu. Press the **<Esc>** key to exit the dialog box.

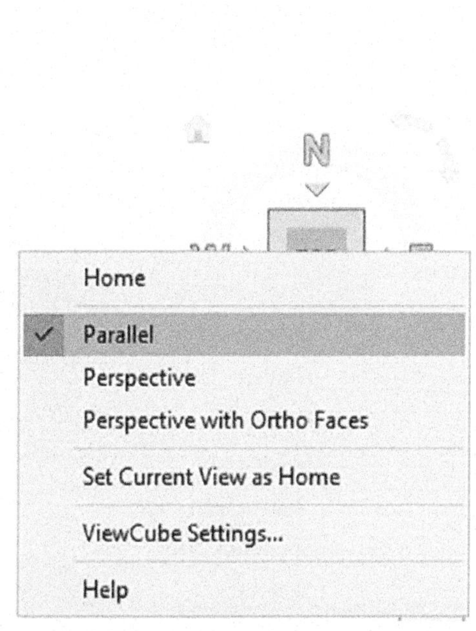

Figure 1-23
Right-click **ViewCube** menu

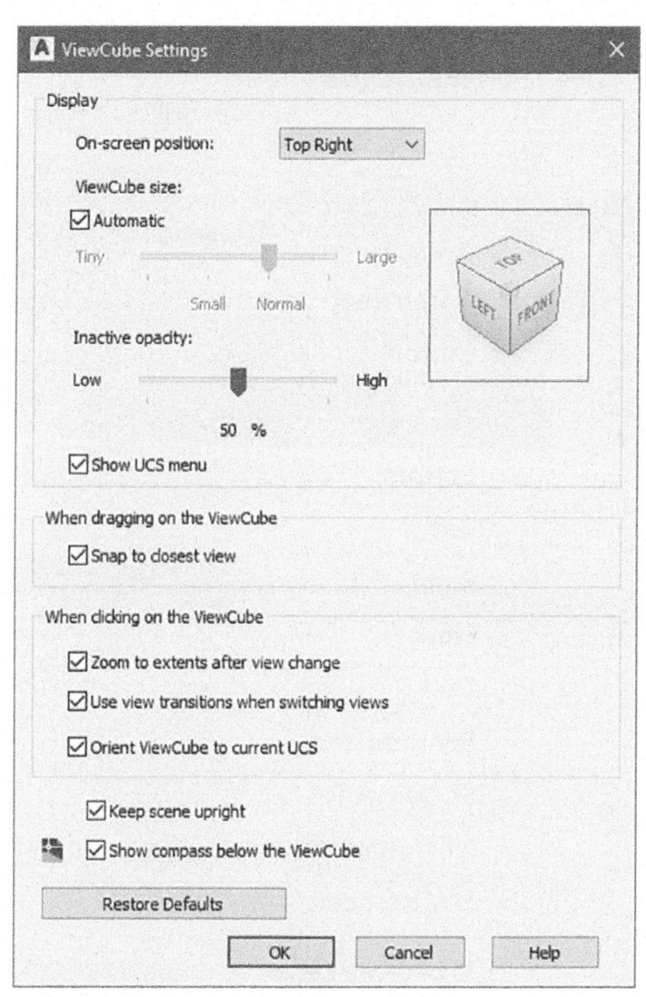

Figure 1-24
ViewCube Settings dialog box

Navigation Bar

navigation bar: An area in the AutoCAD user interface that contains navigation tools that are common across multiple Autodesk programs. The unified navigation tools include Autodesk ViewCube, SteeringWheels, ShowMotion, and 3Dconnexion 3D controllers.

Tools on the ***navigation bar*** with a small down arrow can be expanded to display additional tools. The **NAVBAR** system variable controls appearance of the navigation bar (ON or OFF).

Similarly, the system variable **DISPLAYVIEWCUBEIN2D** (ON or OFF) controls the display of the ViewCube.

SteeringWheels: Used by experienced 3D users to navigate the 3D drawing. There is also a 2D wheel.

Pan: Used in 2D and 3D drawing. Analogous to panning with a camera, using this tool allows you to maintain the current display magnification and see parts of the drawing that may be off the screen and not visible in the drawing window.

Zoom: Used in 2D and 3D drawing, the **Zoom** commands help you control how you view the drawing area on the display screen.

Orbit: Rotates the object in 3D space.

3Dconnexion: Rotates the viewpoint in 3D space. (3Dconnexion is an independent manufacturer of 3D mice.)

Show Motion: Used in 3D to record animation.

Step 9. Click on the button in the bottom right of the navigation bar to view the menu shown in Figure 1-25. Clicking a command to display the check mark adds the command icon to the navigation bar; clicking to remove the check mark removes the command icon from the navigation bar. Press the **<Esc>** key to exit the menu.

You can click on the button in the top right of the navigation bar to close it. You can click the ribbon, **View** tab, **Viewport Tools** panel, and change the display of the ViewCube and the navigation bar (Figure 1-26).

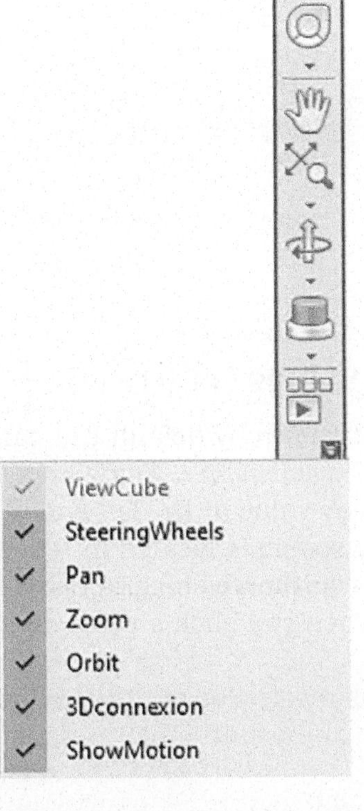

Figure 1-25
Click on the button in the bottom right of the navigation bar to view a menu

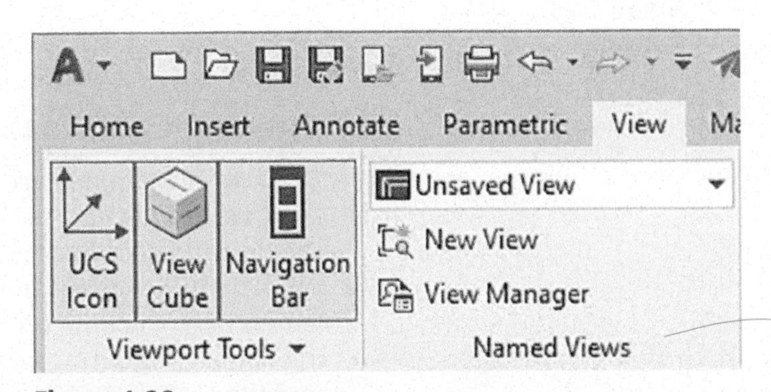

Figure 1-26
You can change the display of the **ViewCube** and the navigation bar

Infocenter

AutoCAD's Infocenter at the top right of the title bar contains links to the program's help system and other resources.

> **Text Input Box:** You can enter a word or phrase in the **Infocenter** text box to search for information (Figure 1-27). Click on the **Search** button to the right of the text box to display the search results in **Autodesk AutoCAD 2022 – Help.** You are connected to the AutoCAD help content, instructional videos, and downloads. You can collapse the text input box by clicking the arrow to the left of the box.

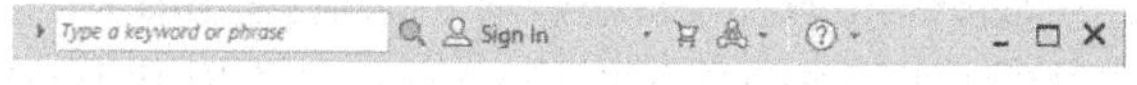

Figure 1-27
Infocenter Search

> **Sign In:** If you have an Autodesk account, this is where you can sign in.
>
> **Autodesk App Store:** Opens the **Autodesk App Store** website.
>
> **Stay Connected:** This provides access to Autodesk product services, support, and the AutoCAD online community.
>
> **Help:** Displays the **Autodesk AutoCAD 2022 – Help** window. The down arrow to the right has additional help information.

Status Bar

The status bar (Figure 1-28) at the bottom of the screen contains the following options. The **Customization** tool at the rightmost end of the status bar allows you to show the tools you want to see on the status bar.

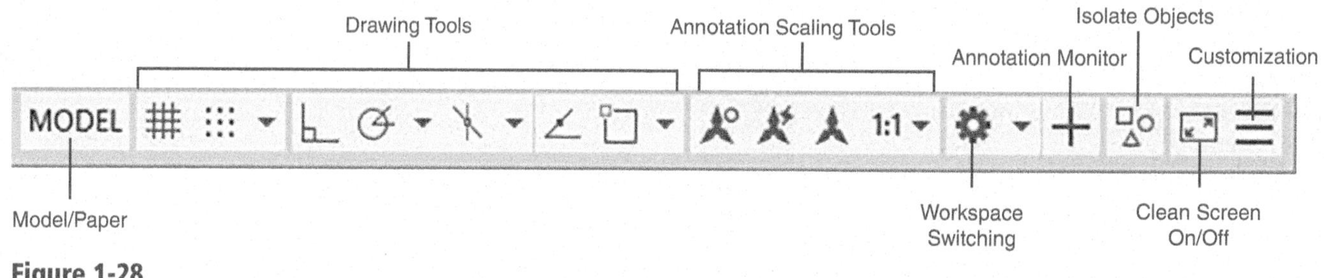

Figure 1-28
Status bar

Drawing Coordinates Values (<Ctrl>+I)

Drawing coordinates are not shown by default but can be turned on using the **Customization** tool of the status bar. Using an x- and y-axis system, the drawing coordinate display value at the left end of the status bar tells you where the cursor on the screen is located in relation to 0,0 (the lower-left corner). Clicking on the coordinates toggles between constantly updating display, updating only when you click a point on screen, or turning updating off.

The drawing tools status toggles (snap, grid, ortho, polar tracking, and so on) are at the middle of the status bar and are represented by icons

Figure 1-29
Drawing tool buttons displayed by clicking **Customization** on the status bar

(Figure 1-28). Click the **Customization** tool at the lower-right end of the status bar to see the icons currently displayed on the status bar (Figure 1-29). For example, the cursor coordinates, which traditionally were on the lower-left end of the status bar, are not shown by default.

The drawing tools status toggles at the bottom of the screen allow you to turn on or off drawing tools that affect your drawing. You can also turn many of the tools off and on using the function keys. The tools and the function keys are as follows:

Infer Constraints (<Ctrl>+<Shift>+I): When this option is on, it controls the application and visibility of geometric constraints such as horizontal, vertical, and perpendicular while you are drawing. To select which constraints you want to use, enter the system variable **CONSTRAINTSETTINGS** to display the dialog box shown in Figure 1-30. It also controls the display of dimensional constraints between geometric objects or points on objects and the order in which constraints are applied to your drawing.

Snap Mode (<F9>): When a command is active and you are specifying points, your graphics cursor (crosshairs) snaps to invisible snap points as you move the cursor across the screen when **Snap Mode** is on. You set the size between snap points.

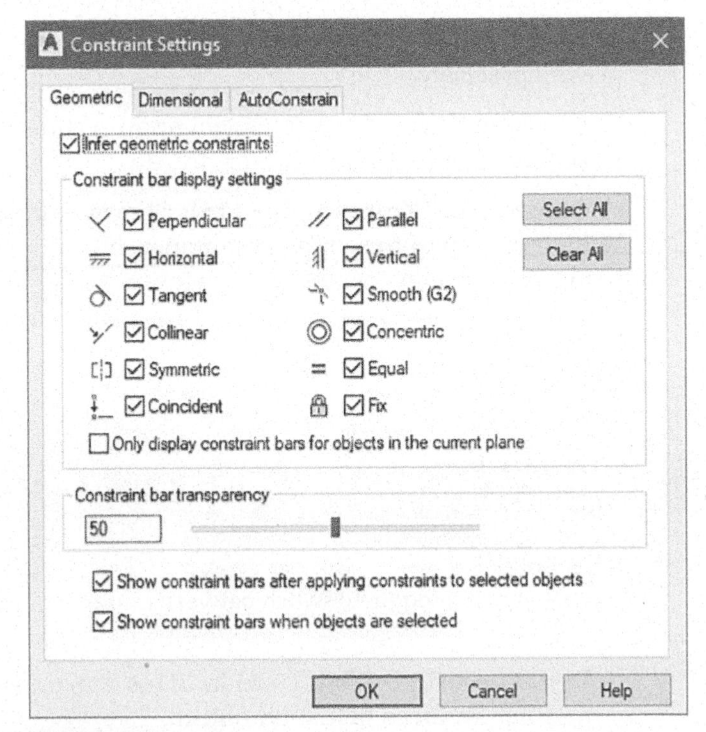

Figure 1-30
Constraint Settings dialog box

Grid Display (<F7>): A visible grid that you see on the screen when the grid is toggled on. You set the size of the grid and can set the appearance of the grid to lines or dots.

Ortho Mode (<F8>): Restricts you to draw only horizontally and vertically when on.

Polar Tracking (<F10>): Shows temporary alignment paths along polar angles when on (Figure 1-31). While the default increment for

PolarSnap is 90 degrees, you can change it easily to 60, 45, 30, 15, and so on as shown in Figure 1-32. You can use the system variable **POLARANG** to reset **PolarSnap**.

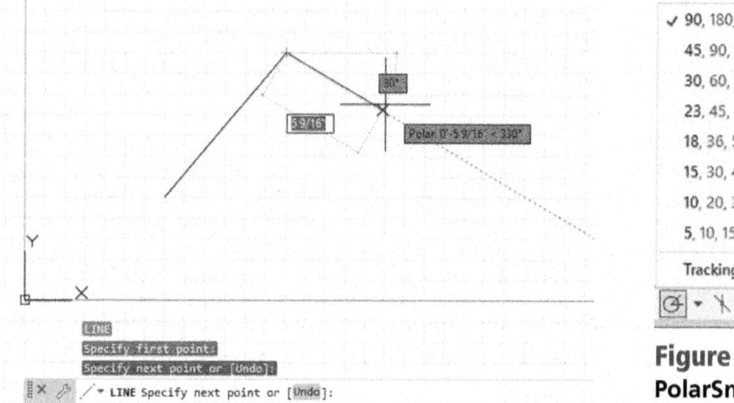

Figure 1-31
Polar angles with **Polar Tracking** on

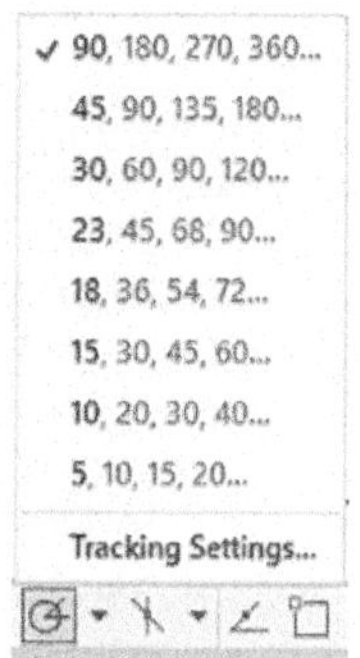

Figure 1-32
PolarSnap angles set from status bar

Isometric Drawing (ISODRAFT): Allows easy switching between the isoplanes for those who use isometric drawings (for example, piping and instrumentation diagrams [Figure 1-33]).

Object Snap (<F3>): Contains command modifiers that help you draw very precisely.

3D Object Snap (<F4>): Object snap setting for drawing in 3D. It contains command modifiers for drawing very accurately in 3D.

Object Snap Tracking (<F11>): Shows temporary alignment paths along object snap points when on.

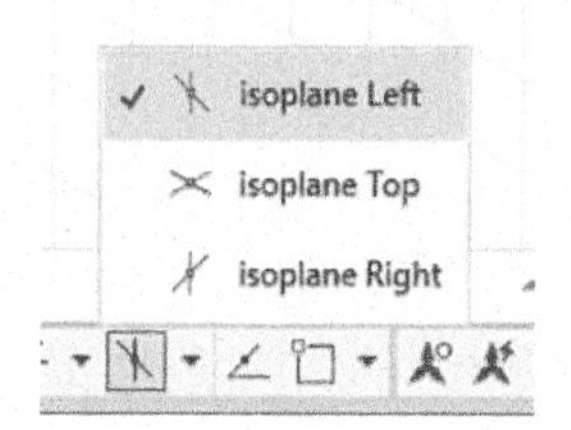

Figure 1-33
Isometric Drawing toggle to switch between isoplanes

Dynamic UCS (<F6>): Used in 3D to move the user coordinate system to different faces of a solid object.

Dynamic Input (<F12>): Gives you information attached to the cursor regarding commands, coordinates, and tooltips. This is the same information that AutoCAD displays in the command line window.

Show/Hide Lineweight: You can assign varying lineweights (widths) to different objects in a drawing. When this toggle is on, the lineweights are displayed on the screen.

Show/Hide Transparency: You can assign varying transparency levels to an object. When this toggle is on, the transparency is displayed on the screen.

Quick Properties (<Ctrl>+<Shift>+P): Every drawing object that you draw has properties such as color, layer, and linetype. When this button is on, the **Quick Properties** window appears when you select an object and allows you to view and change the settings for the properties of the object.

Selection Cycling (<Ctrl>+W): When two drawing objects lie very close to each other or one on top of the other, this helps you select one of the objects. When this toggle is on, you can hold down **<Shift>**+space bar and cycle through the objects.

Annotation Monitor: Associative is a property that belongs to dimensions. Associative dimensions are linked to association points on the object dimensioned. When the association point on the object moves (the object is made larger or smaller), the dimension location, orientation, and text value of the dimension change. When this button is on, dimensions that are disassociated will have a badge beside them.

Model or Paper Space

model space: One of the two primary spaces in which objects are created.

paper space: One of the two spaces in which objects are created or documented. Paper space is used to set up a finished layout for printing or plotting. Often, drawings are plotted in paper space in a drawing title block and border.

The **Model** and **Paper Space** buttons control the visibility of the model and paper space (layout) working environments.

Model space is the drawing window where your drawing is displayed. ***Paper space*** (layout) is the area where you can annotate, lay out, and preview your drawing for printing or plotting.

Quick View Tools

Two Quick View tools can help you change documents and layouts as you work.

Quick View Layouts: Allows you to preview and switch between the current drawing and its layouts.

Quick View Drawings: Allows you to preview and switch between open drawings and their layouts.

Annotation Scaling Tools

The annotation scaling buttons affect annotative objects such as text and dimensions that are added to drawings and need to be scaled when plotted:

Show annotation objects — At current scale: When you have annotative objects on your drawing that support different scales, this button controls their visibility. When it is off, only the annotative objects with the current annotation scale are visible.

Add scales to annotative objects: When this button is on, and the annotation scale is changed, the annotative objects change on the screen to reflect the new scale size. The object then supports two scales.

Annotation scale of the current view: This button allows you to control how annotative text and dimensions appear on the drawing.

Workspace Switching

workspace: A specific arrangement of user interface elements, including their contents, properties, display status, and locations. Workspaces allow the user to quickly switch between specific arrangements of menus, toolbars, and dockable windows as well as many other settings previously specified.

A ***workspace*** is the environment in which you work. It is defined by the menus, toolbars, or palettes that appear on the workspace. The **Workspace** button allows you to switch between defined workspaces.

Lock/Unlock Toolbar and Window Positions

You can add toolbars and windows to your workspace. The **Lock/Unlock** button allows you to lock and unlock the location of these toolbars and windows.

On/Off Hardware Acceleration

When you are working with large drawings or rendering and hiding models, hardware acceleration enhances the graphic performance in AutoCAD.

- **Annotation Monitor:** The **Annotation Monitor** in the drawing tools area of the status bar keeps track of associated and disassociated dimensions. When the **toggle** is **ON**, the cross icon in the status bar is highlighted.
- **Isolate Objects:** You can isolate objects in a drawing or hide them regardless of layer. When objects have been isolated or hidden in the drawing, the **Isolate Objects** button is highlighted.

Clean Screen (<Ctrl>+0 [Zero])

When on, this button clears the screen of the ribbon, toolbars, and dockable windows, excluding the command line, as shown in Figure 1-34.

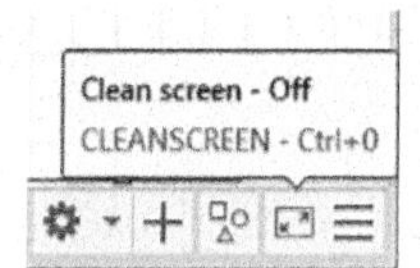

Figure 1-34
Clean Screen tool on the status bar

Modifying and Saving a Workspace

AutoCAD provides you with three different workspaces to choose from when making your own workspace:

Drafting & Annotation: This workspace has the ribbon displayed by default, and the menu bar, toolbars, and tool palettes are off by default.

3D Basics: You use this workspace when you make basic 3D solid models. The basic 3D commands are available. The ribbon containing these basic commands is on by default.

3D Modeling: You use this workspace when you make complex 3D solid models. All the commands and settings used to make, assign materials to, and render solid models are on by default. The ribbon is on by default.

Step 10. Make sure the **Drafting & Annotation** workspace is current, as described next:

Prompt	Response
Type a command:	Click the **Workspace Switching** button on the status bar
The **Workspace Switching** menu appears (Figure 1-35):	If there is a check mark beside **Drafting & Annotation**, it is active If it is active, press **<Esc>** to exit the menu If it is not active, click **Drafting & Annotation** to make it the active workspace

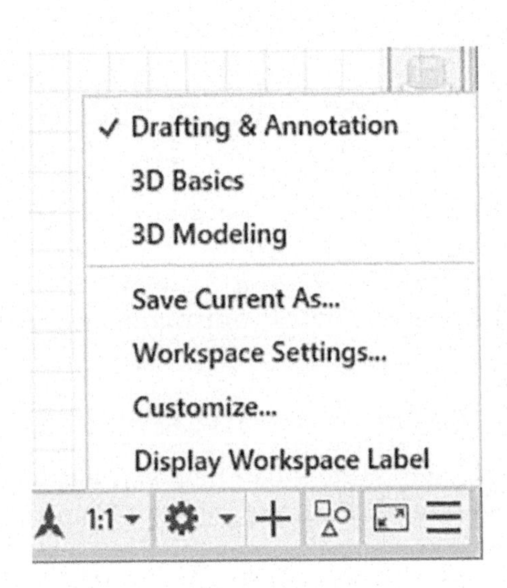

Figure 1-35
Workspace Switching menu

Step 11. Add the menu bar to the AutoCAD screen, as described next:

Prompt	Response
Type a command:	Click the customization button (the down arrow at the right end of the **Quick Access** toolbar) Click **Show Menu Bar** as shown in Figure 1-36

Step 12. Save your workspace, as described next:

Prompt	Response
Type a command:	Click the **Workspace Switching** button on the status bar
The **Workspace Switching** menu appears:	Click **Save Current As...**
The **Save Workspace** text box appears:	Type your name in the **Name:** text box **<Enter>**

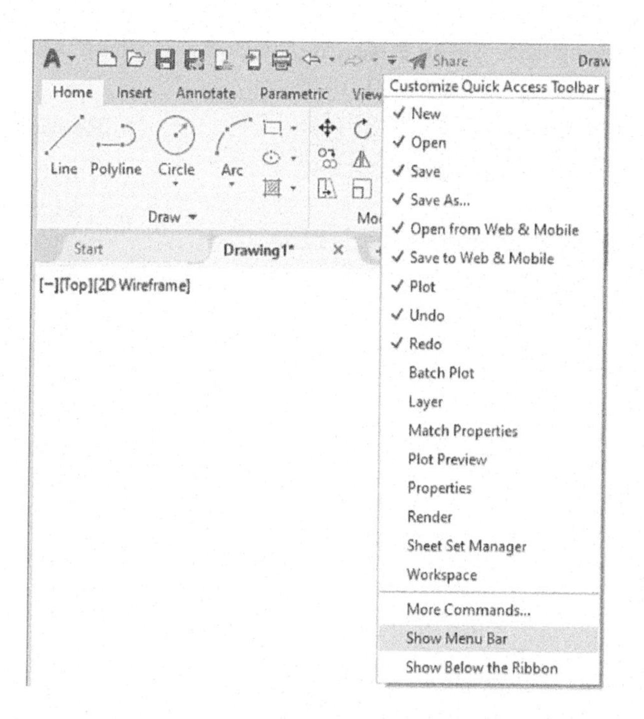

Figure 1-36
Show Menu Bar option

As you become familiar with AutoCAD, you may want to add menus, toolbars, or palettes to your drawing display and keep that display. Click **Save Current As...**, enter your name in the **Name:** text box, and save the modified drawing display as your named workspace again.

Getting Help in AutoCAD 2022

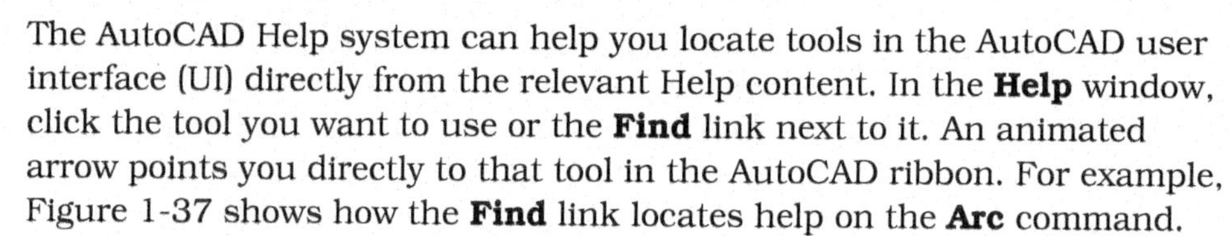

The AutoCAD Help system can help you locate tools in the AutoCAD user interface (UI) directly from the relevant Help content. In the **Help** window, click the tool you want to use or the **Find** link next to it. An animated arrow points you directly to that tool in the AutoCAD ribbon. For example, Figure 1-37 shows how the **Find** link locates help on the **Arc** command.

If the tool is not accessible from the current workspace or is located in a hidden tab or panel, a tooltip in the **Help** window tells you on which ribbon tab and panel you can find it, as shown in Figure 1-38, looking for the **UCS** command.

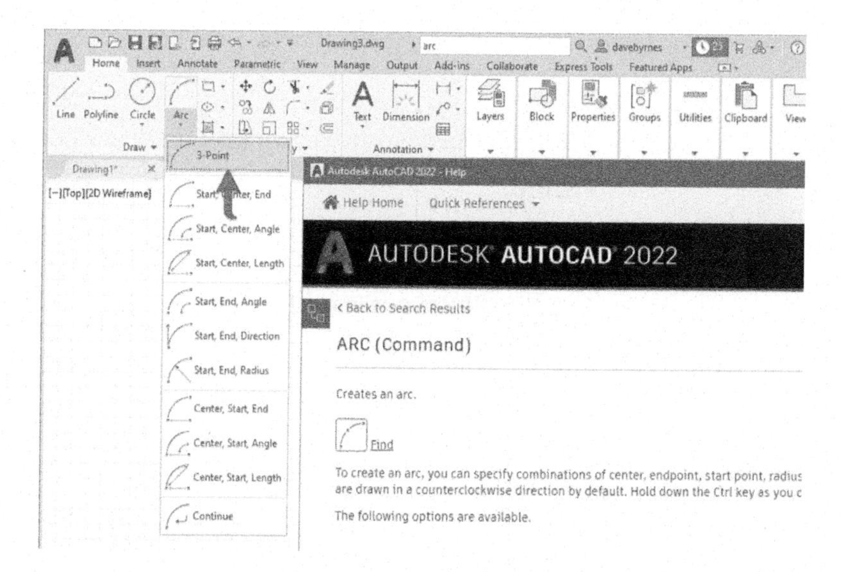

Figure 1-37
Help on the **Arc** command

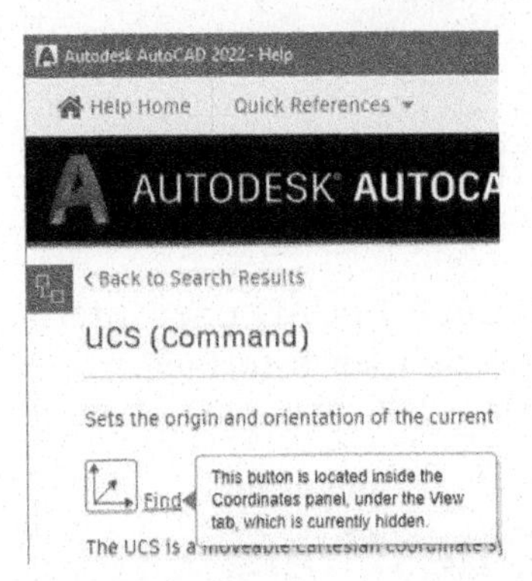

Figure 1-38
Help on the **UCS** (user coordinate system) command

Closing AutoCAD

For now, you will not name or save this exercise. The new workspace is already saved.

Step 13. Click the **Close** button (the **X**) in the upper right corner of the AutoCAD screen if you want to exit AutoCAD.

chapterone

Chapter Summary

This chapter described the AutoCAD user interface and gave you some experience with parts of the user interface. You will now be able to modify and save a workspace so you can begin drawing effectively.

Chapter Test Questions

Multiple Choice

Circle the correct answer.

1. Which of the following is *not* one of the commands in the application menu?
   - a. **Delete**
   - b. **Open**
   - c. **Close**
   - d. **Publish**
2. Which of the following is a ribbon panel?
   - a. **Home**
   - b. **File**
   - c. **Draw**
   - d. **Save**
3. Which of the following icons on the **Modify** panel of the ribbon has a flyout?
   - a. **Move**
   - b. **Copy**
   - c. **Scale**
   - d. **Trim**
4. Ribbon panels with a diagonal arrow in the lower-right corner display which of the following when you click the diagonal arrow?
   - a. Flyouts
   - b. A dialog box or palette
   - c. The **Help** menu
   - d. Options
5. Which of the following displays the name of the command and gives other information relating to it?
   - a. Tooltips
   - b. Flyouts
   - c. Dialog boxes
   - d. Palettes

Matching

Write the number of the correct answer on the line.

a. **Workspace Switching** _____
b. **Status Bar** menu _____
c. **Quick Access** toolbar _____
d. **Quick View Layouts and Drawings** _____
e. **Selection Cycling** _____

1. Allows you to switch between defined workspaces
2. Allows you to preview and switch between layouts and drawings
3. A menu that allows you to turn off and on the visibility of the buttons in the status bar
4. A means of choosing one object when two objects lie directly one on top of each other
5. Contains the **New**, **Open**, **Save**, **Save As...**, **Open from Web & Mobile**, **Save to Web & Mobile**, **Plot**, **Undo**, and **Redo** commands

True or False

Circle the correct answer.

1. **True or False:** The **Quick Access** toolbar can be customized.
2. **True or False:** The **Selection** tab on the **Options** dialog box allows you to change the size of the crosshairs.
3. **True or False:** The **Display** tab on the **Options** dialog box allows you to change the size of the pickbox.
4. **True or False:** The menu bar can be added to the AutoCAD screen by clicking the down arrow to the right of the **Quick Access** toolbar and clicking **Show Menu Bar**.
5. **True or False:** The navigation tools on the right side of the screen allow you to zoom and pan.

List

1. Five components of AutoCAD's graphical user interface.
2. Five tools from **Drawing Tools** toggles on the status bar.
3. Five tabs from the ribbon.
4. Five panels under the **Home** tab of the ribbon.
5. Five commands accessible through the **Application** menu.
6. Five tools from the **Quick Access** toolbar.
7. Five tools under the **Modify** panel, under the **Home** tab of the ribbon.
8. Five tools under the **Draw** panel, under the **Home** tab of the ribbon.
9. Five items that can be added to the status bar using the **Customization** tab.
10. Five ways of executing AutoCAD commands.

Questions

1. How are the tutorials in this book structured?
2. What is the purpose of the **Options** dialog box?
3. What are the four means of inputting or selecting a command?
4. What is the structure of the ribbon?
5. Why would you want to drag a panel from the ribbon, and how do you drag it off and return it to the ribbon?

chapter two

Quick-Start Tutorials: Basic Settings and Commands

CHAPTER OBJECTIVES

- Begin a new AutoCAD drawing and make settings for units, limits, grid, and snap.
- Make layers and assign color, linetype, and lineweight to each layer.
- Use function keys to control grid and snap.
- Use the commands **Save** and **Save As** to save work.
- Use grips to modify objects.
- Use **ORTHO** mode to control drawing horizontal and vertical lines.
- Use annotation scale to control how text and other annotative objects appear on drawings and plots.
- Print/plot drawings from a **Model** tab.
- Correctly use the following commands and settings:

ARC	**MOVE**
CIRCLE	**PAN**
DONUT	**REDO**
DYN	**REDRAW**
ELLIPSE	**REGEN**
ERASE	**SCALE**
GRIDDISPLAY	**Single Line Text**
Highlight	**UNDO**
LINE	**ZOOM**
LTSCALE	

- Correctly use selection set option
- Draw using absolute, relative, polar coordinates, and direct distance entry.

Introduction

The following is a hands-on, step-by-step procedure to complete your first drawing using AutoCAD:

- Tutorial 2-1, Part 1, describes the *settings* that must be made before starting a drawing.

- Tutorial 2-1, Part 2, describes *how to draw using basic commands.*
- Tutorial 2-2 describes *how to print* your drawing.

When you have completed Tutorial 2-1, your drawing will look similar to Figure 2-1.

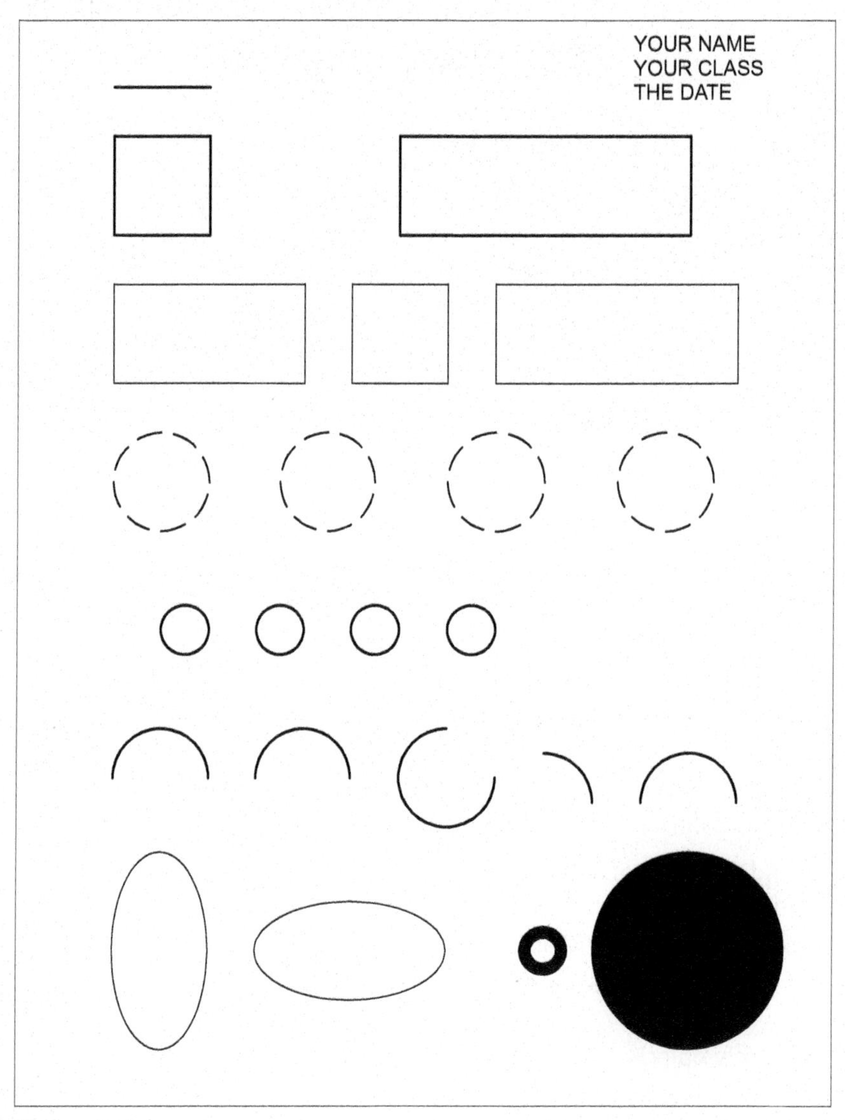

Figure 2-1
Tutorial 2-1 complete

Following the Tutorials in This Book

You are probably using a mouse with a small scroll wheel between the buttons. The left button is the pick button used to select commands and click points on the drawing. The **Response** column item used in the tutorials describes the location of points on the drawing that you have clicked. Figures are provided throughout the chapters to show the location of the points. The points are indicated in bold type in the **Response** column by a **P→**. The **P** is followed by a number; for example, **P1→**, **P2→**. Look at the figure referenced in the step to locate the numbered point on the figure, and click a point in the same place on your drawing.

TUTORIAL 2-1
Part 1, Beginning an AutoCAD Drawing: Saving Your Work; Setting Units, Limits, Grid, and Snap; Creating Layers

Beginning an AutoCAD Drawing

NEW	
Application Menu:	New/ Drawing
Quick Access Toolbar:	
Menu Bar:	File/New
Type a Command:	NEW

When you click **New...** from the **Quick Access Toolbar** or **New** from the application menu button, or the **New** down arrow at the left side of the **Start tab**, AutoCAD allows you to select a template file from the **Template** folder or use the default template file. A template file has settings already established. These settings can include units, limits, grid, snap, and a border and title block. *Templates save time because the settings are already made.*

If you click **New...** and select the **acad.dwt** template, as shown in Figure 2-2, you are in the same drawing environment as when you simply open the AutoCAD program and begin drawing. AutoCAD uses the template acad.dwt for the drawing settings if no other template is selected.

You do not need to click **New...** from the **File** menu. You can stay in the drawing environment that appeared when you started AutoCAD.

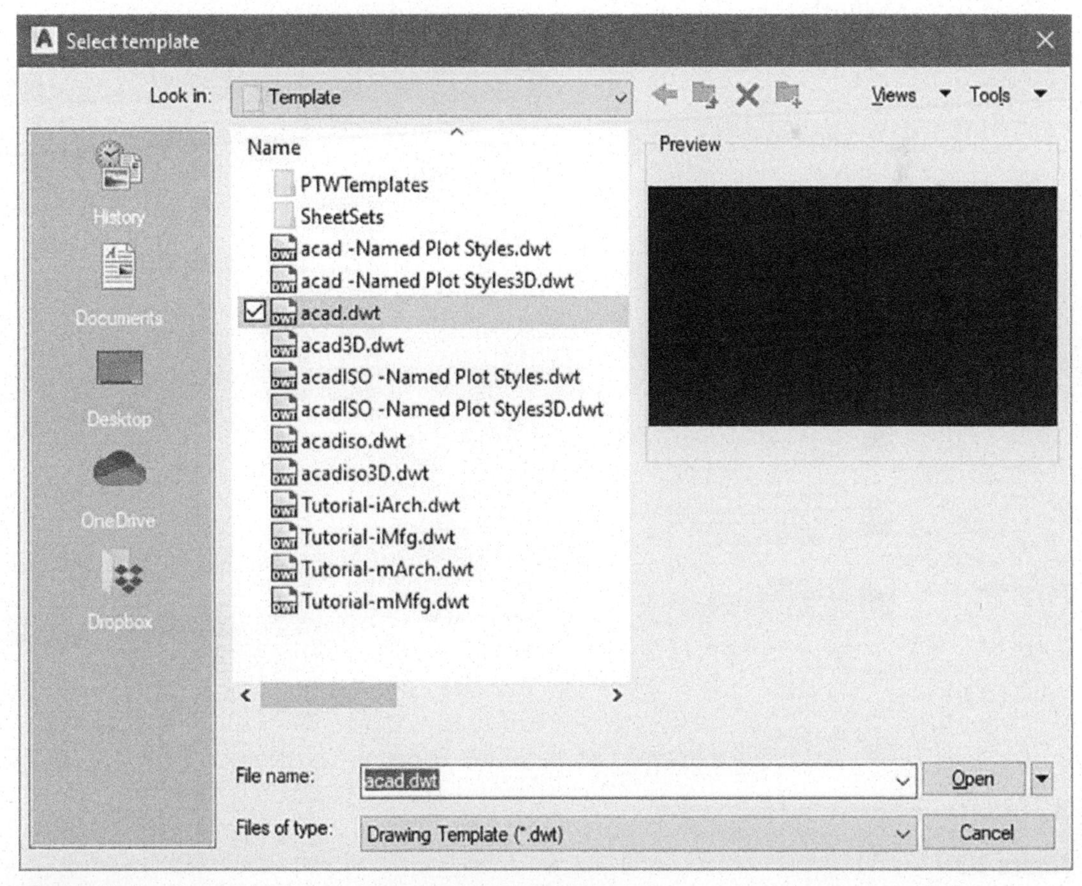

Figure 2-2
Select the **acad.dwt** template for a new drawing

Step 1. If your named workspace is not active, you can select it by using the **Workspace Switching** button in the status bar or in the **Quick Access Toolbar** if **Workspace** is added to the Quick Access tools. You can modify your workspace and save it again as often as you like.

Saving the Drawing

SAVE	
Application Menu:	Save
Quick Access Toolbar:	
Menu Bar:	File/Save
Type a Command:	SAVE
Keyboard:	<Ctrl>+S

SAVE AS	
Application Menu:	Save As
Quick Access Toolbar:	
Menu Bar:	File/Save As
Type a Command:	SAVEAS
Keyboard:	<Ctrl>+<Shift>+S

You must understand two commands, **Save** and **Save As**, and their uses to name and save your work in the desired drive and folder.

Save

Clicking **Save** for a drawing that *you have not yet named activates* the **Save Drawing As** dialog box. You name the drawing by typing a name in the **File name:** input box. You also select a drive and folder where you want the drawing saved.

When you click **Save** for a drawing *that you have named* and already saved, no dialog box appears, the **Qsave** command runs, and the drawing is saved automatically to the drive and folder in which you are working. At this time, the existing drawing file (.dwg) becomes the backup file (.bak), and a new drawing file is created.

Save As

Save As activates the **Save a copy of the drawing** selection box (Figure 2-3) *whether or not the drawing has been named* and allows you to save your drawing using **Save Drawing As** (Figure 2-4) to any drive or folder you choose with a new name if you choose so.

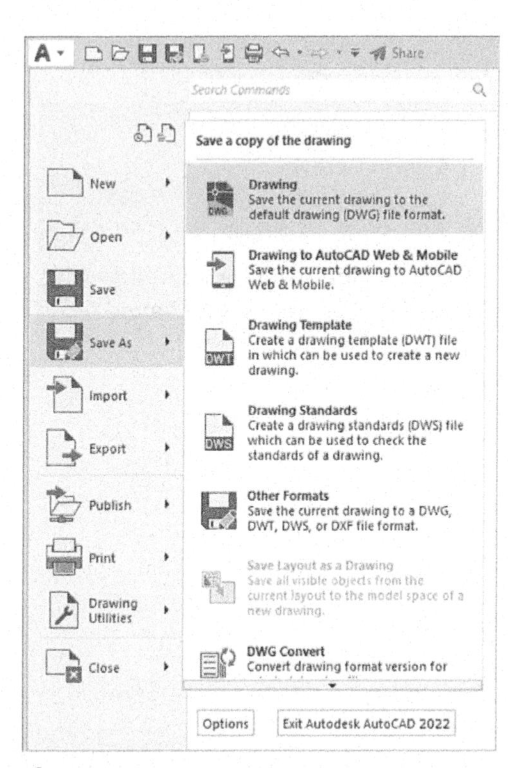

Figure 2-3
Save a copy of the drawing selection box from the **Application** menu

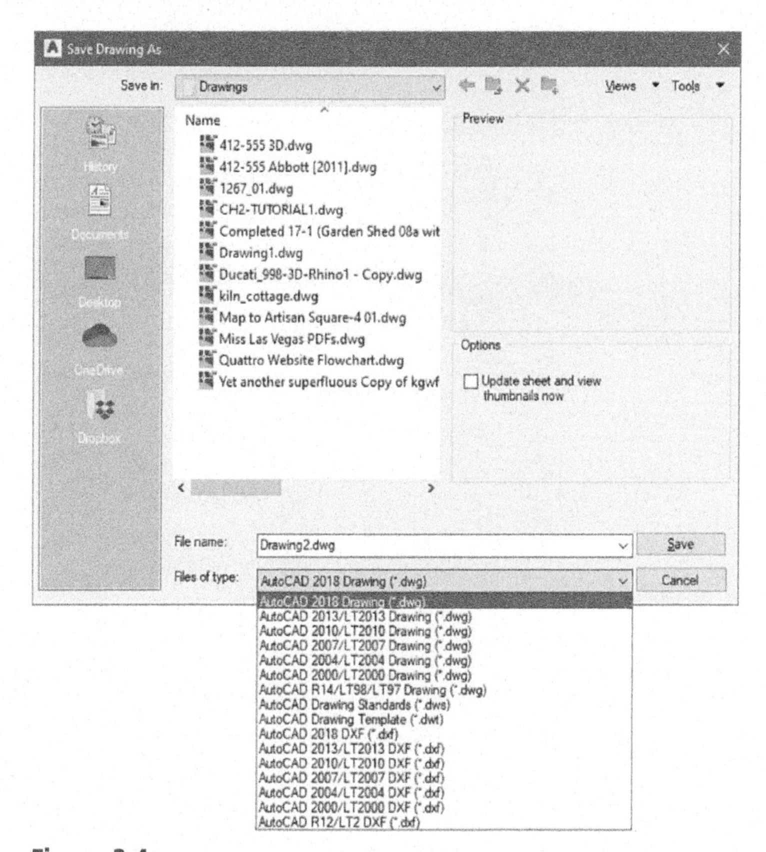

Figure 2-4
Save Drawing As dialog box with file types shown

Some additional features of the **Save As** command are as follows:

- If you use the default drive (the drive on which you are working), and you have opened the drawing from that drive, .dwg and .bak files are created when you have selected the **Create backup copy with each save** check box on the **Open and Save** tab of the **Options** dialog box, as shown in Figure 2-5. To access the **Options** dialog box, type **OP <Enter>**.

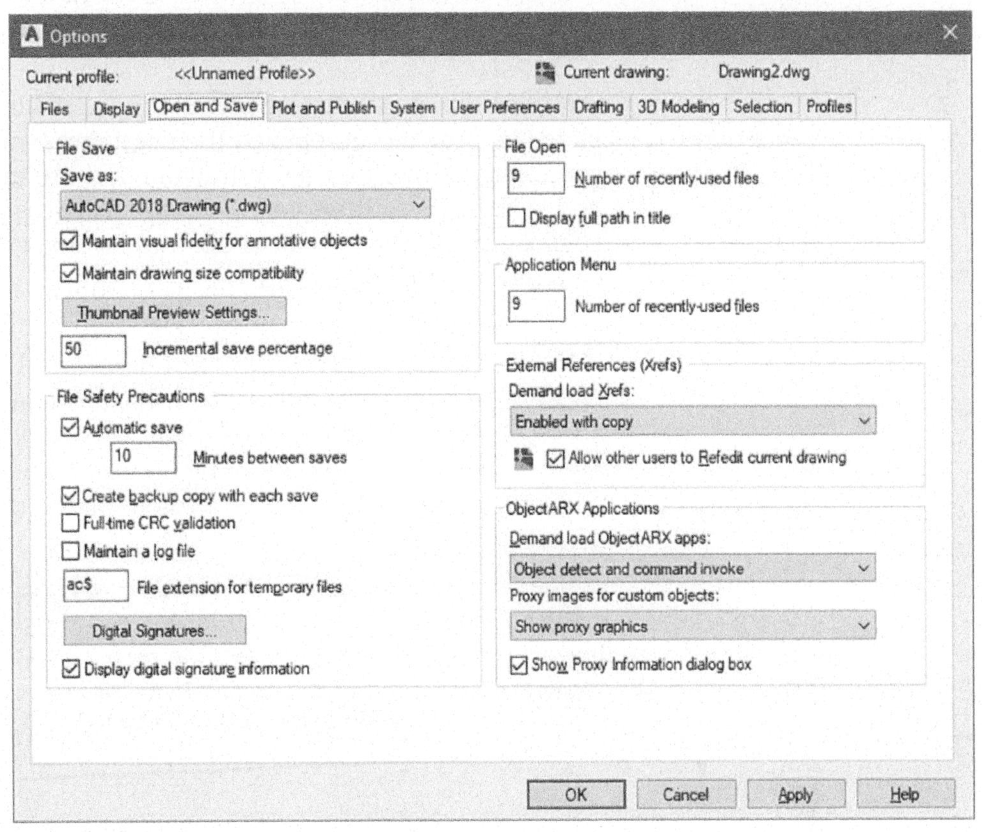

Figure 2-5
Options dialog box, **Open and Save** tab

- If a drive other than the default is specified, only a .dwg file is created.
- To change the name of the drawing, save it under a new name by typing a new name in the **File name:** input box. The drawing is still saved under the original name as well as the new name. You can save the drawing under as many names as you need.
- If the drawing was previously saved, or if a drawing file already exists with the drawing file name you typed, AutoCAD gives you the message *drawing name.dwg already exists. Do you want to replace it?* When you are updating a drawing file, the old .dwg file is replaced with the new drawing, so the answer to click is **Yes**. If you have made an error and do not want to replace the file, click **No**.
- You may save a drawing to as many disks or to as many folders on the hard disk as you want. You should save your drawing in two different places as insurance against catastrophe.

- You can save drawings to an **AutoCAD Web** cloud account. This is where you can store, share, and view your drawings online from any computer, mobile phone, or tablet. **AutoCAD Mobile** is a cloud-based CAD editor from Autodesk that allows you to view, edit, and share your drawings.
- You may save any drawing as another AutoCAD file type (Figure 2-4), as discussed next.

DWT

DWT is a drawing template file. Settings are already established in a template file. Just as you opened the **acad.dwt** template file to start a drawing, you can make settings for a drawing that are unique to your work situation and save those settings as a template file. This saves time, because settings such as units, limits, grid, snap, and layers (which you will learn in this chapter) will already be set.

DWS

DWS is a drawing standards file. It defines standards for layers, dimension styles, linetypes, and text styles. You can associate the standards file with another drawing, check the drawing to see whether the standards differ, and change any differing standards to match the DWS file.

> **NOTE**
>
> AutoCAD automatically names your drawings, using the names **Drawing1, Drawing2,** and so on, if you do not type a name in the **File name:** input box. The name you save the drawing as appears in the AutoCAD title bar.

DXF

DXF is a drawing interchange format file. You use it to share drawing data among other CAD programs. You can open a DXF file, save it as a DWG file, and work with the drawing.

Step 2. Name and save Tutorial 2-1 on the drive and/or folder you want (Figure 2-6), as described next:

Prompt	**Response**
Type a command:	Click **Save** on the **Quick Access Toolbar**
The **Save Drawing As** dialog box appears with the file name highlighted, as shown in Figure 2-6:	Type **CH2-TUTORIAL1** Select the drive and/or folder in which you want to save **CH2-TUTORIAL1** Click **Save**

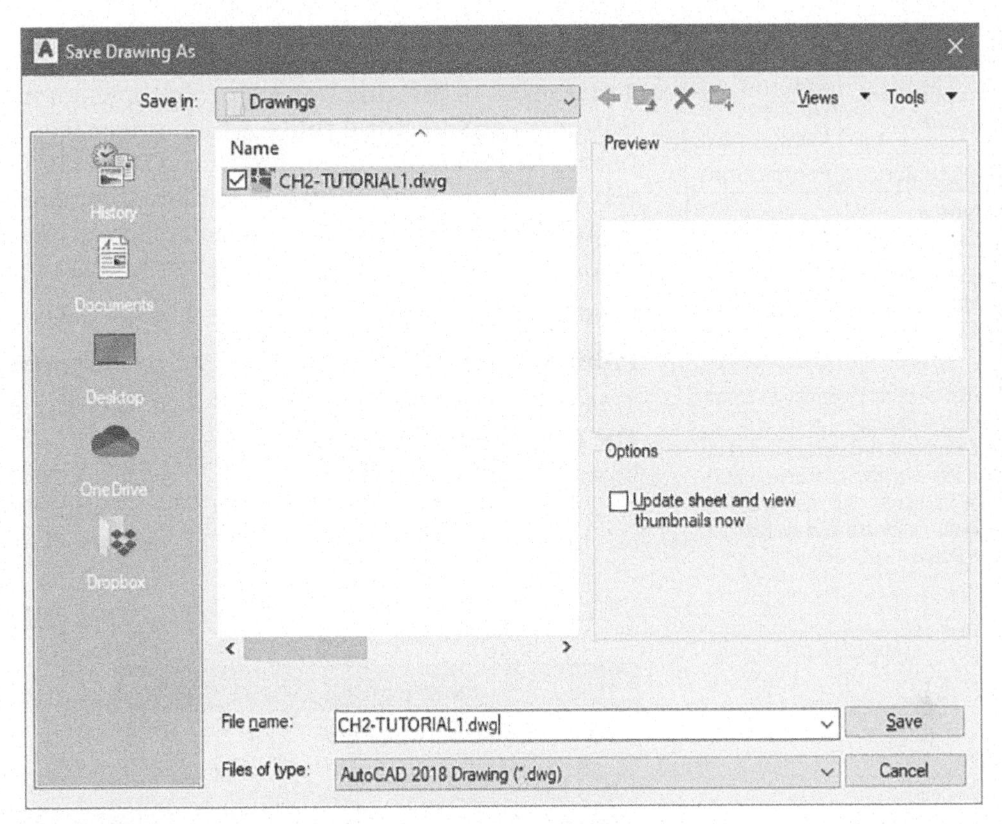

Figure 2-6
Save Drawing As dialog box; save **CH2-TUTORIAL1**

Drawing Name and File Name Extension

The drawing name can be up to 255 characters long and can have spaces. The drawing name cannot have special characters that the AutoCAD or Microsoft Windows programs use for other purposes. The special characters that cannot be used include the less-than and greater-than symbols (<>), forward slashes and backslashes (/ \), backquotes (`), equal signs (=), vertical bars (|), asterisks (*), commas (,), question marks (?), semicolons (;), colons (:), and quotation marks ("). As you continue to learn AutoCAD, other objects will also be named, such as layers. These naming conventions apply to all named objects.

AutoCAD automatically adds the file extension .dwg to the drawing name and .bak to a backup file. The **Files of Type** drop-down below the file name in the **Save Drawing As** dialog box describes the file type.

> **TIP**
>
> If you lose a drawing file, you can rename the drawing's .bak file as a .dwg file and use it as the drawing file. Using Windows Explorer, right-click on the file name and select **Rename** from the menu. Simply keep the name, but change the file extension. If the .dwg file is corrupted, you may give the .bak file a new name and change the extension to .dwg. Don't forget to add the .dwg extension in either case, because *the file will not open without a .dwg extension.*

UNITS	
Application Menu:	Drawing Utilities/ Units
Menu Bar:	Format/Units
Type a Command:	UNITS
Command Alias:	UN

units: A setting referring to drawing units. For example, an inch is a drawing unit. Architectural units utilize feet and fractional units. Decimal, fractional, engineering, and scientific units are also available in the **Drawing Units** dialog box.

Units

Units refers to drawing units. For example, an inch is a drawing unit. In this book, architectural units, which utilize feet and fractional inches, are used. The **Precision:** input box in the **Drawing Units** dialog box allows you to set the smallest fraction to display when showing coordinates and defaults on the screen. There is no reason to change any of the other settings in the **Drawing Units** dialog box at this time.

Step 3. Set drawing units (Figure 2-7), as described next:

Prompt	**Response**
Type a command:	**Units...** (or type **UN <Enter>**)
The **Drawing Units** dialog box appears (Figure 2-7):	Click **Architectural** (for **Type:** under **Length**) Click **0′-0 1/16″** (for **Precision:** under **Length**) Click **OK**

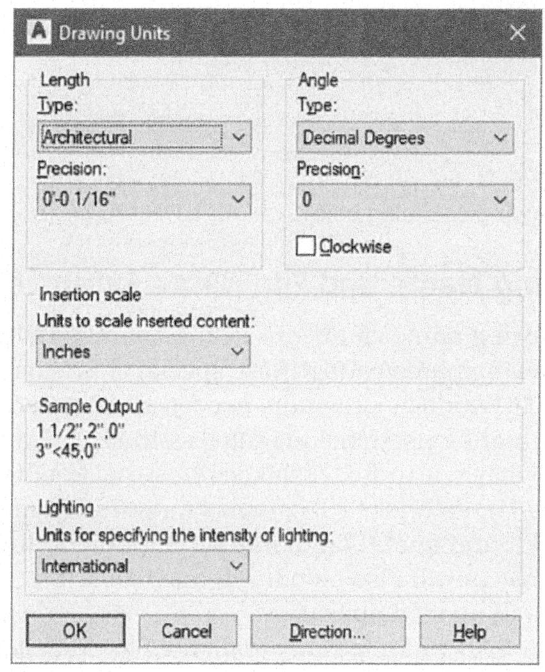

Figure 2-7
Drawing Units dialog box

NOTE

The **Precision:** input box has no bearing on how accurately AutoCAD draws. It allows you to set the smallest fraction to display values shown on the screen, such as coordinates and defaults. No matter what the **Precision:** setting, AutoCAD draws with extreme accuracy.

Controlling Your Drawing

When you begin drawing with AutoCAD, you may perhaps click a tab or drawing tool that you do not need. If you select the **Layout1** or **Layout2** tab at the bottom of your drawing window and are not sure where you are in the drawing, simply select the **Model** tab to return to your drawing. You use the **Layout** tabs for printing or plotting, and they will be described later.

Chapter 2

NOTE

To cancel a command, press **<Esc>** (from the keyboard).

Step 4. Make sure **SNAP** and **GRID** are clicked on in the status bar and that **all other status bar settings** are toggled off.

Drawing Scale

drawing scale: The scale at which drawings are made.

You do not need to set a ***drawing scale*** factor. When using AutoCAD to make drawings, always draw full scale, using real-world feet and inches. You can print or plot full-scale drawings at any scale.

Drawing Limits and the Cartesian Coordinate System

LIMITS	
Menu Bar:	Format/ Drawing Limits
Type a Command:	LIMITS

Drawing limits define the area in which you create your drawing. AutoCAD uses Cartesian (x,y,z) coordinates to locate and identify every object in the drawing space. Limits and coordinates are two of the most fundamental tools in creating drawings.

Step 5. Set drawing limits, as described next:

Prompt	**Response**
Type a command:	Type **LIMITS <Enter>**
Specify lower-left corner or [ON OFF] <0′-0″, 0′-0″>:	**<Enter>**
Specify upper-right corner <1″-0′, 0′-9″>:	Type **8-1/2,11 <Enter>**

TIP

Pressing the space bar is just like pressing the <Enter> key.

drawing limits: The user-defined rectangular area of the drawing covered by lines or dots (when specified) when the grid is on.

Cartesian coordinate system: A coordinate system that has three axes, x, y, and z. The x-axis value is stated first and measures left to right horizontally. The y-axis value is stated second and measures from bottom to top vertically. The z-axis value is stated third and is used in three-dimensional modeling.

Think of ***drawing limits*** as your drawing area, sheet size, or sheet boundaries. This sheet of paper is also called the *workplane*. The workplane is based on a ***Cartesian coordinate system***. A Cartesian coordinate system has three axes, x, y, and z. Here, 8-1/2,11 was set as the drawing limits. In the Cartesian coordinate system, that value is entered as 8-1/2,11 using a comma with no spaces to separate the x- and y-axis coordinates. The x-axis coordinate of a Cartesian coordinate system is stated first (8-1/2) and measures drawing limits from left to right (horizontally). The y-axis coordinate is second (11) and measures drawing limits from bottom to top (vertically). You will be drawing on a vertical 8-1/2″ × 11″ workplane similar to a standard sheet of typing paper. The z-axis is used in 3D.

The lower-left corner, the origin point of the drawing boundaries, is 0,0 and is where the x- and y-axes intersect. The upper-right corner is 8-1/2,11 (Figure 2-8). These are the limits for Tutorial 2-1. To turn the 8-1/2″ × 11″ area horizontally, enter the limits as 11,8-1/2. With units set to Architectural, AutoCAD defaults to inches, so the inch symbol is not required.

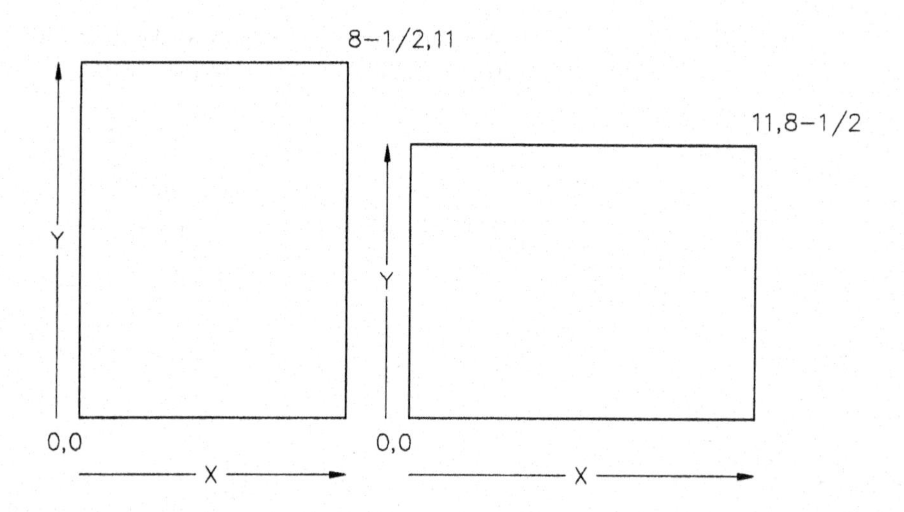

Figure 2-8
Drawing limits

NOTE

The acad.dwt template provides 1′-0″,0′-9″ as the drawing limits for the upper-right corner of the drawing. Remember, to change the upper-right limits, you must type the x-axis coordinate first, a comma, and then the y-axis coordinate second.

The coordinate display numbers in the extreme lower-left corner of the AutoCAD screen tell you where the crosshairs on the screen are located in relation to the 0,0 origin. The coordinate display is off by default. To turn on coordinate display, click **Customization** at the far-right side of the status bar, and then select **Coordinates**. The display updates as you move the cursor.

If you need to change the drawing limits, you may do so at any time by entering new limits to the *Specify upper-right corner:* prompt. Changing the drawing limits will automatically show the grid pattern for the new limits.

Grid

grid: An area consisting of evenly spaced dots or lines to aid drawing. The grid is adjustable. The grid lines or dots do not plot.

The ***grid*** is a visible pattern of lines or dots on the display screen. The grid is not part of the drawing, but it helps in visualizing the size and relationship of the drawing elements. It can also confirm where your limits are. It is never plotted. Pressing function key **<F7>** or **<Ctrl>+G** turns the grid on or off, as does clicking the **GRID** button in the status bar at the bottom of the screen.

GRIDDISPLAY

GRIDDISPLAY is a system variable that controls the grid behavior using the following settings:

0 When **GRIDDISPLAY** is set to **0**, the grid is restricted to the limits that are set. Currently, the limits are set to **8-1/2,11** as shown in Figure 2-9.

1 When **GRIDDISPLAY** is set to **1,** the grid is not restricted to the limits set, as shown in Figure 2-10.

2 This setting turns on the adaptive grid display. That means when you are zoomed out, the density of the grid is limited. To see the difference between a 1″ line zoomed out with **GRIDDISPLAY** set to **0** and **GRIDDISPLAY** set to **2** with **GRID** set to **¼″**, see Figure 2-11.

4 When **GRIDDISPLAY** is set to **4,** the adaptive grid shows additional minor grid lines between the major grid lines.

8 Normally, the grid lies on the drawing plane. When **GRIDDISPLAY** is set to **8,** the grid moves to the x,y plane set by using dynamic UCS to move to the selected 3D surface. Chapter 14 covers Dynamic UCS (DUCS).

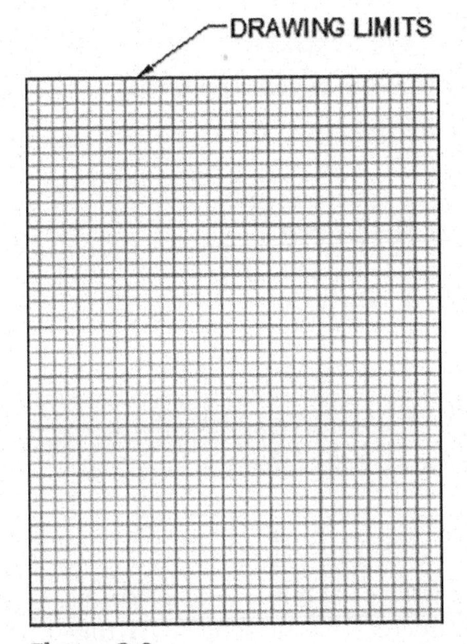

Figure 2-9
GRIDDISPLAY set to **0**

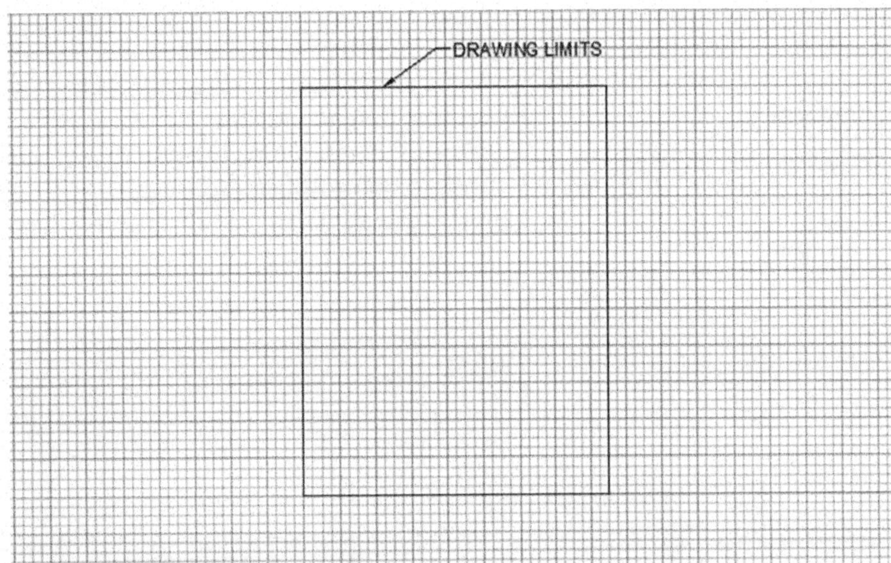

Figure 2-10
GRIDDISPLAY set to **1**

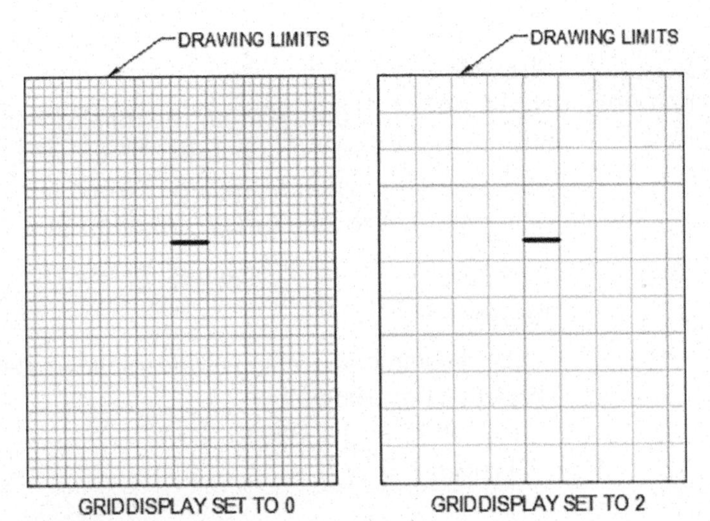

Figure 2-11
Difference between **GRIDDISPLAY** set to **0** and **2** when zoomed out, with **GRID** set to **1/4″**

Step 6. Set **GRIDDISPLAY** to **0** so the grid will be restricted to the area specified by the limits, as described next:

Prompt	Response
Type a command:	Type **GRIDDISPLAY <Enter>**
Enter new value for GRIDDISPLAY <3>:	Type **0 <Enter>**

Step 7. Set the grid spacing, as described next:

GRID	
Menu Bar:	Tools/ Drafting Settings
Keyboard	<F7>
Status Bar:	
Type a Command:	GRID

Prompt	Response
Type a command:	Type **GRID <Enter>**
Specify grid spacing(X) or [ON OFF Snap Major aDaptive Limits Follow Aspect] <0'-0 1/2">:	Type **1/4 <Enter>**
Type a command:	**<Enter>** (to repeat the **GRID** command)
Specify grid spacing(X) or [ON OFF Snap Major aDaptive Limits Follow Aspect] <0'-0 1/4">:	Type **M <Enter>**
Enter the number of grid divisions per major grid line <5>:	Type **4 <Enter>**

You can click the options in the command prompt line. Instead of typing **M** for the option **Major,** *click the option in the command prompt line.*

You have just set a grid spacing of 1/4", where each line is spaced 1/4" vertically and horizontally, with a major grid line every four spaces. By the way, if you see dots for the grid points instead of grid lines, you need to change the system variable **GRIDSTYLE** from **1** to **0** at the command prompt.

Snap

SNAP	
Menu Bar:	Tools/ Drafting Settings
Keyboard	<F9>
Status Bar:	
Type a Command:	SNAP

Snap is an invisible grid on the display screen. When a command is active and you are specifying points, the crosshairs will snap, or lock, to an invisible snap grid when snap is on. When snap is on and points are not being specified, the crosshairs do not snap to a grid.

Step 8. Set the snap spacing, as described next:

Prompt	Response
Type a command:	Type **SN <Enter>**
Specify snap spacing or [ON OFF Aspect Legacy Style Type] <0'-0 1/2">:	Type **1/8 <Enter>**

You have set 1/8" as the snap spacing. With a setting of 1/8", each snap point is spaced 1/8" horizontally and vertically.

Pressing function key **<F9>** or **<Ctrl>+B** turns the snap on or off. The snap can also be turned on or off by selecting either option in response to the prompt *Specify snap spacing or [ON OFF Aspect Style Type]* or by clicking the **SNAP** button at the bottom of the screen. You may turn snap on and off while you are drawing.

Setting the snap spacing the same as the grid spacing or as a fraction of the grid spacing is helpful so the crosshairs snap to every grid point or to every grid point and in between at regular spacings. You can set the snap to snap several times in between the grid points.

Zoom

zoom: The process of moving around the drawing. Zooming in shows you a close-up view of a drawing area. Zooming out shows you a larger viewing area.

Use the **ZOOM** command and its options to change the view of the drawing. **ZOOM** is more fully discussed later in this chapter. Here, you will use the **All** option of the **ZOOM** command.

ZOOM ALL	
Ribbon/ Panel	View/ Navigate/All
Zoom Toolbar:	
Navigation Bar:	
Menu Bar:	View/Zoom/ All
Type a Command:	ZOOM <Enter> ALL<Enter>
Command Alias:	Z<Enter> A<Enter>

Step 9. View the entire drawing area, as described next.

Prompt	Response
Type a command:	**Zoom** (or type **Z <Enter>**)
Specify corner of window, enter a scale factor (nX or nXP), or [All Center Dynamic Extents Previous Scale Window Object] <real time>:	Type **A <Enter>**

The **Zoom-All** command displays the entire drawing limits or extents, whichever is larger. You already know what the limits are by setting the limits of the drawing. Extents is anything you have drawn and may be within or outside your limits. In this instance, **Zoom-All** will provide a view of the drawing limits. With **GRIDDISPLAY** set to **0,** the grid display shows the limits.

Drafting Settings Dialog Box

You can also set snap and grid by using the **Drafting Settings** dialog box (Figure 2-12).

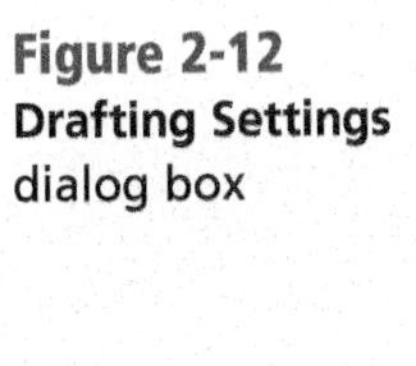

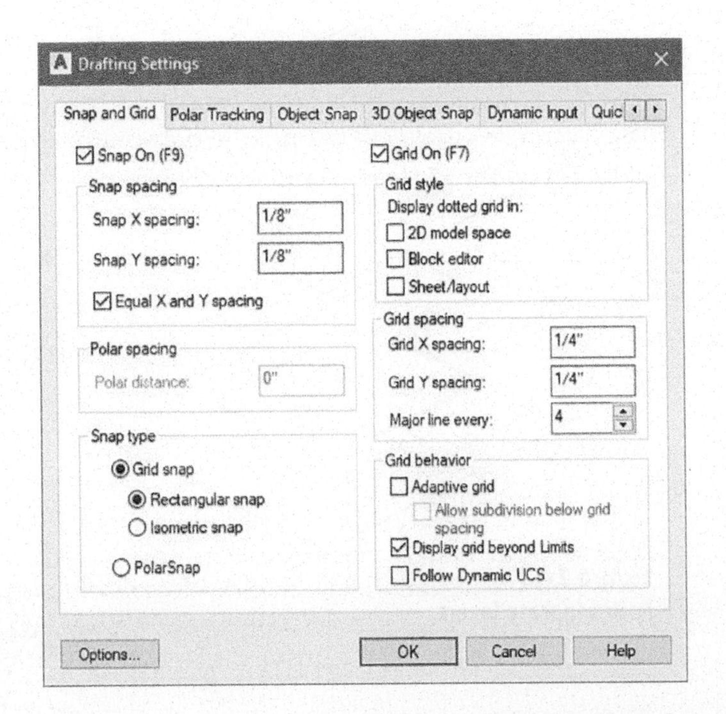

Figure 2-12
Drafting Settings dialog box

To access the **Drafting Settings** dialog box, right-click on **SNAP** or **GRID** in the status bar and click **Snap Settings...** or **Grid Settings...** (or type **DS** for **Drafting Settings** and **<Enter>**). The dialog box is a handy tool to use in setting the snap and grid spacing, but if you are a fair typist, typing these commands from the keyboard is faster.

Layers

layer: A group of drawing objects that are like transparent overlays on a drawing. You can view layers individually or in combination with other layers. Layers can be turned on or off, frozen or thawed, plotted or not plotted, and filtered.

You can place different parts of a project on separate ***layers*** (Figure 2-13). The walls may be on one layer, the fixtures on another, the electrical on a third layer, the furniture on a fourth layer, and so on. No limit exists to the number of layers you may use in a drawing. Each is perfectly aligned with all the others. You may view each layer on the display screen separately, one layer in combination with one or more of the other layers, or all layers together. You may also plot each layer separately or in combination with other layers or plot all layers at the same time. The layer name can be from 1 to 255 characters in length.

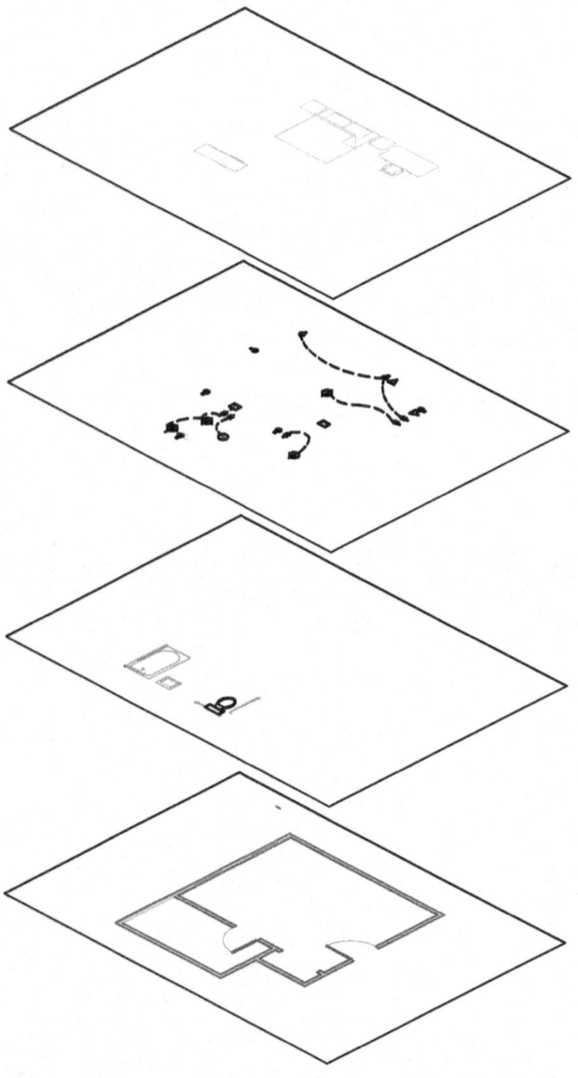

Figure 2-13
Four separate layers

LAYER	
Ribbon/ Panel	Home/ Layers/ Layer Properties
Layers Toolbar:	
Menu Bar:	Layers Toolbar:
Type a Command:	LAYER
Command Alias:	LA

Step 10. Create layers using the **Layer Properties Manager** palette (Figures 2-14 and 2-15), as described next:

Prompt	**Response**
Type a command:	**Layer Properties** (or type **LA <Enter>**)
The **Layer Properties Manager** palette appears:	Click the **New Layer** icon three times (see Figure 2-14)
Layer1, Layer2, Layer3 appear in the **Layer Name** list (Figure 2-15):	Click the box under **Color**, beside **Layer1**

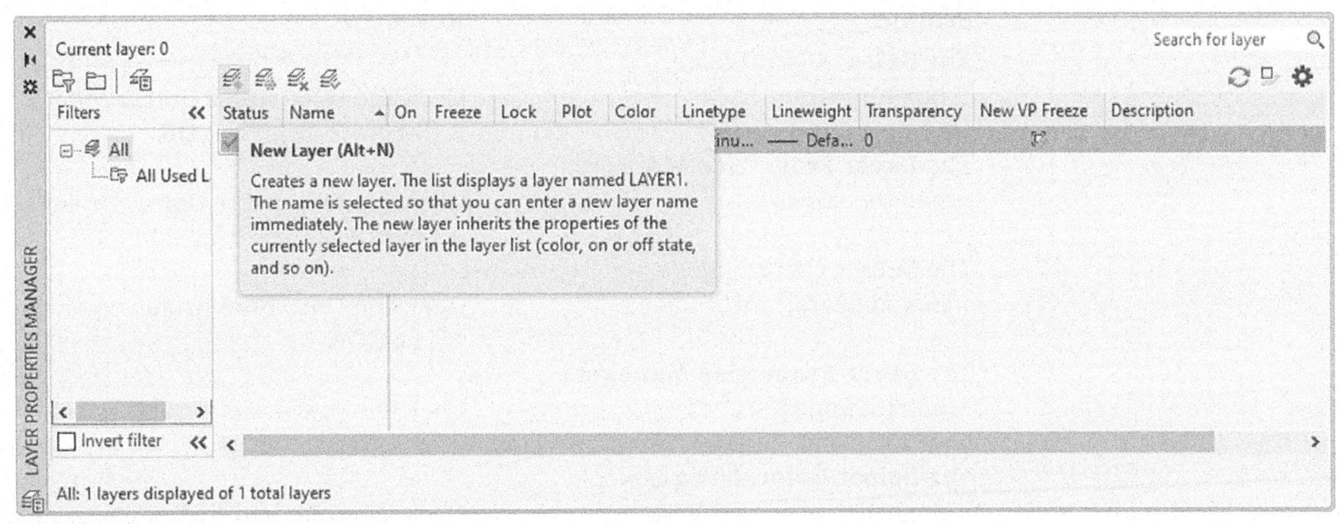

Figure 2-14
Layer Properties Manager palette

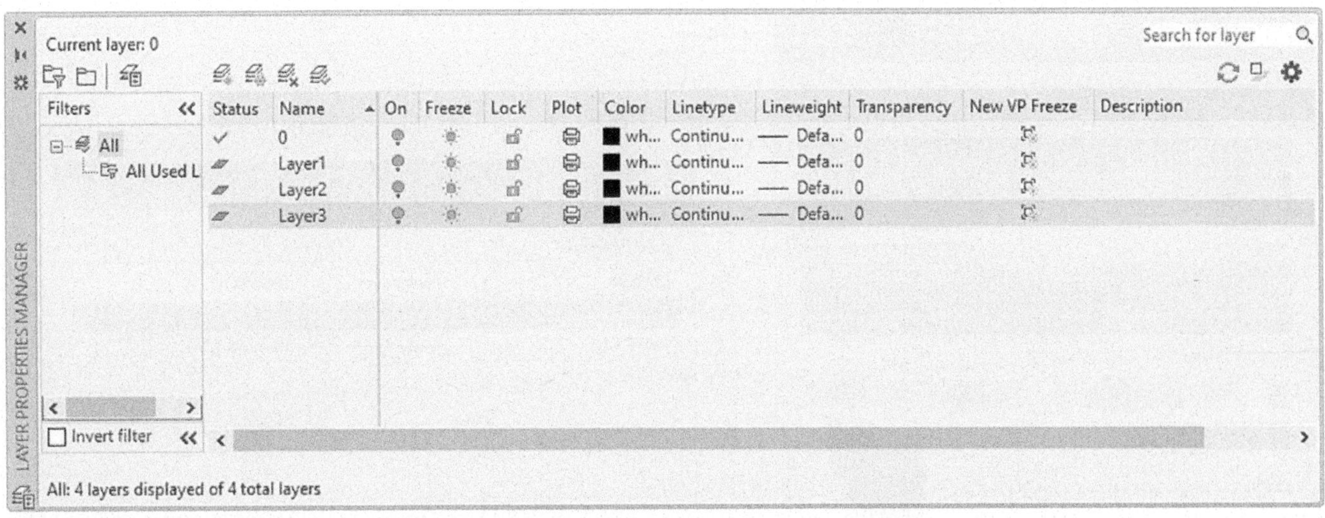

Figure 2-15
Layer1, Layer2, and **Layer3** appear in the **Layer Name** list

> **NOTE**
>
> The standard colors are 1 (red), 2 (yellow), 3 (green), 4 (cyan), 5 (blue), 6 (magenta), and 7 (white or black).

Layer Lists

Layer lists are displayed using natural ordered sort. For example, the layer names 1, 4, 25, 16, 21, 2, 20, 10 are sorted as 1, 2, 4, 10, 16, 20, 21, 25 instead of 1, 10, 16, 2, 20, 21, 25, 4. Natural ordered sort applies to all layer lists, including the Hatch Editor Ribbon tab and Quick Select, just to name a few. You can restore the ASCII sort used in previous releases by changing the new **SORTORDER** system variable to **0**.

Step 11. Assign colors to layers (Figure 2-16), as described next:

Prompt	Response
The **Select Color** dialog box appears:	Click the color **white** (Index color: 7) (Figure 2-16); click **OK**
The **Layer Properties Manager** palette appears:	Click the box under **Color**, beside **Layer2**
The **Select Color** dialog box appears:	Click the color **blue** (Index color: 5); Click **OK**
The **Layer Properties Manager** palette appears:	Click the box under **Color**, beside **Layer3**
The **Select Color** dialog box appears:	Click the color **red** (Index color: 1); Click **OK**

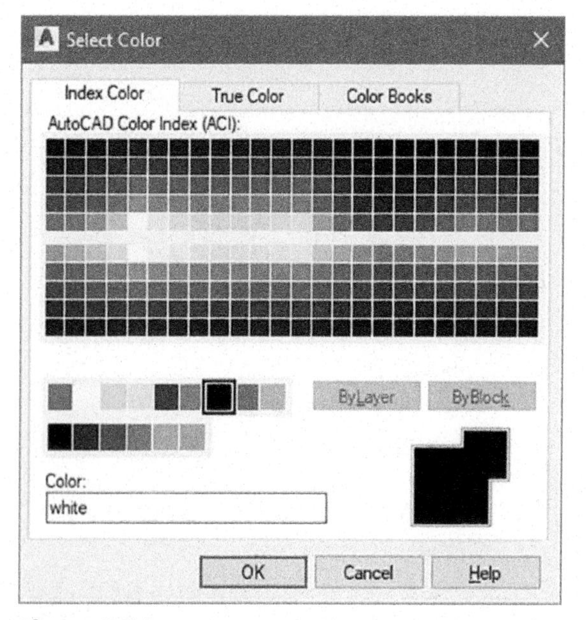

Figure 2-16
Select Color dialog box

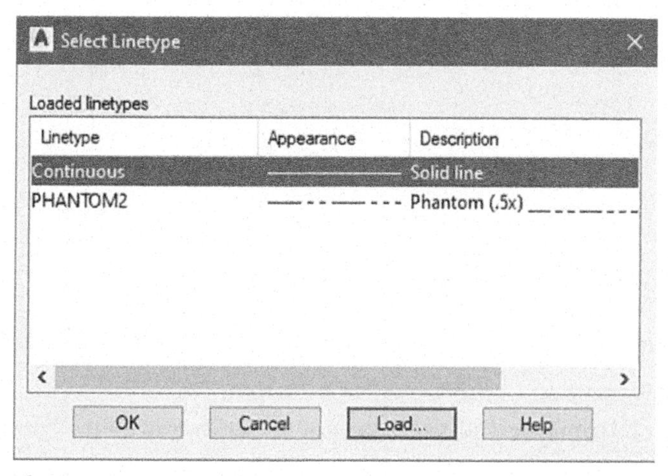

Figure 2-17
Select Linetype dialog box

Step 12. Assign linetypes to layers (Figures 2-17, 2-18, and 2-19), as described next:

Prompt	Response
The **Layer Properties Manager** palette appears:	Click the word **Continuous** under **Linetype**, beside **Layer2**
The **Select Linetype** dialog box appears (Figure 2-17):	Click **Load...** (to load linetypes so they can be selected)
The **Load or Reload Linetypes** dialog box appears:	Scroll down the list of **Available Linetypes** and select **Phantom2**
The **Select Linetype** dialog box reappears:	Click **Phantom2**, and then click **OK**
The **Layer Properties Manager** palette reappears:	Click the word **Phantom2** under **Linetype**, beside **Layer2**
The **Select Linetype** dialog box appears:	Click **Load...**
The **Load or Reload Linetypes** dialog box appears:	Move the mouse to the center of the dialog box and right-click

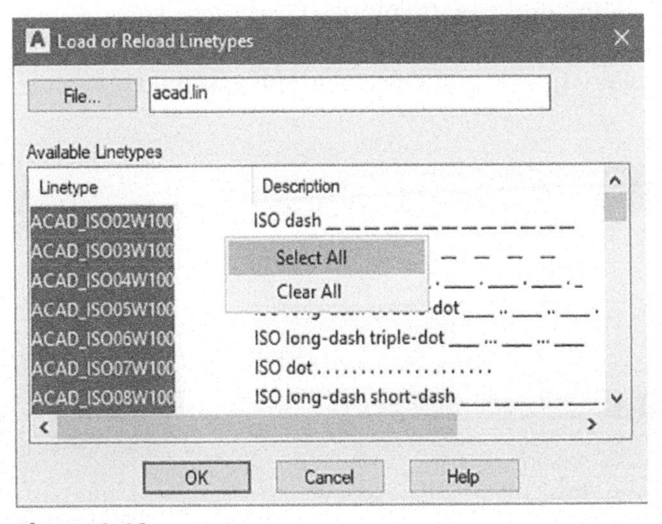

Figure 2-18
Load or Reload Linetypes dialog box

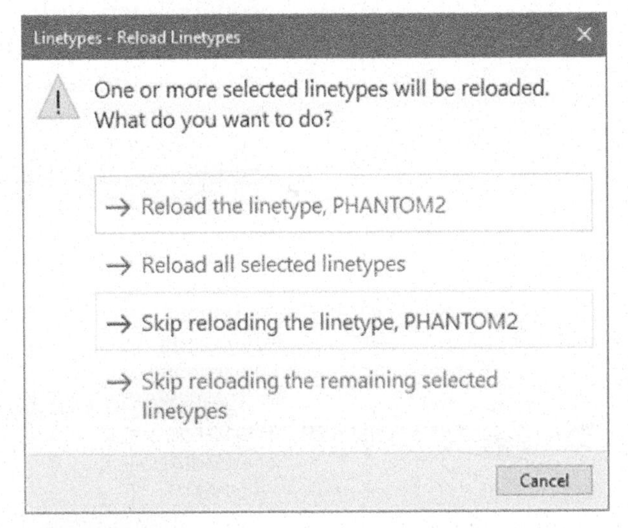

Figure 2-19
Click **Skip reloading the linetype, PHANTOM2.**

Prompt	Response
	Click **Select All** (Figure 2-18)
	Click **OK**
The **Linetypes-Reload Linetypes** dialog box appears:	Click **Skip reloading the linetype, PHANTOM2** (Figure 2-19)

Linetypes

linetype: How a line, arc, polyline, circle, or other item is displayed. For example, a continuous line has a different linetype than a hidden line.

You must load ***linetypes*** before you can select them. You can load individual linetypes, or you can load several by holding down the **<Shift>** key as you select. The AutoCAD library of standard linetypes provides you with three different sizes of each standard linetype other than continuous. For example, the DASHED line has the standard size called **DASHED**, a linetype half the standard size called **DASHED2(.5x)**, and a linetype twice the standard size called **DASHEDX2(2x)**.

Prompt	Response
The **Select Linetype** dialog box appears (Figure 2-20):	Click **DASHED**
	Click **OK**
	Click the close button **(X)** in the upper-left corner of the **Layer Properties Manager** palette

Lineweights

lineweight: A width value that can be assigned to objects such as lines, arcs, polylines, circles, and many other objects that contain features that have width.

Lineweights are expressed in millimeters or inches. The default lineweight initially set for all layers is .25 mm, or .010 inch. Lineweights need to be varied; for example, to show thick lines for walls and thin lines for dimensions, to emphasize something on the drawing, to show existing and new construction, or to show existing and new furniture. Lineweight is an important component for drawing legibility. Lineweights are displayed in pixels on the screen; they plot with the exact width of the assigned lineweight.

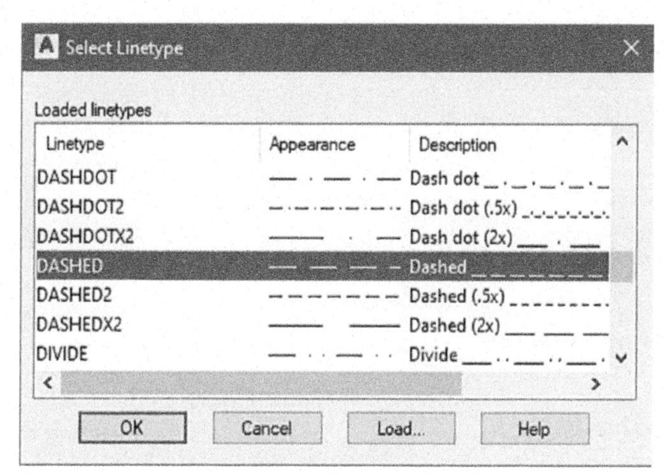

Figure 2-20
Select the **DASHED** linetype

Lineweight Settings Dialog Box

To access the **Lineweight Settings** dialog box (Figure 2-21), enter the **LWEIGHT** command (command alias: **LW**). In this dialog box, you can change the **Units for Listing** from millimeters to inches or reset the default lineweight. You can also adjust the **Model** tab display scale of lineweights by moving the slider to change the scale.

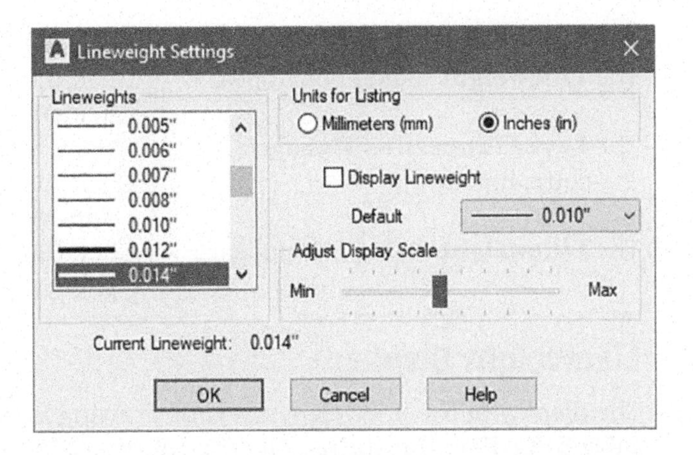

Figure 2-21
Change **Lineweight** settings to inches

Step 13. Set the **Units for Listing** in the **Lineweight Settings** dialog box to **Inches**. The lineweights will read in inches in the **Layer Properties Manager** palette instead of millimeters. If you prefer millimeters, set it to millimeters. Click **OK** to exit the dialog box.

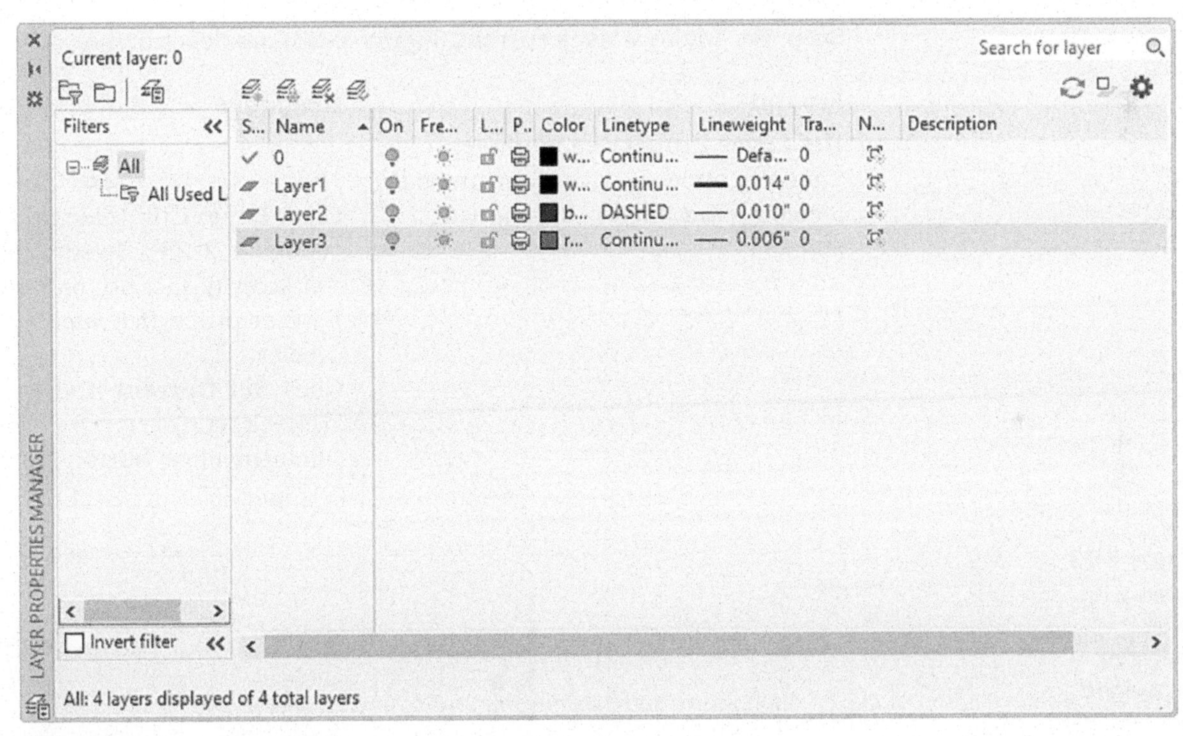

Figure 2-22
Assign lineweights to layers

Step 14. Assign lineweights to layers (Figure 2-22), as described next:

Prompt	**Response**
Type a command:	**Layer Properties** (or type **LA <Enter>**)
The **Layer Properties Manager** palette appears:	Click the word **Default** under **Lineweight**, beside **Layer1**
The **Lineweight** dialog box appears:	Click **0.014″** (.35mm) Click **OK**
The **Layer Properties Manager** palette appears:	Click the word **Default** under **Lineweight**, beside **Layer2**

Prompt	Response
The **Lineweight** dialog box appears:	Click **0.010″** (.25mm) Click **OK**
The **Layer Properties Manager** palette appears:	Click the word **Default** under **Lineweight**, beside **Layer3**
The **Lineweight** dialog box appears:	Click **0.006″** (.15mm) Click **OK**

Lineweight Display

The display of the lineweights in your drawing is controlled by clicking **LWDISPLAY** on the status bar. The **LWDISPLAY** status bar button is turned off by default. Turn it on by clicking **Customization** at the right end of the status bar, and then selecting **LineWeight** from the list. Lineweights are not displayed unless **LWDISPLAY** is on.

Step 15. Turn **LineWeight** on (in the status bar).

Step 16. Make a layer current (Figure 2-23), as described next:

Prompt	Response
The **Layer Properties Manager** palette appears with layer names, colors, and linetypes assigned:	Click **Layer1** (to select it) (Figure 2-23). Be sure to click on a layer name, not on one of the other properties such as lock or color Click **Set Current** (the green check icon) Click the close button **(X)** in the upper-left corner of the palette

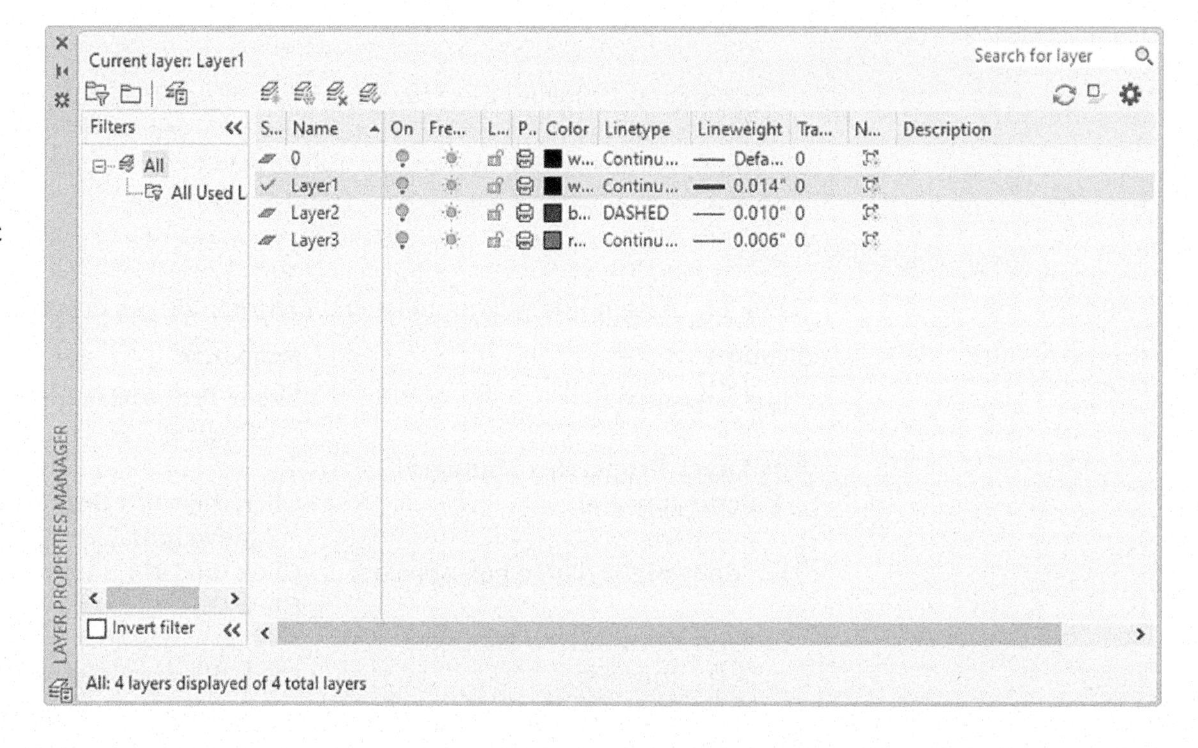

Figure 2-23 Layers with colors, linetypes, lineweights assigned, and Layer1 current

You can also double-click the layer name to set it current. Anything drawn from this point until another layer is set current will be on Layer1.

To change a layer name after using **New Layer** to create layers, click the layer name to highlight it, then slowly left-click the name again in the **Name:** input area, and type over the existing name. You can also click the layer name and then use **Rename** from the right-click menu to rename a layer. You can initially name the layers by clicking **New** and then typing the layer names separated by a comma. When you type the comma, you move to the next layer.

Additional layer control option icons on the **Layer Properties Manager** palette and **Layers** panel of the **Home** tab of the ribbon (Figure 2-24) that can be changed, reading from left to right, are as follows:

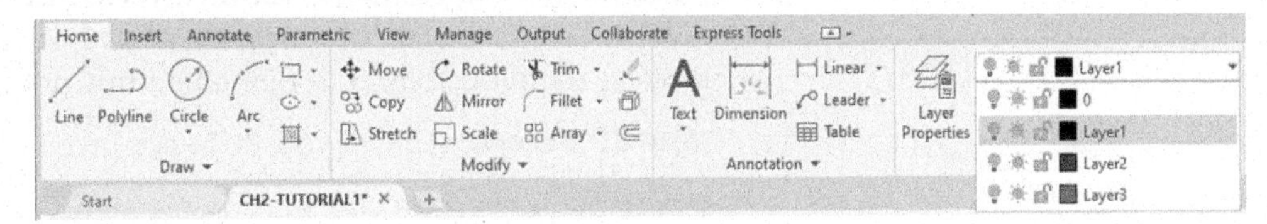

Figure 2-24
Layer status on the **Layers** panel of the **Home** tab of the ribbon

> **NOTE**
>
> When a layer is off or frozen, and it aligns with other layers, it is important not to move objects that align with a frozen or off layer. Objects on the off or frozen layer do not move and will not be aligned with the moved items when you turn on the off layer or thaw the frozen layer. However, when all objects are selected (when you type **ALL <Enter>** to select objects), objects on a layer that is off and thawed will move.

Turn a Layer On or Off for Entire Drawing: This option pertains to the visibility of layers. When a layer is turned off, it is still part of the drawing, but any entity drawn on that layer is not visible on the screen and cannot be plotted. For instance, the building exterior walls layer, interior walls layer, and electrical layer are turned on and all other layers turned off to view, edit, or plot an electrical plan. You can turn one or more layers off and on as required.

Freeze or Thaw a Layer for Entire Drawing: This option also pertains to the visibility of layers. The difference between on/off and freeze/thaw is a matter of how quickly the drawing regenerates on the display screen. If a layer is frozen, it is not visible and cannot be plotted, and AutoCAD spends no time regenerating it. A layer that is turned off is not visible and cannot be plotted, but AutoCAD does regenerate it.

Lock or Unlock a Layer Globally for Entire Drawing: When a layer is locked, it is visible, and you can draw on it. You cannot use any of the **Edit** commands to edit any of the drawing entities on the layer. You cannot accidentally change any entity that is already drawn.

To change the state of any layer, pick the icon to select the alternative state. For example, Figure 2-24 shows that **Layer1** was turned off by picking the lightbulb to turn it off. Additional layer properties that are shown in the **Layer Properties Manager** palette are as follows:

transparency: A setting that makes an object more or less transparent.

Transparency: This option pertains to changing the ***transparency*** versus the opaqueness of objects on a layer. You can enter a transparency value between 0 and 90, inclusive.

Plot Style: Plot styles are created using a plot style table to define various properties such as color, grayscale, and lineweight. A layer's plot style overrides the layer's color, linetype, and lineweight. You use plot styles when you want to plot the same drawing with different settings or different drawings with the same settings.

FOR MORE DETAILS

See Chapter 5 for more on plot styles.

Plot: Allows you to make visible layers nonplottable. For example, you may not want to plot a layer that shows construction lines. When a layer is nonplottable, it is displayed but not plotted.

New VP Freeze: Allows you to freeze layers in a newly created viewport.

Description: Allows you to type a general description of the layer in the area.

If you create some layers that you do not need, delete them by highlighting them and picking the **Delete** icon.

Setting the Annotation Scale

annotation scale: A setting that controls the size of text and other annotative objects on the drawing.

Annotation scale is a setting that controls how text and other annotative objects appear on a drawing. This setting affects annotative objects, such as text and dimensions, that are added to drawings that will be scaled when plotted (for example, scale: 1/4″ = 1′-0″). Each object, such as text or dimensions, *has an annotative property that it must be set to for this setting to apply.*

Step 17. Make sure your annotation scale located in the lower-right corner of the AutoCAD screen is set to the default **1:1** (Figure 2-25).

Figure 2-25
Annotation scale is set to 1:1

Saving the Drawing

As discussed earlier in the chapter, you must save your drawing from time to time. As this drawing has already been saved and named, clicking the **Save** button on the **Quick Access Toolbar**, or entering **Ctrl+S** at the keyboard, invokes the **QSAVE** command.

Step 18. Save the drawing, as described next:

Prompt	Response
Type a command:	**Qsave** (or click the **Save** button on the **Quick Access Toolbar**)
The drawing is saved in the drive and folder selected at the beginning of this exercise.	

NOTE

Make sure you save your drawing often, so you do not lose any of your work.

Using the Mouse and Right-Click Customization

The **Right-Click Customization** dialog box settings control what happens when you click the right mouse button (shown as **<Enter>** in this book). To access the **Right-Click Customization** dialog box, type **OP <Enter>**. Select the **User Preferences** tab of the **Options** dialog box (Figure 2-26). Click the **Right-click Customization...** button in the **Windows Standard Behavior** area, and the **Right-Click Customization** dialog box (Figure 2-27) appears.

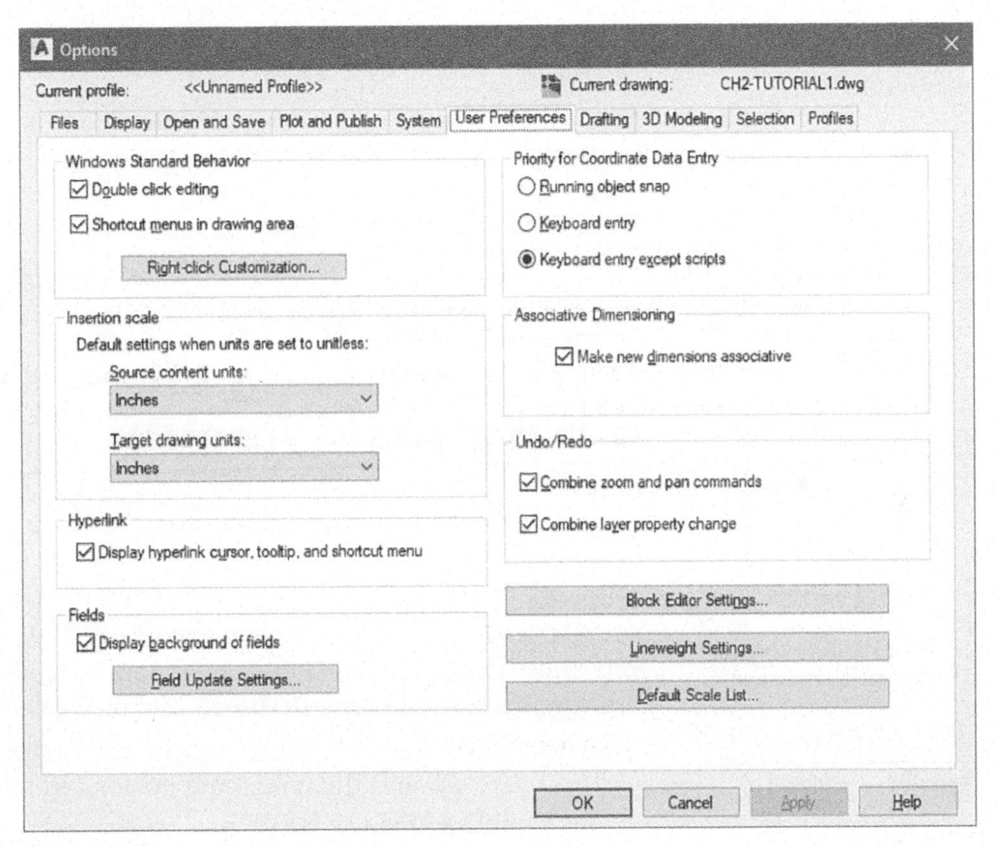

Figure 2-26
Options dialog box with **User Preferences** tab clicked

In the **Response** columns of the exercises, **<Enter>** indicates that you should right-click. Notes in parentheses are used to clarify how **<Enter>** is used; for example, **<Enter>** (to return to the **Line** command prompt). Leave the **Right-Click Customization** dialog box set to the default as shown in Figure 2-27. As you become more familiar with AutoCAD, you may decide to change this setting.

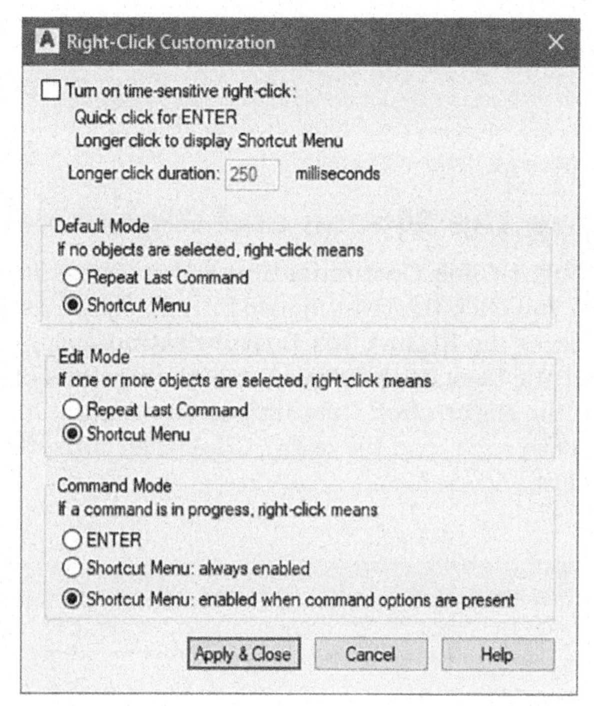

Figure 2-27
Right-Click Customization dialog box

TUTORIAL 2-1
Part 2, Drawing Lines, Circles, Arcs, Ellipses, and Donuts

Ortho

Ortho: A setting that limits pointing device input to horizontal or vertical (relative to the current snap angle and the user coordinate system).

ORTHO MODE	
Keyboard	<F8>
Status Bar:	
Type a Command:	ORTHO

Press the **<F8>** function key to turn ***Ortho*** mode on and off, or click **ORTHOMODE** at the bottom of your screen. **Ortho** mode, when on, helps you draw lines perfectly, horizontally and vertically. It does not allow you to draw at an angle, so turn **Ortho** off and on as needed.

Step 19. Make sure that **SNAP, GRID, ORTHOMODE,** and **LWDISPLAY** are on, and the remaining buttons in the status bar are off. Make sure **Layer1** is current.

Step 20. Complete a **Zoom-All** command to make sure you are looking at the entire 8-1/2″ × 11″ limits of your drawing.

> **TIP**
>
> When **Ortho** mode is on, drawing or editing a drawing part is restricted to horizontal and vertical movements only. Hold down the **<Shift>** key as a temporary override key to turn **ORTHO** off and on. See Appendix B for additional temporary override keys.

LINE	
Ribbon/ Panel	Home/Draw
Draw Toolbar:	
Menu Bar:	Draw/Line
Type a Command:	LINE
Command Alias:	L

Drawing Lines Using the Grid Marks and Snap Increments

Use Figure 2-28 as a guide when locating the lines, squares, and rectangles drawn using the **LINE** command.

Lines can be drawn by snapping to the grid visible on the screen. The snap is set at 1/8″, and the grid is set at 1/4″. The grid provides a visual cue for the snap points that snap on every grid mark and in between every grid mark.

Step 21. Draw a horizontal line 1″ long, using the snap increments and grid marks (Figure 2-28), as described next:

Prompt	**Response**
Type a command:	**Line** (or type **L <Enter>**)
Specify first point:	**P1→** (Do not type "P1." Look at Figure 2-28 and click the point P1→, approximately two grid spaces down (1/2″) and four grid spaces to the right (1″) of the upper-left corner of the page.)

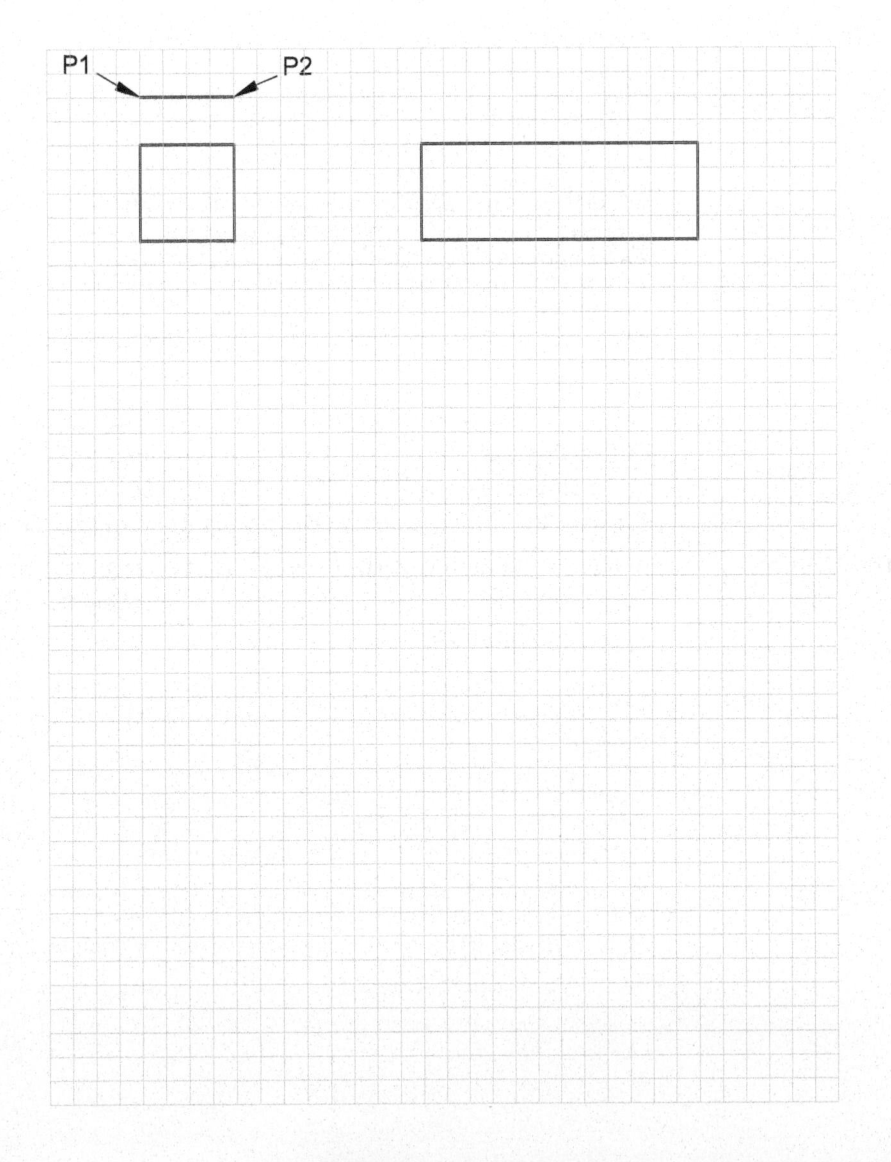

Figure 2-28
Draw a line, a square, and a rectangle

Prompt	Response
Specify next point or [Undo]:	**P2→** (move your cursor four grid marks to the right and click the point **P2→**)
Specify next point or [Undo]:	**<Enter>** When you use a right-click for **<Enter>**, a shortcut menu appears, and you must click **<Enter>** on the shortcut menu to complete the command. When you use the keyboard **<Enter>** key or the space bar, the command is completed, and the shortcut menu does not appear

Erase and Undo

ERASE	
Ribbon/ Panel	Modify/ Erase
Modify Toolbar:	
Menu Bar:	Modify/Erase
Type a Command:	ERASE
Command Alias:	E
Keyboard:	Select, then <Delete>

You can use the **Erase** command to remove objects from your drawing. If you made a mistake, use the **Undo** command to unerase the object. And if you change your mind again, you can use the **Redo** command to restore the deletion.

TIP

You can use the **OOPS** command to unerase the last object that you erased without undoing things that you have done since. **Undo** undoes your last action, whatever it is. So if you erase something, and then move or copy something, and then decide you didn't want to erase the object at all, using **Undo** to delete the object will reverse all the actions you made since you issued **Erase**.

Step 22. Erase the line and bring it back again, as described next:

Prompt	Response
Type a command:	**Erase** (or type **E <Enter>**)
Select objects:	Position the small box that replaces the crosshairs anyplace on the line and click the line
Select objects: 1 found	
Select objects:	**<Enter>** (the line disappears)
Type a command:	Type **U <Enter>** (the line reappears)

NOTE

Use the **Undo** arrow in the **Quick Access** toolbar to reverse the most recent action. Click the arrow to the right of the **Undo** arrow to see a list of actions you can undo. The **Redo** arrow reverses the effect of the **Undo** arrow and has a list of actions you can redo.

Do not be afraid to draw with AutoCAD. If you make a mistake, you can easily erase it using the **ERASE** command. The **UNDO** command will restore everything erased by the **ERASE** command. When you are using the **ERASE** command, a small box replaces the screen crosshairs. The small box is called the *pickbox.*

Step 23. Draw a 1″ square using the snap increments and grid marks and undo the last two lines (Figure 2-29), as described next:

Prompt	**Response**
Type a command:	**Line**
Specify first point:	**P1→** (click a point 1/2″ directly below the left end of the line just drawn)
Specify next point or [Undo]:	**P2→** (Figure 2-29)
Specify next point or [Undo]:	**P3→**
Specify next point or [Close Undo]:	**P4→**
Specify next point or [Close Undo]:	**P5→**

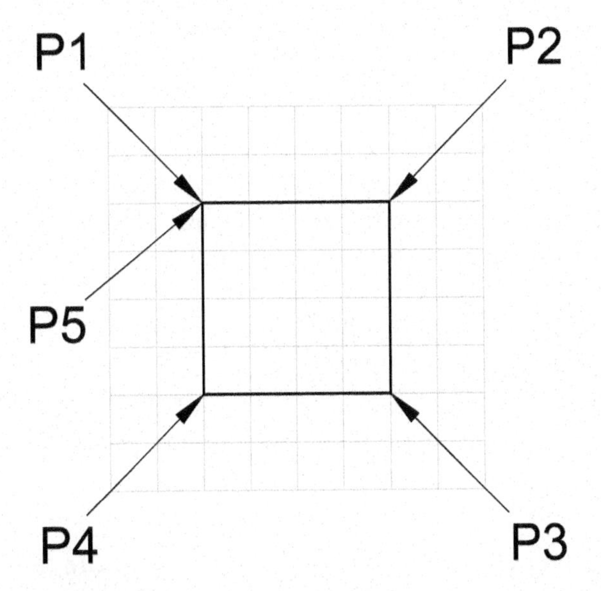

Figure 2-29
Draw a 1″ square using grid marks

Prompt	**Response**
Specify next point or [Close Undo]:	Type **U <Enter>** (move your mouse to see that the line is undone)
Specify next point or [Close Undo]:	Type **U <Enter>**
Specify next point or [Close Undo]:	**<Enter>** (to stop and return to the command prompt)

While in the **LINE** command, if you decide you do not like the last line segment drawn, use the **UNDO** command to erase it and continue on with the *Specify next point or [Close Undo]:* prompt. Clicking more than one undo will backtrack through the line segments in the reverse order in which they were drawn.

Step 24. Complete the square (Figure 2-29), as described next:

Prompt	**Response**
Type a command:	**<Enter>** (to return to the **Line** command prompt)
Specify first point:	**<Enter>** (to see the line attached, turn the grid off and back on)
Specify next point or [Undo]:	**P4→**
Specify next point or [Undo]:	**P5→**
Specify next point or [Close Undo]:	**<Enter>** (to stop)

The **LINE** command has a very handy feature: If you respond to the *Specify first point:* prompt by pressing the **<Enter>** key or the space bar, the line will start at the end of the most recently drawn line.

> **TIP**
>
> Pressing the **<Esc>** key cancels the command selection process and returns AutoCAD to the command prompt. Use **<Esc>** if you get stuck in a command.

Drawing Lines Using Absolute Coordinates

absolute coordinates: Coordinate values measured from an origin point or 0,0 point in the drawing.

Remember, 0,0 is the lower-left corner of the page, the origin point of the Cartesian coordinate system. When you use ***absolute coordinates*** to draw, the x-axis coordinate is entered first and identifies a location on the horizontal axis. The y-axis coordinate is entered second and identifies a location on the vertical axis. The page size is 8-1/2,11. A little adding and subtracting to determine the absolute coordinates will locate the rectangle on the page as follows.

Step 25. Draw a rectangle using absolute coordinates (Figure 2-30), as described next. Remember: **GRID, SNAP, ORTHOMODE,** and **LineWeight** should be on.

Prompt	**Response**
Type a command:	**Line** (move the crosshairs to the center of the screen)
Specify first point:	Type **4,10 <Enter>** (the line begins)
Specify next point or [Undo]:	Type **7,10 <Enter>**
Specify next point or [Undo]:	Type **7,9 <Enter>**
Specify next point or [Close Undo]:	Type **4,9 <Enter>**
Specify next point or [Close Undo]:	Type **C <Enter>**

Step 26. Click on the coordinate display to turn the screen coordinate display on (if needed) and move your pointer to each corner of the square. Watch how the screen coordinate display shows the *x,y* coordinate position of each corner. Compare those coordinates with the coordinates you just typed and entered. They are the same.

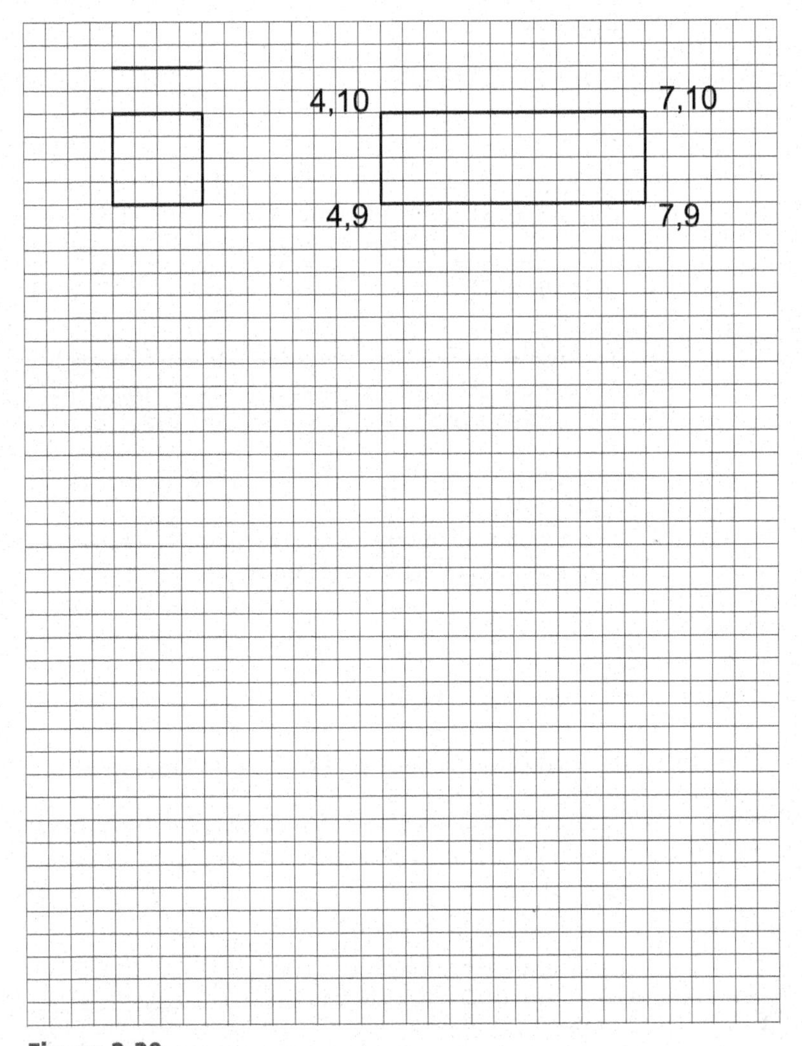

Figure 2-30
Draw a rectangle using absolute coordinates

Drawing Lines Using Relative Coordinates

relative coordinates: Coordinates specified in relation to a previous point picked. Relative coordinates are entered by typing @ followed by the x and y coordinates. For example, after a point is entered to start a line, typing and entering @1,0 will draw the line 1″ in the x direction and 0″ in the y direction.

You use ***relative coordinates*** after a point is entered. (Relative to what? Relative to the point just entered.) After you click a point on the drawing, you enter relative coordinates by typing @, followed by the x,y coordinates. For example, after a point is entered to start a line, typing and entering @1,0 will draw the line from that point 1″ in the x direction, 0″ in the y direction.

Step 27. Set **Layer3** current. Layer3 has a .006″ (.15mm) lineweight.

Step 28. Draw a rectangle using relative coordinates (Figure 2-31), as described next:

Prompt	Response
Type a command:	**Line**
Specify first point:	Click a point on the grid **1/2″** below the lower-left corner of the first square drawn
Specify next point or [Undo]:	Type **@2,0 <Enter>**
Specify next point or [Undo]:	Type **@0,–1 <Enter>**
Specify next point or [Close Undo]:	Type **@–2,0 <Enter>**
Specify next point or [Close Undo]:	Type **C <Enter>**

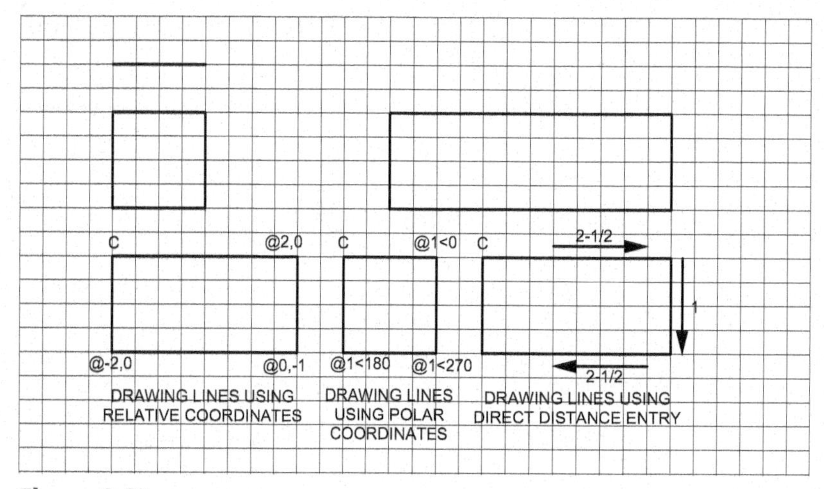

Figure 2-31
Draw a rectangle using relative coordinates, a square using polar coordinates, and a rectangle using direct distance entry

A minus sign (-) is used for negative line location with relative coordinates. Negative is to the left for the x-axis and down for the y-axis.

Drawing Lines Using Polar Coordinates

polar coordinates: Coordinate values that are entered relative to the last point picked. They are typed starting with an @ followed by a distance and angle of direction; the angle is preceded by a < sign.

Absolute and relative coordinates are extremely useful in some situations; however, for many design applications (for example, drawing walls) ***polar coordinates*** or direct distance entry is used. Be sure you understand how to use all types of coordinates.

Polar coordinates are also relative to the last point entered. They are typed starting with an @, followed by a distance and angle of direction. Figure 2-32 shows that the default direction for positive angles is counter-clockwise. The angle of direction is always preceded by a < sign when polar coordinates are entered.

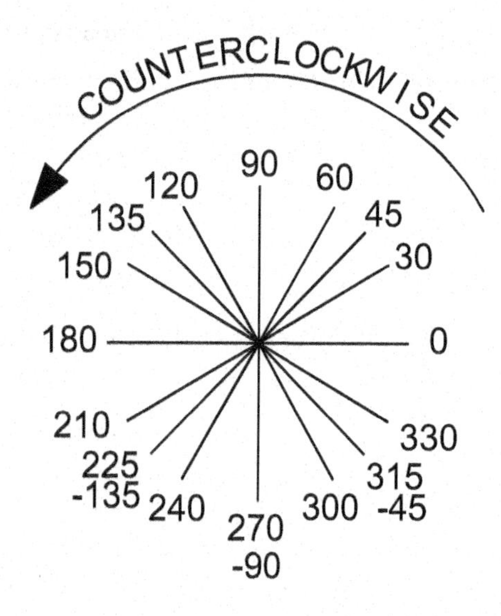

Figure 2-32
Polar coordinate angles

You can change the direction for positive angles to clockwise by selecting the **Clockwise** check box on the **Drawing Units** dialog box. We will use the default counterclockwise direction in this book.

Step 29. Draw a 1″ square using polar coordinates (refer to Figure 2-31), as described next:

Prompt	Response
Type a command:	**<Enter>** (to return to the **Line** command prompt)
Specify first point:	Click a point on the grid **1/2″** to the right of the upper-right corner of the last rectangle drawn
Specify next point or [Undo]:	Type **@1<0 <Enter>**
Specify next point or [Undo]:	Type **@1<270 <Enter>**
Specify next point or [Close Undo]:	Type **@1<180 <Enter>**
Specify next point or [Close Undo]:	Type **C <Enter>**

Chapter 2

Drawing Lines Using Direct Distance Entry

direct distance entry: The process of specifying a second point by first moving the cursor to indicate direction and then entering a distance.

Direct distance entry is a quick, accurate, and easy way to draw lines. It can also be used with any other command that asks you to specify a point. Click on the screen first, then move your mouse in the direction you want to draw, type **the distance**, and press **<Enter>**.

Step 30. Draw a rectangle using direct distance entry (refer to Figure 2-31), as described next:

Prompt	Response
Type a command:	**Line** (with **ORTHO** on)
Specify first point:	Click a point on the grid **1/2″** to the right of the upper-right corner of the square just drawn
Specify next point or [Undo]:	Move your mouse to the right; type **2-1/2 <Enter>**
Specify next point or [Undo]:	Move your mouse down; type **1 <Enter>**

Prompt	Response
Specify next point or [Close Undo]:	Move your mouse to the left; type **2-1/2 <Enter>**
Specify next point or [Close Undo]:	Type **C <Enter>**

TIP

Entering 2.5 is the same as entering 2-1/2. You are still working in inches, and decimal inches are often easier to type than fractional inches.

DYNMODE	
Keyboard:	<F12>
Menu Bar:	Tools/ Drafting Settings
Status Bar:	

DYNMODE

As you gain more experience, you may want to use dynamic input to draw. Click **DYNMODE** at the bottom of your screen to turn dynamic input on and off. When on, **DYNMODE** mode displays three tooltips of command information near your cursor. These are *pointer input, dimension input,* and *dynamic prompts* (for dynamic input settings in the **Drafting Settings** dialog box, see Figure 2-33).

> **NOTE**
>
> You can display the **Dynamic Input** button on the status bar by clicking **Customization** at the right end of the status bar and then clicking on **Dynamic Input**. If you turn **DYNMODE** on by clicking it on the status bar, you will see the dynamic input display attached to the cursor.

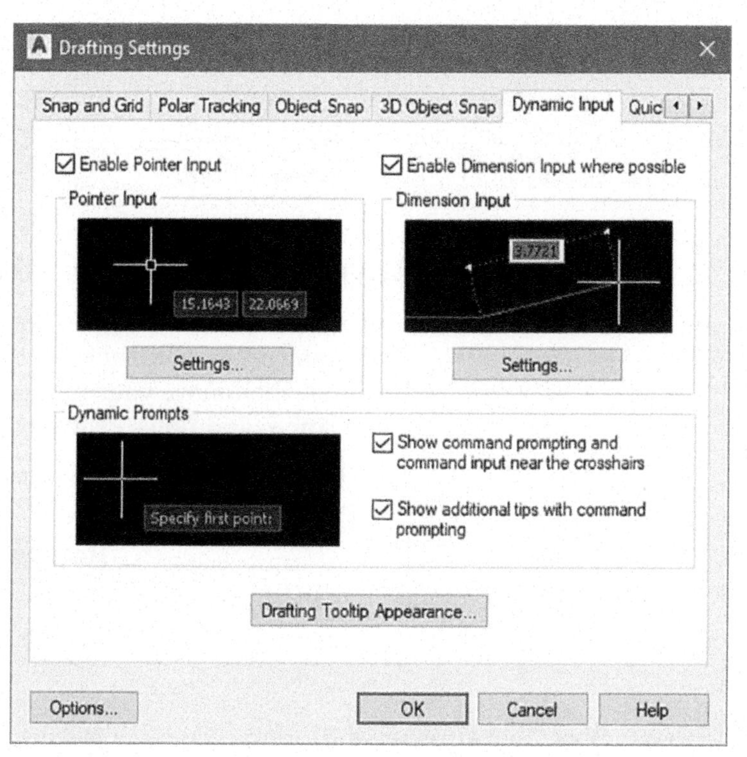

Figure 2-33
Drafting Settings dialog box, **Dynamic Input** tab

When **DYNMODE** is on, you can enter coordinate values into the input fields instead of using the command line. They are entered as follows:

To enter *absolute coordinates*, type the pound sign (#) prefix, type the absolute coordinates, and press **<Enter>** (example: **#4,4 <Enter>**).

Entering *relative coordinates* is the default. To enter relative coordinates, type the relative coordinates without the @ sign and press **<Enter>** (example: **5,3 <Enter>**).

To enter *polar coordinates*, type **the distance from the first point**, press **<Tab>** (to lock the value), type the angle value, and press **<Enter>**.

Right-click **DYNMODE** on the status bar, and then click **Settings...** to access the **Dynamic Input** tab of the **Drafting Settings** dialog box (Figure 2-33). On this tab, you can control the display of the three tooltips near your cursor when **DYNMODE** is on. Hold **<F12>** down to turn **DYN** off temporarily.

CIRCLE	
Ribbon/ Panel	Home/ Draw
Draw Toolbar:	
Menu Bar:	Draw/Circle
Type a Command:	CIRCLE
Command Alias:	C

Circle

In this section, you will add four circles to the shapes in the drawing.

Step 31. Look at Figure 2-34 to determine the approximate location of the four dashed-line circles you will draw.

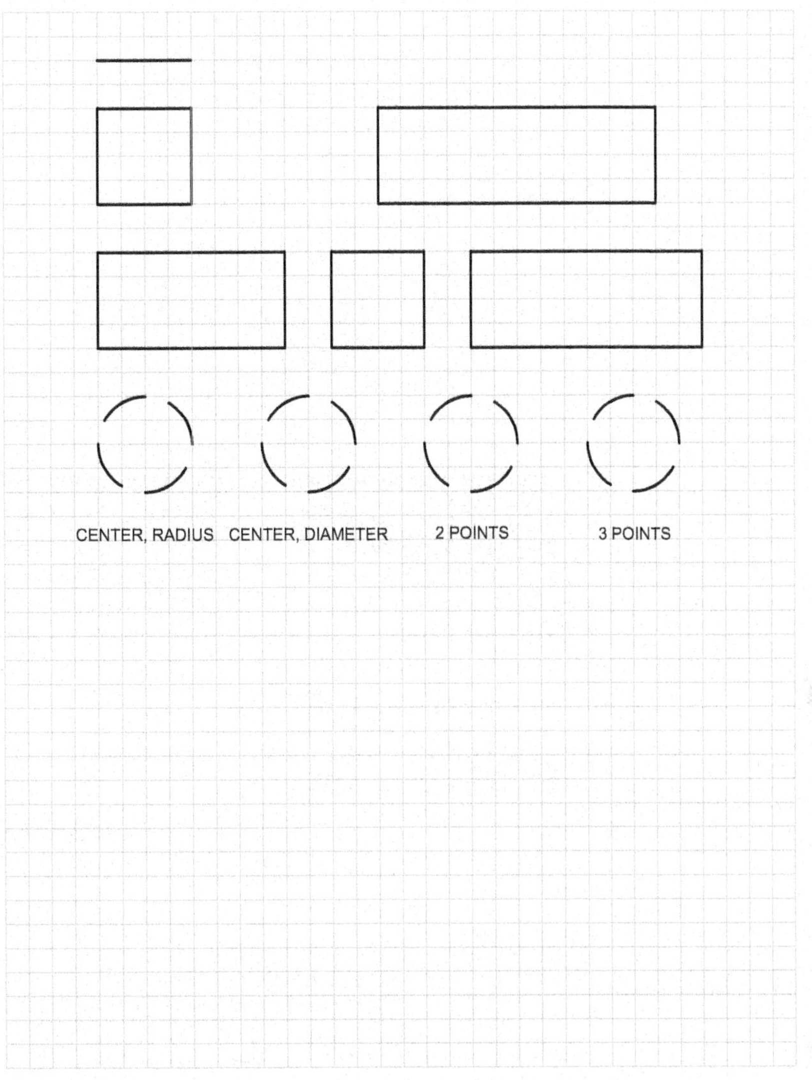

Figure 2-34
The locations of four circles

Step 32. Set **Layer2** current. Layer2 has a dashed linetype.

Step 33. Turn **ORTHO** off; **SNAP**, **GRID**, and **LWT** are on.

Center, Radius

The **Center, Radius** option is the default method of drawing circles. You specify a center point, and then specify a value to define the radius.

Step 34. Draw a circle with a 1/2″ radius (Figure 2-35), as described next:

Prompt	**Response**
Type a command:	**Center, Radius** (or type **C <Enter>**)
Specify center point for circle or [3P 2P Ttr(tan tan radius)]:	**P1→** (Figure 2-35)
Specify radius of circle or [Diameter]:	Type **1/2 <Enter>** (the circle appears)

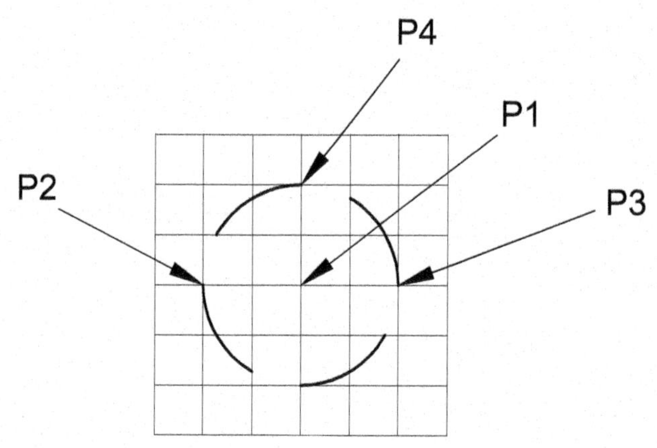

Figure 2-35
Draw the same-size circle using four different methods

Center, Diameter

The **Center, Diameter** option is similar to **Center, Radius**, except that the value you enter after picking the center point becomes the diameter of the circle. Enter **D** to invoke the **Diameter** option, or select the **Circle, Diameter** option from the ribbon.

Step 35. Draw a circle with a 1″ diameter (refer to Figure 2-35), as described next:

Prompt	**Response**
Type a command:	**<Enter>** (to return to the **CIRCLE** command prompt)
Specify center point for circle or [3P 2P Ttr(tan tan radius)]:	**P1→** (Figure 2-35)
Specify radius of circle or [Diameter] <0′-0 1/2″>:	Type **D** **<Enter>** (to specify diameter)
Specify diameter of circle <0′-1″>:	**<Enter>** (the circle appears)

2 Points

You select a center point and enter a value for the previous two options. For the next two options, you define a circle by picking points on its circumference. With the **2 Point** option, the two points you select become the endpoints of the circle's diameter.

Step 36. Draw a 1″-diameter circle by locating the two endpoints of its diameter (Figure 2-35), as described next:

Prompt	**Response**
Type a command:	**2 Point**
Specify center point for circle or [3P 2P Ttr(tan tan radius)]:	Type **2P** **<Enter>**
Specify first endpoint of circle's diameter:	**P2→** (on a grid mark, Figure 2-35)
Specify second endpoint of circle's diameter:	**P3→** (move four grid spaces to the right)

3 Points

When you create a circle using the **3 Point option**, you pick three points on screen, or enter three pairs of x,y coordinates. The circle is drawn through the three points.

Step 37. Draw a 1″-diameter circle by clicking three points on its circumference (Figure 2-35), as described next:

Prompt	Response
Type a command:	**3 Point**
Specify center point for circle or [3P 2P Ttr(tan tan radius)]:	Type **3P <Enter>**
Specify first point on circle:	**P2→** (Figure 2-35)
Specify second point on circle:	**P3→** (move four grid spaces to the right)
Specify third point on circle:	**P4→** (the center of the top of the circle)

You have just learned four different methods of drawing the same-size circle. You can watch the size of the circle change on the screen by moving the pointer, and you can select the desired size by clicking the point that indicates the size.

TTR

The final option of the **CIRCLE** command is **Tan, Tan, Radius**. This stands for tangent, tangent, and radius. A tangent touches a circle at a single point. For example, you can draw a circle that's tangent to two lines by using the **TANgent** object snap and selecting the lines, and then specifying a radius value.

LTSCALE

AutoCAD provides a variety of linetypes that you may use. For example, the DASHED linetype provided by AutoCAD consists of 1/2″ line segments with 1/4″ spaces in between. The given line segment length (1/2″) and spacing (1/4″) for the DASHED linetype are drawn when the global linetype scale factor is set to 1 (the default).

To make the line segment length or spacing smaller, enter a linetype scale factor smaller than 1 but larger than 0 at the **LTSCALE** prompt. To make the line segment length and spacing larger, enter a linetype scale factor larger than 1. Look closely to see the circle's DASHED linetype scale change when the following is entered.

LTSCALE	
Type a Command:	LTSCALE
Command Alias:	LTS

Step 38. Use **LTSCALE** to change the size of the DASHED linetype, as described next:

Prompt	Response
Type a command:	Type **LTSCALE <Enter>**
Enter new linetype scale factor <1.0000>:	Type **1/2 <Enter>**
Regenerating model.	

ZOOM

The most commonly used **ZOOM** commands (**Window**, **All**, **Previous**, **Extents**, and **Realtime**) help you control how you view the drawing area on the display screen. While drawing the lines and circles for this chapter, you have been able to view the entire 8-1/2″ × 11″ drawing limits on the screen. You used the **Zoom-All** command earlier to ensure that view. The **ZOOM** commands are located on the navigation bar and the ribbon (Figure 2-36).

Zoom-Window

The **Zoom-Window** command allows you to pick two opposite corners of a rectangular window on the screen. The cursor changes to form a rubber band that shows the size of the window on the screen. The size of the window is controlled by the movement of the mouse. The part of the drawing inside the windowed area is magnified to fill the screen when the second corner of the window is clicked.

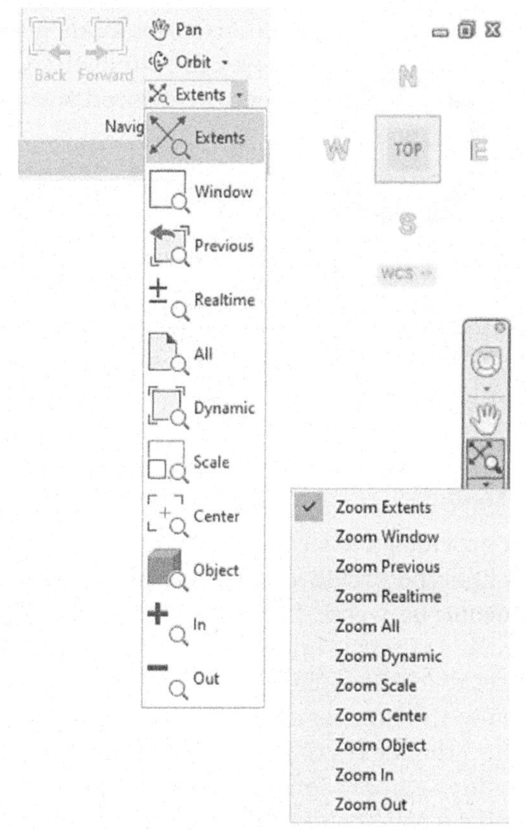

Figure 2-36
ZOOM commands on the ribbon (left) and the navigation bar (right)

> **NOTE**
>
> The **Navigate** panel of the ribbon's **View** tab is not displayed by default. To display it, click the **View** tab to make it current, and then right-click in the empty gray area at the right end of the ribbon. On the pop-up menu, hover over **Show Panels**, and then select **Navigate** to turn it on.

Step 39. Use **Zoom-Window** to look more closely at the four circles (Figure 2-37), as described next:

Prompt	**Response**
Type a command:	Type **Z <Enter>**
Specify corner of window, enter a scale factor (nX or nXP), or [All Center Dynamic Extents Previous Scale Window Object] <real time>:	**P1→** (lower-left corner of the window, Figure 2-37)
Specify opposite corner:	**P2→** (upper-right corner of the window)

Zoom-All

Now that you have a windowed area of the drawing, how do you return to the entire drawing view? The drawing extents include whatever graphics are actually drawn on the page. If only half of the page is full of graphics, the extents will take up half of the page. Sometimes, graphics are drawn outside the limits; this, too, is considered the drawing extents. The limits of the drawing are set with the **Limits** command. *The* **Zoom-All** *command displays the entire drawing limits or extents, whichever is larger.* In this instance, **Zoom-All** will provide a view of the drawing limits.

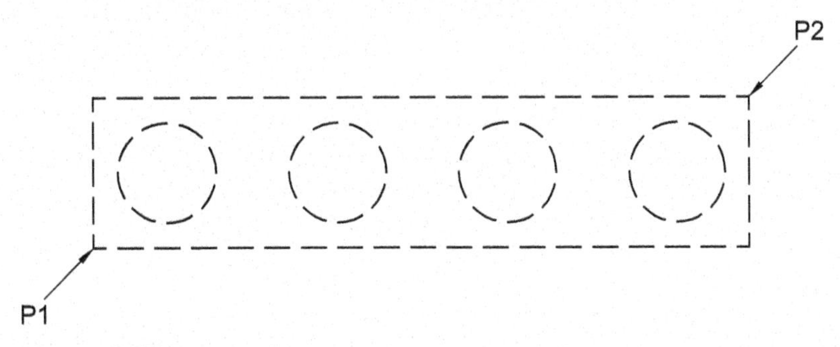

Figure 2-37
Use **Zoom-Window**

Step 40. Use **Zoom-All** to view the entire drawing, as described next:

Prompt	**Response**
Type a command:	**Zoom-All** (or type **Z <Enter>**)
Specify corner of window, enter a scale factor (nX or nXP), or [All Center Dynamic Extents Previous Scale Window Object] <real time>:	Type **A <Enter>**

Zoom-Previous

Zoom-Previous is a very convenient feature. AutoCAD remembers up to 10 previous views. This is especially helpful and saves time if you are working on a complicated drawing.

Step 41. Use **Zoom-Previous** to see the last view of the tangent circles again, as described next:

Prompt	Response
Type a command:	**<Enter>** (to repeat the **ZOOM** command)
Specify corner of window, enter a scale factor (nX or nXP), or [All Center Dynamic Extents Previous Scale Window Object] <real time>:	Type **P <Enter>**

Zoom-Extents

The extents of a drawing include whatever graphics are actually drawn on the page. The **Zoom-Extents** command provides a view of all drawing entities on the page as large as possible to fill the screen.

Step 42. Use **Zoom-Extents** to view the extents of drawing **CH2-TUTORIAL1**.

Zoom-Object

Zoom-Object allows you to select an object or objects and press **<Enter>** to describe the area that will be displayed.

Zoom-Realtime

Press **<Enter>** at the **Zoom** prompt to activate **Zoom-Realtime**. After activating the command, to zoom in or out, hold down the left mouse button and move the mouse up or down to change the magnification of the drawing. Press the right mouse button to access a shortened **Zoom** and **Pan** menu. Click **Exit** or press **<Esc>** to exit the command.

Wheel Mouse. You can also zoom in and out by turning the wheel of a two-button mouse.

PAN	
Ribbon/ Panel	View/ Navigate
Navigation Bar:	
Menu Bar:	View/Pan
Type a Command:	PAN
Command Alias:	P

PAN REALTIME

The **Pan Realtime** command is located on the navigation bar and on the ribbon. **Pan** allows you to maintain the current display magnification and see parts of the drawing that may be off the screen and not visible in the display. Like panning with a camera, **Pan** does not change the magnification of the view.

You may also type **P <Enter>** to activate this command. To move the view of your drawing at the same magnification, hold down the left button on your mouse and move the mouse in any direction to change the view of your drawing.

Wheel Mouse. If you have a wheel mouse, you can pan by pressing down on the wheel and moving the mouse.

Transparent Commands

transparent command: A command that can be used while another command is in progress.

You can use a ***transparent command*** while another command is in progress. Being able to change the display while a command such as **Line** is in progress is convenient. All the **ZOOM** commands and the **PAN** command

REDRAW	
Keyboard:	<F7>
Menu Bar:	View/ Redraw
Type a Command:	REDRAW
Command Alias:	R

REGEN	
Menu Bar:	View/ Regen
Type a Command:	REGEN
Command Alias:	RE

from the navigation bar and the ribbon may be used transparently; you can simply click them.

Commands that do *not* select objects, create new objects, or end the drawing session also usually can be used transparently. You can use the grid and snap settings transparently. After you have entered a command such as **Line**, you can type **'CAL <Enter>** to start the calculator command transparently, type **'P <Enter>** to start the **PAN** command, or type **'grid** to change the grid setting. An apostrophe (') must precede the command name. The >> preceding the command prompt in the command line window indicates the command is being used transparently.

REDRAW

When you pick **Redraw** from the **View** menu or type **R <Enter>**, AutoCAD redraws and cleans up your drawing. Drawing entities affected by editing of other objects are redrawn. Pressing function key **<F7>** twice turns the grid off and on and also redraws the screen.

REGEN

When you click **Regen** from the **View** menu, AutoCAD regenerates the entire drawing.

TIP

Sometimes when you are viewing an entire page and zoom in on a circle, it will be made of small linear segments. When the magnification of the circle was enlarged, to save time AutoCAD did not regenerate the drawing. When the entire page is displayed, fewer linear segments are used to make up the circle. When you type and enter **Regen**, AutoCAD regenerates the circle, making the circle smoother for the larger magnification.

HIGHLIGHT

When you select any object such as a circle or line to erase or move or otherwise modify, the circle or line is highlighted. This highlighting is controlled by the **HIGHLIGHT** system variable. When you type **HIGHLIGHT <Enter>**, the **HIGHLIGHT** command has two responses: enter **1** to turn highlighting on, or **0** to turn highlighting off. You will need to have this variable on so the items selected are confirmed by the highlighting.

Move and Editing Commands Selection Set

MOVE	
Ribbon/ Panel	Home/ Modify
Modify Toolbar:	Move
Menu Bar:	Modify/ Move
Type a Command:	MOVE
Command Alias:	M

You may want to move some of the items on your page to improve the layout of the page. The **MOVE** command allows you to do that.

Step 43. Set **Layer1** current.

Step 44. Use **Zoom-All** to view the entire drawing. Use **Zoom-Realtime** as needed to draw the circles in the next step.

Step 45. Draw a row of four 1/2″-diameter circles, 1″ on center (1″ from the center of one circle to the center of the next circle), as shown in Figure 2-38.

Step 46. Pick **Move** from the ribbon (or type **M <Enter>**).

Step 47. Select a circle by clicking a point on the circle, and move it (Figure 2-39), as described next:

Prompt	**Response**
Select objects:	**P1→** (any point on the circumference of the circle, as shown in Figure 2-39)
Select objects: 1 found Select objects:	**<Enter>** (you have completed selecting objects)
Specify base point or [Displacement] <Displacement>:	**P2→** (the center of the circle—be sure **SNAP** is on)
Specify second point or <use first point as displacement>:	Click a point three grid spaces (3/4″) to the right or with **ORTHO** on, move your mouse to the right; type **3/4 <Enter>**

NOTE

Keep **SNAP** on while moving a drawing entity. Snap from one grid point (base point or displacement) to another (second point).

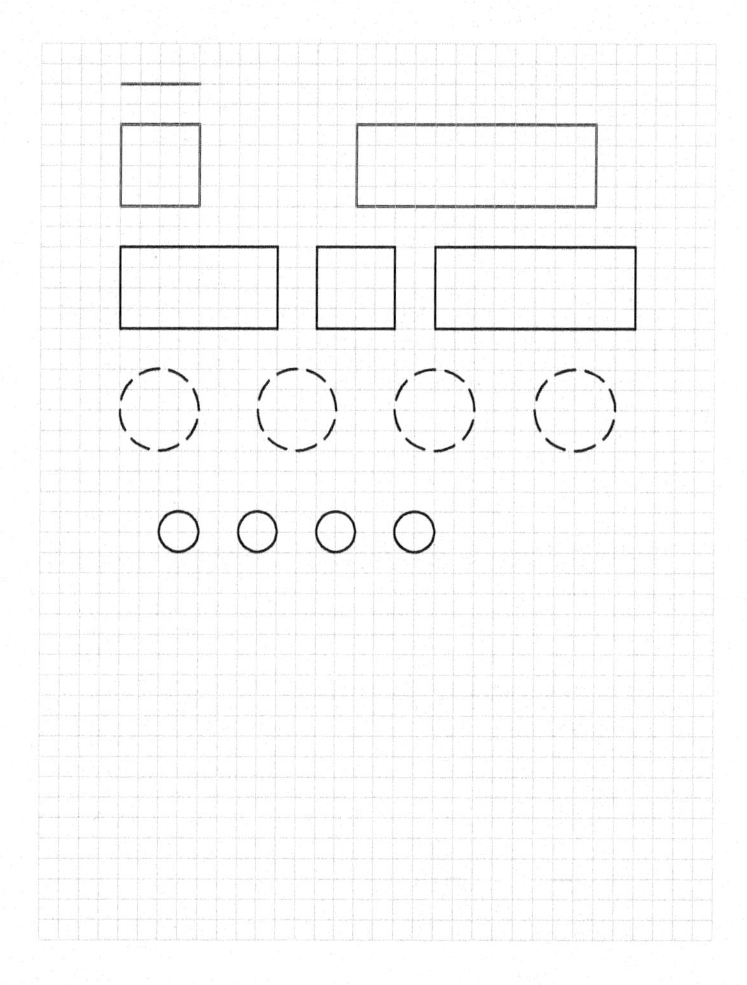

Figure 2-38
Draw a row of four 1/2″-diameter circles, 1″ on center

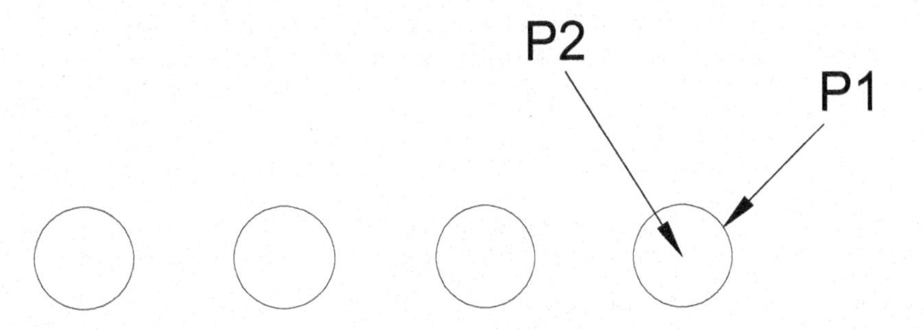

Figure 2-39
Select a circle by clicking a point on the circle, and then move it

Step 48. Select a circle by clicking a point on the circle, and move it using relative coordinates (Figure 2-40), as described next:

Prompt	Response
Type a command:	**<Enter>** (to repeat the **Move** command prompt)
Select objects:	**P1→** (Figure 2-40)
Select objects: 1 found	
Select objects:	**<Enter>**

Figure 2-40
Select a circle by clicking a point on the circle, and move it using relative coordinates

Prompt	Response
Specify base point or [Displacement] <Displacement>:	**P2→** (the center of the circle)
Specify second point or <use first point as displacement>:	Type **@–3/4,0 <Enter>**

NOTE

When you use the **MOVE** command, the base point can be anyplace on the drawing if you give a specific direction and distance for the second point.

You can give the second point of displacement by clicking a point on the screen or by using absolute, relative, or polar coordinates, or direct distance entry.

Step 49. Select items to be edited by using a window, and then remove an item from the selection set (Figure 2-41), as described next:

Prompt	Response
Type a command:	**<Enter>** (to repeat the **Move** command prompt)
Select objects:	**P1→** (Figure 2-41)
Specify opposite corner: 4 found	**P2→**
Select objects:	Type **R** **<Enter>** (or hold down the **<Shift>** key)
Remove objects:	**P3→**

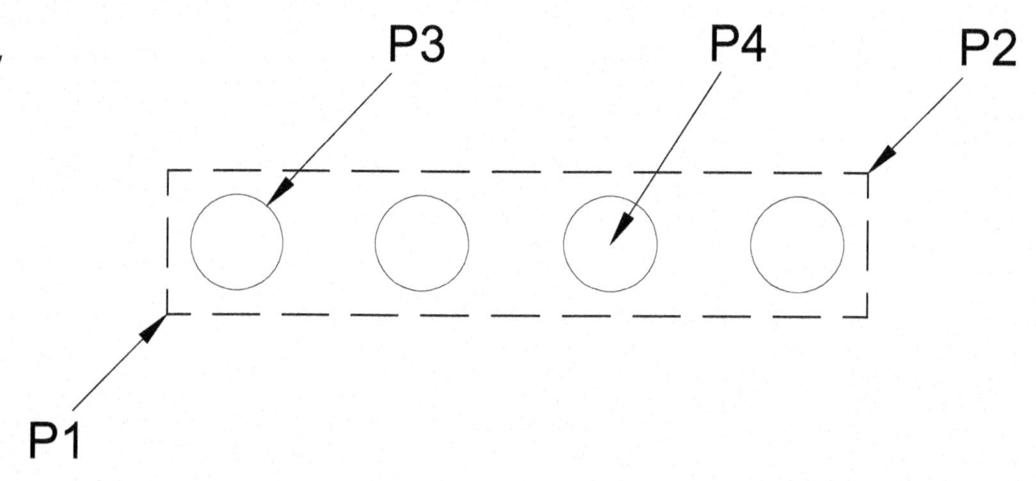

Figure 2-41
Select items to be edited by using a window, and then remove an item from the selection set

Prompt	Response
Remove objects:	**<Enter>**
Specify base point or [Displacement] <Displacement>:	**P4→** (the center of the circle or anyplace on the drawing)
Specify second point or <use first point as displacement>:	With **ORTHO** on, move your mouse down; type **1/2** **<Enter>**

Options for Selecting Objects to Modify

After you pick **Move**, the prompt in the prompt line asks you to *Select objects:*. Also, a pickbox replaces the screen crosshairs. The pickbox helps you select the item or group of items to be moved by positioning the pickbox on the item. The item or group of items selected is called the *selection set*. Many of the AutoCAD **Modify** commands provide the same prompt, the pickbox, and also the same options used to select the object or objects to be edited. To view all the options used to select an object or objects, type and enter a **?** at the *Select objects:* prompt. The options are Window/Last/Crossing/Box/All/Fence/WPolygon/Cpolygon/Group/Add/Remove/Multiple/Previous/Undo/AUto/SIngle/Subobject/Object. We will cover some of the more commonly used options used to select objects.

Window (W) and Crossing Window (C)

The window selection (picking left to right) and crossing window selection (picking right to left) options allow you to pick two opposite corners of a rectangular window on the screen. The crosshairs of the pointer change to form a rubber band that shows the size of the window on the screen. The size of the window is controlled by the movement of the pointer.

With the window selection option, only the parts of the drawing that are *entirely contained within the window* are selected to be edited. If the window covers only a part of a drawing entity, that entity is not selected. You may also type **W <Enter>** at the *Select objects:* prompt to activate the Window response.

When you use the crossing window selection, any part of the drawing that is contained within or *crossed by the crossing window* is included in the selection set. With a crossing window, a drawing entity such as a line or circle does not have to be entirely contained within the window to be selected—it only has to be touched by the crossing window. The colors of both the crossing window and the window are controlled by the **Visual Effect Settings** on the **Selection** tab of the **Options** dialog box.

Picking an empty area on the drawing and moving your mouse to the right creates a window. Picking and moving to the left creates a crossing window.

> **TIP**
>
> Typing **W <Enter>** or **C <Enter>** to activate a window or a crossing window is helpful when the drawing area is dense and clicking an empty area is difficult or impossible.

Step 50. Return the circles to the approximate location shown in Figure 2-38.

All (ALL)

All (ALL) selects all objects on thawed layers.

Fence (F)

Fence (F) allows you to click points that draw a line that selects any objects it crosses.

Remove (R) and Add (A)

The **Remove** option allows you to remove a drawing part from the selection set. If you are in the **Remove** mode and decide to add another drawing part to the selection set, type **A <Enter>** to return to the **Add** mode.

Last (L) and Previous (P)

The **Last** option selects the most recent drawing entity created. The **Previous** option selects the most recent selection set. Both are handy if you want to use several editing commands on the same drawing entity or the same selection set. You may also type and enter **L** or **P** from the keyboard while you are in a command and selecting objects.

Undo (U)

While in an editing command, if you decide you do not want something in a selection set, you may use the **UNDO** command to remove it and continue on with the *Select objects:* prompt. Typing **U <Enter>** backtracks through the selection sets in the reverse order in which they were selected.

Grips

grips: Small squares, rectangles, and triangles that appear on objects you select when no command is active. After selecting the grip, you can move, stretch, rotate, scale, copy, add a vertex, convert a line to an arc, convert an arc to a line, and mirror the objects without entering commands.

Grips are small squares that appear on an object if it is selected with no command active. Grips are very useful and can speed up your use of many of the **Modify** commands.

> **TIP**
>
> If grips appear when you do not want them, press the **<Esc>** key.

Step 51. Use grips to change the size of a circle; then move, scale, and rotate several circles at the same time, as described next:

Prompt	Response
Type a command:	With no command active, click on one of the 1/2″ diameter circles you have drawn
Small blue squares (grips) appear at each quadrant and at the center of the circle:	Click one of the grips at one of the quadrants of the circle
The grip changes color (becomes hot). Specify stretch point or [Base point Copy Undo eXit]:	Move your mouse to see that the size of the circle changes, then type **3/4 <Enter>**

Prompt	Response
The radius of the circle is now 3/4″	Click **Undo** (or type **U <Enter>**) to return the circle to its previous size
Type a command:	Using a window, select all four 1/2″ diameter circles
Grips appear at each quadrant and at the centers of all circles:	Click the grip at the far-left quadrant
The grip changes color (becomes hot). **STRETCH** Specify stretch point or [Base point Copy Undo eXit]:	Press the space bar to advance to the **Move** grip mode in the command area

MOVE
Specify move point or [Base point Copy Undo eXit]: Move your mouse to the right to see that the circles move with your cursor. You can now type the distance to move the circles or you can click the destination point. For now, type **5 <Enter>** to move the circles 5″ to the right

With all circles still displaying grips: Click the grip at the far-left quadrant

The grip changes color (becomes hot).
STRETCH
Specify stretch point or [Base point Copy Undo eXit]: Press the space bar twice to advance to the **Rotate** grip mode

ROTATE
Specify rotation angle or [Base point Copy Undo Reference eXit]: Move your mouse so you can see that the circles are rotated. You can now type an angle or you can click a point to select the angle

For now, type **45 <Enter>** to rotate the circles 45°

Type a command: Click **Undo** twice (or type **U <Enter>** twice) to return the circles to their original position

FOR MORE DETAILS

See Chapters 3 and 14 for more about grips.

NOTE

Hold down the **<Shift>** key to select multiple grips.

UNDO and REDO

UNDO	
Quick Access Toolbar:	
Menu Bar:	Edit/Undo
Type a Command:	UNDO
Command Alias:	U

Understanding how to use the **UNDO** command can be very helpful when drawing with AutoCAD.

When the **Undo** icon on the **Quick Access** toolbar is clicked, the most recent command is undone. To undo more than one command, click the **Undo** icon more than once or use the list provided under the down arrow to undo a group of commands. The **Redo** icon becomes active and *you can immediately use the* Redo *icon or list to redo as many commands as you need. If you resume drawing immediately after using the* Undo *icon, the* Redo *icon does not become active.*

Typing **U** from the keyboard at the command prompt and pressing the **<Enter>** key undoes the most recent command operation. Most of the time,

REDO	
Quick Access Toolbar:	
Menu Bar:	Edit/Redo
Type a Command:	REDO
Keyboard:	<Ctrl>+Y

the operation that is undone is obvious, such as when a line that you have just drawn is undone. The most recent mode settings that are not obvious, such as **Snap**, will be undone also. *Typing* **REDO** *and pressing* **<Enter>** *will redo only one undo, and must immediately follow the* **U** *or* **UNDO** *command.*

When you type and enter **U** from the keyboard, no prompt line appears. If you type **UNDO <Enter>**, the prompt *Enter the number of operations to undo or [Auto Control BEgin End Mark Back] <1>:* appears. The default is <1>. You may enter a number for the number of operations to be undone. For instance, if you enter 5 at the prompt, five operations will be undone. If you decide you went too far, you can type **REDO <Enter>** or select **Redo** from the **Standard** toolbar to restore all five operations.

Typing **U** from the keyboard and pressing the **<Enter>** key is the same as entering the number **1** at the **Undo** prompt. In that instance, **Redo** *will redo only one undo, no matter how many times you typed and entered* **U.**

ARC	
Ribbon/ Panel	Home/ Draw
Draw Toolbar:	
Menu Bar:	Draw/Arc
Type a Command:	ARC
Command Alias:	A

ARC

You can choose from many methods to draw arcs. Whatever the situation, you can select a method to suit your needs. Experiment with the different methods described next and decide which ones you prefer to use. Use Figure 2-42 as a guide when locating the approximate location of the arcs on your drawing.

3-Point

Using the **3-point** method, you can draw an arc clockwise or counterclockwise by specifying the start point, second point, and endpoint of the arc.

Step 52. Draw three arcs using the **3-point** method (Figure 2-43), as described next:

Prompt	Response
Type a command:	**3 Point** (or type **A <Enter>**)
Specify start point of arc or [Center]:	**P1→**
Specify second point of arc or [Center End]:	**P2→** (Figure 2-43)
Specify end point of arc:	**P3→**
Command:	**<Enter>** (repeat **ARC**)
Specify start point of arc or [Center]:	**P4→**
Specify second point of arc or [Center End]:	**P5→**
Specify end point of arc:	**P6→**
Command:	**<Enter>** (repeat **ARC**)
Specify start point of arc or [Center]:	**P7→**
Specify second point of arc or [Center End]:	**P8→**
Specify end point of arc:	**P9→**

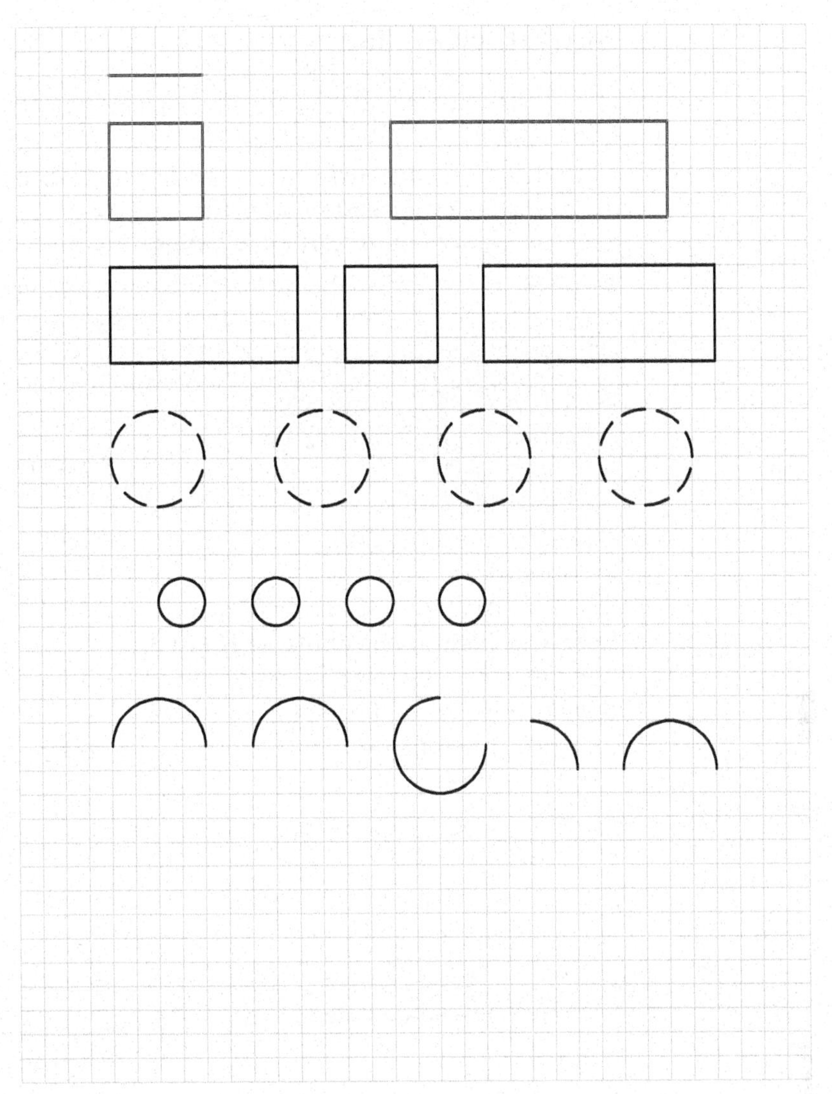

Figure 2-42
Draw arcs

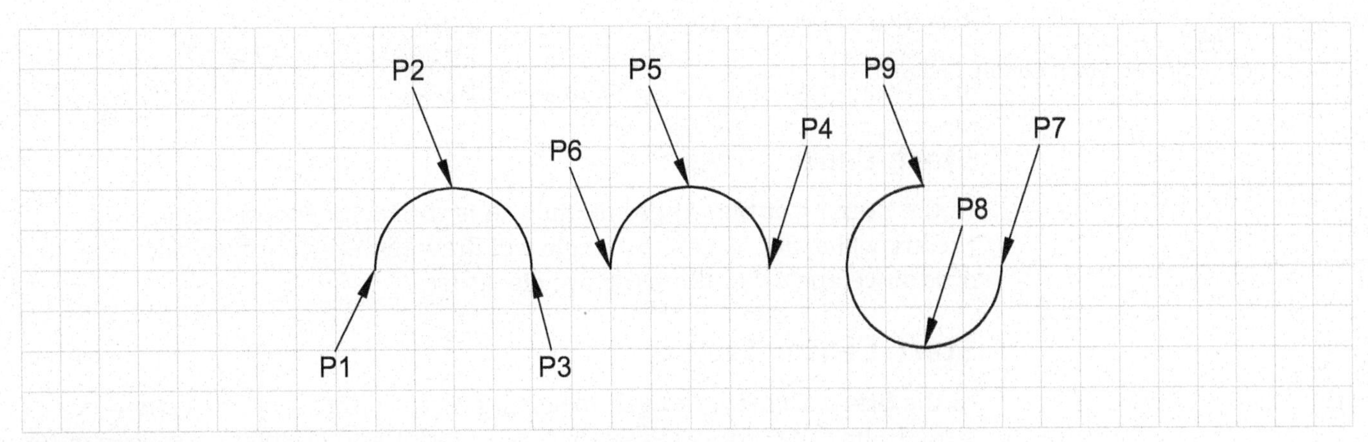

Figure 2-43
Draw arcs using the 3-point method

Start, Center, End

The **Start, Center, End** method allows you to draw an arc only counter-clockwise, by specifying the start, center, and end.

Step 53. Draw two arcs using the **Start, Center, End** method (Figure 2-44), as described next. Click the **Arc** dropdown menu from the **Draw** panel of the ribbon's **Home** tab, then choose **Start, Center, End**:

Prompt	Response
Type a command:	**Arc-Start, Center, End**
Specify start point of arc or [Center]:	**P1→**
Specify second point of arc or [Center End]:_c Specify center point of arc:	**P2→** (Figure 2-44)
Specify end point of arc or [Angle chord Length]:	**P3→**
Command:	**Arc-Start, Center, End**
Specify start point of arc or [Center]:	**P4→** (Figure 2-44)
Specify second point of arc or [Center End]:_c Specify center point of arc:	**P5→**
Specify end point of arc or [Angle chord Length]:	**P6→**

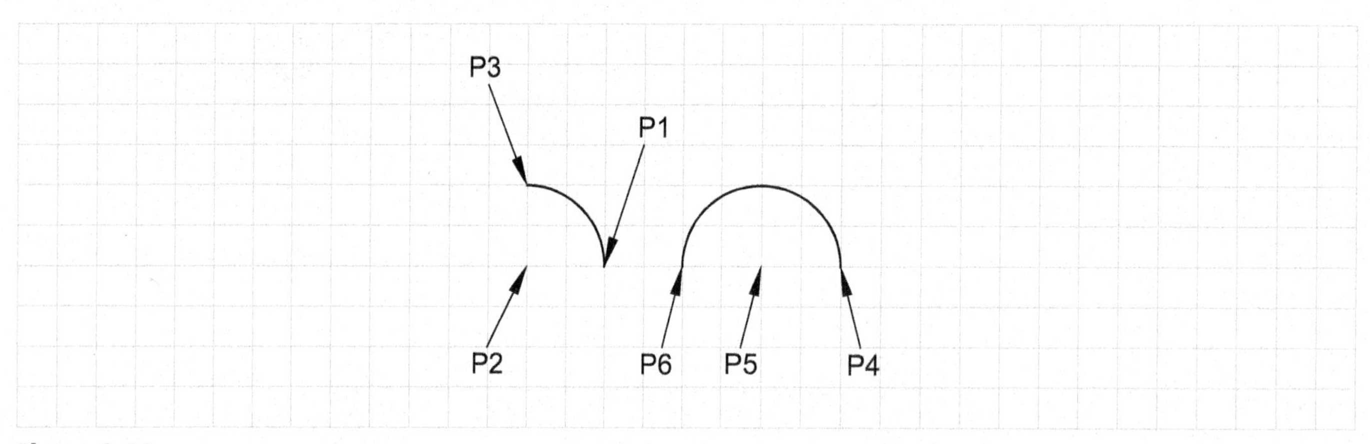

Figure 2-44
Draw arcs using the **Start, Center, End** method

Start, Center, Angle

In the **Start, Center, Angle** method, **A** is the included angle (the angle the arc will span). A positive angle will draw the arc counterclockwise; a negative angle will draw the arc clockwise.

Start, Center, Length

In the **Start, Center, Length** method, **L** is the chord length. A *chord* is a straight line that connects an arc's start point and endpoint. You can enter a positive chord length to draw a minor arc (less than 180°) and a negative chord length to draw a major arc (more than 180°). Both are drawn counterclockwise.

Start, End, Angle

With the **Start, End, Angle** method, after the start point and endpoint of the arc have been picked, a positive angle draws the arc counterclockwise; a negative angle keeps the same start and endpoints but draws the reverse arc or draws clockwise.

Start, End, Direction

In the **Start, End, Direction** method, **Direction** is the specified direction that the arc takes from the start point. The direction is specified in degrees. You can also specify the direction by pointing to a single point. You can draw major, minor, counterclockwise, and clockwise arcs with the **Start, End, Direction** method.

Start, End, Radius

In the **Start, End, Radius** method, **Radius** is the arc radius. When you use this method, enter a positive radius to draw a minor arc (less than 180°) and enter a negative radius to draw a major arc (more than 180°). Both are drawn counterclockwise.

Continue

If you pick **Continue**, a new arc starts tangent at the endpoint of the last arc or line drawn. You need to pick only the endpoint of the new arc to complete it. If an arc is already drawn, pressing the **<Enter>** key has the same effect.

ELLIPSE	
Ribbon/ Panel	Home/ Draw
Draw Toolbar:	
Menu Bar:	Draw/ Ellipse
Type a Command:	ELLIPSE
Command Alias:	EL

ELLIPSE

Look at Figure 2-45 to determine the approximate location of the ellipses drawn with the **ELLIPSE** command.

Axis, End

The minor axis of an ellipse is its smaller axis, and the major axis is the larger axis.

Step 54. Set **Layer3** current.

Step 55. Draw an ellipse by entering points for the minor axis of the ellipse (Figure 2-46), as described next:

Prompt	**Response**
Type a command:	**Ellipse-Axis, End** (or type **EL** **<Enter>**)
Specify axis endpoint of ellipse or [Arc Center]:	**P1→** (Figure 2-46)
Specify other endpoint of axis:	**P2→** With **ORTHO** on, move your mouse to the right; type **1** **<Enter>**
Specify distance to other axis or [Rotation]:	**P3→** With **ORTHO** on, move your mouse up; type **1** **<Enter>**

Figure 2-45
Draw ellipses and donuts

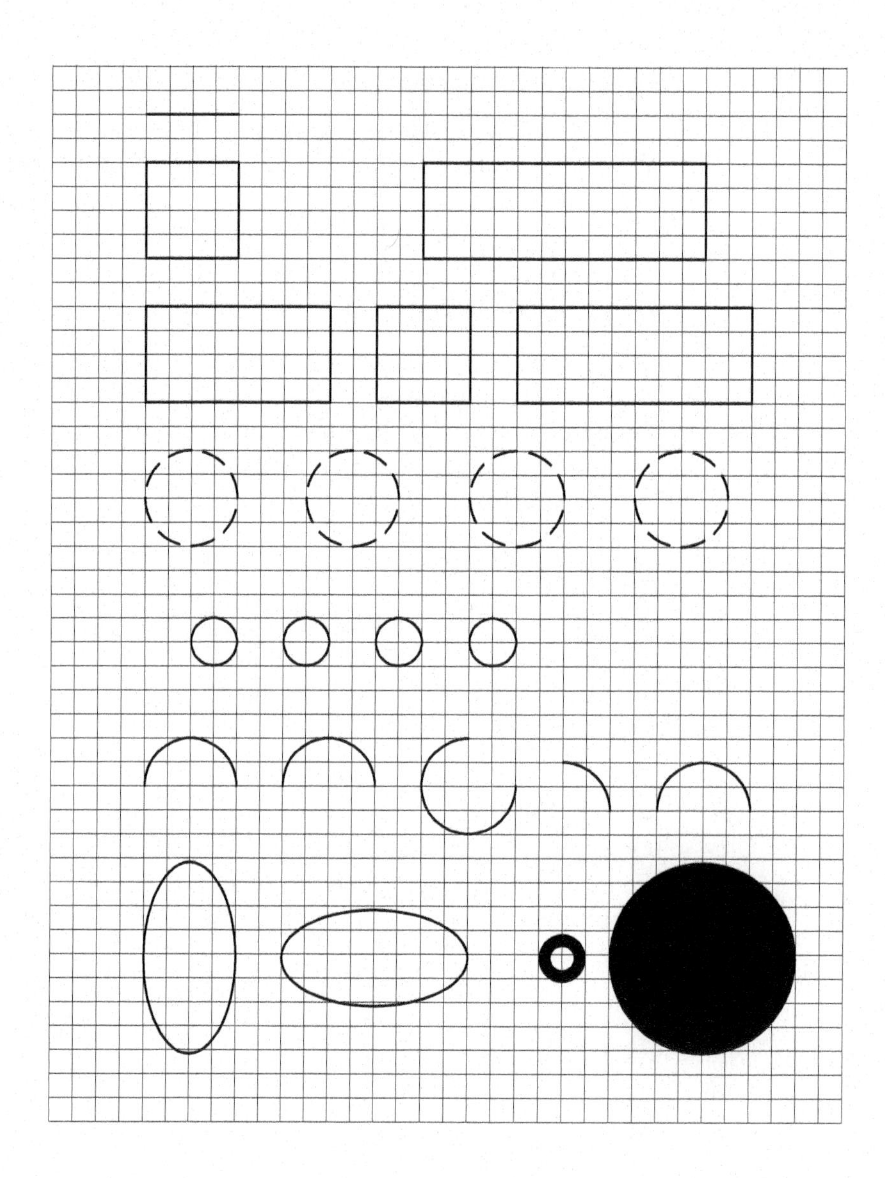

Figure 2-46
Draw an ellipse by entering points for the minor and major axes of the ellipse

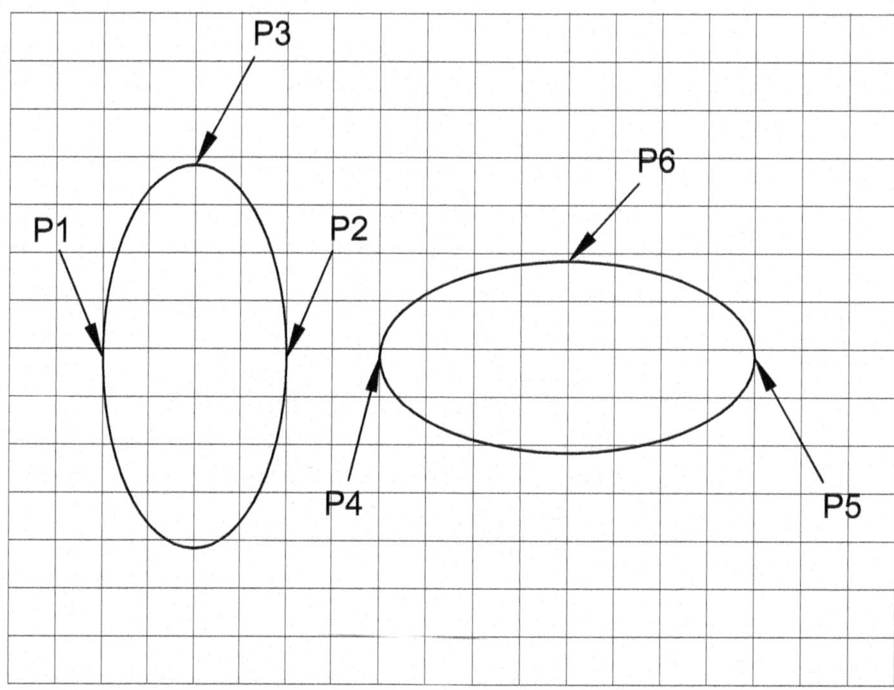

Step 56. Draw an ellipse by entering points for the major axis of the ellipse (Figure 2-46), as described next:

Prompt	Response
Type a command:	**Ellipse-Axis, End**
Specify axis endpoint of ellipse or [Arc Center]:	**P4→** (Figure 2-46)
Specify other endpoint of axis:	**P5→** With **ORTHO** on, move your mouse to the right; type **2 <Enter>**
Specify distance to other axis or [Rotation]:	**P6→** With **ORTHO** on, move your mouse up; type **1/2 <Enter>**

Center

You may also draw an ellipse by specifying the center point, the endpoint of one axis, and the length of the other axis. Type **C** and press **<Enter>** at the prompt *Specify axis endpoint of ellipse or [Arc Center]:* to start with the center of the ellipse. Entering the center point first is similar to the first two methods described, and either the minor or major axis may be constructed first. As with all methods of drawing an ellipse, you can specify the points by clicking a point on the drawing, by typing and entering coordinates, or by direct distance entry.

DONUT	
Ribbon/ Panel	Home/ Draw
Menu Bar:	Draw/ Donut
Type a Command:	DONUT
Command Alias:	DO

DONUT

Look at Figure 2-45 to determine the approximate location of the solid ring and solid circle drawn using the **DONUT** command.

Step 57. Set **Layer1** current.

Step 58. Use the **DONUT** command to draw a solid ring (Figure 2-47), as described next:

Prompt	Response
Type a command:	**DONUT** (or type **DO <Enter>**)
Specify inside diameter of donut <default>:	Type **1/2 <Enter>**
Specify outside diameter of donut <default>:	Type **1 <Enter>**
Specify center of donut or <exit>:	Click a point on the drawing
Specify center of donut or <exit>:	**<Enter>**

Figure 2-47
Use the **DONUT** command to draw a solid ring and a solid circle

Step 59. Use the **DONUT** command to draw a solid circle (Figure 2-47), as described next:

Prompt	Response
Type a command:	**<Enter>** (repeat **DONUT**)
Specify inside diameter of donut <0′-0 1/2″>:	Type **0** **<Enter>** (so there is no center hole)
Specify outside diameter of donut <0′-1″>:	**<Enter>**
Specify center of donut or <exit>:	Click a point on the drawing
Specify center of donut or <exit>:	**<Enter>**

You can use the **DONUT** command to draw solid dots of any size as well as solid rings with different inside and outside diameters.

SCALE	
Ribbon/ Panel	Home/ Modify
Modify Toolbar:	
Menu Bar:	Modify/Scale
Type a Command:	SCALE
Command Alias:	SC

SCALE

The **SCALE** command lets you reduce or enlarge either drawing entities or an entire drawing. The **Copy** option of the **SCALE** command allows you to copy and enlarge or reduce the object at the same time.

Step 60. Use the **SCALE** command to reduce the solid ring (Figure 2-48), as described next:

Prompt	Response
Type a command:	**SCALE** (or type **SC** **<Enter>**)
Select objects:	Window the ring (or click the outside edge of the ring)
Select objects:	**<Enter>**
Specify base point:	Click the center of the ring
Specify scale factor or [Copy Reference]:	Type **.5** **<Enter>**

The relative scale factor of .5 was used to reduce the solid ring. A relative scale factor of 2 would have enlarged the solid ring.

Reference

The **SCALE** command's **Reference** option allows you to scale an object relative to another object, or to a specified distance.

Step 61. Use the **SCALE** command to enlarge the solid donut (Figure 2-48), as described next:

Prompt	Response
Type a command:	**<Enter>** (repeat **SCALE**)
Select objects:	Window the solid donut
Select objects:	**<Enter>**
Specify base point:	Click the center of the solid donut
Specify scale factor or [Copy Reference] <default>:	Type **R** **<Enter>**
Specify reference length <0′-1″>:	**<Enter>** (to accept **1** as the default)
Specify new length or [Points] <0′-1″>:	Type **2** **<Enter>**

The **Reference** option allows you to type and enter a number for the reference (current) length of a drawing entity. You can also enter the reference (current) length by picking two points on the drawing to show AutoCAD the reference (current) length. You can type and enter the new length by using a number, or you can enter it by picking two points on the drawing to show the new length.

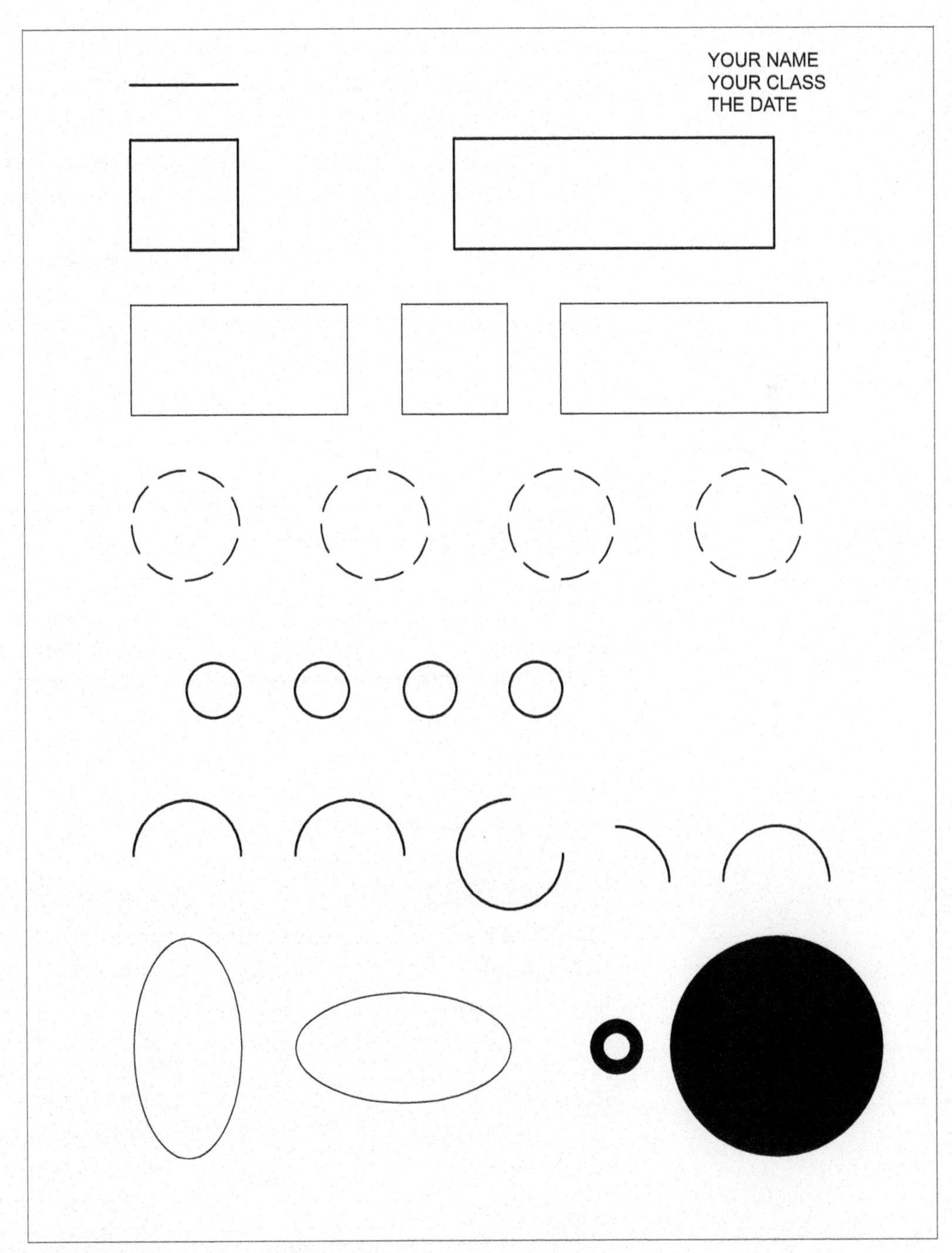

Figure 2-48
Tutorial 2-1, Part 2, complete

SINGLE LINE TEXT	
Ribbon/ Panel	Annotate/Text
Text Toolbar:	
Menu Bar:	Draw/Text/ Single Line Text
Type a Command:	TEXT

Adding Text

Finally, you finish Tutorial 2-1 by labeling it with single-line text.

Step 62. Set **Layer3** current.

Step 63. Add your name, class, and date to the upper-right corner of your drawing as described next:

Prompt	Response
Type a command:	**Single Line Text** (or type **DT <Enter>**)
Specify start point of text or [Justify Style]:	Click a point in the upper-right corner to start typing your name as shown in Figure 2-48
Specify height <default>:	Type **1/8 <Enter>**
Specify rotation angle of text <0>:	**<Enter>** (to accept the 0 default rotation)
The **In-Place Text Editor** appears:	Type **YOUR NAME <Enter> YOUR CLASS <Enter> THE DATE <Enter>**
The **In-Place Text Editor**:	**<Enter>** (to close the **In-Place Text Editor**)

Command History

AutoCAD provides a record of the command history for the current session. Gray highlighted lines of this command history are shown in the command line window. You can change the number of **Lines of Prompt History** displayed by using the command line right-click menu in Figure 2-49.

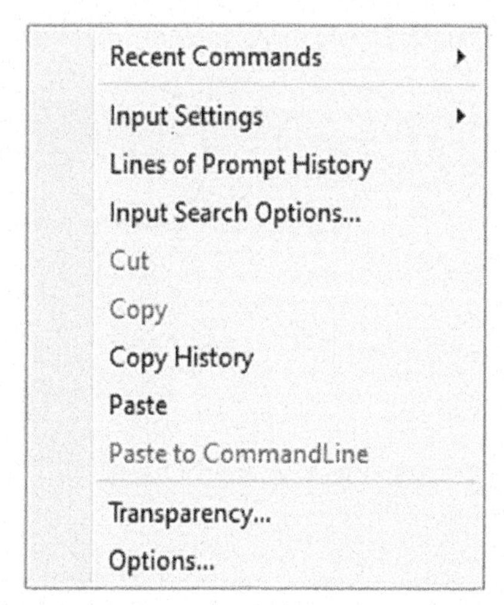

Figure 2-49
Command line right-click menu

Pressing **<F2>** will show you a full command history of the current session that you can scroll through.

Step 64. When you have completed Tutorial 2-1, Part 2 (Figure 2-48), save your drawing in at least two places.

TUTORIAL 2-2

Plot Responses for CH2-TUTORIAL1, Using the Model Tab

PLOT	
Application Menu:	Print/Plot
Ribbon/ Panel	Output/ Plot
Quick Access Toolbar:	
Menu Bar:	File/Plot ...
Type a Command:	PLOT
Keyboard:	<Ctrl>+P

When you start a new drawing, AutoCAD provides a single **Model** tab and two **Layout** tabs at the bottom of the drawing window. Thus far you have been working on the **Model** tab in model space. Model space is the 2D (and also 3D) environment where you create your drawings. You can also plot (or print) from the **Model** tab. Tutorial 2-2 describes how to print from the **Model** tab.

The following is a hands-on, step-by-step tutorial to make a hard copy of **CH2-TUTORIAL1**.

Step 1. Open drawing **CH2-TUTORIAL1** and complete a **Zoom-All** command so it is displayed on the screen.

Step 2. Make sure the **Model** tab is current.

Step 3. Click the **Plot** command from the **Quick Access** toolbar or type **PLOT <Enter>** to access the **Plot** dialog box. Pressing **<Ctrl>+P** will also access the **Plot** dialog box.

Step 4. If you don't see an area labeled **Plot style table (pen assignments)** at the right side of the dialog box, click the **More Options** arrow in the lower-right corner of the **Plot** dialog box to display the entire **Plot** dialog box (Figure 2-50).

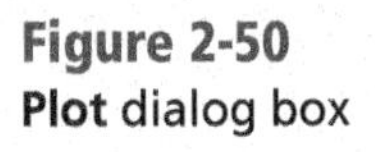

Figure 2-50
Plot dialog box

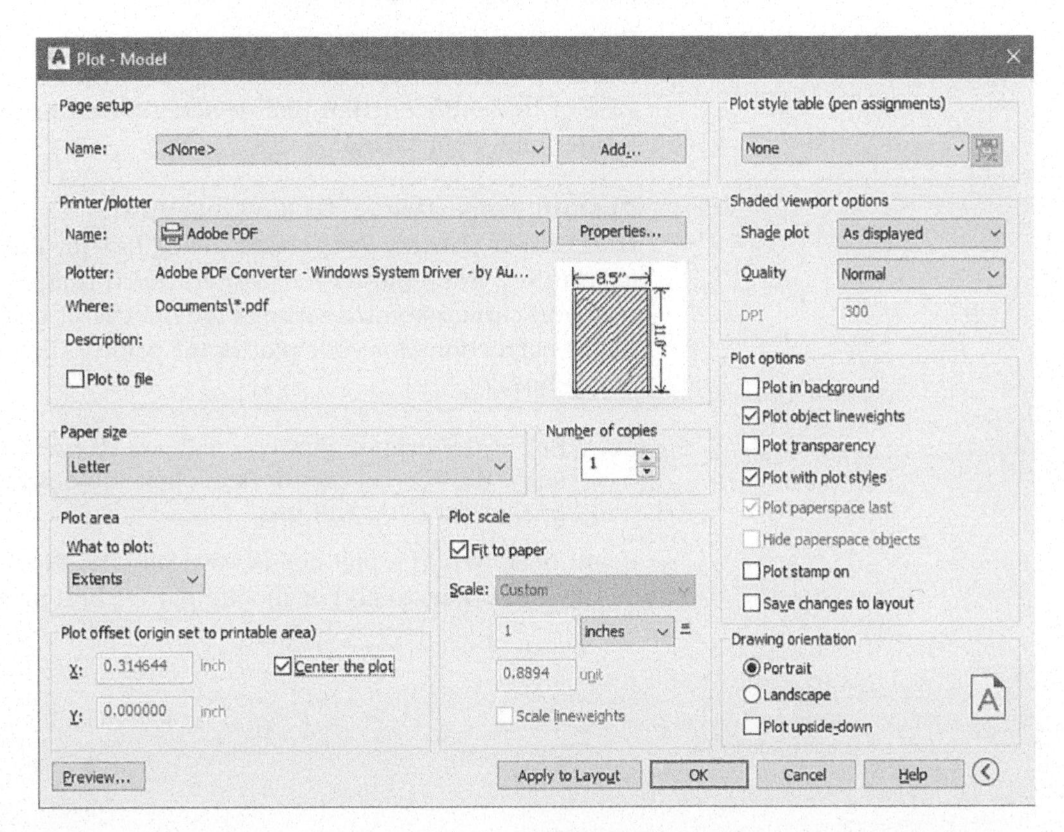

FOR MORE DETAILS

See Chapter 5 for advanced plotting.

Plot - Name

The strip at the top of the dialog box displays the current layout tab name or shows whether the **Model** tab is current. It shows **Model** now because the **Model** tab is current.

Page Setup

The settings that control the final plot output are referred to as *page setups.*

> **Name:** This list box displays any named or saved page setups that you can select to apply to the current page setup.
>
> **Add...:** Clicking this button displays the **Add Page Setup** dialog box. You can specify a name for the new page setup.

Step 5. Set the **Page setup** to **None**.

Printer/Plotter

The **Name:** line displays the current plot device (plotter or printer). Clicking the down arrow displays a list of the available plotting devices in the **Name:** list. You can select the plot device that you want to use.

> **Properties...:** Clicking this button displays the **Plotter Configuration Editor** (Figure 2-51). The **Plotter Configuration Editor** allows you to view or to modify current plot device information. If **None** is in the **Name:** line, **Properties...** is grayed out.
>
> **Custom Properties...:** Clicking this button of the **Plotter Configuration Editor** opens a **Properties** dialog box for the configured plotter (or printer). Each plotter (or printer) has a unique **Properties** dialog box; you can customize settings for the vector colors, print quality, and raster corrections for your plotter (or printer) using the **Properties** dialog box.

Step 6. Select the printer that you will use. If the **Name:** line does not show the correct plot device, click the down arrow and select the printer that you will use.

If you need to add a plot device, you use the **Plotter Manager** (under **File** in the menu bar) to add or modify plotter and printer configuration files.

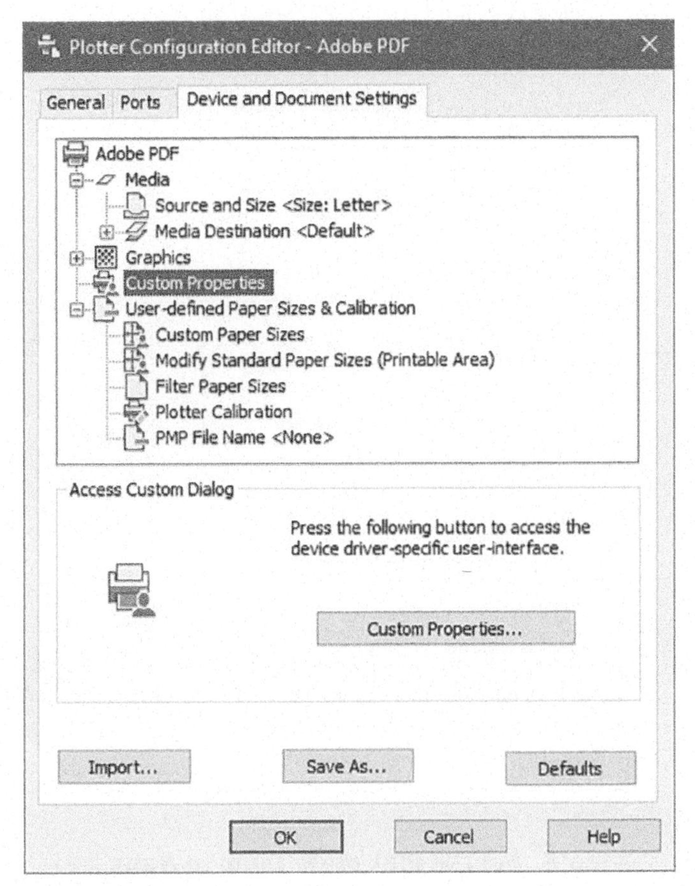

Figure 2-51
Plotter Configuration Editor dialog box

Plot to File

If you do not select the **Plot to file** check box, AutoCAD plots directly from your computer. If there is a cable leading from your computer to the printer or plotter, or if you are plotting from a network, do not select the **Plot to file** check box.

If you do select the **Plot to file** check box, a file is created with the extension .plt. You can save this plot file and transfer it to any computer connected to a plotter or printer.

Browse for Plot File...

When you select **Plot to file** and click **OK**, the **Browse for Plot File** dialog box displays. This dialog box allows you to save the plot file.

Step 7. Select the correct setting for the **Plot to file** check box for your situation.

Plot Style Table (Pen Assignments)

plot style table: A collection of plot styles. Plot styles are made using plot style tables. They apply to objects only when the plot style table is attached to a layout or viewport.

Plot styles allow you to plot the same drawing in different ways. You can use the ***plot style table*** (Figure 2-52) to create, edit, or store plot style files.

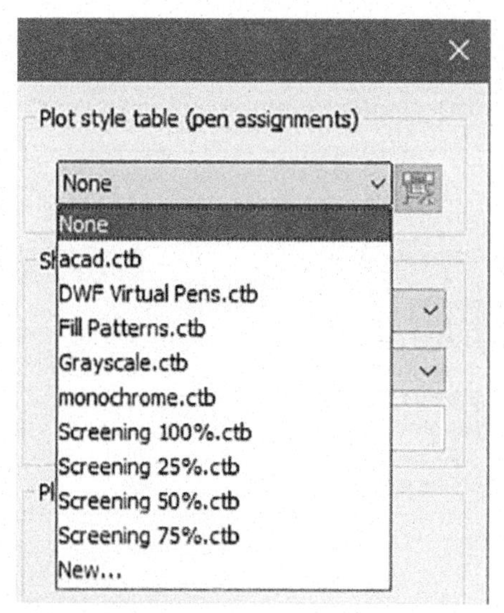

Figure 2-52
Plot style table

FOR MORE DETAILS

See Chapter 5 for more on plot styles.

Step 8. Set the **Plot style table** to **None**.

Paper Size

The **Paper size:** line displays the current paper size. Clicking the down arrow displays the paper sizes the printer (Figure 2-53) or plotter (Figure 2-54) can accommodate; the current size is highlighted. An A, B, D, or E displayed beside the size indicates a standard American National Standards Institute (ANSI) paper size. ARCH displayed beside the size indicates a standard architectural paper size.

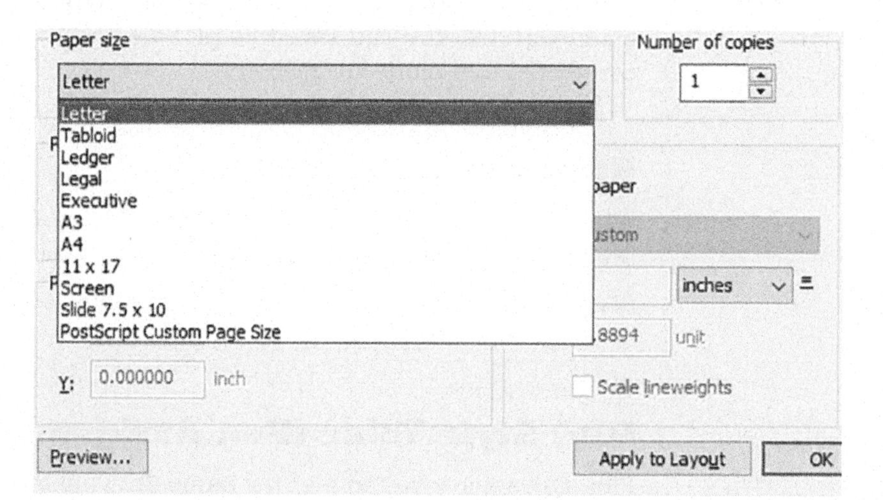

Figure 2-53
Paper sizes for a printer

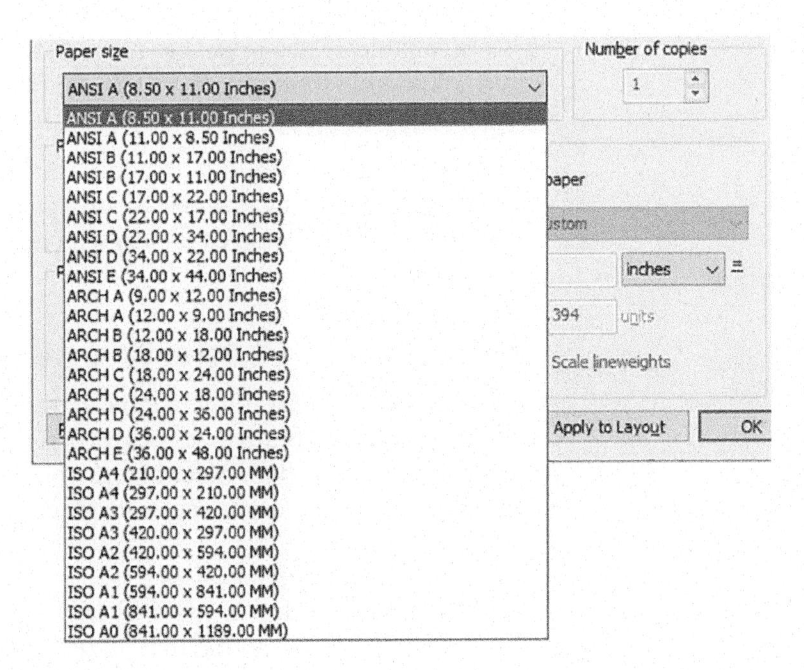

Figure 2-54
Paper sizes for a plotter

Step 9. Select the **Letter** (8.5 × 11 in.) paper size, and **1** for the **Number of copies**.

Plot Area

When you click the Plot Area down arrow, the following options are displayed (**View** will not be displayed because you have not named and saved a view in your drawing):

Display: This option plots the part of the drawing that is displayed on the screen at the time the plot is made.

Extents: This option plots the drawing extents. The drawing extents are whatever graphics are actually drawn, including any graphics that lie outside the limits of the drawing area.

Limits: This option plots the part of the drawing that lies within the drawing limits. The limits for drawing **CH2-TUTORIAL1** are 8-1/2,11.

Window: This selection allows you to pick two corners of a window and plot only the part of the drawing that is within the window. Clicking the **Window <** button clears the **Plot** dialog box so you can view your drawing and use your mouse to click the two corners of a window. AutoCAD then returns to the **Plot** dialog box.

Step 10. Click **Extents** to select the drawing extents as part of the drawing that is to be printed.

Plot Scale

In model space, you draw full scale, so most drawings need to be plotted to scale.

Scale: The **Scale:** line displays the scale at which the drawing will be plotted. If the scale list is gray, click the **Fit to paper** check box to make the scale list selectable. When you click the down arrow, a list of available scales appears. You can select the scale that you want to use. To be able to measure a plotted drawing accurately using a scale, you must enter a specific plotting scale.

Fit to paper: You may respond by selecting **Fit to paper** instead of entering a specific scale. When you select this option, AutoCAD scales the selected plot area as large as possible to fit the specified paper size.

Annotative Property and Annotation Scale

Objects such as text, dimensions, hatches, and leaders can be annotative. To make text annotative, you can turn the annotative property on in the **Text Style** dialog box. Also, before you add the text to your drawing, you must set the annotation scale, located in the lower-right corner of the status bar.

When a drawing such as a large house or building is drawn full scale, the text that is added to the drawing also must be large. For instance, if you want the text of a drawing to be 1/8″ high when plotted at a scale of 1/4″ = 1′-0″, the text that you add while drawing full scale will need to be 6″ high, as shown in the 1/4″ = 1′-0″ scale in Figure 2-55.

ANNOTATION SCALE	TEXT SIZE ON SCALED PLOTTED DRAWINGS	SCALE FACTOR	TEXT SIZE ON FULL-SIZE DRAWINGS
1/8"=1'-0"	1/8"	96	12"
1/4"=1'-0"	1/8"	48	6"
1/2"=1'-0"	1/8"	24	3"
1"=1'-0"	1/8"	12	1-1/2"

Figure 2-55
Examples of annotation scales for text

Annotation scale controls how the text and other annotative objects appear on the drawing. When you make the text annotative and set the annotation scale of the drawing, AutoCAD automatically does the arithmetic for you and controls how the text looks on your screen. When adding the text, you have to enter only the size of the text you want in the plotted drawing, and AutoCAD automatically calculates the size of the text on the drawing using the annotation scale setting.

If you have annotative objects on your drawing and have set the annotation scale, plotting your drawing at the same scale as the annotation scale that you have set is usually best. If there are no annotative objects on your drawing, the annotation scale does not affect anything. If the plot scale and the annotation scale differ, when the plot is initiated, AutoCAD prompts you with *The annotation scale is not equal to the plot scale. Do you wish to Continue?* You can answer with **OK** or **Cancel.**

Step 11. Select a scale of **1:1,** which is 1 plotted inch = 1 drawing unit.

FOR MORE DETAILS

See Chapter 6 for more information about annotative text and Chapter 7 for more information about annotative dimensions.

Plot Offset (Origin Set to Printable Area)

Use the **Plot offset** area to center the plot on the paper, or specify specific horizontal and vertical distances from the lower-left corner of the paper.

Center the plot: To center the drawing on the paper, select the **Center the plot** check box; the plot will be automatically centered on the paper.

X and Y offset: The plot offset specifies the location of the plot, on the paper, from the lower-left corner of the paper. The **X:** input line moves the plotted drawing in the X direction on the paper, and the **Y:** input moves the drawing in the Y direction. You can enter either positive or negative values.

Step 12. Select the **Center the plot** check box.

Notice that the X and Y inputs are automatically calculated to center the selected plotting area (extents) in the paper size (8-1/2″ × 11″).

Shaded Viewport Options

The **Shaded Viewport** options relate to 3D drawings and control how shaded and rendered viewports are plotted. This process is described in Chapters 14 and 15.

Plot Options

Plot options and drawing orientation are visible when you click the **More** arrow at the bottom-right corner of the **Plot** dialog box.

Plot in background: A check mark in this box allows you to continue working while your drawing is being plotted.

Plot object lineweights: A check mark in this box tells AutoCAD to plot the drawing using the lineweights you have assigned to any object in the drawing.

Plot transparency: You can enter a transparency value in the **Layer** dialog box. It is a setting that makes an object more or less transparent. If you have transparent objects in your drawing, this option determines whether the transparency is plotted.

Plot with plot styles: This option allows you to use a plot style. Because you are not using a plot style, this box will not be checked.

Plot paperspace last: Selecting this option means that model space will be plotted first. Usually, paper space drawings are plotted before model space drawings.

Hide paperspace objects: The **Hide paperspace objects** check box refers to 3D objects only. When you use the **Hide** command, AutoCAD hides any surface on the screen that is behind another surface in 3D space. If you want to do the same on your paper space plot, you must select the **Hide paperspace objects** check box. This shows only in the full plot preview window.

Another way to hide in paper space is to select the viewport in which you want to have hidden lines, click **Properties** under **Modify** in the menu bar, and turn **Shade plot** to **Hidden**.

Plot stamp on: Selecting this check box allows you to place signatures and other stamps on the drawing.

Save changes to layout: Selecting this check box allows you to save any changes you have made in the **Plot** dialog box.

Step 13. If the **Plot with plot styles** check box is selected, click it to remove the check mark. Select the **Plot object lineweights** box. (**Plot paperspace last** and **Hide paperspace objects** are grayed out because no **Layout** tabs were used.)

Drawing Orientation

The paper icon represents the orientation of the selected paper size. The letter A icon represents the orientation of the drawing on the paper.

Portrait: This radio button allows you to specify a vertical orientation of the drawing on the page.

Landscape: This radio button allows you to specify a horizontal orientation of the drawing on the page. If a plot shows only half of what should have been plotted, you may need to change the orientation.

Plot upside-down: This check box allows you to plot the drawing, in a portrait or landscape orientation, upside-down.

Step 14. Select the **Portrait** orientation.

Preview...

The **Preview...** button shows you exactly how the final plot will appear on the sheet.

Step 15. Click the **Preview...** button.

Preview your plot for **CH2-TUTORIAL1**, Part 2, Figure 2-56. If there is something wrong with the plot, press the space bar and make the necessary adjustments. If the preview looks OK, press the space bar to end the preview. You may also right-click to access the menu shown in Figure 2-57.

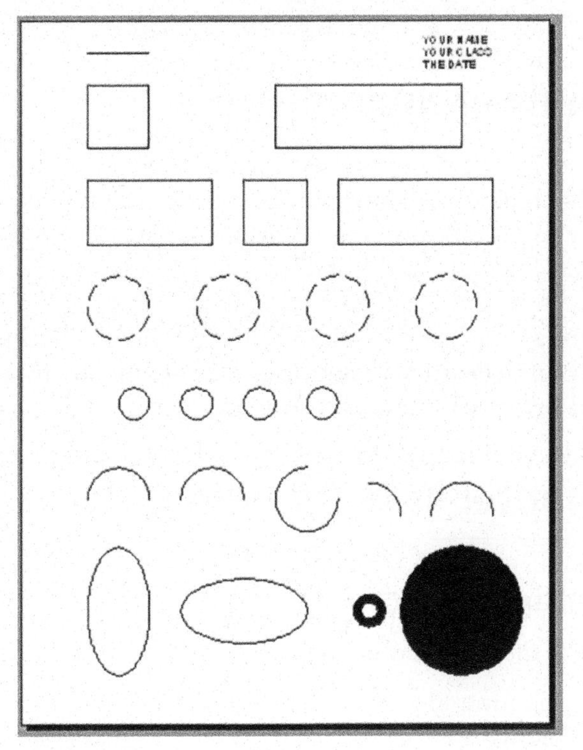

Figure 2-56
Plot preview

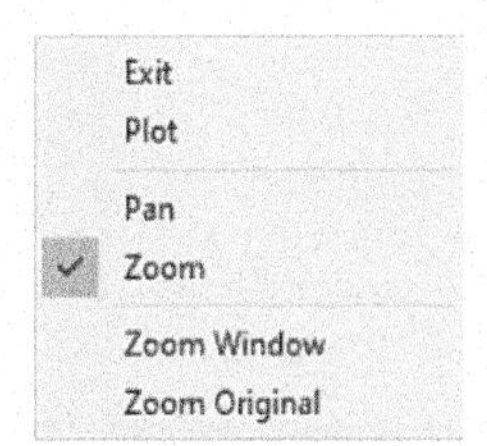

Figure 2-57
Preview right-click menu

Step 16. Click **OK** from the **Plot** dialog box (or click **Plot** from the right-click menu).

The plot proceeds from this point. If you have not created a plot file, remove the completed plot from the printer or plotter. If you have created a .plt file, take your disk to the plot station or send your plot via a network.

Chapter Summary

This chapter provided you the information necessary to set up and begin a new AutoCAD drawing. In addition, you learned to make layers and assign color, linetype, and lineweight to each layer. You also learned how to use the **Save** and **Save as** commands, use basic drawing and editing commands, and print or plot your drawing. Now you have the skills and information necessary to set up and make basic drawings, save your drawings, and print or plot your drawings.

Chapter Test Questions

Multiple Choice

Circle the correct answer.

1. The function key **<F7>** described in this chapter does which of the following?
   a. Flips the screen from the text display
   b. Turns snap on or off
   c. Turns **ORTHO** on or off
   d. Turns grid on or off
2. Which of the following function keys turns snap on or off?
   a. **<F2>**
   b. **<F7>**
   c. **<F8>**
   d. **<F9>**
3. How many layers may you use in a drawing?
   a. 1
   b. 16
   c. 32
   d. An unlimited number
4. AutoCAD provides how many sizes of each standard linetype (except continuous)?
   a. 1
   b. 2
   c. 3
   d. As many as you want
5. When you use the **MOVE** command with a window selection (click left, drag right — not a crossing window):
   a. Everything the window touches is selected
   b. Everything entirely within the window is selected
   c. The last item clicked is selected
   d. Nothing is selected

6. When you use the **MOVE** command with a crossing window selection (click right, drag left):
   a. Everything the window contains or touches is selected
   b. Everything entirely within the window is selected
   c. The last item clicked is selected
   d. Nothing is selected
7. Which of the following are small squares that appear on an object when it is selected with no command active?
   a. Grips
   b. Snaps
   c. Squares
   d. Rectangles
8. When you plot from the **Model** tab, which of the following will produce a plot of the part of the drawing that is displayed on the screen?
   a. **Display**
   b. **Extents**
   c. **Window**
   d. **Limits**
9. When you plot from the **Model** tab, which of the following will produce a plot of the entire drawing, even if part of it is outside the limits?
   a. **Display**
   b. **Extents**
   c. **Window**
   d. **Limits**
10. A drawing that is to be plotted using the **Model** tab so that it fits on a particular size sheet without regard to the scale requires which scale response?
    a. **1:1**
    b. **Full**
    c. **1:2**
    d. **Fit to paper**

Matching

Write the number of the correct answer on the line.

a. **Ortho** ______

b. **Ltscale** ______

c. **Save As...** ______

d. **Extents** ______

e. **GRIDDISPLAY** ______

1. A command that allows you to save drawings with a different name
2. A setting that changes the spacing between dashes in a hidden line
3. A setting that permits you to draw only horizontally or vertically
4. When this setting is zero, the grid shows the limits of the drawing
5. When this area is selected, all of the drawing is plotted even if part of it is outside the drawing limits

True or False

Circle the correct answer.

1. **True or False:** The default lower-left corner of the drawing limits is 8-1/2,11.
2. **True or False:** To make the line segment length and spacing larger for a dashed linetype, enter a number larger than 1 at the **Ltscale** prompt *Enter new linetype scale factor <1.000>.*
3. **True or False:** Direct distance entry can be used only when drawing a line.
4. **True or False:** The **3-point** method of drawing arcs allows you to draw arcs clockwise or counterclockwise.
5. **True or False:** Pressing the **<Esc>** key cancels a command.

List

1. Five types of **Drawing Units** available in AutoCAD.
2. Five **Visual Styles** accessible from the **View** (pull-down) menu.
3. Five ways to access the **PLOT** command.
4. Five color index numbers and their corresponding colors.
5. Five ways of drawing an arc.
6. Five options of the **ZOOM** command.
7. Five ways of accessing the **ELLIPSE** command.
8. Five commands and their respective aliases.
9. Five ways of accessing the **Layer Properties Manager** palette.
10. Five ways of accessing the single-line text command in AutoCAD.

General Questions

1. In what situations would you use the **Ortho** setting?
2. Why would you want to use the **Ltscale** setting?
3. How can the annotation scale be used to make it easier to draw and plot drawings?
4. Which settings on the status bar do you want to use in your workspace?
5. What are all the selection set options, and how can you use them effectively?

chaptertwo

Chapter Projects

Project 2-1: *Drawing Shapes I* [BASIC]

Draw, full size, the shapes shown in Figure 2-58. Use the dimensions shown. Locate the shapes approximately as shown. Use your workspace to make the following settings:

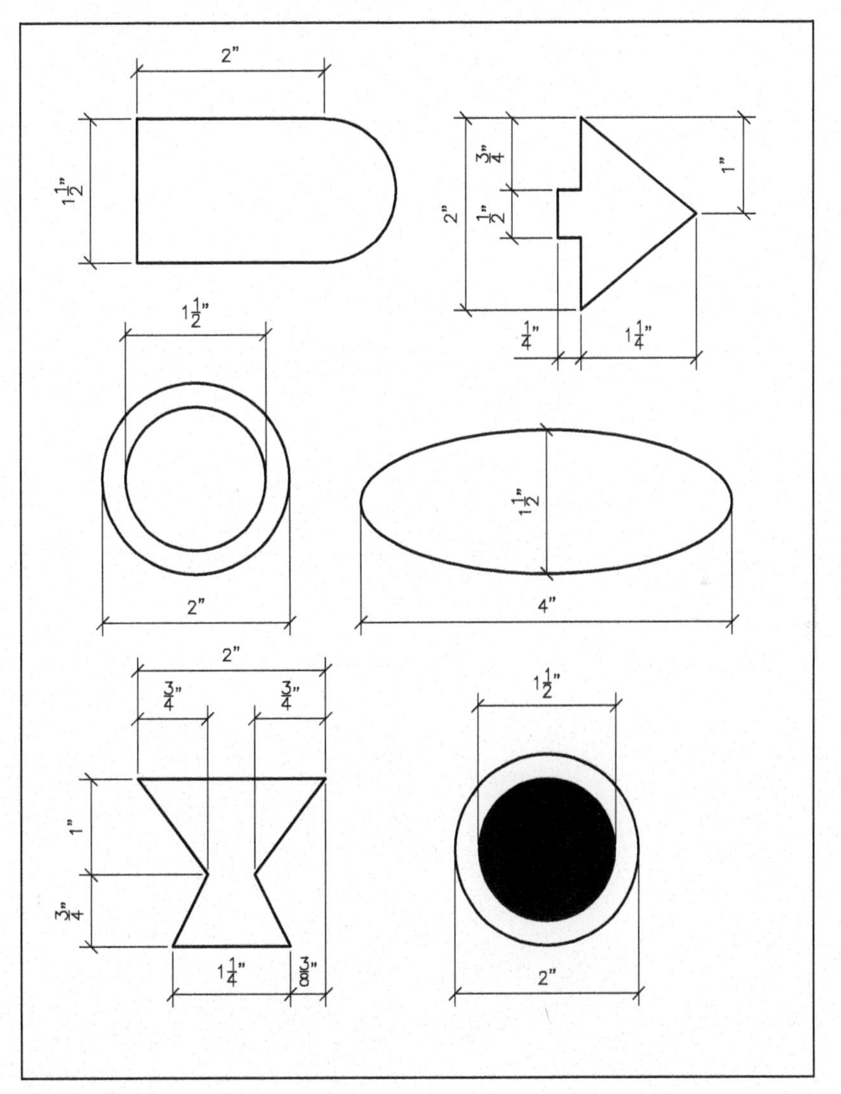

Figure 2-58
Project 2-1: Drawing Shapes I

1. **Use Save As...** to save the drawing with the name **CH2-P1**
2. Set drawing units: **Architectural**
3. Set drawing limits: **8-1/2,11**
4. Set **GRIDDISPLAY**: **0**

5. Set grid: **1/4″**
6. Set snap: **1/8″**
7. Create the following layers:

Layer name	Color	Linetype	Lineweight
Layer1	blue	continuous	.0100 (.25 mm)

Project 2-2: *Drawing a Pattern* **[BASIC]**

Draw the pattern shown in Figure 2-59. Use an architectural scale to measure the pattern and draw it full scale. Use your workspace to make the following settings:

1. Use **Save As...** to save the drawing with the name **CH2-P2**
2. Set drawing units: **Architectural**
3. Set drawing limits: **8-1/2,11**
4. Set **GRIDDISPLAY**: **0**
5. Set grid: **1/4″**
6. Set snap: **1/8″**
7. Create the layers on your own.

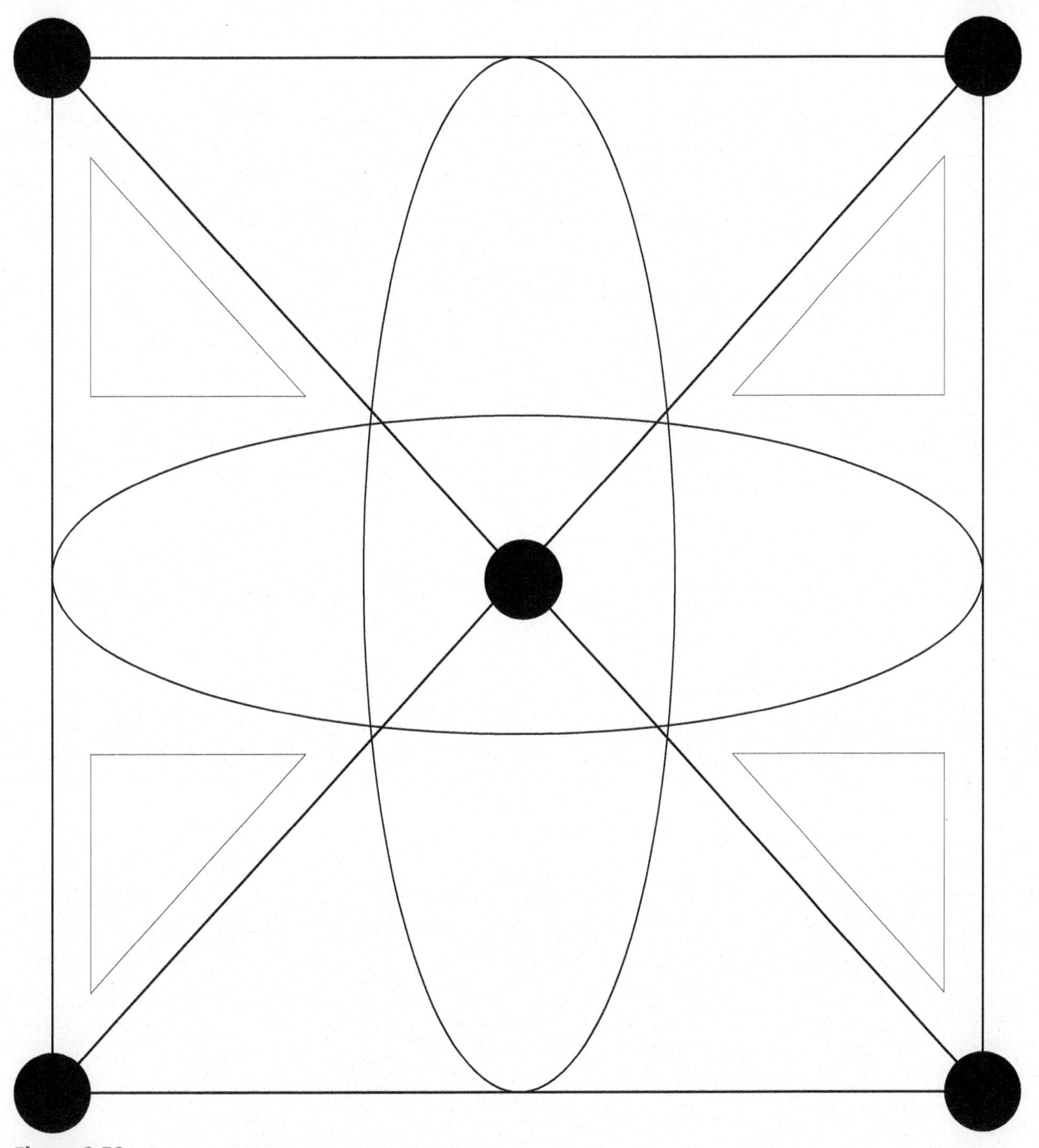

Figure 2-59
Project 2-2: Drawing a pattern (scale: 1″ = 1″)

Project 2-3: *Drawing Shapes II* **[INTERMEDIATE]**

Draw the shapes shown in Figure 2-60. Use an architectural scale to measure the shapes and draw them full scale. Your drawing will be the size shown in the figure. Use your workspace to make the following settings:

1. Use **Save As...** to save the drawing with the name **CH2-P3**
2. Set drawing units: **Architectural**
3. Set drawing limits: **8-1/2,11**
4. Set **GRIDDISPLAY**: **0**
5. Set grid: **1/4"**
6. Set snap: **1/8"**
7. Create the layers on your own.

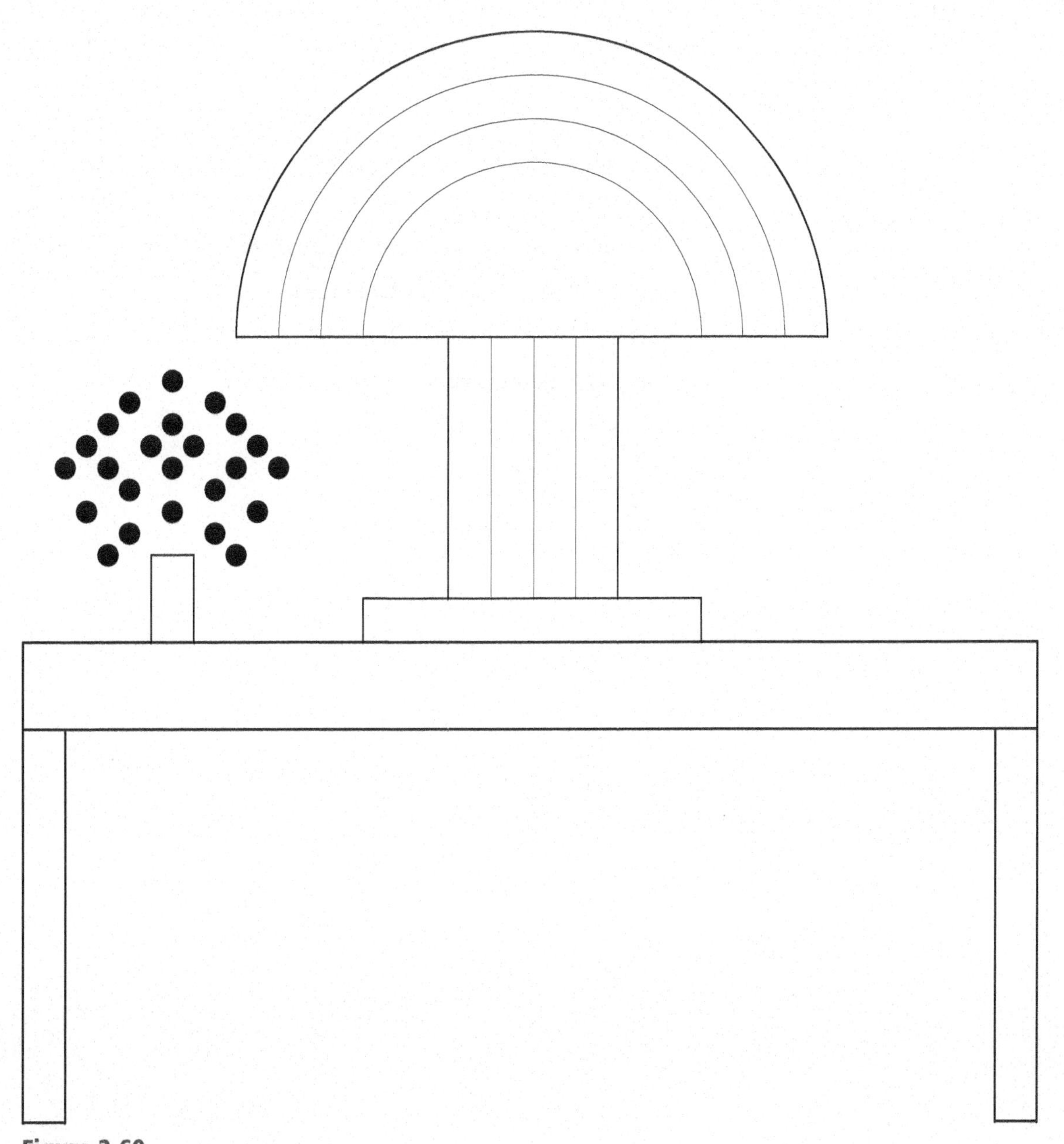

Figure 2-60
Project 2-3: Drawing Shapes II (scale: 1″ = 1″)

Project 2-4: *Drawing a Door* **[INTERMEDIATE]**

Draw the door shape shown in Figure 2-61. Use an architectural scale to measure the figure and draw it full scale. Use your workspace to make the following settings:

1. Use **Save As...** to save the drawing with the name **CH2-P4**
2. Set drawing units: **Architectural**
3. Set drawing limits: **8-1/2,11**
4. Set **GRIDDISPLAY**: **0**
5. Set grid: **1/4"**
6. Set snap: **1/8"**
7. Create the layers on your own.

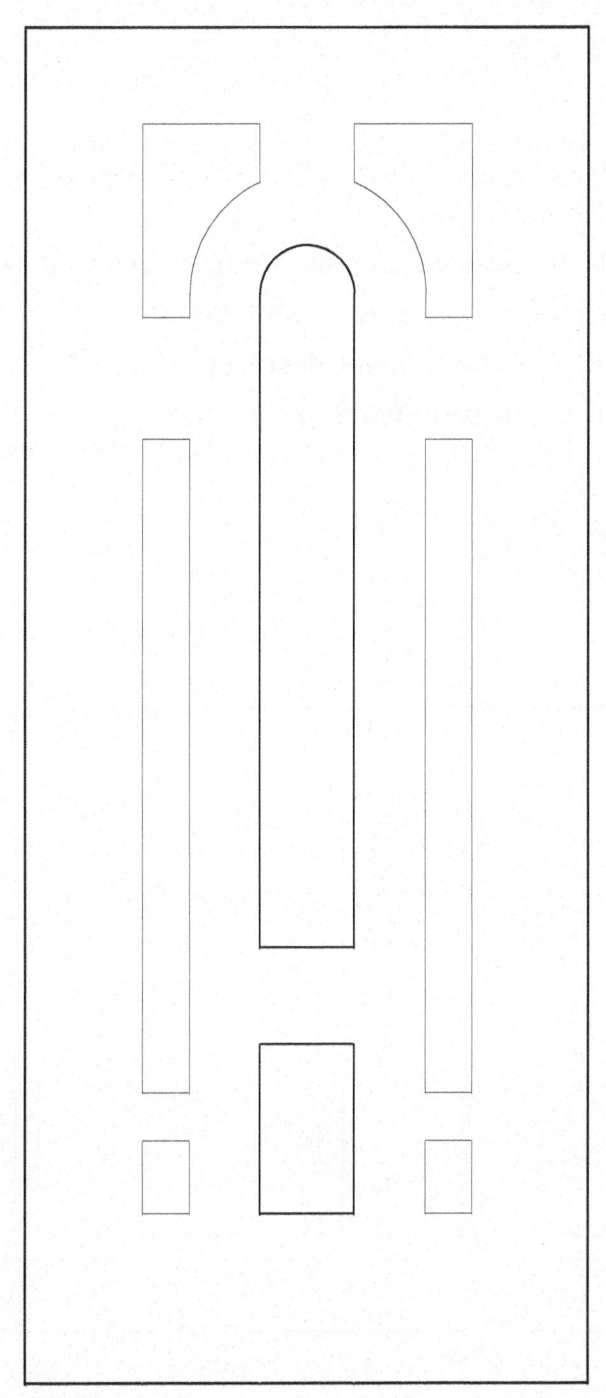

Figure 2-61
Project 2-4: Drawing a door (scale: 1″ = 1″)

Project 2-5: *Drawing Shapes III* [ADVANCED]

Draw the shape shown in Figure 2-62. Use an architectural scale to measure the figure and draw it full scale. Use your workspace to make the following settings:

1. Use **Save As...** to save the drawing with the name **CH2-P5**
2. Set drawing units: **Architectural**
3. Set drawing limits: **8-1/2,11**
4. Set **GRIDDISPLAY**: **0**
5. Set grid: **1/4″**
6. Set snap: **1/16″**
7. Create the layers on your own.

Figure 2-62
Project 2-5: Drawing Shapes III (scale: 1″ = 1)

chapter three

Drawing with AutoCAD: Conference and Lecture Rooms

CHAPTER OBJECTIVES

- Correctly use the following commands and settings:

BREAK	FILLET
CHAMFER	From
COPY	Grips
Distance	HATCH
DIVIDE	ID Point
Drawing Template	MEASURE
EXPLODEEXTEND	MIRROR
OFFSET	Polyline Edit
OSNAP	Rectangle
POINT	RECTANGULAR ARRAY
POLAR ARRAY	ROTATE
POLYGON	Tracking
Polyline	TRIM

- Draw using polar tracking.
- Use Point Style to set the appearance of points.

EXERCISE 3-1
Drawing a Rectangular Conference Room, Including Furniture

In Exercise 3-1, you learn to draw a conference room, including walls and furnishings. When you have completed Exercise 3-1, your drawing will look similar to Figure 3-1.

Step 1. Use your workspace to make the following settings:

1. Use **Save As...** to save the drawing with the name **CH3 EXERCISE1**
2. Set drawing units: **Architectural**

Figure 3-1
Exercise 3-1: Drawing a rectangular conference room, including furniture (scale: 1/4″ = 1′-0″)

NAME
CLASS
DATE

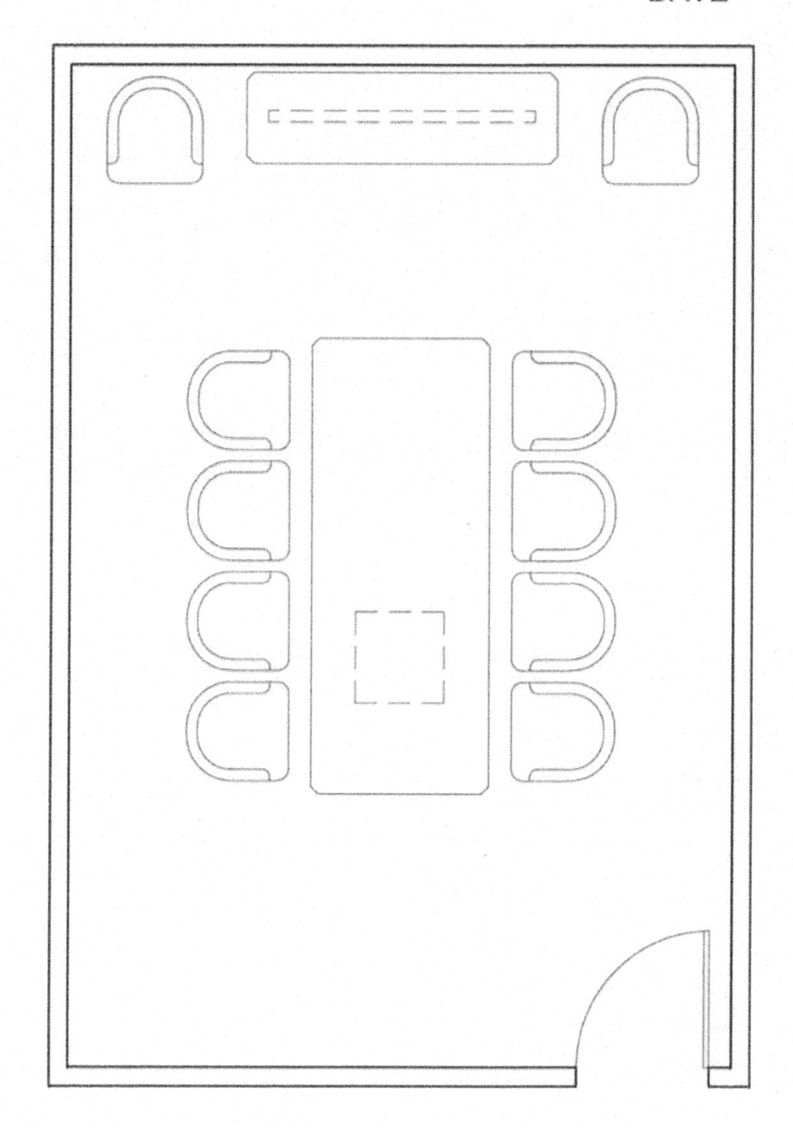

3. Set drawing limits: **25′,35′** (Don't forget the foot marks.)
4. Set **GRIDDISPLAY**: **0**
5. Set grid: **12″**
6. Set snap: **6″**
7. Create the following layers:

Layer name	Color	Linetype	Lineweight
a-anno-text	green	continuous	.006[dp] (.15 mm)
a-door	red	continuous	.004[dp] (.09 mm)
a-wall-intr	blue	continuous	.010[dp] (.25 mm)
i-eqpm-ovhd	red	hidden	.004[dp] (.09 mm)
i-furn	cyan	continuous	.004[dp] (.09 mm)

TIP

You can create the layers by clicking the **New layer** icon and then typing the layer names separated by a comma. When you type the comma, the **Name** list moves to the next layer, and you can type the next layer name.

8. Set layer **a-wall-intr** current.
9. Use **Zoom-All** to view the limits of the drawing.
10. Turn **SNAP**, **GRID**, and **LWDISPLAY** on. The remaining buttons in the status bar are off.

Making a Drawing Template

drawing template: A drawing used to ensure consistency by providing standard styles and settings.

You will be able to use these settings for the remaining tutorials in this chapter. Making a ***drawing template*** of the settings will save you the time of setting up Exercises 3-2, 3-3, and 3-4.

Step 2. Save the drawing as a template on the drive and/or folder in which you want to save (Figures 3-2 and 3-3), as described next:

Prompt	Response
Type a command:	**Save As...**
The **Save Drawing As** dialog box appears:	Click the down arrow in the **Files of type:** input box and click **AutoCAD Drawing Template (*.dwt)**
	Type **Ch3-conference-rm-setup** (in the **File name:** input box so the **Save Drawing As** dialog box appears as shown in Figure 3-2). Notice the text in the **Save in:** input box has changed to **Template**
	Click the down arrow in the **Save in:** input box and highlight the drive and folder in which you want to save
	Click **Save**
The **Template Options** dialog box appears (Figure 3-3):	Type **Setup for Ch3 conference rooms** (as shown in Figure 3-3)
	Click **OK**

NOTE

Remember to save often to avoid losing your work. Backing up your work by saving on two drives is always a good idea.

Figure 3-2
Save the drawing as a template

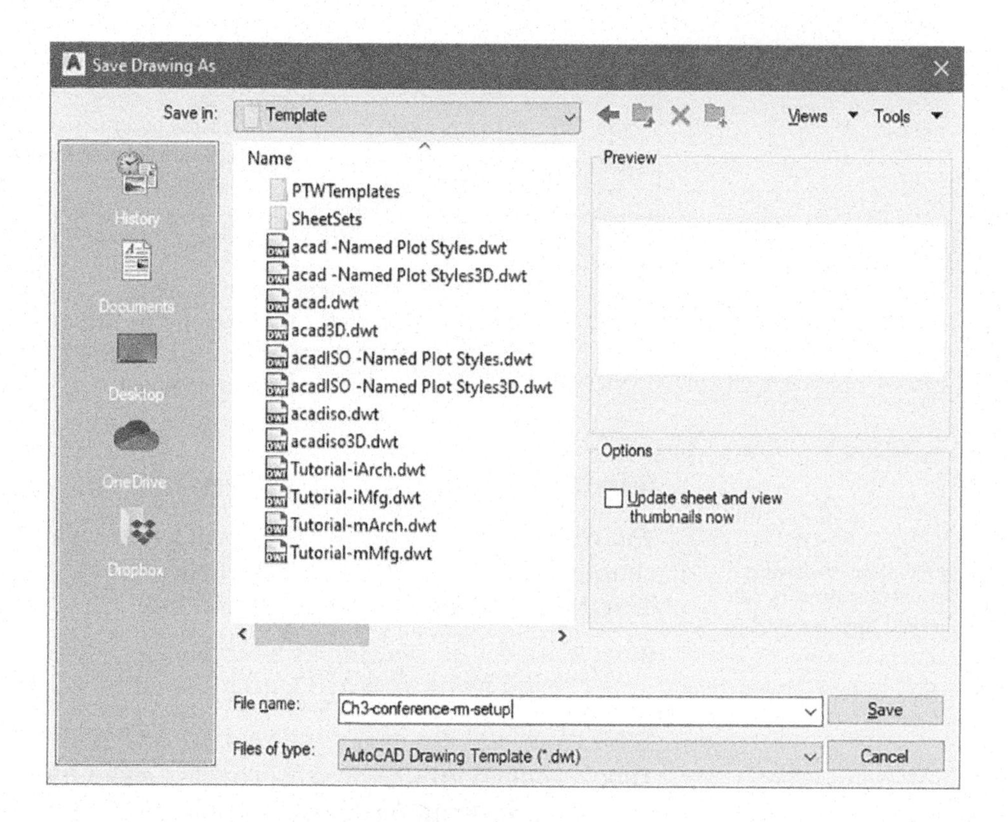

Figure 3-3
Template Options dialog box

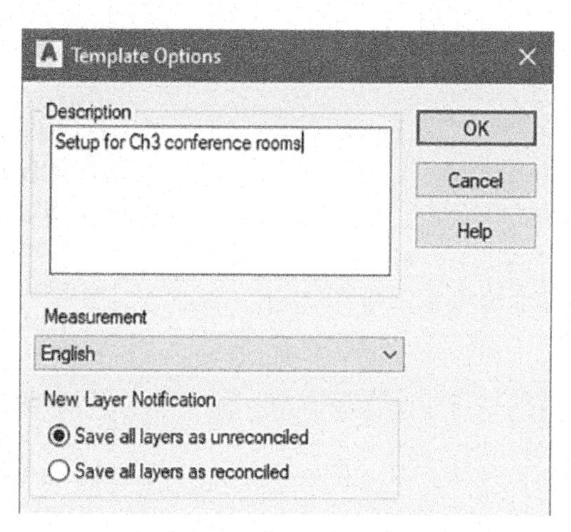

Step 3. The drawing remains as a template in the **Template** folder, so you must save it again as a drawing file. Save the drawing as a drawing file on the drive and/or folder in which you want to save, as described next:

Prompt	**Response**
Type a command:	**Save As...**
The **Save Drawing As** dialog box appears:	Click the down arrow in the **Files of type:** input box and click **AutoCAD 2018 Drawing (*.dwg)**. (Remember, **AutoCAD 2018 Drawing** is the drawing file format used by AutoCAD 2022.)

Prompt	Response
	Click the down arrow in the **Save in:** input box and highlight the drive and folder in which you want to save
	Click **CH3-EXERCISE1** (to appear in the **File name:** input box)
	Click **Save**
The **Save Drawing As** dialog box appears saying *The drawing already exists. Do you want to replace it?*	Click **Yes**

Polyline

polyline: A continuous line or arc composed of one or more segments, the width of which can be changed.

Begin by drawing the conference room walls using the **Polyline** command. A ***polyline*** is different from a regular line in that regardless of the number of segments that make up a polyline, AutoCAD treats a polyline drawn with one operation of the **Polyline** command as a single entity. This is especially helpful when you are drawing walls, because after you draw the outline of a single room or entire building, you can offset the entire polyline to show the thickness of the walls.

POLYLINE	
Ribbon/Panel	Home/ Draw Polyline
Draw Toolbar:	
Menu Bar:	Draw/ Polyline
Type a Command:	PLINE
Command Alias:	PL

Step 4. Use **Polyline** to draw the inside lines of the conference room walls (Figure 3-4), as described next:

Prompt	Response
Type a command:	**Polyline** (or type **PL<Enter>**)
Specify start point:	Type **5′,5′ <Enter>**

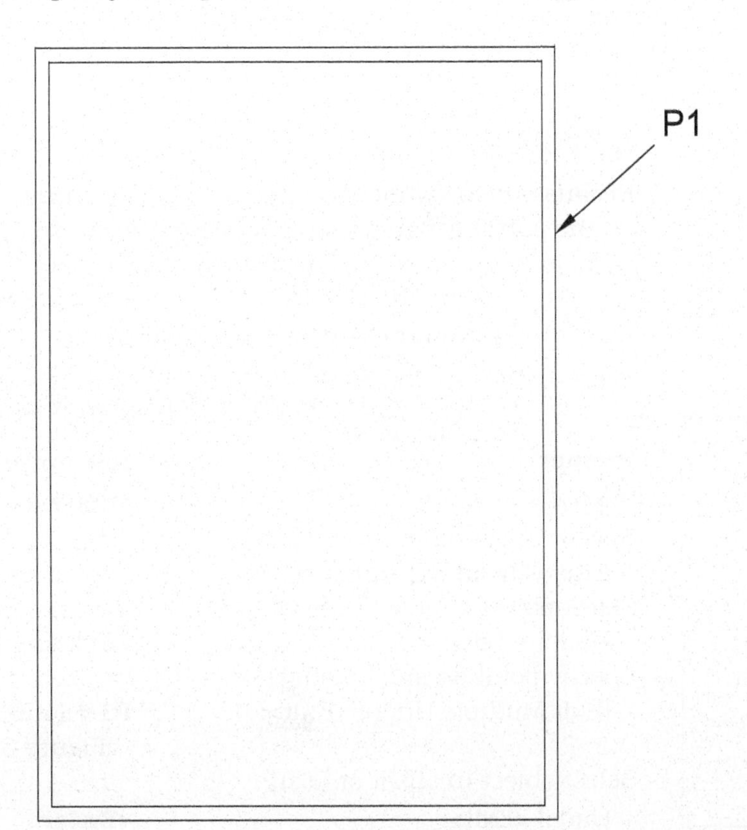

Figure 3-4
Draw the conference room walls

Prompt	Response
	(You have just entered absolute coordinates; the polyline starts 5′ to the right on the x-axis and 5′ up on the y-axis.) Set **ORTHO** on (press **<F8>** or click **ORTHO**)
Current line-width is 0′-0″. Specify next point or [Arc Halfwidth Length Undo Width]:	Move your mouse to the right and type **15′ <Enter>** (direct distance entry)
Specify next point or [Arc Close Halfwidth Length Undo Width]:	Move your mouse up and type **22′ <Enter>**
Specify next point or [Arc Close Halfwidth Length Undo Width]:	Move your mouse to the left and type **15′ <Enter>**
Specify next point or [Arc Close Halfwidth Length Undo Width]:	Type **C <Enter>**

Undo

The **Polyline Undo** option is similar to the **LINE** command. If you do not like the last polyline segment drawn, use the **Undo** option to erase it and continue with the *Specify next point or [Arc Close Halfwidth Length Undo Width]:* prompt.

You can enter any of the capitalized options in the **Polyline** prompt by typing the letters in either upper- or lowercase, or you can simply click the option in the command-line window. The remaining options in the **Polyline** prompt are described later in this chapter.

OFFSET

Because the polyline is treated as a single entity, when you click one point on the polyline, you are able to offset the entire outline of the conference room at once. If the outline of the room had been drawn with the **LINE** command, using the **OFFSET** command would offset each line segment individually, and the corners would not meet.

Step 5. Use the **OFFSET** command to draw the outside line (showing depth) of the conference room walls (Figure 3-4), as described next:

OFFSET	
Ribbon/Panel	Home/ Modify
Draw Toolbar:	
Menu Bar:	Modify/ Offset
Type a Command:	OFFSET
Command Alias:	O

Prompt	Response
Type a command:	**Offset** (or type **O <Enter>**)
Specify offset distance or [Through Erase Layer] <Through>:	Type **5 <Enter>**
Select object to offset or [Exit Undo] <Exit>:	Click anyplace on the polyline
Specify point on side to offset or [Exit Multiple Undo] <Exit>:	**P1→** (outside the rectangle, Figure 3-4)
Select object to offset or [Exit Undo] <Exit>:	**<Enter>**

The four options in the **Offset** prompt are **offset distance**, **Through**, **Erase**, and **Layer**. To complete the conference room wall, 5″ was set as the offset distance. To use any of the other options, type and enter the capital letter shown for the option in the command line or press **<Enter>** to start the **<Through>** default option.

Through

When you start the **Through** option and select the object to be offset, AutoCAD prompts: *Specify through point or [Exit Multiple Undo] <Exit>:*. You respond by clicking a point on the drawing through which you want the object to be offset.

Erase

When you start the **Erase** option, AutoCAD prompts: *Erase source object after offsetting? [Yes No] <No>:*. You can then respond with **Yes** or **No,** and AutoCAD continues by asking you to specify the offset distance, object to offset, and point on side to offset.

Layer

When you start the **Layer** option, AutoCAD prompts: *Enter layer option for offset objects [Current Source] <Source>:*. You can then respond with the selection of current or source layer, and AutoCAD continues by asking you to specify the offset distance, object to offset, and point on side to offset.

EXPLODE

EXPLODE	
Ribbon/ Panel	Home/ Modify
Draw Toolbar:	
Menu Bar:	Modify/ Explode
Type a Command:	EXPLODE
Command Alias:	X

Because the polyline is treated as a single entity, it must be "exploded" before individual line segments can be edited. The **EXPLODE** command splits the solid polyline into separate line segments. After the polyline is exploded into separate line segments, you will be able to add the conference room door.

Step 6. Use the **EXPLODE** command to split the two polylines that make the conference room walls, as described next:

Prompt	**Response**
Type a command:	**Explode** (or type **X <Enter>**)
Select objects:	Click anyplace on the outside polyline
Select objects:	Click anyplace on the inside polyline
Select objects:	**<Enter>**

After you use the **EXPLODE** command, the walls do not look different, but each line segment is now a separate entity.

ID Point

ID POINT	
Ribbon/ Panel	Home/ Utilities
Draw Toolbar:	
Menu Bar:	Tools/ Inquiry/ ID Point
Type a Command:	ID

A useful command, **ID Point** (located under the expanded **Utilities** panel of the **Home** tab on the ribbon) allows you to locate a point on a drawing and have the position of the point displayed in coordinates. AutoCAD remembers the coordinate location of the point. You can initiate a command, such as **LINE,** *immediately* after the **ID Point** command has located a point on the drawing. You can enter the start point of the **LINE** command by using relative or polar coordinates, or you may also use direct distance entry to specify a distance from the established ID point location. Alternatively, you can use the **From** option of the **Osnap** menu (shown later in Figure 3-16 and used in Step 39) to define a reference point and then define the x- and y-offset from that point. The upcoming steps explain this further. Let's continue with the exercise using **ID Point**.

Step 7. Use **Zoom-Window** to magnify the lower-right corner of the conference room where the door will be located.

Step 8. Use **ID Point** to locate a point on the drawing. Use **LINE** to draw the right side of the door opening (Figure 3-5), as described next:

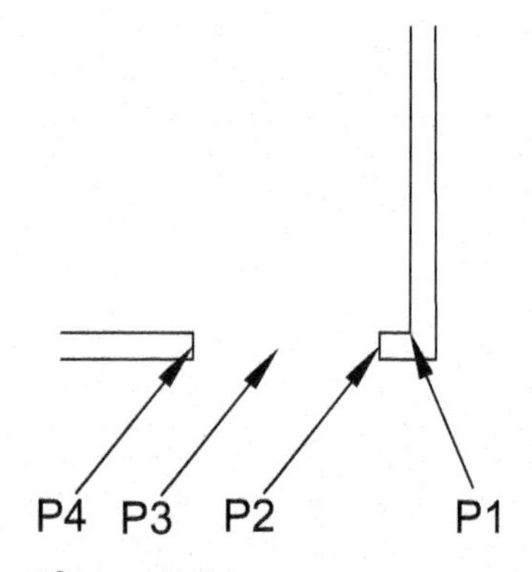

Figure 3-5
Draw the door opening

Prompt	**Response**
Type a command:	**ID Point** (or type **ID <Enter>**)
Specify point:	**P1→** (with **SNAP** on, snap to the inside lower-right corner of the conference room, Figure 3-5)
Point: X = 20′-0″ Y = 5′-0″ Z = 0′-0″	
Type a command:	Type **L <Enter>**
Specify first point:	Type **@6<180 <Enter>** (you have just entered polar coordinates; move your mouse so you can see where the line is attached)
Specify next point or [Undo]:	Type **@5<−90 <Enter>** (using polar coordinates; the line 5″) is extended downward
Specify next point or [Undo]:	**<Enter>**

> **TIP**
>
> Instead of typing **@5<−90 <Enter>**, type **PER <Enter>** and draw the line down until it intersects at a 90° angle with the outside line of the wall. This is an **Object Snap** mode (**Perpendicular**), which is described more fully later in this exercise.

Step 9. Offset the line 3′ to the left to form the door opening, as described next:

Prompt	**Response**
Type a command:	**Offset** (or type **O <Enter>**)
Specify offset distance or [Through Erase Layer] <0′-5″>:	Type **3′ <Enter>**
Select object to offset or [Exit Undo]<Exit>:	**P2→** (the 5″ line you just drew; Figure 3-5)
Specify point on side to offset or [Exit Multiple Undo]<Exit>:	**P3→** (pick to the left)
Select object to offset or [Exit Undo]<Exit>:	**<Enter>**

TRIM

TRIM	
Ribbon/ Panel	Home/ Modify Trim
Draw Toolbar:	
Menu Bar:	Modify/ Trim
Type a Command:	TRIM
Command Alias:	TR

Watch the **Trim** prompts carefully. You cannot pick the objects to trim until you have selected all cutting edges (the edge to which the object is trimmed) and pressed the **<Enter>** key, so that the prompt *Select object to trim or shift-select to extend or [Fence Crossing Project Edge eRase Undo]:* appears. If you are unable to trim an object because it does not intersect a cutting edge, and you have selected **all** as the cutting edges, hold the **<Shift>** key down and click on the entity to extend while still in the **TRIM** command.

NOTE

Press **<Enter>** at the **Trim** prompt *Select objects or <select all>:* to select all objects as cutting edges.

Step 10. Use the **TRIM** command to trim the horizontal wall lines between the two 5″ vertical lines that represent the door opening (Figure 3-5), as described next:

Prompt	Response
Type a command:	**Trim** (or type **TR <Enter>**)
Current settings: Projection = UCS Edge = None, Mode = Quick	
Select object to trim or Shift-select to extend or [cuTting edges Crossing mOde Project eRase]	Click **CuTting edges** in the command-line window, or type **T**
Select objects or <select all>:	**P2→** (the 5″ vertical line; Figure 3-5)
Select objects: 1 found	
Select objects:	**P4→** (the second 5″ vertical line)
Select objects: 1 found, 2 total	
Select objects:	**<Enter>**
Select object to trim or Shift-select to extend or [Fence Crossing Project Edge eRase Undo]:	Click the two horizontal wall lines between **P2→** and **P4→** (Figure 3-5)
	<Enter> (to complete the command)

Step 11. Set layer **a-door** current.

Rectangle

RECTANGLE	
Ribbon/Panel	Home/ Draw
Draw Toolbar:	
Menu Bar:	Draw/ Rectangle
Type a Command:	RECTANG
Command Alias:	REC

Use the Rectangle command to create a door for the floor plan.

Step 12. Draw a 1-1/2″-long by 3′-wide rectangle to represent the door (Figure 3-6):

Prompt	Response
Type a command:	**Rectangle** (or type **REC <Enter>**)
Specify first corner point or [Chamfer Elevation Fillet Thickness Width]:	**P1→** (be sure **SNAP** is on); snap to the upper-right corner of the door opening to begin the rectangle

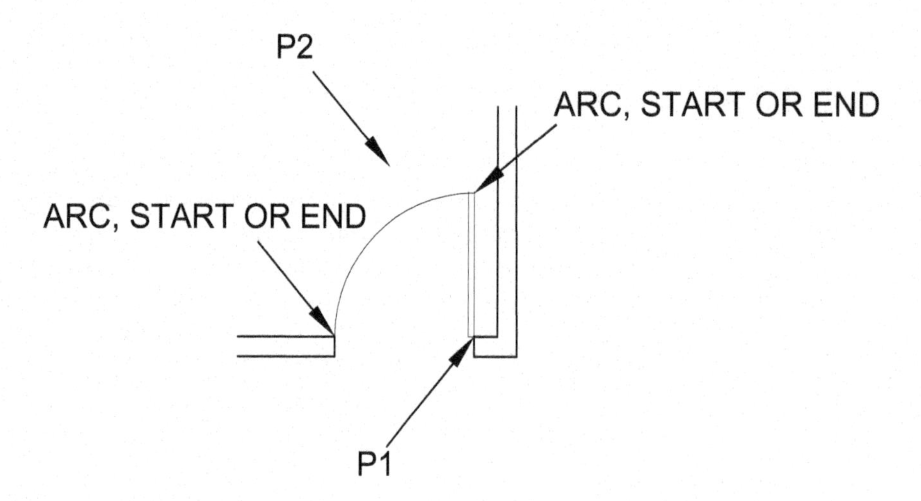

Figure 3-6
Draw the door using **Rectangle** and **Arc-Start, End, Direction** commands

Prompt	**Response**
Specify other corner point or [Area Dimensions Rotation]:	Type **D <Enter>**
Specify length for rectangle <0′-1-1/2″>:	Type **1-1/2 <Enter>**
Specify width for rectangle <3′-0″>:	Type **3′ <Enter>**
Specify other corner point or [Area Dimensions Rotation]:	**P2→** (pick any point to the left of the door symbol so the rectangle appears as shown in Figure 3-6)

Step 13. Use the **Arc-Start, End, Direction** method to draw the door swing arc. Be sure **SNAP** and **ORTHO** are on. The arc can be drawn clockwise or counterclockwise. Move your mouse so the direction of the arc appears, as shown in Figure 3-6.

TIP

The default setting for the **Rectangle** command when the **Dimension** option is selected is:

Default Rotation setting of 0:

Length is the x direction value.
Width is the y direction value.

When you change the Rotation setting to 90:

Length is the y direction value.
Width is the x direction value.

When the rectangle is visible, and the prompt *Specify other corner point:* appears, you change the position of the rectangle by moving your mouse right or left, up or down.

Step 14. Set layer **i-furn** current. Use **Zoom-Extents.**

Step 15. Use the **Polyline** command to draw a credenza (84″ long by 24″ deep) centered on the 15′ rear wall of the conference room, 2″ away from the wall. Locate an ID point by snapping to the inside upper-left corner of the conference room. Start the polyline **@48,-2** (relative coordinates) away from the point. Finish drawing the credenza by using direct distance entry. You can use feet or inches. Remember, AutoCAD defaults to inches in architectural units, so use the foot (′) symbol if you are using feet. Be sure to draw the credenza using one operation of **Polyline** so it is one continuous polyline. Use the **Close** option for the last segment of the polyline (Figure 3-7).

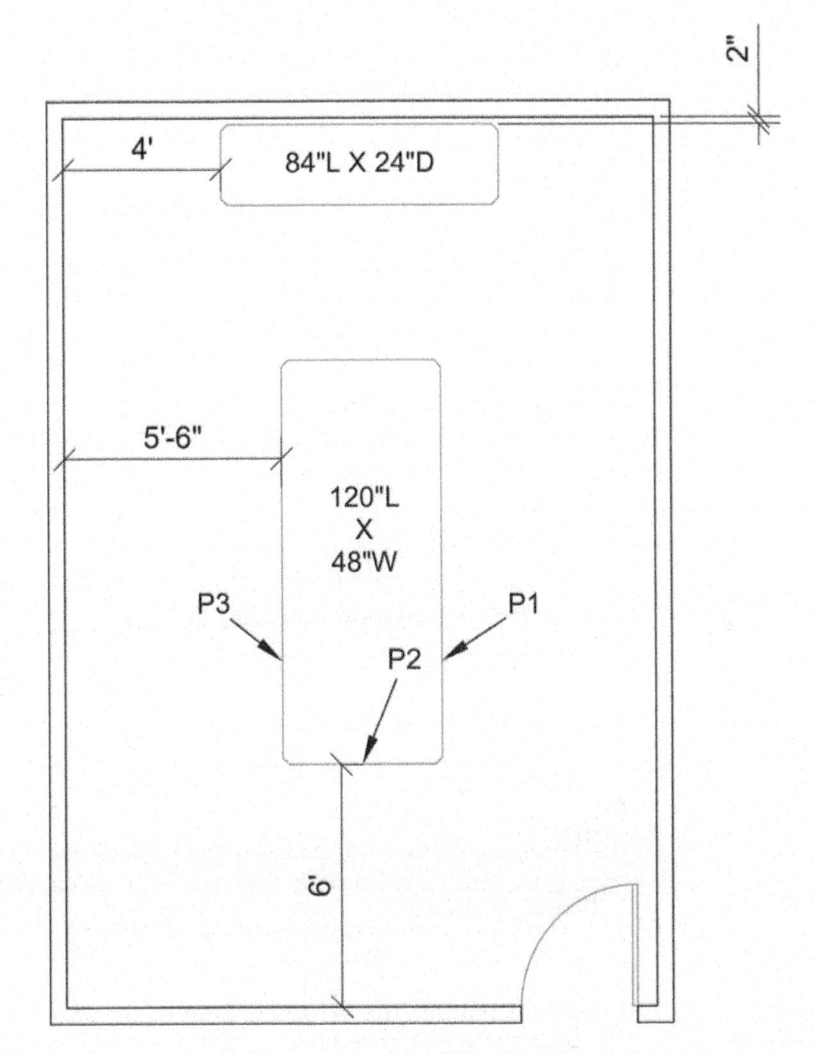

Figure 3-7
Draw a credenza and a conference table; chamfer the corners

Step 16. Draw a conference table 120″ long by 48″ wide using the **LINE** command. You can determine the location of the first point by using **ID Point** or by using grid and snap increments. Use direct distance entry to complete the table. Refer to Figure 3-7 for the location of the table in the room.

Step 17. Zoom in on the table.

CHAMFER

CHAMFER	
Ribbon/ Panel	Home/ Modify (Fillet drop-down) Chamfer
Draw Toolbar:	
Menu Bar:	Modify/ Chamfer
Type a Command:	CHAMFER
Command Alias:	CHA

A **chamfer** is an angle (usually 45°) formed at a corner. The following steps will use the **CHAMFER** command to make the beveled corners of the conference table and credenza.

Step 18. Use the **CHAMFER** command to bevel the corners of the table (Figure 3-7), as described next:

Prompt	**Response**
Type a command:	**Chamfer** (or type **CHA <Enter>**)
(TRIM mode) Current chamfer Dist1 = 0′-0″ Dist2 = 0′-0″	
Select first line or [Undo Polyline Distance Angle Trim mEthod Multiple]:	Type **D <Enter>**
Specify first chamfer distance <0′-0″>:	Type **2 <Enter>**
Specify second chamfer distance <0′-2″>:	**<Enter>**
Select first line or [Undo Polyline Distance Angle Trim mEthod Multiple]:	**P1→** (Figure 3-7)
Select second line or Shift-select to apply corner or [Distance Angle mEthod]:	**P2→**
Type a command:	**<Enter>** (repeat **CHAMFER**)
(TRIM mode) Current chamfer Dist1 = 0′-2″, Dist2 = 0′-2″	
Select first line or [Undo Polyline Distance Angle Trim mEthod Multiple]:	**P2→**
Select second line or Shift-select to apply corner:	**P3→**

NOTE

Type **M <Enter>** (for **Multiple**) at the **Chamfer** prompt so you do not have to repeat the **CHAMFER** command.

Step 19. Chamfer the other corners of the table (Figure 3-7).

Step 20. Zoom in on the credenza.

Polyline

Because you drew the credenza using one operation of the **Polyline** command and used the **Close** option to complete the credenza rectangle, it is treated as a single entity. The **CHAMFER** command **Polyline** option chamfers all corners of a continuous polyline with one click.

Undo

Undo allows you to undo the previous chamfer.

Angle

The Angle option of the **CHAMFER** command allows you to specify an angle and a distance to create a chamfer.

Trim

The Trim option of both the **CHAMFER** and **FILLET** commands allows you to specify that the part of the original line removed by the chamfer or fillet remains as it was. To do this, type **T <Enter>** at the **Chamfer** prompt and **N <Enter>** at the *Trim/No trim <Trim>:* prompt. Test this option on a corner of the drawing so you know how it works. Be sure to return it to the **Trim** option.

mEthod

The **mEthod** option of the **CHAMFER** command allows you to specify whether you want to use the **Distance** or the **Angle** method to specify how the chamfer is to be drawn. The default is the **Distance** method.

Multiple

Multiple allows you you to chamfer multiple corners without repeating the **CHAMFER** command.

Step 21. Use chamfer distance 2″ to chamfer the corners of the credenza (Figure 3-7), as described next:

Prompt	**Response**
Type a command:	**Chamfer**
(TRIM mode) Current chamfer Dist1 = 0′-2″, Dist2 = 0′-2″	
Select first line or [Undo Polyline Distance Angle Trim mEthod Multiple]:	Type **P <Enter>** (accept 2″ distances as previously set)
Select 2D polyline or [Distance Angle mEthod]:	Click anyplace on the credenza
Four lines were chamfered	

> **TIP**
>
> If the last corner of the credenza does not chamfer, this is because the **Close** option of the **Polyline** command was not used to complete the polyline rectangle. Explode the credenza and use the **CHAMFER** command to complete the chamfered corner.

> **NOTE**
>
> While in the **CHAMFER** command, hold down the **<Shift>** key to select any two lines that do not meet, and you can make 90° corners of those two lines. This is the same as a 0 chamfer distance but will work regardless of the chamfer distance set.

When setting the chamfer distance, you can set a different distance for the first and second chamfers. The first distance applies to the first line clicked, and the second distance applies to the second line clicked. You can also set the distance by clicking two points on the drawing.

You can set a chamfer distance of zero and use it to remove the chamfered corners from the table. Using a distance of zero will make 90° corners on the table. Then you can erase the old chamfer lines. This will change the table but not the credenza because it does not work with a polyline. If you have two lines that do not meet to form an exact corner or that overlap, use the **CHAMFER** command with 0 distance to form an exact corner. The **CHAMFER** command will chamfer two lines that do not intersect. It automatically extends the two lines until they intersect, trims the two lines according to the distance entered, and connects the two trimmed ends with the chamfer line.

> **NOTE**
>
> Remember to turn **SNAP** off and on as needed. Turn **SNAP** off when it interferes with selecting an entity. Turn it back on as needed.

Step 22. Zoom in on a portion of the grid outside the conference room walls.

Step 23. Draw a rectangle 26″ wide by 28″ deep using the **POLYLINE** command (Figure 3-8). Be sure to have **SNAP** on when you draw the rectangle. Next, you will edit this rectangle using the **FILLET** command to create the shape of a chair.

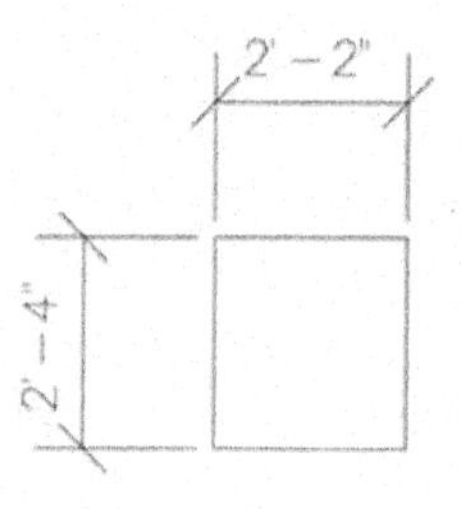

Figure 3-8
Draw a rectangle 26″ wide × 28′ deep using the **POLYLINE** command

FILLET	
Ribbon/Panel	Home/ Modify Fillet
Draw Toolbar:	
Menu Bar:	Modify/ Fillet
Type a Command:	FILLET
Command Alias:	F

FILLET

The **FILLET** command is similar to **CHAMFER**, except the **FILLET** command creates a round instead of an angle.

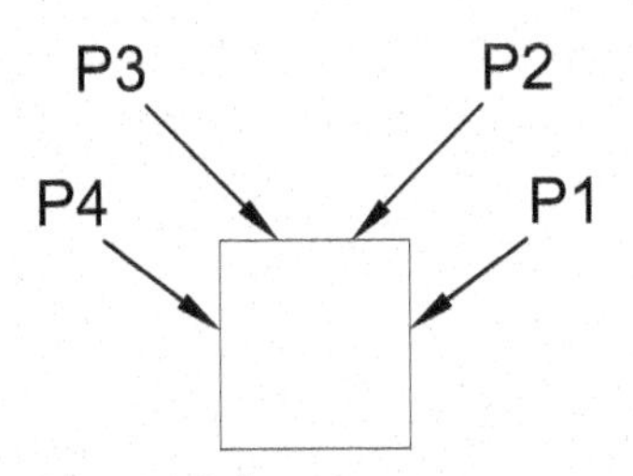

Figure 3-9
Use **FILLET** to create the chair symbol

Step 24. Use the **FILLET** command to edit the back of the rectangle to create the symbol of a chair (Figure 3-9), as described next:

Prompt	Response
Type a command:	**Fillet** (or type **F** **<Enter>**)
Current settings: Mode = TRIM, Radius = 0′-0″	
Select first object or [Undo Polyline Radius Trim Multiple]:	Type **R** **<Enter>**
Specify fillet radius <0′-0″>:	Type **12** **<Enter>**
Select first object or [Undo Polyline Radius Trim Multiple]:	Type **T** **<Enter>**
Enter Trim mode option [Trim No trim]<Trim>:	Type **T** **<Enter>** (verify **Trim** option)
Select first object or [Undo Polyline Radius Trim Multiple]:	**P1→** (Figure 3-9)
Select second object or shift-select to apply corner or [Radius]:	**P2→**
Type a command:	**<Enter>** (repeat **Fillet**)
Current settings: Mode = TRIM, Radius = 1′-0″	
Select first object or [Undo Polyline Radius Trim Multiple]:	**P3→**
Select second object or Shift-select to apply corner or [Radius]:	**P4→**

The **Polyline** option of **Fillet** automatically fillets an entire continuous polyline with one click. Remember to set the fillet radius first.

Fillet will also fillet two circles, two arcs, a line and a circle, a line and an arc, or a circle and an arc.

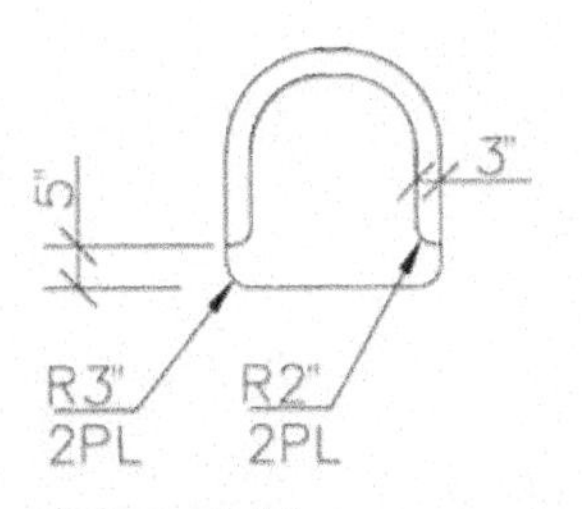

Figure 3-10
Use **OFFSET**, **TRIM**, **EXTEND**, and **FILLET** commands to complete the shape of the chair

Step 25. Use the commands **OFFSET**, **TRIM**, **EXTEND**, and **FILLET** to complete the shape of the chair, as shown in Figure 3-10.

> **NOTE**
>
> When using TRIM, you can invoke the **EXTEND** command by holding down the space bar as you select objects. For more on **EXTEND**, see Chapter 6.

Osnap: An abbreviation of *object snap,* which specifies a snap point at an exact location on an object.

COPY	
Ribbon/Panel	Home/ Modify Copy
Draw Toolbar:	
Menu Bar:	Modify/ Copy
Type a Command:	COPY
Command Alias:	CO or CP

COPY and Osnap-Midpoint

The **COPY** command allows you to copy any part of a drawing either once or multiple times. Object snap modes (***Osnap***), when combined with other commands, help you to draw very accurately. As you become more familiar with the object snap modes, you will use them constantly to draw with extreme accuracy. The following introduces the **Osnap-Midpoint** mode, which helps you snap to the midpoint of a line or arc.

> **NOTE**
>
> Save your drawing often so you do not lose your work.

Step 26. Use the **COPY** command, combined with **Osnap-Midpoint**, to copy the chair you have just drawn (Figure 3-11), as described next:

Prompt	Response
Type a command:	**Copy** (or type **CP <Enter>**)
Select objects:	Click the first corner of a window that will include the chair
Specify opposite corner:	Click the other corner of the window to include the chair
Select objects:	**<Enter>**
Specify base point or [Displacement mOde] <Displacement>:	Type **MID <Enter>**
mid of	**P1→** (Figure 3-11) (Turn **SNAP** off as needed)
Specify second point or [Array] <use first point as displacement>:	**P2→** (be sure **SNAP** is on, and leave enough room to rotate the chair, Figure 3-12)
Specify second point or [Array Exit Undo]<Exit>:	**<Enter>**

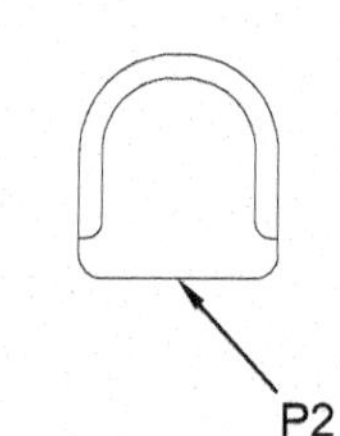

Figure 3-11
Copy the chair using **Osnap-Midpoint**

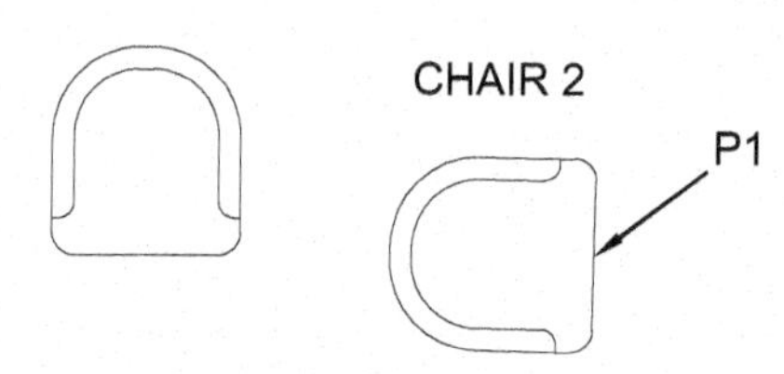

Figure 3-12
The rotated chair

The **Osnap-Midpoint** mode helped you snap very accurately to the midpoint of the line; you used the midpoint of the line that defines the front of the chair as the base point. When using the **COPY** command, carefully choose the base point so that it helps you easily locate the copies.

ROTATE	
Ribbon/Panel	Home/ Modify Rotate
Draw Toolbar:	
Menu Bar:	Modify/ Rotate
Type a Command:	ROTATE
Command Alias:	RO

ROTATE

The **ROTATE** command rotates a selected drawing entity in the counterclockwise direction; 90° is to the left, and 270° (or –90°) is to the right. You select a base point of the entity to be rotated, and the entity rotates about that base point.

> **TIP**
>
> The AutoCAD system variable **ANGDIR** sets the direction of positive angles. If the variable is set to 1, the direction is clockwise and is the same as selecting the **Clockwise** check box on the **Drawing Units** dialog box. When **ANGDIR** is set to 0, the direction is counterclockwise, and the **Clockwise** check box of the **Drawing Units** dialog box is not selected.

Step 27. Use the **ROTATE** command to rotate CHAIR 2 (Figure 3-12), as described next:

Prompt	**Response**
Type a command:	**Rotate** (or type **RO <Enter>**)
Current positive angle in UCS: ANGDIR=counterclockwise ANGBASE=0	
Select objects:	Start the window to include CHAIR 2
Specify opposite corner:	Complete the window to include CHAIR 2
Select objects:	**<Enter>**
Specify base point:	Type **MID <Enter>**
mid of	**P1→** (Figure 3-12)
Specify rotation angle or [Copy Reference]:	Type **90 <Enter>**

NOTE

If part of the entity that is to be rotated lies on the specified base point, that part of the entity remains on the base point while the entity's orientation is changed.

Reference

If you don't know the specific rotation angle, the **Reference** option of the **Rotate** prompt is sometimes easier to use. It allows you to select the object to be rotated and click the base point. Type **R <Enter>** for **Reference.** Then you can enter the *Reference angle:* (current angle) of the object by typing it and pressing **<Enter>**. If you don't know the current angle, you can show AutoCAD the *Reference angle:* by picking the two endpoints of the line to be rotated. You can specify the *New angle:* by typing it and pressing **<Enter>**. If you don't know the new angle, you can show AutoCAD the *New angle:* by picking a point on the drawing.

POINT	
Ribbon/ Panel	Home/Draw (slideout)
Draw Toolbar:	
Menu Bar:	Draw/Point
Type a Command:	POINT
Command Alias:	PO

POINT

The **POINT** command allows you to draw points on your drawing. **Object Snap** recognizes these points as nodes. You use the **Osnap** mode **Node** to snap to points.

You can choose from many different styles of points. The appearance of these points is determined by the **PDMODE** (point definition mode) and **PDSIZE** (point definition size) options within the **POINT** command.

POINT STYLE	
Ribbon/ Panel	Home/ Utilities (slideout) Point Style...
Menu Bar:	Format/Point Style
Type a Command:	PTYPE

Step 28. Use the **Point Style...** command to set the appearance of points, as described next:

Prompt	**Response**
Type a command:	**Point Style...** (or type **PTYPE <Enter>**)
The **Point Style** dialog box appears (Figure 3-13):	Click the **X** box Type **6"** in the **Point Size:** input box Click **OK**

Figure 3-13
Point Style dialog box

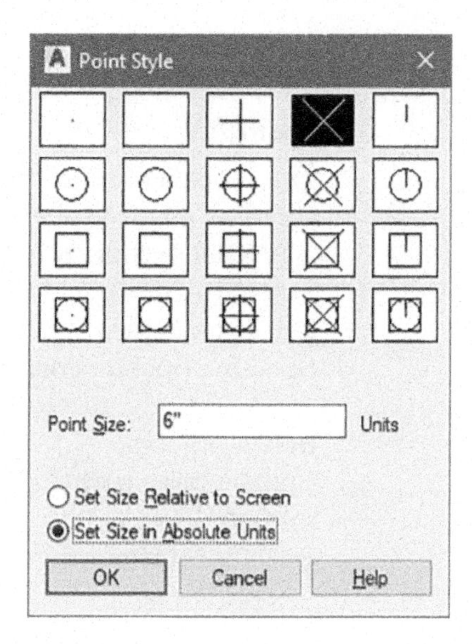

You have just set the points to appear as an X, and they will be 6″ high. The **Point Style** dialog box shows the different types of points available. You may set the size of the point in a size relative to the screen or in absolute units.

Step 29. Use the **OFFSET** command to offset the line that defines the long left side of the conference table. The chairs will be placed 6″ from the edge of the table, so set 6″ as the offset distance. Offset the line outside the table, as shown in Figure 3-14. You will use this line as a construction line to help locate the chairs.

DIVIDE

The **DIVIDE** command indicates the divisions of an entity in equal parts and places point markers along the entity at the dividing points. The **PDMODE** variable has been set to 3 (an X point), so an X will appear as the point marker when you use **DIVIDE.**

DIVIDE	
Ribbon/ Panel	Home/Draw (slideout)
Menu Bar:	Draw/Point/ Divide
Type a Command:	DIVIDE
Command Alias:	DIV

Step 30. Use **DIVIDE** to divide the offset line into eight equal segments (Figure 3-14), as described next:

Prompt	Response
Type a command:	**Divide** (or type **DIV <Enter>**)
Select object to divide:	Click anyplace on the offset line
Enter the number of segments or [Block]:	Type **8 <Enter>** (the X points divide the line into eight equal segments)

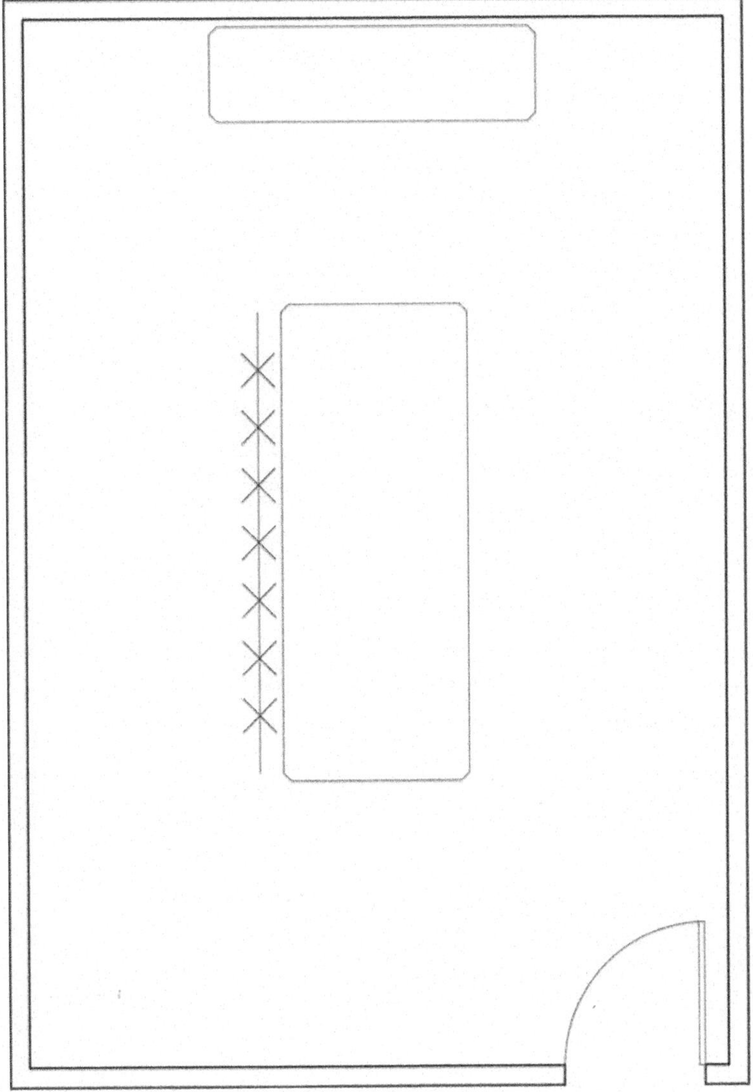

Figure 3-14
Offset the lines defining the long left side of the conference table and use the **DIVIDE** command to show eight equal segments along the line object

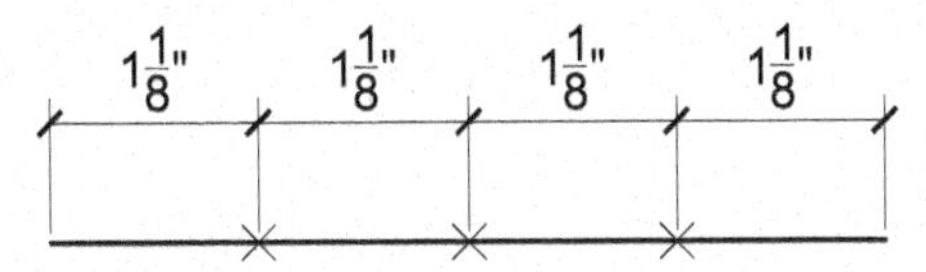

DIVIDE: Four equal parts of a 4-1/2″ line

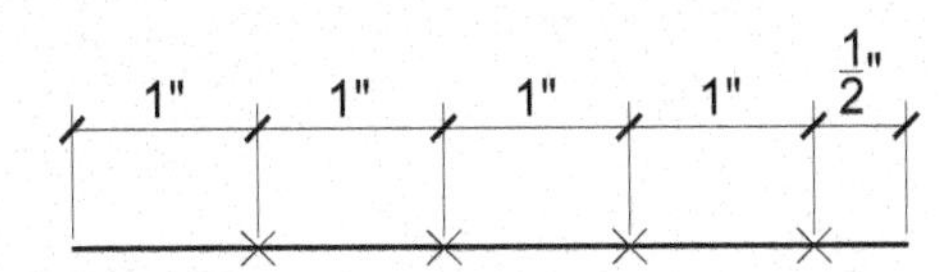

MEASURE: 1″ lengths of a 4-1/2″ line

Figure 3-15
Examples of the **DIVIDE** and **MEASURE** commands

MEASURE

MEASURE	
Ribbon/ Panel	Home/Draw (slideout)
Menu Bar:	Draw/Point/ Measure
Type a Command:	MEASURE

The **MEASURE** command is similar to the **DIVIDE** command (Figure 3-15) except that with **MEASURE,** you specify the distance. **DIVIDE** calculates the interval to divide an entity into a specified number of equal segments. The **MEASURE** command places point markers at a specified distance along an entity.

The measurement and division of a circle start at the angle from the center that follows the current snap rotation. The measurement and division of a closed polyline start at the first vertex drawn. The **MEASURE** command also draws a specified block at each mark between the divided segments.

OSNAP

It is important that you become familiar with and use object snap modes in combination with **DRAW, MODIFY,** and other AutoCAD commands. When an existing drawing object is not located on a snap point, connecting a line or other drawing entity exactly to it is impossible. You may try, and you may think that the two points are connected, but a close examination **(Zoom-Window)** will reveal that they are not. Object snap modes are used in combination with other commands to connect exactly to points of existing objects in a drawing. You need to use object snap modes constantly for complete accuracy.

Activating Osnap

You can activate **Osnap** mode in the following ways:

- Type the **Osnap** abbreviation (first three letters of the object snap mode).
- Press **<Shift>** and right-click in the drawing area, then choose an object snap mode from the **Object Snap** menu that appears (Figure 3-16).
- Right-click **OSNAP** on the status bar, and then click Object Snap **Settings...** (Figure 3-17) to access the **Drafting Settings** dialog box (Figure 3-18). Select the desired **Osnap** mode or modes check boxes.

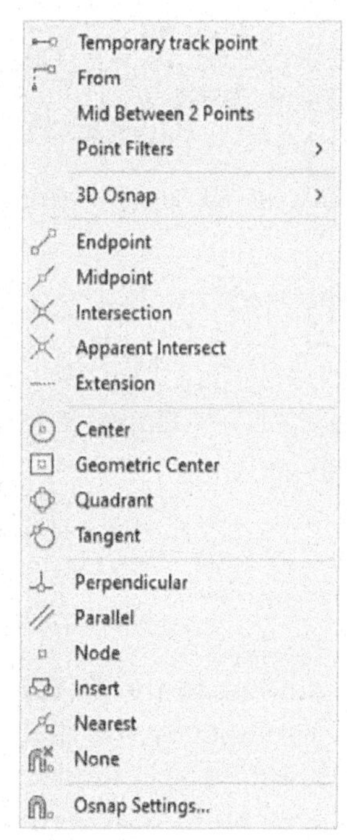

Figure 3-16
Activate the **Osnap** menu by pressing **<Shift>** and right-click in the drawing area

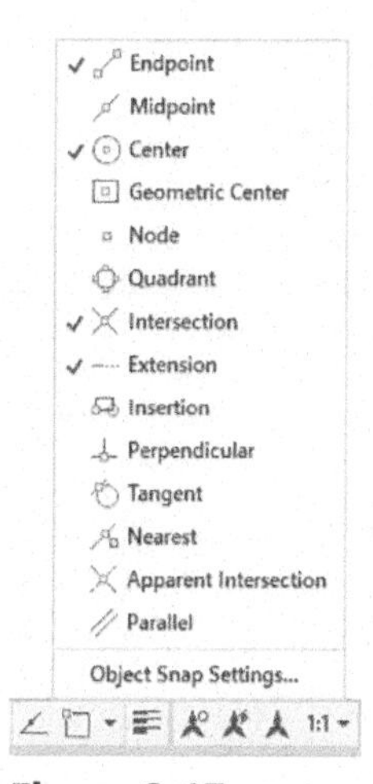

Figure 3-17
Activate **OSNAP** by right-clicking **Object Snap** on the status bar, then clicking **Settings...** to access the **Drafting Settings** dialog box

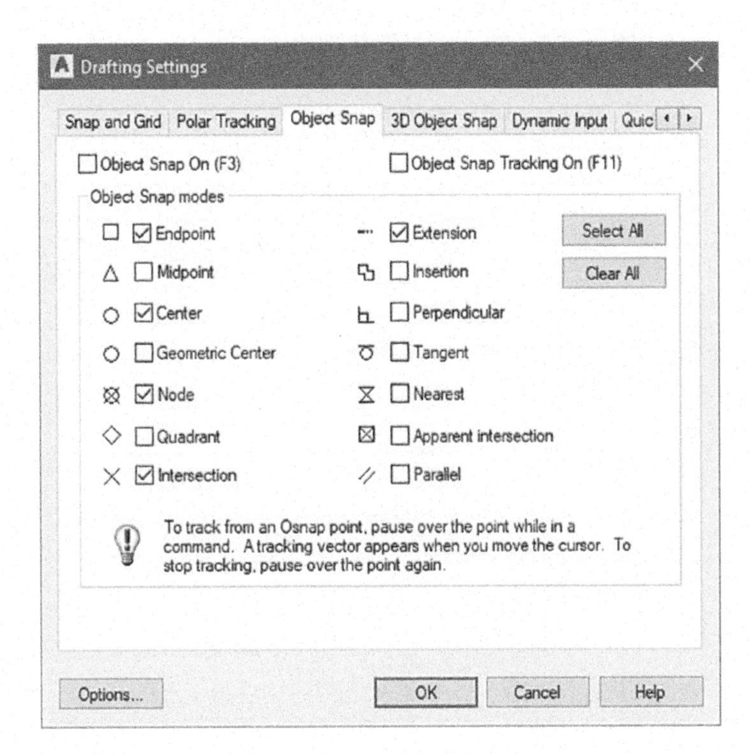

Figure 3-18
Drafting Settings dialog box with **Node** selected

Copy, Osnap-Midpoint, Osnap-Node

Next, you copy the chair several times using different object snap modes.

Step 31. Right-click **Snap cursor to 2D reference points** on the status bar, click **Object Snap Settings...**, and set a running **Osnap** mode of **Node** (Figures 3-17 and 3-18).

Step 32. Make sure **ORTHO** and **SNAP** are off and **OSNAP** is on in the status bar.

Step 33. Use the **COPY** command (combined with **Osnap-Midpoint** and **Osnap-Node**) to copy CHAIR 2 four times on the left side of the conference table (Figure 3-19), as described next:

Prompt	Response
Type a command:	**Copy** (or type **CP <Enter>**)
Select objects:	Click below and to the left of CHAIR 2
Specify opposite corner:	Window CHAIR 2
Select objects:	**<Enter>**
Specify base point or [Displacement mOde] <Displacement>:	Type **MID <Enter>**
mid of	**P1→** (anyplace on the straight line that forms the front of the chair symbol)
Specify second point or [Array] <use first point as displacement>:	**P2→, P3→, P4→, P5→ <Enter>** (Figure 3-19)

The points act as nodes (snapping exactly on the center of the X) when a running **Object Snap** is set.

Step 34. Type **PDMODE <Enter>** at the command prompt. Set the **PDMODE** to **1**, and the drawing is regenerated. The Xs will disappear. You have set the **PDMODE** (point definition mode) to be invisible.

Step 35. Erase the offset line used to locate the chairs on the left side of the table. Use **<F7>** to redraw if it looks as if part of the chairs has been erased.

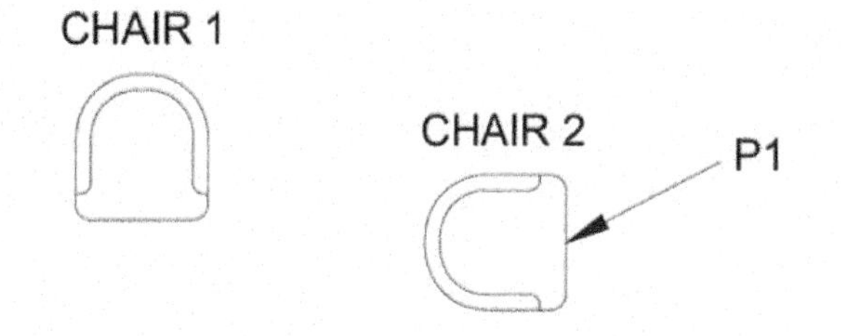

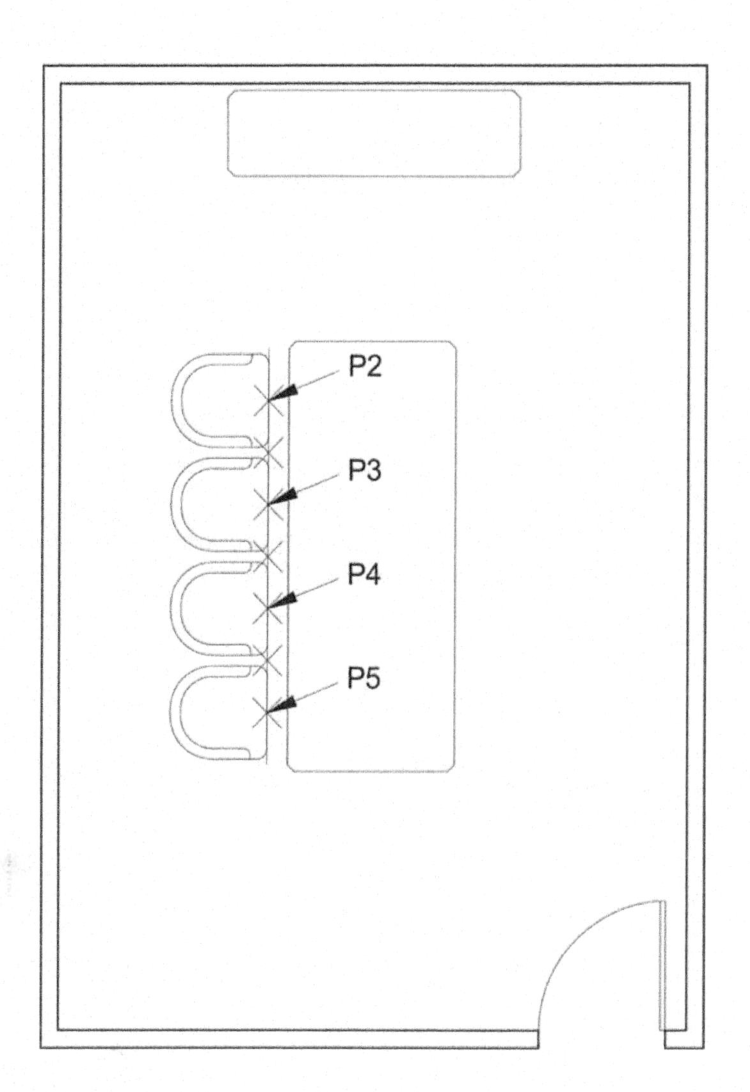

Figure 3-19
Copy CHAIR 2 four times on the left side of the conference table using **Osnap-Midpoint** and **Osnap-Node**

MIRROR	
Ribbon/ Panel	Home/Modify Mirror
Draw Toolbar:	
Menu Bar:	Modify/ Mirror
Type a Command:	MIRROR
Command Alias:	MI

MIRROR

The **MIRROR** command allows you to mirror about an axis any entity or group of entities. The axis can be at any angle.

Step 36. Draw the chairs on the right side of conference table using the **MIRROR** command (Figure 3-20), as described next:

Prompt	**Response**
Type a command:	**MIRROR** (or type **MI <Enter>)**
Select objects:	**P1→**

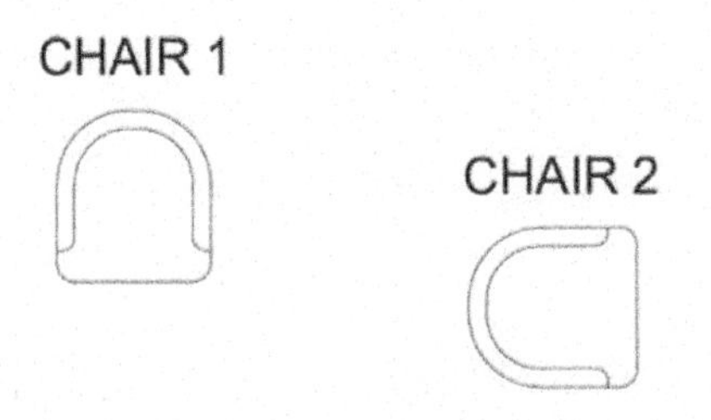

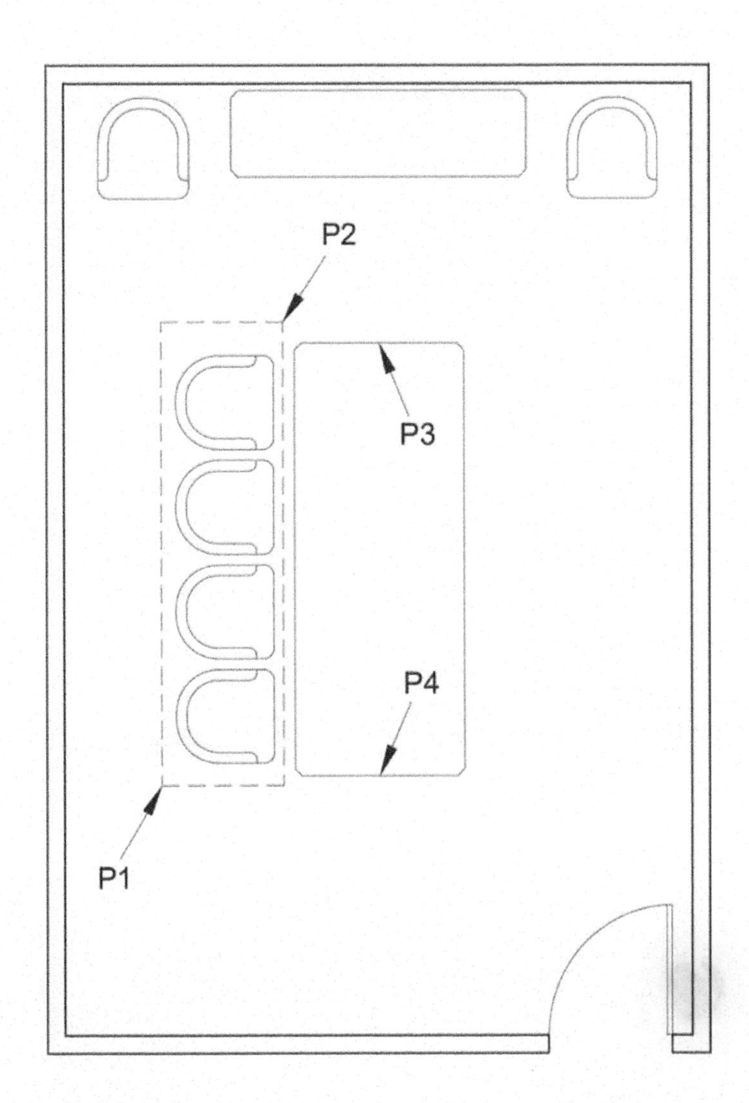

Figure 3-20
Use the **MIRROR** command to copy the four chairs on the left side to the right side, and then copy CHAIR 1 to both sides of the credenza

Prompt	**Response**
Specify opposite corner:	**P2→** (window the chairs on the left side of the conference table)
68 found	
Select objects:	**<Enter>**
Specify first point of mirror line:	Type **MID <Enter>**
mid of	**P3→**
Specify second point of mirror line:	Type **MID <Enter>**
mid of	**P4→**
Erase source objects? [Yes No] <N>:	**<Enter>**

Step 37. Add the chairs on each side of the credenza as shown in Figure 3-20.

Step 38. Set layer **i-eqpm-ovhd** current.

Step 39. Add the 72″ × 3″ recessed projection screen and the 24″ × 24″ ceiling-mounted projector to the plan as shown in Figure 3-21. Let's use the **From** option of the **OSNAP** menu to do this.

Start the **Rectangle** command, **<Shift>** and right-click to open the **OSNAP** menu, select **From**, and then show the inner upper-left corner of the room as the reference point. You will be prompted to define the x- and y-offsets: 4′6″ and −1′, respectively. 72″ and 3″. This fixes one corner of the rectangle for the recessed projection screen. The second corner is fixed by typing in **@72,-3** and pressing **<Enter>**. As for the ceiling-mounted projector, use the inner lower-left corner of the room as the reference, 6′6″ and 8′0″ as the x- and y-offsets to fix the lower-left corner of the rectangle and **@24,24** to fix the second point of the rectangle.

Figure 3-21
Add the projection screen and projector

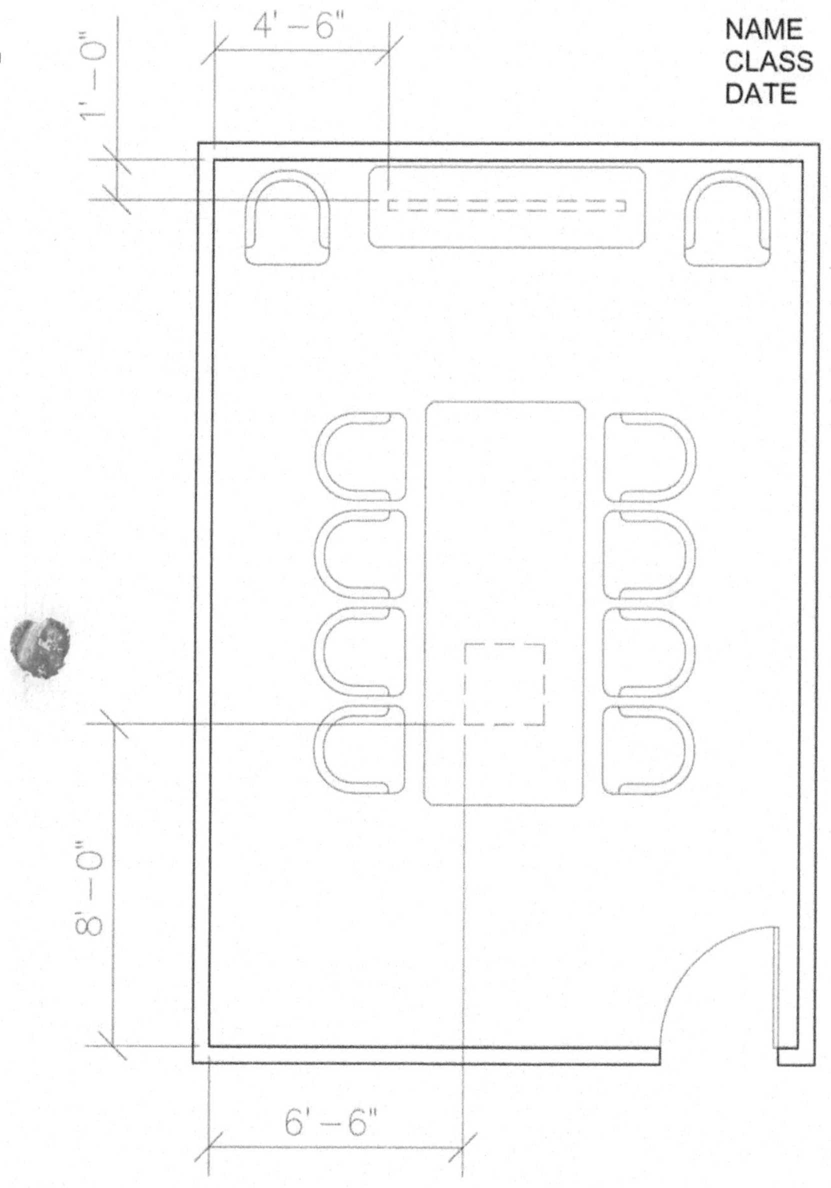

Step 40. Erase the chairs you have drawn outside the conference room walls.

Step 41. Set layer **a-anno-text** current.

> **TIP**
>
> Remember to change the **LTSCALE** setting if your hidden linetype does not show as hidden. To make the line segment length or spacing smaller, enter a linetype scale factor smaller than 1 but larger than 0 at the **LTSCALE** prompt. To make the line segment length and spacing larger, enter a linetype scale factor larger than 1.

Step 42. Use the **Single Line Text** command (type **DT <Enter>**) to type your name, class number, and date, 6″ high in the upper-right corner. When plotted to a scale of 1/4″ = 1′-0″, the 6″-high text will be 1/8″ high.

> **FOR MORE DETAILS**
>
> Chapter 6 describes and covers using annotative text. When adding annotative text, you have to enter only the size of the text you want in the printed drawing, and AutoCAD automatically calculates the size of the text on the drawing.

Step 43. When you have completed Exercise 3-1 (Figure 3-22), save your work in at least two places.

Step 44. Print your drawing from the **Model** tab at a scale of **1/4″ = 1′-0″**.

> **FOR MORE DETAILS**
>
> In Chapter 5 you will use a color-dependent plot style to change layer colors 1 through 7 to the color black when printing and plotting.

Osnap Modes That Snap to Specific Drawing Features

You have already used **Osnap-Midpoint** and **Node.** They are examples of **Osnap** modes that snap to drawing features. **Midpoint** snaps to the midpoint of a line or arc, and **Node** snaps to a point entity.

The following list describes other **Osnap** modes that snap to specific drawing features. AutoCAD **Osnap** modes treat each edge of a solid and each polyline segment as a line. You will use many of these **Osnap** modes while completing the exercises in this book.

Mid Between 2 Points (M2P): Snaps to a point midway between two points that you pick on the drawing.

Endpoint (END): Snaps to the endpoint of a line or arc. The end of the line or arc nearest the point picked is snapped to.

Midpoint (MID): Snaps to the midpoint of a line or arc.

Figure 3-22
Exercise 3-1 complete

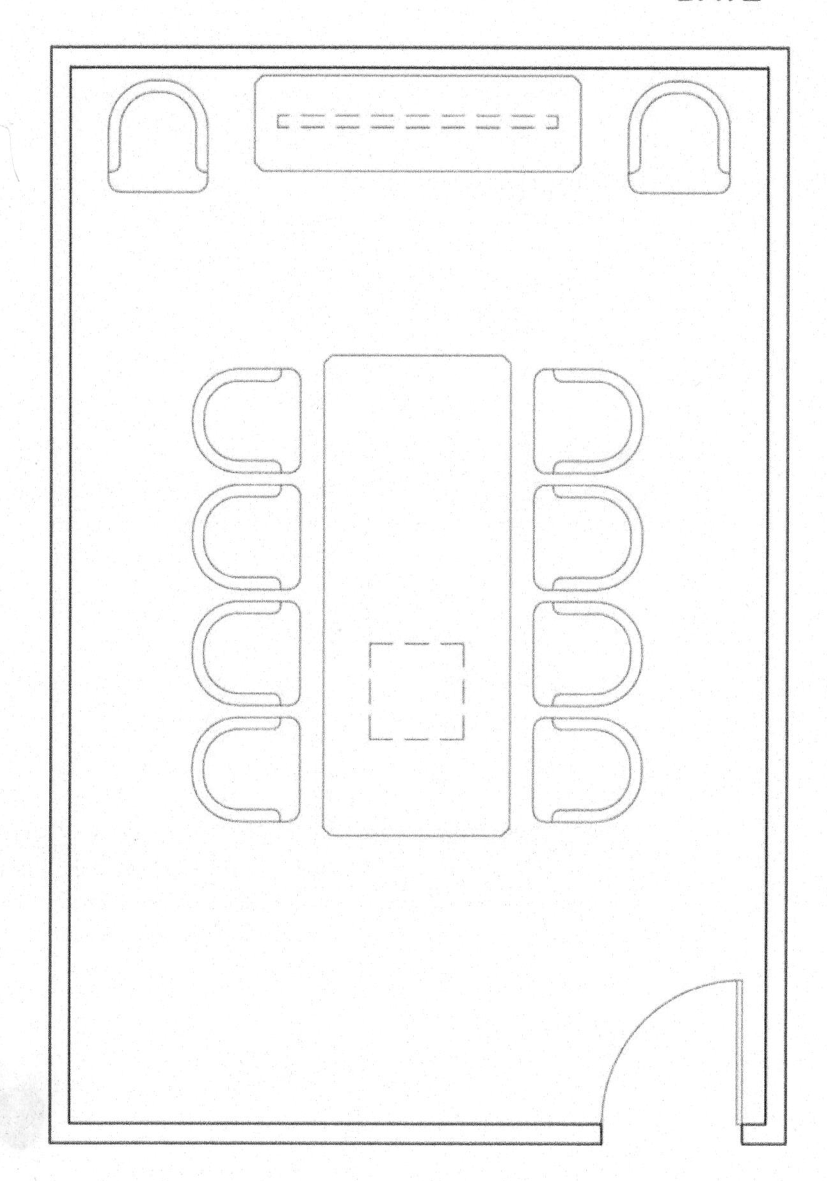

Center (CEN): Snaps to the center of an arc, ellipse, or circle.

Geometric Center (GCEN): Snaps to the centroid of a closed polyline or spline.

Node (NOD): Snaps to a point (**POINT** command).

Quadrant (QUA): Snaps to the closest quadrant point of an arc or circle. These are the 0°, 90°, 180°, and 270° points on a circle, arc, or ellipse.

Intersection (INT): Snaps to the intersection of two lines, a line with an arc or circle, or two circles and/or arcs.

Extension (EXT): Extends a line or arc. With a command and the **Extension** mode active, pause over a line or arc, and after a small plus sign is displayed, slowly move along a temporary path that follows the extension of the line or arc. You can draw objects to and from points on the extension path line.

Insertion (INS): Snaps to the insertion point of text, attribute, or block. (These objects are described in later chapters.)

Perpendicular (PER): Snaps to the point on a line, circle, or arc that forms a 90° angle from that object to the last point. For example, if you are drawing a line, click the first point of the line, and then use **Perpendicular** to connect the line to another line. The new line will be perpendicular to the first pick.

Tangent (TAN): Snaps to the point on a circle or arc that when connected to the last point entered forms a line tangent to (touching at one point) the circle or arc.

Nearest (NEA): Snaps to the point on a line, arc, or circle that is closest to the position of the crosshairs; also snaps to any point (**POINT** command) node that is closest to the crosshairs. You will use this mode when you want to be sure to connect to a line, arc, circle, or point, and cannot use another **Osnap** mode.

Apparent intersect (APP): Snaps to what appears to be an intersection even though one object is above the other in 3D space.

Parallel (PAR): Draws a line parallel to another line. With the **LINE** command active, click the first point of the new line you want to draw. With the **Parallel** mode active, pause over the line you want to draw parallel to, until a small parallel line symbol is displayed. Move the cursor away from but parallel to the original line, and an alignment path is displayed for you to complete the new line.

For the **LINE** command, you can also use the **Tangent** and **Perpendicular** modes when picking the first point of the line. This allows you to draw a line tangent to, or perpendicular to, an existing object.

Running Osnap Modes

You can use individual **Osnap** modes while in another command, as you did with **Midpoint**. You can also set a running **Osnap** mode, as you did with **Node**. A running **Osnap** mode is constantly in effect while you are drawing, until it is disabled. This saves time by eliminating your constant return to the **Osnap** setting.

Clicking **OSNAP** on in the status bar (or pressing function key **<F3>**) will activate any running **Osnap** modes you have set, and clicking it off will disable any running **Osnap** modes you have set.

> **NOTE**
>
> Be sure to disable a running **Osnap** mode when you are through using it. A running **Osnap** mode can interfere with your drawing if it snaps to a point to which you do not intend to snap.

Osnap Settings: Marker, Aperture, Magnet, Tooltip

Note the markers (small symbols) beside each **Object Snap** mode in the **Drafting Settings** dialog box, **Object Snap** tab (Figure 3-18). You control the display of the markers via the **Drafting** tab of the **Options** dialog box (Figure 3-23). Selecting the **Marker** check box adds the marker symbol to the crosshairs. The **AutoSnap Marker Size** slider bar near the bottom of the dialog box specifies the size of the marker.

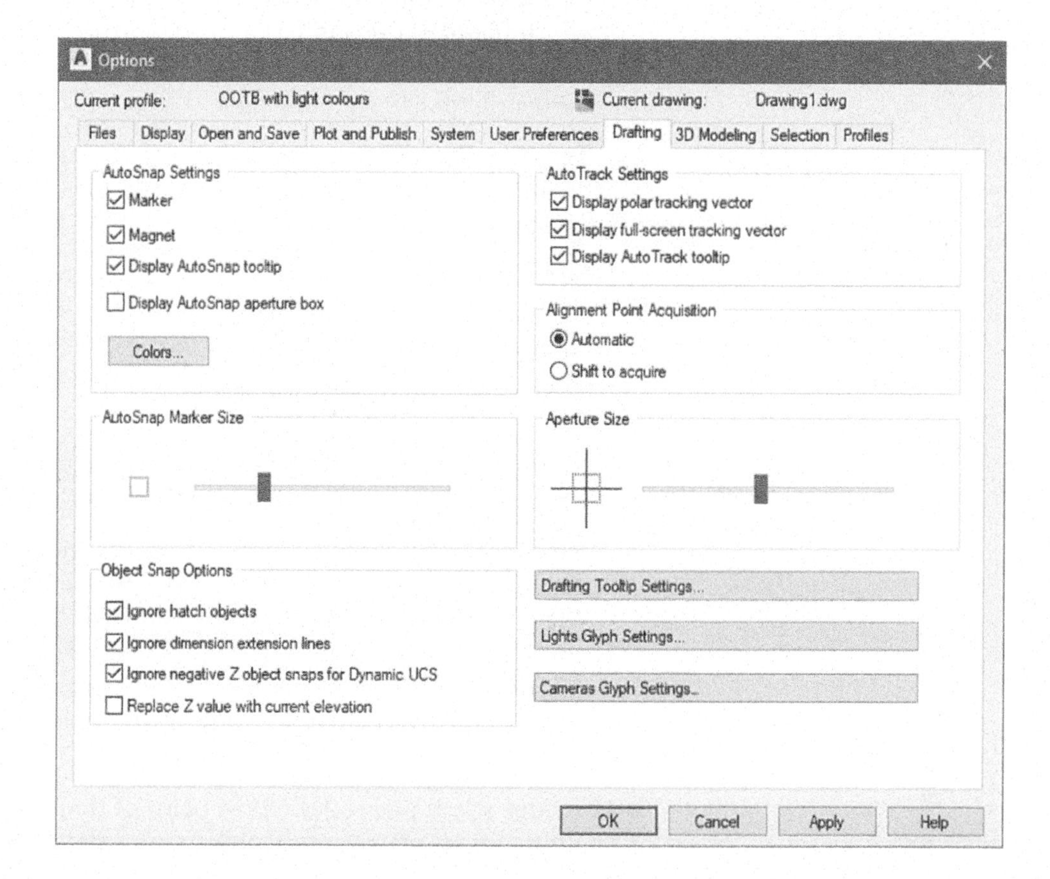

Figure 3-23
Options dialog box, **Drafting** tab

When **Osnap** is activated, you can also add a small target box called an *aperture* to the screen crosshairs. This small box shows the area within which AutoCAD will search for **Object Snap** candidates. Select the **Display AutoSnap aperture box** on the **Drafting** tab of the **Options** dialog box. The **Aperture Size** slider bar on the right side of the dialog box specifies the size of the box.

EXERCISE 3-2
Drawing a Rectangular Lecture Room, Including Furniture

In Exercise 3-2, you draw a lecture room, including walls and furnishings. When you have completed Exercise 3-2, your drawing will look similar to Figure 3-24.

Step 1. Click **Open...**, change the **Files of type:** input box to **Drawing Template (*.dwt)**, and open template **Ch3-conference-rm-setup**, which you previously made at the beginning of Exercise 3-1.

Step 2. Click **Save As...**, change the **Files of type:** input box to **AutoCAD 2018 Drawing (.dwg)**, and save the template as a drawing file named **CH3-EXERCISE2**.

Step 3. Verify the following settings:

1. Drawing units: **Architectural**
2. Drawing limits: **25′,35′**
3. **GRIDDISPLAY**: **0**
4. Grid: **12″**
5. Snap: **6″**
6. Verify the following layers:

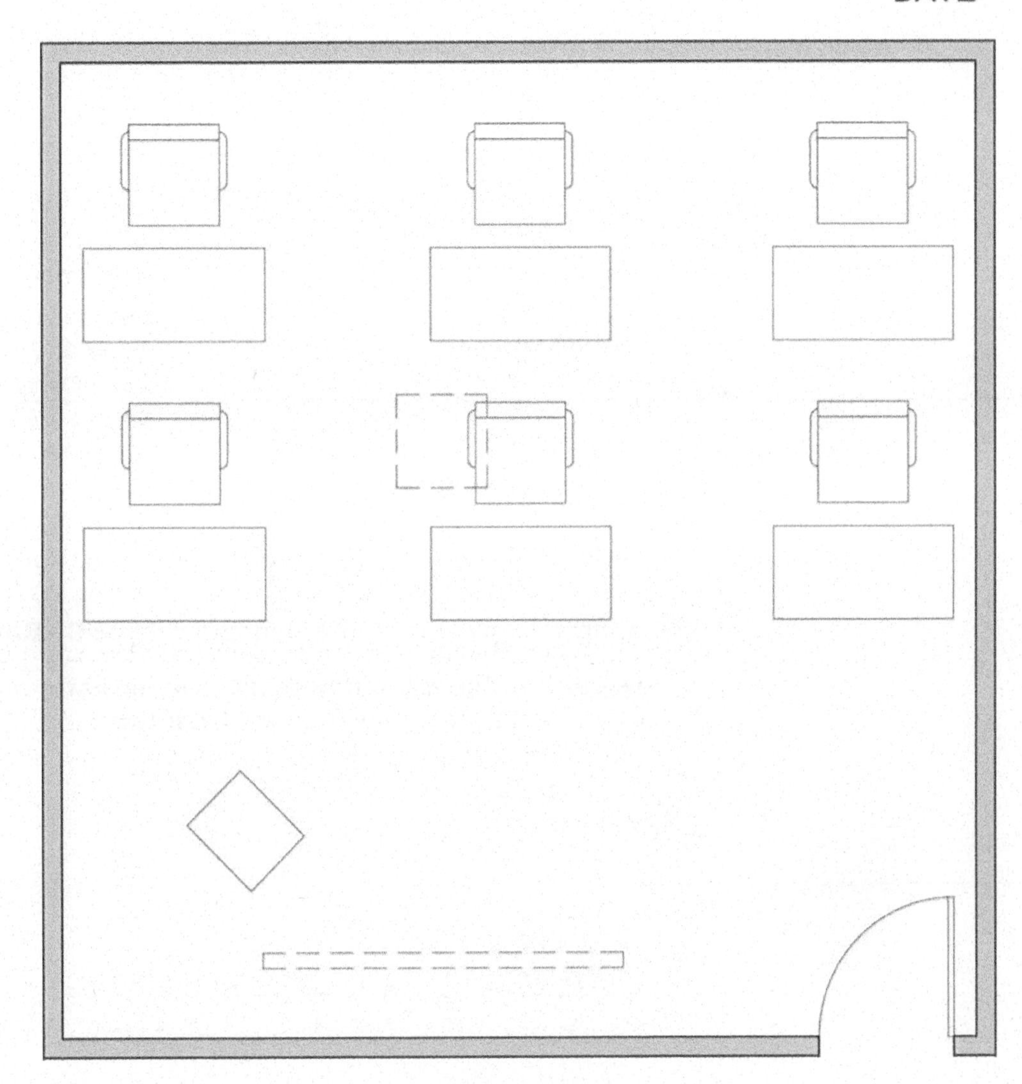

Figure 3-24
Exercise 3-2: Drawing a rectangular lecture room, including furniture (scale: 1/4″ = 1′-0″)

Layer name	Color	Linetype	Lineweight
a-anno-text	green	continuous	.006″ (.15 mm)
a-door	red	continuous	.004″ (.09 mm)
a-wall-intr	blue	continuous	.010″ (.25 mm)
i-eqpm-ovhd	red	hidden	.004″ (.09 mm)

Step 4. Set layer **a-wall-intr** current.

Step 5. Use **Zoom-All** to view the limits of the drawing.

Step 6. Turn **SNAP**, **GRID**, and **LWDISPLAY** on. The remaining buttons in the status bar should be off.

Making Solid Walls Using Polyline and Solid Hatch

In Exercise 3-2 you will use the **LINE** command to draw the lecture room walls; you will then use the **Polyline Edit** command to change the lines to a polyline before you offset the walls. After you have completed drawing the walls, you will use the **HATCH** command to make the walls solid.

Step 7. Use **LINE** to draw the walls of the lecture room (Figure 3-25), as described next:

Prompt	**Response**
Type a command:	**Line** (or type **L <Enter>**)
Specify first point:	**Type 2′,7′ <Enter>**
Specify next point or [Undo]:	Turn **ORTHO** on
	Move your mouse to the right and type **20′6 <Enter>**
Specify next point or [Undo]:	Move your mouse straight up and type **21′ <Enter>**
Specify next point or [Close Undo]:	Move your mouse to the left and type **20′6 <Enter>**
Specify next point or [Close Undo]:	Type **C <Enter>**

Step 8. Use **Zoom-Window** to magnify the lower right corner of the lecture room where the door will be drawn.

Figure 3-25
Use the **LINE** command to draw the lecture room walls

From

From: A command modifier that locates a base point and then allows you to locate an offset point from the base point.

From is a command modifier that locates a base point and then allows you to locate an offset point from that base point. It is similar to **ID Point** but differs in that **From** is used within a command; **ID Point** must be used before the command is activated. You use **From** at a prompt that asks you to locate a point, and it does not work unless a command is active to issue that prompt. Both **From** and **ID Point** are usually used in combination with **Object Snap** modifiers when locating the initial base point.

BREAK

BREAK	
Ribbon/ Panel	Home/ Modify (slideout)
Draw Toolbar:	
Menu Bar:	Modify/Break
Type a Command:	BREAK
Command Alias:	BR

You can use the **BREAK** command to erase a part of a drawing object.

Step 9. Use the **BREAK** command to create an opening for the lecture room door (Figure 3-26), as described next:

Prompt	**Response**
Type a command:	**Break** (or type **BR <Enter>**)
Select object:	Click anyplace on the bottom horizontal line
Specify second break point or [First point]:	Type **F <Enter>** (for first point)
Specify first break point:	Type **FRO <Enter>** (abbreviation for **From**)
Base point:	**Osnap-Intersection**
int of	**P1→** (Figure 3-26)

Figure 3-26
Use the **BREAK** command to make an opening for the lecture room door

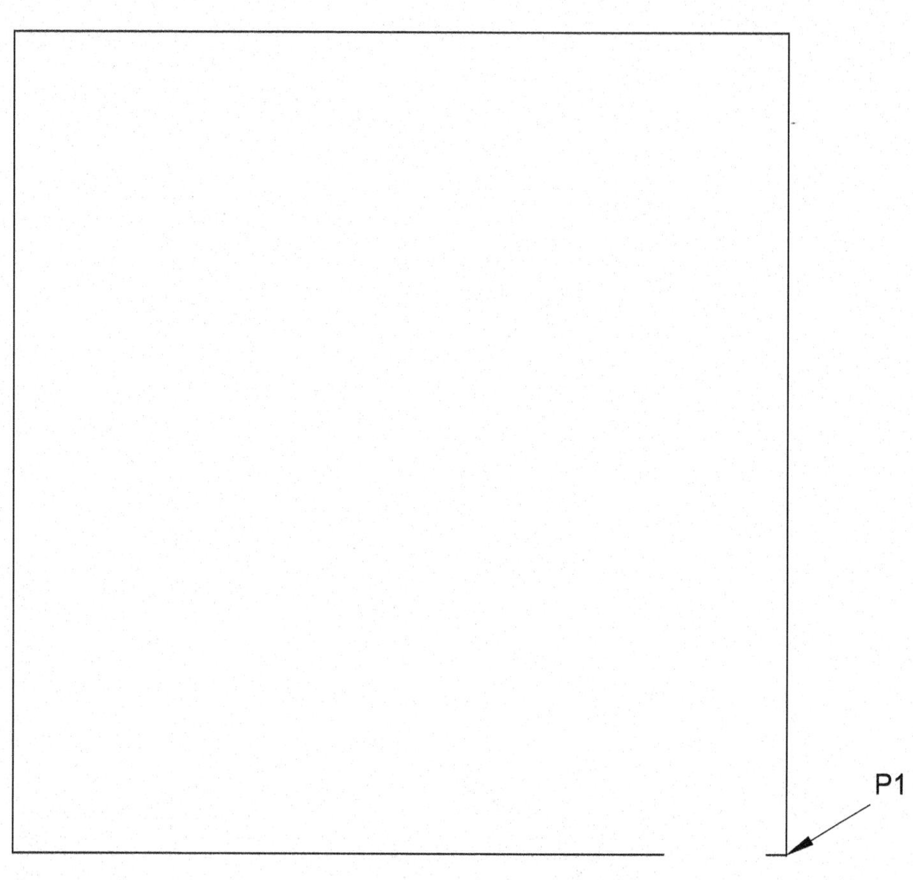

Prompt	Response
<Offset>:	Type **@6<180 <Enter>** (polar coordinate)
Specify second break point:	Type **@36<180 <Enter>** (polar coordinate)

First

When selecting an entity to break, you may use the point entered in the selection process as the first break point, or you may type **F <Enter>** to be able to select the first break point. Using **F <Enter>** allows you to start over in specifically selecting both beginning and ending break points.

@

Sometimes you need only to break an entity and not erase a section of it. In that case, use @ as the second break point. The line will be broken twice on the same point; no segments will be erased from the line.

EDIT POLYLINE	
Ribbon/ Panel	Home/ Modify (slideout) 
Modify IIToolbar:	
Menu Bar:	Modify/ Object/ Polyline
Type a Command:	PEDIT
Command Alias:	PE

Polyline Edit

Edit Polyline is a **Modify** command you use to edit polylines or to change lines into polylines. It can join lines or arcs together and make them a single polyline. You can also use it to change the width of a polyline.

Step 10. Use **Polyline Edit** to change the lines into a polyline, as described next:

Prompt	**Response**
Type a command:	**Polyline Edit** (or type **PE <Enter>**)
Select polyline or [Multiple]:	Click any of the lines drawn
Object selected is not a polyline	
Do you want to turn it into one? <Y>	**<Enter>** (to tell AutoCAD yes, you want to turn it into a polyline)
Enter an option [Close Join Width Edit vertex Fit Spline Decurve Ltype gen Reverse Undo]:	Type **J <Enter>** (for **Join**)
Select objects: 5 found	Type **ALL <Enter>** (to select all the lines)
Select objects:	**<Enter>**
4 segments added to polyline	
Enter an option [Open Join Width Edit vertex Fit Spline Decurve Ltype gen Reverse Undo]:	**<Enter>**

Step 11. Use the **OFFSET** command to offset the polyline 5″ to the **outside** of the current polyline.

Step 12. Use the **LINE** command with a running **Osnap Endpoint** to close the polyline. Type **L <Enter>**. Click **P1→**, **P2→ <Enter><Enter>**. Click **P3→**, **P4→ <Enter>** as shown in Figure 3-27.

Step 13. Use **Zoom-Extents** so you can see the entire drawing graphics.

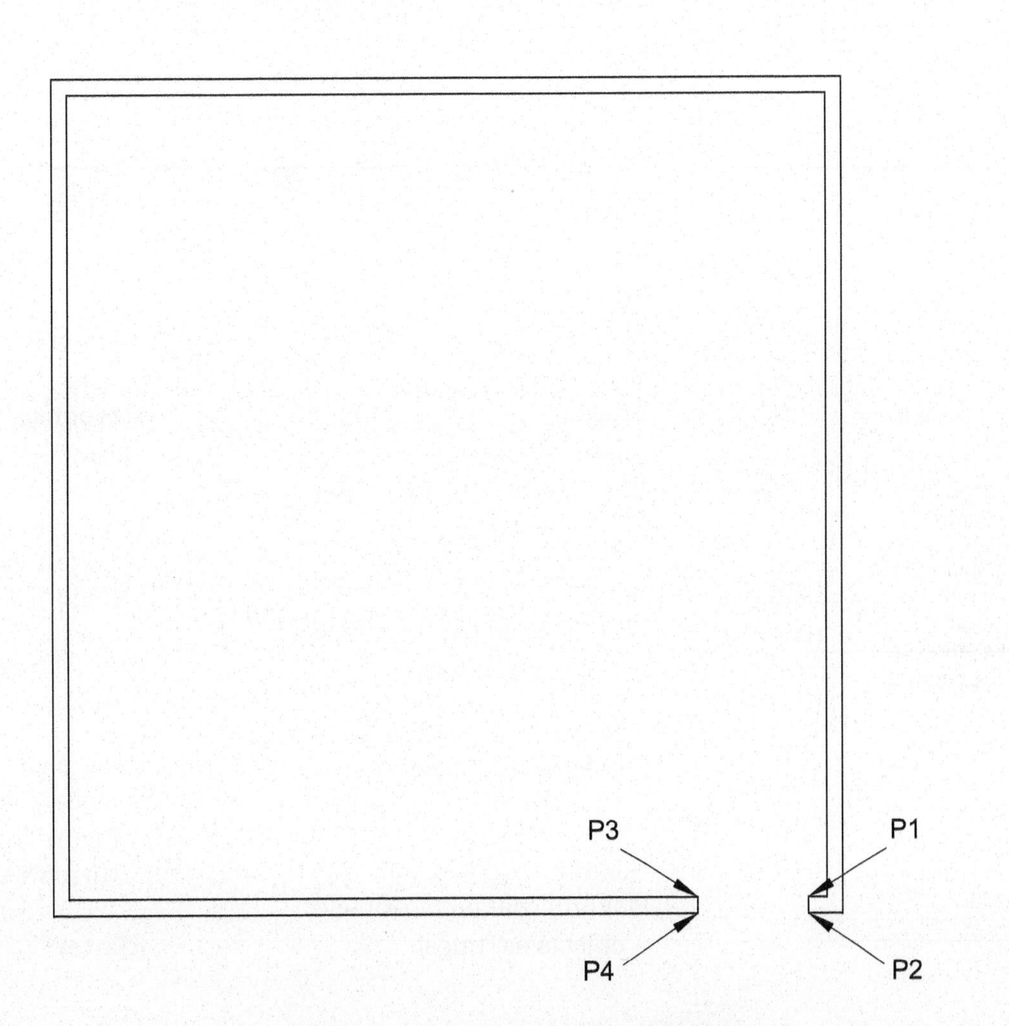

Figure 3-27
Use the **LINE** command to close the ends of the polylines

HATCH

hatch: The process of filling in a closed area with a pattern. Hatching can consist of solid filled areas, gradient-filled areas, or areas filled with patterns of lines, dots, or other objects.

You will use a single ***hatch*** pattern to create solid walls, as shown in Figure 3-24.

FOR MORE DETAILS

See Chapters 8 and 13 for more about the **Hatch and Gradient** dialog box.

Step 14. Create the following new layer and set it as the current layer:

Layer name	Color	Linetype	Lineweight
a-wall-patt-gray	gray (253)	continuous	.004" (.09 mm)

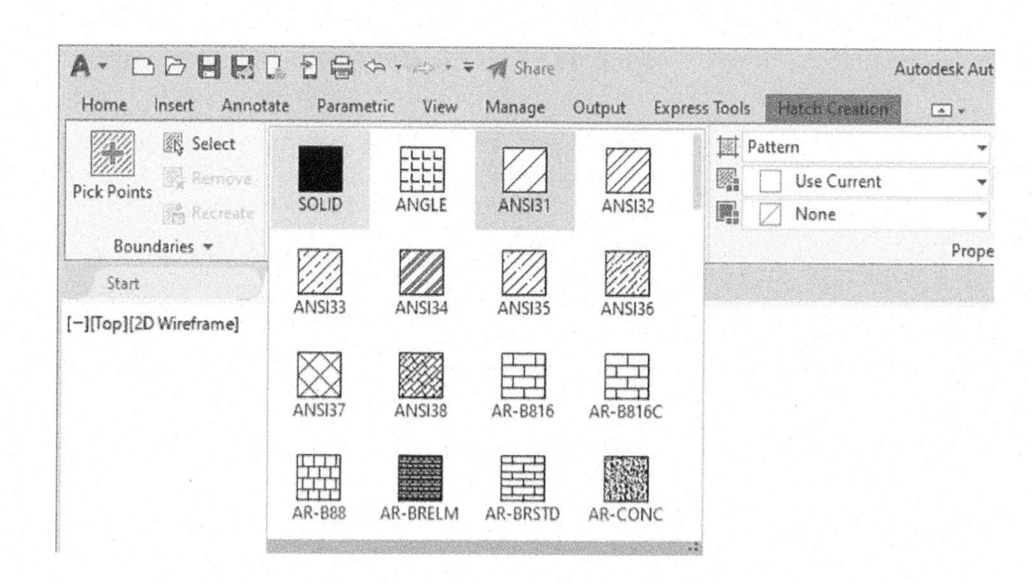

Figure 3-28
Hatch Pattern Gallery with **SOLID** hatch selected

HATCH	
Ribbon/Panel	Home/ Draw
Draw Toolbar:	
Menu Bar:	Draw/ Hatch...
Type a Command:	HATCH
Command Alias:	H

Step 15. Use the **HATCH** command to make the walls solid, as described next:

Prompt	**Response**
Type a command:	**Hatch** (or type **H <Enter>**)
The **Hatch Creation** ribbon tab appears:	Click the down arrow button of the **Hatch Pattern Gallery** (Figure 3-28)
Pick internal point or [Select objects seTtings]:	Click the **SOLID pattern**, as shown in Figure 3-28
Pick internal point or [Select objects seTtings]:	Click **P1→** (any point between the two polylines forming the wall, Figure 3-29—you may have to turn **SNAP** off)
Pick internal point or [Select objects seTtings]:	**<Enter>**

Step 16. Set layer **a-door** current.

Step 17. Draw a 1-1/2″-long by 3′-wide rectangle to represent the door (Figure 3-29). Be sure to use **Osnap-Endpoint** or **Osnap Intersection** to start the rectangle at the upper-right corner of the door opening.

Step 18. Use the **Arc-Start, End, Direction** method to draw the door swing arc. Be sure **OSNAP** and **ORTHO** are on. You can draw the arc clockwise or counterclockwise. Move your mouse so the arc appears as shown in Figure 3-29.

Step 19. Set layer **i-furn** current.

Step 20. Locate the table and chair symbols as shown in Figure 3-30. Use the **LINE** or **Rectangle** command to draw the 48″-long × 24″-wide table. Center a 24″-long × 26″-wide rectangle 6″ from the table to start the chair symbol, as shown in Figure 3-30.

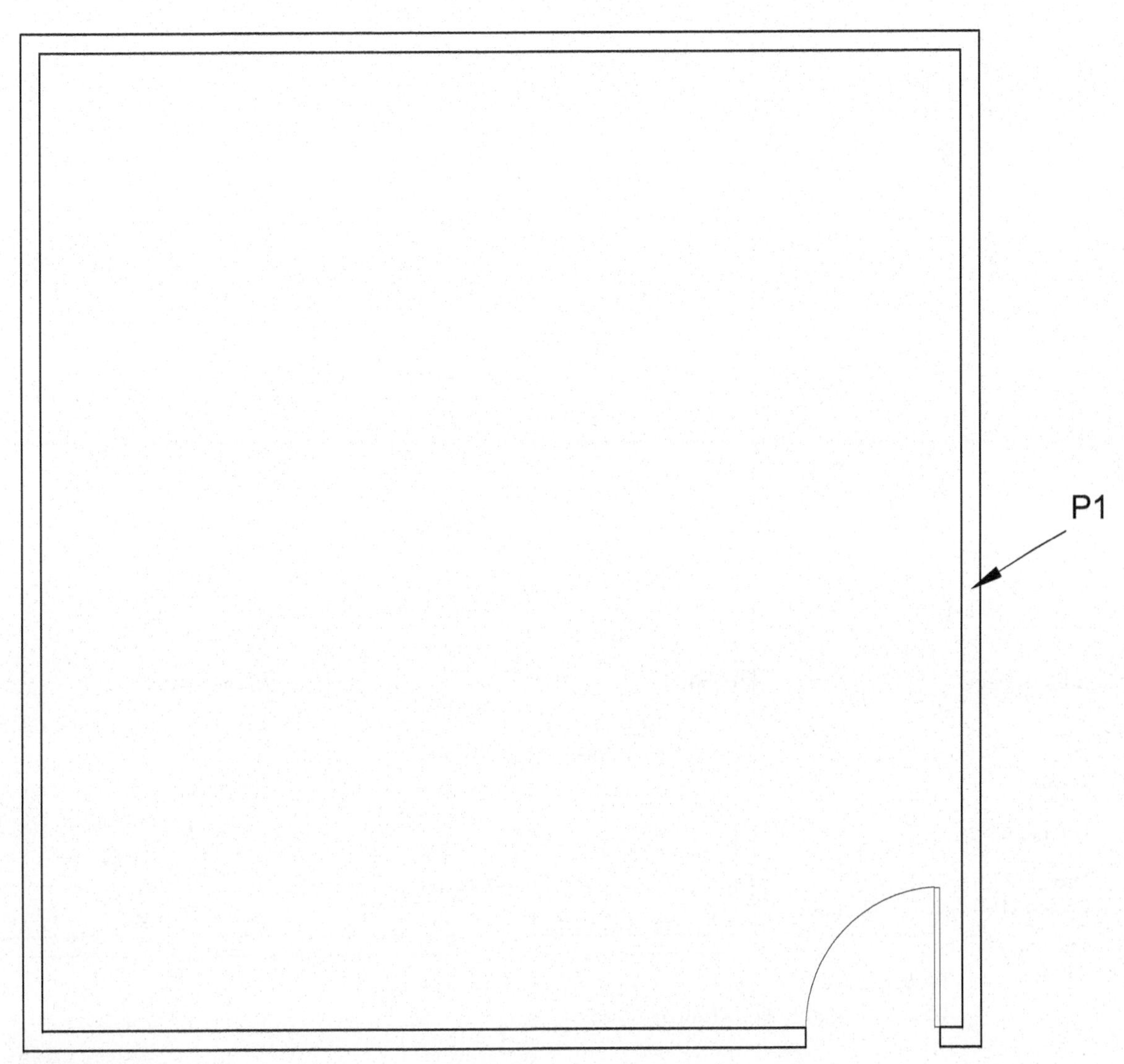

Figure 3-29
Click any point between the two polylines forming the wall to make the walls solid; draw the door

Step 21. Complete the chair symbol as shown in Figure 3-31.

Step 22. Use **Zoom-Extents** after you finish drawing the chair symbol.

RECTANGULAR ARRAY	
Ribbon/ Panel	Home/ Modify Array
Modify Toolbar:	
Menu Bar:	Modify/ Array/ Rectangular Array
Type a Command:	ARRAY
Command Alias:	AR

ARRAY

The **ARRAY** command allows you to make multiple copies of an object in a rectangular or polar (circular) array and along a path, as shown in Figure 3-33. You use the **Rectangular** option in Exercise 3-2; the **Polar** option is described in Exercise 3-3.

> **NOTE**
>
> In the **ARRAY** command, include the original item in the number of rows and columns.

Step 23. Use the **ARRAY** command to make a rectangular pattern of six chairs and tables (Figures 3-32 and 3-33), as described next:

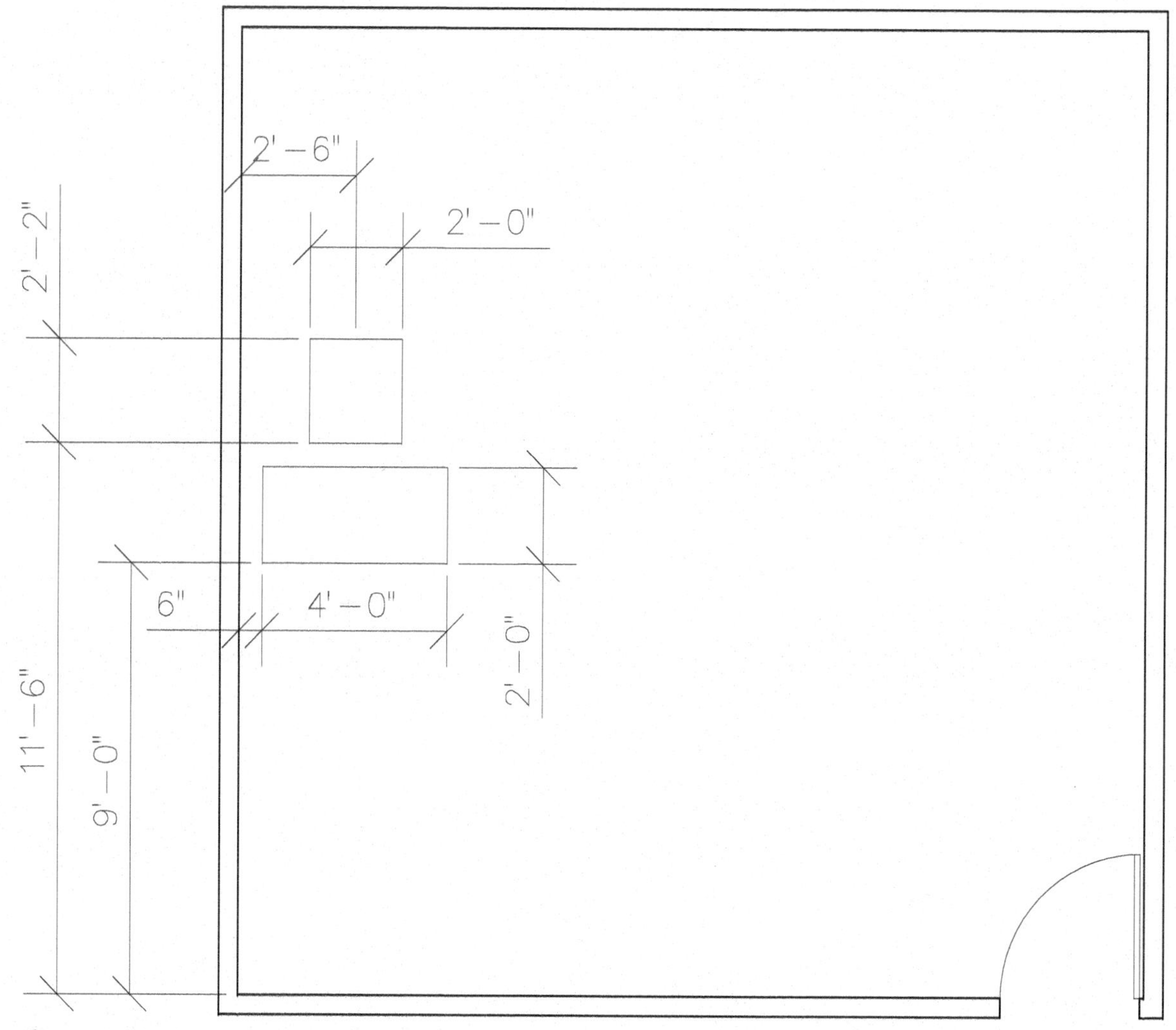

Figure 3-30
Locate the table and chair symbols

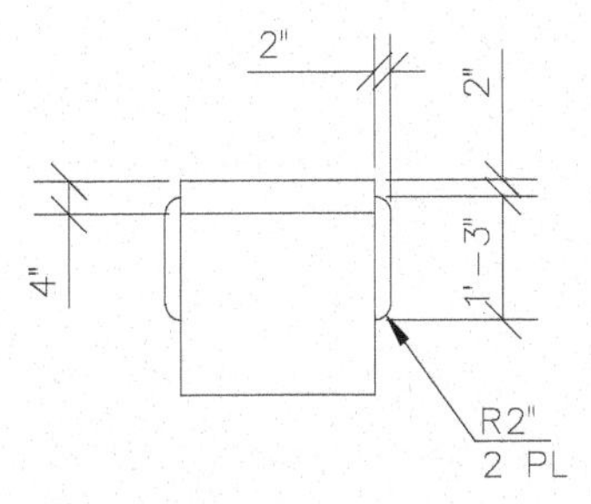

Figure 3-31
Complete the chair symbol

Prompt	Response
Type a command:	**Rectangular Array** (or type **ARRAYRECT <Enter>**)
Select objects:	Click **P1→** to locate the first corner of a window to include the entire chair and table
Specify opposite corner:	Click **P2→** to window the chair and table just drawn
Select objects:	**<Enter>**
	An array preview of the table and chair is shown on the screen. Specify the array type and whether or not it's associative
Type = Rectangular Associative = Yes	
Select grip to edit array or [Associative Base point COUnt Spacing COLumns Rows Levels eXit]<eXit>:	Type **S <Enter>**
Specify the distance between columns or [Unit cell] <6'>:	Type **7'6<Enter>**

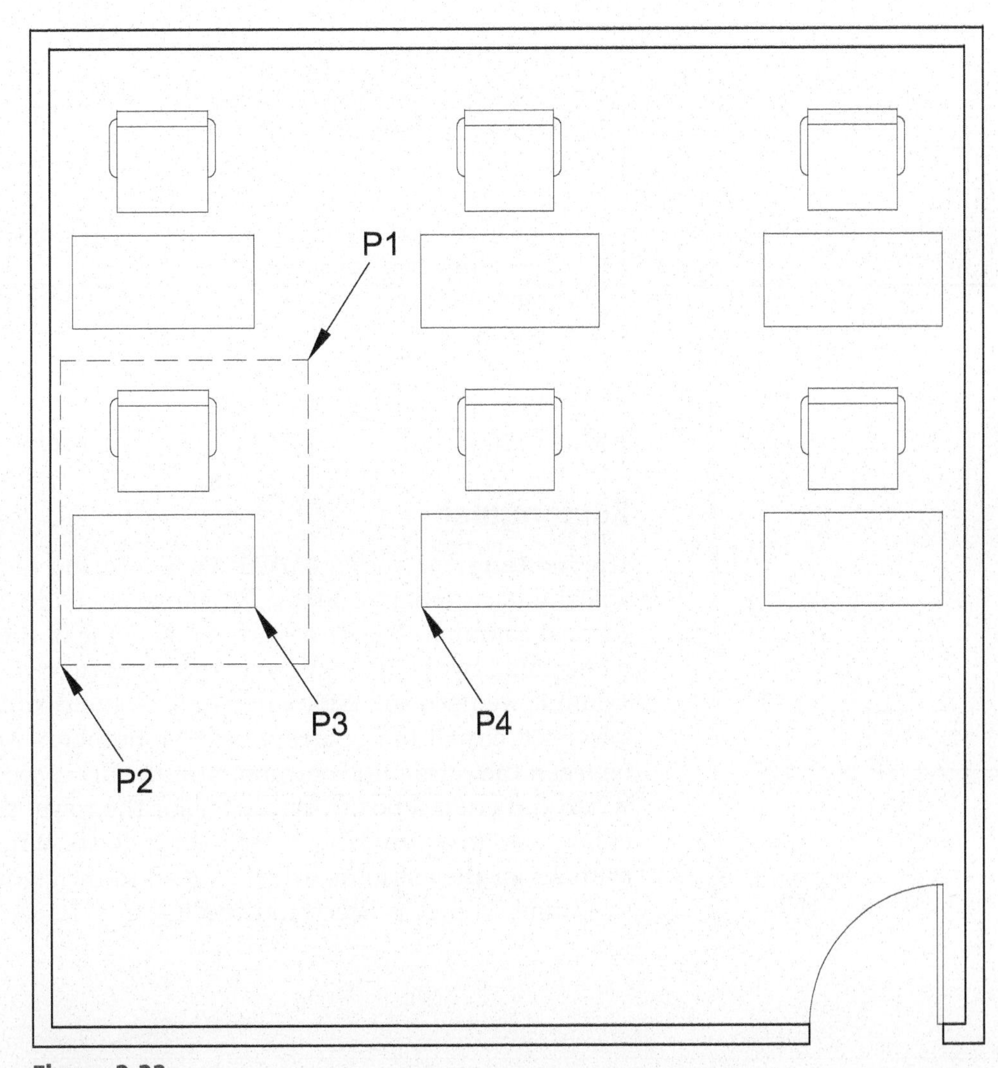

Figure 3-32
Array the tables and chairs; use **Distance** to measure the aisle width

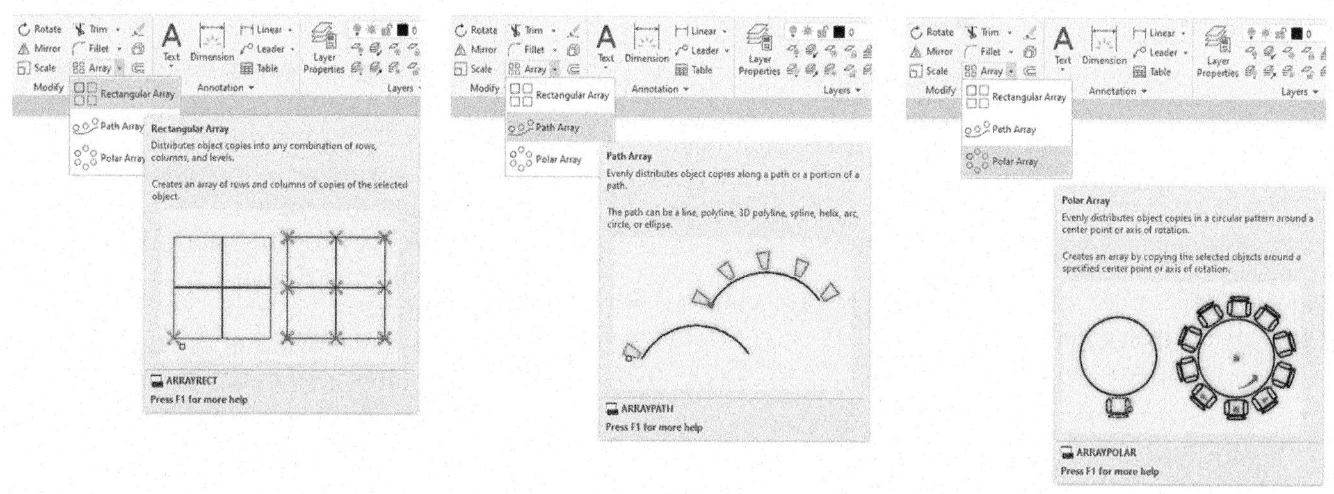

Figure 3-33
The three types of arrays

Prompt	**Response**
Specify the distance between rows <7′>:	Type **6′<Enter>**
Select grip to edit array or [Associative Base point COUnt Spacing COLumns Rows Levels eXit]<eXit>:	Type **COU<Enter>**
Enter the number of columns or [Expression] <4>:	Type **3<Enter>**
Enter the number of rows or [Expression] <3>:	Type **2<Enter>**
Select grip to edit array or [Associative Base point COUnt Spacing COLumns Rows Levels eXit]<eXit>:	**<Enter>**

Rectangular

The **Rectangular** option of **ARRAY** allows you to make multiple copies of an object in a rectangular array. The array is made up of horizontal rows and vertical columns. The direction and spacing of the rows and columns are determined by the distance you specify between each. In the previous example we used the table and chair as the cornerstone element in the lower-left corner of the array. Positive numbers were used for the distance between the rows and columns, and the array went up and to the right. When you enter a positive number for the rows, they proceed up; when you enter a negative number, they proceed down. When you enter a positive number for the columns, they proceed to the right; when you enter a negative number, they proceed to the left.

PATH ARRAY	
Ribbon/ Panel	Home/ Modify Array
Modify Toolbar:	
Menu Bar:	Modify/Array/ Path Array
Type a Command:	ARRAYPATH

Path

The **Path** option of **ARRAY** allows you to make multiple copies of an object evenly distributed along a path or part of a path. The path can be a line, polyline, arc, circle, or ellipse.

ARRAYEDIT	
Ribbon/ Panel	Home/ Modify (slideout)
Modify II Toolbar:	
Menu Bar:	Modify/ Object/ Array
Type a Command:	ARRAYEDIT

ARRAYEDIT

An array must be associative, an option in the array commands, for the **ARRAYEDIT** command to work. When an array is associative, it is treated as a single object and you can edit it by using grips, **Properties**, or **ARRAYEDIT**.

TIP

Items can automatically be added to a path array when you lengthen the path using the **Measure** option of **ARRAYEDIT**.

NOTE

After an object has been selected, you can use the **Array** option of the **COPY** command to make multiple copies of the object.

DISTANCE	
Ribbon/ Panel	Home/ Utilities
Inquiry Toolbar:	
Menu Bar:	Tools/ Inquiry/ Distance
Type a Command:	Distance
Command Alias:	DI

Distance

You can use the **Distance** command to determine measurements.

Step 24. Use the **Distance** command to measure a specified distance (Figure 3-32), as described next:

Prompt	**Response**
Type a command:	**Distance** (or type **DI <Enter>**)
Specify first point:	**Osnap-Intersection**
int of	**P3→** (Figure 3-32)
Specify second point or [Multiple points]:	**Osnap-Intersection**
int of	**P4→** (Figure 3-32)
Distance = 3′8″, Angle in XY Plane = 0, Angle from XY Plane = 0, Delta X = 3′-8″, Delta Y = 0′-0″, Delta Z = 0′-0″	

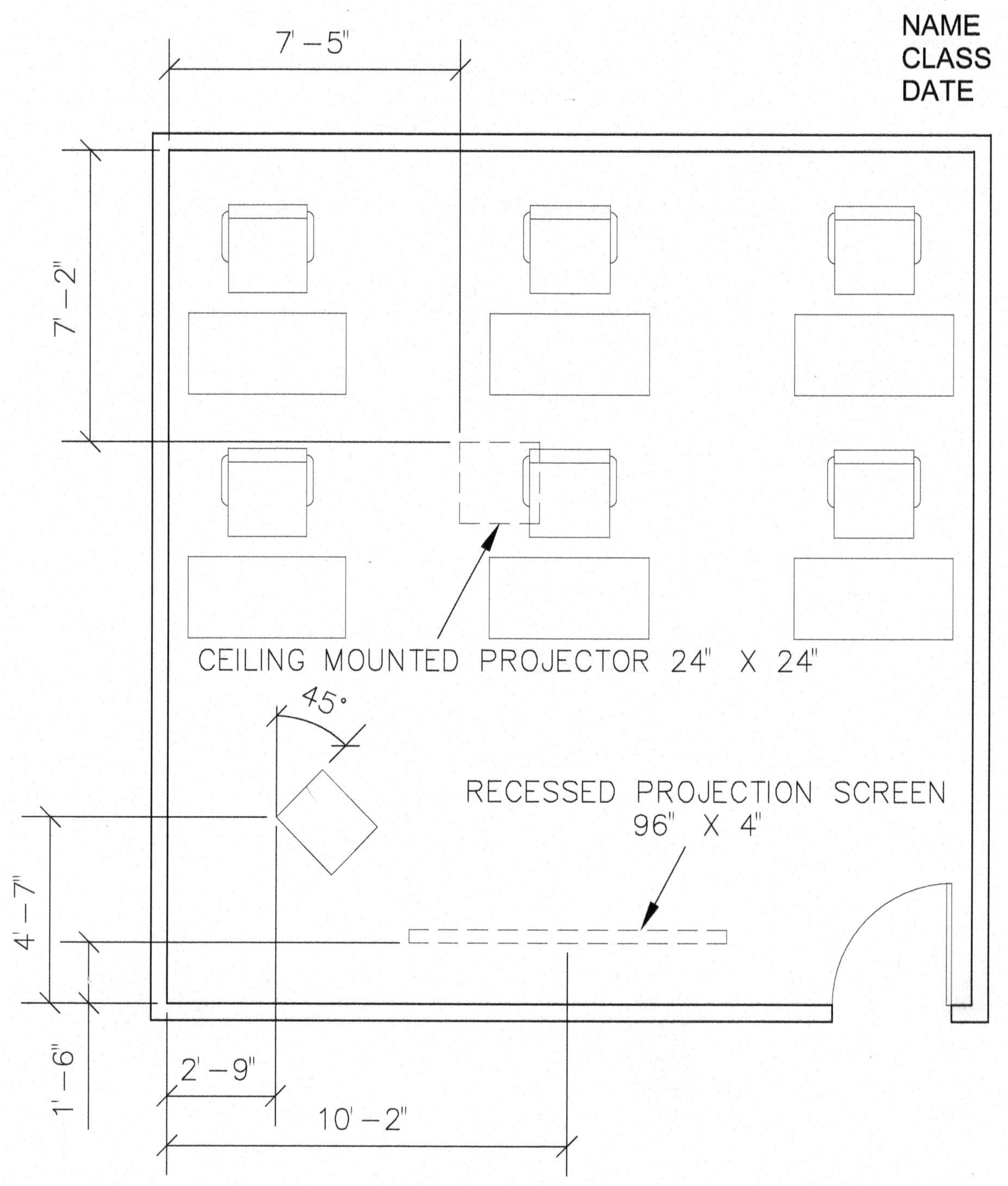

Figure 3-34
Draw the 24″ × 20″ lectern, the 24″ × 24″ ceiling projector, and the 96″ × 4″ recessed projection screen

Step 25. Draw the 24″ × 20″ lectern as shown in Figure 3-34.

Step 26. Set layer **i-eqpm-ovhd** current.

Step 27. Draw the 24″ × 24″ ceiling-mounted projector and the 96″ × 4″ recessed projection screen as shown in Figure 3-34.

Step 28. Set layer **a-anno-text** current.

Step 29. Use the **Single Line Text** command (type **DT <Enter>**) to type your name, class number, and date, 6″ high in the upper-right corner.

Step 30. When you have completed Exercise 3-2 (Figure 3-35), save your work in at least two places.

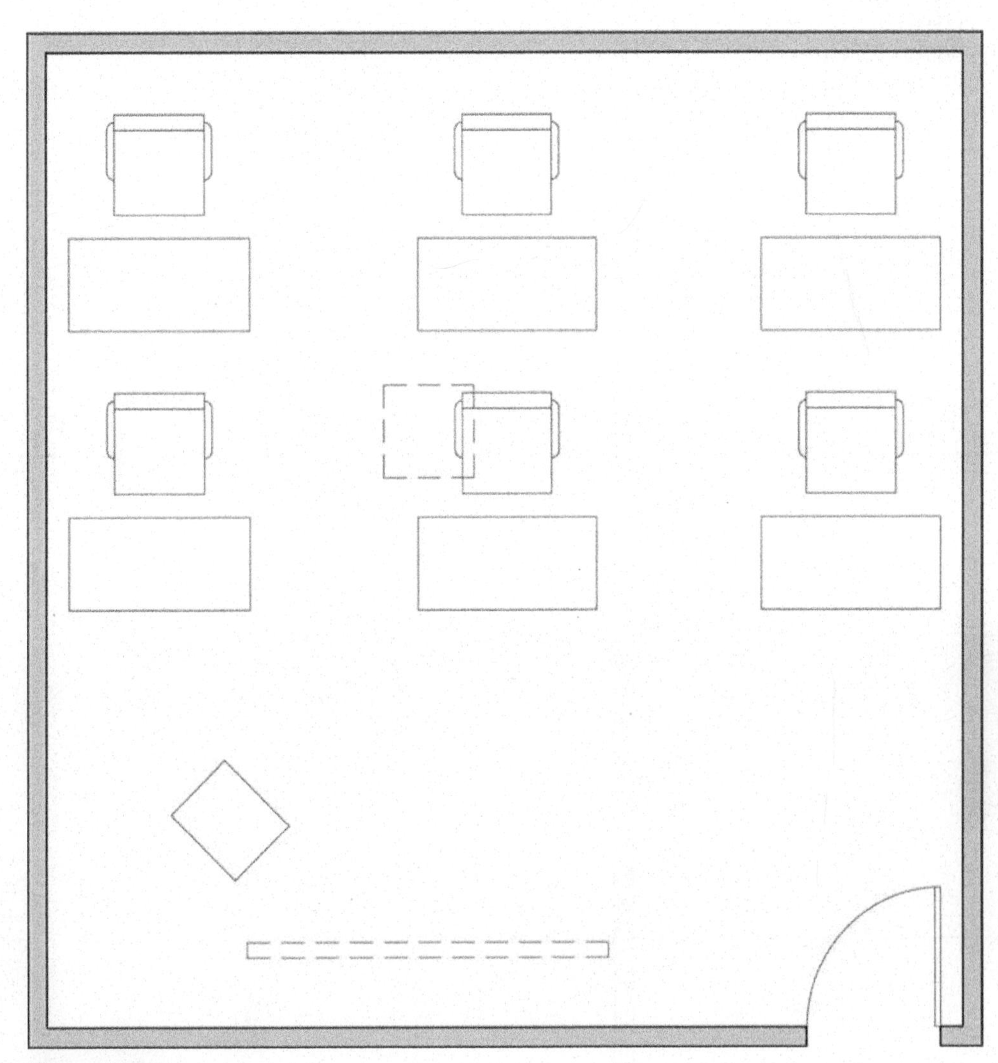

Figure 3-35
Exercise 3-2 complete

As for the dimensions and other annotations shown in Figure 3-34, dimension and multi-leader tools are needed and will be discussed in future exercises.

Step 31. Print your drawing from the **Model** tab at a scale of **1/4″ = 1′-0″**.

EXERCISE 3-3
Drawing a Curved Conference Room, Including Furniture

In Exercise 3-3, you draw a conference room, including walls and furnishings. When you have completed Exercise 3-3, your drawing will look similar to Figure 3-36.

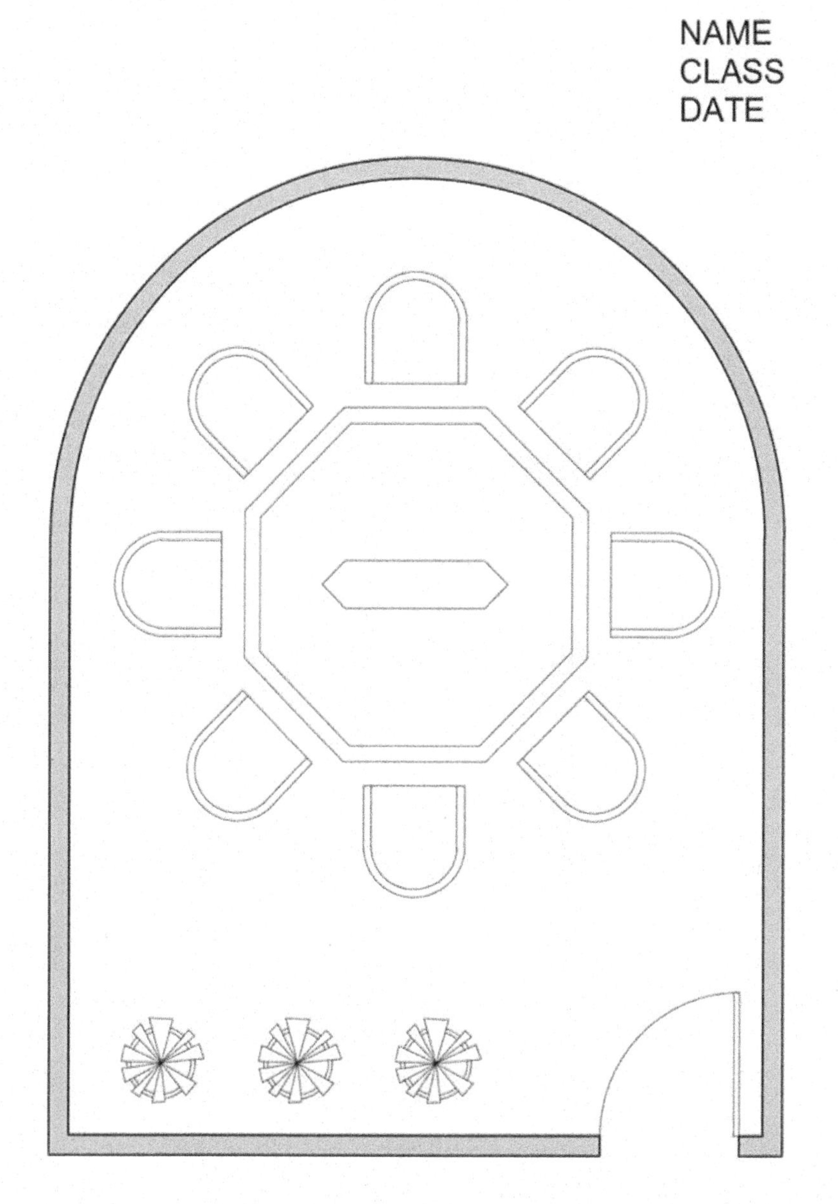

Figure 3-36
Exercise 3-3: Drawing a curved conference room, including furniture (scale: 1/4″ = 1′-0″)

Step 1. Click **Open...**, change the **Files of type:** input box to **Drawing Template (*.dwt)**, and open the **Ch3-conference-rm-setup** template, which you previously made at the beginning of Exercise 3-1.

Step 2. Click **Save As...**, change the **Files of type:** input box to **AutoCAD 2018 Drawing (.dwg)**, and save the template as a drawing file named **CH3-EXERCISE3**.

Step 3. Verify the following settings:

1. Drawing units: **Architectural**
2. Drawing limits: **25′,35′**
3. **GRIDDISPLAY**: **0**
4. Grid: **12″**
5. Snap: **6″**
6. Verify the following layers:

Layer name	Color	Linetype	Lineweight
a-anno-text	green	continuous	.006″ (.15 mm)
a-door	red	continuous	.004″ (.09 mm)
a-wall-intr	blue	continuous	.010″ (.25 mm)
i-eqpm-ovhd	red	hidden	.004″ (.09 mm)
i-furn	cyan	continuous	.004″ (.09 mm)

Step 4. Set layer **a-wall-intr** current.

Step 5. Use **Zoom-All** to view the limits of the drawing.

Step 6. Turn **SNAP**, **GRID**, and **LWDISPLAY** on. The remaining buttons in the status bar should be off.

Polyline

Next, you create the inside walls with polylines, lines, and arcs.

Step 7. Use **Polyline**, **LINE**, and **ARC** to draw the inside lines of the conference room walls (Figure 3-37) as described next:

Prompt	**Response**
Type a command:	**Polyline** (or type **PL <Enter>**)
Specify start point:	Type **5′,5′<Enter>** Set **ORTHO** on
Current line-width is 0′-0″	
Specify next point or [Arc Halfwidth Length Undo Width]:	Move your mouse to the right and type **15′ <Enter>** (direct distance entry)
Specify next point or [Arc Close Halfwidth Length Undo Width]:	Move your mouse up and type **12′6 <Enter>**
Specify next point or [Arc Close Halfwidth Length Undo Width]:	Type **A <Enter>**
Specify endpoint of arc or [Angle CEnter CLose Direction Halfwidth Line Radius Second pt Undo Width]:	Move your mouse to the left and type **15′ <Enter>**

Figure 3-37
Use the **Polyline** command with **LINE** and **ARC** options to draw the inside lines of the conference room walls

Prompt	**Response**
Specify endpoint of arc or [Angle CEnter CLose Direction Halfwidth Line Radius Second pt Undo Width]:	Type **L <Enter>**
Specify next point or [Arc Close Halfwidth Length Undo Width]:	Type **C <Enter>**

NOTE

When a wide polyline is exploded, the width information is lost, and the polyline changes to a line segment.

Width

The **Polyline Width** option allows you to draw wide polylines. The starting and ending points of the polyline are the *center* of the polyline's width.

Half Width

This option specifies the width of the polyline from the center of the polyline to either edge.

Length

The **Length** option in the **Polyline** prompt allows you to draw a polyline segment at the same angle as the previously drawn polyline segment by specifying the length of the new segment.

Close

Using the **Close** option when you are completing a wide polyline is always best. The effect of using **Close** is different from clicking or entering a point to complete the polyline. With the **Close** option, the last corner is completely closed.

Step 8. Use the **OFFSET** command to offset the polyline 5″ to the **outside**, as shown in Figure 3-38.

Step 9. Draw the **3′** door opening as shown in Figure 3-38.

Step 10. Set layer **a-door** current.

Step 11. Use the **Rectangle** command to draw a **1-1/2″**-long by **3′**-wide rectangle to represent the door (Figure 3-38).

Step 12. Use the **Trim** command with the two vertical lines of step 9 as cutting edges and trim the 3′ wide opening in the wall as shown in Figure 3-38.

Step 13. Use the **Arc-Start, End, Direction** method to draw the door swing arc (Figure 3-38). Be sure **SNAP** and **ORTHO** are on.

Step 14. Set layer **i-furn** current.

Figure 3-38
Offset the polyline and draw the door opening and the door

POLYGON

POLYGON: Command that draws a polygon with 3 to 1024 sides.

POLYGON	
Ribbon/ Panel	Home/Draw **(Rectangle** flyout)
Draw Toolbar:	
Menu Bar:	Draw/ Polygon
Type a Command:	POLYGON
Command Alias:	POL

The ***POLYGON*** command draws a regular polygon with 3 to 1024 sides. After you specify the number of sides, the **Polygon** prompt is *Specify center of polygon or [Edge]:*. When you specify the center of the polygon (default option), the polygon can then be inscribed in a circle or circumscribed about a circle. When the polygon is inscribed in a circle, all the vertices lie on the circle, and the edges of the polygon are inside the circle. When the polygon is circumscribed about a circle, the midpoint of each edge of the polygon lies on the circle, and the vertices are outside the circle. A polygon is a closed polyline.

Step 15. Use the **POLYGON** command to draw the conference table (Figure 3-39), as described next:

Prompt	**Response**
Type a command:	**Polygon** (or type **POL <Enter>**)
Enter number of sides <4>:	Type **8 <Enter>**
Specify center of polygon or [Edge]:	**P1→** (Figure 3-39)
Enter an option [Inscribed in circle Circumscribed about circle]<I>:	Type **I <Enter>** (or just **<Enter>** if **I** is the default)
Specify radius of circle:	Type **48 <Enter>**

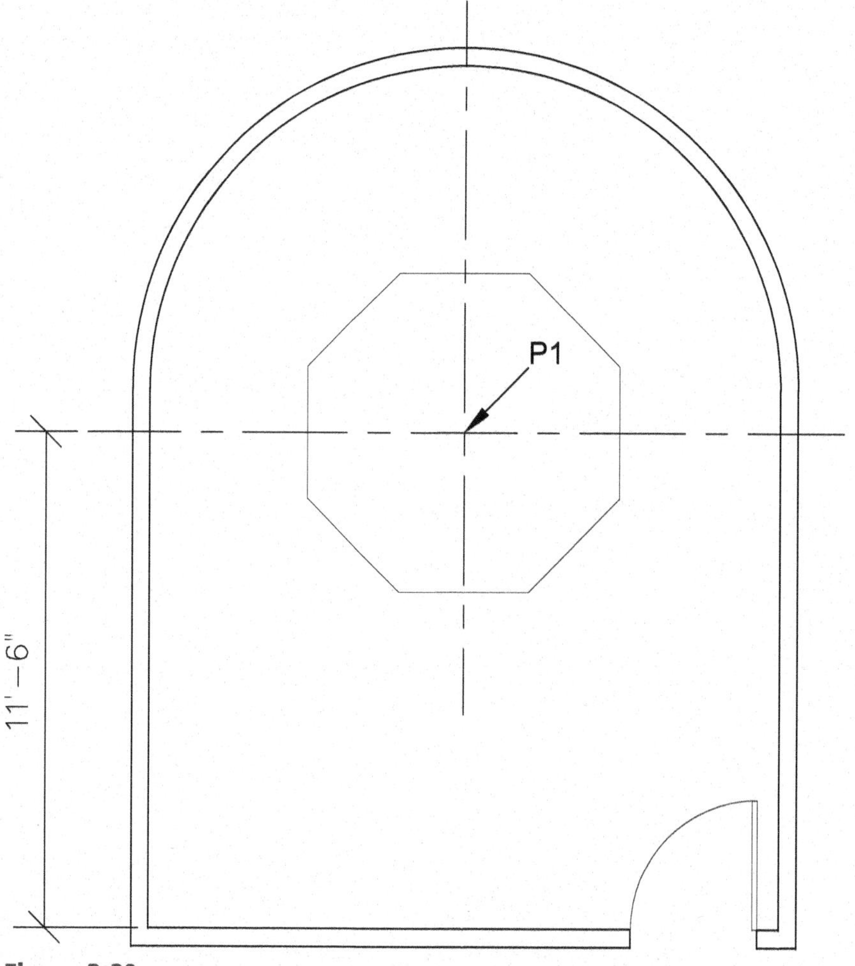

Figure 3-39
Locate the polygon

The method of specifying the radius controls the orientation of the polygon. When you specify the radius with a number, as in the preceding responses, the bottom edge of the polygon is drawn at the current snap angle—horizontal in the polygon just drawn. When you specify the radius of an inscribed polygon with a point, a vertex of the polygon is placed at the point location. When you specify the radius of a circumscribed polygon with a point, an edge midpoint is placed at the point's location.

Edge

When you select the **Edge** option of the prompt, AutoCAD prompts *Specify first endpoint of edge:* and *Specify second endpoint of edge:*. The two points entered at the prompts specify one edge of a polygon that is drawn counterclockwise.

Step 16. Use the **Polyline** or **Rectangle** command to draw a rectangle 36″ long × 12″ wide in the center of the polygon just drawn (Figure 3-40A). This is a good exercise to learn how to specify the center of the polygon as reference point (use **From** followed by **Mid Between 2 Points** from the **Osnap** menu) to construct the rectangle. After defining the center as the reference point, define the upper-left and lower-right corners with **@-18,6** and **@38,-12**, respectively. Try this on your own or ask your instructor to demonstrate it.

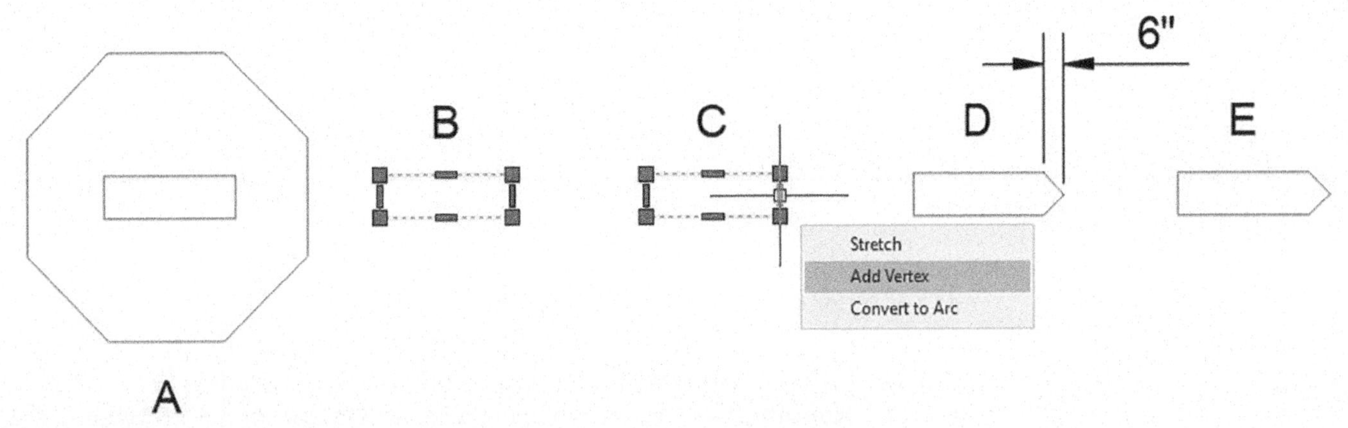

Figure 3-40
Steps for adding a 6″ vertex to the right side of the rectangle

> **NOTE**
>
> If you activate the grips on the vertex just added, you will get the grip option **Remove Vertex** when you hover over the vertex grip.

Grips—Add Vertex

The **Add Vertex** grip is for objects drawn using the **Polyline**, **Rectangle**, or **POLYGON** command. When you hover over a grip, a tooltip displays the options **Stretch**, **Convert to Arc**, **Convert to Line**, and **Add Vertex**, or you can right-click and get a menu that shows all the grip options.

Step 17. Use the **Add Vertex** grip to draw a vertex on the right side of the rectangle just drawn, as described next (Figure 3-40):

Prompt	**Response**
Type a command:	With no command active, click on the rectangle you have drawn
Small blue squares (grips) appear at each midpoint and intersection of the rectangle lines (Figure 3-40B):	Hover over the midpoint grip on the right side of the rectangle (Figure 3-40C)
A tooltip menu is displayed:	Click **Add Vertex**
A vertex appears (Figure 3-40D):	With **ORTHO** on, move your cursor to the right and type **6 <Enter>** (Figure 3-40E)
	Press **<Esc>** to clear the grips

Step 18. Use the **Add Vertex** grip to add a 6″ vertex on the left side of the rectangle (Figure 3-41).

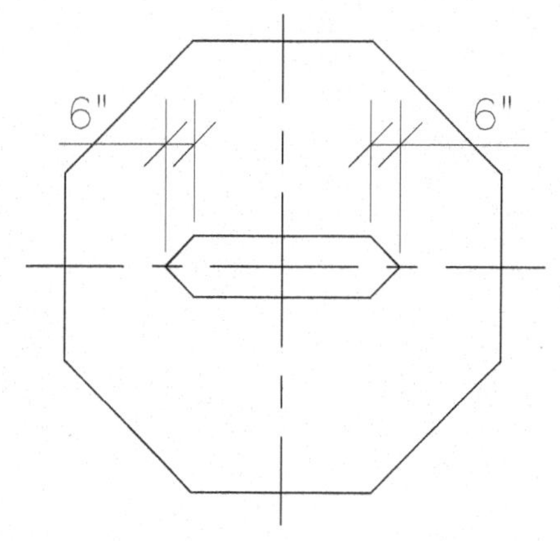

Figure 3-41
Add a 6″ vertex on the left side of the rectangle

Step 19. To begin drawing the chair symbol, use the **Polyline** or **Rectangle** command to draw a rectangle 26″ long × 16″ wide (Figure 3-42A) and 6″ away from the outer edge of the table.

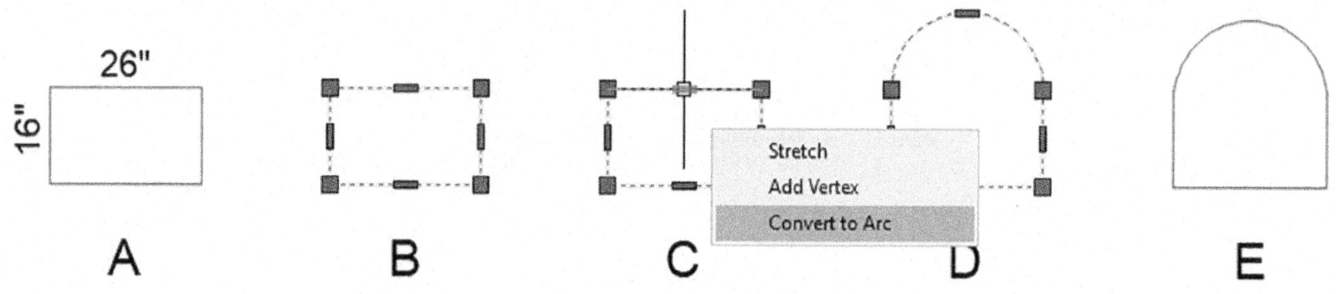

Figure 3-42
Steps in drawing the chair using **Convert to Arc**

Grips—Convert to Arc

The **Convert to Arc** grip is for objects drawn using the **Polyline**, **Rectangle**, or **POLYGON** command.

Step 20. Use the **Convert to Arc** grip to draw the back curved edge of the chair symbol as described next (Figure 3-42):

Prompt	Response
Type a command:	With no command active, click on the rectangle you have drawn
Small blue squares (grips) appear at each midpoint and intersection of the rectangle lines (Figure 3-42B):	Hover over the midpoint grip on the top line of the rectangle (Figure 3-42C)
A tooltip menu is displayed:	Click **Convert to Arc**
An arc appears (Figure 3-42D):	With **ORTHO** on, move your cursor up and type **12 <Enter>**
	Press **<Esc>** to clear the grips (Figure 3-42E)

Step 21. Use the **EXPLODE** command to split the polylines.

Step 22. Use the **OFFSET** command (offset 2″) to draw the **inside** lines of the chair symbol (Figure 3-43).

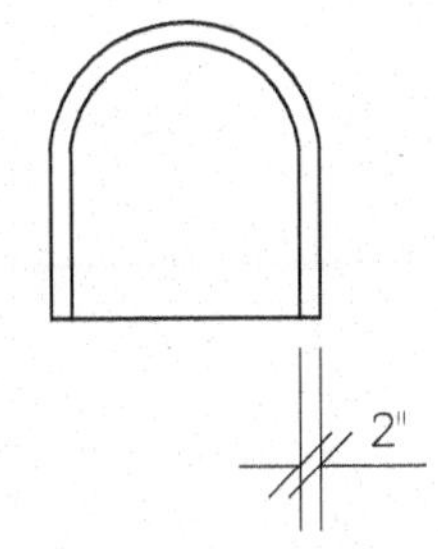

Figure 3-43
Explode the polylines and offset them

> **NOTE**
>
> If you activate the grips on the chair symbol arc before it is exploded, you will get the grip option **Convert to Line** when you hover over the arc grip.

Step 23. The chairs are located 6″ out from the outside edge of the table. Use the **MOVE** command, **Osnap-Midpoint** (to the front of the chair), and **From** to locate the front of the chair 6″ outside the midpoint of an edge of the conference table polygon (Figure 3-44).

You could have avoided the use of the **Move** command in this step by using the .x, .y, and .z (x, y, z filters) to place the rectangle at its correct location 6″ away from the outer edge of the table. Use the Help system of AutoCAD to learn about coordinate filters or ask your instructor to demonstrate them in class.

Figure 3-44
Position the chair and offset the polygon

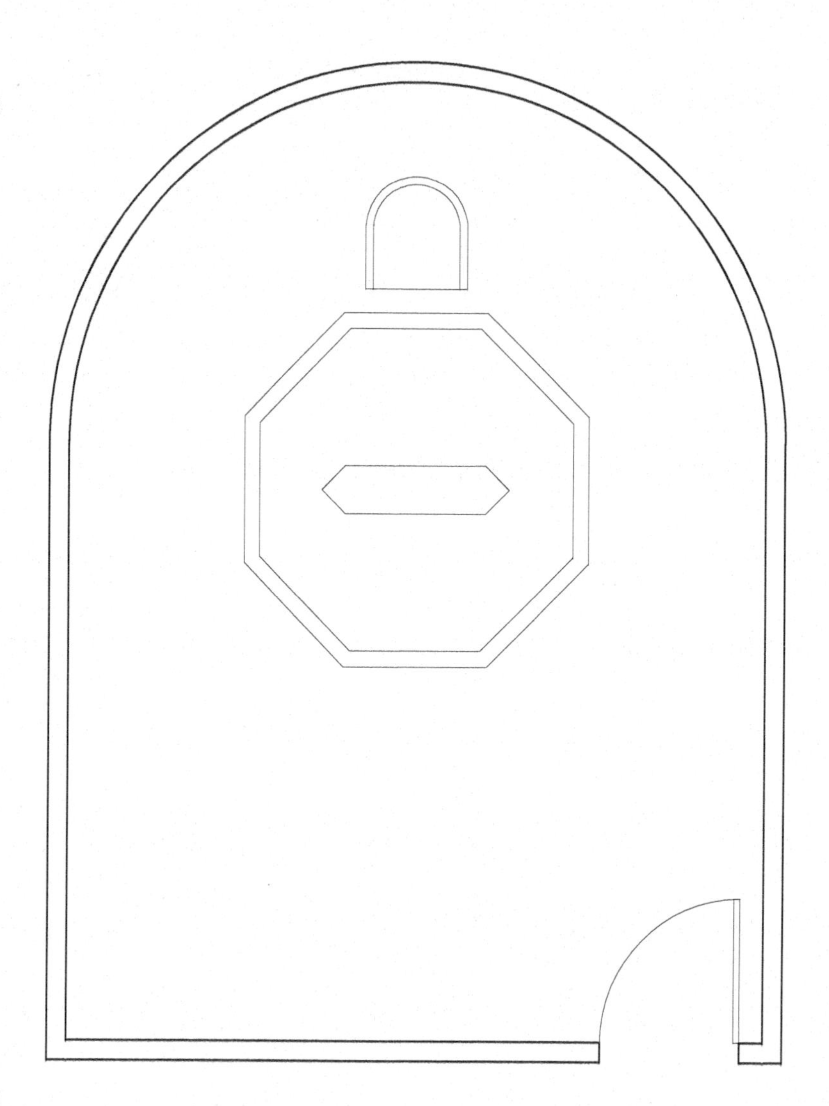

POLAR ARRAY	
Ribbon/ Panel	Home/ Modify Array
Modify Toolbar:	
Menu Bar:	Modify/ Array/Polar Array
Type a Command:	ARRAY
Command Alias:	AR

Polar: The option of the **ARRAY** command that allows you to make multiple copies of an object in a circular array.

Step 24. Use the **OFFSET** command to offset the outside edge of the conference table 4″ to the **inside** to form the 4″ band (Figure 3-44).

Step 25. Use **Zoom-Extents** after you finish drawing the 4″ band.

ARRAY

Polar

The ***Polar*** option of the **ARRAY** command allows you to make multiple copies of an object in a circular array. You can specify a 360° **Angle to fill** to form a full circular array. You can specify an angle less than 360° to form a partial circular array. When you specify a positive angle, the array is rotated counterclockwise (+=ccw). When you specify a negative angle, the array is rotated clockwise (−=cw).

AutoCAD constructs the array by determining the distance from the array's center point to a point on the object selected. *If more than one object is selected, the reference point is on the last item in the selection set.*

Step 26. Use the **POLAR ARRAY** command to make a polar (circular) pattern of eight chairs (Figure 3-45), as described next:

Prompt	Response
Type a command:	**Polar Array** (or type **ARRAYPOLAR <Enter>**)

Figure 3-45
Array the chairs, draw the potted plant and copy it, and hatch the walls

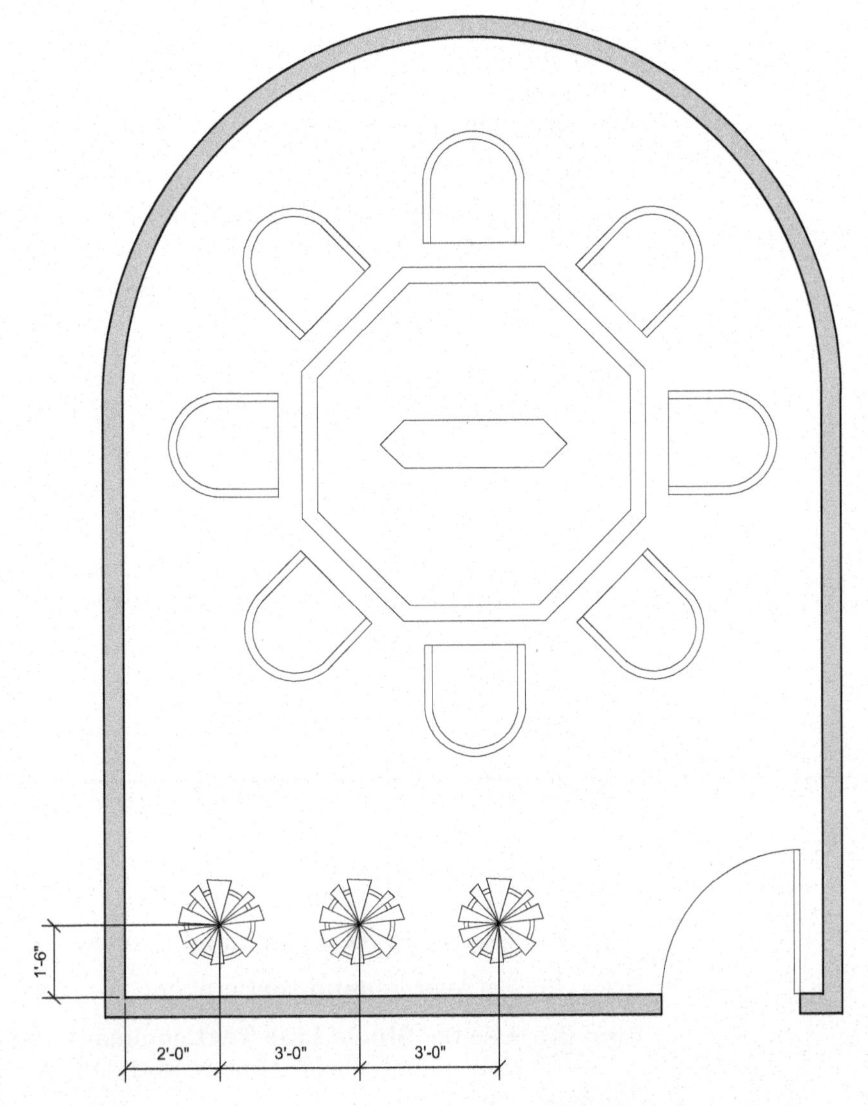

Prompt	Response
Select objects:	Click the first corner for a window to select the chair just drawn
Specify opposite corner:	Window the chair just drawn
Select objects:	**<Enter>**
Specify center point of array [or Base point Axis of rotation]:	Click the center point of the polygon using the **Geometric Center (GCEN)** object snap mode.

Prompt	Response
Select grip to edit array or [ASsociative Base point Items Angle between Fill angle ROWs Levels ROTate items eXit] <eXit>:	Type **I<Enter>**i
Enter number of items in array or [Expression] <6>:	Type **8<Enter>**
Select grip to edit array or [ASsociative Base point Items Angle between Fill angle ROWs Levels ROTate items eXit]<eXit>:	**<Enter>**

Step 27. Use **Zoom-Window** to zoom in on the area of the conference room where the plants and planters are located (Figure 3-45).

Step 28. Use the **CIRCLE** command, **9″** radius, to draw the outside shape of one planter.

Step 29. Use the **OFFSET** command, offset distance **1″**, offset to the **inside** of the planter, to give a thickness to the planter.

Step 30. Use the **LINE** command to draw multisegmented shapes (to show a plant) in the planter (Figure 3-45).

Step 31. Use the **TRIM** command to trim the lines of the pot beneath the plant leaves. Window the entire planter to select the cutting edges, and then select the lines to trim.

Step 32. Use the **COPY** command to draw the next two planters, as shown in Figure 3-45.

Step 33. Create the following new layer and set it as the current layer:

Layer name	Color	Linetype	Lineweight
a-wall-patt-gray	gray (253)	continuous	.004″ (.09 mm)

Step 34. Use the **HATCH** command to make the walls solid (Figure 3-45).

Step 35. Set layer **a-anno-text** current.

Step 36. Use the **Single Line Text** command (type **DT <Enter>**) to type your name, class number, and date, 6″ high in the upper-right corner.

Step 37. When you have completed Exercise 3-3 (Figure 3-46), save your work in at least two places.

Step 38. Print your drawing from the **Model** tab at a scale of **1/4″ = 1′-0″**.

Figure 3-46
Exercise 3-3 complete

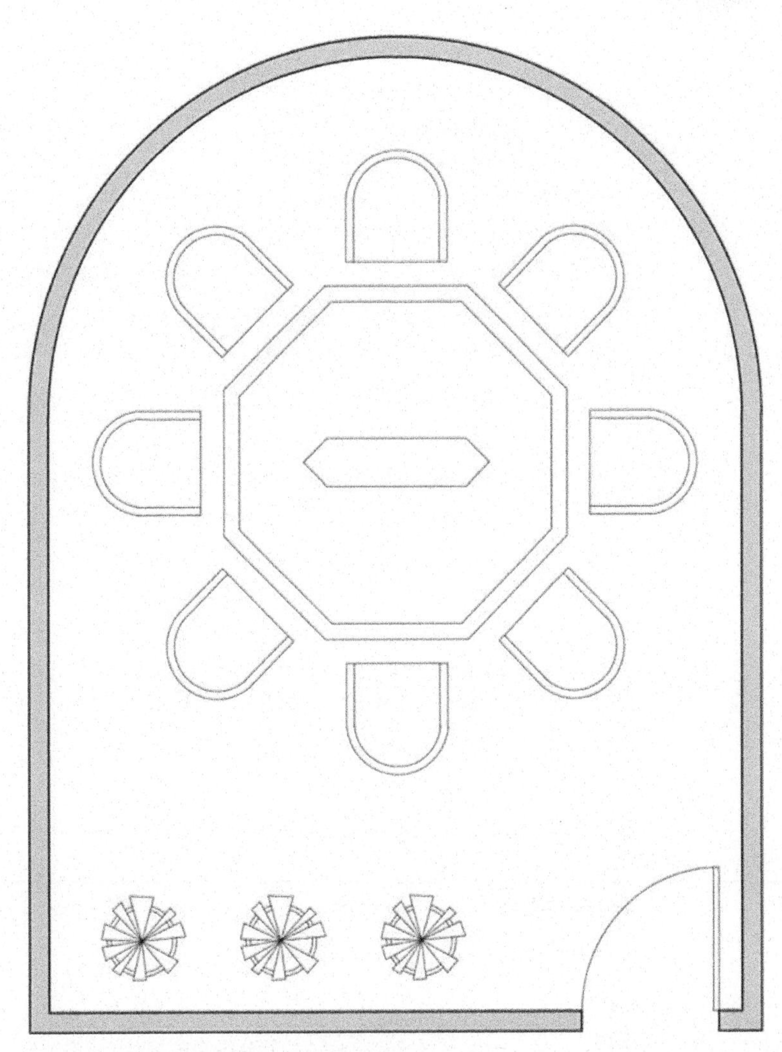

EXERCISE 3-4
Drawing a Conference Room Using Polar Tracking

In Exercise 3-4, you will use polar tracking to draw lines at angles in 15° increments. When you have completed Exercise 3-4, your drawing will look similar to Figure 3-47.

Step 1. Click **Open...**, change the **Files of type:** input box to **Drawing Template (*.dwt)**, and open the **Ch3-conference-rm-setup** template, which you previously created at the beginning of Exercise 3-1.

Step 2. Click **Save As...**, change the **Files of type:** input box to **AutoCAD 2018 Drawing (.dwg)**, and save the template as a drawing file named **CH3-EXERCISE4**.

Figure 3-47
Exercise 3-4: Drawing a conference room using polar tracking (scale 1/4″ = 1′-0″)

NAME
CLASS
DATE

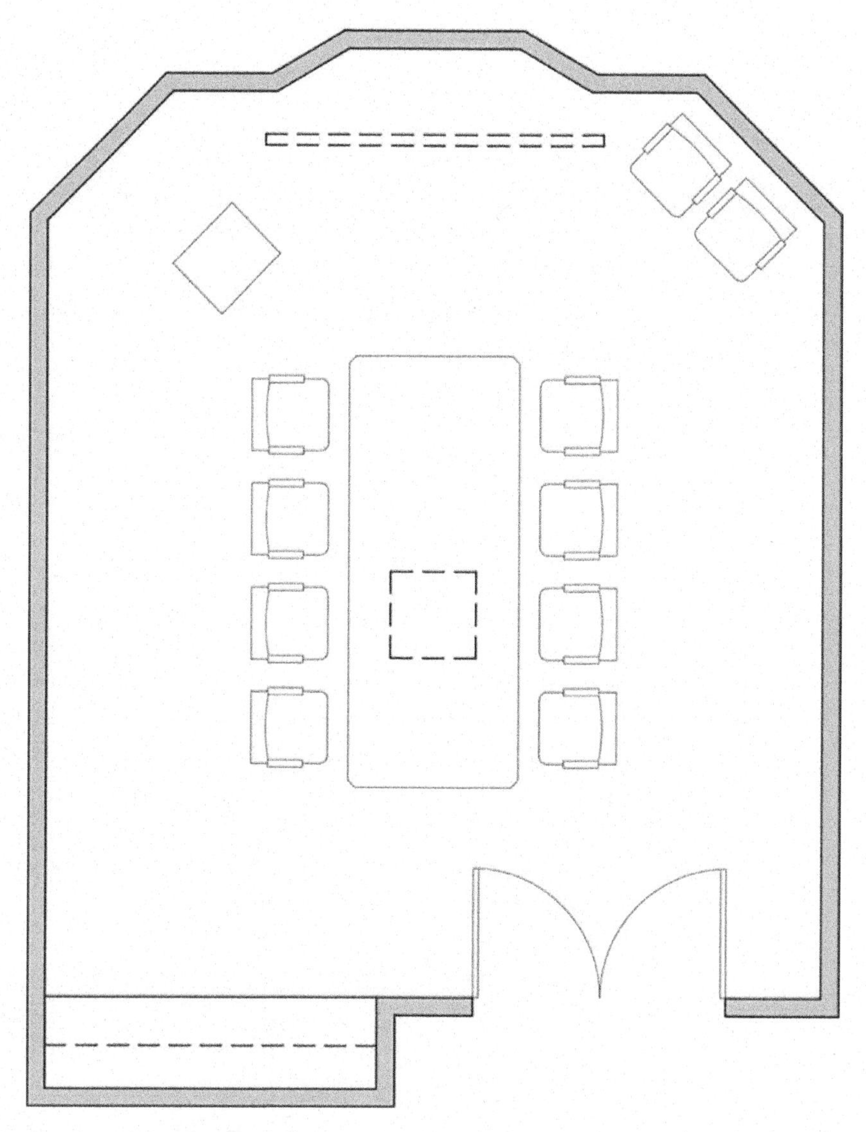

Step 3. Verify the following settings:

1. Drawing units: **Architectural**
2. Drawing limits: **25′,35′**
3. **GRIDDISPLAY**: **0**
4. Grid: **12″**
5. Snap: **6″**
6. Verify the following layers:

Layer name	Color	Linetype	Lineweight
a-anno-text	green	continuous	.006″ (.15 mm)
a-door	red	continuous	.004″ (.09 mm)
a-wall-intr	blue	continuous	.010″ (.25 mm)
i-eqpm-ovhd	red	hidden	.004″ (.09 mm)
i-furn	cyan	continuous	.004″ (.09 mm)

Step 4. Set layer **a-wall-intr** current.

Step 5. Use **Zoom-All** to view the limits of the drawing.

Step 6. Turn **SNAP, GRID,** and **LWDISPLAY** on. The remaining buttons in the status bar should be off.

Polar Tracking

Polar tracking lets you specify angles at which to draw. Polar tracking is similar to Ortho mode, but unlike Ortho, polar tracking merely indicates your specified angles and does not force you to draw horizontally or vertically like Ortho does.

polar tracking: A means of specifying points using your own increment angle.

Step 7. Set ***polar tracking*** angles at 15°, as described next:

Prompt	Response
Type a command:	Place your mouse over **Polar Tracking** on the status bar and right-click
A right-click menu appears:	Click **Tracking Settings...**
The **Drafting Settings** dialog box appears with the **Polar Tracking** tab selected:	Click the list under **Increment angle:** and click **15** (as shown in Figure 3-48)
	Click **OK**

Polar Tracking (<F10>): Shows temporary alignment paths along specific angles of interest (for example, 15 degrees). Although the default increment for PolarSnap is 90 degrees, one can change it easily to 60, 45, 30, 15, and so on, as shown in Figure 3-48. You can use the system variable **POLARANG** to reset PolarSnap.

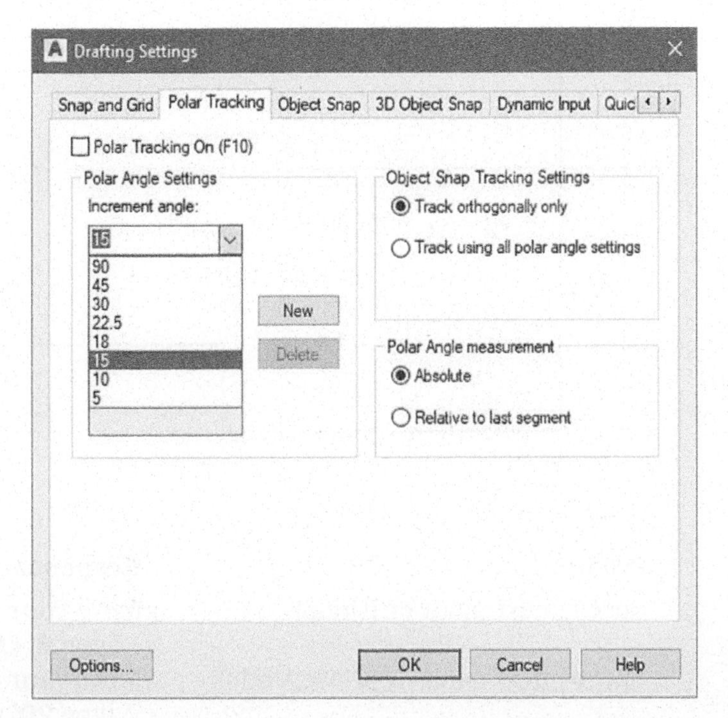

Figure 3-48
Set polar tracking angles

Step 8. Use the **LINE** command with direct distance entry and polar tracking to draw the inside lines of the conference room walls (Figure 3-49), as described next:

Prompt	Response
Type a command:	**Line** (or type **L <Enter>**)
Specify first point:	Type **11′6,4′ <Enter>**
Specify next point or [Undo]:	Turn **ORTHO** on Move your mouse down and type **2′ <Enter>**

Figure 3-49
Measurements for the walls

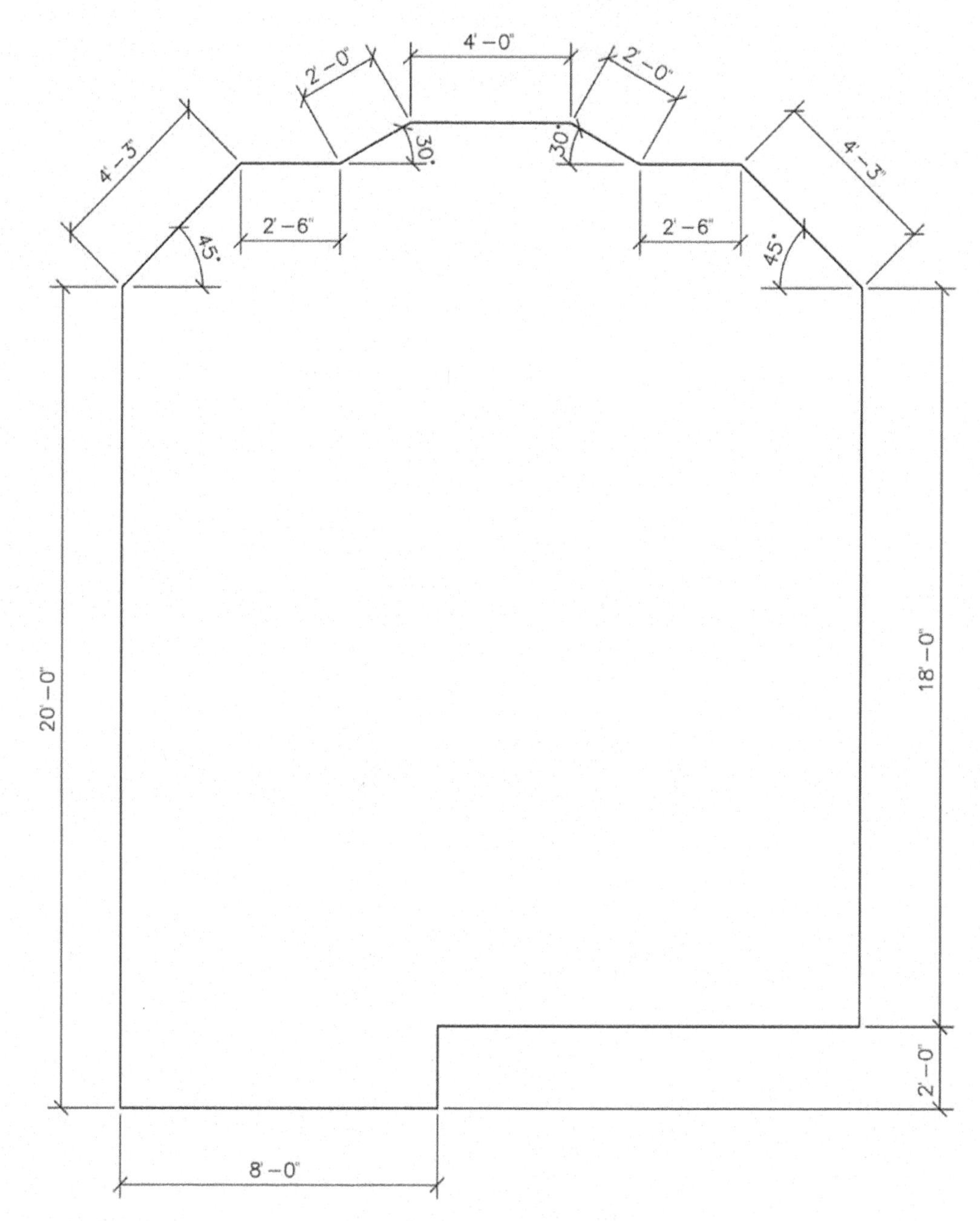

Prompt	Response
Specify next point or [Undo]:	Move your mouse to the left and type **8′ <Enter>**
Specify next point or [Close Undo]:	Move your mouse straight up and type **20′ <Enter>**

Prompt	Response
Specify next point or [Close Undo]:	Turn **POLAR** on (**ORTHO** turns off automatically) Move your mouse so that **45°** shows and type **4'3 <Enter>**
Specify next point or [Close Undo]:	Move your mouse so that **<0°** shows and type **2'6 <Enter>**
Specify next point or [Close Undo]:	Move your mouse so that **<30°** shows and type **2' <Enter>**
Specify next point or [Close Undo]:	Move your mouse so that **<0°** shows and type **4' <Enter>**
Specify next point or [Close Undo]:	Move your mouse so that **<330°** shows and type **2' <Enter>**
Specify next point or [Close Undo]:	Move your mouse so that **<0°** shows and type **2'6 <Enter>**
Specify next point or [Close Undo]:	Move your mouse so that **<315°** shows and type **4'3 <Enter>**
Specify next point or [Close Undo]:	Move your mouse straight down so that **<270°** shows and type **18' <Enter>**
Specify next point or [Close Undo]:	Type **C <Enter>** (to complete the **LINE** command)

Polyline Edit

Next, you join all the lines you created into a single polyline.

Step 9. Use **Polyline Edit** to join all lines into a single polyline, as described next:

Prompt	Response
Type a command:	**Polyline Edit** (or type **PE <Enter>**)
Select polyline or [Multiple]:	Click any of the lines
Object selected is not a polyline	
Do you want to turn it into one? <Y>	**<Enter>**
Enter an option [Close Join Width Edit vertex Fit Spline DecurveLtype gen Reverse Undo]:	Type **J <Enter>**
Select objects:	Type **ALL <Enter>** (or use a crossing window to select all)
12 found	
Select objects:	**<Enter>**
11 segments added to polyline	
Enter an option [Open Join Width Edit vertex Fit Spline Decurve Ltype gen Reverse Undo]:	**<Enter>**

Step 10. Use the **OFFSET** command to offset the polyline 5″ to the **outside**, as shown in Figure 3-50.

Step 11. To split the two polylines that make the conference room walls into separate line segments, place two vertical lines (length: wall thickness = 5″) and location as shown in Figure 3-50. **EXPLODE** both polylines.

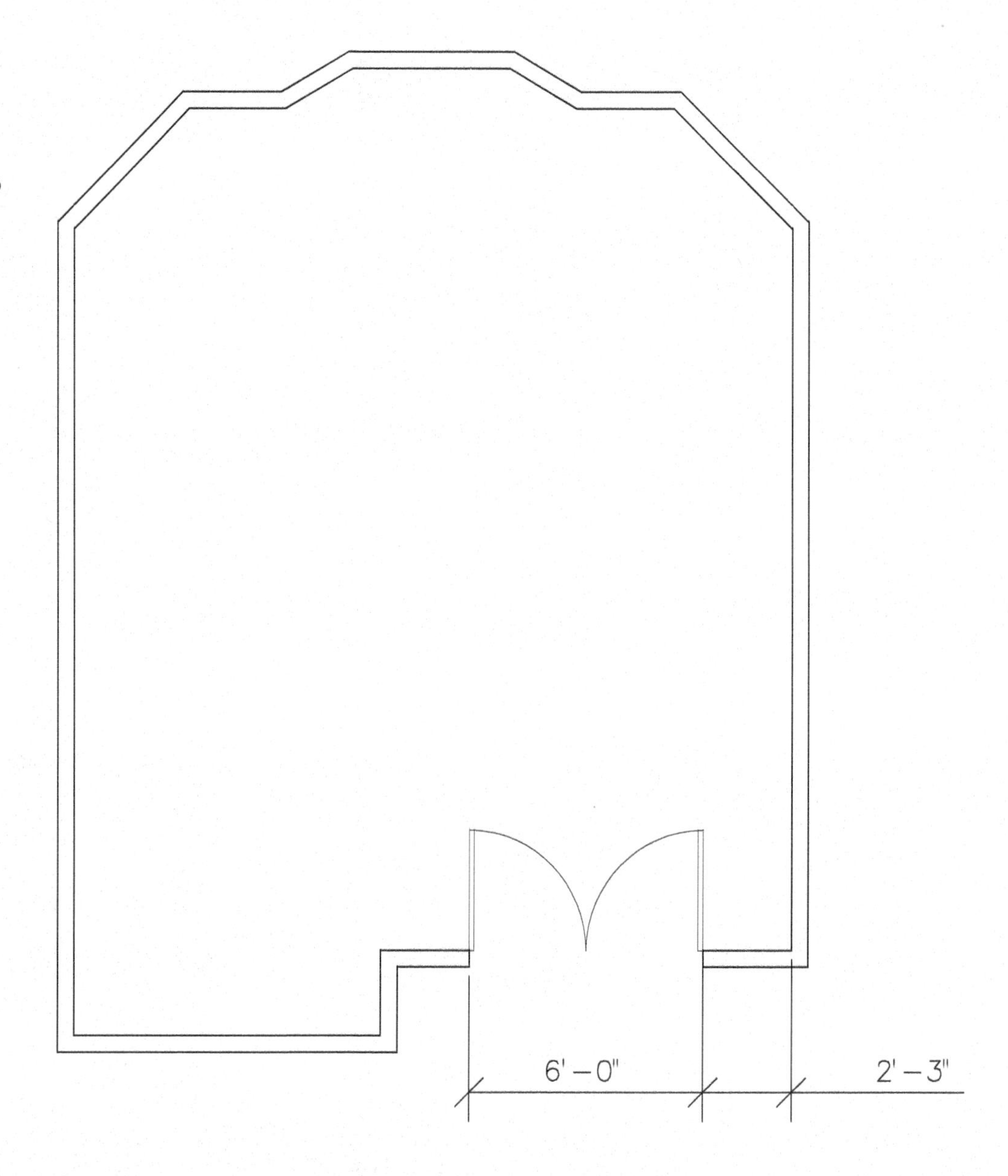

Figure 3-50
Offset the polyline 5″ to the outside, explode both polylines, make the 6′ door opening, and draw the two doors

Step 12. Use the **Trim** command to create the 6′ door opening as shown in Figure 3-50. The two vertical lines of the previous step will be the cutting edges for the **Trim** command.

Step 13. Set layer **a-door** current.

Step 14. Use the **Rectangle** command to draw the two 1-1/2″ × 3′ door symbols (Figure 3-50).

Step 15. Use the **Arc-Start, End, Direction** method to draw the door swing arcs (Figure 3-50).

Step 16. Set layer **i-furn** current.

Specifying Points with Tracking

Tracking, which is similar to the **ID Point** command, allows you to specify points, except that you can activate tracking whenever AutoCAD asks for a point. You can also specify as many points as you need until you arrive at the desired location. You then press **<Enter>** to end the tracking mode.

tracking: A means of reducing, if not eliminating, the number of construction lines you draw by specifying points. Alternatively, use the **From** option of the **Object Snap** menu (shown earlier in Figure 3-16) to define a reference point and then define the x- and y-offset from that point. The upcoming steps explain this further. For now, let's continue with the exercise using ID Point.

Step 17. Draw the table using **Rectangle** and **Osnap-Tracking** (Figure 3-51), as described next:

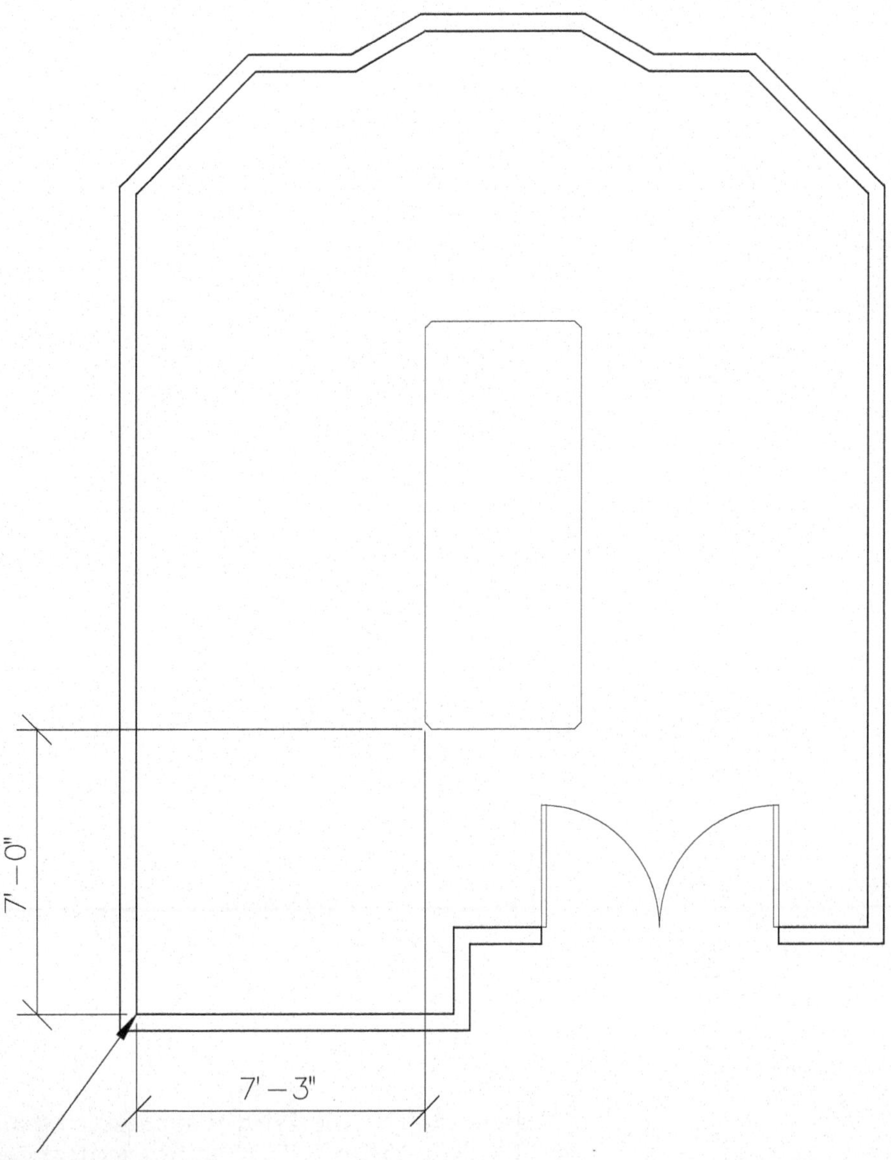

Figure 3-51
Draw the table using **Rectangle** and **Osnap-Tracking**

Prompt	**Response**
Type a command:	**Rectangle** (or type **REC <Enter>**)
Specify first corner point or [Chamfer Elevation Fillet Thickness Width]:	Type **C <Enter>**
Specify first chamfer distance for rectangles <0′-0″>:	Type **2 <Enter>**
Specify second chamfer distance for rectangles <0′-2″>:	**<Enter>**
Specify first corner point or [Chamfer Elevation Fillet Thickness Width]:	Type **TRACK <Enter>**

Prompt	Response
First tracking point:	Type **INT <Enter>** (with **ORTHO** off) in the lower-left inside corner of the room
Next point (Press ENTER to end tracking):	Move your mouse to the right (with **ORTHO** on and **OSNAP** off) and type **7′3 <Enter>**
Next point (Press ENTER to end tracking):	Move your mouse up and type **7′ <Enter>**
Next point (Press ENTER to end tracking):	**<Enter>** (to end tracking)
Specify other corner point or [Area Dimensions Rotation]:	Type **@48,120 <Enter>** (relative coordinates)

Drawing the Chairs around the Conference Table

Step 18. Zoom in on a portion of the grid so you can begin to draw the chair symbol.

Step 19. Draw a rectangle 20″ wide by 22″ deep (change chamfer distance to 0) using the **LINE** or **Rectangle** command (Figure 3-52A).

Step 20. Draw the 2″ × 10″ left chair arm using **Rectangle** and **Tracking** (Figure 3-52B).

Step 21. Use **MIRROR** and **TRIM** to place the right arm and trim the extra lines out (Figure 3-52C).

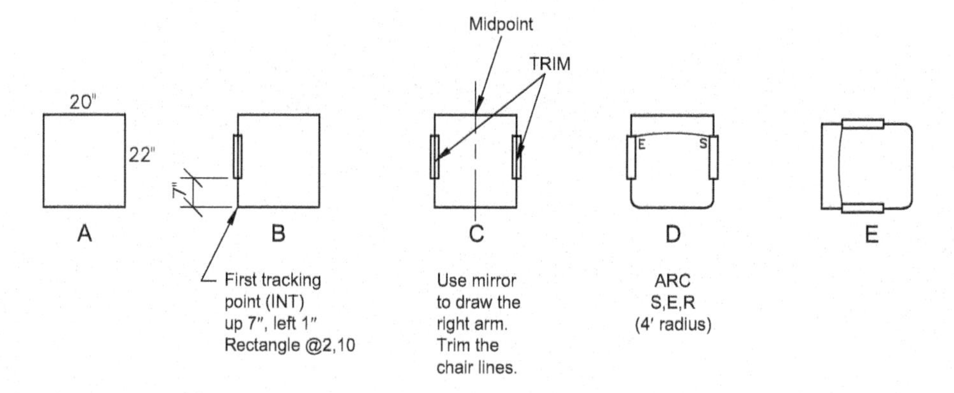

Figure 3-52 Draw the conference room chair

Step 22. Draw a 2″ fillet on the bottom two corners of the chair (Figure 3-52D).

Step 23. Use **Arc-Start, End, Radius** (4′ radius) to complete the chair symbol (Figure 3-52D).

Step 24. Rotate the chair to appear as shown in Figure 3-52E.

Step 25. Explode the table, and then offset the line that defines the long left side of the table 6″ to the outside of the table. Alternatively, place a line 6″ away from the edge of the table to the left, using the **Line** command and **From** option of **Osnap,** as shown in Figure 3-53. Use **Explode** at a minimum, especially when you can avoid it.

Step 26. Set the **Point Style** to **X** and size to **6″**.

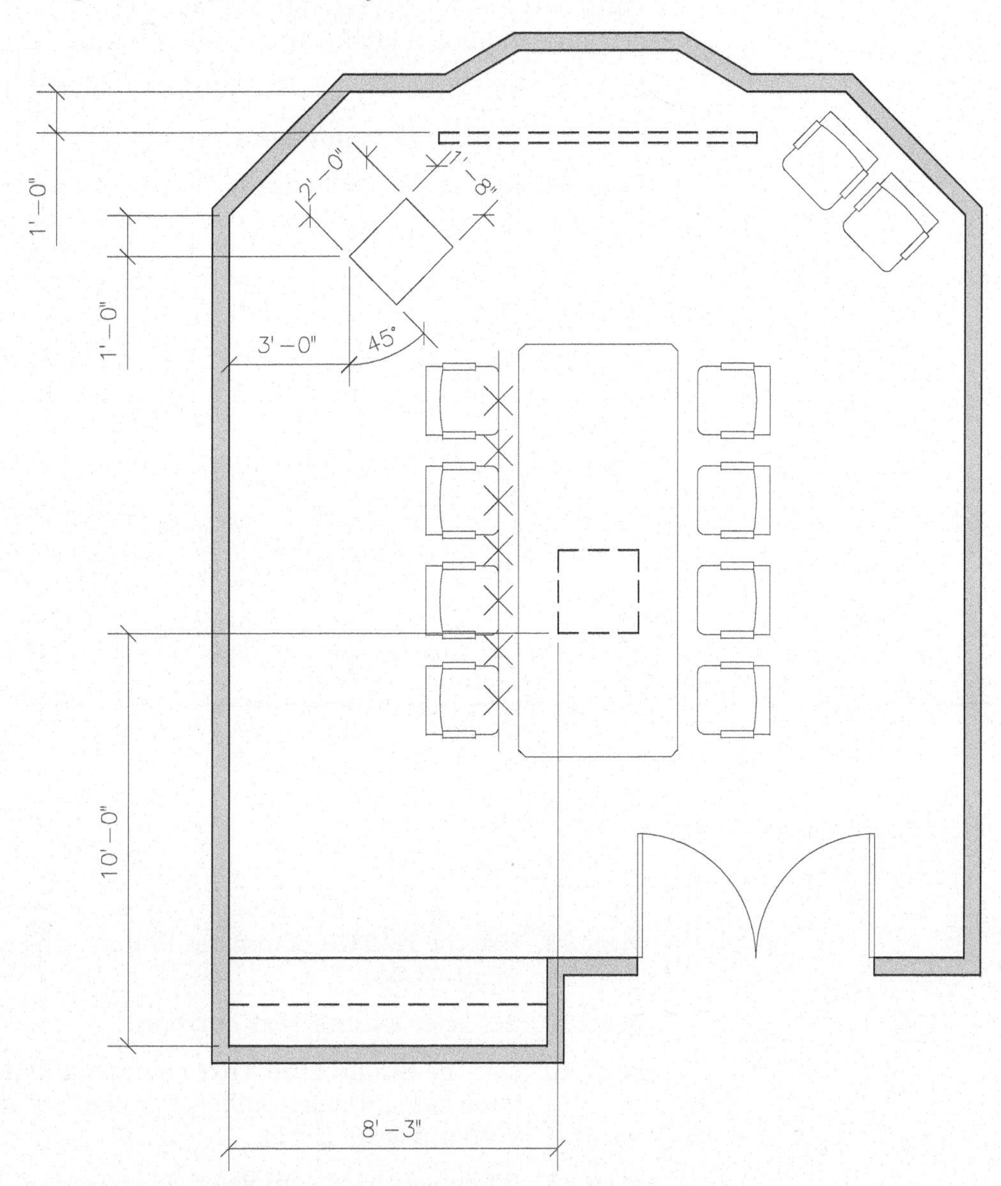

Figure 3-53
Complete the conference room

Step 27. Divide the offset line into eight equal segments.

Step 28. Use **COPY** and **Osnap-Midpoint** to pick up the chair and **Osnap-Node** to copy the chair on the points of the divided line (Figure 3-53).

Step 29. Use the **MIRROR** command to draw the chairs on the right side of the conference table (Figure 3-53).

Step 30. Set **PDMODE** to **1** (invisible).

Step 31. Erase the offset line used to locate the chairs.

Completing the Conference Room

Finish the conference room by adding a lectern, projector screen, and cabinet. Add additional chairs and hatch the walls as shown in Figure 3-53.

Step 32. Draw the 24″ × 20″ lectern as shown in Figure 3-53.

Step 33. Set layer **i-eqpm-ovhd** current.

Step 34. Add the 96″ × 3″ recessed projection screen and the 24″ × 24″ ceiling-mounted projector to the plan as shown in Figure 3-53. Locating the 96″ × 3″ recessed projection screen will require use of the x, y, z-filters and the **Mid Between 2 Points** option of the **Osnap** menu. Ask your instructor to demonstrate it in class.

Step 35. Make the following new layers and draw the lines for the built-in upper and lower cabinets, as shown in Figure 3-53:

Layer name	Color	Linetype	Lineweight
a-flor-case	green	continuous	.006″ (.15 mm)
a-flor-case-uppr	red	hidden line	.004″ (.09 mm)

Step 36. Copy and rotate the two extra chairs in the room, as shown in Figure 3-53.

Step 37. Create the following new layer and set it as the current layer:

Layer name	Color	Linetype	Lineweight
a-wall-patt-gray	gray (253)	continuous	.004″ (.09 mm)

Step 38. Use the **HATCH** command to make the walls solid, as shown in Figure 3-53.

Step 39. Set layer **a-anno-text** current.

Step 40. Use the **Single Line Text** command (type **DT <Enter>**) to type your name, class number, and date, 6″ high in the upper-right corner (Figure 3-54).

Step 41. When you have completed Exercise 3-4 (Figure 3-54), save your work in at least two places.

Step 42. Print your drawing from the **Model** tab at a scale of **1/4″ = 1′-0″**.

Figure 3-54
Exercise 3-4 complete

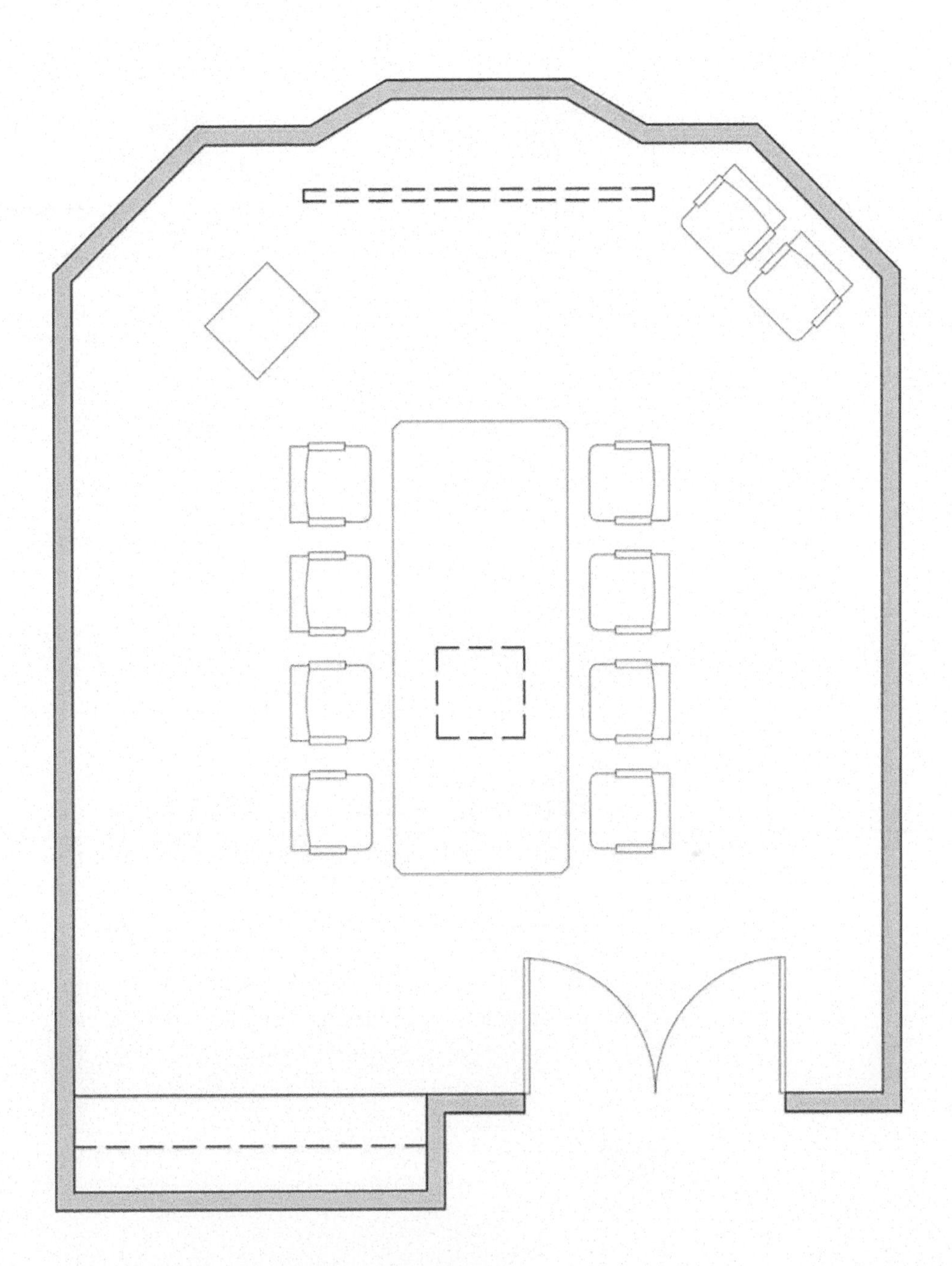

Using Command Preview

Command preview, in the Preview area of the **Selection** tab of the **Options** dialog box (Figure 3-55), enables you to preview the results of **Trim**, **Extend**, **Lengthen**, **Break**, and **MatchProp** operations before actually selecting the objects. The command also enables you to preview **Fillet**, **Chamfer**, and **Offset** operations.

For example, the **Trim** and **Extend** tools provide a preview of the results before you commit the selection. After you select the cutting or boundary edges, you simply pass the cursor over the object you want to trim or extend. A preview of the resulting object is displayed. When you are trimming, the segment to be removed is dimly displayed, and a cursor badge indicates that it will be deleted.

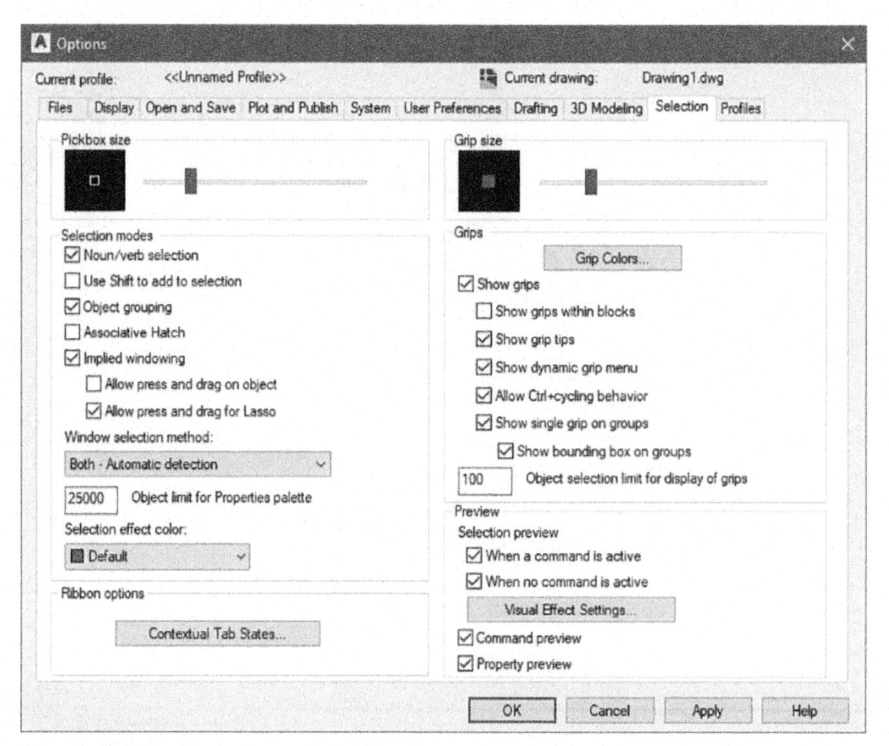

Figure 3-55
Options dialog box, **Selection** tab – **Command preview** option

Choosing Selection Options

In addition to selecting groups of objects using a window or a window crossing, you can also click the cursor in a blank area of the drawing and then drag around the objects to create a lasso selection. **Allow press and drag for Lasso** in the **Options** dialog box on the **Selection** tab enables you to specify the lasso (Figure 3-55). For a traditional rectangular window or crossing selection, click and release to pick each corner of the rectangle.

Chapter Summary

This chapter provided you the information necessary to set up and draw conference and lecture rooms. You learned how to use many of the **Draw**, **Inquiry**, and **Modify** commands. You also learned how to use the command options **Osnap**, **From**, **Tracking**, and **Polar Tracking**, and you learned the uses of a drawing template. Now you have the skills and information necessary to produce conference and lecture rooms.

Chapter Test Questions

Multiple Choice

Circle the correct answer.

1. When the outline of the walls of a room is drawn with a zero-width polyline, which of the following commands can you use to draw most quickly the second line that shows the depth of the walls?

   a. **Line**
   b. **Polyline**
   c. **OFFSET**
   d. **COPY**

2. Which of the following commands do you use to split a solid polyline into separate segments?

   a. **ID Point**
   b. **OFFSET**
   c. **ARRAY**
   d. **EXPLODE**

3. Which of the following commands do you use to locate a point on a drawing and to display the position of that point in absolute coordinates?

   a. **ID Point**
   b. **Inquiry**
   c. **First point**
   d. **Distance**

4. Which of the following commands can you use to draw a rounded corner?

   a. **CHAMFER**
   b. **FILLET**
   c. **OFFSET**
   d. **TRIM**

5. Which of the folloing **Osnap** modifiers do you use to snap to a point entity?

   a. **Perpendicular**
   b. **Endpoint**
   c. **Node**
   d. **Midpoint**

6. Which of the following rotation angles is the same as -90°?

   a. 90
   b. 180
   c. 270
   d. 300

7. Which of the following controls the appearance of the markers used in the **DIVIDE** command?

   a. **Aperture Size (APBOX)**
   b. **Point Style (DDPTYPE)**
   c. **Osnap (OSNAP)**
   d. **Pickbox Size (PICKBOX)**

8. Which of the following do you use to change the size of the target box that appears when using **Modify** commands?

   a. **Aperture (APBOX)** c. **Osnap (PICKBOX)**

   b. **Point Style (DDPTYPE)** d. **Pickbox Size (PICKBOX)**

9. Which of the following commands can you use to join lines or arcs together and make them a single polyline?

   a. **EXPLODE** c. **Polyline**

   b. **Polyline Edit (PEDIT)** d. **CLOSE**

10. Which of the following command options allows you to chamfer the corners of a rectangle using only the **Rectangle** command?

    a. **C** c. **P**

    b. **D** d. **All**

Matching

Write the number of the correct answer on the line.

a. **Osnap** ______

b. **Polyline** ______

c. **TRIM** ______

d. **Tracking** ______

e. **From** ______

1. A setting option that allows you to start a line from the exact endpoint of an existing line
2. A command used to draw a rectangle that can be offset with a single click
3. A command modifier that locates a base point and then allows you to locate an offset point from that base point
4. A command that is used to cut off lines
5. A method of locating points before the start point of a line is specified

True or False

Circle the correct answer.

1. **True or False:** The **Chamfer** command will chamfer two lines that do not intersect.
2. **True or False:** All lines of a square drawn with a polyline can be offset with one use of the **OFFSET** command.
3. **True or False:** You can select all objects in the drawing as cutting edges by pressing **<Enter>** at the prompt *Select objects or <select all>:*.
4. **True or False:** The width of a polyline cannot be changed.
5. **True or False:** The **ID Point** command is used to determine the exact distance from one point to another.

List

1. Five commands under the **Modify** panel of the ribbon with the **Home** tab ON.
2. Five options under the **Polyline** command.
3. Five options under the **Offset** command.
4. Five options of the the **Osnap** toolbar.
5. Five options under the **Chamfer** command.
6. Five ways of launching the **Point** command.
7. Five options under the **Polyline Edit** command.
8. Five ways of launching the **Hatch** command.
9. Five commands accessible upon activating a grip.
10. Five tabs in the **Drafting Settings** window.

Questions

1. How does **DIVIDE** differ from **MEASURE**?
2. When should you use **Osnap?**
3. When should you use **LINE** instead of **Polyline**?
4. When should you use **Polyline Edit**?
5. What is the **ARRAY** command used for and what are its options?

Chapter Projects

Project 3-1: *Rectangular Lecture Room Including Furniture* **[BASIC]**

1. Draw the floor plan of the lecture room as shown in Figure 3-57. Use the dimensions shown in Figure 3-58, or use an architectural scale to measure the floor plan and draw it full scale.

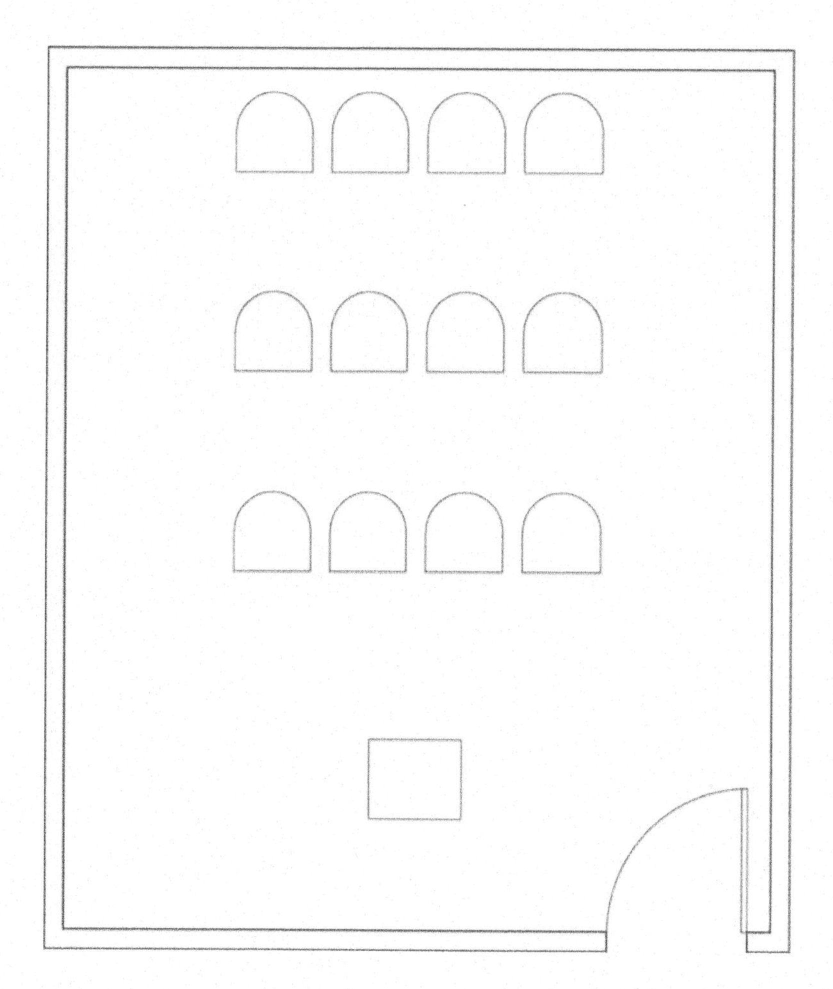

Figure 3-57
Project 3-1: Rectangular lecture room including furniture (scale: 1/4″ = 1′-0″)

2. Use the **Single Line Text** command to type your name, class number, and date, 6″ high in the upper-right corner (Figure 3-57).

3. Print your drawing from the **Model** tab at a scale of **1/4″ = 1′-0″**.

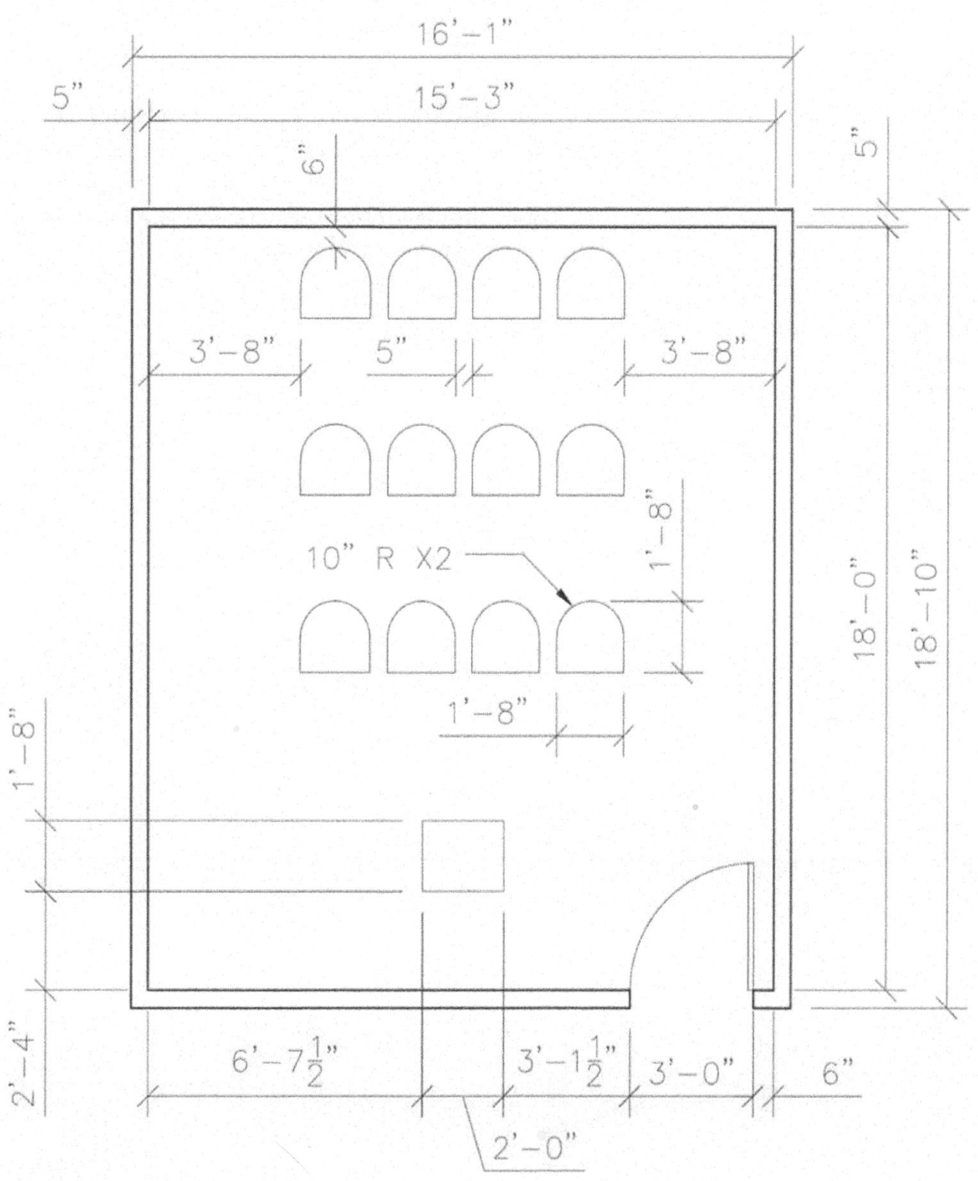

Figure 3-58
Dimensions for Project 3-1 (scale: 1/4″ = 1′-0″)

Project 3-2: *Curved Conference Room Including Furniture* [INTERMEDIATE]

1. Draw the floor plan of the conference room as shown in Figure 3-59. Use the dimensions shown in Figure 3-60, or use an architectural scale to measure the floor plan and draw it full scale. Your drawing will look like Figure 3-59 without the centerline.

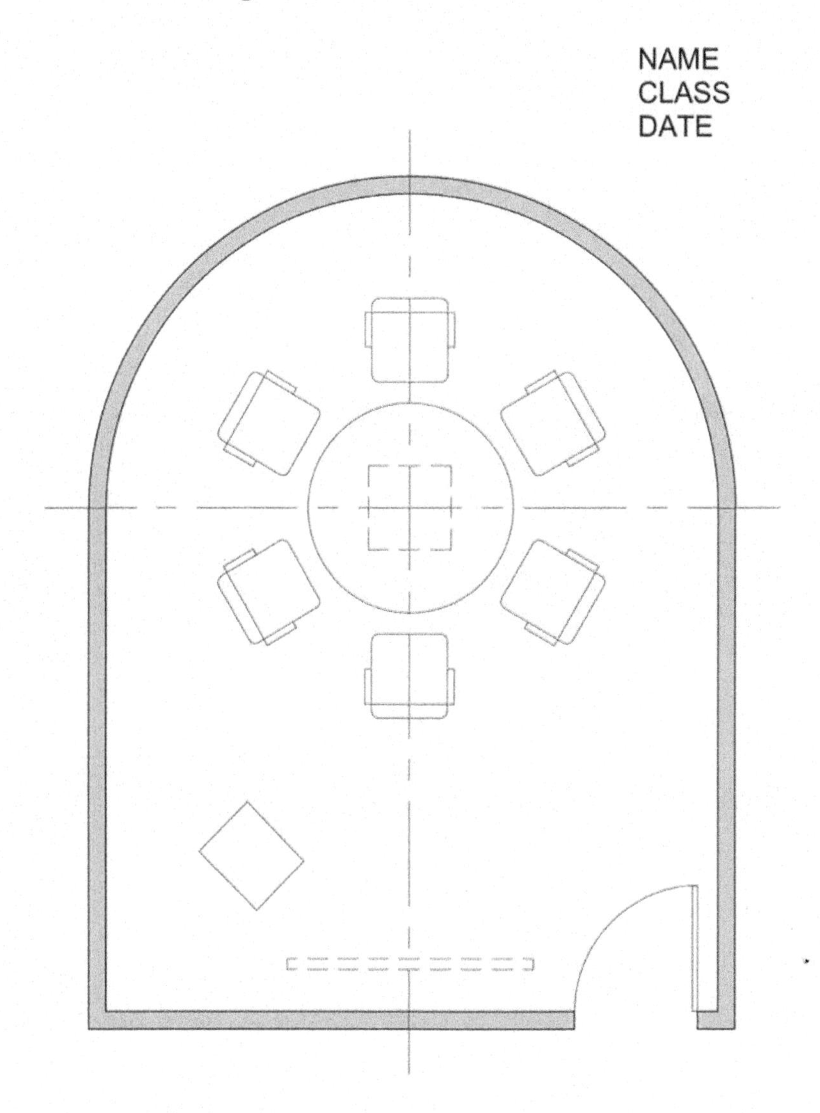

Figure 3-59
Project 3-2: Curved conference room including furniture (scale: 1/4″ = 1′-0″)

2. Use the **Single Line Text** command to type your name, class number, and date, 6″ high in the upper-right corner (Figure 3-59).
3. Print your drawing from the **Model** tab at a scale of **1/4″ = 1′-0″**.

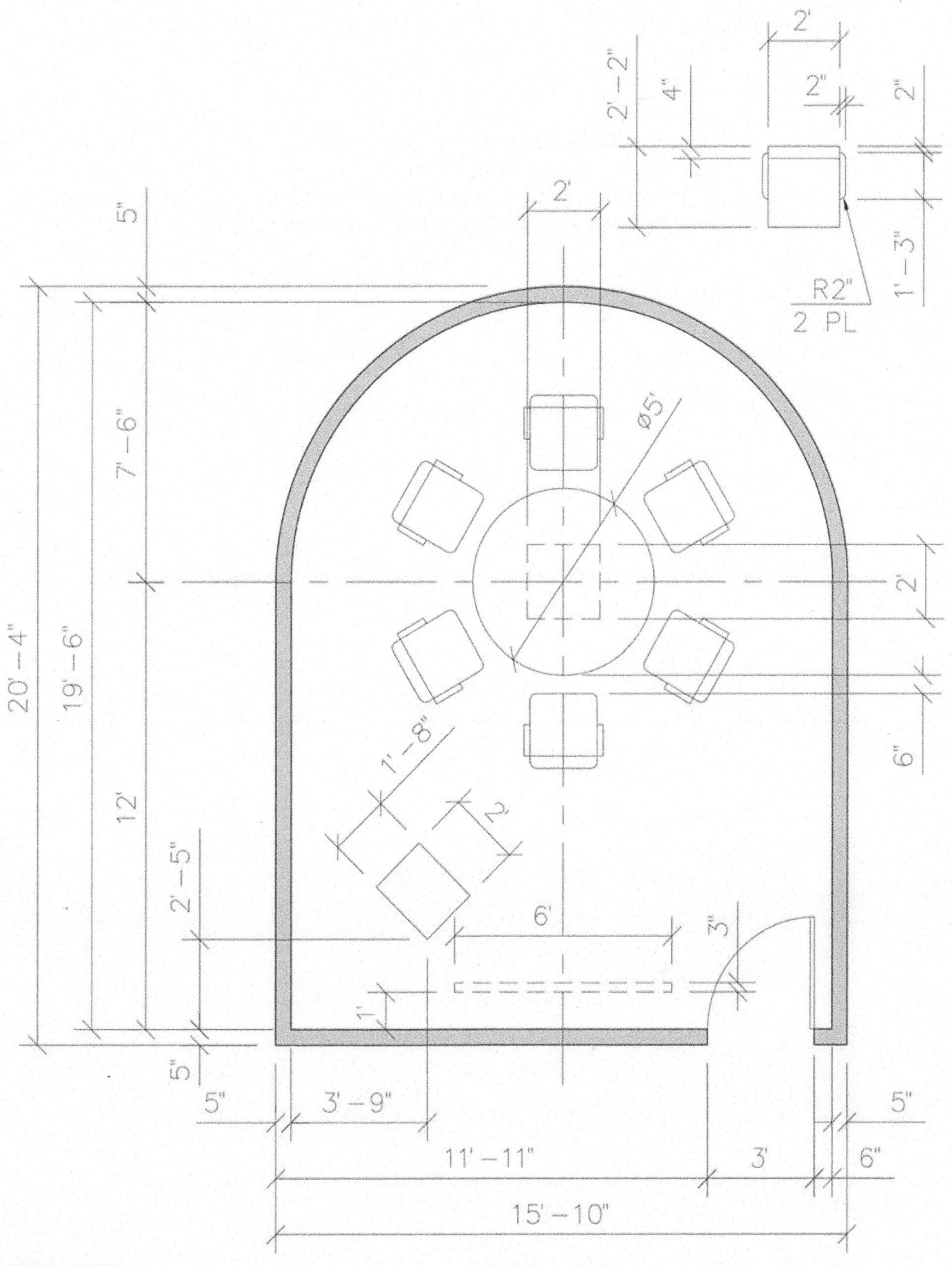

Figure 3-60
Dimensions for Project 3-2 (scale: 1/4" = 1'-0")

Project 3-3: *Video Conference Room Including Furniture* **[BASIC]**

1. Draw the floor plan of the video conference room as shown in Figure 3-61. Use the dimensions shown in Figure 3-62, or use an architectural scale to measure the floor plan and draw it full scale. Your drawing will look like Figure 3-61 without the centerline.

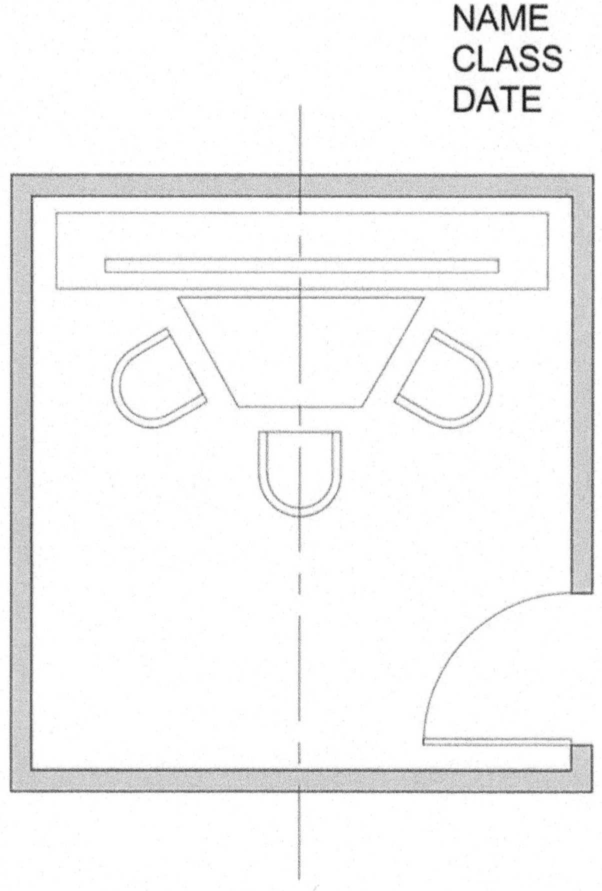

Figure 3-61
Project 3-3: Video conference room including furniture (scale: 1/4″ = 1′-0″)

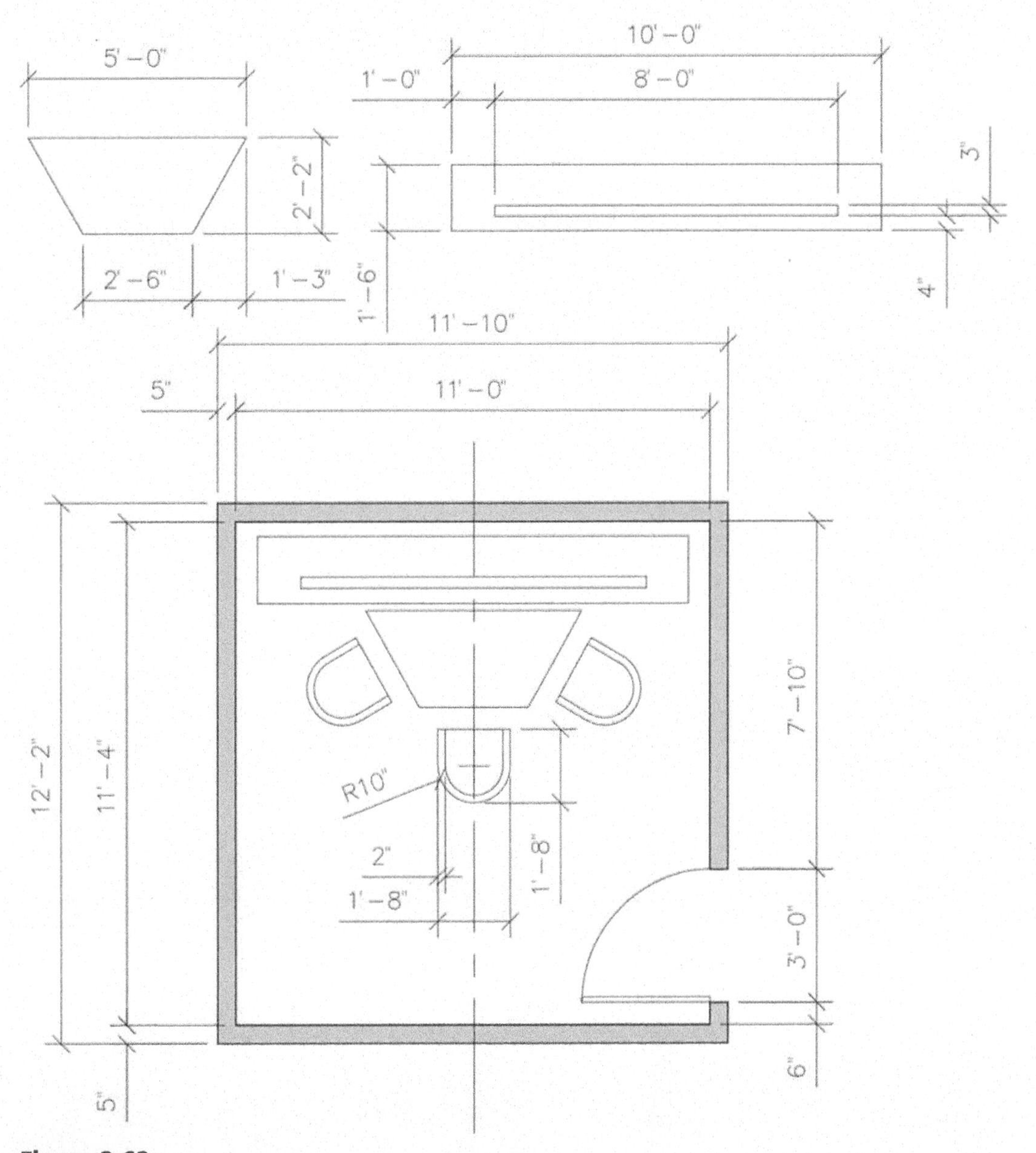

Figure 3-62
Dimensions for Project 3-3 (scale: 1/4″ = 1′-0″)

2. Use the **Single Line Text** command to type your name, class number, and date, 6″ high in the upper-right corner (Figure 3-61).
3. Print your drawing from the **Model** tab at a scale of **1/4″ = 1′-0″**.

Project 3-4: *Rectangular Conference Room Including Furniture* **[INTERMEDIATE]**

1. Draw the floor plan of the conference room as shown in Figure 3-63. Use the dimensions shown in Figure 3-64, or use an architectural scale to measure the floor plan and draw it full scale.

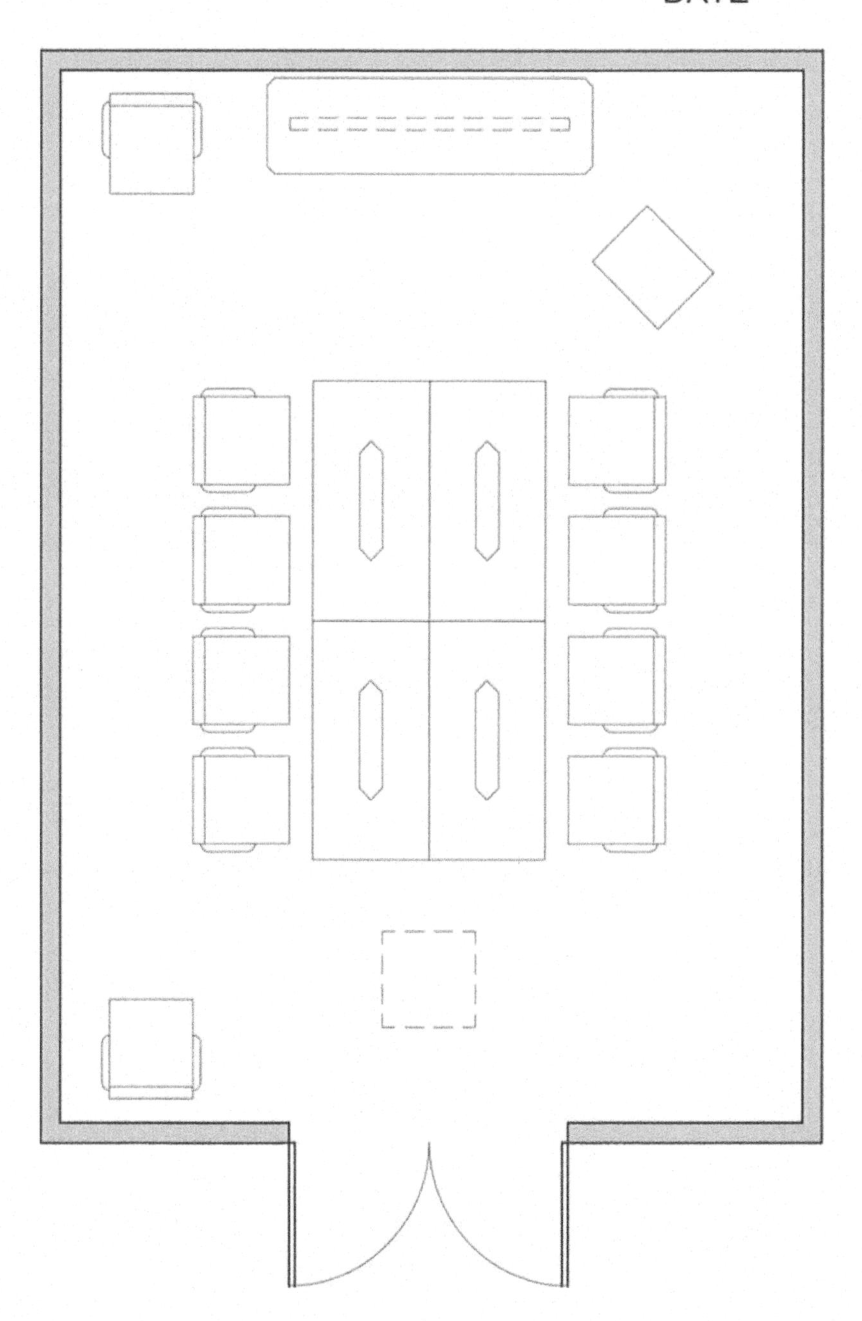

Figure 3-63
Project 3-4: Rectangular conference room including furniture (scale: 1/4″ = 1′-0″)

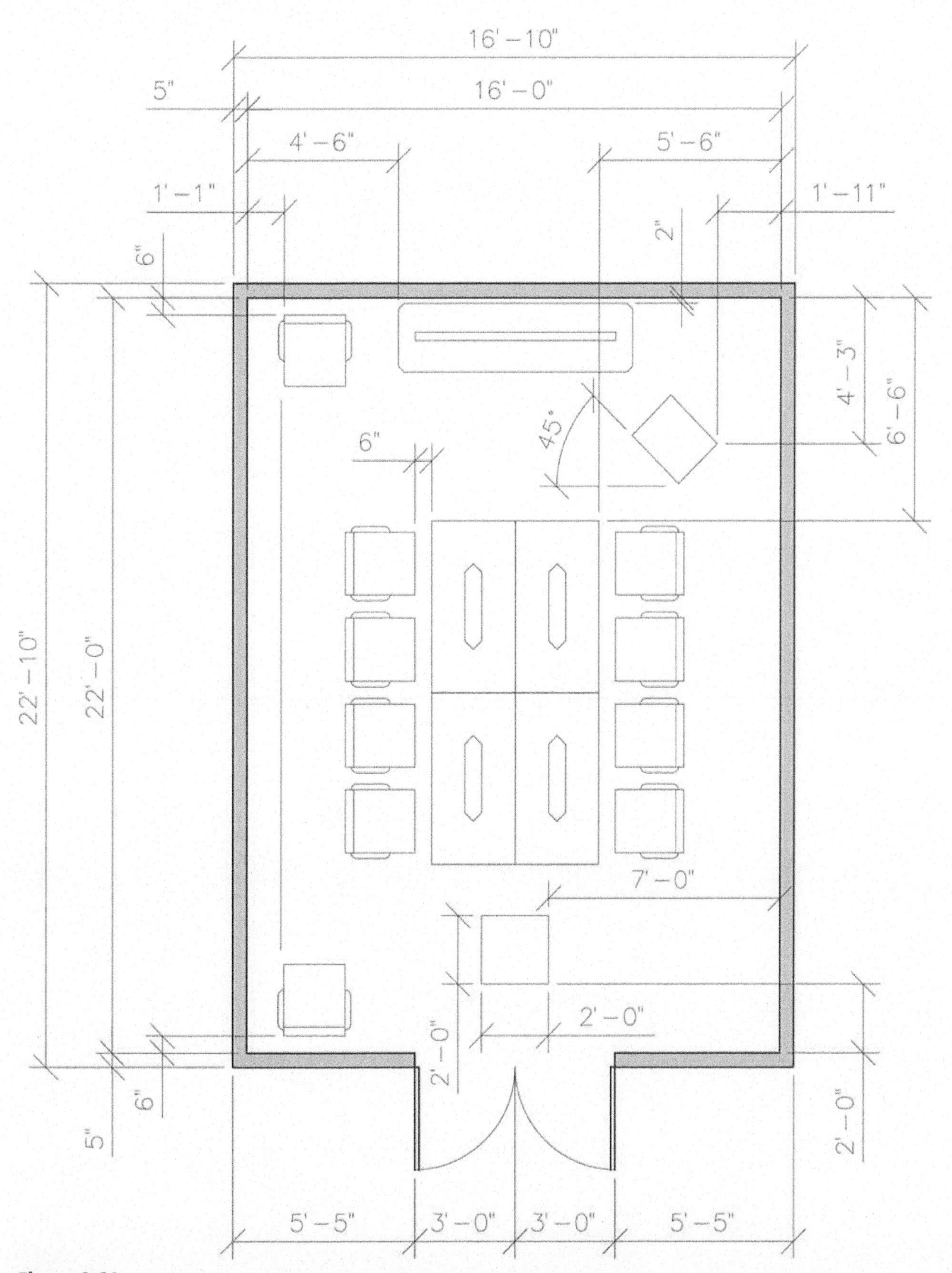

Figure 3-64
Sheet 1 of 2, Dimensions for Project 3-4 (scale: 1/4″ = 1′-0″)

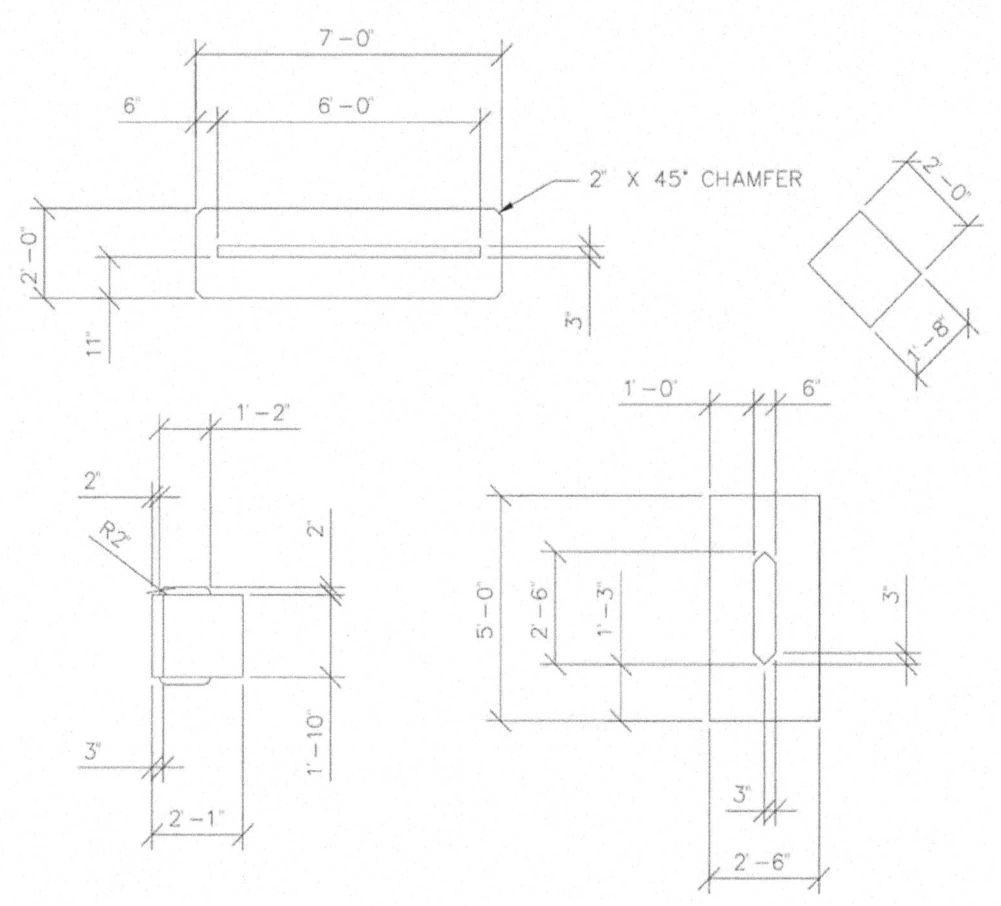

Figure 3-64
Sheet 2 of 2, Dimensions for Project 3-4 (scale: 1/4″ = 1′-0″)

2. Use the **Single Line Text** command to type your name, class number, and date, 6″ high in the upper-right corner (Figure 3-63).

3. Print your drawing from the **Model** tab at a scale of **1/4″ = 1′-0″**.

Project 3-5: *Conference Room with Angles Including Furniture* **[ADVANCED]**

1. Draw the floor plan of the conference room as shown in Figure 3-65. Use the dimensions shown in Figure 3-66, or use an architectural scale to measure the floor plan and draw it full scale.

NAME
CLASS
DATE

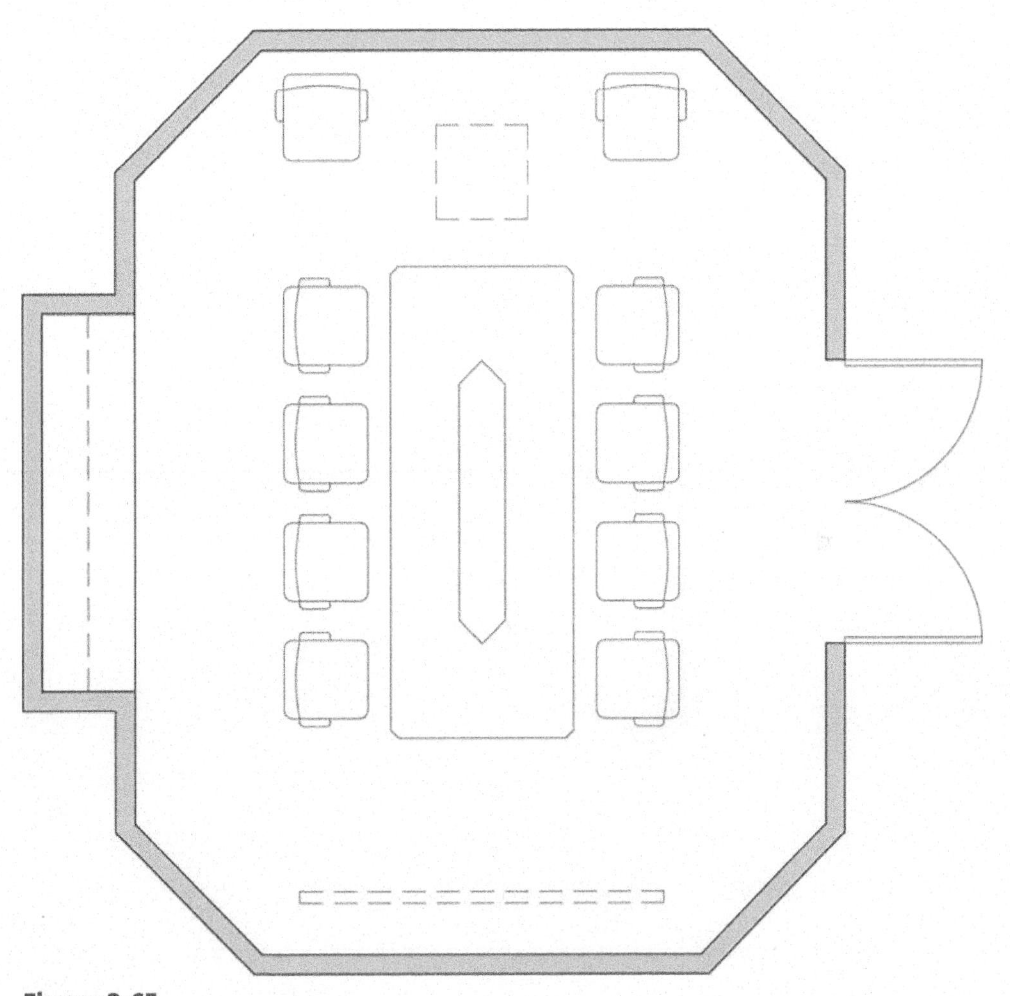

Figure 3-65
Project 3-5: Conference room with angles including furniture (scale: 1/4″ = 1′-0″)

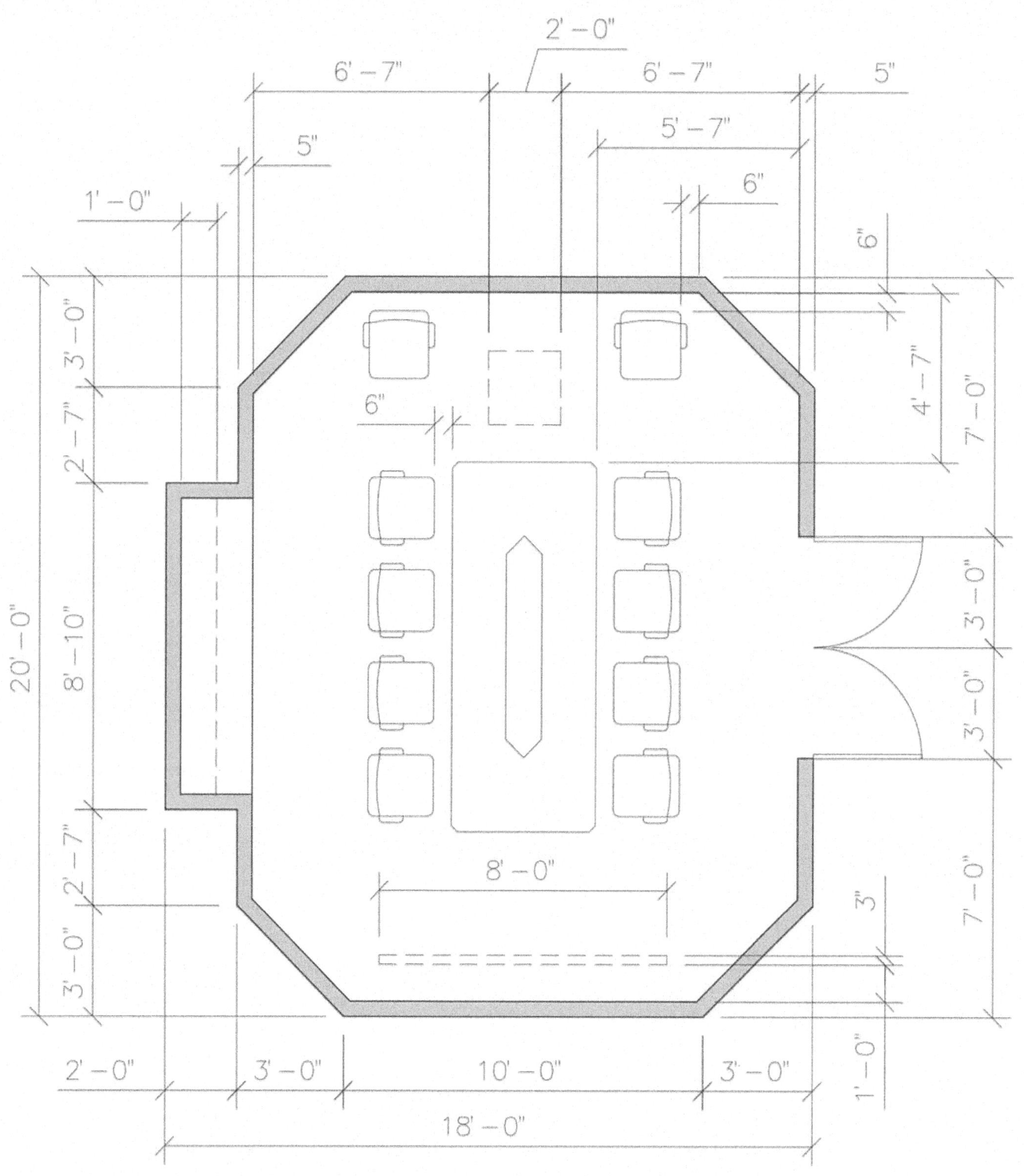

Figure 3-66
Sheet 1 of 2, Dimensions for Project 3-5 (scale: 1/4″ = 1′-0″)

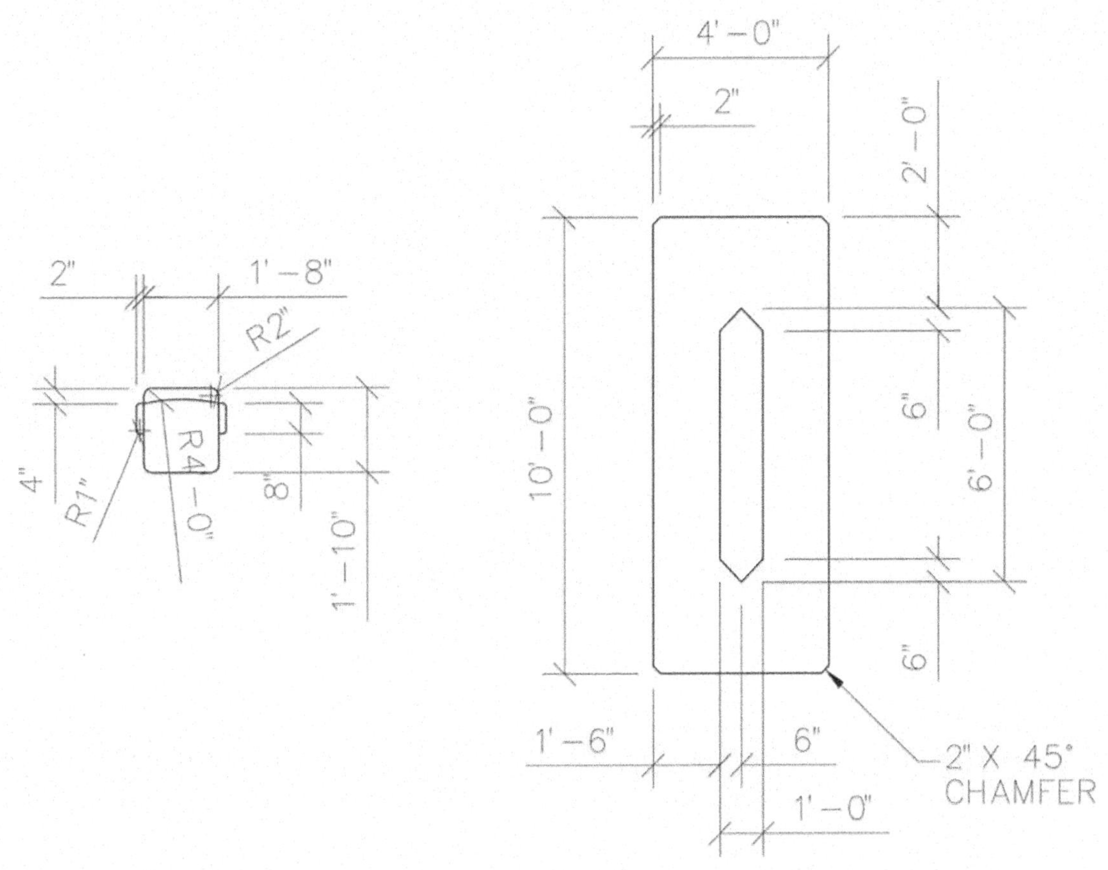

Figure 3-66
Sheet 2 of 2, Dimensions for Project 3-5 (scale: 1/4″ = 1′-0″)

2. Use the **Single Line Text** command to type your name, class number, and date, 6″ high in the upper-right corner (Figure 3-65).
3. Print your drawing from the **Model** tab at a scale of **1/4″ = 1′-0″**.

chapter four

Adding Text and Tables to the Drawing

CHAPTER OBJECTIVES

- Define the terms *style* and *font* and describe the function of each.
- Use **Dtext** (single line text) to draw text.
- Use **TEXTEDIT** to change text contents.
- Use different fonts on the same drawing.
- Place text on several different parts of the drawing with a single command.
- Use the modifiers **Align, Fit, Center, Middle, Right, Top,** and **Style.**
- Use the **Text Style...** dialog box to create condensed, expanded, obliqued, backward, inclined, and upside-down text.
- Use the **Text Style...** dialog box to change any style on the drawing to a different font.
- Use **Properties** to change text characteristics.
- Use standard codes to draw special characters such as the degree symbol, the diameter symbol, the plus–minus symbol, and underscored and overscored text.
- Use **Mtext** (multiline text) to create paragraph text.
- Spell-check your drawing.
- Use the **Table** command to create door and window schedules.

EXERCISE 4-1
Placing Text on Drawings

To make complete drawings with AutoCAD, you need to know how text is added to the drawings. In Exercise 4-1, we examine the following AutoCAD commands, used to place lettering on drawings:

- **Text Style...:** Used to control the appearance of text
- **Single Line Text (Dtext):** Used to draw text that is not in paragraph form
- **Multiline Text (Mtext):** Used to draw text that is in paragraph form

When you have completed Exercise 4-1, your drawing will look similar to the one in Figure 4-1.

Figure 4-1
Exercise 4-1: Placing text on drawings

THIS WAS TYPED
WITH THE HEADING STYLE
AND THE IMPACT FONT
1/4" HIGH

THIS WAS TYPED
WITH THE HAND LETTER STYLE
AND THE CITY BLUEPRINT FONT
3/16" HIGH, CENTERED

VERTICAL STYLE

STANDARD STYLE, FIT

OVERSCORE WITH THE OVERSCORE STYLE

OVERSCORE WITH THE STANDARD STYLE

UNDERSCORE WITH THE STANDARD STYLE

STANDARD CODES WITH THE STANDARD STYLE

±1/16"   45°   Ø1/2

UPSIDE DOWN AND BACKWARD
WITH THE UPSIDE DOWN STYLE,
ARIAL FONT

THIS IS A PARAGRAPH OR MULTLINE TEXT TYPED WITH THE SANS SERF FONT IN TWO COLUMNS, 1/8" HIGH, IN AN AREA THAT MEASURES 5-1/2"W X 1" HIGH JUSTIFIED (JUSTIFIED IS ALIGNED ON BOTH SIDES). THE GUTTER SPACE IS BETWEEN THE TWO COLUMNS.

> **TIP**
>
> If you click **New...** and select the **acad.dwt** template, you will be in the same drawing environment as when you simply open the AutoCAD program and begin drawing. AutoCAD uses the **acad.dwt** template for the drawing settings if no other template is selected.

Step 1. Use your workspace to make the following settings:

1. Use **Save As...** to save the drawing with the name **CH4-EXERCISE1.**
2. Set drawing units: **Architectural**
3. Set drawing limits: **8-1/2,11** (the inch mark is not needed)
4. Set **GRIDDISPLAY**: **0**
5. Set grid: **1/4**
6. Set snap: **1/8**
7. Create the following layers:

Layer name	Color	Linetype	Lineweight
a-anno-text	green	continuous	.006" (.15 mm)
a-area-ttbl	magenta	continuous	.006" (.15 mm)

8. Set layer **a-anno-text** current.
9. Use **Zoom-All** to view the limits of the drawing.

Making Settings for Text Style

Understanding the difference between the terms *style name* and *font name* with regard to text is important:

Style Name

AutoCAD provides in the **Text Style** dialog box (use **ST** for Style to see the **Text Style** dialog box), by default, a style named *Standard*. By default, the Standard style includes the following settings (Figure 4-2):

Font Name:	Arial
Font Style:	Regular
Annotative:	Not checked
Height:	0′–0″
Upside down:	Not checked
Backwards:	Not checked
Vertical:	Not checked
Width Factor:	1
Oblique Angle:	0

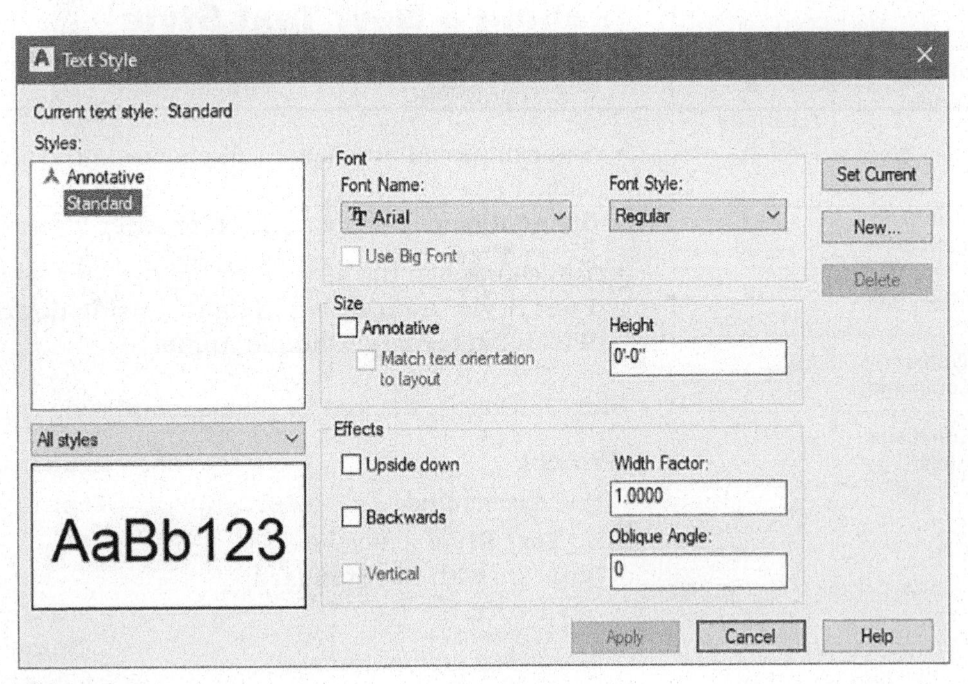

Figure 4-2
The Standard text style default settings

Font Name

font: A distinctive set of letters, numbers, punctuation marks, and symbols.

This is the name of any ***font*** file. A font determines how text looks by defining its typeface, or graphical design. A font has to be installed in either the AutoCAD program (SHX fonts), or in Windows (TrueType fonts) before you can select it and assign it to a style name. AutoCAD assigns the Arial font to the Standard style by default. AutoCAD has two types of fonts available, as shown in Figure 4-3:

1. **TrueType fonts:** The standard font type provided by Microsoft Windows. TrueType fonts have the .ttf file name extension. This extension is *not* shown in the **Text Style** dialog box **Font Name** list.
2. **SHX fonts:** AutoCAD's own set of fonts that have the .shx file name extension. This extension *is* shown in the **Text Style** dialog box **Font Name** list.

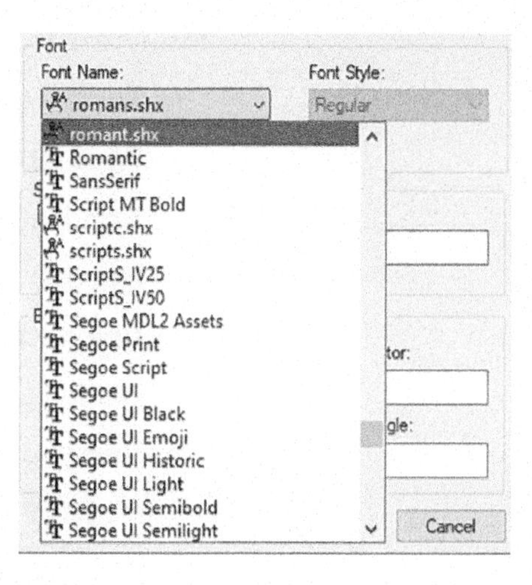

Figure 4-3
Two types of fonts: .shx and .ttf

TEXT STYLE	
Ribbon/ Panel:	Annotate/ Text/
Text Toolbar:	
Menu Bar:	Format/ Text Style...
Type a Command:	STYLE
Command Alias:	ST

Making a New Text Style

By clicking **New...** in the **Text Style** dialog box (Figure 4-2), you can make new text styles.

- You can assign any name you choose to the style name. You may use the same name for the style that is used for the font name, or you may use a different name, single number, or letter for the style name.
- You can assign the settings to the new text style to include **Font Name**, **Font Style**, **Annotative**, **Height**, **Upside down**, **Backwards**, **Vertical**, **Width Factor**, and **Oblique Angle**.

Step 2. Change the font for the Standard style (Figure 4-4), as described next:

Prompt	**Response**
Type a command:	**Text Style...** (or type **ST <Enter>**)
The **Text Style** dialog box appears with the **Standard** style current:	Click **TechnicLite** (in the **Font Name:** list) Click **Apply**

Any text typed while the Standard style is active will now contain the TechnicLite font. Notice the preview area in the lower-left corner that shows you what the font looks like. Notice also that the vertical setting is grayed out, indicating that this font cannot be drawn with one letter above the other.

The other settings should be left as they are. *If you leave the text height set at 0, you will be able to draw different heights of the same style and you will be able to change the height of text if you need to. Leave the text height set to 0 in all cases.* The **Width Factor** allows you to stretch letters so they are wider by making the **Width Factor** greater than 1, and narrower by making the **Width Factor** less than 1. The **Oblique Angle** slants the letters to the right if the angle is positive and to the left if the angle is negative.

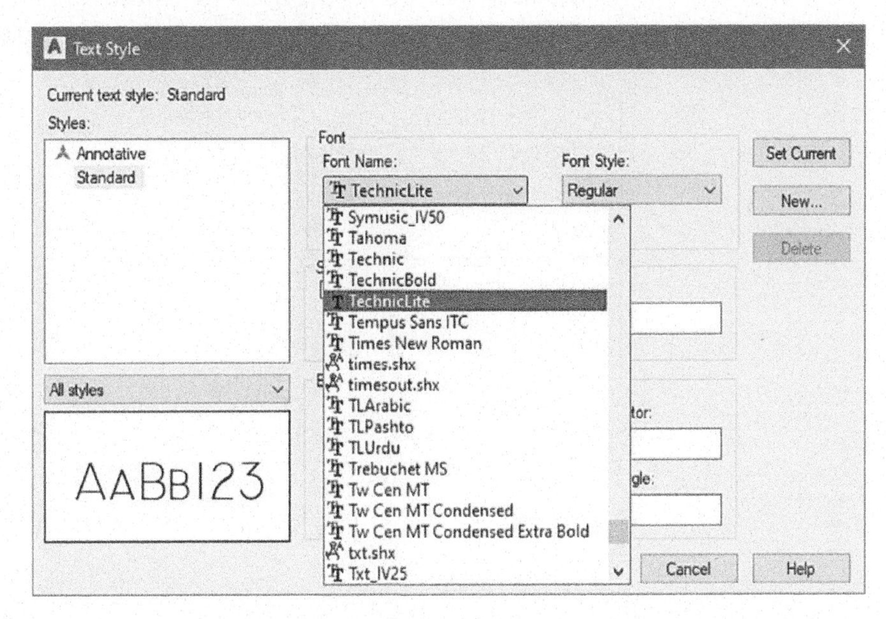

Figure 4-4
Select the **TechnicLite** font for the Standard style

AutoCAD also provides a style named Annotative. You use this style when you have added text to a drawing that will be plotted to scale (for example, 1/4″ = 1′-0″). You can make any style annotative in the **Text Style** dialog box by selecting the **Annotative** check box.

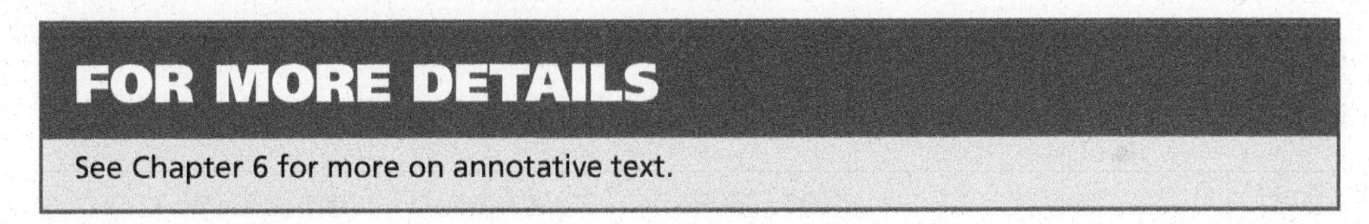

FOR MORE DETAILS

See Chapter 6 for more on annotative text.

Step 3. Make the settings for a new style that will be used on the drawing (Figures 4-5 and 4-6), as described next:

Prompt	Response
The **Text Style** dialog box:	Click **New...** (button on the right)
The **New Text Style** dialog box appears with a **Style Name** that AutoCAD assigns, style1:	Type **HEADING** (to name the style, Figure 4-5)
	Click **OK** (or press **<Enter>**)
The **Text Style** dialog box appears:	Click **romand.shx** (in the **Font Name:** list, Figure 4-6)
	Click **Apply**

Figure 4-5
Name the style, HEADING

Figure 4-6
Select the romand.shx font for the HEADING style

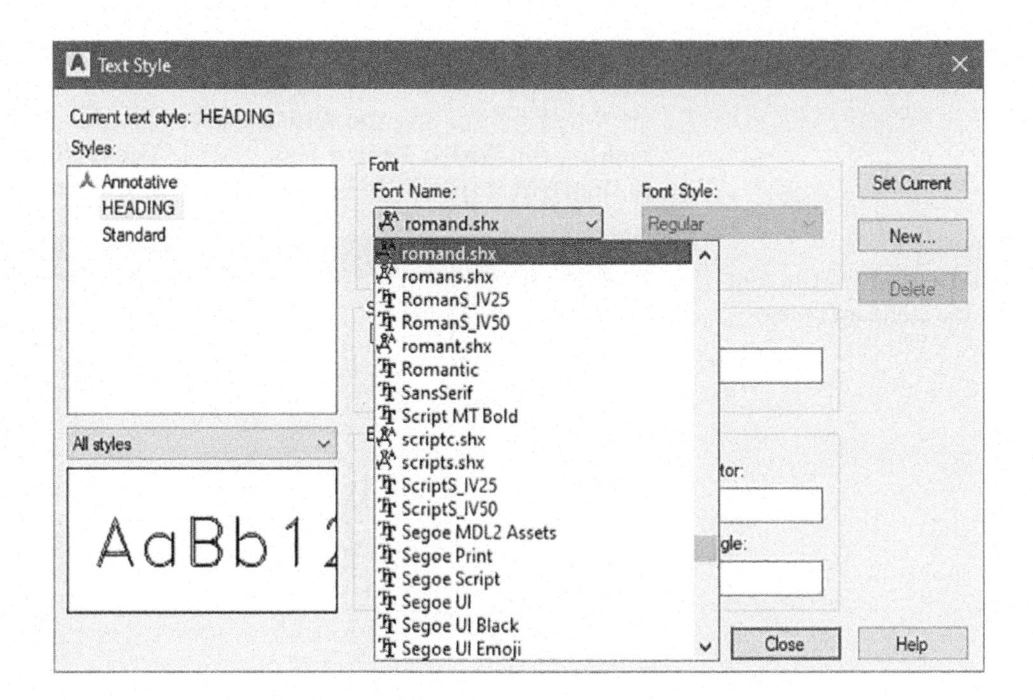

You now have two styles that have been defined on your drawing, Standard and HEADING.

TIP

To locate a font in the **Font Name:** list, hold your cursor over any font name in the list and type the first few letters of the desired font. You can also scroll through the **Font Name:** list by pressing the up or down arrow key on the keyboard or by using the wheel on your mouse.

Step 4. Make the settings for the following new styles (Figure 4-7):

Style Name	Font Name	Other Settings
HAND LETTER	CityBlueprint	None
OVERSCORE	Arial	None
UPSIDEDOWN	Arial	In the **Effects** box, select the **Upside down** check box and the **Backwards** check box.
VERTICAL	romand.shx	In the **Effects** box, select the **Vertical** check box (Figure 4-7). Deselect the **Upside down** and **Backwards** check boxes.

Step 5. Check the **Styles** list to determine whether your list matches the one shown in Figure 4-8.

Step 6. Click the **HEADING** style name and the **Set Current** button to make it current; close the dialog box.

NOTE

If you make a mistake while making the settings for a new style, go back to the **Text Style** dialog box, highlight the style name, change or fix the settings, and click **Apply**.

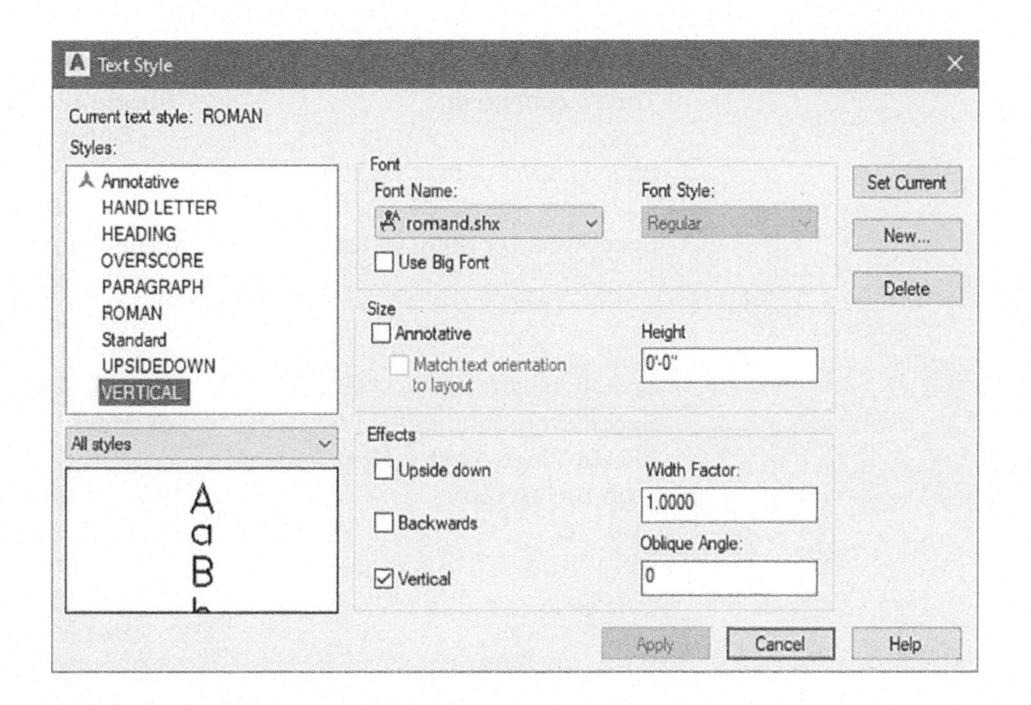

Figure 4-7
Make settings for the VERTICAL style

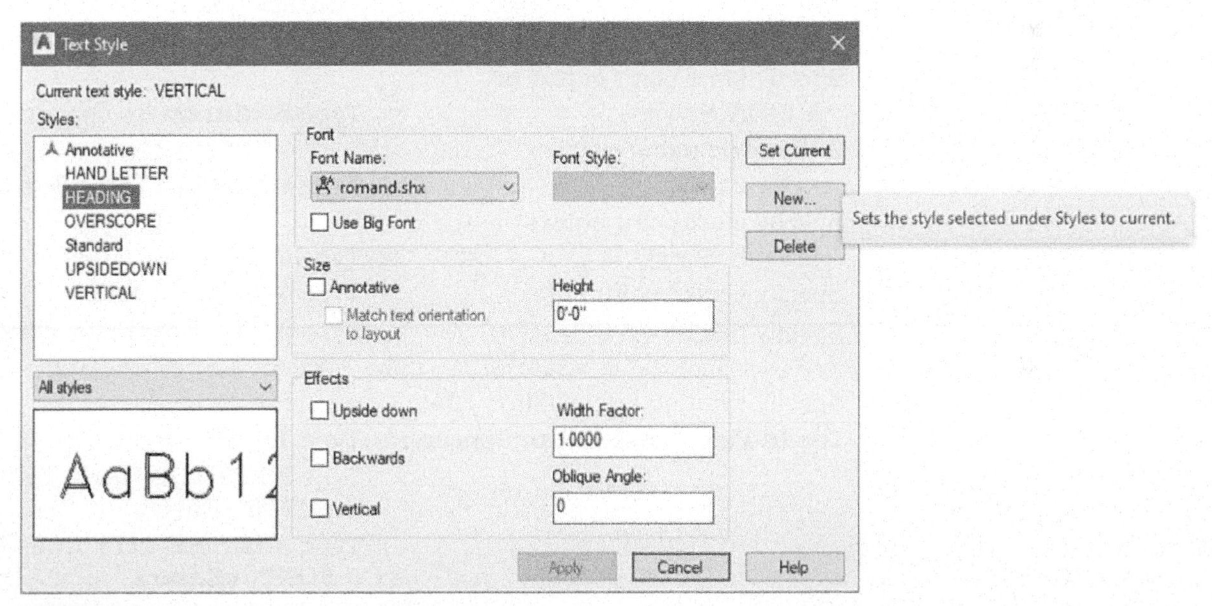

Figure 4-8
Check the **Styles** list and set the HEADING style current

Using the Single Line Text Command to Draw Text

You use the **Single Line Text** command (also known as **Dtext**) to draw text that is not in paragraph form. Although the name of the command might lead you to believe that only a single line can be drawn, that is not the case. To draw one line under another, just press **<Enter>**, and you can draw the next line with the same settings as the first line.

If you are not happy with the location of text, use the **MOVE** command to relocate it.

Step 7. Draw the first two examples at the top of the page using **Single Line Text** (Figure 4-9), as described next:

Prompt	**Response**
Type a command:	**Single Line Text** (or type **DT <Enter>**)
Specify start point of text or [Justify Style]:	Type **C <Enter>** (to center the text)
Specify center point of text:	Type **4-1/4,10 <Enter>** (you are locating the center of the line of text using absolute coordinates, 4-1/4″ to the right and 10″ up)
Specify height <0′-0 3/16″>:	Type **1/4 <Enter>**
Specify rotation angle of text <0>:	**<Enter>**
The **In-Place Text Editor** appears on the screen:	Type **THIS WAS TYPED <Enter>** Type **WITH THE HEADING STYLE, <Enter>** Type **AND THE ROMAND FONT, <Enter>** Type **1/4″ HIGH <Enter>** **<Enter>** (to exit the **Text Editor**) **<Enter>** (repeat **DTEXT**)
Specify start point of text or [Justify Style]:	Type **S <Enter>** (to change styles)
Enter style name or [?] <HEADING>:	Type **HAND LETTER <Enter>**
Specify start point of text or [Justify Style]:	Type **C <Enter>**
Specify center point of text:	Type **4-1/4,8 <Enter>**
Specify height <0′-0 3/16″>:	Type **3/16 <Enter>** (or **<Enter>** to accept a 3/16″ default)
Specify rotation angle of text <0>:	**<Enter>**
The **In-Place Text Editor** appears:	Type **THIS WAS TYPED <Enter>** Type **WITH THE HAND LETTER STYLE <Enter>** Type **AND THE CITY BLUEPRINT FONT, <Enter>** Type **3/16″ HIGH, CENTERED <Enter> <Enter>**

Figure 4-9
First two examples of **Single Line Text**

Figure 4-10
Using the **Fit** option of **Single Line Text**

Step 8. Draw the next block of text using the **Fit** option of **Single Line Text** with the Standard style (Figure 4-10), as described next:

Prompt	**Response**
Type a command:	**Single Line Text** (or type **DT <Enter>**)
Specify start point of text or [Justify Style]:	Type **S <Enter>** (to change styles)
Enter style name or [?] <HAND LETTER>:	Type **STANDARD <Enter>**
Specify start point of text or [Justify Style]:	Type **F <Enter>** (for **Fit**)
Specify first endpoint of text baseline:	Type **1-1/2,6 <Enter>**
Specify second endpoint of text baseline:	Type **7,6 <Enter>**
Specify height <0′-0 3/16″>:	Type **1/2 <Enter>**
The **In-Place Text Editor** appears:	Type **STANDARD STYLE, FIT OPTION <Enter> <Enter>**

Setting the Justify Option

When you activate the **Single Line Text** command, the prompt is *Specify start point of text or [Justify Style]:*. The **Style** option allows you to select a different style (that has already been defined) for the text you are about to draw. *If you type* **J <Enter>**, the prompt then becomes *Enter an option [Align Fit Center Middle Right TL TC TR ML MC MR BL BC BR]:*.

Align: Draws the text between two points that you click. It does not condense or expand the font but instead *adjusts the letter height* so that the text fits between the two points.

Fit: Draws the text between two clicked points as used in the **Align** option, but instead of changing the letter height, **Fit** *condenses or expands the font* to fit between the points.

Center: Draws the text so that the *bottom of the line of lettering* is centered on the clicked point. You may also choose the top or the middle of the line of lettering by typing **TC** or **MC** at the justify prompt.

Middle: Draws the text so that the *middle of the line of lettering* is centered around a clicked point. This is useful when you must center a single line of text in an area such as a box.

Right: Draws the text so that *each line of text is right justified* (ends at the same right margin). You may also select the top or center of the line by typing **TR** or **MR** at the justify prompt.

TL TC TR ML MC MR BL BC BR: These are the alignment options: **Top Left, Top Center, Top Right, Middle Left, Middle Center, Middle Right, Bottom Left, Bottom Center, Bottom Right.** They are used with horizontal text.

Step 9. Draw a line of text using the VERTICAL style (Figure 4-11), as described next:

(Remember that you checked **Vertical** in the **Text Style** dialog box for this text style.)

Figure 4-11
Using the **Vertical** option of **Single Line Text**

THIS WAS TYPED
WITH THE HEADING STYLE
AND THE ROMAND FONT
1/4" HIGH

THIS WAS TYPED
WITH THE HAND LETTER STYLE
AND THE CITY BLUEPRINT FONT
3/16" HIGH, CENTERED

STANDARD STYLE, FIT

VERTICAL STYLE

Prompt	**Response**
Type a command:	**<Enter>** (repeat **DTEXT**)
Specify start point of text or [Justify Style]:	Type **S <Enter>**
Enter style name or [?] <Standard>:	Type **VERTICAL <Enter>**
Specify start point of text or [Justify Style]:	Type **J <Enter>**
Enter an option [Left/Center/Right/Align/Middle]:	Type **L <Enter>**
Specify start point of text or [Justify Style]:	Type **1,6 <Enter>**
Specify height <0'-0" 3/16">:	Type **1/4 <Enter>**
Specify rotation angle of text <0>:	270 **<Enter>**
The **In-Place Text Editor** appears:	Type **VERTICAL STYLE <Enter> <Enter>**

Using Standard Codes to Draw Special Characters

45%%D
45°

Figure 4-12
Degree symbol code

%%C.500
Ø.500

Figure 4-13
Diameter symbol code

%%P.005
±.005

Figure 4-14
Plus–minus symbol code

Figures 4-12 through 4-16 show the use of codes to obtain several commonly used symbols, such as the degree symbol, the diameter symbol, the plus–minus symbol, and underscored and overscored text. The top line of Figure 4-12 shows the code that you must type to obtain the degree symbol following the number 45. Two percent symbols followed by the letter D produce the degree symbol.

Figure 4-13 illustrates that two percent symbols followed by the letter C produce the diameter symbol.

Figure 4-14 shows the code for the plus–minus symbol.

Figure 4-15 shows the code for underscore: two percent symbols followed by the letter U. Notice that the first line contains only one code. The second line contains two codes: one to start the underline and one to stop it.

Figure 4-16 shows the code for overscored text. The same code sequence applies for starting and stopping the overscore.

%%UUNDERSCORE
UNDERSCORE

%%UUNDERSCORE%%U LETTERS
UNDERSCORE LETTERS

Figure 4-15
Underscore code

%%OOVERSCORE
OVERSCORE

%%OOVERSCORE%%O LETTERS
OVERSCORE LETTERS

Figure 4-16
Overscore code

Step 10. Draw five lines containing special codes for the overscore, underscore, plus–minus, degree, and diameter symbols (Figure 4-17), as described next:

Prompt	**Response**
Type a command:	**<Enter>** (repeat **DTEXT**)
Specify start point of text or [Justify Style]:	Type **S <Enter>**
Enter style name or [?] <VERTICAL>:	Type **OVERSCORE <Enter>**
Specify start point of text or [Justify Style]:	Type **1-1/2,5 <Enter>**

THIS WAS TYPED
WITH THE HEADING STYLE
AND THE ROMAND FONT
1/4" HIGH

THIS WAS TYPED
WITH THE HAND LETTER STYLE
AND THE CITY BLUEPRINT FONT
3/16" HIGH, CENTERED

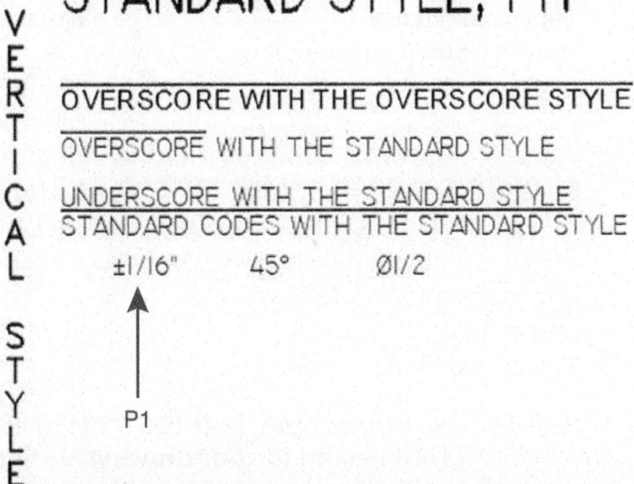

Figure 4-17
Using **Single Line Text** to draw symbols with standard codes

Prompt	Response
Specify height <0′-0 3/16″>:	Type **3/16 <Enter>**
Specify rotation angle of text <0>:	**<Enter>**
The **In-Place Text Editor** appears:	Type **%%OOVERSCORE WITH THE OVERSCORE STYLE <Enter> <Enter>**
Type a command:	**<Enter>** (repeat **DTEXT**)
Specify start point of text or [Justify Style]:	Type **S <Enter>**
Enter style name or [?] <OVERSCORE>:	Type **STANDARD <Enter>**
Specify start point of text or [Justify Style]:	Type **1-1/2,4-1/2 <Enter>**
Specify height <0′-0 1/2″>:	Type **3/16 <Enter>**
Specify rotation angle of text <0>:	**<Enter>**
The **In-Place Text Editor** appears:	Type **%%OOVERSCORE%%O WITH THE STANDARD STYLE <Enter> <Enter>**
Type a command:	**<Enter>** (repeat **DTEXT**)
Specify start point of text or [Justify Style]:	Type **1-1/2,4 <Enter>**
Specify height <0′-0 3/16″>:	Type **3/16 <Enter>**
Specify rotation angle of text <0>:	**<Enter>**
The **In-Place Text Editor** appears:	Type **%%UUNDERSCORE WITH THE STANDARD STYLE <Enter> <Enter>**
Type a command:	**<Enter>** (repeat **DTEXT**)
Specify start point of text or [Justify Style]:	**<Enter>**
The **In-Place Text Editor** appears:	Type **STANDARD CODES WITH THE STANDARD STYLE <Enter> <Enter>**
Type a command:	**<Enter>** (repeat **DTEXT**)
Specify start point of text or [Justify Style]:	Click **P1 <Enter>** (a point in the approximate location as shown in Figure 4-17)
Specify height <0′-0 3/16″>:	**<Enter>** (to accept the 3/16″ default height)
Specify rotation angle of text <0>:	**<Enter>**
The **In-Place Text Editor** appears:	Type **%%P1/16″ <Enter> <Enter>**
Type a command:	

Step 11. Use **Single Line Text (DTEXT)** to add the following text (3/16 height) to your drawing, as shown in Figure 4-17:

45° (45%%D)

(Ø1/2″ (%%C1/2″)

Step 12. Make the style name UPSIDE DOWN current.

> **TIP**
>
> When you are typing using the UPSIDE DOWN style, it does not show as upside down and backward on your screen until you have completed typing the text and pressed the **<Enter>** key twice, once to indicate you do not want a second line of text and once to exit the **DTEXT** command.

Step 13. Use **Single Line Text** to draw the following phrase (3/16 height) upside down and backward with its start point at 7,2-1/2 (Figure 4-18):

UPSIDE DOWN AND BACKWARD <Enter>
WITH THE UPSIDEDOWN STYLE, <Enter>
ARIAL FONT <Enter> <Enter>

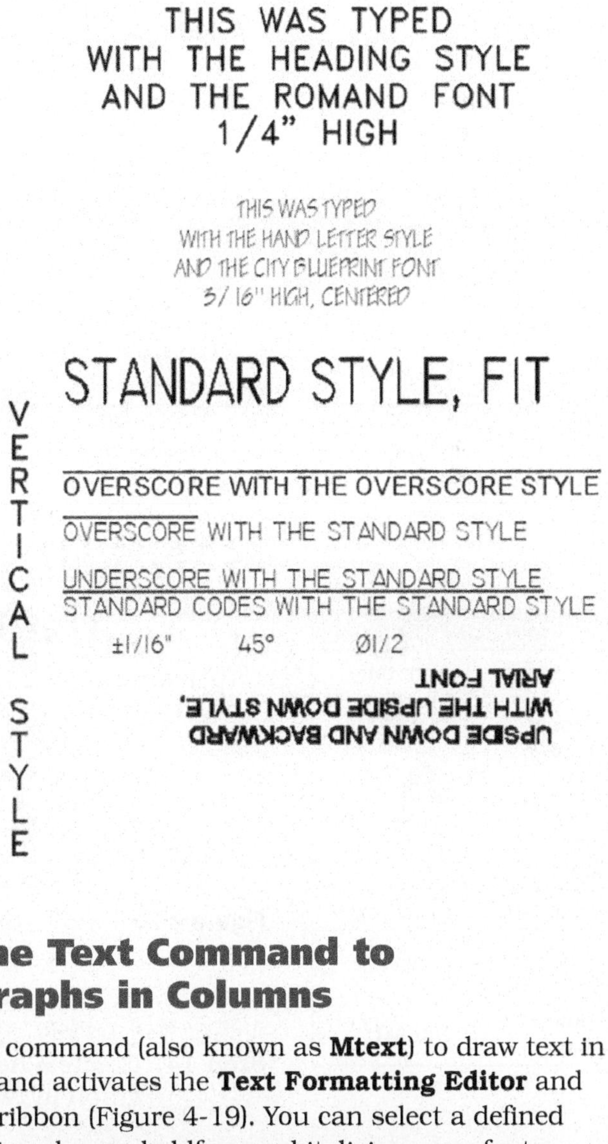

Figure 4-18
Draw a phrase upside down and backward with the UPSIDE DOWN style

Using the Multiline Text Command to Draw Text Paragraphs in Columns

You use the **Multiline Text** command (also known as **Mtext**) to draw text in paragraph form. The command activates the **Text Formatting Editor** and the **Text Editor** tab on the ribbon (Figure 4-19). You can select a defined style, change the text height and case, boldface and italicize some fonts, select a justification style, specify the width of the paragraph (or columns and the space between columns within the paragraph), search for a word

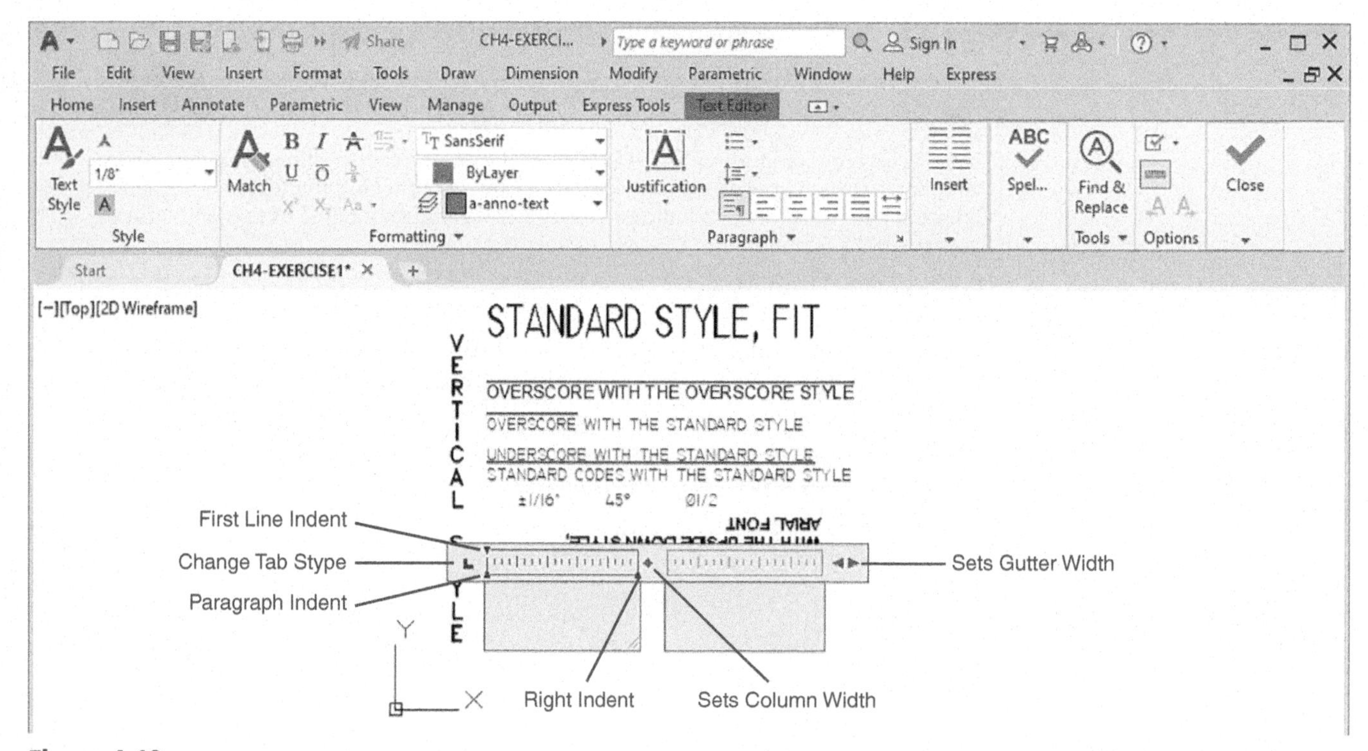

Figure 4-19
Text Formatting Editor with columns and the **Text Editor** tab of the ribbon

and replace it with another, import text, number lines, insert bullets, and select symbols for use on your drawing. In this exercise, you will create a paragraph in two columns using the **SansSerif** font.

sans serif: Any text font that does not contain serifs. Serifs are the small features at the ends of letters and numbers.

Sans serif is a term that means "without serifs." Serifs are the small features at the ends of letters and numbers, as shown in Figure 4-20.

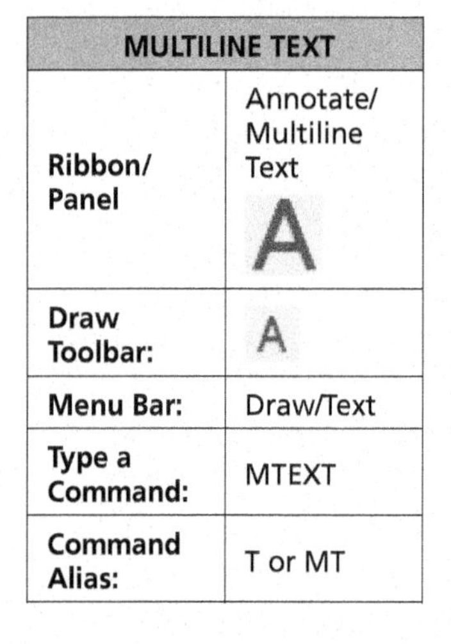

MULTILINE TEXT	
Ribbon/ Panel	Annotate/ Multiline Text
Draw Toolbar:	
Menu Bar:	Draw/Text
Type a Command:	MTEXT
Command Alias:	T or MT

SANS SERIF LETTERING
(NO SERIFS)

SERIF LETTERING
(WITH SERIFS)

These are Serifs

Figure 4-20
Serifs

Step 14. Create a new text style and use **Multiline Text** to draw a paragraph in two columns, as described next:

Prompt	**Response**
Type a command:	Type **ST <Enter>**
The **Text Style** dialog box appears:	Click **New**
The **New Text Style** dialog box appears:	Type **PARAGRAPH** (as the new style name) Click **OK**
The **Text Style** dialog box appears:	Change the **Font Name:** to **SansSerif** Deselect the **Annotative**, **Upside down**, and **Backwards check boxes** (if they are selected) Click **Set Current**
The current style has been modified. Do you want to save your changes?	Click **Yes**
Type a command:	Click **Close** **Multiline Text...** (or type **MT <Enter>**)
Specify first corner:	Type **1-1/2,2 <Enter>**
Specify opposite corner or [Height Justify Linespacing Rotation Style Width Columns]:	Type **H <Enter>**
Specify height <3/16″>:	Type **1/8 <Enter>**
Specify opposite corner or [Height Justify Linespacing Rotation Style Width Columns]:	Type **C <Enter>**
Enter column type [Dynamic Static No columns] <Dynamic>:	Type **S <Enter>**
Specify total width: <1′-6″>:	Type **5-1/2 <Enter>**
Specify number of columns: <2>:	Type **2 <Enter>**
Specify gutter width: <1″>:	Type **1/2 <Enter>**
Specify column height: <2″>:	Type **1 <Enter>**
The **Text Formatting Editor** appears, and the ribbon changes:	Click the **Justify** icon (Figure 4-21) (so the text is flush right and flush left) Type the paragraph shown in Figures 4-21 and 4-23. When you type 1/8 in the paragraph, the characters are stacked, one above the other. Highlight the stacked fraction, right-click, and select **Stack Properties** from the menu to display the **Stack Properties** dialog box. Click **AutoStack...** to display the **AutoStack Properties** dialog box (see Figure 4-22). Deselect the **Enable Autostacking check box**; click **OK** After the paragraph is typed correctly, click **Close Text Editor** (on the ribbon)

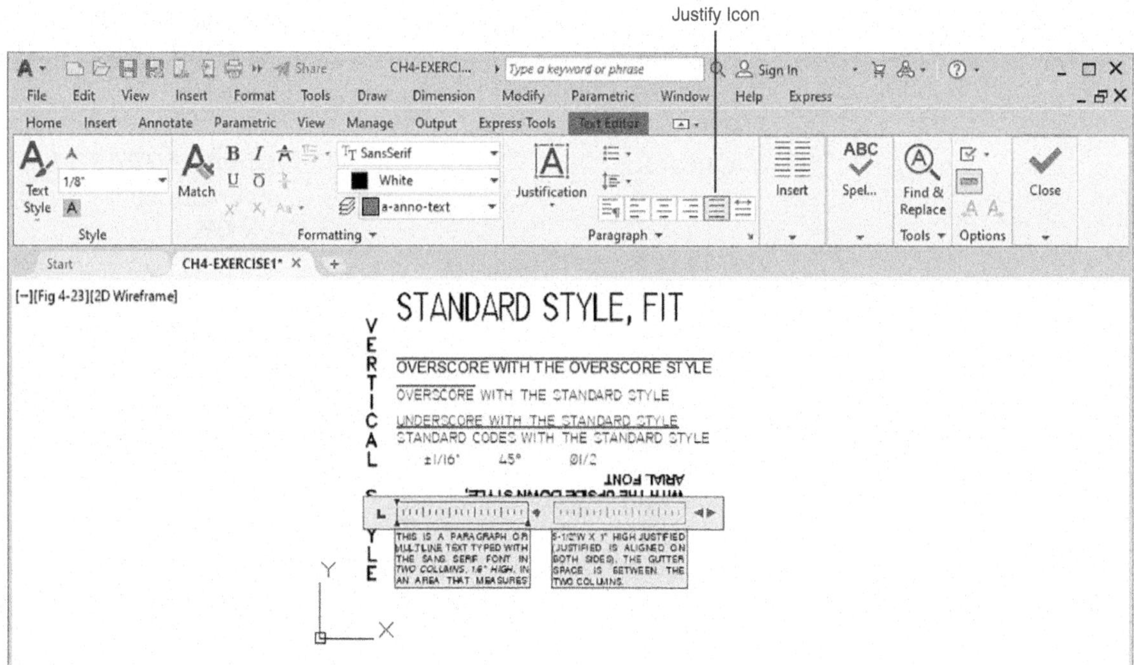

Figure 4-21
Multiline text in two columns with the **Justify** icon clicked

Figure 4-22
Deselecting Autostacking

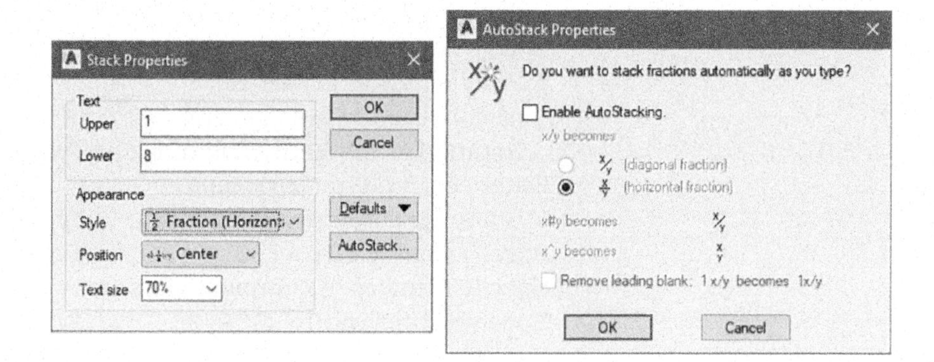

> **TIP**
>
> When the column width and height have been set in the **Text Formatting Editor,** you do not need to press **<Enter>** to go to the next line in the paragraph—this happens automatically as you type.

Changing Text Properties

Sometimes you need to change the text font, height, or content. AutoCAD has several commands that you can use to do this:

Text Style...: Use this command to change the font of a text style that already exists on your drawing.

TEXTEDIT: (same as double-click): Use this command if you want to change only the text contents for single line text. This command allows you to select multiline text to change its contents and several of its properties.

Properties: Use this command to change any of the text's characteristics: properties, justification, style, height, rotation angle, the text content, or any of several other properties.

Figure 4-23
Type multiline text in two columns

Step 15. Use the **Text Style...** command to change the font of text typed with the HEADING name from Romand to Impact (Figure 4-24), as described next:

Prompt	Response
Type a command:	**Text Style...** (or type **ST <Enter>**)
The **Text Style** dialog box appears:	Click **HEADING** (in the **Styles:** list)
	Click **Set Current**
	Click **Impact** (from the **Font Name:** list, Figure 4-24)
	Click **Apply**
	Click **Close**

Notice that everything you typed with the HEADING style name is now still in the HEADING style but changed to the Impact font.

Step 16. Use the **TEXTEDIT** command to change "**AND THE ROMAND FONT**" at the top of the page to "**AND THE IMPACT FONT**" (Figure 4-25), as described next:

TEXTEDIT	
Text Toolbar:	A
Menu Bar:	Modify/ Object/Text
Type a Command:	TEXTEDIT
Command Alias:	ED

Prompt	Response
Type a command:	Double-click **AND THE ROMAND FONT**
The **In-Place Text Editor** appears:	Click to the right of **ROMAND**, backspace over **ROMAND**, and type **IMPACT <Enter>** (Figure 4-25)
Select an annotation object or [Undo]:	**<Enter>**

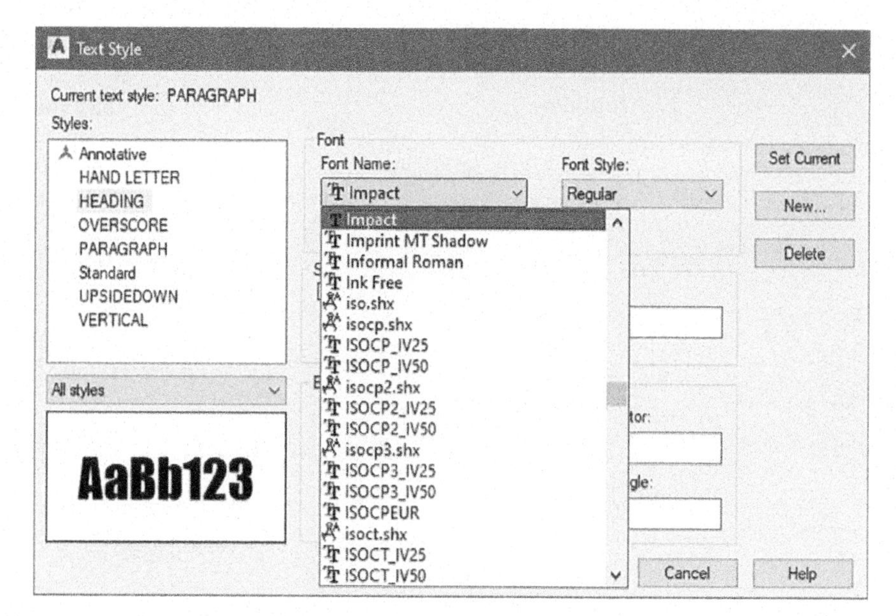

Figure 4-24
Select the Impact font for the HEADING style

THIS WAS TYPED
WITH THE HEADING STYLE
AND THE IMPACT FONT
1/4" HIGH

Figure 4-25
Change text using **TEXTEDIT**

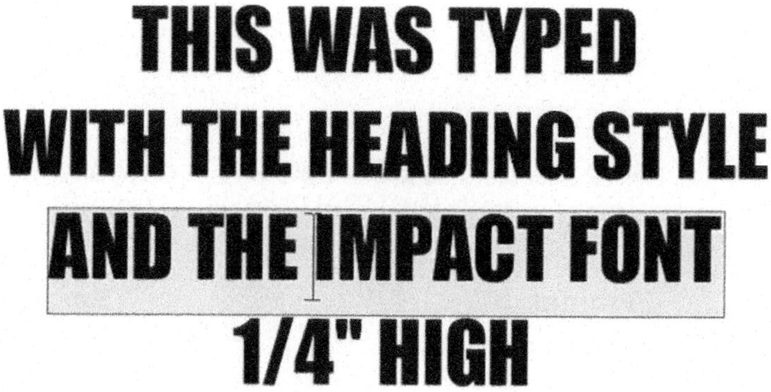

> **NOTE**
>
> Double-click on any text to edit it. If you double-click and nothing happens, go to **Options, Selection** tab, **Selection modes,** and make sure the **Noun/verb** check box is selected.

Step 17. Double-click on the line of text that reads **1/4" HIGH** and change it to **1/4" HIGH, CENTERED**

Step 18. Use **TEXTEDIT** to change the words **TWO COLUMNS, 1/8" HIGH,** to the italic font (Figure 4-26), as described next:

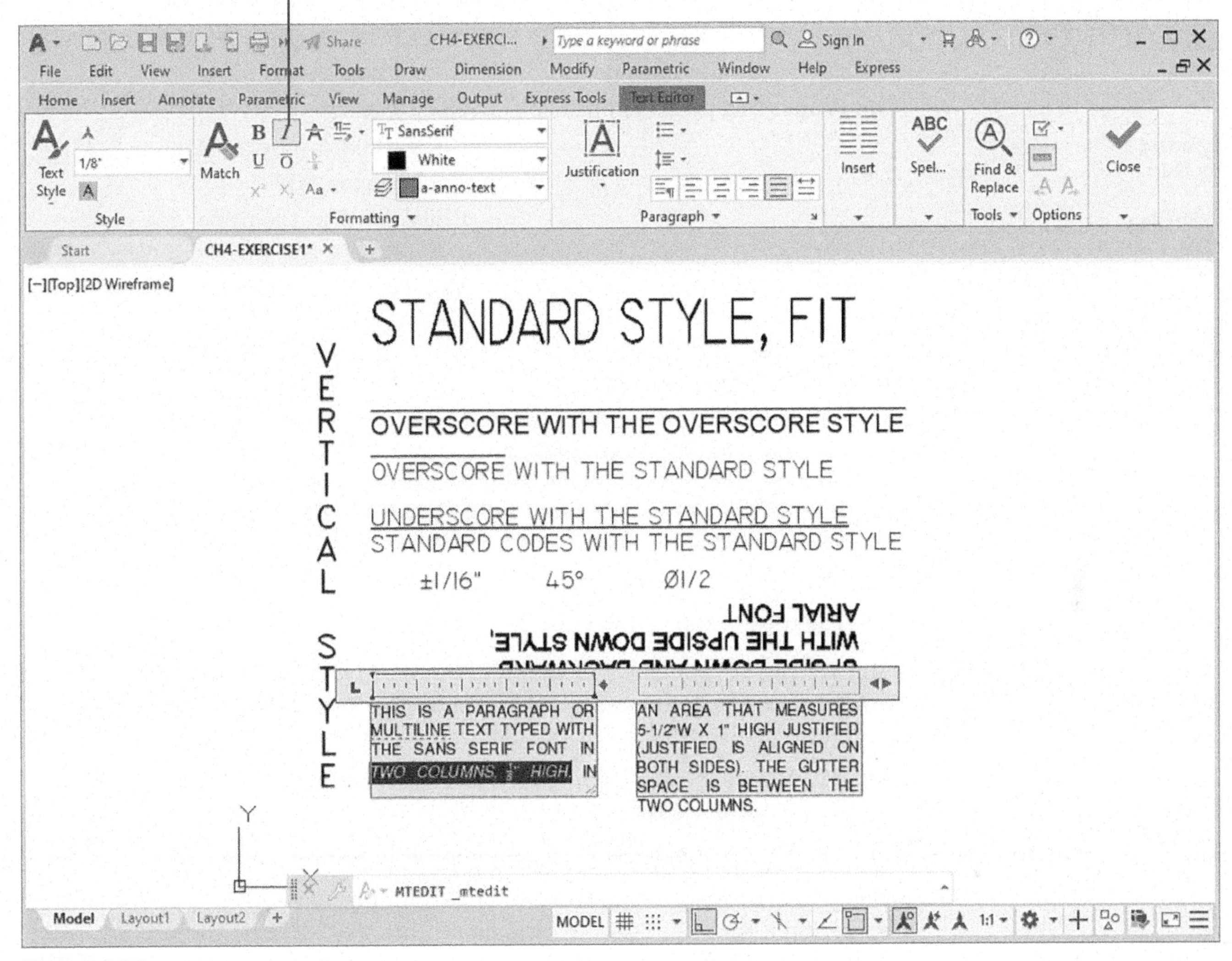

Figure 4-26
Change multiline text to italic

Prompt	Response
Type a command:	Double-click any point on the multiline text
The **Text Formatting Editor** (Figure 4-26) appears:	Click the left mouse button to the left of the word **TWO,** hold it down, and drag it to the end to the word **HIGH** so that **TWO COLUMNS, 1/8″ HIGH** is highlighted, and then click **I** (for italic) on the ribbon
	Click **Close** (on the ribbon)

Step 19. Use the **Properties** palette to change the vertical line of text from layer **a-anno-text** to layer **a-area-ttbl** (Figure 4-27), as described next:

PROPERTIES	
Ribbon/ Panel	View/ Palettes
Standard Toolbar:	
Menu Bar:	Modify/ Properties
Type a Command:	PROPERTIES
Command Alias:	PR
Keyboard:	<Ctrl>+1

Prompt	**Response**
Type a command:	Click the vertical line of text (VERTICAL STYLE) and right-click
The right-click menu appears:	Click **Properties**
The **Properties** palette appears:	Click **Layer**
	Click the down arrow (Figure 4-27)
	Click **a-area-ttbl**
	Click the **X** in the upper-left corner to close
	VERTICAL STYLE is now changed to **a-area-ttbl**

Step 20. Use **Single Line Text**, Standard style, 1/8″ high to place your name in the upper-left corner and class number in the upper-right corner. The start point for your name is 1,10-1/2. Use right-justified text for class number (at the **Dtext** prompt *Specify start point of text or [Justify Style]:* type **R <Enter>.** The right endpoint of the text baseline is 7-1/2,10-1/2.

SPELL CHECK	
Ribbon/ Panel	Annotate/ Text
Text Toolbar:	
Menu Bar:	Tools/ Spelling
Type a Command:	SPELL
Command Alias:	SP

Checking the Spelling

AutoCAD has a spell checker that allows you to check the spelling on your drawing. The **Spell** command is located on the **Text** tab of the **Annotate** panel, or type **SP <Enter>** at the command prompt to access it.

Step 21. When you have completed Exercise 4-1, save your work in at least two places.

Step 22. Print your drawing from the **Model** tab at a scale of **1:1.**

When you create Mtext in AutoCAD 2022, it automatically applies bullets or numbering if these options are enabled in the **Text Editor** ribbon tab. You can use **Manage** (from the menu bar) and **Customize User Interface (CUI)** from the **Customization** panel to add the **Text Editor** contextual tab to the ribbon.

TIP

You can use the **Auto Number** command on the **Express Tools** tab of the ribbon to add numbering to existing Mtext objects. For example, the Mtext shown to the left below becomes that shown to the right below by using the **Auto Number** command and with **Starting number = 1, increment = 1,** added as prefix:

Text sample line one	1 Text sample line one
Text sample line two	2 Text sample line two
Text sample line three	3 Text sample line three
Text sample line four	4 Text sample line four
Text sample line five	5 Text sample line five

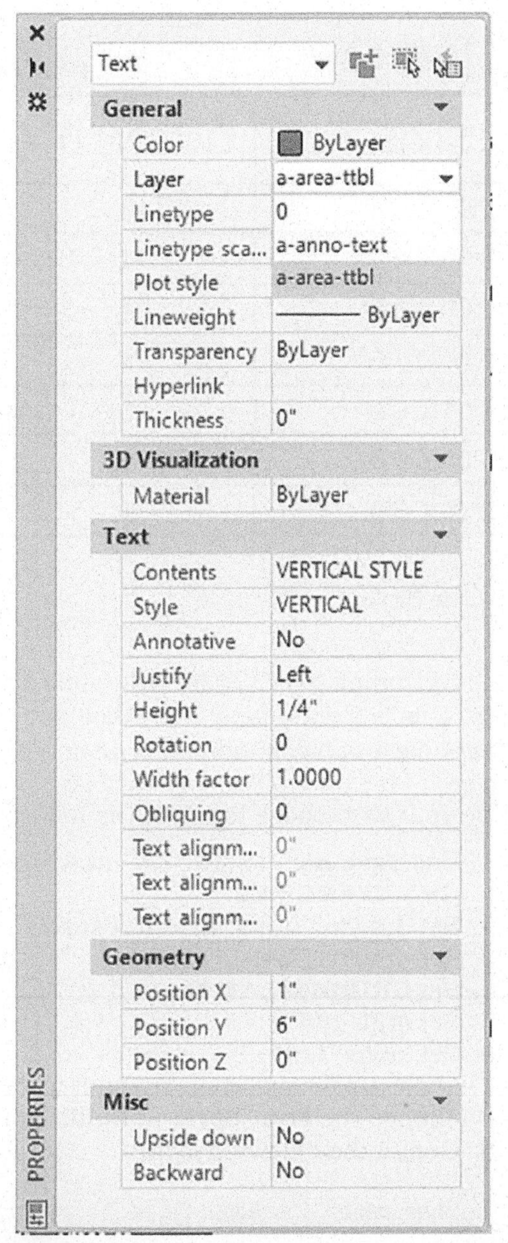

Figure 4-27
Change text to layer **a-area-ttbl**

EXERCISE 4-2 Using the TABLE Command to Create a Door Schedule

The **TABLE** command in AutoCAD 2022 is a tool to create professional-appearing tables such as door schedules, tables for drawing sets, window schedules, and similar items.

DOOR SCHEDULE			
MARK	SIZE	QUANTITY	REMARKS
1	2'0" X 6'8"	8	FLUSH DOOR
2	2'6" X 6'8"	2	FLUSH DOOR
3	2'6" X 6'8"	1	EXT FLUSH DOOR
4	3'0" X 7'0"	1	EXT FLUSH DOOR
5	4'0" X 6'8"	3	DOUBLE DOOR
6	3'0" X 6'8"	1	DOUBLE DOOR
7	9'4" X 6'8"	1	SLIDING DOOR

Figure 4-28
Completed door schedule table (Scale: 1″=1″)

When you have completed Exercise 4-2, your drawing will look similar to Figure 4-28. This is a commonly used means of specifying the number and types of doors used in a commercial or residential building.

Step 1. Use your workspace to make the following settings:

1. Use **Save As...** to save the drawing with the name **CH4-EXERCISE2**.
2. Set drawing units: **Architectural**
3. Set drawing limits: **11,8-1/2**
4. Set **GRIDDISPLAY**: **0**
5. Set grid: **1/4″**
6. Set snap: **1/8″**
7. Make a new text style, name it **Title**, use the **Arial Font**, and change the **Font Style** to **Bold**.
8. Create the following layer:

Layer name	Color	Linetype	Lineweight
a-anno-schd	green	continuous	.006″ (.15 mm)

9. Set layer **a-anno-schd** current.
10. Use **Zoom-All** to view the limits of the drawing.

TABLE	
Ribbon/ Panel	Home/ Annotation Table
Draw Toolbar:	
Menu Bar:	Draw/ Table ...
Type a Command:	TABLE
Command Alias:	TB

Step 2. Use the **TABLE** command to modify the Standard table, as described next:

Prompt	Response
Type a command:	Click **Table** (or type **TB <Enter>**)
The **Insert Table** dialog box (Figure 4-29) appears:	Click the **Launch the Table Style dialog** icon (the icon next to the **Standard Table style** name)

Figure 4-29
Insert Table dialog box

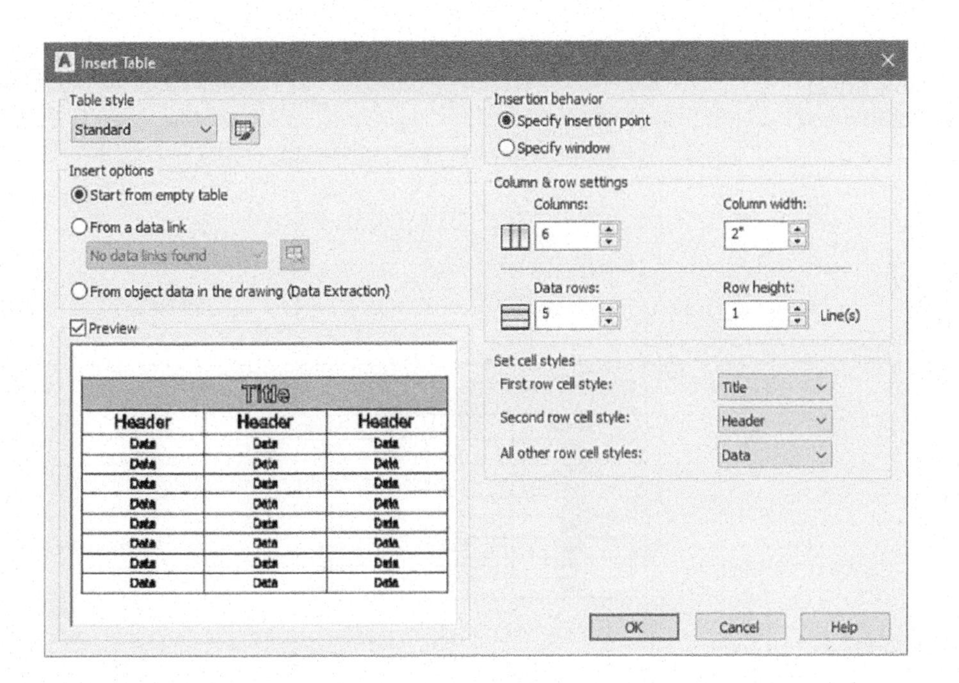

Prompt	**Response**
The **Table Style** dialog box (Figure 4-30) appears:	At this point you could specify a new table name, but for now just modify the Standard table. Click **Modify...**
The **Modify Table Style Standard** dialog box (Figure 4-31) appears:	Three cell styles, **Title, Header, and Data**, are provided within the Standard table Click **Title** under **Cell styles** [Figure 4-31] to make the following settings:

Figure 4-30
Table Style dialog box

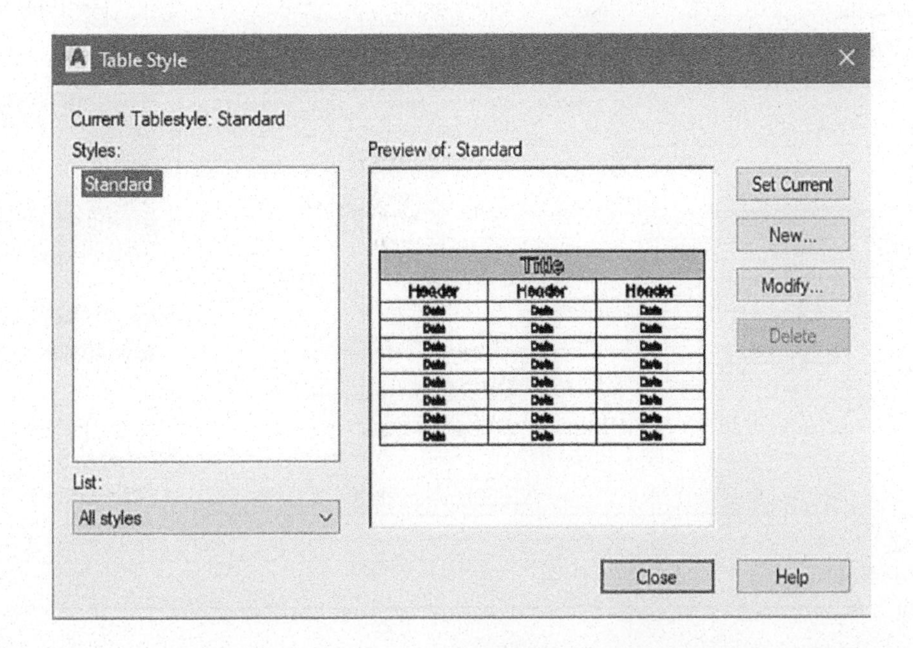

Figure 4-31
Modify Table Style: Standard dialog box

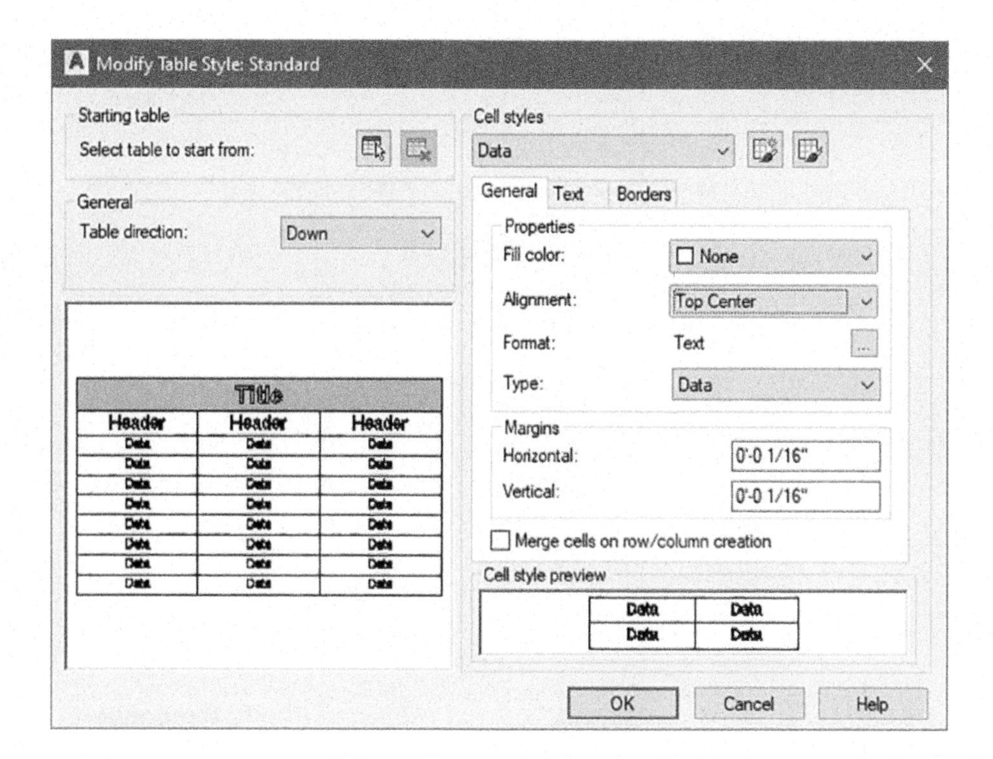

Prompt	**Response**
	Click the **General** tab (Figure 4-32)
	Click the **Fill color:** list down arrow and **Select Color... 9** (a light gray as the background color for the Title cell). You have to click **Select Color...** at the bottom of the list to access the **Index Color** tab (Figure 4-32); click **OK**

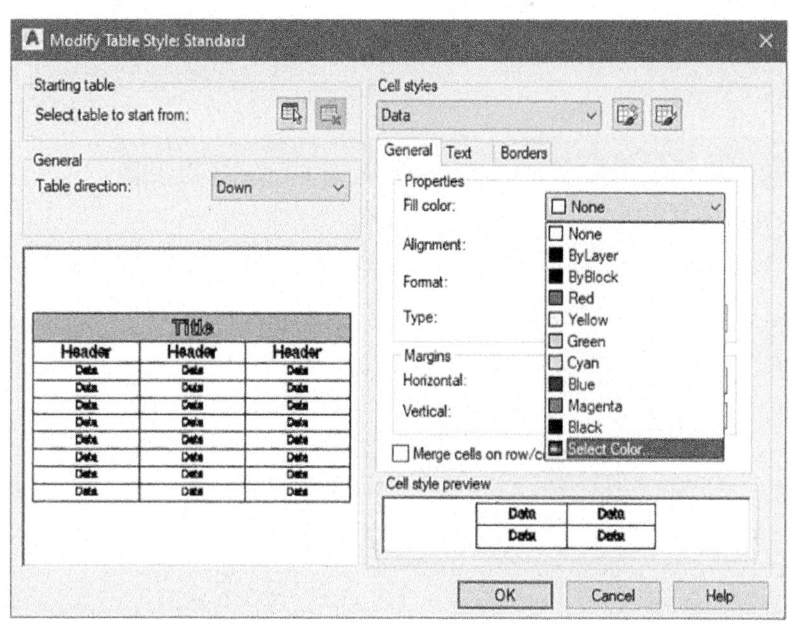

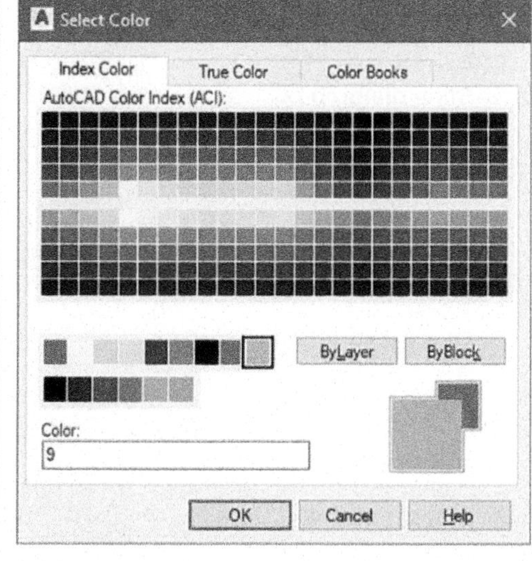

Figure 4-32
Click the **General** tab and **Select Color... 9**

Prompt	Response
	Click the **Text** tab (Figure 4-33)
	Click the **Text style:** list down arrow to set the **Text style: Title** current (Figure 4-33)
	Click **Data** under **Cell styles** (Figure 4-34) to make the following settings:
	Click the **General** tab

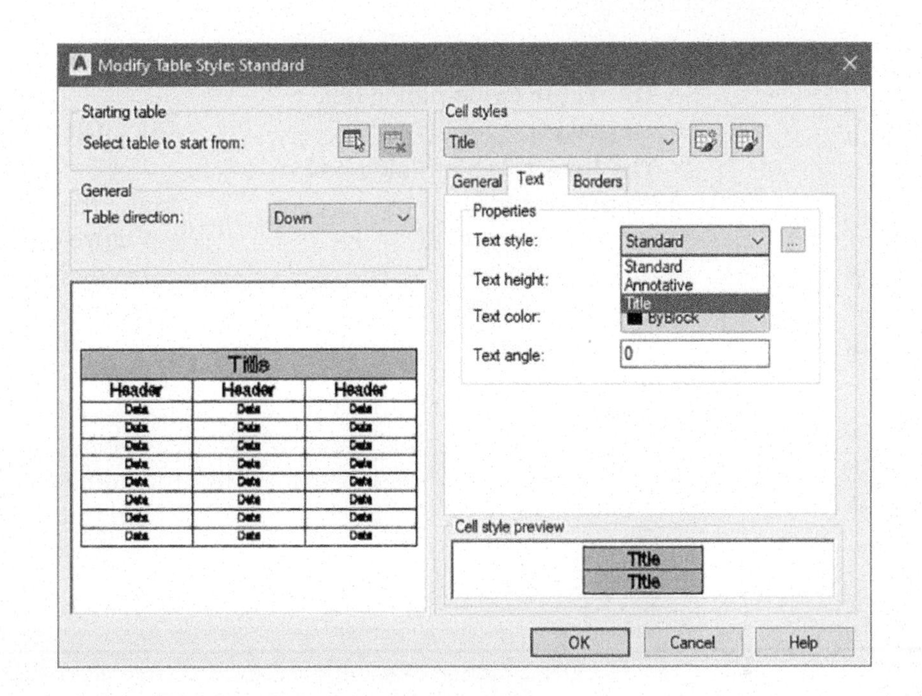

Figure 4-33
Click the **Text** tab and set **Text Style: Title** current

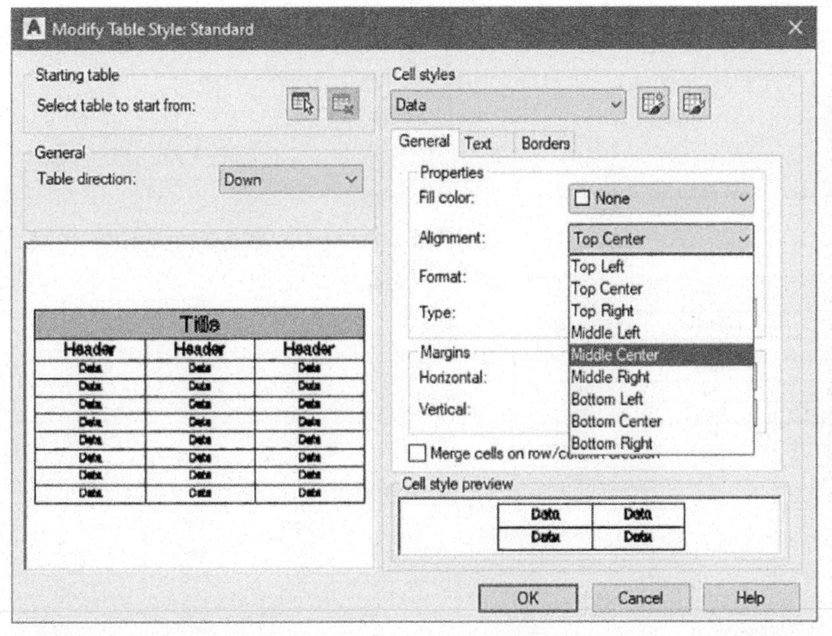

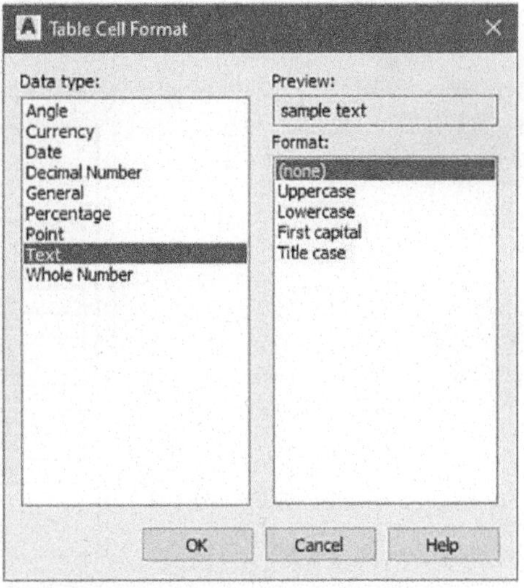

Figure 4-34
Click **Data** under **Cell styles,** click the **Alignment:** list arrow and set alignment to **Middle Center,** and click the ... button to set **Format:** to **Text**

Prompt	Response
	Click the **Alignment:** list down arrow and set the alignment to **Middle Center** (Figure 4-34)
	Beside **Format**, click the **...** button to set the **Table Cell Format:** to **Text** (Figure 4-34); click **OK**
	Click the **Text** tab (Figure 4-35)
	Set **Text height: to 1/8″** (Figure 4-35)
	Click **OK**
The **Table Style** dialog box appears:	Click **Close**
The **Insert Table** dialog box appears:	Make the settings shown in Figure 4-36: **6** columns (you will need only 4, but specify 6 anyway—you will delete 2 of them); set **Column width** at **2″** (you will change the column widths as you create the table); **5** rows (you will need 7, but specify 5 for now—adding rows is very easy); set **Row height:** at **1** if it is not the default; click **OK**

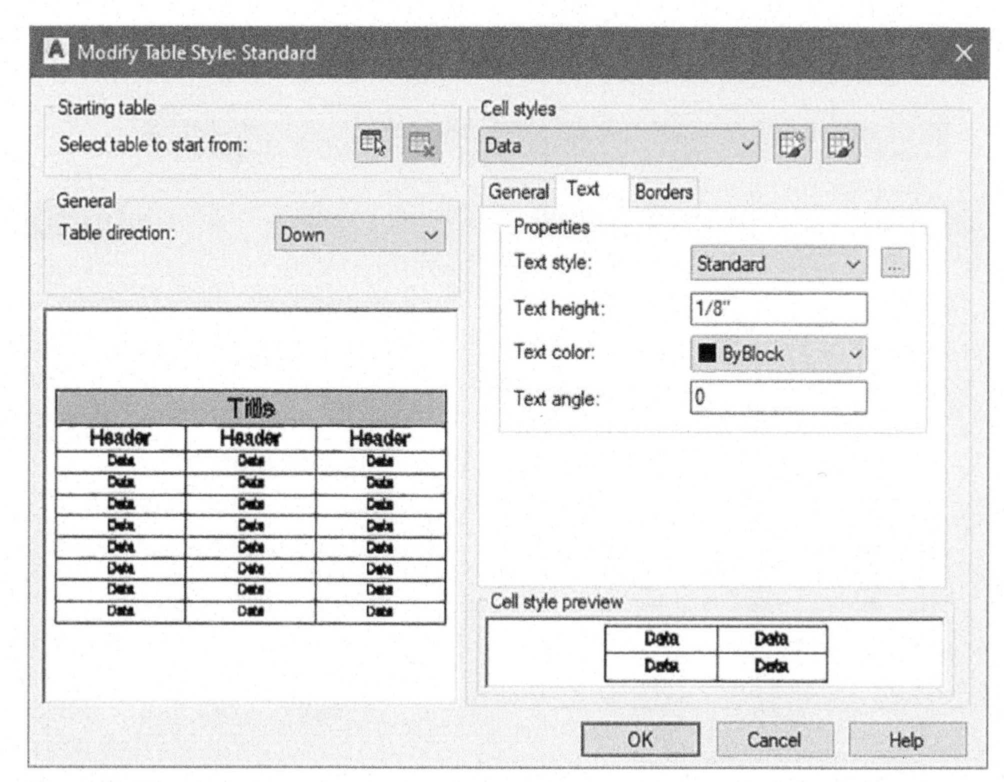

Figure 4-35
Set **Data Text height:** to 1/8″

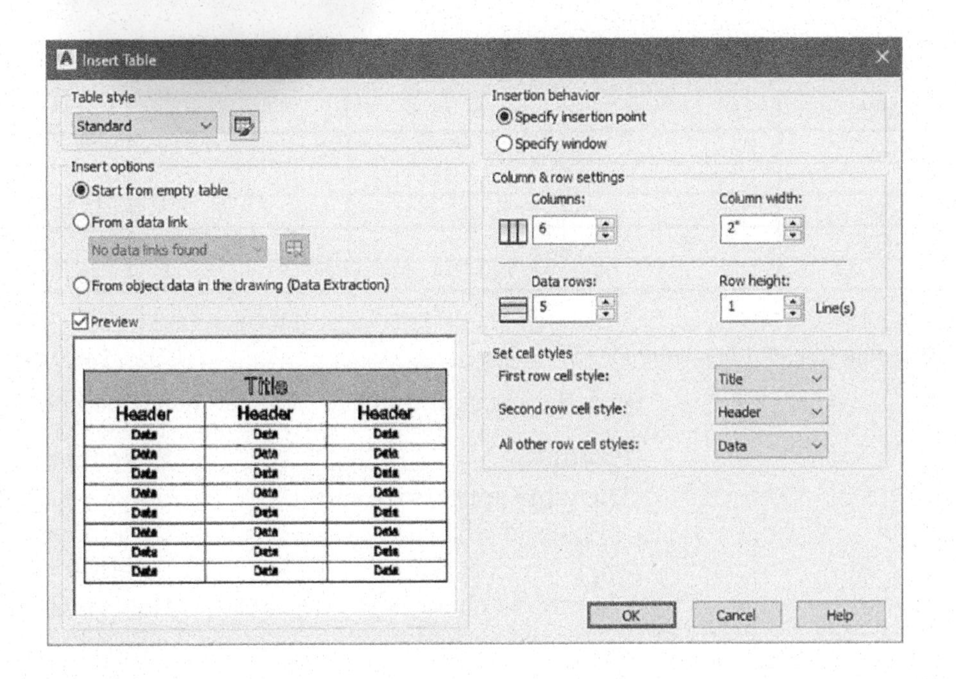

Figure 4-36
Make settings for columns and rows

Step 3. Insert the table and type the title, as described next:

Prompt	**Response**
Specify insertion point:	Click a point to place the table in the approximate center of the page (It will hang outside the drawing limits for now.)
The cursor flashes in the center of the **Title** cell:	Type **DOOR SCHEDULE <Enter>**

Step 4. Create column 1 head and all data in column 1, as described next:

Prompt	**Response**
The cursor moves to the center of the column 1 header cell:	Type **MARK <Enter>**
The cursor moves to the center of the first data cell:	Type **1 <Enter>**
The cursor moves to the center of the second data cell:	Type **2 <Enter>** **3 <Enter>** through **5** (so the table appears as shown in Figure 4-37. If numbers in the data cells are not in the center, click once on each number, then right-click and select **Alignment—Middle Center**. You can also select all the data cells at once using a crossing window and align them all at once.)

DOOR SCHEDULE					
MARK					
1					
2					
3					
4					
5					

Figure 4-37
Door schedule title and first column

Step 5. Insert and delete rows, as described next:

Prompt	**Response**
The table appears as shown in Figure 4-37:	Click once on the **4** data box, as shown in Figure 4-38
The ribbon changes (Figure 4-38):	Hold down the **<Shift>** key (so you can select two rows at the same time), and click the next row below, release the **<Shift>** key, then click **Insert Below** on the **Ribbon Row** panel
	Click the blank box under item **5** and type **6 <Enter>**, and **7 <Enter>**

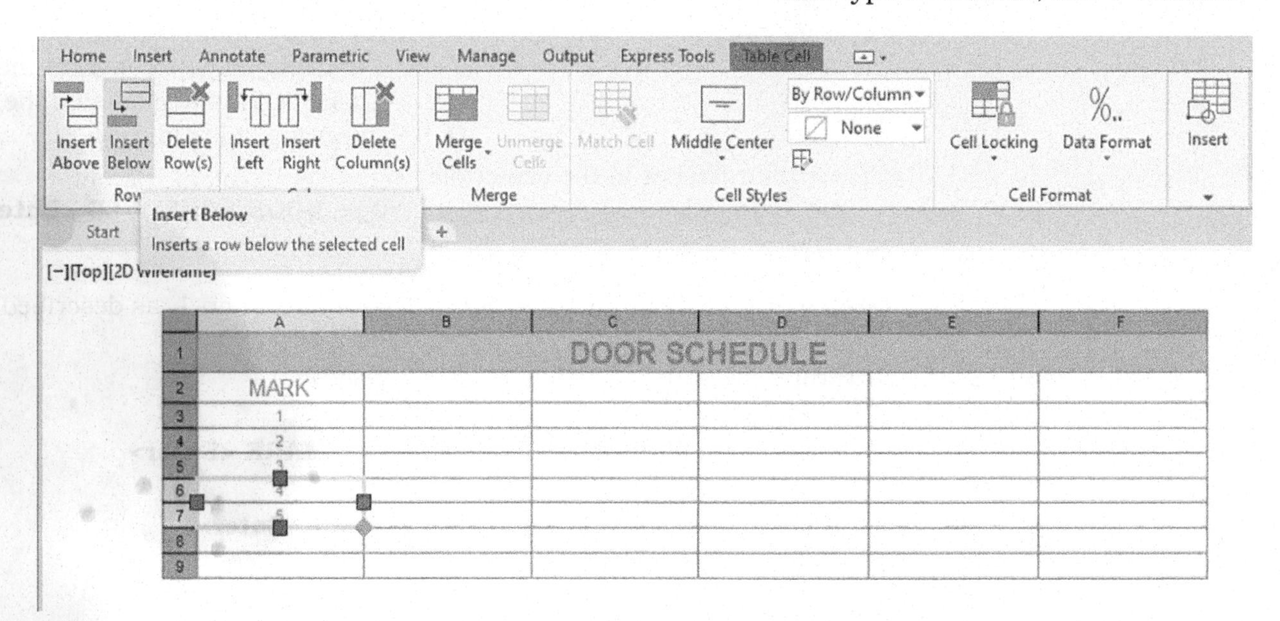

Figure 4-38
Insert two rows below

Step 6. Add the remaining column headers (Figure 4-39), as described next:

Prompt	**Response**
	Double-click the second column head area
The ribbon changes and the cursor flashes in the center of the column 2 header:	Type **SIZE** (do not press **<Enter>**)
	Press the **<Tab>** key

Figure 4-39
Add a column heading

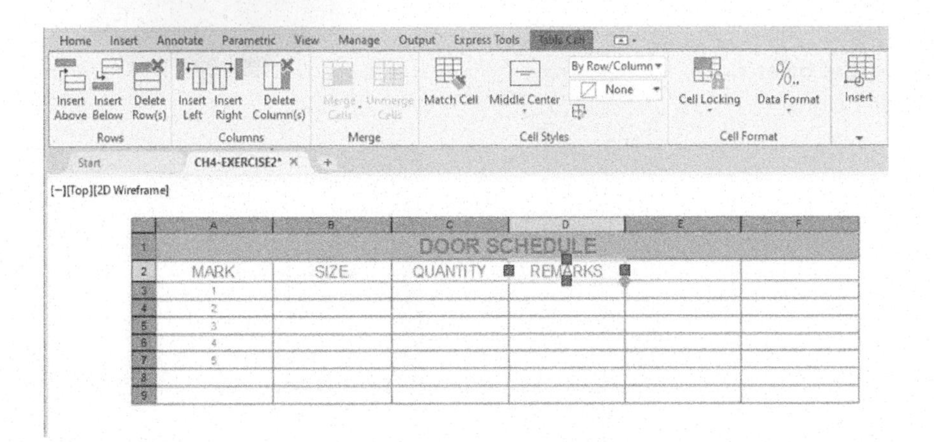

Prompt	Response
The cursor is flashing in the center of the third column header:	Type **QUANTITY** Press the **<Tab>** key
The cursor is flashing in the center of the fourth column header:	Type **REMARKS** Click any point in the screen area

Step 7. Delete unneeded columns (Figure 4-40), as described next:

Prompt	Response
	Click the two columns to the right of the **REMARKS** column (hold down the **<Shift>** key to select the second column) With the two blank columns highlighted, click **Delete Column(s)** (Figure 4-40)

Figure 4-40
Delete columns

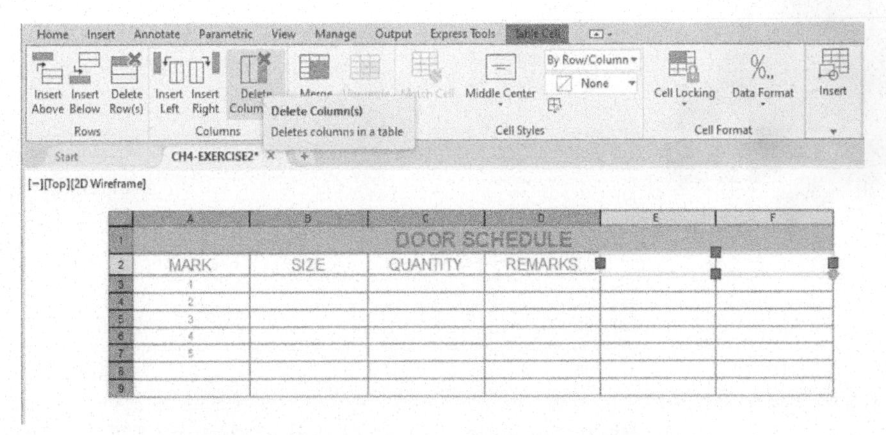

Step 8. Change the width of the columns to fit the data text (Figure 4-41), as described next:

Prompt	Response
	Click once on the first column header **(MARK)** and right-click
The right-click menu appears:	Click **Properties**
The **Properties** palette appears:	Change **Cell width** to **1″** and **Cell height** to **1/2″** (Figure 4-41)

Figure 4-41
Use the **Properties** palette to change cell height

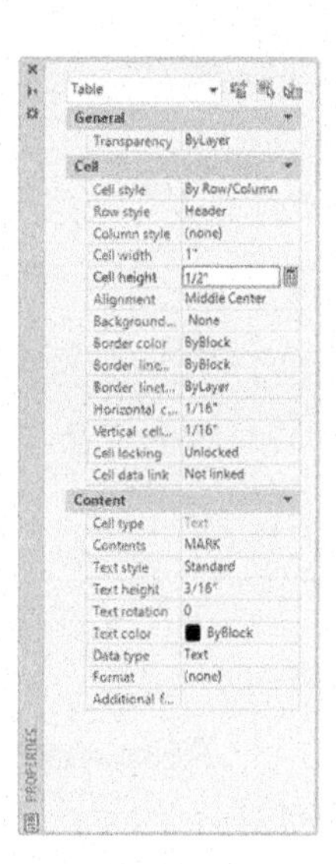

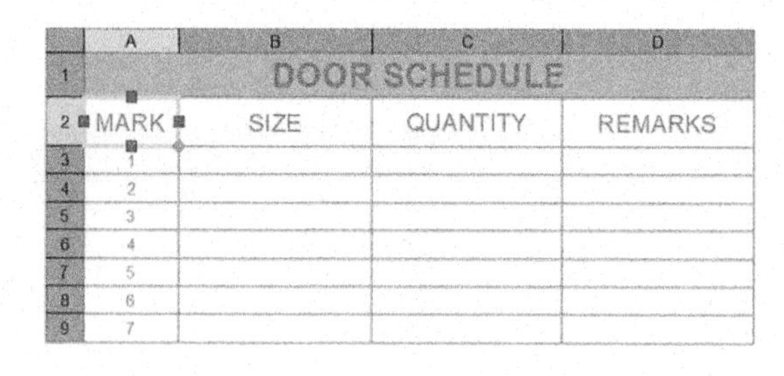

Step 9. Change the width of the remaining columns (Figure 4-42):

Column **2 (SIZE)**—change to **1-1/2"**

Column **3 (QUANTITY)**—change to **1-1/2"**

Column **4 (REMARKS)**—change to **2"**

Close the **Properties** palette.

Figure 4-42
Use the **Properties** palette to change cell width

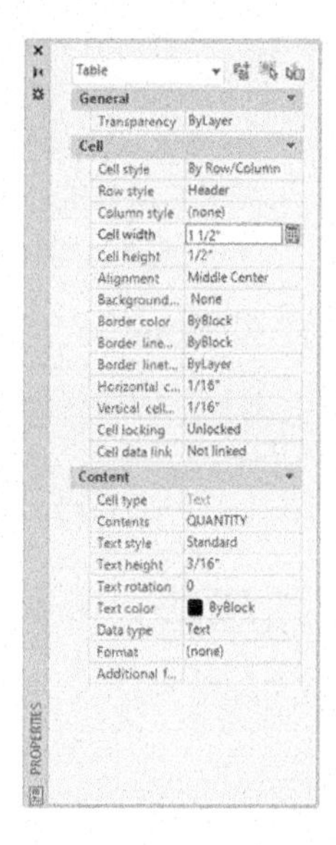

Step 10. Click the first cell under the **SIZE** column header and type **2'0" × 6'8" <Enter>**. Type each remaining door size (Figure 4-43) and press **<Enter>**.

Step 11. Double-click the first cell under the **QUANTITY** column header and type each door quantity (Figure 4-43) and press **<Enter>**.

Step 12. Double-click the first cell under the **REMARKS** column header and type each door description (Figure 4-43) and press **<Enter>**.

Step 13. Align data in the **REMARKS** column middle left (Figures 4-43, 4-44, and 4-45), as described next:

Figure 4-43
Type each door size, quantity, and description; select all data cells in the REMARKS column

DOOR SCHEDULE			
MARK	SIZE	QUANTITY	REMARKS
1	2'0" X 6'8"	8	FLUSH DOOR
2	2'6" X 6'8"	2	FLUSH DOOR
3	2'6" X 6'8"	1	EXT FLUSH DOOR
4	3'0" X 7'0"	1	EXT FLUSH DOOR
5	4'0" X 6'8"	3	DOUBLE DOOR
6	3'0" X 6'8"	1	DOUBLE DOOR
7	9'4" X 6'8"	1	SLIDING DOOR

P1
P2

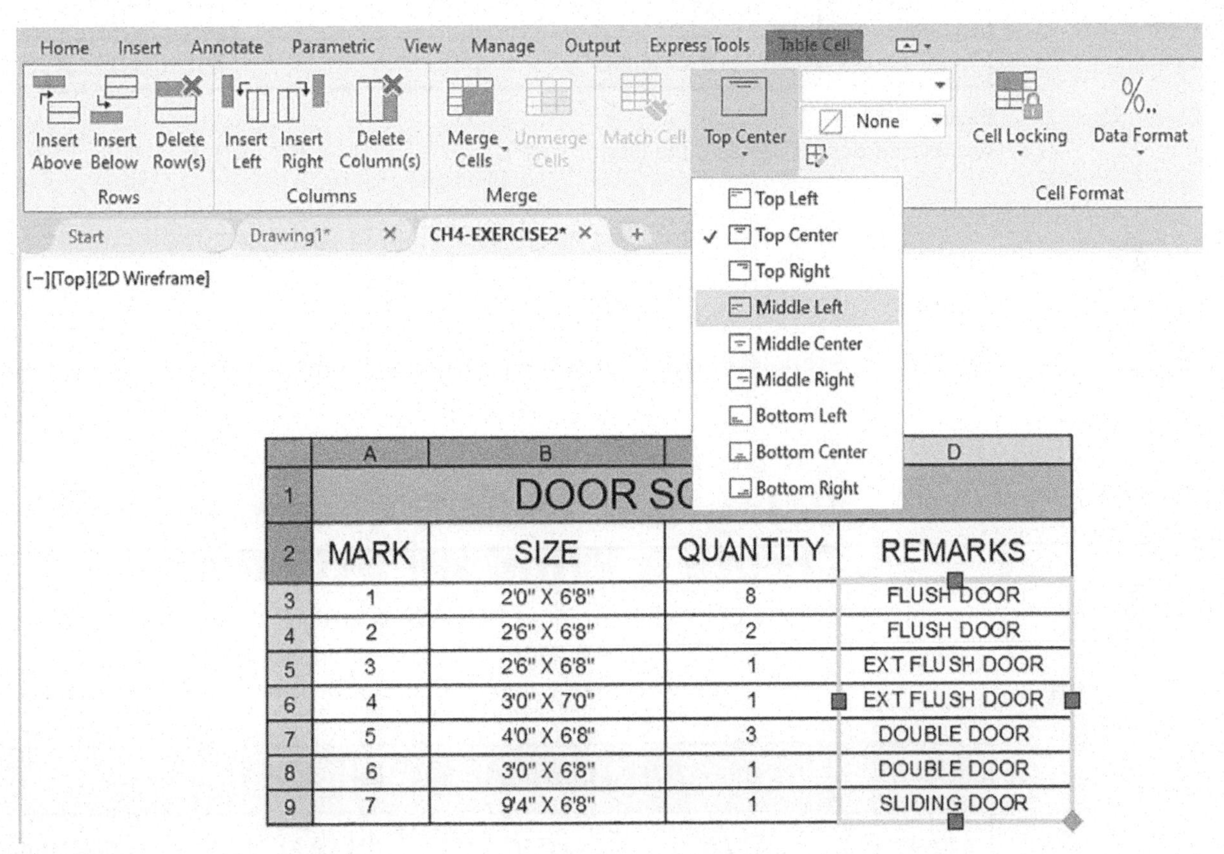

Figure 4-44
Align REMARKS column middle left

Prompt	**Response**
With no command active:	Click **P1→** (Figure 4-43)
Specify opposite corner:	Click **P2→** (to window the data in the **REMARKS** column)
The ribbon changes:	Click **Alignment—Middle Left** (from the **Cell Styles** panel, Figure 4-44)

DOOR SCHEDULE			
MARK	SIZE	QUANTITY	REMARKS
1	2'0" X 6'8"	8	FLUSH DOOR
2	2'6" X 6'8"	2	FLUSH DOOR
3	2'6" X 6'8"	1	EXT FLUSH DOOR
4	3'0" X 7'0"	1	EXT FLUSH DOOR
5	4'0" X 6'8"	3	DOUBLE DOOR
6	3'0" X 6'8"	1	DOUBLE DOOR
7	9'4" X 6'8"	1	SLIDING DOOR

Figure 4-45
Completed door schedule table (Scale: 1″=1″)

Step 14. Type your name **1/8″** high in the upper-right corner.

Step 15. When you have completed Exercise 4-2, save your work in at least two places.

Step 16. Print your drawing from the **Model** tab at a scale of **1:1.**

EXERCISE 4-3
Using the TABLE Command to Create a Window Schedule

When you have completed Exercise 4-3, your drawing will look similar to Figure 4-46. This is a commonly used means of specifying the number and types of windows used in a commercial or residential building.

WINDOW SCHEDULE				
MARK	SIZE	HEIGHT	QUANTITY	REMARKS
A	4' 5-1/8"	4' 2-5/8"	1	METAL FRAME
B	3' 1-1/8"	4' 2-5/8"	9	METAL FRAME
C	6'-0"	4' 2-5/8"	1	METAL FRAME
D	5'-0"	4' 2-5/8"	1	METAL FRAME
E	9'-0"	4' 2-5/8"	1	METAL FRAME

Figure 4-46
Completed window schedule table (Scale: 1″=1″)

Step 1. Use the information described in Exercise 4-2 to complete the window schedule shown in Figure 4-46.

Step 2. You may copy **CH4-EXERCISE2**, save it as **CH4-EXERCISE3**, and make changes as needed to make the new table.

Chapter Summary

In this chapter you learned to add text and tables to drawings. In addition, you learned to make window and door schedules and a title block. Now you have the skills and information necessary to add text to drawings and to make window and door schedules. You also learned to use the **SPELL** command to make sure there are no misspelled words in your drawings.

Chapter Test Questions

Multiple Choice

Circle the correct answer.

1. The command used in this chapter to place line text (text not in paragraph form) on drawings is:

   a. **Single Line Text (Dtext)**
   b. **TXT**
   c. **Multiline Text (Mtext)**
   d. **TEXTEDIT**

2. The command used in this chapter to place paragraph text on drawings is:

   a. **Single Line Text (Dtext)**
   b. **TXT**
   c. **Multiline Text (Mtext)**
   d. **TEXTEDIT**

3. Which of the following could be used as a style name?

   a. SIMPLEX
   b. TITLE
   c. NAMES
   d. All these could be used as a style name.

4. Which of the following is a font name?

   a. SIMPLEX
   b. TITLE
   c. NAMES
   d. All these are font names.

5. When you set the text style, which of the following text height settings will allow you to draw different heights of the same text style?

   a. 1/4
   b. 0′-0″
   c. 1
   d. 100

6. Which of the following **Single Line Text** options draws text between two clicked points and adjusts the text height so that it fits between the two points?

   a. **Fit**
   b. **Align**
   c. **Justify**
   d. **Style**

7. Which of the following **Single Line Text** options draws text between two clicked points and condenses or expands the text to fit between the two points but does not change the text height?

   a. **Fit**
   b. **Align**
   c. **Justify**
   d. **Style**

8. The justification letters **MR** stand for:

a. Middle, Right-justified
b. Margin, Right-justified
c. Midpoint, Left-justified
d. Bottom, Right-justified

9. Which of the following modifiers should you select if you want the bottom of the line of text to end 1/2″ above and 1/2″ to the left of the lower-right corner of the drawing limits?

a. **TL**
b. **BR**
c. **BL**
d. **TR**

10. Which of the following best describes the text properties that can be modified for the title, header, and data cell styles?

a. Style
b. Height
c. Color and angle
d. All of the above

Matching

Write the number of the correct answer on the line.

a. **TABLE** _____
b. Middle Center _____
c. **Single Line Text** _____
d. Standard codes _____
e. **TEXTEDIT** _____

1. The same as double-clicking text
2. A command used to draw text not in paragraph form
3. A command used to make door and window schedules
4. Used to draw commonly used symbols, such as the degree symbol
5. A text alignment description

True or False

Circle the correct answer.

1. **True or False:** You can change from one text style to another from within the **Single Line Text** command.
2. **True or False:** Columns in a table cannot be deleted.
3. **True or False:** The **Properties** command allows you to change text height, contents, properties, justification, and style.
4. **True or False:** The default text style name is Standard, and the default font is Arial.
5. **True or False:** Paragraph text cannot be used in a drawing.

List

1. Five aliases for text placement and editing available in AutoCAD.
2. Five settings for creating a text style.
3. Five text justifications available in AutoCAD upon launching the text command.

4. Five standard codes for special characters such as the degree (°) and percent (%) symbols.
5. Five Unicode control codes for the following special symbols:

   o

   ℄

   ±

   Ø

   ≠

6. Five options of the **Stack Properties** dialog box.
7. Five ways of opening the **Check Spelling** dialog box.
8. Five options of the **New Table Style** dialog box.
9. Five options of the **Table Cell Format** dialog box.
10. Five steps in editing the contents of a cell of a table.

Questions

1. How can tables be modified to contain several lines of headings?
2. When should you use paragraph text?
3. What is **Single Line Text** used for and what are its options?
4. Name the three cell styles that the standard table style provides.
5. What is the best and most efficient way to modify text?

Chapter Projects

Project 4-1: *Lighting Legend* [BASIC]

1. Draw the lighting legend as shown in Figure 4-47. Measure Figure 4-47 using a 1/4″ = 1′-0″ scale and draw it full size.

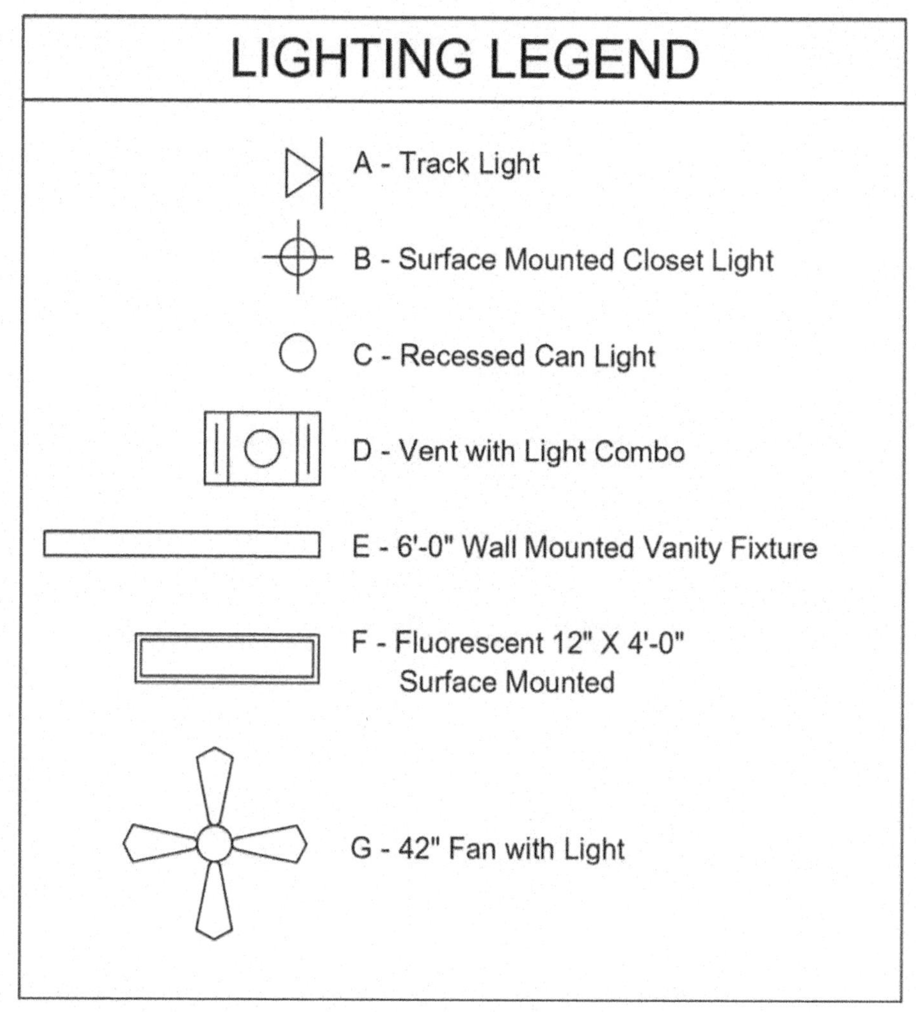

Figure 4-47
Project 4-1: Lighting schedule (Scale: 1/4″ = 1′-0″)

2. Type your name 6″ high in the upper-right corner.
3. Save the drawing in at least two places and print the drawing to Scale: 1/4″=1′-0″.

Project 4-2: *Room Finish Schedule*
[INTERMEDIATE]

1. Use the **TABLE** command to draw the room finish schedule as shown in Figure 4-48. Measure Figure 4-48 and draw it full size.
2. Type your name on the drawing.
3. Save the table in at least two places and print the table at a scale of 1:1, landscape orientation, on an 8-1/2″ × 11″ sheet.

ROOM FINISH SCHEDULE - UNITS											
Rm. No.	Rm. Name	Base North	Base South	Base East	Base West	Walls North	Walls South	Walls East	Walls West	Ceiling Type	Ceiling Height
101	Living Room	WB	WB	WB	WB	-	-	-	-	GYP	VARIES
102	Kitchen	WB	WB	WB	WB	-	-	-	-	GYP	VARIES
103	Dining Area	WB	WB	WB	WB	-	-	-	-	GYP	VARIES
104	Storage Room	WB	WB	WB	WB	-	-	-	-	GYP	8'-0"
105	Corridor	WB	WB	WB	WB	-	-	-	-	GYP	8'-0"
106	Laundry	WB	WB	WB	WB	-	-	-	-	GYP	8'-0"
107	Master Bedroom	TB	TB	TB	TB	-	-	-	-	GYP	7'-0"
108	Master Bath	TB	TB	TB	TB	-	-	-	-	GYP	8'-0"
109	Bedroom	WB	WB	WB	WB	-	-	-	-	GYP	7'-0"
110	Bath	TB	TB	TB	TB	-	-	-	-	GYP	8'-0"
111	Closet	WB	WB	WB	WB	-	-	-	-	GYP	8'-0"
112	Master Closet	WB	WB	WB	WB	-	-	-	-	GYP	8'-0"
113	Garage	WB	WB	WB	WB	-	-	-	-	GYP	8'-0"
114	Garage Storage	WB	WB	WB	WB	-	-	-	-	GYP	8'-0"
115	Wet Bar	WB	WB	WB	WB	-	-	-	-	GYP	VARIES

Figure 4-48
Project 4-2: Room finish schedule (Scale: 1″ = 1″)

Project 4-3: *Door and Frame Schedule*
[ADVANCED]

1. Use the **TABLE** command to draw the door and frame schedule as shown in Figure 4-49. Measure Figure 4-49 and draw it full size.
2. Type your name on the drawing.
3. Save the table in at least two places and print the table at a scale of 1:1, landscape orientation, on an 8-1/2″ × 11″ sheet.

DOOR AND FRAME SCHEDULE							
Door Description	Door Type	Door Material	Frame Width	Frame Height	Frame Thickness	Frame Type	Hardware Sets
Entry Door	1	Aluminum Clad Wood	3'-0"	6'-8"	0'-1 3/4"	ACW	To have (3) spring hinge, 1250 4-1/2 X 4-1/2, 652 ,HAG., (1) entrance lock, D53PD RHO,
							626 SCH., (1) wall stop,WS407CCV, 630 IVE., (1) dead bolt lock B661P, 626 SCH.,
							(1) sweep 315 CN, 628 PEM, and (1) threshold (per door manufacturer's recommendations).
French Door	2	Aluminum Clad Wood	2'-11"	6'-8"	0'-1 3/4"	ACW	To have (6) spring hinge, 1250 4-1/2 X 4-1/2, 652 ,HAG., (1) entrance lock, D53PD RHO,
							626 SCH., (1) wall stop,WS407CCV, 630 IVE., (1) dead bolt lock B661P, 626 SCH.,
							(1) sweep 315 CN, 628 PEM, and (1) threshold (per door manufacturer's recommendations).
Exterior Door	3	Aluminum Clad Wood	2'-0"	6'-8"	0'-1 3/4"	ACW	
Interior Door	4	Hollow Core Wood	2'-8"	6'-8"	0'-1 3/4"	W	To have (3) hinge BB1279 4-1/2 X 4-1/2, 652 HAG., (1) privacy lock D40S RHO, 626 SCH,
							(1) wall stop WS407CCV, 630 IVE., and (1) weatherstrip 297AV head & jambs, 628PEM.
Interior Door	5	Hollow Core Wood	2'-0"	6'-8"	0'-1 3/4"	W	To have (3) hinge BB1279 4-1/2 X 4-1/2, 652 HAG., (1) privacy lock D40S RHO, 626 SCH,
							(1) wall stop WS407CCV, 630 IVE., and (1) weatherstrip 297AV head & jambs, 628PEM.
Closet Door	6	Mirror panels	(2) 1'-11 1/2"	6'-8"	0'-1 3/4"	MR	Manufacturer provided
Closet Door	7	Mirror panels	(2) 1'-11 1/2"	6'-8"	0'-1 3/4"	MR	Manufacturer provided
Laundry Door	8	Wood louvered panels	3'-11"	6'-8"	0'-1 3/4"	W	Manufacturer provided
Shower Door	9	Glass	2'-0"	6'-8"	0'-1 3/4"	G	Manufacturer provided
Laundry Door	10	Aluminum Vinyl	(2) 1'-11 1/2"	6'-8"	0'-1 3/4"	AV	Manufacturer provided
Garage Door	12	Aluminum	10'-0"	7'-0"	0'-1 3/4"	A	Manufacturer provided
Hollow Metal Door	11	Hollow Metal	3'-0"	6'-8"	0'-1 3/4"	HM	To have (3) hinge BB1279 4-1/2 X 4-1/2, 652 HAG., (1) storeroom lock D80PD RHO, 626 SCH, (1) threshold 171A X MS&A, 628 PEM, and (1) wall stop WS407CCV, 630 IVE.

NOTES:
ACW - aluminum clad wood W - wood
MR - Mirror G - Glass HM - hollow metal
A - aluminum AV - aluminum vinyl
General Note: T = tempered glass

Figure 4-49
Project 4-3: Door and frame schedule (Scale: 1″=1″)

5 chapter five

Advanced Plotting: Using Plot Styles, Paper Space, Multiple Viewports, and PDF Files

CHAPTER OBJECTIVES

- Create a color-dependent plot style.
- Print/plot drawings with one viewport from a layout tab.
- Toggle between **PAPER** space and **MODEL** space while in a layout tab.
- Correctly use the following commands:

  Page Setup Manager **MVIEW**
  INSERT-BLOCK **Properties**
  VIEWPORTS (VPORTS) **Convert Plot Styles**
- Print/plot drawings with multiple viewports from a layout tab.
- Print/plot drawings at various scales on the same sheet.
- Print/plot drawings to a PDF file.

Understanding Layer Names, Colors, and Lineweights

Layers, their colors, and lineweights are very significant in plotting and printing. Varying the thickness of different types of lines such as those used to draw walls, doors, text, and furniture can make a drawing much more useful and aesthetically pleasing.

The *AIA CAD Layer Guidelines* have been used as a guide for naming the layers used in this book. Different lineweights have been used to provide drawing legibility in the plans: very heavy, heavy, medium, light, and very light. Colors have been selected to be applied consistently to these layers.

Figure 5-1 shows the lineweights. There are two sets of lineweights: one for A- and B-size sheets and one for C- and D-size sheets. Larger lineweights are used on the C- and D-size sheets to accommodate the larger scale of the drawings.

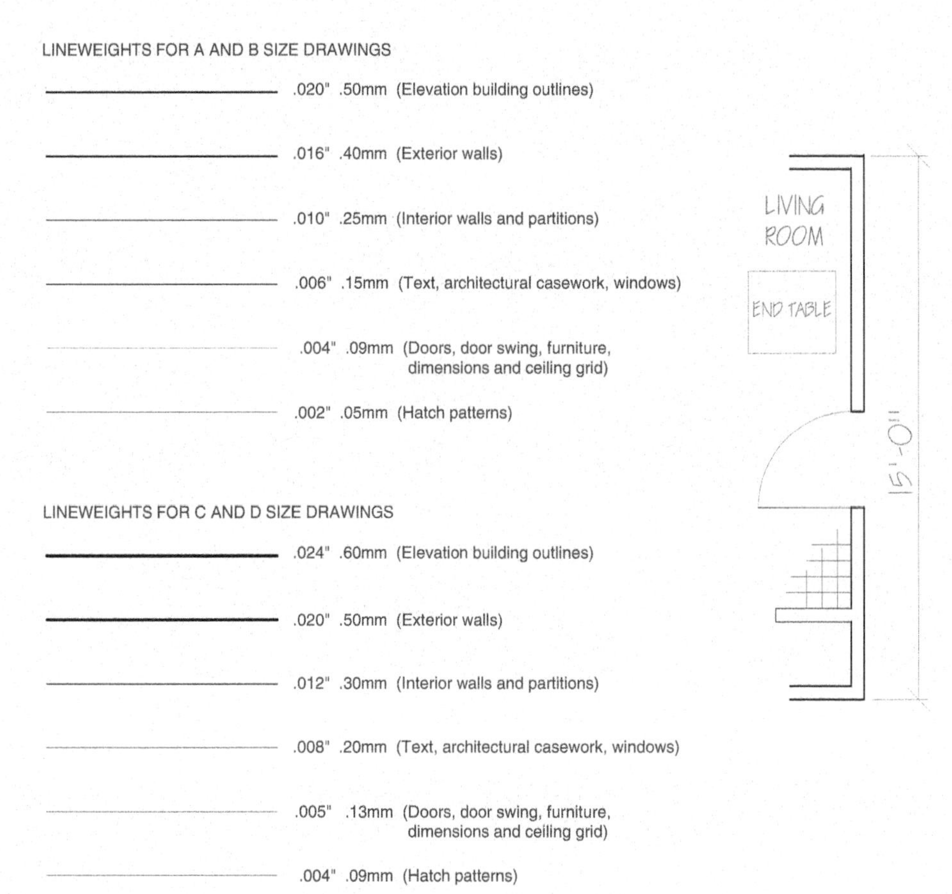

Figure 5-1
Lineweights for A-, B-, C-, and D-size drawings

Figure 5-2 shows the layer names, colors, and lineweights used in this book. This provides a basic outline of layers, colors, and lineweights for architectural plans, which can be adjusted or changed as required for individual needs or preferences.

Choosing a Plot Style

plot style: An object property that makes a collection of settings for color, dithering, gray scale, pen assignments, screening, linetype, lineweight, end styles, join styles, and fill styles. Plot styles are used at plot time.

Plot styles allow you to plot the same drawing in different ways. AutoCAD provides some plot styles, or you can create your own. A plot style contains settings that can override an object's color, linetype, and lineweight. The two types of plot styles are *named* and *color-dependent*.

LAYER NAME	DESCRIPTION	COLOR	LINEWEIGHT A & B SIZE	LINEWEIGHT C & D SIZE
Architectural				
a-anno-area	area calculation	green	.006" (.15mm)	.008" (.20mm)
a-anno-dims	dimensions	red	.004" (.09mm)	.005" (.13mm)
a-anno-revs	revisions	white	.014" (.35mm)	.016" (.40mm)
a-anno-schd	schedules	green	.006" (.15mm)	.008" (.20mm)
a-anno-text	general text	green	.006" (.15mm)	.008" (.20mm)
a-anno-ttbl	border & title block	magenta	.006" (.15mm)	.008" (.20mm)
a-anno-vprt	viewport boundary	green	.006" (.15mm)	.008" (.20mm)
a-clng-susp	suspended elements	red	.004" (.09mm)	.005" (.13mm)
a-door	doors & door swings	red	.004" (.09mm)	.005" (.13mm)
a-fixt	fixtures	green	.006" (.15mm)	.008" (.20mm)
a-fixt-fauc	faucets	white	.002" (.05mm)	.004" (.09mm)
a-flor-case	casework	green	.006" (.15mm)	.008" (.20mm)
*a-flor-case-spec	specialty items (closet rod)	red	.004" (.09mm)	.005" (.13mm)
*a-flor-case-uppr	upper casework	red	.004" (.09mm)	.005" (.13mm)
*a-flor-whch	wheelchair circle	red	.004" (.09mm)	.005" (.13mm)
a-glaz	glass	green	.006" (.15mm)	.008" (.20mm)
a-wall-extr	exterior building wall	white	.016" (.40mm)	.020" (.50mm)
a-wall-head	door & window headers	blue	.010" (.25mm)	.012" (.30mm)
a-wall-intr	interior building wall	blue	.010" (.25mm)	.012" (.30mm)
a-wall-patt-blck	hatch fill	red	.004" (.09mm)	.005" (.13mm)
a-wall-patt-gray	hatch fill	gray(253)	.004" (.09mm)	.005" (.13mm)
Architectural - Elevations				
a-elev-dims	dimensions	red	.004" (.09mm)	.005" (.13mm)
*a-elev-hdln	hidden lines	red	.004" (.09mm)	.005" (.13mm)
a-elev-lwt1	elevation	blue	.010" (.25mm)	.012" (.30mm)
a-elev-lwt2	elevation	white	.002" (.05mm)	.004" (.09mm)
a-elev-otln	building outlines	white	.020" (.50mm)	.024" (.60mm)
a-elev-patt	hatch patterns	white	.002" (.05mm)	.004" (.09mm)
a-elev-text	text	green	.006" (.15mm)	.008" (.20mm)
Architectural –Sections				
a-sect-dims	dimensions	red	.004" (.09mm)	.005" (.13mm)
a-sect-fixt	fixtures	green	.006" (.15mm)	.008" (.20mm)
*a-sect-hdln	hidden lines	red	.004" (.09mm)	.005" (.13mm)
a-sect-lwt1	section	blue	.010" (.25mm)	.012" (.30mm)
a-sect-lwt2	section	white	.002" (.05mm)	.004" (.09mm)
a-sect-patt	hatch patterns	white	.002" (.05mm)	.004" (.09mm)
a-sect-text	text	green	.006" (.15mm)	.008" (.20mm)
Architectural –Details				
a-detl-dims	dimensions	red	.004" (.09mm)	.005" (.13mm)
a-detl-lwt1	detail	blue	.010" (.25mm)	.012" (.30mm)
a-detl-patt	hatch patterns	white	.002" (.05mm)	.004" (.09mm)
a-detl-text	text	green	.006" (.15mm)	.008" (.20mm)
Electrical				
e-anno-symb-lite	symbols	blue	.010" (.25mm)	.012" (.30mm)
e-anno-symb-powr	symbols	blue	.010" (.25mm)	.012" (.30mm)
e-anno-text-lite	text	green	.006" (.15mm)	.008" (.20mm)
e-anno-text-powr	text	green	.006" (.15mm)	.008" (.20mm)
*e-lite-circ	lighting circuits	white	.016" (.40mm)	.020" (.50mm)
Interiors				
i-anno-text-furn	text	green	.006" (.15mm)	.008" (.20mm)
*i-eqpm-ovhd	equipment: overhead	red	.004" (.09mm)	.005" (.13mm)
i-furn	furnishings	cyan	.004" (.09mm)	.005" (.13mm)

All layers have a continuous linetype, except those with an * beside them. The * denotes a layer with a hidden linetype.

Figure 5-2
Layer names, colors, and linetypes

Named Plot Style (STB)

named plot style: A plot style that is organized by a user-defined name. Named plot styles can be assigned to AutoCAD layers or to individual drawing objects.

Named plot styles are assigned to objects and layers. They are saved as an STB file. Color-dependent plot styles are used by a majority of architects and are used in this book.

Color-Dependent Plot Style (CTB)

color-dependent plot style: A plot style that is organized by the AutoCAD Color Index (ACI) number. Color-dependent plot styles are automatically assigned by the color of the AutoCAD object and can be changed to plot any color specified. Color-dependent plot styles are often made to print all colors black.

With a ***color-dependent plot style***, any object that has the same color will be plotted using the same characteristics described in the plot style. For example, you can set the color-dependent plot style for the colors green and blue to be printed black with a lineweight of .006″. The color-dependent plot style can also be set for green and blue to be printed black but with the object lineweight assigned by the layer on which the object was drawn. The plot style allows you to plot with either of the following:

1. Lineweight assigned to the layer
2. Lineweight assigned in the plot style

This same method applies to linetype; for example, all blue lines will print with the object linetype assigned to the layer or with the linetype assigned in the plot style.

In Exercise 5-1 you will make your own color-dependent plot style, then plot a drawing using that plot style in Exercises 5-2, 5-3, and 5-4. This plot style will print or plot object colors 1 (red) through 7 (black) as black with the object lineweight assigned by the layer on which the item was drawn.

EXERCISE 5-1
Make a Color-Dependent Plot Style to Change Colors to Plot Black

ADD COLOR-DEPENDENT PLOT STYLE TABLE	
Menu Bar:	Tools/Wizards/ Add Color-Dependent Plot Style Table ...
Type a Command:	R14PENWIZARD

Step 1. Open drawing **CH3-EXERCISE1**.

Step 2. Add a color-dependent plot style table, as described next:

Prompt	Response
Type a command:	If you have the menu bar displayed, click **Add Color-Dependent Plot Style Table Wizard**, or type **r22penwizard <Enter>** (the command has been renamed **R14PENWIZARD**)
The **Add Color-Dependent Plot Style Table** dialog box (Figure 5-3) appears:	Click **Start from scratch** Click **Next** Type **Your name Color to Black** (in the **File name** box) Click **Next** Click **Plot Style Table Editor...**
The **Plot Style Table Editor** appears (Figure 5-4):	Click **Color 1**, hold down the **<Shift>** key and click **Color 7** to select colors 1 through 7 In the **Properties:** area Click **Black** (in the **Color:** Input) **Use object linetype** and **Use object lineweight** should be active, as shown in Figure 5-4 Click **Save & Close**

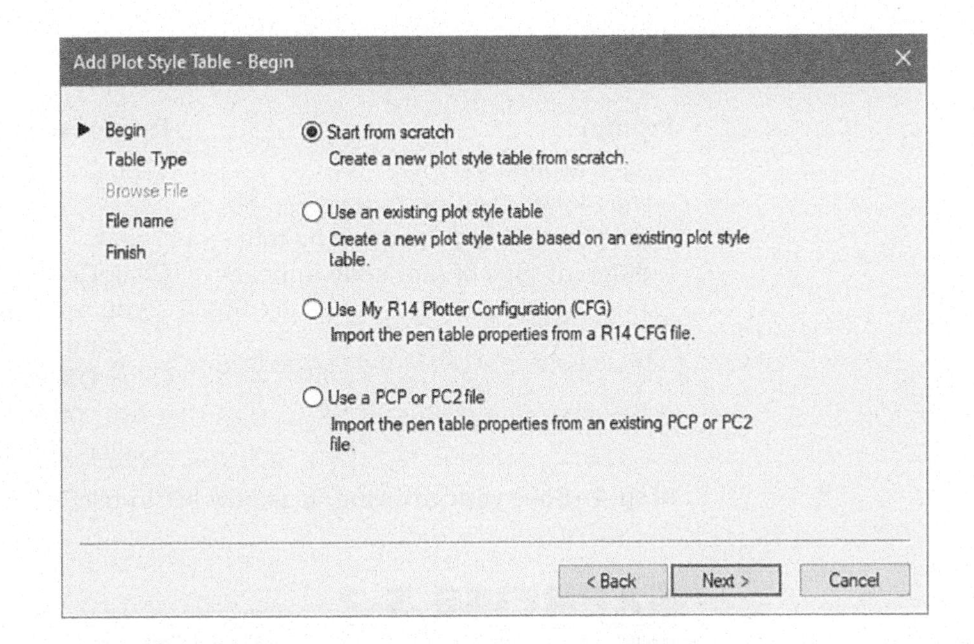

Figure 5-3
Add Color-Dependent Plot Style Table wizard

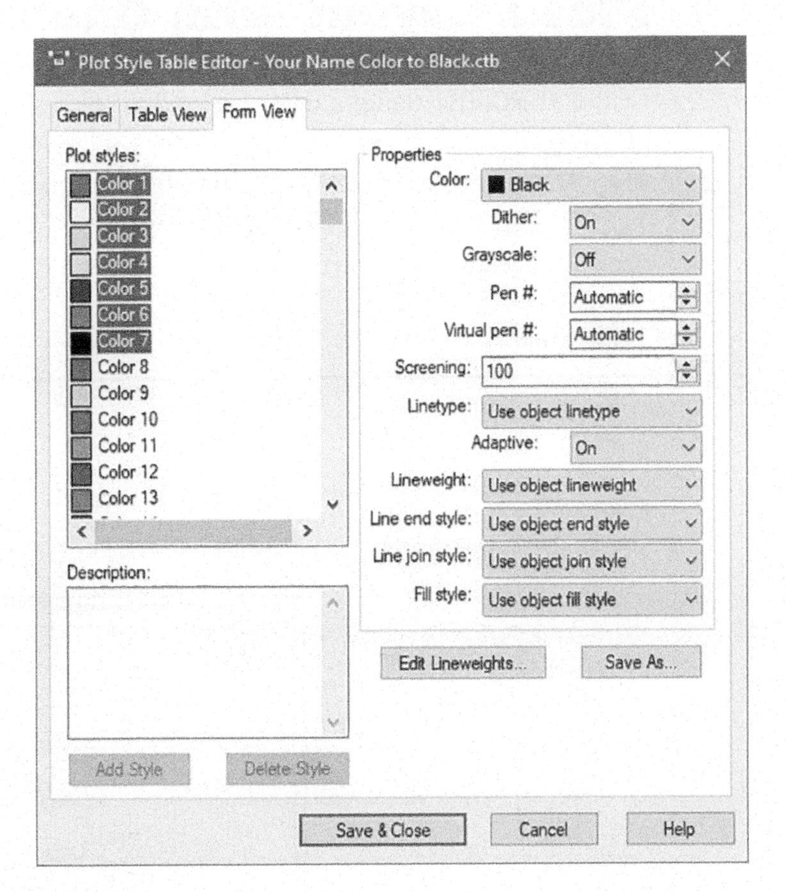

Figure 5-4
Plot Style Table Editor changing colors 1 through 7 to plot black

Prompt	**Response**
The **Add Color-Dependent Plot Style Table-Finish** dialog box appears with **Use this plot style table for the current drawing** check box selected:	Click **Finish**

Step 3. Use the **Convert Plot Styles** command to make sure your drawings are set to use color-dependent plot styles, as described next:

Prompt	Response
Type a command:	Type **CONVERTPSTYLES <Enter>**
A warning indicating that you are converting your drawing to a different type of plot style appears:	Click **Cancel** if the warning shows you are converting the drawing to a named plot style Click **OK** if the warning shows you are converting the drawing to a color-dependent plot style

Step 4. Save your drawing. It is now set to use color-dependent plot styles.

EXERCISE 5-2
Plot a Layout with One Viewport

The following is a hands-on, step-by-step exercise to make a hard copy of CH3-EXERCISE1 using a color-dependent plot style. When you have completed Exercise 5-2, your print will look similar to Figure 5-5.

Step 1. Open drawing **CH3-EXERCISE1** so it is displayed on the screen and save it as **CH5-EXERCISE2**.

Step 2. Create the following new layer and set it as the current layer:

Layer name	Color	Linetype	Lineweight
a-anno-vprt	green	continuous	.006″ (.15 mm)

Figure 5-5
CH5-EXERCISE2 complete

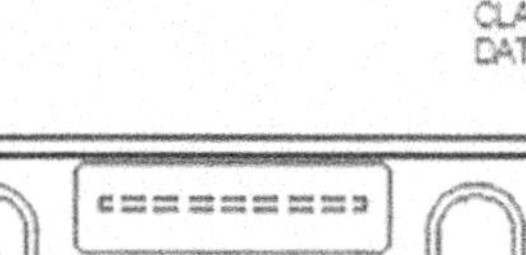

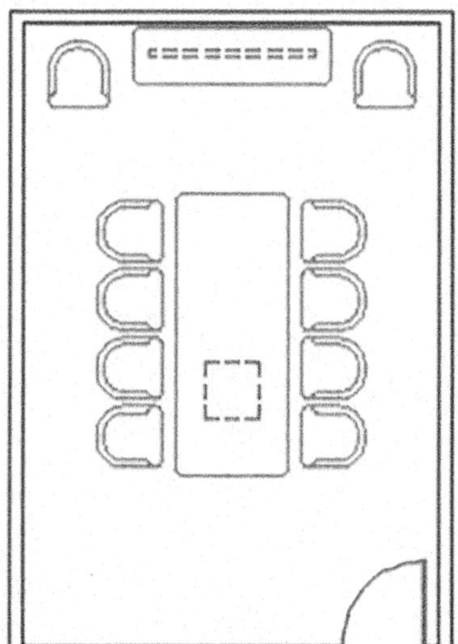

Model, Layout1, and Layout2 Tabs

At the bottom of the drawing window are the **Model**, **Layout1**, and **Layout2** tabs. Model space is the 2D (and also 3D) environment in which you have been working to this point. ***Model space*** is where you create and modify your 2D and 3D models (drawings). You can also print from the **Model** tab. You use a ***layout*** tab to view paper space. ***Paper space*** shows the actual printed or plotted drawing on a real-size piece of paper.

model space: One of the two primary spaces in which objects are made.

layout: A two-dimensional page setup made in paper space that represents the paper size and what the drawing will look like when it is plotted. Multiple layouts can be created for each drawing.

paper space: One of the two spaces in which objects are made or documented. Paper space is used for making a finished layout for printing or plotting. Often, drawings are restored in paper space in a drawing title block and border.

NOTE

While you are on the **Layout1** tab, turning off the grid may be helpful. Click the **PAPER** toggle in the status bar to return to **MODEL**, turn the grid off, and click the **MODEL** toggle to return to **PAPER**.

Step 3. Click the **Layout1** tab at the bottom of drawing CH5-EXERCISE2. You are now in paper space. Notice that the toggle on the status bar shows the paper space icon or reads **PAPER**. Clicking it will change it to **MODEL**. Make sure you are in paper space and the toggle reads **PAPER**.

PAGE SETUP MANAGER	
Ribbon/ Panel	Output/Plot/
Application Menu:	Print/Page Setup
Layouts Toolbar:	
Menu Bar:	File/Page Setup Manager ...
Type a Command:	PAGESETUP

Page Setup Manager

Step 4. Right-click the **Layout1** tab and click **Page Setup Manager....** The **Page Setup Manager** (Figure 5-6) appears.

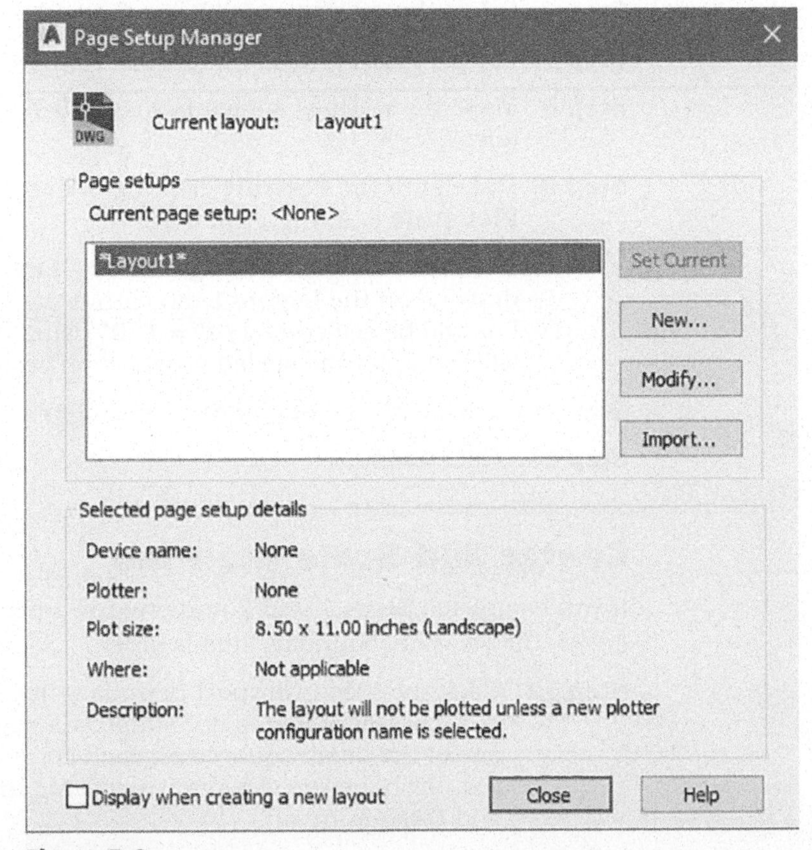

Figure 5-6
Page Setup Manager

Step 5. With **Layout1** in **Page setups** selected, click **Modify....** The **Page Setup** dialog box for **Layout1** appears (Figure 5-7).

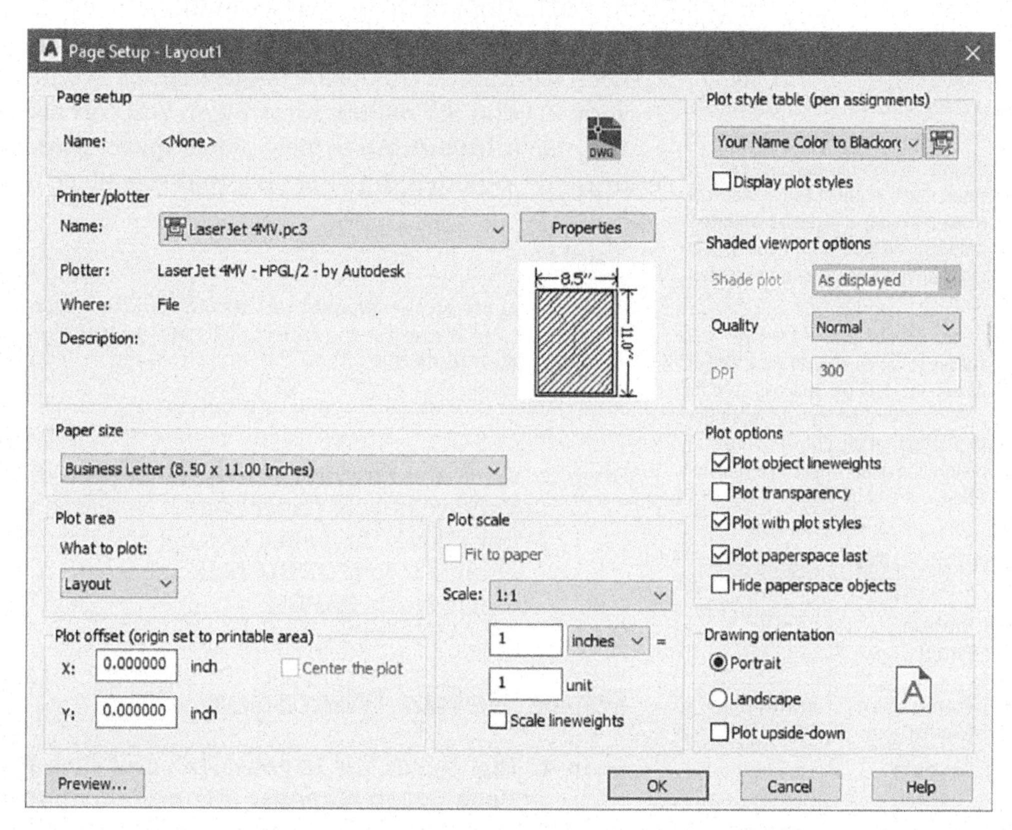

Figure 5-7
Page Setup - Layout1 dialog box

Step 6. Select the printer you will use for a letter-size paper.

Step 7. Set the **Plot style table** to **Your Name Color to Black**.

Step 8. Make the settings shown in Figure 5-7 in the **Page Setup** dialog box.

Step 9. Make sure the **Portrait** drawing orientation is selected and the **Plot scale** is **1:1** (Figure 5-7).

The **Plot scale** on the **Page Setup - Layout1** dialog box is **1:1**. The drawing on the **Layout1** tab within the green viewport boundary line will be scaled to **1/4″ = 1′-0″** using **Properties** in Step 16. You will then plot the scaled viewport on Layout1.

Step 10. Click **OK**. The **Page Setup Manager** appears.

Step 11. Click **Close.**

Center and Scale the Plan

If you completed Steps 1 and 2 and created a new layer with the color green, the viewport boundary line is green.

Step 12. Click the green viewport boundary line to select it. If your viewport boundary line is not shaped as shown in Figure 5-8, click one of the small squares on each corner (called grips). It becomes red. Reshape the viewport by moving the grip. Be sure **ORTHO** and **OSNAP** are off.

You can reshape, resize, move, erase, and copy the viewport.

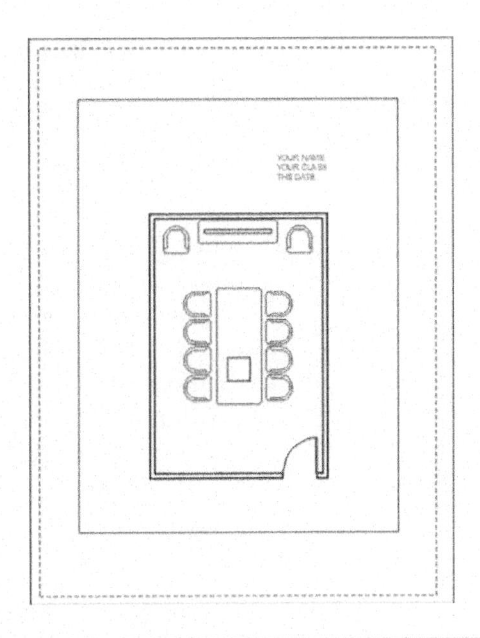

Figure 5-8
Select the viewport boundary

> **NOTE**
>
> The viewport boundary line (green line) comes in on the layer that is current. That's why you created a layer named **a-anno-vprt** for the viewport and assigned the green color to it.

Step 13. If your drawing is not centered in the viewport, click **PAPER** in the status bar to return to **MODEL** (model space). Use the **PAN** or **ZOOM** command to center the drawing. Click **MODEL** to return to **PAPER** (paper space) before continuing with the plot setup.

Step 14. Click the green viewport boundary line to select it (Figure 5-8).

Step 15. Click **Properties** from the **Palettes** panel.

Step 16. Click **Standard scale** in the **Properties** palette (Figure 5-9). Click the arrow to the right of **Standard scale** and scroll down to select

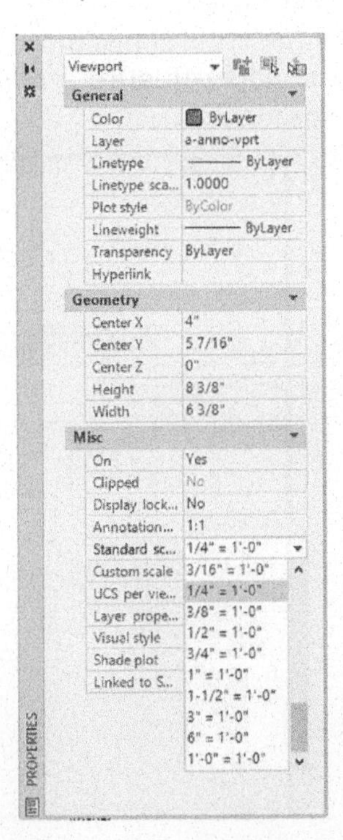

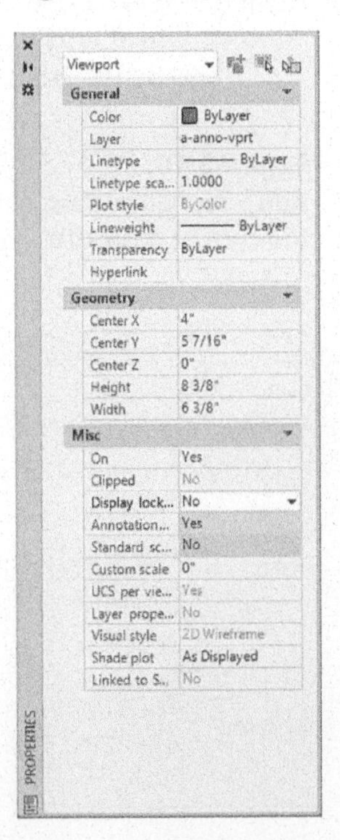

Figure 5-9
Set viewport scale to 1/4″ = 1′-0″ and lock the display

1/4" = 1'-0". This scale is applied to the drawing in the paper space viewport. Click **Display locked** (above the scale) and click **Yes** to lock the display scale for this viewport. Close the **Properties** palette.

Step 17. Turn the **a-anno-vprt** layer off so the viewport boundary line will not print.

When the display is locked, you cannot accidentally zoom in or out while in model space and lose the 1/4" = 1'-0" scale. If you zoom in or out while in paper space, you do not change the scale because you are zooming in or out on the paper only. When the display is locked, you cannot reposition the drawing. If you need to reposition or change the drawing in any way, you must turn the **Viewport** layer back on, select the viewport boundary line, select **Properties**, and unlock the display to make any changes.

TIP

While in a layout tab, you can click the **PAPER** toggle to return to **MODEL** and the **MODEL** toggle to return to **PAPER**. You can also click the **Model** tab to return to the drawing, make any changes, and then click the **Layout** tab to return to the layout tab and paper space.

Complete the Layout

Step 18. Click **PAPER** to return to model space and erase the existing name, class, and date on the upper right of your drawing. Then, click **MODEL** to return to paper space.

TIP

While in a layout, you can type **MS <Enter>** to return to **MODEL** space or type **PS <Enter>** to return to **PAPER** space.

Step 19. Use a text style with the Arial font; set layer **a-anno-text** current; and add your name, your class, and the date in all capitals, 3/16" high, to the paper (Figure 5-10).

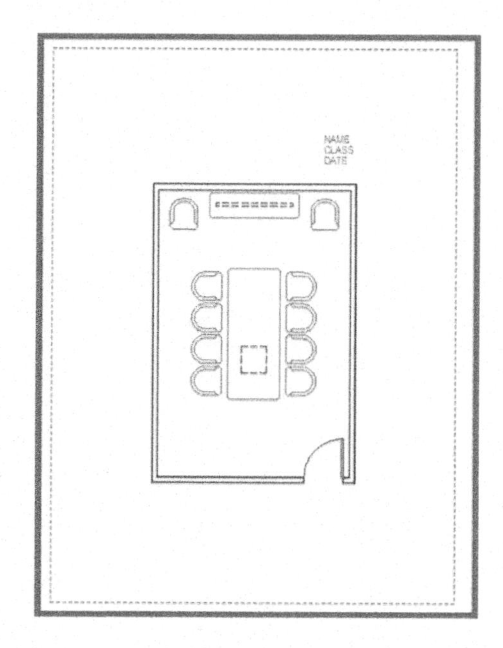

Figure 5-10
Add your name, class, and the current date 3/16" high

NOTE

When you type your name or anything else 3/16″ high in **PAPER** space, it will be printed 3/16″ high when the layout is printed at a scale of 1:1.

PLOT	
Ribbon/Panel	Output/ Plot
Application Menu:	Print/Plot
Quick Access Toolbar:	
Menu Bar:	File/Plot
Type a Command:	PLOT
Keyboard:	<Ctrl>+P

Step 20. While in **PAPER**, change **LTSCALE** as needed to show the **HIDDEN** linetype.

Step 21. Right-click the **Layout1** tab. The right-click menu appears.

Step 22. Click **Rename.** Type **Furniture Plan** for the new layout name. Press **<Enter>**.

Step 23. Right-click the **Furniture Plan** tab. The right-click menu appears.

Step 24. Click **Plot....** The **Plot** dialog box appears.

Step 25. Click **Preview....** If the preview is okay, right-click and click **Plot**. If it is not okay, exit and correct the problem. The plot proceeds from this point.

Step 26. Save the drawing in at least two places.

EXERCISE 5-3
Plot a Layout with Two Viewports

The following is a step-by-step exercise to make a hard copy of CH3-EXERCISE1 and CH3-EXERCISE2 on one sheet of letter-size paper. When you have completed Exercise 5-3, your print will look similar to Figure 5-11.

Step 1. Open drawing **CH3-EXERCISE1** so it is displayed on the screen and save it as **CH5-EXERCISE3**.

Insert an Entire Drawing into a Current Drawing

INSERT BLOCK	
Ribbon/Panel	Insert/Block
Draw Toolbar:	
Menu Bar:	Insert/ Blocks Palette ...
Type a Command:	INSERT
Command Alias:	I

You can use the **Insert-Block** command to insert any drawing into the current drawing and define it as a block in that drawing. Simply use the **Insert-Block** command to insert the drawing. Use the **Browse...** button in the **Insert** dialog box to locate the drawing.

Step 2. Insert **CH3-EXERCISE2** into the current drawing as described next:

Prompt	Response
Type a command:	Type **I <Enter>**
The **BLOCKS** palette appears:	Click the **Select File to Insert** button at the top right of the palette
The **Insert** dialog box appears:	In the **Look in:** dropdown, browse to locate **CH3-EXERCISE2** in your folder and click on it as shown in Figure 5-12 Click **Open**
Drawing **CH3-EXERCISE2** appears at the crosshairs:	Click a point to locate the drawing directly above **CH3-EXERCISE1** (Figure 5-13)

Figure 5-11
CH5-EXERCISE3 complete

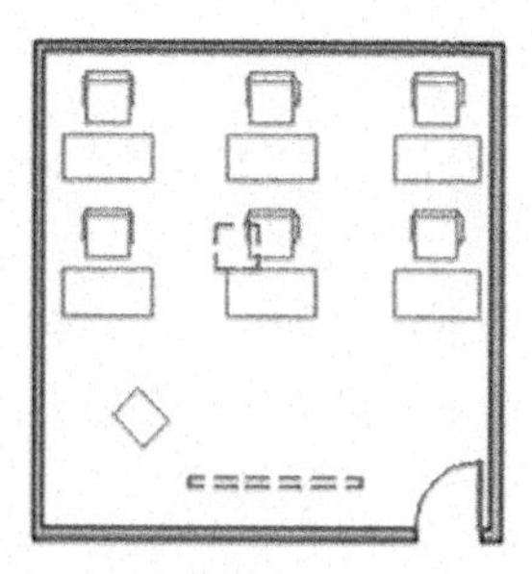

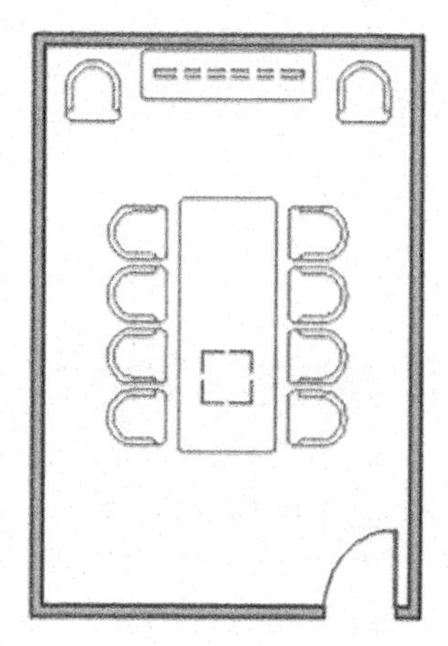

Figure 5-12
Browse to locate CH3-EXERCISE2

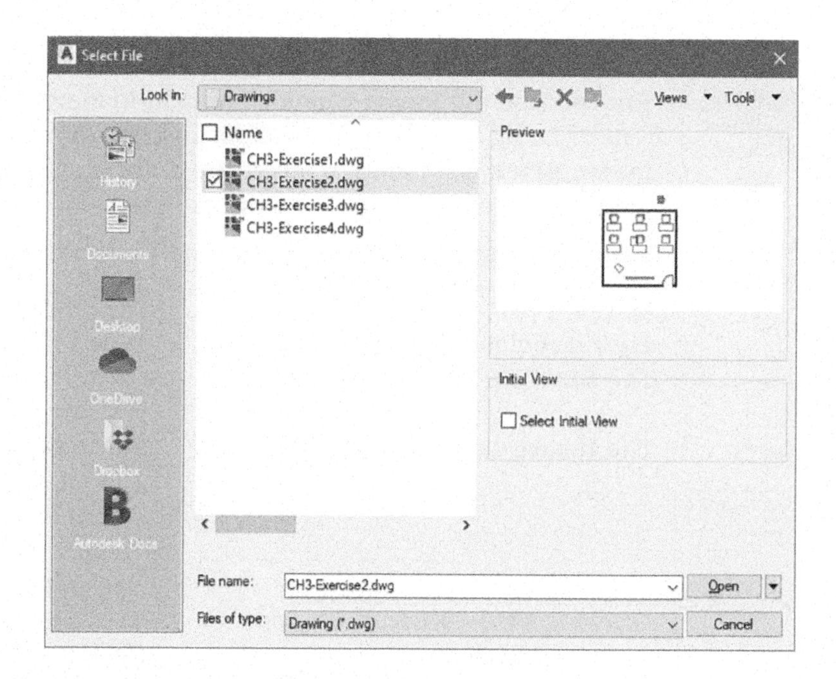

Figure 5-13
INSERT CH3-EXERCISE2 directly above CH3-EXERCISE1

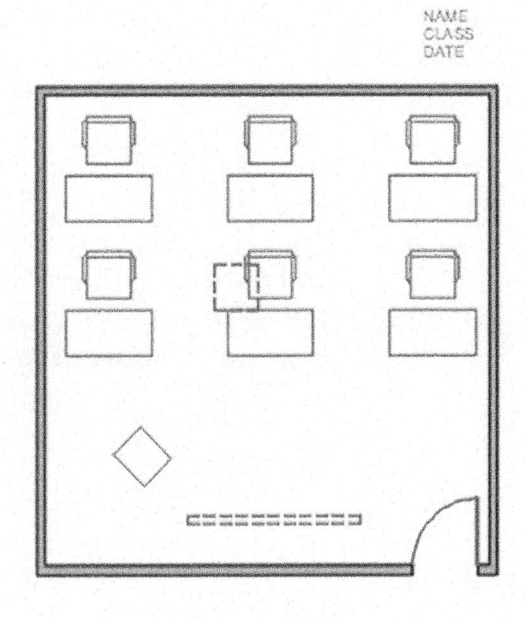

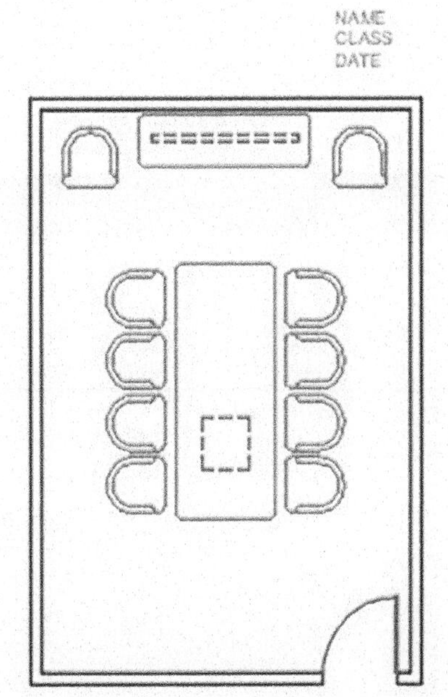

Step 3. The inserted drawing comes in as a single entity. **Explode** the **CH3-EXERCISE2** drawing.

FOR MORE DETAILS

For more about the **Insert-Block** command and the advantages of using blocks, see Chapter 6.

Step 4. Erase the name, class, and date from both drawings.

Step 5. Make sure the **Model** tab is current. Turn the grid off.

Page Setup Manager

Step 6. Create the following new layer and set it as the current layer:

Layer name	Color	Linetype	Lineweight
a-anno-vprt	green	continuous	.006″ (.15 mm)

Step 7. Click the **Layout1** tab at the bottom of the drawing.

Step 8. Right-click the **Layout1** tab and click **Page Setup Manager....** **The Page Setup Manager** appears.

Step 9. Click **Modify....** The **Page Setup** dialog box for Layout1 appears.

Step 10. Select the printer you will use for a letter-size paper.

Step 11. Set the **Plot style table** to **Your Name Color to Black**.

Step 12. Make the settings shown in Figure 5-14 in the **Page Setup** dialog box.

Step 13. Make sure the **Portrait** drawing orientation is selected and the **Plot scale** is **1:1** (Figure 5-14).

Step 14. Click **OK**. The **Page Setup Manager** appears.

Step 15. Click **Close**.

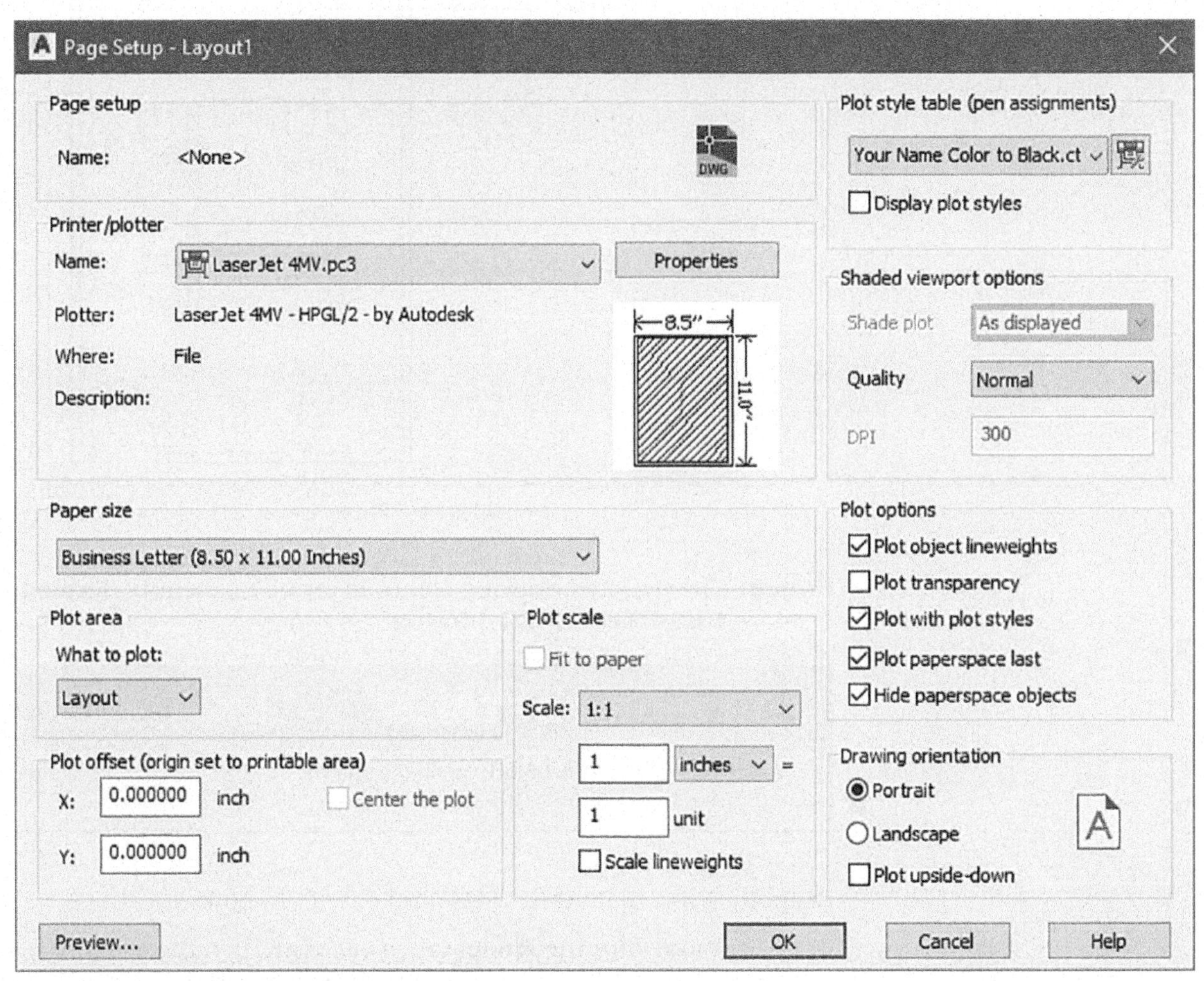

Figure 5-14
Page Setup – Layout1 dialog box

Copy a Viewport

Step 16. If your green viewport boundary line is not shaped as shown in Figure 5-15, use grips to reshape it.

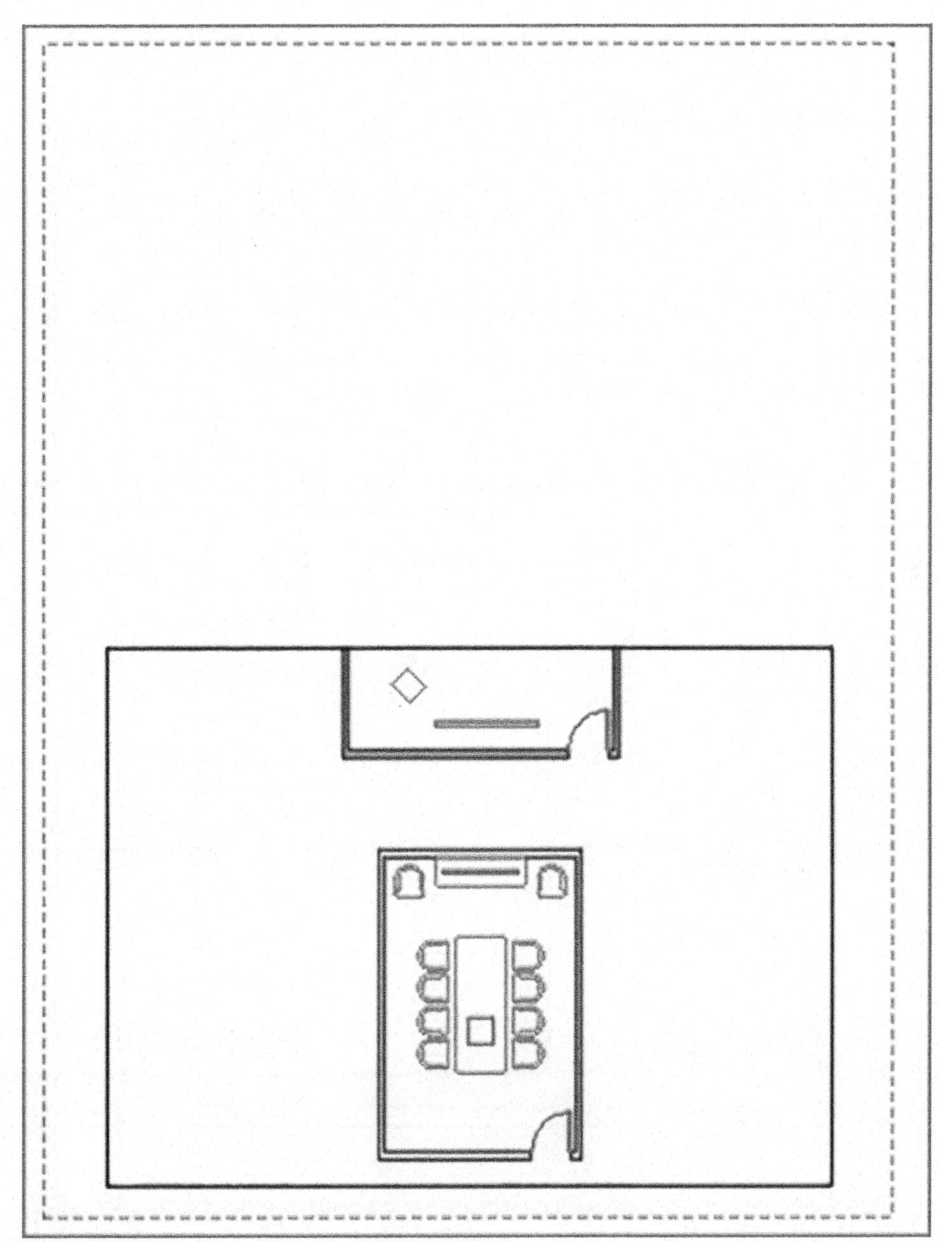

Figure 5-15
Viewport boundary

Step 17. While in **PAPER** space, use the **COPY** command to copy the viewport (click on any point on the green viewport boundary line to select it) to the approximate location shown in Figure 5-16.

Center and Scale the Plans

Step 18. Click the **PAPER** toggle to go to **MODEL**, click inside each viewport to select it, and center **CH3-EXERCISE1** in the bottom viewport and **CH3-EXERCISE2** in the top viewport. Return to **PAPER**.

Figure 5-16
Copy the viewport

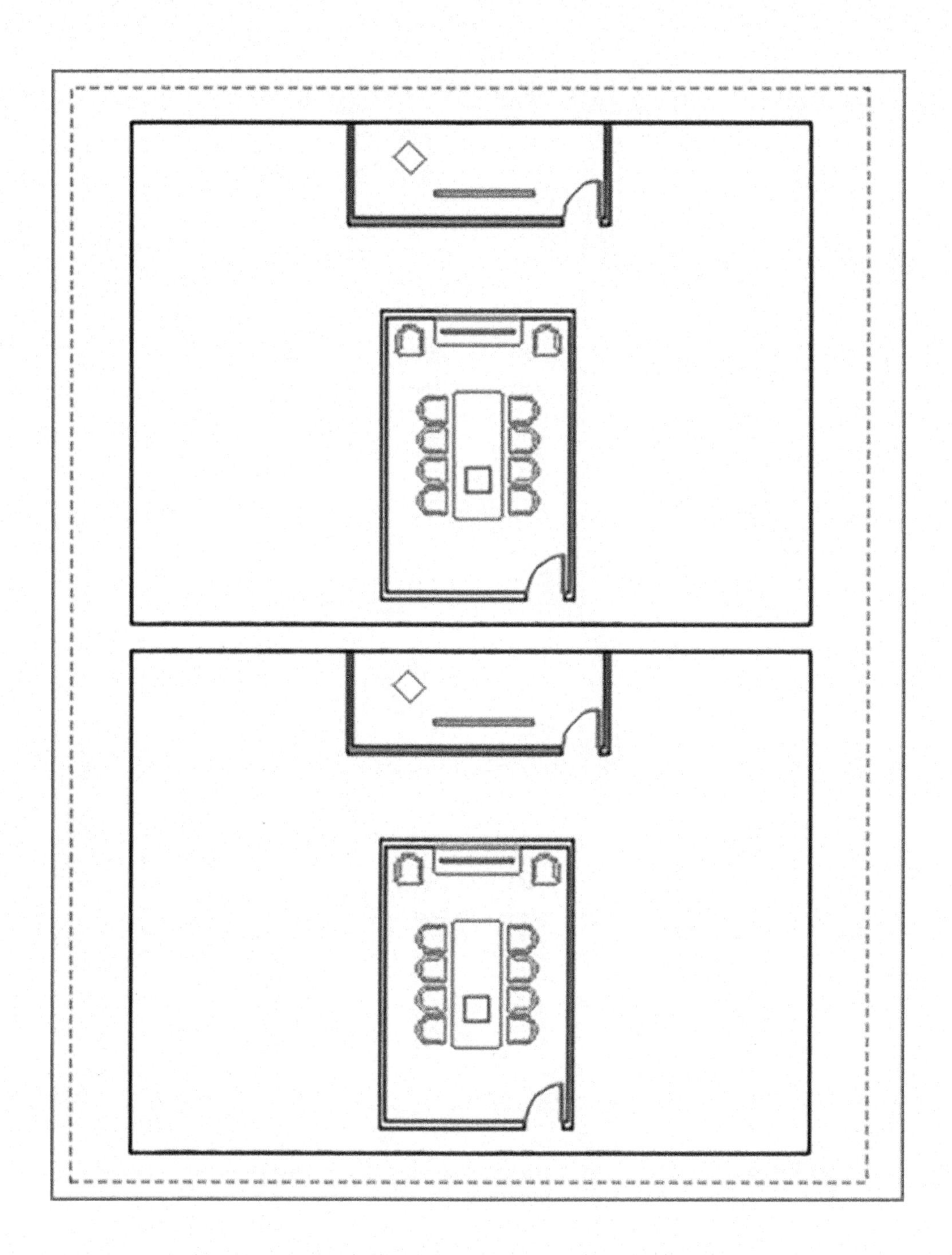

Step 19. While in **PAPER**, click the green viewport boundary line of the bottom viewport to select it and use **Properties** to set the scale of **CH3-EXERCISE1** to **3/16″ = 1′-0″**. While in **PAPER,** you can change the size of the viewport boundary. While in **MODEL,** you can move the drawing to center it. When the drawing is centered and scaled, be sure to lock the display (Figure 5-17).

> **TIP**
>
> You can lock and unlock viewports with the padlock icon on the status bar. And you can set viewport scale on the status bar by selecting the **Scale of the selected viewport** button. You can also set the viewport scale by clicking the down arrow beside the grip at the center of the viewport to open the viewport scale list.

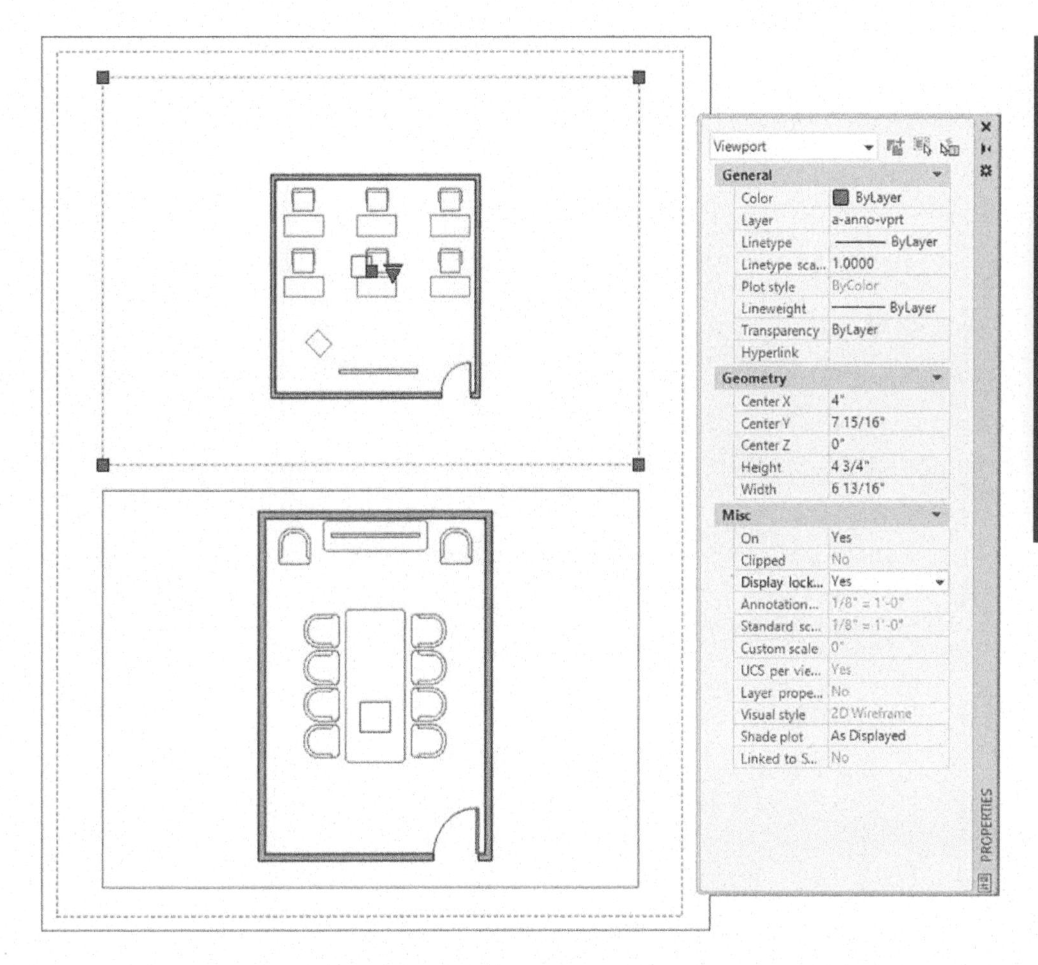

Figure 5-17
Set the scale of the bottom viewport to 3/16″ = 1′-0″. Set the scale of the top viewport to 1/8″ = 1′-0″. Lock the display of both viewports.

Step 20. Set the scale of **CH3-EXERCISE2** in the top viewport to **1/8″ = 1′-0″** (Figure 5-17) and lock the display.

Step 21. Turn the **a-anno-vprt** layer off (the outline of the viewports, shown in green) so they will not print.

> **TIP**
>
> If you accidentally use a **ZOOM** command while in **MODEL** space and change the scale of an unlocked display, turn the **Viewport** layer on. Click on the viewport boundary line and then click the viewport scale in the status bar (or the dropdown arrow in the middle of the viewport), input the scale, and lock the display. Zooming while you are in **PAPER** space will not change the scale of the drawing.

Complete the Layout

Step 22. While in **PAPER**, use a text style with the Arial font; set layer **a-anno-text** current; and add your name, your class, and the date in all capitals, 3/16″ high, to the paper (Figure 5-18).

Step 23. Type the scale of each viewport 1/8″ high and complete as shown in Figure 5-18.

Step 24. While in **PAPER**, change **LTSCALE** as needed to show the **HIDDEN** linetype.

NAME
CLASS
DATE

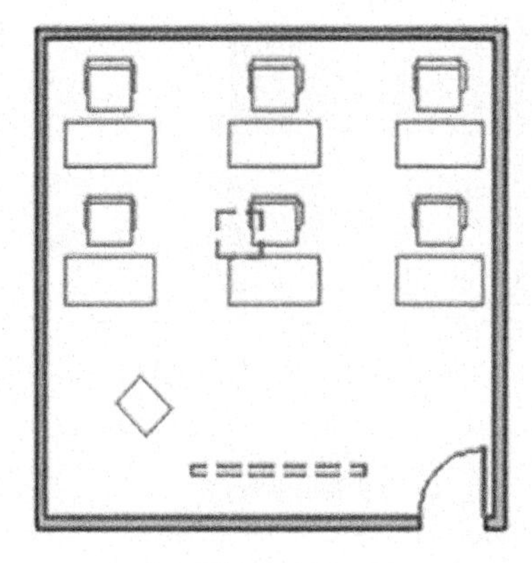

SCALE: 1/8"= 1'-0"

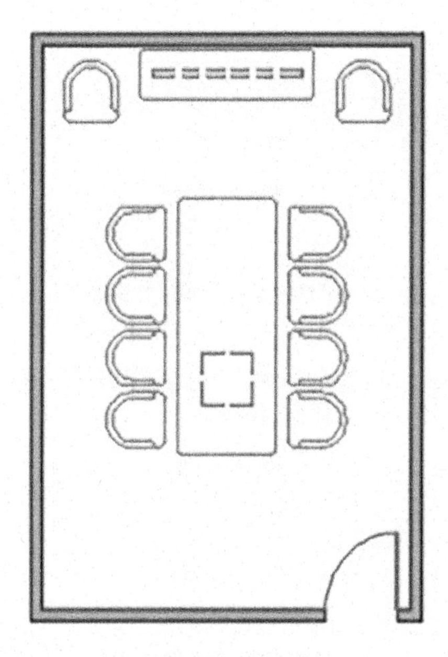

SCALE: 3/16"= 1'-0"

Figure 5-18
CH5-EXERCISE3 complete

Step 25. Rename **Layout1** to **Furniture Plan** for the new layout name.

Step 26. Plot **CH5-EXERCISE3** at a scale of **1:1**. The viewport scales are already set.

Step 27. Save the drawing in two places.

EXERCISE 5-4
Plot a Layout with Four Viewports

The following is a step-by-step exercise to make a hard copy of CH3-EXERCISE1, CH3-EXERCISE2, CH3-EXERCISE3, and CH3-EXERCISE4 on one sheet of letter-size paper. When you have completed Exercise 5-4, your print will look similar to Figure 5-19.

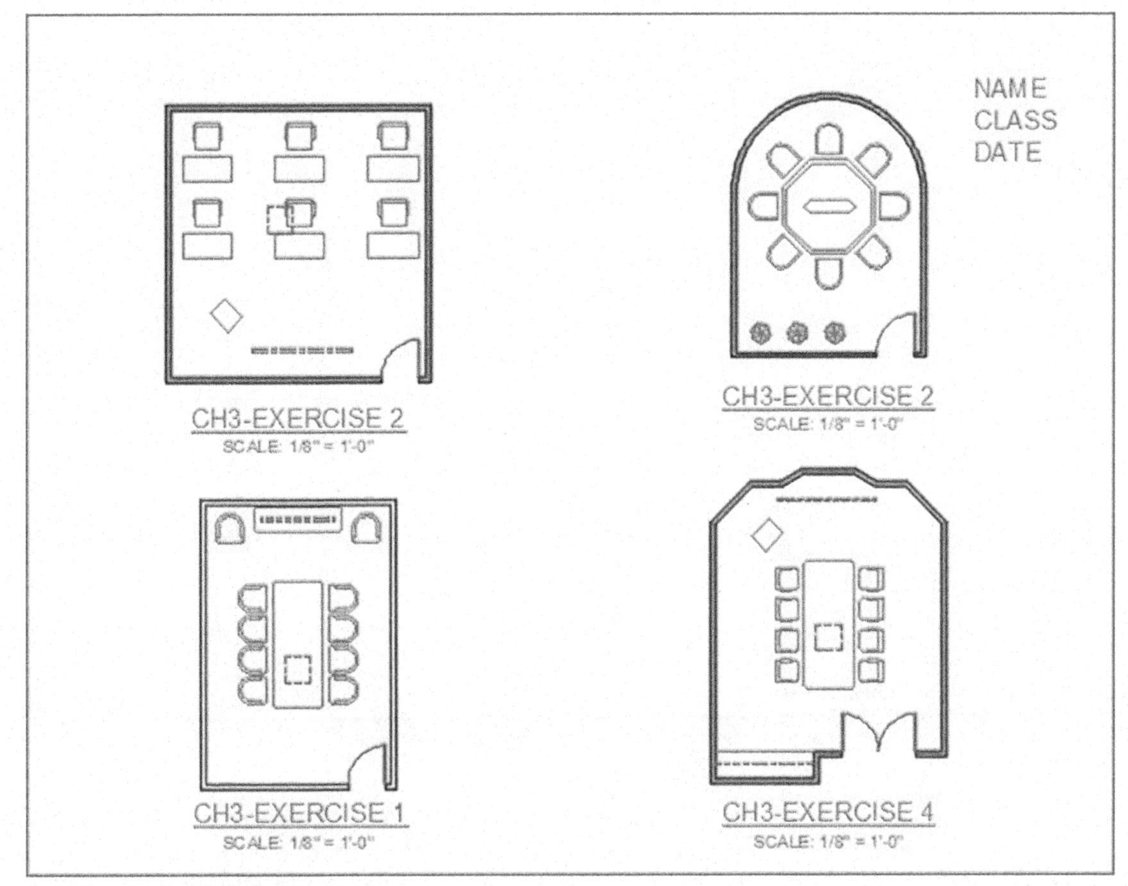

Figure 5-19
CH5-EXERCISE4 complete

Step 1. Open drawing **CH3-EXERCISE1** so it is displayed on the screen and save it as **CH5-EXERCISE4.**

Step 2. Insert **CH3-EXERCISE2**, **CH3-EXERCISE3**, and **CH3-EXERCISE4** into the current drawing.

Step 3. Arrange the four drawings as shown in Figure 5-20.

Step 4. **Explode** each of the inserted drawings.

Step 5. Erase the name, class, and date from all drawings.

Step 6. Make sure the **Model** tab is current. Turn the grid off.

Step 7. Use **Zoom-Extents** to view the extents of the drawing.

Figure 5-20
Arrange the drawings

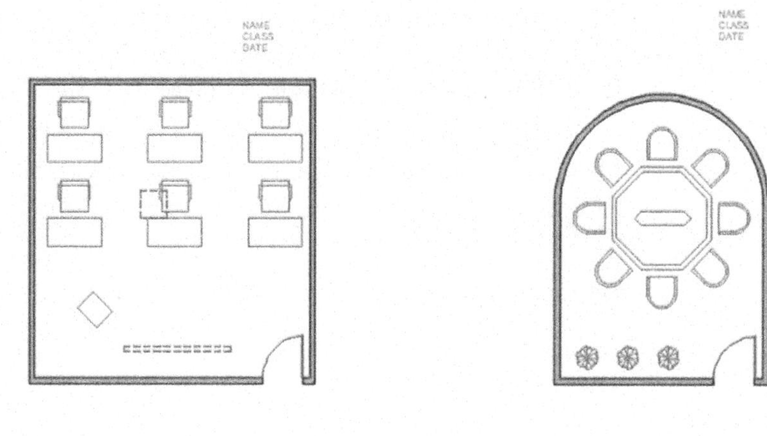

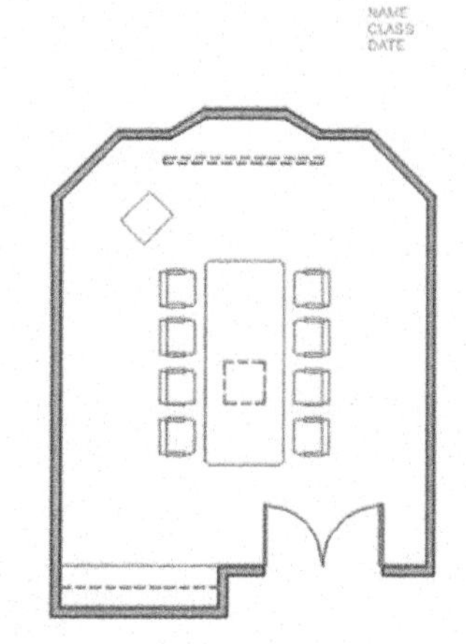

VIEWPORT	
Ribbon/ Panel	View/Model Viewports/ Viewports Configuration
Viewports Toolbar:	
Menu Bar:	View/View-ports/Named Viewports
Type a Command:	VPORTS

Viewports (VPORTS)

MODEL space is where you create your 2D or 3D model (drawing). While in **MODEL** space, you can use the **Viewports** command to divide the display screen into multiple viewports as shown in Figure 5-21. **MODEL** space is limited in that although several viewports may be visible on the display screen, only one viewport can be plotted.

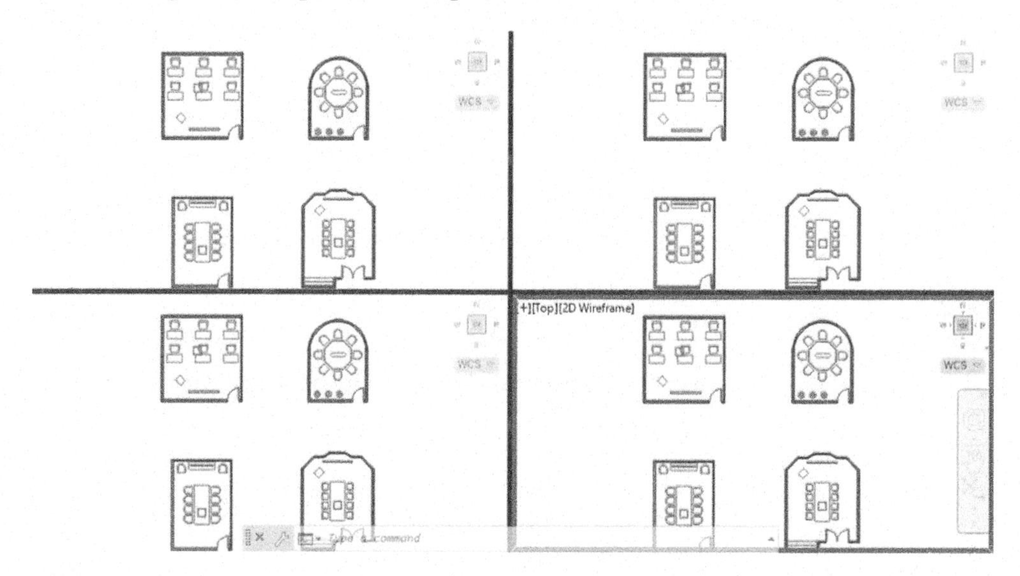

Figure 5-21
The screen is divided into four equal viewports

When you click any of the **layout** tabs, your drawing is in **PAPER** space. **PAPER** space shows a piece of paper on which you can arrange a single drawing (viewport) or as many drawings or views (viewports) as you need. In **PAPER** space you can also plot as many viewports as you need.

Step 8. Divide the screen into four viewports as described next:

Prompt	**Response**
Type a command:	Type **VPORTS <Enter>**
The **Viewports** dialog box appears	Click **Four: Equal** on the **New Viewports** tab and name the viewport configuration **VP4** as shown in the **New name:** text box in Figure 5-22 Click **OK** (the screen divides into four viewports, Figure 5-21)

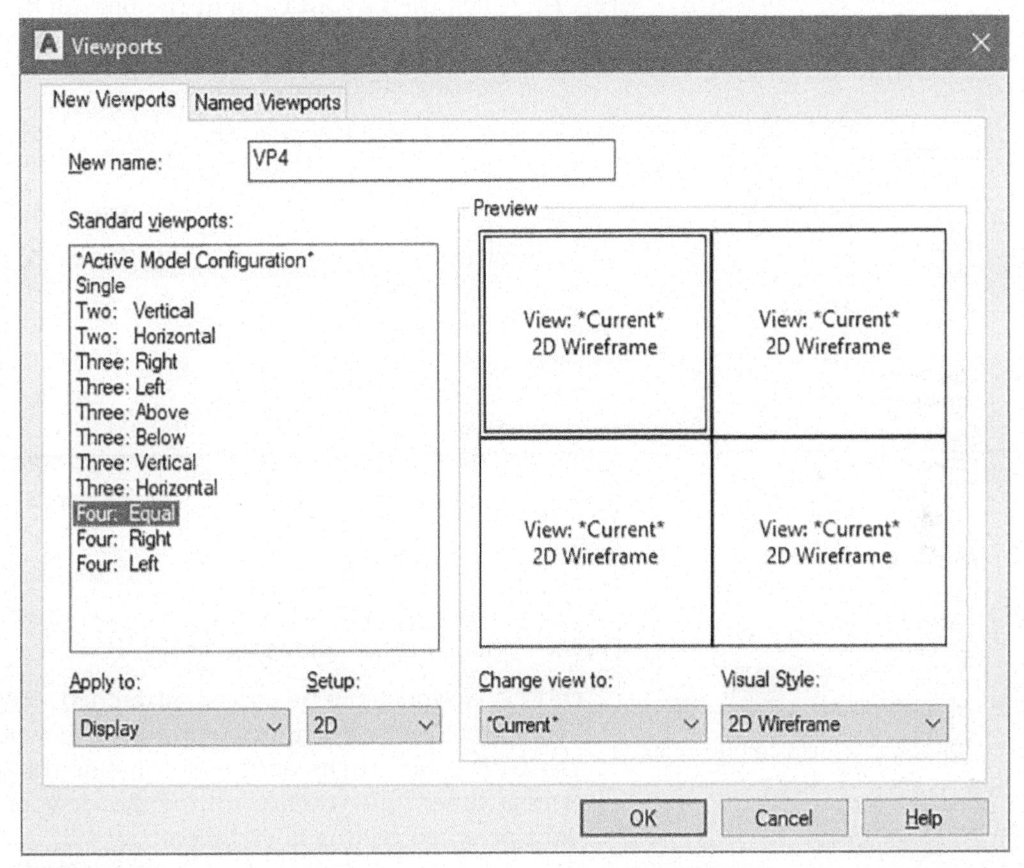

Figure 5-22
Divide the screen into four equal viewports and name the viewport configuration, **VP4**

The active viewport, outlined with a solid line, displays the lines of the cursor when you move the cursor into it. Inactive viewports display an arrow when the cursor is moved into those areas. To make a different viewport active, position the arrow in the desired viewport and click.

The **Viewports** dialog box allows you to name, save, preview, and recall any number of configurations of viewports and change the configuration of the current viewport.

While in **MODEL** space, the model (drawing) is the same in each viewport. If you edit the model in any one viewport, you are doing it in all viewports. You may, however, display a different UCS in each viewport and zoom in or out in a viewport without affecting other viewport magnifications.

Use MVIEW to Restore the Viewport VP4 into Layout1

Step 9. Create the following new layer and set it as the current layer:

Layer name	Color	Linetype	Lineweight
a-anno-vprt	green	continuous	.006″ (.15 mm)

Step 10. Click the **Layout1** tab at the bottom of the drawing.

Step 11. Click on the current green viewport boundary line and erase the existing single viewport.

MVIEW	
Ribbon/ Panel	Home/ Layout tab (paper space only)
Type a Command:	MVIEW
Command Alias:	MV

Step 12. Use the **MVIEW** command to restore the saved model space viewport VP4 into Layout1 as described next:

Prompt	Response
Type a command:	Type **MVIEW <Enter>**
Specify corner of viewport or [ON OFF Fit Shadeplot Lock NEw NAmed Object Polygonal Restore LAyer 2 3 4] <Fit>:	Type **R <Enter>**
Enter viewport configuration name or [?] <*Active>:	Type **VP4 <Enter>**
Specify first corner or [Fit] <Fit>:	**<Enter>** (to accept **Fit** and the viewport configuration VP4 fills the page; Figure 5-23)

You use the **MVIEW** command in a Layout with **PAPER** current. The **MVIEW** options are as follows:

OFF: A viewport can be copied, stretched, erased, moved, or scaled. You cannot edit the drawing within the viewport while in **PAPER** space. The **OFF** option turns off the view inside the viewport and saves regeneration time while you are editing the viewports. You can turn the views back on when editing is complete.

ON: Turns on the **MODEL** space view (drawing inside the viewport).

Shadeplot: Allows you to choose from among five options: **As displayed**, **Wireframe**, **Hidden**, **Visual styles**, and **Rendered**. These are options used in 3D.

Lock: Allows you to lock the scale of a viewport so it does not change when you zoom in or out.

Object: Allows you to create a new viewport by selecting an existing object such as a circle.

Figure 5-23
The viewport configuration fills the page

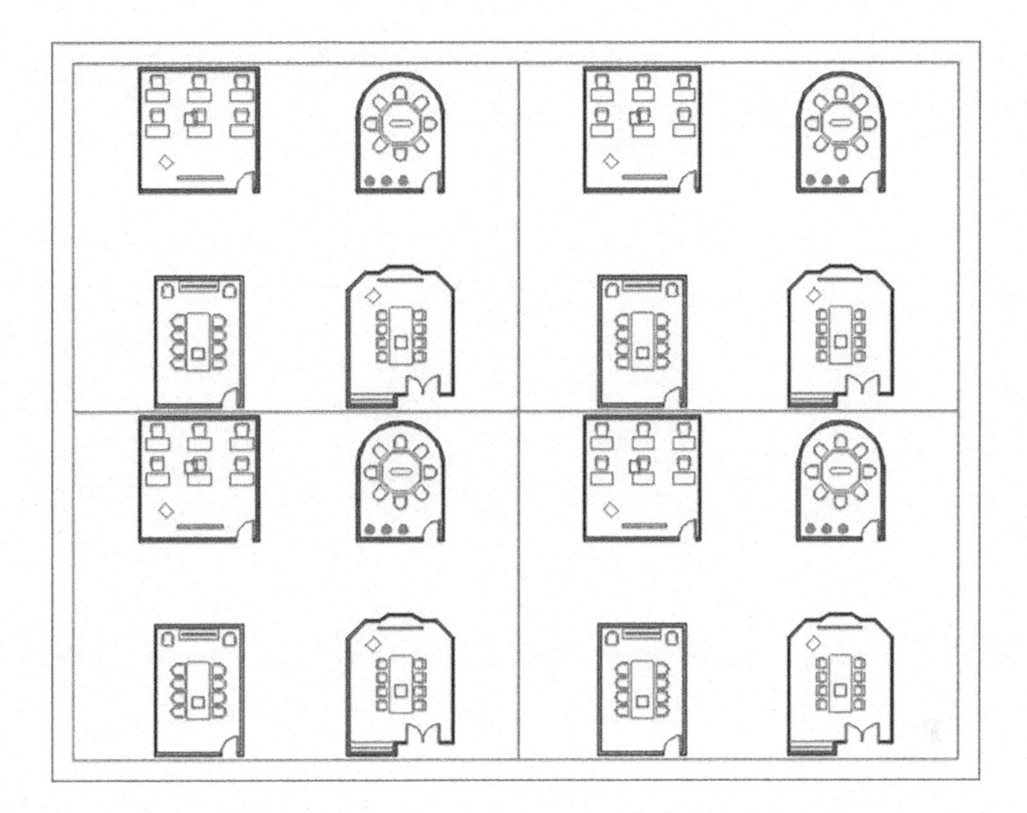

Polygonal: Allows you to draw an irregular-shaped viewport using polyline lines and arcs.

Fit: Creates a single viewport to fill current paper space limits. You can erase other viewports before or after you use the **Fit** option.

Layer: Allows you to remove viewport property overrides.

2,3,4: Creates two, three, or four viewports in a specified area or to fit the current paper space limits.

Restore: Restores saved model space viewports (saved with the **VIEWPORTS** command) into **PAPER** space.

Specify Corner of Viewport: Creates a new viewport defined by picking two corners or by typing the X and Y coordinates of the lower-left and upper-right corners.

Page Setup Manager

Step 13. Right-click the **Layout1** tab and click **Page Setup Manager....** The **Page Setup Manager** appears.

Step 14. Click **Modify....** The **Page Setup** dialog box for Layout1 appears.

Step 15. Select the printer you will use for a letter-size paper.

Step 16. Set the **Plot style table** to **Your Name Color to Black**.

Step 17. Make the settings shown in Figure 5-24 in the **Page Setup** dialog box.

Step 18. Make sure the **Landscape** drawing orientation is selected and the **Plot scale** is **1:1** (Figure 5-24).

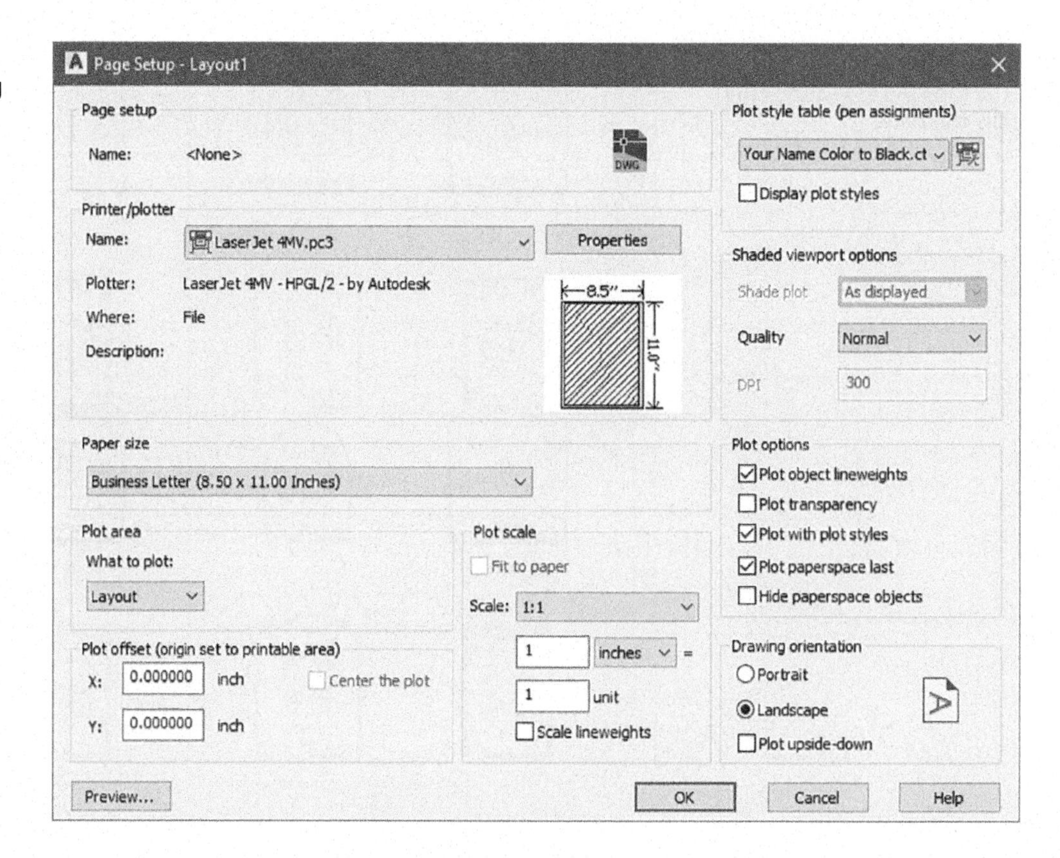

Figure 5-24
Page Setup - Layout1 dialog box

Step 19. Click **OK**. The **Page Setup Manager** appears.

Step 20. Click **Close**.

Center and Scale the Plans

Step 21. Click the **PAPER** toggle to go to **MODEL** and click inside each viewport to select it. Center **CH3-EXERCISE1** in the bottom-left viewport, **CH3-EXERCISE2** in the top-left viewport, **CH3-EXERCISE3** in the top-right viewport, and **CH3-EXERCISE4** in the bottom-right viewport, as shown in Figure 5-25. Return to **PAPER**.

Step 22. While in **PAPER**, click the green viewport boundary line of all the viewports to select them and set the scale of all viewports to **1/8″ = 1′-0″** (Figure 5-25). While in **MODEL**, you can move the drawing to center it. When the drawing is centered and scaled, be sure to lock the display.

Step 23. Turn the **a-anno-vprt** layer off (the outline of the viewports, shown in green) so they will not print.

Complete the Layout

Step 24. While in **PAPER**, use a text style with the Arial font; set layer **a-anno-text** current; and add your name, your class, and the date in all capitals, 3/16″ high, to the paper (Figure 5-25).

Step 25. Type the name of each viewport 3/16″ high, type the scale of each viewport 1/8″ high, and complete as shown in Figure 5-25.

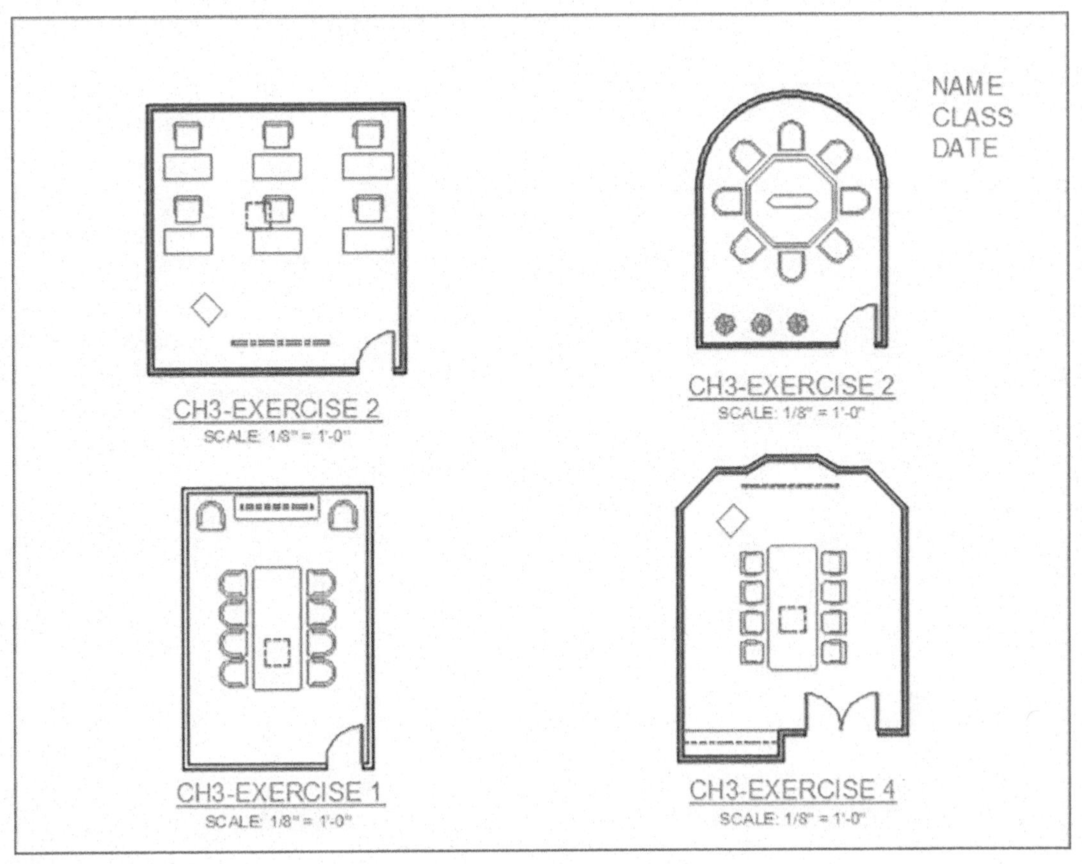

Figure 5-25
CH5-EXERCISE4 complete

Step 26. While in **PAPER**, change **LTSCALE** as needed to show the **HIDDEN** linetype.

Step 27. Plot **CH5-EXERCISE4** at a scale of **1:1**. The viewport scales are already set.

Step 28. Save the drawing in two places.

FOR MORE DETAILS

See Chapter 12 for information about freezing and thawing layers within different viewports.

EXERCISE 5-5
Make PDF Files That Can Be Attached to E-mails and Opened without the AutoCAD Program

PDF (portable document format) files: Files of drawings that are made using the **Plot** dialog box. These files can be opened and read without the use of the AutoCAD program.

Sending files to clients who do not have the AutoCAD program is often necessary. ***PDF (portable document format) files*** can be used to show drawings without sending .dwg files. The following exercise shows you how to do that.

Step 1. Open drawing **CH5-EXERCISE3** and select the **Layout1** tab so it appears on the screen.

Step 2. Make a PDF file from the **CH5-EXERCISE3** drawing, as described next:

Prompt	**Response**
Type a command:	Click **PLOT**
The **Plot - Layout1** dialog box appears:	In the **Printer/plotter Name:** box, click **DWG To PDF.pc3** as shown in Figure 5-26 Check other parts of the **Plot** dialog box to be sure all settings are as shown in Figure 5-26 Click **OK**
The **Browse for Plot File** box appears:	Locate the folder and drive where you want to save the file and change the name to **CH5-EXERCISE5** as shown in Figure 5-27 Click **Save**
The PDF image appears:	If the image is complete, close the program. If not, redo the plot, making any necessary changes such as plotting extents on a larger sheet of paper.

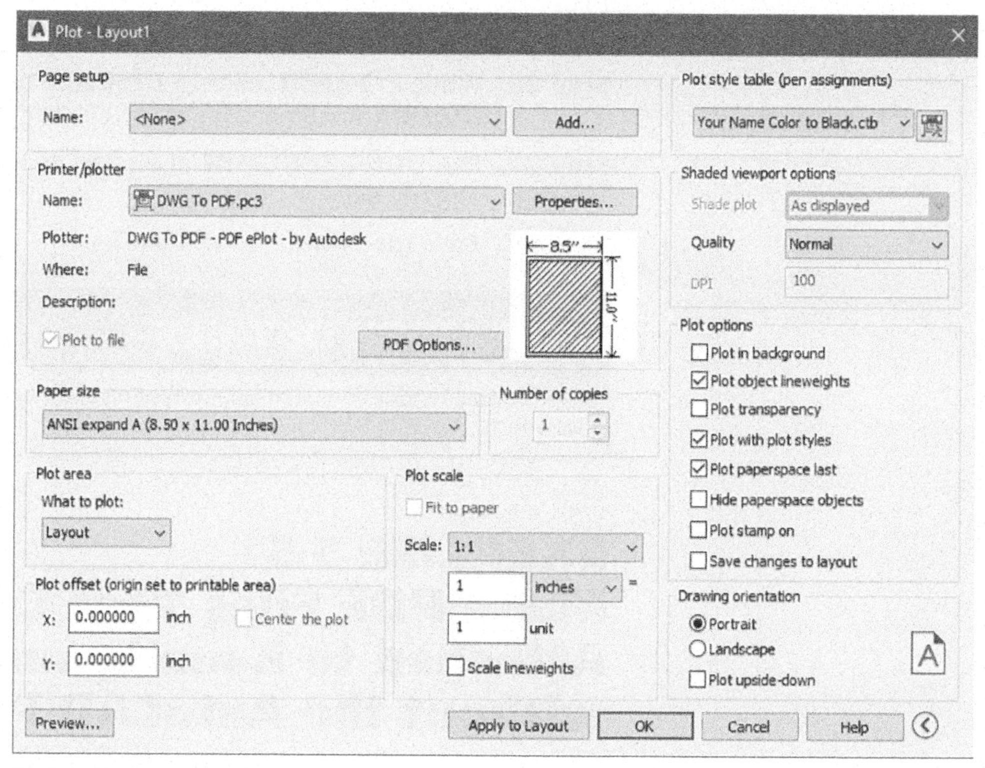

Figure 5-26
Plot - Layout1 dialog box

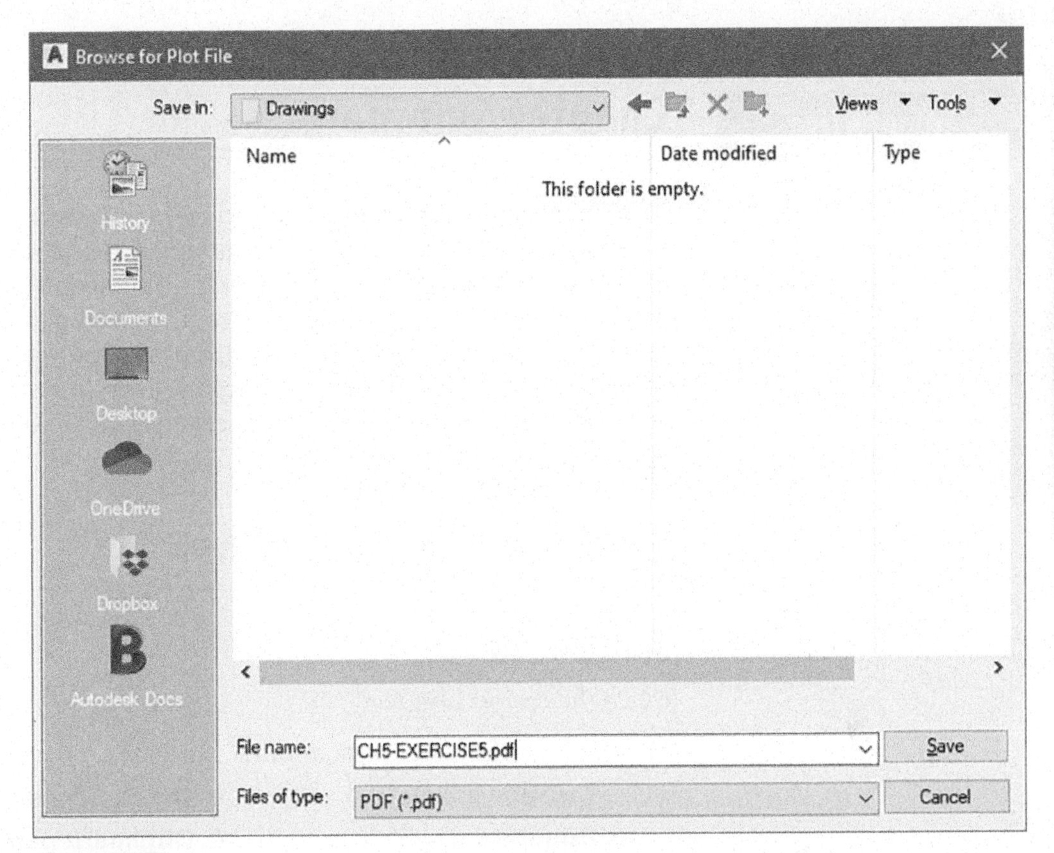

Figure 5-27
Locate the folder to save the PDF file and change the name to **CH5-EXERCISE5**

That's it. You now have a PDF file of your drawing that you can send to anyone, and others can view it whether or not they have AutoCAD.

Chapter Summary

This chapter provided you the information necessary to make a color-dependent plot style, make different layout tabs for your drawings, print or plot drawings with multiple viewports from layout tabs, and print and plot drawings. In addition, you learned to print and plot drawings at various scales on the same sheet and to print drawings to a PDF file. Now you have the skills and information necessary to print and plot drawings in a variety of ways on any of the standard paper sheet sizes or to a PDF file that can be viewed without AutoCAD.

Chapter Test Questions

Multiple Choice

Circle the correct answer.

1. Which of the following contains the **Plot...** command?
   a. **Utilities** panel
   b. **Annotate** panel
   c. **Quick Access** toolbar
   d. **Clipboard** panel
2. Properties that can be set in a plot style table are:
   a. Color
   b. Linetype
   c. Lineweight
   d. All the above
3. When a viewport is restored into a layout (**PAPER** space), what color is the viewport boundary line?
   a. The color of the furniture layer
   b. The color of the current layer
   c. The color of the text layer
   d. None of the above
4. Which tab in the **Viewports** dialog box must be current for you to name the new viewport?
   a. **New Viewports**
   b. **New Name Viewports**
   c. **Standard Viewports**
   d. **Named Viewports**
5. Which of the following is **not** an option for the **MVIEW** command?
   a. **Polygonal**
   b. **OFF**
   c. **Select**
   d. **Layer**
6. Which of the following is a configuration option in the **Viewports** dialog box?
   a. **Two: Vertical**
   b. **Four: Below**
   c. **Five: Horizontal**
   d. **Two: Above**
7. Which of the following **MVIEW** options allows you to draw an irregular-shaped viewport?
   a. **Layer**
   b. **Circle**
   c. **Fit**
   d. **Polygonal**

8. When you click a viewport boundary in **PAPER** space, what command allows you to set the scale of the viewport?

a. **Scale**
b. **Properties**
c. **Viewport**
d. **Insert**

9. When you are using the **Plot...** command to plot a layout tab that has a single viewport that is already scaled to 1/2″ = 1′-0″, in the **Plot** dialog box, use a **Plot scale** of:

a. **1:1**
b. **1:2**
c. **1:48**
d. **Fit to paper**

10. Which of the following is **not** one of the three tabs at the bottom of the drawing window (when **Model** and **Layout** tabs are displayed)?

a. **Model**
b. **Layout1**
c. **Layout2**
d. **Model2**

Matching

Write the number of the correct answer on the line.

a. Plot style ______
b. Layout tab ______
c. PDF files ______
d. Drawing orientation ______
e. Viewports ______

1. An area in **PAPER** space containing views of a drawing
2. Color-dependent
3. Used to view **PAPER** space
4. A drawing that can be viewed without AutoCAD
5. Landscape

True or False

Circle the correct answer.

1. **True or False:** Named and color-dependent are the two different types of plot styles.
2. **True or False:** You can reshape, resize, move, erase, and copy a viewport.
3. **True or False:** While working on a layout tab, you can only work in **PAPER** space.
4. **True or False:** You can make a color-dependent plot style to allow you to plot with the lineweights that are assigned to the layers in the drawing.
5. **True or False:** You can make a color-dependent plot style to allow you to plot all colors in the drawing as black.

List

1. Five ways of accessing **Page Setup Manager** in paper space.
2. Five options from the **Page Setup** window after you select **Modify** from **Page Setup Manager**.
3. Five ways of accessing the **Plot/print** command.
4. Five ways of inserting an entire drawing into the current drawing.

5. Five standard drawing sheet sizes based on the U.S. customary system.
6. Five operations that can be performed on a **PAPER** space viewport.
7. Five options from the **Plot Style Table Editor**.
8. Five MODEL **space** viewport configurations.
9. Five shortcuts for space switching (**MODEL/PAPER**) and the related system parameters.
10. Five options from the **Viewports** dialog box in **MODEL** space.

Questions

1. How does a named plot style differ from a color-dependent plot style?
2. In Exercise 5-4, with four drawings, why is the layout plotted at a scale of 1:1?
3. Why would you want to have a drawing with multiple viewports?
4. Why would you want to plot drawings at different scales on the same sheet?
5. What are PDF files used for and how can they be done quickly and efficiently?

Chapter Projects

Project 5-1: *Make a PDF File (Using Project 3-1)* [BASIC]

1. Open Project 3-1.
2. Use the procedure described in Exercise 5-5 to make a PDF file of Project 3-1.

Project 5-2: *Plot a Single Viewport to Scale and a Color-Dependent Plot Style (Using Project 3-2)* [INTERMEDIATE]

1. Open Project 3-2.
2. Use the procedure described in Exercise 5-2 (with one viewport) to plot Project 3-2.

Project 5-3: *Plot Two Viewports at Two Different Scales and a Color-Dependent Plot Style (Using Projects 3-1 and 3-2)* [ADVANCED]

1. Open Project 3-1 and insert Project 3-2.
2. Use the procedure described in Exercise 5-3 (with two viewports) to plot Projects 3-1 and 3-2.

6

chaptersix

Drawing the Floor Plan: Walls, Doors, and Windows

CHAPTER OBJECTIVES

- Correctly use the following commands and settings:

Annotative Text
AutoCAD Design Center
BLOCK
COLOR
Edit Multiline
EXTEND
HATCH
INSERT
Linetype
Lineweight
LIST
Make Object's Layer Current
Match Properties
Multiline
Multiline Style
OSNAP
PROPERTIES
RECTANGLE
RECTANGULAR ARRAY
WBLOCK

The Tenant Space Project

Exercise 6-1 contains step-by-step instructions for using **Multiline** (a command that allows up to 16 lines to be drawn at a time) to draw the exterior and interior walls of a tenant space. The exercise also contains step-by-step instructions for inserting windows and doors into the plan.

Chapters 7, 8, 9, and 11 provide step-by-step instructions to complete the tenant space project started in this chapter. Each chapter will use the building plan drawn in this chapter to complete a part of the project as described next.

Chapter 7: You will dimension the tenant space and calculate the square footage.

Chapter 8: You will draw elevations, sections, and details.

Chapter 9: You will draw furniture, assign attributes (furniture specifications), and add the furniture to the plan.

Chapter 11: You will draw the reflected ceiling plan and voice/data/power plan.

EXERCISE 6-1
Tenant Space Floor Plan

When you have completed Exercise 6-1, the tenant space floor plan, your drawing will look similar to Figure 6-1.

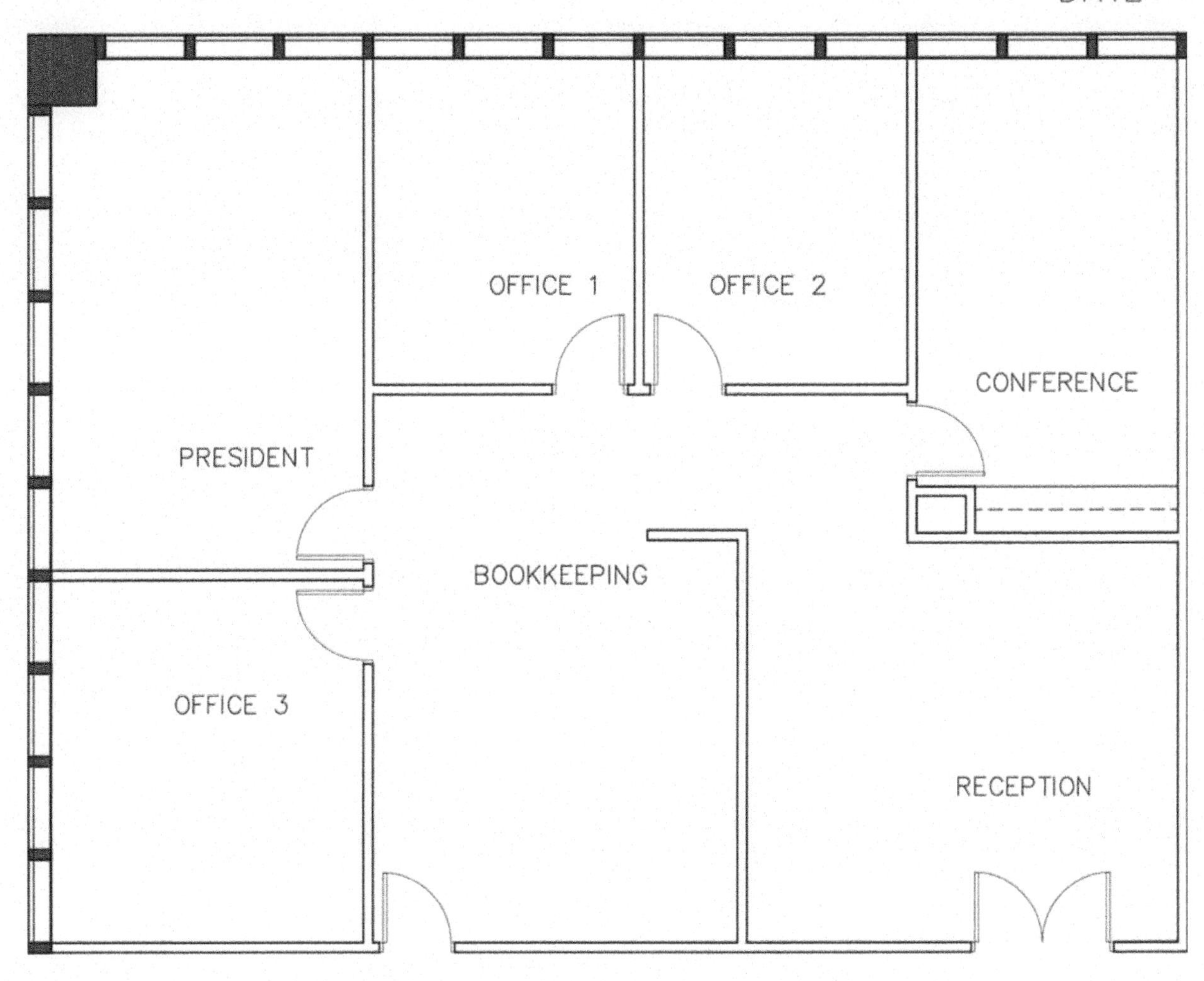

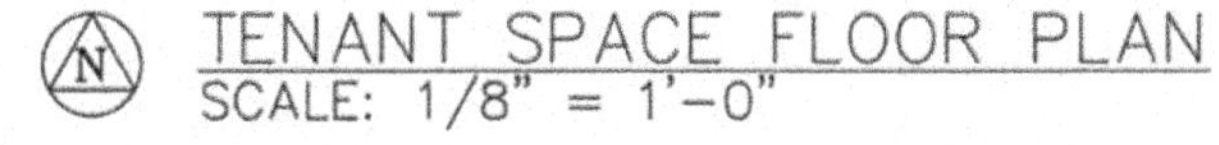

Figure 6-1
Exercise 6-1: Tenant space floor plan (scale: 1/8″ = 1′-0″)

Step 1. Use your workspace to make the following settings:

1. Use **Save As...** to save the drawing with the name **CH6-EXERCISE1**
2. Set drawing units: **Architectural**
3. Set precision: **1/32″**
4. Set drawing limits: **75′,65′**
5. Set **GRIDDISPLAY**: **0**
6. Set grid: **12″**

7. Set snap: **6″**
8. Create the following layers. Be sure to type and enter a comma after each layer name. The cursor will move to the next line so you can type the next layer name:

Layer name	Color	Linetype	Lineweight
a-anno-text	green	continuous	.006″ (.15 mm)
a-door	red	continuous	.004″ (.09 mm)
a-wall-intr	blue	continuous	.010″ (.25 mm)
a-flor-case	green	continuous	.006″ (.15 mm)
a-flor-case-uppr	green	hidden	.006″ (.15 mm)
a-glaz	green	continuous	.006″ (.15 mm)
a-wall-extr	white	continuous	.016″ (.40 mm)
a-wall-intr	blue	continuous	.010″ (.25 mm)
a-wall-patt-blck	red	continuous	.004″ (.09 mm)

9. Set layer **a-wall-extr** current.
10. Use **Zoom-All** to view the limits of the drawing.

NOTE

If you cannot see the entire name of the layer, right-click on one of the titles such as **Name, Color,** or **Linetype** to open a right-click menu. Click **Maximize all columns** in the right-click menu to be able to see the entire layer name you have typed.

RECTANGLE

RECTANGLE	
Ribbon/ Panel	Home/Draw
Draw Toolbar:	
Menu Bar:	Draw/ Rectangle
Type a Command:	RECTANG
Command Alias:	REC

The following part of Exercise 6-1 uses the **RECTANGLE** and **HATCH** commands to draw the window mullions and the 3′-square corner column located in the northwest corner of the tenant space.

Step 2. Use the **RECTANGLE** command to draw the 3′-square corner column (Figure 6-2), as described next:

Prompt	**Response**
Type a command:	**RECTANG** (or type **REC <Enter>**)
Specify first corner point or [Chamfer Elevation Fillet Thickness Width]:	Type **17′,51′ <Enter>**
Specify other corner point or [Area Dimensions Rotation]:	Type **@3′,-3′ <Enter>** (be sure to include the minus)

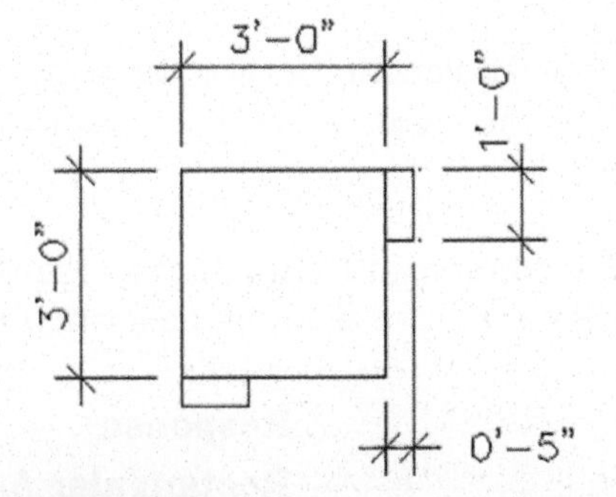

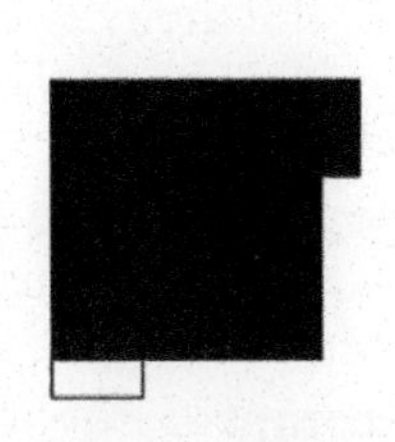

Figure 6-2
Use the **RECTANGLE** and **HATCH** commands to draw the corner column and two mullions

Step 3. Zoom in close around the column and use the **RECTANGLE** command to draw the two separate mullions (5″ × 12″) that are on the east and south sides of the column just drawn, as shown in Figure 6-2. Use snap and relative coordinates (click the top-right corner for the first point, then **@5,-12** for the other corner points) to draw the mullion much like you just drew the corner column. Remember, with relative coordinates, enter the x-axis value first, then a comma, then the y-axis value.

Step 4. Set layer **a-wall-patt-blck** current.

HATCH

Step 5. Use the **HATCH** command to make the corner column solid (Figure 6-2), as described next:

Prompt	Response
Type a command:	**HATCH** (or type **H <Enter>**)
Pick internal point or [Select objects seTtings]:	Type **T <Enter>**
The **Hatch and Gradient** dialog box appears:	Select **SOLID** at the top of the **Pattern** list and click **Add: Pick points**
Pick internal point or [Select objects seTtings]:	Click any point inside the square
Pick internal point or [Select objects seTtings]:	**<Enter>**
The area is hatched.	

Step 6. Use the **HATCH** command to make the mullions solid. Hatch one mullion, and then exit the **HATCH** command before hatching the second mullion so you can array them separately.

ARRAY

The **Rectangular** option of **ARRAY** allows you to make copies of an object in a rectangular pattern. The array is made up of horizontal rows and vertical columns.

You specify the direction and spacing of rows and columns:

When you specify a positive number for the distance between rows, the array is drawn up. When you specify a negative number, the array is drawn down.

When you specify a positive number for the distance between columns, the array is drawn to the right. When you specify a negative number, the array is drawn to the left.

Step 7. Use the **ARRAY** command to finish drawing the mullions on the north exterior wall (Figure 6-3), as described next:

Prompt	Response
Type a command:	**Rectangular Array** (or type **ARRAYRECT<Enter>**)

Prompt	Response
Select objects:	Click a crossing window to select the mullion rectangle and hatch pattern on the east side of the column **<Enter>**
Type = Rectangular; Associative = Yes Select grip to edit array or [Associative Base point COUnt Spacing COLumns Rows Levels eXit]<eXit>:	Type **S <Enter>**
Specify the distance between columns or [Unit cell] <7 1/2″>:	Type **4′ <Enter>**
Specify the distance between rows <1′-6″>:	Type **1 <Enter>**

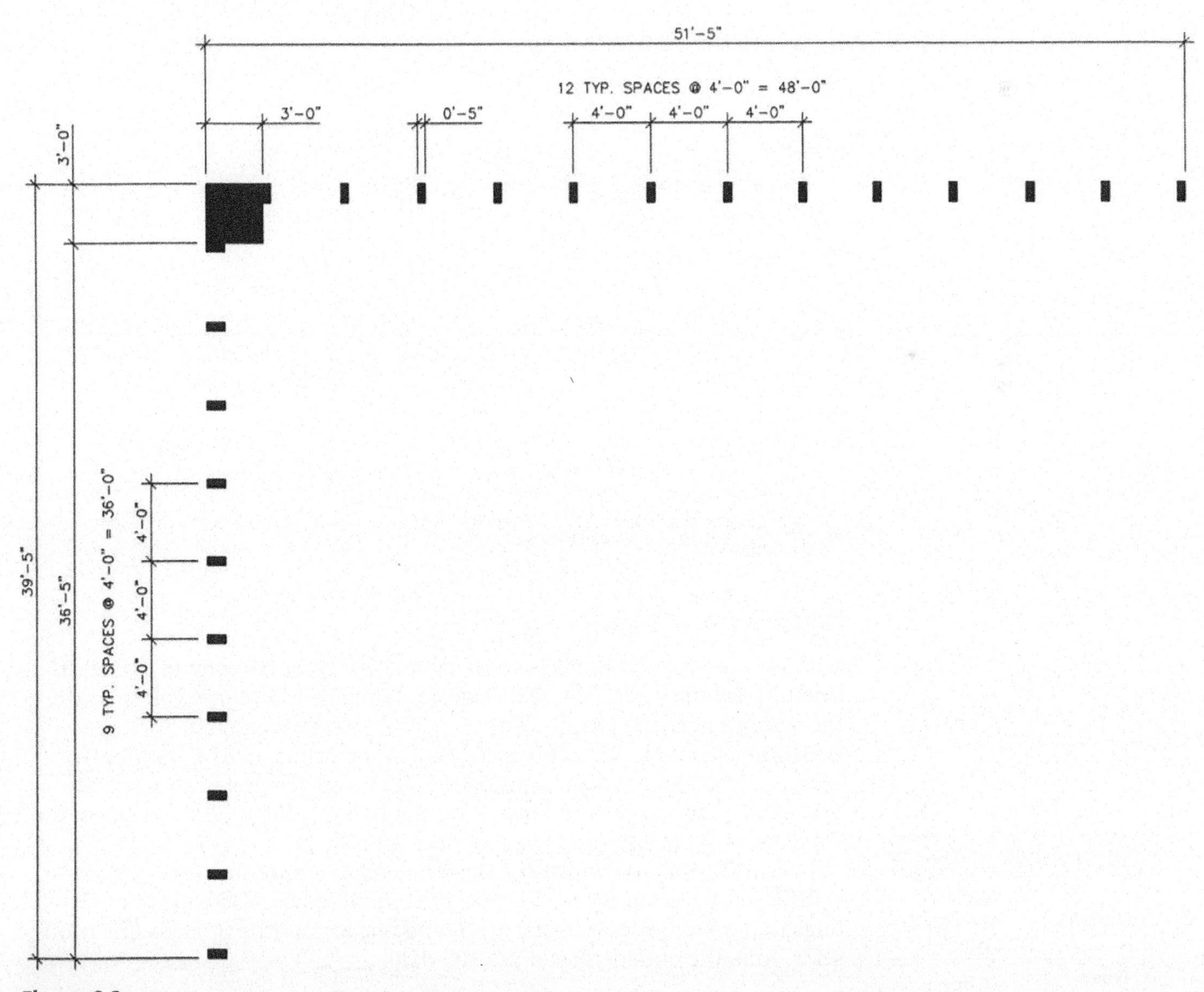

Figure 6-3
Use the **ARRAY** command to finish drawing the mullions

Prompt	Response
Select grip to edit array or [Associative Base point COUnt Spacing COLumns Rows Levels eXit]<eXit>:	Type **COU <Enter>**
Enter the number of columns or [Expression] <4>:	Type **13 <Enter>**
Enter the number of rows or [Expression] <3>:	Type **1 <Enter>**
Select grip to edit array or [Associative Base point COUnt Spacing COLumns Rows Levels eXit]<eXit>:	**<Enter>**

Step 8. Use the **ARRAY** command to draw the remaining mullions on the west exterior wall, as shown in Figure 6-3. Specify **1** for the distance between columns, **-4′** for the distance between rows, **1** for the number of columns, and **10** for the number of rows.

> **NOTE**
>
> When you start **ARRAYRECT**, AutoCAD defaults to showing you a default array of three rows and four columns. You must change the number of rows and columns and the distance between them for the array to complete.

Step 9. Draw the walls using **Multiline**. It is helpful if the column and mullions are not solid. Set **FILL** off (or **FILLMODE** to **0**) and regenerate the drawing (type in **REGEN** and **<Enter>**) so that the columns and mullions are not solid.

Step 10. Zoom to extents and use the **Distance** command (type **DI <Enter>**) with **OSNAP** to verify that all your measurements are correct.

Step 11. Set layer **a-wall-extr** current.

Multiline Style

With the column and mullions now completed, you are ready to use **Multiline** to draw the walls. The **Multiline Style** dialog box allows you to make the settings necessary to draw up to 16 lines at the same time with the **Multiline** command. You can specify color and linetype for any of the 16 lines and end caps for each multiline. You can specify the walls as solid (background fill) or not. You must add the name of the multiline style to the list of current styles before you can draw with it.

MULTILINE STYLE	
Menu Bar:	Format/ Multiline Style...
Type a Command:	MLSTYLE

Next, you will use **Multiline Style** to create a multiline style named THREE for the north exterior wall of the tenant space. You will make settings to have one line at 0, one at 9″, and one at 12″ (the 3″ glass line is offset 3″ from the outside line of the 12″ wall).

Step 12. Use **Multiline Style...** to make the settings for a new style named THREE (Figures 6-4 and 6-5), as described next:

Prompt	**Response**
Type a command:	**Multiline Style...** (or type **MLSTYLE <Enter>**)
The **Multiline Style** dialog box appears with **Standard** highlighted:	Click **New...**
The **Create New Multiline Style** dialog box appears:	Type **THREE** in the **New Style Name** box Click **Continue**

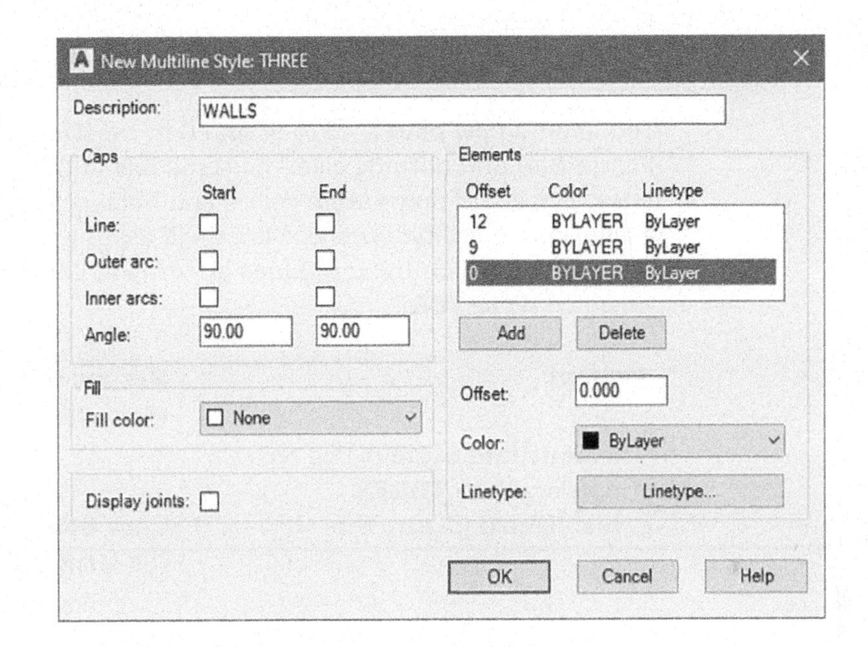

Figure 6-4
WALLS style THREE and elements with offsets of 0″, 9″, and 12″

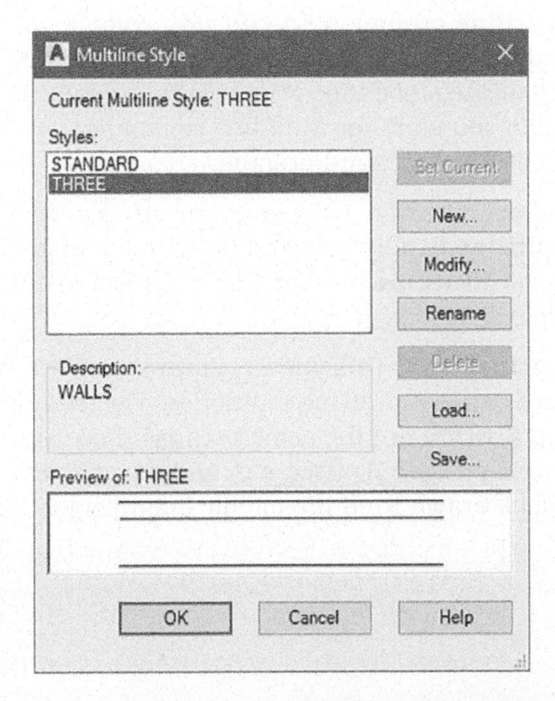

Figure 6-5
Multiline style named THREE

Prompt	**Response**
The **New Multiline Style: THREE** dialog box appears:	Type **WALLS** in the **Description:** box
	Highlight **0.500** in the **Offset:** input box (below the **Add** and **Delete** buttons) and type **9**
	Click **Add**
	Highlight **0.000** in the **Offset:** input box and type **12**
	Click **Add**
	If necessary, scroll down the **Elements** list box to look. If you have a –0.5 offset, click **–0.5** in the list, and click **Delete** to delete an unnecessary offset.

You should now have a 12, a 9, and 0 in the **Elements** list, as shown in Figure 6-4, and nothing else—no scroll bar to the right indicating more lines. You could now assign colors and linetypes to the lines. If you do not assign colors or linetypes, the lines will assume the color and linetype of the layer on which the multilines are drawn. Leave colors and linetypes assigned **BYLAYER**.

Prompt	**Response**
	Click **OK**
The **Multiline Style** dialog box appears with **THREE** highlighted (Figure 6-5)	Click **Set Current**
	Click **OK**

Multiline Command

multiline: A method of drawing as many as 16 lines at the same time with or without end caps.

MULTILINE	
Menu Bar:	Draw/ Multiline
Type a Command:	MLINE
Command Alias:	ML

The **Multiline** prompt is *Specify start point or [Justification Scale STyle]:*. The ***Multiline*** command uses the current multiline style to draw up to 16 lines at the same time with or without end caps.

When you start the Multiline command, you see the following three options at the command prompt:

Style: You can set any style current that has been defined with the **Multiline Style** command if it is not already current (type **ST <Enter>** at the **Multiline** prompt, and then type the style name **<Enter>** and begin drawing).

Justification: This option allows you to select top, zero, or bottom lines to begin drawing multilines. The default is **Top**. In this case **Zero** and **Bottom** are the same because there are no negative offsets. If you have a positive 3 offset, a 0, and a negative 3 offset, your three lines will be drawn from the middle line with justification set to zero.

Scale: This option allows you to set the scale at which lines will be drawn. If your multiline style has a 10 offset, a 6 offset, and a 0, and you set the scale at .5, the lines will be drawn 5″ and 3″ apart. The same style with a scale of 2 draws lines 20″ and 12″ apart.

NOTE

You cannot have spaces in the style name, but spaces are okay in the description.

Step 13. Use **Multiline** to draw the north exterior wall of the tenant space (Figure 6-6), as described next:

Prompt	**Response**
Type a command:	**Multiline** (or type **ML <Enter>**)
Current settings: Justification = Top, Scale = 1.00, Style = THREE	
Specify start point or [Justification Scale STyle]:	**Osnap-Intersection**
of	**P1→** (Figure 6-6)
Specify next point:	Turn **ORTHO** on. Move your mouse to the right and type **48′ <Enter>**
Specify next point or [Undo]:	**<Enter>**

Step 14. Create a new multiline style with the name **THREE-WEST; Start With THREE; Description: WALLS**; and offsets of **0**, **3**, and **12**. Just change the 9 to 3. Set this style current (Figure 6-7).

Step 15. Use **Multiline** with a justification of **Bottom** to draw the west wall of the tenant space with the THREE-WEST multiline style. Use **Osnap-Intersection** and click **P2→** (Figure 6-6) to start the multiline and make the line **36′** long (subtract 2′5″ from the dimension on the right side of Figure 6-6 to account for the 3′-square corner column and the 5″ mullion).

Step 16. Next, draw the interior walls. Keep layer **a-wall-extr** current. You will change the layer on which the interior walls are drawn to **a-wall-intr** in this exercise with the **PROPERTIES** command.

Step 17. Create a new multiline style with the name **TWO**; Start With the **STANDARD** style; **Description: INTERIOR WALLS;** and offsets of **0** and **5** (Figure 6-8). Set this style current.

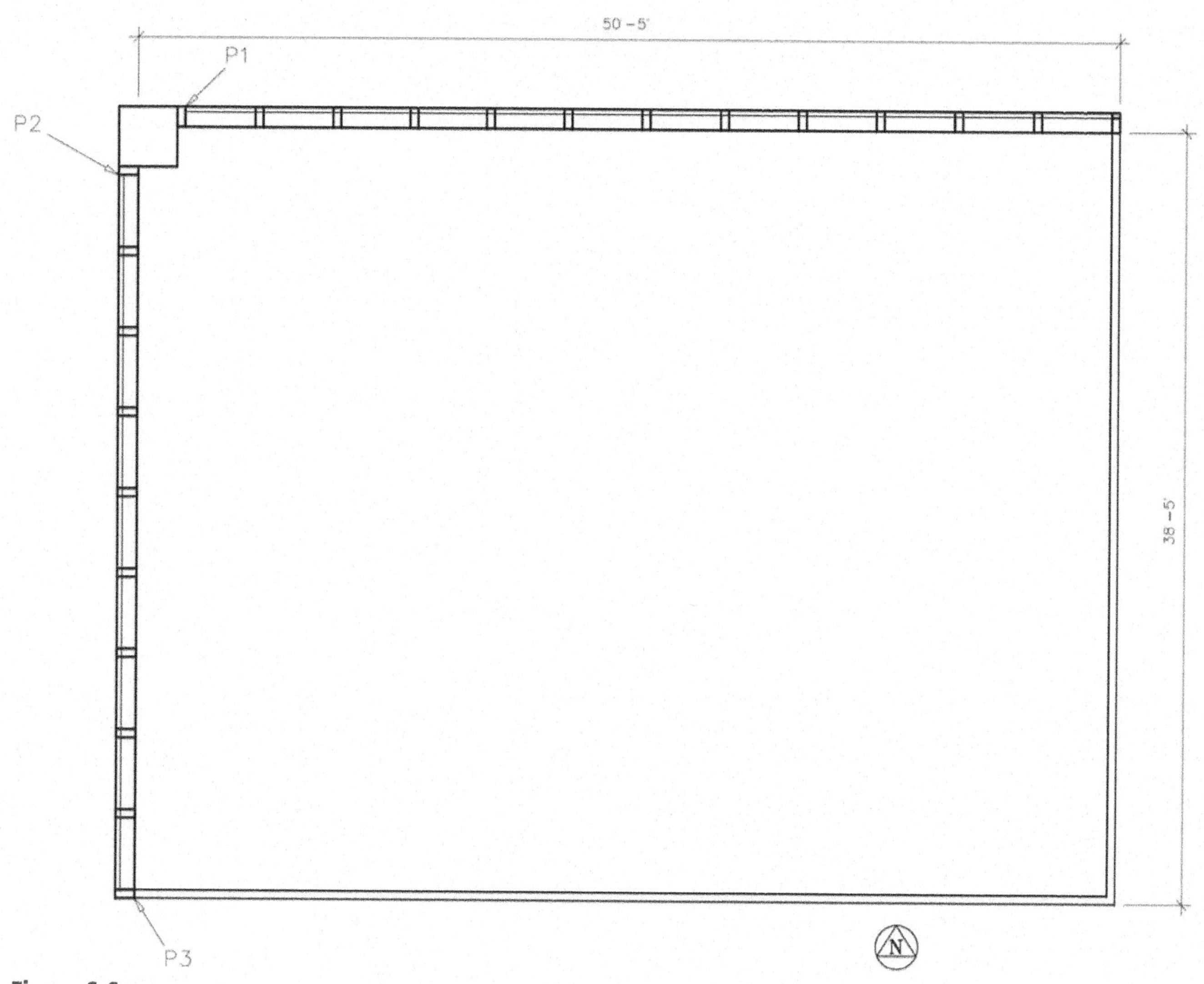

Figure 6-6
Use **Multiline** to draw exterior walls with the multiline styles THREE and TWO

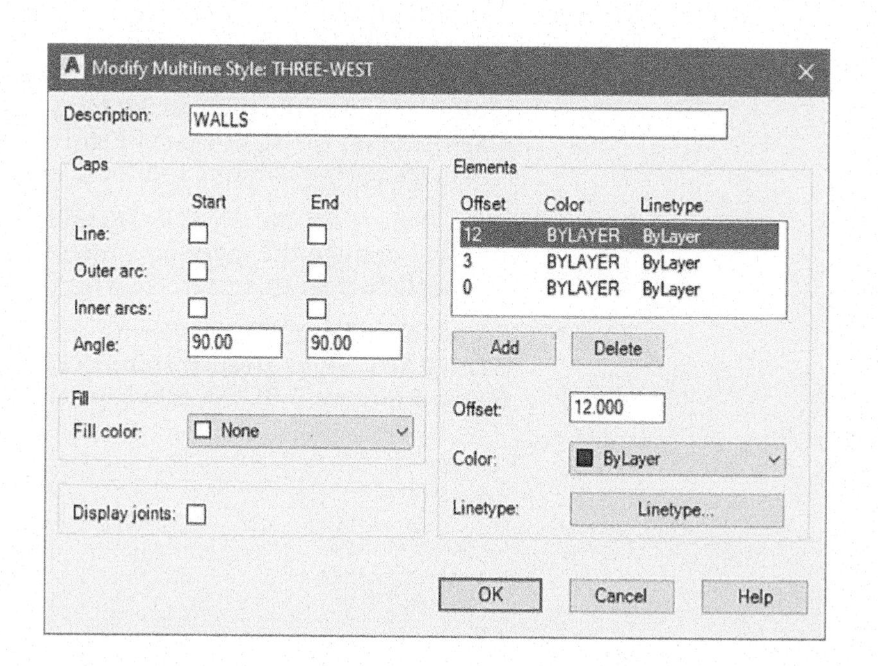

Figure 6-7
Make a new multiline style named THREE-WEST

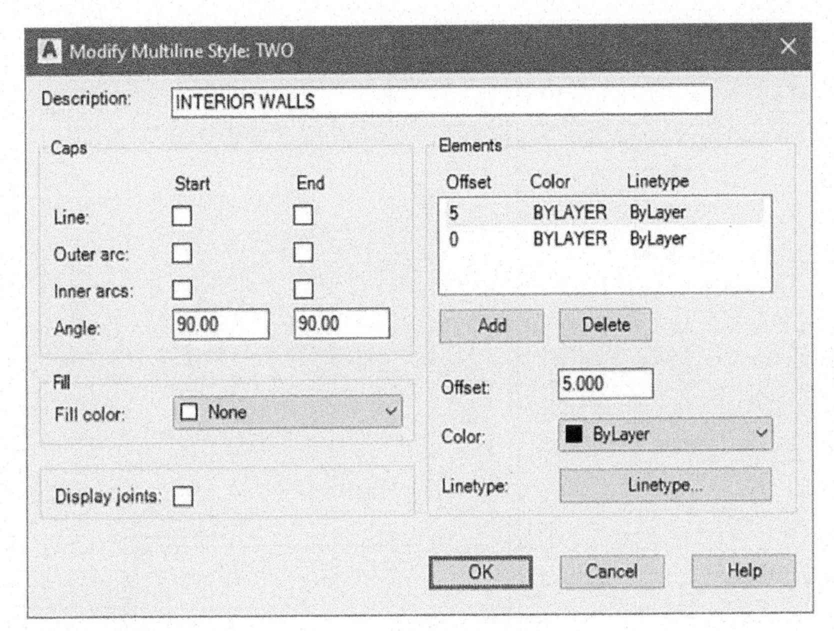

Figure 6-8
Make a new multiline style named TWO

Step 18. Use **Multiline** with a justification of **Bottom** to draw the south and east walls of the tenant space. Use **Osnap-Intersection** and click **P3→** (Figure 6-6). Make the line to the right **50′5″** and the line up **38′5″**.

Step 19. Use **Multiline** with the multiline style **TWO** to draw **5″**-wide horizontal and vertical interior walls inside the tenant space (Figure 6-9), as described next:

Prompt	**Response**
Type a command:	**Multiline** (or type **ML** **<Enter>**)
Current settings: Justification = Bottom, Scale = 1.00, Style = TWO	
Specify start point or [Justification Scale STyle]:	**Osnap-Intersection**
of	Click **P1→** (Figure 6-9)

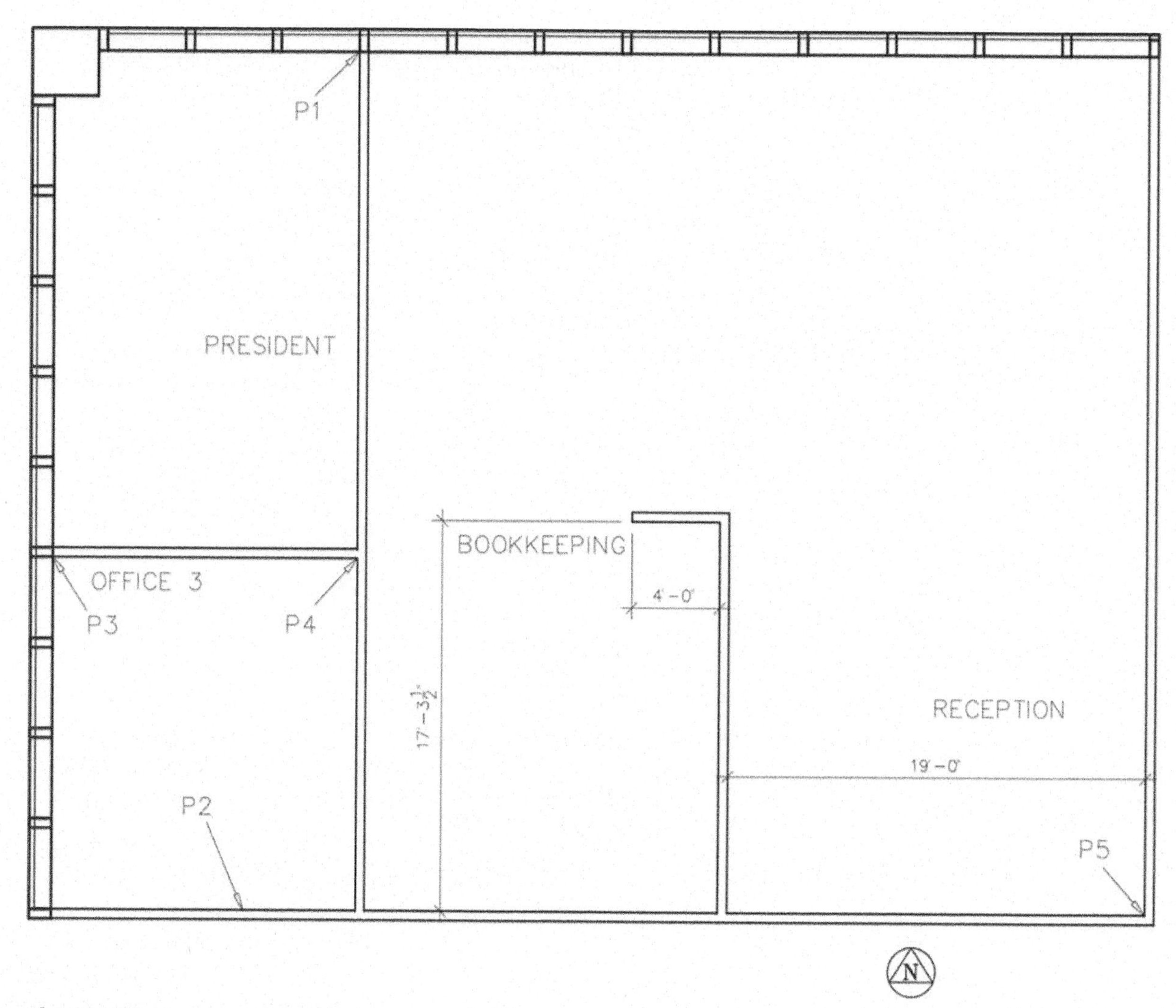

Figure 6-9
Use **Multiline** to draw interior walls

Prompt	**Response**
Specify next point:	**Osnap-Perpendicular** (turn **SNAP** off as needed)
to	**P2→**
Specify next point or [Undo]:	**<Enter>** (you will edit the intersection later)
Type a command:	**<Enter> (repeat MLINE)**
Current settings: Justification = Bottom, Scale = 1.00, Style = TWO:	
Specify start point or [Justification Scale STyle]:	**Osnap-Intersection**
of	**P3→**
Specify next point:	**Osnap-Perpendicular**
to	**P4→**
Specify next point or [Undo]:	**<Enter>** (you will edit the intersection later)

Step 20. Create a new multiline style that uses the settings of the **TWO** style but adds an end cap at the end of the line. Then use **Multiline** and **From** to draw the wall that separates the reception and bookkeeping areas (Figures 6-9 and 6-10), as described next:

Prompt	Response
Type a command:	**Multiline Style...**
The **Multiline Style** dialog box appears:	Click **TWO** and click **New...**
The **Create New Multiline Style** dialog box appears:	Type **TWO-CAP-END** in the **New Style Name** box; click **Continue**
The **New Multiline Style: TWO-CAP-END** dialog box appears:	In the **Caps** area, click the **End** check box in the **Line:** row to select it, as shown in Figure 6-10 Click **OK**
The **Multiline Styles dialog box** appears with **TWO-CAP-END** highlighted:	Click **Set Current;** click **OK**
Type a command:	Type **ML <Enter>**
Current settings: Justification = Bottom Scale = 1.00 Style = TWO-CAP-END	
Specify start point or [Justification Scale STyle]:	**From** (or type **FRO <Enter>**)
Base point:	**Osnap-Endpoint**
of	**P5→** (Figure 6-9)
<Offset>:	Type **@19′<180 <Enter>**
Specify next point:	Turn **ORTHO** on; move your mouse up and type **17′8-1/2 <Enter>**
Specify next point or [Undo]:	Move your mouse to the left and type **4′5 <Enter>**
Specify next point or [Close/Undo]:	**<Enter>** (you will edit the intersection next)

Figure 6-10
Add an end cap to the interior walls

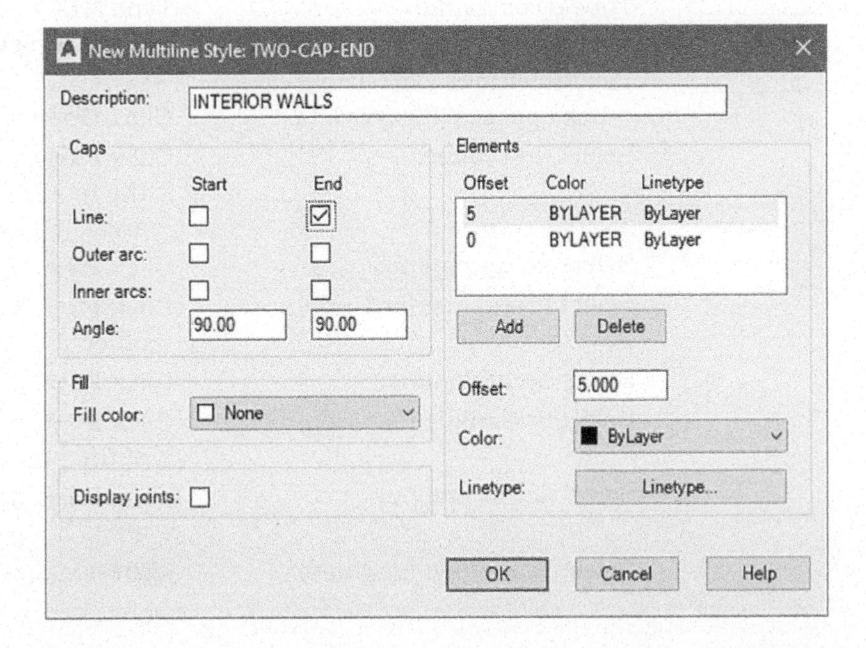

Look at the **Fill color:** area in Figure 6-10. When you select a color from the list, the walls are drawn with a solid fill and can be filled with any color.

Edit Multiline Command

The **Edit Multiline** command allows you to change the intersections of multilines in a variety of ways, as shown in Figure 6-11. Just click the change you want, and then click the two multilines whose intersection you want to change.

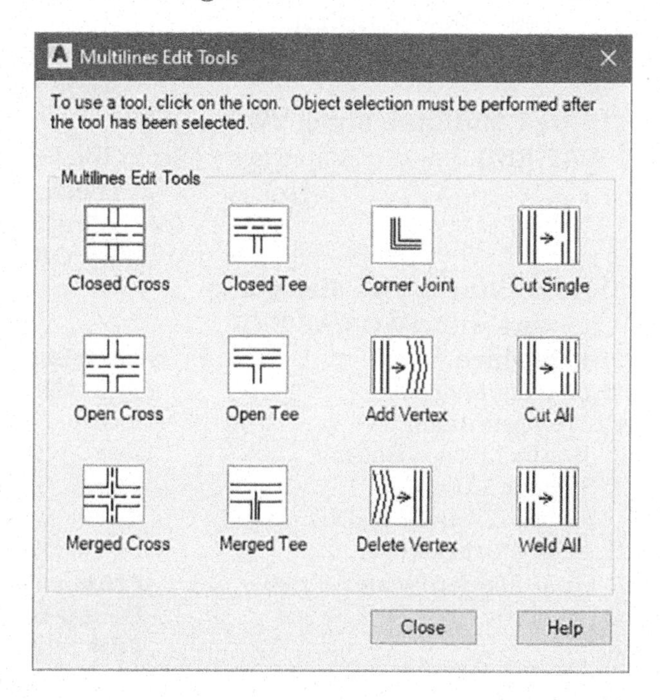

Figure 6-11
Multilines Edit Tools dialog box

EDIT MULTILINE	
Menu Bar:	Modify/ Object/ Multiline ...
Type a Command:	MLEDIT

Step 21. Use **Edit Multiline** to trim the intersections of the multilines forming the interior walls to an Open Tee (Figures 6-11 and 6-12), as described next:

Prompt	Response
Type a command:	Type **MLEDIT <Enter>** or double-click any multiline
The **Multilines Edit Tools** dialog box appears (Figure 6-11):	Click **Open Tee**
Select first mline:	Click **P1→**, the vertical wall separating the reception and bookkeeping areas (Figure 6-12)
Select second mline:	Click **P2→**, the south horizontal wall
Select first mline (or Undo):	Click **P3→**, the interior vertical wall of office 3
Select second mline:	Click **P2→**, the south horizontal wall
Select first mline (or Undo):	Click **P4→**, the interior horizontal wall of the president's office
Select second mline:	Click **P3→**, the interior vertical wall of office 3
Select first mline (or Undo):	**<Enter>**

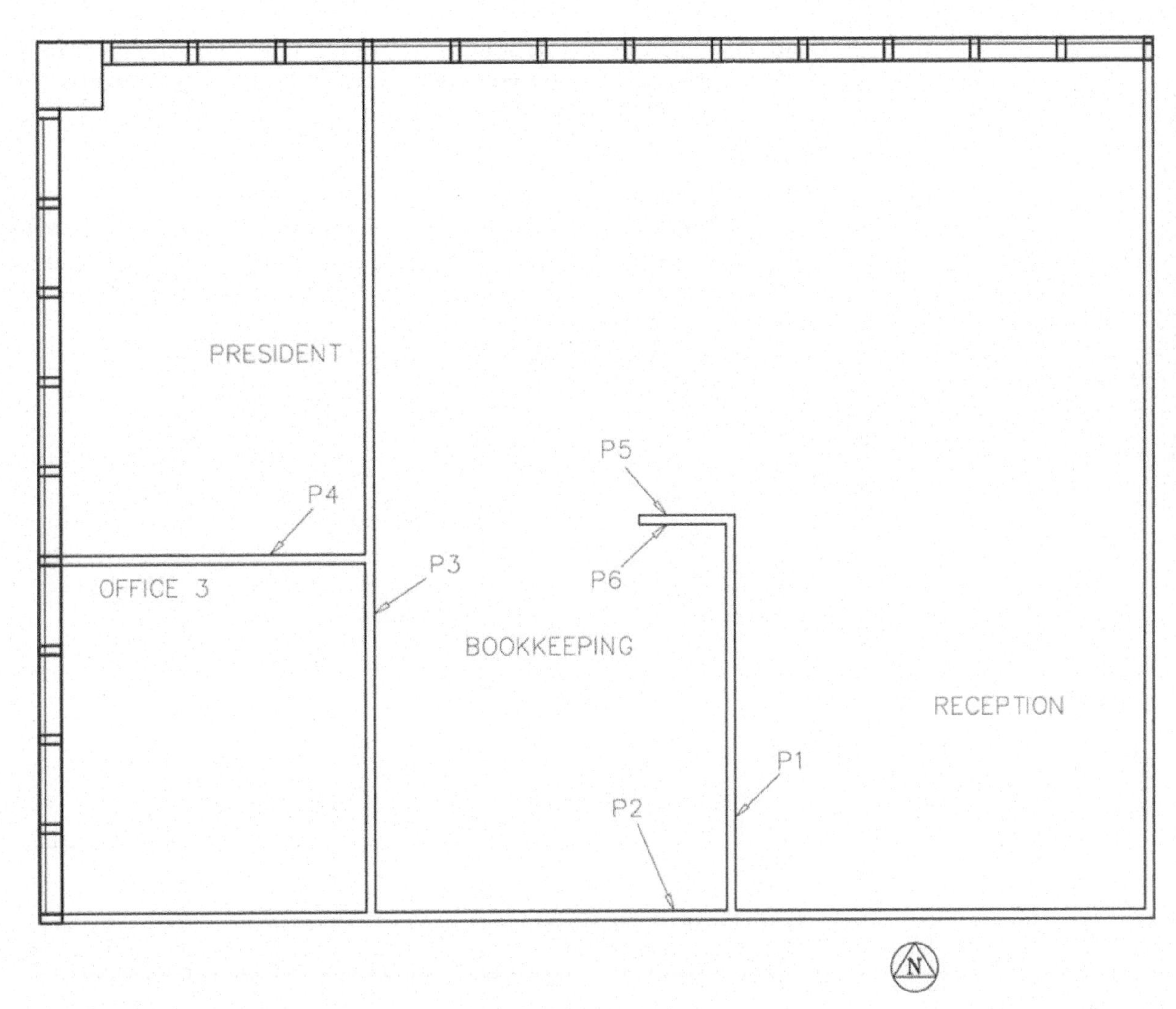

Figure 6-12
Using the **EXTEND** command

EXTEND	
Ribbon/ Panel	Modify/ Extend
Draw Toolbar:	
Menu Bar:	Modify/ Extend
Type a Command:	EXTEND
Command Alias:	EX

EXTEND

The **EXTEND** command allows you to lengthen an existing multiline or line segment to meet a specified boundary edge. As an example, Figure 6-12 shows the multiline **P3** selected as the boundary edge; press **<Enter>**, then click **P5** as the multiline to extend. The multiline junction **EXTEND** options are **Closed**, **Open**, and **Merged**. **Closed** does not trim the line at the wall intersection. **Open** and **Merged** do trim the line.

You can also **EXPLODE** the multiline (not recommended as the MLEDIT tools work only on multilines). When you explode the multiline, it becomes separate line segments. You can then use the **EXTEND** command to lengthen existing lines. Figure 6-12 shows the line selected as **P3** for the boundary edge and **P5** and **P6** as the lines to extend. You would then have to erase the end cap.

properties: All the attributes of an object such as color, layer, linetype, linetype scale, lineweight, and thickness.

PROPERTIES

The ***Properties*** palette (Figure 6-13) allows you to change any property that can be changed.

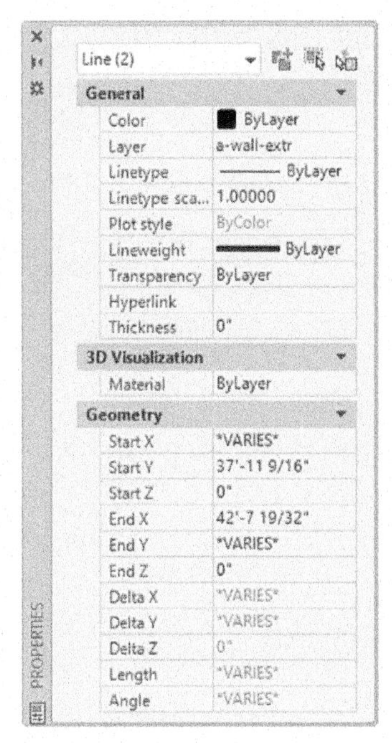

Figure 6-13
Properties palette

Step 22. Use the **PROPERTIES** command to change the layer of the interior walls from the **a-wall-extr** layer to the **a-wall-intr** layer, as described next:

Prompt	Response
Type a command:	**Properties**
The **Properties** palette appears:	Use a crossing window to select all the interior walls including the east and south interior walls.
The **Properties** palette lists all the interior wall properties:	Click **Layer...** Click the down arrow Click **a-wall-intr** Close the dialog box and press **<Esc>**

To change a property using the **Properties** palette, select the object and then either enter a new value or select a new value from a list. You can leave the **Properties** palette open, and you can also right-click on the title bar of the **Properties** palette to dock it.

Step 23. Explode the outside wall line of the exterior north and west walls of the tenant space.

Step 24. Use the **PROPERTIES** command to change the layer property of the glass line (the middle line on the north and west walls) from the **a-wall-extr** layer to the **a-glaz** layer.

> **TIP**
>
> When the **QP (Quick Properties)** toggle is **ON** in the status bar, the quick properties palette appears when you click on an object. You can use the quick properties palette to view and change an object's layer as well as other properties of the object.

LIST	
Ribbon/ Panel	Home/ Properties (slideout) List
Inquiry Toolbar:	
Menu Bar:	Tools/ Inquiry
Type a Command:	LIST
Command Alias:	LI

LIST

After you have changed the property of an entity and would like to confirm the change, or if you need additional information about an entity, using the **LIST** command is helpful. Depending on the type of entity selected, the **LIST** command provides a screen display of the data stored for the entity.

Step 25. Use the **LIST** command to examine the data stored for one of the glass lines, as described next.

Prompt	Response
Type a command:	**List** (or type **LI <Enter>**)
Select objects:	Click only one of the glass lines **<Enter>**
Information appears:	Press **<F2>** (to exit the command)

COLOR

To access the **Select Color** dialog box (Figure 6-14), click **Select Colors...** on the **Properties** panel (or type **COL <Enter>**). You can set colors in the following ways:

Set Color ByLayer: We have discussed and used color by assigning color to a layer, thus controlling the color **ByLayer**. The object is drawn with a layer current and inherits the color assigned to the layer.

The **Select Color** dialog box sets the color for drawing. When you select **ByLayer**, the objects are drawn with the color of the layer on which they are drawn.

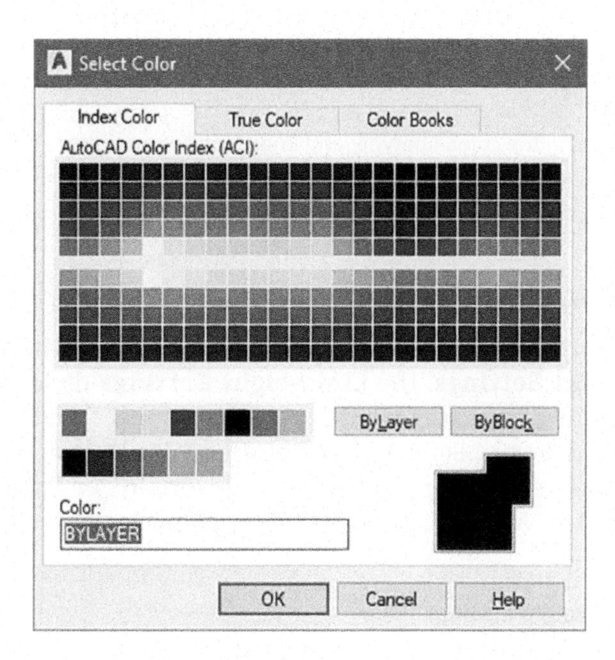

Figure 6-14
Select Color dialog box

Set Color Individually: You can also set the color property of objects individually. When you select a color, such as red, in the **Select Color** dialog box, the objects subsequently drawn are red. The objects will be red regardless of the layer that is current when they are drawn.

To keep your drawing simple, when you need a new color, create a layer and assign the new color to that layer.

Set Color ByBlock: You can draw library parts that are blocks on the **0** layer, which is the same as setting the color, lineweight, and linetype properties to **ByBlock**. The following examples explain the reason for this.

EXAMPLE 1

A door (library part) is drawn on a layer named **DOOR** that is assigned the color red, and **WBLOCK** creates a new drawing file of the door. The door block is inserted into a new project. Because the block was originally drawn on a layer named **DOOR** (color red), the layer name is dragged into the new drawing layer listing, and the door will be red, regardless of the layer current in the new drawing. (You learn about the **WBLOCK** command later in this chapter.)

EXAMPLE 2

A door (library part) is drawn on Layer 0, **WBLOCK** makes a new drawing file of the door, and the door drawing is inserted into a new project. Because the block was originally drawn on Layer 0, the door is generated on the drawing's current layer and inherits all properties of that layer. Before drawing any entity that will be used as a block, you need to decide how you will use it in future drawings; that will determine how color, lineweight, and linetype are assigned.

Linetype

When you select the **Linetype** command from the **Home** tab's **Properties** panel, the **Linetype Manager** dialog box appears. Like the **Color** command, you can set the linetype property **ByLayer**, individually, or **ByBlock**.

> **NOTE**
>
> Setting the color, linetype, and lineweight of an object individually is possible. But generally, creating a new layer and assigning the new color, linetype, or lineweight to the layer is preferable.

Lineweight

If you right-click the **Lineweight...** button on the status bar and click **Lineweight Settings**, the **Lineweight Settings** dialog box (Figure 6-15) appears. (You may need to click **Customize** and select the **LineWeight check box**.) Like with the **Color** and **Linetype** commands, you can set the lineweight property **ByLayer**, individually, or **ByBlock**. Click **LWDISPLAY** on the status bar to display lineweight properties.

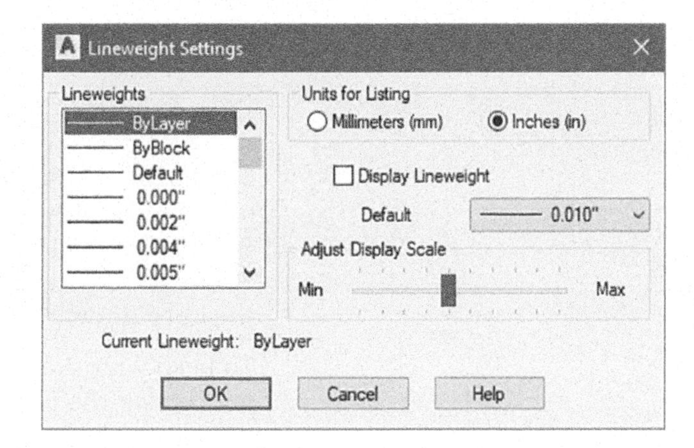

Figure 6-15
Lineweight Settings dialog box

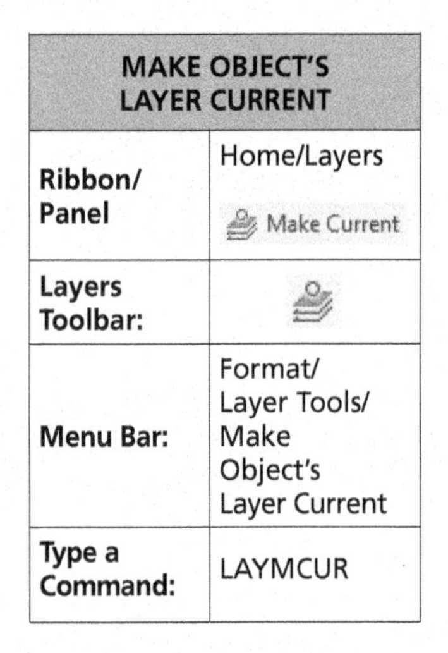

MAKE OBJECT'S LAYER CURRENT	
Ribbon/ Panel	Home/Layers Make Current
Layers Toolbar:	
Menu Bar:	Format/ Layer Tools/ Make Object's Layer Current
Type a Command:	LAYMCUR

Make Object's Layer Current

Make Object's Layer Current is another useful command on the **Layers** panel. When you activate this command and pick any object, the layer that object is on becomes current.

MATCH PROPERTIES	
Ribbon/ Panel	Home/ Properties
Standard Toolbar:	
Menu Bar:	Modify/ Match Properties
Type a Command:	MATCHPROP

Match Properties

When you select the **Match Properties** command from the **Properties** panel, or type and enter **MATCHPROP** at the command prompt, the prompt is *Select source object:*. At that prompt, you can select the object whose properties you want to copy, and a paintbrush is attached to the cursor. The prompt changes to *Select destination object(s) or [Settings]:*, and you can then select the object to which you want to copy the properties.

When you type and enter the **Settings** option to the **Match Properties** prompt, the **Property Settings** dialog box appears (Figure 6-16). Figure 6-16 shows the properties that you can copy. By default, all properties are selected and show a check mark in the box beside the property name. Click to remove the check mark if you do not want a property copied.

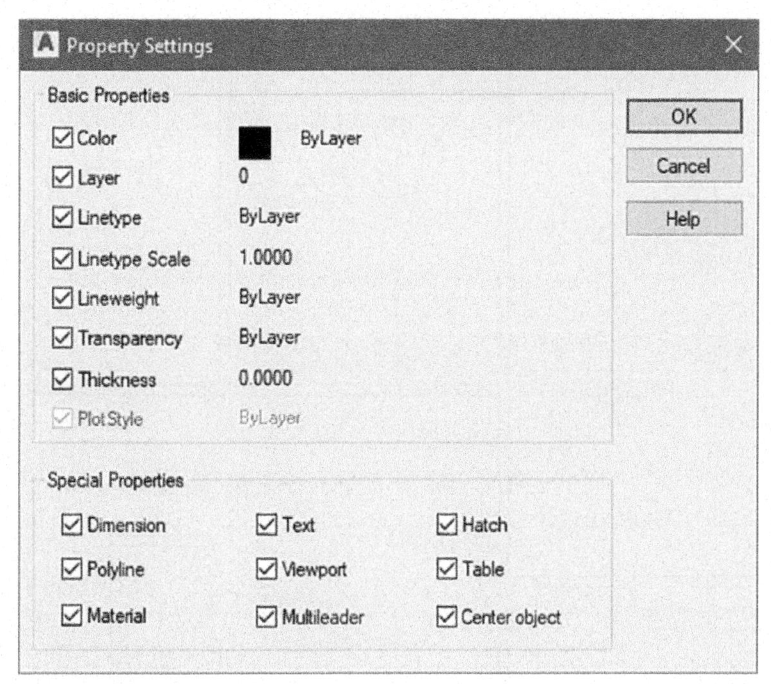

Figure 6-16
Property Settings dialog box

Step 26. Set layer **a-wall-intr** current. Use **Multiline** with the correct multiline style current to finish drawing the interior walls of the tenant space. Use the dimensions shown in Figure 6-17. Use MLEDIT tools of Figure 6-11 as much as possible to finish the interior walls. However, you can use the **Modify** commands (**Extend, Trim, Edit Multiline**, and so on) to fix the multiline. To prepare for the insertion of the doors, the interior walls are to be opened a distance of 3′4″ for single and 6′4″ for double doors. Use the Cut All tool of **MLEDIT** or the **Trim** command to complete this using the dimensions provided in Figure 6-21. Finally, use the **LINE** command to cap the walls at the breaks.

Step 27. Set **FILL** on (or FILLMODE to 1) and regenerate the drawing.

Step 28. Use the dimensions shown in Figure 6-18 to draw the two door types—single door and double door—that will be defined as blocks and inserted into the tenant space. Draw the lines representing the doors, door frames, and the arcs showing the door swings on the **a-door** layer. Pick any open space on your drawing and draw each door full size. In the following part of this exercise, you use the **BLOCK** and **WBLOCK** commands to define the doors as blocks and to save the blocks as new drawings.

Block

The **Block** command allows you to define any part of a current drawing as a block. You can insert copies of the block only into that drawing. You cannot use copies of a block defined with the **Block** command in any other drawing without using the AutoCAD **DesignCenter** (described in Chapter 10).

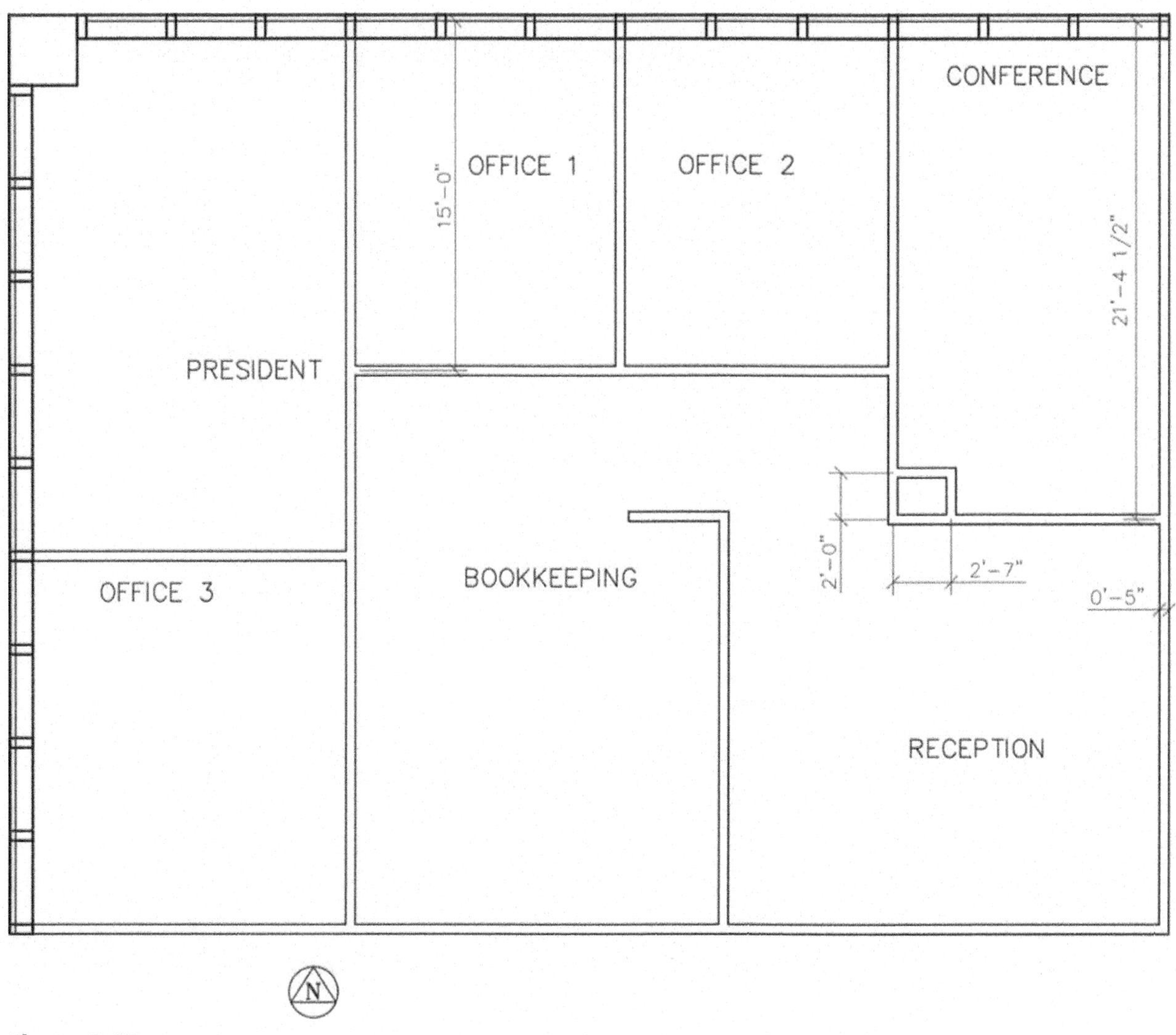

Figure 6-17
Use **Multiline** to finish drawing the interior walls

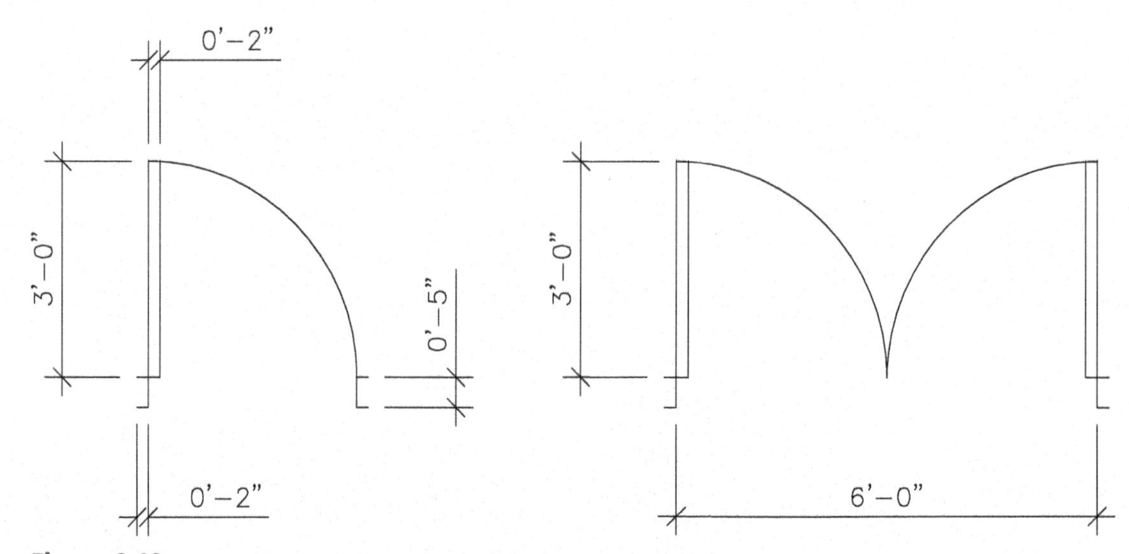

Figure 6-18
Two door types that you will define as blocks and insert into the tenant space

BLOCK	
Ribbon/ Panel	Home/Block
Draw Toolbar:	
Menu Bar:	Draw/Block/ Make
Type a Command:	BLOCK
Command Alias:	B

Step 29. Use the **Block** command to define the single-door drawing as a block named **DOOR** stored in the current drawing (Figure 6-19), as described next:

Prompt	Response
Type a command:	**Block...** (or type **B <Enter>**)
The **Block Definition** dialog box appears:	Type **DOOR** in the **Name:** input box Click the **Delete** option button under **Objects** Click the **Pick point** button
Specify insertion base point:	**Osnap-Endpoint**
of:	**P1→** (Figure 6-19)
The **Block Definition** dialog box appears:	Click the **Select objects** button
Select objects:	Click a point to locate the first corner of a selection window
Specify opposite corner:	Window only the single-door drawing
Select objects:	**<Enter>**
The **Block Definition** dialog box appears:	Make all settings as shown in Figure 6-19; click **OK**
The single-door symbol is gone and is now defined as a block within your drawing.	

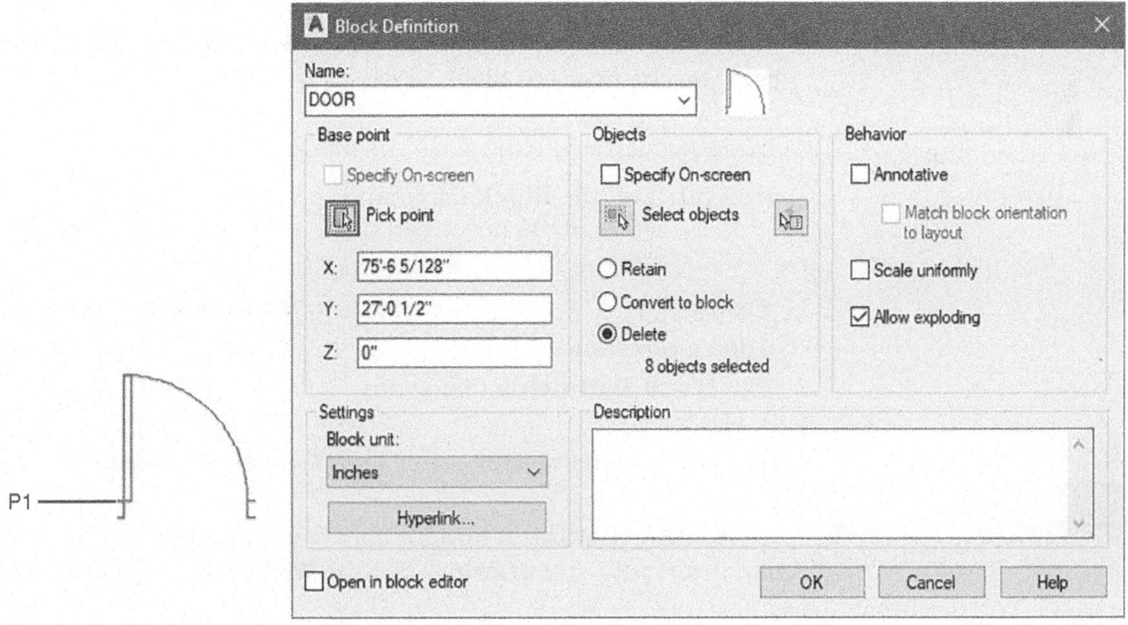

Figure 6-19
Make a block of the door; name it **DOOR**

The three option buttons in the **Objects** area of the **Block Definition** dialog box specify what happens to the selected object (in this instance, the door) after you create the block are:

Retain: The door symbol will remain in the drawing but will not be a block.

Convert to block: The door symbol will remain in the drawing and will be saved as a block.

Delete: The door symbol will be deleted.

The four check boxes in the **Behavior** area of the **Block Definition** dialog box (Figure 6-19) specify the following:

Annotative: You can use annotative blocks for inserting objects such as elevation reference symbols that contain a circle (balloon) and numbers. When you insert the annotative balloon and number block into a drawing, the sizes change according to the annotation scale. They are always the same size when plotted, regardless of the scale of the plotted drawing, if the annotation scale is the same as the plot scale. In this chapter we do not annotate the blocks because the tenant space is drawn full scale, and we want the door plotted sizes to change depending on the plotted scale.

Match block orientation to layout: When you select the **Annotative** check box, this option specifies that the orientation of the block in paper space viewports matches the orientation of the layout.

Scale uniformly: When you select this option, the block is uniformly scaled in x, y, and z planes—**do not check this box**.

Allow exploding: Selecting this check box enables the block to be exploded.

A block name can be 1 to 255 characters long. It may include only letters, numbers, and three special characters—$ (dollar sign), - (hyphen), and _ (underscore).

You use the **Insert** command later in this exercise to insert copies of the DOOR block into your drawing. *The Specify insertion base point:* is the point on the inserted block to which the crosshairs attach. It allows you to position copies of the block exactly into the drawing. It is also the point around which you can rotate the block when you insert it.

Step 30. Use the **Block** command to view a listing of the block just created, as described next.

Prompt	**Response**
Type a command:	**Block ...** (or type **B <Enter>**)
The **Block Definition** dialog box appears:	Click the down arrow below **Name:**
The block name appears:	Click **<Cancel>**

WBLOCK	
Ribbon/ Panel	Insert/ Block Definition
Type a Command:	WBLOCK
Command Alias:	W

When you want to build a library of parts defined as blocks that you can insert into any drawing, use the **WBLOCK** command, described next.

Wblock

The **WBLOCK** command allows you to define any part of a drawing or an entire drawing as a block. Blocks created with the **WBLOCK** command become drawing files with a .dwg extension, just like any other AutoCAD drawing. They can be stored on any disk, drive, or network and you can then insert them into any drawing.

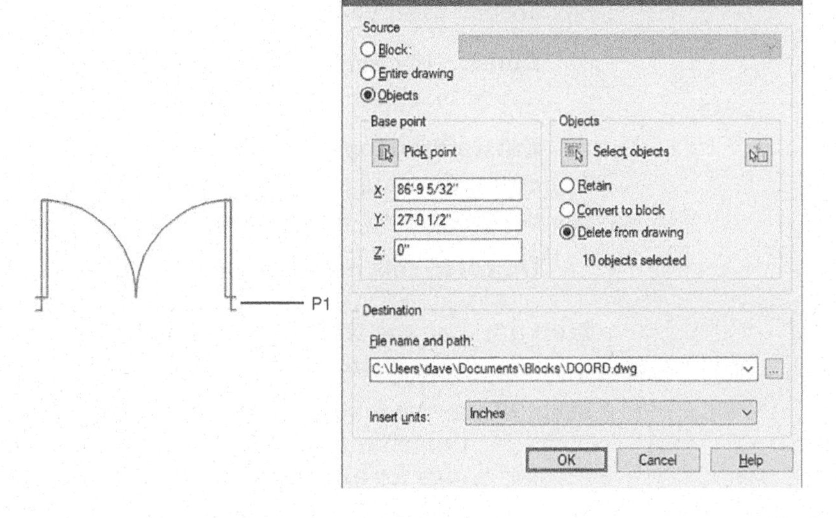

Figure 6-20
Write Block dialog box for DOORD drawing

Step 31. Create a new folder named **Blocks** in which to store your wblocked drawings.

Step 32. Use **WBLOCK** to save the double-door drawing as a block on your hard drive or on a network (Figure 6-20), as described next:

Prompt	Response
Type a command:	Type **W <Enter>**
The **Write Block** dialog box appears:	Type **DOORD** (to replace the "new block" name in the **File name and path:** input box) Click the **...** button (to the right of **File name and path:**) to browse for files or folders and select the path where you want to save
The **Browse for Drawing File** dialog box appears:	Click the down arrow in the **Save in:** input box to select the drive and folder where you want to save the double-door drawing Click **Save**
The **Write Block** dialog box appears:	Click the **Delete from drawing** button Click the **Pick point** button
Specify insertion base point:	**Osnap-Endpoint**
of	**P1→** (Figure 6-20)
The **Write Block** dialog box appears:	Click the **Select objects** button
Select objects:	Window the entire double-door drawing
Select objects:	**<Enter>**
The **Write Block** dialog box appears:	Click **OK**

The double-door drawing disappears and is saved as a new drawing file with a .dwg file extension.

You can recall copies of the DOORD drawing and insert them into any other drawing. It is obvious that building a library of parts that you can insert into any drawing saves time.

The three option buttons in the **Source** area of the **Write Block** dialog box specify what you are defining:

Block: This helps define a block that is stored in a current drawing as a new block outside the current drawing.

Entire drawing: You can define not only parts of a drawing but also an entire drawing as a block. Use 0,0,0 as the base point when defining an entire drawing as a block.

Objects: This option allows you to select an object to define as a block.

Step 33. Use the **WBLOCK** command to write the **DOOR** block stored in your current drawing to a disk and folder of your choice.

Step 34. In the following part of this exercise, you will insert the doors into the tenant space. Before inserting the doors, you must add openings for all doors to the drawing. Each single door is 3′4″ wide, including the 2″ frame, so each opening for a single door is 3′4″ wide. As shown in Figure 6-21, the dimension from the corner of each room to the outside edge of the single door frame is 3-1/2″. The dimensions shown in Figure 6-21 for the door to office 1 apply to all single-door openings.

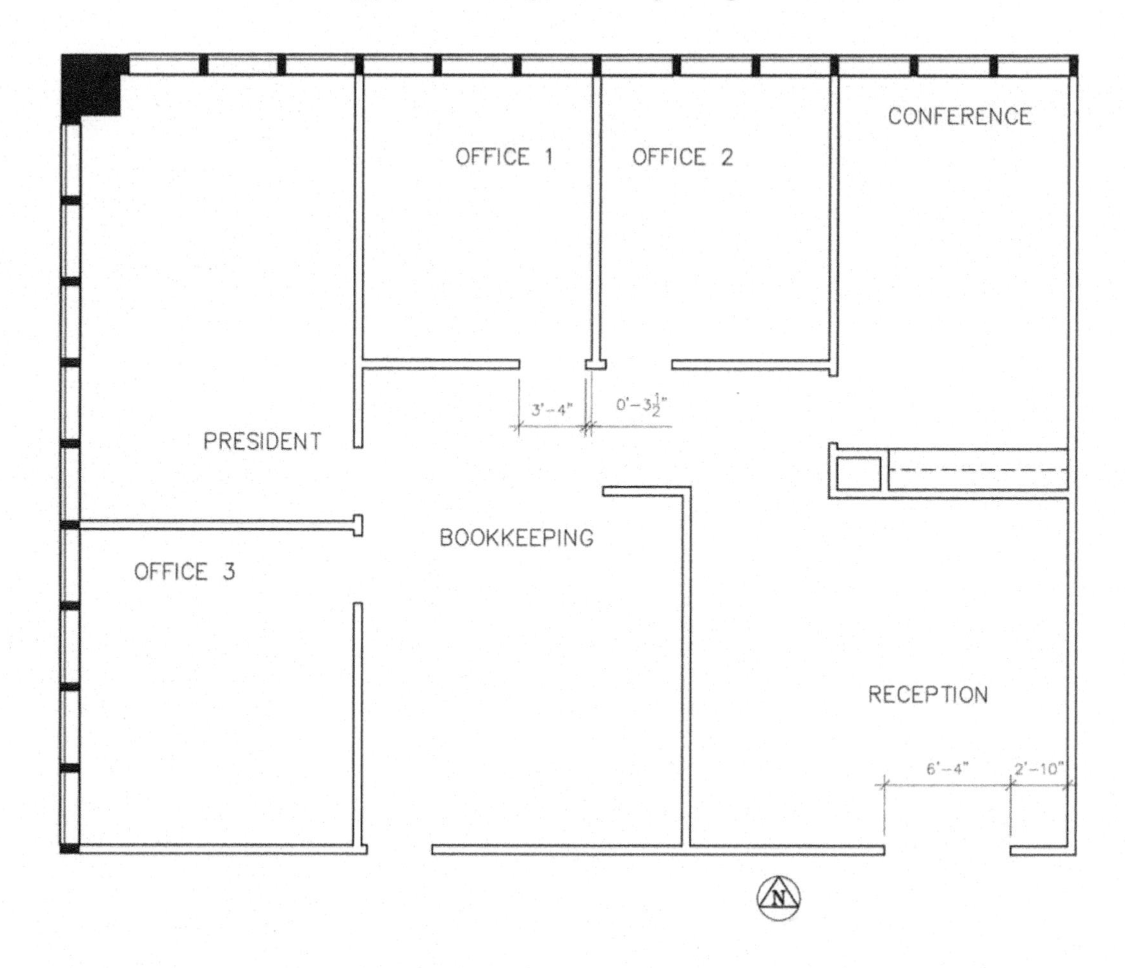

Figure 6-21
Use the dimensions shown to draw the openings for all doors

Insert

The **Insert** command allows you to insert the defined blocks into your drawing. You may use it to insert a block defined with either the **Block** command or the **WBLOCK** command.

NOTE

Do not confuse the **Insert** command described here with the **Insert** object snap mode. **INS** object snap allows you to snap to the insertion point of text or a block entity.

In the following part of the exercise you use the **Insert** command to insert the DOOR block into the tenant space. Don't forget to zoom in on the area of the drawing on which you are working. Remember also that the insertion point of the DOOR block is the upper-left corner of the door frame.

Step 35. Use the **Insert** command to insert the block named DOOR into office 2 (Figures 6-22 and 6-23), as described next:

Prompt	Response
Type a command:	**Insert ...** (or type **I <Enter>**)
The **BLOCKS** palette opens with the **Current Drawing** tab active. Blocks defined in the current drawing appear in the **Current Drawing Blocks** area. Under **Options**, make sure there is a check mark beside Insertion Point (Figure 6-22).	Drag the **DOOR** block from the **Current Drawing Blocks** area into the drawing. The crosshairs are attached to the insertion point defined when the block was created.
Specify insertion point or [Base-point Scale Rotate]:	**Osnap-Intersection**
of	**P1→** (Figure 6-23)

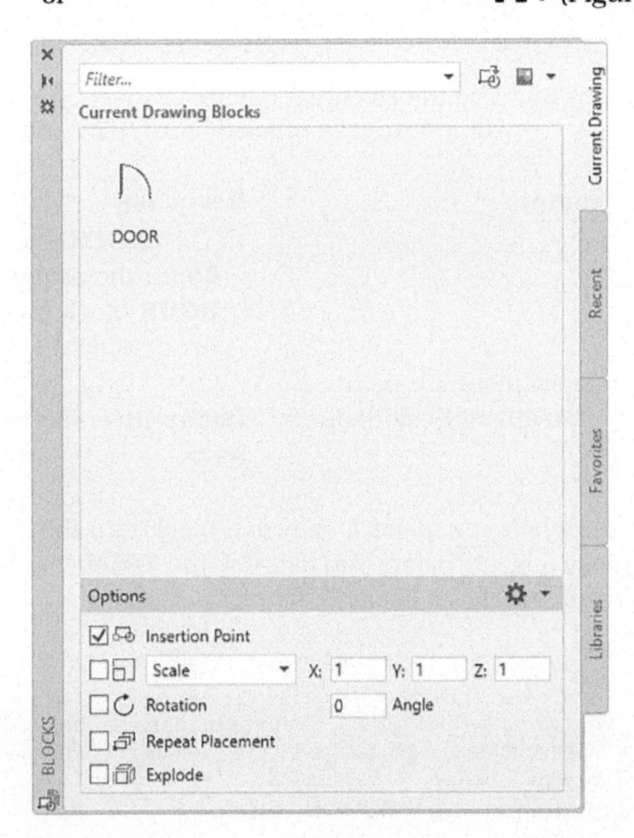

Figure 6-22
Use the **BLOCKS** palette **Current Drawing** tab to insert the block named DOOR

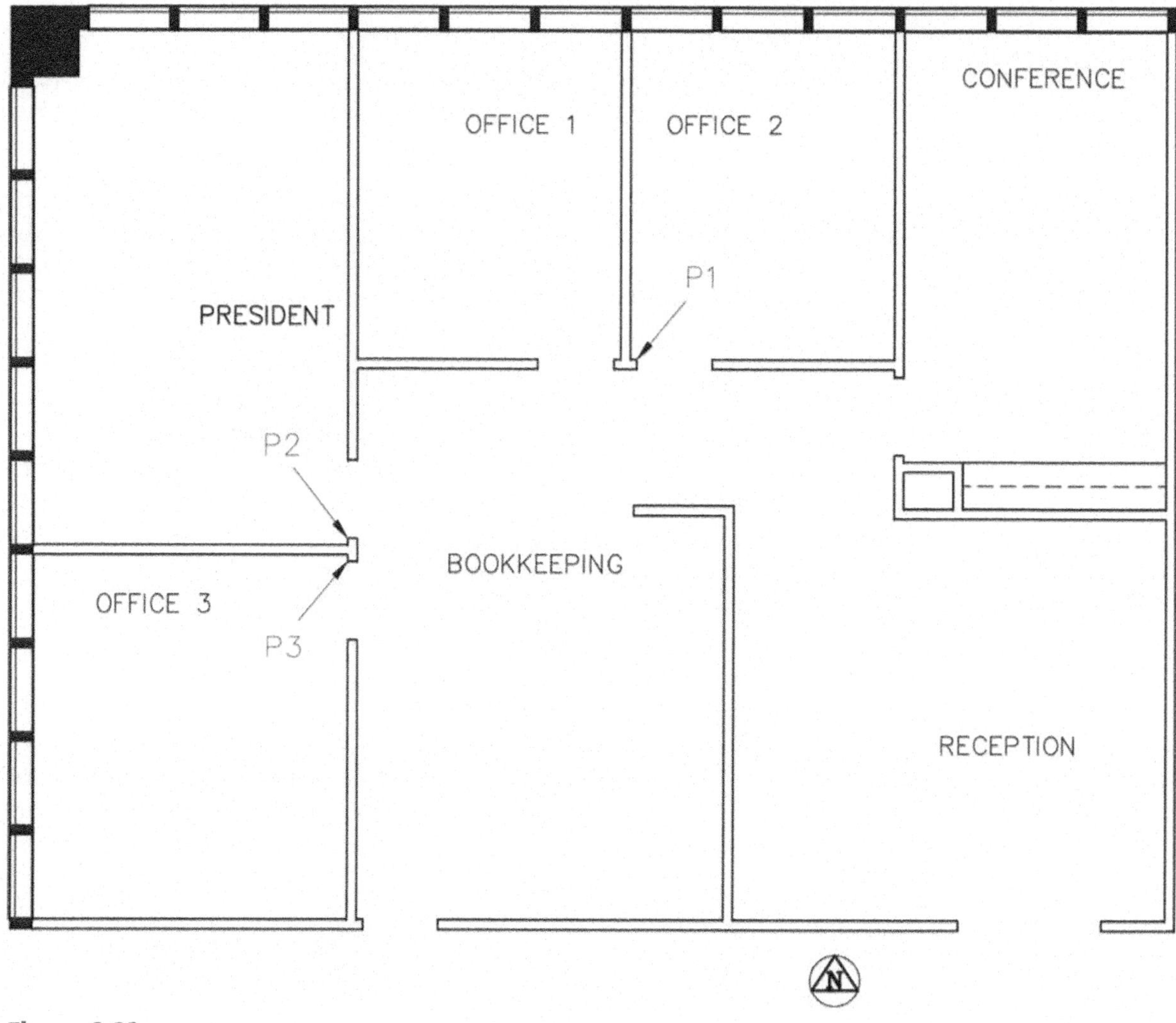

Figure 6-23

Step 36. Use the **BLOCKS** palette to insert the block named DOOR into the president's office (Figure 6-23), as described next:

Prompt	Response
	In the **BLOCKS** palette under **Options**, type **90** (in the **Angle:** input box) and drag the **DOOR** block toward the door opening of the president's office.
Specify insertion point or [Basepoint Scale Rotate]:	**Osnap-Intersection**
of	**P2→**

When you insert a copy of a block into the drawing, it is inserted as a single object. Before you can use the **TRIM** command or edit a copy of a block, you must explode the block.

> **NOTE**
>
> When you explode a block, it returns to separate objects. If you want a block to be inserted already exploded, select the **Explode** check box in the lower-left corner of the **BLOCKS** palette.

NOTE

Door blocks originally drawn on the **a-door** layer will be on that layer in the drawing, regardless of which layer is current when you insert the blocks into the drawing.

Insertion Point

The insertion point of the incoming block is the point you defined as the base point when you defined the door objects as a block. In the preceding exercises, you used **Osnap-Intersection** to position copies of the block exactly into the drawing. You can also use the **ID** command or **From** (on the **Osnap** menu) when inserting a block. Use the **ID** command to identify a point on the drawing, and then initiate the **Insert** command after the point has been located. You can then enter the *Insertion point:* of the block by using relative or polar coordinates to specify a distance from the established point location.

X Scale Factor, Y Scale Factor

The X and Y scale factors provide flexibility in how the copy of the block will appear when you insert it. The default X and Y scale factor is 1. A scale factor of 1 inserts the block as it was originally drawn.

You can type and enter new scale factors in response to the prompts. AutoCAD multiplies all X and Y dimensions of the block by the X and Y scale factors entered. By default, the Y scale factor equals the X scale factor, but you can enter a different Y scale factor separately.

You can enter negative X or Y scale factors to insert mirror images of the block. When the X scale factor is negative, the Y scale factor remains positive. When the Y scale factor is negative, the X scale factor remains positive. Either a negative X or Y scale factor will work in the following example, but we will use negative X.

Step 37. Using the **BLOCKS** palette and a negative X scale factor, rotate the angle of the block to insert the block named **DOOR** into office 3 (Figure 6-23), as described next:

Prompt	Response
	Type **-1** (in the **X Scale** input box); type **90** (in the **Rotation Angle:** input box)
	Drag the **DOOR** block into the drawing area
	Osnap-Intersection
of	**P3→** (Figure 6-23)

Step 38. Continue using the **BLOCKS** palette to complete the insertion of all doors in the tenant space. The **DOORD** block was not saved as a block in the current drawing when you used **WBLOCK** to create it. Click the **Insert Block** button at the top of the **BLOCKS** palette, to the immediate right of the **Filter...** text box, to open the **Select File to Insert** dialog box. Navigate to your **Blocks** folder and select **DOORD**. The double door block is attached to the crosshairs at the defined insertion point. (Figure 6-24).

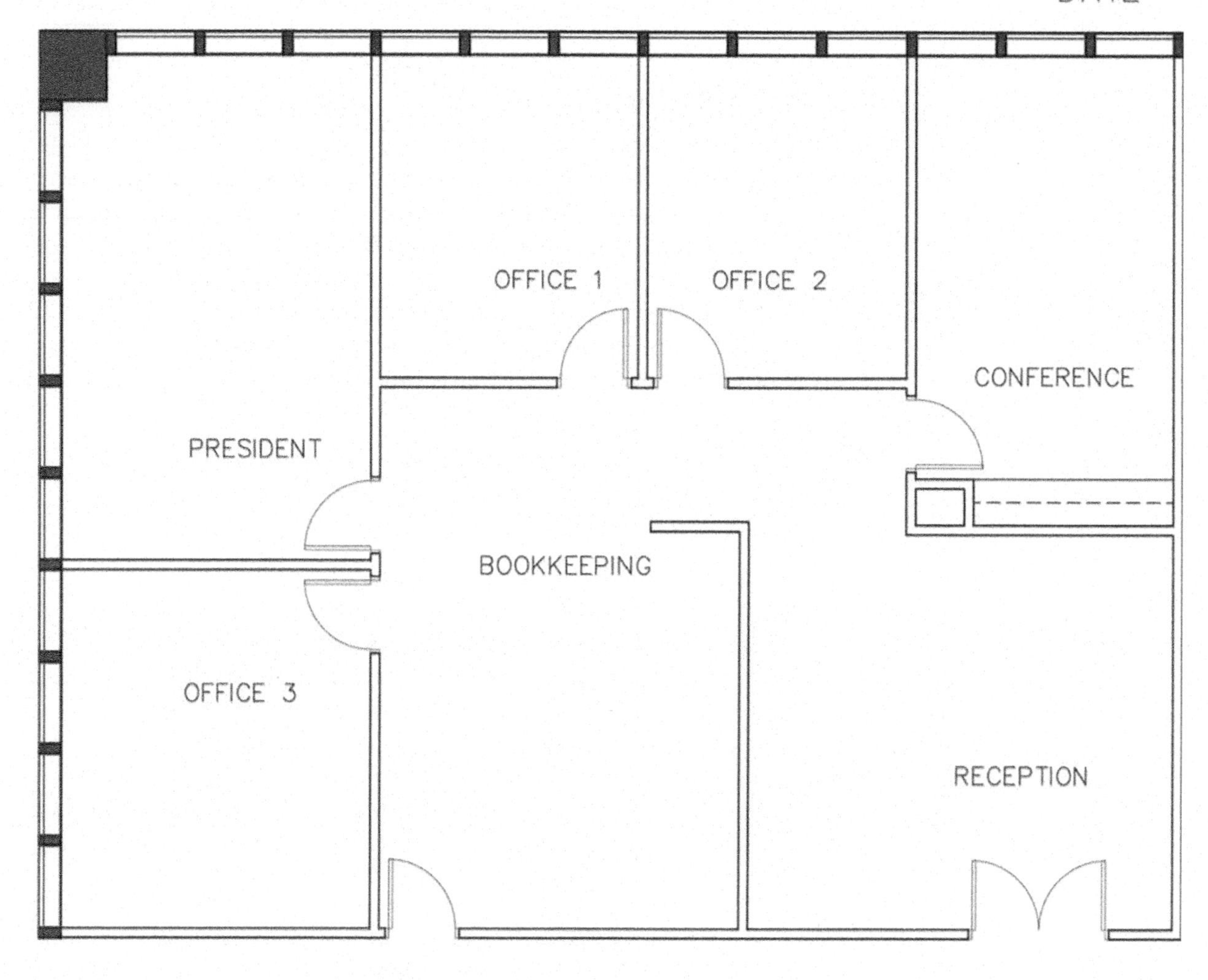

Figure 6-24
Exercise 6-1: Tenant space floor plan (scale: 1/8″ = 1′-0″)

Step 39. Set layer **a-flor-case** current. Draw a line to show the conference room base cabinets, 24″ deep. Set layer **a-flor-case-uppr** current. Draw a line to show the upper cabinets, 12″ deep. Set **LTSCALE** to show the **HIDDEN** line of the upper cabinets (Figure 6-24).

Step 40. Set layer **a-anno-text** current.

Step 41. In the **Text Style** dialog box, change the text style **Standard** to the **romans** font and set the **Standard Style** current.

Using Annotative Text

When the tenant space floor plan is drawn full scale, the text on the full-scale screen drawing must be large so it can be seen on the screen. For example, if you want text to be 1/8″ high on the paper drawing that is printed at 1/8″ = 1′-0″, the text will be 12″ high on the full-scale drawing on the screen (a scale factor of 96).

annotative text: Text that has a property that allows it to change as the scale of the entire drawing changes.

Annotation scale controls how the text and other annotative objects appear on the drawing. When you make the text ***annotative*** and set the annotation scale of the drawing in the lower-right corner of the status bar, AutoCAD automatically does the arithmetic for you and controls how the text looks on your screen. When adding the text, you have to enter only the height of the text you want in the plotted drawing (paper height), and AutoCAD calculates the height of the text on the full-scale screen drawing using the annotation scale setting.

Step 42. In the **Text Style** dialog box, select the **Annotative** check box under **Size** to make sure the annotative property is set to on for the **Standard Style** (Figure 6-25).

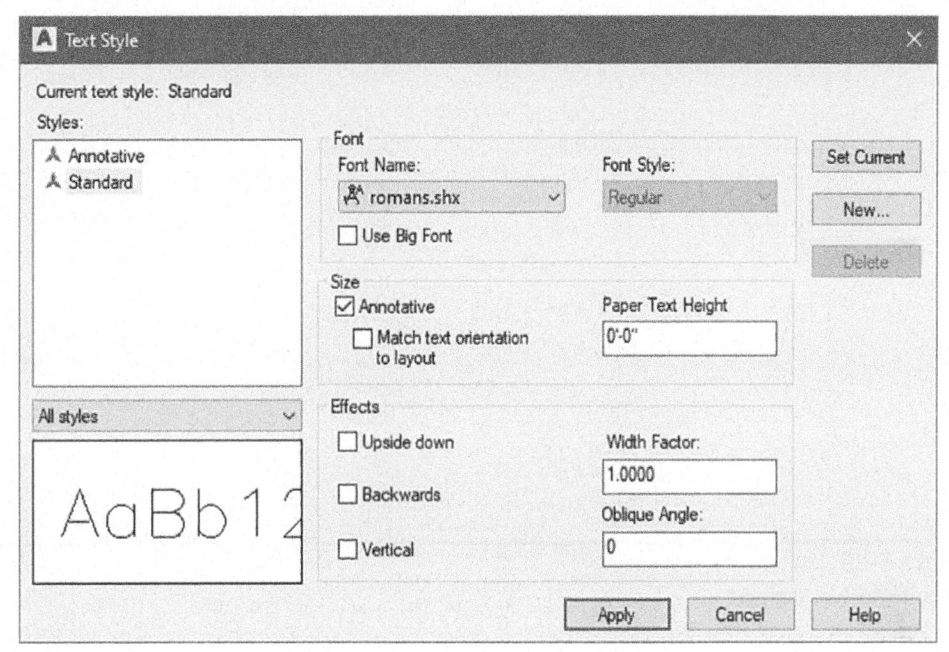

Figure 6-25
Text Style dialog box with **romans** font and **Annotative** selected

Step 43. Set the drawing annotation scale to **1/8″ = 1′-0″** (located in the lower-right area on the AutoCAD screen (Figure 6-26).

Step 44. Use **Dtext**, height **3/32″** to type the identifying name in each room. Use the approximate locations shown in Figure 6-24; you can move the names as needed when you insert furniture into the drawing.

Step 45. Use **Dtext**, height **1/8″** to type your name, class, and date in the upper-right area, as shown in Figure 6-24.

Step 46. Use **Dtext**, height **1/8″** to type the underlined text TENANT SPACE FLOOR PLAN.

Step 47. Use **Dtext**, height **3/32″** to type the drawing scale.

Step 48. Draw the North arrow similar to the North arrow on Figure 6-24. Use a **2′-2″**–diameter circle. Make a new text style named **North Arrow**, RomanT font, not annotative, and set it current. Use **Dtext** to make an **8″-high** letter **N** in the circle.

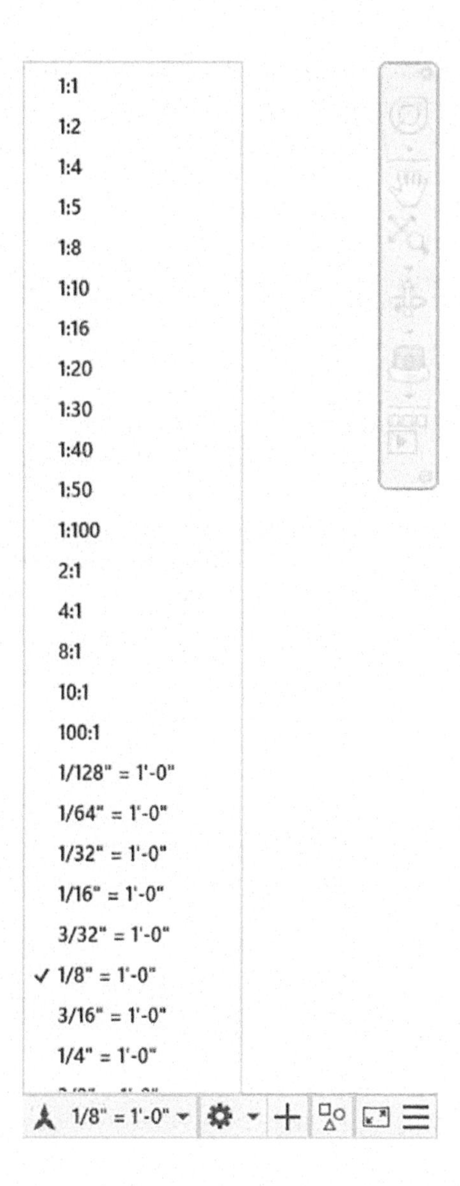

Figure 6-26
Set annotation scale to 1/8″ = 1′-0″

Inserting Entire Drawings as Blocks

You can insert into the current drawing any drawing that has not been defined as a block and define it as a block within that drawing. Simply use the **BLOCKS** palette to insert the drawing. Use the **Select File to Insert** button at the top of the **BLOCKS** palette to locate the drawing.

Advantages of Using Blocks

The use of blocks in drawings has many advantages that can save you time:

- A library of drawing parts allows an often-used part to be drawn once instead of many times.
- You can combine blocks with customized menus to create a complete applications environment around AutoCAD that provides the building and furnishings parts that are used daily.
- After you define a block and insert it into the drawing, you can update all references to that block by redefining the block.
- Because AutoCAD treats a block as a single object, less disk space is used for each insertion of a block.

Step 49. When you have completed Exercise 6-1, save your work in at least two places.

Step 50. Print the tenant space floor plan at a scale of **1/8″ = 1′-0″**.

EXERCISE 6-2
Hotel Room 1 Floor Plan

In Exercise 6-2, you will draw a hotel room floor plan. You will use the AutoCAD **DesignCenter** to insert existing fixtures such as a tub, toilet, sink, and faucet into the floor plan. You'll use lineweights to make the drawing more attractive and use a solid hatch pattern with a gray color to make the walls solid. When you have completed Exercise 6-2, your drawing will look similar to Figure 6-27 without dimensions.

Step 1. Use your workspace to make the following settings:

1. Use **Save As...** to save the drawing with the name **CH6-EXERCISE2**.
2. Set drawing units: **Architectural**
3. Set drawing limits: **40′,40′**
4. Set **GRIDDISPLAY: 0**
5. Set grid: **12″**
6. Set snap: **6″**
7. Create the following layers, and then set layer **a-wall-intr** current:

Layer Name	Description	Color	Linetype	Lineweight
a-anno-text	text	green	continuous	.006″ (.15 mm)
a-door	doors and door swings	red	continuous	.004″ (.09 mm)
a-fixt	bathroom fixtures	green	continuous	.006″ (.15 mm)
a-fixt-fauc	sink faucet	white	continuous	.002″ (.05 mm)
a-flor-case	closet shelf	green	continuous	.006″ (.15 mm)
a-flor-case-spec	closet rod	red	hidden	.004″ (.09 mm)
a-flor-whch	wheelchair circle	red	hidden	.004″ (.09 mm)
a-glaz	glass	green	continuous	.006″ (.15 mm)
a-wall-extr	exterior building wall	white	continuous	.016″ (.40 mm)
a-wall-intr	interior building wall	blue	continuous	.010″ (.25 mm)
a-wall-patt-gray	hatch fill	gray (253)	continuous	.004″ (.09 mm)

Step 2. Use the correct layers and the dimensions shown in Figure 6-27 to draw the exterior and interior walls, window glass, doors, closet shelf, and closet rod of the hotel room. Your drawing will look similar to Figure 6-28.

Step 3. Set layer **a-wall-patt-gray** current and use the **HATCH** command to shade the walls of the hotel room as shown in Figure 6-27.

Step 4. Set layer **a-fixt** current.

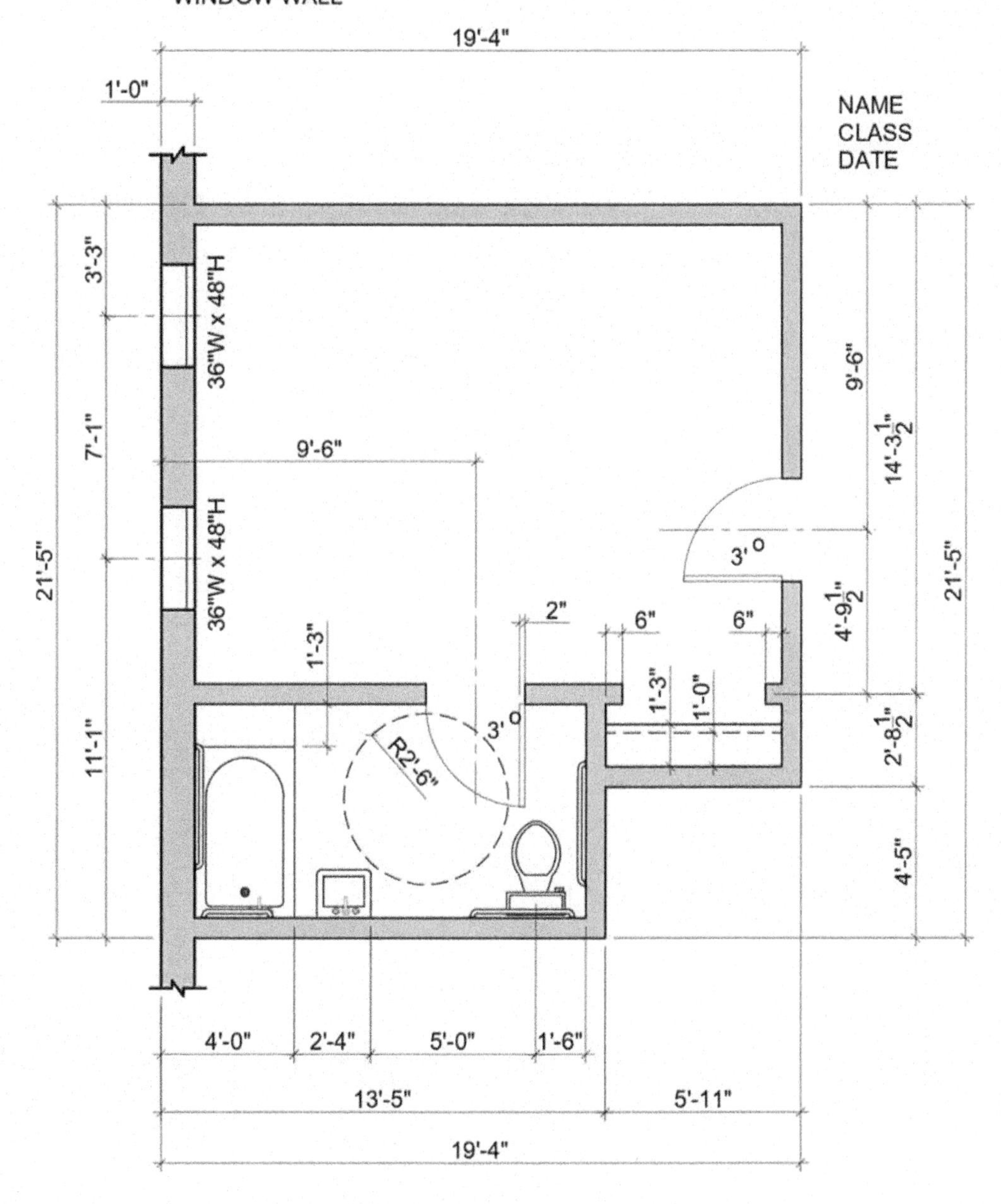

Figure 6-27
Exercise 6-2: Hotel room 1 floor plan (scale: 3/16″ = 1′-0″)

DESIGNCENTER	
Ribbon/ Panel	View/ Palettes
Standard Toolbar:	
Menu Bar:	Tools/ Palettes/ DesignCenter
Type a Command:	ADCENTER
Command Alias:	DC
Keyboard:	<Ctrl>+2

AutoCAD DesignCenter

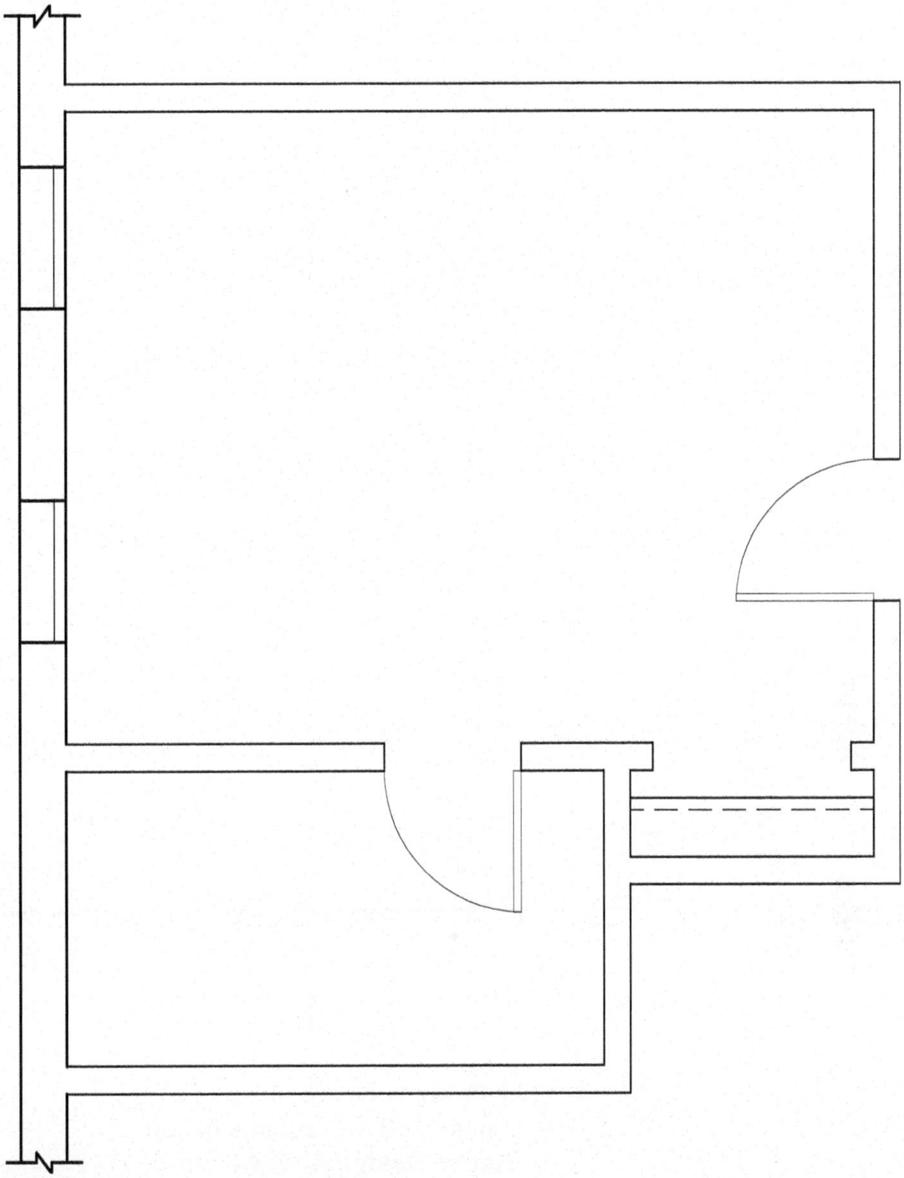

Figure 6-28
Draw exterior and interior walls, doors, closet shelf, and rod

Step 5. Open the AutoCAD **DesignCenter** and locate the **2D Architectural House Designer** blocks drawing (Figure 6-29), as described next:

Prompt	**Response**
Type a command:	**DesignCenter** (or type **DC <Enter>**)

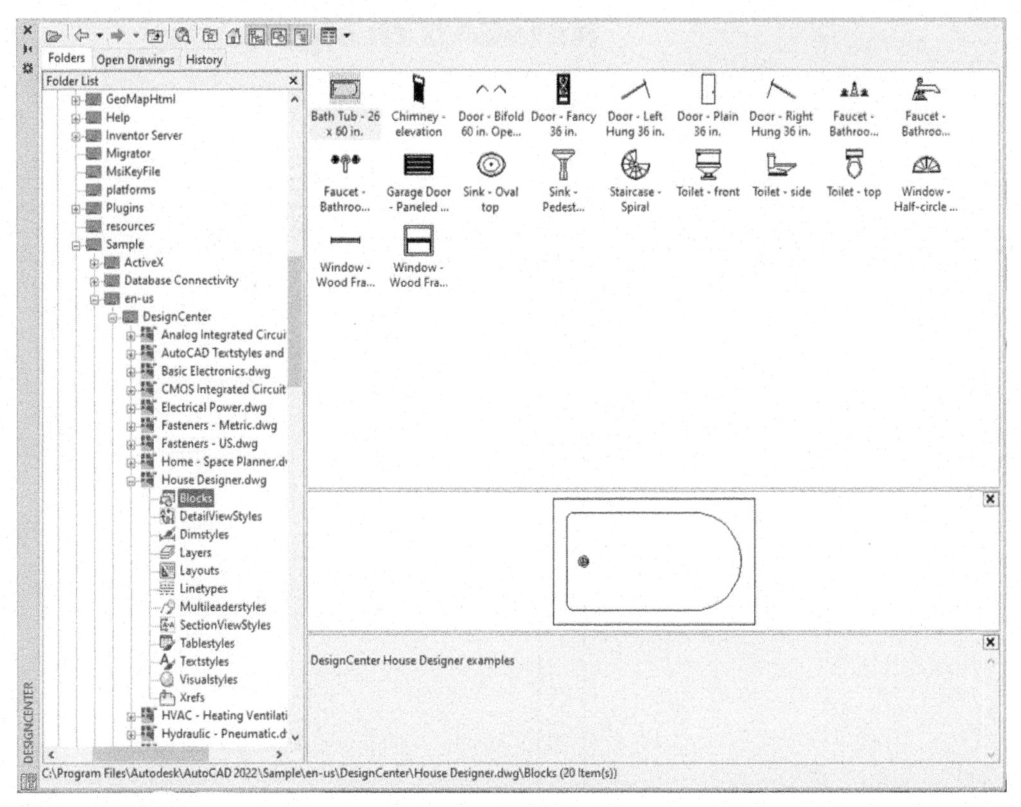

Figure 6-29
Select the **Bath Tub - 26 × 60 in.** from the **DesignCenter**

Prompt	Response
The **DesignCenter** appears:	Look at the file path at the bottom of Figure 6-29. Use the same or similar path to locate the **DesignCenter** folder Click **House Designer.dwg**
The **DesignCenter** shows the blocks and other items in the **House Designer.dwg** (Figure 6-29). Your **DesignCenter** may appear different, depending on what is selected in the **Views** icon or **Tree View** toggle at the top of the **DesignCenter**.	Click the **+** symbol beside **House Designer.dwg**, and then click **Blocks**
All the predefined blocks for the drawing appear.	Click **Bath Tub - 26 × 60 in.** (click and hold down the left mouse button and drag and drop the bathtub into the drawing) (*Note:* The bathtub size is 36″ × 60″)

Step 6. Rotate the tub and use **Osnap-Intersection** to locate the tub (Figure 6-30). Add a line to show the tub seat (Figure 6-31).

Figure 6-30
Insert the bathtub

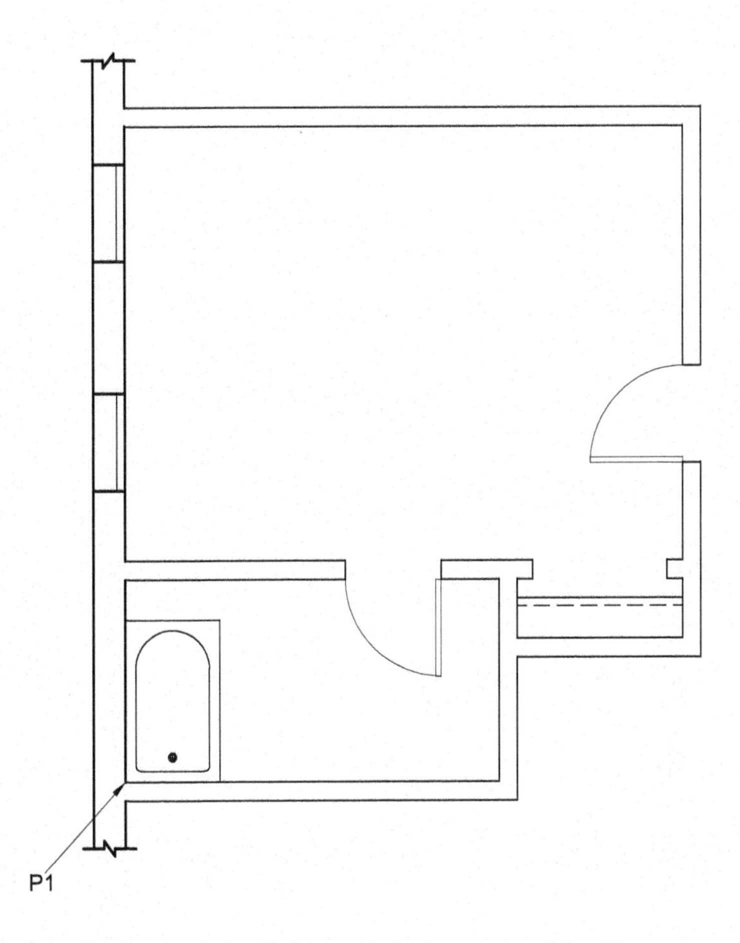

Figure 6-31
Bathroom dimensions for Exercise 6-2: Hotel room 1 floor plan (scale: 3/16″ = 1′-0″)

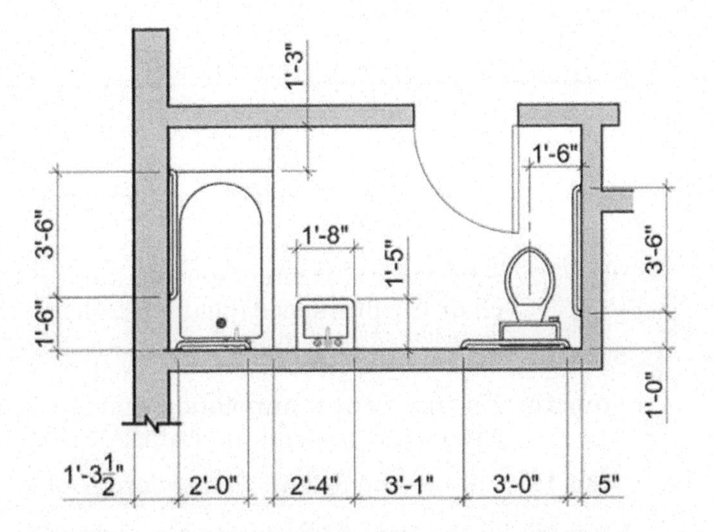

Step 7. Insert the toilet in the location shown 2″ from the south wall (Figure 6-31). Locate the toilet symbol in the **DesignCenter, House Designer.dwg, Blocks, Toilet - top.**

Step 8. Draw the sink using the dimensions shown in Figure 6-32.

Step 9. Set layer **a-fixt-fauc** current and insert the top view of the faucet in the locations shown (Figure 6-31) in the bathtub and sink. You will have to insert it on the **a-fixt-fauc** layer because the faucet is so detailed the lines will flow together unless they are very thin. Locate the faucet symbol in the **DesignCenter, House Designer.dwg, Blocks, Faucet - Bathroom top.**

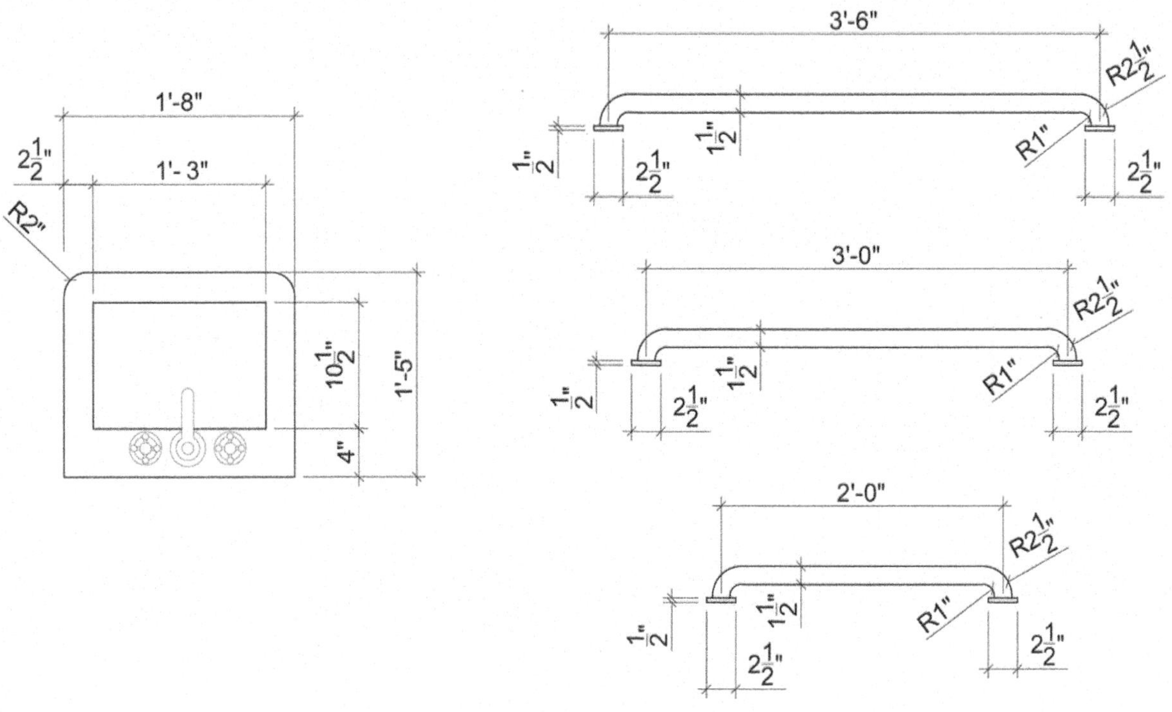

Figure 6-32
Sink and grab bar dimensions

Step 10. Draw the grab bars on the **a-fixt** layer, using the dimensions shown in Figures 6-31 and 6-32.

Step 11. Trim the toilet, sink, faucet, and tub seat lines that show through the grab bars. You will have to explode the blocks before you can trim. When the blocks are exploded, they will return to the **0** layer. Window the exploded blocks and put them back on the green **a-fixt** layer so they will plot with the correct lineweight.

Step 12. Set layer **a-flor-whch** current and draw the 60″-diameter wheelchair turning space (Figure 6-27).

Step 13. Set layer **a-anno-text** current.

Step 14. Set the drawing annotation scale to **1/4″ = 1′-0″** (located in the lower-right area on the AutoCAD screen).

Step 15. Change the text style **Standard** to the **CityBlueprint** font.

Step 16. In the **Text Style** dialog box, select the **Annotative** check box under **Size** to make sure the annotative property is on.

Step 17. Use **Dtext**, height **1/8″** to type your name, class, and date in the upper-right area (Figure 6-27).

Step 18. Use **Dtext**, height **3/16″** to type the underlined text HOTEL ROOM 1 FLOOR PLAN.

Step 19. Use **Dtext**, height **1/8″** to type the drawing scale.

Step 20. When you have completed Exercise 6-2, save your work in at least two places.

Step 21. Print the hotel room 1 floor plan at a scale of **1/4″ = 1′-0″**.

Chapter Summary

This chapter provided you the information necessary to set up and draw floor plans. In addition you learned to create and insert blocks and to use the **DesignCenter**. You also learned how to use annotative text, **Multiline, HATCH, ARRAY, RECTANGLE**, and other commands relating to floor plans. Now you have the skills and information necessary to produce floor plans that you can use in interior design.

Chapter Test Questions

Multiple Choice

Circle the correct answer.

1. What is the maximum number of lines you can draw at the same time with **Multiline?**

   a. 2 c. 12
   b. 4 d. 16

2. Which of the following **Multiline** justification options can you use to draw a three-line multiline that has a 3 offset, a 0, and a -3 offset, using the middle line?

   a. Top c. Zero
   b. Right d. Left

3. When you have created a new multiline style, what must you pick in the **Multiline Style** dialog box to set the new style current?

   a. **Set Current** c. **Save...**
   b. **Load** d. **Add**

4. Which of the following must you select first when using the **EXTEND** command?

   a. The correct layer c. Object to extend
   b. The correct color d. Boundary edge

5. Which of the following may not be changed with the **PROPERTIES** command?

   a. Color c. Layer
   b. Linetype d. Drawing name

6. Which of the following commands tells you the layer a line is on and its length?

   a. **Status** c. **DIST**
   b. **LIST** d. **Area**

7. If you insert a block with the **Explode check box** select in the **Insert** dialog box, which of the following is true?
    a. The block must be exploded before it can be edited.
    b. Each element of the block is a separate object.
    c. AutoCAD will not accept the block name.
    d. The block comes in smaller than originally drawn.
8. The **WBLOCK** command does which of the following?
    a. Creates a drawing file on any disk, drive, or network
    b. Creates a drawing on the hard drive only
    c. Creates blocks of parts of the current drawing only
    d. Uses only named blocks on the current drawing
9. Which scale factor can you use to create a mirror image of a block with the **Insert** command?
    a. Negative X, Negative Y
    b. Positive X, Positive Y
    c. Negative X, Positive Y
    d. Mirrored images cannot be created with the **Insert** command.
10. Which of the following commands attaches a paintbrush to the cursor so you can copy properties from one object to another?
    a. **Match Properties**
    b. **Copy Prop**
    c. **Make Object's Layer Current**
    d. **PROPERTIES**

Matching

Write the number of the correct answer on the line.

a. **ARRAY** _____

b. **EXTEND** _____

c. **Multiline Edit** _____

d. **Multiline** _____

e. **LIST** _____

1. A command that allows you to draw up to 16 lines at a time
2. A command that allows objects to be copied in rows and columns
3. A command that tells you what line a layer is on and its length
4. A command that you can use to modify a multiline without exploding it
5. A command that allows you to change the length of a line so it touches a boundary edge

True or False

Circle the correct answer.

1. **True or False:** When you create a block using the **Block** command and the **Retain Objects** box is selected, the objects selected remain on the screen.
2. **True or False: You can use Multiline Edit** on exploded multilines.
3. **True or False:** One advantage of using blocks is that you have to draw the object only once.
4. **True or False:** If you want your annotative text to be 1/8″ high on a drawing printed at a scale of 1/8″ = 1′-0″, your text will measure 8″ high when you are drawing full scale.
5. **True or False:** You must pick the boundary edge first before lines can be extended.

List

1. Five ways of accessing the **RECTANGLE** command.
2. Five parameters needed to construct a **Rectangular Array**.
3. Five parameters to specify under **Element** when you define a new **Multiline Style**.
4. Five tools of the **Multilines Edit Tools** dialog box.
5. Five ways of accessing the **LIST** command.
6. Five entity properties **MatchProp** can match between the source and destination objects.
7. Five ways of accessing the **Block** command.
8. Five parameters to specify when inserting a block into a drawing.
9. Five ways of accessing AutoCAD's Design Center.
10. Five advantages of using blocks.

Questions

1. In what situations would you use the **Multiline** command?
2. For what purpose would you want to use the **ARRAY** command?
3. How can objects drawn on the same layer be a different color?
4. What can the **LIST** command tell you about an object?
5. How can you use the **HATCH** command in drawing a floor plan?

Chapter Projects

Project 6-1: *Hotel Room 2 Floor Plan* [BASIC]

1. Draw the floor plan of hotel room 2 as shown in Figure 6-33. Use the dimensions shown or use an architectural scale to measure the floor plan and draw it full scale. Your drawing should look similar to Figure 6-33 without dimensions.
2. Plot or print the drawing to scale.

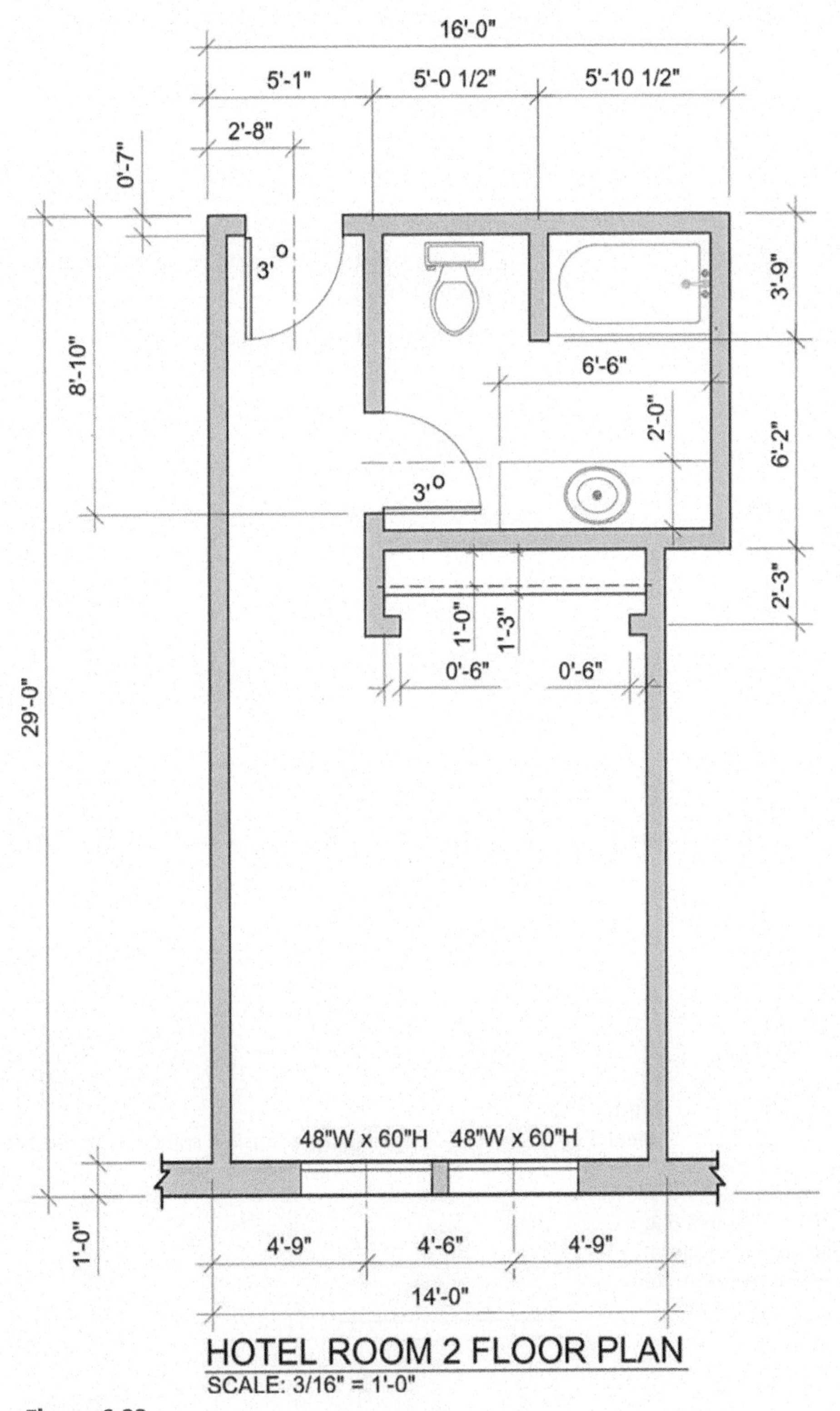

Figure 6-33
Project 6-1: Hotel room 2 floor plan (scale: 3/16″ = 1′-0″)

Project 6-2: *Wheelchair-Accessible Commercial Restroom Floor Plan* **[INTERMEDIATE]**

1. Draw the floor plan of the commercial restroom shown in Figure 6-34. Use the dimensions shown in Figure 6-34 (Sheets 1 and 2) or use an architectural scale to measure the floor plan and draw it full scale. Your drawing should look similar to Figure 6-34 (Sheet 1) without dimensions.
2. Plot or print the drawing to scale.

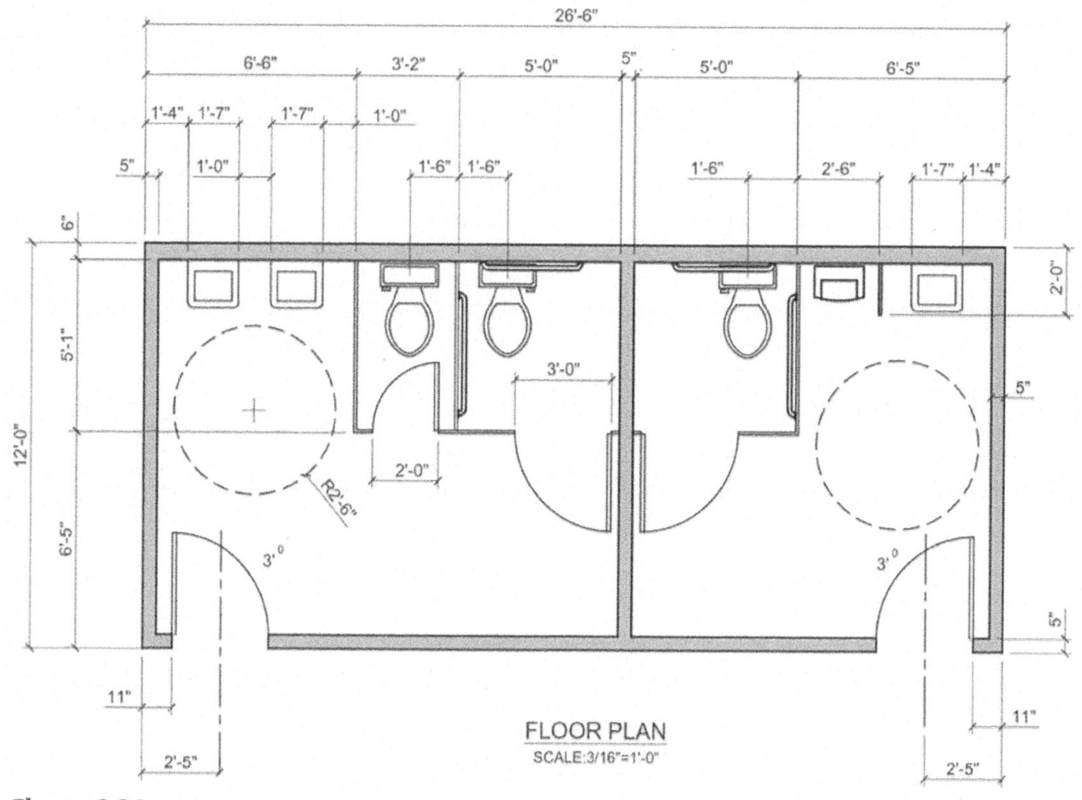

Figure 6-34
Sheet 1 of 2, Project 6-2: Wheelchair-accessible commercial restroom floor plan (scale: 3/16″ = 1′-0″)

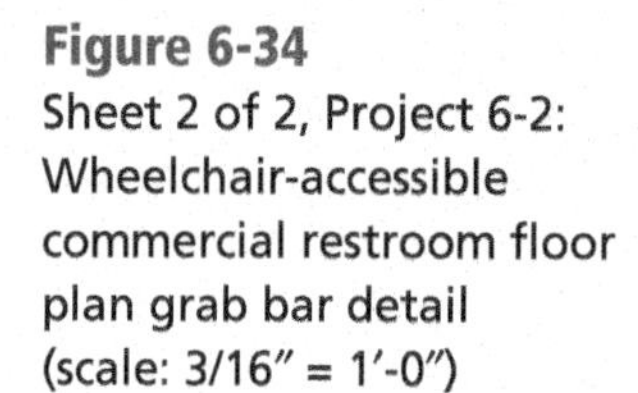
Figure 6-34
Sheet 2 of 2, Project 6-2: Wheelchair-accessible commercial restroom floor plan grab bar detail (scale: 3/16″ = 1′-0″)

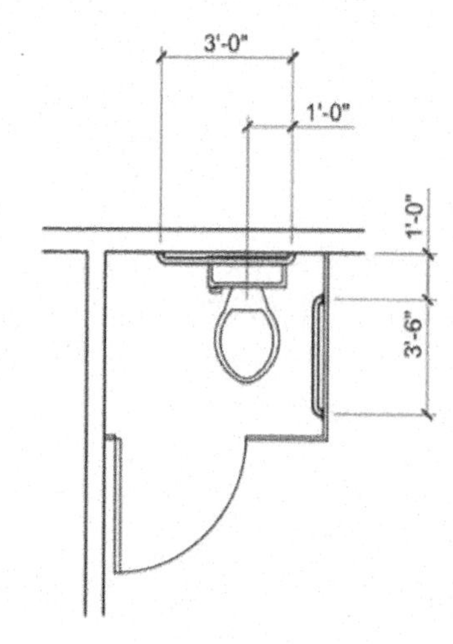

chapter seven

Dimensioning and Area Calculations

CHAPTER OBJECTIVES

- Understand the function of dimension variables.
- Set dimension variables.
- Save and restore dimension styles.
- Correctly use the following commands and settings:

Aligned Dimensioning	**Baseline Dimensioning**	**DIMASSOC**	**Grips**
Align Text	**CAL**	**DIMBREAK**	**Linear Dimensioning**
AREA	**Continue Dimensioning**	**DIMDLE**	**MATCHPROP**
		DIMEDIT	**Oblique**
		Dimension Edit	**Override**
		Dimension Style	**QDIM**
		DIMSCALE	**REVCLOUD**
		DIMSPACE	**STATUS**
		DIMTXT	**Update**

Eight Basic Types of Dimensions

You can create eight basic types of dimensions using AutoCAD. They are linear, aligned, arc length, ordinate, radius, jogged, diameter, and angular. They are listed in the **Dimension** menu of the menu bar, or you can create them by entering three characters: **D**, followed by the first two letters of the dimension type you want. For example, **DDI** is the command alias shortcut for **DIMDIAMETER**, **DAN** for **DIMANGULAR** and so forth. You can also create multiple dimension types by clicking the **Dimension** button on the **Dimensions** panel of the **Annotate** tab of the ribbon (see Figure 7-1).

You can activate each dimension type shown in Figure 7-2 automatically by hovering over the drawing object to be dimensioned, or by selecting one of the following from the drop-down list:

Linear: For dimensioning the length of horizontal, vertical, and angled lines

Figure 7-1
The **Dimensions** panel of the ribbon's **Annotate** tab

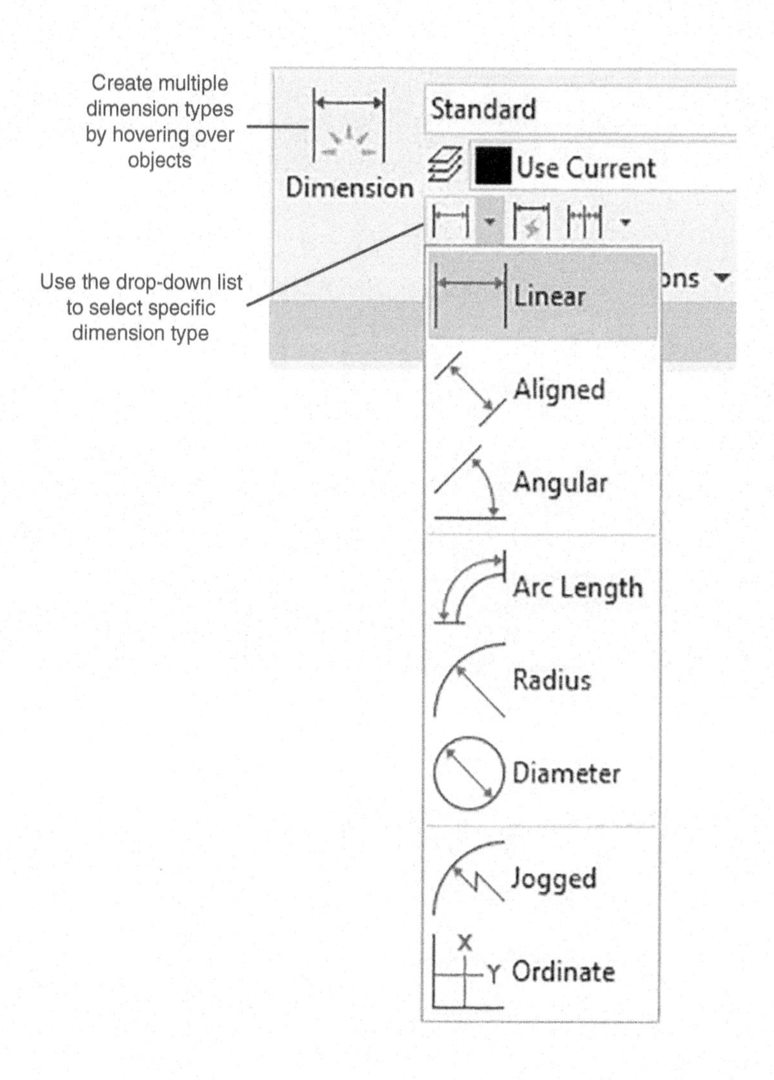

Aligned: For showing the length of features that are drawn at an angle

Arc Length: For dimensioning the length of an arc

Ordinate: To display the X or Y distance from the defined 0,0 point of a feature

Radius: To create radius dimensioning for arcs and circles

Jogged: To create jogged radius dimensioning for arcs and circles

Diameter: To create diameter dimensioning for arcs and circles

Angular: For dimensioning angles

Additionally, you can draw leaders and center marks by selecting **Multileader** or **Center Mark**.

You control the appearance of these eight basic types of dimensions, leaders, and center marks when they are drawn and plotted by settings called *dimension variables*.

Using Dimension Variables

dimension variables: A set of numeric values, text strings, and settings that control dimensioning features.

Dimension variables are settings that determine what your dimensions look like on your drawing. For instance, as shown in Figure 7-3, setting the

Figure 7-2
Basic types of dimensions

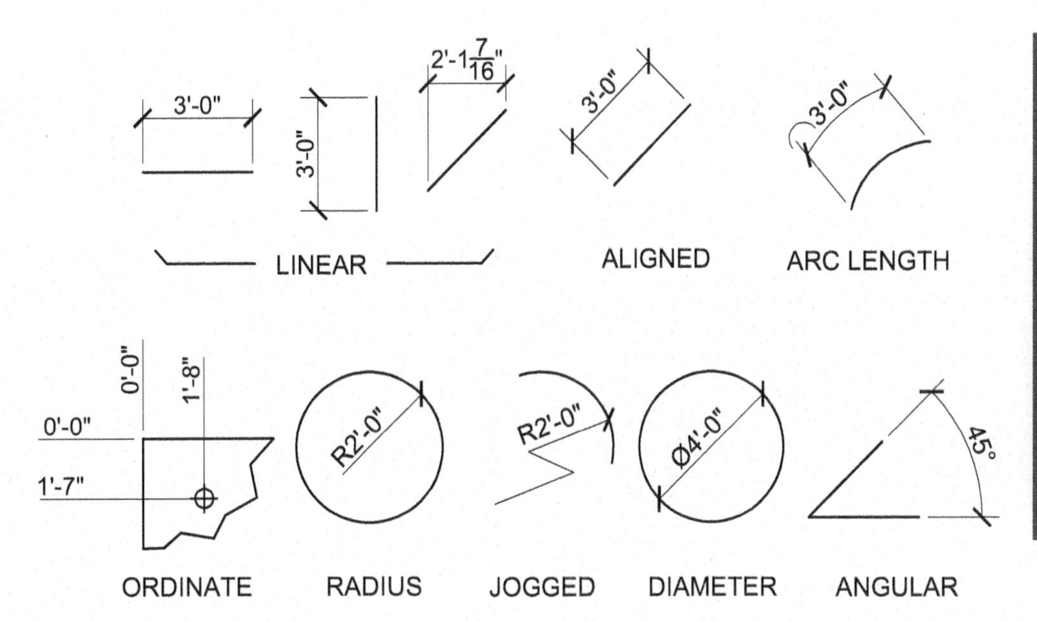

dimension variables determines the size of a tick mark, how far the dimension line extends beyond the tick, how far the extension line extends beyond the dimension line, and so on.

You can display a list of dimension variables by switching to the text screen (note that the command line window must be docked). Enter **SETVAR** (for set variable). At the **Enter variable name or [?]:** prompt, enter **?**. Then at the **Enter variable(s) to list <*>:** prompt, enter **DIM***. The **AutoCAD Text Window** appears with a listing of all dimension variables. (You will have to press **<Enter>** several times to see them all.)

Figure 7-3
Dimension terms and variables

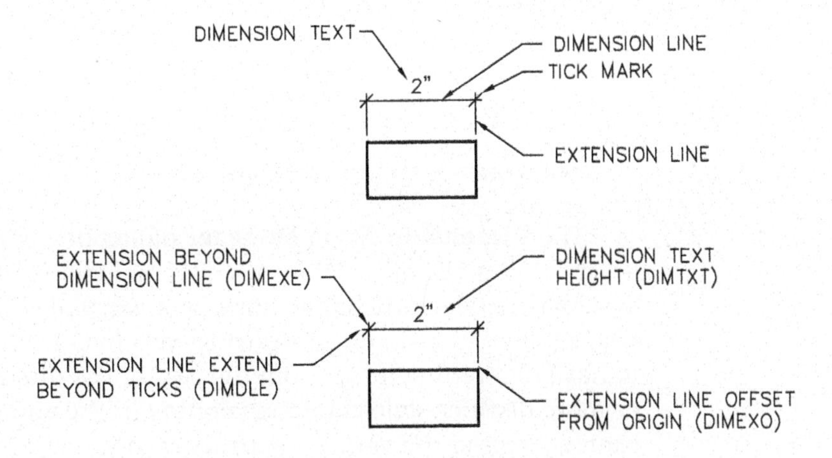

Figure 7-4 presents a complete list of AutoCAD 2022's dimension variables, their default values, and a brief description of each.

DIMADEC	0.0000	Controls number of decimal places in angular dimensions
DIMALT	OFF	Enables or disables alternate units
DIMALTD	2.0000	Alternate unit decimal places
DIMALTF	25.4000	Multiplier value for alternate dimensions
DIMALTRND	0.0000	Rounding of alternate dimensions
DIMALTTD	2.0000	Alternate tolerance decimal value in alternate dimensions
DIMALTTZ	0.0000	Zero suppression in tolerance values
DIMALTU	2.0000	Controls alternate unit format
DIMALTZ	0.0000	Controls zero suppression in alternate dimensions
DIMANNO	0.0000	Controls whether current dimension style is annotative
DIMAPOST		Text prefix or suffix for alternate units
DIMARCSYM	0.0000	Controls display of arc symbol in arc length dimensions
DIMASSOC	2.0000	Controls associativity of dimensions
DIMASZ	0.1800	Specifies size of dimension and leader arrows
DIMATFIT	3.0000	Controls spacing of dimension elements in limited space
DIMAUNIT	0.0000	Controls unit format for angular dimensions
DIMAZIN	0.0000	Controls zero suppression in angular dimensions
DIMBLK	""	Controls both arrow symbols on dimensions
DIMBLK1	""	Controls arrow symbol on first end of dimension
DIMBLK2	'	Controls arrow symbol on second end of dimension
DIMCEN	0.0900	Controls center mark on radial and diameter dimensions
DIMCLRD	0.0000	Specifies colors of dimension lines, arrows, and leaders
DIMCLRE	0.0000	Specifies colors of extension lines, centerlines, and center marks
DIMCLRT	0.0000	Specifies color of dimension text
DIMCONSTRAINTICON	3.0000	Displays lock icon on dimensions with constraints
DIMCONTINUEMODE	1.0000	Specifies current or existing style for continued dimensions
DIMDEC	4.0000	Number of decimal places in primary dimensions
DIMDLE	0.0000	Specifies distance extension line extends beyond dimension line for oblique-stroke arrows
DIMDLI	0.3800	Specifies separation of dimensions in baseline dimensions
DIMDSEP	"."	Specifies decimal separator character
DIMEXE	0.1800	Specifies distance extension line extends beyond dimension line
DIMEXO	0.0625	Specifies distance between extension line and origin point
DIMFRAC	0.0000	Specifies fraction format for architectural dimension units
DIMFXL	1.0000	Specifies length of extension line between dimension line and origin point
DIMFXLON	OFF	Specifies whether or not extension lines are fixed length
DIMGAP	0.0900	Specifies length of gap when a dimension line is broken by another dimension line
DIMJOGANG	45.0000	Specifies angle of "break" segment in jogged radius dimensions
DIMJUST	0.0000	Controls spacing of horizontal dimension text
DIMLAYER	"use current"	Specifies a default layer for all dimensions
DIMLDRBLK	""	Specifies arrow type of leaders
DIMLFAC	1.0000	Specifies scale factor for dimension measurements
DIMLIM	OFF	Controls whether or not dimensions show a limit range
DIMLTEX1	""	Specifies linetype for first extension line
DIMLTEX2	""	Specifies linetype for second extension line
DIMLTYPE	""	Specifies linetype for dimension line
DIMLUNIT	2.0000	Specifies units type for all dimensions except angular
DIMLWD	-2.0000	Assigns lineweights to dimension lines
DIMLWE	-2.0000	Assigns lineweights to extension lines
DIMPICKBOX	5.0000	Specifies size of selection target from within the DIM prompt
DIMPOST	""	Specifies prefix or suffix to dimension text
DIMRND	0.0000	Specifies rounding value for dimensions
DIMSAH	OFF	Controls display of dimension arrows
DIMSCALE	1.0000	Applies a scale factor to all dimensions
DIMSD1	OFF	Suppress first dimension line
DIMSD2	OFF	Suppress second dimension line
DIMSE1	OFF	Suppress first extension line
DIMSE2	OFF	Suppress second extension line
DIMSOXD	OFF	Suppress arrows if extension lines too close together
DIMSTYLE	"Standard"	Displays unit type - Architectural or ISO
DIMTAD	0.0000	Places dimension text above or vertically centered on dimension line
DIMTDEC	4.0000	Sets decimal places for tolerances
DIMTFAC	1.0000	Tolerance text height scale factor
DIMTFILL	0.0000	Controls dimension text backgrounds
DIMTFILLCLR	0.0000	Sets background color for dimension text
DIMTIH	ON	Sets dimension text inside extension lines to horizontal or aligned with dimension line
DIMTIX	OFF	Places dimension text between extension lines
DIMTM	0.0000	Sets minus tolerance value
DIMTMOVE	0.0000	Sets options for moving dimension text
DIMTOFL	OFF	Forces dimension line inside extension lines
DIMTOH	ON	Sets dimension text outside extension lines is horizontal or aligned with dimension line
DIMTOL	OFF	Enables tolerance dimensions
DIMTOLJ	1.0000	Controls vertical justification for tolerance values
DIMTP	0.0000	Sets plus tolerance value
DIMTSZ	0.0000	Sets dimension tick size
DIMTVP	0.0000	Controls vertical position of dimension text if DIMTAD is off
DIMTXSTY	"Standard"	Displays text style for dimensions
DIMTXT	0.1800	Sets height of dimension text
DIMTXTDIRECTION	OFF	Specifies direction in which dimensions are read
DIMTXTRULER	ON	Displays ruler when editing dimension text
DIMTZIN	0.0000	Suppresses zeros in tolerance dimensions
DIMUPT	OFF	Controls user-located text options
DIMZIN	0.0000	Controls zero suppression in primary units

Figure 7-4
AutoCAD's dimension variables

The **Dimension Style Manager** dialog box (Figure 7-5) allows you to set most dimension variables using a dialog box. It allows you to name the dimension style and change dimension variables using tabs on the dialog box. While dimensioning a drawing, you may want some of the dimensions to have different settings from the rest of the dimensions. You can use two or more distinct styles of dimensioning in the same drawing. You may save each style (and the variable settings for that style) separately and recall them when needed.

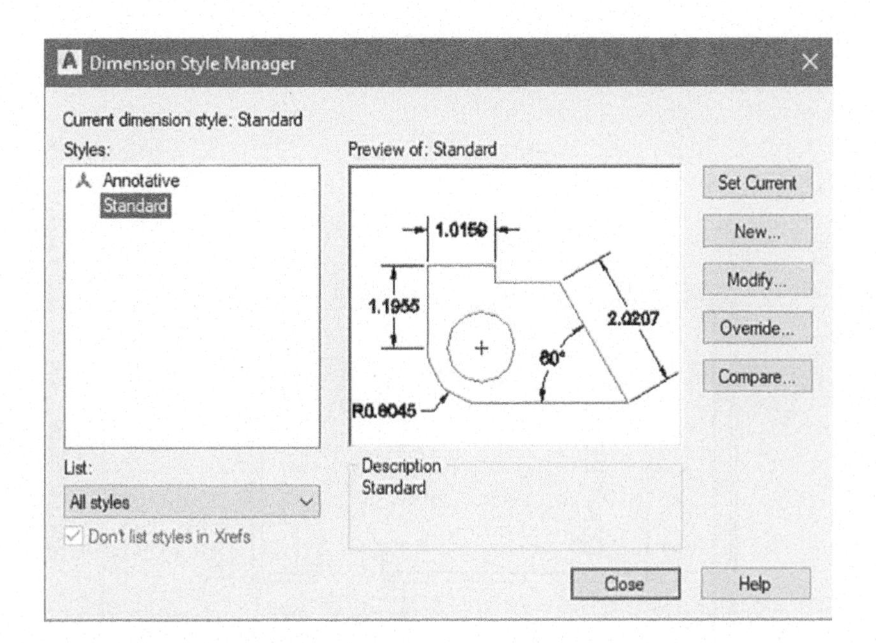

Figure 7-5
Dimension Style Manager

EXERCISE 7-1
Dimensioning the Tenant Space Floor Plan Using Linear Dimensions

Exercise 7-1 provides instructions for setting the dimension variables for the tenant space floor plan drawn in Exercise 6-1, saving the dimension variables, and dimensioning the exterior and interior of the tenant space floor plan using linear dimensions. When you have completed Exercise 7-1, your drawing will look similar to Figure 7-6.

> **NOTE**
>
> In **EXERCISE 12-1** and **EXERCISE 12-2,** you will freeze layers to make a presentation that displays the dimensioned floor plan, furniture plan, reflected ceiling plan, and the voice/data/power plan. This will work only if you have saved **CH6-EXERCISE1, CH7-EXERCISE1, CH9-EXERCISE1**, and **CH11-EXERCISE1** as a single drawing.

Step 1. Begin drawing **CH7-EXERCISE1** by opening existing drawing **CH6-EXERCISE1** and saving it as **CH7-EXERCISE1** on the hard drive or network drive, as described next:

Prompt	Response
Type a command:	Click **Open...**
The **Select File** dialog box appears:	Locate **CH6-EXERCISE1** Double-click **CH6-EXERCISE1**
CH6-EXERCISE1 opens	
Type a command:	**Save As...**

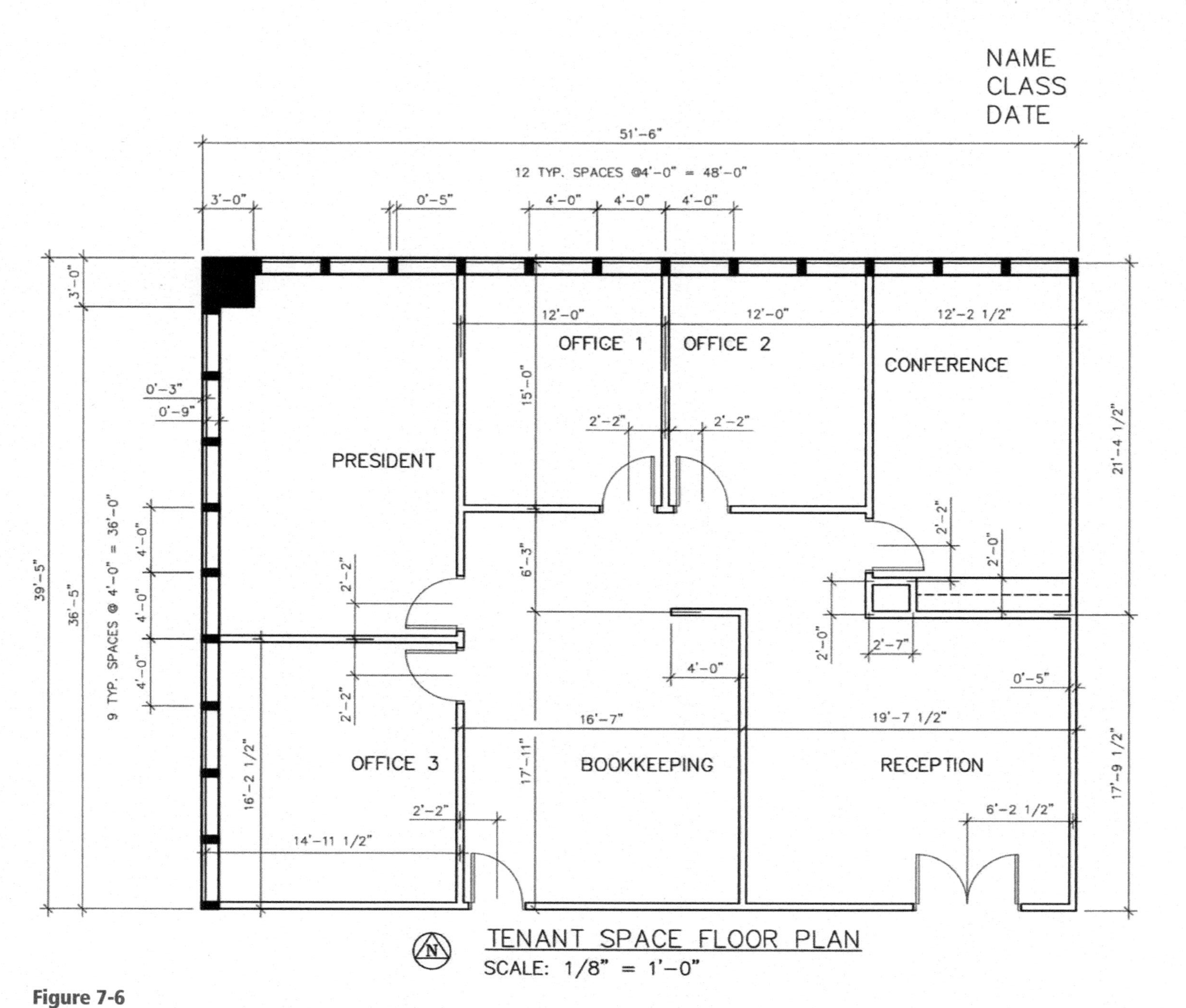

Figure 7-6
Exercise 7-1: Dimensioning the tenant space floor plan using linear dimensions (scale: 1/8" = 1'-0")

Prompt	Response
The **Save Drawing As...** dialog box appears:	Type **CH7-EXERCISE1** (replace **CH6-EXERCISE1** in the **File Name:** input box) Click the correct drive and folder Click **Save**

You are now working on the hard drive or network with a drawing named **CH7-EXERCISE1**.

Step 2. Verify that **UNITS** is set to **Architectural**, as described next:

Prompt	Response
Type a command:	**Type UN <Enter>**
The **Drawing Units** dialog box appears:	Select **Architectural** in the **Type:** input box Select **0′-0 1/32″** in the **Precision:** input box Click **OK**

> **NOTE**
>
> Be sure to select **32** as the denominator of the smallest fraction to display when setting drawing units so that the dimension variable settings will display the same fraction if they are set in 32nds.

There are two different ways to set dimension variables: by entering the name of the dimension variable in the command line window, or by using the **Dimension Style Manager** dialog box. The following describes the two ways to set dimension variables.

Setting the Dimension Variables Using the Command Prompt

Step 3. Use **STATUS** to view the current status of all the dimension variables and change the setting for **DIMDLE**, as described next:

Prompt	Response
Type a command:	Type **SETVAR <Enter>**
Enter variable name of [?]:	Enter a question mark
Enter variable(s) to list <*>:	Type **DIM* <Enter>**
The dimension variables appear in the **AutoCAD Text Window**	Press **<Enter>** to see how the variables are currently set. Close the **AutoCAD Text Window**
Type a command:	Type **DLE <Enter>** (dimension line extension)
Enter new value for dimension variable <default>:	Type **1/16 <Enter>**

Setting the Dimension Variables Using the Dimension Style Manager Dialog Box

The **Dimension Style Manager** (type **D** and **<Enter>**) dialog box (Figure 7-7) allows you to change dimension variables using tabs on the dialog box. The default dimension style is **Standard**. Notice that there is a *style override* to the **Standard** dimension style. The override was created when you just typed a new setting for **DIMDLE**, using the command line. You can also create an override using the dialog box (see the **Override...** button). A dimension style override changes a dimension system variable without changing the current dimension style. All dimensions created in the style include the override until you delete the override, save the override to the current style or a new style, or set another style current.

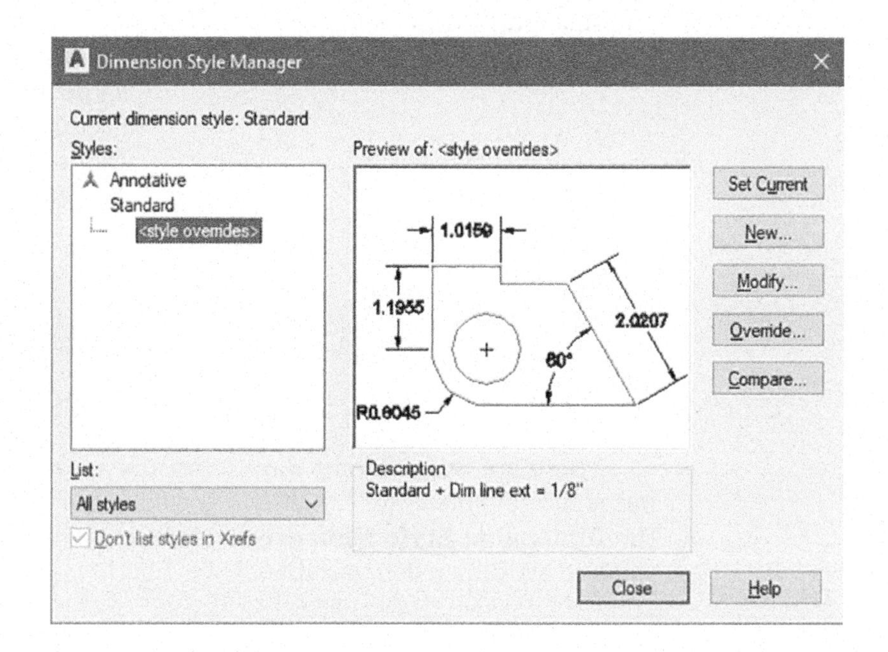

Figure 7-7
Dimension Style Manager showing a style override

You can use the **Modify...** button to modify the existing **Standard** style, or you can name a new style and make that style current when you begin dimensioning. In this exercise you will create a new style that has several dimension variables that are different from the **Standard** style.

DIMENSION STYLE	
Ribbon/ Panel	Annotate/ Dimensions/ <dialog box launcher>
Dimension Toolbar:	
Menu Bar:	Dimension/ Dimension Style...
Type a Command:	DIMSTYLE
Command Alias:	D

Step 4. Use the **Dimension Style Manager** to create a new style (Figures 7-7 through 7-13), as described next:

Prompt	**Response**
Type a command:	**Dimension Style...** (or type **DDIM** **<Enter>**)
The **Dimension Style Manager** dialog box (Figure 7-6) appears:	Click **New...**
The **Create New Dimension Style** dialog box (Figure 7-7) appears:	Type **STYLE1** in the **New Style Name:** input box
	Click **Start With: Standard** (Figure 7-8)
	Click **Continue** (or press **<Enter>**)

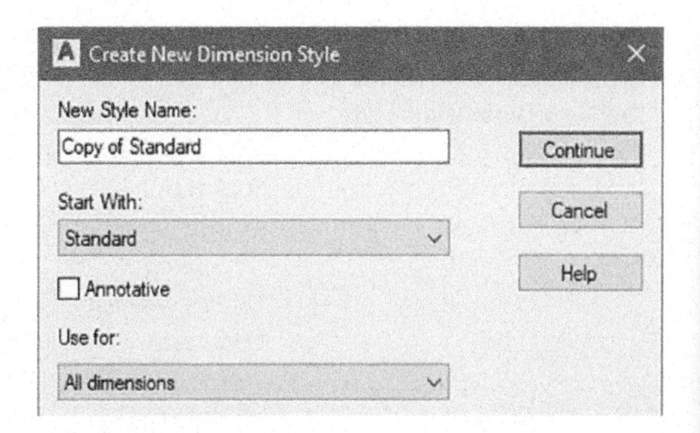

Figure 7-8
Create New Dimension Style dialog box

Prompt	**Response**
The **New Dimension Style** dialog box appears:	Click **the Primary Units** tab (Figure 7-9) (setting the **Primary Units** first will allow you to view how dimensions will appear as you set other variables)
The **Primary Units** tab displays:	Select **Architectural** in the **Unit format:** input box
	Select **0′-0 1/2″** in the **Precision:** input box
	Set all other variables for this tab as shown in Figure 7-9
	Click the **Symbols and Arrows** tab (Figure 7-10)

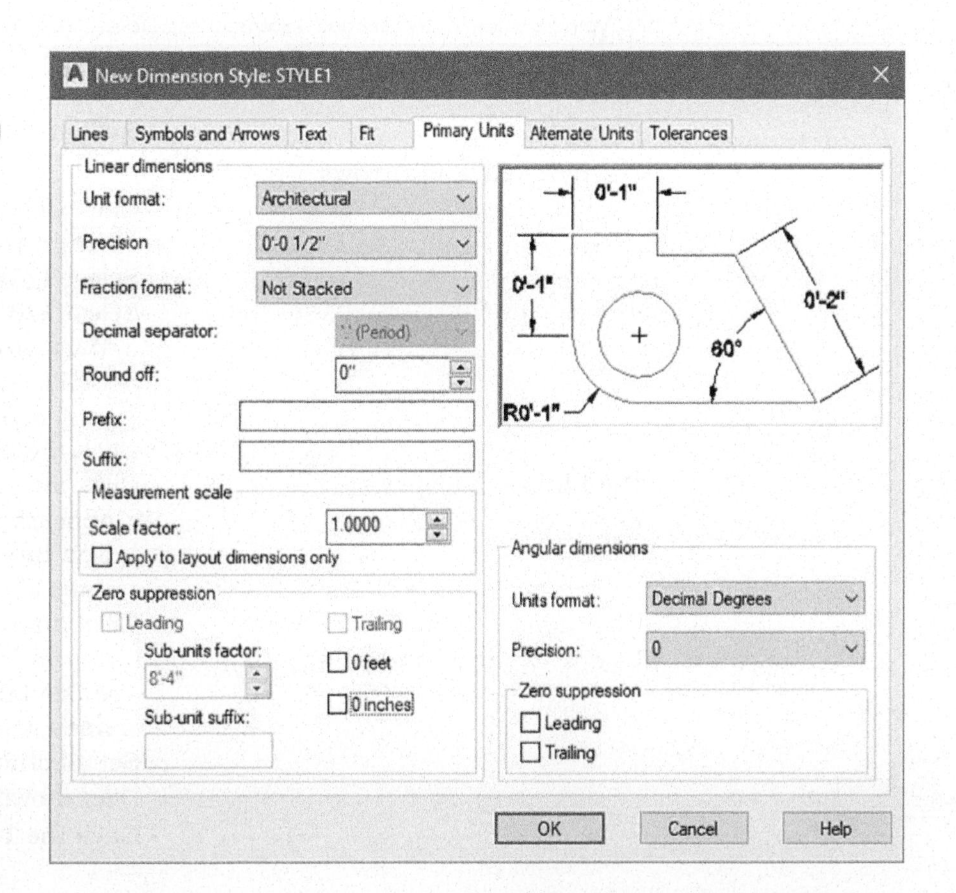

Figure 7-9
Primary Units tab of the **New Dimension Style** dialog box

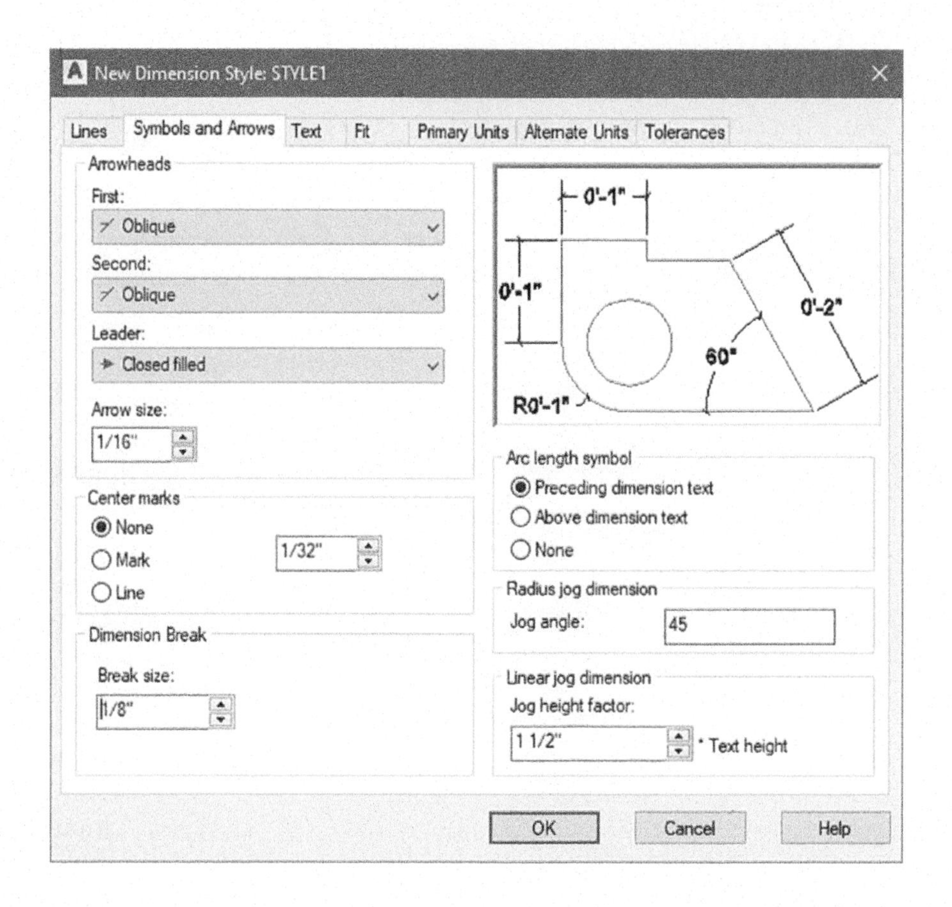

Figure 7-10
Symbols and Arrows tab of the **New Dimension Style** dialog box

> **TIP**
>
> Typing a value in the text box is sometimes quicker than using the up and down arrows.

Prompt	Response
The **Symbols and Arrows** tab displays:	Click **Oblique** in the **Arrowheads: First:** list
	Select **1/16″** in the **Arrow size:** list
	Select **1/32″** in the **Center marks: Mark** size list
	Set all other variables for this tab as shown in Figure 7-10
	Click the **Lines** tab (Figure 7-11)
The **Lines** tab displays:	Click an arrow so that **1/16″** appears in the **Extend beyond dim lines:** box in the **Extension lines** area
	Click an arrow so that **1/16″** appears in the **Extend beyond ticks:** box in the **Dimension lines** area
	Set all other variables for this tab as shown in Figure 7-11
	Click the **Text** tab

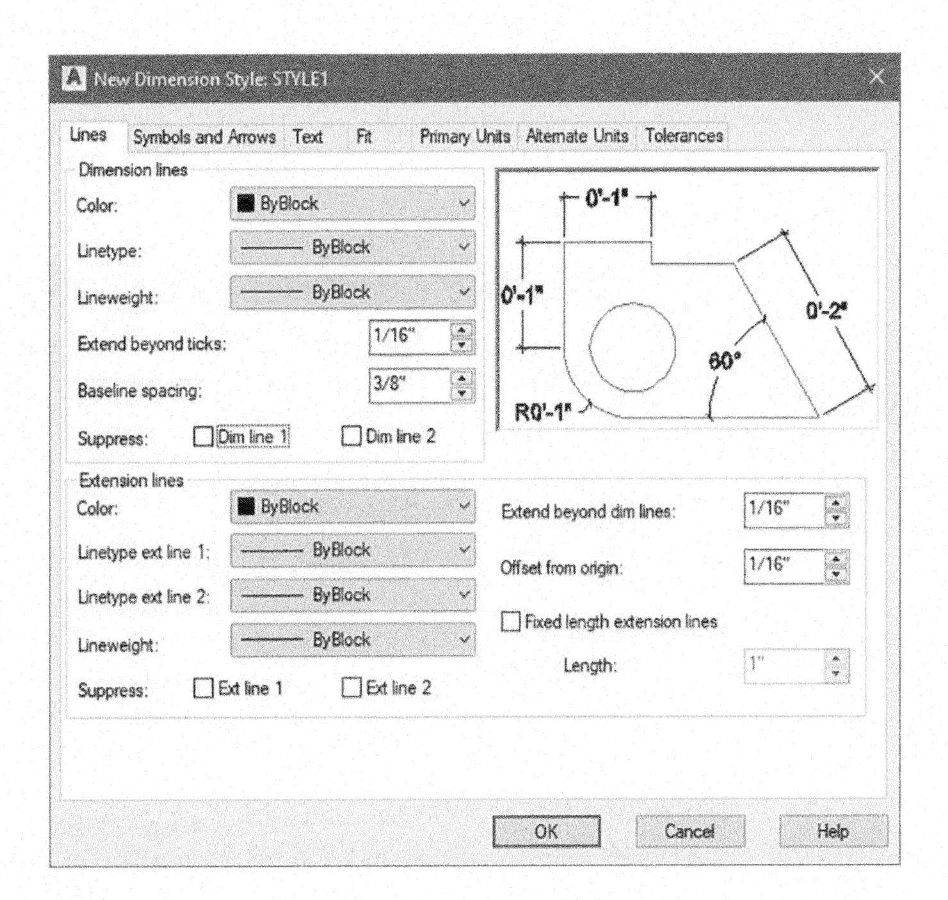

Figure 7-11
Lines tab of the **New Dimension Style** dialog box

Prompt	**Response**
The **Text** tab displays:	Click **1/16″** in the **Text height:** box (Figure 7-12)
	Click **Above** in the **Vertical:** box of the **Text placement** area (this places dimension text above the dimension line)
	Click **0′-0 1/32″** in the **Offset from dim line:** box in the **Text Placement** area
	Click the **Aligned with dimension line** option button in the **Text alignment** area
	Click the three dots (ellipsis) to the right of the **Standard Text style:** input box
The **Text Style** dialog box appears:	Check to make sure the **Standard** text style with the **simplex.shx** font is set current
	Set all other variables for this tab as shown in Figure 7-12
	Click the **Fit** tab

> **NOTE**
>
> If you want a thicker tick, select **Architectural tick** in the **Arrowheads: First:** list on the **Symbols and Arrows** tab.

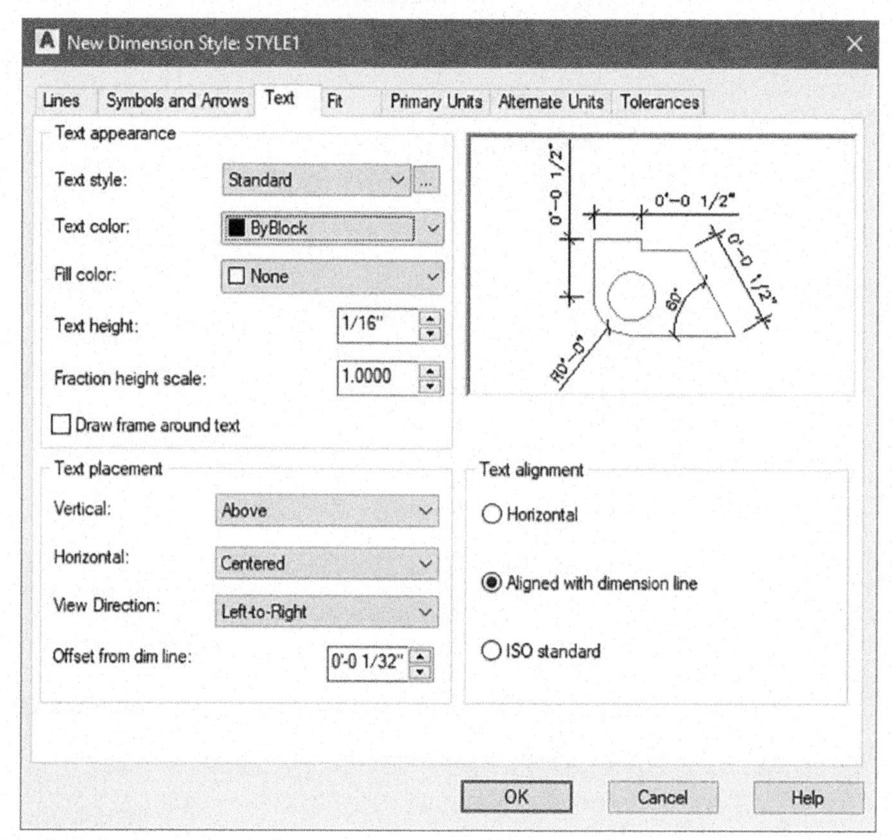

Figure 7-12
Text tab of the **New Dimension Style** dialog box

Prompt	**Response**
The **Fit** tab displays:	Click the **Either text or arrows (best fit)** option button in the **Fit options** area (Figure 7-13) Select the **Annotative** check box Set all variables for this tab as shown in Figure 7-13 Click **OK**

Figure 7-13
Fit tab of the **New Dimension Style** dialog box

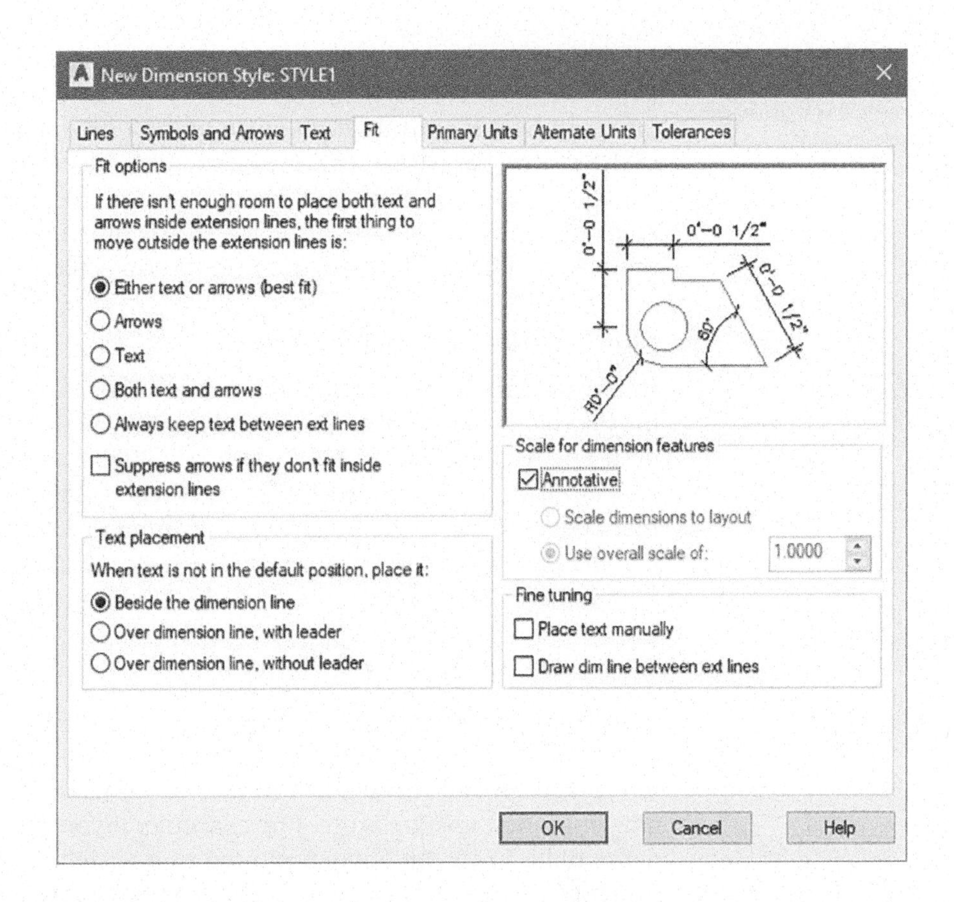

Prompt	**Response**
The **AutoCAD Alert** dialog box appears:	Click **OK**
The **Dimension Style Manager** appears with **STYLE1** highlighted:	Click **Set Current** (to set **STYLE1** current)
	Click **Close**

Using the Fit Tab to Scale for Dimension Features

In the preceding section, you set dimension variables that govern the sizes, distances, and spacing of dimension elements. It is important to understand how the value that is entered for a variable that governs a size, distance, or spacing of a dimension element relates to your drawing as it appears on the screen and when the drawing is plotted. You control this via the following settings, as shown on the **Fit** tab in Figure 7-13.

Annotative

When the tenant space floor plan is drawn full scale, the dimensions on the full-scale screen drawing must be large so they can be seen on the screen. For example, if you want the dimension text to be 1/8″ high on the paper drawing that is printed at 1/8″ = 1′-0″, the dimension text will be 12″ high on the full-scale drawing on the screen (a scale factor of 96).

annotative: A property belonging to objects, such as text, dimensions, and hatch patterns, that is commonly used to annotate drawings.

Annotation scale controls how the dimensions and other ***annotative*** objects appear on the drawing. When you make the dimension style annotative and set the annotation scale of the drawing in the lower-right corner of the status bar, AutoCAD automatically does the arithmetic for you and controls how the dimensions look on your screen. When you add dimensions, AutoCAD calculates the size of the dimension variables on the full-scale screen drawing using the annotation scale setting.

Scale Dimensions to Layout

Drawings can be dimensioned in either model space, with the actual drawing geometry, or in paper space, through scaled viewports. Some companies do it one way, and some do it the other. If you create dimensions in a paper space layout, selecting **Scale dimensions to layout** sizes dimension elements according to the scale of the printed drawing, which is usually 1:1. If you create dimension in model space, you will probably use the second option and set an overall scale as described next.

Use Overall Scale of: (DIMSCALE)

The **Use overall scale of:** setting is also referred to as the *overall scale factor* and the variable **DIMSCALE**. When a drawing such as the tenant space or a large house is drawn full scale, the dimensions that are added to the drawing must also be large. For example, if you want the text of the dimensions to be 1/16″ high when plotted at a scale of 1/8″ = 1′-0″, the text of the dimensions that you add while dimensioning full scale will be 6″ high. **DIMSCALE** is the variable that controls the overall scale factor, or how the dimension parts appear on the screen display while you are drawing full scale and how they appear when plotted. For example, if you decide that the dimension text (**DIMTXT**) will be 1/16″ high when a drawing is plotted, enter **1/16″** for the text height value (**DIMTXT**). If you plan to plot the drawing at 1/8″ = 1′-0″, set the overall scale factor (**DIMSCALE**) to **96** (1/8″ = 12″, 1 = 96). While you are drawing full scale, the text height will be 1/16″ = 96″, or 6″ high on the screen. When the drawing is plotted at 1/8″ = 1′-0″, the entire drawing, including the dimension text, is reduced by a scale factor of 96 (6″ ÷ 96 = 1/16″).

The overall scale factor (**DIMSCALE**) for a drawing that is plotted at 1/4″ = 12″ is 48 (1/4 = 12, 1 = 48). For a plotting ratio of 1/2″ = 12″, the overall scale factor (**DIMSCALE**) is 24 (1/2 = 12, 1 = 24).

> **TIP**
>
> Start a drawing, set the dimension variables, and save the drawing as a template for future dimensioning projects.

Step 5. Create the following new layer and set it as the current layer:

Layer name	Color	Linetype	Lineweight
a-anno-dims	Red	continuous	.004″ (.09 mm)

Step 6. Make sure the **Annotation Scale** is set to 1/8″ = 1′-0″.

Linear and Continue Dimensioning

Linear dimensions are the most basic type of AutoCAD dimension. Linear dimensions are either horizontal or vertical, or they can be rotated if you specify the angle for the dimension line. After a dimension is created, you can use the **Continue** option to create a string of dimensions, as shown in Figure 7-15.

Step 7. Using **Linear**, dimension the column and one mullion on the north exterior wall of the tenant space floor plan (Figure 7-14), as described next:

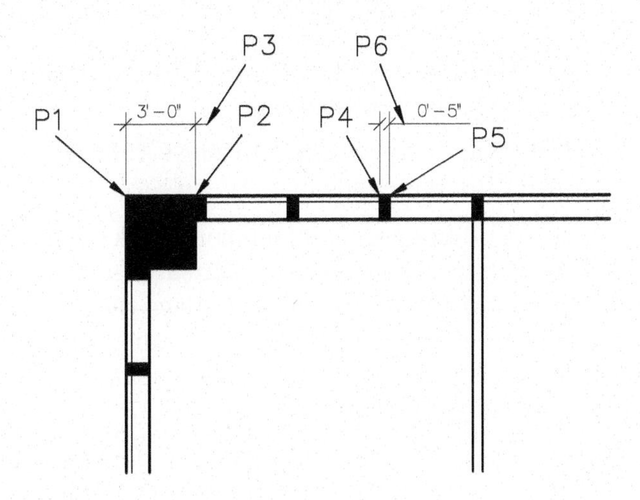

Figure 7-14
Linear dimensioning

DIMENSION: LINEAR	
Ribbon/ Panel	Annotate/ Dimensions
Dimension Toolbar:	
Menu Bar:	Dimension/ Linear
Type a Command:	DIMLINEAR
Command Alias:	DLI

Prompt	Response
Type a command:	**Linear** (or type **DLI <Enter>**)
DIMLINEAR Specify first extension line origin or <select object>:	**P1→** (with **SNAP** on)
Specify second extension line origin:	**P2→**
Specify dimension line location or [Mtext Text Angle Horizontal Vertical Rotated]:	**P3→** (on snap, three grid marks up, with 12″ grid)
Type a command:	**<Enter>** (repeat **Linear**)
DIMLINEAR Specify first extension line origin or <select object>:	**Osnap-Intersection**
of	**P4→**
Specify second extension line origin:	**Osnap-Intersection**
of	**P5→**
Specify dimension line location or [Mtext Text Angle Horizontal Vertical Rotated]:	**P6→** (on snap, three grid marks up)

In the **Linear** command, after the second extension line origin is selected, the prompt reads: *Specify dimension line location or [Mtext Text Angle Horizontal Vertical Rotated]:*.

Before you pick a dimension line location, you may type the first letter of any of the options in the brackets and press **<Enter>** to activate it. These options are as follows:

Mtext: To activate the **Multiline Text** command for dimensions requiring more than one line of text.

Text: To replace the default text with a single line of text. To suppress the text entirely, press the space bar.

Angle: To rotate the text of the dimension to a specific angle.

Horizontal: To specify that you want a horizontal dimension; this is normally not necessary.

Vertical: To specify that you want a vertical dimension; this is normally not necessary.

Rotated: To specify by entering a rotation angle that you want to rotate the entire dimension.

Using other specific dimension types such as **Aligned**, **Diameter**, or **Ordinate** is the same as using **Linear**. First choose the type of dimension you want, then select points and place the dimension. However, using the **Dimension** command (**Dimensions** panel of the **Annotate** tab, or simply type **DIM <Enter>**) and placing dimensions from the **Dim:** prompt is simpler and more efficient.

Step 8. Using the **Dimension** button, dimension horizontally (center to center) the distance between four mullions on the north exterior wall of the tenant space (Figure 7-15), as described next. (Before continuing, zoom in or pan over to the four mullions to be dimensioned.)

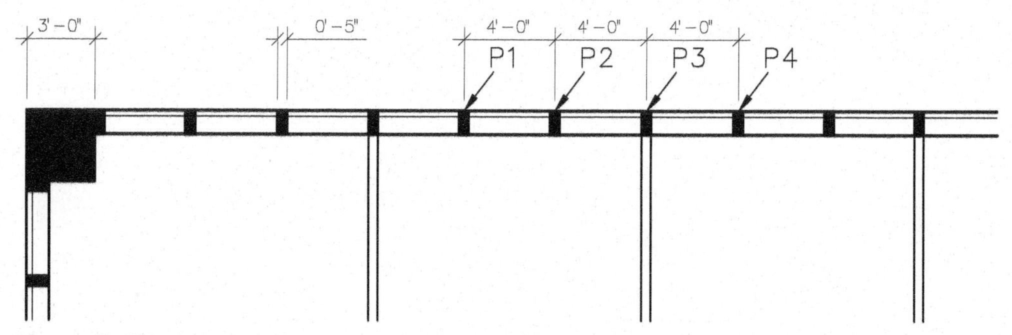

Figure 7-15
Linear dimensioning with the **Dimension** command to draw horizontal dimensions

Prompt	**Response**
Type a command:	**Dimension** (from the **Dimensions** panel) or type **DIM <Enter>**
DIM Select objects or specify first extension line origin or [Angular Baseline Continue Ordinate AliGn Distribute Layer Undo]:	**Osnap-Midpoint**
of	**P1→**
DIM Specify second extension line origin or [Undo]:	**Osnap-Midpoint**
of	**P2→**

DIMENSION: CONTINUE	
Ribbon/ Panel	Annotate/ Dimensions
Dimension Toolbar:	
Menu Bar:	Dimension/ Continue
Type a Command:	DIMCONTINUE
Command Alias:	DCO

Prompt	**Response**
DIM Specify dimension line location or second line for angle [Mtext Text text Undo]:	Click a point on snap, three grid marks up, to align with previous dimensions
DIM Select objects or specify first extension line origin or [Angular Baseline Continue Ordinate AliGn Distribute Layer Undo]:	Click **Continue** in the command prompt window, or type **C <Enter>**
DIM Specify first extension line origin to continue:	**Osnap-Midpoint**
of	**P3→**
Specify second extension line origin or [Select/Undo] <Select>:	**Osnap-Midpoint**
of	**P4→**
Specify second extension line origin or [Select/Undo] <Select>:	**<Enter>**
Select continued dimension:	**<Enter>** (to complete the command)

NOTE

You may change the dimension string at the prompt *Specify dimension line location by typing T <Enter>*, then typing new dimensions from the keyboard and pressing **<Enter>**.

Step 9. Using **Dimension**, add vertical dimensions (center to center) to show the distance between four mullions on the west exterior wall of the tenant space (Figure 7-16), as described next. (Before continuing, zoom in on the four mullions to be dimensioned.)

Prompt	**Response**
Type a command:	**Dimension** (from the **Dimensions** panel) or type **DIM <Enter>**
DIM Select objects or specify first extension line origin or [Angular Baseline Continue Ordinate AliGn Distribute Layer Undo]:	**Osnap-Midpoint**
of	Click the first mullion (dimension south to north)
DIM Specify second extension line origin or [Undo]:	**Osnap-Midpoint**
of	Pick the second mullion
DIM Specify dimension line location or second line for angle [Mtext Text text Undo]:	Pick a point on snap, three grid marks to the left, similar to previous dimension line locations

Prompt	Response
DIM Select objects or specify first extension line origin or [Angular Baseline Continue Ordinate AliGn Distribute Layer Undo]:	Click **Continue** in the command prompt window, or type **C <Enter>**
Specify a second extension line origin or [Undo Select]<Select>:	**Osnap-Midpoint**
of	Pick the third mullion
Specify a second extension line origin or [Undo Select]<Select>:	**Osnap-Midpoint**
of	Pick the fourth mullion
Specify a second extension line origin or [Undo Select]<Select>:	**<Enter>**
Select continued dimension:	**<Enter>**

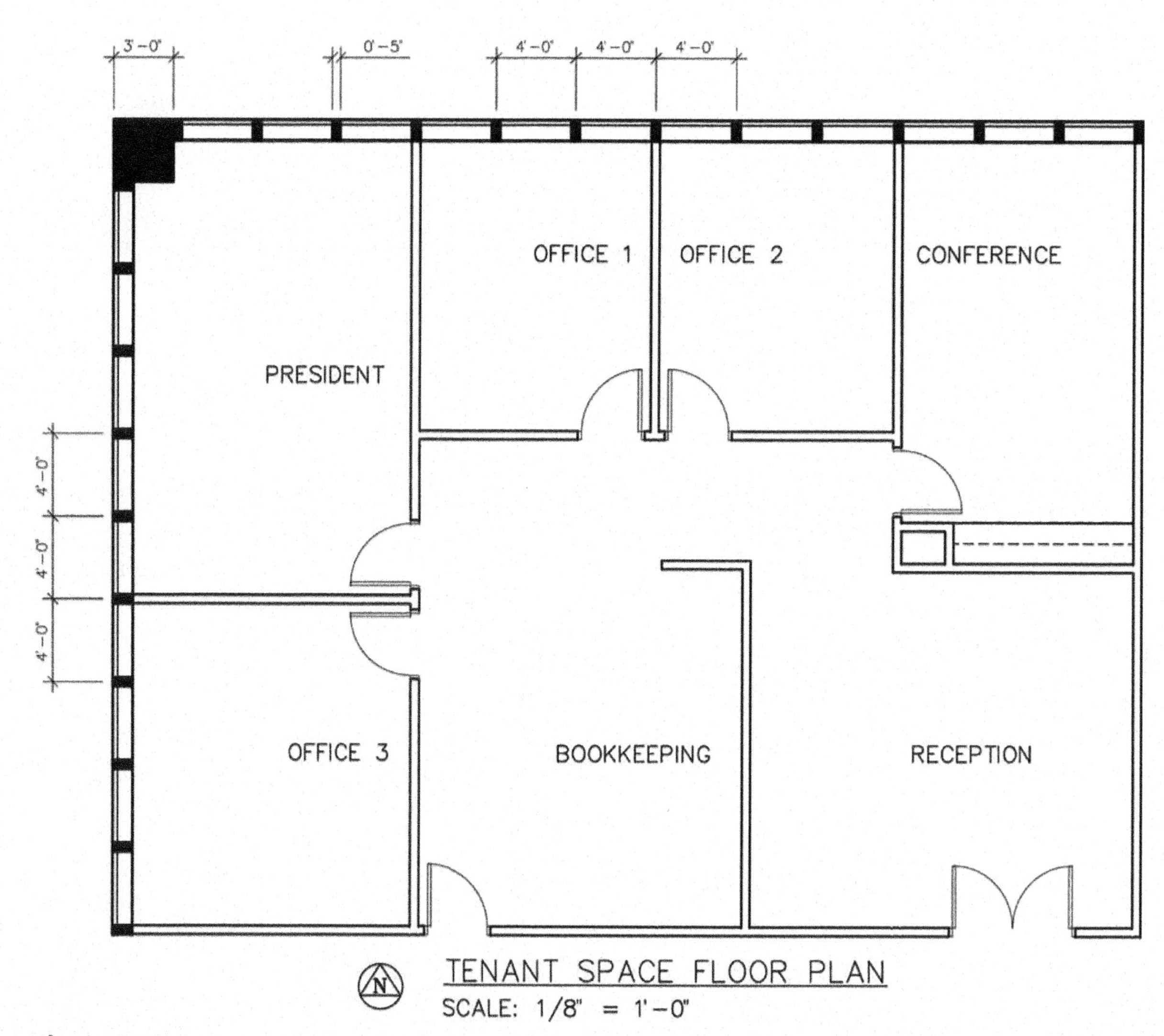

Figure 7-16
Linear dimensioning with the **Dimension** command's **Continue** option to draw vertical dimensions (scale: 1/8″ = 1′-0″)

TIP

Use **OSNAP** commands to select extension line origins. Set a running **Osnap** mode.

Aligned Dimensioning

DIMENSION: ALIGNED	
Ribbon/ Panel	Annotate/ Dimensions
Dimension Toolbar:	
Menu Bar:	Dimension/ Aligned
Type a Command:	DIMALIGNED
Command Alias:	DAL

When you use the **Aligned** option, you can select the first and second extension line origin points of a line that is at an angle, and the dimension line will run parallel to the origin points. You can also simply hover over the object and click to place the dimension. Figure 7-17 shows an example of aligned dimensioning.

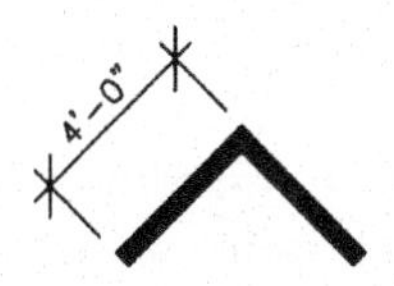

ALIGNED

Figure 7-17
Dimensioning with the **Dimension** command's **Aligned** option

Baseline Dimensioning

With linear dimensioning, after the first segment of a line is dimensioned, picking the **Baseline** option in the **Dimension** command automatically continues the next linear dimension from the baseline (first extension line) of the first linear dimension. The new dimension line is offset to avoid drawing on top of the previous dimension. The **DIMDLI** variable controls the size of the offset. Figure 7-18 shows linear dimensioning with the **Baseline** command.

Figure 7-18
Dimensioning with the **Dimension** command's **Baseline** option

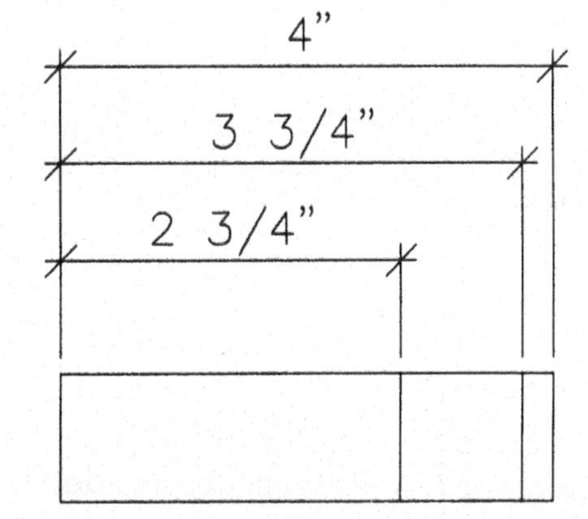

TIP

When erasing construction lines, avoid selecting definition points; otherwise, the dimension associated with that point will be erased.

Step 10. Use **DTEXT**, centered, to add the text **12 TYP. SPACES @ 4′-0″ = 48′-0″** to the north side of the plan (Figure 7-19). Place it two grid marks (on a 12″ grid) above the dimension line of the mullion's dimension. Set the text height to **1/16″** (text is annotative).

> **NOTE**
>
> When stacking dimension lines, locate the first dimension line farther from the object being dimensioned than subsequent dimension lines are from each other. For example, locate the first dimension line three grid marks from the object and the second dimension line two grid marks from the first dimension line.

Step 11. Use **Dimension** to dimension the overall north exterior wall of the tenant space. You may snap to the tick (intersection) of a previous dimension (Figure 7-19).

Step 12. Use **DTEXT**, centered, to add the text **9 TYP. SPACES @ 4′-0″ = 36′-0″** to the west side of the plan (Figure 7-19). Place it two grid marks (on a 12″ grid) above the dimension line of the mullions dimension. Set the text height to **1/16″** and the rotation angle to **90**.

Step 13. Use **Dimension** to dimension from the southwest corner of the tenant space to the southern corner of the column. At the **DIM** prompt, click **Continue** or type **C <Enter>** to continue the dimension to the outside northwest corner of the building (Figure 7-19).

Step 14. Use the **Dimension** command's **Baseline** option to dimension the overall west exterior wall of the tenant space (Figure 7-19). Select the extension line of the vertical dimension at the southwest corner, and then click the northwest corner of the column.

Step 15. Set a running **Osnap** mode of **Nearest**.

Step 16. Dimension from the middle of the west wall of Office 2 to the center of the door in Office 2. Use the **<Shift>** key and right-click to get the **Osnap** menu and pick **Mid Between 2 Points** to complete the dimension (Figure 7-19), as described next:

Prompt	**Response**
Type a command:	**DIMLINEAR** (or **DLI**)
Specify first extension line origin or <select object>:	**<Shift>** + right-click Click **Mid Between 2 Points** (Figure 7-20)
Specify first extension line origin or <select object>: _m2p First point of mid:	Click **P1→** (left side of wall symbol)
Second point of mid:	Click **P2→** (right side of wall symbol)
Specify second extension line origin:	**<Shift>** + right-click Click **Mid Between 2 Points**
Specify second extension line origin: _m2p First point of mid:	Click **P3→** (left side of door opening)
Second point of mid:	Click **P4→** (right side of second wall)
Specify dimension line location or [Mtext Text Angle Horizontal Vertical Rotated]:	Pick a point to locate the dimension

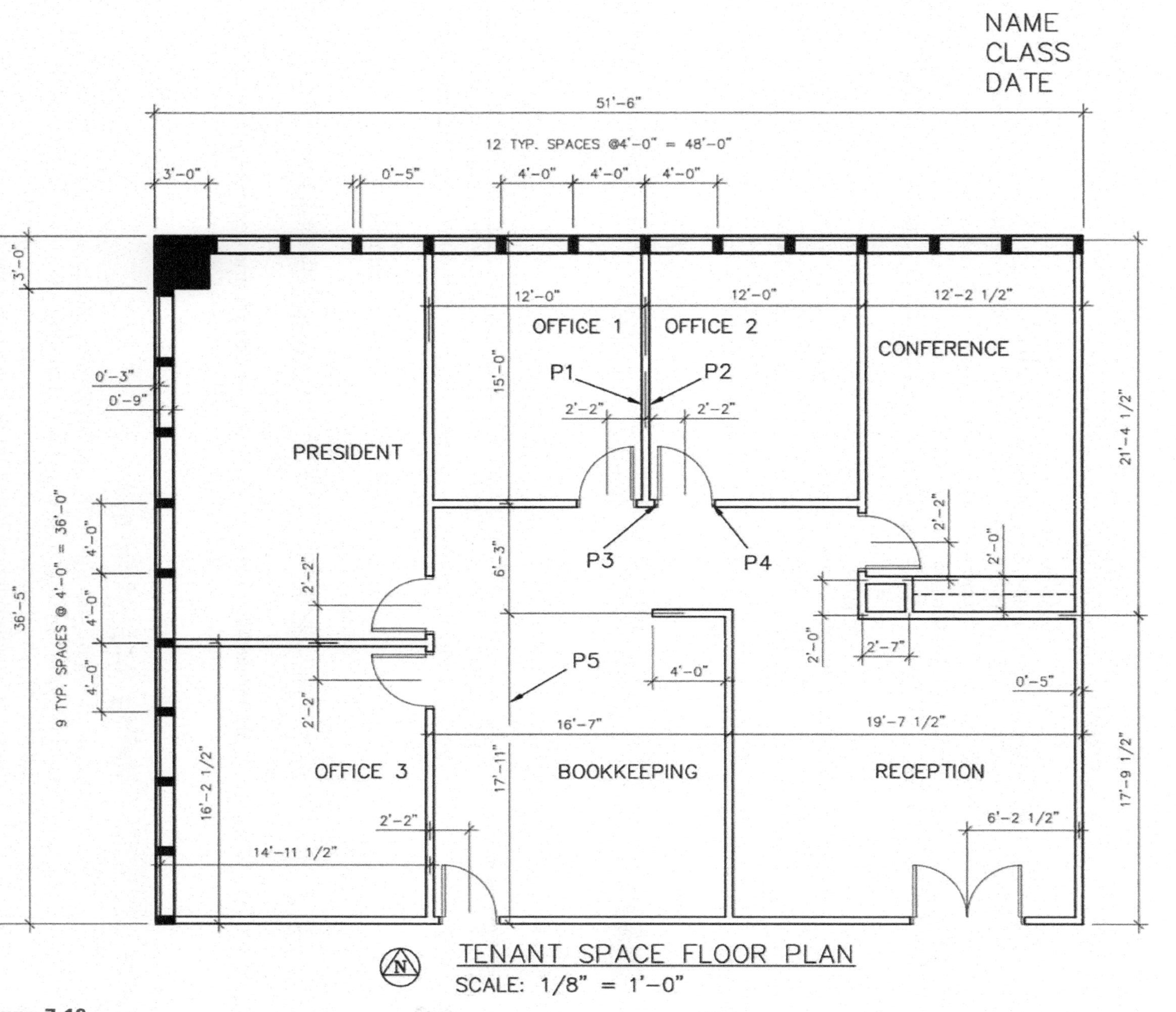

Figure 7-19
Exercise 7-1 complete (scale: 1/8" = 1'-0")

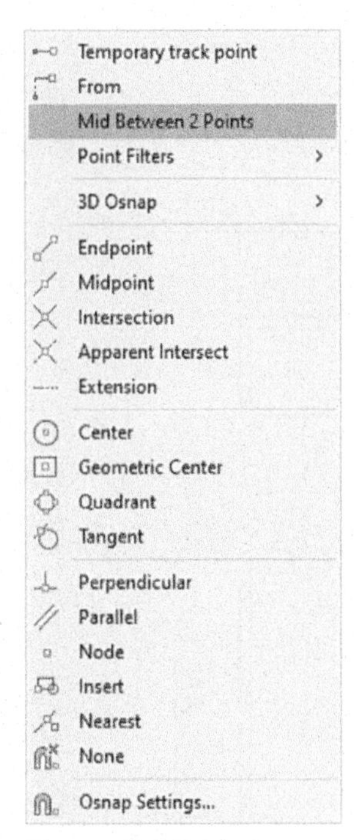

Figure 7-20
Mid Between 2 Points

Step 17. Complete the dimensioning using the **Linear** dimension commands and the appropriate **Osnap** modifiers. When you are dimensioning from left to right, any outside dimension line and text will be placed to the right. Dimensioning from right to left draws any outside dimension line and text to the left.

Adding a Dimension Break

It's considered bad form for dimension lines to cross each other. To avoid such a crossing, you can specify a break in one dimension line where a second dimension line crosses over it. The dimension break moves dynamically, so if the second dimension line moves, the break in the first line moves with it.

DIMENSION BREAK	
Ribbon/ Panel	Annotate/ Dimensions
Dimension Toolbar:	
Menu Bar:	Dimension/ Dimension Break
Type a Command:	DIMBREAK

Step 18. Add a dimension break in the vertical dimension line in the bookkeeping area that crosses over another dimension line, as described next (Figure 7-19):

Prompt	**Response**
Type a command:	Select **DIMBREAK** from the **Dimensions** panel of the **Annotate** tab
Select dimension to add/remove break or [Multiple]:	**P5→** (Figure 7-19)
Select object to break dimension or [Auto Manual Remove]<Auto>:	**<Enter>**
1 object modified	
Dimension disassociated	
The break is added	

You can add a break to a dimension line, extension line, or to a multileader (described in Chapter 8). When you issue the **DIMBREAK** command, you select the dimension line you want to break, and optionally select one of the following options:

Multiple: Allows you to select more than one dimension line that you want to break

Manual: Allows you to pick the first and second break point for the break

Remove: Allows you to select the dimension and remove the break from that dimension

Using Adjust Space

DIMENSION: LINE SPACE	
Ribbon/ Panel	Annotate/ Dimensions
Dimension Toolbar:	
Menu Bar:	Dimension/ Dimension Space
Type a Command:	DIMSPACE

You can use **Adjust Space (DIMSPACE)** to make the spacing between parallel dimension lines equal. This command asks you to select a base dimension—the dimension you do not want to move. The command then asks you to select dimensions that are parallel to the base dimension and that you want to space equally. After you have selected the dimensions, press **<Enter>**. You can then enter a distance (for example, 24″), or you can press **<Enter>** and the dimensions will be automatically spaced—the automatic space is twice the height of the dimension text.

If you have a series of dimensions that you want to align, enter a **0** for the spacing value, and they will align.

Step 19. Move your name, class, and date outside any dimension lines, if needed.

Step 20. When you have completed Exercise 7-1, save your work in at least two places.

Step 21. Print Exercise 7-1 at a scale of **1/8″ = 1′-0″**.

EXERCISE 7-2
Revisions and Modifying Dimensions
Setting the DIMASSOC Dimension Variable

The **DIMASSOC** dimension variable is not stored in a dimension style, but it does affect how dimensions behave in relation to the object being dimensioned. It has three states:

0 **DIMASSOC** is off. This setting creates exploded dimensions. Each part of the dimension (arrowheads, lines, text) is a separate object.

1 **DIMASSOC** is on. This setting creates dimensions that are single objects but are not associated with the object being dimensioned. When the dimension is created, definition points are formed (at the ends of extension lines, for example). If these points are moved, as with the **Stretch** command, the dimension changes, but it is not directly associated with the object being dimensioned.

2 **DIMASSOC** is on. This setting creates **associative dimension** objects. The dimensions are single objects, and one or more of the definition points on the dimension are linked to association points on the object. When the association point on the object moves, the dimension location, orientation, and text value of the dimension change. For example, check **DIMASSOC** to make sure the setting is **2** (type **DIMASSOC <Enter>**. If the value is not 2, type **2 <Enter>**). Draw a 2′ diameter circle and dimension it using the **Diameter** dimensioning command. With no command active, click any point on the circle so that grips appear at the quadrants of the circle. Click any grip to make it hot, and move the grip. The dimension changes as the size of the circle changes.

The **Annotation Monitor** toggle in the status bar keeps track of associated dimensions. When the **Annotation Monitor** toggle is **ON**, dimensions that are disassociated will have a badge beside them. When you pick or right-click the badge, a menu appears with commands that allow you to reassociate or delete the dimension. When the **Annotation Monitor toggle** is **ON**, the tool button is highlighted.

Exercise 7-2 describes commands that you can use to modify dimensions and make a revision cloud. When you have completed Exercise 7-2, your drawing will look similar to Figure 7-21.

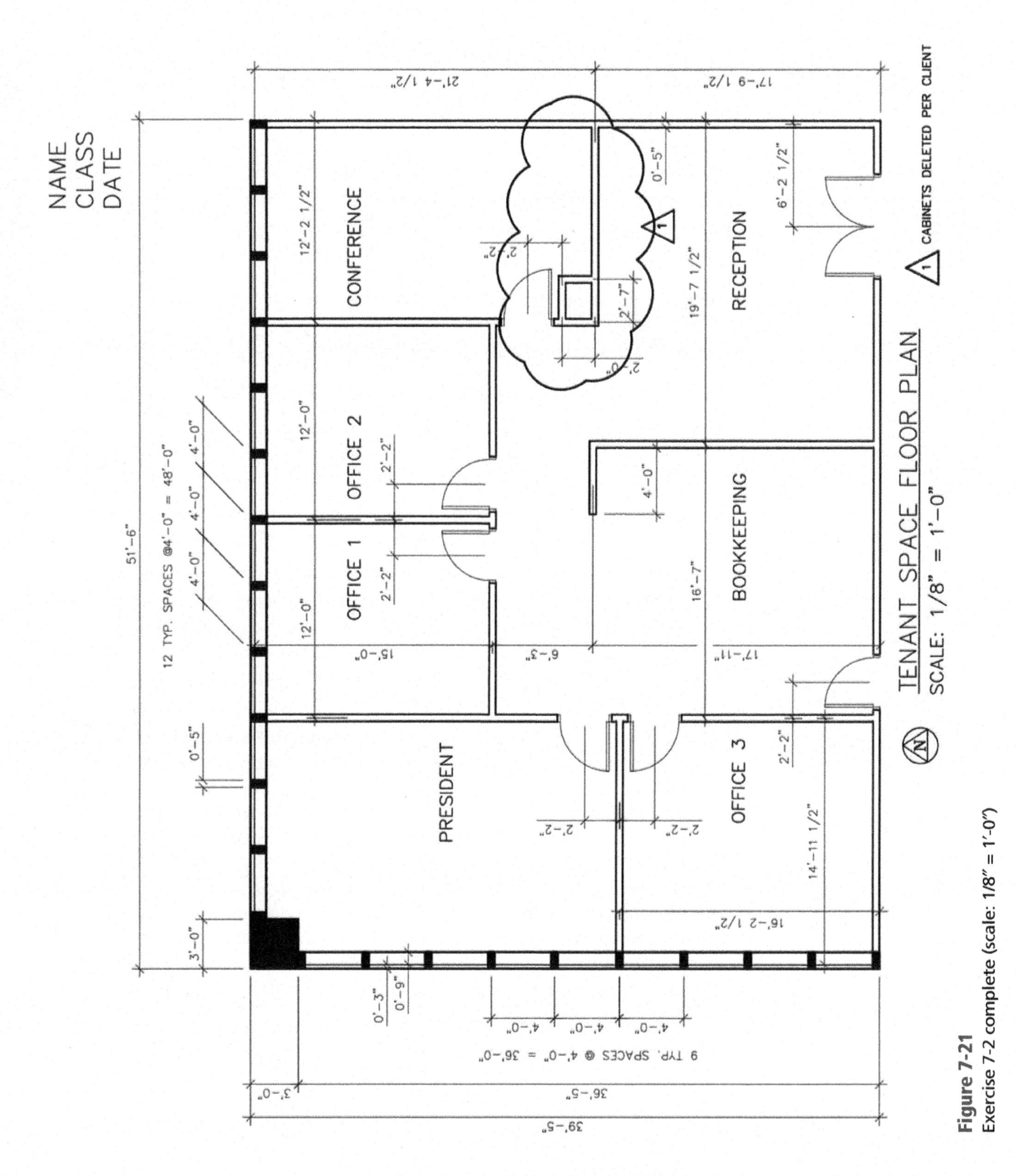

Figure 7-21
Exercise 7-2 complete (scale: 1/8" = 1'-0")

Step 1. Open drawing **CH7-EXERCISE1** and save it as **CH7-EXERCISE2** to the hard drive or network drive.

Understanding Associative Dimension Commands

When the **DIMASSOC** variable is on, each dimension that is drawn is created as a block. That means that the extension lines, dimension lines, ticks or arrows, text, and all other parts of the dimensions are entered as a single object. When **DIMASSOC** is on and set to **2**, the dimensions drawn are called *associative dimensions*. When **DIMASSOC** is off, the extension lines, dimension lines, and all other parts of the dimension are drawn as separate entities.

Four dimension options—**Oblique**, **Align Text**, **Override**, and **Update**—can be used only if **DIMASSOC** was on while you drew the dimensions. The following sections describe these commands.

Oblique

DIMENSION: OBLIQUE	
Ribbon/ Panel	Annotate/ Dimensions
Menu Bar:	Dimension/ Oblique
Type a Command:	DIMEDIT/ Oblique

Dimension lines are always parallel to the object or distance being dimensioned, and extension lines are usually perpendicular to the dimension line, but in rare cases you can specify an oblique angle of the extension lines. One typical use of obliqued extension lines is in 2D isometric drawing, as described in Chapter 13.

Step 2. Create an oblique angle for the extension lines of the four mullions on the north exterior wall of the tenant space (Figure 7-22), as described next:

Prompt	Response
Type a command:	On the **Annotate** tab, click the down arrow beside the **Dimensions** panel to expand the panel. Click **Oblique**
Select objects:	Pick the extension lines of the mullion dimensions on the north exterior wall until they are all highlighted
Select objects:	**<Enter>**
Enter obliquing angle (press **<Enter>** for none):	Type **45 <Enter>**
The extension lines of the mullion dimensions appear as shown in Figure 7-22.	

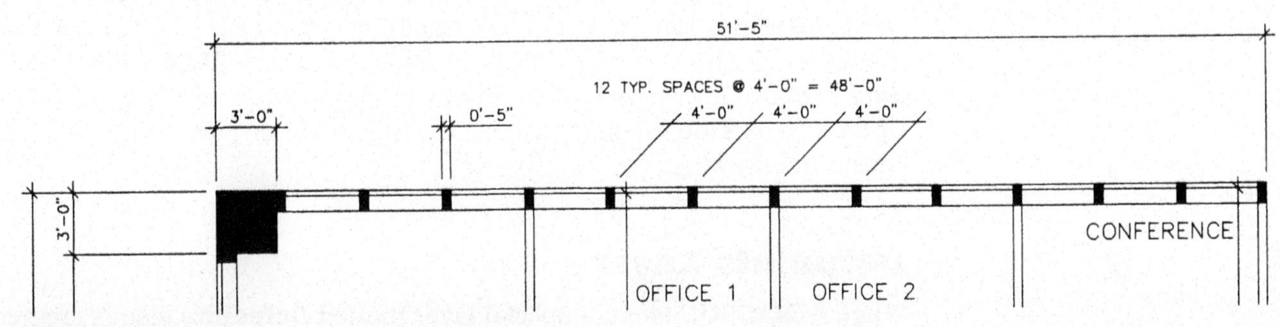

Figure 7-22
Using the **Dimension** command's **Oblique** option

ALIGN DIMENSION TEXT	
Ribbon/ Panel	Annotate/ Dimensions <slideout>
Dimension Toolbar:	
Menu Bar:	Dimension/ Align Text
Type a Command:	DIMTEDIT
Command Alias:	DIMTED

DIMENSION OVERRIDE	
Ribbon/ Panel	Annotate/ Dimensions <slideout>
Menu Bar:	Dimension/ Override
Type a Command:	DIMOVERRIDE
Command Alias:	DIMOVER

DIMENSION UPDATE	
Ribbon/ Panel	Annotate/ Dimensions
Dimension Toolbar:	
Menu Bar:	Dimension/ Update
Type a Command:	DIMSTYLE/ Apply

Align Text (Home-Angle-Left-Center-Right)

You can change the position or rotation angle along the dimension line of the dimension text with options of the Align Text option of the Dimension Text Edit command.

Step 3. Change the placement of the text for the overall dimension on the west exterior wall of the tenant space to flush right, and return it to the center position, as described next.

Prompt	**Response**
Type a command:	Pick **Right Justify** from the expanded **Dimensions** panel (or type **DIMTEDIT <Enter>**)
Select dimension:	Pick the dimension text **39′-5″**
The text moves to the right side of the dimension line (if the dimension line was drawn bottom to top, the dimension moves to the bottom).	
Type a command:	**Center Justify**
Select dimension:	Pick the same dimension **<Enter>**
The text moves back to the center of the dimension line.	

The **Left** option left justifies the text along the dimension line. The **Angle** option allows you either to type a new text angle (and press **<Enter>**) or to pick two points to show AutoCAD the new text angle. The **Home** option returns the dimension text to its home position.

Override

The **Override** command is helpful when you are in the middle of dimensioning a project or have completed dimensioning a project and decide that you need to change one or more of the dimension variables in a named style. You can find the **Override** option of the **Dimensions** command on the expanded **Dimensions** panel. It is used to change one or more dimension variables for selected dimensions but does not affect the current dimension style.

Update

Update differs from **Override** in that it updates dimensions using the current settings of the dimension style. For example, if you decide that a dimension variable needs to be changed in a dimension style, change the variable. You may click the **Save** button in the **Dimension Styles** dialog box to save the changed variable to the dimension style. If you do not save the changed variable, AutoCAD prompts you with an **ALERT** dialog box, *Save changes to current style?*, when you change dimension styles. Use **Update** to include the new variable settings in all or part of the dimensions within the drawing.

Defpoints Layer

When **DIMASSOC** is on, a special layer named **Defpoints** also is created. Definition points for dimensions are drawn on the **Defpoints** layer. They are small points on the drawing that are not plotted but are used to create the dimension. When the dimension is updated or edited, the definition points are redefined. Note: Elements on the **Defpoints** layer are not displayed on the final print.

Using the PROPERTIES Palette

You can use the **PROPERTIES** palette to change the properties of any dimension, as shown in Figure 7-23. Begin by selecting the dimension to be modified, click **Properties** from the **Modify** panel on the ribbon, right-click and click **Properties**, or press **<Ctrl>+1**. The **Properties** palette appears. Clicking the arrows to the right of the **Property** group displays a list of those items that you can change. To change dimension text, click **Text override** (below **Measurement**) and type the new text in the box to the right.

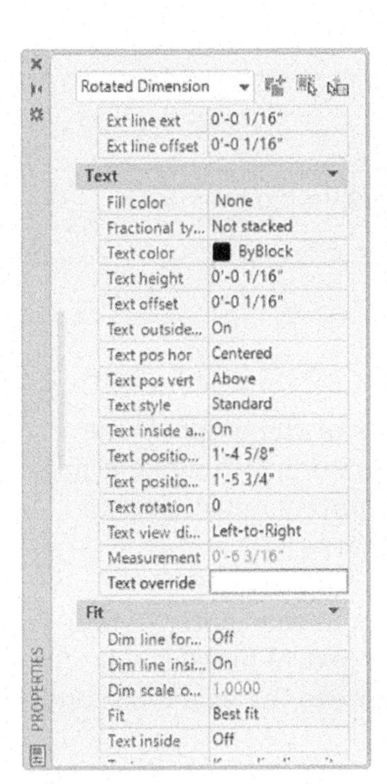

Figure 7-23
Use the **Properties** palette to change dimension text

Accessing Match Properties

When you select the **Match Properties** command or type and enter **MATCHPROP** at the command prompt, the prompt is *Select source object:*. At that prompt you can select the dimension whose properties you want to copy, and a paintbrush is attached to the cursor. The prompt changes to *Select destination object(s) or [Settings]:*, and you can then select the dimension to which you want to copy the properties.

When you type and enter the **Settings** option at the **Match Properties:** prompt, the **Property Settings** dialog box appears. Properties that can be copied are shown in the **Property Settings** dialog box. By default, all properties are selected and show a check in the box beside the property name. You can copy some or all of the properties of a dimension. If you do not want a property copied, click to deselect that property in the **Property Settings** dialog box.

Using Grips

Grips are small, solid-filled squares that appear on an object when you click on the object. Grips are particularly useful in modifying the placement of dimension text and the location of extension and dimension lines. The following steps introduce you to grip-editing.

Step 4. Practice using grips, as described next:

Prompt	**Response**
Type a command:	Click the **14'-11 1/2"** dimension in Office 3
Five squares appear on the dimension: one at the end of each extension line, one at the center of each tick, and one in the center of the dimension text:	Click the grip in the center of the dimension text
The grip changes color (becomes hot): Specify stretch point or [Base point Copy Undo eXit]:	With **SNAP** and **ORTHO** on, move your mouse up and click a point two grid marks up

Prompt	Response
The dimension is stretched up two grid marks:	Click the same grip to make it hot, move your mouse to the right, and click a point two grid marks to the right

TIP

To use multiple grips and to keep the shape of the dimension or any object with which you are using grips, hold down the **<Shift>** key before selecting the grips to make them hot.

Prompt	Response
The dimension text moves two grid marks to the right:	Click the grip at the origin of the first extension line to make it hot, and then move your mouse up two grid marks
The origin of the first extension line moves up two grid marks:	Click the grip in the center of the dimension text to make it hot, and then press the space bar one time
The prompt changes to Specify move point or [Base point Copy Undo eXit]:	Move your cursor two grid marks down and click a point
The entire dimension moves down two grid marks:	Press **<Esc>**
The grips disappear:	Type **U <Enter>**, and continue pressing **<Enter>** until the dimension is returned to its original state

To use grips, select a grip to act as the base point. Then, select one of the **Grip** modes—**Stretch**, **Move**, **Rotate**, **Scale**, or **Mirror**. You can cycle through these modes by pressing **<Enter>** or the space bar, or right-click to see all the modes and options.

Drawing a Revision Cloud

REVISION CLOUD	
Ribbon/ Panel	Home/Draw <slideout>
Draw Toolbar:	
Menu Bar:	Draw/ Revision Cloud
Type a Command:	REVCLOUD

Any change on a plan is submitted with a change order. You use a revision cloud to identify any area of a plan that has been changed. The cloud is coordinated with a note in the title block that gives a brief description of the change.

Step 5. Create the following new layer and set it as the current layer:

Layer name	Color	Linetype	Lineweight
a-anno-revs	white	Continuous	.014″ (.35 mm)

Step 6. Erase the two lines that represent the cabinets in the conference room.

Step 7. Draw a revision cloud to identify the area on the plan that has been changed (Figure 7-24), as described next:

Prompt	Response
Type a command:	Expand the **Draw** panel of the **Home** tab and click **Revision Cloud** or type **REVCLOUD** **<Enter>**
Minimum arc length: 0′-0″ Maximum arc length: 0′-0 1/2″ Style: Normal Type: Rectangular	
REVCLOUD Specify first corner point or [Arc length Object Rectangular Polygonal Freehand Style Modify] <Object>:	Type **A** **<Enter>**
Specify minimum length of arc <0′- 0 1/2″>:	Type **3′** **<Enter>**

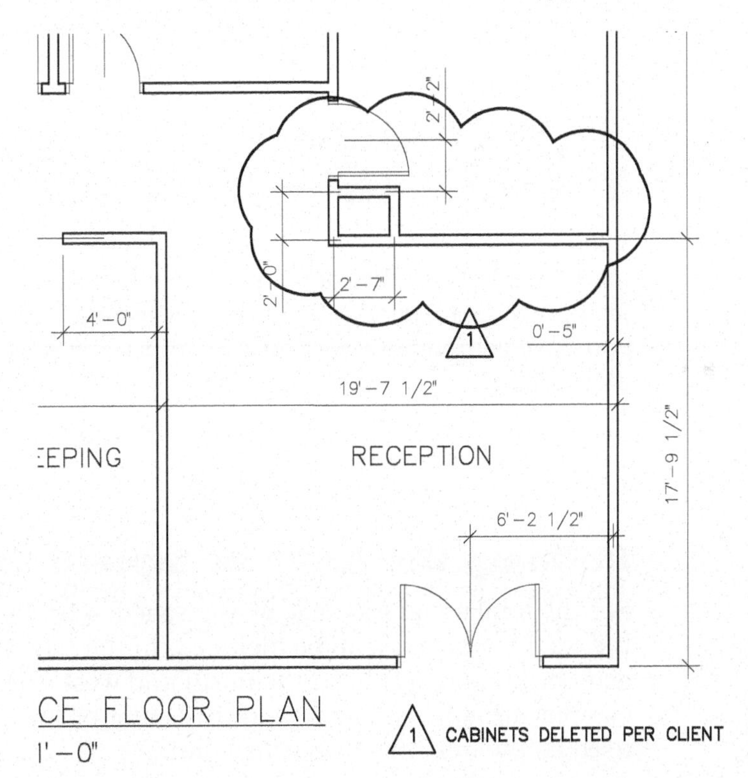

Figure 7-24
Draw a revision cloud to identify an area that has been changed

Prompt	Response
REVCLOUD Specify first corner point or [Arc length Object Rectangular Polygonal Freehand Style Modify] <Object>:	Click and hold down the button
Guide crosshairs along cloud path...	Guide your cursor along the cloud path until the cloud is finished
Revision cloud finished	

Revision clouds can be sized and shaped by selecting any of the following options. You will usually have to fiddle with the length of arcs to make the revision cloud look suitable.

Arc Length: Allows you to set an approximate arc length in the revision cloud. AutoCAD creates a minimum and maximum arc length based on what you specify.

Object: Allows you to select an object to convert to a revision cloud. You can convert a circle, ellipse, polyline, or spline to a revision cloud.

Style: Allows you to select a style named **Calligraphy**, which gives the appearance of a revision cloud drawn with a pen.

Step 8. Use grips to move any dimensions that are hidden by the cloud or to edit individual arcs in the revision cloud.

Step 9. Set layer **a-anno-text** current and add the 2′-2″ triangle, revision number, and revision note to the plan (Figure 7-24).

Step 10. When you have completed Exercise 7-2, save your work in at least two places.

Step 11. Print Exercise 7-2 at a scale of **1/8″ = 1′-0″**.

EXERCISE 7-3
Tenant Space Total Square Footage

Exercise 7-3 provides step-by-step instructions for using the **AREA** command to compute the total square footage of the tenant space floor plan. It also provides instructions for using the **CAL** (calculator) command. When you have completed Exercise 7-3, your drawing will look similar to Figure 7-25.

Step 1. Open drawing **CH7-EXERCISE1** and save it as **CH7-EXERCISE3** to the hard drive.

Defining the Area for Square Footage

AREA	
Ribbon/ Panel	Home/ Utilities/ Measure
Measuremt Tools Toolbar:	
Menu Bar:	Tools/ Inquiry/Area
Type a Command:	AREA

For the total square footage of any space to be computed, you must identify the exact area that is to be included. In the tenant space, the face of the exterior building glass on the north and west walls is used as the building's exterior measuring points, and the center of the south and east walls is used as the interior measuring points.

Step 2. Freeze layers **a-anno-dims** and **Defpoints**.

Step 3. Create the following new layer and set it as the current layer:

Layer name	Color	Linetype	Lineweight
a-anno-area	green	Continuous	.006″ (.15 mm)

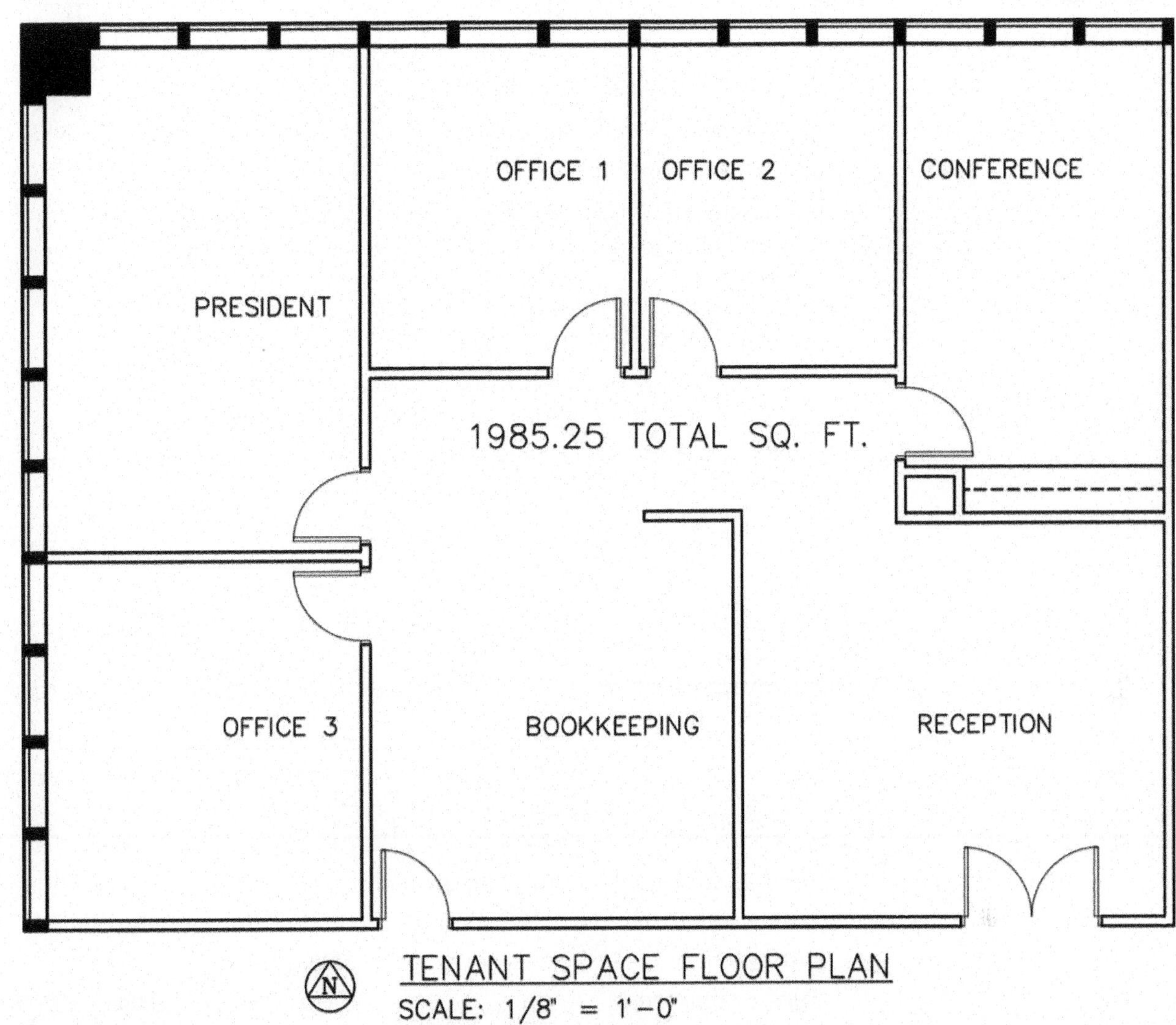

Figure 7-25
Exercise 7-3: Tenant space total square footage

Step 4. Type **FILL <Enter>**, then **OFF <Enter>** so that the column and mullions are not solid. Regenerate the drawing (type **RE <Enter>**).

Step 5. To be able to select the defining points of the exact area, as described earlier, use the **LINE** command to draw separate lines in each corner of the tenant space to which you can snap using **Osnap-Intersection** and **Osnap-Midpoint**. Figure 7-26 shows each corner with the added lines.

Figure 7-26
Defining points of the exact area included in the total square footage of the tenant space

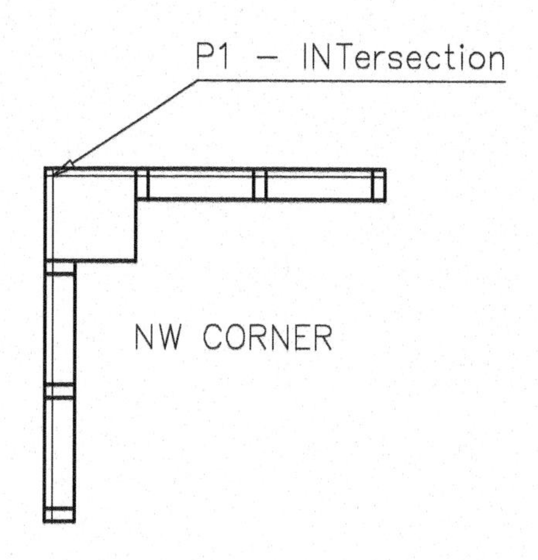

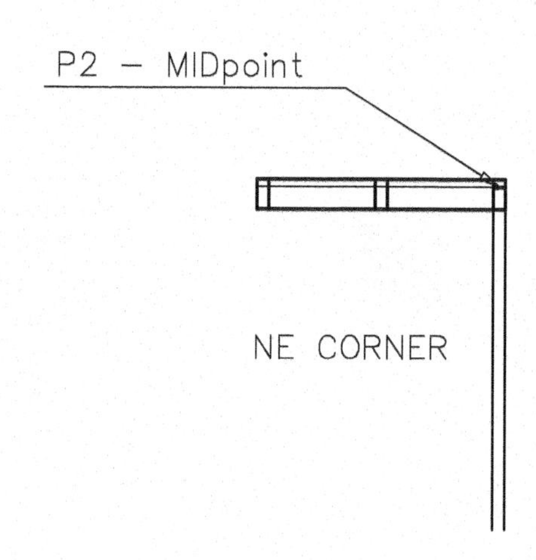

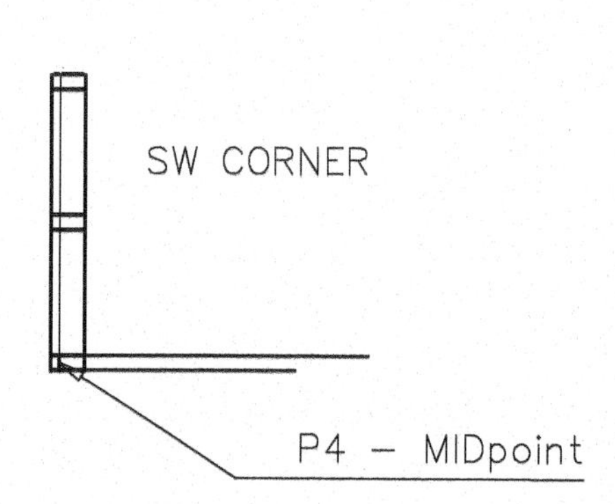

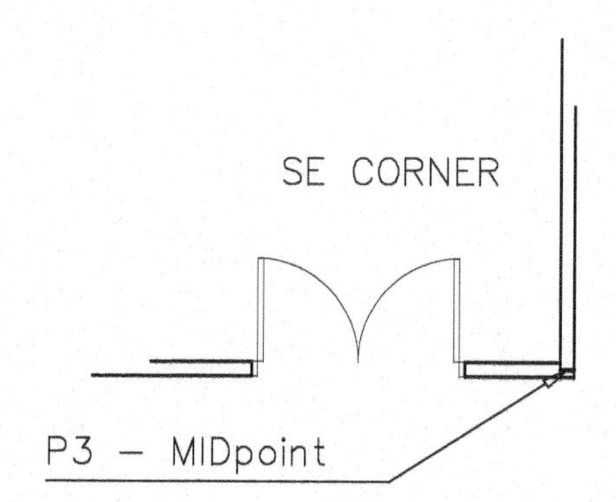

Step 6. Compute the total square footage of the tenant space (Figure 7-26), as described next:

Prompt	**Response**
Type a command:	**Area** (or type **AREA <Enter>**)
Specify first corner point or [Object Add area Subtract area]: <Object>:	**Osnap-Intersection**
	Zoom a window around the northwest corner
of	**P1→** (Figure 7-26)
	Zoom a window around the northeast corner
Specify next point or [Arc Length Undo]:	**Osnap-Midpoint**
of	**P2→**
	Zoom a window around the southeast corner
Specify next point or [Arc Length Undo]:	**Osnap-Midpoint**
of	**P3→**
	Zoom a window around the southwest corner

Prompt	Response
Specify next point or [Arc Length Undo Total] <Total>:	**Osnap-Midpoint**
of	**P4→**
Specify next corner point or [Arc Length Undo Total]<Total>:	**<Enter>**
Area = 285876.25 square in. (1985.2517 square ft), Perimeter = 179'-10"	
Type a command:	Use the **DTEXT** command **1/8"** high (annotative text) to write the number of total square feet on the drawing (Figure 7-25)

Options of the AREA command let you build on the areas of the drawing you originally selected. You can add to the selection or take away from it. You can also find the area of a selected closed object.

Add area: When you pick **Add**, the **AREA** command is placed in an add mode. You must pick **Add** before specifying the first space (of all the spaces to be added together). When you specify the first space, the area information appears. When you specify the second space, its individual area information appears along with the total area information of the two spaces together. Each subsequent space specified appears as an individual area total and is added to the running total.

Subtract area: When pick **Subtract**, each subsequent space specified appears as an individual area total and is subtracted from the running total.

Object: This option allows you to compute the area of a selected circle, ellipse, polygon, solid, or closed polyline. For a circle, the area and circumference appear. When you pick a wide, closed polyline, the area defined by the center line of the polyline appears (the polyline width is ignored). **Object** is the fastest way to find the area of a closed polyline.

Step 7. Turn **FILL** on.

Step 8. Regenerate the drawing (type **RE <Enter>**).

Using the Cal Calculator

AutoCAD provides a handy calculator that functions much like many handheld calculators. The following uses the add and divide features of the calculator. You may want to try other features on your own.

Use **CAL** to add three figures: += add

-= subtract

×= multiply

/= divide

TIP

You can use CAL within any command, such as **LINE** or **MOVE**, to specify a point. This avoids having to add and subtract dimensions beforehand. You must add an apostrophe before the **CAL** (**'CAL**) to use it within a command.

Prompt	**Response**
Type a command:	Type **CAL <Enter>**
>>Expression:	Type: **2'6 + 6'2 + 4'1 <Enter>**
12'-9"	

NOTE

AutoCAD's QUICKCALC command displays a calculator palette that you can use for scientific calculations, unit conversion, and basic calculations. You can also use the calculator transparently by entering 'CALC.

Step 9. When you have completed Exercise 7-3, save your work in at least two places.

Step 10. Print Exercise 7-3 at a scale of **1/8" = 1'-0"**.

chapterseven

Chapter Summary

This chapter provided you the information necessary to dimension floor plans. In addition, you learned to set dimension variables, edit dimensions, update dimensions, make revisions, and calculate total square footage using the **AREA** command. Now you have the skills and information necessary to produce dimensioned floor plans that you can use in interior design.

Chapter Test Questions

Multiple Choice

Circle the correct answer.

1. A complete list of current dimension variables and settings appears when you type which of the following at the *Setvar:* prompt?

a. **DIM***
b. **DIMSTYLE**
c. **STATUS**
d. **UPDATE**

2. Which of the following dimension variables controls the height of text used in the dimension?

a. **DIMSTYLE**
b. **DIMASZ**
c. **DIMTIX**
d. **DIMTXT**

3. Which tab on the **New Dimension Style** dialog box would you use to change a tick to a closed, filled arrowhead?

a. **Lines**
b. **Symbols and Arrows**
c. **Fit**
d. **Primary Units**

4. Which tab on the **New Dimension Style** dialog box would you use to change the appearance of the dimension text from one text style to another?

a. **Lines**
b. **Fit**
c. **Text**
d. **Primary Units**

5. Which tab on the **New Dimension Style** dialog box would you use to change the overall scale factor from 96 to 48?

a. **Symbols and Arrows**
b. **Primary Units**
c. **Text**
d. **Fit**

6. Which tab on the **New Dimension Style** dialog box would you use to set the distance that the dimension line extends beyond the tick?

a. **Lines**
b. **Symbols and Arrows**
c. **Text**
d. **Fit**

7. Which tab on the **New Dimension Style** dialog box would you use to make a setting to always display the dimension text horizontally on the page?

   a. **Lines** c. **Text**
   b. **Fit** d. **Primary Units**

8. If a full-size drawing is to be plotted at a plotting ratio of 1/8″ = 12″, the **DIMSCALE** value should be set to:

   a. 1 c. 12
   b. 48 d. 96

9. A Defpoints layer is created when a dimension is drawn with which of the following variables set to on?

   a. **DIMSTYLE** c. **DIMTAD**
   b. **DIMTOH** d. **DIMASSOC**

10. To find the area of a closed polyline most quickly, which of the **AREA** command options should you use?

   a. **Object** c. **Subtract**
   b. **Poly** d. **First point**

Matching

Write the number of the correct answer on the line.

a. **AREA** ______
b. **Revision Cloud** ______
c. Definition point ______
d. Defpoints ______
e. Grips ______

1. When this is erased, the associated dimension will be erased also
2. A command that calculates the total square footage of a room
3. Squares that appear on a dimension when it is clicked with no command active
4. A layer that is created when **DIMASSOC** is on
5. A command that allows you to draw a feature that shows a change has been made on the drawing

True or False

Circle the correct answer.

1. **True or False:** The seven tabs in the **New Dimension Style** dialog box are **Lines**, **Symbols and Arrows**, **Text**, **Fit**, **Primary Units**, **Alternate Units**, and **Tolerances**.
2. **True or False:** You use ordinate dimensioning to show the length of features that are drawn at an angle.
3. **True or False:** The two styles available in the **Revision Cloud** command are **Normal** and **Calligraphy**.

4. **True or False:** The five **Grip** modes you can cycle through are **Stretch**, **Copy**, **Rotate**, **Move**, and **Mirror**.
5. **True or False:** You must set **Units** to **Architectural** and **Precision** to 1/32″ for dimension variables to display in 32nds of an inch.

List

1. Five types of dimensions.
2. Five dimension variables and their functions from **Dimension Style Manager**.
3. Five components of a dimension.
4. Five ways of accessing **Dimension Style Manager**.
5. Five dimension commands available when **DIMASSOC** is on while the dimension is placed.
6. Five ways of creating **Linear** dimensions.
7. Five commands on the ribbon's **Home** tab/**Utilities** panel.
8. Five options under the **AREA (MeasureGeom)** command.
9. Five **Unit Conversion** parameters of the **QUICKCALC** command.
10. Five ways of accessing the **Oblique** dimension command.

Questions

1. In what situations would you use the **AREA** command?
2. For what purpose would you use annotative dimensions?
3. Which dimensioning variables will you most likely change from the default setting?
4. How many ways are there to edit dimensions?
5. Name and describe the eight types of dimensions.

Chapter Projects

Project 7-1: *Hotel Room 2 Dimensioned Floor Plan* **[BASIC]**

1. Set dimension variables for the hotel room floor plan.
2. Create a new layer for dimensions, and dimension the hotel room floor plan (Figure 7-27).
3. Locate the first row of dimensions farther from the drawing (for example, 2′) than the first row of dimensions is from the second row of dimensions (for example, 1′6″). Consistently space each row of dimensions on all four sides of the drawing.
4. Plot or print the drawing to scale.

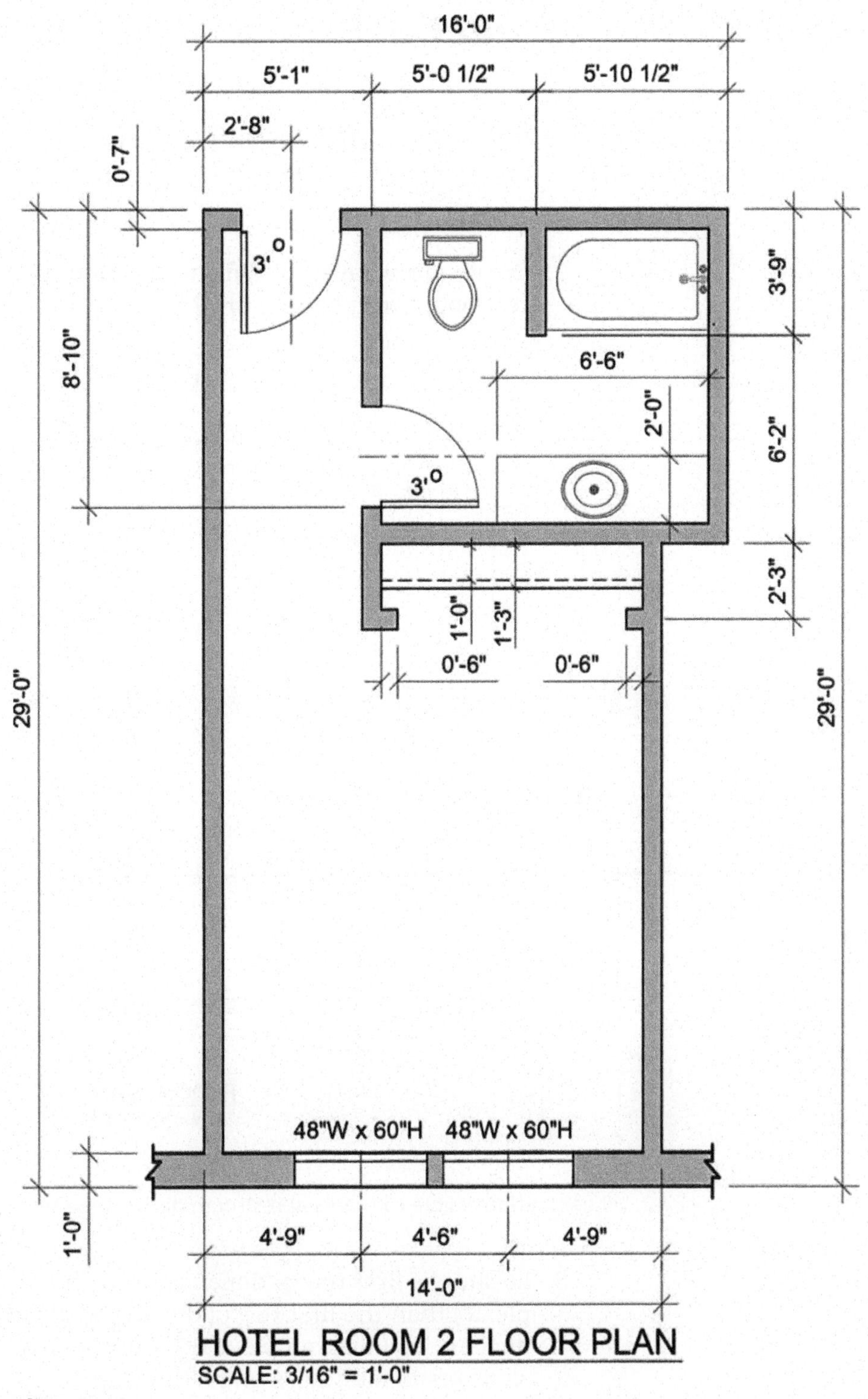

Figure 7-27

Project 7-1: Hotel room 2 dimensioned floor plan (scale: 3/16″ = 1′-0″)

Project 7-2: *Wheelchair-Accessible Commercial Restroom Dimensioned Floor Plan* [INTERMEDIATE]

1. Set dimension variables for the commercial restroom floor plan.
2. Create a new layer for dimensions, and dimension the commercial restroom floor plan (Figure 7-28).

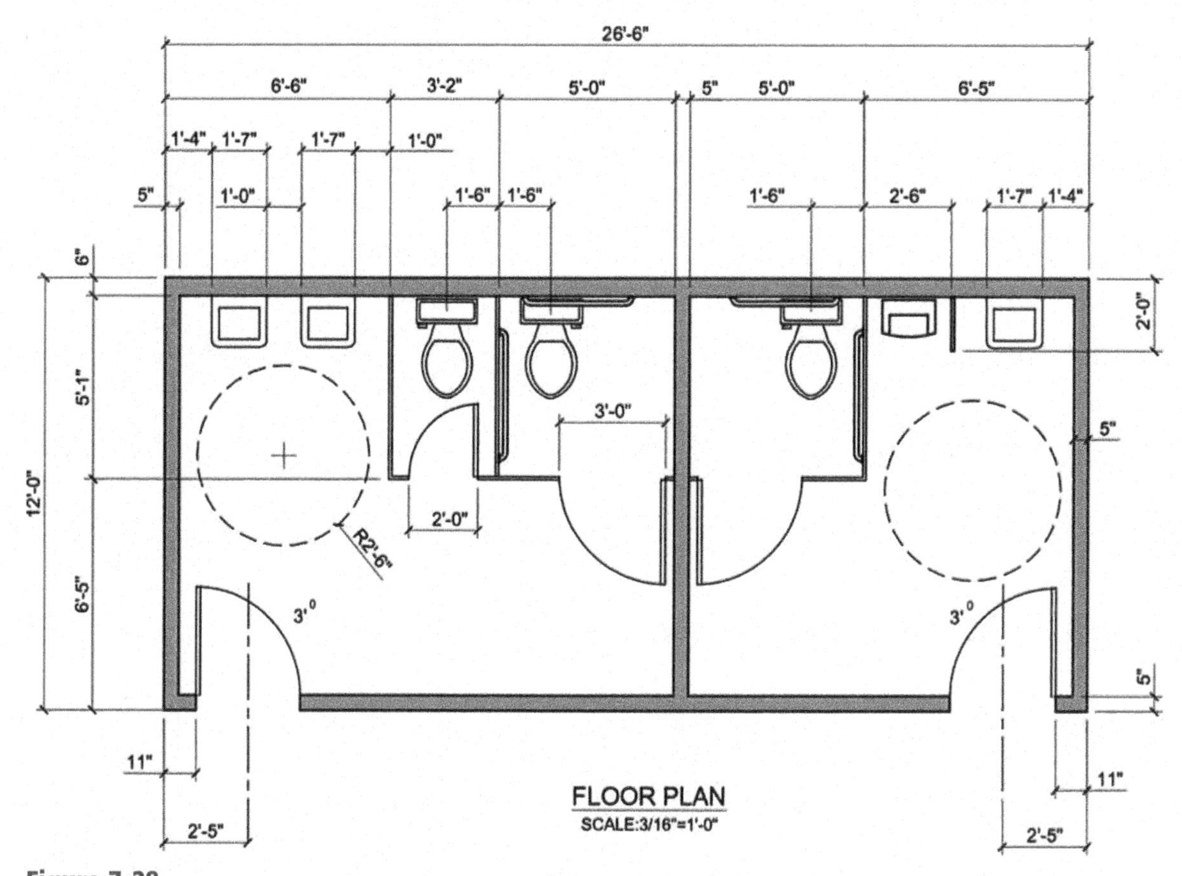

Figure 7-28
Project 7-2: Wheelchair-accessible commercial restroom dimensioned floor plan (scale: 3/16″ = 1′-0″)

3. Locate the first row of dimensions farther from the drawing (for example, 2′) than the first row of dimensions is from the second row of dimensions (for example, 1′6″). Consistently space each row of dimensions on all four sides of the drawing.
4. Plot or print the drawing to scale.

chaptereight

Drawing Elevations, Sections, and Details

CHAPTER OBJECTIVES

- Correctly use the following commands and settings:

Edit Hatch	**MIRROR**	**Multileader Style**	**STRETCH**
HATCH	**Multileader**	**Object Snap Tracking**	**UCS**
		Point Filters	**UCS Icon**

Introduction

The AutoCAD program makes it possible to produce clear, accurate, and impressive drawings of elevations, sections, and details. Many of the commands you have already learned are used in this chapter, along with some new commands.

EXERCISE 8-1
Tenant Space: Elevation of Conference Room Cabinets

In Exercise 8-1, an elevation of the south wall of the tenant space conference room is drawn. The south wall of the tenant space conference room has built-in cabinets that include a refrigerator and a sink. When you have completed Exercise 8-1, your drawing will look similar to Figure 8-1.

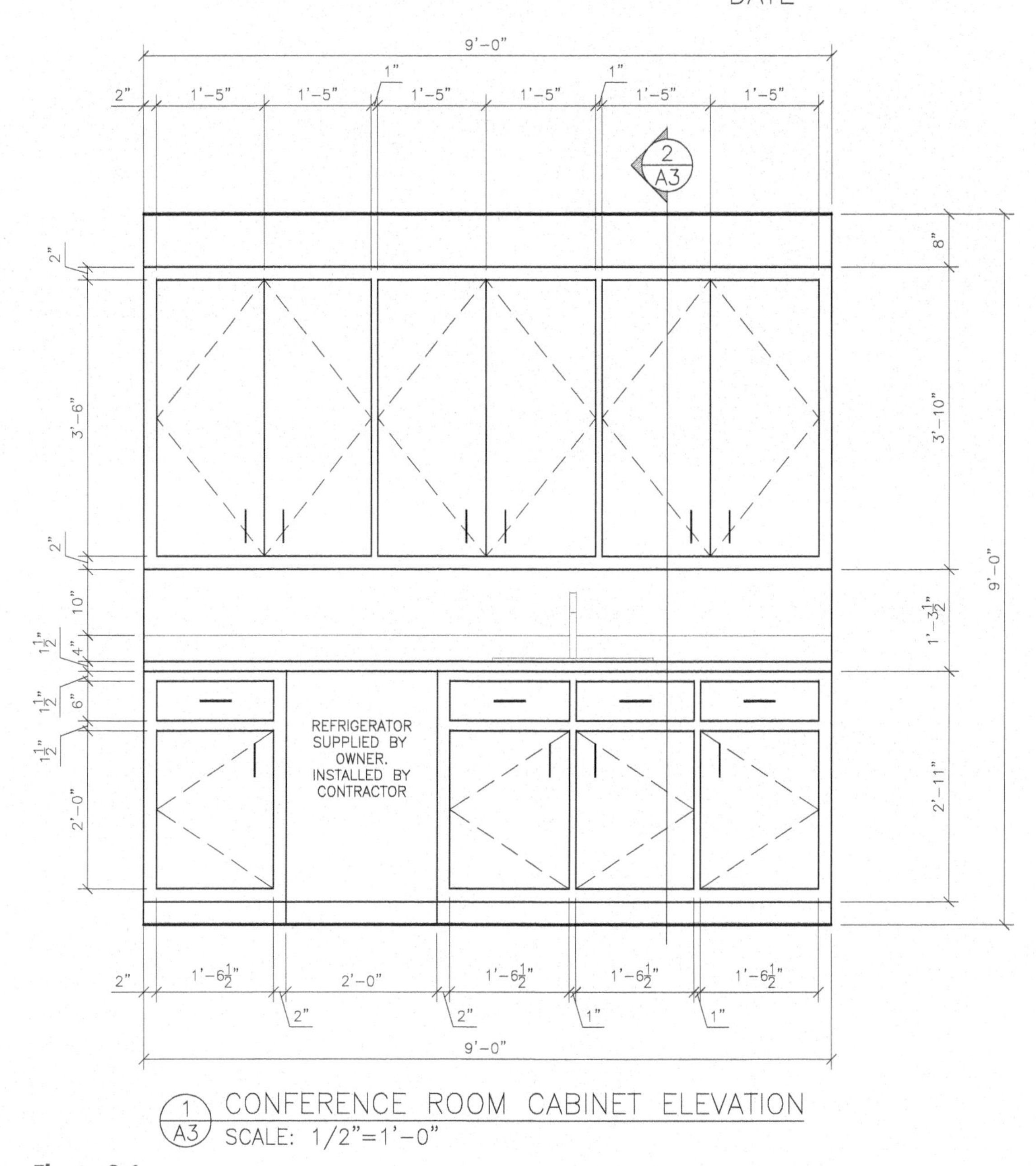

Figure 8-1
Exercise 8-1: Tenant space, elevation of conference room cabinets (scale: 1/2′ = 1′-0″)

Step 1. Use your workspace to make the following settings:

1. Use **Save As...** to save the drawing on the hard drive with the name **CH8-EXERCISE1**.
2. Set drawing units: **Architectural**
3. Set drawing limits: **25′,24′**
4. Set **GRIDDISPLAY**: **0**
5. Set grid: **12″**
6. Set snap: **6″**
7. Create the following layers:

Layer name	Color	Linetype	Lineweight
a-elev-dims	red	continuous	.004″ (.09 mm)
a-elev-hdln	red	hidden	.004″ (.09 mm)
a-elev-lwt1	blue	continuous	.010″ (.25 mm)
a-elev-lwt2	white	continuous	.002″ (.05 mm)
a-elev-otln	white	continuous	.016″ (.40 mm)
a-elev-patt	white	continuous	.002″ (.05 mm)
a-elev-text	green	continuous	.006″ (.15 mm)

8. Set layer **a-elev-lwt1** current.
9. Use **Zoom-All** to view the limits of the drawing.

UCS

UCS	
Ribbon/ Panel	View/ Coordinates
UCS Toolbar:	
Menu Bar:	Tools/ New UCS
Type a Command:	UCS

While you were drawing with AutoCAD in previous chapters, the UCS icon was located in the lower-left corner of your drawings. A coordinate system is simply the X, Y, and Z coordinates used in your drawings. For 2D drawings, only the X and Y coordinates are meaningful. The Z coordinate is used for a three-dimensional model.

Notice that the 2D UCS icon (Figure 8-2) has a W on it. The *W* stands for *world coordinate system.* Notice also that the default 3D UCS icon shows a box at the origin when viewed in either 2D or 3D. This is the AutoCAD fixed coordinate system, which is common to all AutoCAD drawings. Your version of AutoCAD uses the 3D icon by default, showing only x- and y-axes, so the W is not visible.

Figure 8-2
2D model space, 3D model space, and paper space UCS icons

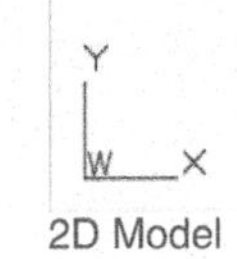

2D Model Space Icon

Z Y X

3D Model Space Icon

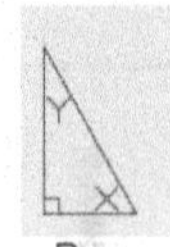

Paper Space Icon

user coordinate system: A user-defined variation of the world coordinate system. Variations in the coordinate system range from moving the default drawing origin (0,0,0) to another location to changing orientations for the x-, y-, and z-axes. It is possible to rotate the world coordinate system on any axis to make a UCS with a different two-dimensional XY plane.

You use the **UCS** command to set up a new **user coordinate system.** When you type **UCS** from the command prompt, the prompt is *Specify origin of UCS or [Face NAmed OBject Previous View World X Y Z ZAxis] <World>:.* The Z coordinate is described and used extensively in the chapters that cover 3D modeling. The UCS command options that apply to two dimensions are listed next: x-, y-, and z-axes. Rotating the world coordinate system on any axis to make a UCS with a different two-dimensional XY plane is possible.

Specify origin of UCS: Allows you to create a new UCS by selecting a new origin and a new x-axis. If you select a single point, the origin of the current UCS moves without changing the orientation of the x- and y-axes.

NAmed: When this option is entered, the prompt *Enter an option [Restore Save Delete?]* appears. It allows you to restore, save, delete, and list named user coordinate systems.

OBject: Allows you to define a new UCS by pointing to a drawing object such as an arc, point, circle, or line.

Previous: Makes the previous UCS current.

World: The AutoCAD fixed coordinate system, which is common to all AutoCAD drawings. In most cases you will want to return to the world coordinate system before plotting any drawing.

Step 2. Use the **UCS** command to change the origin of the current UCS, as described next:

Prompt	**Response**
Type a command:	Type **UCS <Enter>**
Specify origin of UCS or [Face NAmed OBject Previous View World X Y Z ZAxis] <World>	Type: **8′,12′ <Enter>**
Specify point on x-axis or <Accept>:	**<Enter>**

NOTE

You can change the UCS so you can move 0,0 to any point on your drawing to make it more convenient to locate points.

The origin for the current user coordinate system is now 8′ in the X direction and 12′ in the Y direction. The UCS icon may not have moved from where 0,0 was originally located. The **UCS Icon** command, described next, is used to control the orientation and visibility of the UCS icon.

UCS Icon

You can choose from two model space UCS icons to use: one for 2D drawings and one for 3D drawings. The default is the 3D icon, which you will probably use for both 2D and 3D. You use the **UCS Icon** command to control the visibility and orientation of the UCS icon (Figure 8-2). The UCS icon appears as lines (most often located in the lower-left corner of an AutoCAD drawing) that show the orientation of the x-, y-, and z-axes of the current UCS. It appears as a triangle in paper space. The **UCS Icon** command options are *ON OFF All Noorigin ORigin Properties:*. The **UCS Icon** command options follow.

ON: Allows you to turn on the UCS icon if it is not visible.

OFF: Allows you to turn off the UCS icon when it gets in the way. This has nothing to do with the UCS location—only the visibility of the UCS icon.

All: Allows you to apply changes to the UCS icon in all active viewports. (Chapter 12 describes the **Viewports** command, which allows you to create multiple viewports.)

Noorigin: When **Noorigin** is current, the UCS icon is displayed at the lower-left corner of the screen.

ORigin: Forces the UCS icon to be displayed at the origin of the current UCS. For example, when you click **USC Icon - Origin**, the new UCS that you just created will appear in its correct position. If the origin of the UCS is off the screen, the icon is still displayed in the lower-left corner of the screen.

Properties: When you select **Properties**, the **UCS Icon** dialog box appears (Figure 8-3). This box allows you to select the 2D or 3D model space icon and to change the size and color of model space and paper space (**Layout** tab) icons.

NOTE

The **Coordinates** panel is hidden in the **Ribbon View** tab by default. Right-click on the **View** tab to show the **Coordinates** panel.

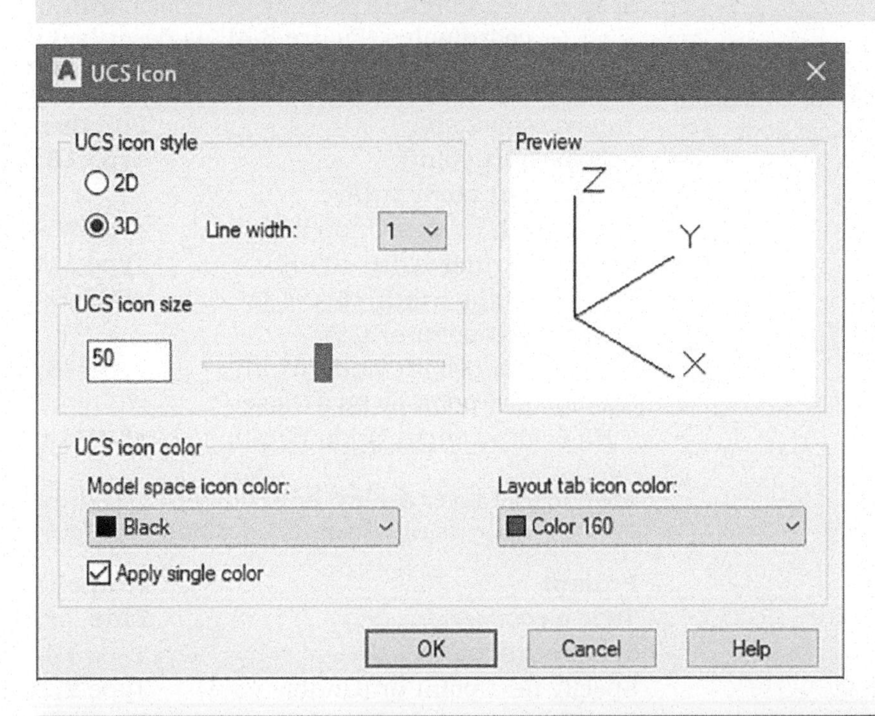

Figure 8-3
UCS Icon dialog box

FOR MORE DETAILS

See Chapters 14 and 15 for more on **UCS** and **UCSICON**.

Step 3. If the UCS icon did not move, use the **UCS Icon** command to force the UCS icon to be displayed at the origin of the new, current UCS, as described next:

UCSICON	
Ribbon/ Panel	UCS Icon View/ Coordinates
Menu Bar:	UCS Icon View/ Display/UCS Icon
Type a Command:	UCSICON

Prompt	**Response**
Type a command:	Type **UCSICON <Enter>**
Enter an option [ON OFF All Noorigin ORigin Selectable Properties] <ON>:	In the command prompt window, click ORigin or type **OR <Enter>** (the UCS icon moves to the 8′,12′ coordinate location)

Draw the Upper Cabinets

Step 4. Using absolute coordinates, draw a rectangle forming the first upper cabinet door. Start the drawing at **(2,2)** (two inches above and two inches to the right of the new UCS), Figure 8-4, as described next:

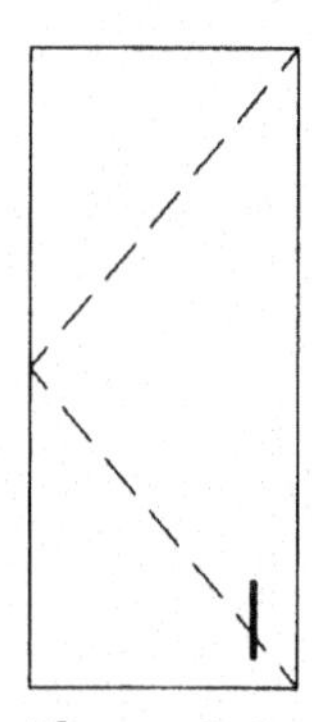

Figure 8-4
Draw the lines forming the first upper cabinet door

Prompt	**Response**
Type a command:	**Rectangle** (or type **REC <Enter>**)
Specify first corner point or [Chamfer Elevation Fillet Thickness Width]:	Type **2,2 <Enter>**
Specify other corner point or [Area Dimensions Rotation]:	Type **19,44 <Enter>**

Step 5. Use **Polyline** to draw the door hardware using absolute coordinates (Figure 8-4), as described next:

Prompt	**Response**
Type a command:	**Polyline** (or type **PL <Enter>**)
Specify start point:	Type **16,4 <Enter>**
Specify next point or [Arc Halfwidth Length Undo Width]:	Type **W <Enter>**
Specify starting width <0′-0″>:	Type **1/4 <Enter>**
Specify ending width <0′-0 1/4″>:	**<Enter>**
Specify next point or [Arc Halfwidth Length Undo Width]:	Type **16,9 <Enter>**
Specify next point or [Arc Close Halfwidth Length Undo Width]:	**<Enter>**

Step 6. Set layer **a-elev-hdln** current and draw the dashed lines of the door using absolute coordinates (Figure 8-4), as described next:

Prompt	**Response**
Type a command:	**Line** (or type **L <Enter>**)
Specify first point:	Type **19,3′8 <Enter>**
Specify next point or [Undo]:	Type **2,23 <Enter>**
Specify next point or [Undo]:	Type **19,2 <Enter>**
Specify next point or [Close Undo]:	**<Enter>**

Step 7. Change the linetype scale of the Hidden linetype to make it appear as dashes, change the linetype to **Hidden2**, or both. A large linetype scale such as 12 is needed. (Type **LTSCALE <Enter>**, then type **12 <Enter>**.)

Mirror

MIRROR	
Ribbon/ Panel	Home/ Modify
Modify Toolbar:	
Menu Bar:	Modify/Mirror
Type a Command:	MIRROR
Command Alias:	MI

The **MIRROR** command allows you to mirror about an axis any entity or group of entities. The axis can be at any angle.

Step 8. Draw the **second upper cabinet door**, using the **MIRROR** command to copy the cabinet door just drawn (Figure 8-5), as described next:

Prompt	**Response**
Type a command:	**Mirror** (or type **MI <Enter>**)
Select objects:	**P1→**
Specify opposite corner:	**P2→**
Select objects:	**<Enter>**
Specify first point of mirror line:	**P3→** (with **ORTHO** and **OSNAP-INTERSECTION** on)
Specify second point of mirror line:	**P4→**
Erase source objects? [Yes No] <N>:	**<Enter>** (to complete command)

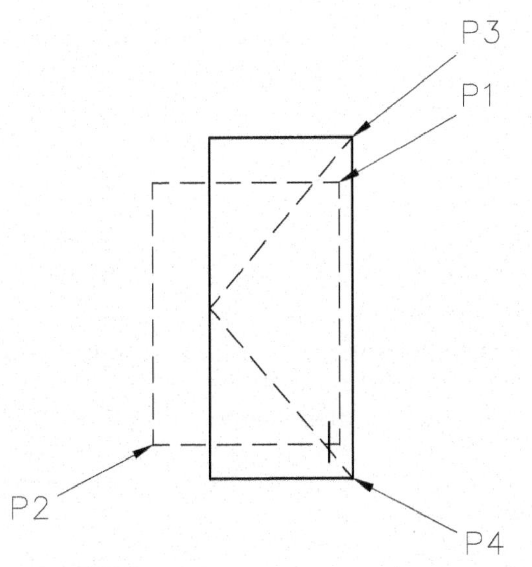

Figure 8-5
Use the **MIRROR** command to copy the cabinet door

> **NOTE**
>
> If you want to mirror a part of a drawing containing text but do not want the text to be a mirror image, change the **MIRRTEXT** system variable setting to **0**. This allows you to mirror the part and leave the text "right reading." When **MIRRTEXT** is set to **1**, the text is given a mirror image. To change this setting, type **MIRRTEXT <Enter>**, then type **0 <Enter>**.

Step 9. Set layer **a-elev-lwt1** current. Using relative coordinates, draw a rectangle forming the outside of the upper cabinet. Start the rectangle at the **0,0** location of the new UCS (Figure 8-6), as described next:

Prompt	**Response**
Type a command:	**Rectangle** (or type **REC <Enter>**)
Specify first corner point or [Chamfer Elevation Fillet Thickness Width]:	Type **0,0 <Enter>**
Specify other corner point or [Area Dimensions Rotation]:	Type **@9′,3′10 <Enter>**

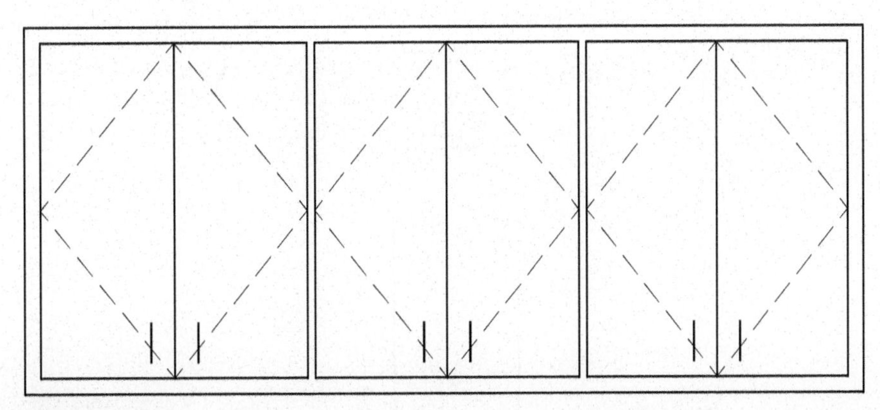

Figure 8-6
Draw the upper cabinets

Step 10. Copy the first two **upper cabinet doors** 2′11″ and 5′10″ to the right (Figure 8-6) as described next:

Prompt	**Response**
Type a command:	**Copy** (or type **CP <Enter>**)
Select objects:	Use a window to select the first two upper cabinet doors
Select objects:	**<Enter>**
Specify base point or [Displacement mOde] <Displacement>:	Click any point
Specify second point or [Array] <use first point as displacement>:	With **ORTHO** on, move your mouse to the right and type **2′11 <Enter>**
Specify second point or [Array Exit Undo] <Exit>:	Move the mouse to the right and type **5′10 <Enter>**
Specify second point or [Exit Undo] <Exit>:	**<Enter>**

Draw the Lower Cabinets

Step 11. Use the **MIRROR** command to draw the **first lower cabinet door** (Figure 8-7), as described next:

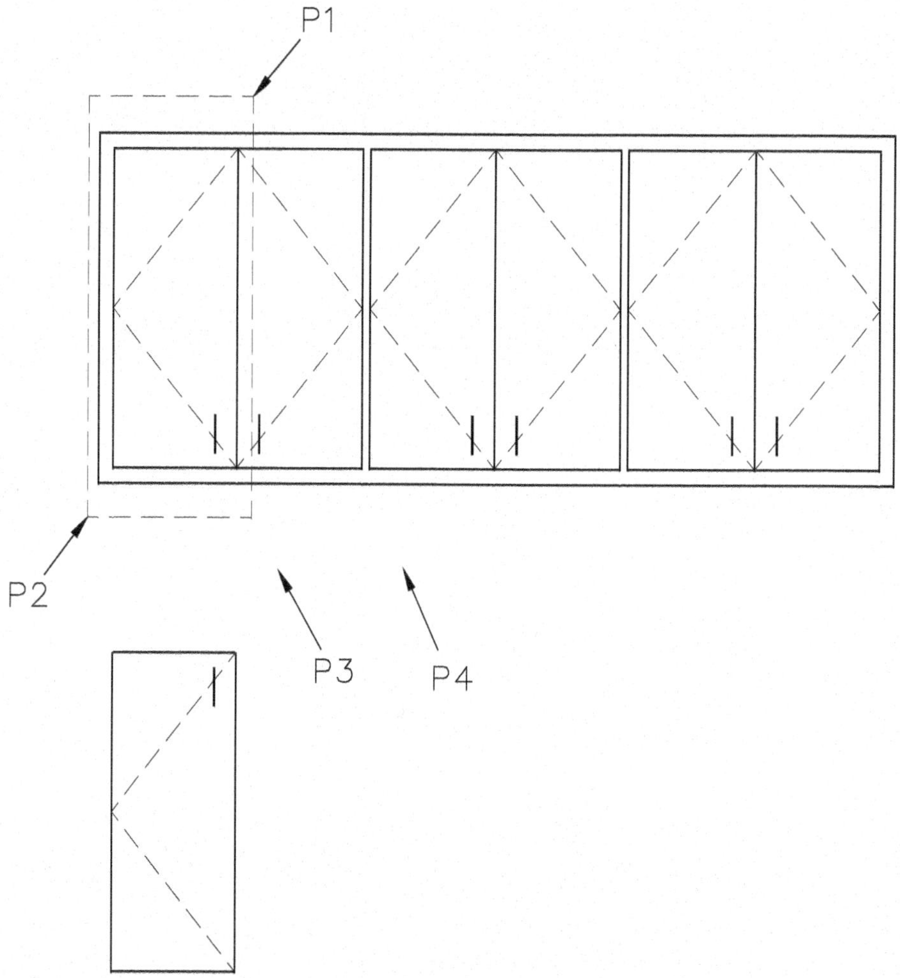

Figure 8-7
Use the **MIRROR** command to draw the first lower cabinet door

P1
P2
P3
P4

Prompt	Response
Type a command:	**Mirror** (or type **MI <Enter>**)
Select objects:	**P2→** (left to right)
Specify opposite corner:	**P1→**
Select objects:	**<Enter>**
Specify first point of mirror line:	**P3→** (with **ORTHO** and **SNAP** on; the lower cabinets will be moved to the accurate location later)
Specify second point of mirror line:	**P4→**
Erase source objects? [Yes No] <N>:	**<Enter>** (the lower cabinet is now too high and too narrow)

Stretch

STRETCH	
Ribbon/ Panel	Home/ Modify
Modify Toolbar:	
Menu Bar:	Modify/ Stretch
Type a Command:	STRETCH
Command Alias:	S

You can use the **STRETCH** command to stretch entities to make them longer or shorter. You can also use it to move entities that have other lines attached to them without removing the attached lines (described later in this exercise). **STRETCH** requires you to use a crossing window to select objects. As with many other **Modify** commands, you may select objects initially, then remove or add objects to the selection set before you perform the stretch function.

Step 12. Use the **STRETCH** command to change the height of the **first lower cabinet door** just drawn (Figure 8-8), as described next:

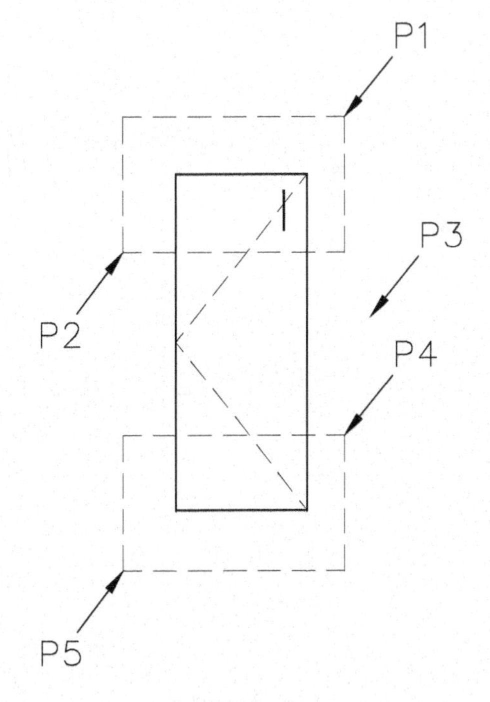

Figure 8-8
Use the **STRETCH** command to change the height of the first lower cabinet door

Prompt	Response
Type a command:	**Stretch** (or type **S <Enter>**)
Select objects to stretch by crossing-window or crossing-polygon... Select objects:	**P1→**
Specify opposite corner:	**P2→**
Select objects:	**<Enter>**

Prompt	Response
Specify base point or [Displacement] <Displacement>:	**P3→** (any point)
Specify second point or <use first point as displacement>:	Type **@9<270 <Enter>** (or with **ORTHO** on, move your mouse down and type **9 <Enter>**) (the upper door height, 3′6″, minus the lower door height, 2′, divided by 2; take half off the top of the door and half off the bottom)
Type a command:	**Stretch** (or press **<Enter>**)
Select objects to stretch by crossing-window or crossing-polygon... Select objects:	**P4→**
Specify opposite corner:	**P5→**
Select objects:	**<Enter>**
Specify base point or [Displacement] <Displacement>:	**P3→** (any point)
Specify second point or <use first point as displacement>:	Type **@9<90 <Enter>** (or move your mouse up and type **9 <Enter>**). The lower cabinet door should now be 18″ shorter than the upper cabinet door from which it was mirrored (3′6″ minus 18″ equals 2′, the cabinet door height)

Step 13. Use the **STRETCH** command to change the width of the **first lower cabinet door** (Figure 8-9), as described next:

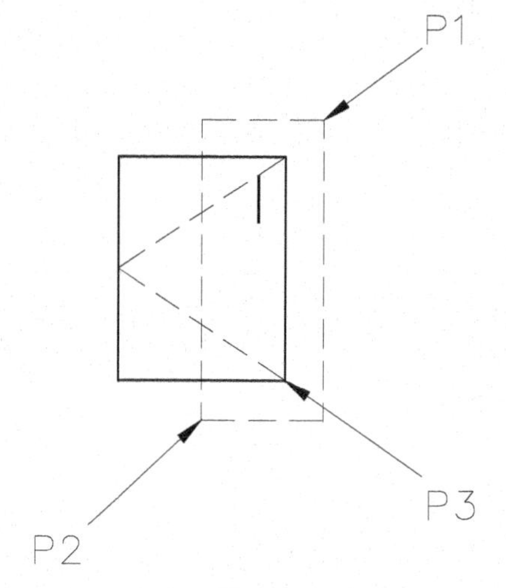

Figure 8-9
Use the **STRETCH** command to change the width of the cabinet door

Prompt	Response
Type a command:	**Stretch**
Select objects to stretch by crossing-window or crossing-polygon... Select objects:	**P1→**
Specify opposite corner:	**P2→**
Select objects:	**<Enter>**

Prompt	**Response**
Specify base point or [Displacement] <Displacement>:	**P3→** (any point)
Specify second point or <use first point as displacement>:	Type **@1-1/2<0 <Enter>** (or move the mouse to the right and type **1-1/2 <Enter>**) (the upper door width, 1′5″, plus 1-1/2″, equals the lower door width, 1′6-1/2″)

Step 14. Save the current UCS used to draw the upper cabinets, as described next:

Prompt	**Response**
Type a command:	Type **UCS <Enter>**
Specify origin of UCS or [Face NAmed OBject Previous View World X Y Z ZAxis] <World>:	Type **S <Enter>**
Enter name to save current UCS or [?]:	Type **UPPER <Enter>**

Step 15. Create a new UCS origin for drawing the lower cabinets by moving the existing UCS origin **–4′2-1/2″** in the Y direction, as described next.

Prompt	**Response**
Type a command:	**<Enter>** (repeat **UCS**)
Specify origin of UCS or [Face NAmed OBject Previous View World X Y Z ZAxis] <World>:	Type **O <Enter>**
Specify new origin point <0,0,0>:	Type **0,-4′2-1/2 <Enter>** (be sure to include the minus)

Step 16. Move the **lower cabinet door** to a point 2″ above and 2″ to the right of the origin of the current UCS (Figure 8-10), as described next:

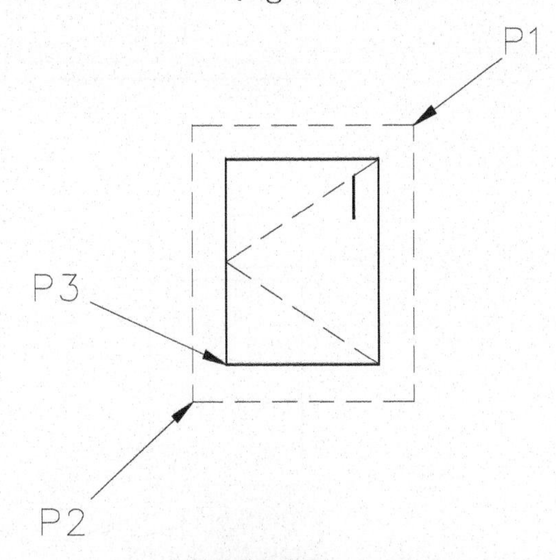

Figure 8-10 Move the lower cabinet door to a point 2″ above and 2″ to the right of the origin of the current UCS

Prompt	**Response**
Type a command:	**Move** (or type **M <Enter>**)
Select objects:	**P1→** (Figure 8-10)

Prompt	Response
Specify opposite corner:	**P2→**
Select objects:	**<Enter>**
Specify base point or [Displacement] <Displacement>:	**Osnap-Intersection**
of	**P3→**
Specify second point or <use first-point as displacement>:	Type **2,2 <Enter>**

Step 17. Using relative coordinates, draw a rectangle forming the drawer above the lower cabinet door (Figure 8-11), as described next:

Prompt	Response
Type a command:	**Rectangle** (or type **REC <Enter>**)
Specify first corner point or [Chamfer Elevation Fillet Thickness Width]:	Type **FRO <Enter> Osnap-Intersection**
Base point:	Click the upper-left corner of the lower cabinet door
<Offset>:	Type **@1-1/2<90 <Enter>**
Specify other corner point or [Area Dimensions Rotation]:	Type **@1′6-1/2,6 <Enter>**

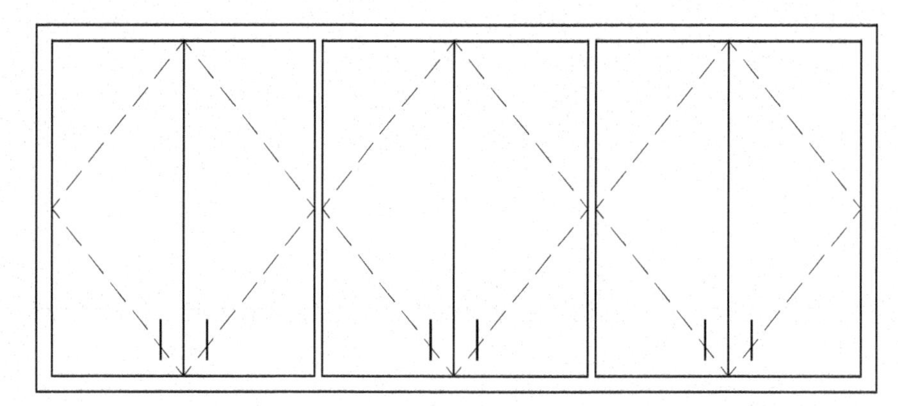

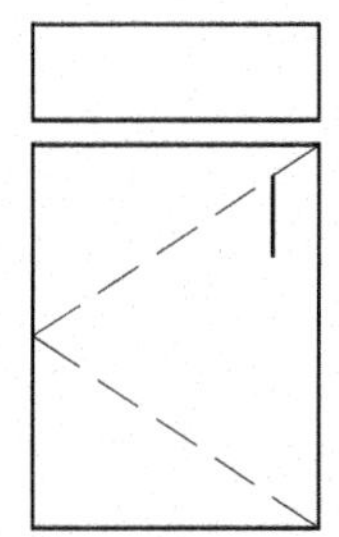

Figure 8-11
Draw the drawer

Step 18. Copy the door handle from the handle midpoint to the midpoint of the bottom line of the drawer, rotate it 90°, and move it up 3″ as shown in Figure 8-12.

Figure 8-12
Copy the door handle, rotate it, and move it

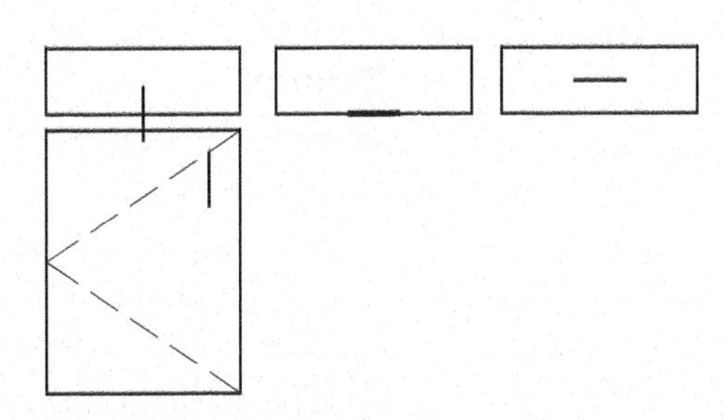

Step 19. Explode the upper cabinet outer rectangle. Offset the bottom line of the rectangle several times and change two lines to other layers (Figure 8-13) as described next:

Offset the bottom line of the rectangle down **10″** and change it to the **a-elev-lwt2** layer.

Offset the bottom line of the rectangle down **14″**.

Offset that line down **1-1/2″**.

Offset that line down **2′11″**.

Offset that line down **3-1/2″** and change the offset line to the **a-elev-otln** layer.

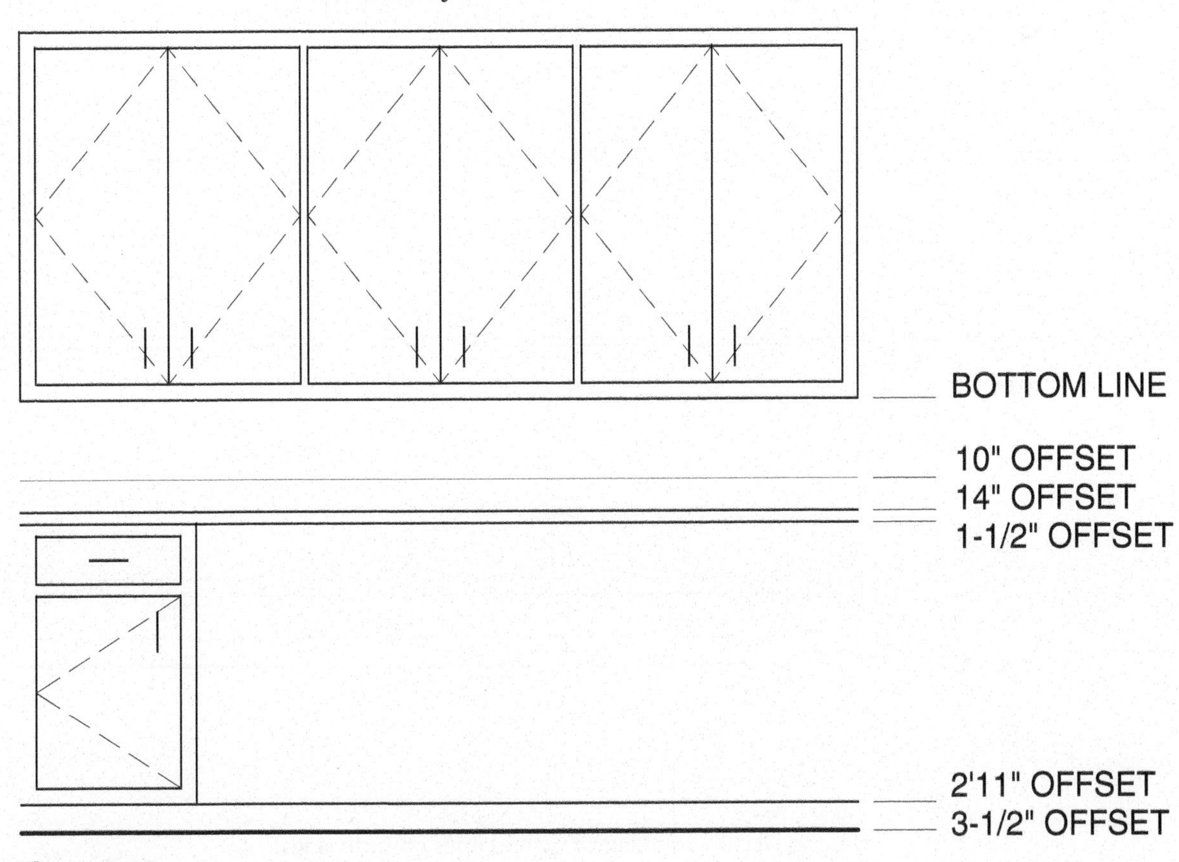

Figure 8-13
EXPLODE the upper cabinet outer rectangle and offset the bottom line

Step 20. Use zero radius **Fillet** to extend lines on both sides of the cabinets as described next:

Prompt	**Response**
Type a command:	**Fillet** (or type **F** <Enter>)
Select first object or [Undo Polyline Radius Trim Multiple]:	Type **M** <Enter>

Prompt	Response
Select first object or [Undo Polyline Radius Trim Multiple]:	Click **P1→** (Figure 8-14)
Select second object or Shift-select to apply corner or [Radius]:	Click **P2→**
Select first object or [Undo Polyline Radius Trim Multiple]:	Click **P3→**
Select second object or Shift-select to apply corner or [Radius]:	Click **P4→**
Select first object or [Undo Polyline Radius Trim Multiple]:	**<Enter>**

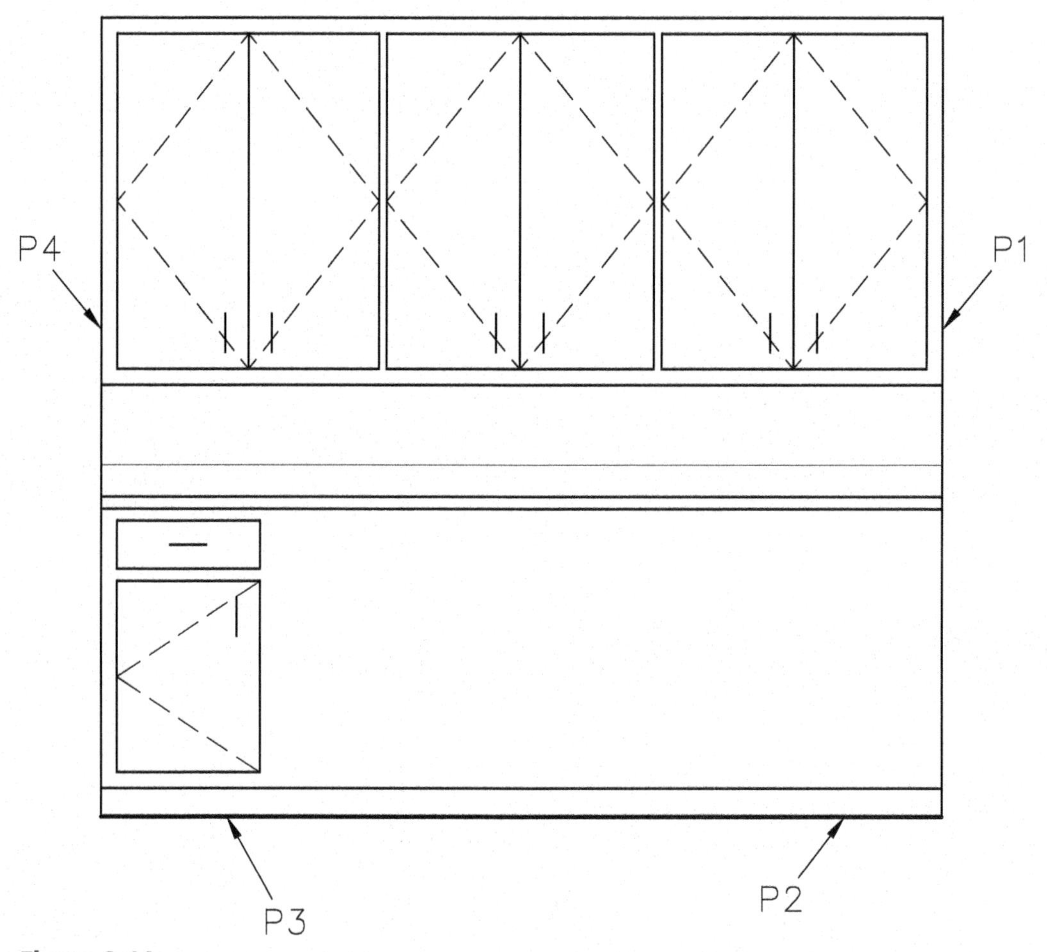

Figure 8-14
Use the **FILLET** command to extend lines on both sides

Step 21. Use the **MIRROR** command to draw the door and drawer on the right side of the lower cabinet (Figure 8-15).

Step 22. Use the **COPY** command to copy the door and drawer on the left 3′10 - 1/2″ to the right (Figure 8-16).

Step 23. Use the **COPY** command to copy the door and drawer on the far right 1′7 - 1/2″ to the left.

Figure 8-15
Use the **MIRROR** command to draw the door and drawer on the far right

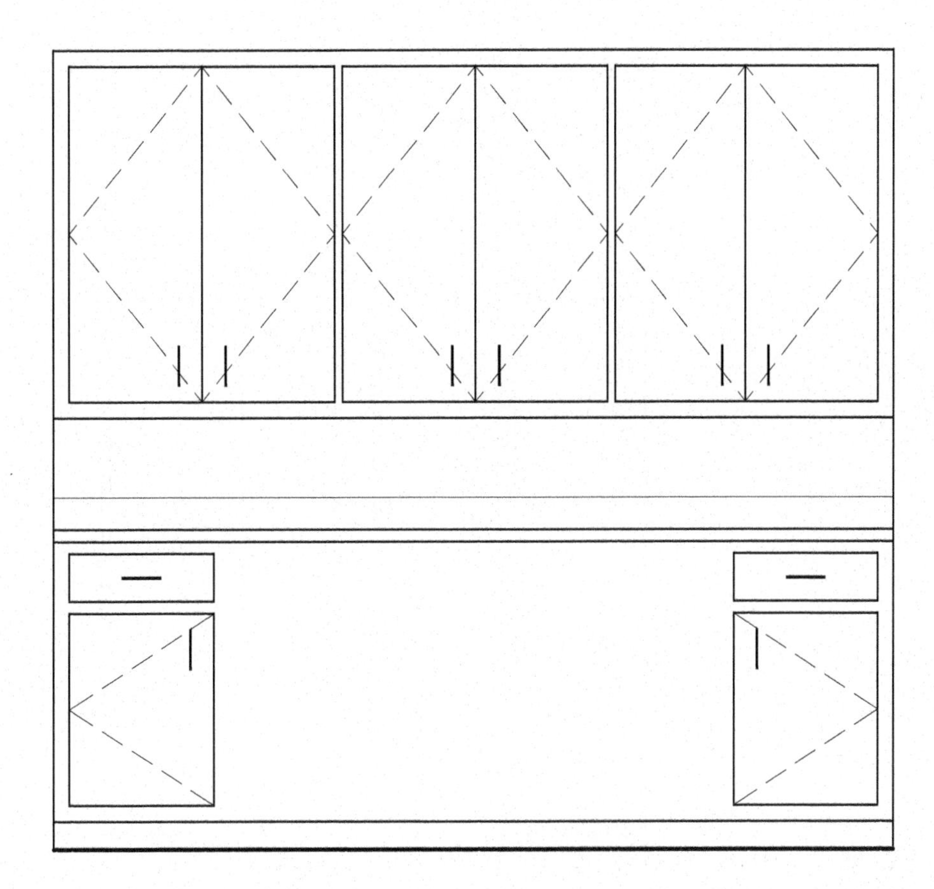

Figure 8-16
COPY drawers and doors; **OFFSET** and **TRIM** lines to form the refrigerator

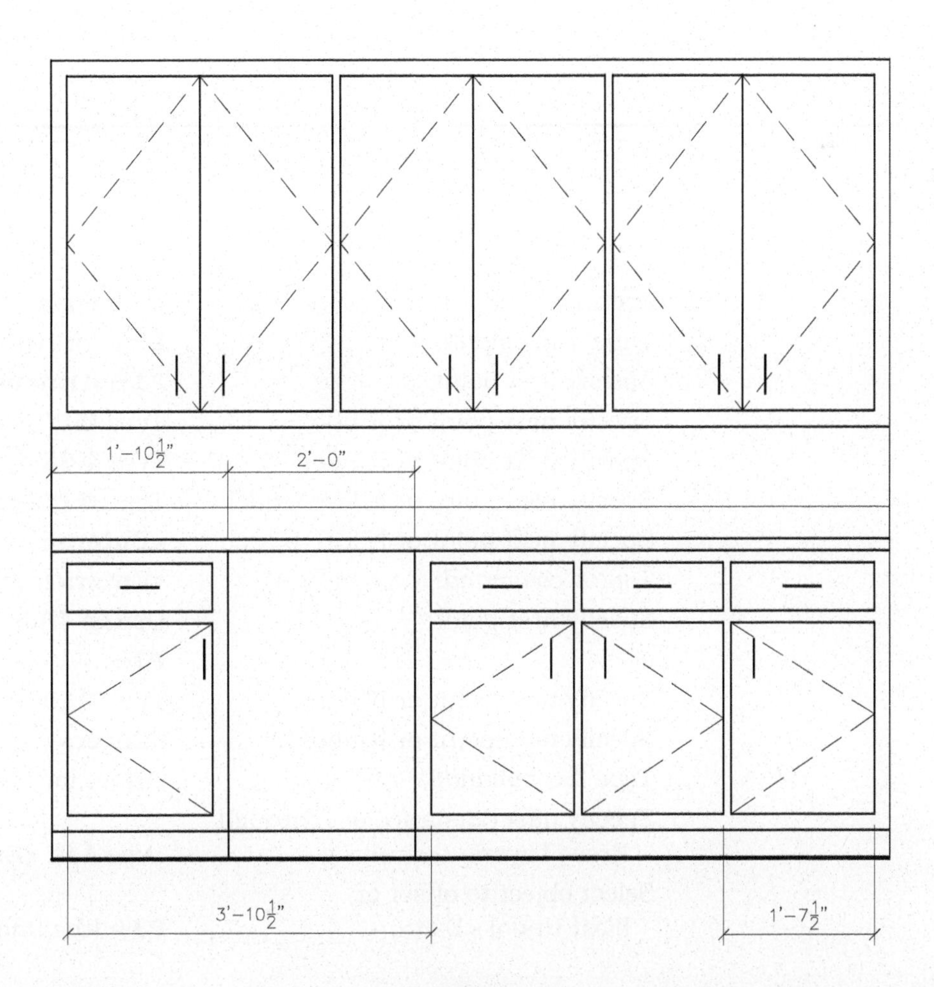

Step 24. Offset the cabinet line on the far left, 1′10 - 1/2″ to the right. Offset that line 2′0″ to the right to form the refrigerator. Trim lines as needed (Figure 8-16).

Step 25. Set layer **a-elev-lwt2** current. Draw the sink in the approximate location shown in Figure 8-17 (the **STRETCH** command will be used later to move the sink to the correct location), as described next:

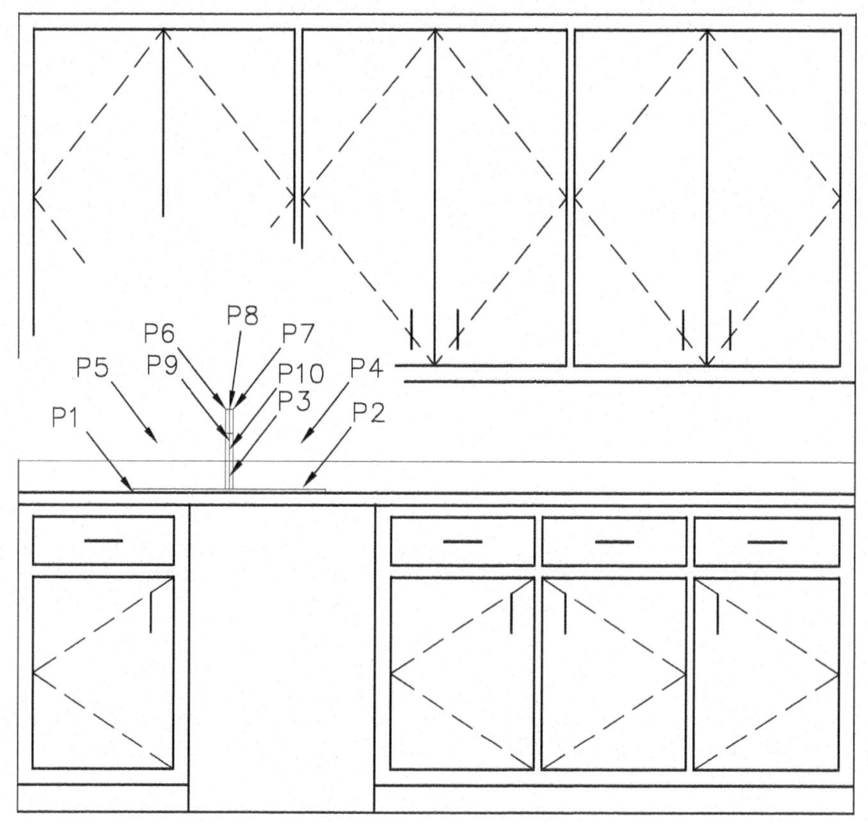

Figure 8-17
Draw the sink in the approximate location shown

Prompt	**Response**
Type a command:	**Line** (or type **L <Enter>**)
Specify first point:	**P1→ (Osnap-Nearest)**
Specify next point or [Undo]:	Type **@1/2<90 <Enter>**
Specify next point or [Undo]:	Type **@25<0 <Enter>**
Specify next point or [Close Undo]:	Type **@1/2<270 <Enter>**
Specify next point or [Close Undo]:	**<Enter>**
Type a command:	**<Enter>** (repeat **LINE**)
Specify first point:	**Osnap-Midpoint**
of	**P2→**
Specify next point or [Undo]:	Type **@10<90 <Enter>**
Specify next point or [Undo]:	**<Enter>**
Type a command:	**Offset** (or type **O <Enter>**)
Specify offset distance or [Through Erase Layer] <default>:	Type **1/2 <Enter>**
Select object to offset or [Exit Undo] <Exit>:	**P3→** (the line just drawn)

Prompt	Response
Specify point on side to offset or [Exit Multiple Undo] <Exit>:	**P4→** (to the right)
Select object to offset or [Exit Undo] <Exit>:	**P3→**
Specify point on side to offset or [Exit Multiple Undo] <Exit>:	**P5→** (to the left)
Select object to offset or [Exit Undo] <Exit>:	**<Enter>**
Type a command:	**Line**
Specify first point:	**Osnap-Endpoint**
of	**P6→**
Specify next point or [Undo]:	**Osnap-Endpoint**
of	**P7→**
Specify next point or [Undo]:	**<Enter>** (to complete the command)
Type a command:	**Offset**
Specify offset distance or [Through Erase Layer] <0′-1/2″>:	Type **3 <Enter>**
Select object to offset or [Exit Undo] <Exit>:	**P8→**
Specify point on side to offset or [Exit Multiple Undo] <Exit>:	**P10→**
Select object to offset or [Exit Undo] <Exit>:	**<Enter>**
Type a command:	**Erase** (or type **E <Enter>**)
Select objects:	**P9→** (the center vertical line)
Select objects:	**<Enter>**

Step 26. Trim out the line of the backsplash where it crosses the faucet.

Step 27. You can use the **STRETCH** command to move entities that have other lines attached to them without removing the attached lines. Use **STRETCH** to move the sink to its correct location (Figure 8-18), as described next:

Prompt	Response
Type a command:	**Stretch** (or type **S <Enter>**)
Select objects to stretch by crossing-window or crossing-polygon... Select objects:	**P2→**
Specify opposite corner:	**P1→**
Select objects:	**<Enter>**
Specify base point or [Displacement], Displacement:	**Osnap-Midpoint**
of	**P3→**
Specify second point or <use first point as displacement>:	**P4→** (with **ORTHO** on, pick a point directly above the space between the two center doors, Figures 8-18 and 8-19)

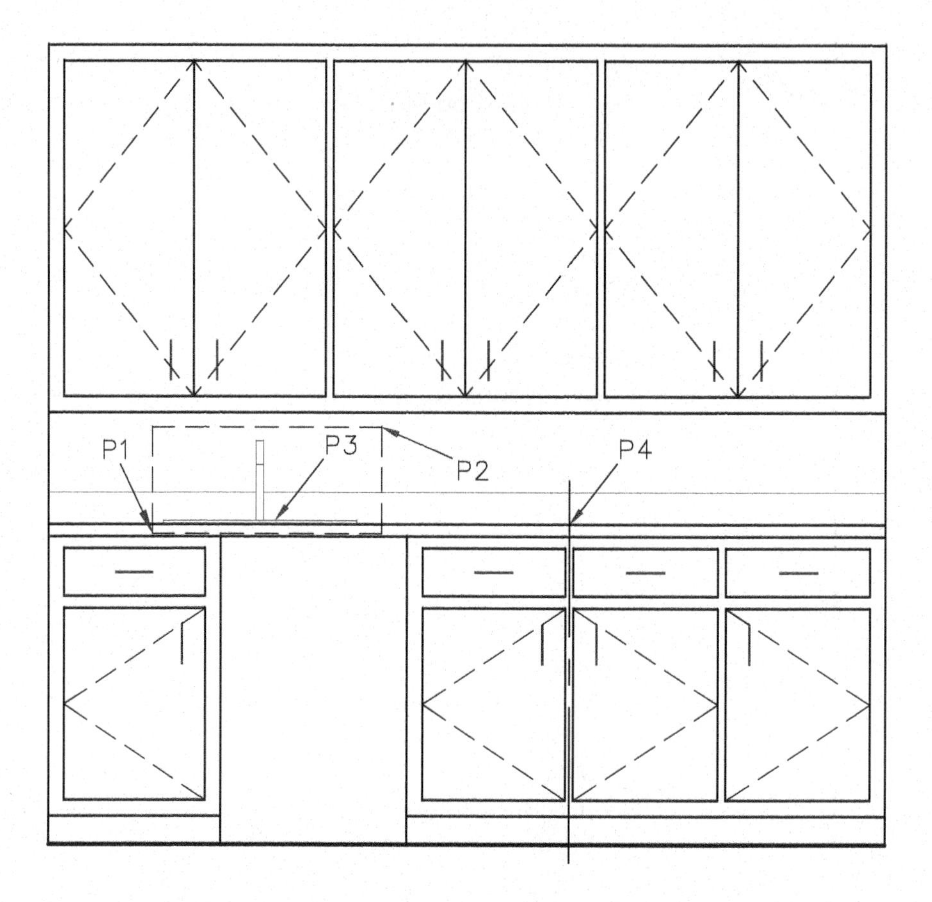

Figure 8-18
Use the **STRETCH** command to move the sink to its correct location

Complete the Drawing

Step 28. Use the **OFFSET** and **EXTEND** commands to draw the ceiling line above the cabinets (Figure 8-19). Change the ceiling line to the **a-elev-otln** layer.

Step 29. Use the **UCS** command to save the current UCS, and name it **LOWER**. Set the UCS to **World**.

Step 30. Set the drawing annotation scale to **1/2″ = 1′-0″**.

Step 31. Set layer **a-elev-text** current.

Step 32. Change the text style to **Standard** with the **romans** font.

Step 33. In the **Text Style** dialog box, select the box beside **Annotative** under **Size** to make sure the annotative property is set to on.

Step 34. Use **DTEXT**, height **1/16″** to place the note on the refrigerator.

Step 35. Use **DTEXT**, height **1/8″** to type your name, class, and the current date in the upper right area.

Step 36. Use **DTEXT**, height **1/8″** to type the underlined text **CONFERENCE ROOM CABINET ELEVATION**.

Step 37. Add the elevation and section symbols to the elevation drawing, as shown in Figure 8-19. Use a **4″** radius circle and **3/32″** high text.

Step 38. Use **DTEXT**, height **3/32″** to type the drawing scale.

Step 39. Set layer **a-elev-dims** current.

Step 40. Set the dimensioning variables.

Step 41. Add the dimensions as shown in Figure 8-19.

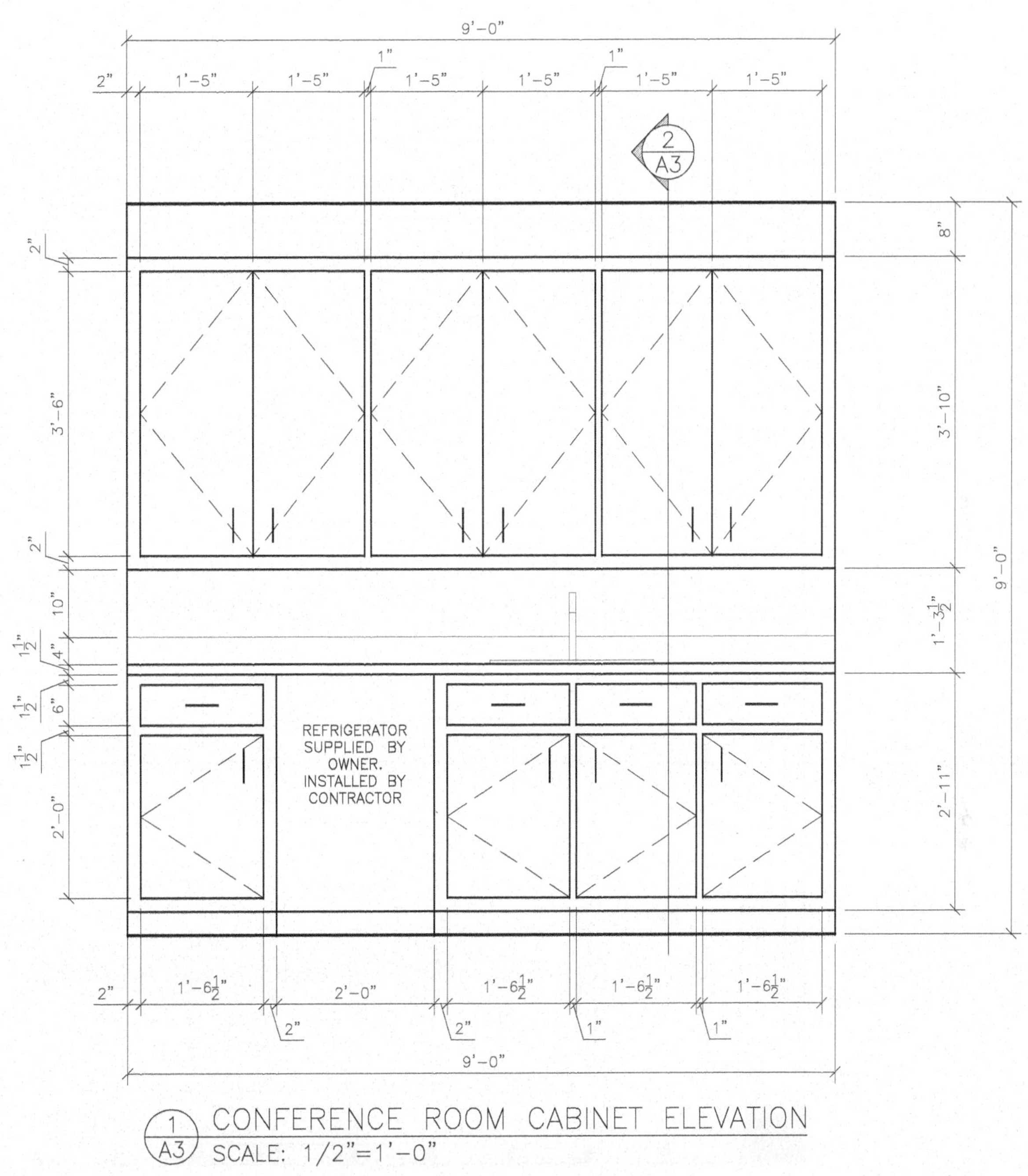

Figure 8-19
Complete the elevation drawing (scale: 1/2″ = 1′-0″)

Step 42. When you have completed Exercise 8-1, save your work in at least two places.

Step 43. Print Exercise 8-1 at a scale of **1/2″ = 1′-0″**.

Step 44. Add the elevation symbol, as shown in Figure 8-20, to the conference room on your tenant space floor plan drawing (CH7-EXERCISE1.dwg). Use a **1′**-radius circle and **1/16″**-high text (annotative).

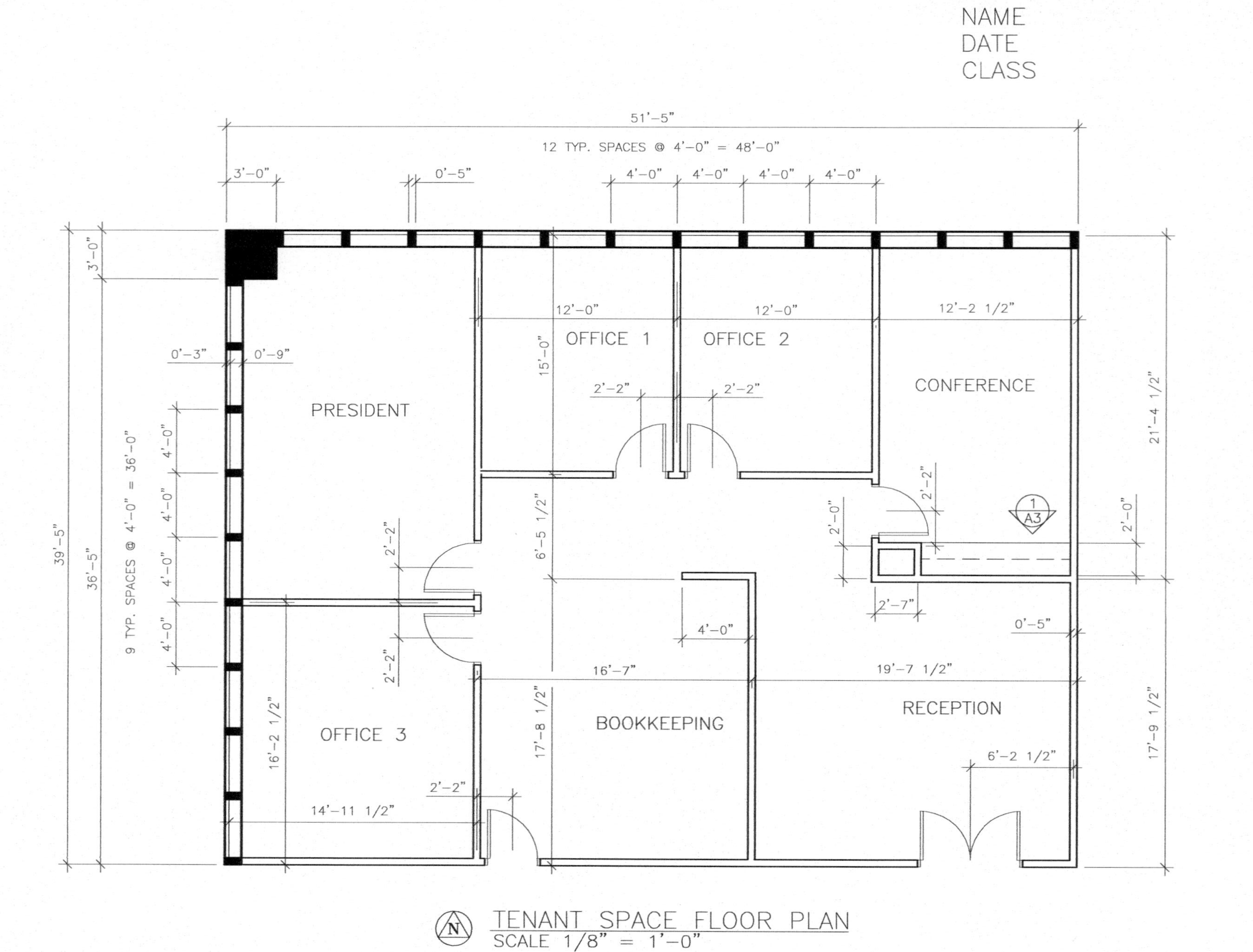

Figure 8-20
Tenant space floor plan with elevation symbol (scale: 1/8" = 1'-0")

EXERCISE 8-2
The Multileader Command

multileader: A leader with multiple leader lines. These leaders can be customized to show index numbers inside circles, hexagons, and other polygons.

You can use the ***Multileader*** command in a variety of ways. With **Multileader,** you can draw a leader arrowhead first, tail first, or content first. You can align the text or balloons after you have drawn them. You can gather balloons so you have several balloons on the same leader, and you can add or delete leaders. In Exercise 8-2, you use all these options.

Step 1. Use your workspace to make the following settings:

1. Set drawing units: **Architectural**
2. Set drawing limits: **8-1/2,11**
3. Set **GRIDDISPLAY**: **0**
4. Set grid: **1/2″**
5. Set snap: **1/8″**
6. Create the following layers:

Layer name	Color	Linetype	Lineweight
Circles	magenta	continuous	.010″ (.25 mm)
Leaders	red	continuous	.004″ (.09 mm)

7. Set the **Circles** layer current.
8. Use the **Standard** text style with the Arial font.
9. Make sure **ATTDIA** is set to **0**.
10. Save the drawing as **CH8-EXERCISE2**.

Circles to Be Used with Multileaders

Step 2. Draw all the 1/4″-radius circles shown in Figure 8-21 in the approximate locations shown. Space the circles 1″ apart so you have space for the leaders. Draw the concentric circles as shown in the lower left. Radii for the concentric circles are 1/4″, 3/8″, 1/2″, and 5/8″.

Step 3. Set the **Leaders** layer current.

Multileader Standard Style

MULTILEADER STYLE	
Ribbon/ Panel	Home/ Annotation
Multileader Toolbar:	
Type a Command:	MLEADER-STYLE
Command Alias:	MLS

Step 4. Open the **Multileader Style Manager** dialog box and make the settings for the Standard style as described next:

Prompt	Response
Type a command:	**Multileader Style** (or type **MLS** **<Enter>**)
The **Multileader Style Manager** appears with the Standard style current:	Click **Modify...**
The **Modify Multileader Style: Standard** dialog box appears:	Click the **Content** tab. Make the settings shown in Figure 8-22 if they are not there already:
	Multileader type: **Mtext**
	Text height: **3/16**

Figure 8-21
Draw 1/4″-radius circles and 1/4″-, 3/8″-, 1/2″-, and 5/8″-radius concentric circles

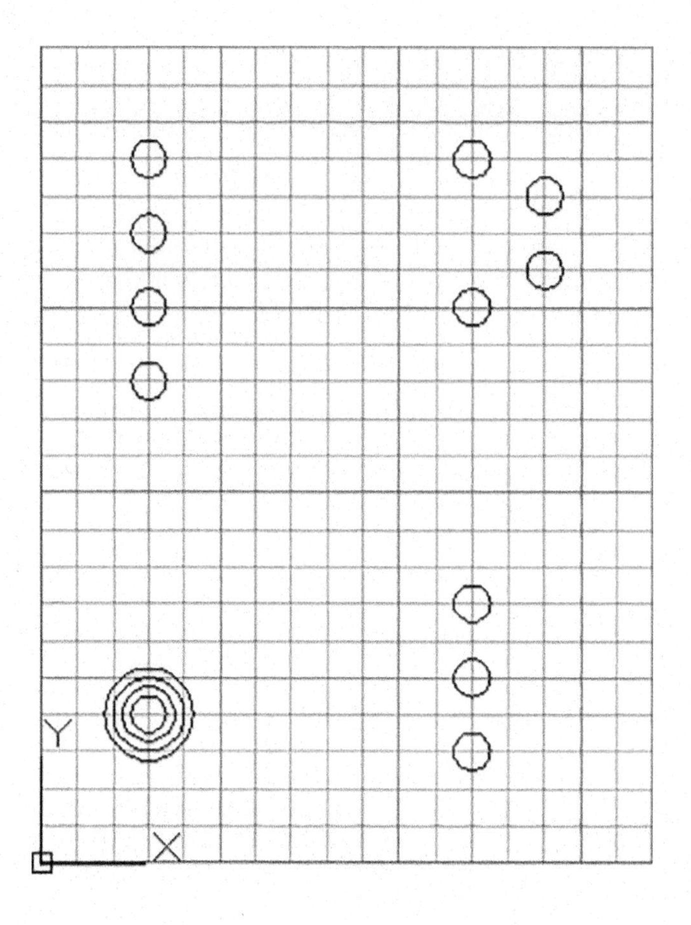

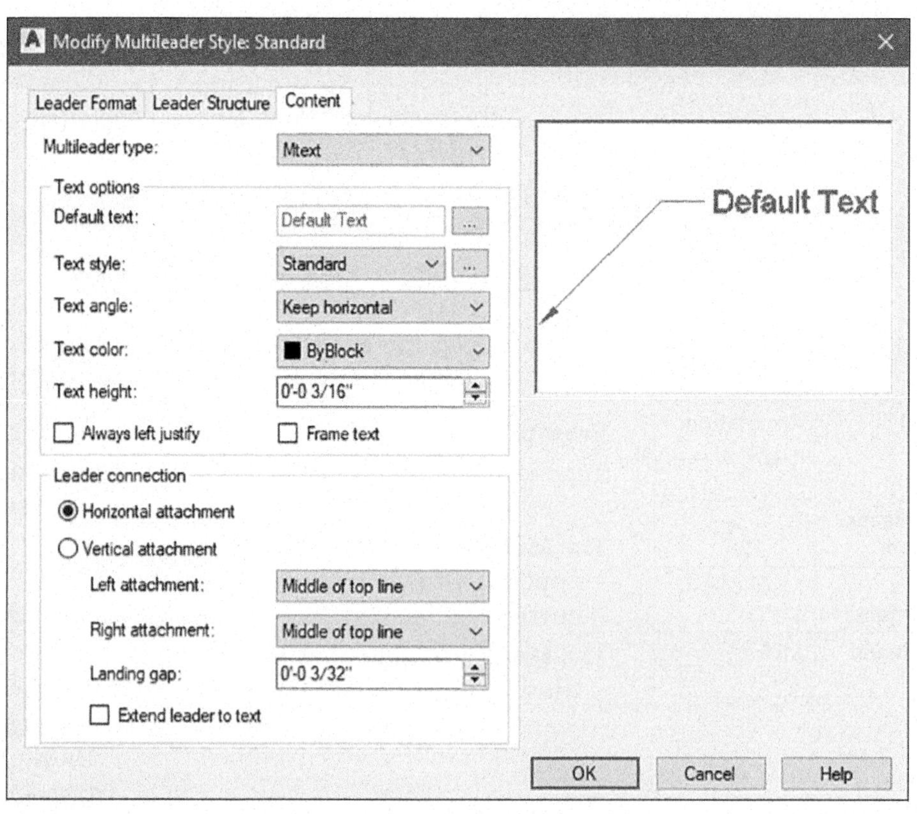

Figure 8-22
Modify Multileader Style: Standard dialog box, **Content** tab

Prompt	Response
	Left attachment: **Middle of top line**
	Right attachment: **Middle of top line**
	Landing gap: **3/32** (The landing is the horizontal line of the leader, and the landing gap is the distance between the landing and the text.)
	Click the **Leader Structure** tab (Figure 8-23) and make the following settings:
	Landing distance: **3/8″**
	Scale: **1**
	Click the **Leader Format** tab (Figure 8-24), and make the following settings:
	Type: **Straight**
	Arrowhead Symbol: **Closed filled**
	Arrowhead Size: **3/16″**
	Click **OK**
The **Multileader Style Manager** with the **Standard** style highlighted appears:	Click **Set Current**
	Click **Close**

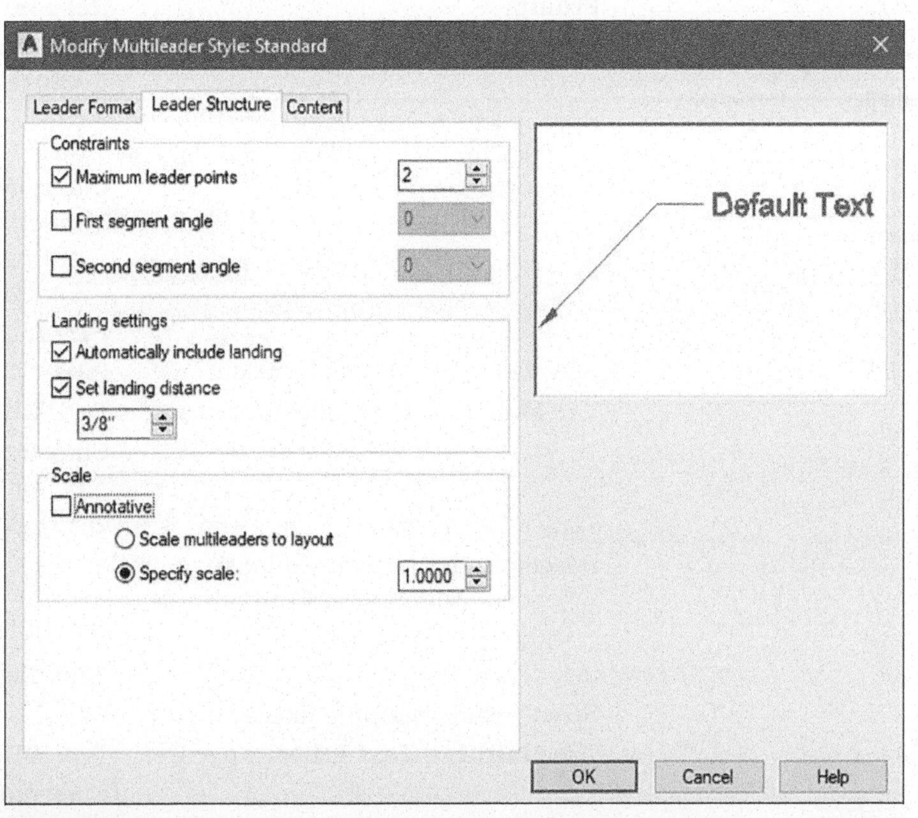

Figure 8-23
Modify Multileader Style: Standard dialog box, **Leader Structure** tab

Figure 8-24
Modify Multileader Style: Standard dialog box, **Leader Format** tab

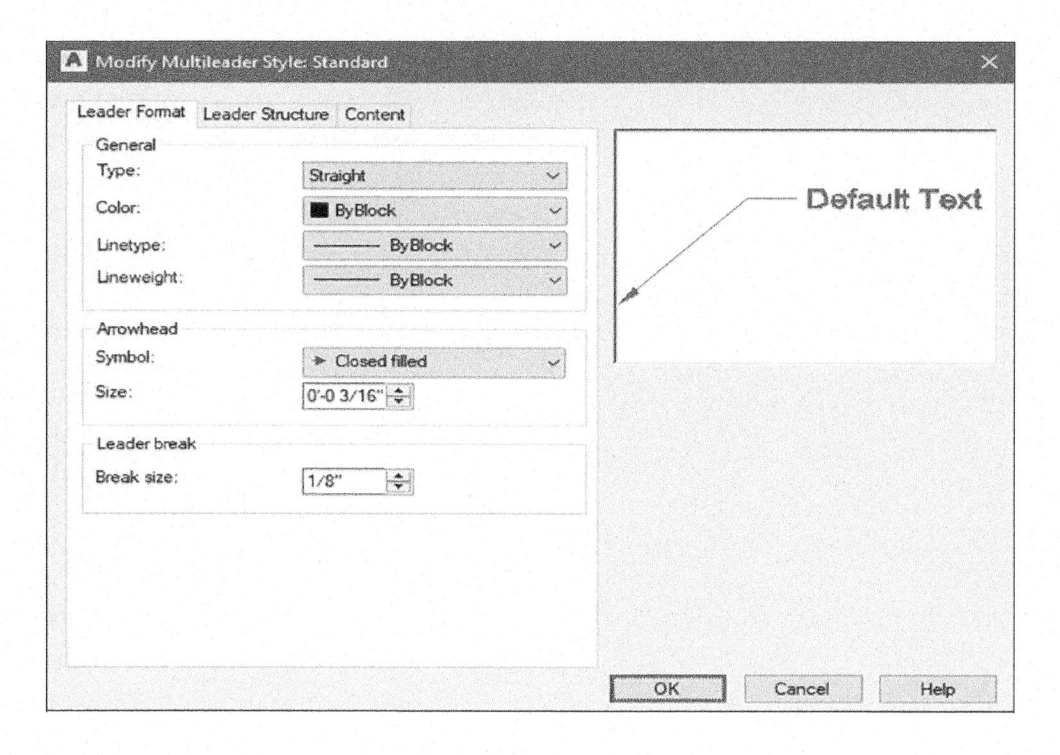

Multileader

MULTILEADER	
Ribbon/ Panel	Home/ Annotation
Multileader Toolbar:	
Menu Bar:	Dimension/ Multileader
Type a Command:	MLEADER
Command Alias:	MLD

Step 5. Draw four multileaders using the **Standard** multileader style. Draw two leaders arrowhead first, one leader landing first, and one leader content first, as described next:

Prompt	**Response**
Type a command:	**Multileader** (or type **MLEADER <Enter>**)
Specify leader arrowhead location or [leader Landing first Content first Options] <Options>:	**Osnap-Nearest** (The arrow should touch the outside of the circle but point toward the center of the circle.)
to	**P1→** (Figure 8-25)
Specify leader landing location:	**P2→**
The **Multiline Text Editor** appears:	Type **CIRCLE1**
	Click anywhere outside the text editor to place the text
Type a command:	**<Enter>**
Specify leader arrowhead location or [leader Landing first Content first Options] <Options>:	**Osnap-Nearest**
to	**P3→** (Figure 8-25)
Specify leader landing location:	**P4→**
The **Multiline Text Editor** appears:	Type **CIRCLE2**
	Click outside the text editor
Type a command:	**<Enter>**

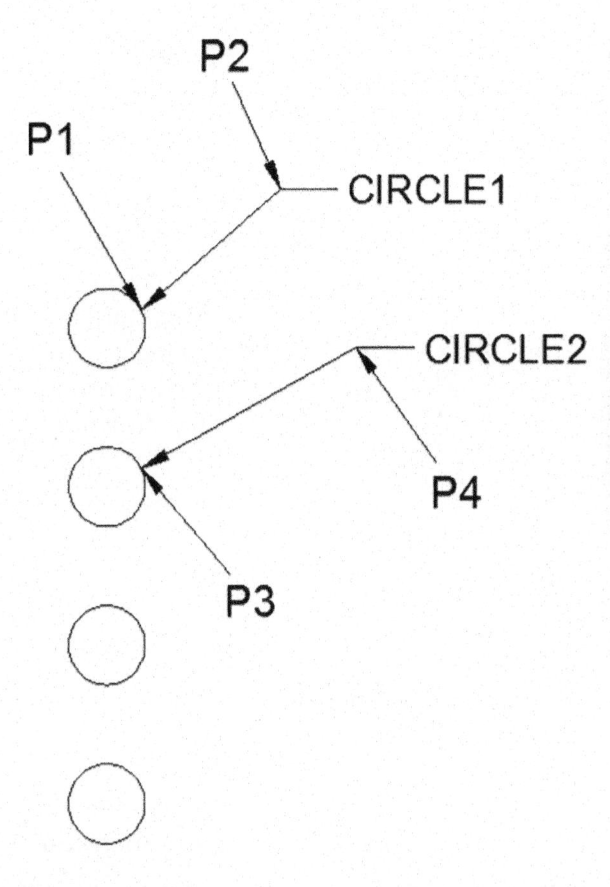

Figure 8-25
Draw two leaders arrowhead first with the **Standard** multileader style

Prompt	**Response**
Specify leader arrowhead location or [leader Landing first Content first Options] <Options>:	Type **L <Enter>** (to select **Landing** first)
Specify leader landing location or [leader arrowHead first Content first Options] <Options>:	**P2→** (Figure 8-26)

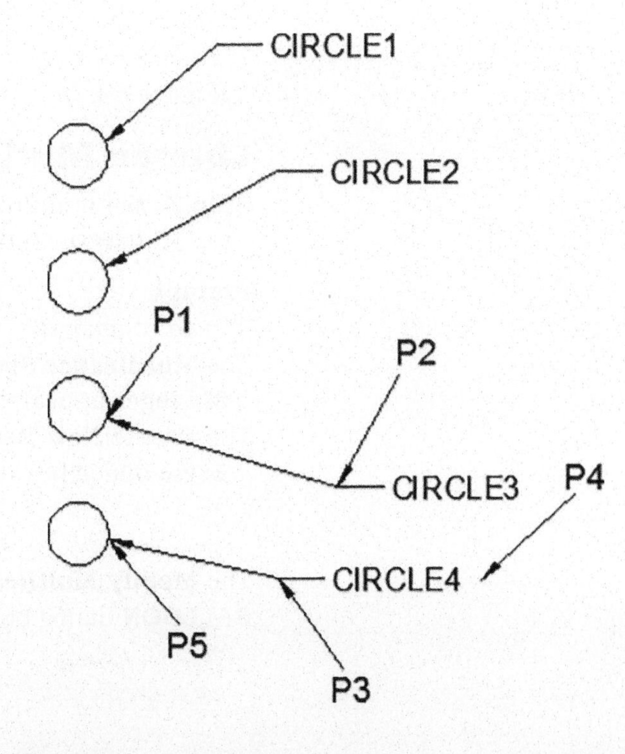

Figure 8-26
Draw one leader landing first (P1, P2); draw another leader content first (P3, P4, P5)

Prompt	**Response**
Specify leader arrowhead location:	**P1→ (Osnap-Nearest)**
The **Multiline Text Editor** appears:	Type **CIRCLE3** Click outside the text editor
Type a command:	**<Enter>**
Specify leader landing location or [leader arrowHead first Content first Options] <Options>:	Type **C <Enter>**
Specify first corner of text or [leader arrowHead first leader Landing first Options] <Options>:	**P3→**
Specify opposite corner:	**P4→**
The **Multiline Text Editor** appears:	Type **CIRCLE4** Click outside the text editor
Specify leader arrowhead location:	**P5→** (**Osnap-Nearest**)

Multileader Align

MULTILEADER ALIGN	
Ribbon/ Panel	Home/ Annotation/ Leader dropdown
Multileader Toolbar:	
Type a Command:	MLEADER-ALIGN
Command Alias:	MLA

Step 6. Align the leaders so all the text starts at the same distance from the left, as described next:

Prompt	**Response**
Type a command:	**Align Multileaders** (or type **MLA <Enter>**)
Select multileaders:	Use a window to select all four leaders (the window can include the circles also)
Specify opposite corner: 4 found	
Select multileaders:	**<Enter>**
Current mode: Use current spacing Select multileader to align to or [Options]:	Click the top leader (CIRCLE1)
Specify direction:	With **ORTHO** on, click a point below the bottom leader (CIRCLE4)
The leaders are aligned (Figure 8-27).	

Change Multileader Style

Step 7. Set a multileader style so the text appears inside a circle, as described next:

Prompt	**Response**
Type a command:	**Multileader Style** (or type **MLS <Enter>**)
The **Multileader Style Manager** appears:	Click **New...**
The **Create New Multileader Style** dialog box appears:	Type **BALLOON** in the **New style name**: text box (Figure 8-28) Click **Continue**
The **Modify Multileader Style**: **BALLOON** dialog box appears:	Click the **Content** tab Click **Block** in the **Multileader type**: list Click **Circle** in the **Source block:** list (Figure 8-29)

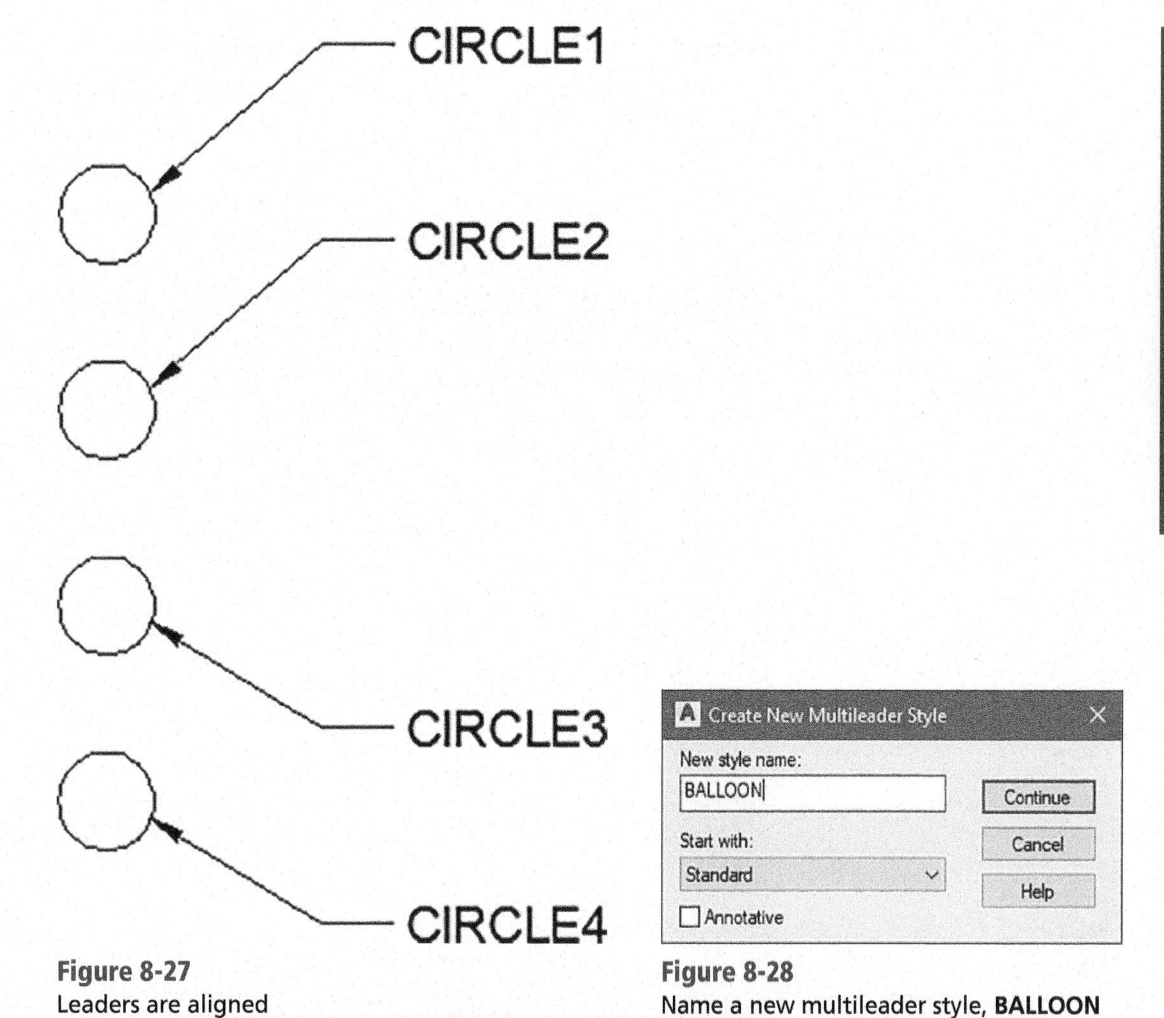

Figure 8-27
Leaders are aligned

Figure 8-28
Name a new multileader style, **BALLOON**

Figure 8-29
Select **Block** for **Multileader type, Circle** for the **Source block**, and **2″** for the **Scale**

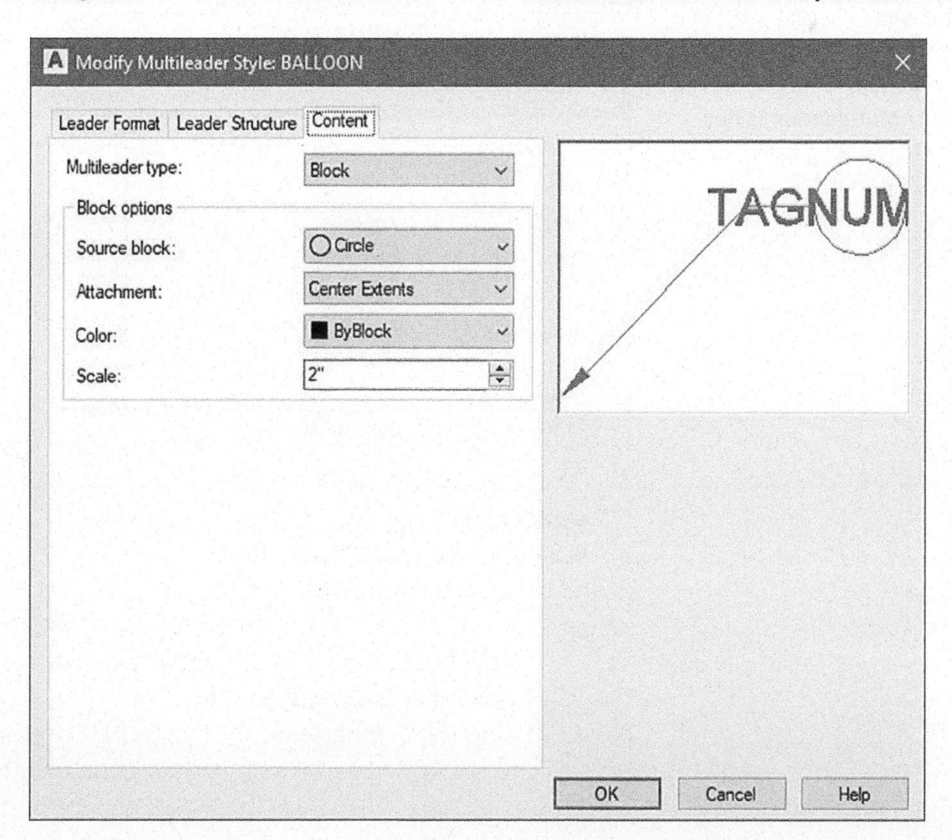

Prompt	Response
	Type **2** in the **Scale:** text box
	Click the **Leader Structure** tab
	Click the **Specify scale:** option button
	Type **1** in the **Specify scale:** text box (Figure 8-30)

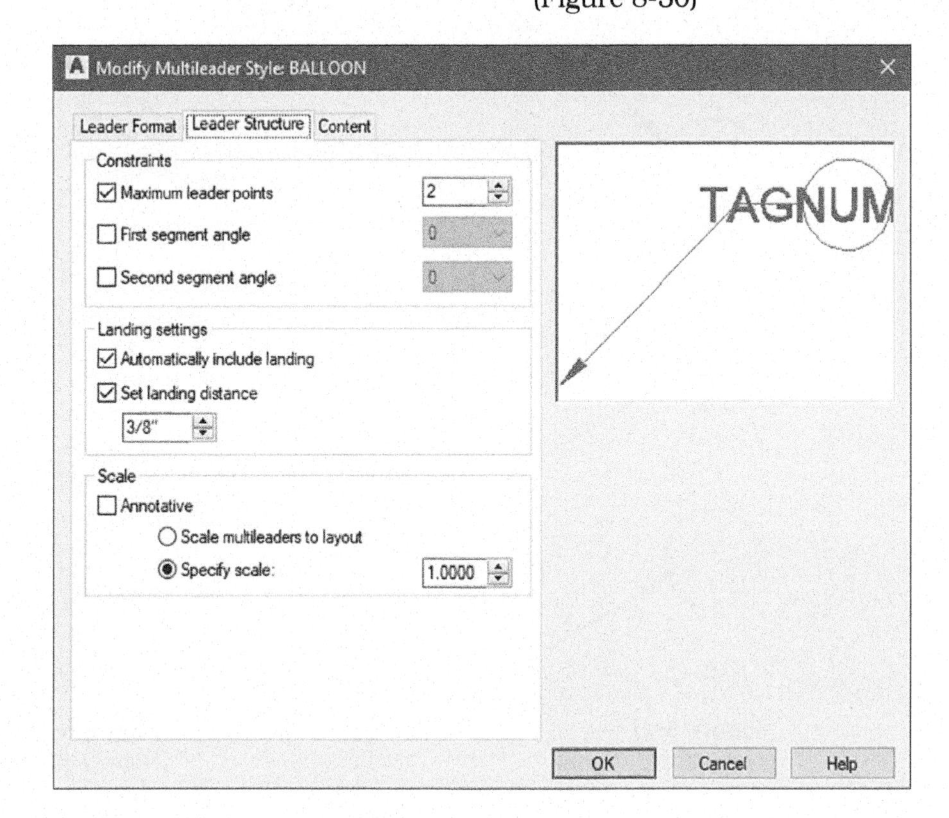

Figure 8-30
Modify Multileader Style: BALLOON dialog box, **Leader Structure** tab

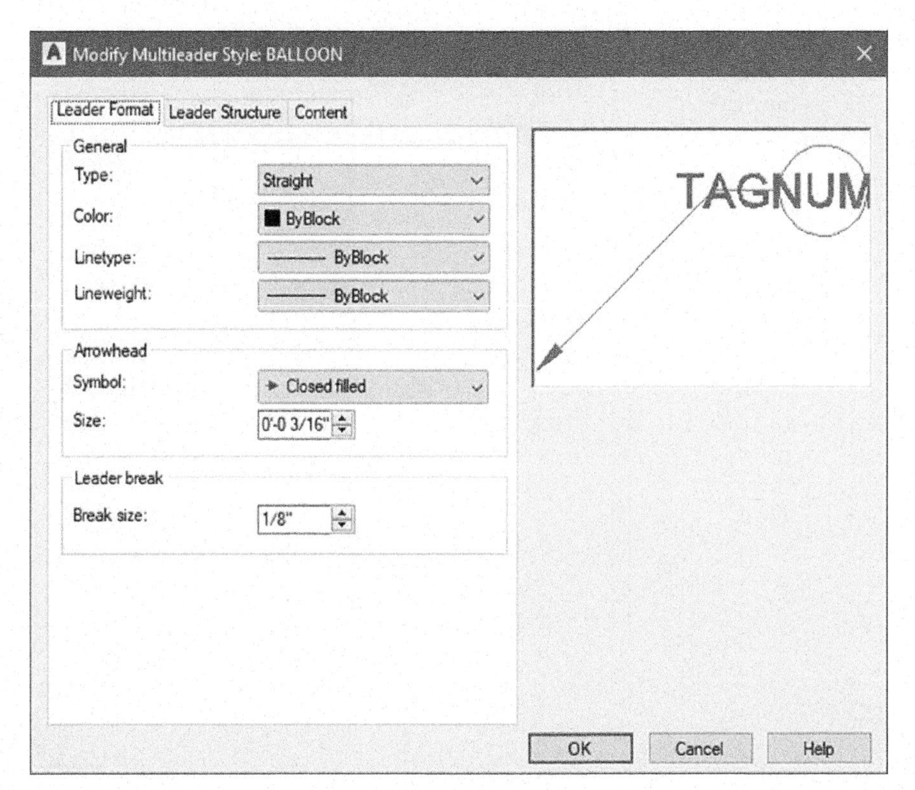

Figure 8-31
Modify Multileader Style: BALLOON dialog box, **Leader Format** tab

Prompt	Response
	Click the **Leader Format** tab and change the arrowhead size to **3/16** (Figure 8-31)
	Click **OK**
The **Multileader Style Manager** appears with the BALLOON Style highlighted:	Click **Set Current**
	Click **Close**

Step 8. Draw four multileaders using the BALLOON multileader style. Draw all four with the content first (Figure 8-32), as described next:

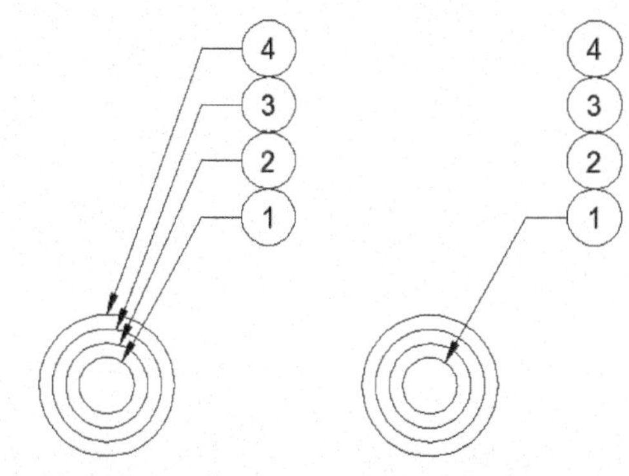

Figure 8-32
Collected content attached to one leader

Prompt	Response
Type a command:	**Multileader** (or type **MLEADER <Enter>**)
Specify insertion point for block or [leader arrowHead first leader Landing first Options] <Options>:	A circle appears on your cursor
	Click a snap point on the drawing to locate the center point of the circle, containing the number 1 (Figure 8-32)
Enter attribute values	
Enter tag number <TAGNUMBER>:	Type **1 <Enter>**
Specify leader arrowhead location:	**Osnap-Nearest**
to	Click a point on the 1/4″-radius circle (the arrow should touch the outside of the circle but point toward the center of the circle)
Type a command:	**<Enter>**
Specify insertion point for block or [leader arrowHead first leader Landing first Options] <Options>:	Click a snap point to locate the center point of the circle containing the number 2 (Figure 8-32)

Prompt	**Response**
Enter attribute values	
Enter tag number <TAGNUMBER>:	Type **2 <Enter>**
Specify leader arrowhead location:	**Osnap-Nearest**
to	Click a point on the 3/8″-radius circle (pointing toward the center is not important on the circles containing the numbers 2, 3, and 4)
Type a command:	**<Enter>**
Specify insertion point for block or [leader arrowHead first leader Landing first Options] <Options>:	Click the center point of the circle containing the number 3 (Figure 8-32)
Enter attribute values	
Enter tag number <TAGNUMBER>:	Type **3 <Enter>**
Specify leader arrowhead location:	**Osnap-Nearest**
to	Click a point on the 1/2″-radius circle
Type a command:	**<Enter>**
Specify insertion point for block or [leader arrowHead first leader Landing first Options] <Options>:	Click the center point of the circle containing the number 4 (Figure 8-32)
Enter attribute values	
Enter tag number <TAGNUMBER>:	Type **4 <Enter>**
Specify leader arrowhead location: <Osnap on>	**Osnap-Nearest**
to	Click a point on the 5/8″-radius circle
Type a command:	**<Enter>**

Multileader Collect

MULTILEADER COLLECT	
Ribbon/ Panel	Home/ Annotation/ Leader dropdown
Multileader Toolbar:	
Type a Command:	MLEADER-COLLECT
Command Alias:	MLC

Step 9. Collect the four leaders so all the balloons are attached to one leader, as described next (Figure 8-32):

Prompt	**Response**
Type a command:	Collect multileaders (or type **MLC <Enter>**)
Select multileaders:	Select all four leaders
Select multileaders:	**<Enter>**
Specify collected multileader location or [Vertical Horizontal Wrap] <Horizontal>:	Type **V <Enter>**
Specify collected multileader location or [Vertical Horizontal Wrap] <Vertical>:	Move your mouse so you can see one leader attached to the number 1 balloon. Click a point to locate the balloons, as shown in Figure 8-32

Step 10. Set a running **Osnap-Nearest**.

Multileader Add

MULTILEADER ADD	
Ribbon/ Panel	Home/ Annotation/ Leader dropdown
Multileader Toolbar:	
Type a Command:	AIMLEADER EDITADD

Step 11. Draw a multileader and add three leaders to it, as described next, Figures 8-33 and 8-34:

Prompt	Response
Type a command:	**Multileader** (or type **MLEADER <Enter>**)
Specify insertion point for block or [leader arrowHead first leader Landing first Options] <Options>:	A circle appears on your cursor. Click a snap point on the drawing to locate the center point of the circle containing the number 5 (Figure 8-33)
Enter attribute values	
Enter tag number <TAGNUMBER>:	Type **5 <Enter>**
Specify leader arrowhead location:	Click a point on the top circle, **Osnap-Nearest** (Figure 8-33)
Type a command:	**Add Leader** (or type **AIMLEADEREDITADD <Enter>**)
Select a multileader:	Click the multileader you just drew
1 found	
Specify leader arrowhead location or [Remove leaders]:	Click a point on the next circle, **Osnap-Nearest** (Figure 8-34)
Specify leader arrowhead location or [Remove leaders]:	Click a point on the next circle, **Osnap-Nearest**
Specify leader arrowhead location or [Remove leaders]:	Click a point on the last circle, **Osnap-Nearest <Enter>**

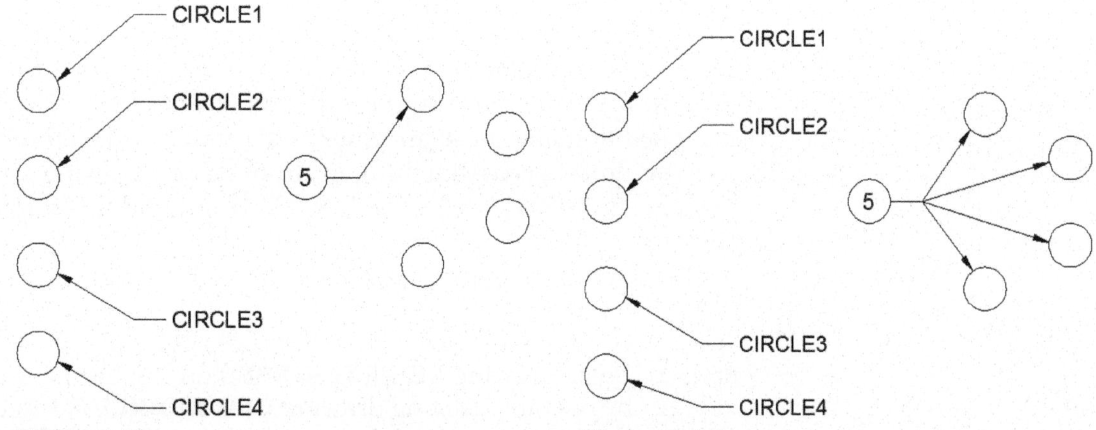

Figure 8-33
Draw the multileader for the number 5

Figure 8-34
Draw one leader and add three more

Step 12. Make a new multileader style with the following settings:

1. Name it **HEX** (start with a copy of **BALLOON**).
2. Change the **Source block:** to a **Hexagon**.
3. Set the **HEX** style current.

Step 13. Draw one leader with a **6** in the hexagon and add two leaders to it as shown in Figure 8-35.

Figure 8-35
Exercise 8-2 Complete

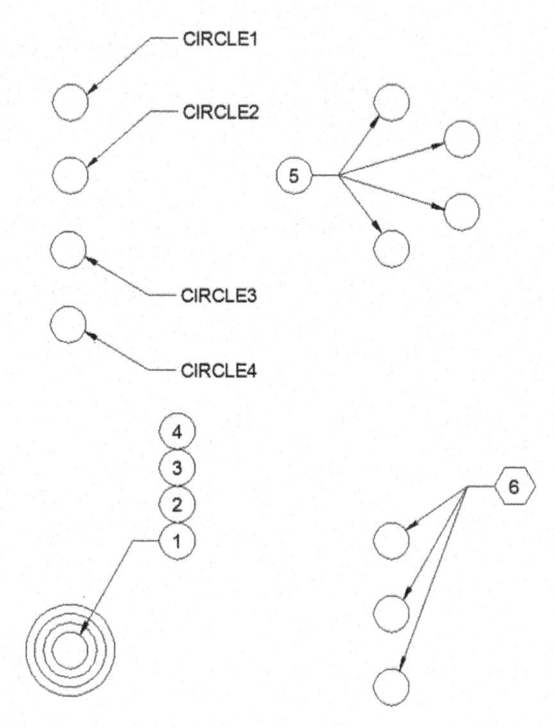

Step 14. Save your drawing in two places.

Step 15. Print the drawing at a scale of **1:1**.

EXERCISE 8-3
Tenant Space: Section of Conference Room Cabinets with Hatching

In Exercise 8-3, you will draw a sectional view of the built-in cabinets on the south wall of the tenant space conference room. The sectional view of the south wall of the cabinets (Figure 8-36) shows many construction details that elevation and plan views cannot. Sectional views are imaginary cuts through an area. You use hatched lines to show where the imaginary saw used to make these imaginary cuts touches the cut objects.

You do this crosshatching in AutoCAD by drawing hatch patterns. Exercise 8-3 will describe the **HATCH** command, used to draw hatch patterns.

When you have completed Exercise 8-3, your drawing will look similar to Figure 8-36.

Step 1. Begin drawing **CH8-EXERCISE3** on the hard drive or network drive by opening existing drawing **CH8-EXERCISE1** and saving it to the hard drive or network drive with the name **CH8-EXERCISE3**. You can use all the settings and text created for Exercise 8-1.

Step 2. Reset drawing limits, grid, and snap as needed.

Step 3. Create the following layers by renaming the existing layers and adding the **a-sect-fixt** layer:

Layer Name	Description	Color	Linetype	Lineweight
a-sect-dims	dimensions, dimension notes	red	continuous	.004″ (.09 mm)
a-sect-fixt	sink	green	continuous	.006″ (.15 mm)
a-sect-hdln	sink hidden lines	red	hidden	.004″ (.09 mm)
a-sect-lwt1	section lines except for those under lwt2	blue	continuous	.010″ (.25 mm)
a-sect-lwt2	recessed standards, 1/4″ upper and lower cabinet plywood backing	white	continuous	.002″ (.05 mm)
a-sect-patt	hatch patterns	white	continuous	.002″ (.05 mm)
a-sect-text	text	green	continuous	.006″ (.15 mm)

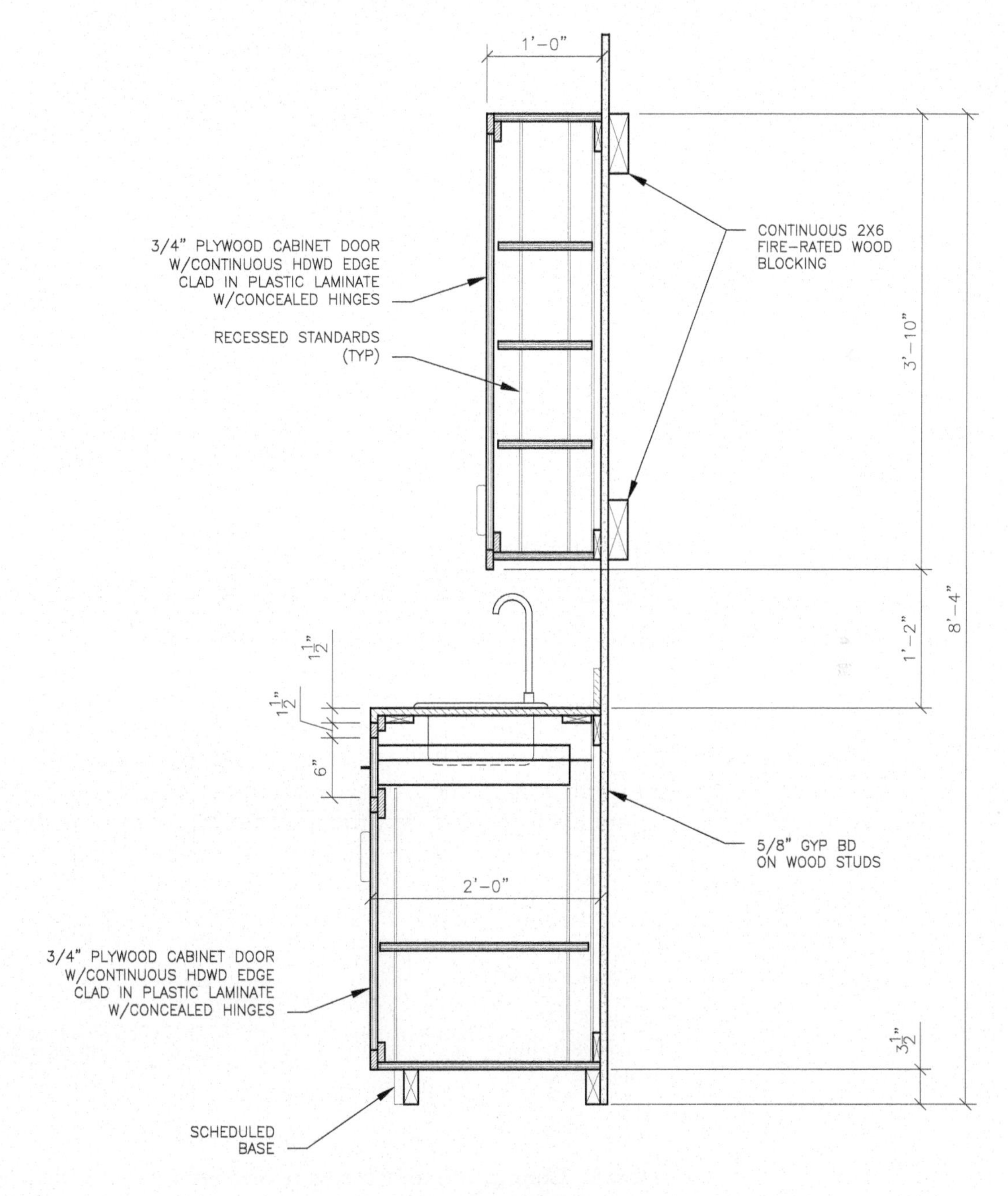

Figure 8-36
Exercise 8-3: Tenant space, section of conference room cabinets with hatching (scale: 3/4″ = 1′-0″)

Step 4. After looking closely at Figure 8-37, you may want to keep some of the conference room elevation drawing parts. Use **Erase** to eliminate the remainder of the drawing.

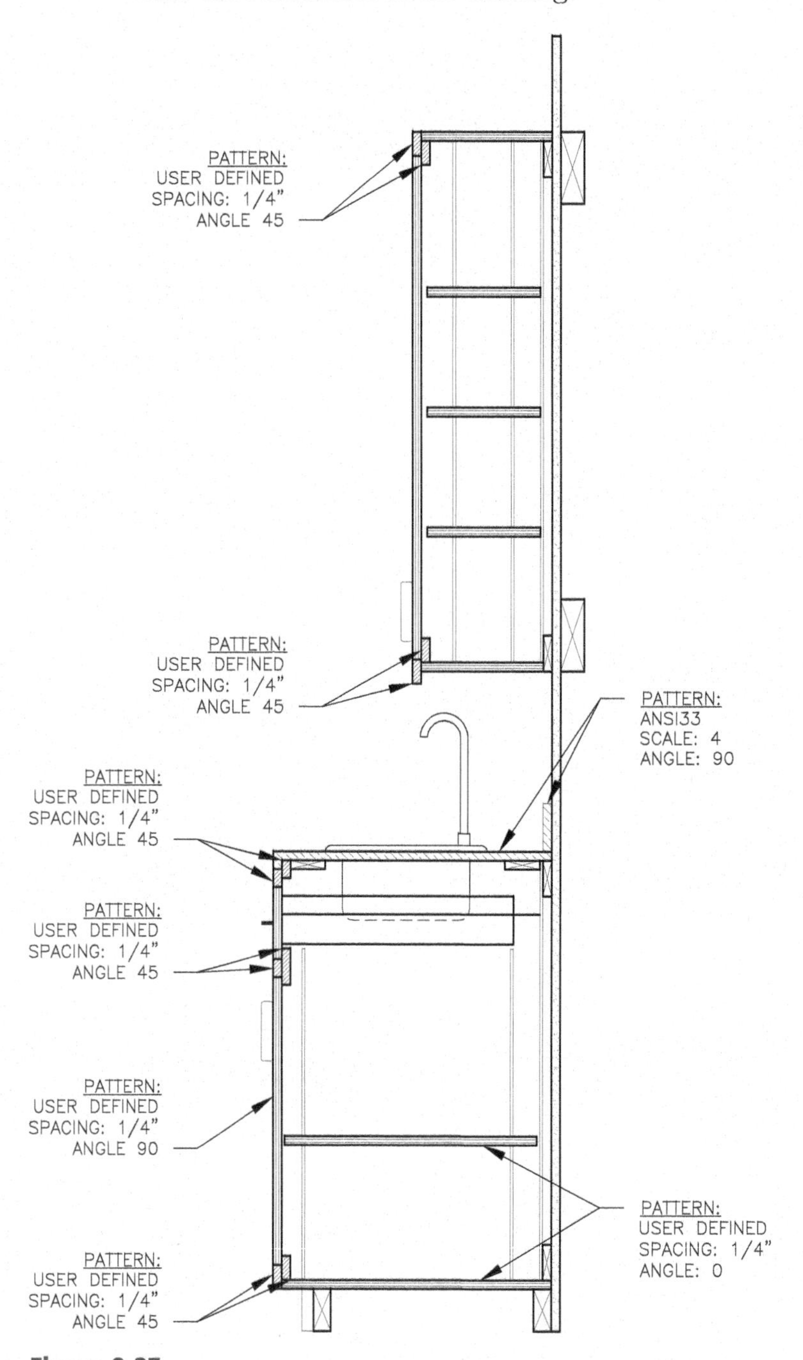

Figure 8-37
Exercise 8-3: Tenant space, section of conference room cabinets before hatching (scale: 3/4" = 1'-0")

Step 5. Change the underlined text to read CONFERENCE ROOM CABINET SECTION, change the top number in the balloon, and change the drawing scale to read as shown in Figure 8-37.

Step 6. Set the drawing annotation scale to **3/4" = 1'-0"**.

Step 7. Use the correct layers and the dimensions shown in Figure 8-37 to draw the sectional view of the south wall of the tenant space conference room cabinets *before using* the **HATCH** command. Draw the section full size (measure features with an architectural scale of 3/4″ = 1′ to find the correct size). Include the text and the dimensions. Note that the sink, faucet and hardware are generic. Duplicate them, or find similar objects by searching for fixtures on the Internet. Your drawing will look similar to Figure 8-37 when it is completed prior to your adding hatch patterns.

Step 8. When the cabinet section is complete with text and dimensions, freeze the **a-sect-dims** and **a-sect-text** layers so they will not interfere with drawing the hatch patterns.

Prepare to Use the Hatch Command with the Add: Select Objects Boundary Option

When you use the **HATCH** command two options are available for selecting the **boundary** of the area you will hatch; those two options are **Add: Pick points** and **Add: Select objects**. The **Add: Select objects** option requires additional preparation.

The most important aspect of using the **HATCH** command *when you use **Select objects** to create the boundary* is to define clearly the boundary of the area to be hatched. If the boundary of the hatching area is not clearly defined, some of the hatch pattern may go outside the boundary area, or the boundary area may not be completely filled.

Before you use the **HATCH** command in this manner, all areas to which hatching will be added must be prepared so that none of their boundary lines extend beyond the area to be hatched. When the views on which you will draw hatching have already been drawn, using the **BREAK** or **BREAKATPOINT** command is often necessary to break the boundary lines into line segments that clearly define the hatch boundaries. Use the **BREAK** command when you want a visible gap in the selected object. You can also use the **BREAKATPOINT** command to break a single object into segments without visible gaps between the segments.

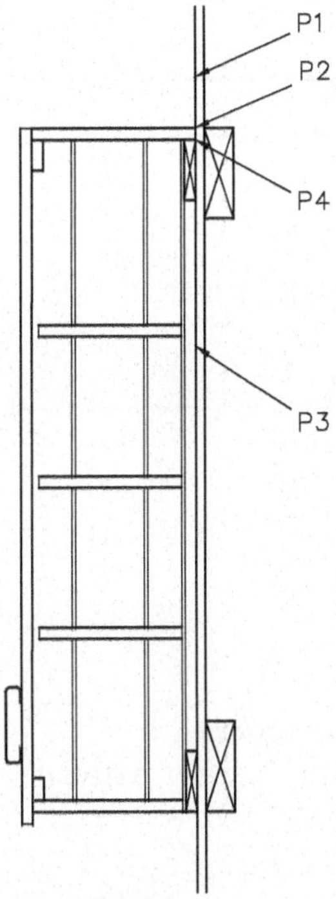

Step 9. Use the **BREAKATPOINT** command to help clearly define the right edge of the horizontal plywood top of the upper cabinets (Figure 8-38), as described next:

Prompt	**Response**
Type a command:	From the expanded **Modify** panel on the **Home** tab, click **Break at Point**
Select object:	**P1→** (to select the vertical line)
BREAKATPOINT Specify break point:	**P2→** (use **Osnap-Intersection**)
Type a command:	**<Enter>** (repeat **BREAKATPOINT**)
Select object:	**P3→** (to select the vertical line)
BREAKATPOINT Specify break point:	**P4→** (use **Osnap-Intersection**)
	The line is broken into three segments

You have just used the **BREAKATPOINT** command to break the vertical line so that it is a separate line segment that clearly defines the right edge of the plywood top area.

Figure 8-38
Use the **BREAKATPOINT** command to define clearly the right edge of the horizontal top area of the upper cabinets

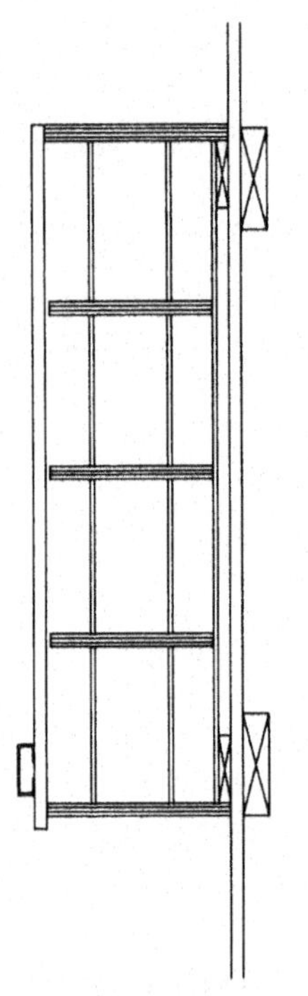

Figure 8-39
Upper cabinets with hatch patterns drawn

Step 10. Use the **BREAKATPOINT** command to define the bottom-left edge of the plywood top boundary. Break the vertical line at the intersection of the bottom of the left edge (Figure 8-39).

Step 11. When the boundary of the plywood top is clearly defined, the top, bottom, right, and left lines of the top are separate line segments that do not extend beyond the boundary of the plywood top. To check the boundary, pick and highlight each line segment. Use the **BREAKATPOINT** command on the top horizontal line of the plywood top, if needed (Figure 8-39).

Step 12. Use the **BREAKATPOINT** command to prepare the three plywood shelves and the plywood bottom of the upper cabinet boundaries for hatching (Figure 8-39).

Step 13. The **HATCH** command will also not work properly if the two lines of an intersection do not meet; that is, if any small gap exists. If you need to check the intersections of the left side of the plywood shelves to make sure they intersect properly, do this before continuing with the **HATCH** command.

TIP

You may prefer to draw lines on a new layer over the existing ones to form the enclosed boundary area instead of breaking, as described in this procedure. You may erase these additional lines easily with a window after you turn off all layers except the one to be erased. This is sometimes faster and allows the line that was to be broken to remain intact.

TIP

If a small gap exists at the intersection of two lines, change the gap tolerance (**HPGAPTOL**) system variable. Type **HPGAPTOL <Enter>** at the command prompt. Any gaps equal to or smaller than the value you specify in the hatch pattern gap tolerance are ignored, and the boundary is treated as closed. You can also use the **CHAMFER** command (0 distance) or the **FILLET** command (0 radius) to connect two lines to form a 90° angle.

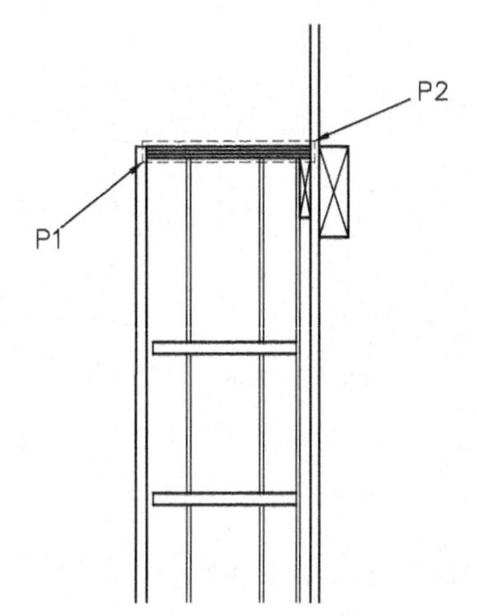

Figure 8-40
Use the **HATCH** command with the **Select Objects <Boundary>** option to draw a uniform horizontal-line hatch pattern on the plywood top of the upper cabinets

Use the Hatch Command with the Add: Select Objects Boundary Option

Step 14. Set layer **a-sect-patt** current.

Step 15. Use the **HATCH** command with the **Add: Select objects** boundary option to draw a uniform horizontal-line hatch pattern on the plywood top of the upper cabinets (Figure 8-40), as described next:

Prompt	Response
Type a command:	**Hatch** (or type **H <Enter>**
Pick internal point or [Select objects seTtings]:	**T <Enter>**)

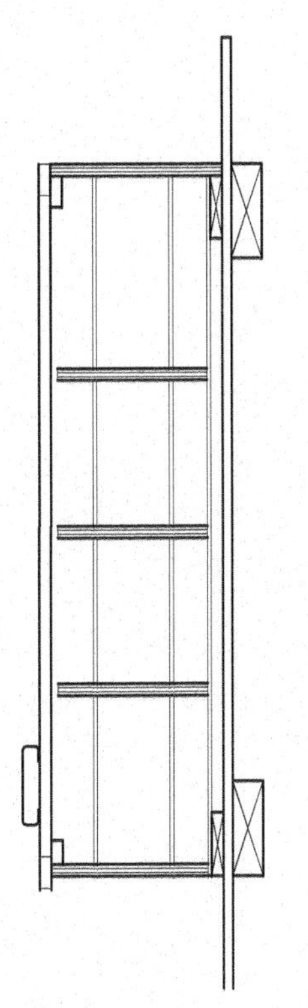

Figure 8-41
Draw a hatch pattern on the three plywood shelves and the plywood bottom of the upper cabinet

Prompt	Response
The **Hatch and Gradient** dialog box appears:	Click **User-defined** in the **Type:** area of **Type and pattern**: Angle: **0** Spacing: **1/4"** Click **Add: Select objects**
Select objects or [picK internal point setTings]:	(Figure 8-39) Click **P1→**
Specify opposite corner:	Click **P2→**
Select objects or [picK internal point seTtings]:	
(A preview of your hatching appears):	**<Enter>** (if the correct hatch pattern was previewed; if not, click **<Esc>** and fix the problem)

NOTE

Although the **Pick points** method of creating hatch boundaries is often much easier, you must know how to use **Select objects** as well. There are instances when **Pick points** just does not work.

The plywood top of the upper cabinet is now hatched.

Step 16. Use the same hatching procedure to draw a hatch pattern on the three plywood shelves and the plywood bottom of the upper cabinet, as shown in Figure 8-41.

TIP

Turn off or freeze the text and dimension layers if they interfere with hatching.

Use the Hatch Command with the Add: Pick Points Boundary Option

When you use the **Add: Pick points** boundary option to create a boundary for the hatch pattern, AutoCAD allows you to pick any point inside the area, and the boundary is automatically created. You do not have to prepare the boundary of the area as you did with the **Select objects** boundary option, but you have to make sure there are no gaps in the boundary.

Step 17. Use the **HATCH** command with the **Pick points** boundary option to draw a uniform vertical-line hatch pattern on the upper cabinet door (Figure 8-42), as described next:

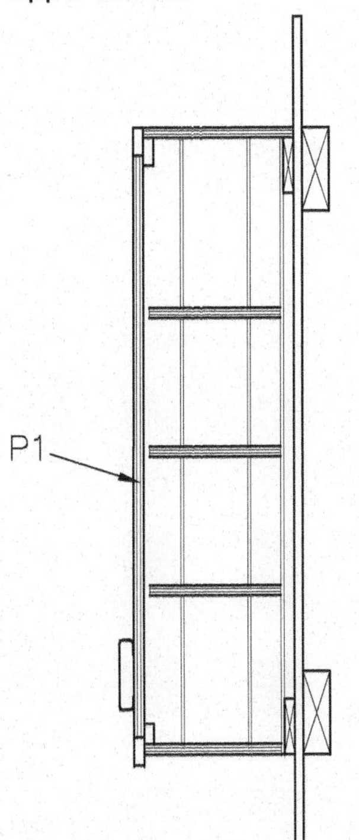

Figure 8-42
Use the **HATCH** command with the **Pick points** boundary option to draw a uniform vertical-line hatch pattern on the upper cabinet door

Prompt	Response
Type a command:	**Hatch** (or type **H <Enter>**)
Pick internal point or [Select objects seTtings]:	Type **T**
The **Hatch and Gradient** dialog box appears:	Click **User-defined** in the **Type:** area of **Type and pattern**: Angle: **90** Spacing: **1/4"** Click **Add: Pick points**

Prompt	Response
Pick internal point or [Select objects seTtings]:	Click **P1→** (inside the door symbol)
Pick internal point or [Select objects seTtings]:	
(A preview of your hatching appears):	**<Enter>** (if the correct hatch pattern was previewed; if not, click **<Esc>** and fix the problem)

TIP

You may have to draw a line across the top of the 5/8″ gypsum board to create the hatch pattern on the gypsum board.

Step 18. Use the **HATCH** command with the **Pick points** boundary option to draw the AR-SAND hatch pattern on the 5/8″ gypsum board (Figures 8-43, 8-44, and 8-45), as described next:

Prompt	Response
Type a command:	**Hatch**
Pick internal point or [select objects seTtings]:	Type **T <Enter>**
The **Hatch and Gradient** dialog box appears:	Click **Predefined** (in the **Type:** area) Click **...** (to the right of the **Pattern:** list box)
The **Hatch Pattern Palette** appears:	Click the **Other Predefined** tab Click **AR-SAND** (Figure 8-43) Click **OK**

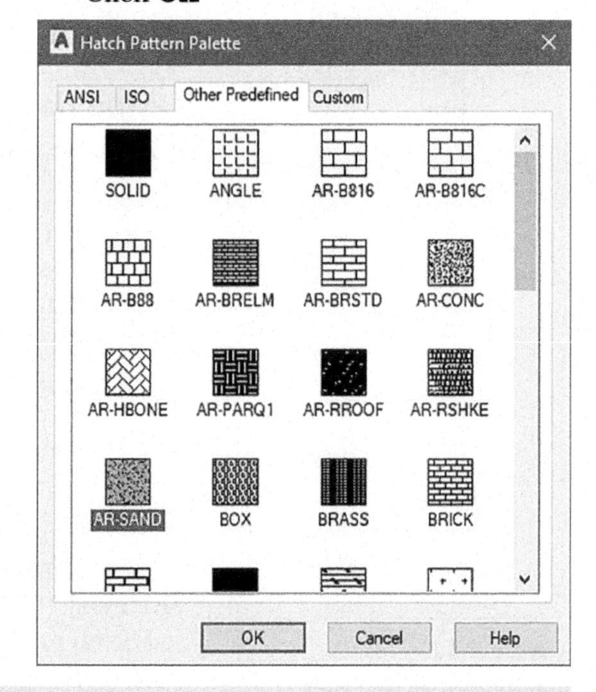

Figure 8-43
Select AR-SAND

NOTE

When **Associative** is selected in the **Hatch and Gradient** dialog box, you can pick any point on the hatch pattern to erase it.

Prompt	Response
The **Hatch and Gradient** dialog box appears (Figure 8-43):	Click **0** (in the **Angle** box) Type **3/8"** (in the **Scale:** box) Click **Add: Pick points**
Pick internal point or [Select objects seTtings]:	Click any point inside the lines defining the 5/8" gypsum board boundary (Figure 8-44)
Pick internal point or [Select objects seTtings]:	**<Enter>**

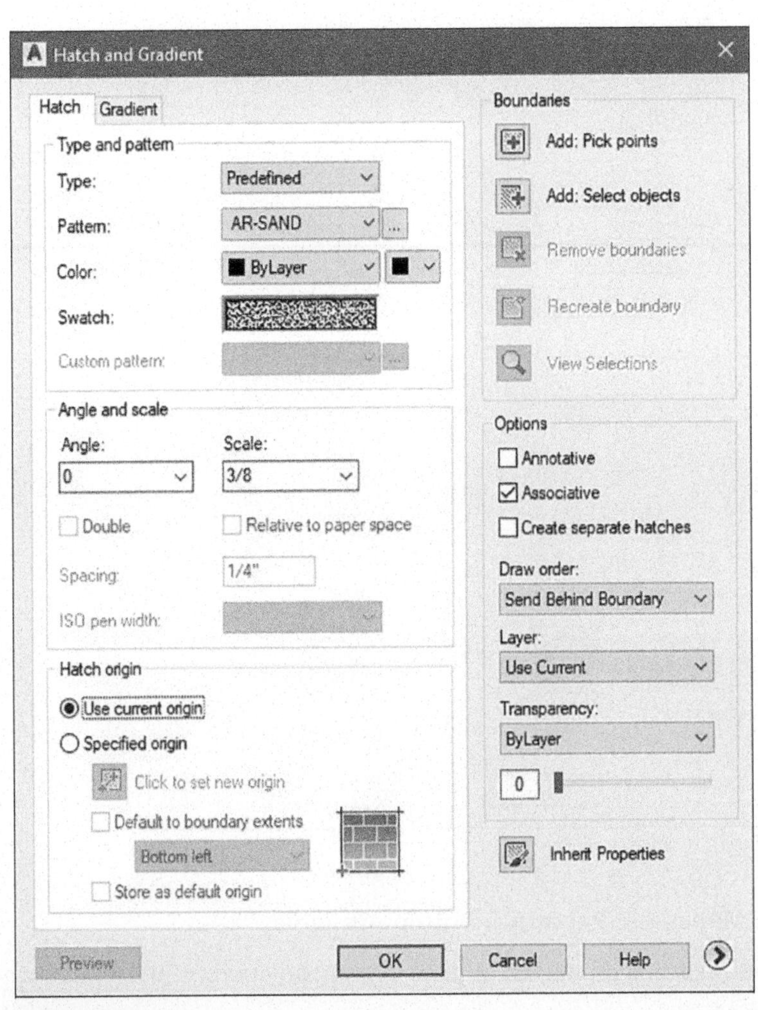

Figure 8-44
Specify scale for AR-SAND

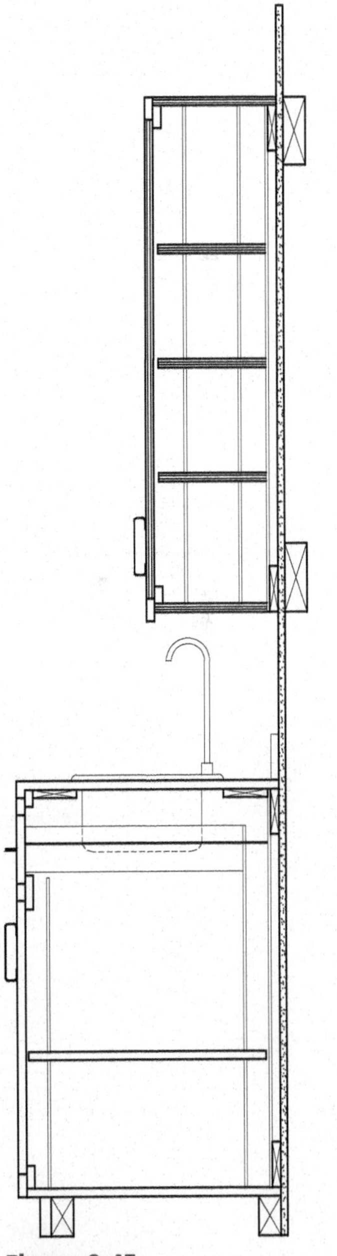

Figure 8-45
Use the **HATCH** command to draw the AR-SAND hatch pattern on the 5/8" gypsum board

The 5/8″ gypsum board is now hatched. (If you get an error message, try 1/2″ for scale in the **Scale:** box or draw a line across the top of the gypsum board.)

Hatch; Hatch and Gradient Dialog Box; Hatch Tab

Type and Pattern

When you activate the **HATCH** command (type **H <Enter>**, then **T <Enter>**) the **Hatch and Gradient** dialog box with the **Hatch** tab selected appears (Figure 8-46). As listed in the **Type and Pattern:** list boxes, the pattern types can be as follows:

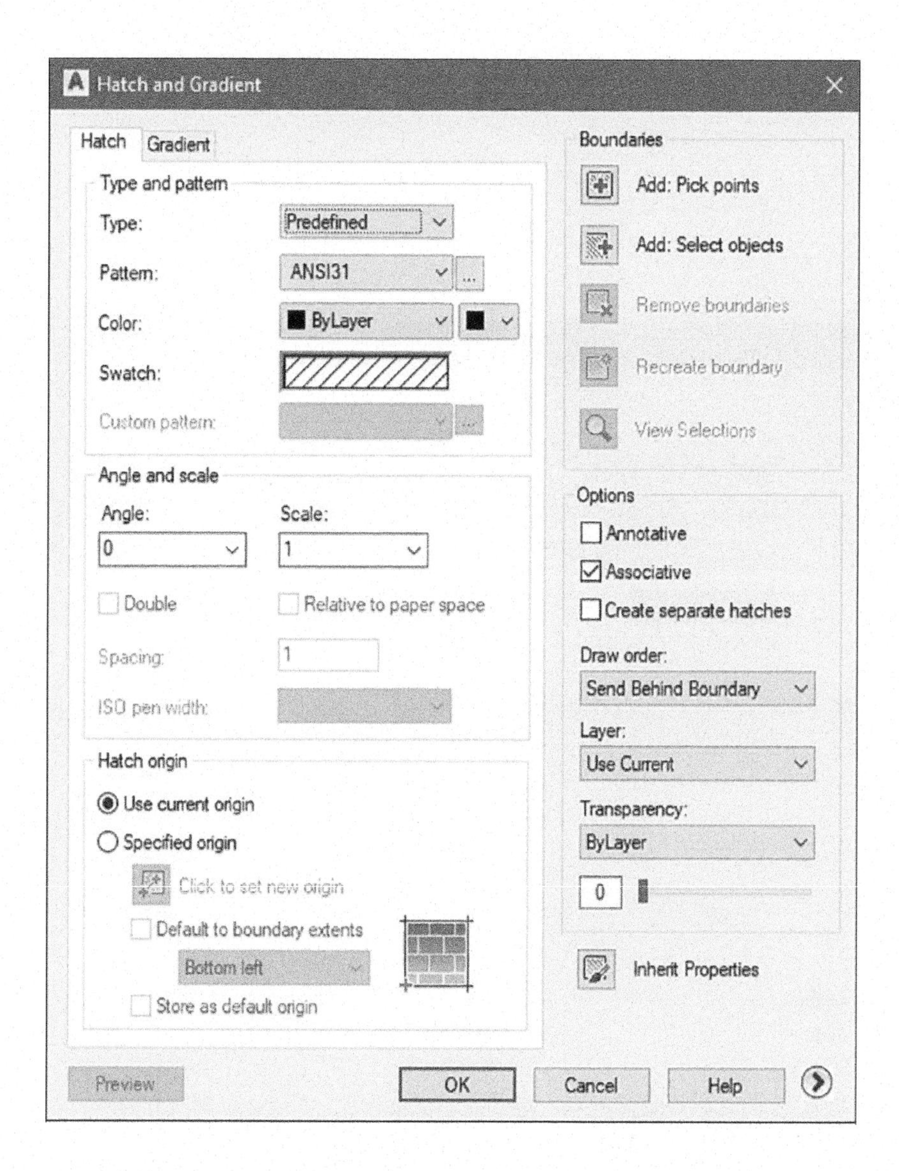

Figure 8-46
Hatch and Gradient dialog box, **Hatch** tab

Predefined: Makes the **Pattern...** button available.

User-defined: Defines a pattern of lines using the current linetype.

Custom: Specifies a custom pattern from the ACAD.pat file or any other PAT file.

To view the predefined hatch pattern options, click the ellipsis (...) to the right of the **Pattern:** list box. The **Hatch Pattern Palette** appears (Figure 8-47). Other parts of the **Hatch and Gradient** dialog box are as follows:

Pattern: Specifies a predefined pattern name.

Color: Allows you to use the current color or to choose another color for the hatch.

Background color: The list box to the right of the **Color** box allows you to specify a background color for a hatch. The default color is none.

Custom pattern: This list box shows a custom pattern name. This option is available when you select **Custom** in the **Type:** area.

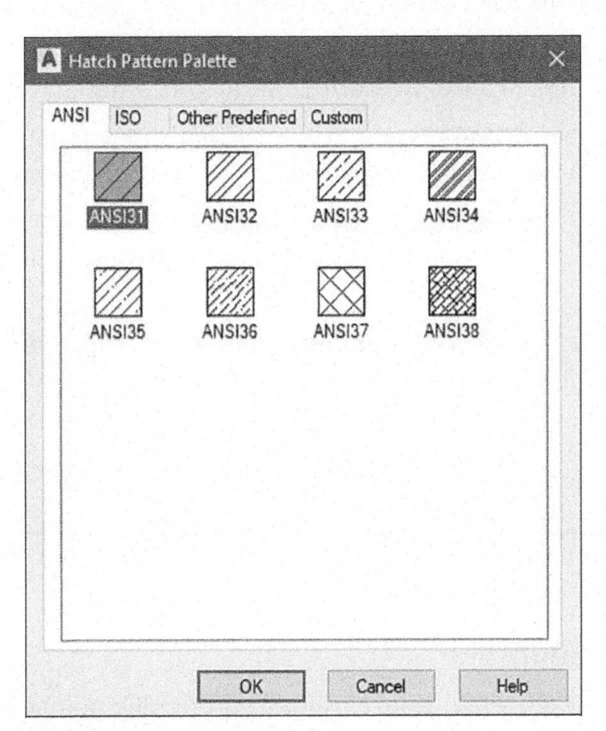

Figure 8-47
Hatch Pattern Palette

Angle and Scale

Angle: This allows you to specify an angle for the hatch pattern relative to the x-axis of the current UCS.

Scale: This allows you to enlarge or shrink the hatch pattern to fit the drawing. It is not available if you have selected **User-defined** in the **Type:** list box.

Double: When you check this box, the area is hatched with a second set of lines at 90° to the first hatch pattern (available when you have selected **User-defined** pattern type).

Relative to paper space: This option scales the pattern relative to paper space so you can scale the hatch pattern to fit the scale of your paper space layout.

Spacing: This allows you to specify the space between lines on a user-defined hatch pattern.

ISO pen width: If you select one of the 14 ISO (International Organization for Standardization) patterns at the bottom of the list of hatch patterns and on the **ISO** tab of the **Hatch Pattern Palette**, this option scales the pattern based on the selected pen width. Each of these pattern names begins with ISO.

Hatch Origin

Hatch Origin controls where the hatch pattern originates. Some hatch patterns, such as brick, stone, and those used as shingles, need to start from a particular point on the drawing. By default, all hatch origins are the same as the current UCS origin.

Use current origin: This option uses 0,0 as the origin by default. In most cases, this will be what you want.

Specified origin: This specifies a new hatch origin. When you click this option, the following options become available:

Click to set new origin: When you click this box, you are then prompted to pick a point on the drawing as the origin for the hatch pattern.

Default to boundary extents: This option allows you to select a new origin based on the rectangular extents of the hatch. Choices include each of the four corners of the extents and its center.

Store as default origin: This option sets your specified origin as the default.

Preview button: Allows you to preview the hatch pattern before you apply it to a drawing.

Boundaries

Add: Pick points: Allows you to pick points inside a boundary to specify the area to be hatched.

Add: Select objects: Allows you to select the outside edges of the boundary to specify the area to be hatched.

Remove boundaries: Allows you to remove from the boundary set objects defined as islands by the **Pick points** option. You cannot remove the outer boundary.

Recreate boundary: Allows you to create a polyline or a region around the hatch pattern.

View Selections: Displays the currently defined boundary set. This option is not available when no selection or boundary has been made.

Options

Annotative: You can make the hatch annotative by selecting the box beside **Annotative** under **Options** in the dialog box. To add the annotative hatch to your drawing, set the desired annotation scale for your drawing, and then hatch the object (using type, pattern, angle, and scale) so you can see that the hatch is the correct size and appearance. If you change the plotting scale of your drawing, you can change the size of the hatch pattern by changing the annotation scale, located in the lower-right corner of the status bar.

Associative: When a check appears in this button, the hatch pattern is a single object and stretches when you stretch the area that has been hatched.

Create separate hatches: When you select this check box, you can create two or more separate hatch areas by using the **HATCH** command only once. You can erase those areas individually.

Draw order: The **Draw order:** list allows you to place hatch patterns on top of or beneath existing lines to make the drawing more legible.

Layer: This option allows you to use the current layer for the hatch or to choose any other predefined layer.

Transparency: This option allows you to use the current transparency setting for the hatch or to choose another setting.

Inherit Properties: This option allows you to pick an existing hatch pattern to use on another area. The pattern picked must be associative (attached to and defined by its boundary).

More Options

When you click the **More Options** arrow in the lower-right corner of the **Hatch and Gradient** dialog box, the following options (Figure 8-48) appear.

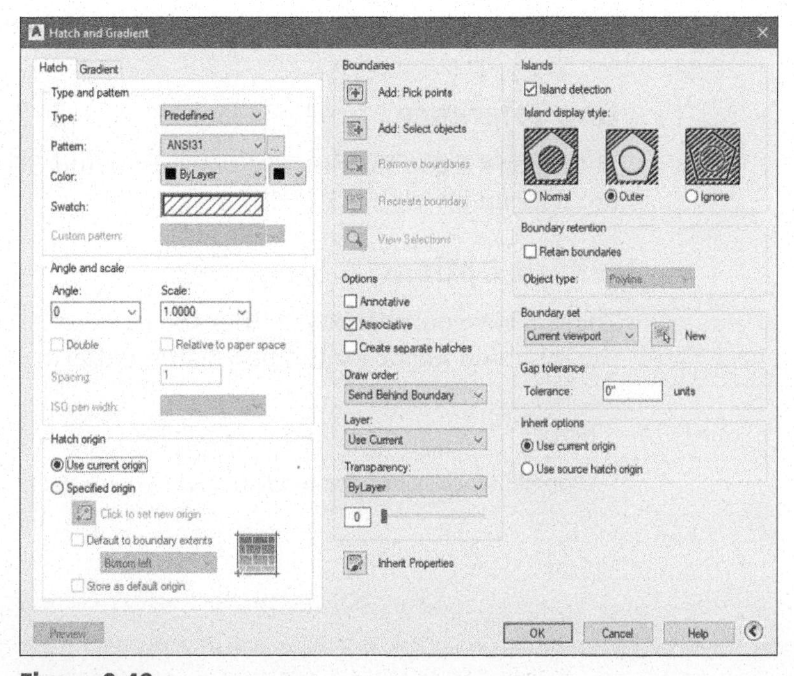

Figure 8-48
Hatch and Gradient dialog box, more options

Islands

Figure 8-48 shows the following **Island display style** options:

Normal: When you select this option (and a selection set is composed of areas inside other areas), alternating areas are hatched, as shown in the **Island display style:** area.

Outer: When you select this option (and a selection set is composed of areas inside other areas), only the outer area is hatched, as shown in the **Island display style:** area.

Ignore: When you select this option (and a selection set is composed of areas inside other areas), all areas are hatched, as shown in the **Island display style:** area.

Boundary Retention

Retain boundaries: This specifies whether the boundary objects will remain in your drawing after hatching is completed.

Object type: This allows you to select either a polyline or a region if you choose to retain the boundary.

Boundary Set

List box: This box allows you to select a boundary set from the current viewport or an existing boundary set.

New: When you click this option, the dialog box temporarily closes and you are prompted to select objects to create the boundary set. AutoCAD includes only objects that can be hatched when it constructs the new boundary set. AutoCAD discards any existing boundary set and replaces it with the new boundary set. If you don't select any objects that can be hatched, AutoCAD retains any current set.

Gap Tolerance

This allows a gap tolerance of between 0 and 5000 units to hatch areas that are not completely enclosed.

Inherit Options

These allow you to choose either the current hatch origin or the origin of the inherited hatch for the new hatch pattern.

NOTE

Chapter 13 fully covers the **Gradient** tab (Figure 8-48).

NOTE

When you double-click on a hatch pattern, **Hatch Editor** appears on the ribbon. The **Hatch Editor** has most of the features of the **Hatch Edit** dialog box.

Edit Hatch

Select **Edit Hatch...** or type **HE <Enter>** and click on a hatch pattern to access the **Hatch Edit** dialog box (Figure 8-49). You can edit the pattern, angle, scale, origin, and draw order of the hatch pattern.

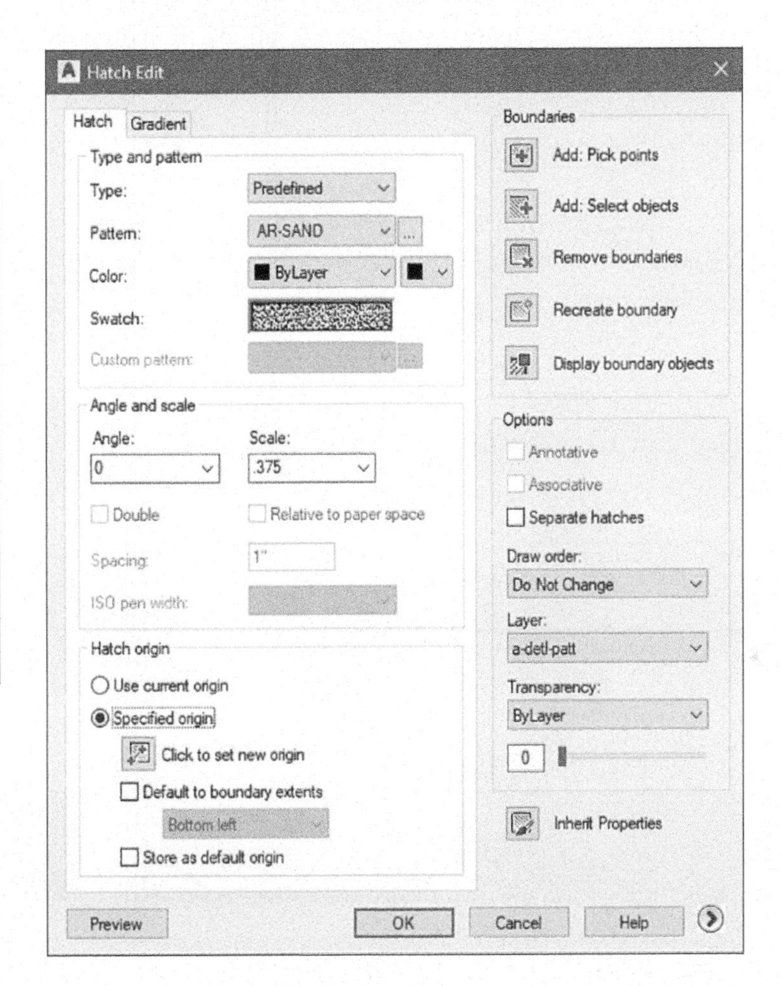

Figure 8-49
Hatch Edit dialog box

EDIT HATCH	
Ribbon/ Panel	Home/ Modify
Modify II Toolbar:	
Menu Bar:	Modify/ Object/ Hatch ...
Type a Command:	HATCHEDIT
Command Alias:	HE

Step 19. Using the patterns described in Figure 8-50, draw hatch patterns by using the **Pick points** option on the lower cabinets and the end views of wood in the upper cabinets.

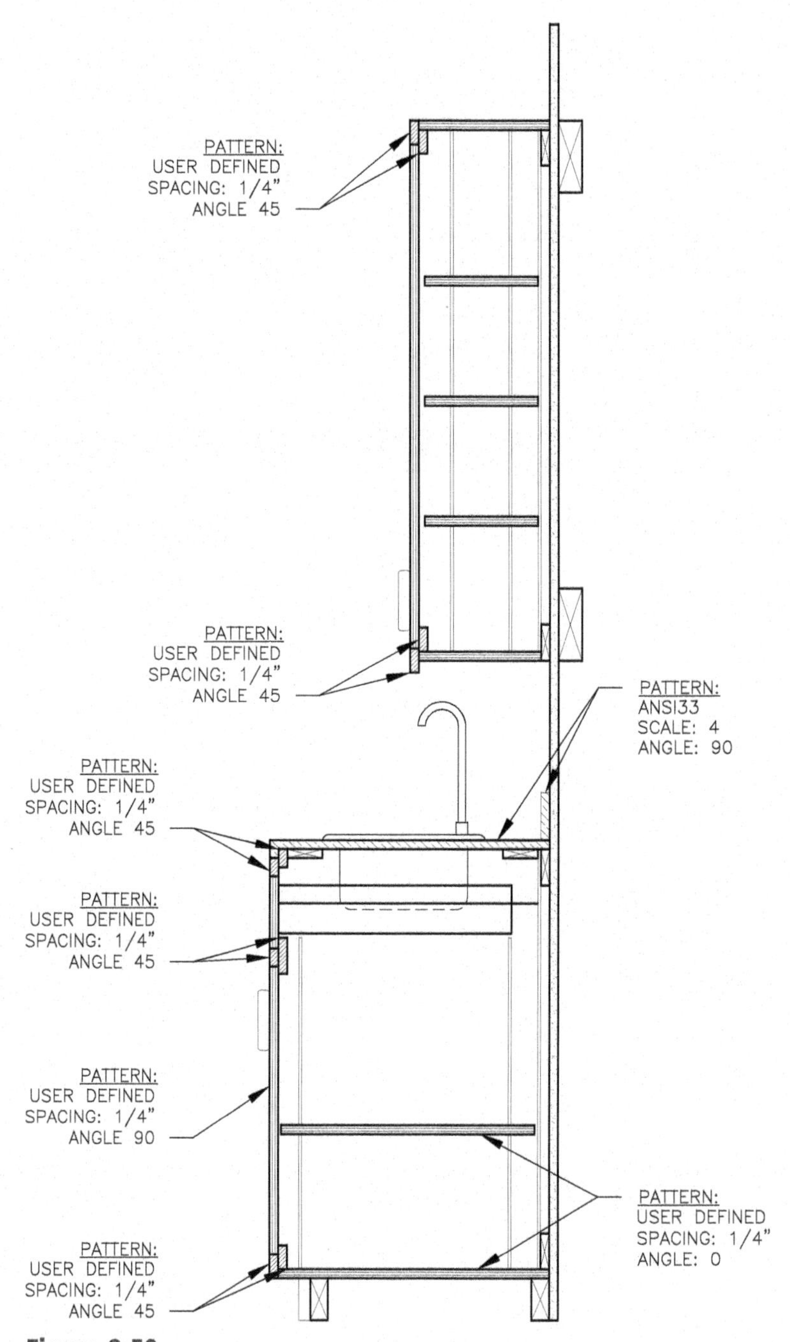

Figure 8-50
Draw the hatch patterns on the upper and lower cabinets as shown

Step 20. Thaw frozen layers.

Step 21. When you have completed Exercise 8-3 (Figure 8-51), save your work in at least two places.

Step 22. Print Exercise 8-3 at a scale of **3/4″ = 1′-0″**.

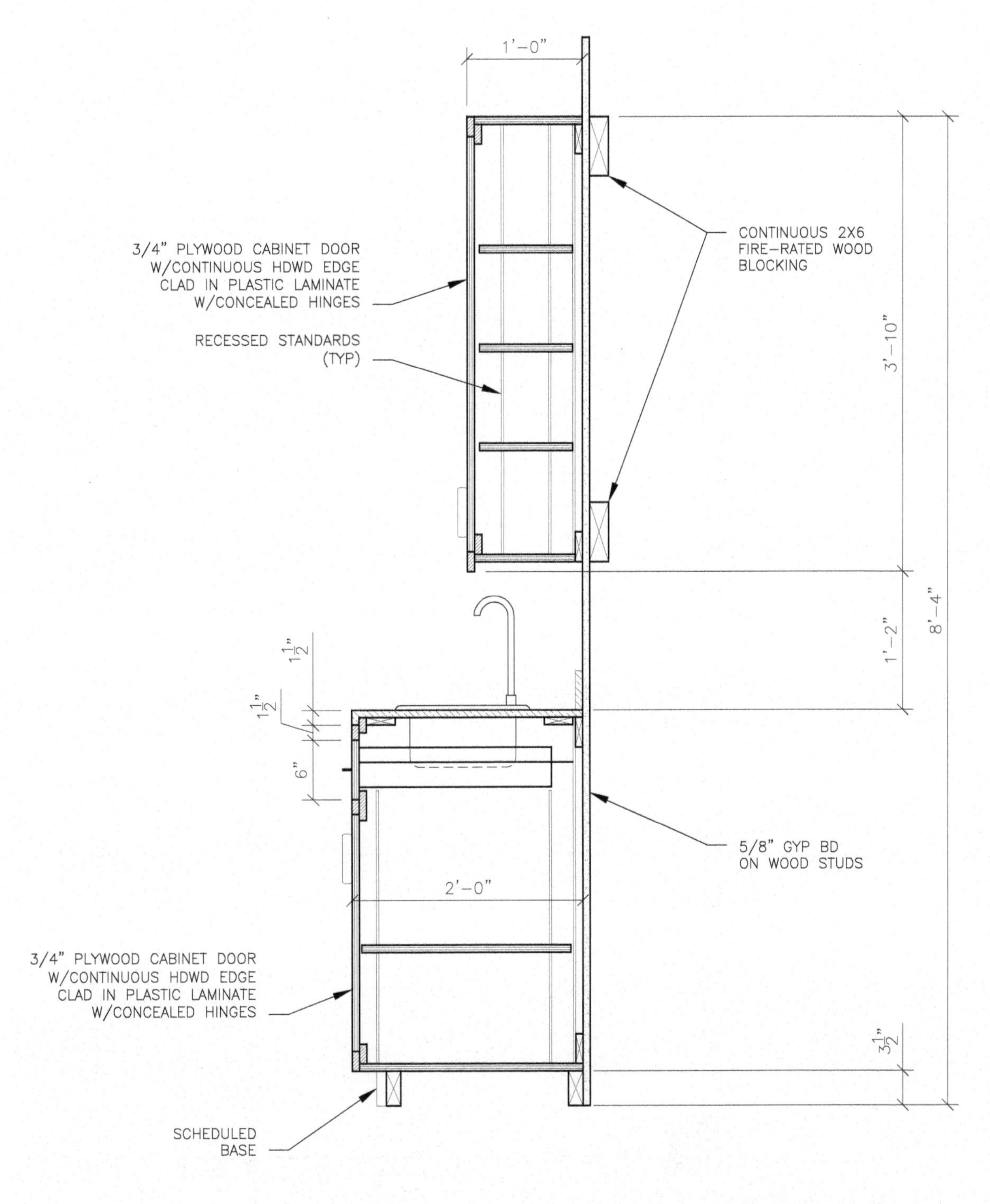

Figure 8-51
Exercise 8-3: Completed section drawing (scale: 3/4" = 1'-0")

Step 23. Add the section symbol as shown in Figure 8-52 to your TENANT SPACE FLOOR PLAN drawing (CH7-EXERCISE1.dwg). Use a **1'**-radius circle and **1/16"**-high text (annotative). You may need to move two dimensions as shown and add a layer for the cutting plane line below the symbol. Use **PHANTOM 2** linetype and **.004"** lineweight, color **red**.

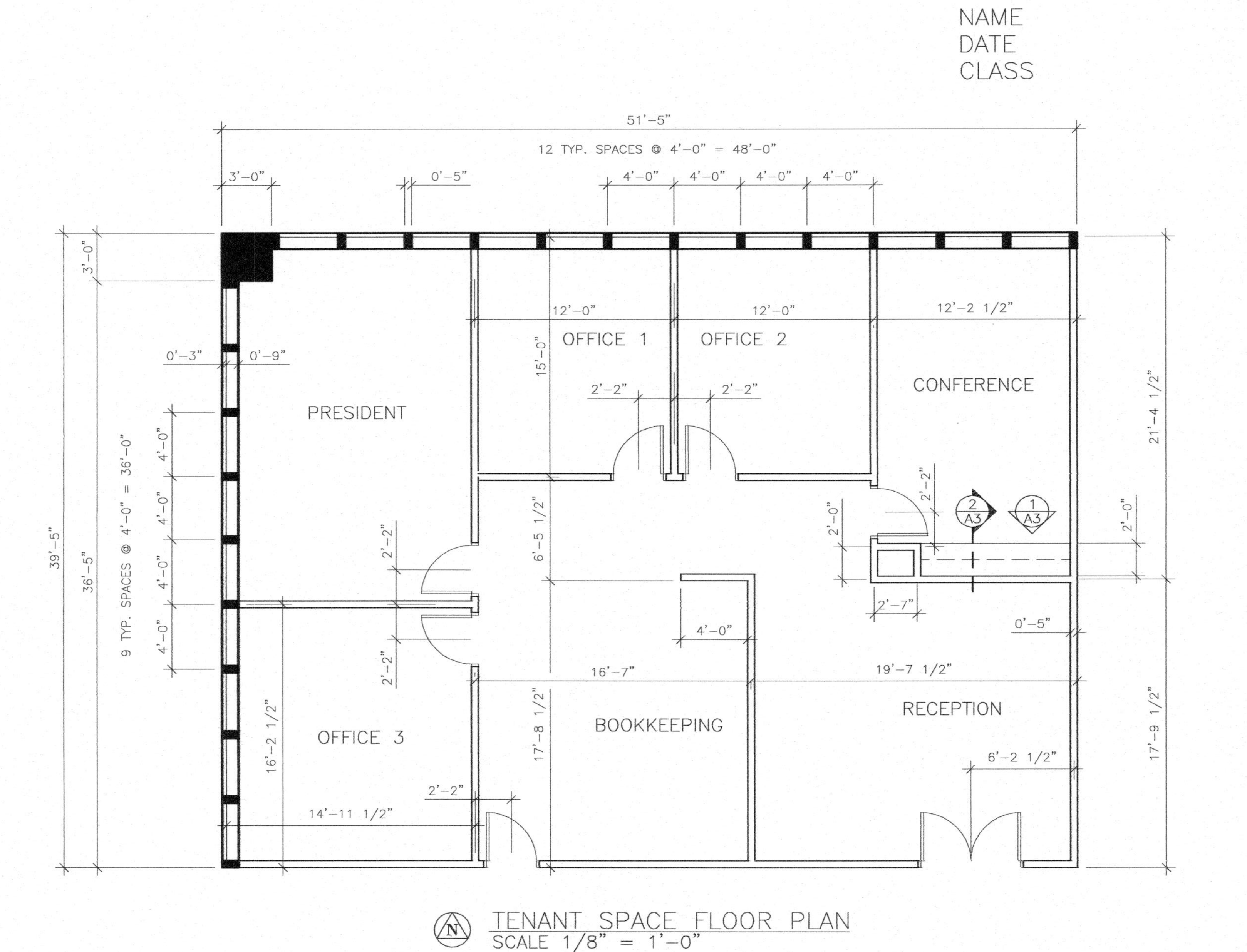

Figure 8-52
Tenant space floor plan with elevation and section symbols (scale: 1/8" = 1'-0")

EXERCISE 8-4
Detail of Door Jamb with Hatching

In Exercise 8-4, you will draw a detail of a door jamb. When you have completed Exercise 8-4, your drawing will look similar to Figure 8-53.

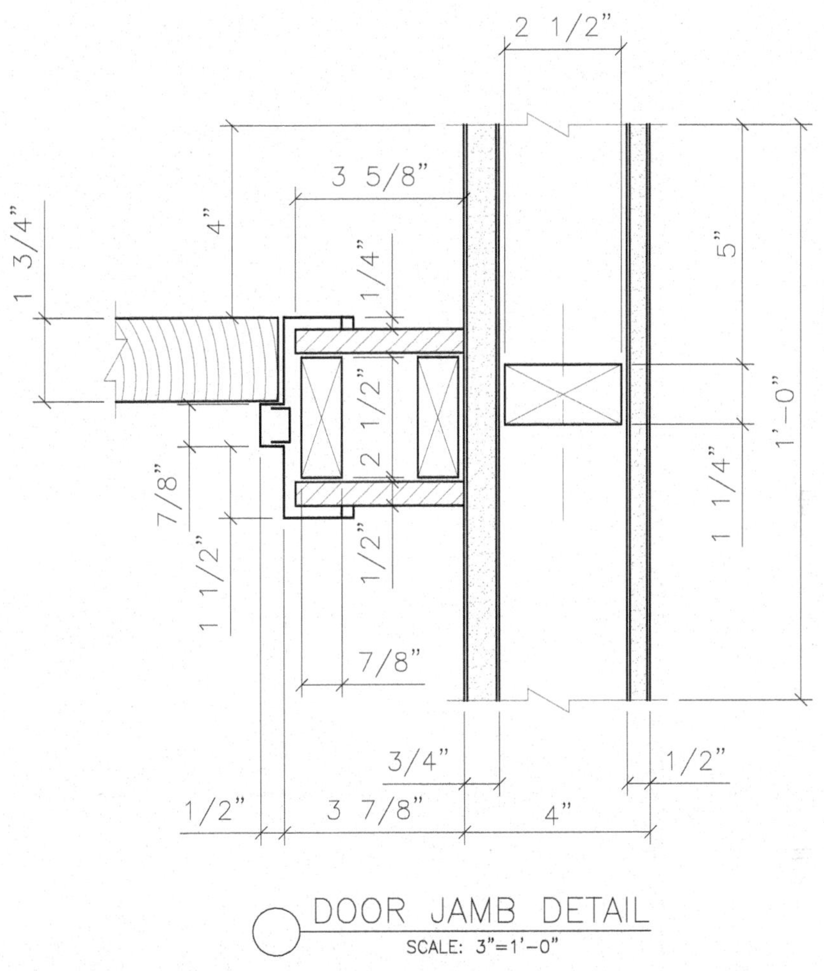

Figure 8-53
Exercise 8-4: Detail of a door jamb with crosshatching (scale: 3″ = 1′-0″)

Step 1. Use your workspace to make the following settings:

1. Use **Save As...** to save the drawing on the hard drive with the name **CH8-EXERCISE4**.
2. Set drawing units, limits, grid, and snap.
3. Create the following layers:

Layer name	Color	Linetype	Lineweight
a-detl-lwt1	blue	continuous	.010″ (.25 mm)
a-detl-dims	red	continuous	.004″ (.09 mm)
a-detl-patt	white	continuous	.002″ (.05 mm)
a-detl-text	green	continuous	.006″ (.15 mm)

4. Set layer **a-detl-lwt1** current.

Step 2. Using the dimensions shown in Figure 8-53, draw all the door jamb components. Drawing some of the components separately and copying or moving them into place will be helpful. Measure any dimensions not shown with a scale of **3″ = 1′-0″**.

Step 3. Set layer **a-detl-patt** current, and draw the hatch patterns as described in Figure 8-54. Use a spline and array it to draw the curved wood grain pattern.

Figure 8-54
Exercise 8-4: Hatch patterns

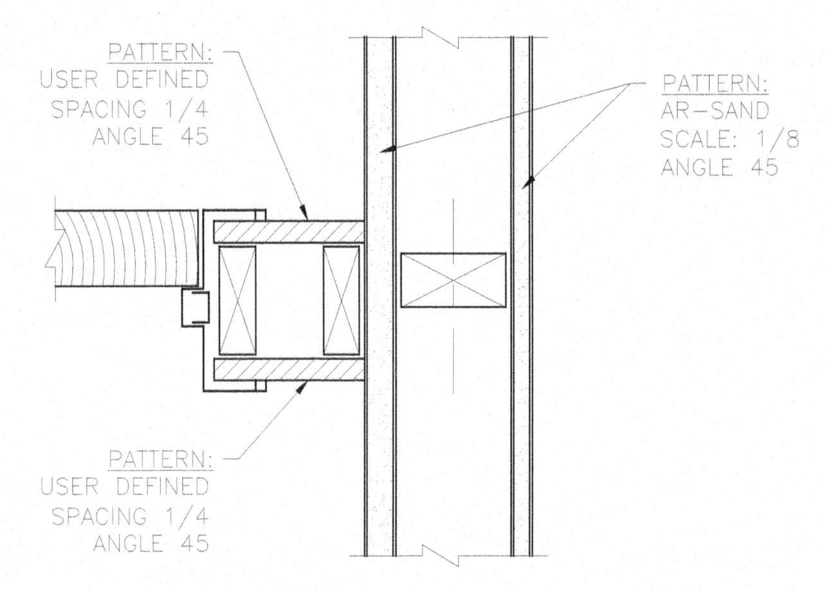

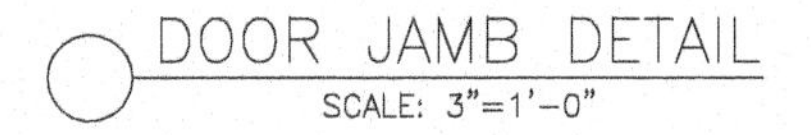

Step 4. Set layer **a-detl-dims** current, set the dimensioning variables, and draw the dimensions as shown in Figure 8-53.

Step 5. Set layer **a-detl-text** current, and add the name of the detail as shown in Figure 8-53. Add your name, class, and current date in the upper right.

Step 6. Save the drawing in two places.

Step 7. Print the drawing at a scale of **3″ = 1′-0″**.

EXERCISE 8-5
Use Point Filters and Object Snap Tracking to Make an Orthographic Drawing of a Conference Table

point filters: A method of entering a point by which the X, Y, and Z coordinates are given in separate stages. Any one of the three coordinates can be first, second, or third.

Object Snap Tracking: A setting that allows you to specify points by hovering your pointing device over object snap points.

In Exercise 8-5, you will use the AutoCAD features called **point filters** and **Object Snap Tracking**. These features are helpful when you are making 2D drawings showing the top, front, and side views of an object. All the features in these views must line up with the same features in the adjacent view. When you have completed Exercise 8-5, your drawing will look similar to Figure 8-55.

Figure 8-55
Exercise 8-5: Use point filters and **Object Snap Tracking** to draw three views of a dining table (scale: 1/2″ = 1′-0″)

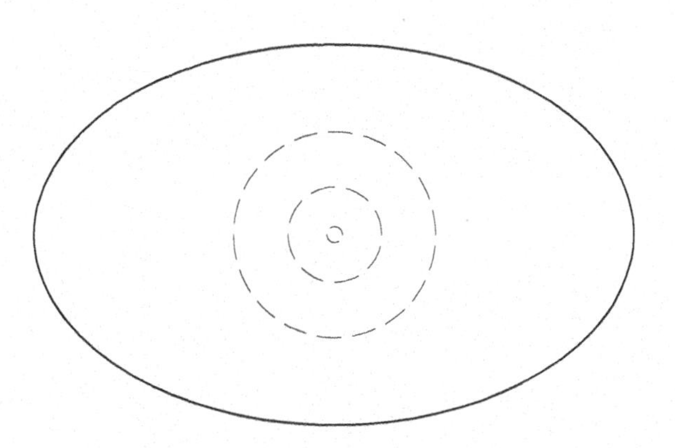

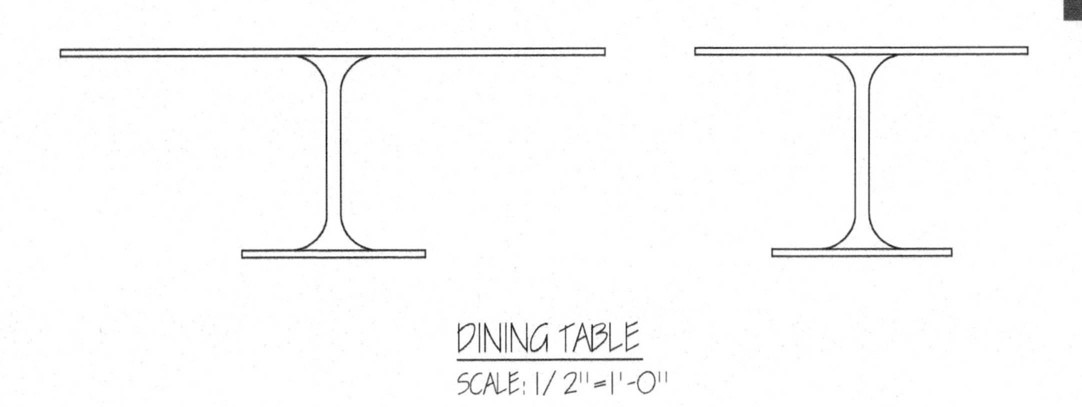

DINING TABLE
SCALE: 1/2"=1'-0"

Step 1. Use your workspace to make the following settings:

1. Set drawing units: **Architectural**
2. Set drawing limits: **16′,14′**
3. Set **GRIDDISPLAY**: **0**
4. Set grid: **2″**
5. Set snap: **1″**
6. Create the following layers:

Layer name	Color	Linetype	Lineweight
Layer1	blue	continuous	.010″ (.25 mm)
Layer2	red	Hidden2	.004″ (.09 mm)
Layer3	green	continuous	.006″ (.15 mm)

7. Set **Layer2** current.
8. Set **LTSCALE**: **8**.
9. Save the drawing as **CH8-EXERCISE5**.

Step 2. Draw the base and column of the table (hidden line), as shown in the top view (Figure 8-56), as described next:

Prompt	**Response**
Type a command:	**Circle-Center, Diameter** (not **Radius**)
Specify center point for circle or [3P 2P Ttr (tan tan radius)]:	Type **4′,9′ <Enter>**

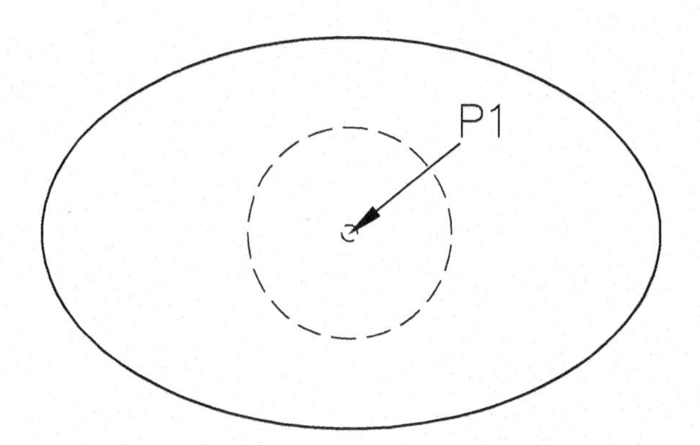

Figure 8-56
Draw the top view of the base, column, and top of the table

Prompt	Response
Specify diameter of circle <default>:	Type **2′2 <Enter>**
Type a command:	**Circle-Center, Diameter** (not **Radius**)
Specify center point for circle or [3P 2P Ttr (tan tan radius)]:	Type **4′,9′** (the same center as the first circle)
Specify diameter of circle <default>:	Type **2 <Enter>**

Step 3. Set **Layer1** current.

Step 4. Draw the elliptical top of the table (continuous linetype), as shown in the top view (Figure 8-56), as described next:

ELLIPSE	
Ribbon/ Panel	Home/Draw
Draw Toolbar:	
Menu Bar:	Draw/Ellipse
Type a Command:	ELLIPSE
Command Alias:	EL

Prompt	Response
Type a command:	**Ellipse-Center**
Specify center of ellipse:	**Osnap-Center**
of	**P1→**
Specify endpoint of axis:	With **ORTHO** on, move your mouse up and type **2′ <Enter>**
Specify distance to other axis or [Rotation]:	Type **39 <Enter>**

Point Filters

Step 5. Use point filters to draw the front view of the top of this elliptical table (Figure 8-57), as described next:

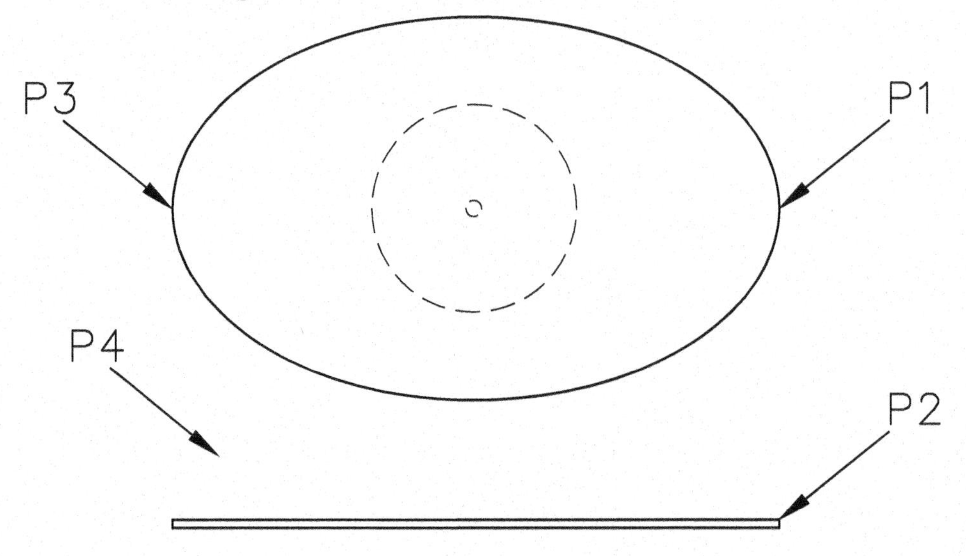

Figure 8-57
Draw the front view of the top of the table using point filters

Prompt	**Response**
Type a command:	**Line**
Specify first point:	Type **.X <Enter>**
of	**Osnap-Quadrant**
of	**P1→** (Figure 8-57)
(need YZ):	**P2→** (with **SNAP** on, pick a point in the approximate location shown in Figure 8-57)
Specify next point or [Undo]:	Type **.X <Enter>**
of	**Osnap-Quadrant**
of	**P3→**
(need YZ):	**P4→** (with **ORTHO** on, pick any point to identify the Y component of the point; **ORTHO** makes the component of the new point the same as the Y component of the previous point)
Specify next point or [Close Undo]:	With **ORTHO** on, move your mouse straight down, and type **1 <Enter>**
Specify next point or [Close Undo]:	Type **.X <Enter>**
of	**Osnap-Endpoint**
of	(Figure 8-57) **P2→**
(need YZ):	With **ORTHO** on, move your mouse to the right, and pick any point
Specify next point or [Close Undo]:	Type **C <Enter>**

Object Snap Tracking

Step 6. Set running **Osnap** modes of **Endpoint**, **Quadrant**, and **Intersection** and turn **OSNAP** and **Object Snap Tracking** on.

Step 7. Use **Object Snap Tracking** and **Offset** to draw the front view of the column (Figure 8-58), as described next:

Prompt	**Response**
Type a command:	**Line**
Specify first point:	Move your mouse to the right quadrant shown as **P1→** (Figure 8-58) but do not click

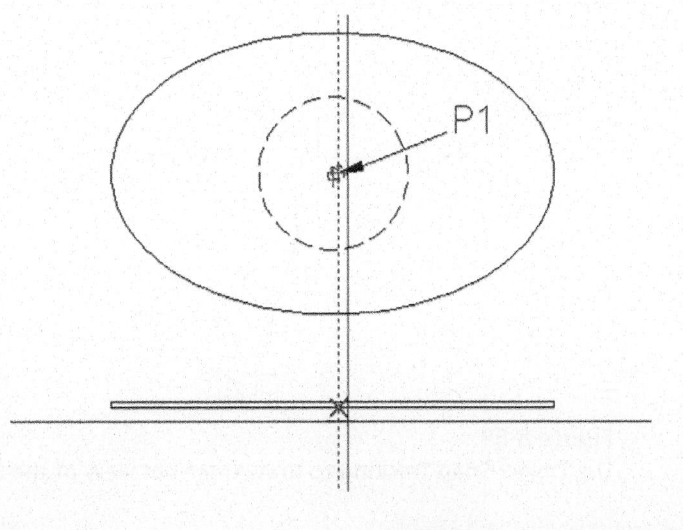

Figure 8-58
Use **Object Snap Tracking** to draw the front view of the column

Prompt	**Response**
	Hold it until the quadrant symbol appears, move your mouse straight down until the dotted line shows the intersection symbol on the bottom line of the tabletop as shown, and then click the intersection point (Figure 8-58)
Specify next point or [Undo]:	With **ORTHO** on, move your mouse straight down and type **27 <Enter>**
Specify next point or [Undo]:	**<Enter>**
Type a command:	**Offset** (or type **O <Enter>**)
Specify offset distance or [Through Erase Layer] <Through>:	Type **2 <Enter>**
Select object to offset or [Exit Undo] <Exit>:	Click **P1→** (Figure 8-59)
Specify point on side to offset or [Exit Multiple Undo] <Exit>:	Click **P2→** (any point to the left of the 27″ line)
Select object to offset or [Exit Undo] <Exit>:	**<Enter>**

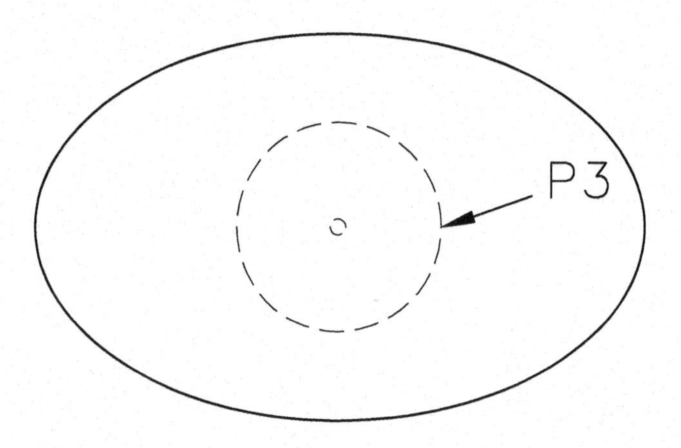

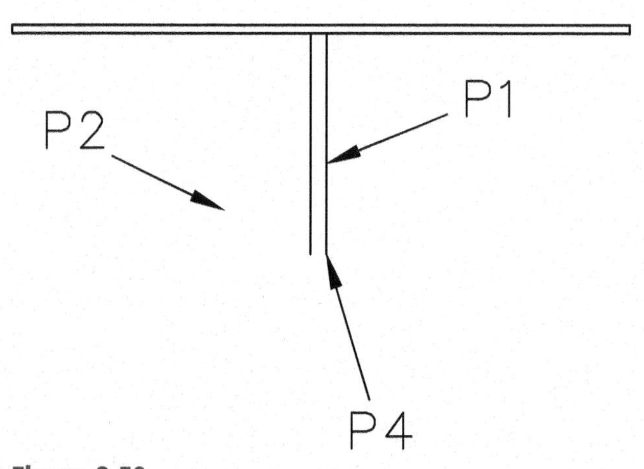

Figure 8-59
Use **Object Snap Tracking** to draw the front view of the base

Step 8. Use **Object Snap Tracking** to draw the front view of the base (Figure 8-59), as described next:

Prompt	**Response**
Type a command:	**Line**
Specify first point:	Move your mouse to the quadrant shown as **P3→** (Figure 8-59) but do not click Hold it until the quadrant symbol appears and move your mouse to **P4→** (do not click). The dotted line shows the endpoint symbol. Move your mouse back to the vertical dotted tracking line and click
Specify next point or [Undo]:	With **ORTHO** on, move your mouse straight down and type **1 <Enter>**
Specify next point or [Undo]:	With **ORTHO** on, move your mouse to the left and type **26 <Enter>**
Specify next point or [Close Undo]:	With **ORTHO** on, move your mouse straight up and type **1 <Enter>**
Specify next point or [Close Undo]:	Type **C <Enter>**

Step 9. Use **Object Snap Tracking** to draw the right-side view of the table with the **LINE** and **COPY** commands (Figure 8-60). Be sure to get depth dimensions from the top view.

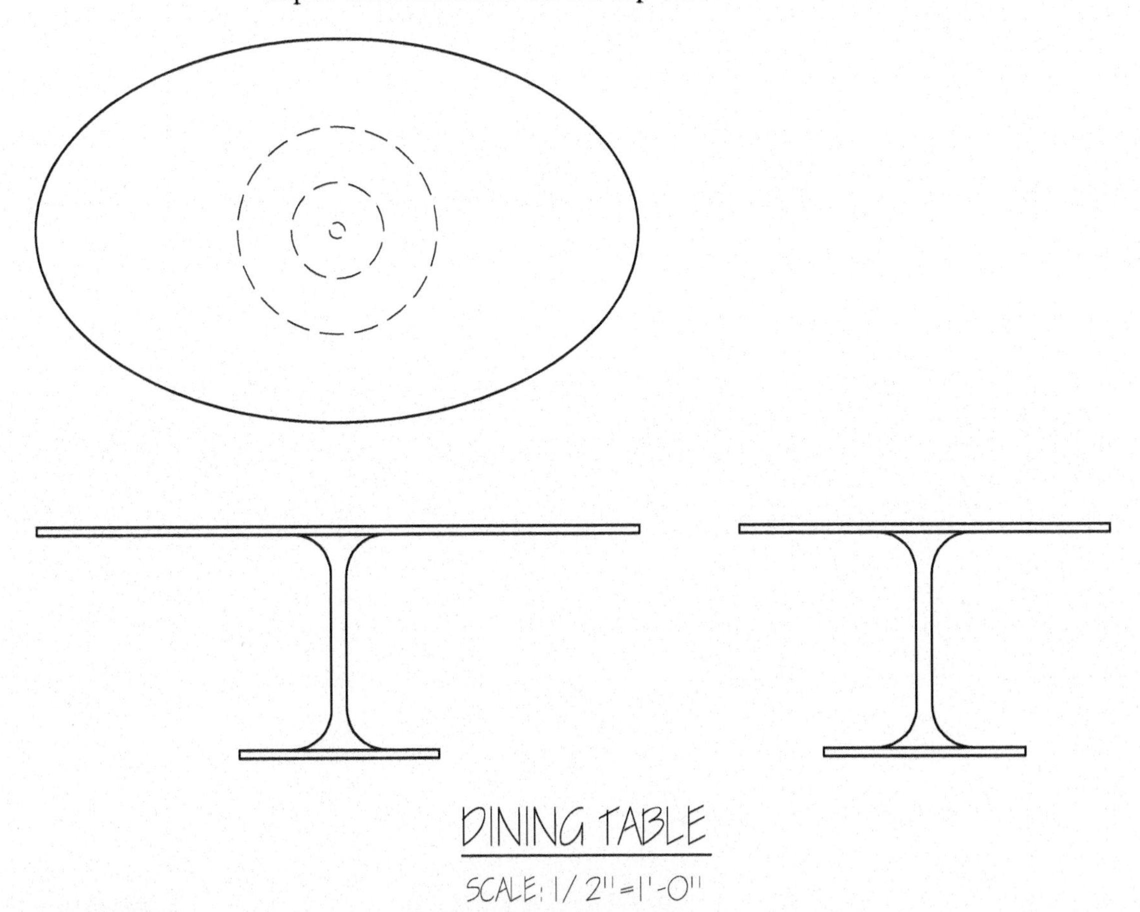

Figure 8-60
Draw the right-side view using **COPY**, **LINE**, and **Object Snap Tracking**. Complete front and right-side views with a 5″ no trim radius and the **TRIM** command

Step 10. Use a **5″**-radius fillet (no trim) and trim to complete front and right-side views.

Step 11. Set **Layer3** current. Label the drawing as shown in Figure 8-55. Add your name, class, and current date in the upper right.

Step 12. Save your drawing in two places.

Step 13. Print the drawing at a scale of **1/2″ = 1′-0″**.

chaptereight

Chapter Summary

This chapter provided you the information necessary to set up and draw interior elevations, sections, and details. You used the **UCS** and **UCS Icon** commands extensively in drawing the elevations. In addition, you explored the **Multileader** command in detail, and you used point filters and **Object Snap Tracking** to draw 2D views. Now you have the skills and information necessary to produce elevations, sections, and drawing details that you can use in interior design sales pieces, information sheets, contract documents, and other similar types of documents.

Chapter Test Questions

Multiple Choice

Circle the correct answer.

1. The **W** on the **2D UCS** icon indicates which of the following?

   a. face
   c. world
   b. view
   d. object

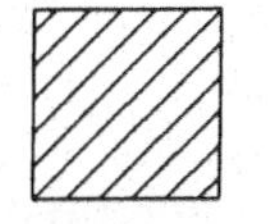

Figure 8-61

2. Which of the following angles produces the user-defined pattern shown in Figure 8-61?

   a. 45
   c. 0
   b. 90
   d. 135

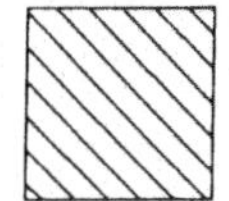

Figure 8-62

3. Which of the following angles produces the user-defined pattern shown in Figure 8-62?

   a. 45
   c. 0
   b. 90
   d. 135

4. Which of the following commands can you use to correct a hatch pattern that extends outside a hatch boundary, after you have exploded it?

   a. **ARRAY**
   c. **MOVE**
   b. **COPY**
   d. **TRIM**

5. When you select the **Noorigin** option of the **UCS Icon**, where is the **UCS Icon** displayed?

   a. The lower-left corner of the screen.
   b. It is turned off.
   c. It moves to the new UCS origin.
   d. It rotates.

6. Which of the following tabs do you use to set the landing distance of a **multileader**?

   a. Leader Format
   c. Content
   b. Leader Structure
   d. Attachment

7. You can use the **Multileader Collect** command to:
   a. Align leaders
   b. Add leaders
   c. Change a circle to a hexagon
   d. Attach multiple balloons to one leader
8. Which setting allows you to mirror an image without mirroring the text?
   a. **MIRRTEXT = 1**
   b. **MIRRTEXT = 0**
   c. **MIRRTEXT = 3**
   d. **DTEXT-STYLE = 0**
9. The **STRETCH** command is best used for:
   a. Stretching an object in one direction
   b. Moving an object along attached lines
   c. Shrinking an object on one direction
   d. All the above
10. Which of the following is an option in the **Boundaries** area of the **Hatch and Gradient** dialog box?
   a. Find boundaries
   b. Subtract boundaries
   c. Remove boundaries
   d. Define boundaries

Matching

Write the number of the correct answer on the line.

a. **UCS** ______
b. **STRETCH** ______
c. **Hatch Editor** ______
d. **HPGAPTOL** ______
e. **Point Filters** ______

1. Appears on the ribbon when you double-click on a hatch pattern.
2. A command used to move entities without removing attached lines
3. A setting that allows a small space in the hatch boundary
4. A method of entering a point by which the X and Y coordinates are given separately
5. A command that is used to move coordinates 0,0 to another point on the drawing

True or False

Circle the correct answer.

1. **True or False:** The **Coordinates** panel is hidden in the **View** tab of the ribbon by default.
2. **True or False:** You can draw a **multileader** with content first only.
3. **True or False:** You must clearly define the boundary of the area to be hatched when you use the **Add: Select Objects** option of the **Hatch** command.
4. **True or False: Origin** is the name of the **UCS Icon** command option that forces the UCS icon to be displayed at the 0,0 point of the current UCS.
5. **True or False:** Picking any point on an associative 35-line hatch pattern with the **ERASE** command and then pressing **<Enter>** will erase it.

List

1. Five ways of accessing the **UCS** command.
2. Five commands of the **Modify** panel under the **Draw Ribbon** tab.
4. Five options of the **Osnap** menu that begin with *M* or *N*.
5. Five options available after you launch the **UCS** command.
6. Five ways of accessing the **Multileader Style** dialog box.
7. Five ways of accessing the **Multileader** command.
8. Five options of the **Multileader Style Manager/Modify** dialog box.
9. Five options under the **Multileader** command.
10. Five options of the **Hatch and Gradient** dialog box.

Questions

1. What is a user coordinate system and how is it used?
2. What are predefined hatch patterns and how are they used?
3. How are point filters and **Object Snap Tracking** similar?
4. When would you use multileaders?
5. How were the **STRETCH** and **MIRROR** commands used in this chapter, and how could you use them in the future?

Chapter Projects

Project 8-1: *Detail Drawing of a Bar Rail* [BASIC]

1. Draw the bar rail detail shown in Figure 8-63. Measure the drawing with an architectural 1/2 scale and draw it full size (1:1) using AutoCAD.

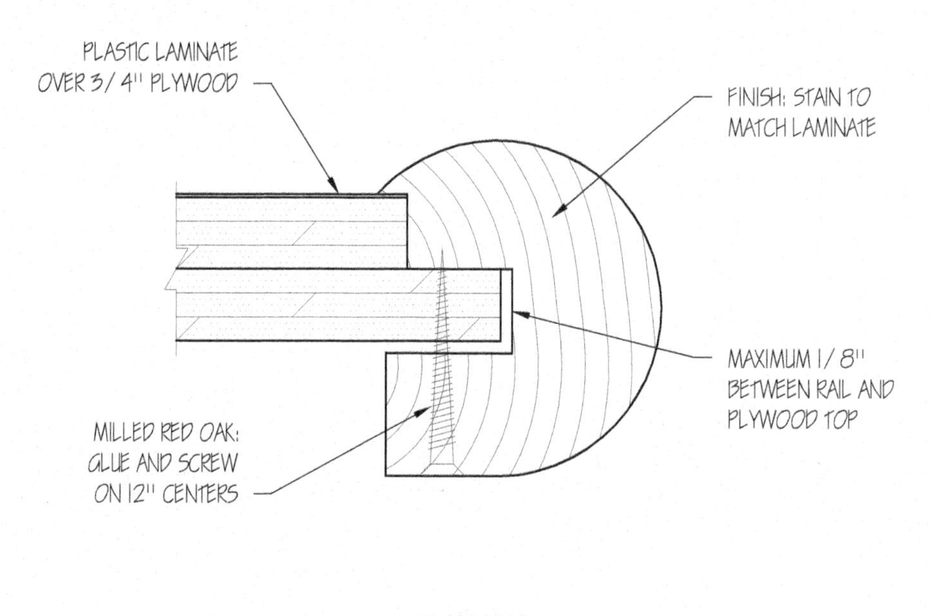

Figure 8-63
Project 8-1: Bar rail detail

2. Set your own drawing limits, grid, and snap. Create your own layers with varying lineweights as needed.
3. Label the drawing as shown in Figure 8-63 in the City Blueprint font. Add your name, class, and the current date in the upper right.
4. Save the drawing in two places and print the drawing at a scale of 1:2.

Project 8-2: *Wheelchair-Accessible Commercial Restrooms Elevation* **[INTERMEDIATE]**

Figure 8-64 shows the floor plan of the commercial restrooms with the elevations indicated. The line of text at the bottom of Figure 8-65 shows where the **House Designer** drawing is located in the AutoCAD **DesignCenter**. The front view of the toilets, urinals, sinks, grab bars, faucets, and toilet paper holders are blocks contained within this drawing or are searchable online. Just double-click on any of these blocks to activate the **INSERT** command and insert these blocks into your elevation drawing as needed. You may need to modify the sink, and you will have to draw the mirror and paper towel holder.

> **TIP**
>
> If you find useable blocks by searching online, saving them so you can use them for other drawings is a good idea. You can use the **Libraries** tab on the **BLOCKS** palette to save your own library of furniture and fixture blocks.

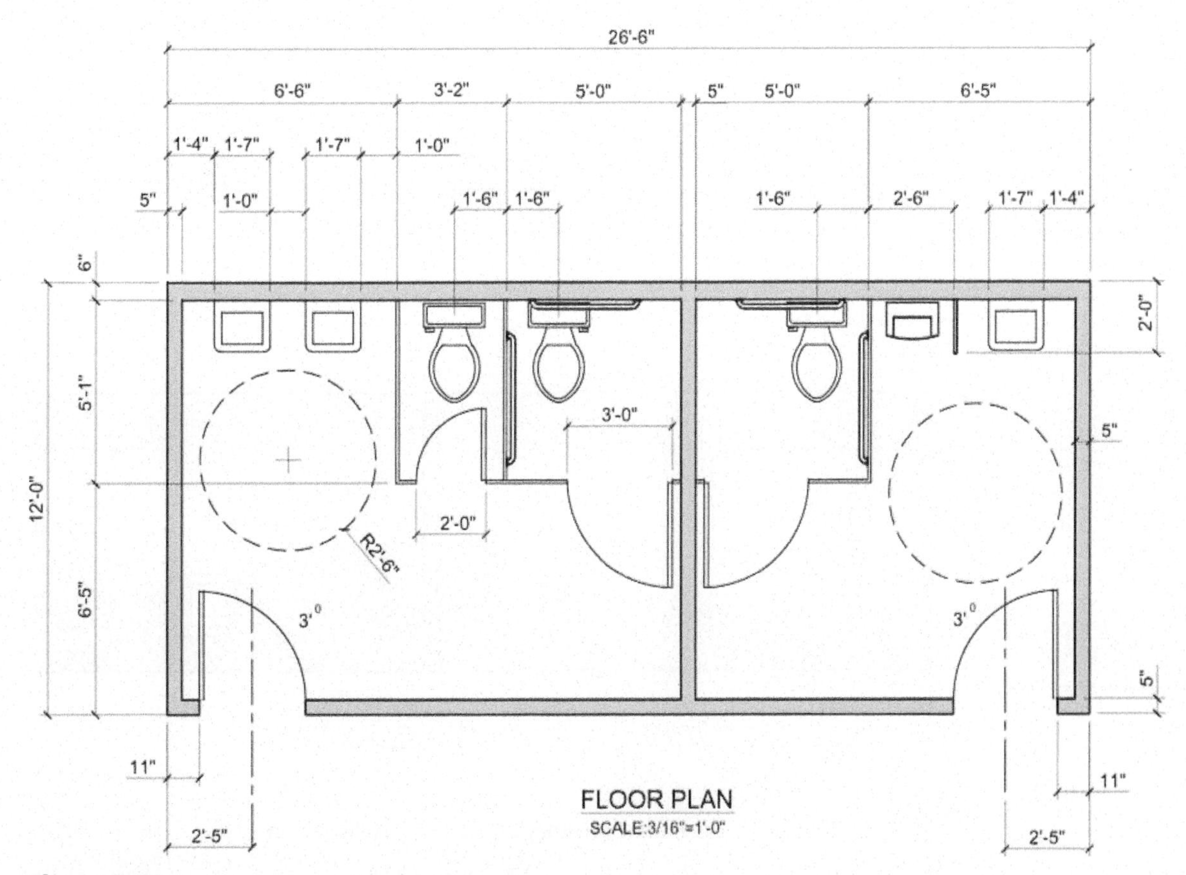

Figure 8-64
Project 8-2: Floor plan of the wheelchair-accessible commercial restrooms (scale: 3/16″ = 1′-0″)

Figure 8-65
Project 8-2: **House Designer** blocks in the **DesignCenter**

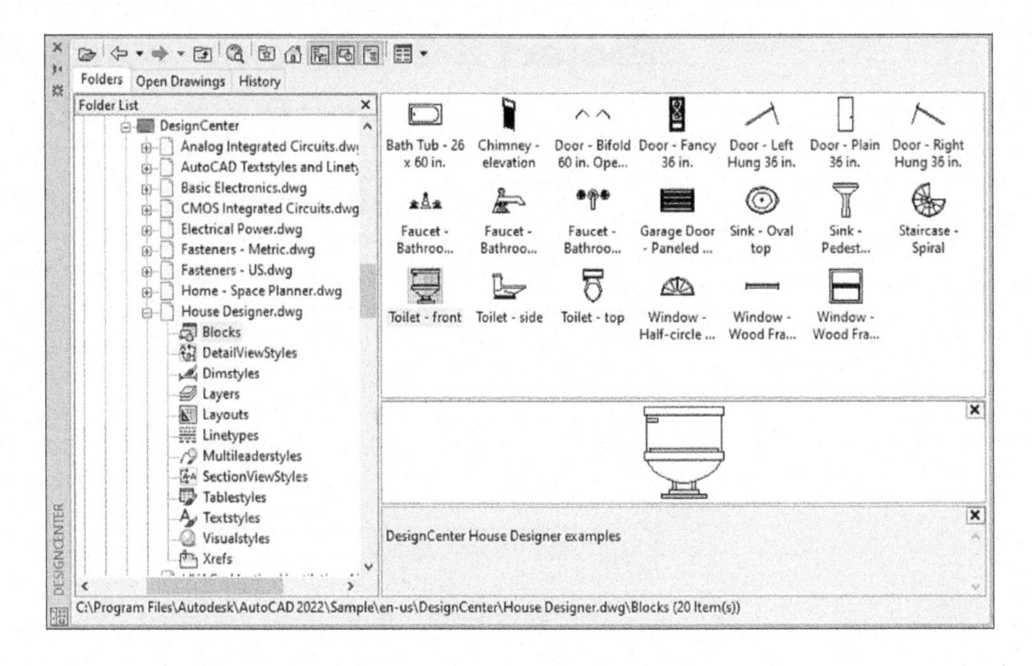

Draw elevation 1 of the commercial wheelchair-accessible restrooms as shown in Figure 8-66. Use the dimensions shown and draw it full scale without dimensions. Use lineweights to make the drawing more attractive and a solid hatch pattern with a gray color to make the walls solid. Use the same gray color for the layer on which you draw the ceramic tile. When you have completed Project 8-2, your drawing will look similar to Figure 8-66. You may locate drawings of the sinks and urinal that are a little different from those shown on this drawing. If so, use them. Just be sure they are located correctly. Add dimensions as required. Save the drawing in two places and print the drawing to scale.

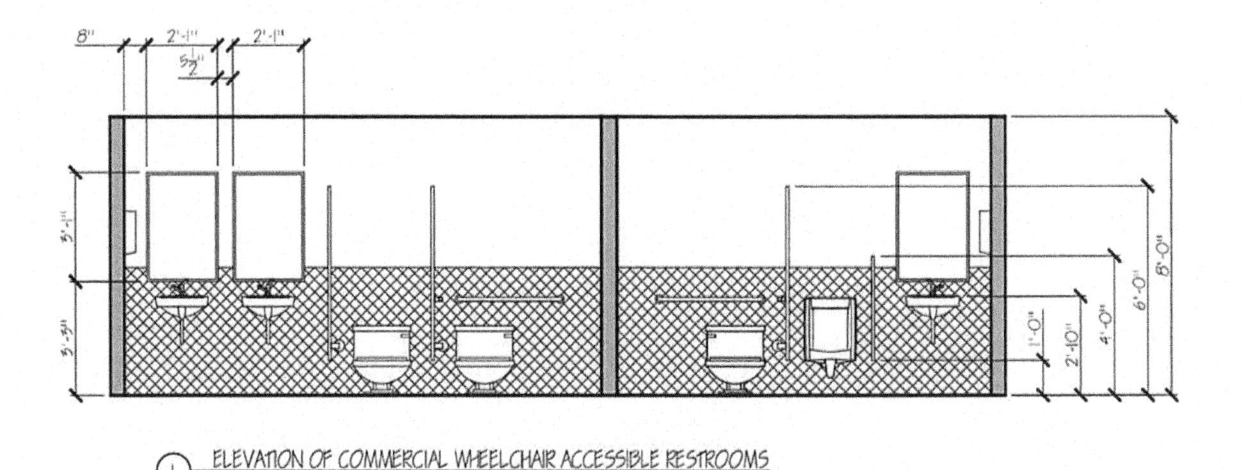

Figure 8-66
Project 8-2: Wheelchair-accessible commercial restrooms elevation (scale: 3/16″ = 1′-0″)

Project 8-3: *Drawing a Mirror and Sections of a Mirror from a Sketch* **[ADVANCED]**

1. Use the dimensions shown to draw the mirror in Figure 8-67 using AutoCAD.

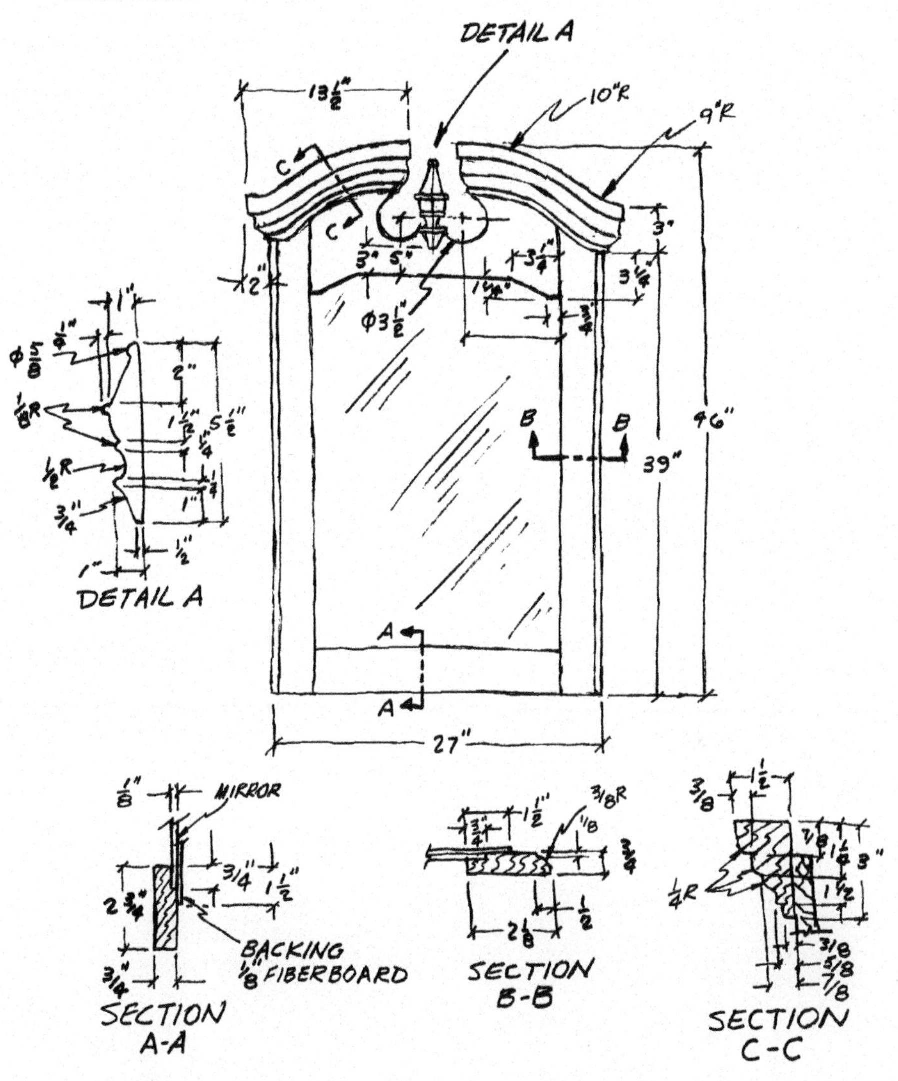

Figure 8-67
Project 8-3: Mirror

2. Set your own drawing limits, grid, and snap. Create your own layers as needed.
3. Do not place dimensions on this drawing, but do show the cutting plane lines and label them as shown.
4. Do not draw Detail A. This information is shown so you can draw that part.
5. Draw and label sections A-A, B-B, and C-C in the approximate locations shown on the sketch. Use the ANSI31 hatch pattern for the sectional views, or draw splines and array them to show wood. Do not show dimensions.
6. Save the drawing in two places and print the drawing to scale.

chapter**nine**

Drawing the Furniture Installation Plan, Adding Specifications, and Extracting Data

CHAPTER OBJECTIVE

- Correctly use the following commands and settings:

ATTDIA system variable
Attribute Display (ATTDISP)
Block Attribute Manager (BATTMAN)
Data Extraction
Define Attributes (ATTDEF)
Edit Text (TEXTEDIT)
Insert
Modify Attribute Global (-ATTEDIT)
Modify Attribute Single (EATTEDIT)
Properties
Quick Properties
Synchronize Attributes (ATTSYNC)
Write Block (WBLOCK)

Introduction

This chapter describes the AutoCAD commands that allow you to add specifications to furnishings and how to extract the specifications from the drawing. These commands are especially important because they reduce the amount of time it takes to count large amounts of like furniture pieces (with specifications) from the plan. Many software programs are available that you can use with AutoCAD to save even more time. These programs provide furniture symbols already drawn and programs that extract specification information in a form that suits your individual needs. Although you may ultimately combine one of these programs with the AutoCAD program, learning the commands included in this chapter will help you to understand how they interact with AutoCAD.

EXERCISE 9-1
Tenant Space Furniture Installation Plan with Furniture Specifications

When you have completed Exercise 9-1, your drawing will look similar to Figure 9-1.

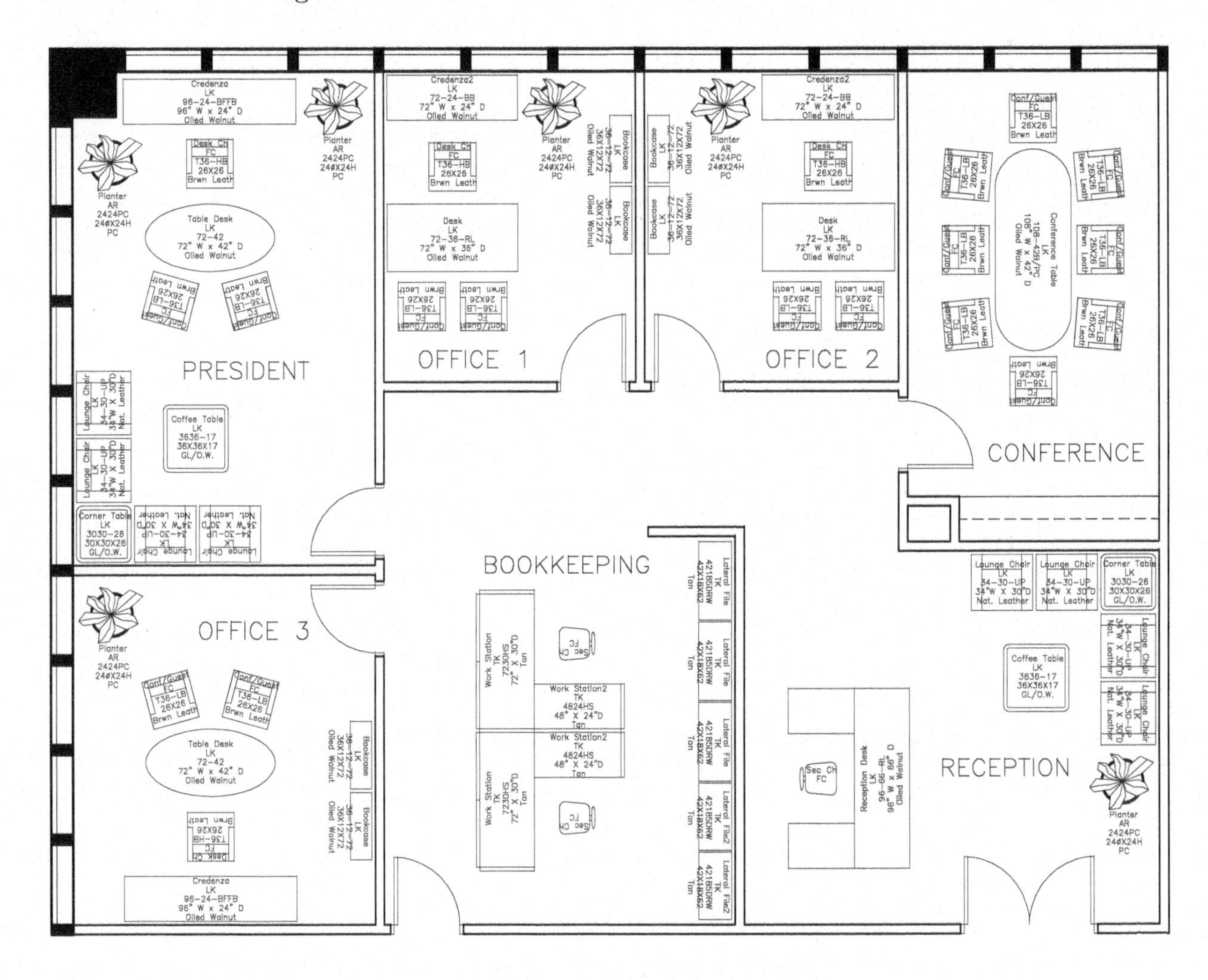

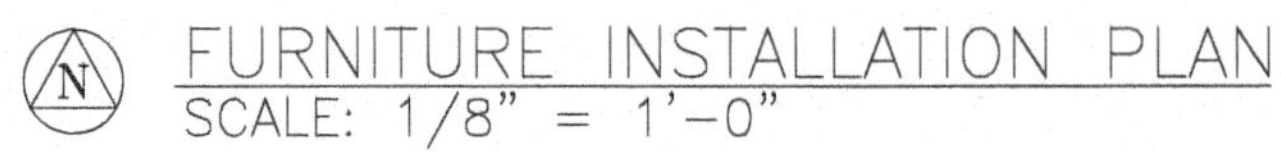

Figure 9-1
Exercise 9-1: Tenant space furniture installation plan with furniture specifications (scale: 1/8″ = 1′-0″)

> **NOTE**
>
> In **EXERCISE 12-1** and **EXERCISE 12-2,** you will freeze layers to make a presentation that displays the dimensioned floor plan, furniture plan, reflected ceiling plan, and voice/data/power plan. This will work only if you have saved **CH6-EXERCISE1, CH7-EXERCISE1, CH9-EXERCISE1,** and **CH11-EXERCISE1** as individual drawing files.

Step 1. Use your workspace to make the following settings:

1. Begin drawing **CH9-EXERCISE1** on the hard drive or network drive by opening existing drawing **CH7-EXERCISE1** and saving it as **CH9-EXERCISE1**.
2. Set **Layer0** current.
3. Freeze layers **a-anno-dims**, **Defpoints**, and **a-anno-area**.

Draw the Furniture Symbols

NOTE

Remember, the furniture and the attributes that you add to the furniture are drawn on **Layer0**, so they assume the characteristics of the layer on which you insert them.

Step 2. You must draw the furniture symbols in plan view as shown in Figure 9-2 before you add specifications. Reference the tenant space reception furniture symbols as shown in Figures 9-3, 9-4, 9-5, and 9-6 to draw each piece full scale on your drawing. Pick any open space on your drawing to draw the furniture. Draw each symbol on **Layer0**. Blocks will be made of each symbol, so it does not matter where you draw the furniture on the plan.

Define Attributes... (ATTDEF)

DEFINE ATTRIBUTES	
Ribbon/ Panel	Home/ Block
Menu Bar:	Draw/Block/ Define Attributes ...
Type a Command:	ATTDEF
Command Alias:	ATT

attribute: An attribute is a label that attaches data to a block. It consists of a tag and a value.

The **Define Attributes...** command allows you to add attributes (in this case, specifications) to the furniture symbols drawn in plan view. After you add the attributes, a block is made of the symbol. When you insert the block into a drawing, the specifications appear on the drawing if you have defined them as visible (attributes can be visible or invisible). You can then extract the attribute information from the drawing using the **Data Extraction...** dialog box.

As shown in Figures 9-3, 9-4, 9-5, and 9-6, each piece of furniture in the tenant space has five ***attributes***. An attribute is made up of two parts: the *tag* and the *value*. The tag is used to name the attribute but does not appear on the inserted drawing. It does appear on the drawing while you are defining attributes and before it is made into a block. The tag is used when the attribute information is extracted from the drawing. The attribute tag may contain any characters, but no spaces, and it is automatically converted to uppercase.

The value is the actual specification, such as Reception Desk, LK, 96-66-RL, 96″W × 66″D, and Oiled Walnut. The attribute value may contain any characters, and it may also have spaces. The value appears on the drawing after you insert it as a block. It appears exactly as it was entered.

Seven optional modes are available for the value of **ATTDEF**; you set them at the beginning of the attribute definition:

Invisible: This value is not displayed on the screen when you insert the block. You may want to use the **Invisible** mode for pricing, or you may want to make some attributes invisible so that the drawing does not become cluttered.

Constant: This value is fixed and cannot be changed. For example, if you use the same chair throughout a project but the fabric varies, then the furniture manufacturer value of the chair will be constant, but the finish value will vary. You cannot edit a constant value.

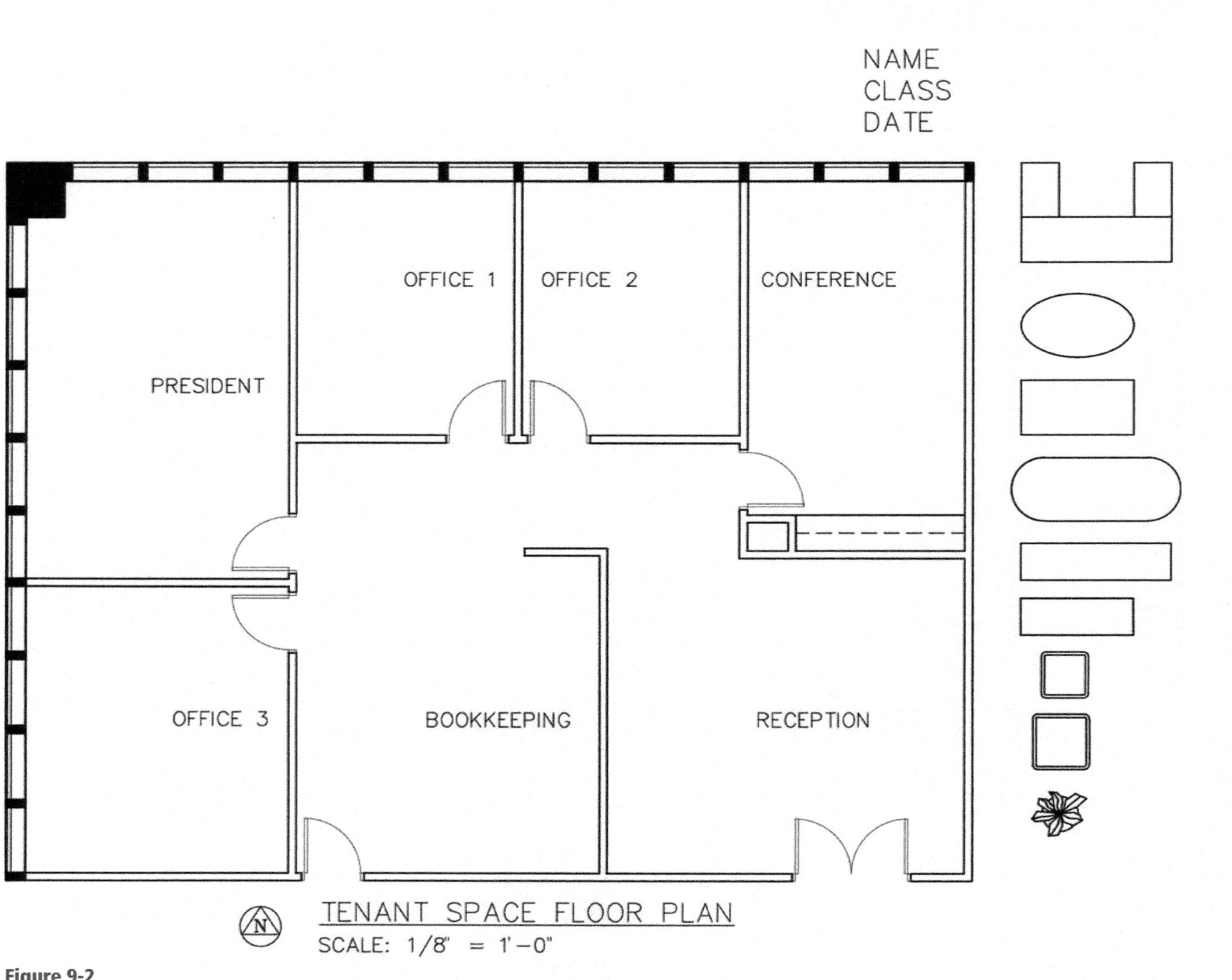

Figure 9-2
Draw furniture symbols outside (or inside) the tenant space floor plan (scale: 1/8″ = 1′-0″)

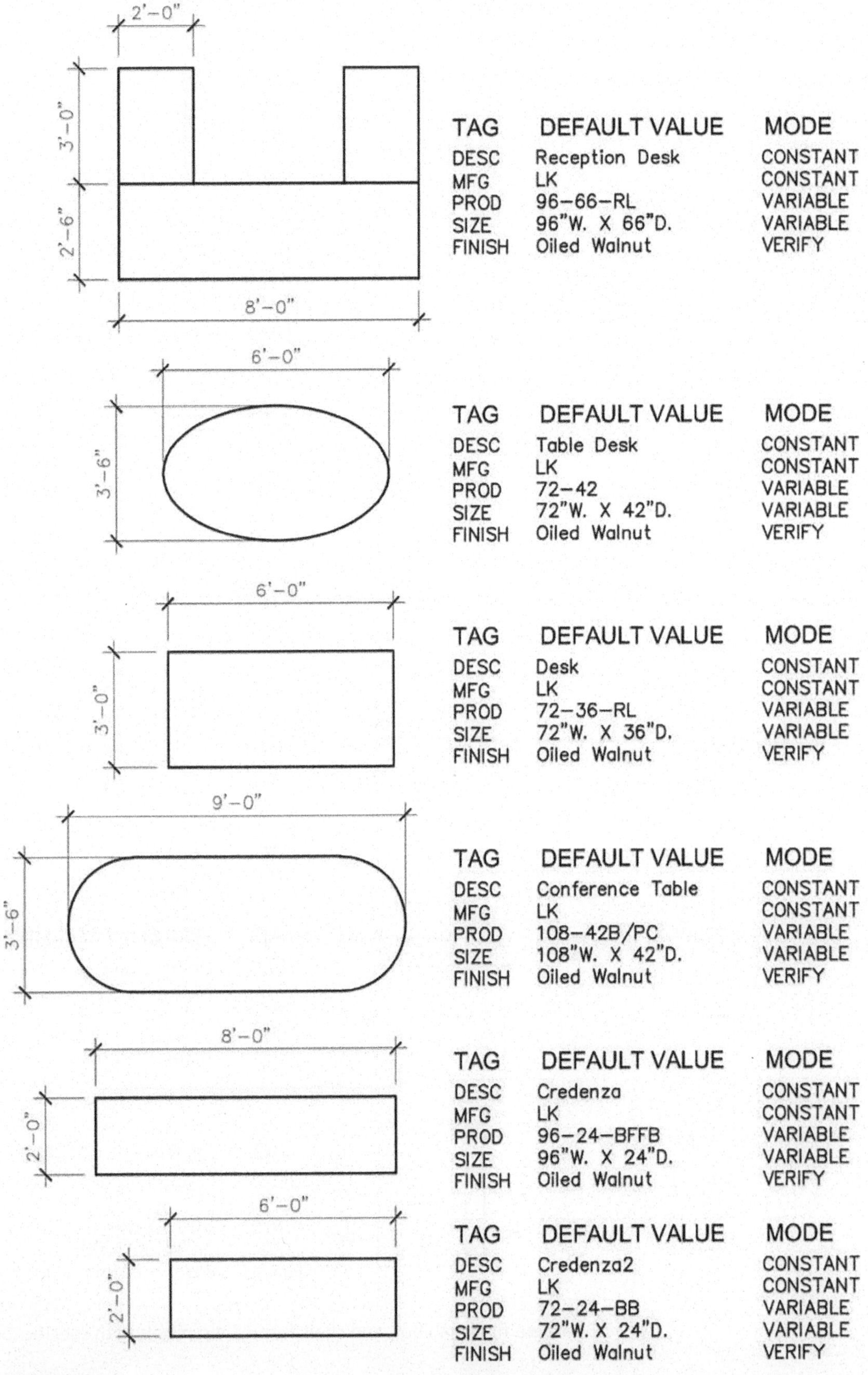

Figure 9-3
Desk, table, and credenza furniture symbols with specifications (scale: 1/4" = 1'-0")

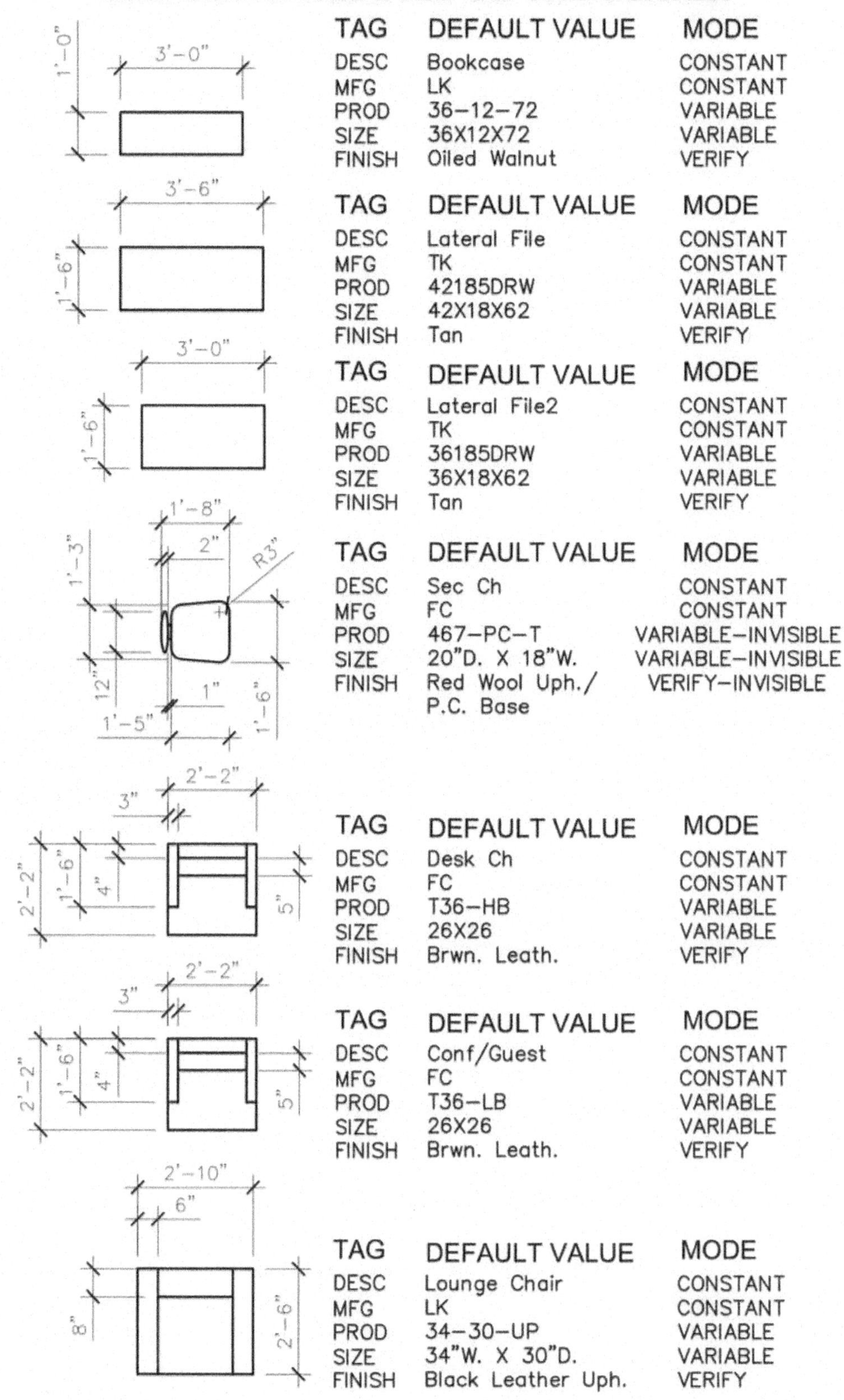

Figure 9-4
Bookcase filing cabinet, and chair furniture symbols with specifications (scale: 1/4″ = 1′-0″)

MAKE SURE YOU DRAW THE FURNITURE AND THE ATTRIBUTES ON THE 0 LAYER

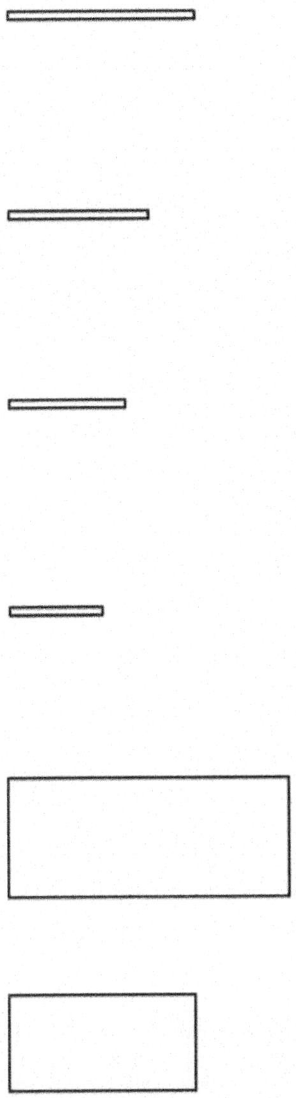

TAG	DEFAULT VALUE	MODE
DESC	Panel 48	CONSTANT–INVISIBLE
MFG	TK	CONSTANT–INVISIBLE
PROD	T4812TS	VARIABLE–INVISIBLE
SIZE	48" X 2" 62"H	VARIABLE–INVISIBLE
FINISH	Rose Fabric	VERIFY–INVISIBLE

TAG	DEFAULT VALUE	MODE
DESC	Panel 36	CONSTANT–INVISIBLE
MFG	TK	CONSTANT–INVISIBLE
PROD	T3612TS	VARIABLE–INVISIBLE
SIZE	48" X 2" 62"H	VARIABLE–INVISIBLE
FINISH	Rose Fabric	VERIFY–INVISIBLE

TAG	DEFAULT VALUE	MODE
DESC	Panel 30	CONSTANT–INVISIBLE
MFG	TK	CONSTANT–INVISIBLE
PROD	T3012TS	VARIABLE–INVISIBLE
SIZE	48" X 2" 62"H	VARIABLE–INVISIBLE
FINISH	Rose Fabric	VERIFY–INVISIBLE

TAG	DEFAULT VALUE	MODE
DESC	Panel 24	CONSTANT–INVISIBLE
MFG	TK	CONSTANT–INVISIBLE
PROD	T2412TS	VARIABLE–INVISIBLE
SIZE	24" X 2" 62"H	VARIABLE–INVISIBLE
FINISH	Rose Fabric	VERIFY–INVISIBLE

TAG	DEFAULT VALUE	MODE
DESC	WS 72 X 30	CONSTANT
MFG	TK	CONSTANT
PROD	7230HS	VARIABLE
SIZE	72" X 30"D.	VARIABLE
FINISH	Tan.	VERIFY

TAG	DEFAULT VALUE	MODE
DESC	WS 48 X 24	CONSTANT
MFG	TK	CONSTANT
PROD	4824HS	VARIABLE
SIZE	48" X 24"D.	VARIABLE
FINISH	Tan.	VERIFY

Figure 9-5
Partition panel and workstation furniture symbols with specifications (scale: 1/4″ = 1′-0″)

Verify: This mode allows the value to be variable and allows you to check the value you have entered. You may enter changes in the value as needed when you insert the block.

Preset: This mode allows the value to be variable. It is similar to **Constant**, but unlike a constant value, you can change the preset value.

Variable: If none of the above modes is selected, the value is variable. The **Variable** mode allows you to change the value.

Figure 9-6
Coffee table, corner table, and planter symbols with specifications (scale: 1/4″ = 1′-0″)

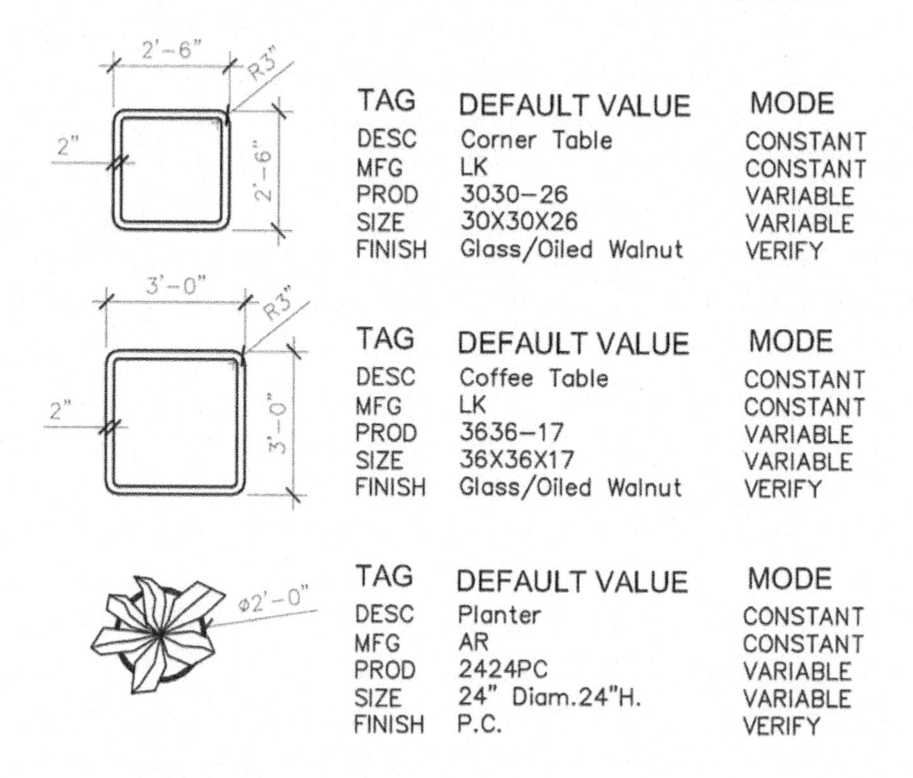

Lock Position: This option locks the attribute location inside the block. This feature is useful when you use dynamic blocks.

Multiple Lines: This option allows the attribute value to contain multiple lines of text. When you select this option, you can specify a boundary width for the attribute.

Step 3. Keep **Layer0** current.

Step 4. Create a new text style named **Attribute** with the romans font. Do not make it annotative. Set it current.

Step 5. Zoom in on the reception desk.

Constant Attribute

Step 6. Use **Define Attributes...** to define the attributes of the reception desk. Make the first two attributes of the reception desk Constant (Figure 9-7), as described next:

Prompt	**Response**
Type a command:	**Define Attributes...** (or type **ATT** **<Enter>**)
The **Attribute Definition** dialog box Appears (Figure 9-7):	Click **Constant** (so a check appears in that **Mode** check box)
The **Prompt:** text box is grayed (if the attribute is constant, there can be no prompt).	Type **DESC** in the **Tag:** box

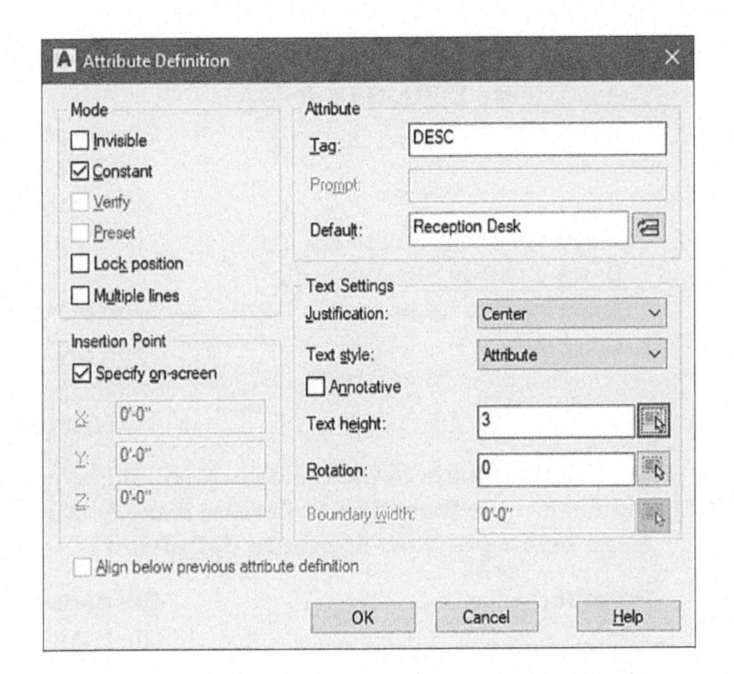

Figure 9-7
Use **Define Attributes...** to define the first constant attribute

Prompt	**Response**
	Type **Reception Desk** in the **Default:** (value) box
	Click the down arrow in the **Justification** box and click **Center**
	Text style: **Attribute**
	Type **3** in the **Text height:** box

All other parts of the dialog box should be as shown in Figure 9-7.

Annotative: An attribute can be annotative. The annotative attribute is always the same size when plotted, regardless of the scale of the plotted drawing, if the annotation scale is the same as the plot scale. In this chapter we do not annotate the attributes because the furniture is drawn full scale, and we want the plotted attribute size to change depending on the plotted scale.

Prompt	**Response**
	Click **OK**
Specify start point:	**P1→** (Figure 9-8)
The first attribute is complete; the attribute tag appears on the drawing.	
Type a command:	**<Enter>** (repeat **ATTDEF**)

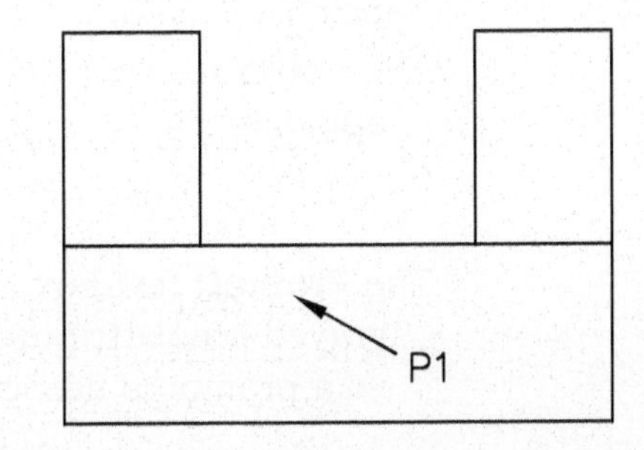

Figure 9-8
Specify the start point of the first attribute

Prompt	Response
The **Attribute Definition** dialog box appears:	**Constant** is selected already; if not, click **Constant** (so a check appears in that **Mode** check box)
The **Prompt:** text box is grayed (if the attribute is constant, there can be no prompt).	Type **MFG** in the **Tag:** box
	Type **LK** in the **Default:** (value) box
	Select the **Align below previous attribute definition** check box

All other parts of the dialog box should be as shown in Figure 9-9. Notice that the **Insertion Point** and **Text Settings** areas are grayed when **Align below previous attribute definition** is selected.

Prompt	Response
	Click **OK**
The second attribute is complete; the attribute tag appears on the drawing.	

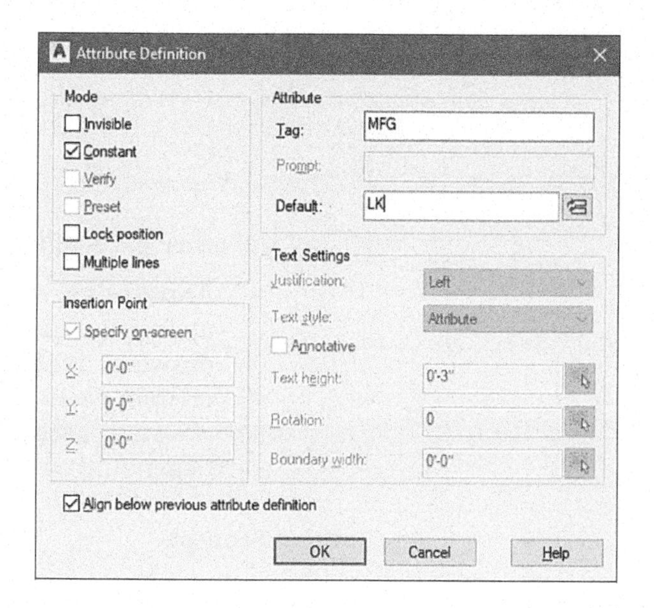

Figure 9-9
Define the second **Constant** attribute

Variable Attribute

Step 7. Make the third and fourth attributes Variable and the fifth one Verify as described next.

Prompt	Response
Type a command:	**<Enter>** (repeat **ATTDEF**)
The **Attribute Definition** dialog box appears:	Clear all the check marks in the **Mode** area (the third attribute is variable)
The **Prompt:** text box is no longer grayed (this attribute is variable, so a prompt is needed).	Type **PROD** in the **Tag:** box

Prompt	Response
	Type **Enter product number** in the **Prompt:** box
	Type **96-66-RL** in the **Default:** (value) box
	Select the **Align below previous attribute definition** check box

The dialog box should be as shown in Figure 9-10.

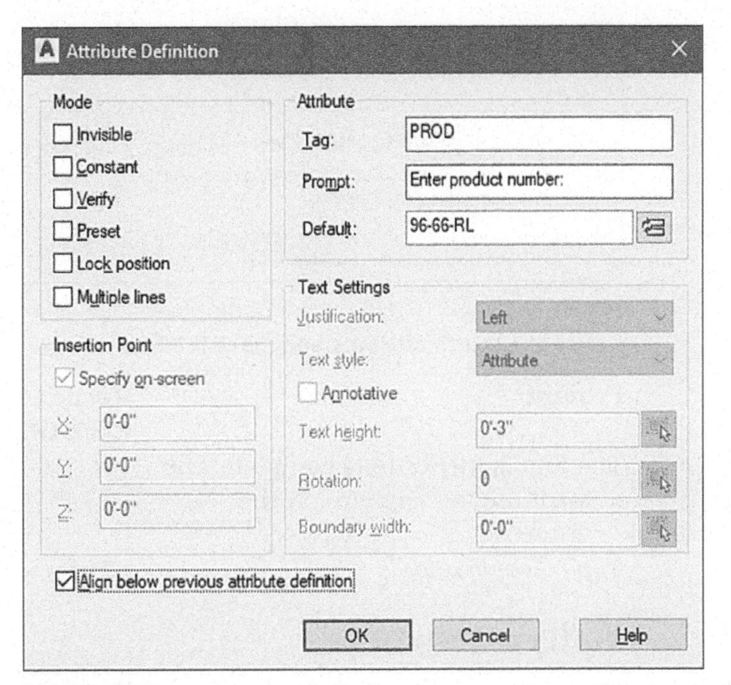

Figure 9-10
Define the third attribute and make it **Variable**

Prompt	Response
	Click **OK**
The third attribute is complete; the attribute tag appears on the drawing.	
Type a command:	**<Enter>** (repeat **ATTDEF**)
The **Attribute Definition** dialog box appears:	
This attribute also is variable, so there should be no check marks in the **Mode** boxes.	Type **SIZE** in the **Tag:** box
	Type **Enter size** in the **Prompt:** box
	Type **96″ W × 66″ D** in the **Default:** (value) box
	Click **Align below previous attribute definition** (so a check appears in that **Mode** check box)

The dialog box should be as shown in Figure 9-11.

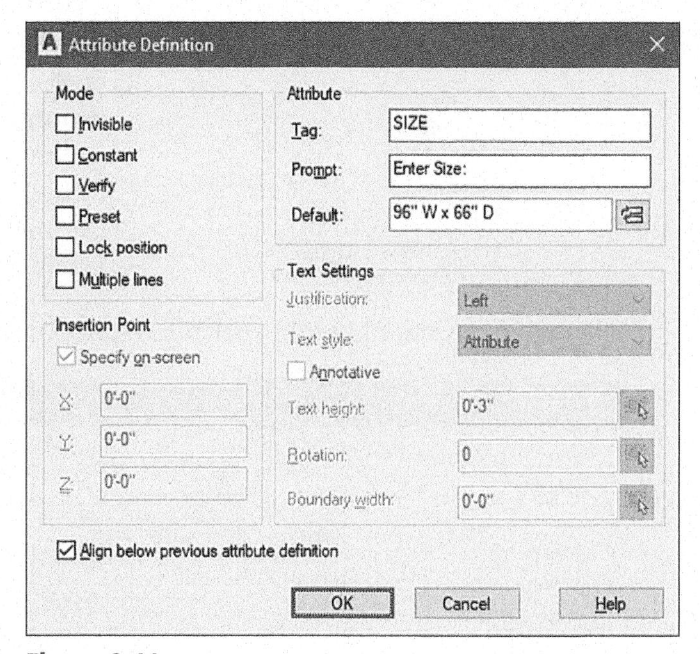

Figure 9-11
Define the fourth attribute and make it **Variable**

Prompt	**Response**
	Click **OK**
The fourth attribute is complete; the attribute tag appears on the drawing.	
Type a command:	**<Enter>** (repeat **ATTDEF**)

Verify Attribute

Prompt	**Response**
The **Attribute Definition** dialog box appears: This attribute also is variable and should be one that is verified (so you have two chances to make sure it is correct).	Select the **Verify** check box for the **Mode**
	Type **FINISH** in the **Tag:** box
	Type **Enter finish** in the **Prompt:** box
	Type **Oiled Walnut** in the **Default:** (value) box
	Select the **Align below previous attribute definition** check box (so a check mark appears in that **Mode** area)

The dialog box should be as shown in Figure 9-12.

Prompt	**Response**
	Click **OK**
The fifth attribute is complete; that attribute tag appears on the drawing.	

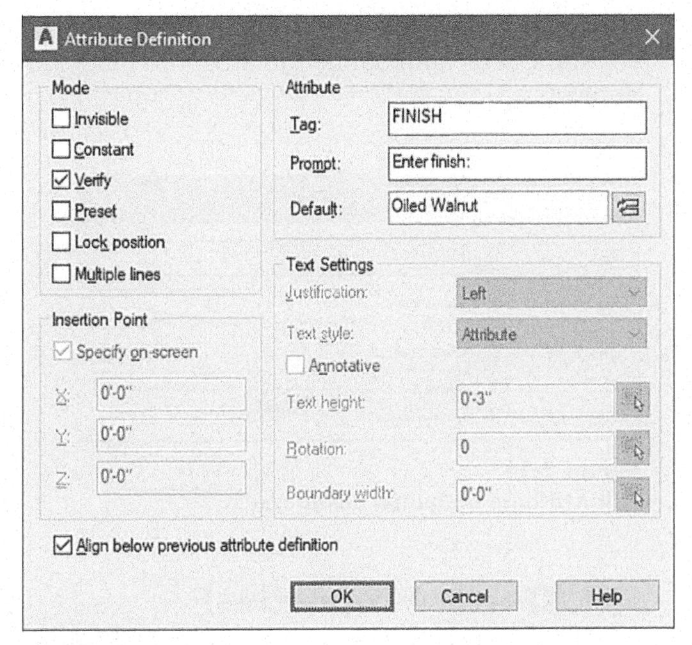

Figure 9-12
Define the fifth attribute and make it a **Verify** one

When you have completed defining the five attributes, your drawing of the reception desk will look similar to the desk shown in Figure 9-13.

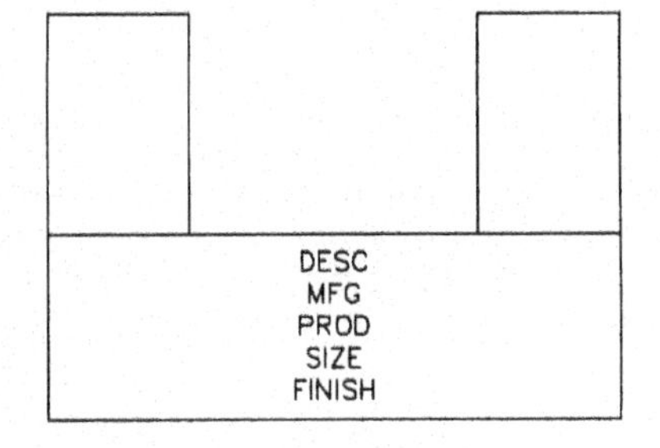

Figure 9-13
Reception desk with attribute tags

> **NOTE**
>
> If you are not happy with the location of the attribute tags, use the **MOVE** command to relocate them before using the **BLOCK** command.

EDIT TEXT	
Text Toolbar:	
Menu Bar:	Modify/ Object/ Text/Edit ...
Type a Command:	TEXTEDIT
Command Alias:	ED

Edit Text (TEXTEDIT)

Did you make a mistake while typing the attribute tag, attribute prompt, or default attribute value? The **Edit Text** command allows you to use the **Edit Attribute Definition** dialog box (Figure 9-14) to correct any typing mistakes you may have made while defining the attributes. Type **ED <Enter>**, and then click the tag to activate the **Edit Attribute Definition** dialog box. The **Edit Text** prompt is *Select an annotation object or [Undo]:*. When you pick a tag, the **Edit Attribute Definition** dialog box appears and allows you to change the attribute tag, prompt, or default value for a Variable, Verify, or Preset attribute. You can change the tag and the default (actually the value) for a constant attribute; adding a prompt for an attribute defined as constant does not change the attribute mode, and the prompt does not appear.

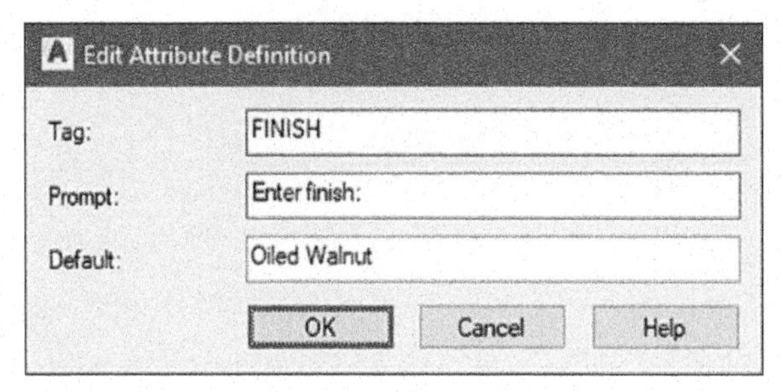

Figure 9-14
Edit Attribute Definition dialog box

QP (Quick Properties)

When the **QP (Quick Properties)** toggle is **ON** in the status bar, the **Quick Properties** palette appears when you click on an attribute tag. The **Quick Properties** palette is similar to the **Edit Text** command and can also be used to view and change an attribute tag's color, layer, text style, and height (Figure 9-15).

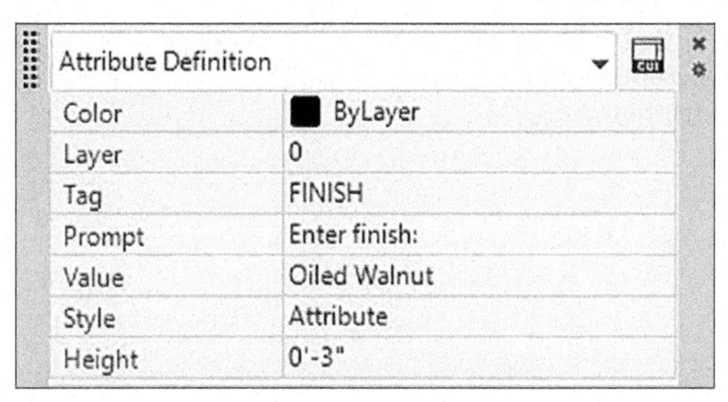

Figure 9-15
Quick Properties palette

Properties Palette

The **Properties** palette (Figure 9-16) allows you to change any property that can be changed.

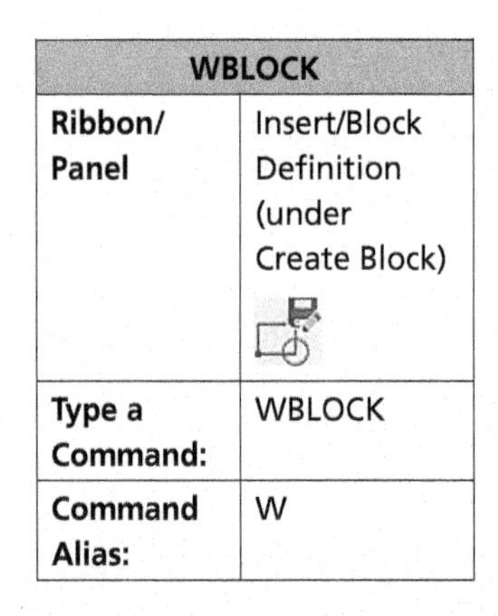

WBLOCK	
Ribbon/ Panel	Insert/Block Definition (under Create Block)
Type a Command:	WBLOCK
Command Alias:	W

WBLOCK the Furniture with Attributes Symbol

Step 8. Use the **Write Block** command (Figure 9-17) to save the reception desk as a drawing (.dwg) file. Save the reception desk to the folder of your choice. Name the wblock **Reception Desk**. Use the insertion base point as shown in Figure 9-18. Orient the desk as shown in Figure 9-18.

Figure 9-16
Properties palette

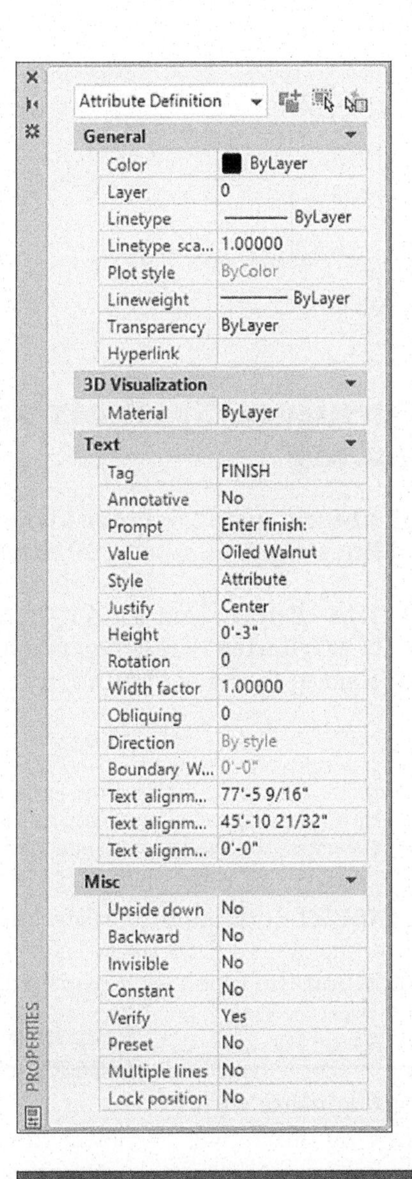

Figure 9-17
Write Block dialog box

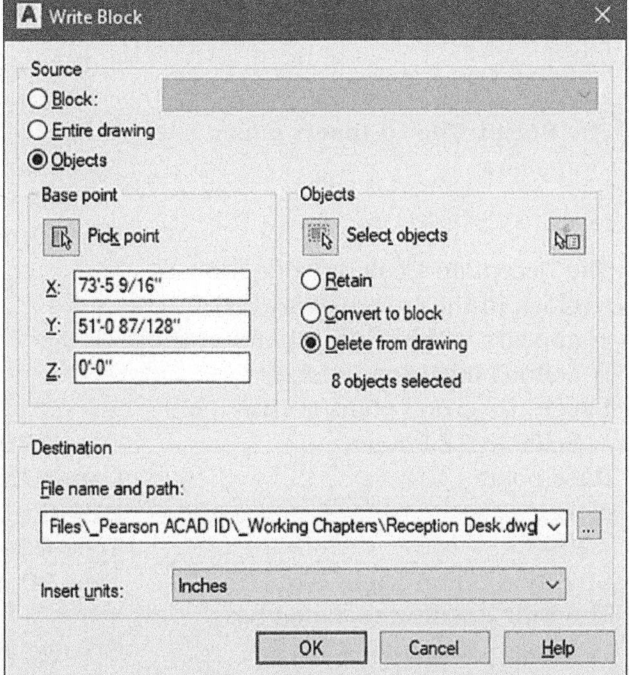

Figure 9-18
Save the reception desk as a drawing (.dwg) file to the folder named **Blocks**

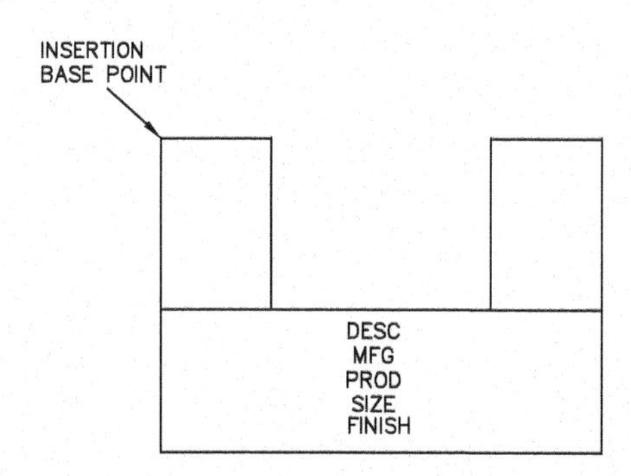

INSERT BLOCK	
Ribbon/ Panel	Insert/Block
Draw Toolbar:	
Menu Bar:	Insert/Blocks Palette ...
Type a Command:	INSERT
Command Alias:	I

Insert the Furniture Symbols with Attributes into the Drawing

Step 9. Create the **i-furn** layer. Set **color** to **cyan**, **linetype** to **Continuous**, and **lineweight** to **.004" (.09 mm)**. Set layer **i-furn** current.

Step 10. Type **ATTDIA <Enter>** and set **ATTDIA** to **1**. With **ATTDIA** set to **1**, the **Edit Attributes** dialog box is used for the attributes. When **ATTDIA** is set to **0**, the command prompts are used.

NOTE

If you want to be prompted for the attribute values in the order you create them, you must select them one by one in that order when you create a block or use WBLOCK. If you select them with a window, they will prompt you in reverse order.

Step 11. Use the **INSERT** command to insert the Reception Desk wblock into the tenant space floor plan. Use **From** (on the **Osnap** menu) to help position the block, as described next:

Prompt	**Response**
Type a command:	**INSERT** (or type **I <Enter>**)
The **BLOCKS** palette appears with the **Current Drawing** tab active:	Select the Insertion Point and Rotation check boxes (Figure 9-19). Click the **Browse** button to the right of the **Filter...** text box at the top of the **BLOCKS** palette
The **Select File to Insert** dialog box appears:	Locate and click the **Reception Desk** file Click **Open**
The Reception Desk drawing (now a block in the current drawing) appears with the crosshairs at the defined insertion point	
Specify insertion point or [Basepoint Scale X Y Z Rotate]:	Type **FRO <enter>**
Base point:	**Osnap-Endpoint**
of	**P1→** (Figure 9-20)
<Offset>:	Type **@24,30 <Enter>**
Specify rotation angle <0>:	Type **90 <Enter>**
The **Edit Attributes** dialog box appears (Figure 9-21):	Change anything that needs to be changed and click **OK**

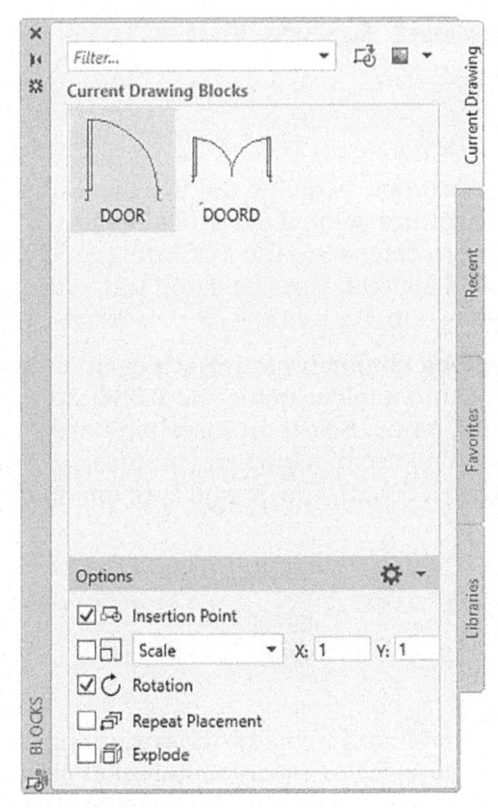

Figure 9-19
Insert dialog box

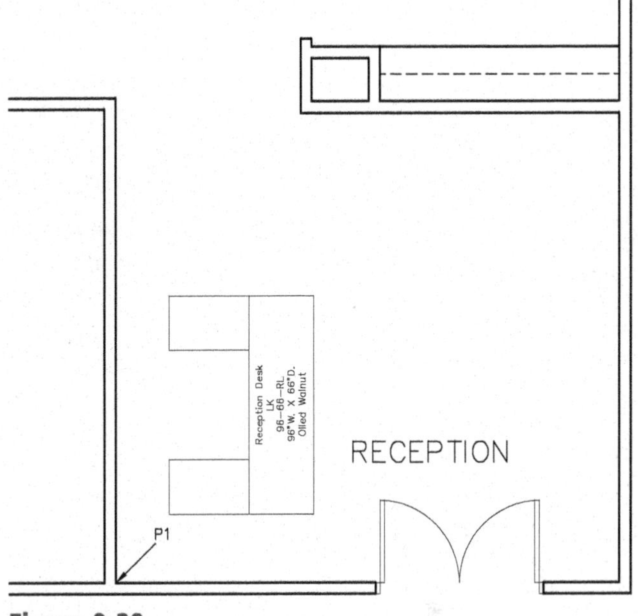

Figure 9-20
Use the **INSERT** command to open the **BLOCKS** palette and insert the reception desk block into the tenant space floor plan

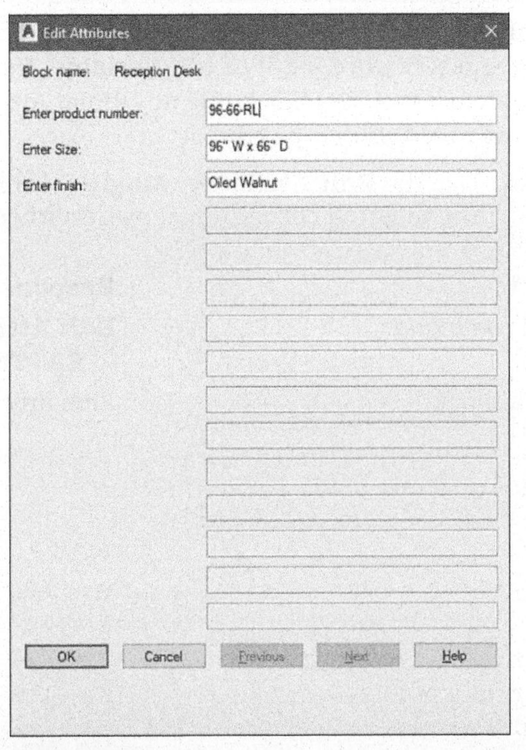

Figure 9-21
Edit Attributes dialog box

Complete the Tenant Space Furniture Installation Plan

Step 12. Keep **Layer0** current.

Step 13. Use **Define Attributes...** to define the five attributes for each of the remaining furniture symbol drawings. Refer to Figures 9-3, 9-4, 9-5, and 9-6 to determine the attribute tag, default value, and mode for each symbol. Use the same text settings for all attributes, as shown in Figures 9-7, 9-9, 9-10, 9-11, and 9-12.

Step 14. Use the **Write Block** command to wblock each of the furniture symbol drawings into a folder using the **DESC** value as the wblocked drawing name. Select an insertion base point that is helpful in positioning the block when you insert it into the drawing. Refer to Figures 9-3, 9-4, 9-5, and 9-6; for example:

DESC VALUE	WBLOCK NAME
Reception Desk	Reception Desk
Table Desk	Table Desk

Step 15. Use the **INSERT** command to insert the remaining furniture symbols into the tenant space furniture installation plan (Figure 9-22). Locate the furniture approximately as shown. After you insert a block, you can copy or move it to a different location.

Some of the values that appeared on the corner table are too long; they go outside the table symbol. You will fix these next.

Edit Attribute, Single...

EDIT ATTRIBUTES SINGLE	
Ribbon/ Panel	Insert/Block
Modify II Toolbar:	
Menu Bar:	Modify/ Object/ Attribute/ Single ...
Type a Command:	EATTEDIT

The **Edit Attribute, Single...** command uses the **Enhanced Attribute Editor** dialog box (Figure 9-23) to edit **Variable**, **Verify**, and **Preset Attributes** values of each inserted block one at a time. Attributes defined with the **Constant** mode cannot be edited.

Step 16. Use the **Edit Attribute, Single...** command to edit the values on the inserted corner table, as described next:

Prompt	**Response**
Type a command:	**Edit Attribute...** (or type **EATTEDIT <Enter>**)
Select a block:	Pick any place on the corner table

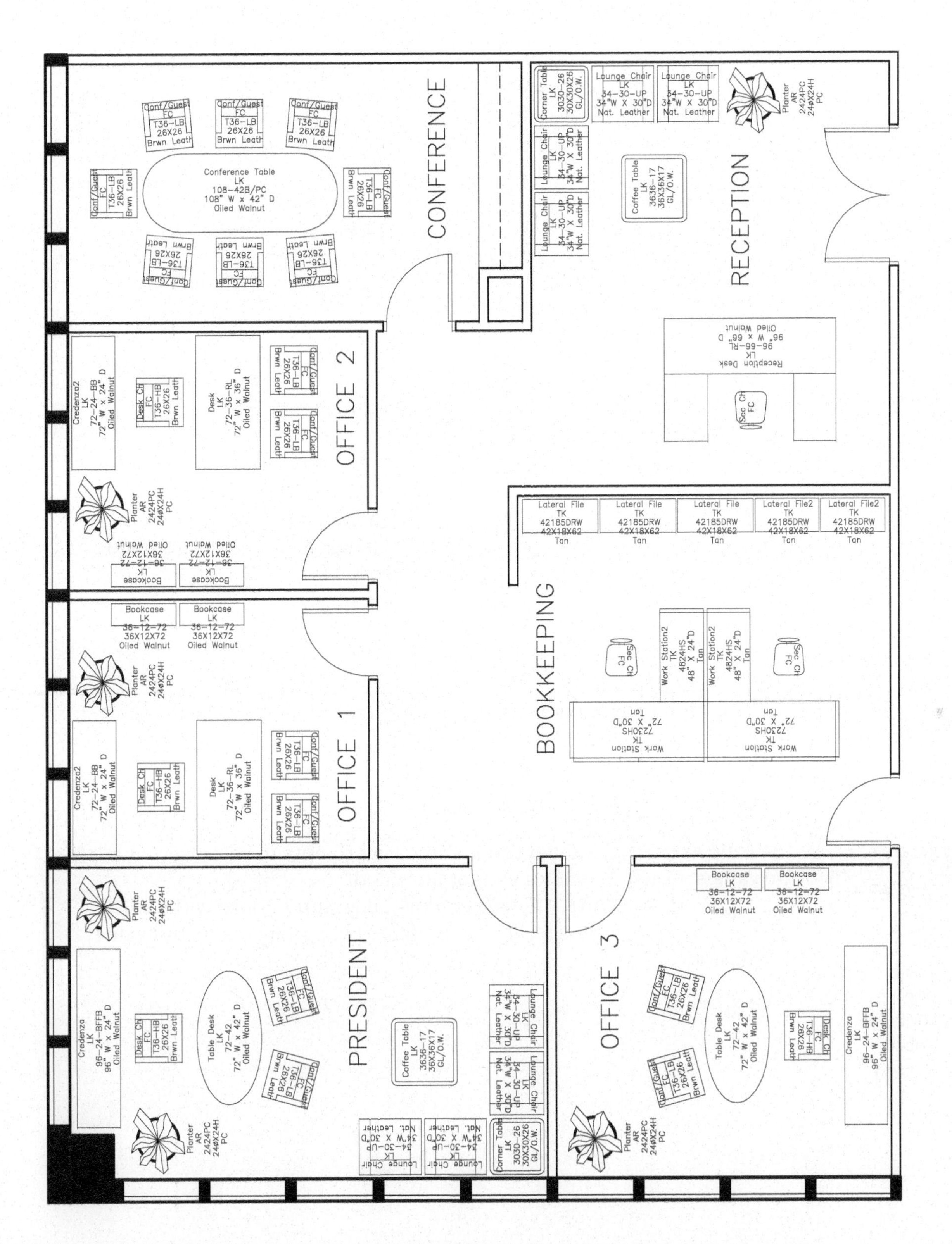

Figure 9-22
Tenant space furniture installation plan

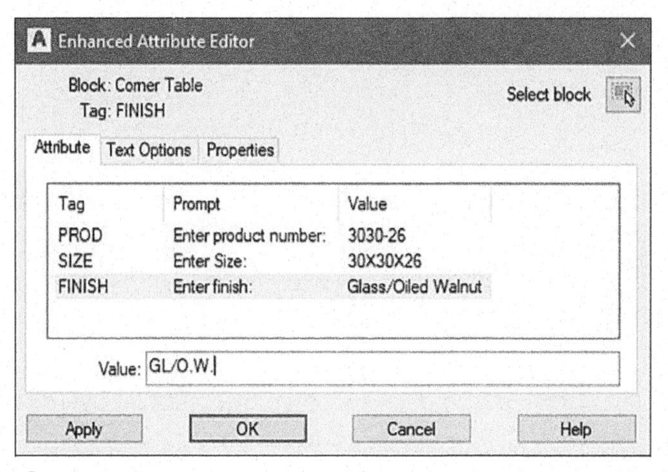

Figure 9-23
Enhanced Attribute Editor dialog box

Prompt	Response
The **Enhanced Attribute Editor** dialog box appears (Figure 9-23):	Use the dialog box to change the **FINISH** value to **GL/O.W.** Highlight the attribute and change the value in the **Value:** text box
	Click **Apply**
	Click **OK**

The values that appear on the corner table now fit within the table symbol (Figure 9-24).

Edit Attribute, Global

EDIT ATTRIBUTES GLOBAL	
Ribbon/ Panel	Insert/Block
Menu Bar:	Modify/ Object/ Attribute/ Global
Type a Command:	-ATTEDIT
Command Alias:	-ATE

The **Edit Attribute, Global** command uses prompts to edit inserted attribute values. Constant values cannot be edited.

The **Edit Attribute, Global** prompts allow you to narrow the value selection by entering a specific block name, tag specification, and value specification.

Figure 9-24
Tenant space reception area (scale: 1/4″ = 1′-0″)

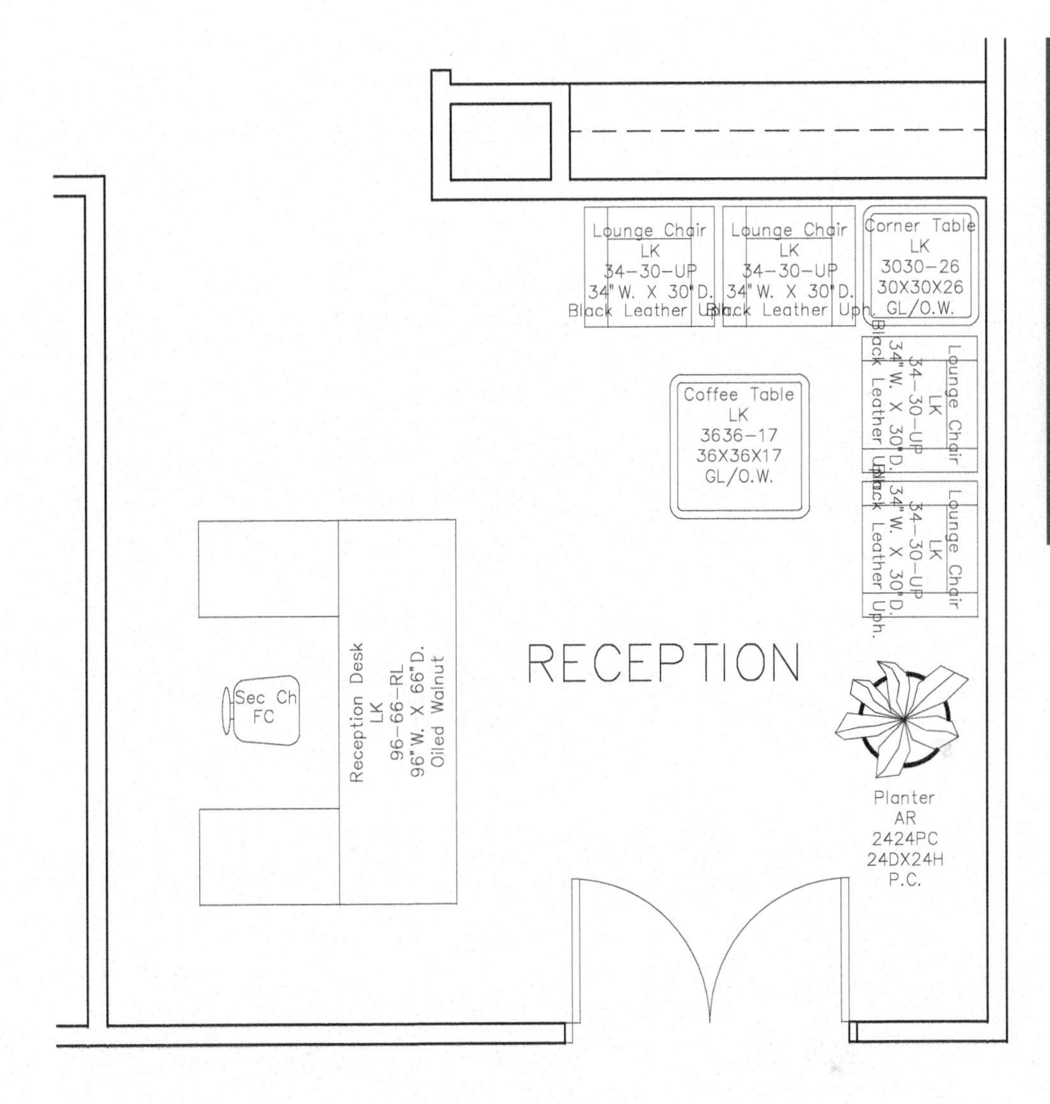

Only visible attributes can be edited when you respond with **Yes** to the prompt *Edit attributes one at a time?*. If you respond with **No** to the prompt, you can edit visible and invisible attribute value text strings.

Let's use the **Edit Attribute, Global** command to edit a value on the eight lounge chairs all at once.

Step 17. Use the **Edit Attributes** command to edit the text string of the FINISH value on all the lounge chairs at once, as described next:

Prompt	**Response**
Type a command:	**Edit Attributes Multiple** (or type **-ATTEDIT <Enter>**) (be sure to include the dash)
Edit attributes one at a time? [Yes No] <Y>	Type **N <Enter>**
Edit only attributes visible on screen? [Yes No] <Y>	**<Enter>**
Enter block name specification <*>:	Type **Lounge Chair <Enter>**
Enter attribute tag specification <*>:	Type **FINISH <Enter>**
Enter attribute value specification <*>:	Type **Black Leather Uph. <Enter>**

Prompt	Response
Select Attributes:	Click the Black Leather Uph. attribute on all four chairs in the reception area and the four lounge chairs in the president's office **<Enter>**
8 attributes selected.	
Enter string to change:	Type **Black Leather Uph. <Enter>**
Enter new string:	Type **Nat. Leath. <Enter>**

Type and enter the block name, tag, and value exactly. You may also enter **No** in response to the prompt *Edit only attributes visible on screen?*, and you may also change invisible attribute values.

> **TIP**
>
> When the **QP (Quick Properties)** toggle is **ON** in the status bar, the **Quick Properties** palette appears when you click on an inserted block's attribute value. You can use the **Quick Properties** palette to view and change an inserted block's Values, Layer, Name, and Rotation, individually or globally. The **Properties** palette allows you to change any property that can be changed.

Attribute Display (ATTDISP)

ATTRIBUTE DISPLAY	
Ribbon/ Panel	Home/Block/ Retain Attribute Display
Menu Bar:	View/Display/ Attribute Display
Type a Command:	ATTDISP

The **Attribute Display (ATTDISP)** command allows you to turn on the invisible attributes of the secretarial chair. The prompt is *Enter attribute visibility setting [Normal ON OFF] <Normal>:*.

ON: Pick **ON** to make the invisible attributes appear. Try this, and you will be able to see the invisible attributes of the secretarial chair.

OFF: Pick **OFF** to make all the attributes on the drawing invisible. Try this, and you will see that all the attributes are not visible.

Normal: Pick **Normal** to make visible attributes defined as **Visible** and to make invisible attributes defined as **Invisible**. Set **Normal** as the default.

Redefining an Inserted Block with Attributes Using the BLOCK Command

As described in Chapter 6, you can redefine a block using the **BLOCK** command. When you redefine a block that has attributes assigned using the **BLOCK** command, previous insertions of the block are affected as follows:

- Old constant attributes are lost and are replaced by new constant attributes, if any.
- Variable attributes remain unchanged, even if the new block definition does not include those attributes.
- New variable attributes are not added.

Future insertions of the block will use the new attributes. You must erase previous insertions of the block and insert them again to use the new attributes.

Block Attribute Manager (BATTMAN)

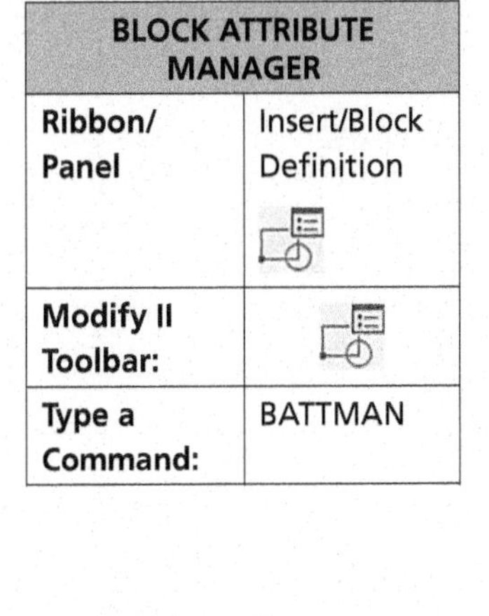

BLOCK ATTRIBUTE MANAGER	
Ribbon/ Panel	Insert/Block Definition
Modify II Toolbar:	
Type a Command:	BATTMAN

The **Block Attribute Manager** allows you to locate blocks in the drawing and edit attributes within those blocks in the current drawing. You can also remove attributes from blocks and change the order in which you are prompted for attribute values when inserting a block (Figure 9-25).

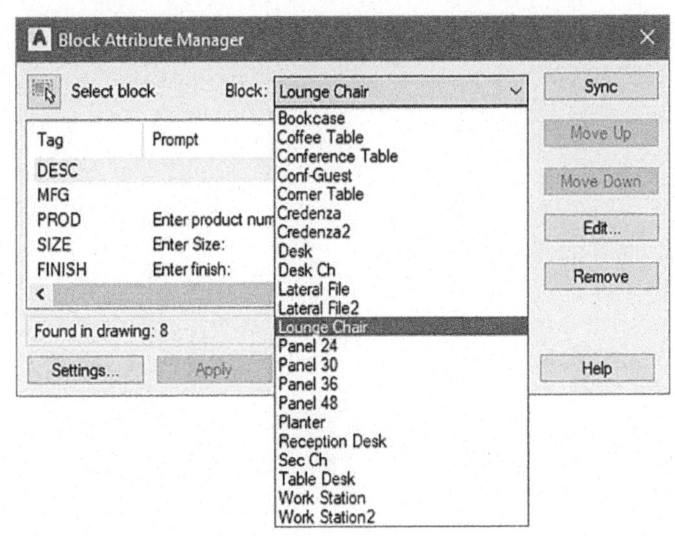

Figure 9-25
Block Attribute Manager

Synchronize Attributes (ATTSYNC)

SYNCHRONIZE ATTRIBUTES	
Ribbon/ Panel	Insert/Block Definition
Modify II Toolbar:	
Type a Command:	ATTSYNC

When you redefine a block (for example, the shape and attributes) using the **BLOCK** or **BEDIT** command, the redefined symbol or shape changes in all existing instances of the redefined block. The attributes do not change. The **Synchronize Attributes** command allows you to select each block whose attributes you want to update to the current redefined attributes.

Step 18. Change the underlined title text to read as shown in Figure 9-26.

Step 19. When you have completed Exercise 9-1, save your work in at least two places.

Step 20. Print Exercise 9-1 to scale.

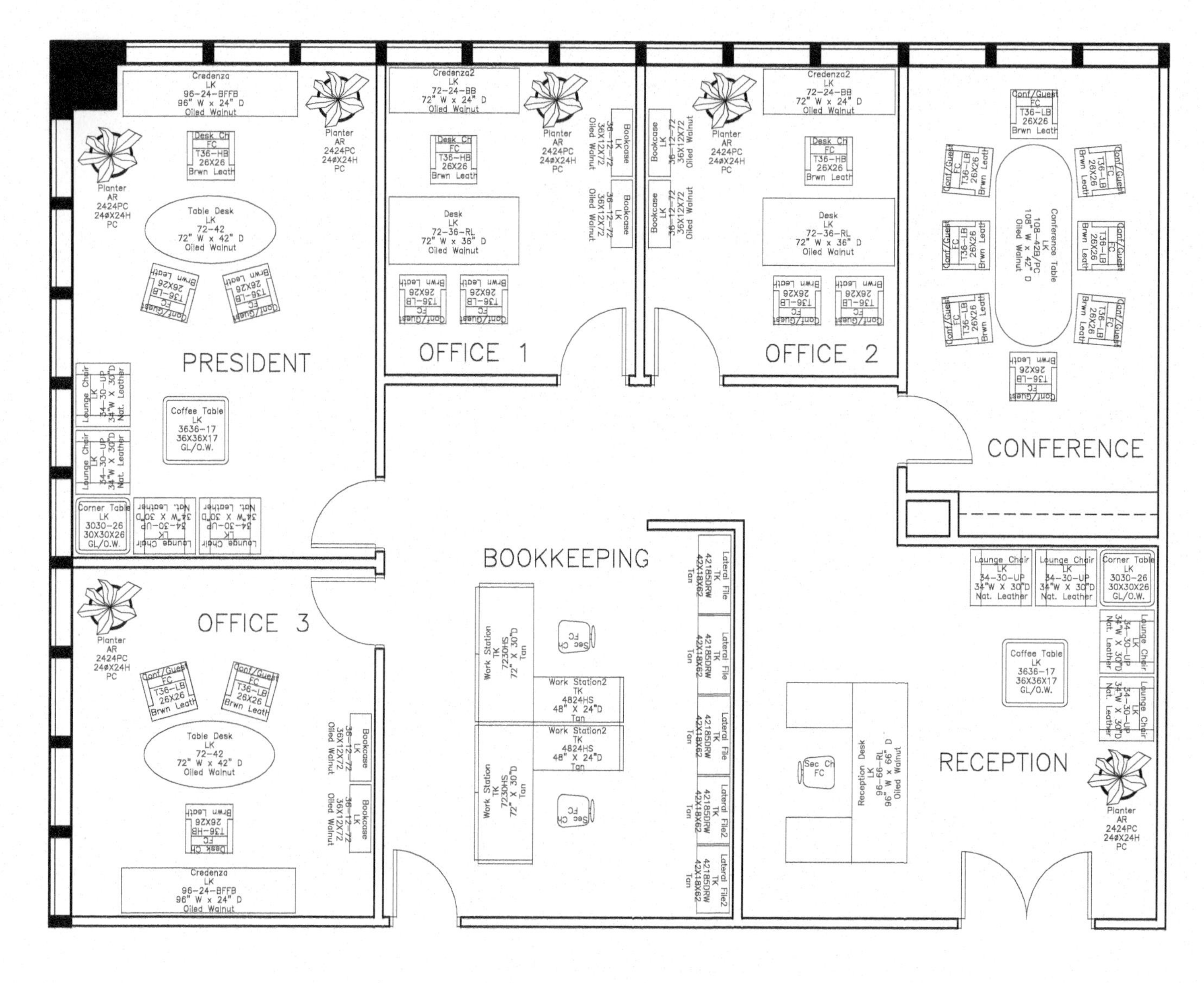

Figure 9-26
Tenant space furniture installation plan with furniture specifications (scale: 1/8″ = 1′-0″)

EXERCISE 9-2
Extracting Attributes from the Tenant Space Furniture Installation Plan

When you have completed Exercise 9-2, your drawing will look similar to Figure 9-27.

Step 1. Begin drawing **CH9-EXERCISE2** on the hard drive or network drive by opening the existing drawing **CH9-EXERCISE1** and saving it as **CH9-EXERCISE2**.

Step 2. Set layer **a-anno-text** current.

Figure 9-27
Exercise 9-2 complete

FURNITURE TOTALS						
Count	Name	DESC	FINISH	MFG	PROD	SIZE
6	Bookcase	Bookcase	Oiled Walnut	LK	36-12-72	36X12X72
2	Coffee Table	Coffee Table	GL/O.W.	LK	3636-17	36X36X17
1	Conference Table	Conference Table	Oiled Walnut	LK	108-42B/PC	108" W x 42" D
16	Conf-Guest	Conf/Guest	Brwn Leath	FC	T36-LB	26X26
2	Corner Table	Corner Table	GL/O.W.	LK	3030-26	30X30X26
2	Credenza	Credenza	Oiled Walnut	LK	96-24-BFFB	96" W x 24" D
2	Credenza2	Credenza2	Oiled Walnut	LK	72-24-BB	72" W x 24" D
2	Desk	Desk	Oiled Walnut	LK	72-36-RL	72" W x 36" D
4	Desk Ch	Desk Ch	Brwn Leath	FC	T36-HB	26X26
3	Lateral File	Lateral File	Tan	TK	42185DRW	42X18X62
2	Lateral File2	Lateral File2	Tan	TK	42185DRW	42X18X62
8	Lounge Chair	Lounge Chair	Nat. Leather	LK	34-30-UP	34"W X 30"D
2	Panel 24	Panel 24	Rose Fabric	TK	T2412TS	24" X 2" X 62"H
3	Panel 30	Panel 30	Rose Fabric	TK	T3012TS	30" X 2" X 62"H
4	Panel 36	Panel 36	Rose Fabric	TK	T3612TS	36" X 2" X 62"H
1	Panel 48	Panel 48	Rose Fabric	TK	T4812TS	48" X 2" X 62"H
6	Planter	Planter	PC	AR	2424PC	24øX24H
1	Reception Desk	Reception Desk	Oiled Walnut	LK	96-66-RL	96" W x 66" D
3	Sec Ch	Sec Ch	Red Wool Uph/PC Base	FC	467-PC-T	20" D X 18"W
2	Table Desk	Table Desk	Oiled Walnut	LK	72-42	72" W x 42" D
2	Work Station	Work Station	Tan	TK	7230HS	72" X 30"D
2	Work Station2	Work Station2	Tan	TK	4824HS	48" X 24"D

Step 3. Prepare the drawing to accept the extracted attributes in a tabular form as follows:

1. Make a new layout using the **Create Layout** wizard (on the **Insert** menu or type **LayoutWizard** and **<ENTER>**):

Begin:	Name it **Furniture Totals**
Printer:	Select a printer
Paper Size:	**Letter (8.5″ × 11″)**
Orientation:	**Landscape**
Title Block:	**None**
Define Viewports:	**Single**
Viewport Scale:	**1:1**
Pick Location:	Click **Next>**
Finish:	Click **Finish**

2. Erase the viewport border created on the new layout so this layout will contain nothing but the table with the extracted attributes (Figure 9-27).
3. Make sure the **Furniture Totals** layout tab is selected, to continue.

Data Extraction...

DATA EXTRACTION	
Ribbon/ Panel	Insert/ Linking & Extraction
Modify II Toolbar:	
Menu Bar:	Tools/Data Extraction ...
Type a Command:	DATA EXTRACTION
Command Alias:	DX

You can use the **Data Extraction** wizard to produce a parts list or bill of materials directly from a drawing that contains blocks with attributes. The drawing you made in this chapter is an excellent example of this type of drawing. With the **Data Extraction** wizard, you can extract existing attributes and create a table as described in this exercise.

Step 4. Extract attributes from this drawing using the **Data Extraction...** command and create a table on the blank **Furniture Totals** layout, as described next:

Prompt	**Response**
Type a command:	**Extract Data...** (or type **DX** **<Enter>**)
The **Data Extraction** wizard (Figure 9-28) appears:	With the **Create a new data extraction** button selected, click **Next**

Figure 9-28
Data Extraction Wizard - Begin (Page 1 of 8)

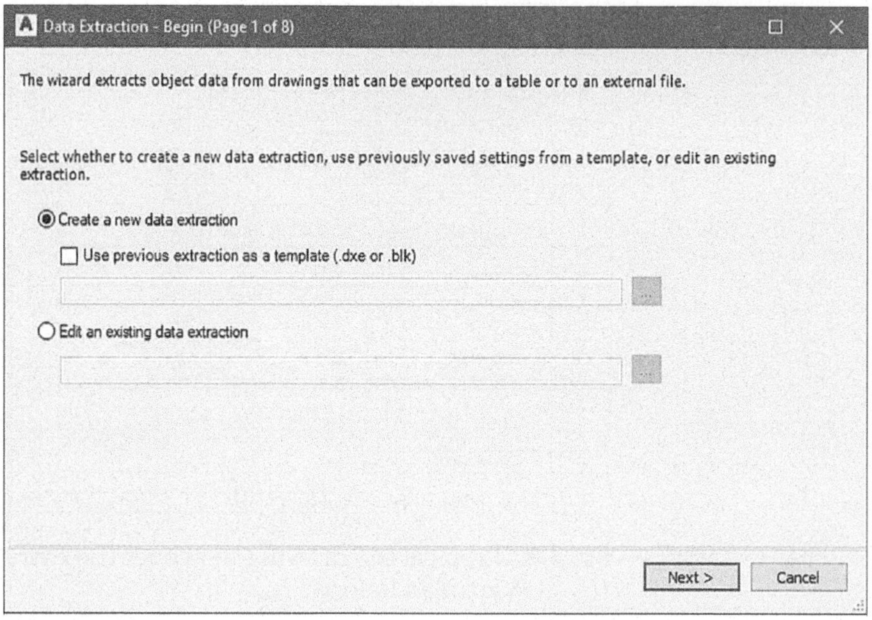

Data Extraction - Begin (Page 1 of 8)

The wizard extracts object data from drawings that can be exported to a table or to an external file.

Select whether to create a new data extraction, use previously saved settings from a template, or edit an existing extraction.

(•) Create a new data extraction

[ ] Use previous extraction as a template (.dxe or .blk)

( ) Edit an existing data extraction

Next > | Cancel

Prompt	Response
The **Save Data Extraction As** dialog box appears:	Select the folder where your drawings are stored and name the file **FURNITURE TOTALS** Click **Save**
The **Data Extraction - Define Data Source (Page 2 of 8)** appears:	Click **Next>**
Select Objects (Page 3 of 8) appears:	Clear the **Display all object types** check box. Select the **Display blocks with attributes only** and **Display objects currently in-use only** check boxes. Have the **Display blocks only** radio button on (Figure 9-29) Click **Next>**
Select Properties (Page 4 of 8) appears:	Under **Category filter**, select only the **Attribute** check box. Under **Properties**, select the check boxes for all five attributes (Figure 9-30) Click **Next>**
Refine Data (Page 5 of 8) appears:	Right-click on the column name for any blank columns if there are any and click **Hide Column** (Figure 9-31) Click **Next>**
Choose Output (Page 6 of 8) appears:	Select the **Insert data extraction table into drawing** check box Click **Next**
Table Style (Page 7 of 8) appears:	Select the **Use property names as additional column headers** check box. Type **FURNITURE TOTALS** in the **Enter a title for your table:** box (Figure 9-32)

Data Extraction - Select Objects (Page 3 of 8)

Select the objects to extract data from:

Objects

	Object	Display Name	Type
☑	Bookcase	Bookcase	Block
☑	Coffee Table	Coffee Table	Block
☑	Conference Table	Conference Table	Block
☑	Conf-Guest	Conf-Guest	Block
☑	Corner Table	Corner Table	Block
☑	Credenza	Credenza	Block
☑	Credenza2	Credenza2	Block
☑	Desk	Desk	Block

Preview

Display options

☐ Display all object types

◉ Display blocks only

○ Display non-blocks only

☑ Display blocks with attributes only

☑ Display objects currently in-use only

< Back   Next >   Cancel

Figure 9-29
Data Extraction - Select Objects (Page 3 of 8)

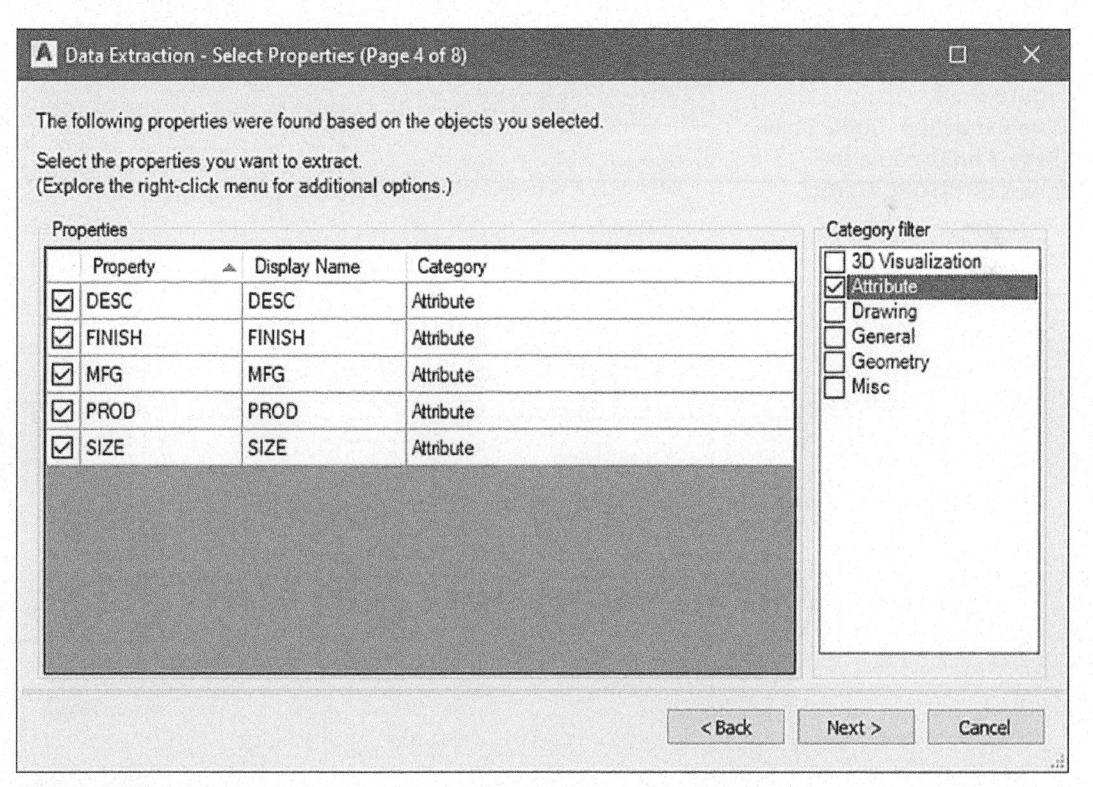

Figure 9-30
Data Extraction - Select Properties (Page 4 of 8)

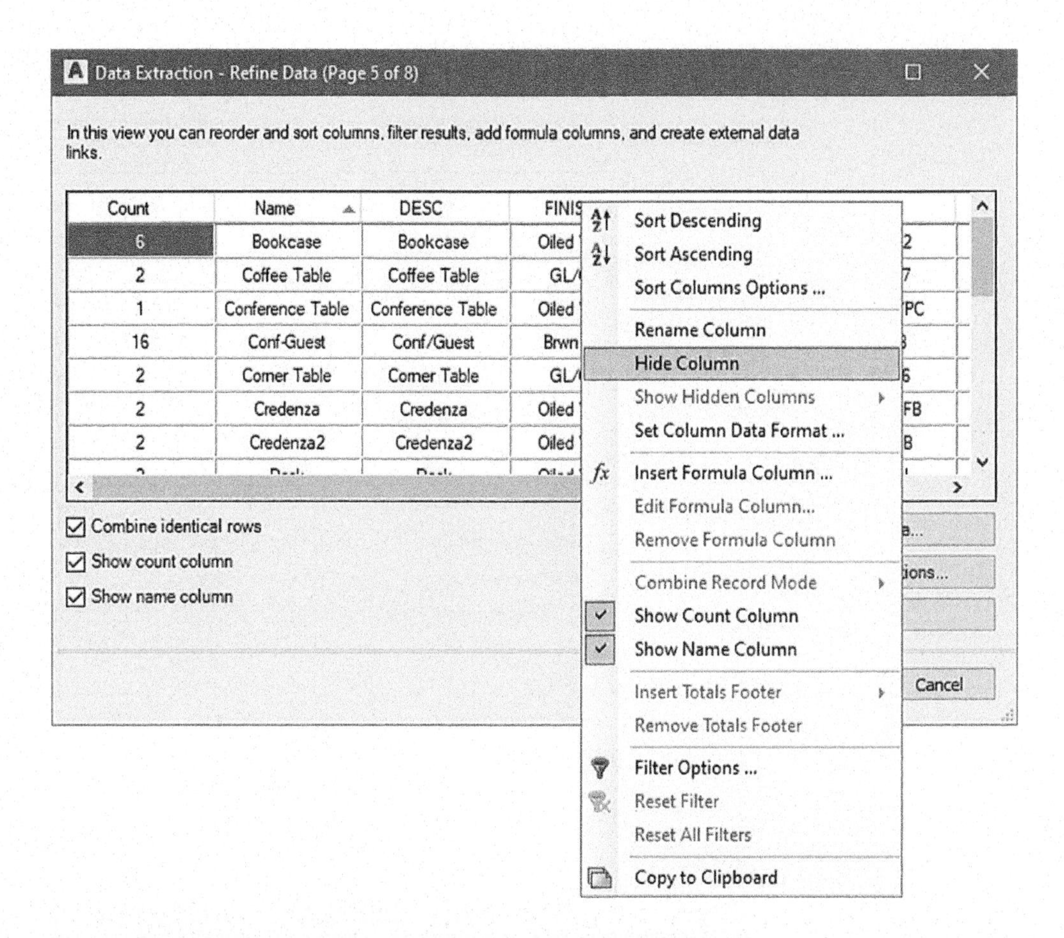

Figure 9-31
Data Extraction - Refine Data (Page 5 of 8); hide any blank columns

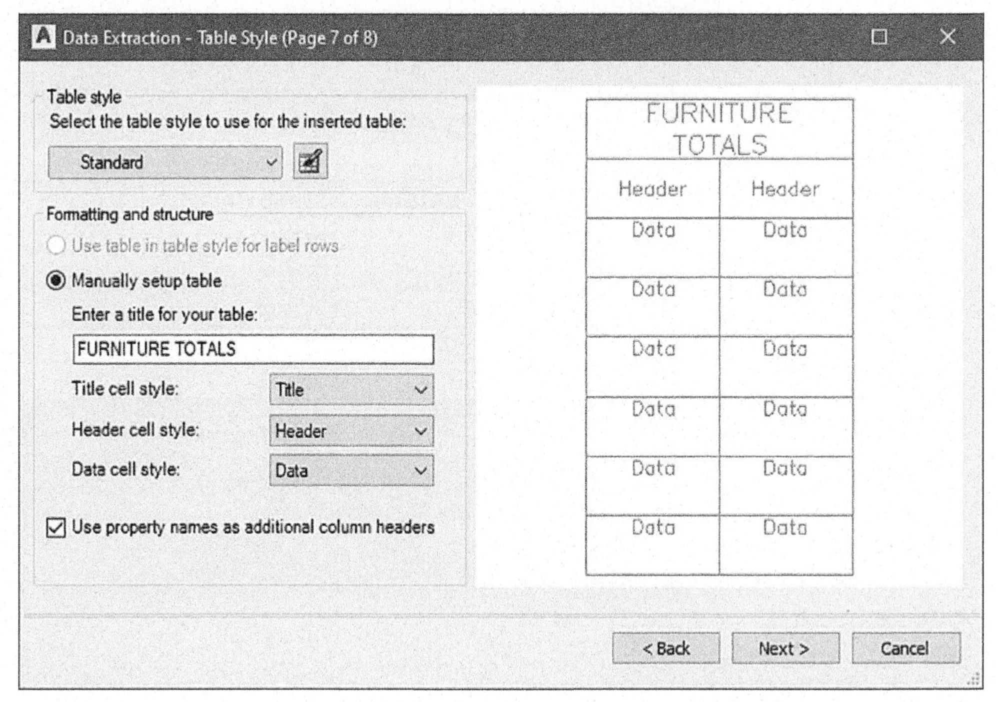

Figure 9-32
Data Extraction - Table Style (Page 7 of 8); name the table **FURNITURE TOTALS**

Prompt	**Response**
	Click **Next**
Finish (Page 8 of 8) appears:	Click **Finish**
Specify insertion point:	Click **a point** to locate the table

Step 5. Align DESC, FINISH, Name, PROD, and SIZE columns middle left (Figure 9-33), as described next:

Prompt	**Response**
Type a command:	Click the open area to the right in the first cell under the **Name** column to start a crossing window and move your mouse to the left and down so your crossing window selects all cells in the **Name** column but DOES NOT CROSS THE BOTTOM LINE OF THE TABLE
	Select **Middle Left** (Figure 9-33) on the ribbon **Table Cell** tab, **Cell Styles** panel

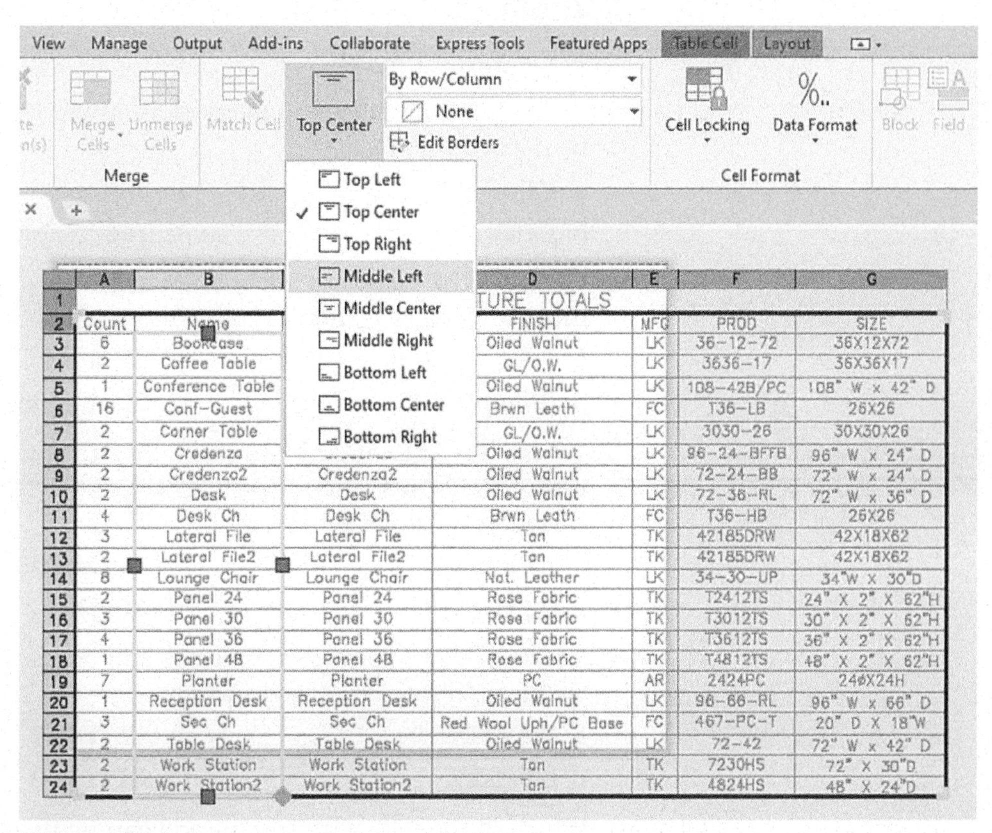

Figure 9-33
Align columns middle left

Step 6. Align the DESC, FINISH, PROD, and SIZE columns middle left.

Step 7. Use the **Reference** option of the **SCALE** command to scale the long side (the horizontal side) of the table to **10″**.

Step 8. Move the table if necessary so it is centered in the viewport.

Step 9. When you have completed Exercise 9-2, add your name, class, and current date to the drawing and save your work in at least two places.

Step 10. Print the Furniture Totals layout at a scale of **1:1** on an **11″ × 8-1/2″** sheet.

9 chapternine

Chapter Summary

This chapter provided you the information necessary to set up and draw furniture installation plans. In addition, you learned to assign attributes and extract data from furniture installation plans. Now you have the skills and information necessary to produce furniture installation plans that can be used in interior design. You also are able to extract data that can be used to count and specify furniture.

Chapter Test Questions

Multiple Choice

Circle the correct answer.

1. In which of the following parts of an attribute definition may spaces **not** be used?

   a. Value   c. Prompt
   b. Default value   d. Tag

2. Which of the following parts of an attribute appear on the inserted furniture symbol when the attribute mode is not **Invisible**?

   a. Tag   c. Value
   b. Prompt   d. Block name

3. To use the **Edit Attributes** dialog box to change or accept default values of attributes when inserting wblocks, which of the following system variables must be set to 1?

   a. **ATTREQ**   c. **ATTMODE**
   b. **ATTDIA**   d. **AUPREC**

4. Which of the following commands can be used to make invisible all the visible attributes on the drawing?

   a. **WATTEDIT**   c. **ATTEDIT**
   b. **ATTEXT**   d. **ATTDISP**

5. Which of the following commands can be used to edit variable, verify, and preset attribute values of an inserted block using a dialog box?

   a. **ATTEXT**   c. **EATTEDIT**
   b. **ATTDEF**   d. **ATTDISP**

Matching

Write the number of the correct answer on the line.

a. **Data Extraction** ______

b. **Define Attributes...** ______

1. A command that allows you to assign attributes to a furniture symbol
2. A command that can be used to produce a parts list or bill of materials

c. **WBLOCK** ______

d. **ATTDISP** ______

e. Value ______

3. A command that is used to save a part of a drawing with defined attributes
4. A part of an attribute that appears on an inserted block
5. A command that makes all attributes appear visible

True or False

Circle the correct answer.

1. **True or False:** AutoCAD can automatically align an attribute definition below one that was defined with the previous **Define Attributes... (ATTDEF)** command.
2. **True or False:** The **Edit Attribute, Single... (EATTEDIT)** command uses the **Enhanced Attribute** dialog box to edit variable, verify, and preset attribute values of one inserted block at a time.
3. **True or False:** The existing variable attributes on a drawing become constant when a block with attributes is redefined.
4. **True or False:** The **Synchronize Attributes (ATTSYNC)** command does *not* allow you to select each redefined block whose attributes you want to update to the current redefined attributes.
5. **True or False:** The **Properties** palette is used to extract attributes from a drawing.

List

1. Five ways of accessing a block's **Define Attributes...** command.
2. Five **Mode** options in the **Attribute Definition** dialog box.
3. Five **Attribute** fields in the **Attribute Definition** dialog box.
4. Five ways of accessing a block's **Edit Attributes** command.
5. Five options of the **Attribute Definition** dialog box when the **Quick Properties** toggle in **ON**.
6. Five ways of accessing the **Insert Block** command.
7. Five command line key-ins that begin with "ATT."
8. Five ways of accessing the **Block Attribute Manager (BATTMAN)**.
9. Five ways of accessing the **Data Extraction** command.
10. Five reasons why blocks with attributes and **Data Extraction** from a drawing are desirable.

Questions

1. What are attributes and when should they be used?
2. How can blocks with attributes be used to make a furniture installation plan?
3. What are the uses of the **Data Extraction** command?
4. How can tables made with the **Data Extraction** command be aligned and otherwise edited?
5. What are the modes that an attribute can have and how are they used?

Chapter Projects

Project 9-1: *Hotel Room 2 Furniture Plan*
[BASIC]

1. Begin CH9-P1 on the hard drive or network drive by opening the existing hotel room 2 floor plan (Project 7-1) and saving it as **CH9-P1**. Your final drawing will look similar to Figure 9-34.

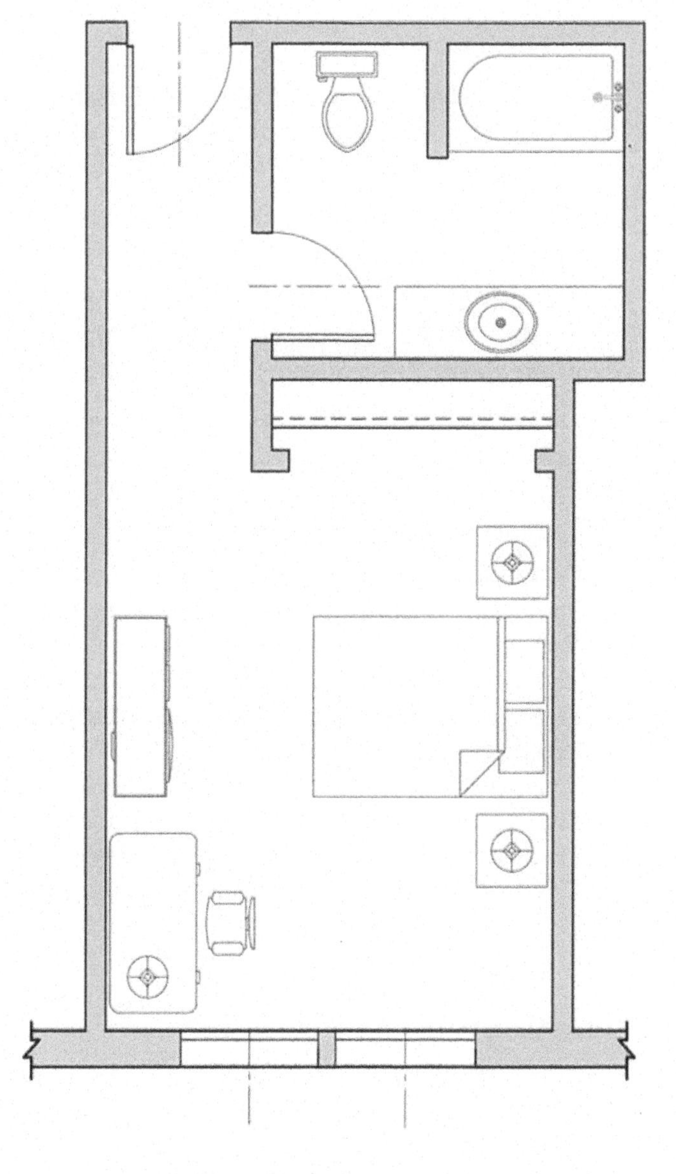

FURNITURE PLAN
SCALE: 3/16" = 1'-0"

Figure 9-34
Project 9-1: Hotel room 2 furniture plan (scale: 3/16″ = 1′-0″)

2. Set the **i-furn** layer current and turn off any layers that are not needed.

3. Select furniture from the **DesignCenter**. Place the furniture in the approximate locations shown in Figure 9-34. You will find all this furniture in the **Home - Space Planner** drawing. Use a 3/16″ = 1′-0″ architectural scale to measure any furniture you do not find, and draw it full scale.

4. Save the drawing in two places and plot or print the drawing to scale.

Project 9-2: *Hotel Room 1 Furniture Plan*
[BASIC]

1. Begin CH9-P2 on the hard drive or network drive by opening the existing hotel room 1 floor plan (Exercise 6-2) and saving it as **CH9-P2**. Your final drawing will look similar to Figure 9-35.

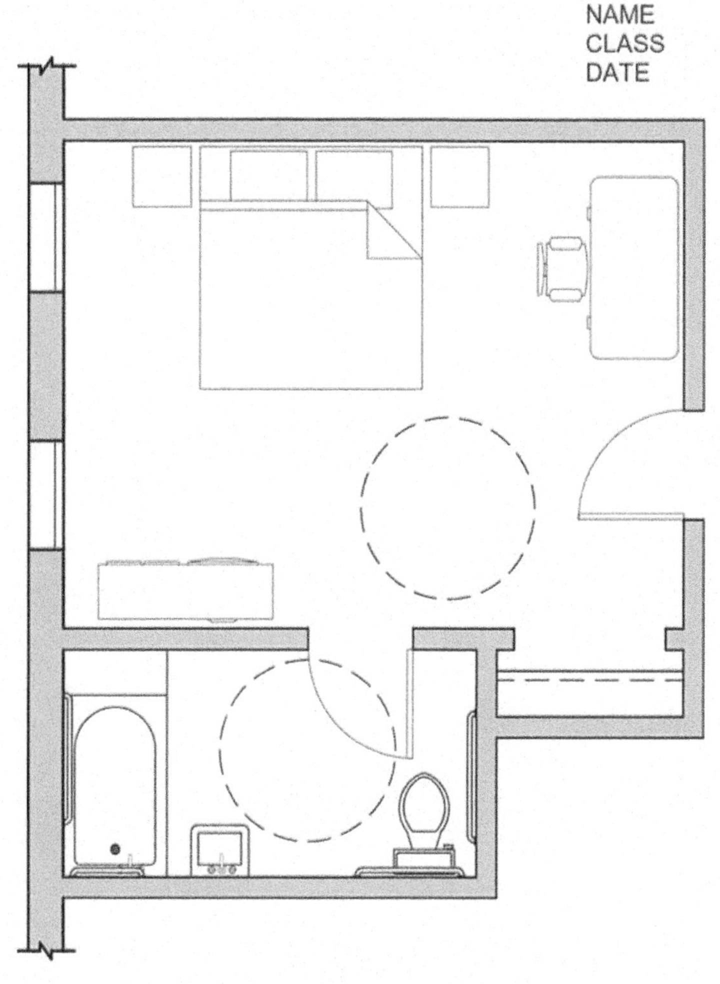

Figure 9-35
Project 9-2: Hotel room 1 furniture plan (scale: 1/4″ = 1′-0″)

2. Set the **i-furn** layer current and turn off any layers that are not needed.
3. Select furniture from the **DesignCenter**. Place the furniture in the approximate locations shown in Figure 9-35. You will find all this furniture in the **Home - Space Planner** drawing.
4. Save the drawing in two places and plot or print the drawing to scale.

chapter ten

DesignCenter, Dynamic Blocks, and External References

CHAPTER OBJECTIVES

- Correctly use the following commands and settings:

Attach External Reference (XATTACH)
Block Editor (BE)
DesignCenter (DC)
(Xref Bind) XBIND
External Reference (XREF)
Set Base Point (BASE)

Introduction

In this chapter, you will use the AutoCAD **DesignCenter** to copy layers and blocks (furniture) from one drawing to another. You will also make blocks that perform actions dynamically. Finally, you will use external reference commands that allow you to attach drawings to other drawings so that they appear in the primary, or host, drawing without becoming part of it.

EXERCISE 10-1
Reception Area Furniture Installation Plan Using DesignCenter

When you have completed Exercise 10-1, your drawing will look similar to Figure 10-3 without dimensions.

Step 1. Use your workspace to make the following settings:

1. Use **Save As...** to save the drawing with the name **CH10-EXERCISE1**.
2. Set drawing units: **Architectural**
3. Set drawing limits: **44′,34′**
4. Set **GRIDDISPLAY**: **0**
5. Set grid: **12″**
6. Set snap: **6″**

The DesignCenter

DesignCenter: A floating palette that allows you to use existing blocks and other named objects from other drawing files. Drag and drop blocks, layers, linetypes, lineweights, text and dimension styles, and external references from any existing drawing. Search for drawings and other files.

AutoCAD's ***DesignCenter*** allows you to do the following:

- Use existing blocks arranged in categories that AutoCAD has provided.
- Use blocks, layers, linetypes, text and dimension styles, and external references from any existing drawing using the drag-and-drop technique.
- Examine drawings and blocks as either drawing names or pictures.
- Search for drawings and other files.

Step 2. Open DesignCenter and examine it, as described next:

DESIGNCENTER	
Ribbon/ Panel	View/ Palettes
Standard Toolbar:	
Menu Bar:	Tools/ Palettes/ Design Center
Type a Command:	ADCENTER
Command Alias:	DC
Keyboard:	<Ctrl>+2

Prompt	**Response**
Type a command:	**DesignCenter** (or press **<Ctrl+2>**, or type **DC <Enter>**)
The **DesignCenter** palette appears:	Look at the bottom of Figure 10-1. Use the same or similar path to locate the **DesignCenter** folder Click **Home - Space Planner.dwg**
DesignCenter shows the blocks and other items in the **Home - Space Planner.dwg** (Figure 10-1). Your **DesignCenter** may appear different, depending on what is selected in the **Views** icon or **Tree View Toggle** at the top of DesignCenter.	Click **Blocks**
All the predefined blocks for the drawing appear.	

You can now click on any of these drawings, hold down the left mouse button, drag the drawing into the current drawing, and drop it. However, do not do that for this exercise. You will use layers and blocks from CH9-EXERCISE1 to complete CH10-EXERCISE1. Let's look at the parts of DesignCenter.

DesignCenter Tabs

The tabs at the top of DesignCenter allow you to access all the following options of DesignCenter:

Folders tab: Shows you the folders existing on the hard drive of your computer.

Open Drawings tab: Shows you the drawings that are currently open.

History tab: Shows you a list of the most recently opened drawings.

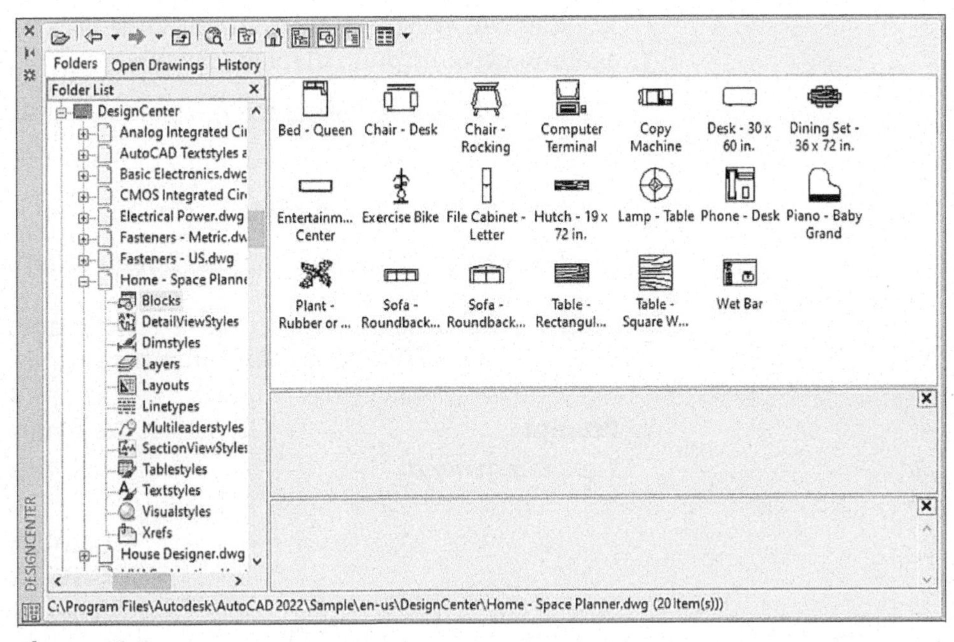

Figure 10-1
The **DesignCenter Home - Space Planner** drawing

DesignCenter Buttons

Now, examine the buttons above the tabs. They are listed next, starting from the first one on the left. Click the **Folders** tab to display all the icons.

Load: Allows you to load drawings and other items that you want to use in your current drawing.

Back: Returns you to the previous screen.

Forward: Sends you forward from a screen obtained from clicking back.

Up: Sends you to the next higher folder structure.

Search: Allows you to search for and locate data you need.

Favorites: Shows what you have in the **Favorites** folder. You can save your most-often-used items here.

Home: Returns you to the default starting folder.

Tree View Toggle: Displays and hides the tree view. The tree view shows the structure of the files and folders in the form of a chart, the area on the left.

Preview: Allows you to look at a preview of any selected item. If there is no preview image saved with the selected item, the **Preview** area will be empty.

Description: Shows a text description of any selected item.

Views: Provides you with different display formats for the selected items.

You can select a view from the **View** list or choose the **View** button again to cycle through display formats:

Large Icons: Shows the names of loaded items with large icons.

Small Icons: Shows the names of loaded items with small icons.

List: Shows a list of loaded items.

Details: Places a name for each item in an alphabetical list.

Step 3. Use DesignCenter to load **i-furn**, **a-door**, and **a-wall-intr** layers from **CH9-EXERCISE1** into the new drawing, as described next:

Prompt	**Response**
Type a command:	Click **Load**
	Click locate drawing **CH9-EXERCISE1** and double-click **CH9-EXERCISE1**
	Click **Layers** (on the left)
The display (Figure 10-2) appears:	Click layer **a-door**, hold down the pick button, drag it into the current drawing (to the right of DesignCenter), and release the pick button
	Repeat the previous for layers **i-furn** and **a-wall-intr**
	Close DesignCenter

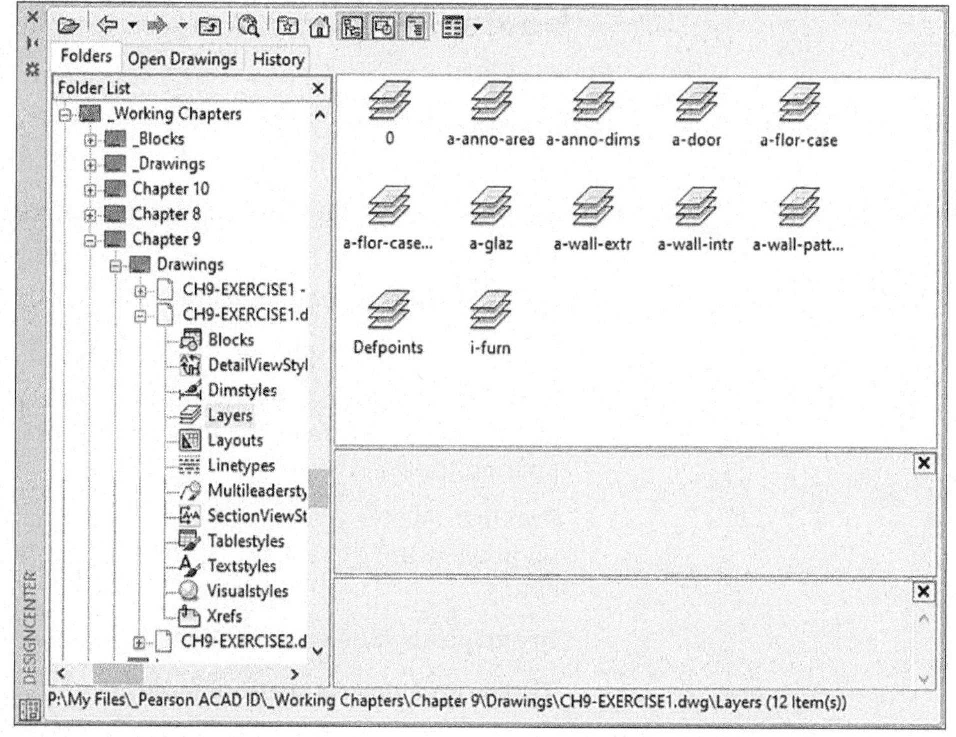

Figure 10-2
Layers in CH9-EXERCISE1

Step 4. Set layer **a-wall-intr** current.

Step 5. Use **Polyline** to draw the outside walls of the reception area using the dimensions from Figure 10-3. Set an offset of 5″ for the wall thickness.

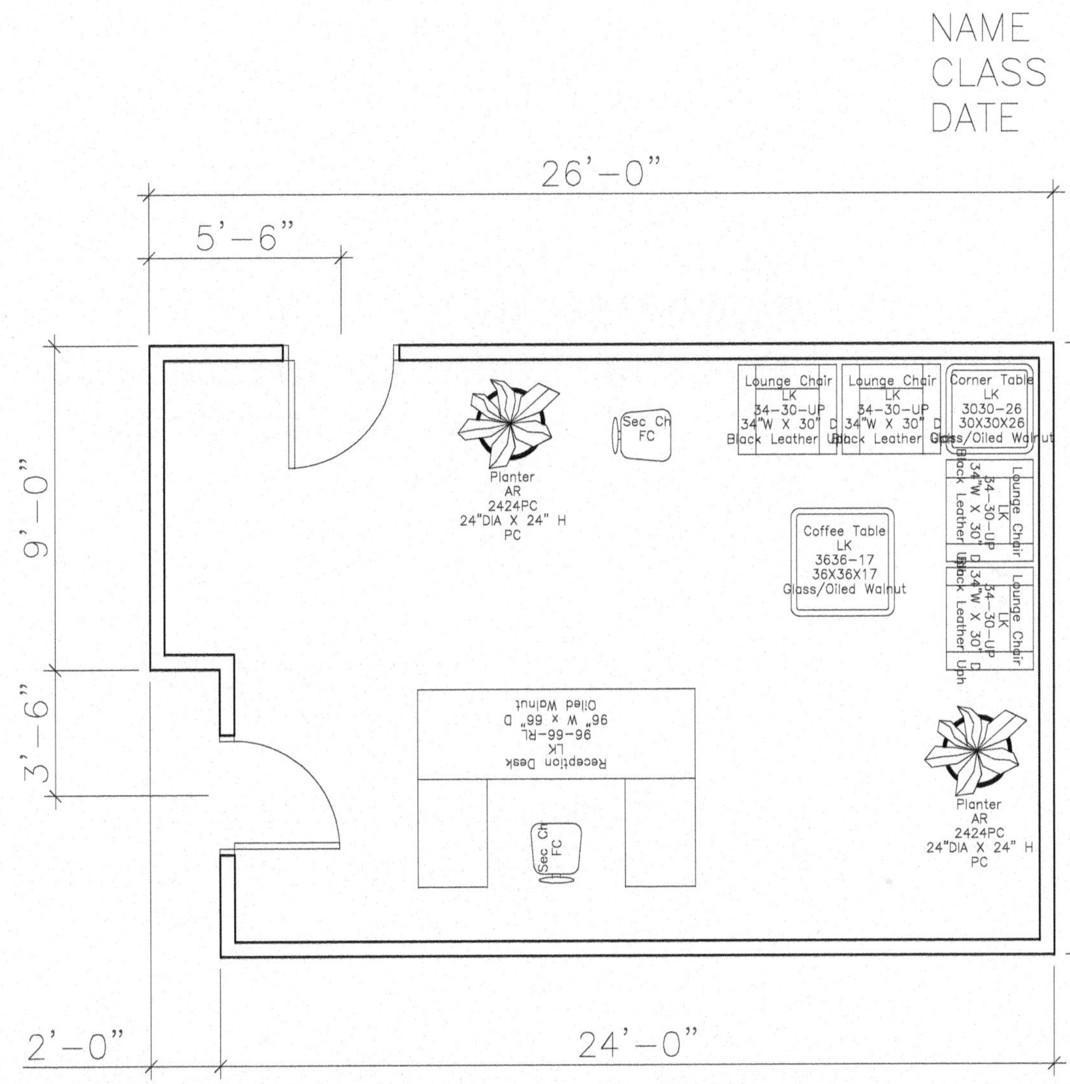

NAME
CLASS
DATE

26'-0"
5'-6"
9'-0"
3'-6"
17'-0"
2'-0"
24'-0"

Lounge Chair LK 34-30-UP 34"W X 30" D Black Leather Uph
Corner Table LK 3030-26 30X30X26 Glass/Oiled Walnut
Sec Ch FC
Planter AR 2424PC 24"DIA X 24" H PC
Coffee Table LK 3636-17 36X36X17 Glass/Oiled Walnut
Reception Desk LK 96-66-RL 96" W x 66" D Oiled Walnut

Figure 10-3
Dimensions for Exercise 10-1 (scale: 3/16″ = 1′-0″)

Step 6. Set layer **a-door** current.

Step 7. Open DesignCenter and click **Blocks** under **CH9-EXERCISE1.** Find the block named **DOOR** and drag and drop it into the current drawing.

Step 8. Use the **MIRROR** and **ROTATE** commands if necessary to correctly position the door.

Step 9. Place doors in the correct locations using the dimensions from Figure 10-3.

Step 10. Use the **TRIM** command to trim the walls from the door openings.

Step 11. Set layer **i-furn** current.

Step 12. Click **Blocks** under **CH9-EXERCISE1;** find the blocks named **Planter, Corner Table, Coffee Table, Reception Desk, Sec Ch,**

and **Lounge Chair**; and drag and drop them into the current drawing.

Step 13. Place furniture in the approximate locations shown in Figure 10-3.

Step 14. When you have completed Exercise 10-1, add your name, class, and the current date to the drawing in the upper right and save your work in at least two places.

Step 15. Print Exercise 10-1 to scale.

EXERCISE 10-2 Training Room Furniture Installation Plan Using DesignCenter and Dynamic Blocks

When you have completed Exercise 10-2, your drawing will look similar to Figure 10-4.

Step 1. Use your workspace to make the following settings:

1. Open drawing **CH3-EXERCISE2** and save it to the hard drive with the name **CH10-EXERCISE2**.
2. Erase all furniture and the door so that only the walls remain.
3. Set layer **a-door** current.

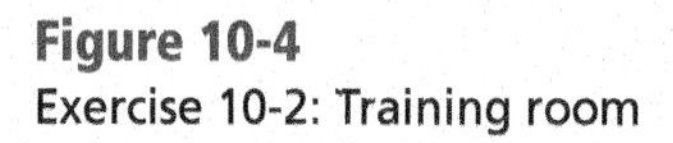

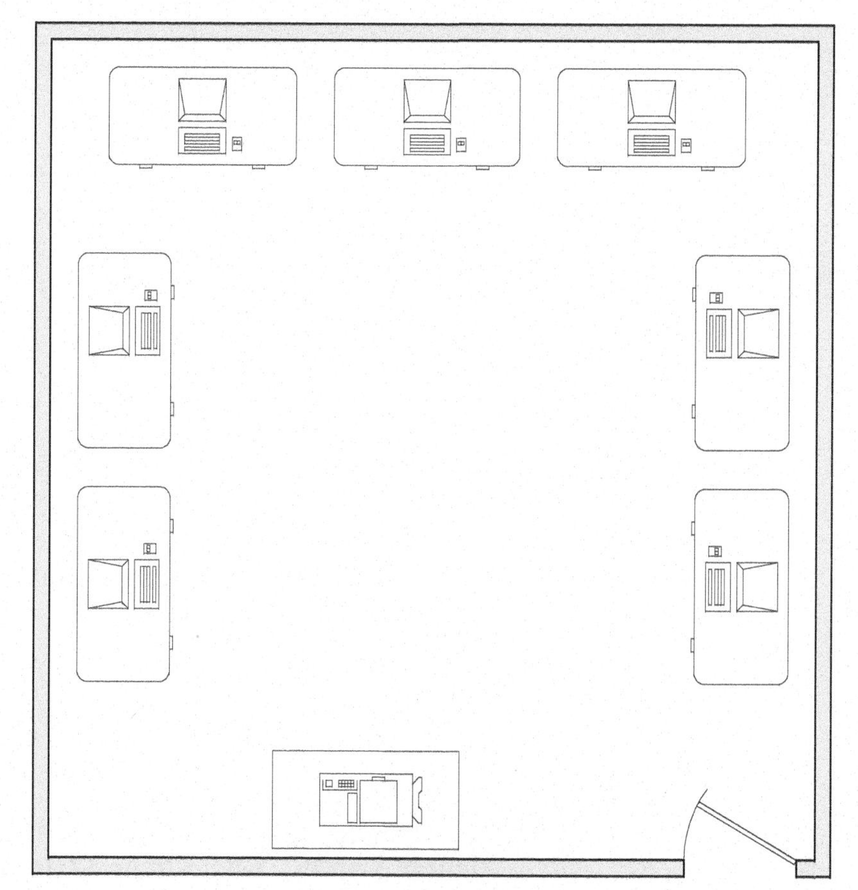

Figure 10-4
Exercise 10-2: Training room

Step 2. Use a block from the **DesignCenter - House Designer** drawing to draw a new door, as described next:

Prompt	Response
Type a command:	**DesignCenter** (or type **DC <Enter>**)
DesignCenter appears	Look at the bottom of Figure 10-5; use the same or similar path to locate the **DesignCenter** folder
	Click **House Designer.dwg**
The available items in the **House Designer** drawing appear:	Double-click **Blocks** and click **Large Icons** in the **Views** list, as shown in Figure 10-6
	Click **Tree View Toggle** to remove the tree view
	Click on the **Door - Right Hung 36 in.** icon and continue to hold down the left mouse button (Figure 10-7). Drag the door off DesignCenter and use **Osnap-Endpoint** to place it as shown in Figure 10-8

Step 3. Set the **i-furn layer** current.

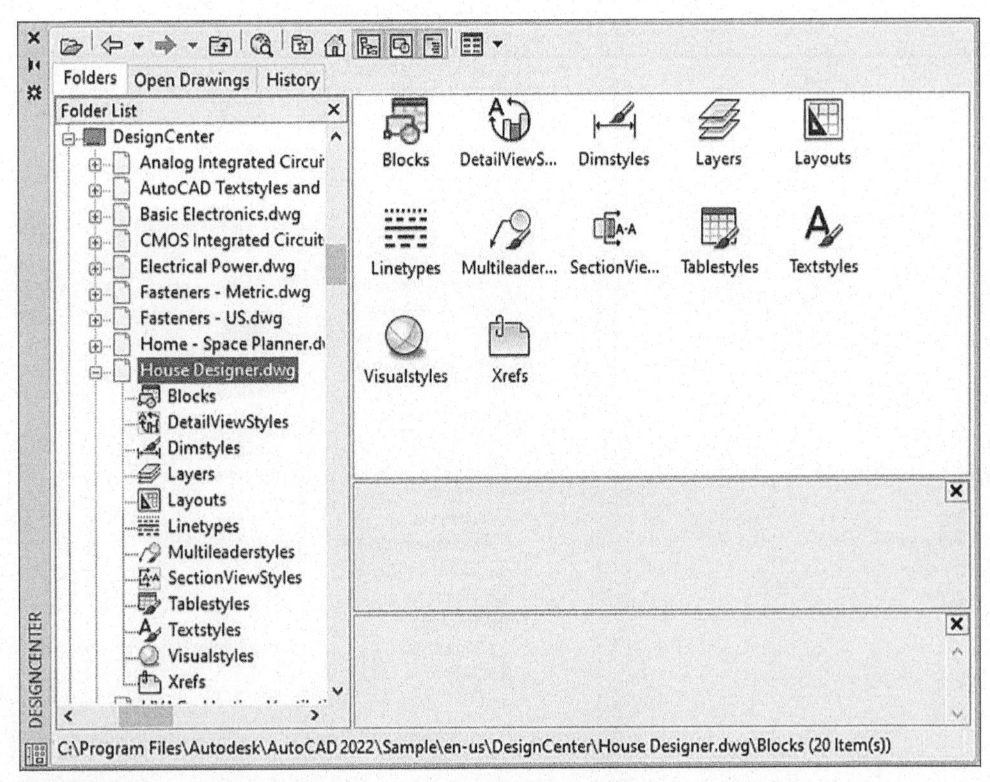

Figure 10-5
Locate **House Designer** blocks

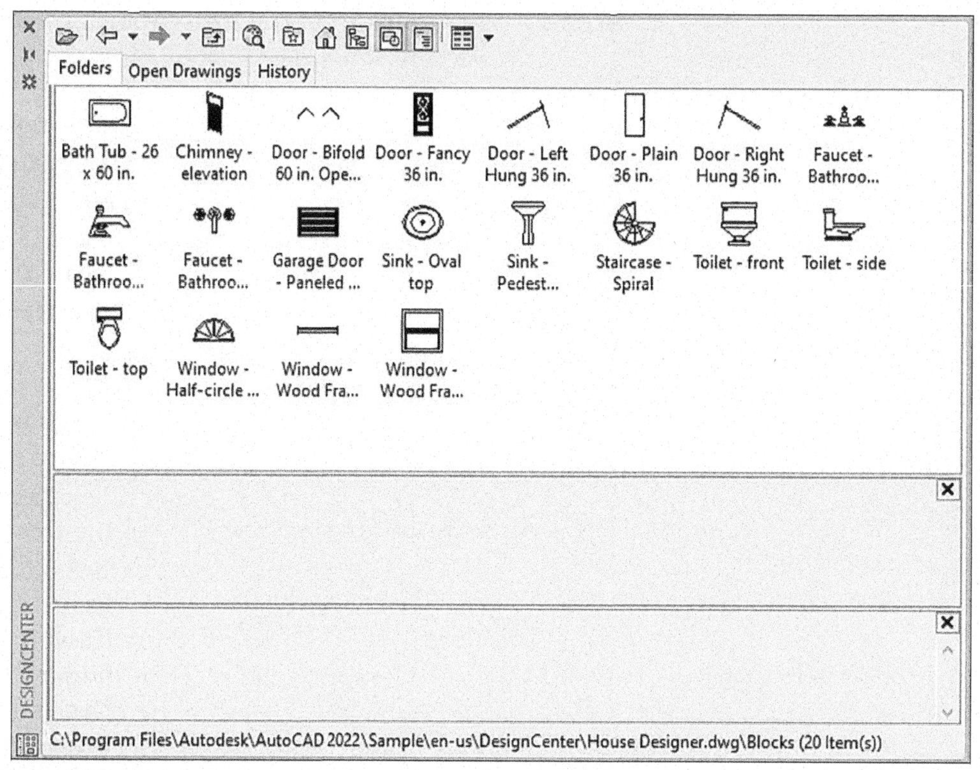

Figure 10-6
Click **Blocks** and **Large Icons** in the **Views** list. Click **Tree View Toggle**

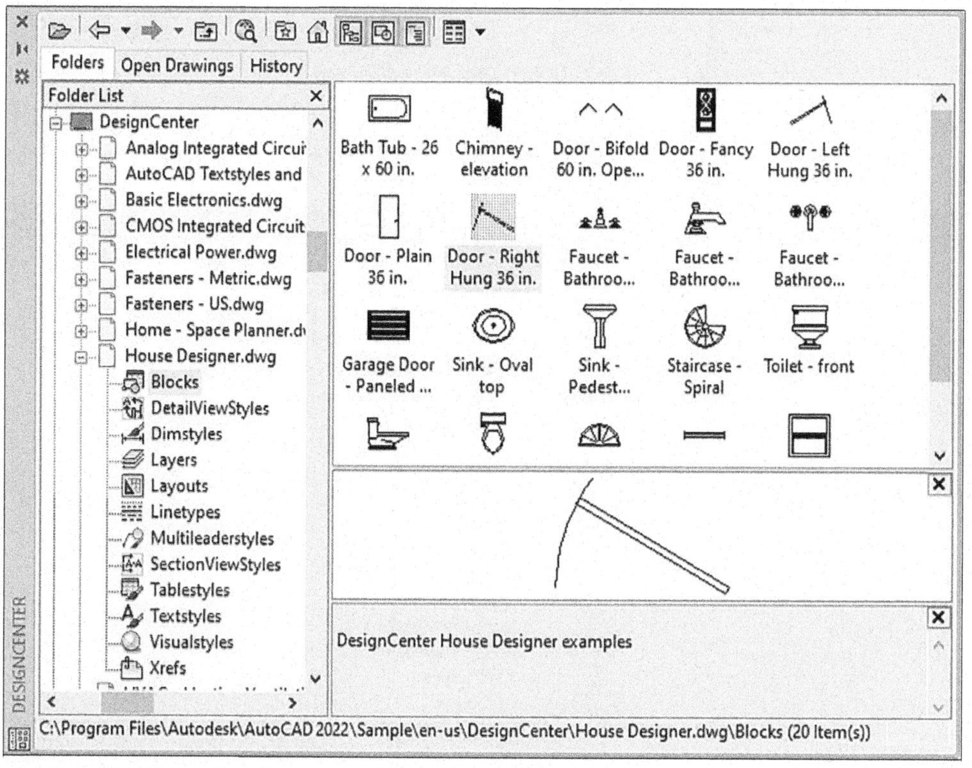

Figure 10-7
Click the **Door - Right Hung 36 in.** Hold down the left mouse button and drag the door off DesignCenter

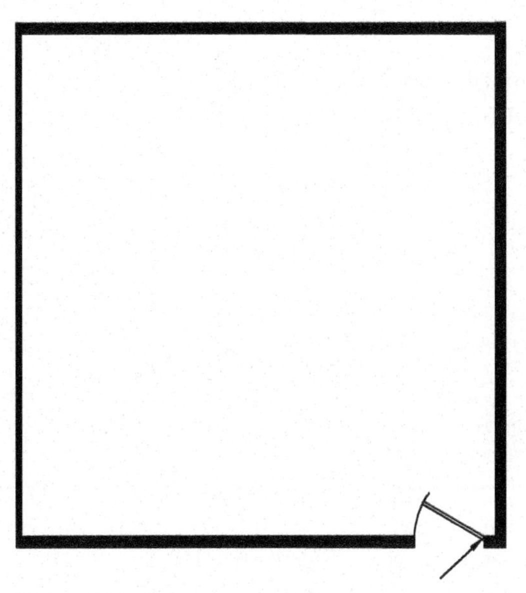

Figure 10-8
Use **Osnap-Endpoint** to place the door in the opening

Step 4. Drag and drop blocks from the **Home - Space Planner** drawing to create furniture in the training room, as described next:

Prompt	Response
Type a command:	Click **Tree View Toggle** to return to tree view
The left side of **DesignCenter** opens up again:	Double-click **Home - Space Planner.dwg** (Figure 10-9)

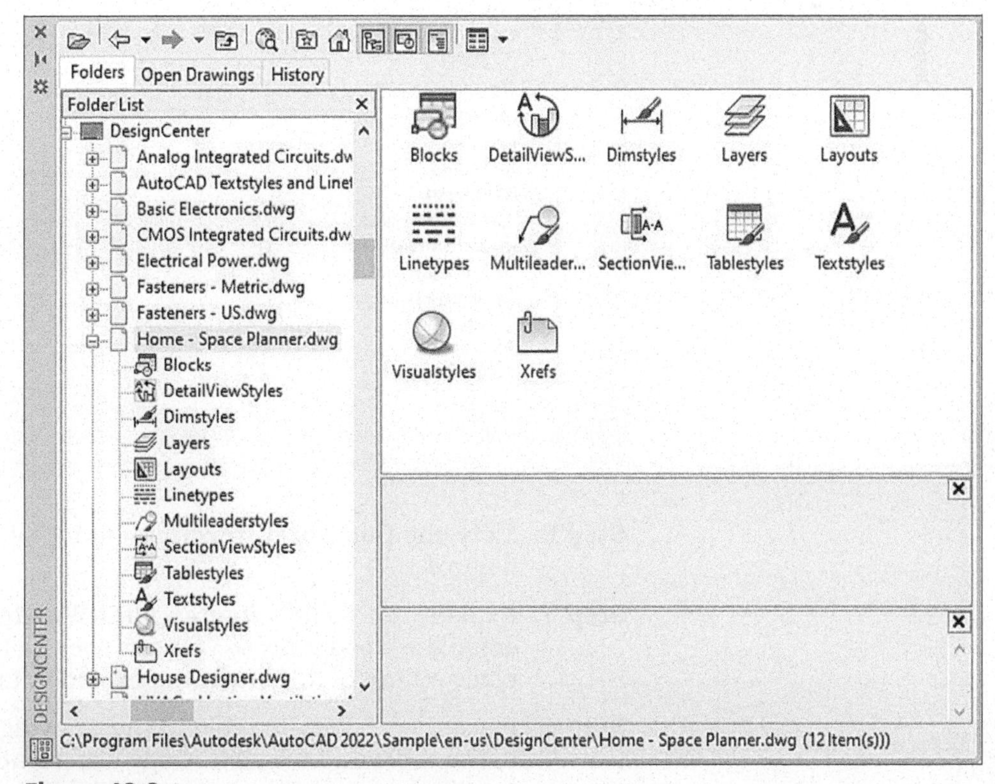

Figure 10-9
Open **Home - Space Planner** drawing

Prompt	Response
The available items in the **Home - Space Planner.dwg** appear:	Click **Blocks**
	Click on the **Desk - 30** × **60 in.** icon and continue to hold down the left mouse button as you drag the **Desk** off DesignCenter and place it on the drawing

> **TIP**
>
> To minimize DesignCenter, click on the **Auto-hide** button (the two triangles below the **X**) in the upper-left corner.

Step 5. Drag and drop the following blocks from the **Home - Space Planner** drawing (Figure 10-10):

1. **Computer Terminal**
2. **Copy Machine**
3. **Table - Rectangular Woodgrain 60 × 30 in.**

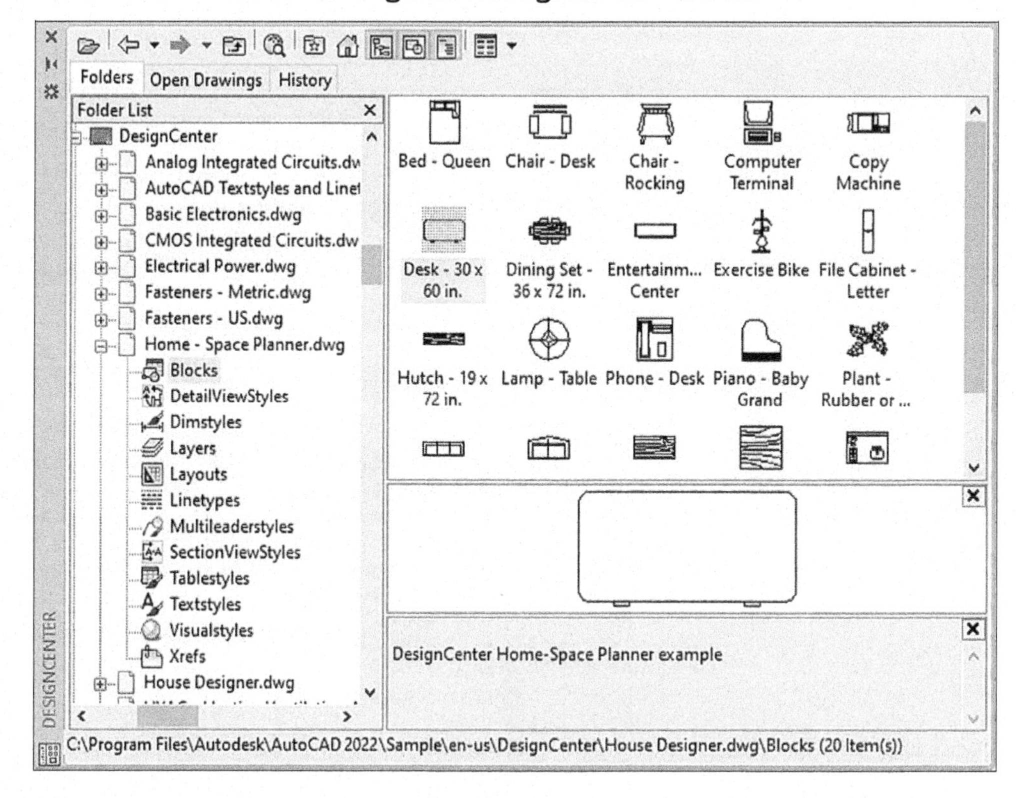

Figure 10-10
Home - Space Planner drawing blocks

Step 6. Move the **Computer Terminal** on top of the **Desk - 30 × 60 in.** (Figure 10-11).

Step 7. Explode the **Table - Rectangular Woodgrain 60 × 30 in.** and erase the woodgrain so you can see the items you are going to place on top of it. Return the exploded table to the **i-furn** layer.

Step 8. Place the woodgrain table in the drawing. Move the **Copy Machine** to the table and rotate it. Copy and rotate the desk and computer terminal so your drawing looks like Figure 10-11.

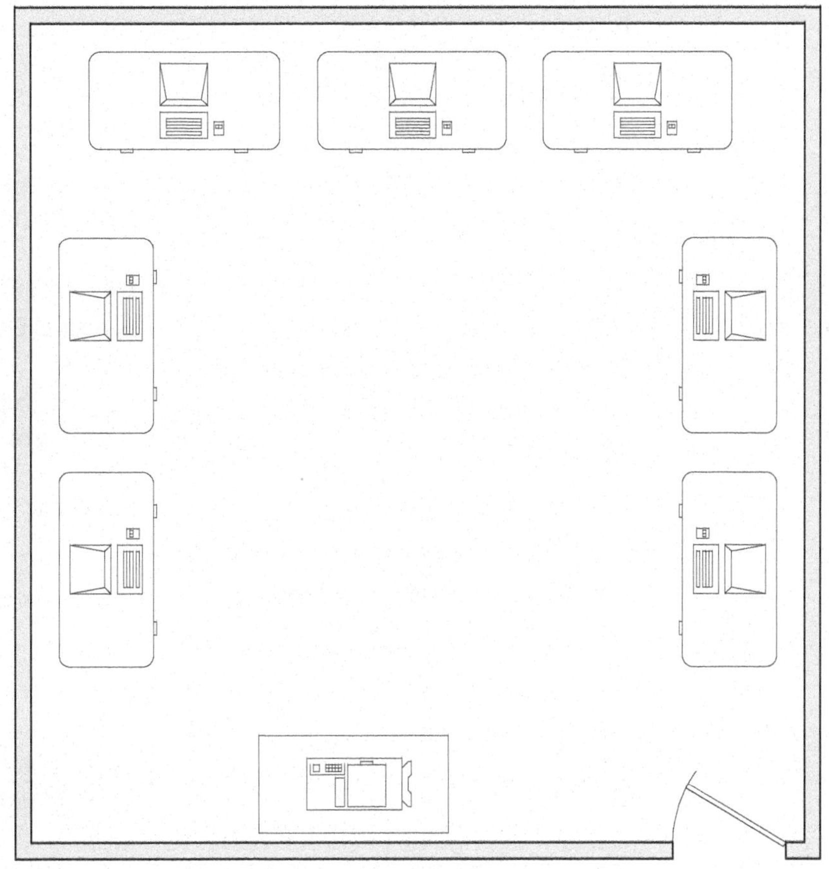

Figure 10-11
Desk, computer, copy machine, and rectangular woodgrain table with woodgrain erased

Use Block Editor to Make Dynamic Blocks

dynamic block: The user-defined collection of drawing objects that can be changed without exploding the block.

You can move part of an inserted ***dynamic block*** within the dynamic block (such as a chair within a chair-and-desk combination) without exploding the block. You can change a dynamic block insertion without exploding it. You must explode a standard inserted block before you can change it. You can also change the size of the dynamic block as you work. For example, if the desk is needed in a variety of sizes, you can define it as a dynamic block that has a parameter (a feature) that allows the width, depth, or both to be changed without exploding the block or redefining it.

BLOCK EDITOR	
Ribbon/ Panel	Insert/Block Definition/ Block Editor
Menu Bar:	Tools/ Block Editor
Type a Command:	BEDIT
Command Alias:	BE

You use the **Block Editor** to create dynamic blocks. The **Block Editor** allows you to add the elements that make a block dynamic. You can create a block from scratch, or you can add dynamic features to an existing block.

In the following part of this exercise you will redefine the existing woodgrain table as a dynamic block that can change size. You will add dynamic blocks of desk chairs that can be visible or invisible. You will also redefine the existing right-hung 36-in. door as a dynamic block that can flip from one side of the wall to the other. Start with the woodgrain table.

> **TIP**
>
> While in the **Block Editor**, you can zoom in and out.

Step 13. Use the **Block Editor** to add a linear parameter to the woodgrain table (so you can easily change the length) as described next:

Prompt	Response
Type a command:	**Block Editor** (or type **BE <Enter>**)
The **Edit Block Definition** dialog box appears:	Click **Table - Rectangular Woodgrain 60 × 30 in.** (Figure 10-12)
	Click **OK**
The table appears with woodgrain. You are in the **Block Editor** environment—notice the **Block Editor** tab in the ribbon is highlighted.	Erase the woodgrain
	Click the **Parameters** tab of the **Block Authoring Palettes**
	Click **Linear**
Specify start point or [Name Label Chain Description Base Palette Value set]:	Click **Osnap-Endpoint**, the upper-left corner of the table
Specify endpoint:	Click **Osnap-Endpoint**, the upper-right corner of the table

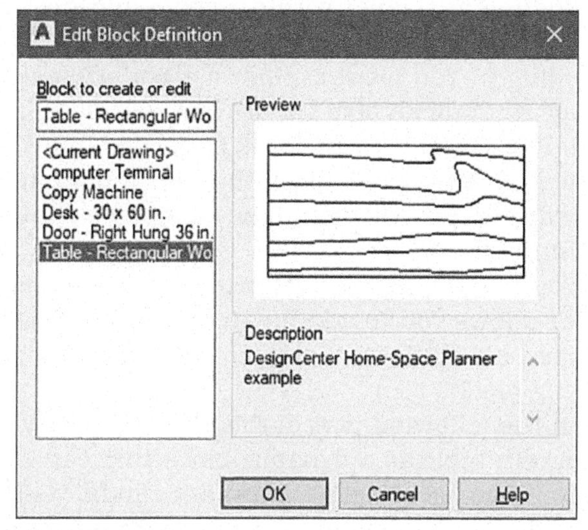

Figure 10-12
Click **Table - Rectangular Woodgrain 60 × 30 in.** in the list of blocks

Prompt	Response
Specify label location:	Click to place the label (**Distance1**) as shown in Figure 10-13
	Click the **Actions** tab of the **Block Authoring Palettes**
	Click **Stretch**
Select parameter:	Click **Distance1** (on the top of the table)
Specify parameter point to associate with action or enter [sTart point Second point] <Start>:	Click the arrow on the upper-right corner of the table
Specify first corner of stretch frame or [CPolygon]:	Click **P1→** (Figure 10-14)
Specify opposite corner:	Click **P2→** (Figure 10-14)
Specify objects to stretch:	Click **P3→**
Select objects:	Click **P4→**
Select objects:	Click **P5→**
Select objects:	**<Enter>**

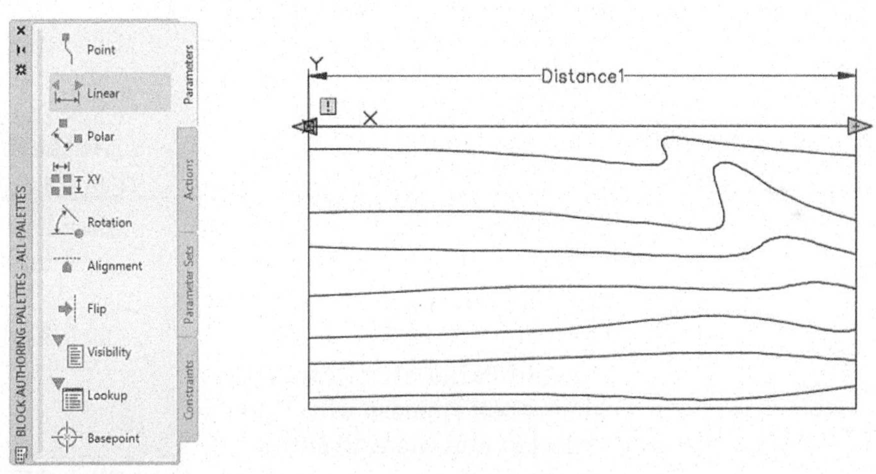

Figure 10-13
Add a linear parameter to the table length

Step 14. Add a lookup parameter and a lookup action that will appear when the block is inserted (so you can just click a number, and the block becomes longer or shorter) as described next:

Prompt	Response
	Click the **Parameters** tab of the **Block Authoring Palettes**
	Click **Lookup**

Figure 10-14
Add the stretch action to the linear parameter

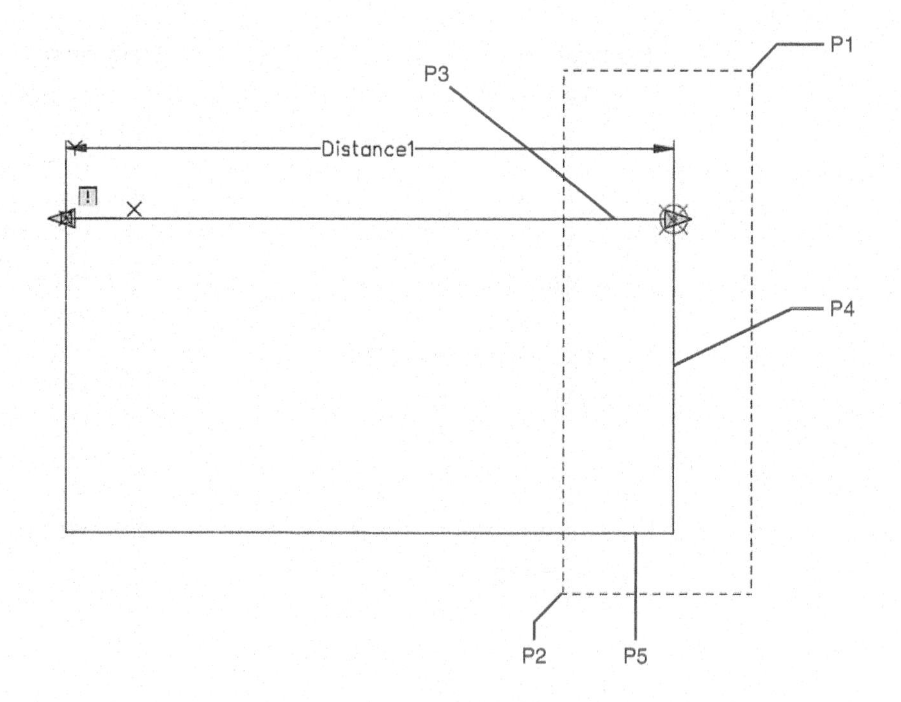

Prompt	**Response**
Specify parameter location or [Name Label Description Palette]:	Click a point close to the table above it (Figure 10-15)
	Click the **Actions** tab of the **Block Authoring Palettes**
	Click **Lookup**
Select parameter:	Click the **Lookup1** parameter you just made
The **Property Lookup Table** appears:	Click **Add Properties...**
The **Add Parameter Properties** dialog box appears with **Linear** selected and the **Add input properties** check box selected.	Click **OK**

Figure 10-15
Locating parameters and actions

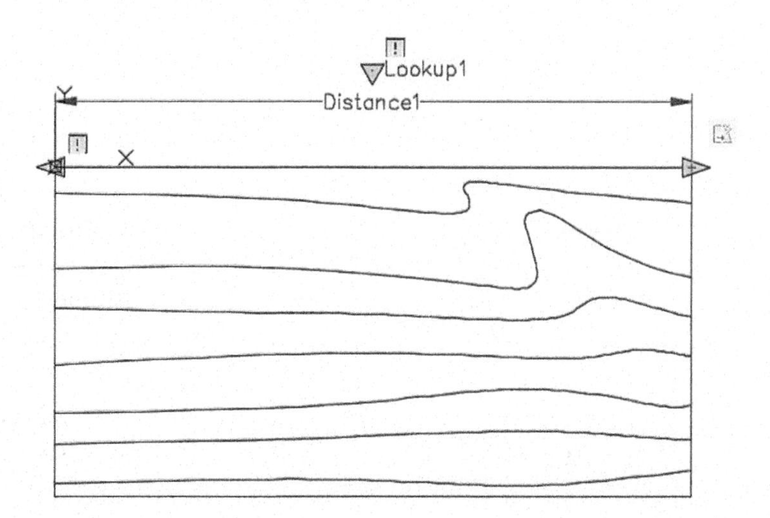

Prompt	Response
The **Property Lookup Table** appears:	Type the properties shown in Figure 10-16; be sure both columns are identical, and then press **<Enter>**
	Click **Audit** (if both columns are identical, you will get the message that no errors were found)
	Click **Close**
	Click **OK** (to exit the **Property Lookup Table**)
	Click **Save Block As** (or type **BSAVEAS <Enter>**)
The **Save Block As** dialog box appears:	In the **Block Name** box, type **Table 5′-5′6″-6′**
	Click **OK**

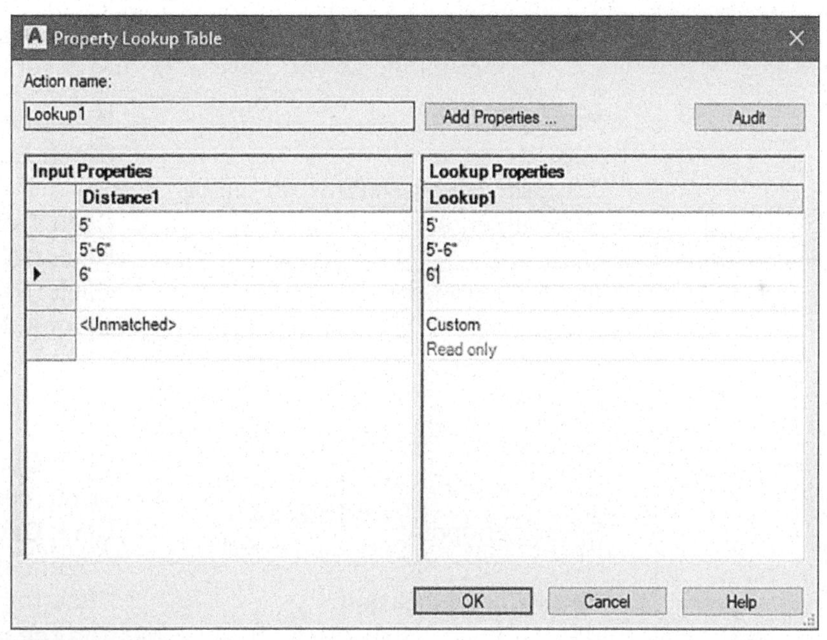

Figure 10-16
Lookup properties for **Lookup1** action

Step 15. Click **Close Block Editor** and insert your dynamic block as described next:

Prompt	Response
The **Block Editor** is open.	Type **BC <Enter>** or **Close Block Editor**
The current drawing appears:	**Erase** the copier table (do not erase the copier)
Type a command:	Type **I <Enter>**
The **Insert** dialog box appears:	Select: **Table 5′-5′6″-6′**
	Click **OK**

Prompt	Response
Specify insertion point or [Basepoint Scale X Y Z Rotate]:	Click a point to replace the copier table you just erased and press **<Enter>**. Click any point on a line of the inserted table
	Click the **Lookup** symbol, Figure 10-17 (to see the three sizes)

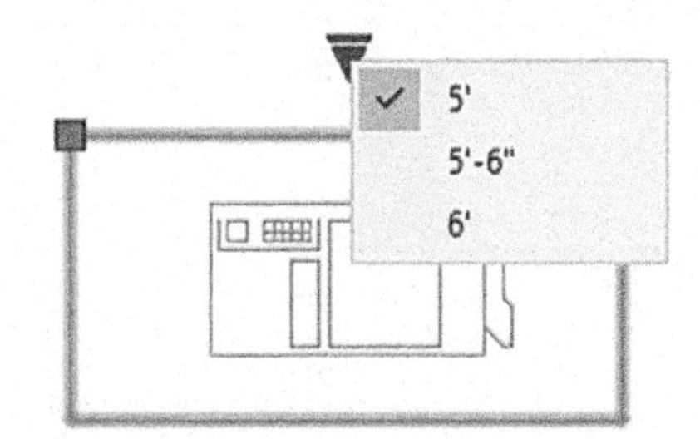

Figure 10-17
Insert the dynamic block and click the **Lookup** symbol

Step 16. You can now click on any of the three numbers, and the block changes length. Change the length to **5′6″**.

Step 17. Press the **<Esc>** key to get rid of the block parameters.

Step 18. Add a linear parameter to make the depth of the copier table dynamic so you have 2′-6″ and 3′ table depths, as described next:

Prompt	Response
Type a command:	**Block Editor** (or type **BE <Enter>**)
The **Edit Block Definition** dialog box appears:	Click **Table 5′-5′6″-6′**
	Click **OK**
The table appears:	Click the **Parameters** tab of the **Block Authoring Palettes**
	Click **Linear**
Specify start point or [Name Label Chain Description Base Palette Value set]:	Click **Osnap-Endpoint**, the lower-right corner of the table
Specify endpoint:	Click **Osnap-Endpoint**, the upper-right corner of the table
Specify label location:	Click to place the label (**Distance2**) on the right side of the table (Figure 10-18)

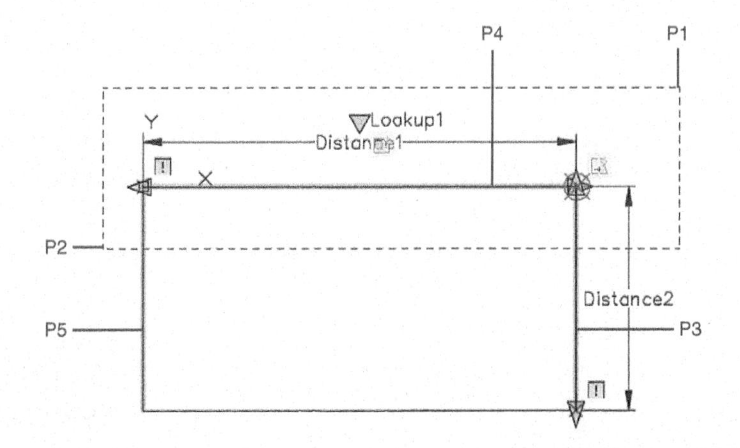

Figure 10-18
Add the stretch and lookup actions to the linear parameter **Distance2**

Prompt	Response
	Click the **Actions** tab of the **Block Authoring Palettes**
	Click **Stretch**
Select parameter:	Click **Distance2** (on the right side of the table)
Specify parameter point to associate with action or enter [sTartpoint Second point] <Start>:	Click the arrow on the upper-right corner of the table
Specify first corner of stretch frame or [CPolygon]:	Click **P1→** (Figure 10-18)
Specify opposite corner:	Click **P2→** (Figure 10-18)
Specify objects to stretch:	Click **P3→**
Select objects: 1 found	Click **P4→**
Select objects: 1 found, 2 total	Click **P5→**
Select objects: 1 found, 3 total	**<Enter>**

Step 19. Add a lookup parameter and a lookup action that will appear when the block is inserted (so you can just click a number, and the block becomes more or less deep), as described next:

Prompt	Response
	Click the **Parameters** tab of the **Block Authoring Palettes**
	Click **Lookup**
Specify parameter location or [Name Label Description Palette]:	Click a point above and to the left of the table (Figure 10-18)
	Click the **Actions** tab of the **Block Authoring Palettes**
	Click **Lookup**
Select parameter:	Click the **Lookup2** parameter you just made
The **Property Lookup Table** appears:	Click **Add Properties...**
The **Add Parameter Properties** dialog box appears with **Linear** selected and the **Add input properties** check box selected:	Click **Linear1**
	Click **OK**
The **Property Lookup Table** appears:	Type the properties shown in Figure 10-19; be sure both columns are identical and click **<Enter>**
	Click **Audit** (if both columns are identical, you will get the message that no errors were found)
	Click **Close**
	Click **OK** (to exit the **Property Lookup Table**)
	Click **Save Block As** (or type **BSAVEAS <Enter>**)

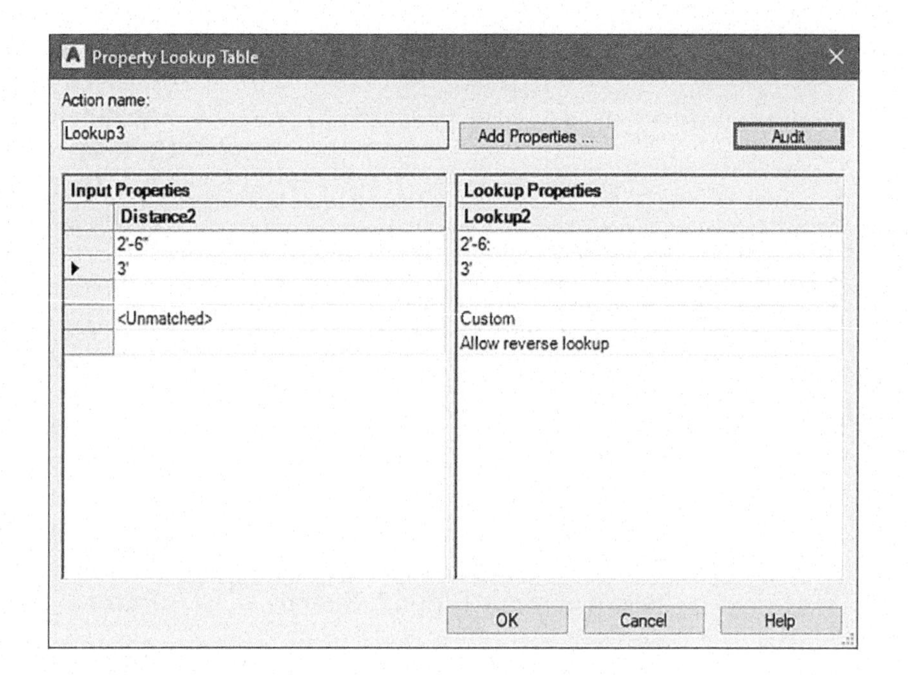

Figure 10-19
Lookup properties for **Lookup3** action

Prompt	Response
The **Save Block As** dialog box appears:	Click **Table 5′-5′6″-6′** (so it appears in the **Block Name** area)
	Click **OK**
The AutoCAD warning appears:	
Block name: is already defined as a block.	
What do you want to do?	Click **Redefine block**
The AutoCAD warning appears:	
Block—Save parameter changes?	Click **Save the changes**

Step 20. On your own, close the **Block Editor**, erase the previous **Table 5′-5′6″-6′** block, and insert the new dynamic block.

Step 21. Click any point on the inserted copier table and click the **Lookup** symbol showing depth.

Step 22. You can now click on any of the two numbers, and the block changes depth. Change the length to 5′6″ and the depth to 3′. The table is now 5′6″ × 3′ (Figure 10-20).

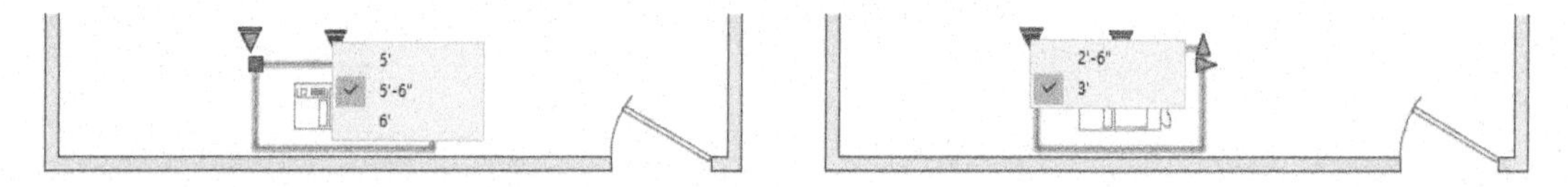

Figure 10-20
Lookup symbols for depth and length

Step 23. Press the **<Esc>** key to get rid of the block parameters.

Step 24. Make the **Sec Ch** and **Desk Ch** blocks dynamic so you can make one or the other invisible by clicking on it, as described next:

1. Open **DesignCenter** (type **DC <Enter>**). Use the **Folders** tab to open your drawing **CH9-EXERCISE1**.
2. Locate the two blocks **Sec Ch** and **Desk Ch** and insert both of them into the current drawing, **CH10-EXERCISE2**.

3. Explode both drawings and erase the attribute tags.
4. Rotate the chairs so they both face the same direction (Figure 10-21).
5. Make a block of the **Desk Ch** drawing with the name **chair1**.
6. Make a block of the **Sec Ch** drawing with the name **chair2**.
7. Open the **Block Editor**, select **chair1** (Figure 10-22), and click **OK**.

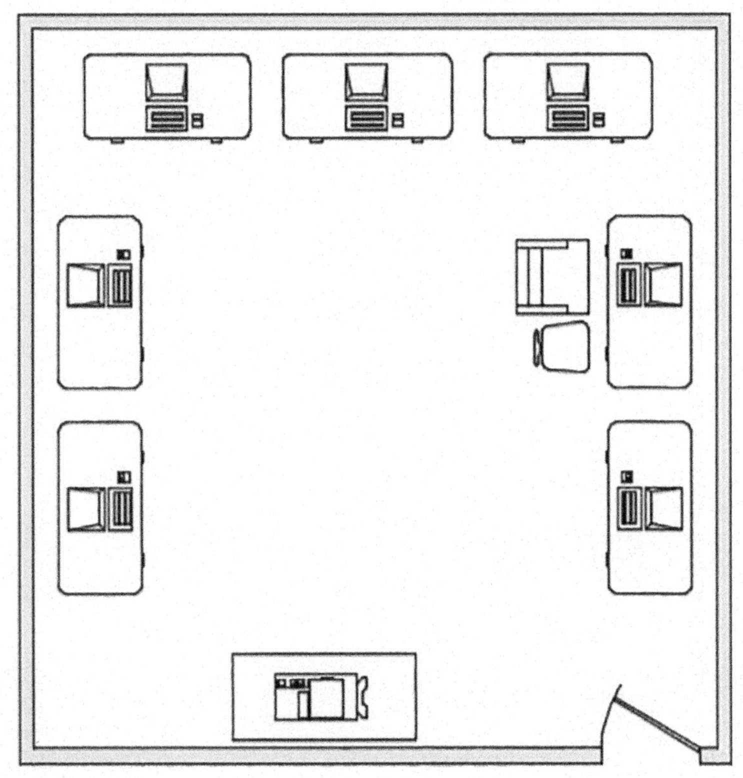

Figure 10-21
Insert **Desk Ch** and **Sec Ch** blocks, explode them, and erase the attribute tags

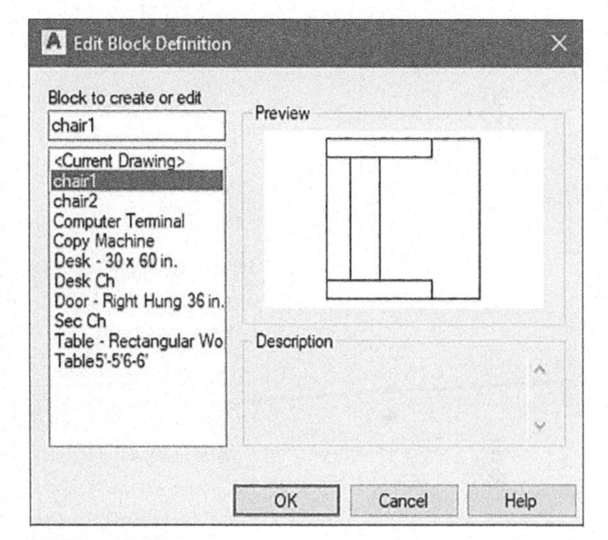

Figure 10-22
Select **chair1** to edit

8. Click the **Parameters** tab of the **Block Authoring Palettes**, click the **Visibility** parameter, and place the parameter below the chair (Figure 10-23). (Placing it below the chair will make it easy to find after the block is inserted again.)
9. Click **Visibility States** on the **Visibility** panel on the ribbon.
10. Click **New**, click **Hide all existing objects in new state** (Figure 10-24), and click **OK** (to exit the **New Visibility State** dialog box).
11. Click **OK** (to exit the **Visibility States** dialog box—you are still in the **Block Editor**).
12. Click **Save Block As** and save and redefine the dynamic block as **chair1**. Close the **Block Editor**.
13. Erase the existing chair1 block if not it is not deleted.
14. Insert **chair1** in the approximate location shown in front of a desk (Figure 10-25). Click on **chair1** and test your **Visibility** parameter, **VisibilityState0**, and **VisibilityState1**. Chair1 should be visible for State0 and invisible for State1.
15. Repeat items 7 through 13 for **chair2**.

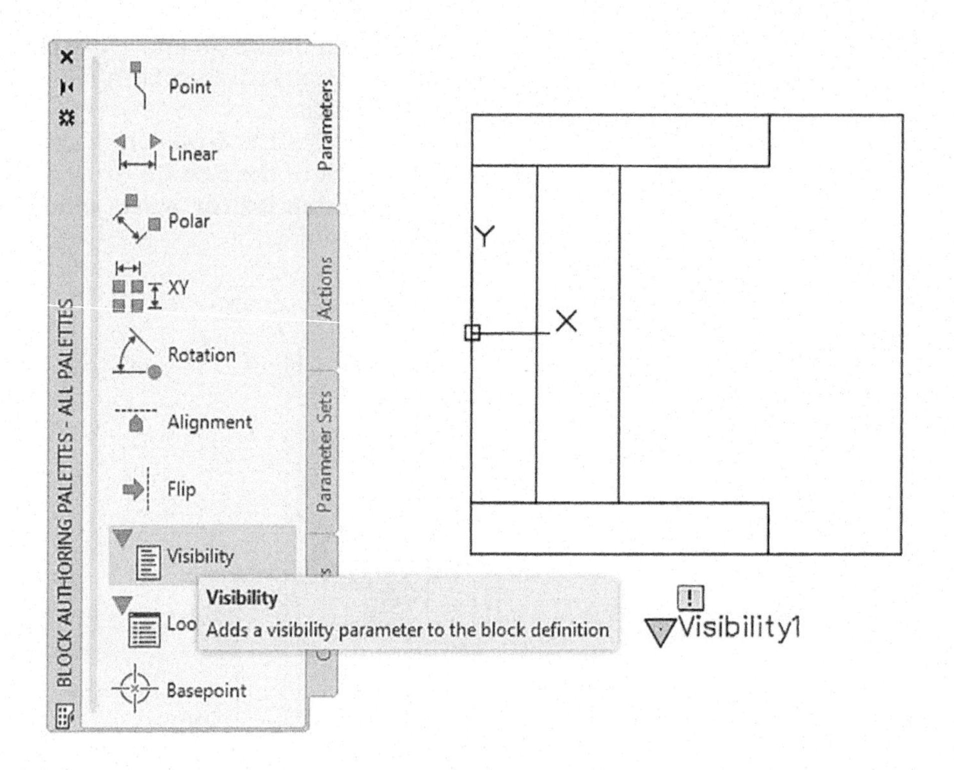

Figure 10-23
Select the **Visibility** parameter and locate it as shown

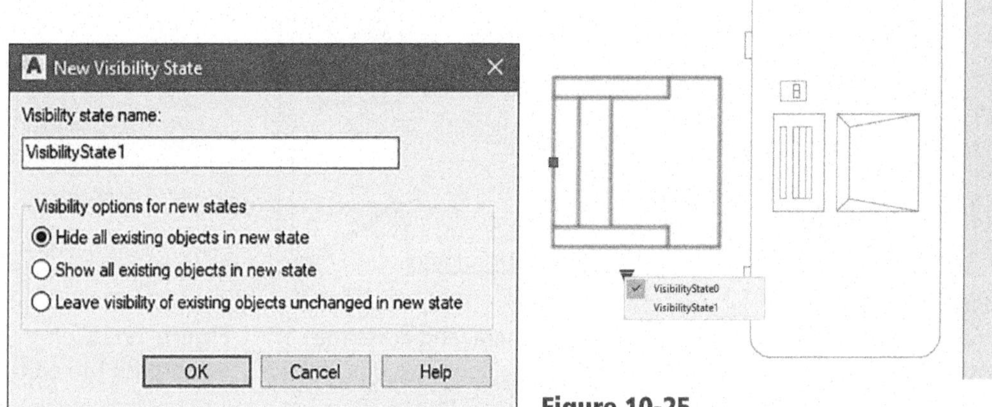

Figure 10-24
Make a **Visibility State** that shows chair1

Figure 10-25
Chair1 inserted with two visibility states—visible and invisible

16. Insert **chair2** so it is positioned as shown in Figure 10-26.
17. Copy **chair1** and **chair2** so each desk has the two chairs.
18. Select all **chair1s** and use the **Properties** command to change the **Visibility State** to 1 (invisible) as shown in Figure 10-27.
19. Make all **chair2s** visible as shown in Figure 10-27.

> **NOTE**
>
> To make an invisible block visible again, open the **Block Editor** and erase the existing visibility parameter on the block. You can then save and redefine the block with no parameter, or you can add a new visibility parameter and save and redefine the block.

Step 25. Make the door a dynamic block so it will open in or out, as described next:

1. Open the **Block Editor**, select **Door - Right Hung 36 in.**, and click **OK**.

2. Draw a line from **P1→** (Figure 10-28) **2-1/2″** straight down. (This line goes to the middle of the wall, so the flip action will flip the door to either side of the room.)
3. Click the **Parameters** tab of the **Block Authoring Palettes**; click the **Flip** parameter.
4. Click **P2→** (Figure 10-28, the lower end of the 2-1/2″ line) as the base point of the reflection line. With **ORTHO** on, click any point to the left of the base point as the endpoint of the reflection line.
5. Locate the label (Figure 10-28).
6. Click the **Actions** tab of the **Block Authoring Palettes**, click **Flip action**, click the **Flip state** parameter, and then select the entire door and press **<Enter>**.
7. Save the dynamic block as **Door - Right Hung 36 in.** to redefine the block and close the **Block Editor**.

Figure 10-26
Both chairs with visibility parameters

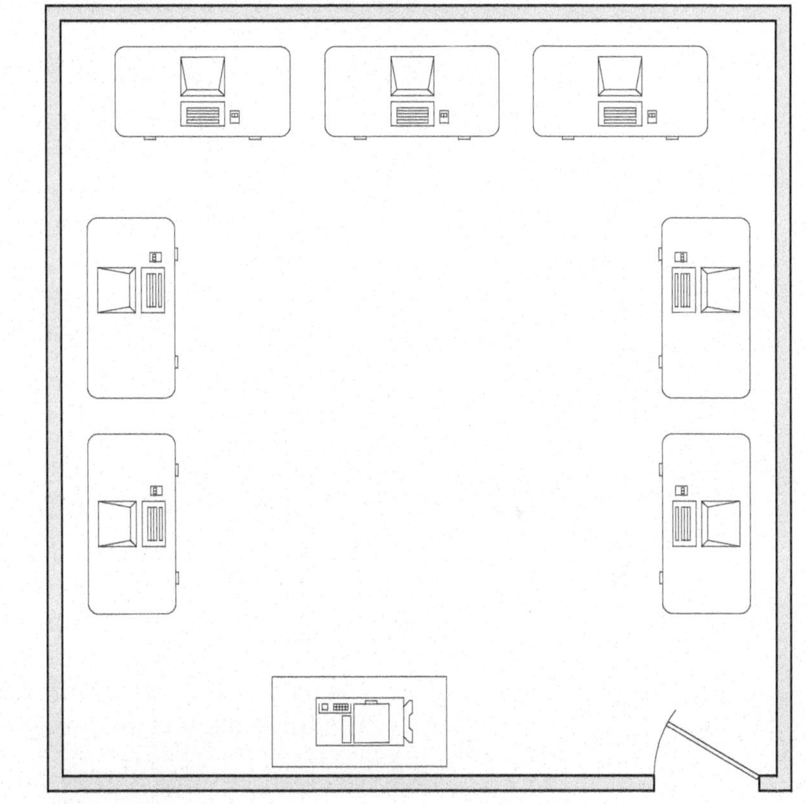

Figure 10-27
Chair1 set to invisible, chair2 set to visible

Figure 10-28
Add the flip parameter and flip action to the door

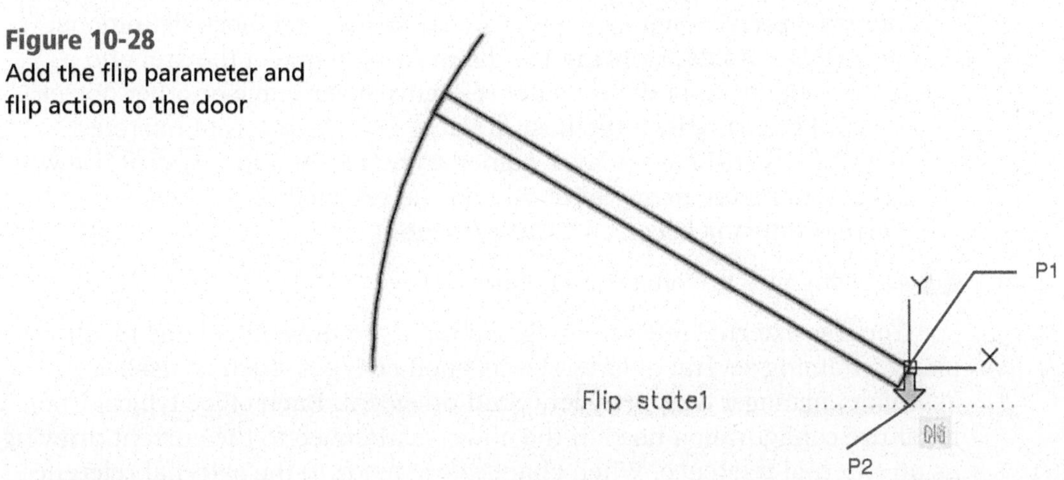

8. Click any point on the door so the flip action is available, flip the door so you see that it works, and then leave it as shown in Figure 10-27.

Step 26. When you have completed Exercise 10-2, add your name, class, and current date to the drawing in the upper right and save your work in at least two places.

Step 27. Print Exercise 10-2 to scale.

EXERCISE 10-3 Attach an External Reference to an Office Plan

XATTACH (Attach External Reference)

Before you start the **XATTACH** command, your primary (or host) drawing must be open. When you activate the **XATTACH** command, the **Select Reference File** dialog box opens and allows you to select the drawing that you want to attach. When you select and open a drawing to be attached as an ***external reference*** to your host drawing, the **External Reference** dialog box opens. The **External Reference** dialog box allows you to specify whether the xref will be an attachment or an overlay:

external reference (xref): A drawing file that is attached to another drawing. External references have the advantage that the host drawing always contains the most recent version of the external reference.

Attachment: An attached xref that is then attached to another drawing becomes a nested xref with all of its features fully recognized.

Overlay: An overlay is ignored when the drawing on which it is overlaid is then attached as an xref to another drawing.

The **XATTACH** command allows you to attach an external reference (xref) drawing to the current, or host, drawing. For each drawing, the data are stored in their own separate file. Any changes made to the external reference drawing are reflected in the host drawing each time the host drawing is loaded into the **Drawing Editor**.

The three distinct advantages to using external references are:

1. The host drawing always contains the most recent version of the external reference.

2. There are no conflicts in layer names and other similar features (called *named objects*), such as linetypes, text styles, and block definitions. AutoCAD automatically inserts the drawing name of the xref and a slash (/) in front of the external reference layer name or other object name. For example, if the host drawing and the external reference (named **CHAIR**) have a layer named **Symbol**, then the current drawing layer retains the name **Symbol**, and the external reference layer in the current drawing becomes **CHAIR/symbol**.

3. Drawing files are often much smaller.

You use external references, for example, for drawing a large furniture plan containing several different levels of office types, such as assistant, associate, manager, vice president, and president. Each office typical (the furniture configuration used in the office) is attached to the current drawing as an external reference. When changes are made to the external reference

Chapter 10

drawing of the manager's office (as a result of furniture substitution, for example), the change is reflected in each instance of a manager's office in the host large furniture plan when it is loaded into the **Drawing Editor**.

External Reference (XREF)

EXTERNAL REFERENCE	
Ribbon/ Panel	Insert/ Reference
Reference Toolbar:	
Menu Bar:	Insert/External References ...
Type a Command:	XREF
Command Alias:	XR

When you activate the **XREF** command, the **External Reference** palette appears. After an external reference has been attached to your drawing, you can right-click on the external reference drawing name to select from the following options:

Attach...: Allows you to attach any drawing as an external reference to the current drawing. There is no limit to the number of external references that you can attach to your drawing. This is the same command as **XATTACH.**

Detach: Lets you remove unneeded external references from your drawing.

Reload: Allows you to update the current drawing with an external reference that has been changed since you began the current drawing. You do not have to exit the current drawing to update it with an external reference that you or someone else changed while in the current drawing.

Unload: Temporarily clears the external reference from the current drawing until the drawing is reloaded.

Bind...: The **Insert** option in the **Bind** dialog box creates a block of the external reference in the current drawing and erases any reference to it as an external reference. The **Bind** option binds the selected xref to the drawing and renames layers in a manner similar to that of the attached xref. This is the same command as **XBIND**.

XBIND

EXTERNAL OBJECT BIND	
Reference Toolbar:	
Type a Command:	XBIND

The **XBIND** (**External Bind**) command allows you to bind a selected subset of an external reference's dependent symbols to the current drawing. For example, if you did not want to create a block of the entire external reference but wanted permanently to add only a dimension style of the external reference to the drawing, you could use **XBIND**.

Features of External References

- An external reference cannot be exploded.
- An external reference can be changed into a block with the **Bind...** option and then exploded. The advantage of using the external reference is then lost. You use the **Bind** option if you want to send a client a disk or file containing only the host drawing without including the referenced data as external reference files.
- External references can be nested. This means you can use a host drawing containing external references as an external reference on another host drawing. No limit exists to the number of drawings you can nest like this.
- An xref icon appears in the lower-right corner of the screen when xrefs are attached to a drawing.

The following steps show you how to attach an xref to your drawing.

Step 1. Draw the floor plan shown in Figure 10-29 and save it as **CH10-EXERCISE3.**

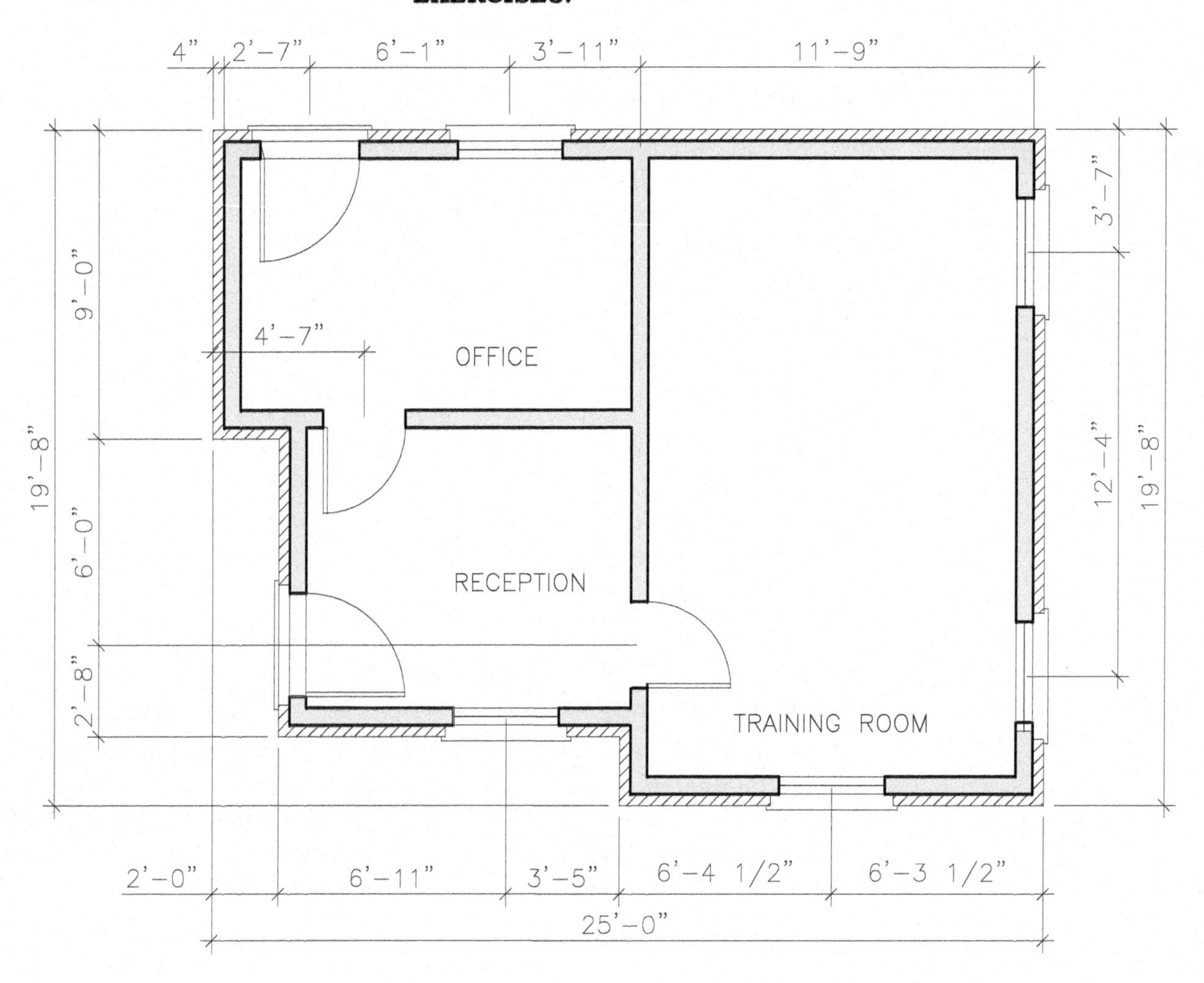

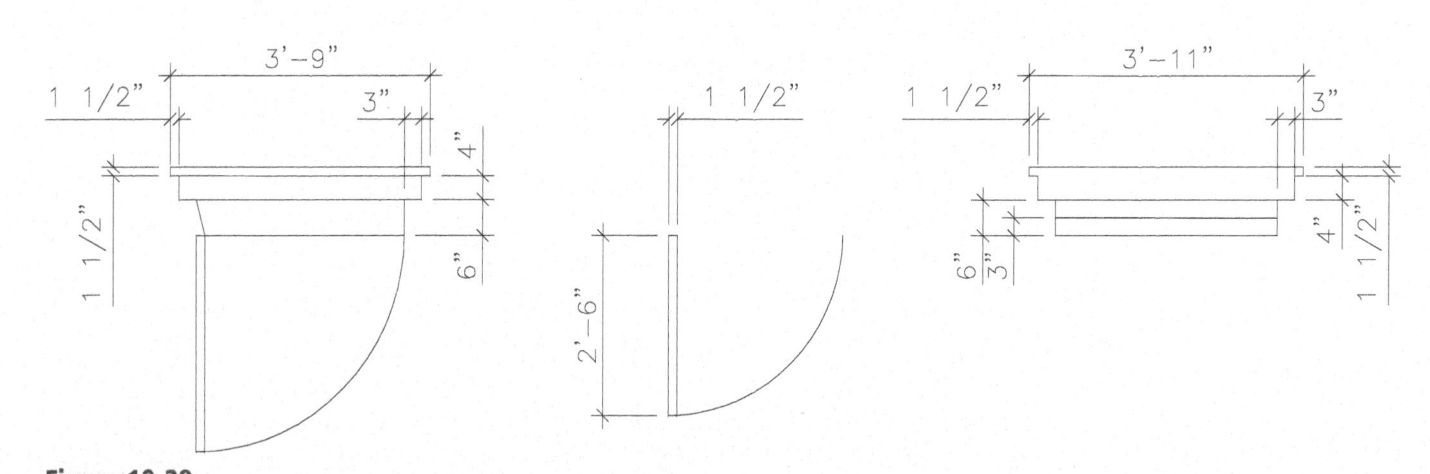

Figure 10-29
Exercise 10-3: Floor plan dimensions (scale: 3/16″ = 1′-0″). Door and window detail dimensions (scale: 3/8″ = 1′-0″)

Step 2. Start a new drawing and draw the typical workstation shown in Figure 10-30. Estimate any dimension not shown.

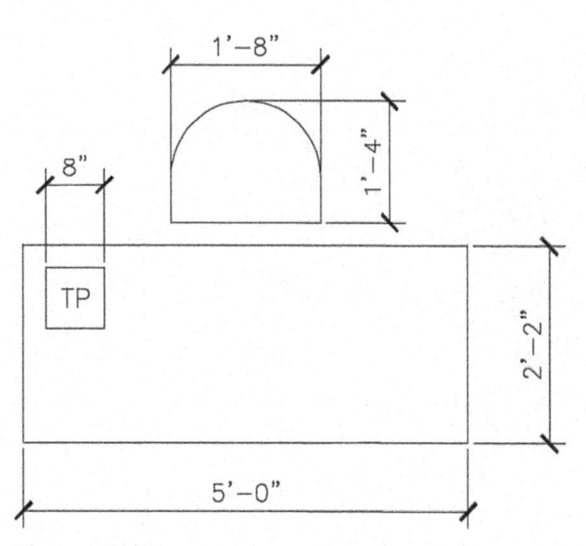

Figure 10-30
Exercise 10-3: Typical workstation dimensions

SET BASE POINT	
Ribbon/ Panel	Insert/Block Definition/ <slideout>
Menu Bar:	Draw/Block/ Base
Type a Command:	BASE

Step 3. Use the **Set Base Point** command (or type **BASE**) to select the midpoint on the arc of the chair as the insertion point for the workstation.

Step 4. Save the typical workstation drawing as **WS10-1** in the same folder with **CH10-EXERCISE3**. Exit the drawing.

Step 5. Open the floor plan drawing **CH10-EXERCISE3**.

Step 6. Attach the workstation to the floor plan drawing, as described next:

ATTACH EXTERNAL REFERENCE	
Ribbon/ Panel	Insert/ Reference
Reference Toolbar:	
Menu Bar:	Insert/ DWG Reference
Type a Command:	XATTACH
Command Alias:	XA

Prompt	**Response**
Type a command:	**XATTACH**
The **Select Reference File** dialog box (Figure 10-31) appears:	Locate drawing **WS10-1** and click on it Click **Open**
The **Attach External Reference** dialog box (Figure 10-32) appears:	Click **OK**
Specify insertion point or [Scale X Y Z Rotate PScale PX PY PZ PRotate]:	Click **P1→** (Figure 10-33)

That's all there is to attaching an external reference to another drawing.

Step 7. Copy the external reference to four other locations on the floor plan as shown in Figure 10-34 (the exact location is not important).

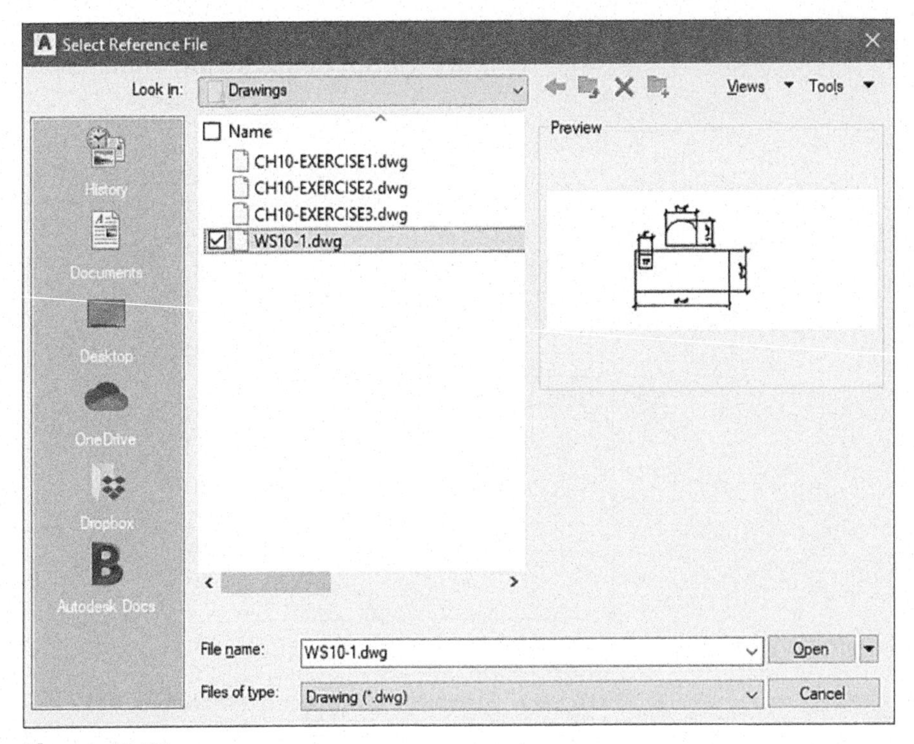

Figure 10-31
Locate drawing **WS10-1** and select it

Step 8. Save your drawing (**CH10-EXERCISE3**) to the same folder or disk as **WS10-1**. Exit the drawing.

You have been informed that all the workstations must now have a computer.

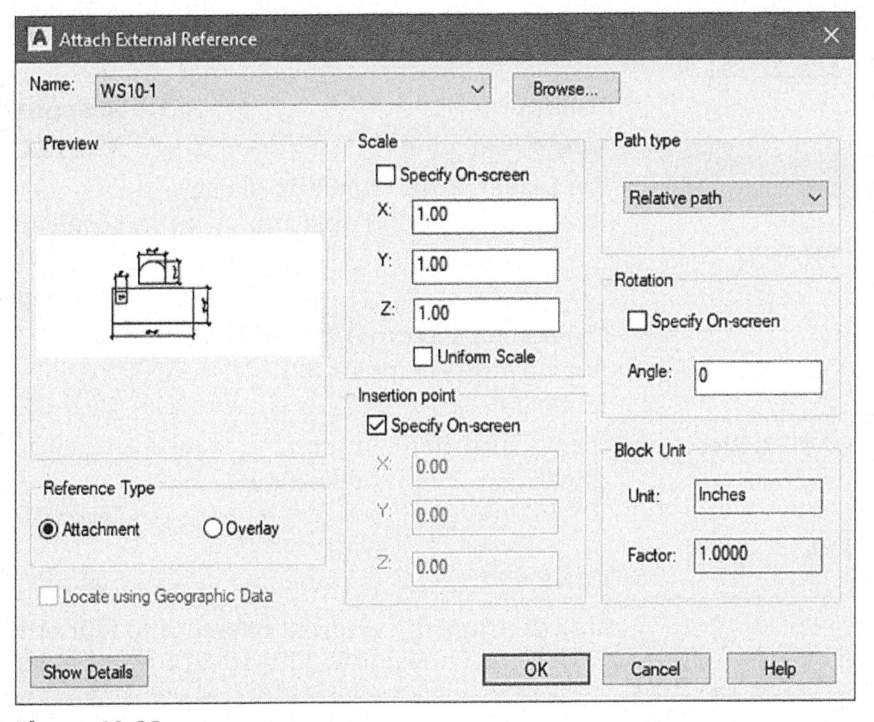

Figure 10-32
Attach External Reference dialog box with **WS10-1** selected

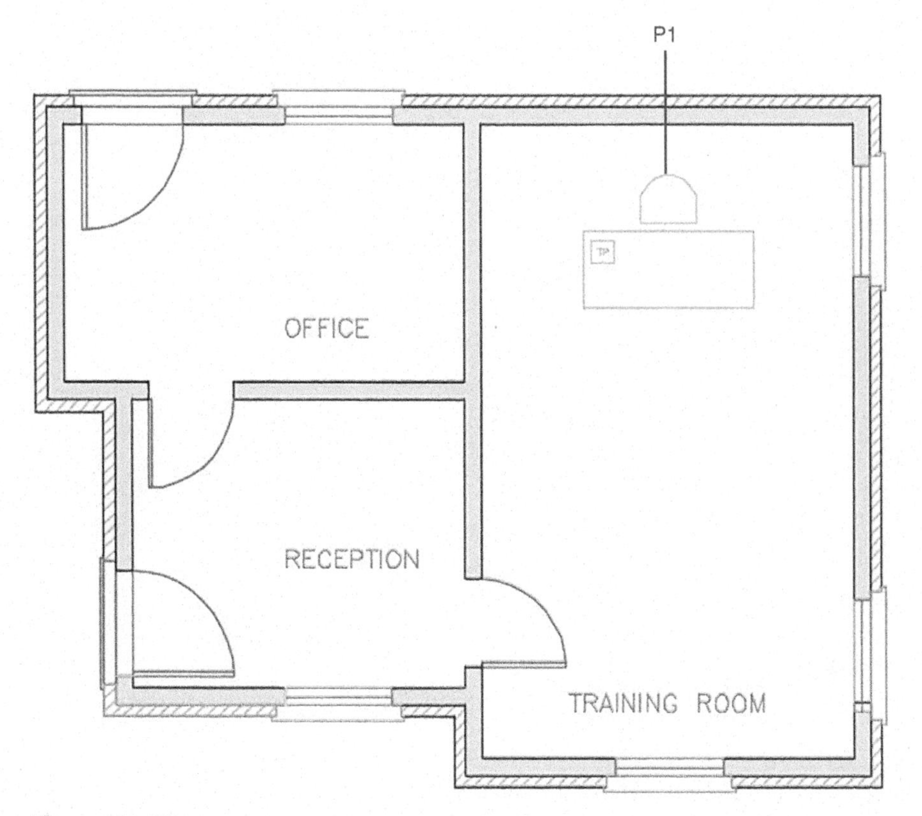

Figure 10-33
Attach the external reference

Step 9. Open drawing **WS10-1** and draw a computer approximately the size shown in Figure 10-35 and label it. Save the new workstation drawing in the same place from which it came.

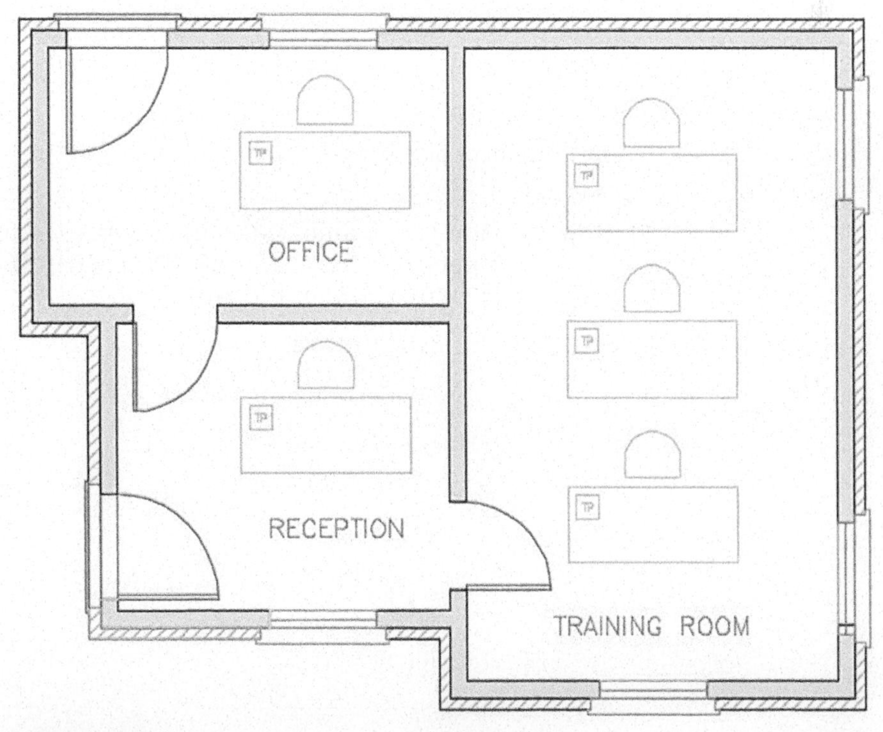

Figure 10-34
Copy the external reference to four other locations

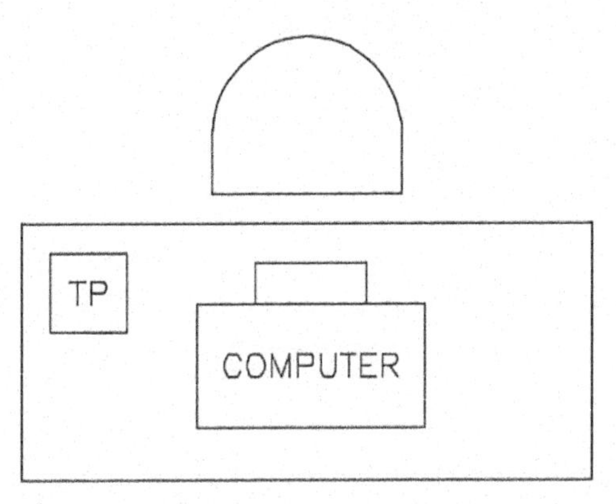

Figure 10-35
The new workstation

Step 10. Open drawing **CH10-EXERCISE3**. It should appear as shown in Figure 10-36.

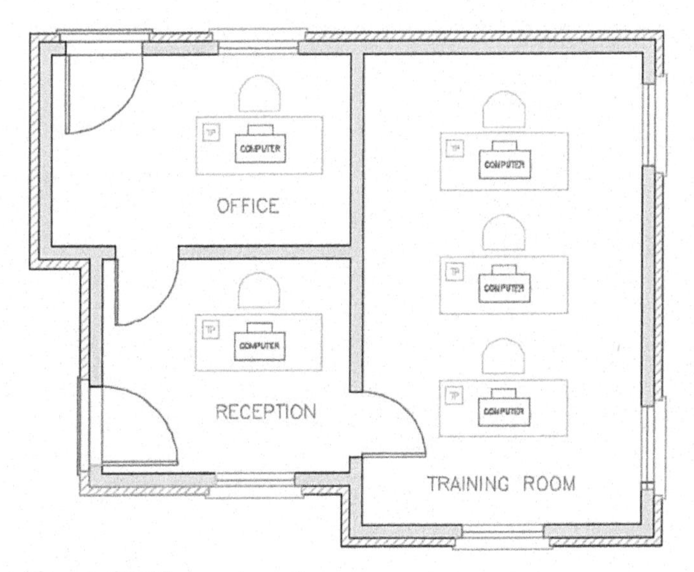

Figure 10-36
The office floor plan with new workstations

Step 11. Add your name, class, and current date to the drawing in the upper right and save **CH10-EXERCISE3** in the same folder or disk from which it came.

Step 12. Print the drawing to scale.

Chapter Summary

This chapter described the AutoCAD **DesignCenter,** dynamic blocks, and external references. It showed you how to use DesignCenter to take blocks, layers, linetypes, and text and dimension styles from any existing drawing using drag and drop and place them in the current drawing. It also showed you how to make external references and dynamic blocks. You will now be able to use these commands to make drawings quickly and efficiently.

Chapter Test Questions

Multiple Choice

Circle the correct answer.

1. The **History** tab on DesignCenter allows you to do which of the following?
   a. Look at a preview of a selected item
   b. Return to the previous screen
   c. Display a list of the most recently opened drawings
   d. Search for data using the **Search** command

2. Which of the following opens the **Block Editor**?
   a. **BOPEN**
   b. **BE**
   c. **BLOCKE**
   d. **BED**

3. Which of the following closes the **Block Editor**?
   a. **BCL**
   b. **CLOSE**
   c. **BC**
   d. **EDCL**

4. Which of the following **External Reference** options allows you to make a block of an external reference in the current drawing?
   a. **Reload**
   b. **Bind**
   c. **Attach...**
   d. **Detach**

5. How many external references can you nest on a host drawing?
   a. 1
   b. 16
   c. 32
   d. Unlimited

Matching

Write the number of the correct answer on the line.

a. External reference ______
b. Dynamic block ______
c. **DesignCenter** ______
d. **Block Authoring Palettes** ______

1. An inserted file that can have varying size parameters attached
2. A host drawing always contains the most recent version of this attached file
3. Can be used to copy blocks from one drawing to another
4. Used for adding parameters to dynamic blocks

True or False

1. **True or False:** DesignCenter allows you to drag and drop blocks, layers, linetypes, and text and dimension styles from an existing drawing into the current drawing.
2. **True or False:** You cannot add dynamic features to an existing block.
3. **True or False:** Dynamic block parameters and actions can be added to a block using the **Block Editor**.
4. **True or False:** Unneeded external references cannot be removed from a drawing.
5. **True or False:** Only two visibility options are available in the **New Visibility State** dialog box.

List

1. Five ways of accessing DesignCenter.
2. Five buttons above the tabs in DesignCenter.
3. Five types of items available from the **DesignCenter/Home Designer** list.
4. Five options from **Block Authoring Palettes/Adding a lookup parameter**.
5. Five ways of accessing the **XREF** command.
6. Five ways of accessing **Attach Ext Ref**.
7. Five **XREF** command options that do not make a block of the XREF in your current drawing.
8. Five features of XREFs.
9. Five block-related commands.

Questions

1. What is DesignCenter used for?
2. How can dynamic blocks be used effectively?
3. What are the uses of parameters and their actions?
4. How can external references be used to keep the same office configurations consistent?

Chapter Projects

Project 10-1: *Dynamic Block (Table and Chair) with Stretch and Move Actions* [BASIC]

1. Draw the table with the phone and the computer as shown in Figure 10-37. The phone and the computer terminal are found in DesignCenter in the **Home - Space Planner** drawing. The table measures 6′ × 2′-8″.
2. Copy the chair from one of the drawings you completed in Chapter 3. Place the chair at the midpoint of the table in the X direction and 6″ up.
3. Block the entire drawing with the name **table with chair**.
4. Access the **Block Editor** (type **BE <Enter>**) and add a linear parameter and a lookup parameter to the table.
5. Add a stretch action and a lookup action to the table as shown in Figure 10-38, similar to those in Exercise 10-2. The lengths of the table should be 8′ and 10′.
6. Add a point parameter and a lookup parameter to the chair.
7. Add a move action and a lookup action to the chair as shown in Figure 10-39. The chair should move 1′ and 2′.
8. Save the block and exit the **Block Editor**.
9. Insert the table with chair block and test it. Move the chair 1′ using the lookup action when you stretch the table to 8′ with its lookup action. Move the chair 2′ when you stretch the table 10′.

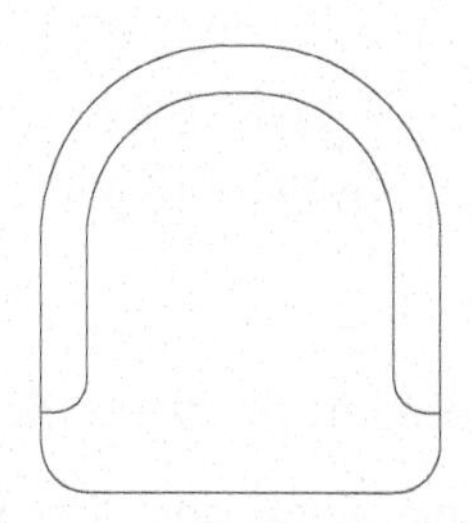

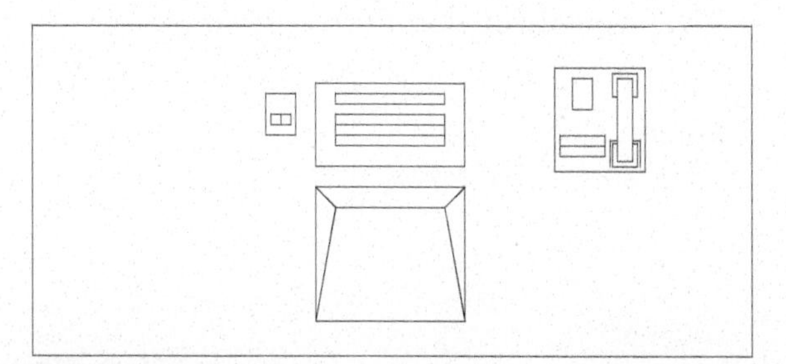

Figure 10-37
The table with chair block

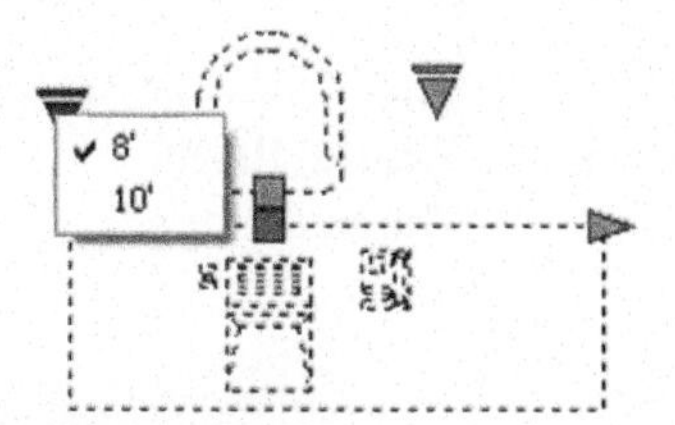

Figure 10-38
The **stretch** and **lookup** actions

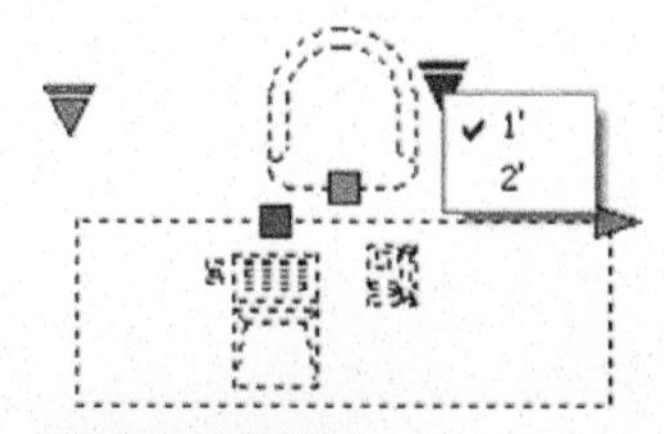

Figure 10-39
The **move** and **lookup** actions

Project 10-2: *Dynamic Block (Bed)* [BASIC]

1. Insert the Bed-queen as shown in Figure 10-40 and explode it. (You will find it in DesignCenter in the **Home - Space Planner** drawing.)
2. Block the entire drawing with the name **bed.**
3. Access the **Block Editor** (type **BE <Enter>**) and add two linear parameters and two lookup parameters to the bed.
4. Add two stretch actions and two lookup actions to the bed as shown in Figure 10-41 similar to those in Exercise 10-2. The lengths of the bed should be 75″ and 80″. The widths of the bed should be 54″, 60″, and 76″.

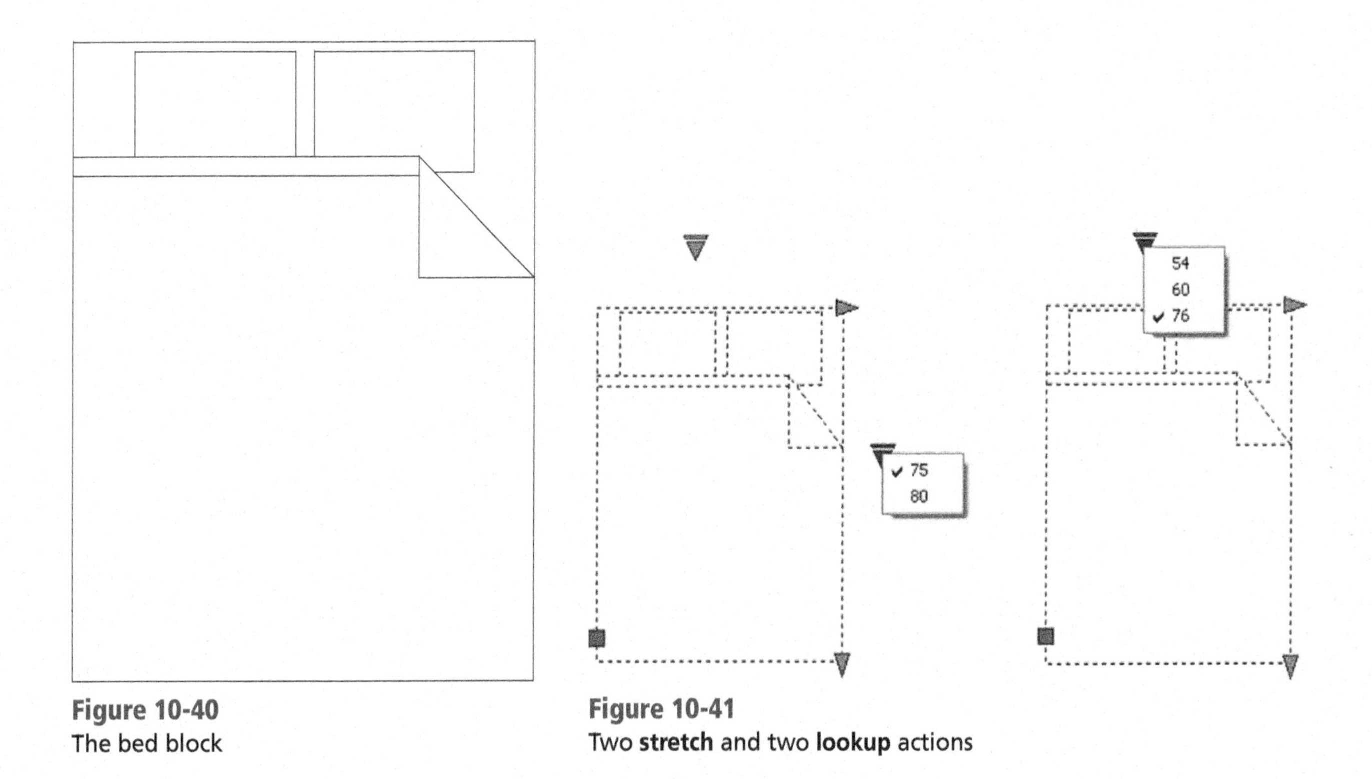

Figure 10-40
The bed block

Figure 10-41
Two **stretch** and two **lookup** actions

5. Save the block and exit the **Block Editor**.
6. Insert the bed block and test it. You should have a dynamic block that gives you three standard bed sizes:

   Full size is 54″ × 75″
   Queen size is 60″ × 80″
   King size is 76″ × 80″

Project 10-3: *Condo Floor Plan with External References* **[ADVANCED]**

1. Draw full size the floor plan of the condo as shown in Figure 10-42. Use a 1/8″ architect's scale to measure any features that do not have dimensions. The scale is 1/8″ = 1′-0″.

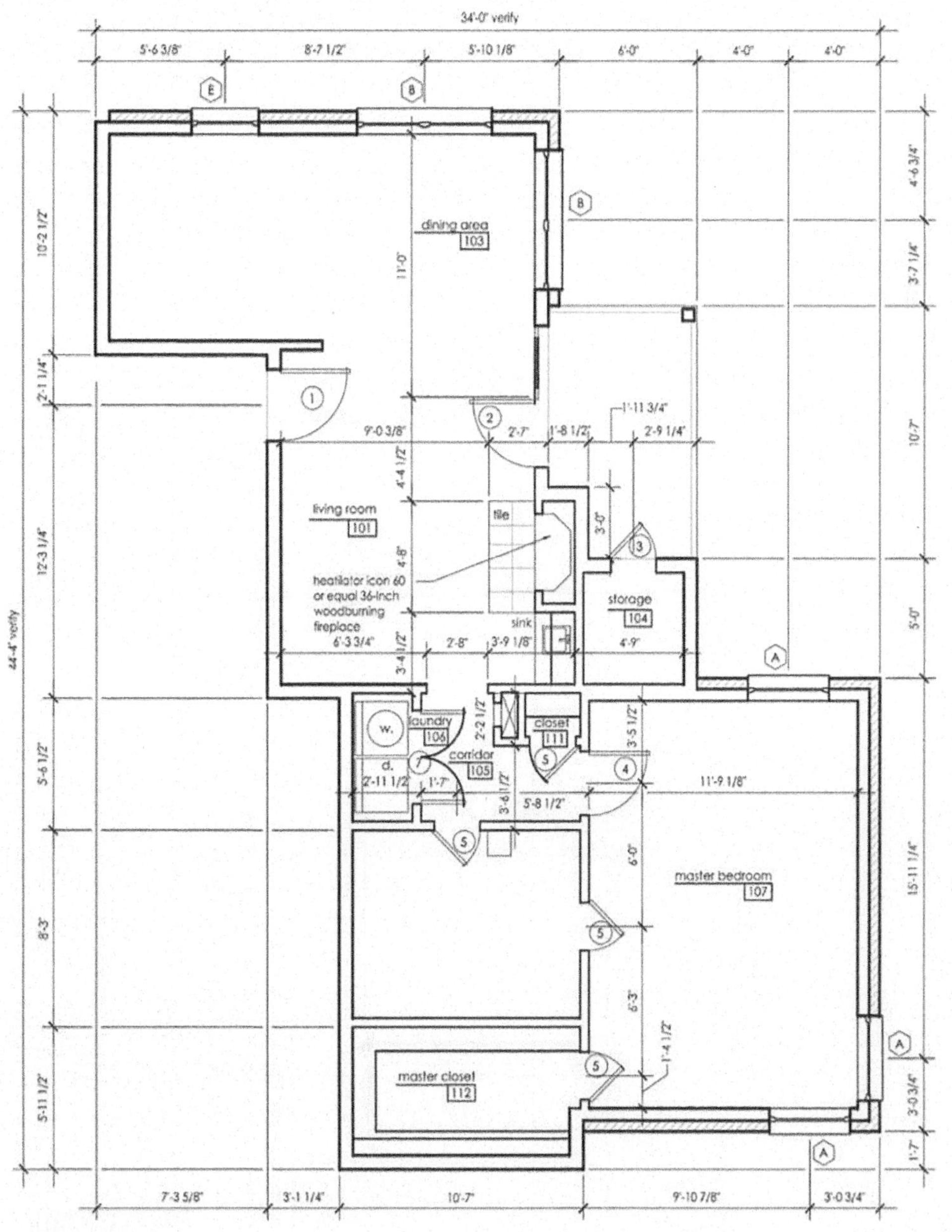

Figure 10-42
Condo floor plan (scale: 1/8″ = 1′-0″)

2. Draw full size the original xref kitchen as shown in Figure 10-43. The scale of this figure is 1/4″ = 1′-0″.

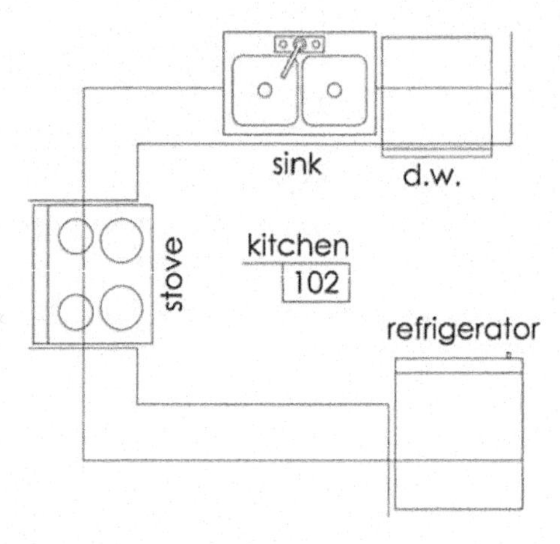

Figure 10-43
Original xref kitchen (scale: 1/4″ = 1′-0″)

3. Attach the original xref kitchen to the condo floor plan as shown in Figure 10-44 and close the condo drawing.

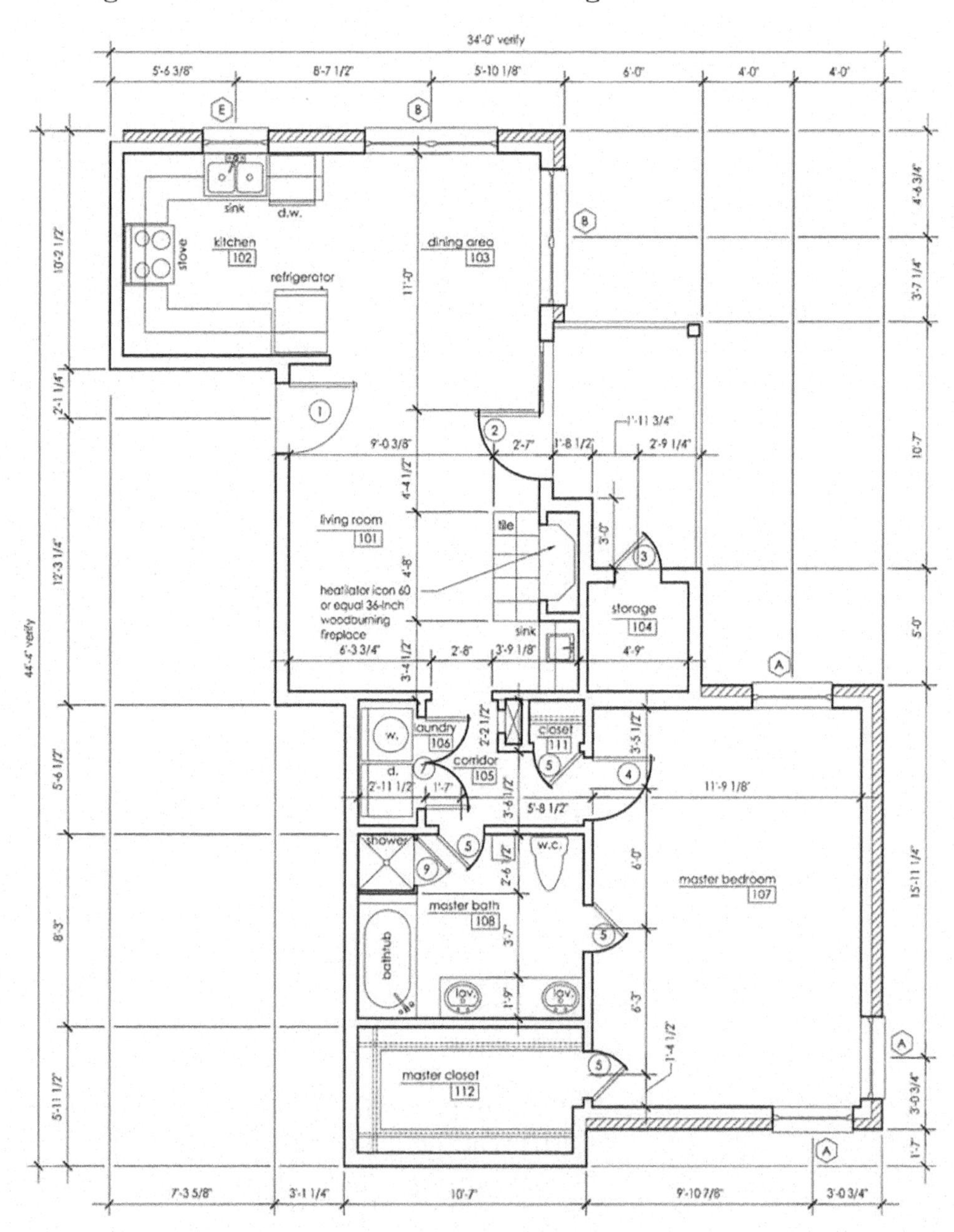

Figure 10-44
Condo floor plan with original xrefs attached (scale: 1/8″ = 1′-0″)

4. Make changes to the original xref kitchen as shown in Figure 10-45. The scale of this figure is 1/4″ = 1′-0″. You will find the new sink, stove, and refrigerator in the **Kitchen** drawing in DesignCenter.

5. Draw full size the original xref bathroom as shown in Figure 10-46. The scale of this figure is 1/4″ = 1′-0″.

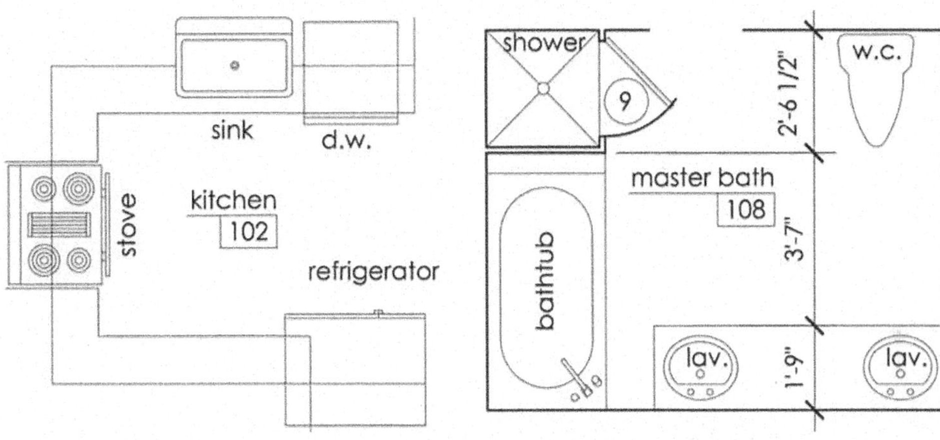

Figure 10-45
Revised xref kitchen (scale: 1/4″ = 1′-0″)

Figure 10-46
Original xref bathroom (scale: 1/4″ = 1′-0″)

6. Attach the original xref bathroom to the condo floor plan as shown in Figure 10-46 and close the condo drawing.

7. Make changes to the original xref bathroom as shown in Figure 10-47. The scale of this figure is 1/4″ = 1′-0″. You will find the new toilet, tub, and sinks in the **House Designer** drawing in DesignCenter.

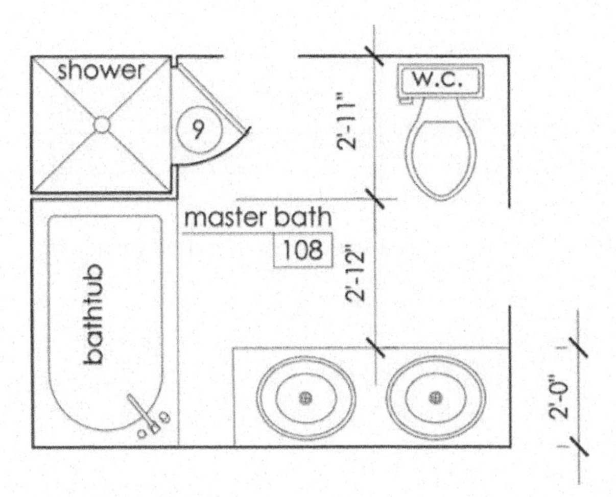

Figure 10-47
Revised xref bathroom (scale: 1/4″ = 1′-0″)

8. Open the condo floor plan. Your drawing should appear as shown in Figure 10-48. You may need to reload the xrefs.

9. Save the drawing in at least two places and print the drawing to scale.

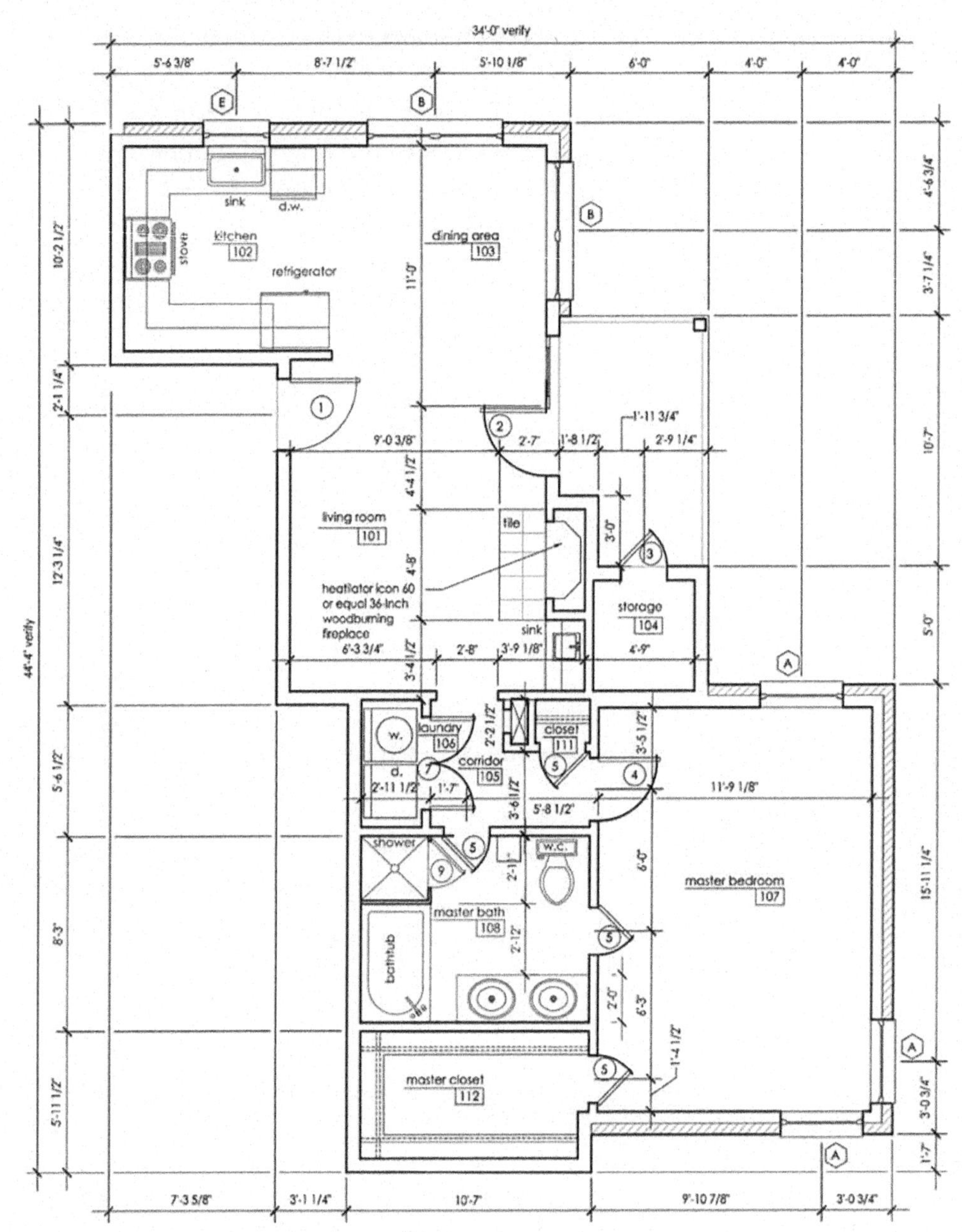

Figure 10-48
Condo floor plan with revised xrefs attached (scale: 1/8″ = 1′-0″)

chapter eleven

Drawing the Reflected Ceiling Plan and Voice/Data/Power Plan

CHAPTER OBJECTIVES

- Draw a reflected ceiling plan.
- Draw a voice/data/power plan.
- Draw a power/communication/lighting plan

Introduction

In this chapter, you use previously learned commands to draw the tenant space reflected ceiling plan in Exercise 11-1, Part 1, and the tenant space voice/data/power plan in Exercise 11-1, Part 2. This chapter provides helpful guidelines for drawing Exercise 11-1, Parts 1 and 2.

reflected ceiling plan: A drawing showing all the lighting symbols and other items such as exit signs that attach to the ceiling in their correct locations in the space. The plan also shows all the switching symbols needed to turn the lights on and off.

The ***reflected ceiling plan*** shows all the lighting symbols and other items such as exit signs that attach to the ceiling in their correct locations in the space. The plan also shows all the switching symbols needed to turn the lights on and off.

The voice/data/power plan shows symbols for telephones (voice), computers (data), and electrical outlets (power).

EXERCISE 11-1

Part 1, Tenant Space Lighting Legend and Reflected Ceiling Plan

lighting legend: A collection of symbols and text that identify lights and other lighting items such as switches.

In Exercise 11-1, Part 1, you will wblock each lighting symbol and then insert each symbol into the tenant space reflected ceiling plan. When you have completed Exercise 11-1, Part 1, your reflected ceiling plan drawing will look similar to Figure 11-1.

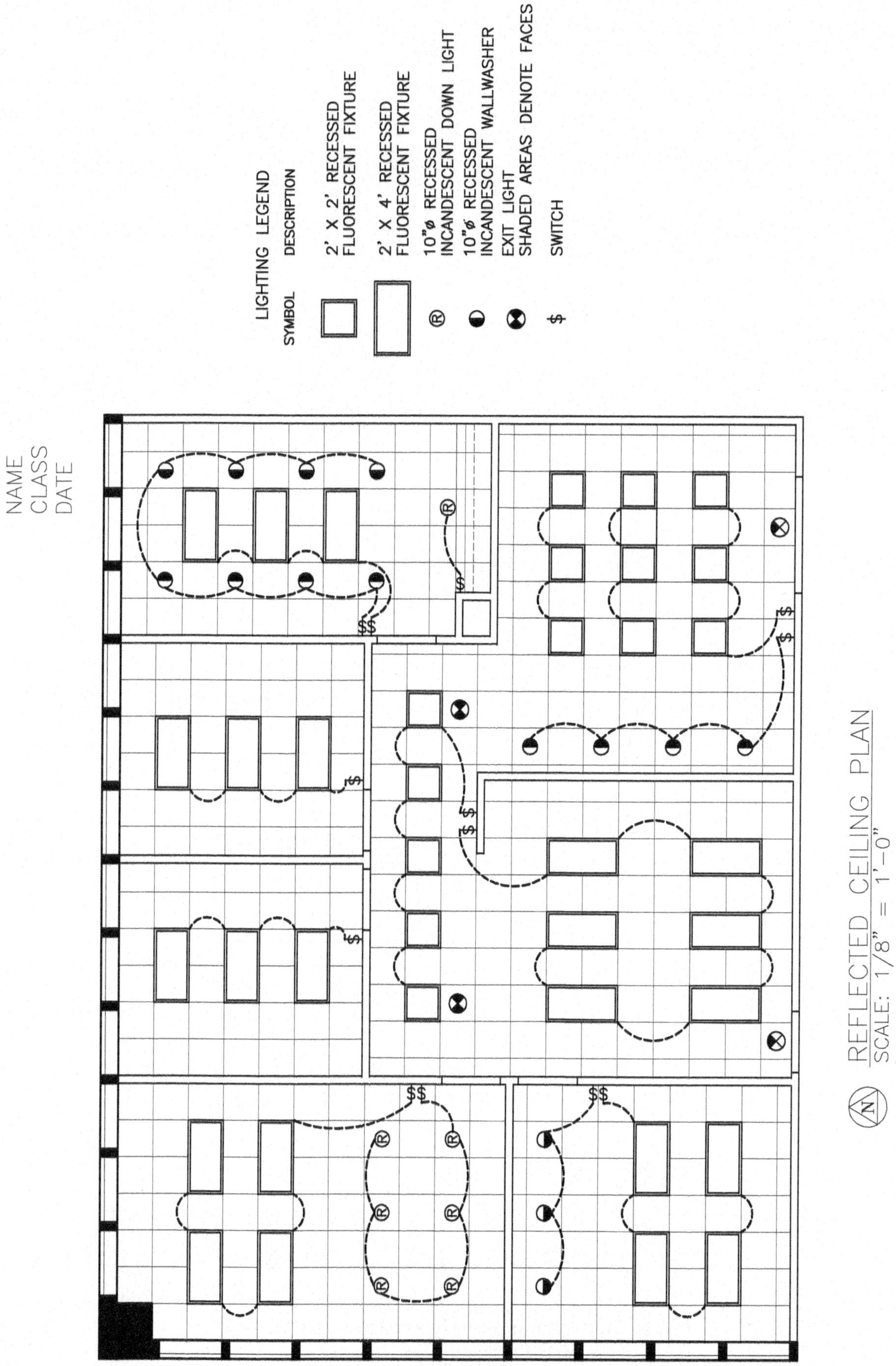

NAME
CLASS
DATE

LIGHTING LEGEND

SYMBOL	DESCRIPTION
☐	2' X 2' RECESSED FLUORESCENT FIXTURE
▭	2' X 4' RECESSED FLUORESCENT FIXTURE
Ⓡ	10"ø RECESSED INCANDESCENT DOWN LIGHT
◐	10"ø RECESSED INCANDESCENT WALLWASHER
⊗	EXIT LIGHT SHADED AREAS DENOTE FACES
$	SWITCH

REFLECTED CEILING PLAN
SCALE: 1/8" = 1'-0"

Figure 11-1
Exercise 11-1: Part 1, Tenant space reflected ceiling plan (scale: 1/8" = 1'-0")

Step 1. Create the following new layers:

Layer name	Color	Linetype	Lineweight
a-clng-susp	red	continuous	.004″ (.09 mm)
e-anno-symb-lite	blue	continuous	.010″ (.25 mm)
e-anno-symb-powr	blue	continuous	.010″ (.25 mm)
e-anno-text-lite	green	continuous	.006″ (.15 mm)
e-anno-text-powr	green	continuous	.006″ (.15 mm)
e-lite-circ	white	hidden	.016″ (.40 mm)

Tenant Space Lighting Legend Symbols

Step 2. Draw each lighting symbol, as shown in Figure 11-2, on the **e-anno-symb-lite** layer, full size. Wblock each symbol to a new folder named **Lighting Symbols**. Identify a logical insertion point, such as a corner of a rectangle or center of a circle.

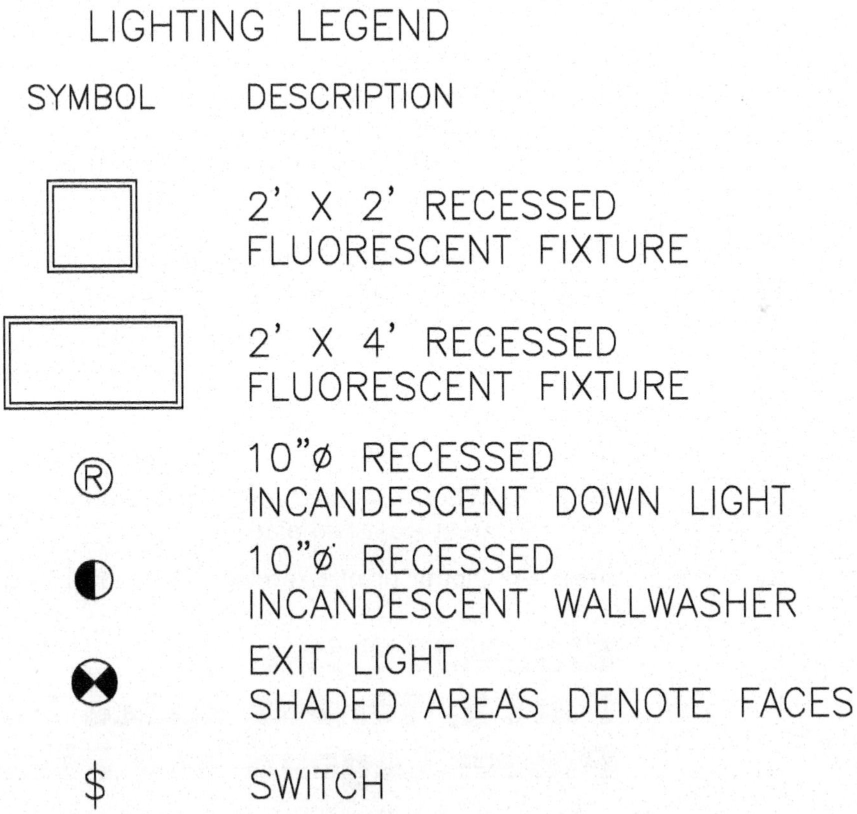

Figure 11-2
Exercise 11-1: Part 1, Tenant space lighting legend (scale: 1/4″ = 1′-0″)

LIGHTING LEGEND

SYMBOL	DESCRIPTION
	2' X 2' RECESSED FLUORESCENT FIXTURE
	2' X 4' RECESSED FLUORESCENT FIXTURE
Ⓡ	10"Ø RECESSED INCANDESCENT DOWN LIGHT
	10"Ø RECESSED INCANDESCENT WALLWASHER
	EXIT LIGHT SHADED AREAS DENOTE FACES
$	SWITCH

Tenant Space Reflected Ceiling Plan

NOTE

In **EXERCISE 12-1** and **EXERCISE 12-2**, you will freeze layers to make a presentation that displays the dimensioned floor plan, furniture plan, reflected ceiling plan, and voice/data/power plan. This will work only if you have saved **CH6-EXERCISE1**, **CH7-EXERCISE1**, **CH9-EXERCISE1**, and **CH11-EXERCISE1** as a single drawing.

Step 3. Begin drawing **CH11-EXERCISE1-REFLECTED CEILING** on the hard drive or network drive by opening the existing drawing **CH9-EXERCISE1** and saving it as **CH11-EXERCISE1-REFLECTED CEILING**.

Step 4. Freeze all the layers that are not needed to draw the reflected ceiling plan.

Step 5. Set layer **a-wall-head** current. Draw lines across the door openings as shown in Figure 11-1.

Step 6. Set layer **a-clng-susp** current and draw the 2′ × 2′ separate balanced ceiling grid in each area as shown in Figure 11-1.

Step 7. Insert the lighting legend symbols, full scale, into the location shown on the tenant space reflected ceiling plan in Figure 11-1.

Step 8. Set layer **e-anno-text-lite** current.

Step 9. Add the text to the lighting legend as shown in Figure 11-1, and make it annotative. The words LIGHTING LEGEND are 3/32″ high text; the remaining text is all 1/16″ high.

Step 10. Prepare the ceiling grid for insertion of the 2′ × 4′ recessed fixture symbols by using the **ERASE** command to erase the ceiling grid lines that will cross the centers of the symbols.

Use the **COPY** command and an **Osnap** modifier to copy the lighting symbols from the legend and place them on the plan as shown in Figure 11-1.

The wallwasher, 2′ × 4′ fixture, and switch symbols appear on the reflected ceiling plan in several different orientations. Copy each symbol and rotate the individual symbols into the various positions, then use **COPY** to draw the additional like symbols in the correct locations on the plan.

Step 11. Set layer **e-lite-circ** current. Use the **ARC** command to draw the symbol for the circuitry. Adjust **LTSCALE** as needed so lines appear as dashed.

Step 12. Change the title text to read as shown in Figure 11-1.

Step 13. When you have completed Exercise 11-1, Part 1, save your work in at least two places.

Step 14. Plot or print Exercise 11-1, Part 1 to scale.

EXERCISE 11-1
Part 2, Tenant Space Voice/Data/Power Legend and Plan

In Exercise 11-1, Part 2, you will wblock each voice, data, and power symbol and then insert each symbol into the tenant space voice/data/power plan. When you have completed Exercise 11-1, Part 2, your voice/data/power plan drawing will look similar to Figure 11-3.

Tenant Space Voice/Data/Power Legend Symbols

Step 1. Draw each voice, data, and power symbol, as shown in Figure 11-4, on the **e-anno-symb-powr** layer, full size. Wblock each symbol to a new folder named **Voice Data Power Symbols**. Identify a logical insertion point, such as the tip of a triangle or center of a circle.

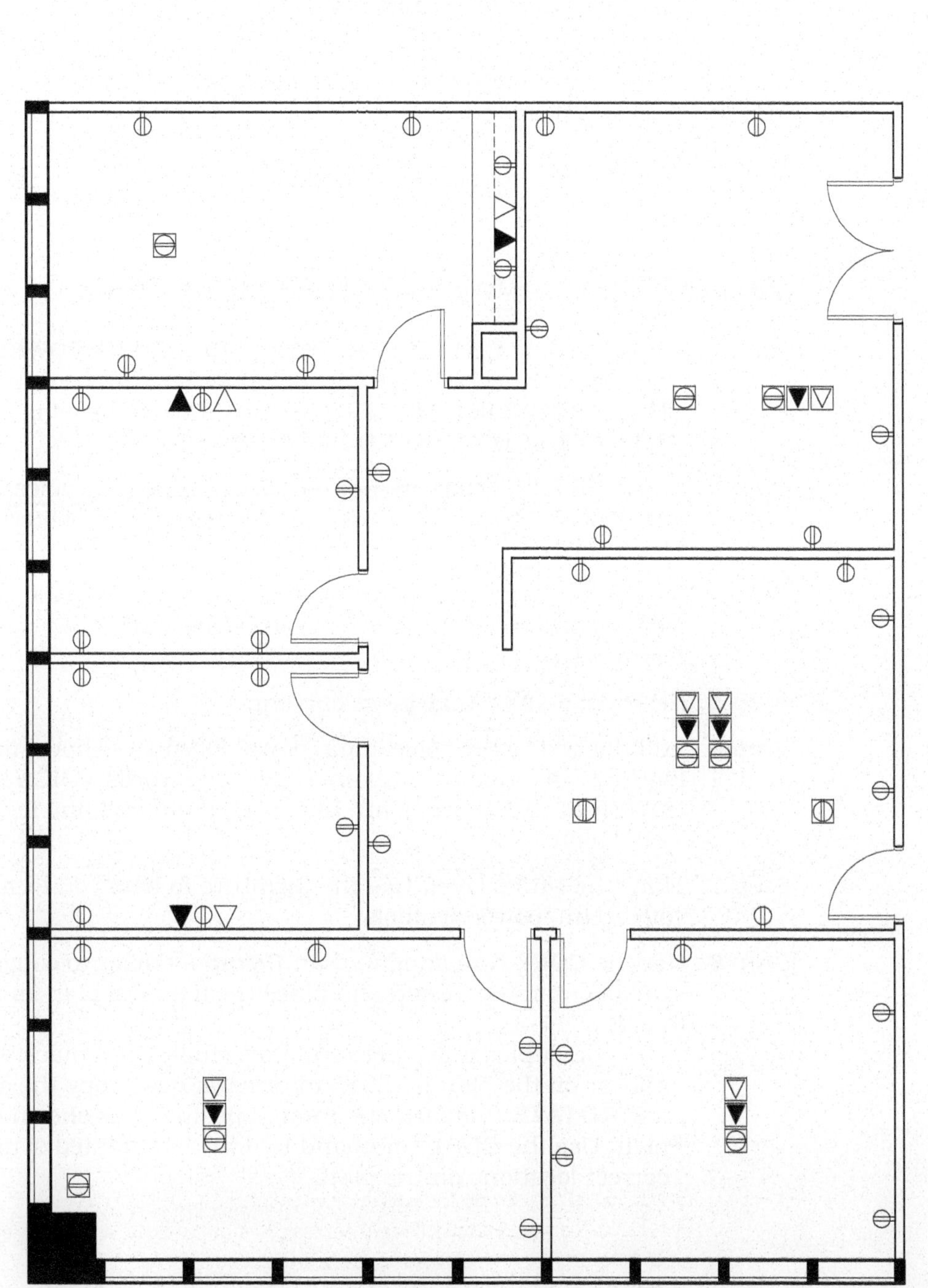

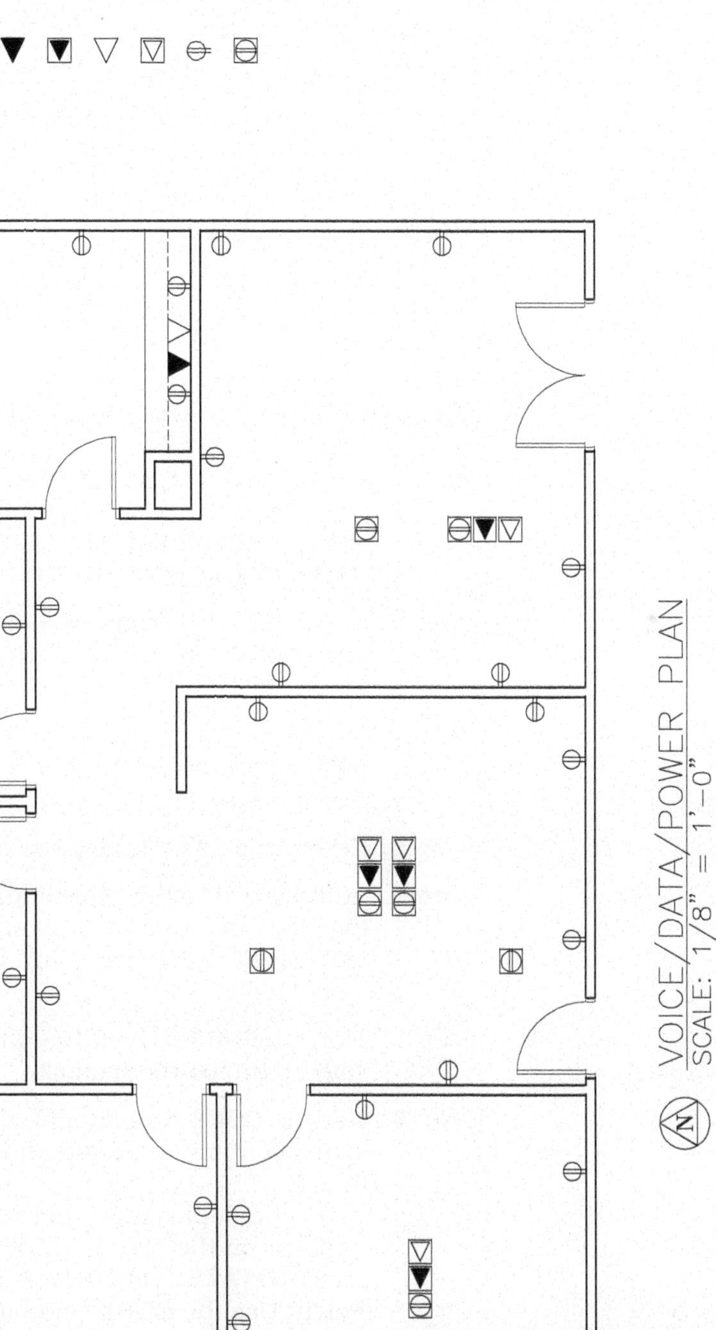

Figure 11-3
Exercise 11-1: Part 2, Tenant space voice/data/power plan (scale: 1/8" = 1'-0")

Figure 11-4
Exercise 11-1: Part 2, Tenant space voice/data/power legend (scale: 1/4″ = 1′-0″)

VOICE/DATA/POWER LEGEND

SYMBOL	DESCRIPTION
	TELEPHONE OUTLET
	FLOOR TELEPHONE OUTLET
	DATA OUTLET
	FLOOR DATA OUTLET
	DUPLEX RECEPTACLE
	FLOOR DUPLEX RECEPTACLE

Tenant Space Voice/Data/Power Plan

voice/data/power plan: A drawing showing all symbols for telephones (voice), computers (data), and electrical outlets (power), and the locations of all these items.

Step 2. Begin drawing **CH11-EXERCISE1-VOICE-DATA-POWER** on the hard drive or network drive by opening the existing drawing **CH11-EXERCISE1-REFLECTED CEILING** and saving it as **CH11-EXERCISE1-VOICE-DATA-POWER**.

Step 3. Freeze all layers that are not required to draw the voice/data/power plan. Thaw any layers that are required, as shown in Figure 11-3.

Step 4. Insert the voice/data/power legend symbols, full scale, in the location shown on the tenant space voice/data/power plan in Figure 11-3.

Step 5. Set layer **e-anno-text-powr** current.

Step 6. Add the text to the voice/data/power legend as shown in Figure 11-4, and make it annotative. The words VOICE/DATA/POWER LEGEND are 3/32″ high text; the remaining text is all 1/16″ high.

Step 7. Thaw the **i-furn** layer. Use the furniture to help you locate the voice/data/power symbols.

Step 8. Use the **COPY** command and an **Osnap** modifier to copy the symbols from the legend and place them on the plan as shown in Figure 11-3.

The duplex receptacle and floor duplex receptacle symbols appear on the plan in different orientations. Copy the symbol and use **ROTATE** to match the rotated positions as shown on the plan. Use the **COPY** command to draw like rotated symbols in the correct locations on the plan.

Osnap-Mid Between 2 Points and picking the two endpoints of the two lines in the duplex receptacle is helpful. Use this point to locate the duplex receptacle along the walls when using the **COPY** command. Use **Osnap-Center** to help locate the floor receptacle symbol.

Step 9. Freeze the **i-furn** layer.

Step 10. Change the title text to read as shown in Figure 11-3.

Step 11. When you have completed Exercise 11-1, Part 2 save your work in at least two places.

Step 12. Plot or print Exercise 11-1, Part 2, to scale.

Chapter Summary

This chapter provided you the information necessary to set up and draw reflected ceiling plans and voice/data/power plans. In drawing these plans you have enhanced your skills in using commands and settings such as **WBLOCK, Annotation Scale, Linetype Scale, Lineweight, COPY, BLOCK, INSERT, MOVE, TEXT, SCALE, Polyline, Polyline Edit**, and other commands. Now you have the skills and information necessary to produce reflected ceiling plans, voice/data/power plans, and power/communication/lighting plans.

Chapter Test Questions

Multiple Choice

Circle the correct answer.

1. Which of the following plans would most likely contain a symbol for a duplex receptacle?
   a. Reflected ceiling plan
   b. Voice/data/power plan
   c. Circuitry plan
   d. None of the above

2. Which of the following plans would most likely contain a symbol for a fluorescent fixture?
   a. Reflected ceiling plan
   b. Voice/data/power plan
   c. Circuitry plan
   d. None of the above

3. Which of the following plans would most likely contain a symbol for a telephone outlet?
   a. Reflected ceiling plan
   b. Voice/data/power plan
   c. Circuitry plan
   d. None of the above

4. Which of the following would most likely contain a symbol for an exhaust fan?
   a. Reflected ceiling plan
   b. Voice/data/power plan
   c. Circuitry plan
   d. None of the above

5. Which of the following linetypes was used to show circuitry?
   a. Continuous
   b. Center
   c. Hidden
   d. Dash-Dot

Matching

Write the number of the correct answer on the line.

a. Voice/data/power plan _____
b. Reflected ceiling plan _____
c. Circuitry _____
d. Mid Between 2 Points _____
e. **INSERT** _____

1. A plan that shows all the lights in an office
2. A plan that shows all the telephone outlets in an office
3. An object snap mode
4. A command that is used to add a block from a symbol library to a drawing
5. A hidden line, arc, or polyline used to show which switch connects to which light

True or False

Circle the correct answer.

1. **True or False:** A reflected ceiling plan contains all the symbols needed for power.
2. **True or False:** A voice/data/power plan contains all the symbols needed for power.
3. **True or False:** Drawing symbols on the correct layer is not really necessary.
4. **True or False:** The width of a polyline can be changed.
5. **True or False:** The appearance of a hidden linetype can be changed with the **LTSCALE** command.

List

1. Five parameters that control a polar array.
2. Five plot area selection options in Plot window.
3. Five essential steps in using **WBLOCK**.
4. Five options of the **Polyline** command.
5. Five options of the **Lengthen** command.
6. Five options of the **Zoom** command.
7. Five options of the navigation bar.
8. Five ways of accessing the plot command.
9. Five **LINE/MLINE** commands.
10. Five parameters that control a rectangular array.

Questions

1. How does a reflected ceiling plan differ from a voice/data/power plan?
2. Why is it necessary to have both reflected ceiling plans and voice/data/power plans?

Chapter Projects

Project 11-1: *Hotel Room 2 Power/Communication/Lighting Legend and Plan* [BASIC]

1. Draw the hotel room power/communication/lighting symbols as shown in Figure 11-5. Do not redraw any symbols you have already drawn and wblocked to a folder. Use an architect's scale to measure the symbols and draw them full scale.

POWER/COMMUNICATION/LIGHTING LEGEND

SYMBOL	DESCRIPTION
	DUPLEX RECEPTACLE
GFIC	DUPLEX RECEPTACLE WITH GROUND FAULT INTERRUPTER CIRCUIT
	TELEPHONE OUTLET
	DATA OUTLET
TV	CABLE TV OUTLET
S/A	SMOKE ALARM – WIRE DIRECT W/BATTERY BACK–UP
	CEILING-MOUNTED LIGHT FIXTURE
	WALL-MOUNTED LIGHT FIXTURE
EX	EXHAUST FAN/LIGHT COMBINATION
$	SWITCH

Figure 11-5
Project 11-1: Hotel room 2 power/communication/lighting legend (scale: 1/4″ = 1′-0″)

2. Complete the hotel room power/communication/lighting plan as shown in Figure 11-6.
3. Plot or print the drawing to scale.

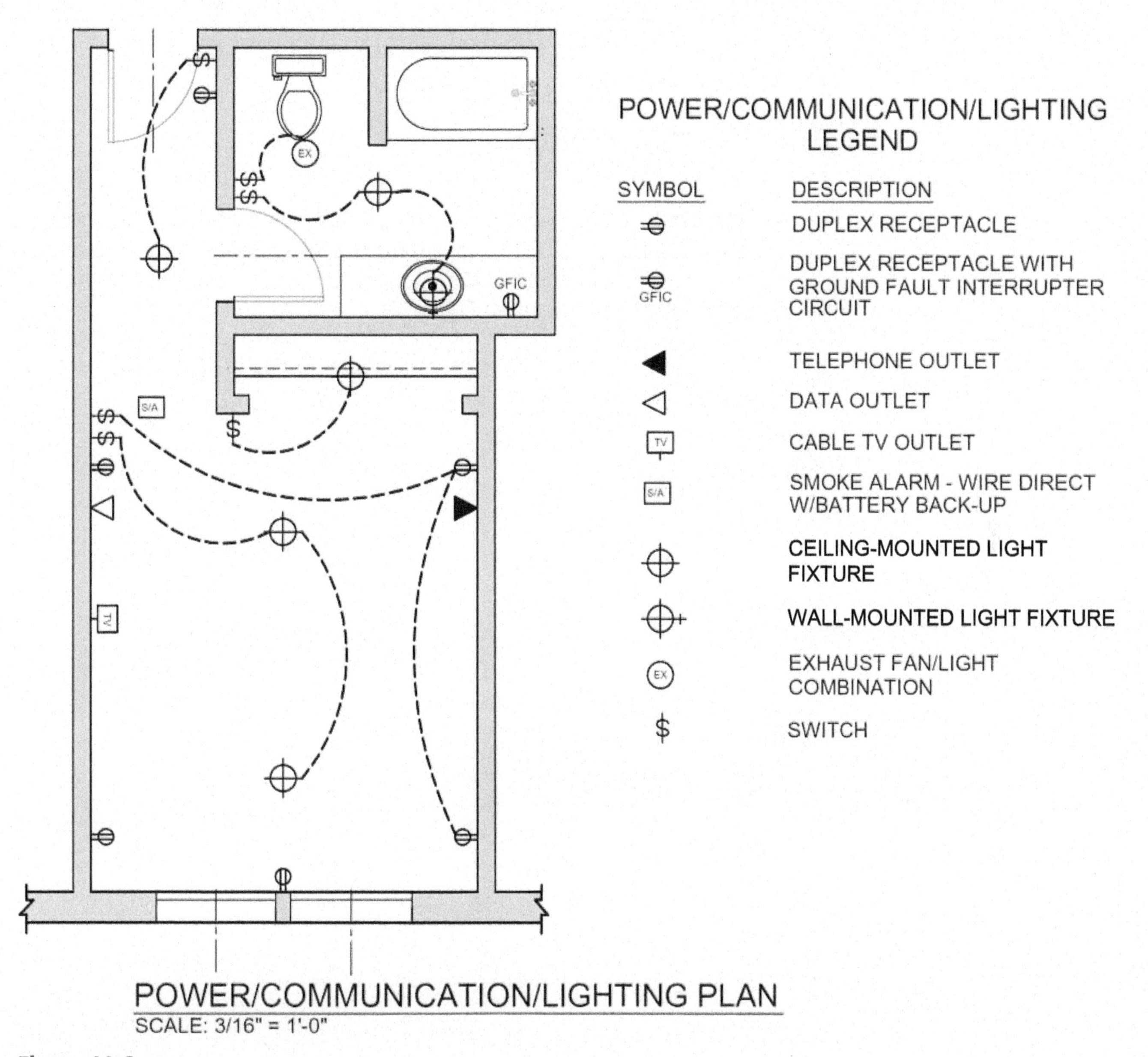

Figure 11-6
Project 11-1: Hotel room 2 power/communication/lighting plan (scale: 3/16″ = 1′-0″)

Project 11-2: *Wheelchair-Accessible Commercial Restroom Lighting Legend and Plan* **[INTERMEDIATE]**

1. Draw the wheelchair-accessible commercial restroom lighting symbols as shown in Figure 11-7. Do not redraw any symbols you have already drawn and wblocked to a folder. Use an architect's scale to measure the symbols and draw them full scale.

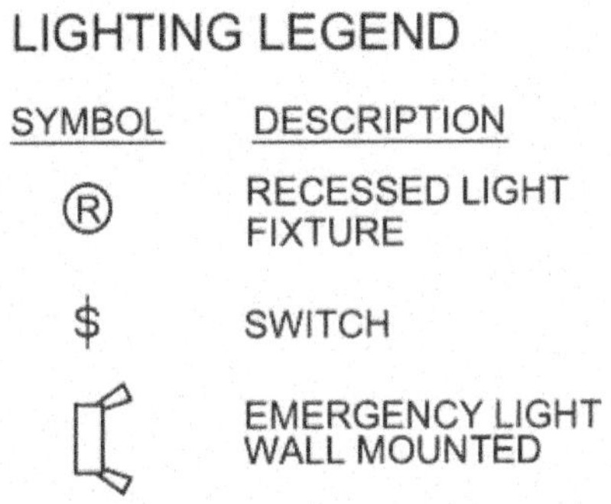

Figure 11-7
Project 11-2: Wheelchair-accessible commercial restroom lighting legend (scale: 3/16″ = 1′-0″)

LIGHTING LEGEND

SYMBOL	DESCRIPTION
Ⓡ	RECESSED LIGHT FIXTURE
$	SWITCH
	EMERGENCY LIGHT WALL MOUNTED

2. Complete the wheelchair-accessible commercial restroom lighting plan as shown in Figure 11-8.
3. Plot or print the drawing to scale.

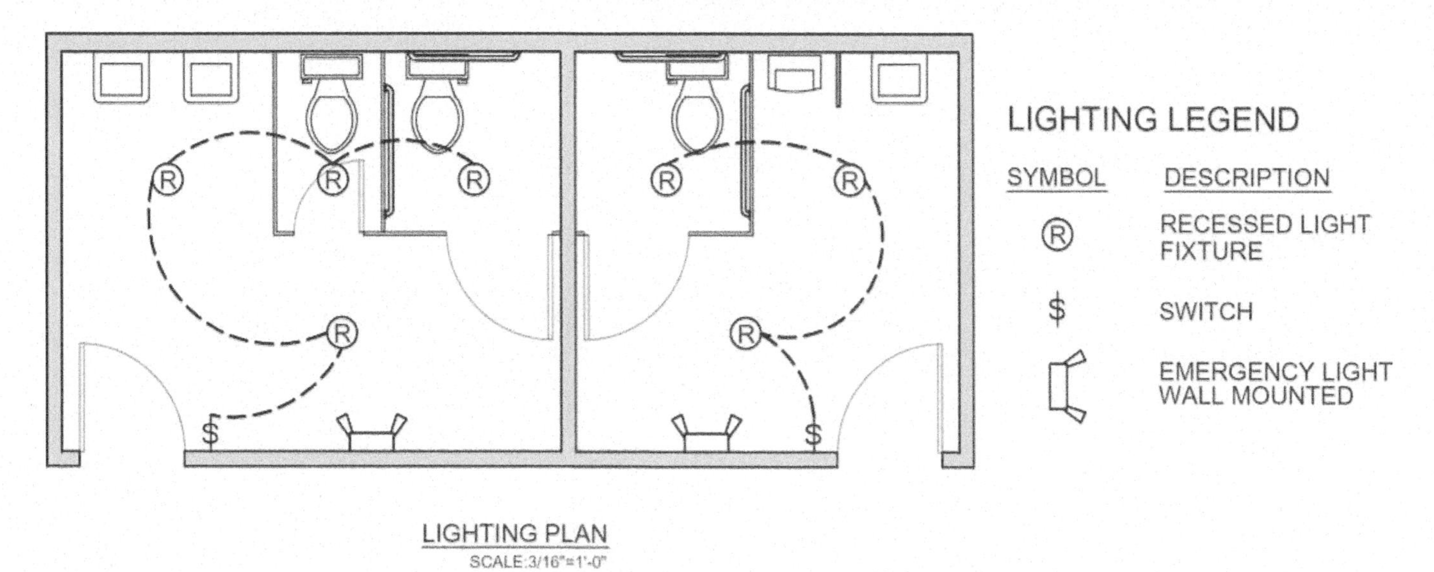

Figure 11-8
Project 11-2: Wheelchair-accessible commercial restroom lighting plan (scale: 3/16″ = 1′-0″)

chapter twelve

Creating Presentations with Layouts and Making a Sheet Set

CHAPTER OBJECTIVES

- Make new layout tabs and rename them.
- Scale and lock viewports.
- Use the **Layer Properties Manager VP Freeze** column to freeze layers in different viewports.
- Correctly use the following commands and settings:

Create Layout Wizard	**Page Setup Manager**
Layer Properties Manager	**Paper Space**
Model Space	**Properties**
MVSETUP	**Quick View Layouts**
New Sheet Set	**Sheet Set Manager**

At some point, you will need to present your drawings in a polished fashion. In this chapter, you create multiple layout views using the **MVSETUP** command, and explore AutoCAD's Sheet Set feature to package a group of drawings.

EXERCISE 12-1
Make a Printed Presentation of the Tenant Space Project by Combining Multiple Plans on One Sheet of Paper

When you have completed Exercise 12-1, your drawing will look similar to Figure 12-1. **Exercise 12-1** and **Exercise 12-2** will work only if you have saved **CH6-EXERCISE1**, **CH7-EXERCISE1**, **CH9-EXERCISE1**, and **CH11-EXERCISE1** as individual drawing files. In both exercises, you will freeze layers to make a presentation that displays the dimensioned floor plan, furniture plan, reflected ceiling plan, and voice/data/power plan.

Figure 12-1
Exercise 12-1 complete

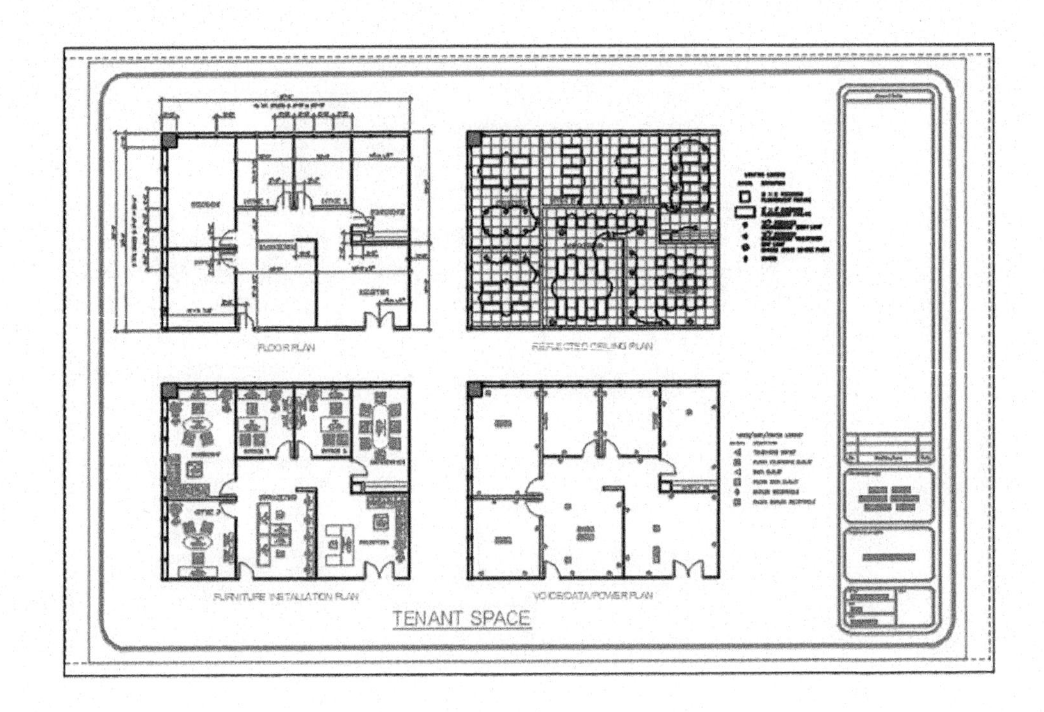

Step 1. Open existing drawing **CH11-EXERCISE1-VOICE-DATA-POWER**; save it as **CH12-EXERCISE1**.

Step 2. **Erase** the north arrow, title text, scale, your name, class, and date.

Step 3. Use **Zoom-All** to view the entire drawing.

Step 4. Turn the **Grid OFF**.

Step 5. Create the following new layer and set it as the current layer:

Layer name	Color	Linetype	Lineweight
a-anno-ttbl	magenta	continuous	.008″ (.20 mm) (for a D-size drawing)

viewports: Windows in either model space or paper space. Two types of viewports are available in AutoCAD, tiled and untiled. Tiled viewports are those that exist in model space with **TILEMODE** on. Untiled viewports exist in either model space or paper space with **TILEMODE** off.

CREATE LAYOUT WIZARD	
Menu Bar:	Tools/Wizards/ Create Layout ...
Type a Command:	LAYOUT WIZARD

Use Create Layout Wizard to Set Up Four Viewports on a Single Sheet

Step 6. Use the **Create Layout** wizard to create a presentation of the Tenant Space Project consisting of four viewports and an architectural title block, as described next:

Prompt	Response
Type a command:	Click **Create Layout Wizard** or type **LAYOUTWIZARD <Enter>**
The **Create Layout-Begin** wizard appears with the name **Layout 3**	Type **Tenant Space Project** Click **Next**
The **Printer** option appears:	Click **DWF6 ePlot.pc3** (or a plotter that plots ARCH D size [36.00 × 24.00 inches]) Click **Next**
The **Paper Size** option appears:	Click **ARCH D (36.00 × 24.00 inches)** in the **Paper Size** list Click **Next**

Prompt	Response
The **Orientation** option appears:	Click **Landscape** Click **Next**
The **Title Block** option appears:	Click **Architectural Title Block.dwg** Click **Next**
The **Define Viewports** option appears:	Click **Array** in the **Viewport setup** list (Figure 12-2) Click **3/16" = 1'-0"** in the **Viewport scale:** input box Type **2** in the **Rows:** input box Type **2** in the **Columns**: input box Type **0.1** in the **Spacing between rows:** input box Type **0.1** in the **Spacing between columns:** input box Click **Next**
The **Pick Location** option appears:	Click **Select location:**
Specify first corner:	Type **2,2 <Enter>**
Specify opposite corner:	Type **28,22 <Enter>**
The **Finish** option appears:	Click **Finish** You are now in **PAPER** space

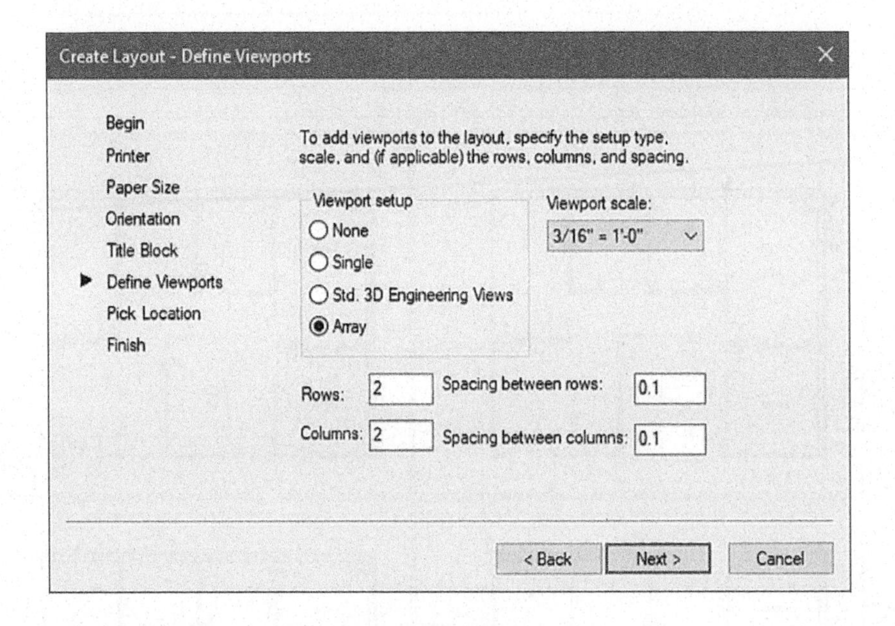

Figure 12-2
Create Layout – Define Viewports dialog box

Complete the Title Block

The **hidden line border** in the **Tenant Space Project Layout tab** shows the plottable area of your plotter, as shown in Figure 12-3. If the title block is too large and extends outside the plottable area, you can either explode and edit the size of the title block or use the **SCALE** command to reduce the title block size.

Step 7. While in **PAPER** space, reduce the size of the title block to fit within the plottable area (Figure 12-4).

Figure 12-3
Hidden line border shows the plottable area of your plotter

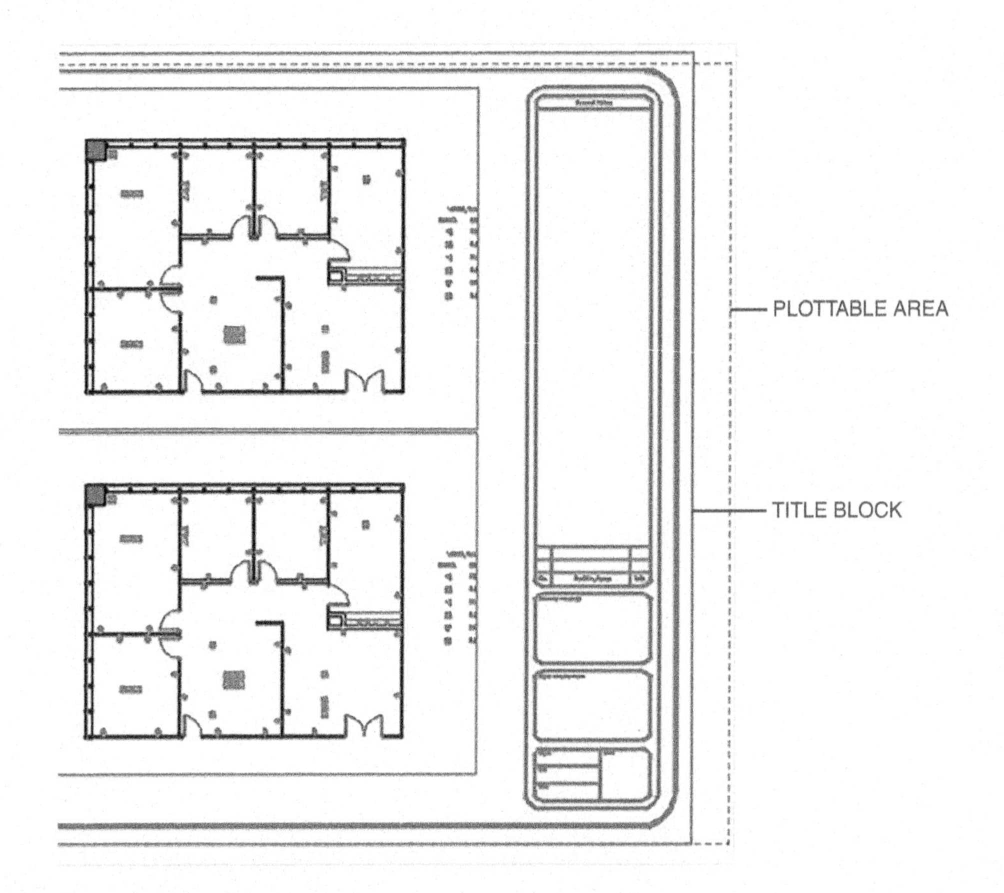

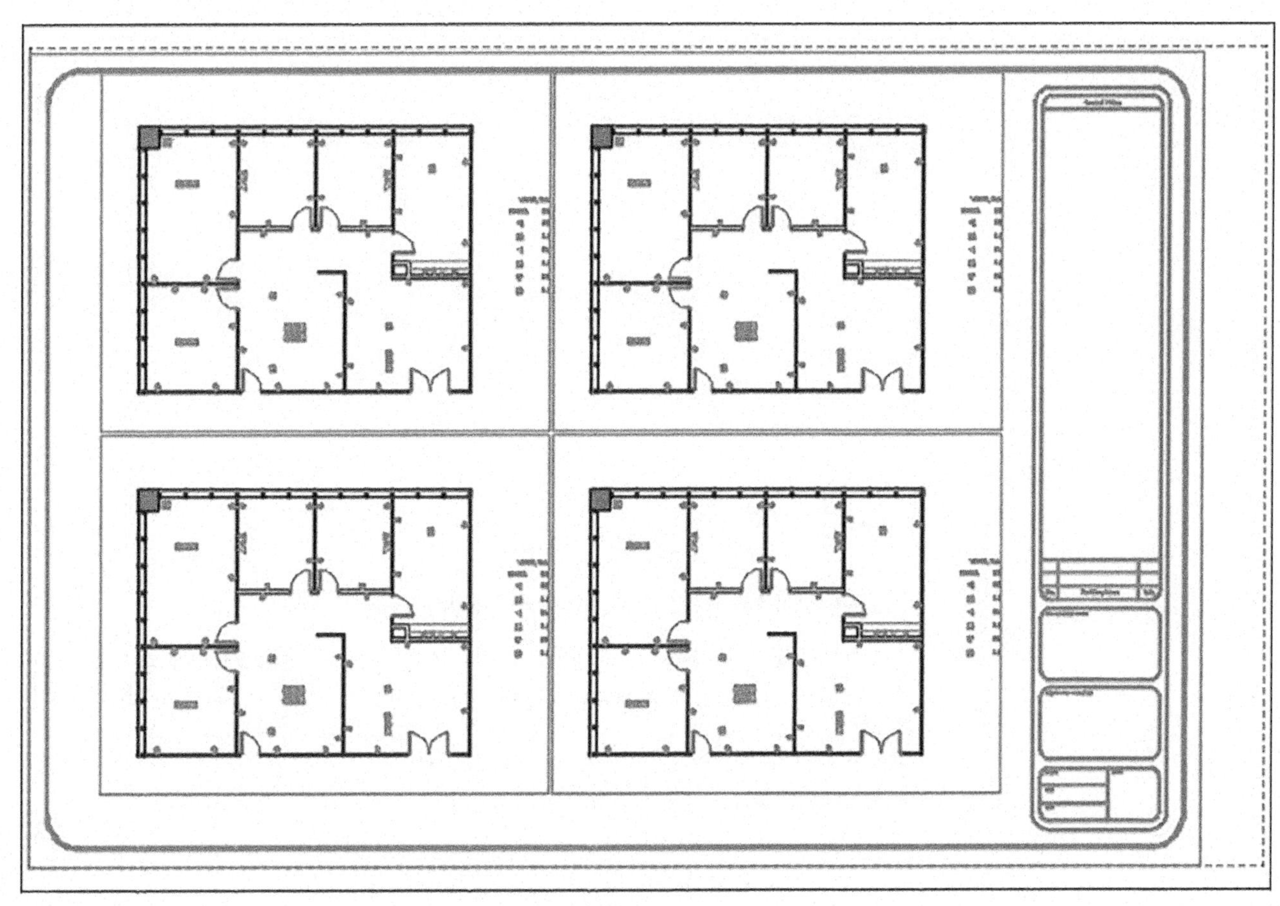

Figure 12-4
Reduce the title block to fit within the plottable area and center viewports inside the title block

Step 8. While in **PAPER** space, use the **MOVE** command to center the four viewports in the title block (Figure 12-4). Click the edge of any viewport boundary to move it or select all four viewports by using a crossing window.

Step 9. While in **PAPER** space, click the viewport boundary edge and use **GRIPS** to make any of the four viewport boundaries larger or smaller, as needed (Figure 12-5).

Step 10. While in **MODEL** space, use the **PAN** command to center the drawings within the four viewports. In **PAPER** space, use **PAN** to center the viewports within the drawing area. (Figure 12-5).

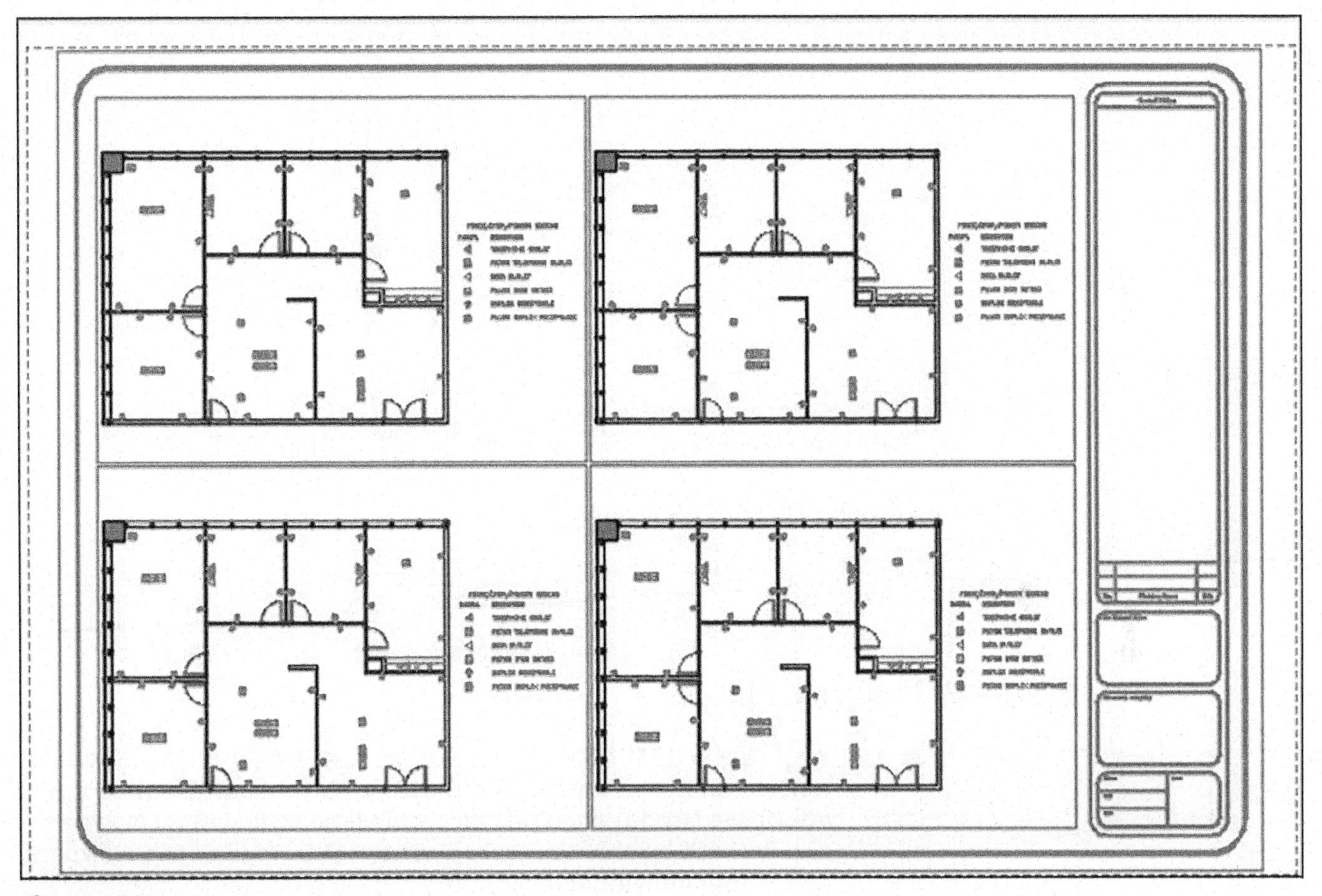

Figure 12-5
Make viewports larger or smaller using **Grips** and use **Pan** to center drawings within viewports

Step 11. While in **PAPER** space, make a new text style (not annotative), set the **a-anno-text** layer current, and complete the title block as described next (Figure 12-6):

YOUR NAME *(3/16″ high, Arial font, Center justification)*

COURSE NUMBER *(3/16″ high, Arial font, Center justification)*

SCHOOL NAME *(3/16″ high, Arial font, Center justification)*

TENANT SPACE *(3/16″ high, Arial font, Center justification)*

CH12-EXERCISE1 *(1/8″ high, Arial font, Left justification)*

DATE *(1/8″ high, Arial font, Left justification)*

3/16″ = 1′–0″ *(1/8″ high, Arial font, Left justification)*

Figure 12-6
Complete the title block

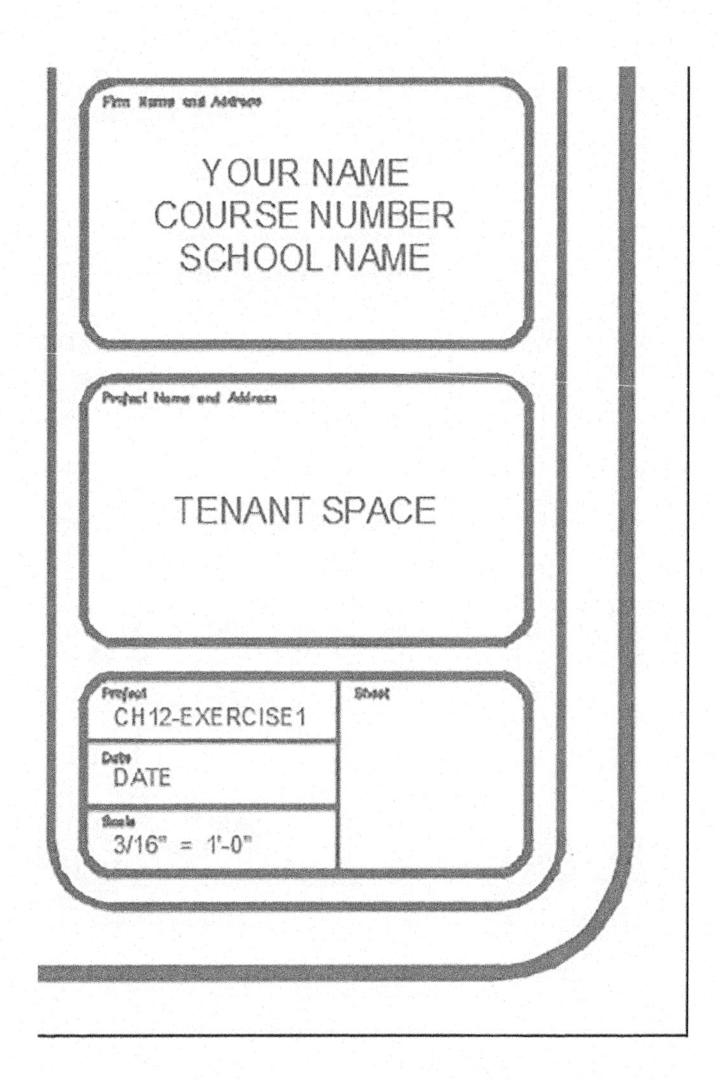

Use Layer Properties Manager to Freeze Viewport Layers

Step 12. While in tiled **MODEL** space, use the **Layer Properties Manager** to thaw all frozen layers and to turn all layers on. When all layers are thawed and turned on, they will all be visible in all viewports, and you will be able to create a unique drawing in each viewport by turning individual layers off.

Step 13. Click the **Tenant Space Project** tab to return to the layout. While in **MODEL** space, use the **Layer Properties Manager** to freeze layers in the upper-left viewport so only the dimensioned floor plan is visible as described next (Figures 12-7 and 12-8):

Figure 12-7
Use the **Layer Properties Manager** to freeze layers using the **VP Freeze** column

Name	On	Freeze	VP Freeze
0			
a-anno-area			
a-anno-dims			
a-anno-ttbl			
a-clng-susp			
a-door			
a-flor-case			

Figure 12-8
Freeze the non-required layers in all viewports

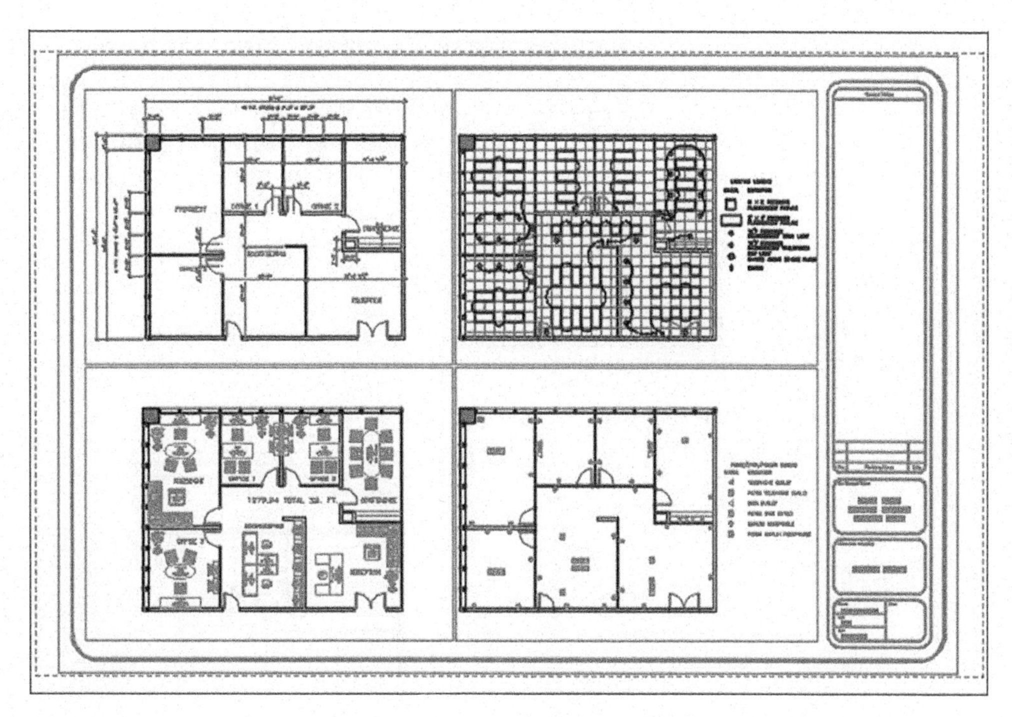

Prompt	**Response**
Type a command:	Click the upper-left viewport to make it active; type **LA <Enter>**
The **Layer Properties Manager** appears:	In the **VP Freeze** column, click the **Freeze/Thaw** symbol to freeze all layers not used to view the dimensioned floor plan in the upper-left viewport (Figure 12-7)

> **TIP**
>
> Position the **viewport** and the **Layer Properties Manager** palette on your display screen so you can watch both. When you freeze a layer, you can see it go away in the floor plan.

Step 14. Click the lower-left viewport to make it active. Use the **Layer Properties Manager** to freeze layers in the lower-left viewport so only the **Furniture Installation Plan** is visible (Figure 12-8).

Step 15. Click the upper-right viewport to make it active. Use the **Layer Properties Manager** to freeze layers in the upper-right viewport so only the **Reflected Ceiling Plan** is visible (Figure 12-8).

Step 16. Click the lower-right viewport to make it active. Use the **Layer Properties Manager** to freeze layers in the lower-right viewport so only the **Voice/Data/Power Plan** is visible (Figure 12-8).

> **TIP**
>
> There will be occasions when you will want to select or deselect all layers at the same time. To do that, position the cursor in an open area in the dialog box, right-click, and then click **Select All** or **Clear All**.

Scale and Center the Plans

Step 17. While in **PAPER** space, click the boundary line of all viewports, click **Properties,** and set a standard scale of **3/16″** = **1′-0″** in all four viewports, as shown in Figure 12-9.

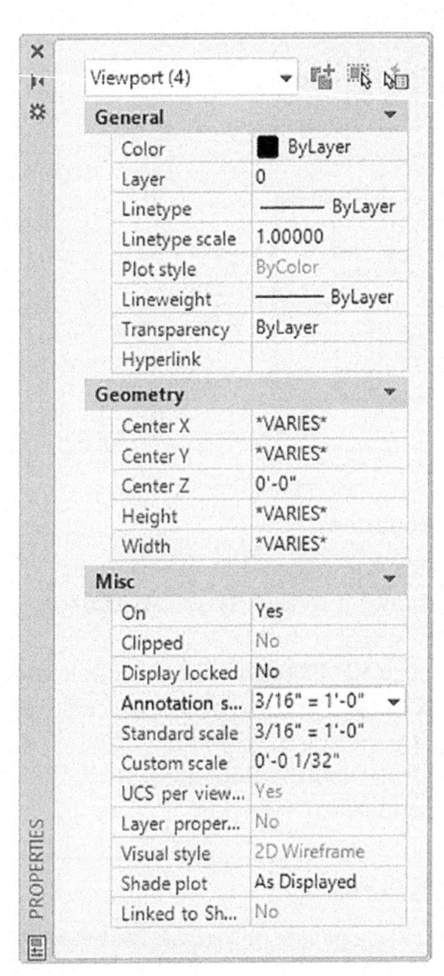

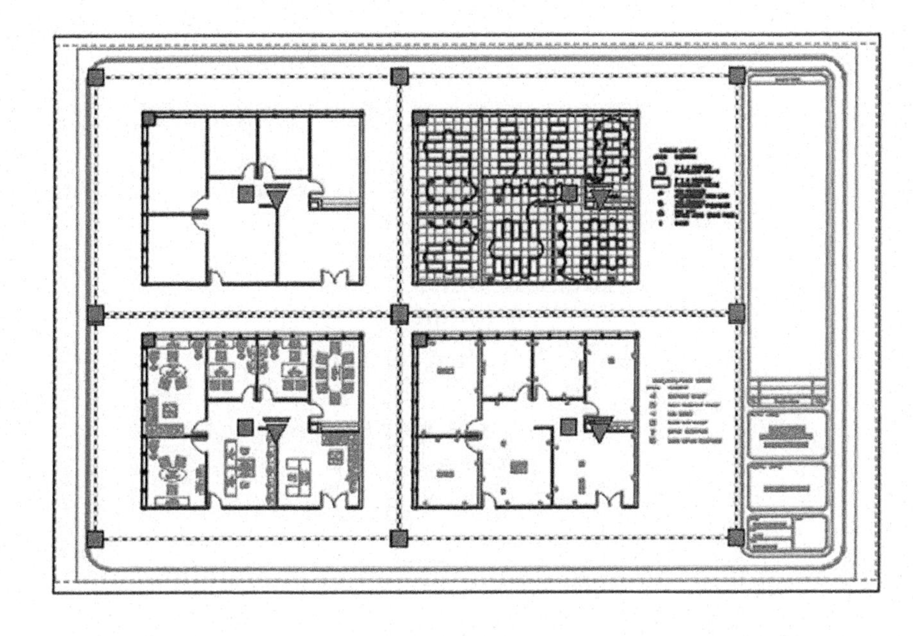

Figure 12-9
Use **Properties** to set a scale of 3/16″ = 1′-0″ in all viewports

Step 18. While in **MODEL** space, use **PAN** to center images in each viewport. Do not zoom in or out while in **MODEL** space. If you do zoom in or out while in **MODEL** space, you will have to reset the scale of the drawing. You will lock the display in Step 21.

Using MVSETUP to Align the Plans

You can use the **MVSETUP** command to align the model space views horizontally and vertically within each viewport.

Step 19. While in **MODEL** space, use the **MVSETUP** command to align the plans in the viewports as described next (Figure 12-10):

Prompt	**Response**
Type a command:	Type **MVSETUP <Enter>**
Enter an option [Align Create Scale viewports Options Title block Undo]:	Type **A <Enter>**

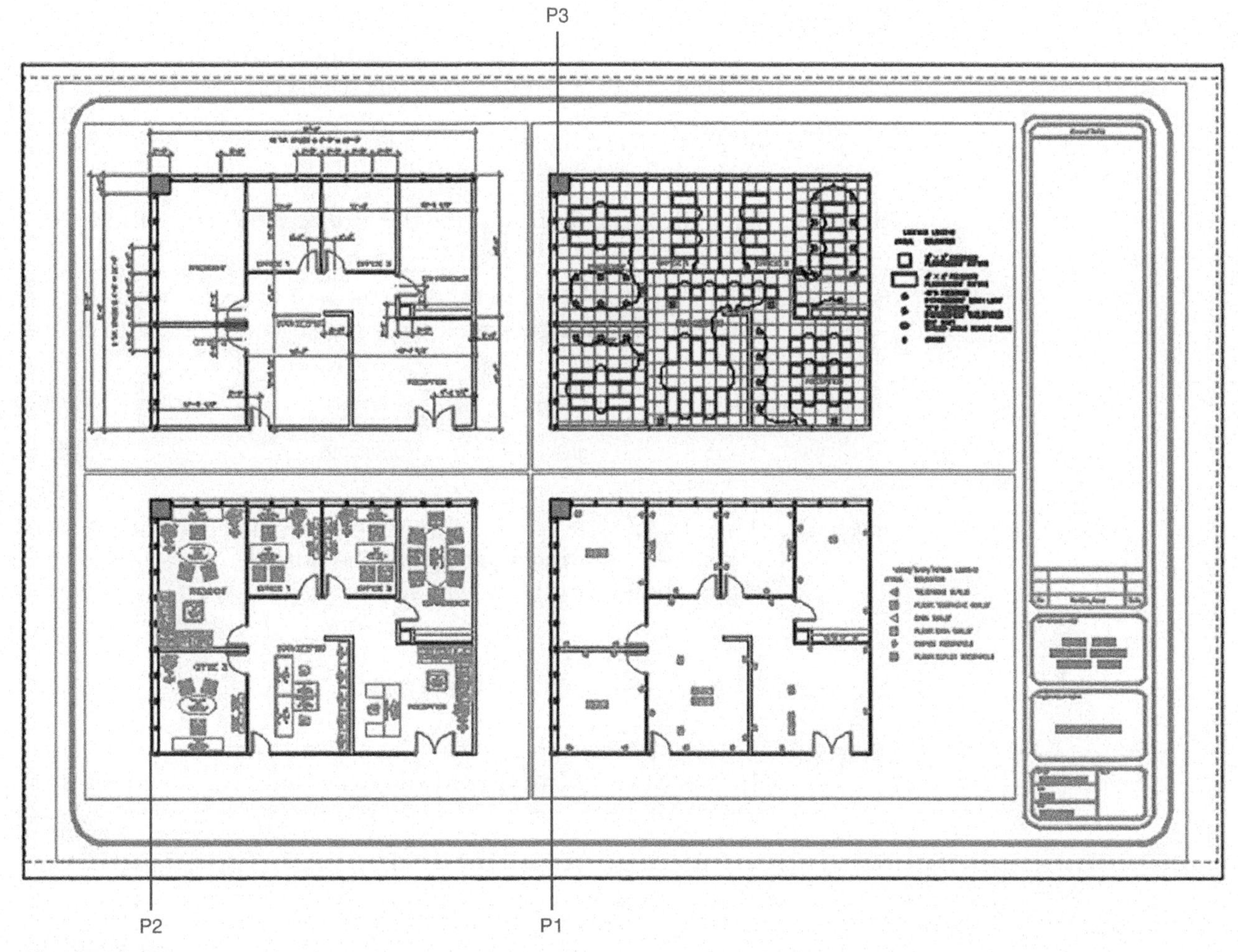

Figure 12-10
Use **MVSETUP** to align viewports horizontally and vertically

Prompt	Response
Enter an option [Angled Horizontal Vertical Alignment Rotate view Undo]:	Type **H <Enter>**
	Click the lower-right viewport to make it active
	Osnap-Intersection
of	**P1→** (Figure 12-10)
Specify point in viewport to be panned:	Click the lower-left viewport to make it active
	Osnap-Intersection
of	**P2→** (Figure 12-10)
Enter an option [Angled Horizontal Vertical Alignment Rotate view Undo]:	Type **V <Enter>**
	Click the upper-right viewport to make it active
	Osnap-Intersection
of	**P3→** (Figure 12-10)
Specify point in viewport to be panned:	Click the lower-right viewport to make it active

Prompt	Response
	Osnap-Intersection
of	**P1→** (Figure 12-10)

Step 20. Align, horizontally and vertically, any remaining **MODEL** space views that need to be aligned.

Step 21. While in **PAPER** space, use the **Properties** command to lock the display of all four viewports.

Step 22. Create the following new layer. In the **Plot** column of the **Layer Properties Manager**, click the printer icon to set it to **NoPlot**.

Layer name	Color	Linetype	Lineweight
a-anno-vprt	green	continuous	.006″ (.15 mm)

Step 23. While in **PAPER** space, change the outside edges of the four viewports to the **a-anno-vprt** layer. The outside edges of the viewports will no longer print but will still be visible.

Complete the Presentation

Step 24. While in **PAPER** space with the **a-anno-text** layer current, label the views using **Dtext** with the Arial font, 1/4″ high, as shown in Figure 12-11.

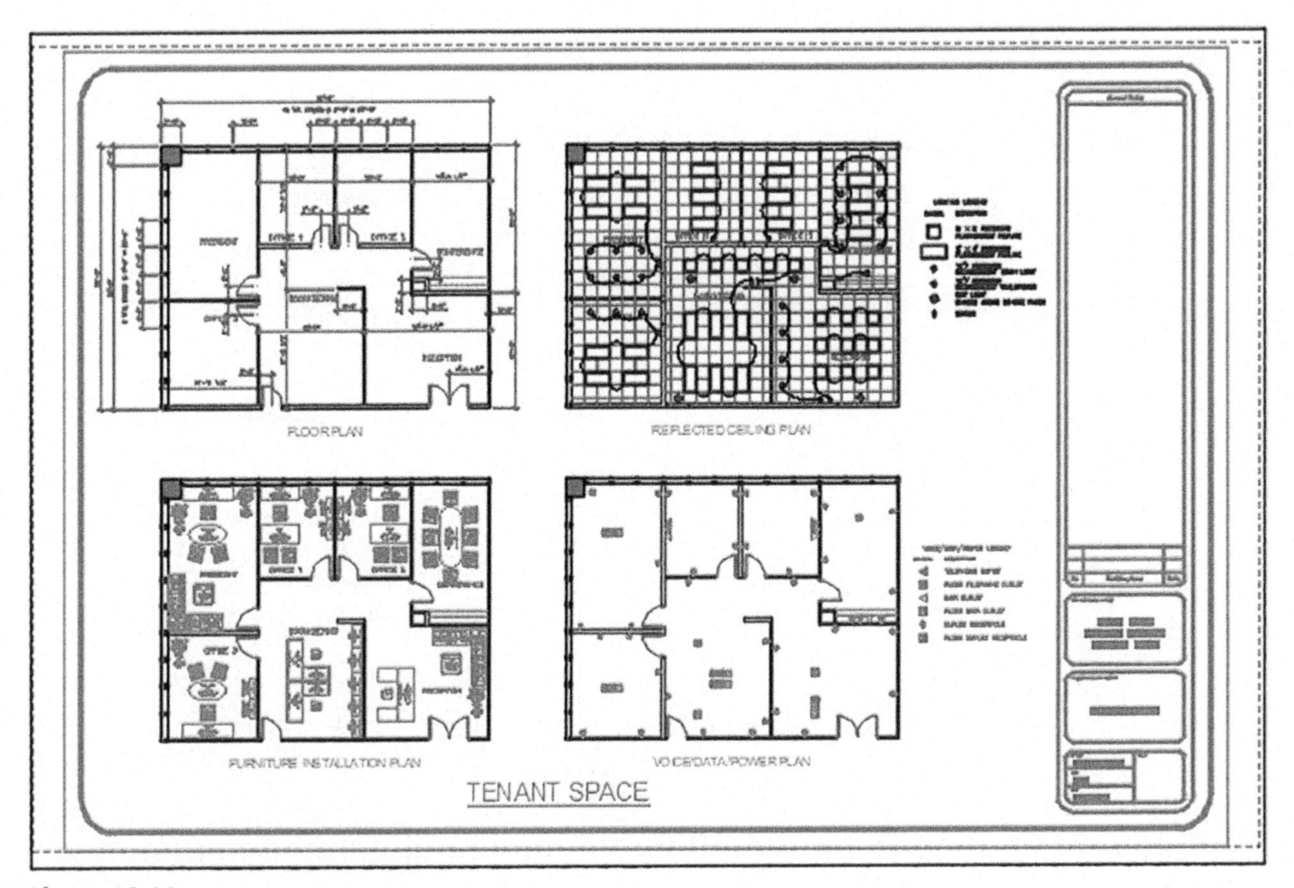

Figure 12-11
Exercise 12-1 complete

Step 25. Use the same font, 1/2″ high, to label the entire drawing **TENANT SPACE**.

Step 26. Make a color-dependent plot style set for all colors to plot black. Set it current.

Step 27. When you have completed Exercise 12-1, save your work in at least two places.

Step 28. Plot Exercise 12-1. Verify the information in the **Tenant Space Project layout** tab, **Page Setup Manager**, and plot the layout at a scale of **1:1**.

EXERCISE 12-2
Making a Four-Sheet Presentation of the Tenant Space Project Using a Sheet Set

When you have completed Exercise 12-2, your drawings will look similar to the four separate sheets shown in Figure 12-12 A–D.

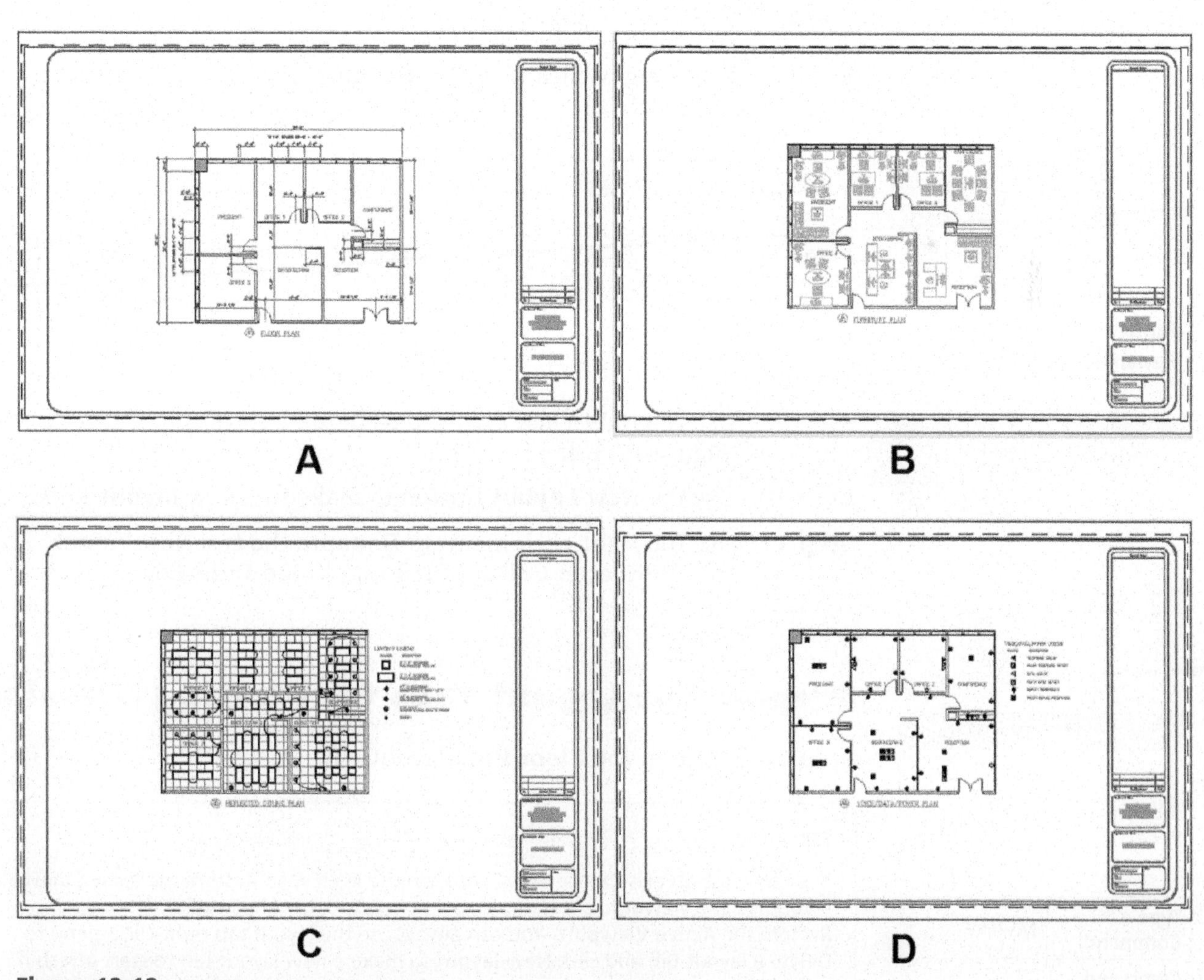

Figure 12-12
Exercise 12-2 complete

Step 1. Open existing drawing **CH11-EXERCISE1-VOICE-DATA-POWER**; save it as **CH12-EXERCISE2**.

Step 2. **Erase** your name, class, and date.

Step 3. Use **Zoom-All** to view the entire drawing.

Step 4. Turn the **Grid OFF**.

Step 5. While in the **MODEL** tab, use the **Layer Properties Manager** to thaw all frozen layers and to turn all layers on. When all layers are thawed and turned on, they will all be visible in all viewports, and you will be able to create a unique drawing in each layout viewport by freezing individual layers.

Step 6. Change the layer lineweights to the **D-size sheet** lineweights as described in Chapter 5.

Step 7. Create the following new layer and set it as the current layer:

Layer name	Color	Linetype	Lineweight
a-anno-vprt	green	continuous	.006″ (.15 mm)

Make New Layout Tabs and Rename the New Layout Tabs

Step 8. Use the right-click menu to **Rename** Layout1 to **Floor Plan** (Figure 12-13).

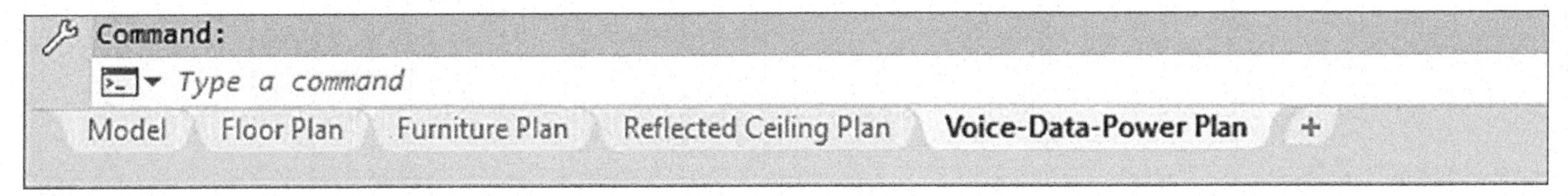

Figure 12-13
Rename layout tabs

Step 9. Use the right-click menu to **Rename** Layout 2 to **Furniture Plan** (Figure 12-13).

Step 10. Use the **New Layout** button to make two **New layout** tabs.

Step 11. Use the right-click menu to **Rename** the two **New layout** tabs **Reflected Ceiling Plan** and **Voice-Data-Power Plan** (Figure 12-13).

Prepare the Layout Tabs for Plotting Drawings

MVIEW	
Ribbon/ Panel	Layout/ Layout Viewports
Type a Command:	MVIEW
Command Alias:	MV

Step 12. Click on the **Floor Plan** layout tab.

> **TIP**
>
> You can erase an existing viewport. You can use **MVIEW** to **Restore the Active Viewport** if you find the viewport is missing from a layout tab. Use the **MVIEW, Fit** option to **Restore the Active Viewport**. You can always use the layout tab right-click menu to **Delete** a layout tab and click **New layout** to make a new layout tab to start afresh if needed.

Step 13. Right-click the **Floor Plan** tab and click **Page Setup Manager....** The **Page Setup Manager** appears with **Floor Plan** highlighted in the **Current page setup** list.

Step 14. Click **Modify....** The **Page Setup – Floor Plan** dialog box appears.

Step 15. Click **DWF6 ePlot.pc3** or the plotter you will use for **ARCH D (36.00 × 24.00 Inches)** paper.

Step 16. Make the settings shown for the **Page Setup – Floor Plan** dialog box as shown in Figure 12-14. Click **OK** and click **Close.**

Step 17. While in **PAPER** space, click the viewport boundary line and use grips to make the viewport size similar to Figure 12-15.

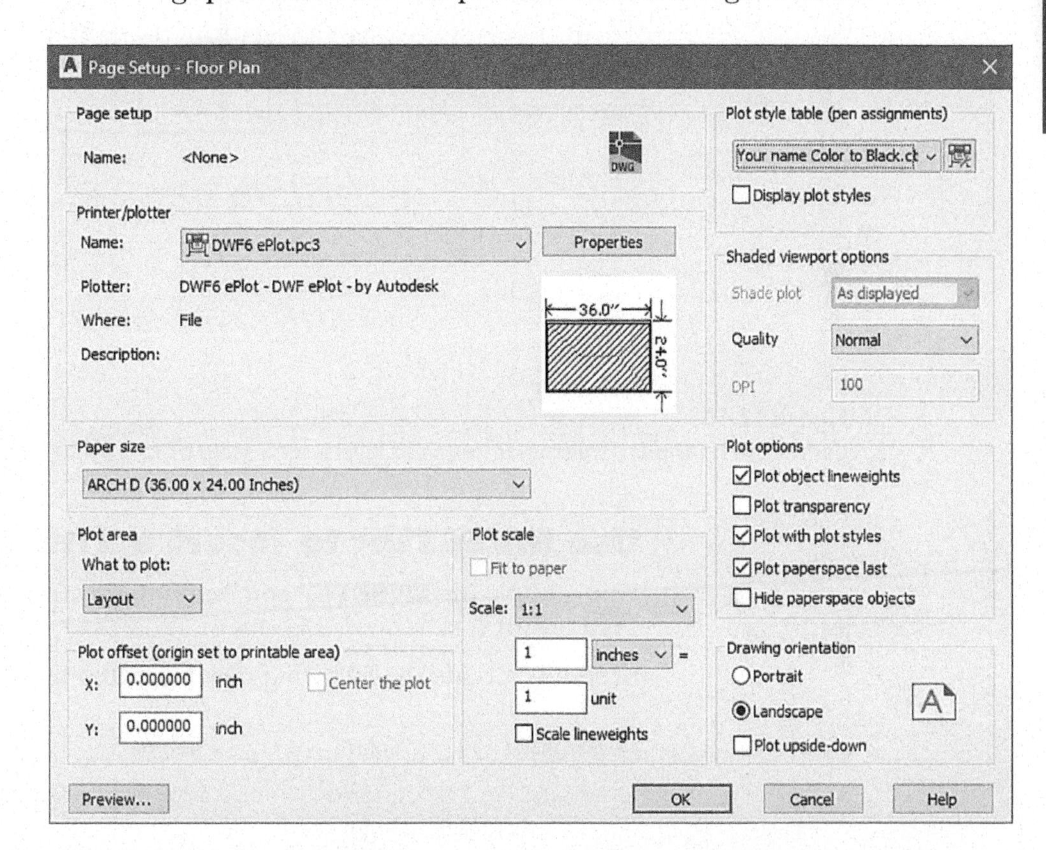

Figure 12-14
Settings for **Page Setup – Floor Plan**

Step 18. While in **MODEL** space, use the **PAN** and **Zoom** commands to center the drawing within the viewport (Figure 12-15).

Step 19. While in **MODEL** space, use the **Layer Properties Manager, VP Freeze** to freeze layers in the *current viewport only* so only the dimensioned Floor Plan is visible, as shown in Figure 12-15.

Step 20. **Erase** the Scale text, keep the North arrow, and center the title **FLOOR PLAN**.

Step 21. While in **PAPER** space, click the boundary line of the viewport, click **Properties,** and set a standard scale of **1/4" = 1'-0"** in the viewport, as shown in Figure 12-15, and lock the display.

Step 22. While in **PAPER** space, set the **LTSCALE** as needed to see the dashed linetype.

Step 23. Repeat Steps 12 through 22 for the **Furniture Plan**, **Reflected Ceiling Plan**, and **Voice-Data-Power Plan** layout tabs.

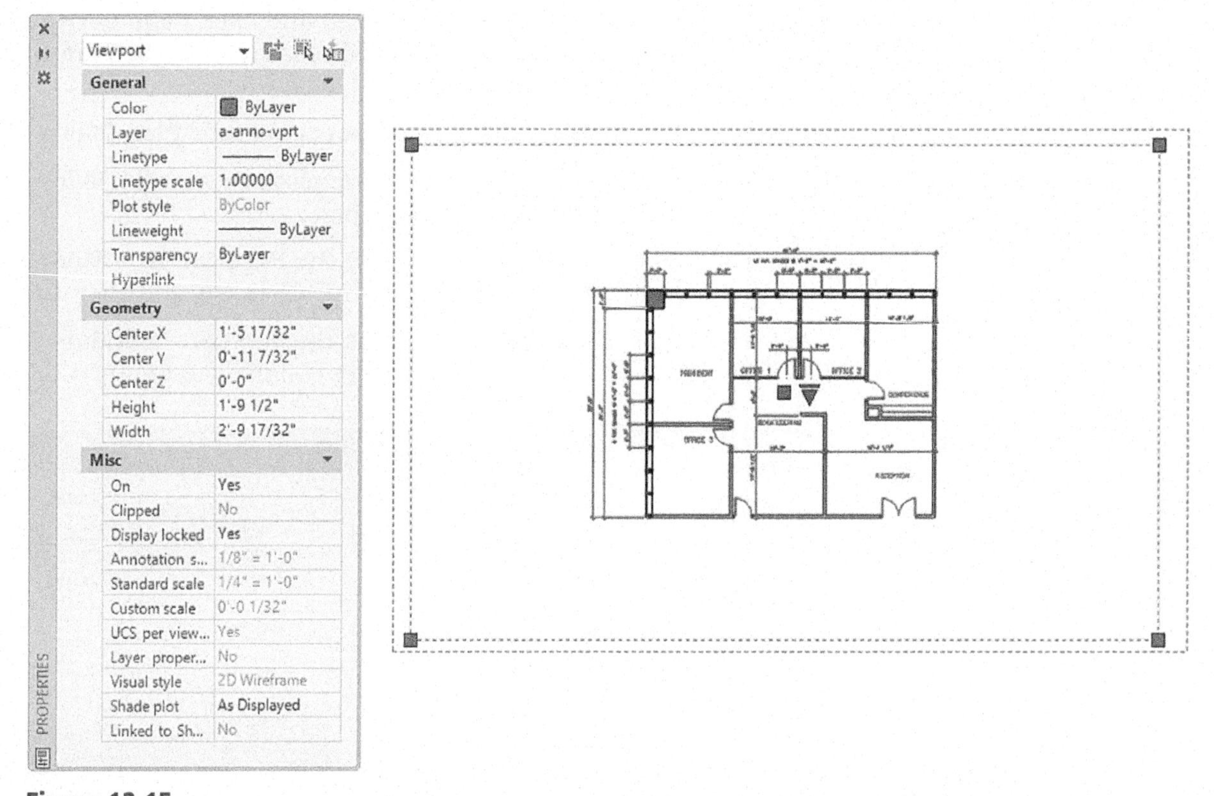

Figure 12-15
Center the floor plan, freeze non-required layers, set a scale of 1/4″ = 1′0″, and lock the display

Use MVSETUP to Insert a Title Block

You can use the **MVSETUP** command to insert a title block into the **Floor Plan** layout tab.

Step 24. Create the following new layer and set it as the current layer:

Layer name	Color	Linetype	Lineweight
a-anno-ttbl	magenta	continuous	.008″ (.20 mm) (for a D-size drawing)

Step 25. While in **PAPER** space, use the **MVSETUP** command to insert an architectural title block as described next (Figure 12-16):

Prompt	Response
Type a command:	Type **MVSETUP <Enter>**
Enter an option [Align Create Scale viewports Options Title block Undo]:	Type **T <Enter>**
Enter title block option [Delete objects Origin Undo Insert] <Insert>:	**<Enter>** (to accept Insert)
Enter number of title block to load or [Add Delete Redisplay]:	Type **12 <Enter>**
Create a drawing named arching.dwg? <Y>:	Type **N <Enter>**

The hidden line border in the Layout tab shows the *plottable area* of your plotter, as shown in Figure 12-16. If the title block is too large and extends outside the plottable area, you can either explode and edit the size of the title block or use the **SCALE** command to reduce the title block size.

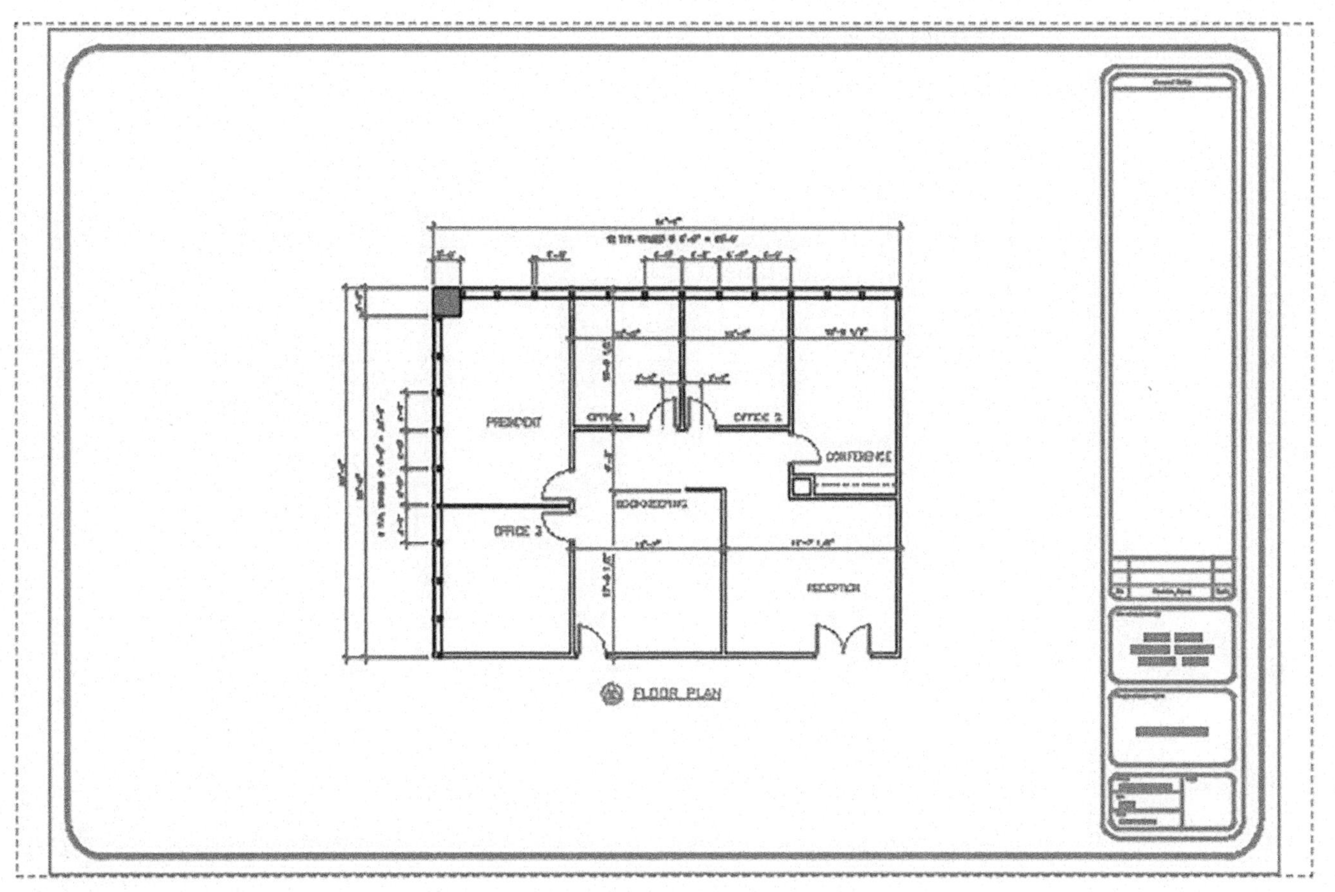

Figure 12-16
Insert the architectural title block, scale it if needed, and complete the title block

Step 26. While in **PAPER** space, reduce the size of the title block to fit within the plottable area. Erase the four lines around the outside of the title block (Figure 12-16).

Step 27. While in **PAPER** space, make a new text style, set the **a-anno-text** layer current, and complete the title block as described next (Figure 12-16):

YOUR NAME *(3/16" high, Arial font, Center justification)*

COURSE NUMBER *(3/16" high, Arial font, Center justification)*

SCHOOL NAME *(3/16" high, Arial font, Center justification)*

TENANT SPACE *(3/16" high, Arial font, Center justification)*

CH12-EXERCISE2 *(1/8" high, Arial font, Left justification)*

DATE *(1/8" high, Arial font, Left justification)*
1/4" = 1'-0" *(1/8" high, Arial font, Left justification)*

Step 28. While in **PAPER** space, make sure the viewport is on the **a-anno-vprt** layer and turn the **a-anno-vprt** layer **OFF**. The outside edges of the viewport will no longer be visible and will not print (Figure 12-16).

Step 29. While in **PAPER** space, **WBLOCK** the title block you just completed and **INSERT** it into the **Furniture Plan**, **Reflected Ceiling Plan**, and **Voice-Data-Power Plan** layout tabs to complete each layout tab.

Quick View Tools

The **Quick View Layouts** tool in the status bar allows you to preview and switch between the current drawing and its layouts. The **Quick View Drawings** tool in the status bar allows you to preview and switch between open drawings and their layouts.

Step 30. Type **QVLAYOUT <Enter>** to display the **Model** tab and all four layout tabs (Figure 12-17).

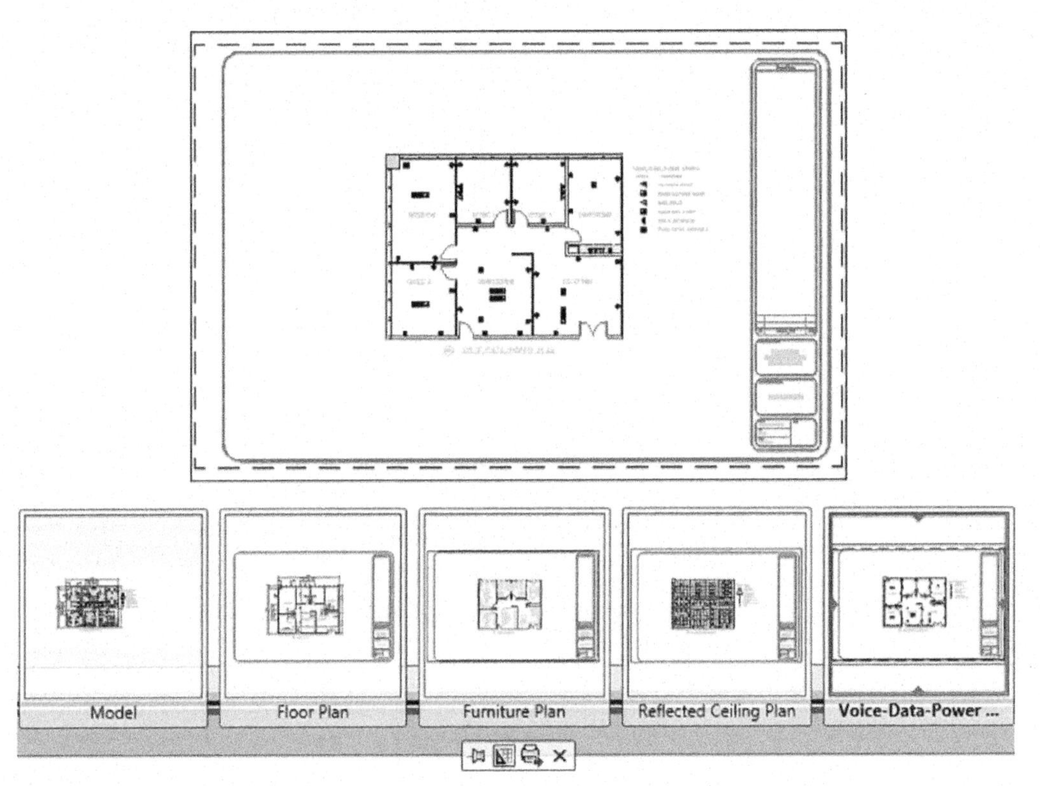

Figure 12-17
Use **Quick View Layouts** to display the **Model** tab and all four layout tabs

When you click **Quick View Layouts**, the model space and paper space layouts in the current drawing are displayed as thumbnail images (Figure 12-17). If you click an image of a layout, it becomes the current layout. You can also click the **Plot** or **Publish** icon on the image to plot or publish each individual layout.

> **TIP**
>
> You can also simply hover over the drawing tab at the top of the drawing area. You will see previews of all layouts in any drawing, complete with **Plot** and **Publish** buttons.

New Sheet Set and Sheet Set Manager

NEW SHEET SET	
Application Menu:	New/
Menu Bar:	File/New Sheet Set ...
Type a Command:	NEWSHEETSET

Use the **New Sheet Set** command to organize layouts into one set when you have several different drawings that you want to package together. Save all the drawings into a separate folder and use the **New Sheet Set** command to organize the layouts of each drawing into a single sheet set. Name the sheet set and save it as a .dst file type within the **New Sheet Set** command. Use the **Sheet Set Manager** to open sheet sets. You can plot, publish, eTransmit, and ZIP sheet sets.

Step 31. Make a new folder labeled **Tenant Space Sheet Set** in the drive in which you want to save the drawing. Save drawing **CH12-EXERCISE2** in the new folder. Be sure to save the drawing instead of copying the drawing so AutoCAD recognizes the completed layout tabs.

Step 32. Make a new sheet set with the name **TENANT SPACE PROJECT**, as described next:

Prompt	Response
Type a command:	**New Sheet Set...** (or type **NEWSHEETSET <Enter>**)
The **Create Sheet Set - Begin** tab appears:	Click **Existing drawings** Click **Next**
The **Create Sheet Set - Sheet Set Details** tab appears:	Type **TENANT SPACE PROJECT** in the **Name of new sheet set:** input box (Figure 12-18)
Click the **ellipsis (...)** button to the right of **Store sheet set data file (.dst) here:**	Click the **Tenant Space Sheet Set** folder Click **Open** Click **Next**
The **Create Sheet Set - Choose Layouts** tab appears:	Click **Browse**
The **Browse for Folder** dialog box appears:	Click the **Tenant Space Sheet Set** folder Click **OK**
The layouts in the drawings in that folder appear as shown in Figure 12-19:	Click **Next**

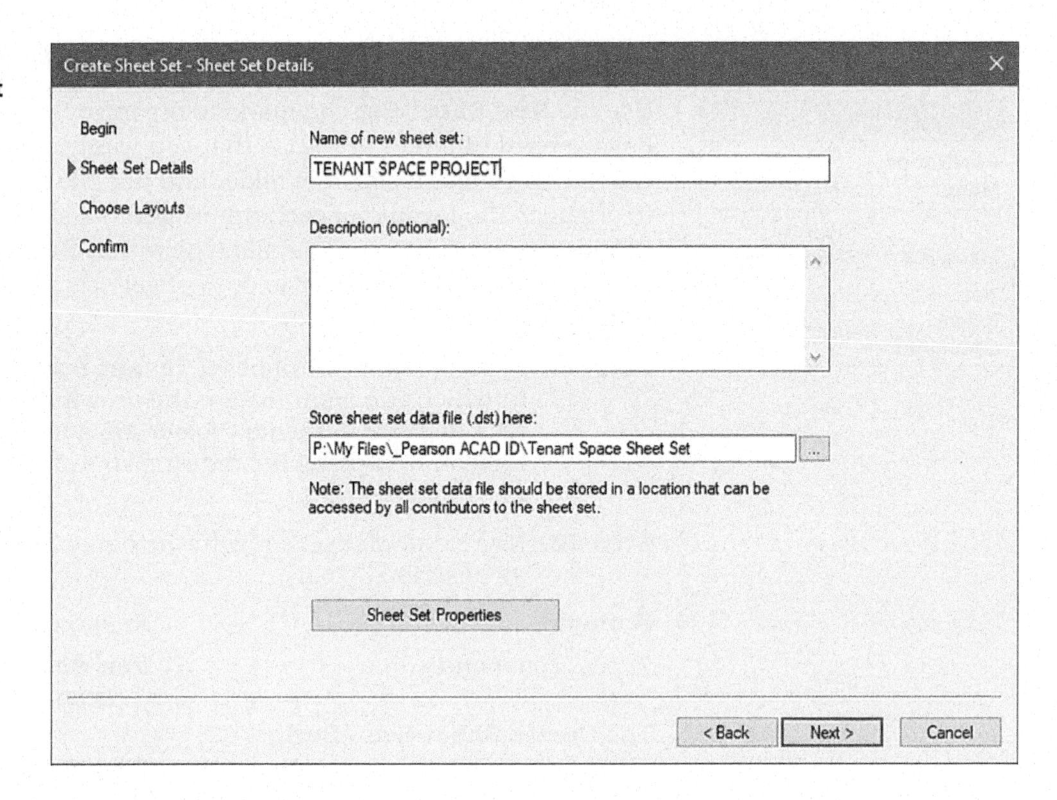

Figure 12-18
Create Sheet Set – Sheet Set Details tab

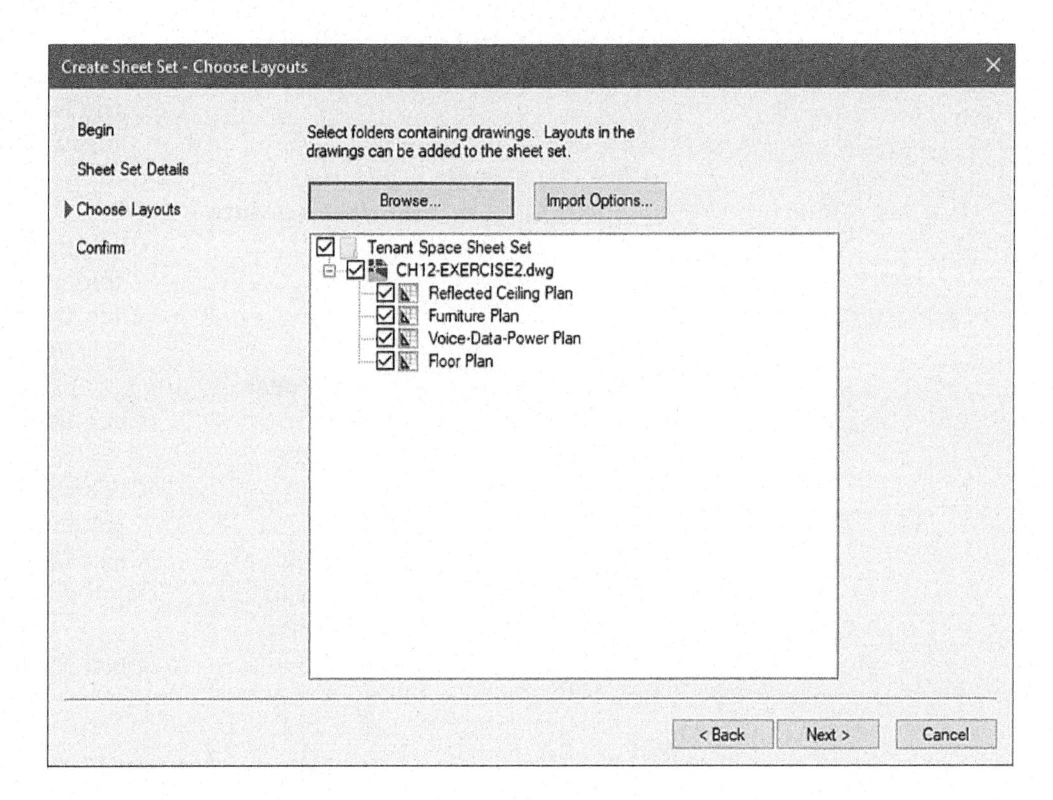

Figure 12-19
Create Sheet Set – Choose Layouts tab

Prompt	Response
The **Create Sheet Set – Confirm** tab appears (Figure 12-20):	Click **Finish**
The **Sheet Set Manager** palette appears with the sheet list.	

Figure 12-20
Create Sheet Set – Confirm tab

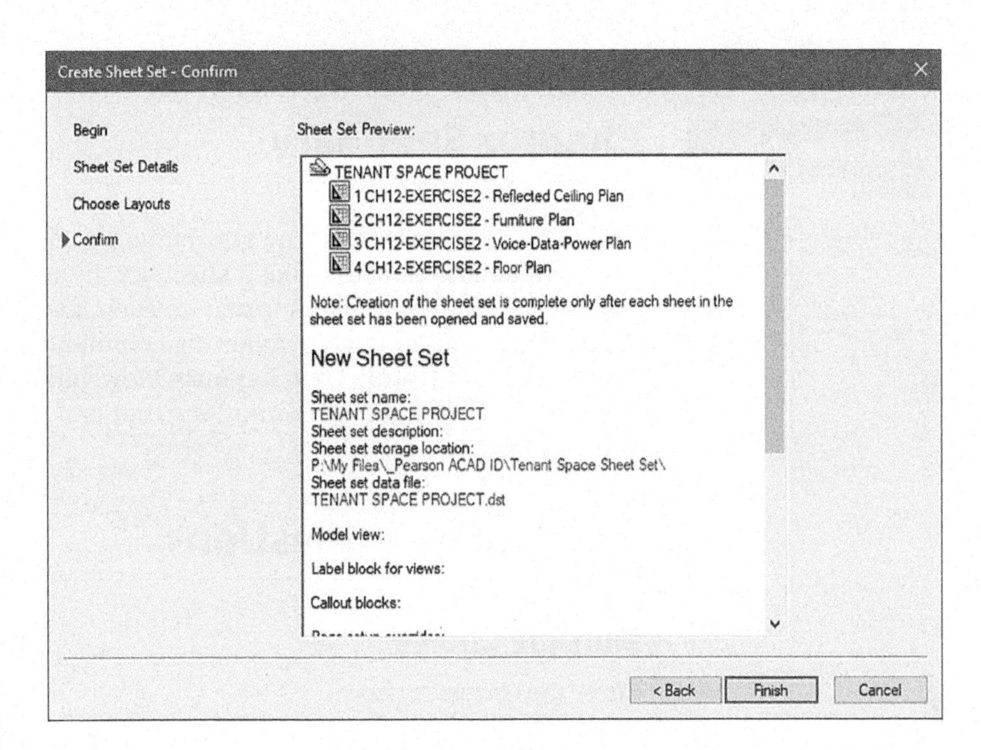

SHEET SET MANAGER	
Ribbon/ Panel	View/Palettes
Standard Toolbar:	
Menu Bar:	Tools/ Palettes/ Sheet Set Manager
Type a Command:	SHEETSET
Command Alias:	SSM
Keyboard:	<Ctrl>+4

Step 33. Hold your mouse over any sheet that needs to be renumbered or renamed and right-click. Use the **Rename and Renumber...** command to correct any numbers or names, so your sheets appear as shown on the right in Figure 12-21.

Step 34. If you need to rearrange the order of the sheets, click and hold on the sheet name, drag it to the desired location (a black line appears), and release the mouse button.

Step 35. With the **Sheet Set Manager** open, test your sheet set by double-clicking on each sheet in the drawing set.

Step 36. When you have completed Exercise 12-2, save your work in at least two places.

Step 37. **Plot** Exercise 12-2. Plot each layout at a scale of **1:1**.

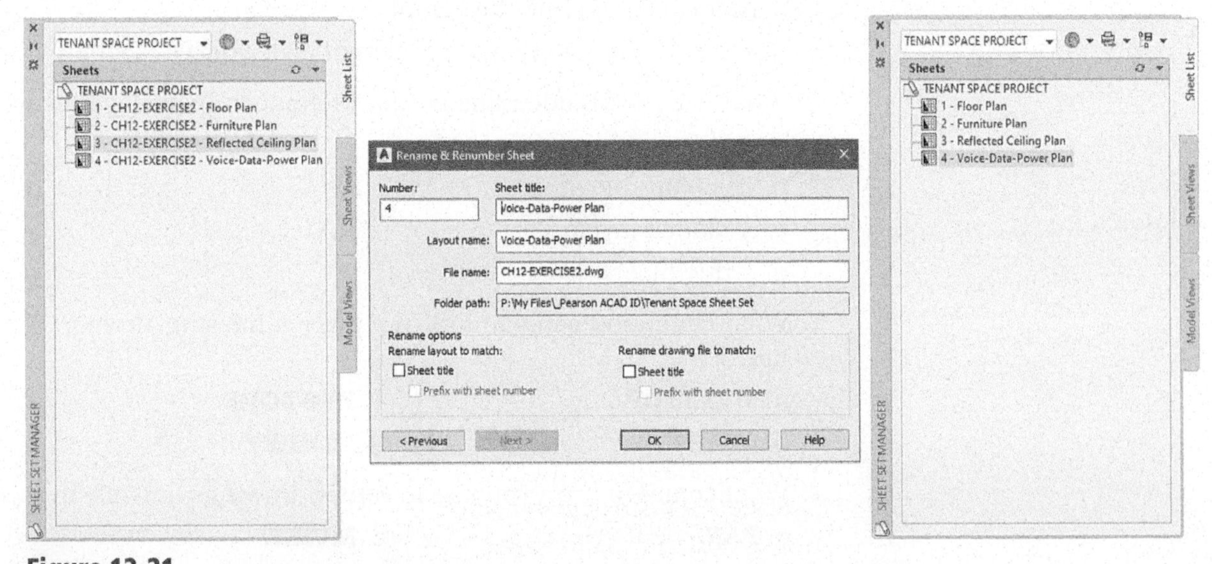

Figure 12-21
Rename and renumber sheets. Correct order is on the right

Chapter Summary

This chapter provided you the information necessary to make presentations with layouts and how to make a sheet set. In addition, you learned to make layouts with different layers frozen on each layout; to use model space and paper space; and to use the following commands: **Create Layout Wizard**, **MVSETUP**, and **Quick View Layouts**. Now you have the skills and information necessary to make presentations that can be used in interior design and architecture.

Chapter Test Questions

Multiple Choice

Circle the correct answer.

1. Which of the following is a characteristic of paper space?
   a. Models are created.
   b. Dimensions are added to a floor plan.
   c. A title block is added.
   d. Attributes are assigned to furniture.
2. What command do you use to insert an architectural title block around a paper space layout?
   a. **MVIEW**
   b. **VPORTS**
   c. **MVSETUP**
   d. **Properties**
3. The **Create Layout Wizard** command does not do which of the following?
   a. Turn viewports on and off
   b. Scale viewports
   c. Allow you to name the layout
   d. Allow you to specify the corners of a viewport's location
4. What does the hidden line border in a paper space layout represent?
   a. A viewport boundary
   b. The plottable area
   c. A hidden layer
   d. A title block
5. What command can you use to replace a missing viewport in a layout tab?
   a. **MVSETUP**
   b. **MVIEW**
   c. **RESTORE**
   d. **MODIFY**
6. What command can you use to center drawings in while in model space?
   a. **PAN**
   b. **RESTORE**
   c. **MVIEW**
   d. **Properties**

7. What command can you use to set a standard scale of 1/4″ - 1′ in paper space viewports?

   a. **Paper Space**
   b. **Model Space**
   c. **Properties**
   d. **Tilemode**

8. Which of the following can you use to align objects in adjacent viewports accurately in model space?

   a. **MVIEW**
   b. **MOVE**
   c. **VPORTS**
   d. **MVSETUP**

9. Which of the following commands do you use to open a sheet set after it has been made?

   a. **MVSETUP**
   b. **Properties**
   c. **Sheet Set Manager**
   d. **Create Layout Wizard**

10. Which of the following settings in the **Properties** palette do you use to lock the scale of a viewport?

    a. **Display Locked**
    b. **UCS per viewport**
    c. **Clipped**
    d. **ON or OFF**

Matching

Write the number of the correct answer on the line.

a. **Sheet Set**_____
b. **Quick View Layouts**_____
c. **VP Freeze**_____
d. **Model Space**_____
e. **Paper Space**_____

1. The space where a title block is placed around a floor plan
2. The space where a floor plan is made
3. A command used to organize multiple layouts into a single package
4. A command used to display multiple layouts as thumbnail images
5. A column in the **Layer Properties Manager** palette

True or False

Circle the correct answer.

1. **True or False:** A viewport boundary cannot be enlarged.
2. **True or False:** Model space may be active when you are working with paper space viewports.
3. **True or False:** A viewport boundary can be moved to a layer that is turned **OFF** so it will not print.
4. **True or False:** The **MVSETUP** command cannot be used to align objects in adjacent viewports.
5. **True or False:** Sheets in a sheet set can be renamed and renumbered.

List

1. Five ways of accessing the **Layers Properties Manager**.
2. Five layer tools from the **Layers Properties Manager** window.
3. Five wild-card characters in the **Search** box of the **Layers Properties Manager**.
4. Five layer options in the **Layers Properties Manager** window.
5. Five prompts for the **MVSETUP** command in model space.
6. Five steps to rotate a **Layout View** using **MVSETUP**.
7. Five options of the **Layout** command.
8. Five layout-related commands.
9. Five view configurations available after the **VPORTS** command is executed.
10. Five view configurations available after the **MVIEW** command is executed.

Questions

1. Why are sheet sets used?
2. When would you use several viewports on a single sheet for a presentation?
3. Why does AutoCAD have model space and paper space?
4. How can you use Quick View Layouts?
5. How can you use the **Properties** command while making layouts?

Chapter Project

Project 12-1: *Hotel Room 2 Presentation Sheet* [BASIC]

1. Open the hotel room 2 power/communication/lighting plan and follow the steps listed for CH12-EXERCISE1.
2. Complete the hotel room 2 presentation sheet as shown in Figure 12-22.

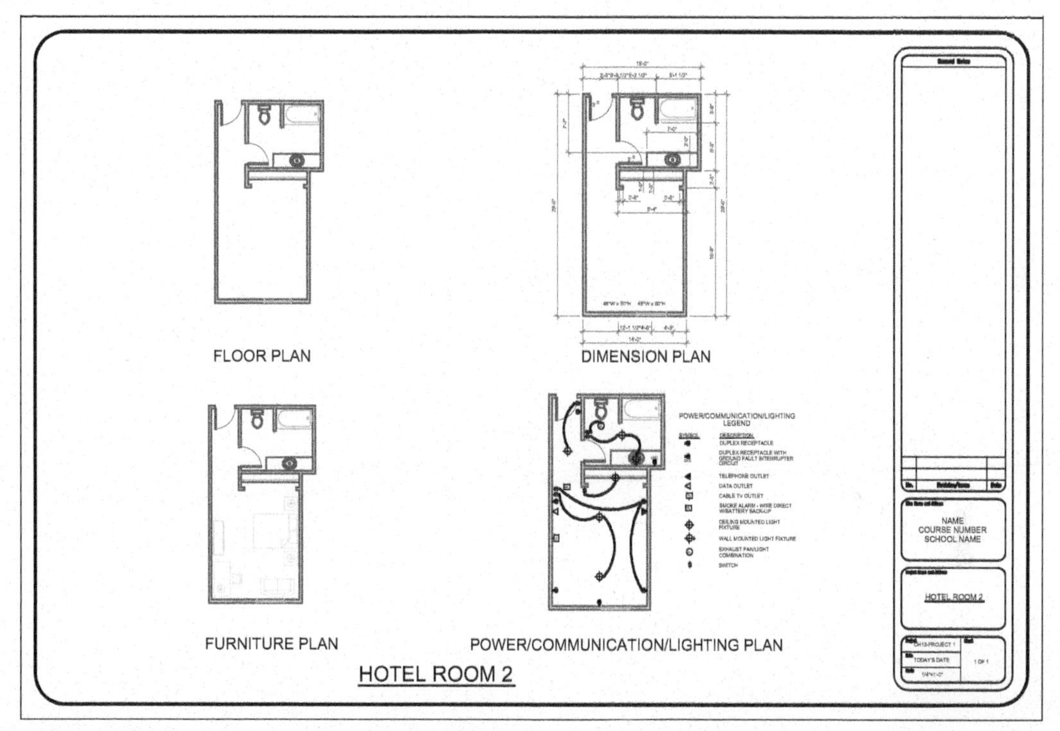

Figure 12-22
Project 12-1: Hotel room 2 presentation sheet

3. Save the drawing in two places and plot or print the drawing to scale.

chapter thirteen

Isometric Drawing and Gradient Hatch Rendering

CHAPTER OBJECTIVES

- Make 2D isometric drawings to scale from 2D orthographic projection drawings.
- Correctly use the following commands and settings:

  ELLIPSE-Isocircle
  SNAP-Style Iso
- Use the **<Ctrl>+E** or **<F5>** key to change from one isoplane to another.
- Use gradient hatch patterns to render isometric drawings.

Axonometric Drawing

axonometric: Forms of 2D drawing that represent 3D objects. The three axonometric drawing forms are isometric, dimetric, and trimetric.

The forms of ***axonometric*** drawing are isometric, dimetric, and trimetric, as shown in Figure 13-1. The trimetric form has the most pleasing appearance because each of the three axes uses a different scale. Dimetric uses the same scale on two axes, and isometric uses the same scale on all three axes. Isometric drawing is the axonometric drawing form covered in this book.

Isometric Drawing

isometric: A 2D drawing method that is used to give the appearance of three dimensions.

Isometric drawing is commonly used to show how objects appear in three dimensions. This drawing method is a two-dimensional one that is used to give the appearance of three dimensions. It is not a 3D modeling form such as those covered in later chapters. In 3D modeling, you actually create 3D objects that can be viewed from any angle and can be placed into a perspective mode.

You can make isometric drawings quickly and easily using AutoCAD software. After you make the proper grid and snap settings, the drawing itself proceeds with little difficulty. The three isometric axes are 30° right, 30° left, and vertical.

Figure 13-1
Axonometric drawing projections

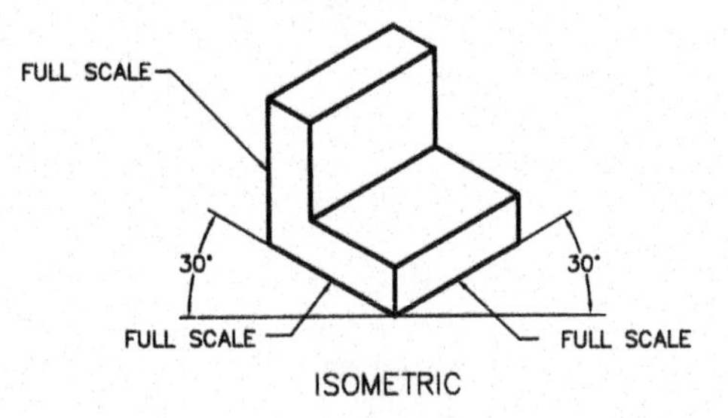

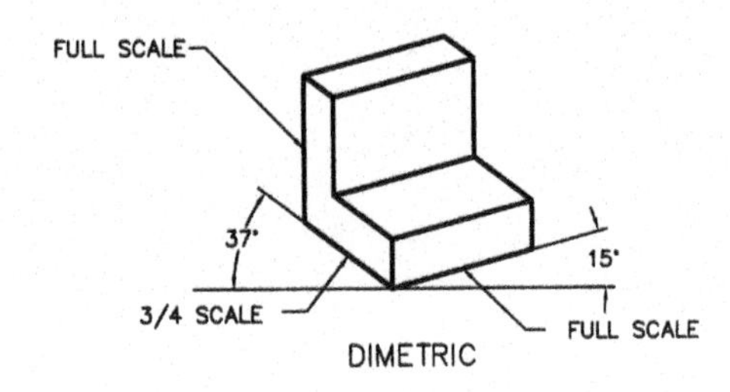

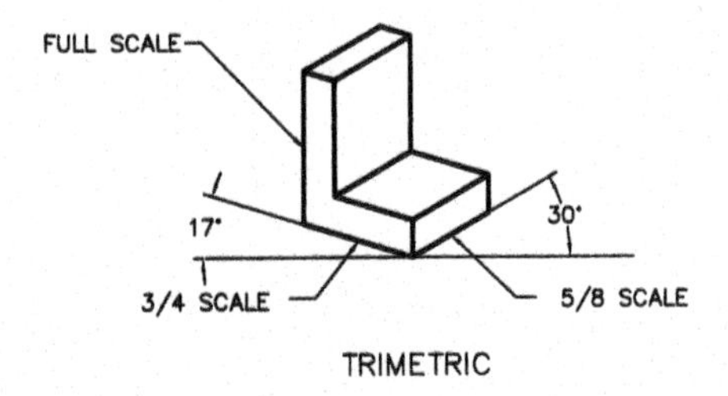

EXERCISE 13-1
Fundamentals of Isometric Drawing

You will draw seven isometric shapes in this exercise to get acquainted with the fundamentals of making isometric drawings using AutoCAD. We will begin with a simple isometric box so that you can become familiar with drawing lines on an isometric axis. All seven of these shapes are drawn on the same sheet and plotted on one 8 1/2″ × 11″ sheet. When you have completed Exercise 13-1, your drawing will look similar to Figure 13-2.

Step 1. Use your workspace to make the following settings:

1. Use **Save As...** to save the drawing with the name **CH13-EXERCISE1**.
2. Set drawing units: **Architectural**
3. Set drawing limits: **11′, 8′6″** (be sure to use the foot symbol)
4. Set snap for an isometric grid, as described next:

Prompt	**Response**
Type a command:	Type **SN <Enter>**
Specify snap spacing or [ON OFF Aspect Legacy Style Type] <0″-0 1/2″>:	Type **S <Enter>**

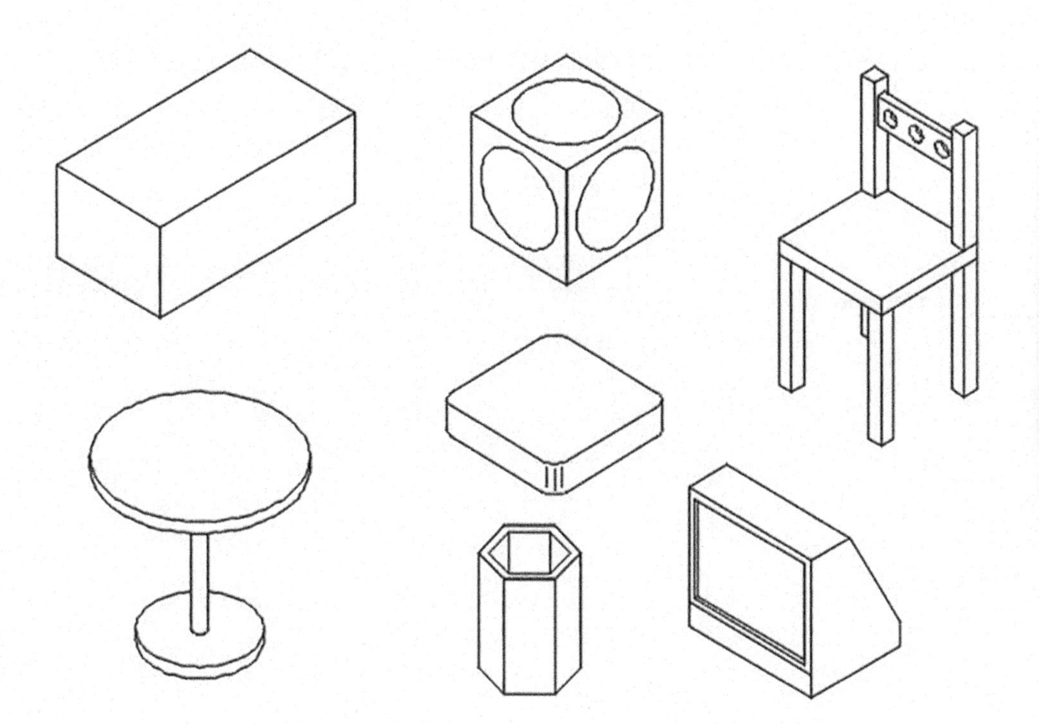

Figure 13-2
Exercise 13-1 complete

Prompt	**Response**
Enter snap grid style [Standard Isometric] <S>:	Click **Isometric** in the command line window or type **I <Enter>** (I for isometric)
Specify vertical spacing <0″–6″>:	Type **1 <Enter>** (if 1″ is not the default)

When you want to exit the isometric grid, type **SN <Enter>** and click **Style** in the command line window, or type **S <Enter>** and click **Standard** or type **S <Enter>** again to select the standard grid. Keep the isometric grid for this exercise.

Isometric Drawing (<ISODRAFT>) button on the status bar allows easy switching between the standard and isometric styles, as well as switching between isometric planes.

5. Set **GRIDDISPLAY**: **0**
6. Set grid Y spacing: **3″**
7. Create the following layer:

Layer name	Color	Linetype	Lineweight
Layer1	blue	continuous	.0070″ (.18 mm)

8. Set **Layer1** current.
9. Use **Zoom-All.**
10. Use the **Drafting Settings** dialog box to display the dot grid in 2D model space. You access the **Drafting Settings** dialog box by right-clicking on **SNAP** or **GRID** on the status bar, and then clicking **Snap Settings...** (Figure 13-3) or **Grid Settings**.

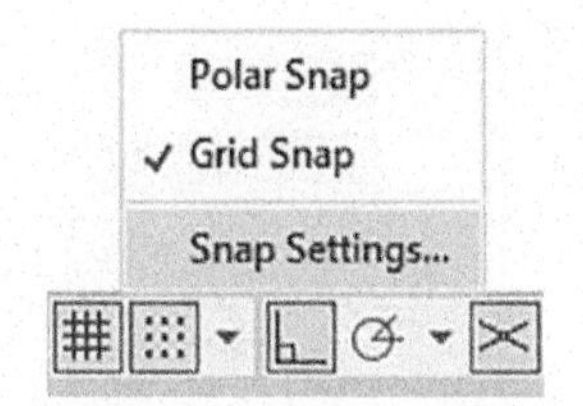

Figure 13-3
Accessing the **Drafting Settings** dialog box

Drafting Settings Dialog Box

When the isometric 1″ snap and 3″ grid are set, **GRIDDISPLAY** is set to **0**, and the dot grid is set, the **Drafting Settings** dialog box displays as shown in Figure 13-4.

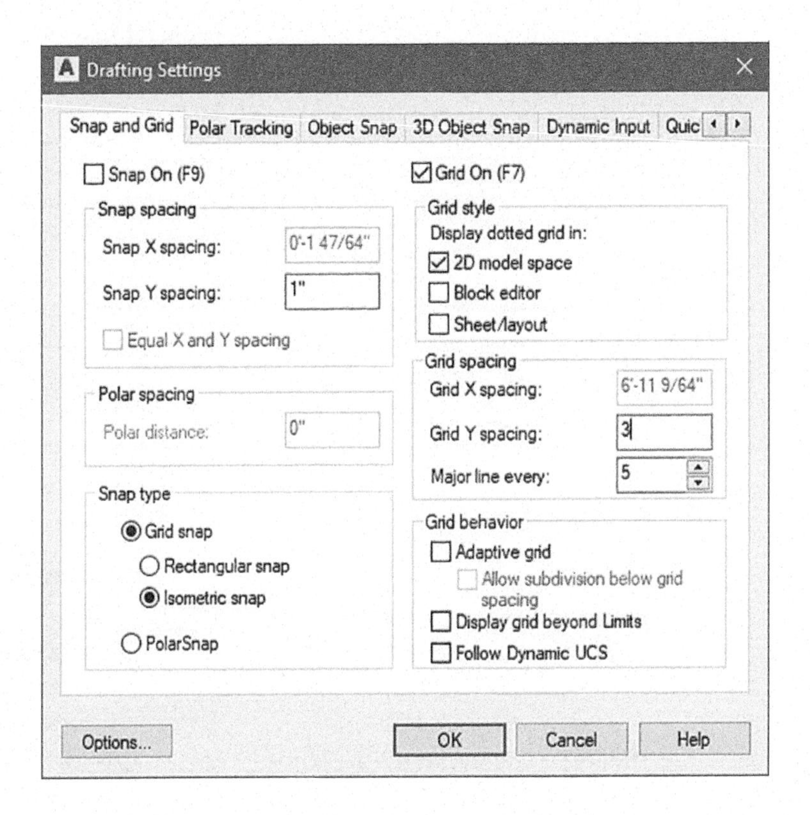

Figure 13-4
Drafting Settings dialog box

Shape 1: Drawing the Isometric Rectangle

Drawing shape 1 (Figure 13-5) helps you become familiar with drawing lines using isometric polar coordinates.

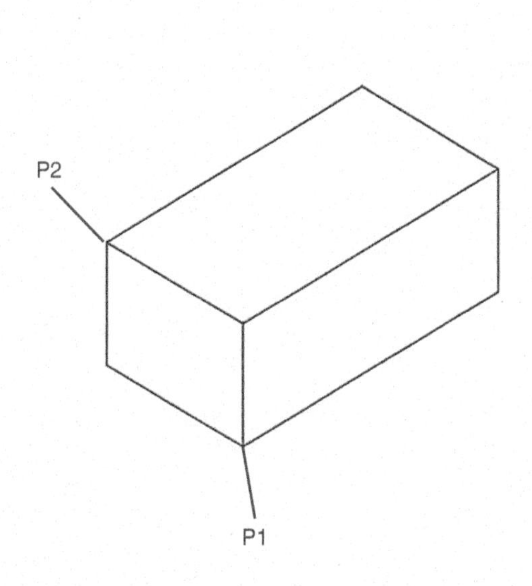

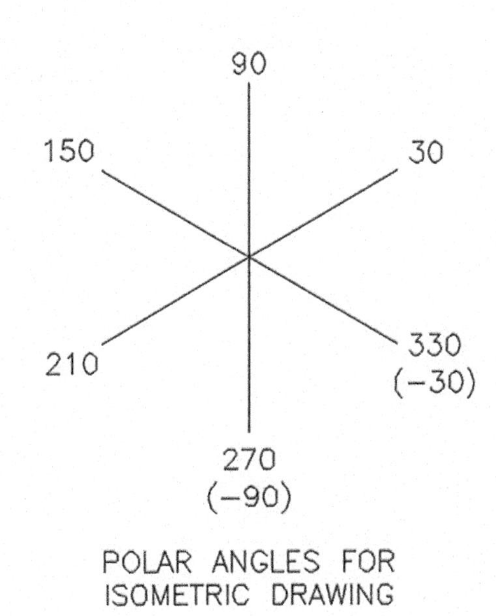

Figure 13-5
Shape 1: Drawing the isometric rectangle

Step 2. Draw the right face of an isometric rectangular box measuring 12″ × 16″ × 30″ using isometric polar coordinates, as described next:

Prompt	Response
Type a command:	**Line** (or type **L <Enter>**)
Specify first point:	**P1→** (Figure 13-5) (absolute coordinates 1′6-3/16″, 4′10-1/2″—this is an isometric snap point)
Specify next point or [Undo]:	Type **@30<30 <Enter>**
Specify next point or [Undo]:	Type **@12<90 <Enter>**
Specify next point or [Close Undo]:	Type **@30<210 <Enter>**
Specify next point or [Close Undo]:	Type **C <Enter>**

Step 3. Draw the left face of the isometric rectangular box, as described next:

Prompt	Response
Type a command:	**<Enter>** (repeat **LINE**)
Specify first point:	**P1→** (Figure 13-5) (**Osnap-Endpoint**)
Specify next point or [Undo]:	Type **@16<150 <Enter>**
Specify next point or [Undo]:	Type **@12<90 <Enter>**
Specify next point or [Close Undo]:	Type **@16<330 <Enter>**
Specify next point or [Close Undo]:	**<Enter>**

Step 4. Draw the top of the isometric rectangular box, as described next:

Prompt	Response
Type a command:	**<Enter>** (repeat **LINE**)
Specify first point:	**P2→**
Specify next point or [Undo]:	Type **@30<30 <Enter>**
Specify next point or [Undo]:	Type **@16<-30 <Enter>**
Specify next point or [Close Undo]:	**<Enter>**

Shape 2: Drawing Isometric Ellipses

When using polar coordinates to draw lines in isometric, you can ignore isoplanes. Isoplanes are isometric faces—top, right, and left. Pressing **<Ctrl>+E** toggles your drawing to the correct isoplane—top, right, or left. You can also use the function key **<F5>** to toggle to the correct isoplane.

Shape 2 (Figure 13-6) has a circle in each of the isometric planes of a cube. When drawn in isometric, circles appear as ellipses. You must use the isoplanes when drawing isometric circles using the **ELLIPSE** command. The following part of the exercise starts by drawing a 15″ isometric cube.

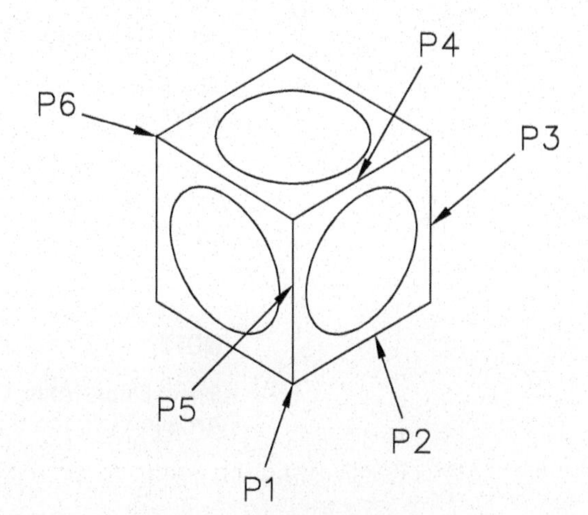

Figure 13-6
Shape 2: Drawing an isometric cube with an ellipse in each isoplane

ISOPLANE TOGGLE	
Type a Command:	ISOPLANE
Status Bar:	
Keyboard	<F5> or <Ctrl>+E

Step 5. Draw the right face of a 15″ isometric cube using direct distance entry, as described next:

Prompt	**Response**
Type a command:	Toggle to the right isoplane (press **<F5>** until **<Isoplane Right>** appears) and click **Line** (or type **L <Enter>**)
Specify first point:	**P1→** (absolute coordinates 6′3/4″,5′3″)
Specify next point or [Undo]:	With **ORTHO** on, move your mouse upward 30° to the right, and type **15 <Enter>**
Specify next point or [Undo]:	Move the mouse straight up and type **15 <Enter>**
Specify next point or [Close Undo]:	Move the mouse downward **210°** to the left and type **15 <Enter>**
Specify next point or [Close Undo]:	Type **C <Enter>**

Step 6. Use the **MIRROR** command to draw the left face of the isometric cube, as described next:

Prompt	**Response**
Type a command:	**Mirror** (or type **MI <Enter>**)
Select objects:	**P2→**, **P3→**, **P4→ <Enter>** (Figure 13-6)
Specify first point of mirror line:	**P1→** (be sure **ORTHO** is on) (**Osnap-Endpoint**)
Specify second point of mirror line:	**P5→** (press **<F5>** to be sure you are in either the right or left isoplane)
Erase source objects? [Yes No]<N>:	**<Enter>**

Step 7. Complete the top face of the isometric cube, as described next:

Prompt	**Response**
Type a command:	Toggle to the top isoplane and click **Line** (or type **L <Enter>**)
Specify first point:	**P6→** (**Osnap-Endpoint**)
Specify next point or [Undo]:	Move the mouse upward **30°** to the right and type **15 <Enter>**
Specify next point or [Undo]:	Move the mouse downward **330°** to the right and type **15 <Enter>**
Specify next point or [Close Undo]:	**<Enter>**

NOTE

If you do not have the isometric snap style active, the **ELLIPSE** command will not prompt you with **Isocircle** as one of the options for the command.

NOTE

Select **Ellipse-Axis, End** if you select from the ribbon. Neither **Ellipse-Center** nor **Ellipse-Arc** allows you to draw an isometric ellipse.

Step 8. Draw an isometric ellipse (6″ radius) that represents a circle in the left isoplane, as described next:

Prompt	**Response**
Type a command:	**Ellipse Axis, End** (or type **EL <Enter>**)
Specify axis endpoint of ellipse or [Arc Center Isocircle]:	Type **I <Enter>**
Specify center of isocircle:	**Osnap-Mid Between 2 Points**
First point of mid:	**P1→**
Second point of mid:	**P6→**
Specify radius of isocircle or [Diameter]:	Press the **<F5>** function key until the command line reads **<Isoplane Left>**, and then type **6 <Enter>**

When you type and enter **D** in response to the prompt *Specify radius of isocircle or [Diameter]:*, you can enter the diameter of the circle. The default is radius.

Step 9. Follow a similar procedure to draw ellipses in the right and top isoplanes. Be sure to specify **Isocircle** after you have selected the **ELLIPSE** command, and be sure you are in the correct isoplane before you draw the ellipse. Use **<F5>** to toggle to the correct isoplane.

When you have completed this part of the exercise, you have the essentials of isometric drawing. Now you are going to apply these essentials to a more complex shape.

> **TIP**
>
> After you become familiar with isometric angles and toggling to isoplanes, use direct distance entry with **ORTHO** on to draw lines. Just move your mouse in the isometric direction and type the number that tells AutoCAD how far you want to go. You may choose to watch the dynamic display of distance and polar angles and simply pick the desired point.

Shape 3: Drawing a Chair with Ellipses That Show the Thickness of a Material

Step 10. Draw the right side of the front chair leg, as described next:

Prompt	**Response**
Type a command:	Toggle to the right isoplane and click **Line** (or type **L <Enter>**) (be sure **ORTHO** is on)
Specify first point:	**P1→** (Figure 13-7) (pick a point in the approximate location [**9′-7/8″, 4′11″**] shown in Figure 13-2)
Specify next point or [Undo]:	With **ORTHO** on, move your mouse straight down **270°** and type **1′5 <Enter>**
Specify next point or [Undo]:	Move your mouse upward **30°** to the right and type **2 <Enter>**
Specify next point or [Close Undo]:	Move your mouse straight up **90°** and type **1′5 <Enter>**
Specify next point or [Close Undo]:	**<Enter>**

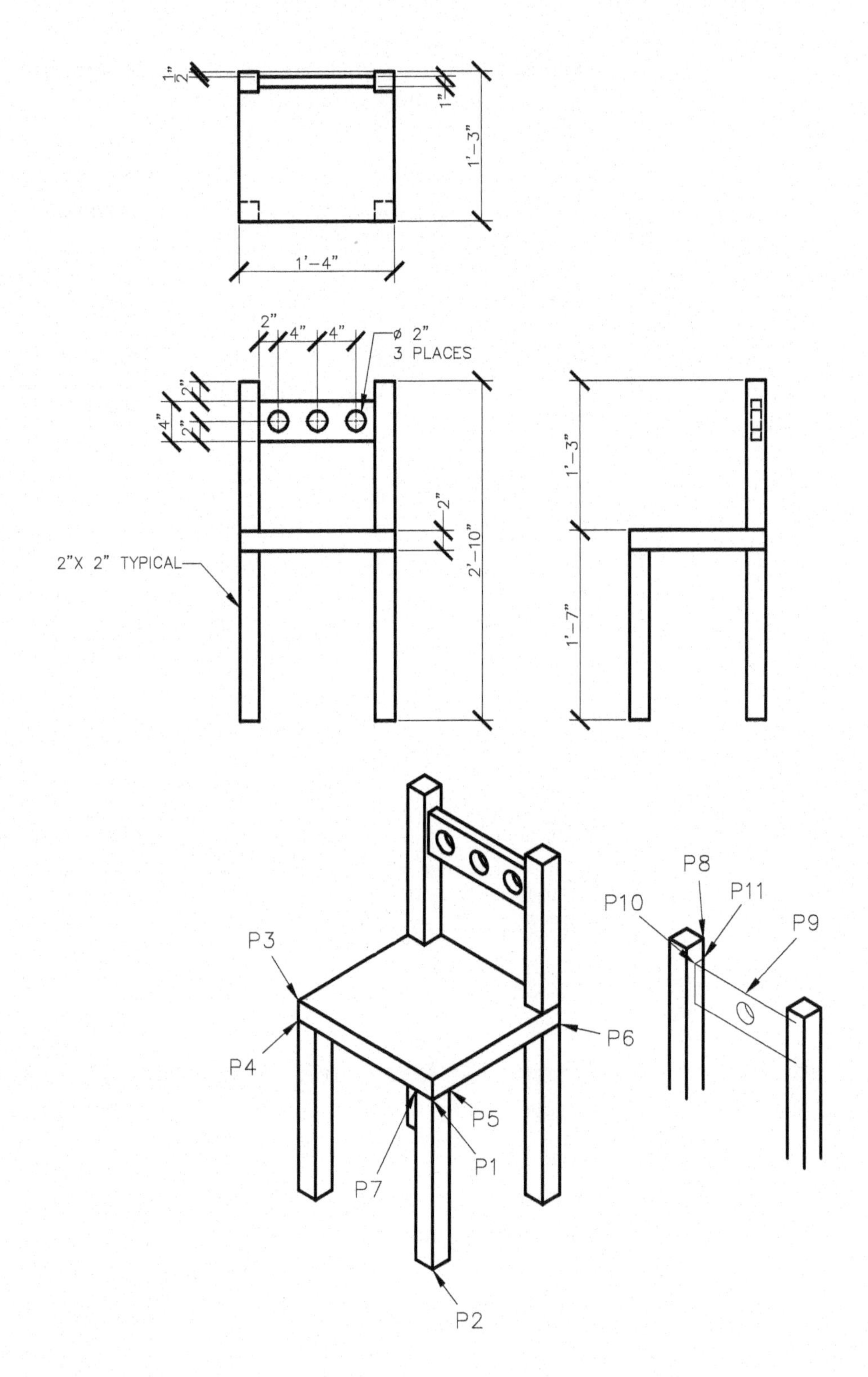

Figure 13-7
Shape 3: Drawing a chair with ellipses that show the thickness of a material

Step 11. Draw the left side of the front chair leg, as described next:

Prompt	**Response**
Type a command:	Toggle to the left isoplane and click **Line** (or type **L <Enter>**)
Specify first point:	**P2→** (**Osnap-Endpoint**) (Figure 13-7)
Specify next point or [Undo]:	Move your mouse upward **150°** to the left and type **2 <Enter>**

Prompt	Response
Specify next point or [Undo]:	Move your mouse straight up **90°** and type **1′5 <Enter>**
Specify next point or [Close Undo]:	**<Enter>**

Step 12. Draw the chair seat, as described next:

Prompt	Response
Type a command:	**Line** (or type **L <Enter>**)
Specify first point:	**P1→** (**Osnap-Endpoint**) (Figure 13-7)
Specify next point or [Undo]:	Move your mouse **150°** upward to the left and type **1′4 <Enter>**
Specify next point or [Undo]:	Move your mouse straight up and type **2 <Enter>**
Specify next point or [Close Undo]:	Move your mouse **330°** downward to the right and type **1′4 <Enter>**
Specify next point or [Close Undo]:	Type **C <Enter>**
Type a command:	**<Enter>** (to begin the **LINE** command)
Specify first point:	**P1→** (**Osnap-Endpoint**)
Specify next point or [Undo]:	Toggle to the right isoplane and with **ORTHO** on, move your mouse **30°** upward to the right and type **1′3 <Enter>**
Specify next point or [Undo]:	Move your mouse straight up and type **2 <Enter>**
Specify next point or [Close Undo]:	Move your mouse **210°** downward to the left and type **1′3 <Enter>**
Specify next point or [Close Undo]:	**<Enter>** (to end the **LINE** command)
Type a command:	**<Enter>** (to begin the **LINE** command)
Specify first point:	**P3→** (**Osnap-Intersection**)
Specify next point or [Undo]:	Toggle to the top isoplane. and with **ORTHO** on, move your mouse **30°** upward to the right and type **1′3 <Enter>**
Specify next point or [Close Undo]:	Move your mouse **330°** downward to the right and type **1′4 <Enter>**
Specify next point or [Close Undo]:	**<Enter>**

Step 13. Copy the front leg to the other three positions.

1. Using the **COPY** command, select the lines of the front leg. Use **P5→** (**Osnap-Endpoint**) (Figure 13-7) as the base point and **P6→** (**Osnap-Intersection**) as the second point of displacement.
2. Using the **COPY** command, select both legs on the right side. Use **P7→** (**Osnap-Endpoint**) (Figure 13-7) as the base point and **P4→** (**Osnap-Intersection**) as the second point of displacement.
3. Use the **TRIM** and **ERASE** commands to delete any unnecessary lines.

Step 14. Use the **LINE** command to draw one of the upright posts, and use the **COPY** command to copy it to the other position. Follow the dimensions shown in Figure 13-7.

Step 15. Draw the 1″ × 4″ × 12″ piece containing the three holes, as described next:

Prompt	Response
Type a command:	**Line** (or type **L <Enter>**)
Specify first point:	Type **FRO <Enter>**
Base point:	Click **P8→** (**Osnap-Intersection**) (Figure 13-7)
<Offset>:	Type **@2<–90 <Enter>**
Specify next point or [Undo]:	Type **@1<210 <Enter>**
Specify next point or [Undo]:	Type **@12<-30 <Enter>**
Specify next point or [Close Undo]:	**<Enter>**
Type a command:	Toggle to the left isoplane, and with **ORTHO** off, click **Ellipse Axis, End** (or type **EL <Enter>**)
Specify axis endpoint of ellipse or [Arc Center Isocircle]:	Type **I <Enter>**
Specify center of isocircle:	Type **FRO <Enter>**
Base point:	Click **P9→** (**Osnap-Midpoint**)
<Offset>:	Type **@2<–90 <Enter>**
Specify radius of isocircle or [Diameter]:	Type **1 <Enter>**
Type a command:	**COPY** (or type **CP <Enter>**)
Select objects:	Click the ellipse just drawn
Select objects:	**<Enter>**
Specify base point or [Displacement mOde] <Displacement>:	Click **P10→** (**Osnap-Endpoint**)
Specify second point or <use first point as displacement>:	Click **P11→** (**Osnap-Endpoint**)
Specify second point or [Exit Undo] <Exit>:	**<Enter>**

Step 16. Trim the copied ellipse so that only the part within the first ellipse remains.

Step 17. Copy the hole described by the ellipses **4″ 330°** downward to the right and **4″ 150°** upward to the left.

Step 18. Draw a **4″** line straight down from **P10→ (Endpoint)** and a **12″** line **330°** downward to the right from the end of the 4″ line.

Step 19. Draw a **12″** line **330°** downward to the right from **P11→ (Endpoint)**.

Step 20. Use the **MOVE** command to move the 1″ × 4″ × 12″ piece and three holes **210°** downward to the left **1/2″**.

Step 21. Use **TRIM, EXTEND** and draw a line on the back to complete the drawing.

Shape 4: Drawing a Shape That Has a Series of Isometric Ellipses Located on the Same Centerline

Shape 4 (Figure 13-8), similar to a round table, will help you become familiar with drawing a shape that has a series of ellipses located on the same centerline. Five ellipses must be drawn. You can locate the centers of two of them, the extreme top and bottom ellipses, by using endpoints of the centerline.

The following part of the exercise begins by having you draw a centerline through the entire height of the object.

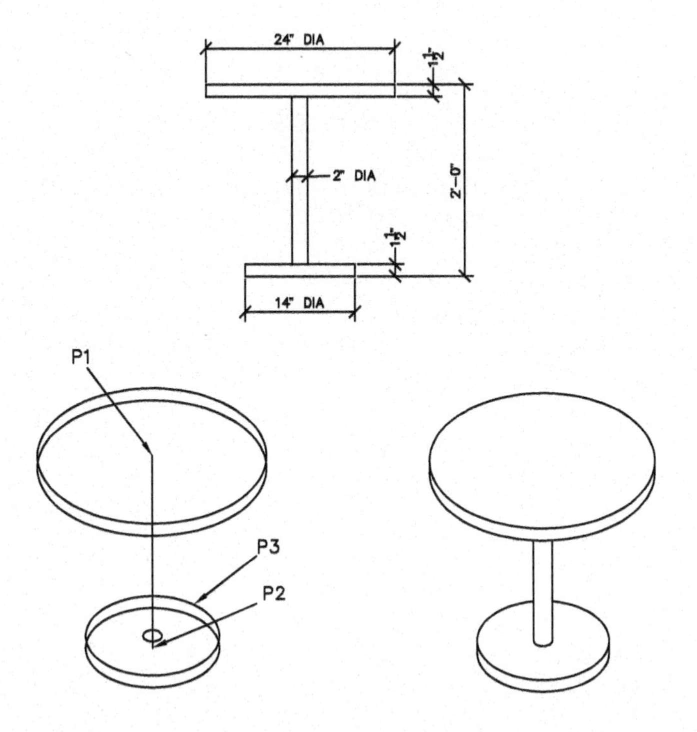

Figure 13-8
Shape 4: Drawing a shape that has a series of isometric ellipses located on the same centerline

Step 22. Begin to draw a shape containing several ellipses of different sizes located on the same centerline by drawing the centerline, as described next:

Prompt	**Response**
Type a command:	**Line** (or type **L <Enter>**)
Specify first point:	**P1→ (1′11-7/16,1′4-1/2)**
Specify next point or [Undo]:	With **ORTHO** on, move your mouse straight up and type **24 <Enter>**
Specify next point or [Undo]:	**<Enter>**

Step 23. Draw five ellipses:

1. Toggle to the top isoplane and use **Endpoint** to locate the center of the uppermost isometric ellipse on the endpoint of the vertical line. Draw it with a diameter of **24″**.

> **NOTE**
>
> Although you can use **Osnap-Nearest** to end an isometric line on another line, the position is not exact. A more exact method is to draw the line beyond where it should end and trim it to the correct length.

2. Draw a second **24″-diameter** isometric ellipse by copying the 24″ ellipse **1-1/2″** straight down.
3. Draw the **14″-diameter** ellipse using the bottom endpoint, **P2→**, of the vertical line as its center. Copy the 14″-diameter ellipse **1-1/2″** straight up.
4. Draw the **2″-diameter** ellipse at the center of the copied 14″-diameter ellipse using **Osnap-Center, P3→**, to locate its center.

Step 24. To draw the 2″ column, toggle to the right or left isoplane (the top isoplane does not allow you to draw vertical lines using a mouse if **ORTHO** is on). Turn **ORTHO** (**<F8>**) on. Draw a vertical line from the quadrant of one side of the 2″-diameter ellipse to just above the first 24″-diameter ellipse. Draw a similar line to form the other side of the column.

Step 25. With **ORTHO** (**<F8>**) on and toggled to the right or left isoplane, draw vertical lines from the quadrants of the ellipse segments to connect each side of the top and bottom ellipses, as shown in Figure 13-9.

Figure 13-9
Shape 4: Drawing tangents to the ellipses

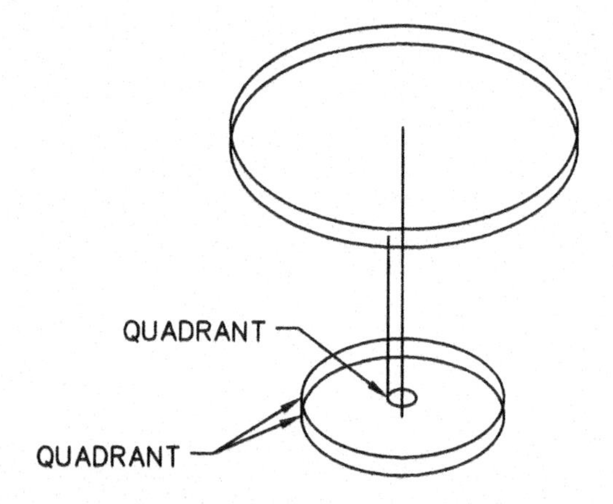

Step 26. Use **TRIM** and **ERASE** to remove unneeded lines. The drawing is complete, as shown in the lower-right corner of Figure 13-8.

Shape 5: Isometric Detail with Rounded Corners

The fifth drawing (Figure 13-10) in this exercise is a shape that has rounded corners. Rounded corners are common in many items. In 2D drawing, the **FILLET** command allows you to obtain the rounded corners quickly and easily. This is not so in isometric. Drawing shape 5 will help you become familiar with how rounded corners must be constructed with isometric ellipses.

Figure 13-10
Shape 5: Isometric detail with rounded corners

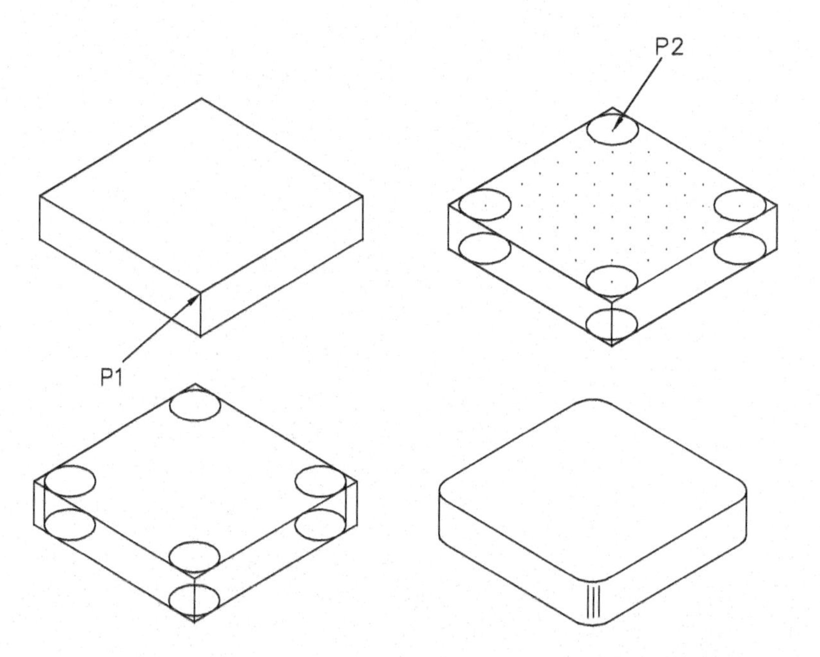

Step 27. Turn **ORTHO** and **SNAP** on and toggle to the top isoplane. Draw an **18″ × 18″**-square shape in the top isoplane (Figure 13-10), as described next:

Prompt	**Response**
Type a command:	**Line** (or type **L <Enter>**)
LINE Specify first point:	**P1→** (on a grid mark) (**5′11,3′3**)
Specify next point or [Undo]: <Isoplane Top> <Ortho on>	Move your mouse upward **30°** to the right and type **18 <Enter>**
Specify next point or [Undo]:	Move your mouse upward **30°** to the left and type **18 <Enter>**
Specify next point or [Close Undo]:	Move your mouse downward **30°** to the left and type **18 <Enter>**
Specify next point or [Close Undo]:	Type **C <Enter>**

Step 28. Copy the 18″ × 18″-square **4″** down as described next:

1. Copy the front two edges of the square to form the bottom of the shape. Copy using **@4<270** (4″ is the depth) as the polar coordinates for the second point of displacement.
2. Draw lines connecting the top and bottom edges. (These lines are for reference only. You may skip this step if you choose.)

Step 29. Draw a **2″-radius** ellipse in the top isoplane, as described next:

Prompt	**Response**
Type a command:	**Ellipse** (or type **EL <Enter>**) (toggle to the top isoplane)
Specify axis endpoint of ellipse or [Arc Center Isocircle]:	Type **I <Enter>**
Specify center of isocircle:	**P2→** (count **2″** in both the **330** and **210** directions from the corner to locate the center of the ellipse. Make sure **SNAP** is on.)
Specify radius of isocircle or [Diameter]:	Type **2 <Enter>**

Step 30. Copy the ellipse just drawn to the other four top corners, locating them in a similar manner.

Step 31. Copy the front three ellipses **4″** in the **270** direction to form corners in the bottom plane. Make sure **SNAP** is on.

Step 32. Draw lines connecting the two outside ellipses using **Osnap-Quadrant**.

Step 33. Use the **TRIM** and **ERASE** commands to remove the extra lines.

Step 34. Add highlights on the front corner to complete the drawing.

Shape 6: A TV Shape with an Angled Back

While drawing in isometric, you will often need to draw angles. To do that, you will need to locate both ends of the angle and connect them. You will not be able to draw any angle otherwise, such as the 62° angle shown in Figure 13-11.

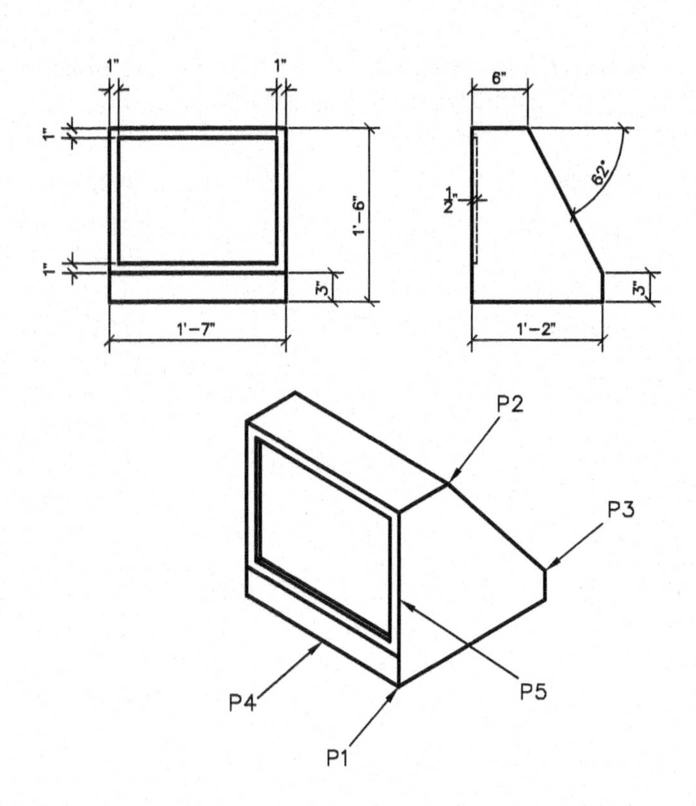

Figure 13-11
Shape 6: A TV shape with an angled back

Step 35. Draw the right side of Figure 13-11, as described next:

Prompt	Response
Type a command:	**Line** (or type **L <Enter>**)
Specify first point:	**P1→** (**8′9-5/8″,9″**)
Specify next point or [Undo]:	Toggle to the right isoplane, and with **ORTHO** on, move your mouse **30°** upward to the right and type **1′2 <Enter>**
Specify next point or [Undo]:	Move your mouse straight up and type **3 <Enter>**
Specify next point or [Close Undo]:	**<Enter>**
Type a command:	**<Enter>** (to get the **LINE** command back)
Specify first point:	**P1→** (again) **(Endpoint)**
Specify next point or [Undo]:	Move your mouse straight up and type **1′6 <Enter>**
Specify next point or [Close Undo]:	Move your mouse **30°** upward to the right and type **6 <Enter>**
Specify next point or [Undo]:	**P3→ (Endpoint)**
Specify next point or [Close Undo]:	**<Enter>**

Step 36. Draw the left side and top of Figure 13-11, as described next:

Prompt	Response
Type a command:	**Line** (or type **L <Enter>**)
Specify first point:	Click **P1→** (Figure 13-11)
Specify next point or [Undo]:	Toggle to the left isoplane and with **ORTHO** on, move your mouse **150°** upward to the left and type **1′7 <Enter>**

Prompt	Response
Specify next point or [Undo]:	Move your mouse straight up and type **1′6 <Enter>**
Specify next point or [Close Undo]:	Toggle to the top isoplane, move your mouse **30°** upward to the right, and type **6 <Enter>**
Specify next point or [Close Undo]:	Click **P2→**
Specify next point or [Close Undo]:	**<Enter>**
Type a command:	**COPY** (or type **CP <Enter>**)
Select objects:	Click **P4→**
Select objects:	**<Enter>**
Specify base point or [Displacement mOde] <Displacement>:	Click any point
Specify second point or <use first point as displacement>:	Toggle to the left isoplane, move your mouse straight up, and type **3 <Enter>**
Specify second point or [Exit Undo] <Exit>:	Move your mouse straight up and type **4 <Enter>**
Specify second point or [Exit Undo] <Exit>:	Move your mouse straight up and type **1′5 <Enter>**
Specify second point or [Exit Undo] <Exit>:	Move your mouse straight up and type **1′6 <Enter>**
Specify second point or [Exit Undo] <Exit>:	**<Enter>**
Type a command:	**<Enter>** (to repeat the **COPY** command)
Select objects:	Click **P5→**
Select objects:	**<Enter>**
Specify base point or [Displacement mOde] <Displacement>:	Click any point
Specify second point or <use first point as displacement>:	Move your mouse **150°** upward to the left and type **1 <Enter>**
Specify second point or [Exit Undo] <Exit>:	Move your mouse **150°** upward to the left and type **1′6 <Enter>**
Specify second point or [Exit Undo] <Exit>:	**<Enter>**

Step 37. Use the **TRIM** command to trim unnecessary lines.

Step 38. Use the **COPY** command to draw the two lines forming the inside edge of the TV screen. Copy them **1/2″, 30°** upward to the right.

Step 39. Draw a line at the intersection of those copied lines.

Step 40. Use the **TRIM** command to trim unnecessary lines. The drawing is complete.

Shape 7: Isometric Detail: A Hexagonal-Shaped Vase

The final shape in this exercise combines several features (Figure 13-12).

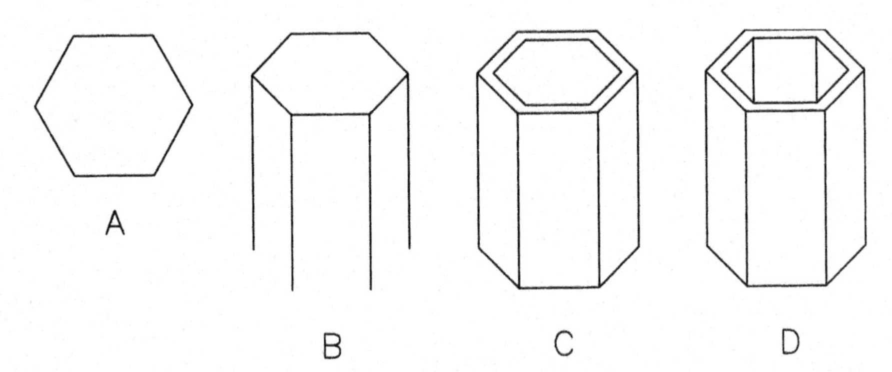

Figure 13-12
Shape 7: Isometric detail: A hexagonal-shaped vase

Step 41. Draw the hexagonal shape of the vase (Figure 13-12A), as described next:

Prompt	Response
Type a command:	**Polygon** (or type **POL <Enter>**)
Enter number of sides <4>:	Type **6 <Enter>**
Specify center of polygon or [Edge]:	Click a point on a grid mark in the approximate location shown in Figure 13-2 (with **SNAP** on)
Enter an option [Inscribed in circle Circumscribed about circle] <1>:	Type **C <Enter>**
Specify radius of circle:	Type **6 <Enter>**

Now you have a hexagon that cannot be used in isometric drawing. To use it, you must block the hexagon, and then insert it with different X and Y values. *Be sure to toggle to the top isoplane when you insert the hexagonal block.*

Step 42. Block and insert the hexagon (Figure 13-12B), as described next:

Prompt	Response
Type a command:	**Block** (or type **B <Enter>**)
The **Block Definition** dialog box appears:	Type **HEX** in the **Name:** input box; make sure **Delete** is selected Click **Pick point**
Specify insertion base point:	Click the center of the hexagon
The **Block Definition** dialog box appears:	Click **Select objects**
Select objects:	Click any point on the hexagon
Select objects:	**<Enter>**
The **Block Definition** dialog box appears:	Click **OK**
The hexagon disappears:	
Type a command:	**Insert-Block...** (or type **I <Enter>**)
The **BLOCKS** palette appears and displays all blocks created in the current drawing (Figure 13-13):	The **HEX** block appears in the **Current Drawing Blocks** area

Prompt	Response
	Click the **Insertion Point**, **Scale**, and **Rotation** check boxes. After you select them, you will be prompted to enter values
	Double-click the **HEX** block in the **BLOCKS** palette. The block is attached to the crosshairs
	Follow the command line window prompts to specify the block parameters. For the **Y** scale factor, enter **.58** (this is a very close approximation to the isometric scale factor)
Specify insertion point or [Basepoint Scale X Y Z Rotate]:	Pick the location of the isometric hexagon as shown in Figure 13-2 (**SNAP** on) (**5′7-9/16″,2′-4″**)

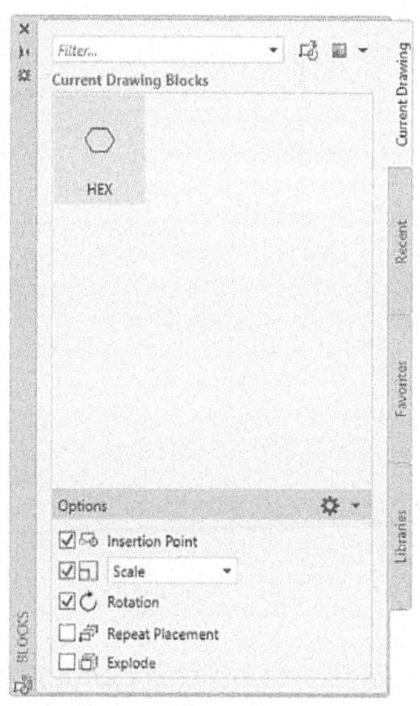

Figure 13-13
The **Current Drawing** tab of the **BLOCKS** palette displays blocks created in the current drawing

Step 43. Draw **1′-3″** vertical lines from each of the visible corners of the hexagon in the **270** direction (Figure 13-12B). (You can draw one line and copy it three times.)

Step 44. Using **Osnap-Endpoint**, draw lines to form the bottom of the hexagon (Figure 13-12C).

Step 45. Copy the HEX block and pick the same point for the base point and second point of displacement so that the copied HEX lies directly on top of the first HEX.

Step 46. Use the **Scale** command to scale the copied HEX to a **.8** scale factor. Be sure to click the center of the HEX block as the base point.

Step 47. Draw vertical lines on the inside of the vase, as shown in Figure 13-12D.

Step 48. When you have completed Exercise 13-1, save your work in at least two places.

Step 49. Plot or print the drawing on an **8-1/2″** × **11″** sheet of paper; use **Fit to paper**.

EXERCISE 13-2
Tenant Space Reception Desk in Isometric

The tenant space reception desk is drawn in isometric in Exercise 13-2. When you have completed Exercise 13-2, your drawing will look similar to Figure 13-14.

Step 1. Use your workspace to make the following settings:

1. Use **Save As...** to save the drawing on the hard drive with the name **CH13-EXERCISE2**.
2. Set drawing units: **Architectural**
3. Set drawing limits: **15′,15′**
4. Set snap: **Style-Isometric-1″**

5. Set **GRIDDISPLAY**: **0**
6. Set grid: **4′**
7. Create the following layer:

Layer name	Color	Linetype	Lineweight
Layer1	green	continuous	Default

8. Set **Layer1** current.
9. Use **Zoom-All**.

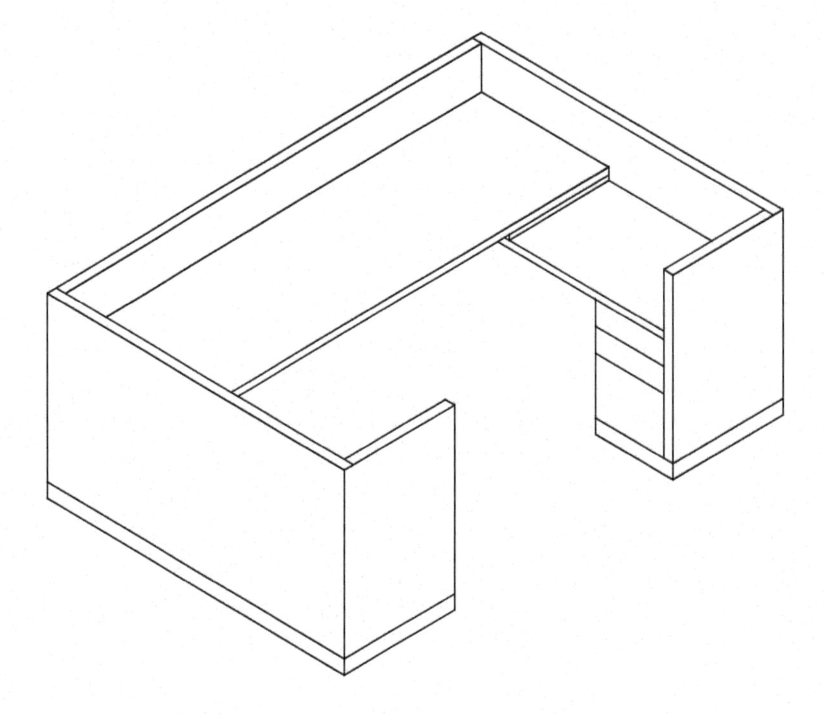

Figure 13-14
Exercise 13-2 complete

This exercise is a series of straight lines, all of which are on the isometric axes. Follow the step-by-step procedure described next so that you get some ideas about what you can and cannot do when using the isometric drawing method. To draw an isometric view of the reception desk (Figure 13-14), use the dimensions shown in Figure 13-16.

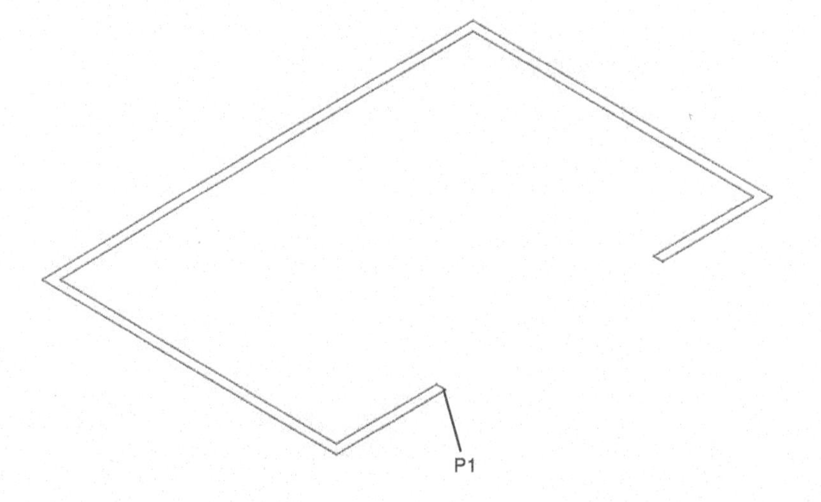

Figure 13-15
Drawing the top edge of the panels

TIP

You can also use direct distance entry to specify distances when you copy if you toggle to the correct isoplane.

Step 2. Set **SNAP** and **ORTHO** on. Toggle to the top isometric plane. Draw the top edge of the panels (Figure 13-14), as described next:

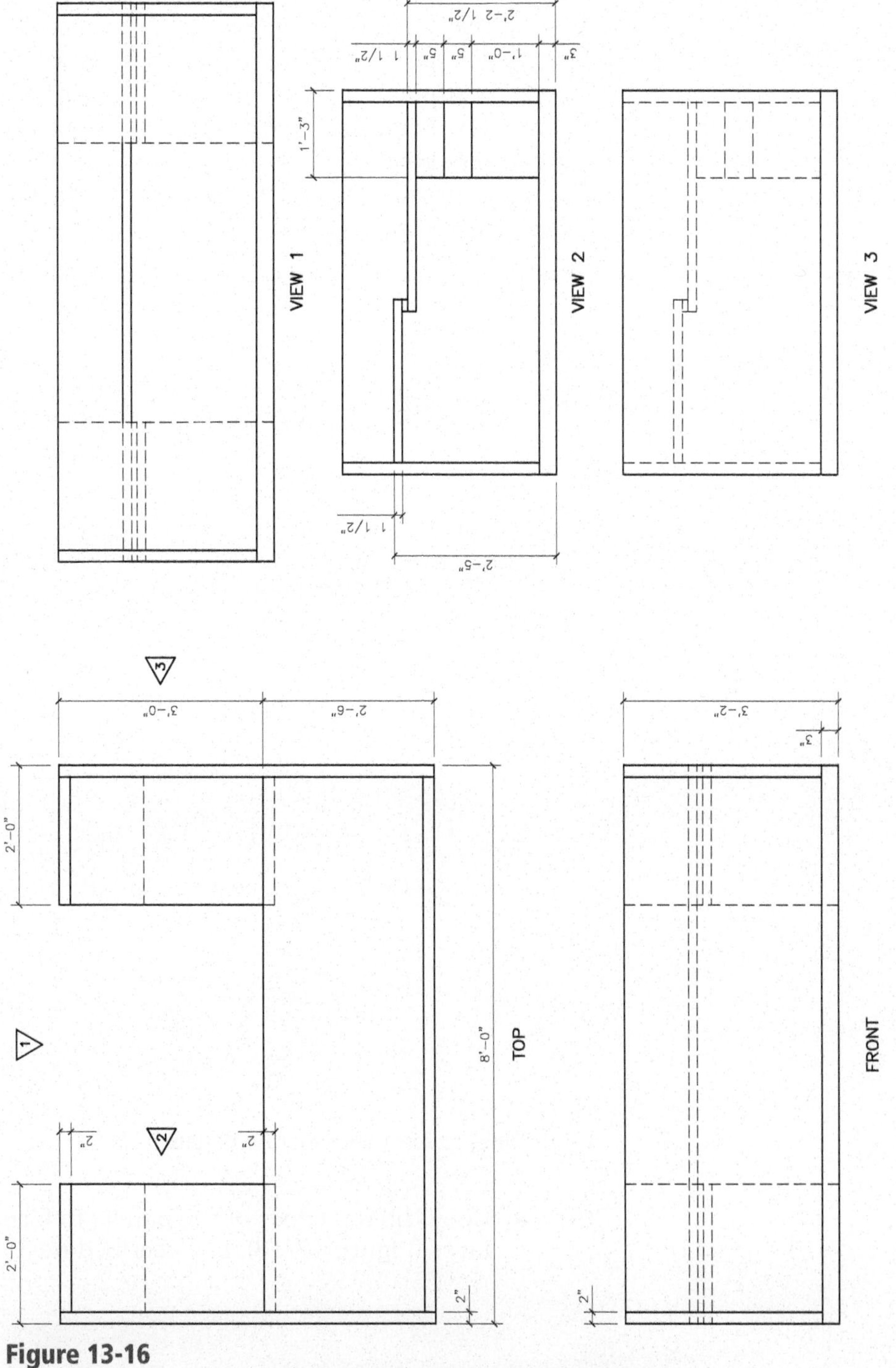

Figure 13-16
Dimensions of the tenant space reception desk (scale: 3/8″ = 1′-0″)

Prompt	Response
Type a command:	**Line** (or type **L <Enter>**)
Specify first point:	**P1→** (Figure 13-15) (absolute coordinates **8′1,7′4**)
Specify next point or [Undo]:	Type **@24<210 <Enter>** (or move the mouse downward **30°** to the left and type **24 <Enter>**)
Specify next point or [Undo]:	Type **@66<150 <Enter>**
Specify next point or [Close Undo]:	Type **@96<30 <Enter>**
Specify next point or [Close Undo]:	Type **@66<-30 <Enter>**
Specify next point or [Close Undo]:	Type **@24<210 <Enter>**
Specify next point or [Close Undo]:	Type **@2<150 <Enter>**
Specify next point or [Close Undo]:	Type **@22<30 <Enter>**
Specify next point or [Close Undo]:	Type **@62<150 <Enter>**
Specify next point or [Close Undo]:	Type **@92<210 <Enter>**
Specify next point or [Close Undo]:	Type **@62<330 <Enter>**
Specify next point or [Close Undo]:	Type **@22<30 <Enter>**
Specify next point or [Close Undo]:	Type **C <Enter>**

Step 3. Use the **EXTEND** command to extend the inside lines of the panels to form the separate panels (Figure 13-17), as described next:

Prompt	Response
Type a command:	**Extend** (or type **EX <Enter>**)
Select objects or [mOde] <select all>:	**<Enter>** (Select all objects as boundary edges)
Select object to extend or shift-select to trim or [Boundary edges Fence Crossing mOde Project Edge]:	**P3→**, **P4→**, **P5→**, **P6→ <Enter>**

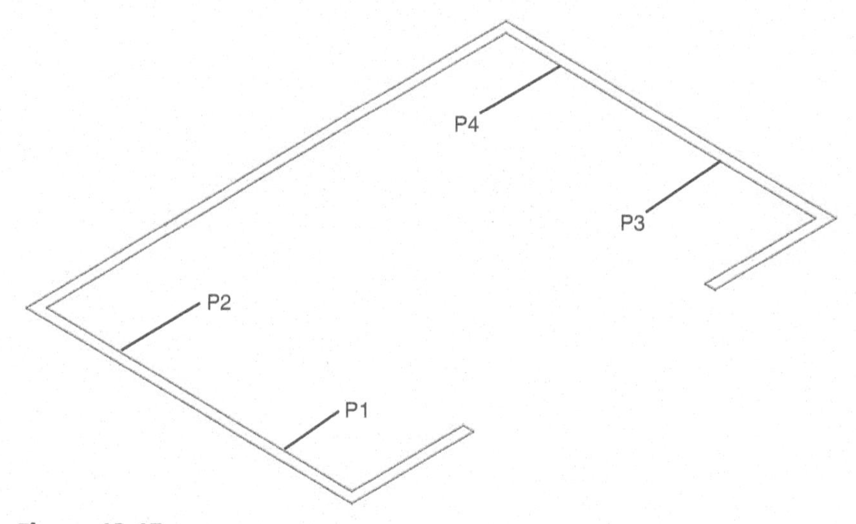

Figure 13-17
Extend lines to form the separate panels

Step 4. Copy the top edges of the panels to form the lower kickplate surfaces (Figure 13-18), as described next:

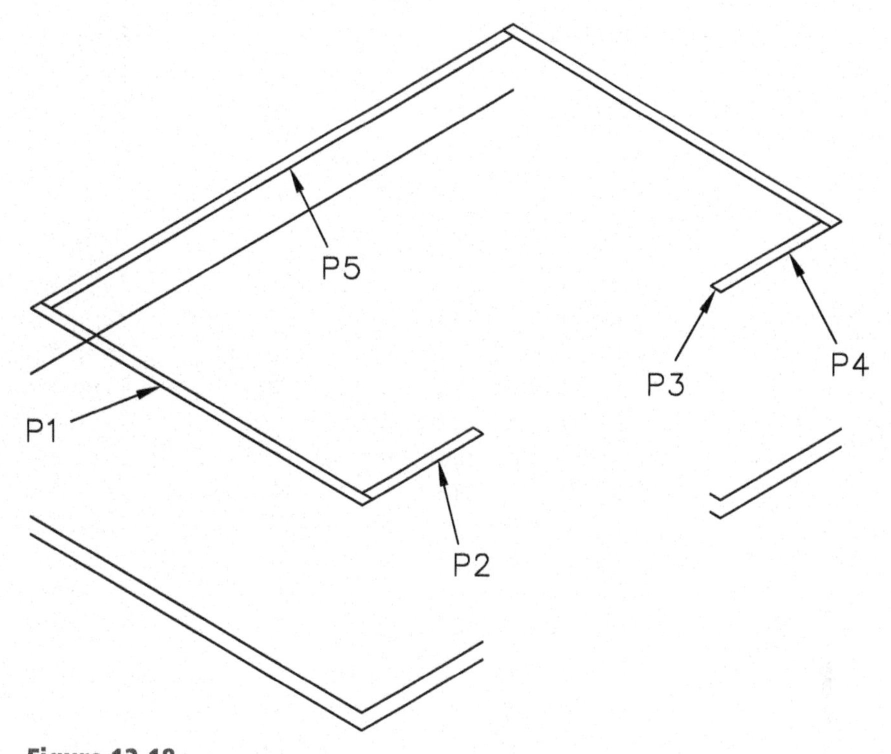

Figure 13-18
Copy the top edges to form the lower kickplate surfaces and the edge of the main work surface

Prompt	**Response**
Type a command:	**Copy** (or type **CP <Enter>**)
Select objects:	**P1→**, **P2→**, **P3→**, **P4→** (Figure 13-18)
Select objects:	**<Enter>**
Specify base point or [Displacement mOde] <Displacement>:	**P1→** (any point is OK)
Specify second point or <use first point as displacement>:	Type **@35<270 <Enter>**
Specify second point or [Exit Undo] <Exit>:	Type **@38<270 <Enter>**
Specify second point or [Exit Undo] <Exit>:	**<Enter>**

Step 5. Repeat the **COPY** command to draw the edge of the main work surface against the inside of the panel (Figure 13-19), as described next:

Prompt	**Response**
Type a command:	**<Enter>**
Select objects:	**P5→**
Select objects:	**<Enter>**
Specify base point or [Displacement mOde] <Displacement>:	**P5→** (any point is okay)
Specify second point or <use first point as displacement>:	Type **@9<270 <Enter>**

Step 6. Set a running **Osnap** mode of **Endpoint** and draw vertical lines connecting top and bottom outside lines and the inside corner above the work surface (Figure 13-19).

Figure 13-19
Draw the vertical lines connecting top and bottom edges; draw the work surfaces

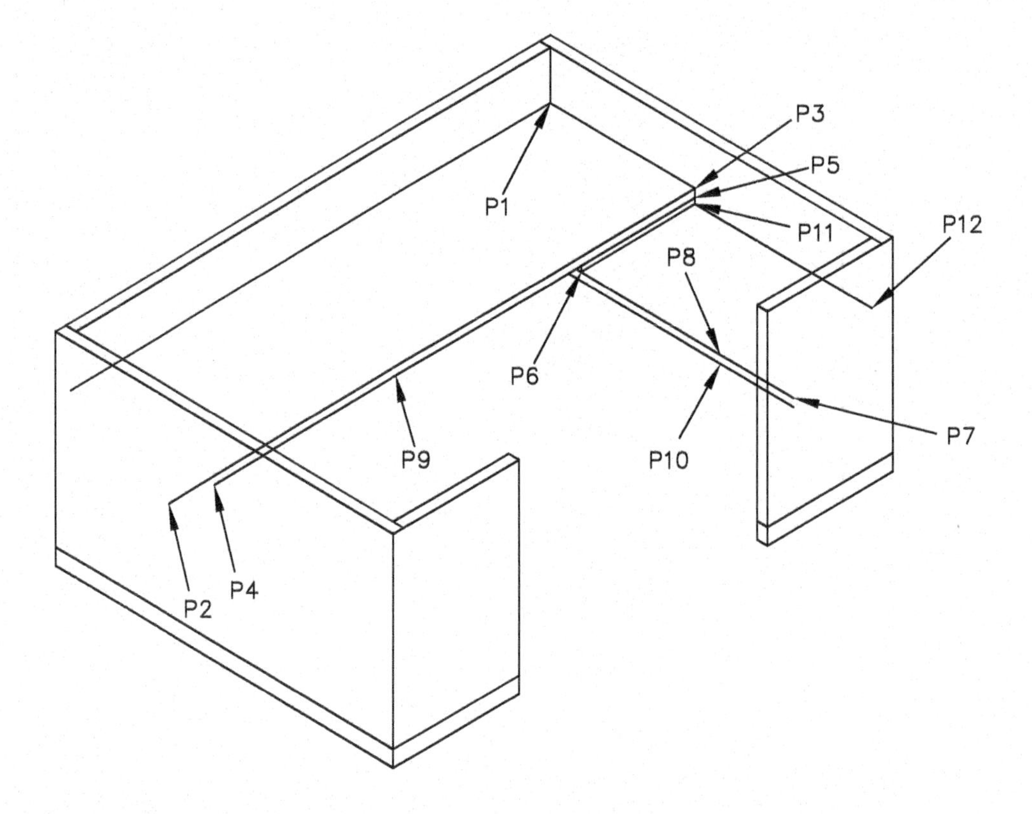

Step 7. Draw the work surfaces (Figure 13-19), as described next:

Prompt	Response
Type a command:	**Line** (or type **L <Enter>**)
Specify first point:	**Osnap-Endpoint, P1→**
Specify next point or [Undo]:	Type **@28<330 <Enter>**
Specify next point or [Undo]:	**P2→** (with **ORTHO** on and the top isoplane active, move your mouse downward **30°** to the left and pick any point beyond the inside of the left partition; you can trim these later)
Specify next point or [Close Undo]:	**<Enter>**
Type a command:	**<Enter>** (repeat **LINE**)
Specify first point:	**Osnap-Endpoint, P3→**
Specify next point or [Undo]:	Type **@1-1/2<270 <Enter>**
Specify next point or [Undo]:	**P4→** (pick another point outside the left partition)
Specify next point or [Close Undo]:	**<Enter>**
Type a command:	**<Enter>** (repeat **LINE**)
Specify first point:	**Osnap-Endpoint, P5→**
Specify next point or [Undo]:	Type **@1<270 <Enter>**
Specify next point or [Undo]:	Type **@22<210 <Enter>**
Specify next point or [Close Undo]:	Type **@1<90 <Enter>**
Specify next point or [Close Undo]:	**<Enter>**
Type a command:	**<Enter>** (repeat **LINE**)
Specify first point:	**Osnap-Endpoint, P6→** (Figure 13-19)
Specify next point or [Undo]:	**P7→** (move the mouse downward **30°** to the right and pick a point outside the right rear panel)

Prompt	**Response**
Specify next point or [Undo]:	**<Enter>**
Type a command:	**<Enter>** (repeat **LINE**)
Specify first point:	**Osnap-Endpoint, P11→**
Specify next point or [Undo]:	**P12→** (pick a point outside the right rear panel) **<Enter>**
Type a command:	**Copy** (or type **CP <Enter>**)
Select objects:	**P8→**
Select objects:	**<Enter>**
Specify base point or [Displacement mOde] <Displacement>:	**P8→** (any point)
Specify second point or <use first point as displacement>:	Type **@1-1/2<270 <Enter>**
Type a command:	**Extend** (or type **EX <Enter>**)
Select objects or <select all>:	**P9→ <Enter>**
Select object to extend or [Fence Crossing Project Edge Undo]:	**P8→**, **P10→ <Enter>**

Step 8. Trim lines that extend outside the panels (Figure 13-20), as described next:

Prompt	**Response**
Type a command:	**Trim** (or type **TR <Enter>**)
Select objects or [mOde] <select all>:	**P1→**, **P2→**, **P3→ <Enter>**
Select object to trim or shift-select to extend or [Fence Crossing Project Edge eRase Undo]:	**P4→**, **P5→**, **P6→**, **P7→**, **P8→**, **P9→ <Enter>**

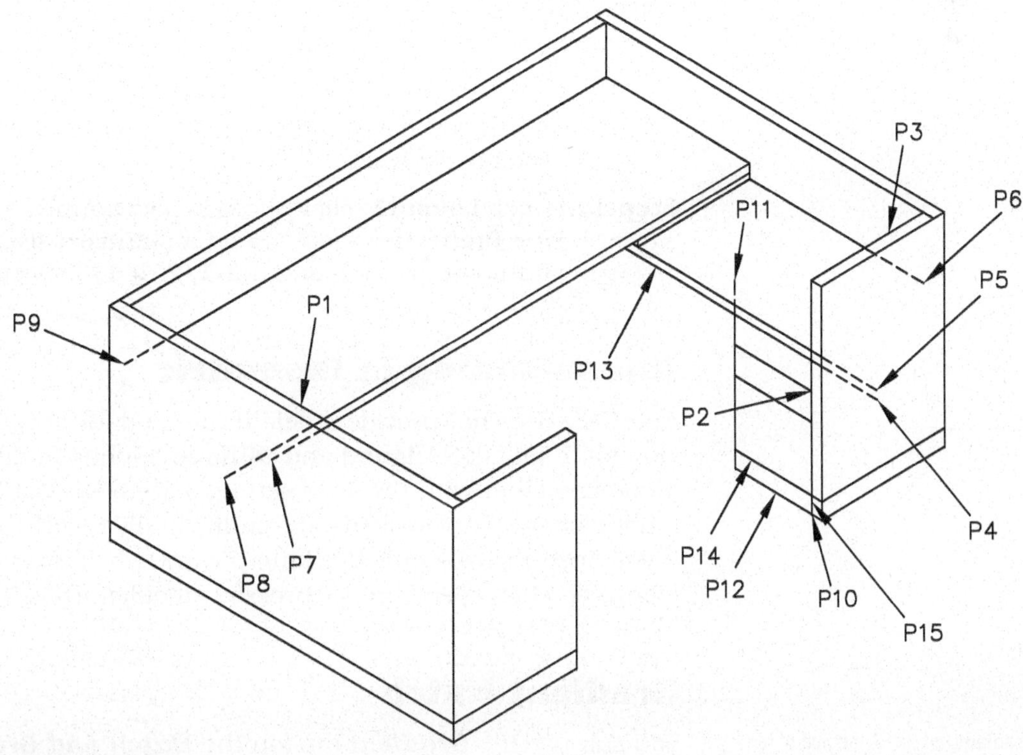

Figure 13-20
Trim lines and draw the drawer pedestal

Step 9. Draw the drawer pedestal (Figure 13-20), as described next:

Prompt	**Response**
Type a command:	**Line** (or type **L <Enter>**)
Specify first point:	**Osnap-Endpoint, P10→**
Specify next point or [Undo]:	Toggle to the left isoplane and type **@15<150 <Enter>**
Specify next point or [Undo]:	**P11→** (with **ORTHO** on, pick a point above the bottom edge of the desktop)
Specify next point or [Close Undo]:	**<Enter>**
Type a command:	**Copy** (or type **CP <Enter>**)
Select objects:	**P12→** (Figure 13-20)
Select objects:	**<Enter>**
Specify base point or [Displacement mOde] <Displacement>:	**P12→** (any point)
Specify second point or <use first point as displacement>:	Type **@3<90 <Enter>**
Specify second point or [Exit Undo] <Exit>:	Type **@15<90 <Enter>**
Specify second point or [Exit Undo] <Exit>:	Type **@20<90 <Enter>**
Specify second point or [Exit Undo] <Exit>:	**<Enter>**

Step 10. Trim the extra lines, as described next:

Prompt	**Response**
Type a command:	**Trim** (or type **TR <Enter>**)
Select objects or <select all>:	**P13→**, **P14→ <Enter>**
Select object to trim or shift-select to extend or [Fence Crossing Project Edge eRase Undo]:	**P15→**, **P11→ <Enter>**

Step 11. When you have completed Exercise 13-2, save your work in at least two places.

Step 12. Click **Layout1**, click the viewport boundary, right-click, and use the **Properties** menu to set a standard scale of **1/2″ = 1′**. Plot or print the drawing on an **8-1/2″ × 11″** sheet of paper.

Dimensioning in Isometric

AutoCAD does not provide a default method for proper isometric dimensioning. Using the **Aligned** and **Oblique** options in dimensioning and using an inclined font with the style setting solve only part of the problem. You must construct arrowheads and individually insert them for each isoplane. If you spend a little time blocking the arrowheads and customizing your menu, you can speed up the process significantly.

Gradient Hatch

gradient hatch: A method of rendering 2D drawings that is similar to air-brush rendering.

You can use the ***Gradient*** tab (on the ***Hatch and Gradient*** dialog box) to render 2D drawings such as the isometric drawings in this chapter (Figure 13-21). The appearance of these renderings is similar to air-brush renderings. The three means you can use to change the pattern appearance are as follows:

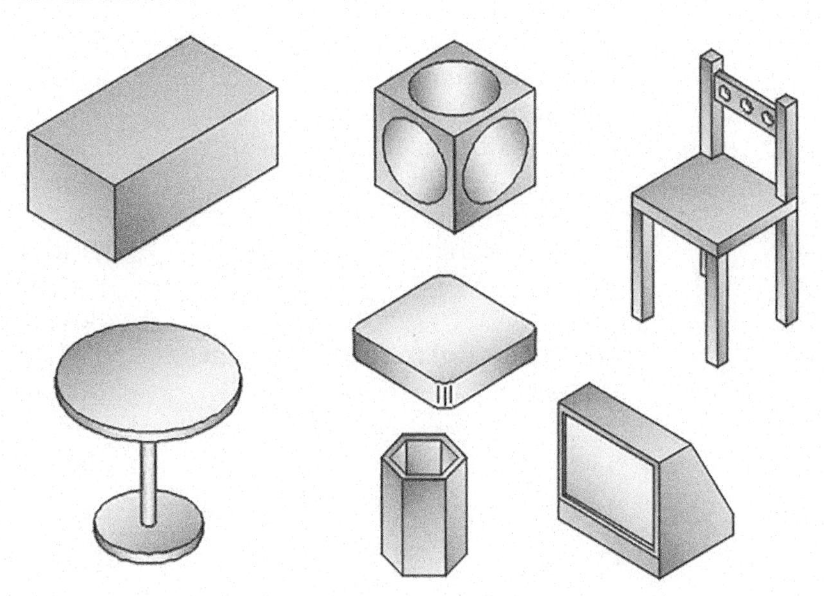

Figure 13-21
Exercise 13-3 complete

1. Select one of the nine pattern buttons.
2. Select the **Centered** check box (or deselect **Centered**).
3. Change the angle of the pattern.

In addition, you can select a color and vary its shade.

In general, follow these guidelines:

- When selecting a gradient pattern, place it on left and right isoplanes at a 60° angle to a horizontal line. Top isoplanes can vary from a horizontal pattern (90° of rotation) to 30°.
- Use the center pattern on the top row to shade holes. This pattern should be at a 0° angle in the top isoplane, 120° in the left isoplane, and 60° in the right isoplane. The **Centered** check box should be deselected so that the pattern shows a darker area on one side of the hole than on the other side.
- Do not be too concerned about where the light is coming from. Consider that there are varying sources of light. Just try to keep light areas next to dark ones and do not be afraid to experiment with any of the nine patterns. Some figures will be challenging and will require several tries before the rendering looks right.
- Use the **Draw order** option to **Send to back** all your gradient patterns so that the lines of the drawing show in front of the gradient patterns.

EXERCISE 13-3
Using Gradient Patterns to Render the Shapes of Exercise 13-1

Step 1. Open drawing **CH13-EXERCISE1**.

Step 2. Save the drawing as **CH13-EXERCISE3**.

Step 3. Open the **Hatch and Gradient** dialog box and select a color, as described next:

Prompt	Response
Type a command:	**Hatch...** (or type **H <Enter>**)
The **Hatch Creation** panel appears on the ribbon:	Click the arrow in the lower right of the **Options** panel
The **Hatch and Gradient** dialog box appears:	With the **Gradient** tab selected, click the ellipsis (**...**) to the right of the one color swatch
The **Select Color** dialog box appears:	Click the **Index Color** tab Click a color (for now, type **42 <Enter>**) in the **Color**: box Click **OK**

Step 4. Hatch the top plane of shape 1 (Figure 13-23), as described next:

Prompt	Response
The **Hatch and Gradient** dialog box appears:	Click the first pattern from the left on the top row to select it Deselect the **Centered** check box Change the **Angle** to **300** Click **Send to back** (in the **Draw order** list) so the lines are visible Click **Add: Pick points** (see Figure 13-22)

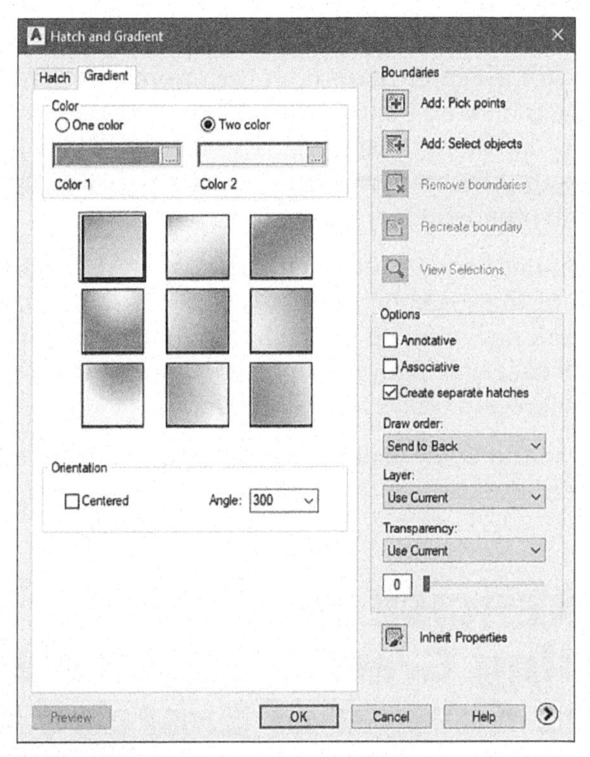

Figure 13-22
Gradient tab, **Hatch and Gradient** dialog box with gradient settings

Prompt	**Response**
Pick internal point or [Select objects seTtings]:	Click any point inside the top plane of shape 1. The gradient hatch fills the top plane
Pick internal point or [Select objects seTtings]:	Type **T <Enter>**
The **Hatch and Gradient** dialog box appears:	Click **Preview**

Figure 13-23
Apply gradient hatch patterns to shape 1

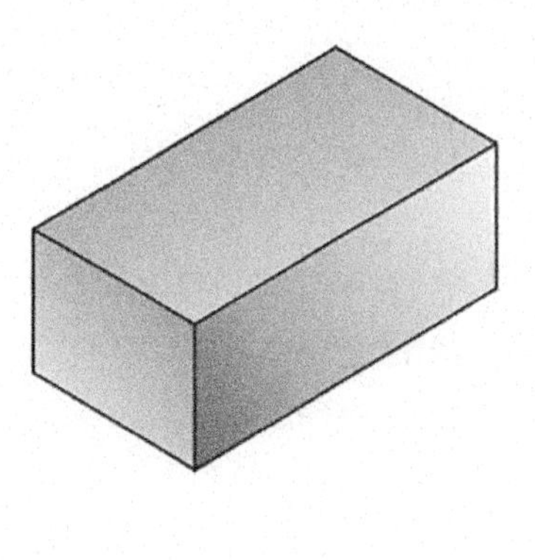

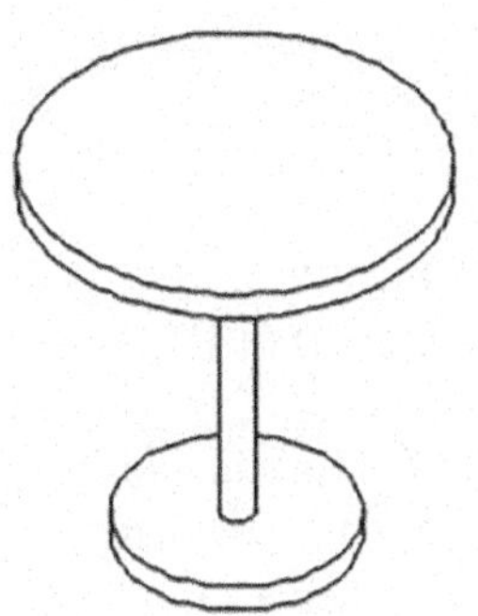

Prompt	**Response**
Pick or press Esc to return to dialog or <Right-click to accept hatch>:	Right-click (if the pattern looks right) **<Enter>** or press **<Esc>** and fix the dialog box
Type a command:	**<Enter>** (repeat **HATCH**) and Type **T <Enter>**

Step 5. Hatch the left plane of shape 1 (Figure 13-23), as described next:

Prompt	**Response**
The **Hatch and Gradient** dialog box appears:	Click the first pattern from the left on the top row to select it Deselect the **Centered** check box Change the **Angle** to **225** Click **Send to back** Click **Add: Pick points**

Prompt	Response
Pick internal point or [Select objects seTtings]:	Click any point inside the left plane of shape 1
Pick internal point or [Select objects seTtings]:	Type **T <Enter>**
The **Hatch and Gradient** dialog box appears:	Click **Preview**
Pick or press <**Esc**> to return to dialog or <Right-click to accept hatch>:	Right-click (if the pattern looks right) **<Enter>** or press **<Esc>** and fix the dialog box
Type a command:	**<Enter>** (repeat **HATCH**) and Type **T <Enter>**

Step 6. Hatch the right plane of shape 1 (Figure 13-23), as described next:

Prompt	Response
The **Hatch and Gradient** dialog box appears:	Click the first pattern from the left on the top row to select it Deselect the **Centered** check box Change the **Angle** to **30** Click **Send to back** Click **Add: Pick points**
Pick internal point or [Select objects seTtings]:	Click any point inside the right plane of shape 1
Pick internal point or [Select objects seTtings]:	Type **T <Enter>**
The **Hatch and Gradient** dialog box appears:	Click **Preview**
Pick or press <**Esc**> to return to dialog or <Right-click to accept hatch>:	Right-click (if the pattern looks right) **<Enter>** or press **<Esc>** and fix the dialog box

Step 7. Hatch the top planes of shape 4 (Figure 13-24), as described next:

Prompt	Response
Type a command:	**<Enter>** and click the arrow in the lower right of the **Options** panel
The **Hatch and Gradient** dialog box appears:	Click the second pattern from the left on the top row to select it Select the **Centered** check box Change the **Angle** to **300** Click **Send to back** Click **Add: Pick points**

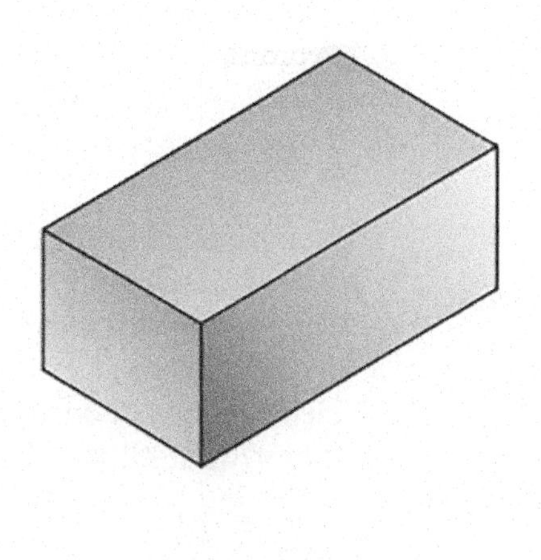

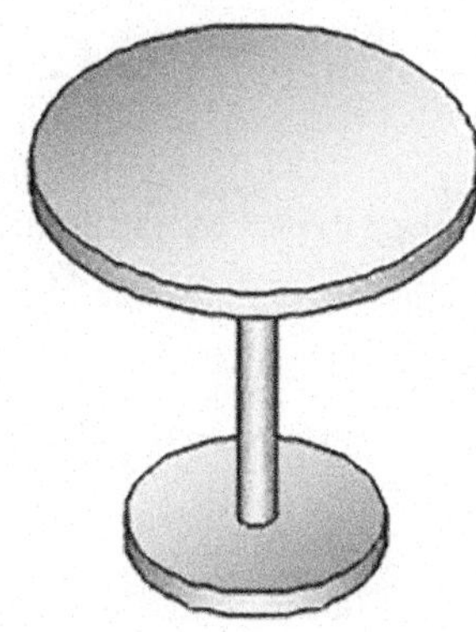

Figure 13-24
Gradient hatch patterns for shape 4

Prompt	**Response**
Pick internal point or [Select objects seTtings]:	Click any point inside the top plane of shape 4, and then click any point inside the top plane of the base, as shown in Figure 13-24
Pick internal point or [Select objects seTtings]:	Type **T <Enter>**
The **Hatch and Gradient** dialog box appears:	Click **Preview**
Pick or press **<Esc>** to return to dialog or <Right-click to accept hatch>:	Right-click (if the pattern looks right) **<Enter>** or press **<Esc>** and fix the dialog box

Step 8. Hatch the cylindrical planes of shape 4 (Figure 13-24), as described next:

Prompt	**Response**
Type a command:	**<Enter>** and click the arrow in the lower right of the **Options** panel
The **Hatch and Gradient** dialog box appears:	Click the second pattern from the left on the top row to select it Check the **Centered** box Change the **Angle** to **0** Click **Send to back** Click **Add: Pick points**

Prompt	Response
Pick internal point or [Select objects seTtings]:	Click any point inside the top edge of the tabletop (Figure 13-24)
Pick internal point or [Select objects seTtings]:	Type **T <Enter>**
The **Hatch and Gradient** dialog box appears:	Click **Preview**
Pick or press <**Esc**> to return to dialog or <Right-click to accept hatch>:	Right-click (if the pattern looks right) **<Enter>** or press **<Esc>** and fix in the dialog box

Step 9. Use the same settings in the **Hatch and Gradient** dialog box to apply patterns to the post and the base edge. You will have to do each one separately because the areas to be hatched are quite different in size. (You can also select **Create separate hatches** on the **Gradient** tab.)

Step 10. Use the **Inherit Properties** option to hatch shape 5 (Figure 13-25), as described next.

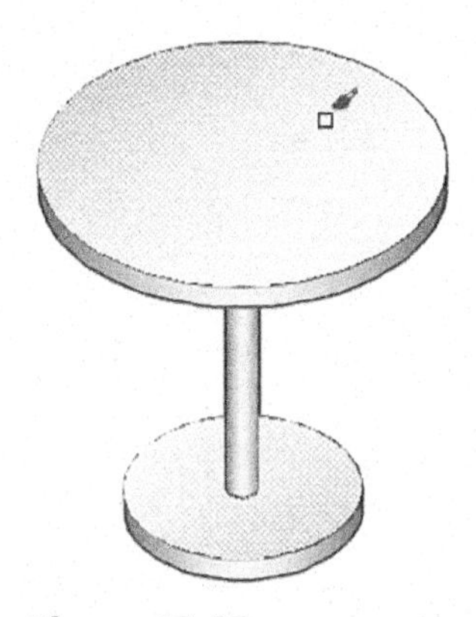

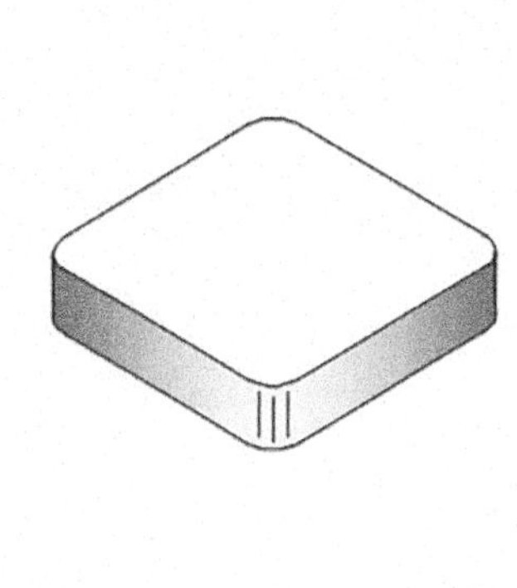

Figure 13-25
Use **Inherit Properties** to hatch shape 5—select **Associative Hatch Object**

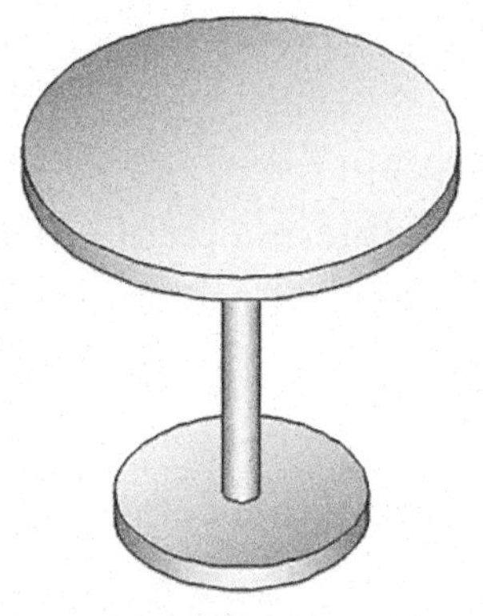

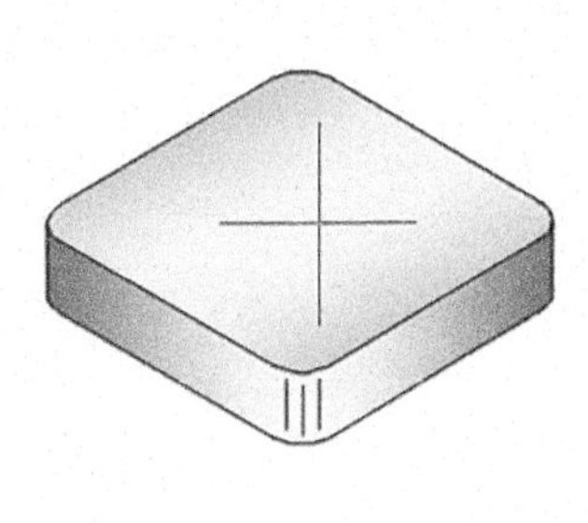

Figure 13-26
Select internal point

Prompt	Response
Type a command:	**H <Enter>** Click the arrow in the lower right of the **Options** panel
The **Hatch and Gradient** dialog box appears:	Click **Inherit Properties**
Select hatch object:	Click the top surface of shape 4 (Figure 13-25)
Pick internal point or [Select objects seTtings]:	Click the top surface of shape 5 (Figure 13-26)
Pick internal point or [Select objects seTtings]:	Type **T <Enter>** Click **Send to back** Click **OK <Enter>**

Prompt	**Response**
Type a command:	**<Enter>** (repeat **HATCH**); click the arrow in the lower-right corner of the **Options** panel
The **Hatch and Gradient** dialog box appears:	Click **Inherit Properties**
Select hatch object:	Click the post pattern of shape 4
Pick internal point or [Select objects seTtings]:	Click the unshaded surface of shape 5
Pick internal point or [Select objects seTtings]:	Type **T <Enter>**
	Click **OK**

Step 11. Use **Inherit Properties** to select hatch patterns from shapes 1 and 5 to complete shape 3.

Step 12. Use **Inherit Properties** and any other patterns you need to shade the remaining shapes so your final drawing looks similar to Figure 13-21.

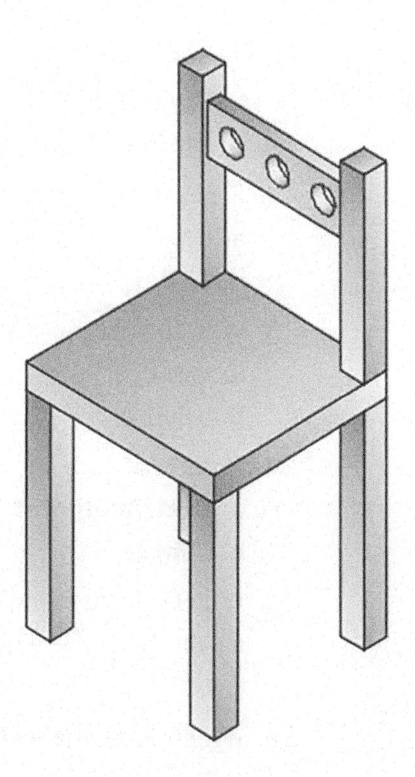

Figure 13-27
Gradient hatch patterns for shape 3

Step 13. Put your name in the lower-right corner and plot the drawing at a scale of **1″ = 1′**. Be sure the **Shade plot:** input box shows **As Displayed**.

Chapter Summary

This chapter provided you the information necessary to set up and draw isometric drawings. In addition, shading of these drawings was demonstrated, and the exercises drawn in isometric were rendered using gradient hatch patterns. Now you have the skills and information necessary to produce isometric drawings that you can use in interior design sales pieces, information sheets, contract documents, and other similar types of documents.

Chapter Test Questions

Multiple Choice

Circle the correct answer.

1. From which of the following dialog boxes are the isometric snap and grid obtained?

   a. **Layer Control...** c. **Grid On/Off**
   b. **Drafting Settings...** d. **UCS Control**

2. From which of the **Snap** options is the isometric snap obtained?

   a. **ON** c. **Rotate**
   b. **OFF** d. **Style**

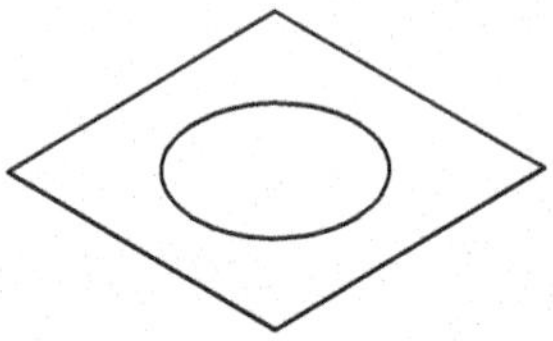

3. Which isoplane was used to draw the ellipse shown in Figure 13-28?

   a. Top c. Right
   b. Left d. It was not drawn on an isoplane.

Figure 13-28

4. From which of the **Ellipse** prompts is the isometric ellipse obtained?

   a. **<Axis endpoint 1>** c. **Isocircle**
   b. **Center** d. **Rotation**

5. Which of the following is **not** one of the normal isometric axes?

   a. 30 c. 90
   b. 60 d. 210

6. Which isoplane was used to draw the ellipse shown in Figure 13-29?

   a. Top c. Right
   b. Left d. It was not drawn on an isoplane.

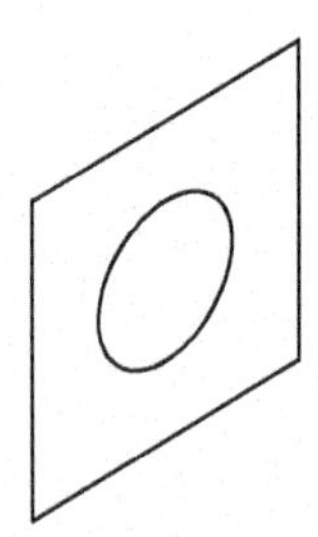

Figure 13-29

7. Which tab on the **Hatch and Gradient** dialog box allows you to apply patterns shown in Figure 13-23?

   a. **Gradient** c. **Hatch**
   b. **Advanced** d There is no such tab.

8. Which key(s) toggle from one isoplane to another?

   a. **<F5>** c. **<Ctrl>+C**
   b. **<F9>** d. **<F7>**

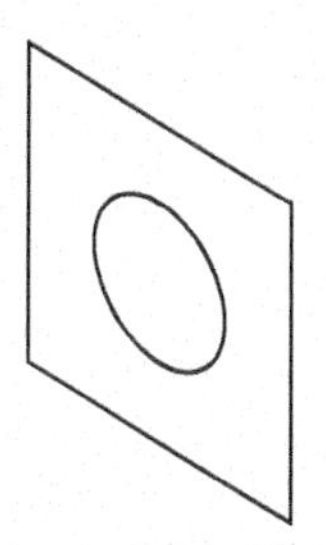

Figure 13-30

9. Which of the following is the same as –30°?
   a. 60°
   b. 150°
   c. 210°
   d. 330°

10. Which isoplane was used to draw the ellipse shown in Figure 13-30?
    a. Top
    b. Left
    c. Right
    d. It was not drawn on an isoplane.

Matching

Write the number of the correct answer on the line.

a. **Draw order** ______
b. Top, right, left ______
c. A 2D drawing method giving the appearance of three dimensions ______
d. Direct distance entry ______
e. 3D objects that can be viewed from any angle ______

1. Isometric drawing
2. 3D models
3. Isometric isoplanes
4. A means of making lines appear more prominent than gradient patterns
5. A means of drawing lines in isometric with **ORTHO** on

True or False

Circle the correct answer.

1. **True or False:** The function key **<F7>** may be used to turn the isometric grid on and off.
2. **True or False:** The syntax **@5.25"<30** draws a line 5.25" long at an angle upward to the right.
3. **True or False:** The top isoplane will **not** allow vertical lines to be drawn with a mouse when **ORTHO** is on.
4. **True or False:** The **Draw order:** option **Send to back** cannot be used to make lines appear more prominent than a gradient hatch pattern.
5. **True or False:** To draw a line at an angle that is **not** on an isometric axis, locate both ends of the line first, then draw the line.

List

1. Five options of the **Snap** command.
2. Five steps in drawing isometric circles.
3. Five steps for dimensioning in isometric drawings.
4. Five ways of accessing the Hatch command.
5. Five Hatch Settings parameters.
6. Five Properties/Options from the Hatch/Gradient window.
7. Five predefined Hatch Patterns representing materials.

8. Five Gradient Settings parameters.
9. Five isometric angles.
10. Five ways of setting up for an isometric drawing.

Questions

1. What is isometric drawing, and how is it used?
2. What is the quickest and best method for drawing isometric lines?
3. Why are isometric ellipses used to draw holes and cylinders?
4. Why must angles in isometric be drawn by locating the ends of the angle instead of drawing a line at a specific angle?
5. How can gradient hatching be used to render shapes other than isometric shapes?

Chapter Projects

Project 13-1: *Using Gradient Patterns to Render the Reception Desk of Exercise 13-2* [BASIC]

1. Open **CH13-EXERCISE2** and use gradient hatch patterns to shade this drawing so it looks similar to Figure 13-31. When you have completed the hatching, put your name in the lower-right corner and plot this drawing at a scale of **1/2″ = 1′-0″**. Be sure the **Shade plot:** input box shows **As Displayed**.
2. Save your drawing in at least two places with the name **CH13-P1**.

Figure 13-31
Project 13-1 completed

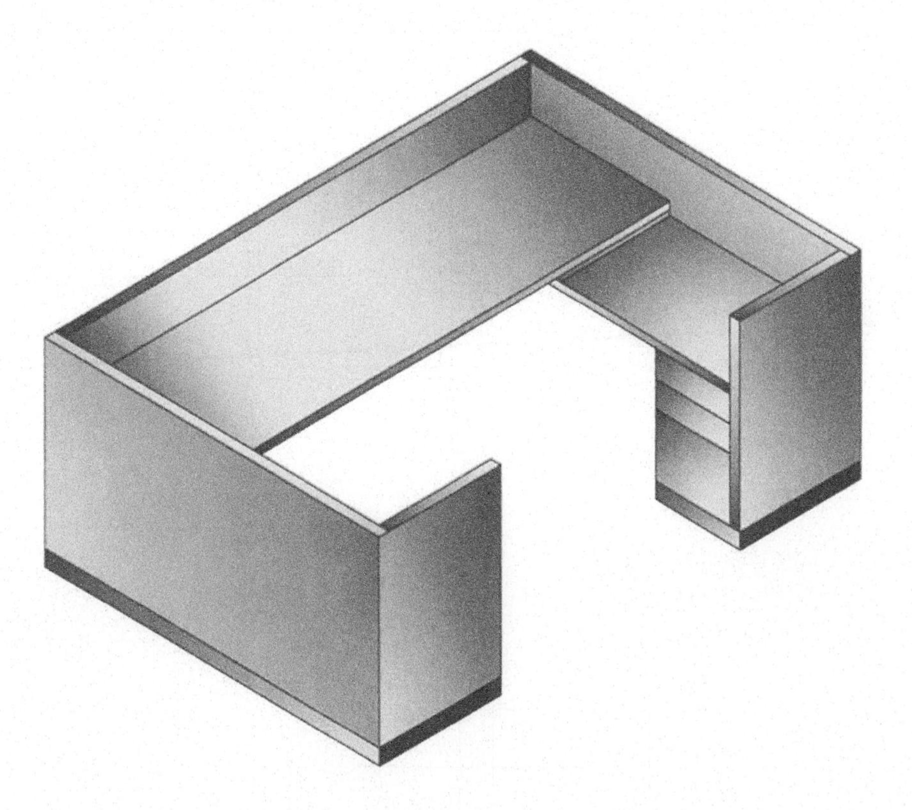

Project 13-2: *Tenant Space Reception Seating Area Isometric* **[INTERMEDIATE]**

1. Make an isometric drawing, full size, of the chairs, coffee table, and corner table to show the entire reception room seating area. Use the dimensions shown in Figure 13-32.

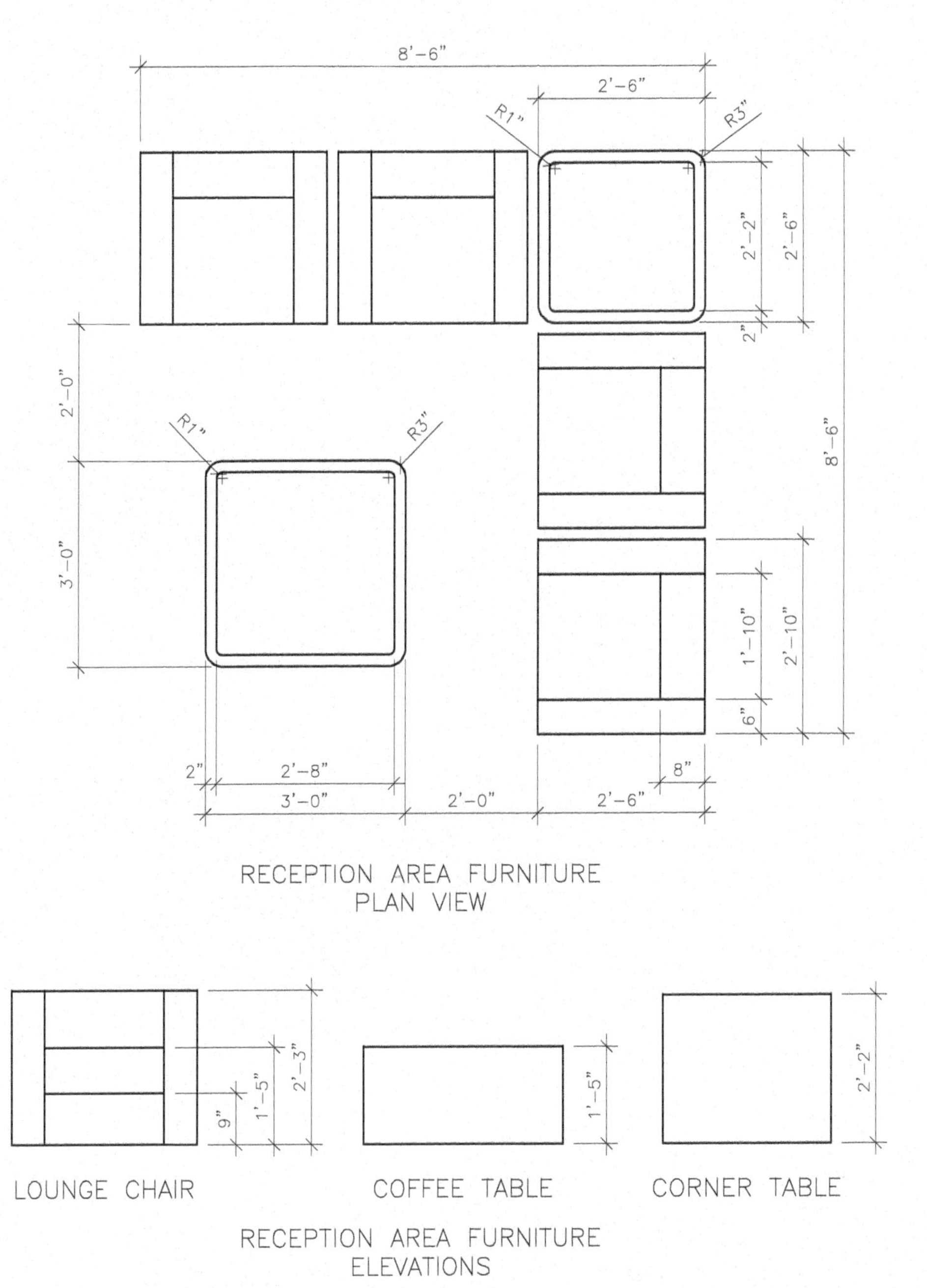

Figure 13-32
Project 13-2: Tenant space reception seating dimensions (scale: 3/8″ = 1′-0″)

2. Click **Layout1**, click the viewport boundary, and use **Properties** from the **Modify** menu to set a standard scale of **1/2″** = **1′**. Plot or print the drawing on an **8-1/2″** × **11″** sheet of paper.

3. Save your drawing in at least two places with the name **CH13-P2.**

Project 13-3: *Tenant Space Conference Chair in Isometric* **[ADVANCED]**

1. Make an isometric drawing, full size, of the conference room chair. Use the dimensions shown in Figure 13-33.

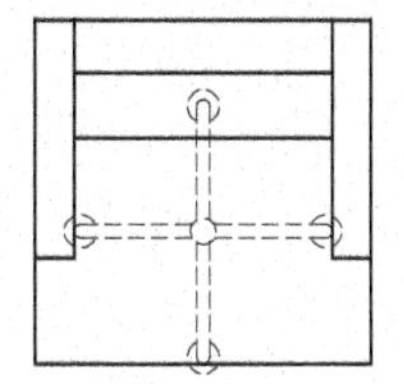

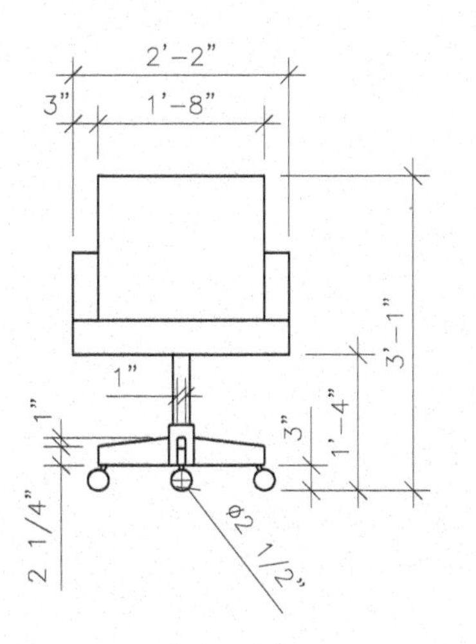

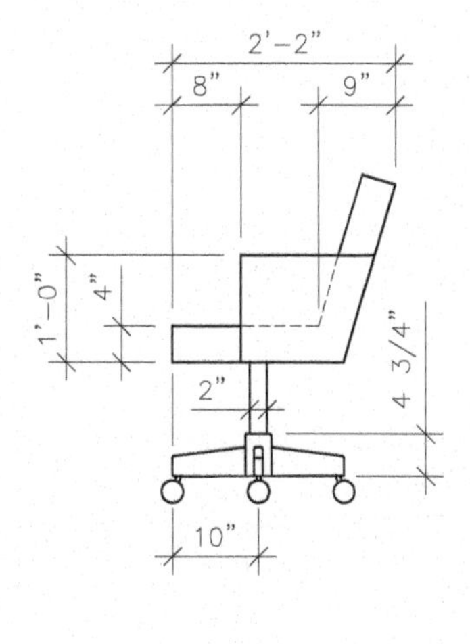

Figure 13-33
Project 13-3: Tenant space conference chair dimensions (scale: 3/8″ = 1′-0″)

2. Click **Layout1**, click the viewport boundary, and use **Properties** from the **Modify** menu to set a standard scale of **1/2″** = **1′**. Plot or print the drawing on an **8-1/2″** × **11″** sheet of paper.
3. Save your drawing in at least two places with the name **CH13-P3.**

chapter fourteen
Solid Modeling

CHAPTER OBJECTIVES

- Use the 3D workspace to create solids.
- Draw the following primitive solids: box, sphere, wedge, cone, cylinder, torus, pyramid, helix, polysolid, and planar surface.
- Make settings to display solids smoothly.
- Use SteeringWheels and ViewCube to change views of a model.
- Draw extruded solids.
- Draw revolved solids.
- Rotate solids about the x-, y-, or z-axis.
- Form chamfers and fillets on solid edges. Join two or more solids.
- Subtract one or more solids from another solid.
- Use the **SOLIDEDIT** command to change existing solids.
- Form a solid model from the common volume of two intersecting solids.
- Obtain perspective views of complex solid models.
- Use **ORBIT** and **RENDER** to render solids and print the rendered model.

Introduction

AutoCAD provides four means of creating 3D models: basic 3D using elevation and thickness, surface modeling, solid modeling, and mesh modeling. Basic 3D has very limited uses. Mesh modeling is used to create solids that have flowing freeform shapes. Basic 3D and mesh modeling are not covered in this book. Solid modeling creates solids that are much more useful and easier to modify than basic 3D. A solid may be a single object called a *primitive*, or it may be a combination of objects called a *composite*.

Creating Primitive Shapes with Solid Commands

A *primitive* solid is a single solid shape that has had nothing added to or subtracted from it. There are 10 solid primitives (box, sphere, wedge, helix, planar surface, polysolid, cone, cylinder, torus, and pyramid) that are the basic shapes often used in solid modeling. You draw them via 10 commands:

BOX
CONE
CYLINDER
HELIX
Planar Surface (PLANESURF)
POLYSOLID
PYRAMID
SPHERE
TORUS
WEDGE

You may also use the **POLYSOLID** command to convert lines, arcs, and polylines into a wall with width and height.

AutoCAD also allows you to form solids by extruding (adding height), sweeping (extruding along a path), lofting (selecting cross-sectional areas), and revolving (rotating about an axis) 2D drawing entities such as polylines, circles, ellipses, rectangles, polygons, and donuts. The commands that extrude, sweep, loft, and revolve drawing entities to form solids are:

EXTRUDE
REVOLVE
SWEEP
LOFT

Creating Composite Solids with Solid Commands

Composite solids are formed by joining primitive solids, other solids, or a combination of the two. These combinations may also be added to or subtracted from other solids to form the composite model needed. This chapter describes the following commands used to create composite solids:

UNION: Allows you to join several solids to form a single solid.

INTERSECT: Allows you to create composite solids from the intersection of two or more solids. **INTERSECT** creates a new solid by calculating the common volume of two or more existing solids.

SUBTRACT: Allows you to subtract solids from other solids.

INTERFERE: Temporarily displays the common volume of two objects or groups of objects; unlike **INTERSECT**, it does not destroy the original objects.

Editing Solids with Solid Commands

In addition to regular AutoCAD editing commands like **COPY** and **ERASE**, there are four specific solid editing commands:

SLICE: Used to create a new solid by cutting the existing solid into two pieces and removing or retaining either or both pieces.

SECTION: Used to create the cross-sectional area of a solid. That area may then be hatched using the **HATCH** command with any pattern you choose. Be sure the section is parallel with the current UCS when you hatch the area.

THICKEN: Used to make a surface thicker.

SOLIDEDIT: Used to change solid objects by extruding, moving, rotating, offsetting, tapering, copying, coloring, separating, shelling, cleaning, checking, or deleting features such as holes, surfaces, and edges.

Controlling UCS in Three Dimensions

Understanding and controlling the UCS is extremely important in creating 3D models. The UCS is the *location and orientation* of the origin of the x-, y-, and z-axes. If you are going to draw parts of a 3D model on a slanted surface, you can create a slanted UCS. If you are going to draw a 3D object, such as the handles on the drawer pedestal, you can locate your UCS so that it is flush with the front plane of the pedestal. You can then make an extrusion from that construction plane and easily create the handles in the correct location.

Chapter 8 described the UCS command options **Origin**, **OBject**, **Previous**, **Restore**, **Save**, **Delete**, **World**, and **?**. The options described in this chapter are **Move**, **Origin**, **3point**, **OBject**, **View**, and **X Y Z**.

Dynamic UCS

You can draw on any face of a 3D solid without changing UCS orientation with one of the UCS options by activating **Dynamic UCS (UCSDETECT)** on the status bar. The UCS then changes automatically when your cursor is over a face of an object, and dynamic UCS is on.

Viewing Solids

3D Views Menu Options

Viewpoint Presets: The **Viewpoint Presets** dialog box (Figure 14-1) appears when you type **VP <Enter>**.

From X Axis: Chart: This option specifies the viewing angle from the x-axis. The button allows you to type the angle; the chart above it allows you to specify a new angle by clicking the inner region on the circle. You can think of the chart, consisting of a square with a circle in it, as a viewpoint looking down on top of an object:

270	Places your view directly in front of the object.
315	Places your view to the right and in front of the object.
0	Places your view on the right side of the object.
45	Places your view to the right and behind the object.
90	Places your view directly behind the object.
135	Places your view to the left and behind the object.
180	Places your view on the left side of the object.
225	Places your view to the left and in front of the object.

Figure 14-1
Navigation tools

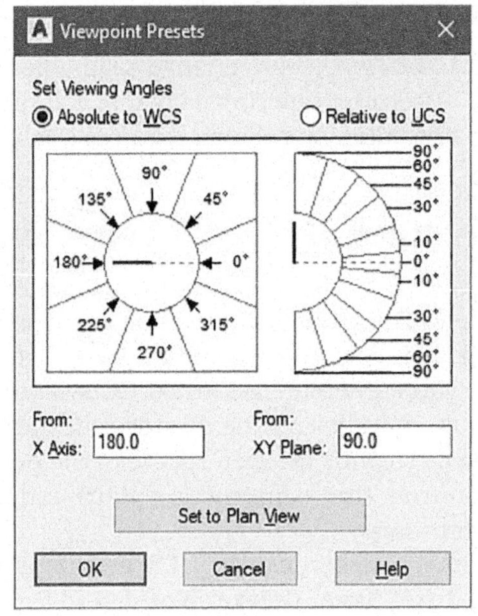

Viewpoint Presets

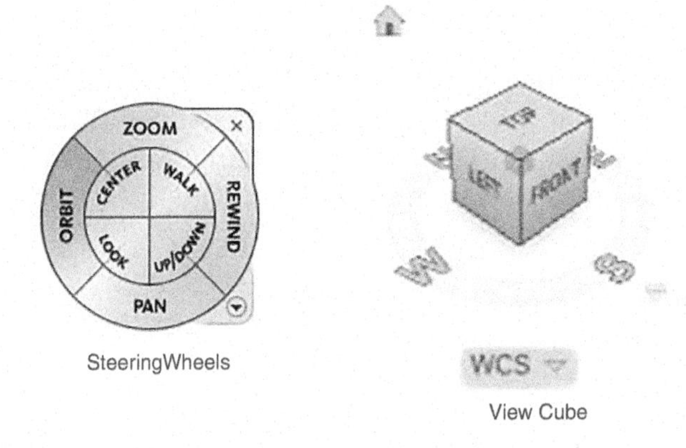

SteeringWheels

View Cube

From XY Plane: Chart: Specifies the viewing angle from the XY plane. The button allows you to type the angle, and the chart above it allows you to specify a new angle by clicking the inner region on the half circle. Consisting of two semicircles, the chart allows you to specify whether the viewpoint is to be above or below the object:

0	Places your view directly perpendicular to the chosen angle. For example, a view of 270 on the left chart and 0 on the right chart places the viewpoint directly in front of the object.
10 to 60	Places your view above the object.
90	Places your view perpendicular to the top view of the chosen angle.
–10 to –60	Places your view below the object.
–90	Places your view perpendicular to the bottom view of the chosen angle.

Set to Plan View: Sets the viewing angles to plan view (270,90) relative to the selected UCS.

Now, let's look at other **3D Views** menu options (Figure 14-2):

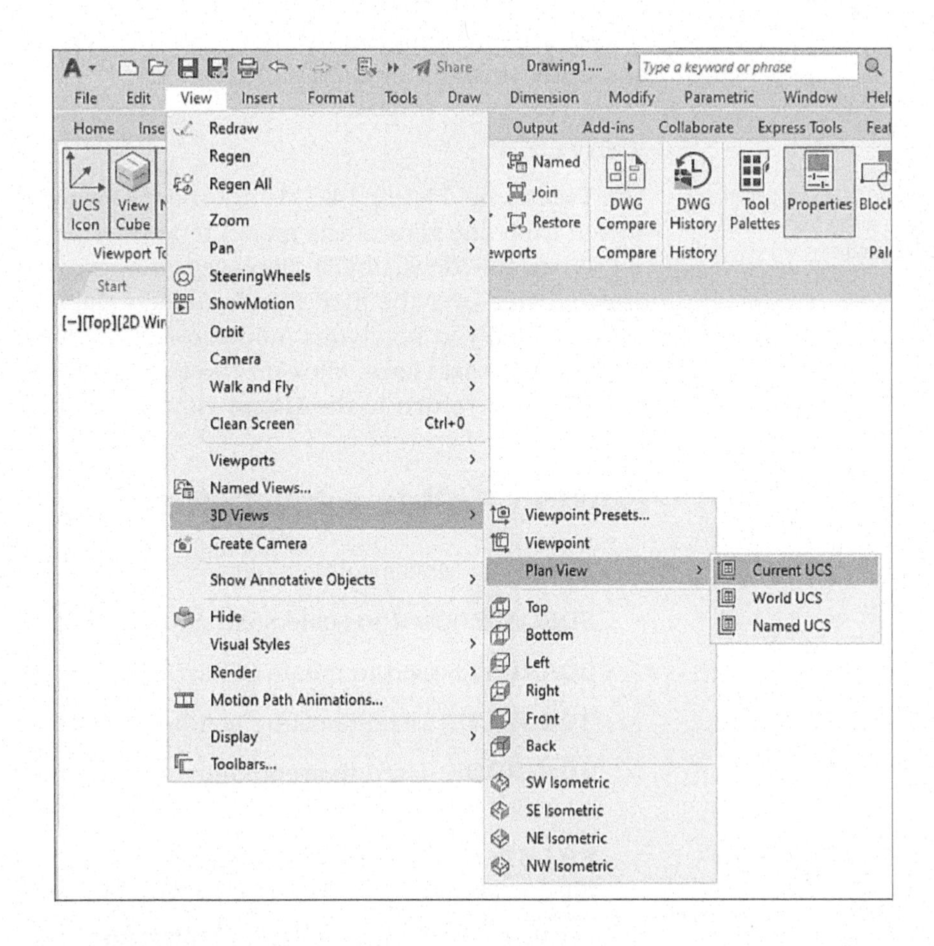

Figure 14-2
The **3D Views** cascading menu

Plan View: Allows you to select the plan view of the current UCS, the World UCS, or a saved and named UCS.

SW Isometric: Gives you an isometric view from the front, to the left, above.

SE Isometric: Gives you an isometric view from the front, to the right, above.

NE Isometric: Gives you an isometric view from the back, to the right, above.

NW Isometric: Gives you an isometric view from the back, to the left, above.

FLY: Changes your view of a 3D model so that it is as if you were flying through the model.

Orbit: A command that allows you to obtain a three-dimensional view in the active viewport.

ORBIT: Allows you to control the viewing of a 3D model using an orbit.

WALK: Changes your view of a 3D model so that it is as if you were walking through the model.

SteeringWheels: Circular tools that are divided into sections. Each section on the SteeringWheel is a tool that allows you to pan, zoom, or show the motion of the current view of the model.

SteeringWheels

SteeringWheels, Figure 14-1, are circular tools that are divided into sections. Each section on the SteeringWheel is a tool that allows you to pan, zoom, or show the motion of the current view of a model.

SteeringWheels can save you time because they combine several of the common navigation tools so they all appear on the wheel. Several different wheels are available you can use. You can change the size, transparency, and other settings for each of the wheels.

ViewCube

ViewCube: A 3D viewing tool that you can use to switch from one view of a model to another.

The ***ViewCube***, Figure 14-1, is another 3D viewing tool that you can use to switch from one view of the model to another.

When the ViewCube is displayed, it appears in one of the corners of the drawing area over the model and displays the current viewpoint of the model. When you hold your mouse over the ViewCube, you can switch to one of the preset views, click on the cube, and move your mouse to rotate the model, or return to the **Home** view of the model.

Editing Solids with Other Commands

3DMOVE: Moves solids easily.

3DSCALE: Used to scale solid objects in three dimensions.

3DARRAY: Used to create 3D arrays of objects.

3DROTATE: Used to rotate solids about the x-, y-, or z-axis.

3DMIRROR: Used to create mirror images of solids about a plane specified by three points.

FILLET: Used to create fillets and rounds. Specify the radius for the fillet, and then click the edge or edges to be filleted.

CHAMFER: Used to create chamfers. Specify the distances for the chamfer, and then click the edge or edges to be chamfered.

ALIGN: Used to move a solid so that a selected plane on the first solid is aligned with a selected plane on a second solid.

EXPLODE: Used to explode a solid into regions or planes. (*Example*: An exploded solid box becomes six regions: four sides, a top, and a bottom.) Use care with **EXPLODE**. When you explode a solid, you destroy it as a solid shape.

Controlling Solids Display

FACETRES: Used to make shaded solids and those with hidden lines removed appear smoother. Values range from 0.01 to 10.0. The default value is 0.5. Higher values take longer to regenerate but look better. Four is a good compromise. If you change this value, you can update the solid to the new value by using the **SHADE** or **HIDE** command again.

ISOLINES: Sets the number of lines on rounded surfaces of solids. Values range from 0 to 2047. The default value is 4. Twenty is a good middle ground. If you change this value, you can update the solid to the new value by regenerating the drawing.

EXERCISE 14-1
Part 1, Drawing Primitive Solids

Exercise 14-1, Parts 1 through 6, provides step-by-step instructions for using the solid commands just described. On completion of this chapter and mastery of the commands included in the chapter, you will have a sound foundation for learning solid modeling.

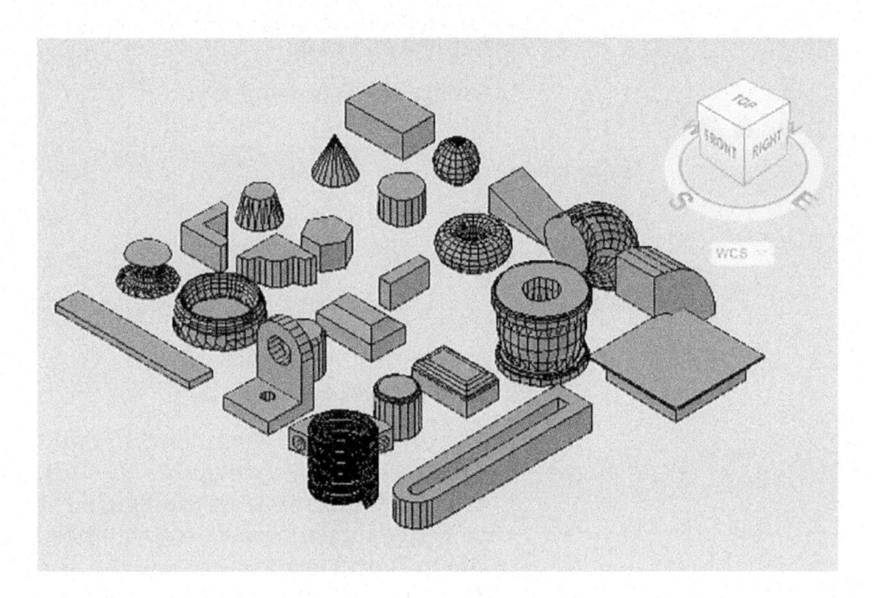

Figure 14-3
Exercise 14-1 complete

When you have completed Exercise 14-1, Parts 1 through 6, your drawing will look similar to Figure 14-3.

Step 1. Make a new workspace for all your 3D drawings as described next:

1. Click **3D Modeling** (Figure 14-4) on the **Workspace Switching** button (in the lower right of the screen). Close the palettes on the right to give yourself more room.
2. If the **Model** and **Layout** tabs are not visible at the left end of the status bar in the **3D Modeling** workspace, type **LAYOUT-TAB <Enter>** and set the value to **1** to display the tabs.
3. Click **3D Modeling-Save Current As...** (Figure 14-5) and type **YOUR NAME-3D** (in the **Name:** box), and then click **Save**.

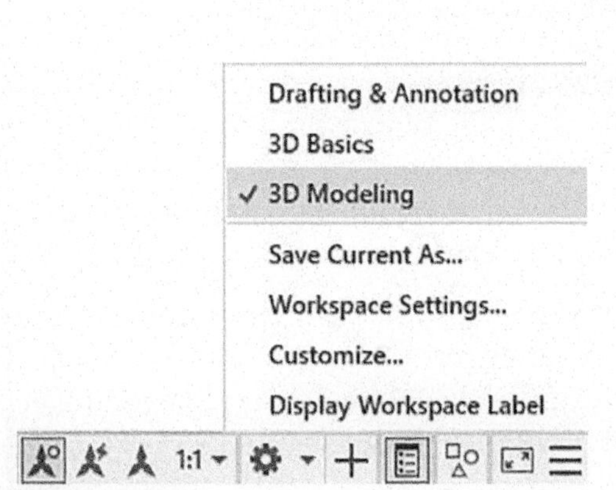

Figure 14-4
3D Modeling workspace

Figure 14-5
Save the workspace

Step 2. Use your new 3D workspace to make the following settings:

1. Use **Save As...** to save the drawing on the hard drive with the name **CH14-EXERCISE1**
2. Set drawing units: **Architectural**
3. Set drawing limits: **11,8-1/2**
4. Set **GRIDDISPLAY: 0**
5. Set grid: **1/2**
6. Set snap: **1/16**
7. Create the following layers:

Layer name	Color	Linetype	Lineweight
3d-m	magenta	continuous	default
3d-r	red	continuous	default
3d-g	green	continuous	default

8. Set layer **3d-m** current.
9. Use the **VPORTS** command to make two vertical viewports. Use **Zoom-All** in both viewports to start, and then zoom in closer so your view is similar to the figures shown. Either viewport may be active as you draw. You will need to use **Zoom-All** occasionally in both viewports to see the entire drawing.
10. Click **[Top]** on the **View Control** at the top-left corner of the viewport, and select **SE Isometric** from the menu (Figure 14-6) to set a viewpoint for the right viewport.
11. Set **FACETRES** to **4** (type **FACETRES <Enter>).**
12. Set **ISOLINES** to **20** (type **ISOLINES <Enter>).**

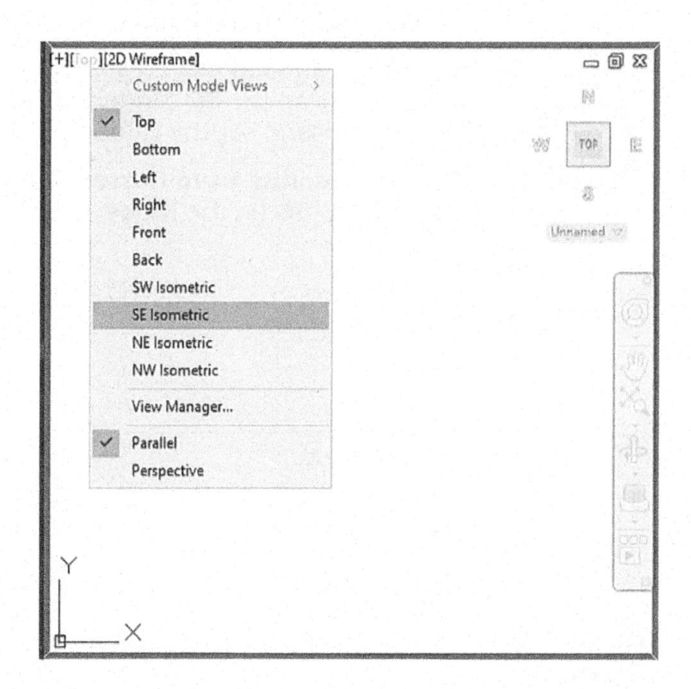

Figure 14-6
Set the **View Control** to **SE Isometric**

BOX	
Ribbon/ Panel	3D Tools/ Modeling
Modeling Toolbar:	
Menu Bar:	Draw/ Modeling/ Box
Type a Command:	BOX

Box

Step 3. Draw a solid box, **1 1/4″ × 3/4″ × 1/2″** height (Figure 14-7), as described next:

Prompt	**Response**
Type a command:	**Box** (or type **BOX <Enter>**)
Specify first corner or [Center]<0,0,0>:	Type **1/2,7-1/2 <Enter>**
Specify other corner or [Cube Length]:	Type **@1-1/4,3/4 <Enter>**
Specify height or [2Point]:	Type **1/2 <Enter>**

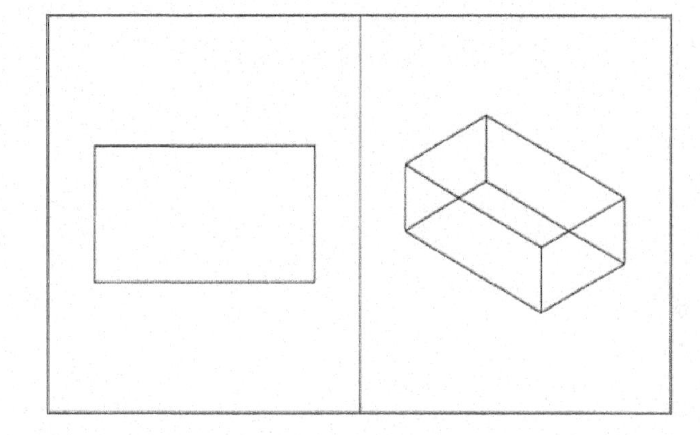

Figure 14-7
Draw a solid box

Center: Allows you to draw a box by first locating its center.

Cube: Allows you to draw a cube by specifying the length of one side.

Length: Allows you to draw a box by specifying its length (X), width (Y), and height (Z).

Sphere

Step 4. Draw a solid sphere, **3/8″** radius (Figure 14-8), as described next:

Prompt	**Response**
Type a command:	**Sphere** (or type **SPHERE <Enter>**)
Specify center point or [3P 2P Ttr]:	Type **2-3/4,7-3/4 <Enter>**
Specify radius or [Diameter]:	Type **3/8 <Enter>**

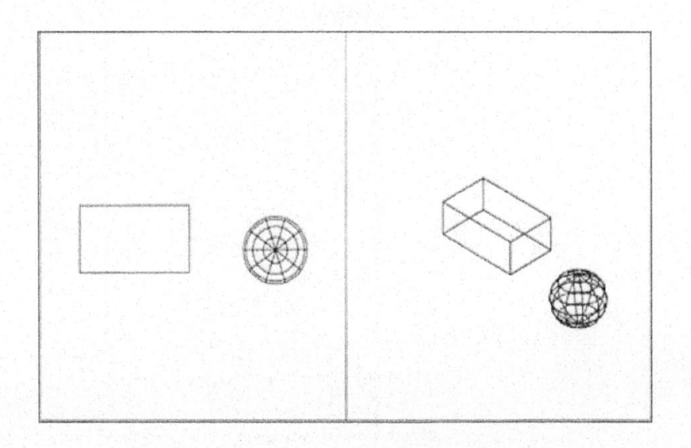

Figure 14-8
Draw a solid sphere

WEDGE	
Ribbon/ Panel	3D Tools/ Modeling
Modeling Toolbar:	
Menu Bar:	Draw/ Modeling/ Wedge
Type a Command:	WEDGE
Command Alias:	WE

Wedge

Step 5. Draw a solid wedge, **3/4″ × 1 1/4″ × 1/2″** height (Figure 14-9), as described next:

Prompt	**Response**
Type a command:	**Wedge** (or type **WE <Enter>**)
Specify first corner or [Center]:	Type **3-3/4,7-1/2 <Enter>**
Specify other corner or [Cube Length]:	Type **@1-1/4, 3/4 <Enter>**
Specify height or [2Point]<1/2″>:	Type **1/2 <Enter>**

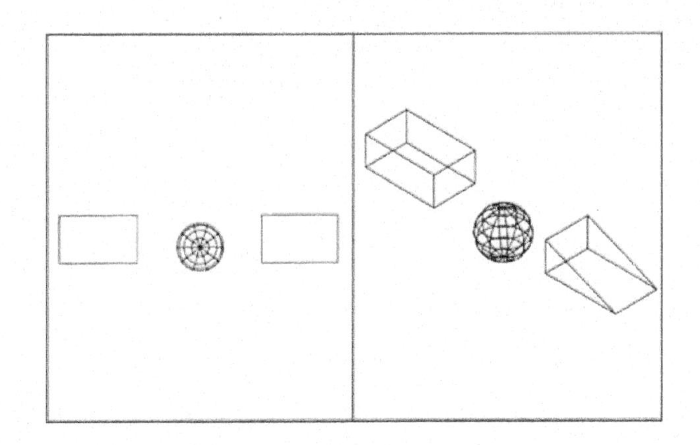

Figure 14-9
Draw a solid wedge

CONE	
Ribbon/ Panel	3D Tools/ Modeling
Modeling Toolbar:	
Menu Bar:	Draw/ Modeling/ Cone
Type a Command:	CONE

Cone

Step 6. Draw a solid cone, **3/8″** radius, **3/4″** height (Figure 14-10), as described next:

Prompt	**Response**
Type a command:	**Cone** (or type **CONE <Enter>**)
Specify center point of base or [3P 2P Ttr Elliptical]:	Type **1-1/4,6-1/2 <Enter>**
Specify base radius or [Diameter]<0′-3/8″>:	Type **3/8 <Enter>**
Specify height or [2Point Axis endpoint Top radius] <0′-0 1/2″>:	Type **3/4 <Enter>**

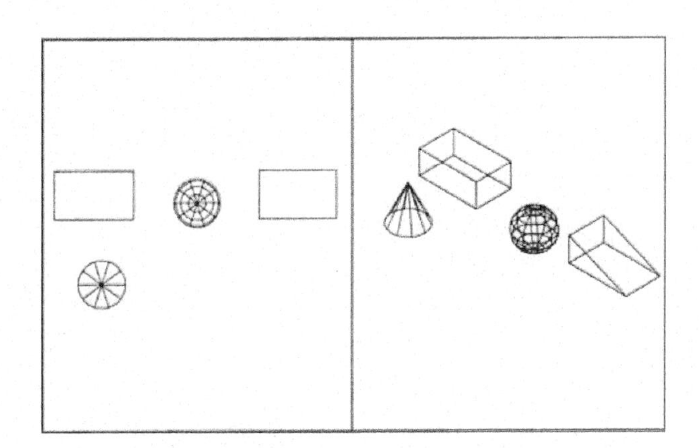

Figure 14-10
Draw a solid cone

CYLINDER	
Ribbon/ Panel	3D Tools/ Modeling
Modeling Toolbar:	
Menu Bar:	Draw/ Modeling/ Cylinder
Type a Command:	CYLINDER
Command Alias:	CYL

Cylinder

Step 7. Draw a solid cylinder, **3/8″** radius, **1/2″** height (Figure 14-11), as described next:

Prompt	**Response**
Type a command:	**Cylinder** (or type **CYL <Enter>**)
Specify center point of base or [3P 2P Ttr Elliptical]:	Type **2-3/4,6-1/2 <Enter>**
Specify base radius or [Diameter] <default>:	Type **3/8 <Enter>**
Specify height or [2Point Axis endpoint]<default>:	Type **1/2 <Enter>**

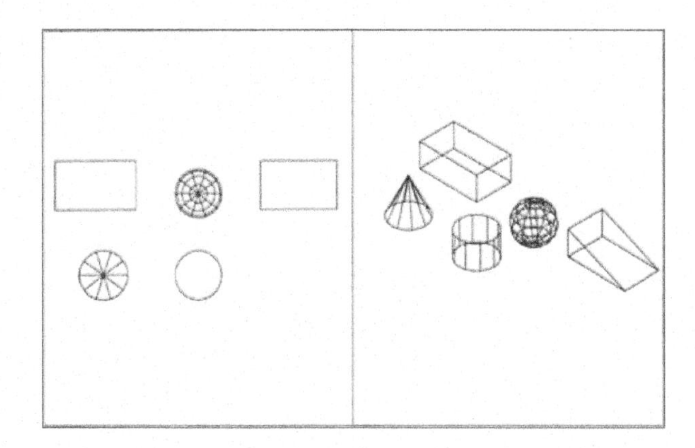

Figure 14-11
Draw a solid cylinder

TORUS	
Ribbon/ Panel	3D Tools/ Modeling
Modeling Toolbar:	
Menu Bar:	Draw/ Modeling/ Torus
Type a Command:	TORUS
Command Alias:	TOR

Torus

Step 8. Draw a solid torus (a 3D donut), **3/8″** torus radius, **1/4″** tube radius (Figure 14-12), as described next:

Prompt	**Response**
Type a command:	**Torus** (or type **TOR <Enter>**)
Specify center point or [3P 2P Ttr]:	Type **4-3/8,6-1/2 <Enter>**
Specify radius or [Diameter]:	Type **3/8 <Enter>**
Specify tube radius or [2Point Diameter]:	Type **1/4 <Enter>**

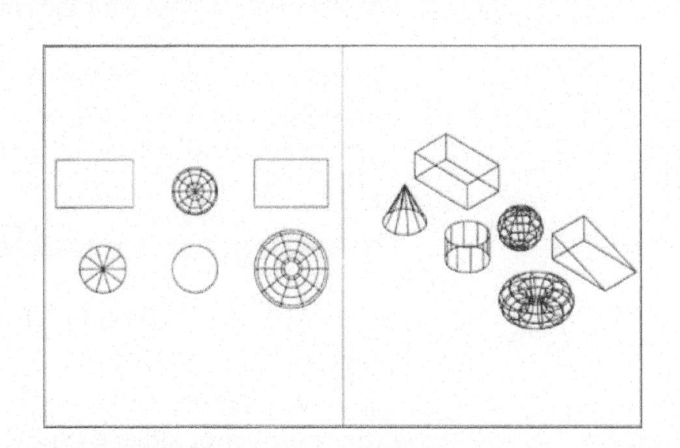

Figure 14-12
Draw a solid torus

The radius of the torus is the distance from the center of the 3D donut to the center of the tube that forms the donut. The radius of the tube is the radius of the tube forming the donut.

EXERCISE 14-1
Part 2, Using Extrude to Draw Extruded Solids

Drawing an Extruded Circle

Step 9. Draw a circle (Figure 14-13), as described next:

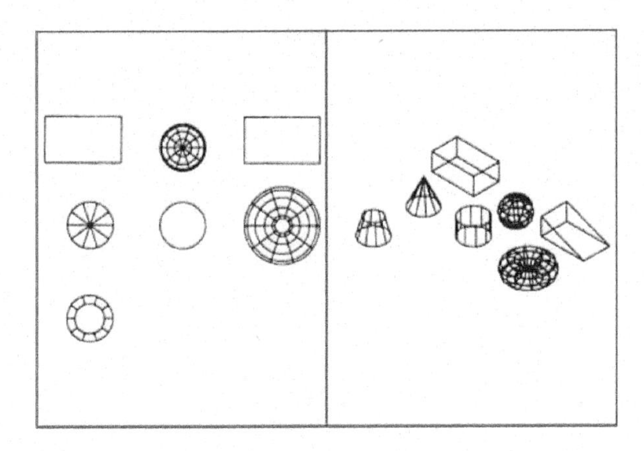

Figure 14-13
Extruding and tapering a circle

Prompt	Response
Type a command:	Type **C <Enter>**
Specify center point of circle or [3P 2P Ttr (tan radius)]:	Type **1-1/4,5 <Enter>**
Specify radius of circle or [Diameter]:	Type **3/8 <Enter>**

EXTRUDE	
Ribbon/ Panel	3D Tools/ Modeling
Modeling Toolbar:	
Menu Bar:	Draw/ Modeling/ Extrude
Type a Command:	EXTRUDE
Command Alias:	EXT

Step 10. Extrude the circle, **1/2″** height, **15°** extrusion taper angle (Figure 14-13), as described next:

Prompt	Response
Type a command:	**Extrude** (or type **EXT <Enter>**)
Select objects to extrude or [MOde]:	Click the circle
Select objects to extrude or [MOde]:	**<Enter>**
Specify height of extrusion or [Direction Path Taper angle Expression]:	Type **T <Enter>**
Specify angle of taper for extrusion or [Expression] <0′-1″>:	Type **15 <Enter>**
Specify height of extrusion or [Direction Path Taper angle Expression] <0′-1″>:	Type **1/2 <Enter>**

Drawing an Extruded Polygon

Step 11. Draw a polygon (Figure 14-14), as described next:

Prompt	Response
Type a command:	**Polygon** (or type **POL <Enter>**)
Enter number of sides <4>:	Type **6 <Enter>**
Specify center of polygon or [Edge]:	Type **2-3/4,5 <Enter>**
Enter an option [Inscribed in circle Circumscribed about circle <I>]:	Type **C <Enter>**
Specify radius of circle:	Type **3/8 <Enter>**

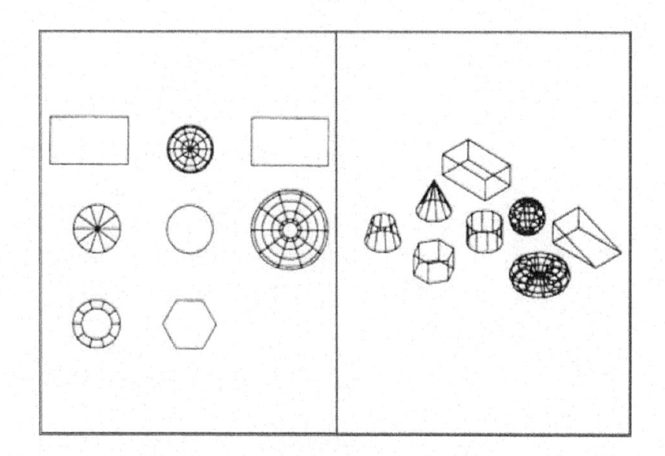

Figure 14-14
Extruding a polygon

PRESSPULL	
Ribbon/ Panel	3D Tools/ Solid Editing
Modeling Toolbar:	
Type a Command:	PRESSPULL

Step 12. Extrude the polygon, **1/2″** height, using the **PRESSPULL** command (Figure 14-14), as described next:

Prompt	**Response**
Type a command:	**Presspull** (or type **PRESSPULL <Enter>**)
Select object or bounded area:	Click any point inside the polygon (in the **SE Isometric** viewport)
Specify extrusion height or [Multiple]:	Move your mouse up and type **1/2 <Enter>**

Drawing an Extruded Rectangle

Step 13. Draw a rectangle (Figure 14-15), as described next:

Prompt	**Response**
Type a command:	**Rectangle** (or type **REC <Enter>**)
Specify first corner point or [Chamfer Elevation Fillet Thickness Width]:	Type **4-1/4,4-1/2 <Enter>**
Specify other corner point or [Area Dimensions Rotation]:	Type **@1/4,7/8 <Enter>**

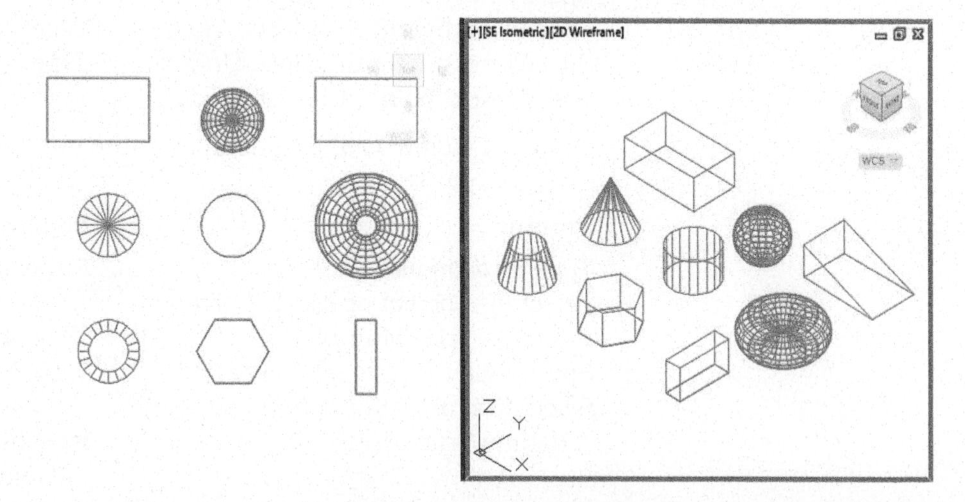

Figure 14-15
Extruding a rectangle

Step 14. Extrude the rectangle, **1/2″** height, **0°** extrusion taper angle (Figure 14-15), as described next:

Prompt	Response
Type a command:	**Extrude** (or type **EXT <Enter>** or use **PRESSPULL**)
Select objects to extrude or [MOde]:	Click the rectangle
Select objects to extrude or [MOde]:	**<Enter>**
Specify height of extrusion or [Direction Path Taper angle Expression] <0′-1″>:	Type **1/2 <Enter>**

Drawing an Extruded Structural Angle

Step 15. Draw the outline of the cross section of a structural angle (Figure 14-16), as described next:

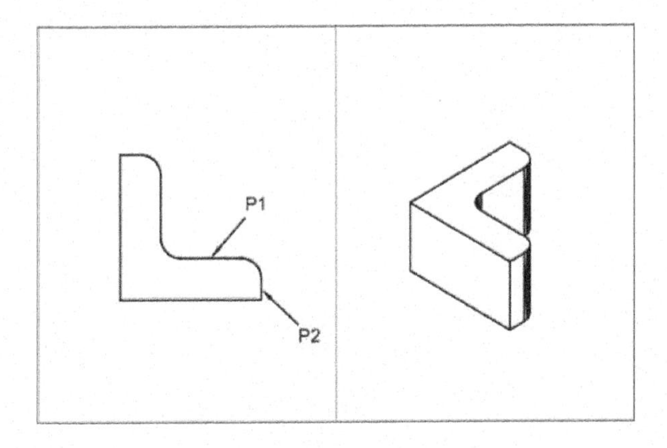

Figure 14-16
Extruding a structural steel angle

Prompt	Response
Type a command:	Type **L <Enter>**
Specify first point:	Type **1,3 <Enter>**
Specify next point or [Undo]:	Type **@7/8,0 <Enter>** (or turn **ORTHO** on and use direct distance entry)
Specify next point or [Undo]:	Type **@0,1/4 <Enter>**
Specify next point or [Close Undo]:	Type **@-5/8,0 <Enter>**
Specify next point or [Close Undo]:	Type **@0,5/8 <Enter>**
Specify next point or [Close Undo]:	Type **@-1/4,0 <Enter>**
Specify next point or [Close Undo]:	Type **C <Enter>**

Step 16. Add a **1/8″**-radius fillet to the outline (Figure 14-16), as described next:

Prompt	Response
Type a command:	**Fillet** (or type **F <Enter>**)
Select first object or [Undo Polyline Radius Trim Multiple]:	Type **R <Enter>**
Specify fillet radius <0′-0 1/2″>:	Type **1/8 <Enter>**
Select first object or [Undo Polyline Radius Trim Multiple]:	**P1→** (use the **Zoom-Window** command if needed to allow you to pick the necessary lines)
Select second object or shift-select to apply corner:	**P2→**

TIP

Type **M <Enter>** before you select the first object for the fillet so you can fillet all corners without repeating the command.

TIP

After typing **M <Enter>**, specifying the radius, and clicking the first two objects, hold down the **<Shift>** key and click the next two lines to get a zero-radius fillet.

Step 17. Draw **1/8″**-radius fillets (Figure 14-16) at the other two intersections shown.

Step 18. Use **JOIN** to combine all the lines and fillets into a single entity (Figure 14-16), as described next:

Prompt	**Response**
Type a command:	Click **Join** from the extended **Modify** panel, or type **JOIN <Enter>**
Select source object or multiple objects to join at once:	Drag a selection window around the lines forming the structural angle
Select objects to join:	**<Enter>**

Step 19. Extrude the cross section of the structural angle, **1/2″** height, **0°** extrusion taper angle (Figure 14-16), as described next:

Prompt	**Response**
Type a command:	**Extrude** (or type **EXT <Enter>**) or use **PRESSPULL**
Select objects to extrude or [MOde]:	Click the rectangle
Select objects to extrude or [MOde]:	**<Enter>**
Specify height of extrusion or [Direction Path Taper angle Expression] <0′-1″>:	Type **1/2 <Enter>**

TIP

PRESSPULL works well for **EXTRUDE** in cases where the extrusion is just up or down. In addition, you do not have to have a single polyline.

Drawing an Extruded Shape

Step 20. Draw the shape shown as Figure 14-17 in the approximate location shown in Figure 14-3. When you draw the shape, be sure that you draw only what is needed. If you draw extra lines, the **Join** command cannot join the lines into a single polyline.

Step 21. Use the **Join** command to join all lines and arcs into a single polyline or use **PRESSPULL** without joining all lines.

Step 22. Extrude the figure to a height of **1/2**.

> **FOR MORE DETAILS**
>
> See Chapter 15 for more on revolving.

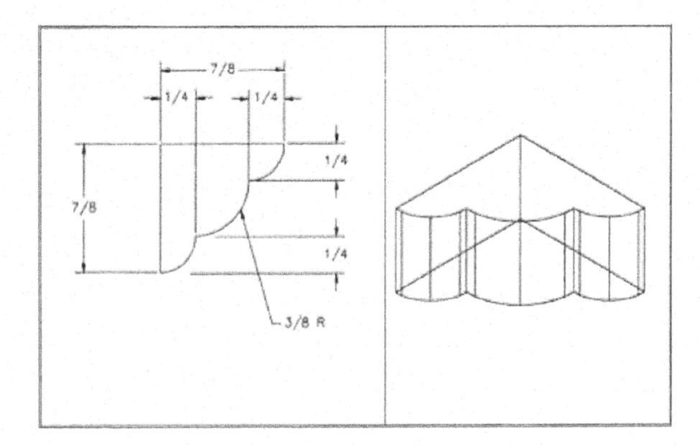

Figure 14-17
Extruding a molding shape

EXERCISE 14-1
Part 3, Using REVOLVE to Draw Revolved Solids; Using 3DROTATE to Rotate Solids about the X-, Y-, and Z-Axes

Drawing Revolved Shape 1

Step 23. Draw two circles (Figure 14-18), as described next:

Prompt	**Response**
Type a command:	Type **C <Enter>**
Specify center point for circle or [3P 2P Ttr (tan radius)]:	Type **6-1/4,7-3/4 <Enter>**

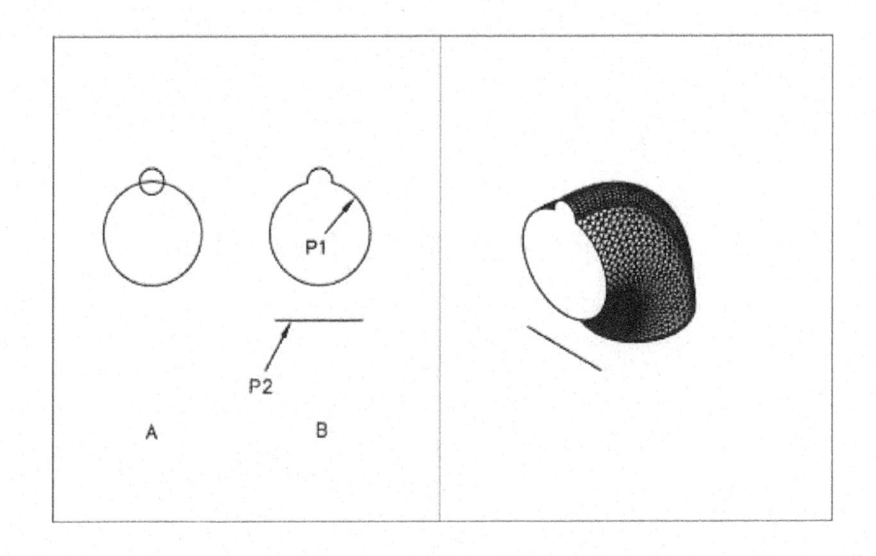

Figure 14-18
Revolving a shape 90°

Prompt	Response
Specify radius of circle or [Diameter]:	Type **1/2 <Enter>**
Type a command:	**<Enter>**
Specify center point for circle or [3P 2P Ttr (tan tan radius)]:	Type **6-1/4,8-1/4 <Enter>**
Specify radius of circle or [Diameter] <0′-1/2″>:	Type **1/8 <Enter>**

Step 24. Use the **TRIM** command to trim parts of both circles (Figures 14-18A and 14-18B), as described next:

Prompt	Response
Type a command:	**Trim** (or type **TR <Enter>**)
Select cutting edges...	
Select objects or <select all>:	**<Enter>**
Select object to trim or shift-select to extend or [Fence Crossing Project Edge eRase Undo]:	Trim the circles as shown in Figure 14-18A (use **Zoom-Window** to get in closer if needed **<Enter>**

Step 25. Join all segments of the circles into one polyline (Figure 14-18B), as described next:

Prompt	Response
Type a command:	**Join** (or type **JOIN <Enter>**)
Select source object or multiple objects to join at once:	Drag a selection window around the circles forming the shape

Step 26. Draw the axis of revolution (Figure 14-18), as described next:

Prompt	Response
Type a command:	**Line** (or type **L <Enter>**)
Specify first point:	Type **6,6-3/4 <Enter>**
Specify next point or [Undo]:	With **ORTHO** on, move your mouse to the right and type **5/8 <Enter>**
Specify next point or [Undo]:	**<Enter>**

REVOLVE	
Ribbon/ Panel	3D Tools/ Modeling
Modeling Toolbar:	
Menu Bar:	Draw/ Modeling/ Revolve
Type a Command:	REVOLVE
Command Alias:	REV

Step 27. Use **REVOLVE** to form a revolved solid created by revolving a single polyline 90° counterclockwise about an axis (Figure 14-18B), as described next:

Prompt	Response
Type a command:	**Revolve** (or type **REV <Enter>**)
Select objects to revolve or [MOde]:	**P1→** (Figure 14-18B)
Select objects to revolve or [MOde]:	**<Enter>**
Specify axis start point or define axis by [Object X Y Z] <Object>:	**<Enter>**
Select an object:	**P2→** (be sure to click the left end of the line for counterclockwise rotation)
Specify angle of revolution or [STart angle/Reverse/EXpression]<360>:	Type **90 <Enter>**

Drawing a Revolved Rectangle

Step 28. Draw a rectangle (Figure 14-19), as described next:

Prompt	**Response**
Type a command:	**Rectangle** (or type **REC <Enter>**)
Specify first corner point or [Chamfer Elevation Fillet Thickness Width]:	Type **7-3/8,7-3/8 <Enter>**
Specify other corner point or [Area Dimensions Rotation]:	Type **@7/8,7/8 <Enter>**

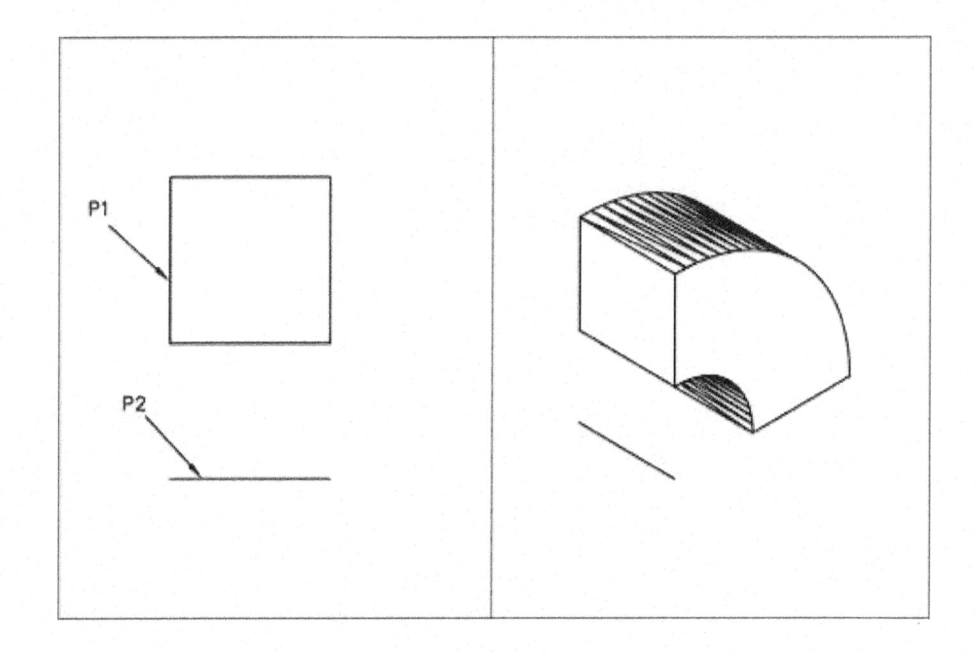

Figure 14-19
Revolving a rectangle

Step 29. Draw the axis of revolution (Figure 14-19), as described next:

Prompt	**Response**
Type a command:	Type **L <Enter>**
Specify first point:	Type **7-3/8,6-3/4 <Enter>**
Specify next point or [Undo]:	Move your mouse to the right and type **3/4 <Enter>** (be sure **ORTHO** is on)
Specify next point or [Undo]:	**<Enter>**

Step 30. Use the **REVOLVE** command to form a revolved solid created by revolving the rectangle 90° counterclockwise about an axis (Figure 14-19), as described next:

Prompt	**Response**
Type a command:	**Revolve**
Select objects to revolve or [MOde]:	**P1→ <Enter>**
Select objects to revolve or [MOde]:	**<Enter>**
Specify axis start point or define axis by [Object X Y Z] <Object>:	**<Enter>**
Select an object:	**P2→** (Click the left end of the line)
Specify angle of revolution or [STart angle Reverse EXpression]<360>:	Type **90 <Enter>**

Drawing a Revolved Paper Clip Holder

Step 31. Draw the cross-sectional shape of the object shown in Figure 14-20 using the **LINE** and **ARC** commands in the left viewport in the approximate locations shown in Figure 14-3.

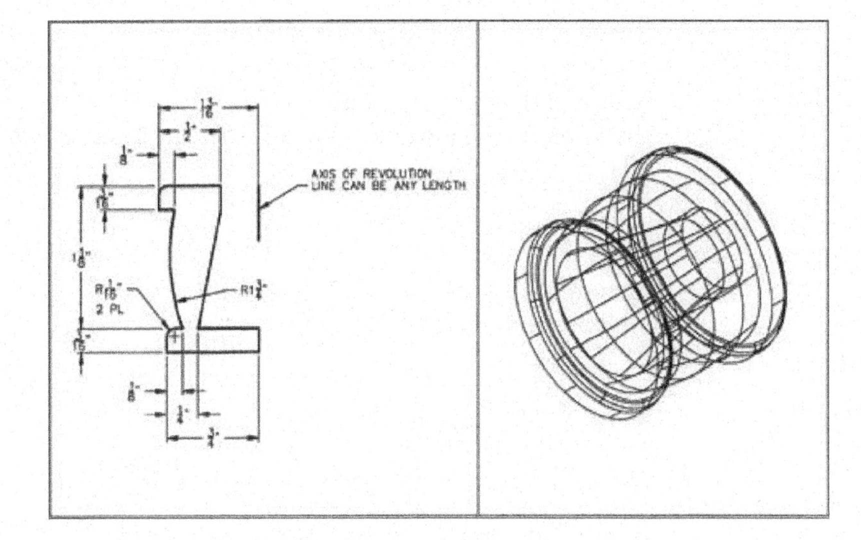

Figure 14-20
Revolving a paper clip holder

Step 32. Use the **Join** command to join all entities of the shape into a single closed polyline.

Step 33. Locate the axis of revolution for the shape in the position shown.

Step 34. Use **REVOLVE** to revolve the shape full circle about the axis.

> **FOR MORE DETAILS**
>
> See Chapter 15 for more on extruding.

Using 3DROTATE

Step 35. Use **3DROTATE** to rotate the paper clip holder **90°** about the x-axis so that it assumes the position shown in Figure 14-21, as described next:

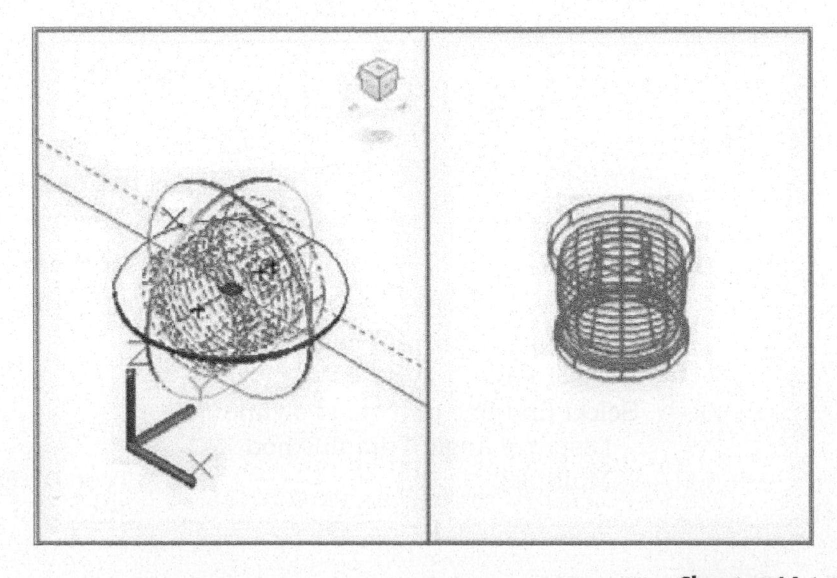

Figure 14-21
Rotating an object about the x-axis

Prompt	Response
Type a command:	Type **3DROTATE <Enter>**
Select objects:	Click the paper clip holder
Select objects:	**<Enter>**

When you have confirmed object selection, the **3D Rotate Gizmo** appears (there are also separate gizmos for **3D Move** and **3D Scale**). The **UCS icon** also changes to a three-dimensional icon, color-coded to the three axes, where **X** is red, **Y** is green, and **Z** is blue. The same three colors, indicating the same three axes, appear on the **3D Rotate Gizmo**.

Specify base point:	Move the crosshairs over the red circle of the gizmo and click when it is highlighted
Specify rotation angle or [Base point Copy Undo Reference eXit]:	Type **90 <Enter>**

EXERCISE 14-1
Part 4, Using CHAMFER and FILLET to Form Chamfers and Fillets on Solid Edges

Chamfering and Filleting the Top Four Edges of Two Separate Boxes

Step 36. Use **BOX** to draw two boxes measuring **1-1/4″** × **3/4″** × **1/2″** height for each, in the approximate locations shown in Figure 14-3.

Step 37. Chamfer the top four edges of the first box (Figure 14-22), as described next:

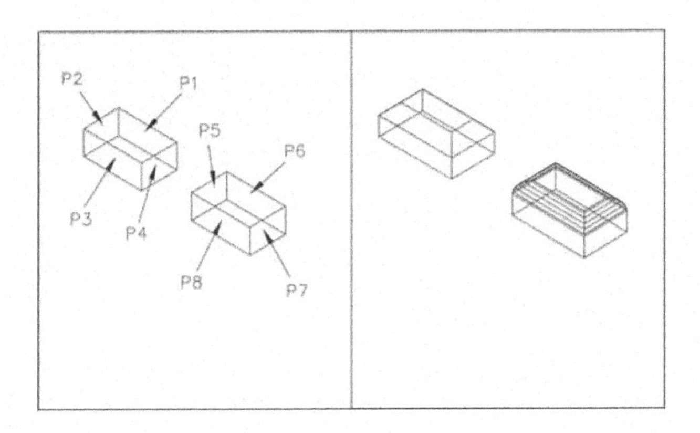

Figure 14-22
Chamfering and filleting solid edges

Prompt	Response
Type a command:	**Chamfer** (or type **CHA <Enter>**)
(TRIM mode) Current chamfer Dist1 = 0′-0″, Dist2 = 0′-0″	
Select first line or [Undo Polyline Distance Angle Trim mEthod Multiple]:	Type **D <Enter>**

Prompt	**Response**
Specify first chamfer distance <0′-0″>:	Type **3/16 <Enter>**
Specify second chamfer distance <0′-0 3/16″>:	**<Enter>**
Select first line or [Undo Polyline Distance Angle Trim mEthod Multiple]:	**P1→** (Figure 14-22)
Base surface selection...	
Enter surface selection option [Next OK (current)] <OK>:	

If the top surface of the box turns dotted, showing it as the selected surface, continue. If one of the side surfaces is selected, type **N <Enter>** until the top surface is selected.

Prompt	**Response**
Enter surface selection option [Next OK (current)] <OK>:	**<Enter>**
Specify base surface chamfer distance <0′-0 3/16″>:	**<Enter>**
Specify other surface chamfer distance <0′-0 3/16″>:	**<Enter>**
Select an edge or [Loop]:	**P1→, P2→, P3→, P4→** (Figure 14-22)
Select an edge or [Loop]:	**<Enter>**

Step 38. Fillet the top four edges of the second box (Figure 14-22), as described next:

Prompt	**Response**
Type a command:	**Fillet** (or type **F <Enter>**)
Current settings: Mode = TRIM, Radius = 0′-0 1/8″	
Select first object or [Undo Polyline Radius Trim Multiple]:	**P5→** (Figure 14-22)
Enter fillet radius <0′-0 1/8″>:	Type **3/16 <Enter>**
Select an edge or [Chain Loop Radius]:	**P6→, P7→, P8→** (Figure 14-22)
Select an edge or [Chain Loop Radius]:	**<Enter>**

Chamfering and Filleting the Top Edge of Two Separate Cylinders

Step 39. Draw two cylinders using **CYLINDER** with a radius of **3/8″** and a height of **3/4″** in the approximate location shown in Figure 14-23 (in front of the two boxes).

Step 40. Chamfer the top edge of the first cylinder (Figure 14-23) using chamfer distances of **1/16″**. Click **P1→** when you select edges to be chamfered.

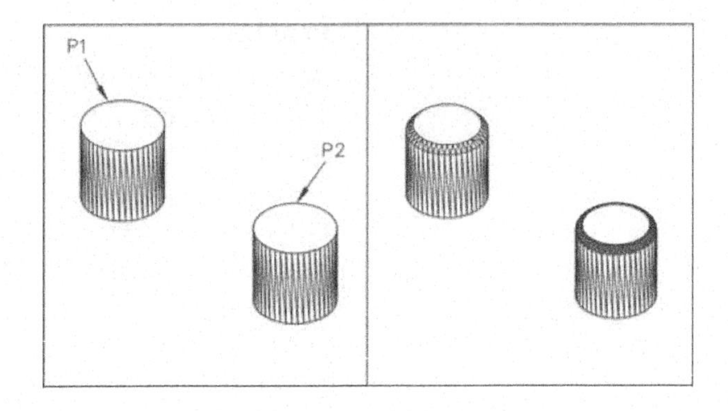

Figure 14-23
Chamfering and filleting cylinders

Step 41. Fillet the top edge of the second cylinder (Figure 14-23) using a fillet radius of **1/16″**. Click **P2→** when you select edges to be filleted.

The edges of the cylinders should appear as shown in Figure 14-23.

EXERCISE 14-1

Part 5, Using UNION to Join Two Solids; Using SUBTRACT to Subtract Solids from Other Solids

Drawing Solid Shape 1

Step 42. Draw solid shape 1 (the base of the shape) and a cylinder that will be the hole in the base (Figure 14-24) with UCS set to **World**, as described next:

Prompt	Response
Type a command:	Type **UCS <Enter>**
Specify origin of UCS or [Face NAmed OBject Previous View World X Y Z ZAxis] <World>:	**<Enter>**
Type a command:	**Box**
Specify corner of box or [Center] <0,0,0>:	Type **4-1/2,3/4 <Enter>**
Specify corner or [Cube Length]:	Type **@1,1 <Enter>**

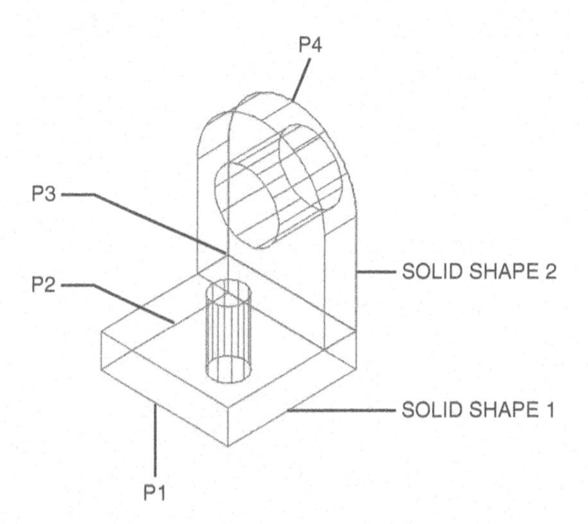

Figure 14-24
Drawing a composite solid

Prompt	Response
Specify height:	Type **1/4 <Enter>**
Type a command:	**Cylinder**
Specify center point of base or [3P 2P Ttr Elliptical]:	Type **.X <Enter>**
of	**Osnap-Midpoint**
of	**P1→**
(need YZ):	**Osnap-Midpoint**
of	**P2→**
Specify base radius or [Diameter]:	Type **1/8 <Enter>**
Specify height or [2Point Axis endpoint]:	Type **1/2 <Enter>** (make the height of the hole tall enough so you can be sure it goes through the model)

Drawing Solid Shape 2

Step 43. Set the **UCS Icon** command to **ORigin** so you will be able to see the UCS icon move when the origin is relocated (type **UCSICON <Enter>**, then **OR <Enter>**).

Step 44. Rotate the UCS **90°** about the x-axis, and move the origin of the UCS to the upper-left rear corner of the box (Figure 14-24), as described next:

Prompt	Response
Type a command:	Click the right viewport (so the UCS changes there and not in the left viewport)
Type a command:	Type **UCS <Enter>**
Specify origin of UCS or [Face NAmed OBject Previous View World X Y Z ZAxis] <World>:	Type **X <Enter>**
Specify rotation angle about X axis <90>:	**<Enter>**
Type a command:	Type **UCS <Enter>**
Specify origin of UCS or [Face NAmed OBject Previous View World X Y Z ZAxis] <World>:	Type **O <Enter>**
Specify new origin point <0,0,0>:	**Osnap-Endpoint**
	P3→ (Figure 14-24)

Step 45. Draw solid shape 2 (the vertical solid) and a cylinder that will be the hole in the vertical solid (Figure 14-24), as described next:

Prompt	Response
Type a command:	**Polyline** (or type **PL <Enter>**)
Specify start point:	Type **0,0 <Enter>**
Specify next point or [Arc Close Halfwidth Length Undo Width]:	With **ORTHO** on, move your mouse right and type **1 <Enter>**
Specify next point or [Arc Close Halfwidth Length Undo Width]:	Move your mouse up and type **3/4 <Enter>**

Prompt	Response
Specify next point or [Arc Close Halfwidth Length Undo Width]:	Type **A <Enter>**
Specify endpoint of arc or [Angle Enter CLose Direction Halfwidth Line Radius Second pt Undo Width]:	Move your mouse left and type **1 <Enter>**
Specify endpoint of arc or [Angle CEnter CLose Direction Halfwidth Line Radius Second pt Undo Width]:	Type **CL <Enter>**
Type a command:	**Extrude** (or type **EXT <Enter>**)
Select objects to extrude:	Click the polyline just drawn
Select objects to extrude:	**<Enter>**
Specify height of extrusion or [Direction Path Taper angle]:	Type **1/4 <Enter>**
	<Enter>
Type a command:	**Cylinder**
Specify center point of base or [3P 2P Ttr Elliptical]:	**Osnap-Center**
of	**P4→**
Specify base radius or [Diameter]:	Type **1/4 <Enter>**
Specify height or [2point Axis endpoint]:	Type **1/2 <Enter>**

The cylinder is longer than the thickness of the upright piece so you can be sure that the hole goes all the way through it.

Make sure the base of the cylinder is located on the back surface of the upright piece. If the cylinder is located on the front surface of the upright piece, move the cylinder **3/8** in the negative Z direction.

UNION	
Ribbon/ Panel	3D Tools/ Solid Editing
Modeling Toolbar:	
Menu Bar:	Modify/Solid Editing/ Union
Type a Command:	UNION
Command Alias:	UNI

SUBTRACT	
Ribbon/ Panel	3D Tools/ Solid Editing
Modeling Toolbar:	
Menu Bar:	Modify/Solid Editing/ Subtract
Type a Command:	SUBTRACT
Command Alias:	SU

Joining with Union

Step 46. Join the base and the vertical shape together to form one model, as described next:

Prompt	Response
Type a command:	**Union** (from **Modify-Solid Editing**) (or type **UNI <Enter>**)
Select objects:	Click the base (Shape 1) and the vertical solid (Shape 2).
Select objects:	**<Enter>**

Using Subtract

Step 47. Subtract the holes from the model, as described next:

Prompt	Response
Type a command:	**Subtract** (from **Modify-Solid Editing**) (or type **SU <Enter>**)
Select solids, surfaces, and regions to subtract from...	

HIDE	
Ribbon/ Panel	View/Visual Styles
Menu Bar:	View/Hide
Type a Command:	HIDE
Command Alias:	HI

Prompt	Response
Select objects:	Click any point on the model
Select objects:	**<Enter>**
Select solids, surfaces, and regions to subtract...	
Select objects:	Click the two cylinders
Select objects:	**<Enter>**

Performing a Hide

Step 48. Perform a **Hide** to be sure the model is correct (Figure 14-25), as described next:

Prompt	Response
Type a command:	**Hide** (or type **HI <Enter>**)

The model should appear as shown in Figure 14-25.

Step 49. Return to the World UCS.

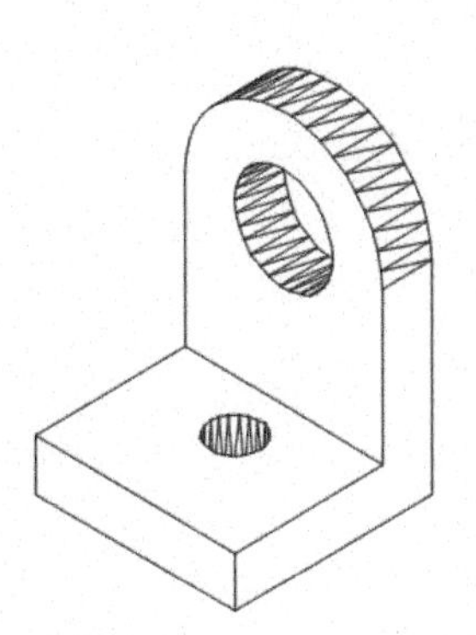

Figure 14-25
The completed model after a hide

> **NOTE**
>
> The **HIDE** command renders a hidden line view in the selected viewport. After the hidden line view appears, you cannot edit the static view. To revert to regular AutoCAD tools, you must do a **REGEN**, a **REDRAW**, or a **ZOOM**. You can also change to a live hidden line view by using the viewport controls in the top-left corner of the viewport.

SWEEP	
Ribbon/ Panel	3D Tools/ Modeling
Modeling Toolbar:	
Menu Bar:	Draw/Modeling/ Sweep
Type a Command:	SWEEP

EXERCISE 14-1

Part 6, Using Sweep, Helix, Subtract, Loft, Planar Surface, Thicken, and Polysolid to Draw Solid Shapes

The commands in this part of Exercise 14-1 are extremely powerful. You use **SWEEP** and **SUBTRACT** in the first shape and **HELIX**, **SWEEP**, and **SUBTRACT** in the second shape.

Sweeping an Object

The **SWEEP** command gives you the ability to create a new solid by sweeping an object along a path. You have the options of selecting a base point, scaling the object as it is swept along the path, and twisting the object as it is swept.

Step 50. Draw an arc on the **3d-g** layer in the approximate location shown in Figure 14-26. It should be about 1-1/2″ long and approximately the shape shown, and make a duplicate of the arc in the same location. Use the **COPY** command to make an identical copy by clicking any point as the base point, then typing **@ <Enter>**, then **<Enter>** again to exit the command.

Figure 14-26
Draw an arc, a circle, and a square

Step 51. Draw a **1/8″**-radius circle in the approximate location shown in Figure 14-26.

Step 52. Draw a **3/8″** square using the **RECTANGLE** command in the approximate location shown on the **3d-g** layer.

Step 53. Use the **SWEEP** command to create the shape shown in Figure 14-27, as described next:

Prompt	Response
Type a command:	**Sweep** (or type **SWEEP <Enter>**)
Select objects to sweep or [MOde]:	Click any point on the circle
Select objects to sweep or [MOde]:	**<Enter>**
Select sweep path or [Alignment Base point Scale Twist]:	Click any point on the arc
Turn off the **3d-m** layer.	

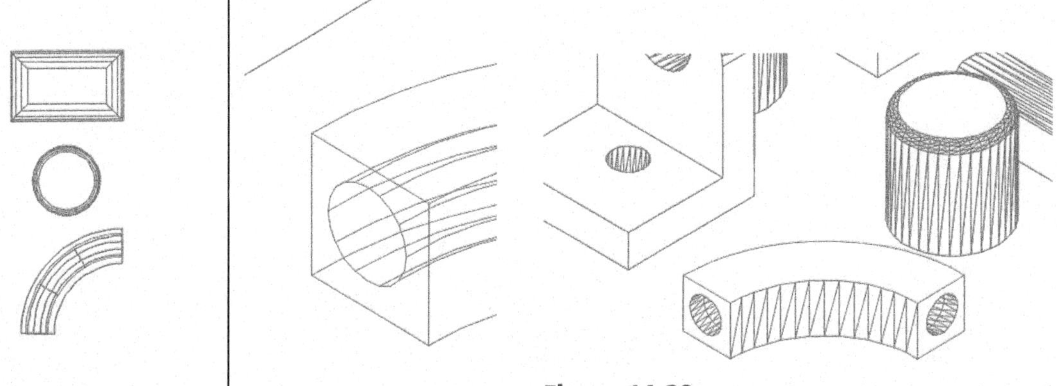

Figure 14-27
Sweeps with layers **3d-m** and **3d-g** on

Figure 14-28
Use **SUBTRACT** to create a hole in the swept square

> **NOTE**
>
> By default, the primitive objects you create for paths and profiles of 3D objects are deleted when you create a solid object from them. This is why you had to create a copy of the arc in Step 50, so you would have a path for both sweeps. If you want to retain the primitive objects, reset the system variable **DELOBJ** from **3** to **0**. Creating these primitives on a separate layer that you can turn off when you don't need it is easy.

Prompt	Response
Type a command:	**SWEEP**
Select objects to sweep or [MOde]:	Click any point on the square
Select objects to sweep or [MOde]:	**<Enter>**
Select sweep path or [Alignment Base point Scale Twist]:	Click any point on the arc
Turn layer **3d-m** on and set it current.	

The sweeps appear as shown in Figure 14-27.

Step 54. Use the **SUBTRACT** command to create a hole throughout the swept square and use the **HIDE** command to check the shape (Figure 14-28), as described next:

Prompt	Response
Type a command:	**Subtract** (or type **SU <Enter>**)
Select solids and regions to subtract from:	
Select objects:	Click any point on the swept square

HELIX	
Ribbon/ Panel	Home/Draw (slideout)
Modeling Toolbar:	
Menu Bar:	Draw/Helix
Type a Command:	HELIX

Prompt	Response
Select solids and regions to subtract:	
Select objects:	Click any point on the swept circle
Type a command:	**Hide** (or type **HI <Enter>**)
Change the swept model to layer **3d-m**.	

Step 55. Use the **HELIX** command to make a helix, as described next:

Prompt	Response
Type a command:	**Helix** (or type **HELIX <Enter>**)
Specify center point of base:	Click a point in the approximate location shown in Figure 14-29
Specify base radius or [Diameter] <0′-0″>:	Type **1/2 <Enter>**
Specify top radius or [Diameter] <0′-0 1/2″>:	**<Enter>**
Specify helix height or [Axis endpoint Turns turn Height tWist] <0′-1/2″>:	Type **T <Enter>**
Enter number of turns <3.0000>:	Type **6 <Enter>**
Specify helix height or [Axis endpoint Turns turn Height tWist] <0′-1″>:	Type **1-1/4 <Enter>**

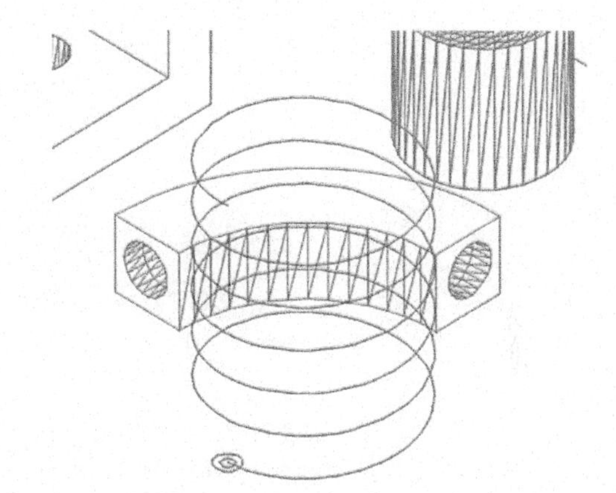

Figure 14-29
Draw the helix and 1/16″-radius and 1/32″-radius circles on the helix endpoint

Step 56. Draw a **1/16″**-radius circle and a **1/32″**-radius circle on the endpoint of the base of the helix (Figure 14-29).

Step 57. Use the **SWEEP** command to sweep the circles around the helix, as described next:

Prompt	Response
Type a command:	**SWEEP** (or type **SWEEP <Enter>**)
Select objects to sweep:	Click both the **1/16″**- and the **1/32″**-radius circles
Select objects to sweep or [MOde]:	**<Enter>**
Select sweep path or [Alignment Base point Scale Twist]:	Click any point on the helix

Step 58. Use the **SUBTRACT** command to subtract the inner swept circle from the outer swept circle (Figure 14-30), as described next:

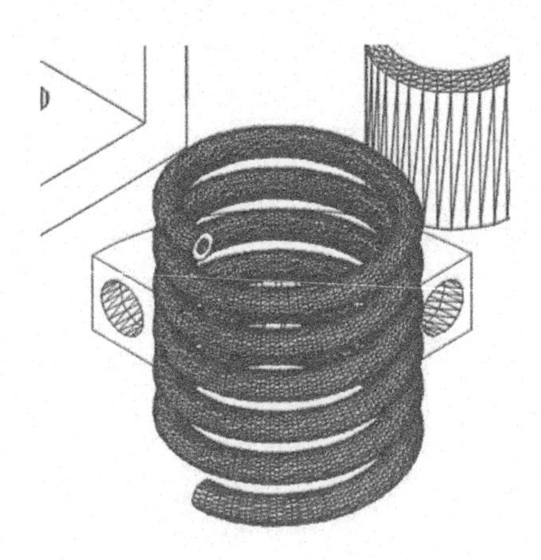

Figure 14-30
Inner swept circle subtracted from outer swept circle

Prompt	**Response**
Type a command:	**SUBTRACT** (or type **SU <Enter>**)
Select solids and regions to subtract from...	Click the **1/16″**-radius swept circle
Select objects:	**<Enter>**
Select objects: Select solids and regions to subtract...	Click the **1/32″**-radius swept circle
Select objects:	**<Enter>**

LOFT	
Ribbon/ Panel	3D Tools/ Modeling
Modeling Toolbar:	
Menu Bar:	Draw/ Modeling/ Loft
Type a Command:	LOFT

Using Loft

The **LOFT** command gives you the ability to create a 3D solid or surface by selecting a set of two or more cross-sectional areas.

If you select two or more closed cross-sectional areas, a solid is created.

If you select two or more open cross-sectional areas, a surface is created.

You cannot use both open and closed cross-sectional areas in a set. You have to choose one or the other.

When you make a lofted shape, you can use the **Loft Settings** dialog box to control the shape of the surface or solid.

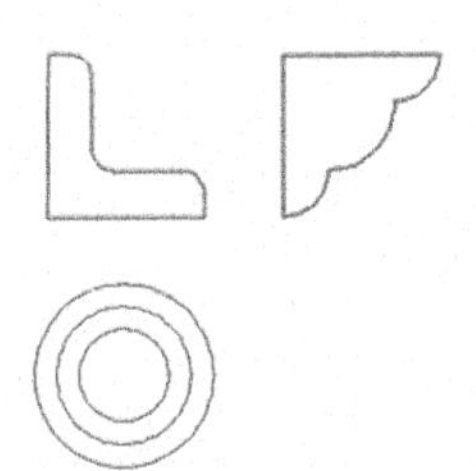

Figure 14-31
Draw 1/4″-, 3/8″-, and 1/2″-radius circles

Step 59. Draw three circles (**1/2″** radius, **3/8″** radius, and **1/4″** radius) in the approximate location shown in Figure 14-31.

Step 60. Move the **1/4″**-radius circle up **1/4″** in the **Z** direction. You may use the **MOVE** command and type **@0,0,1/4 <Enter>** for the second point of displacement or in the 3D view (with **ORTHO** on) click on the circle, click the center grip, move your mouse up, and type **1/4 <Enter>**.

Step 61. Move the **3/8″**-radius circle up **1/2″** in the **Z** direction.

Step 62. Use the **LOFT** command to create a lofted solid and use the **HIDE** command to check it (Figure 14-32), as described next:

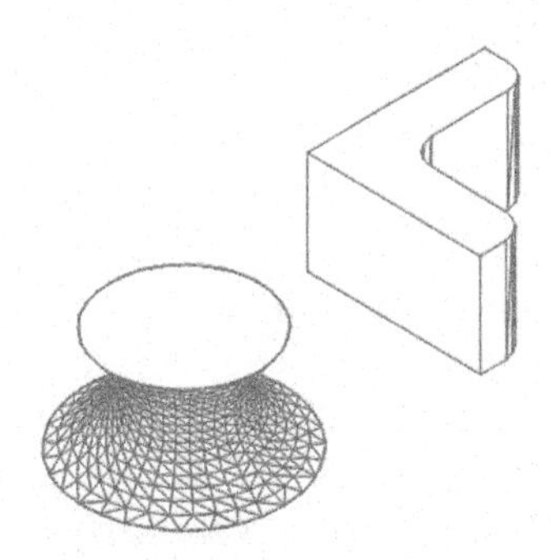

Figure 14-32
Lofted shape complete

Prompt	**Response**
Type a command:	**Loft** (or type **LOFT <Enter>**)
Select cross-sections in lofting order or [POint Join multiple edges MOde]:	Click the **1/2″**-radius circle (the one on the bottom)

Prompt	Response
Select cross-sections in lofting order or [POint Join multiple edges MOde]:	Click the **1/4″**-radius circle (the next one up)
Select cross-sections in lofting order or [POint Join multiple edges MOde]:	Click the **3/8″**-radius circle (the one on top)
Select cross-sections in lofting order or [POint Join multiple edges MOde]:	**<Enter>**
Enter an option [Guides Path Cross sections only Settings] <Cross sections only>:	**<Enter>**
Type a command:	**Hide** (or type **HI <Enter>**)

Creating a Bowl-Shaped Object

The **LOFT** command also enables you to create a bowl-shaped object, as described next:

Step 63. Draw three circles (**3/4″**-radius, **5/8″**-radius, and **1/2″**-radius) in the approximate location shown in Figure 14-33.

Step 64. Move the **1/2″**-radius circle up **1/8″** in the **Z** direction.

Step 65. Move the **5/8″**-radius circle up **1/2″** in the **Z** direction.

Step 66. Use the **LOFT** command to create the bowl, but pick the circles in a different order: Click the one on the bottom first, the one on the top next, and the one in between the two others last.

Step 67. Use the **HIDE** command to check its shape (Figure 14-34).

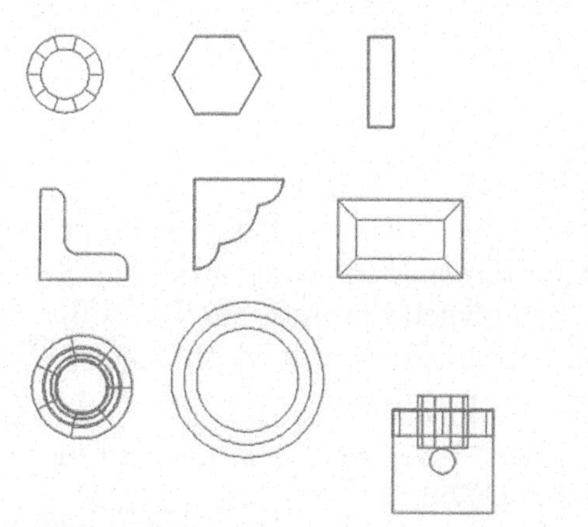

Figure 14-33
Draw 1/2″-, 5/8″-, and 3/4″-radius circles

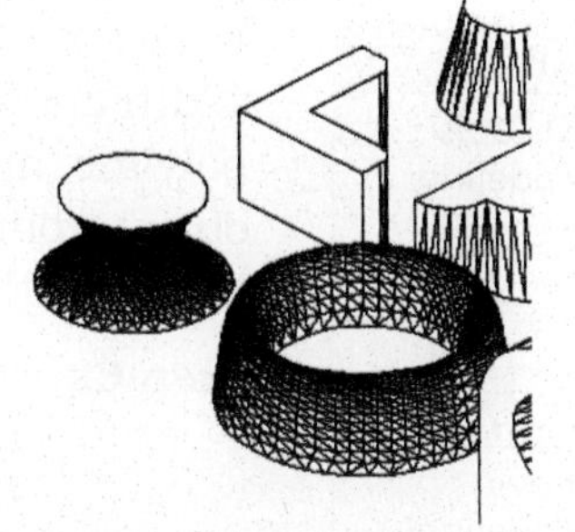

Figure 14-34
Lofted bowl shape complete

PLANAR SURFACE	
Ribbon/ Panel	3D Tools/ Surfaces
Modeling Toolbar:	
Menu Bar:	Draw/ Modeling/ Surfaces/ Planar
Type a Command:	PLANESURF

Using Planar Surface

You can use the **Planar Surface (PLANESURF)** command to make a surface using one of the following:

Select one or more objects that form an enclosed area.

Draw a rectangle so that the surface is created parallel to the rectangle.

THICKEN	
Ribbon/ Panel	3D Tools/ Surfaces
Type a Command:	THICKEN

Step 68. Draw a planar surface and thicken it (Figure 14-35), as described next:

Prompt	Response
Type a command:	**Planar Surface** (or type **PLANESURF <Enter>**)

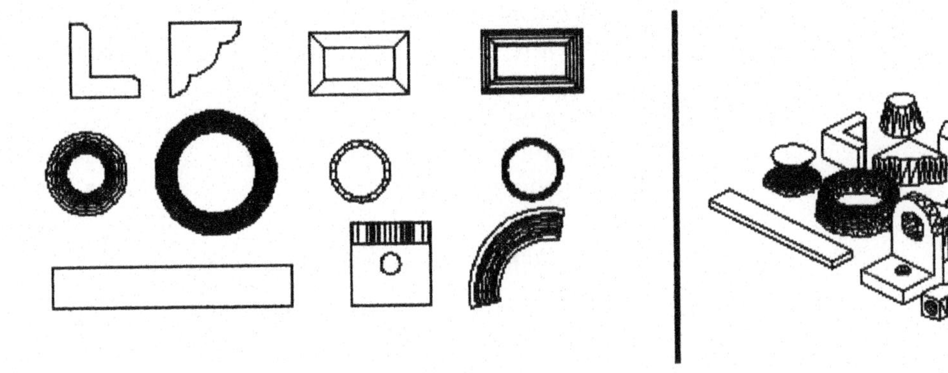

Figure 14-35
Draw the planar surface and thicken it

Prompt	Response
Specify first corner or [Object] <Object>:	Click the lower-left corner in the approximate location shown in Figure 14-35
Specify other corner:	Type **@3,1/2 <Enter>**
Type a command:	**Thicken** (or type **THICKEN <Enter>**)
Select surfaces to thicken:	Click the planar surface
Select surfaces to thicken:	**<Enter>**
Specify thickness <0′-0″>:	Type **1/8 <Enter>**

Using POLYSOLID

POLYSOLID	
Ribbon/ Panel	3D Tools/ Modeling
Modeling Toolbar:	
Menu Bar:	Draw/ Modeling/ Polysolid
Type a Command:	POLYSOLID
Command Alias:	PSOLID

You can use the **POLYSOLID** command to draw walls by specifying the wall width and its height. You can also create a polysolid from an existing line, polyline, arc, or circle. If the width and height have been set, clicking on an object from the polysolid prompt such as a line or an arc will change it to a polysolid that is the height and width of the polysolid setting.

Step 69. Draw a polysolid that has a height of **1/2″** and a width of **1/4″** (Figure 14-36), as described next. (Be sure you are in the World UCS.)

Prompt	Response
Type a command:	**Polysolid** (or type **POLYSOLID <Enter>**)
Specify start point or [Object Height Width Justify] <Object>:	Type **H <Enter>**
Specify height <0′-0″>:	Type **1/2 <Enter>**
Specify start point or [Object Height Width Justify] <Object>:	Type **W <Enter>**
Specify width <0′-0″>:	Type **1/4 <Enter>**

Figure 14-36
Draw a polysolid with a height of 1/2″ and a width of 1/4″

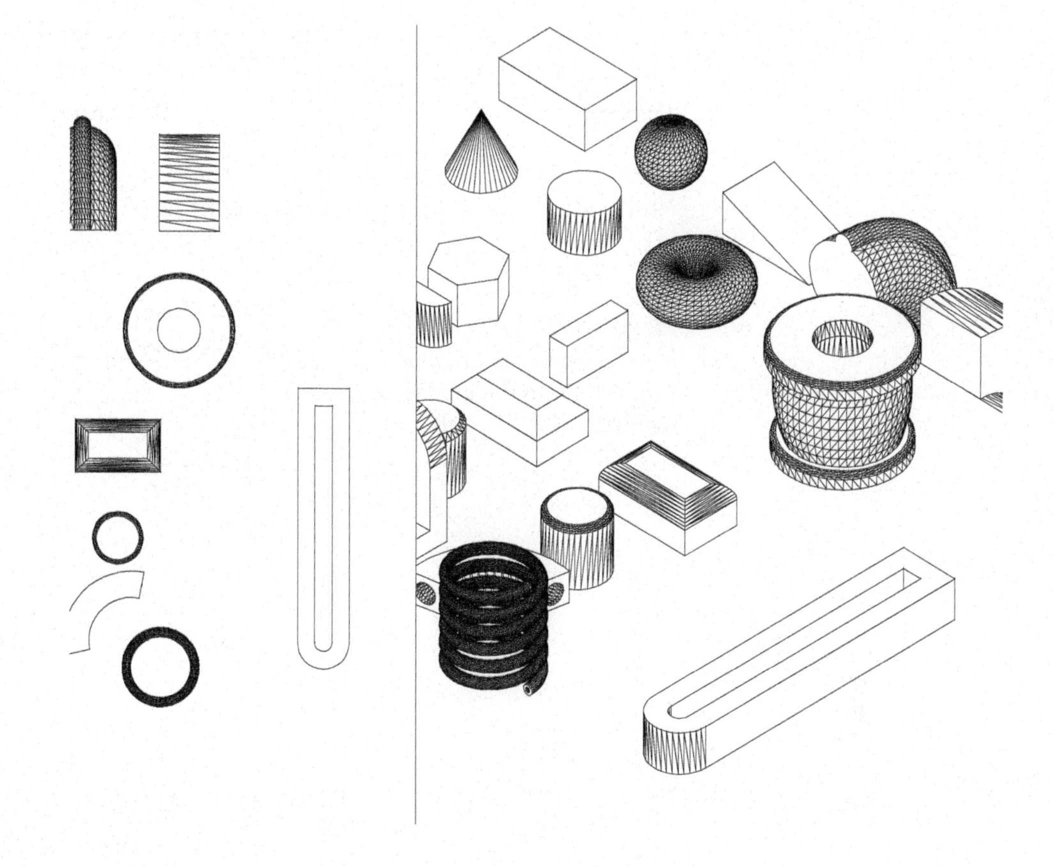

Prompt	Response
Specify start point or [Object Height Width Justify] <Object>:	Type **8-1/2,4 <Enter>**
Specify next point or [Arc Undo]: <Ortho on>	With **ORTHO** on move your mouse down and type **3 <Enter>**
Specify next point or [Arc Undo]:	Type **A <Enter>**
Specify endpoint of arc or [Close Direction Line Second point Undo]:	Move your mouse to the left and type **1/2 <Enter>**
Specify next point or [Arc Close Undo]:	
Specify endpoint of arc or [Close Direction Line Second point Undo]:	Type **L <Enter>**
Specify next point or [Arc Close Undo]:	Move your mouse up and type **3 <Enter>**
Specify next point or [Arc Close Undo]:	Type **C <Enter>**
Type a command:	**Hide** (or type **HI <Enter>**)

EXERCISE 14-1
Part 7, Using Intersection to Form a Solid Model from the Common Volume of Two Intersecting Solids

Drawing the solid model in Exercise 14-1, Part 7, demonstrates another powerful tool that you can use to form complex models.

In this exercise, you will draw two separate solid shapes (in this case, you copy the same shape and rotate it so the two shapes are at right angles to each other) and move them so that they intersect. You use **INTERSECTION** to combine the shapes to form one solid model from the common volume of the two intersecting solids. Figure 14-37 shows the two separate solid shapes and the solid model that is formed from the common volume of the two solid shapes.

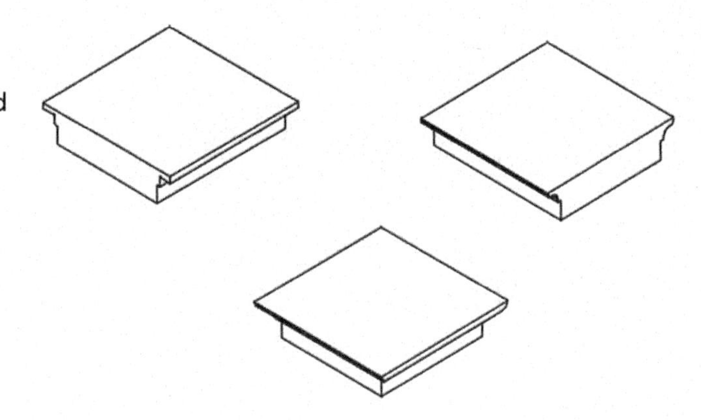

Figure 14-37
Two shapes and the shape formed from the intersected volume of the two shapes

You will also use this shape in Exercise 15-2 to form the cornices at the top of the columns (Figure 15-7).

Drawing Two Extruded Shapes at Right Angles to Each Other

Step 70. Zoom out so you can draw the full-size shapes shown in Figure 14-38 in the left viewport. In an open area of the screen, draw Figure 14-38 using **Polyline** and **FILLET** commands. Use **Polyline** to draw the shape with square corners shown in the top half of the figure, and then use 1″-radius fillets to form the rounded corners.

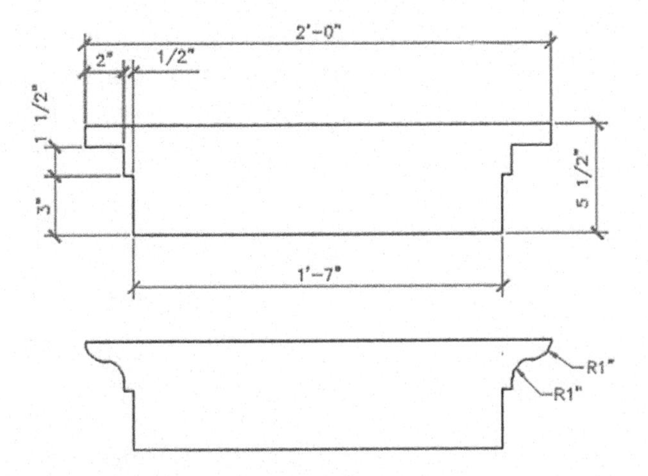

Figure 14-38
Dimensions for the extruded shapes

Step 71. Use the **SCALE** command to scale the polylines to **1/12** their size. (This is a scale of **1″ = 1′-0″**. In Exercise 15-2, you will scale this model to its original size.)

Step 72. In the right viewport, set UCS to **World** and use **3DROTATE** to rotate both shapes **90°** about the x-axis.

Step 73. Use **3DROTATE** to rotate the rounded corner shape **90°** about the z-axis (Figure 14-39).

Step 74. Extrude both shapes **2** (Figure 14-40) (or use **PRESSPULL** to extrude both shapes 2).

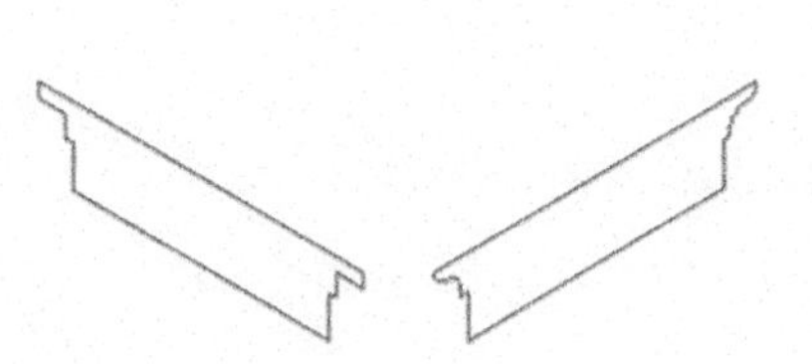

Figure 14-39
Two shapes rotated 90° to each other

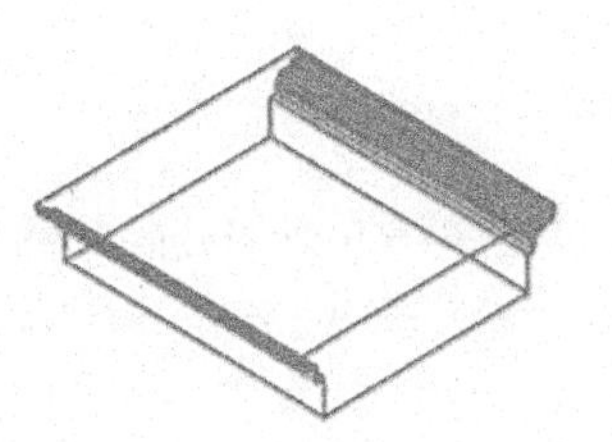

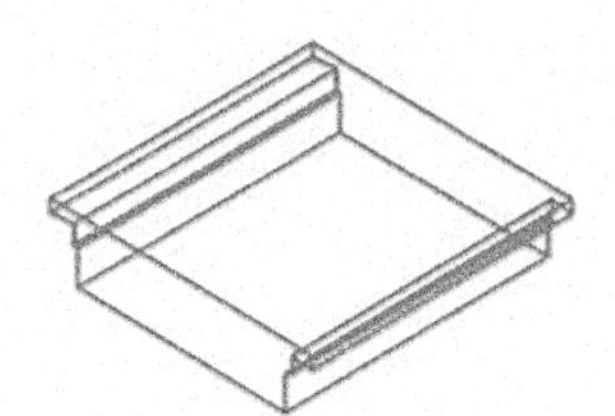

Figure 14-40
Both shapes extruded

Step 75. Use the **MOVE** command to move the solid on the left to intersect with the other solid (Figure 14-41), as described next:

Figure 14-41
Moving one shape to intersect with the other

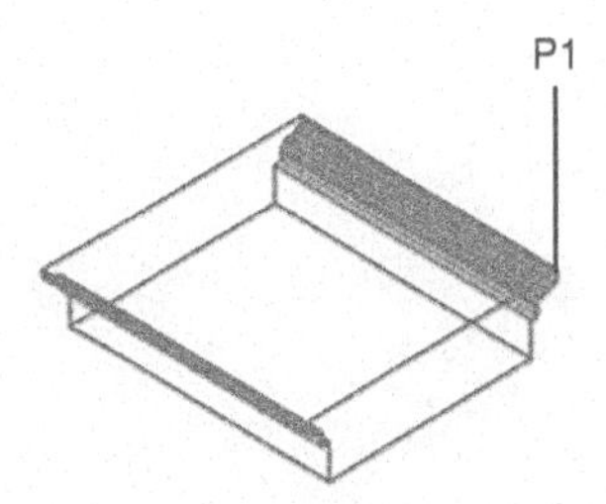

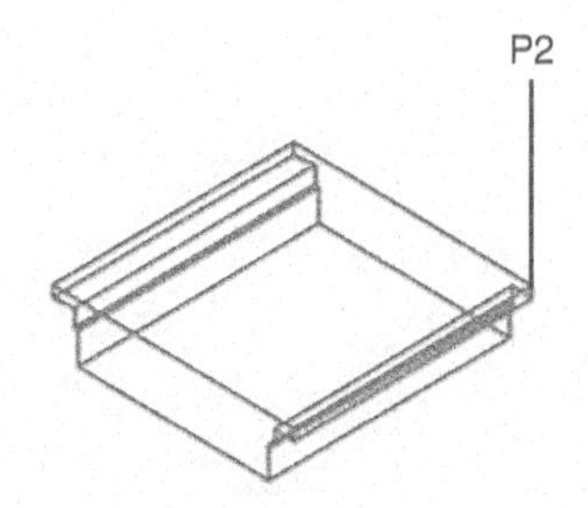

INTERSECT	
Ribbon/ Panel	3D Tools/ Solid Editing
Modeling Toolbar:	
Menu Bar:	Modify/Solid Editing/ Intersect
Type a Command:	INTERSECT
Command Alias:	IN

Prompt	Response
Type a command:	**Move**
Select objects:	Click the shape on the left
Select objects:	**<Enter>**
Specify base point or [Displacement] <Displacement>:	**Osnap-Endpoint**
of	**P1→**
Specify second point or <use first point as displacement>:	**Osnap-Endpoint**
of	**P2→**

Using Intersect

Step 76. Use **INTERSECT** to form a solid model from the common volume of the two intersecting solids (Figure 14-42), as described next:

Prompt	Response
Type a command:	**Intersect** (from **Modify-Solid Editing**) (or type **IN <Enter>**)
Select objects:	Click both shapes **<Enter>**
2 solids intersected	

The display should appear as shown in Figure 14-42.

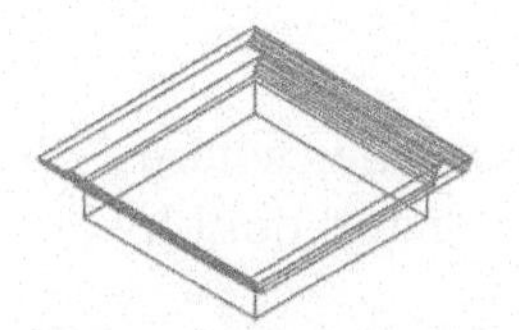

Figure 14-42
The shape formed from the intersected shapes

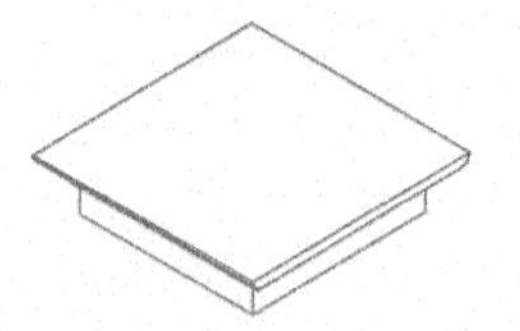

Figure 14-43
The intersected solid after a **HIDE**

Step 77. Perform a **Hide** to be sure the solid model is correct (Figure 14-43), as described next:

Prompt	Response
Type a command:	**Hide** (or type **HI <Enter>**)

The display should appear as shown in Figure 14-43.

Step 78. Make sure the UCS is set to **World** so you will not be surprised at the position the model will assume when it is inserted.

Wblocking the Intersected Model

You should now Wblock the intersected model so you can use it in Exercise 15-2 to form the cornices at the tops of the columns (see Chapter 15's Figure 15-7).

Step 79. Use **WBLOCK** to save the model to a disk (Figure 14-44), as described next:

Prompt	Response
Type a command:	Type **W <Enter>**
The **Write Block** dialog box appears:	Click the three dots to the far right of the **File name and path:** input box

Figure 14-44
Wblocking the intersected shape

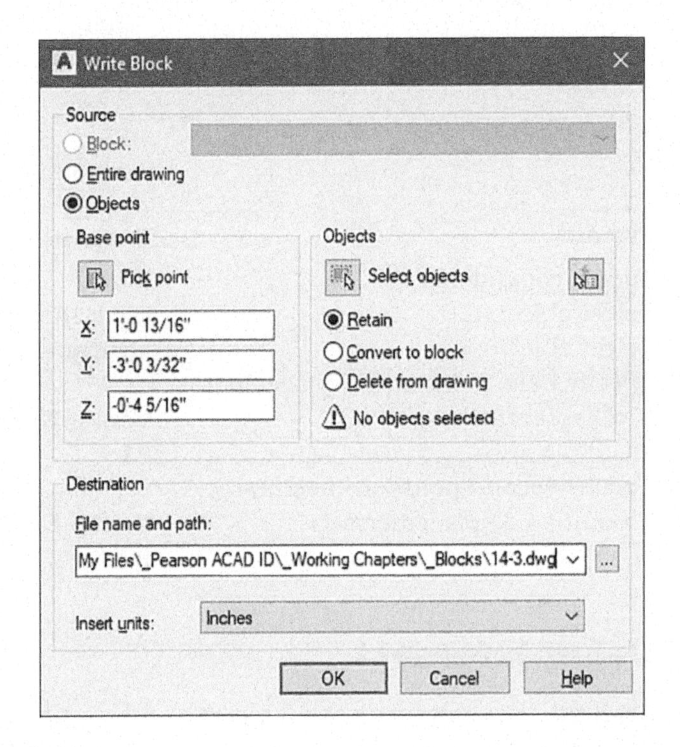

Prompt	Response
	Locate the disk and folder where you store drawings and double-click the folder
The **Browse for Drawing File** dialog box appears:	Type **14-3** in the **File name:** input box, and then click **Save**
	Click **Pick point**

Prompt	Response
Specify insertion base point:	Type **END <Enter>**
of	Click the bottom corner of the intersected shape using **Osnap-Endpoint**. It will be the lowest point on the display.
The **Write Block** dialog box appears:	Click **Select Objects**
Select objects:	Click the intersected shape
Select objects:	**<Enter>**
The **Write Block** dialog box appears:	If **Retain** is not on, click that option button Click **OK**

The shape now exists on your disk as 14-3.dwg, and it is also on the current drawing.

Completing Exercise 14-1

Step 80. Use the **MOVE** command to move the intersected shape to the approximate location shown in Figure 14-3.

Step 81. Use the **VPORTS** command to return to a single viewport of the 3D viewport (Figure 14-3).

Step 82. Click **Visual Styles Manager** (Figure 14-45) and double-click **Conceptual** to shade the drawing, as shown in Figure 14-46.

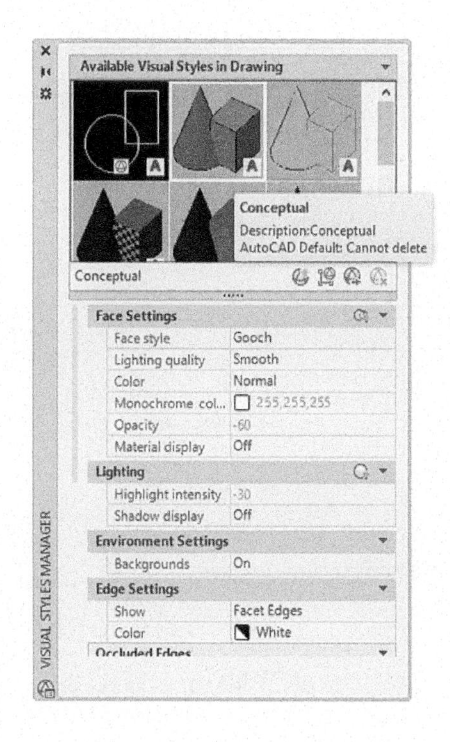

Figure 14-45
Visual Styles Manager

Figure 14-46
Rendered image of Exercise 14-1

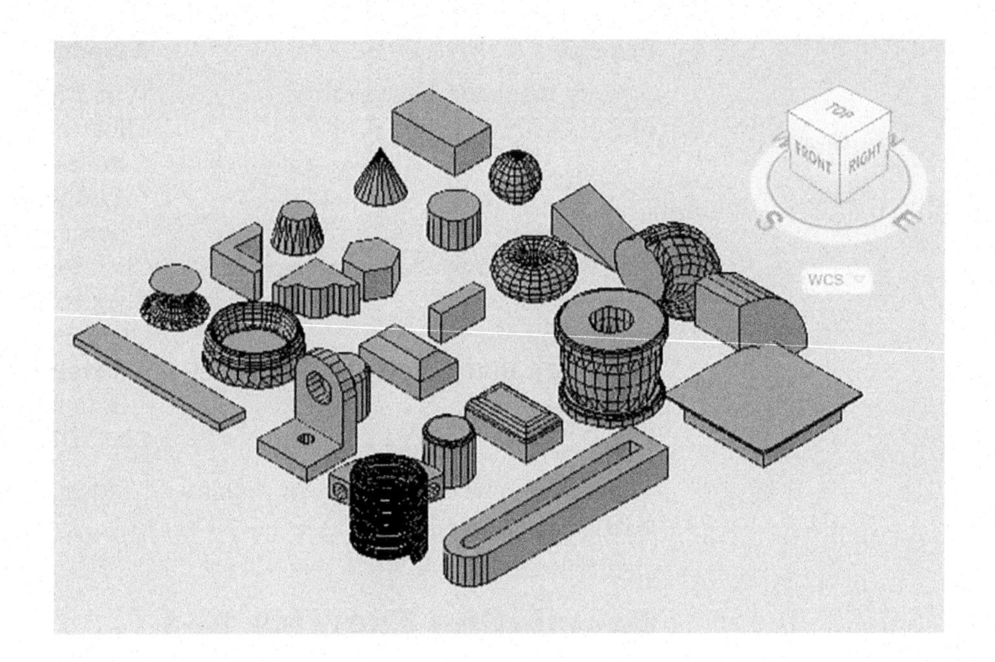

Step 83. Save the drawing in two places.

Step 84. Plot the 3D viewport from the **Model** tab on a standard size sheet of paper. Be sure to click **Conceptual** from the **Shade plot:** list in the **Plot** dialog box so the final plot appears as shown in Figure 14-46.

Chapter Summary

This chapter provided you the information necessary to set up and draw solid models. Now you have the skills and information necessary to produce solid models that you can use in interior design presentations, views of proposed spaces, contract documents, and other similar types of documents.

Chapter Test Questions

Multiple Choice

Circle the correct answer.

1. Which of the following is **not** a **SOLID** command used to draw solid primitives?

a. **BOX**
b. **CYLINDER**
c. **RECTANGLE**
d. **WEDGE**

2. Which of the following is used to make rounded corners on a solid box?

a. **FILLET**
b. **EXTRUDE**
c. **CHAMFER**
d. **ROUND**

3. Which is the last dimension called for when the **BOX** command is activated?

a. Height
b. Width
c. Length
d. First corner of box

4. Which is the first dimension called for when the **SPHERE** command is activated?

a. Segments in X direction
b. Radius
c. Segments in Y direction
d. Center of sphere

5. Which of the following **cannot** be extruded with the **EXTRUDE** command?

a. Polylines
b. Circles
c. Polygons
d. Solids

6. Which of the following commands is used to join several lines into a single polyline?

a. **JOIN**
b. **UNION**
c. **OFFSET**
d. **EXTRUDE**

7. Which of the following is used to make a solid by revolving a polyline about an axis?

a. **REVOLVE**
b. **EXTRUDE**
c. **ROUND**
d. **FILLET**

8. Which of the following adjusts the smoothness of objects rendered with the **HIDE** command?

   a. **SURFTAB1**
   b. **SEGS**
   c. **ISOLINES**
   d. **FACETRES**

9. Which of the following allows you to rotate an object around an x-, y-, or z-axis?

   a. **ROTATE**
   b. **3DROTATE**
   c. **SOLROT**
   d. **OFFSET**

10. Which of the following sets the number of lines on rounded surfaces of solids?

   a. **FACETRES**
   b. **ISOLINES**
   c. **FILLET**
   d. **INTERFERE**

Matching

Write the number of the correct answer on the line.

a. Solid modeling _____
b. SteeringWheel _____
c. **Torus** _____
d. **Polysolid** _____
e. **INTERSECT** _____

1. A solid command used to create a solid from the common volume of two intersecting solids
2. A solid shape similar to a donut
3. A navigation tool
4. A method of drawing that allows you to view an object from any angle
5. A command used to draw a solid shape

True or False

Circle the correct answer.

1. **True or False:** Boxes made with the **BOX** command and combined with the **UNION** command cannot be made into a solid object.
2. **True or False:** A polysolid can have width and height.
3. **True or False:** A **torus** is a solid object.
4. **True or False: Intersect** is **not** a solid command.
5. **True or False: SUBTRACT** is the command used to subtract solids from other solids.

List

1. Five solid primitives.
2. Five key-in commands to create the above primitives.
3. Five methods for constructing surfaces or solids from other geometry.
4. Five solid creation commands under the **3D Solid** tab and **Solid/Boolean** panel.
5. Five drawing entities that can be used as a loft cross section.
6. Five drawing entities that can be used as a loft path.

7. Five commands containing **Rotate**.
8. Five prompts to answer when executing the **PolySolid** command.
9. Five commands/system variables to smooth the display of a 3D object.
10. Five view styles.

Questions

1. What is solid modeling and how is it used?
2. What are the settings that control how a solid is displayed?
3. What are the commands that can be used to create solid models?
4. When should solid models be rendered?
5. How should lights be placed when solid models are rendered?

Chapter Projects

Project 14-1: *Drawing Solid Models of Eight Objects* [BASIC]

1. Draw solid models of the eight objects shown in Figure 14-47. Use the dimensions shown in the top and front views of A through H:

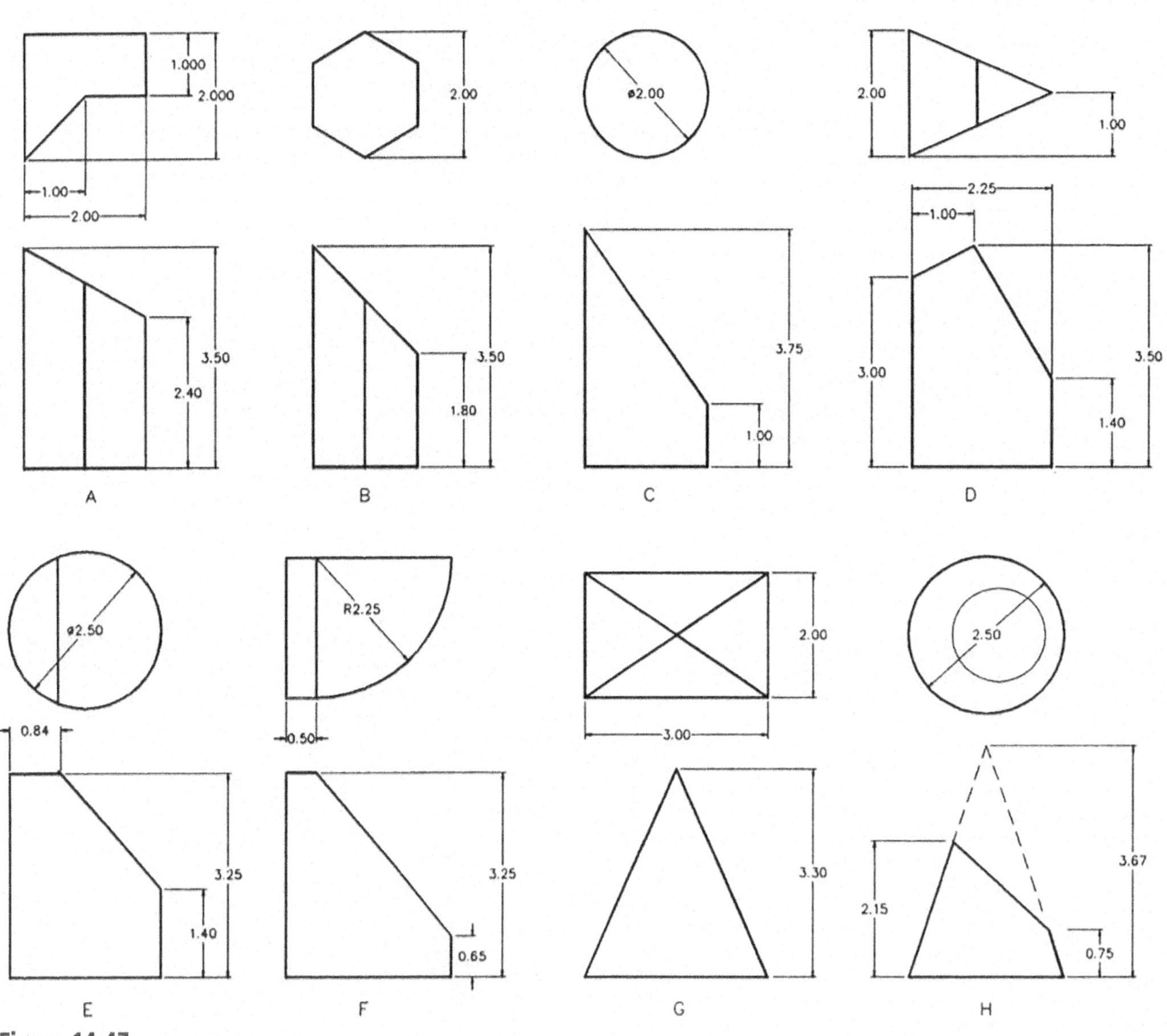

Figure 14-47
Project 14-1: Draw solid models of eight objects

Draw the top view, join it to form a continuous polyline, and extrude it to the height shown in the front view.

Rotate the UCS **90°** about the x-axis, draw a rectangle at the angle shown in the front view, extrude it, move it in the Z direction so it covers the area of the extruded top view that must be removed, and subtract it from the extruded top view.

2. Arrange the objects so that they are well spaced on the page and take up most of a **9″ × 7″** area on an **11″ × 8-1/2″** sheet. Use the **HIDE** command to remove hidden lines.
3. Your final drawing should show eight solid objects in a viewpoint similar to Figure 14-46 (Exercise 14-1).
4. Click **Layout1**, place your name in the lower-right corner in **1/8″** letters, use **Shade plot - As displayed,** and plot or print the drawing on an **11″ × 8-1/2″** sheet at a scale of **1 = 1**.
5. Save your drawing in two places with the name **CH14-P1**.

Project 14-2: *Drawing a Solid Model of a Lamp Table* **[INTERMEDIATE]**

1. Draw a solid model of the lamp table shown in Figure 14-48. Measure the top and front views using a scale of **1″ = 1′-0″** to obtain the correct measurements for the model.

Figure 14-48
Project 14-2: Create a solid model of a table (scale: 1″ = 1′-0″)

2. Use **REVOLVE** for the table pedestal. Use **Polyline** and **EXTRUDE** for one table leg and duplicate it with **Polar Array**. The tabletop can be an extruded circle or a solid cylinder.
3. Use **Orbit** to obtain a perspective view of your final model and click **Layout1** before you plot.
4. Place your name in the lower-right corner in **1/8″** letters using simplex or an architectural font.
5. Plot the drawing at a scale of **1 = 1** on an **11″ × 8-1/2″** sheet.
6. Return to the **Model** tab (World UCS current) and **WBLOCK** the lamp table to a disk with the name **TABLE**.
7. Save your drawing with the name **CH14-P2**.

Project 14-3: *Drawing a Solid Model of the Tenant Space Reception Seating* [BASIC]

1. Draw the chair coffee table and corner table with a series of boxes (Figure 14-49).

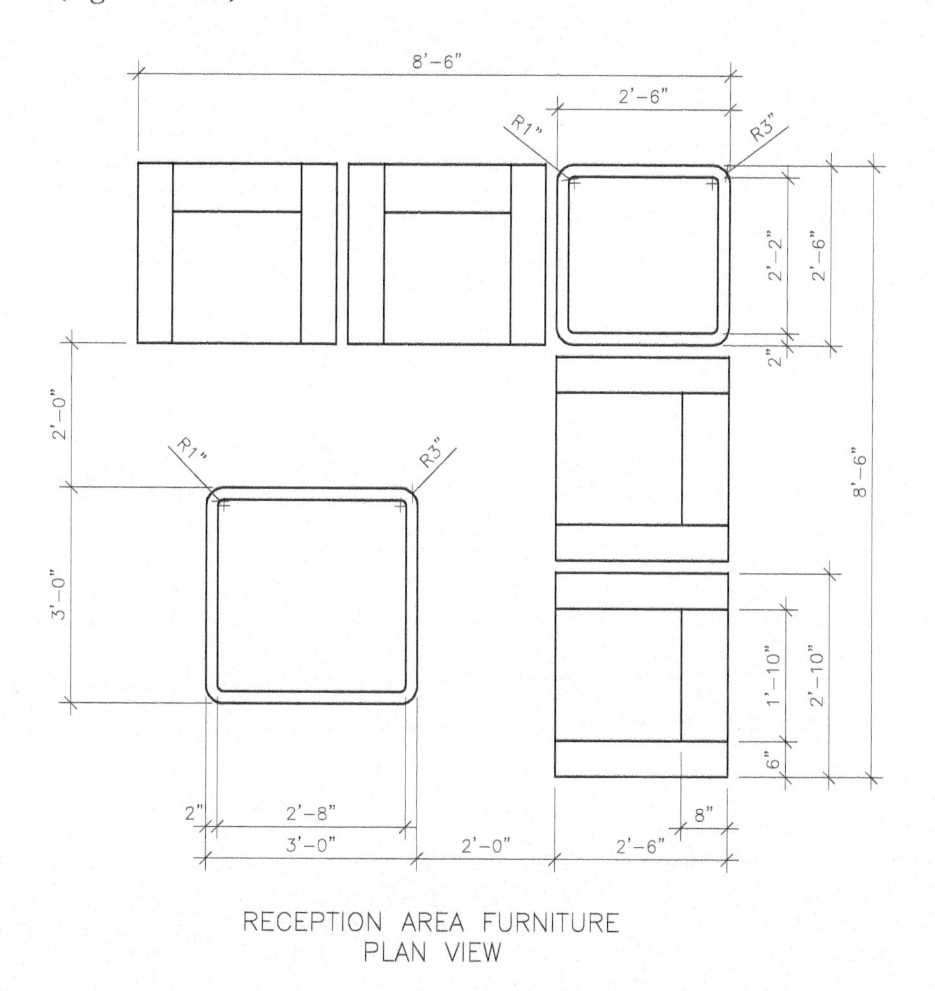

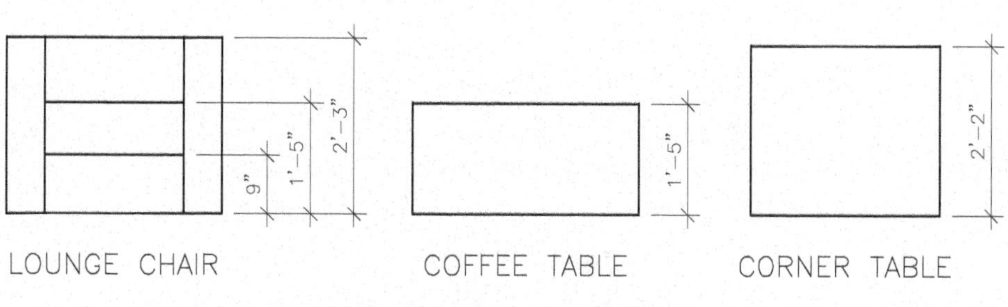

Figure 14-49
Project 14-3: Tenant space reception seating dimensions (scale: 3/8" = 1'-0")

2. Fillet the vertical edges of the coffee table and corner table.

3. Use the **RECTANGLE** command with **1″** fillets to draw the coffee table and corner table inlays. Extrude the rectangles **1″** and place them so they are flush with the top of the tables. Subtract the extruded rectangles from the tables and replace them with other extruded rectangles that are slightly smaller to form the inlays.
4. Use **Orbit** to obtain a perspective view of your final model and click **Layout1** before you plot.
5. Place your name in the lower-right corner in **1/8″** letters using simplex or an architectural font.
6. Plot the drawing at a scale of **1** = **1** on an **11″** × **8-1/2″** sheet.
7. Save your drawing in two places with the name **CH14-P3**.

Project 14-4: *Drawing a Solid Model of a Lamp and Inserting It into the Lamp Table Drawing* **[ADVANCED]**

1. Draw the lamp and the shade from the dimensions shown in Figure 14-50. Use your 1-1/2″ architect's scale for any dimensions not shown.

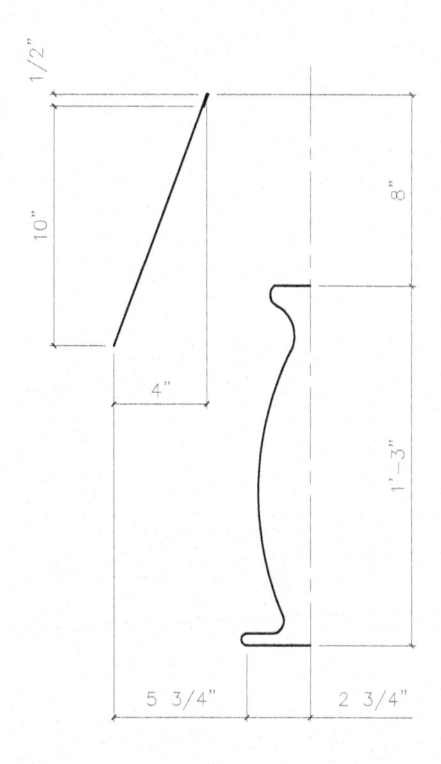

Figure 14-50
Project 14-4: Overall dimensions of the lamp (scale: 1-1/2″ = 1′)

2. Revolve the two polylines to form the lamp.
3. Rotate the lamp **90°** about the x-axis so it is in an upright position.
4. With the World UCS current, **WBLOCK** the lamp to a disk with the name **LAMP**. Use the center of the bottom of the lamp as the insertion point.
5. Insert the lamp from the disk into the lamp table. Center the base of the lamp onto the tabletop as shown in Figure 14-51.

Figure 14-51
Project 14-4: Combine solid models

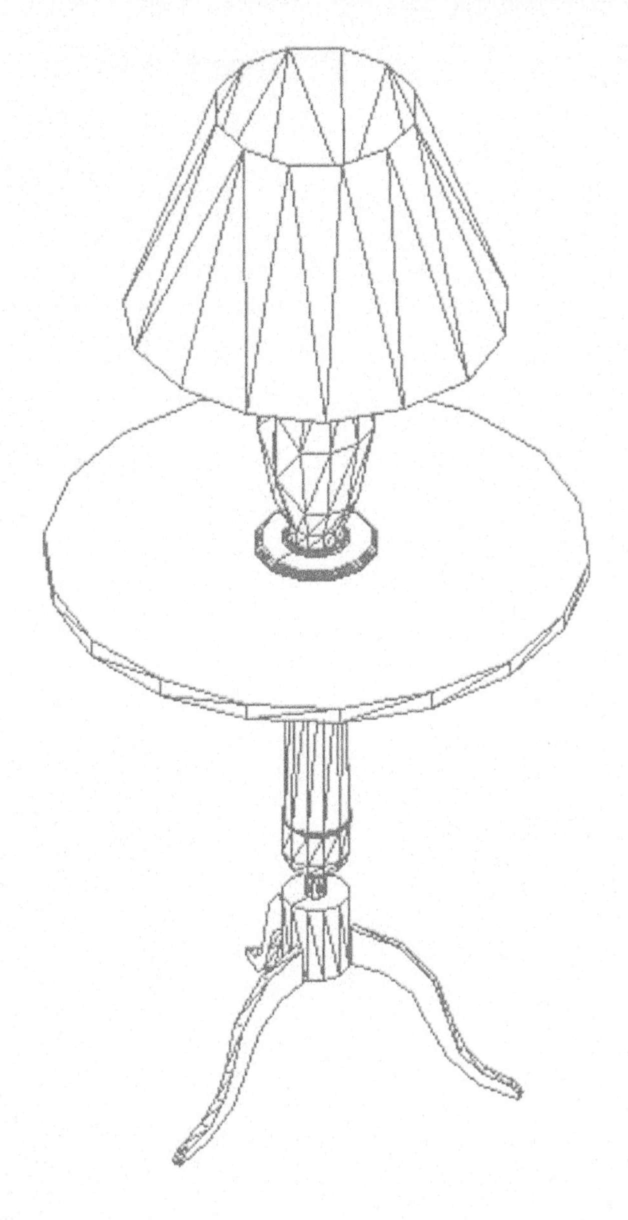

6. Use **Orbit** to obtain a perspective view of your final model and click **Layout1** before you plot.
7. Place your name in the lower right corner in **1/8"** letters using simplex or an architectural font.
8. Plot the drawing at a scale of **1 = 1** on an **11"** × **8-1/2"** sheet.
9. Save your drawing in two places with the name **CH14-P4**.

chapter fifteen

Advanced Modeling

CHAPTER OBJECTIVES

- Correctly use the following commands and settings:

Animation	**LIGHT**
BACKGROUND	**MATERIALS**
Landscape	**Materials Library**
Orbit	**RENDER**
Print 3D models	

- Use solid modeling commands to build solid models of rooms with furniture.
- Build solid models on your own from sketches.

Introduction

This chapter presents more complex models using the **Solids** commands from Chapter 14.

This chapter also covers the **RENDER** and **Animation** commands, which allow you to use lights, attach materials, and apply backgrounds so that you can create a photo-realistic rendering of a 3D scene and produce an animated file. Although there are many means of locating lights in a 3D scene, you will use the endpoints of lines and other objects in these exercises to place lights. You will use the existing materials in the materials library and existing backgrounds to begin using the **RENDER** commands.

You will also make a solid model of a room with furniture and build solid models from sketches.

The first two exercises, creating a chair and a patio, will give you the complex models needed to assign materials, place lights, render, and create an animated file.

EXERCISE 15-1
Creating a Solid Model of Chair 2

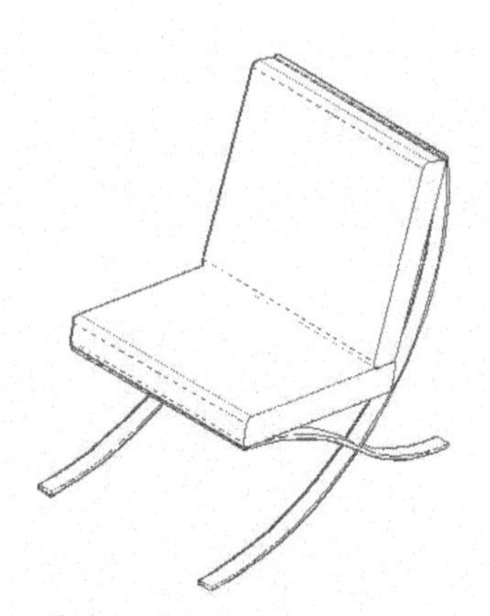

Figure 15-1
Exercise 15-1 complete

In this exercise you will create a solid model of a chair (Figure 15-1). You will insert this chair into the structure that you will create in Exercise 15-2. The **Prompt/Response** format is not used in this exercise. The steps are listed with suggested commands for creating this model.

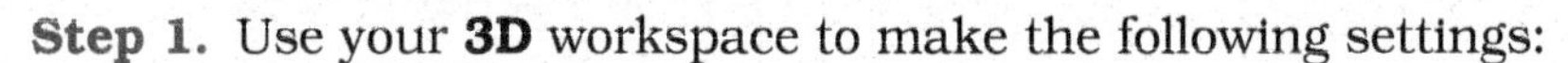

Step 1. Use your **3D** workspace to make the following settings:

1. Use **Save As...** to save the drawing on the hard drive with the name **CH15-EXERCISE1**.
2. Set drawing units: **Architectural**
3. Set drawing limits: **5,5**
4. Set **GRIDDISPLAY**: **0**
5. Set grid: **1**
6. Set snap: **1/4**
7. Create the following layers:

Layer name	Color	Linetype
a-anno-text	green	continuous
a-door	red	continuous
a-wall-intr	blue	continuous
Fabric	magenta	continuous
Metal	green	continuous

8. Set layer **Fabric** current.
9. Use the **VPORTS** command to make two vertical viewports. Use **Zoom-All** in both viewports to start, and then zoom in closer as needed. You will find it easier to draw in the left viewport and use the right viewport to determine whether the model is proceeding as it should.
10. Use **SW Isometric** to select a view for the right viewport.
11. Set **FACETRES** to **4**; set **ISOLINES** to **20**.

Step 2. Draw two **32″ × 5″** cushions using the dimensions from Figure 15-2.

Figure 15-2
Two construction lines, one horizontal 50″ and one vertical 51″; two 32″ × 5″ rectangles, one horizontal rotated –10° and one vertical rotated 20°

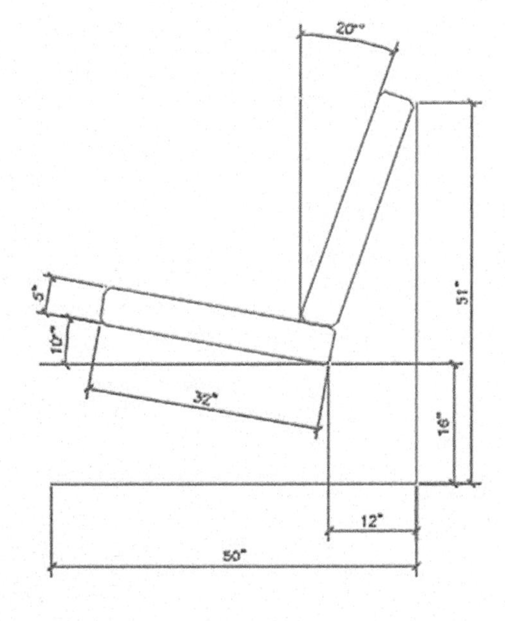

1. Draw two temporary construction lines near the bottom of your drawing in the left viewport. With **ORTHO** on, draw the first line **50"** to the right; draw the second line **51"** up (Figure 15-2).
2. Use **RECTANGLE** to draw the bottom cushion in a horizontal position **16"** above the temporary horizontal construction line and **12"** to the left of the vertical construction line. Use the **Fillet** option of the **RECTANGLE** command to create the **1"** fillet on all four corners at the same time. (Use the **From** option **@-12,16** from the intersection of the construction lines. Draw the rectangle to the left and up **@-32,5**.)
3. Use **RECTANGLE** to draw the back cushion in a vertical position, and fillet all four corners.
4. Use **ROTATE** to rotate the bottom cushion **–10°** and the back cushion **–20°**.
5. Move the back cushion so it sits on the right endpoint of the bottom and use **STRETCH** to form the bottom of the back cushion so it fits flush against the bottom cushion.

Step 3. Draw chair legs and back support (Figure 15-3).

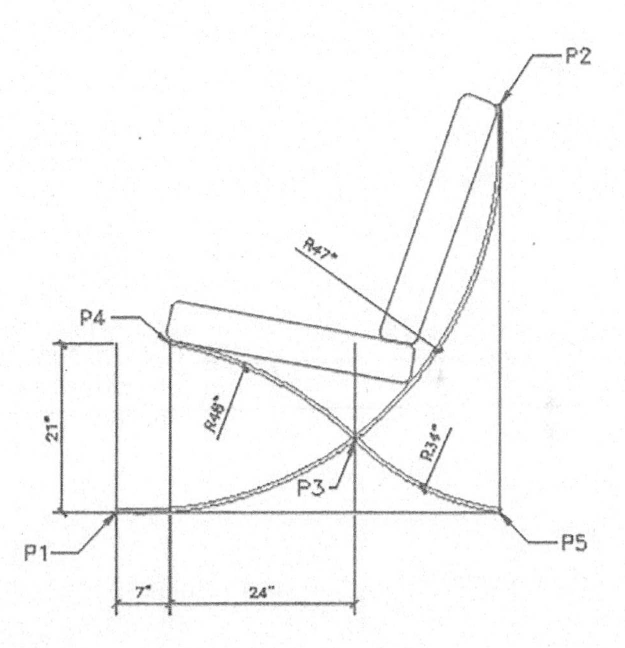

Figure 15-3
Draw three arcs; use **Join** to join the two smaller arcs

1. Set layer **Metal** current.
2. Draw temporary construction lines to locate the beginning and ending points of the three arcs; from the left end of the 50" construction line, draw a **21"** line straight up, and then offset it **7"** to the right. Offset that line **24"** to the right.
3. Use **Arc, Start-End-Radius** to draw the three arcs. First arc: start point **P1→**, endpoint **P2→**, radius **47"**. Second arc: start point **P3→**, endpoint **P4→**, radius **48"**. Third arc: start point **P3→**, endpoint **P5→**, radius **34"**.
4. Use **JOIN** to join the arcs with the 34" and 48" radii.
5. Use **OFFSET** to offset the joined arcs **1/2"** up.
6. Use **OFFSET** to offset the arc with the 47" radius **1/2"** to the left.
7. Use the **LINE** command to draw lines at the ends of all arcs so that the two metal legs have a thickness.
8. Use **JOIN** to join all parts of each leg so they can be extruded.

Step 4. Draw chair supports.

1. Draw the three supports in Figure 15-4 in the locations shown.

Figure 15-4
Draw three 2″ × 1/2″ rectangles; move and rotate them into position

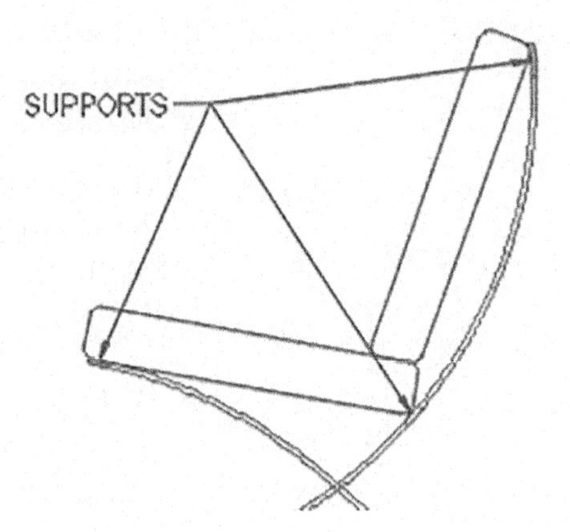

2. Use the **RECTANGLE** command to draw the **2″ × 1/2″** supports in either a vertical or horizontal position, as needed.
3. Use the **ROTATE** and **MOVE** commands to locate the supports in the positions shown.

Step 5. Extrude cushions, legs, and supports.

1. Set layer **Fabric** current so the extruded cushions will be on that layer.
2. Use the **EXTRUDE** command to extrude the two cushions **36″**.
3. Set layer **Metal** current.
4. Use the **EXTRUDE** command to extrude the polylines forming the legs **2-1/2″**.
5. Use the **EXTRUDE** command to extrude the supports **31″**. In the right viewport, use the **View Cube** to rotate the viewpoint so you can see all three supports.
6. Use the control at the top left of the right viewport to change the **Visual Style** from **2D Wireframe** to **Hidden** so the drawing appears as shown in Figure 15-5.

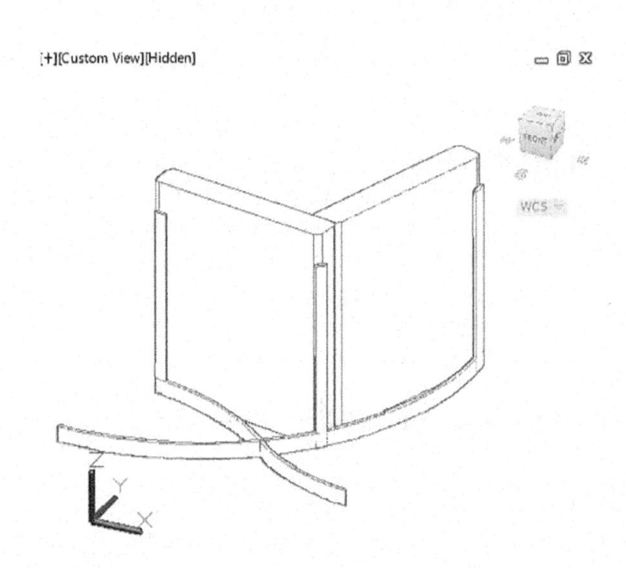

Figure 15-5
Extrude cushions 36″, legs 2-1/2″, and supports 31″

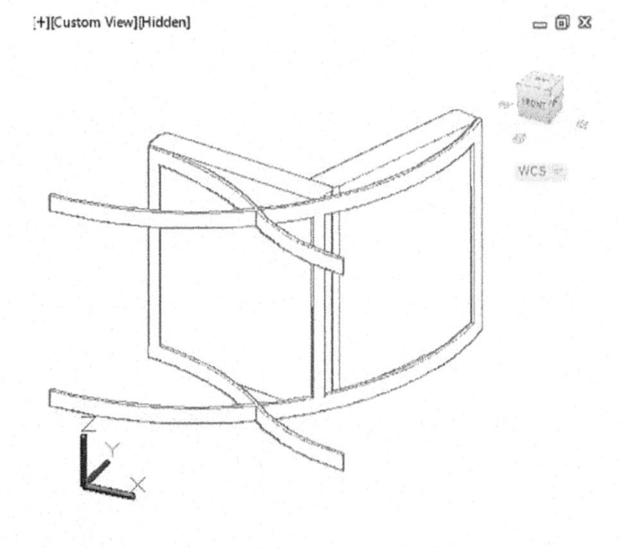

Figure 15-6
Supports moved, legs copied, and all metal parts joined with the **UNION** command

Step 6. Move supports so they sit on top of the legs (Figure 15-6).

1. Use the **MOVE** command to move the three supports **2-1/2″** in the positive **Z** direction (second point of displacement will be **@0,0,2-1/2**).

Step 7. Join the extruded legs to form a single piece.

1. Use the **UNION** command to join the two extruded legs to form a single piece.

Step 8. Add the other set of legs and join legs and supports.

1. Use the **COPY** command to copy the legs **33-1/2″** in the positive **Z** direction (the second point of displacement will be **@0,0,33-1/2**).
2. Use the **UNION** command to join both sets of legs and the three supports into a single object.

Step 9. Rotate the chair to the upright and forward position.

1. Use the **3DROTATE** command to rotate the chair **90°** about the x-axis. Click one of the lowest points of the end of one of the chair legs as the **Point** on the x-axis.

Step 10. Remove hidden lines.

1. Make sure the **Visual Style** is set to **Hidden** so the chair appears as shown in Figure 15-1.

Step 11. Wblock the drawing.

1. Use the **WBLOCK** command to save the drawing on a disk with the name **CH15-EXERCISE1**. Use the bottom of the front of the left leg as the insertion point. Click **Retain** to keep the drawing on the screen.
2. Make a layout in paper space. Use **PROPERTIES** to set a scale of **1/2″ = 1′-0″**.
3. Place your name in the upper-right corner of the viewport **3/16″** high, simplex font.
4. Save the drawing as **CH15-EXERCISE1**.

Step 12. Plot.

1. Plot or print the drawing at a scale of **1 = 1** from paper space (the **Layout1** tab) in the center of an **8-1/2″ × 11″ sheet**. Click **Hidden** in the **Shade plot:** list. (If the **Shade plot** drop-down option is gray, close the **Plot** dialog box, click the viewport boundary, and use the **PROPERTIES** command to change **Shade plot** to **Hidden**, then plot.)

EXERCISE 15-2
Creating a Solid Model of a Patio

In this exercise you will create a solid model of a patio area and insert your chair into it (Figure 15-7). The **Prompt/Response** format is not used in this exercise. The steps are listed with suggested commands for creating this model.

Step 1. Use your **3D** workspace to make the following settings:

1. Use **Save As...** to save the drawing on the hard drive with the name **CH15-EXERCISE2**.

Figure 15-7
Exercise 15-2 complete

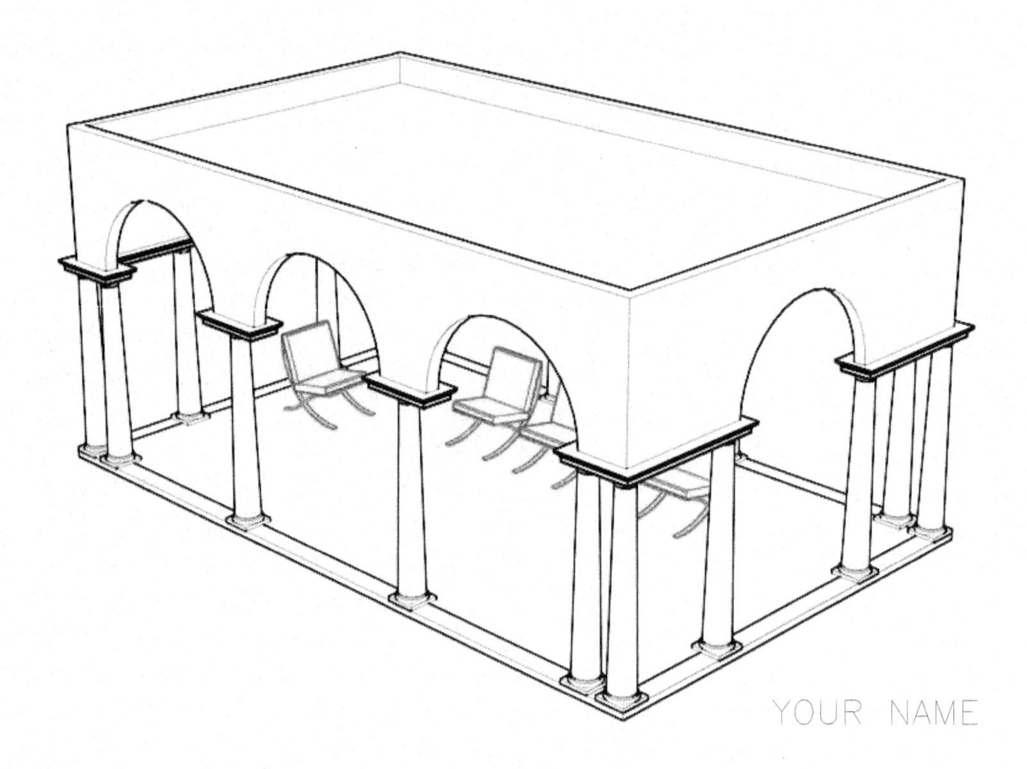

2. Set drawing units: **Architectural**
3. Set drawing limits: **50,40**
4. Set **GRIDDISPLAY**: **0**
5. Set grid: **2′**
6. Set snap: **6**
7. Create the following layers:

Layer name	Color	Linetype
Border	red	continuous
Column	white	continuous
Cornice	white	continuous
Roof	white	continuous
Pad	red	continuous

8. Set layer **Pad** current.
9. Use the **VPORTS** command to make two vertical viewports. Use **Zoom-All** in both viewports to start, and then zoom in closer as needed. You will find it easier to draw in the left viewport and use the right viewport to determine whether the model is proceeding as it should.
10. Use **SE Isometric** to set a viewpoint for the right viewport.
11. Set **FACETRES** to **4**; set **ISOLINES** to **20**. Let's begin at the bottom and work up.

Step 2. Draw the concrete pad with a border around it.

The concrete pad and the border must be two separate objects extruded to a height of **4″**. Draw the outside edge of the border and extrude it, draw the inside edge and extrude it, and subtract it from the outside edge. Finally, draw the pad and extrude it (Figure 15-8).

1. Use the **RECTANGLE** command to draw a rectangle measuring **39′ × 24′**. Start the first corner at absolute coordinates **6′,8′**.
2. Offset the first rectangle **1′** to the inside.
3. Use the **OFFSET** command to offset the **37′ × 22′** rectangle **1/2″** to the inside to form the concrete pad with a **1/2″** space between it and the border.
4. Use the **EXTRUDE** command to extrude all three rectangles **4″**.
5. Use the **SUBTRACT** command to subtract the inside of the border (the 1′-offset extruded rectangle) from the outside of the border. You will have to zoom a window so you can get close enough to pick the correct rectangle to subtract.
6. Put the border on the **Border** layer.

Step 3. Draw the base of the columns.

Draw the base of the columns on the lower-left corner of the drawing. You will copy them after placing the columns on them (Figure 15-9):

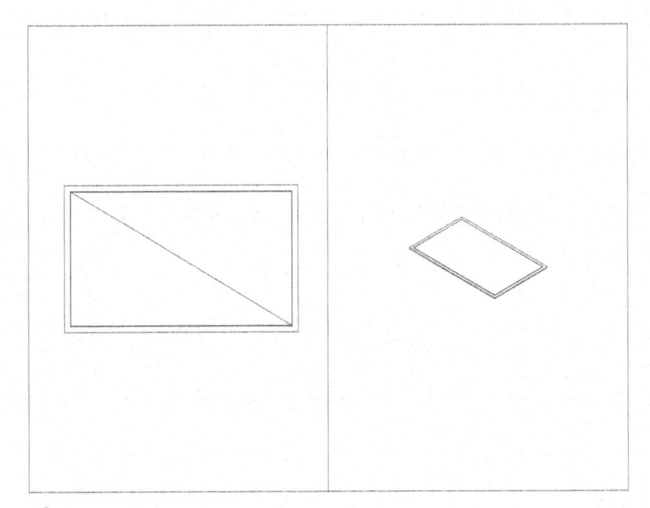

Figure 15-8
The concrete pad with a 1′ border

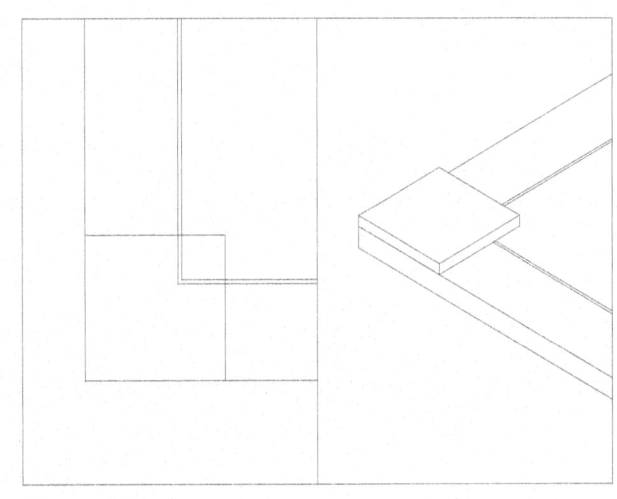

Figure 15-9
Draw the base of the column

1. Set layer **Column** current.
2. Zoom in on the lower-left corner of the drawing, as shown in Figure 15-9, in both viewports.
3. Use **BOX** to draw the column base. The box measures **18″ × 18″ × 2″** height. Locate the corner of box on the lower-left corner of the border as shown. Use **Osnap-Endpoint** to click the first corner, then **@18,18** to specify the other corner.

Step 4. Draw the columns.

Draw the column and rotate it so it sits on top of the base (Figures 15-10, 15-11, 15-12, 15-13, and 15-14):

Figure 15-10
Dimensions for drawing the column

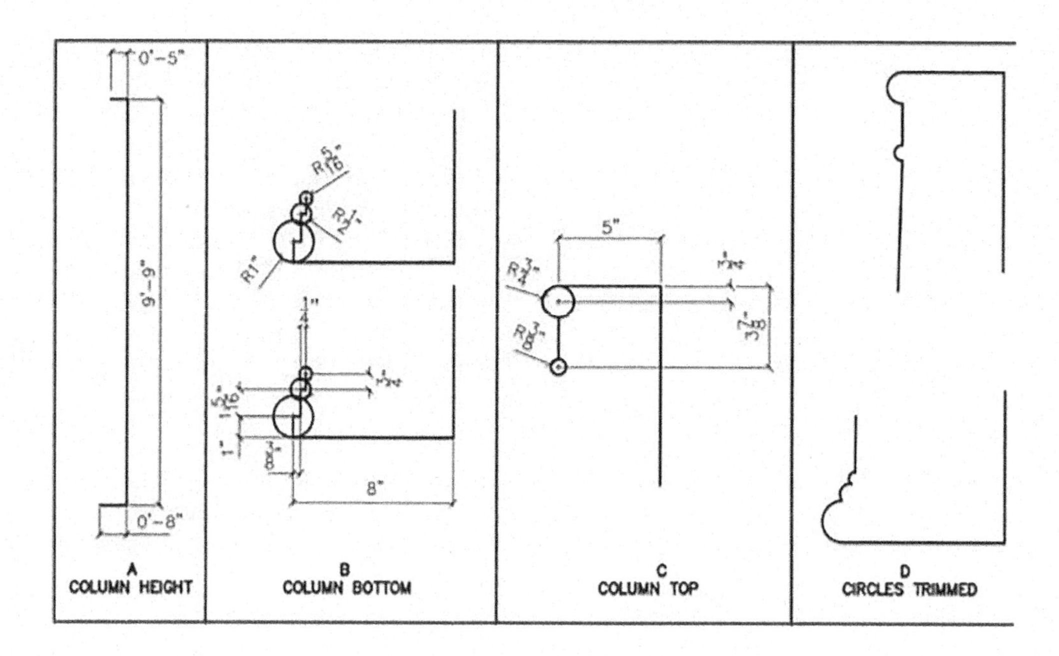

Figure 15-11
The column revolved

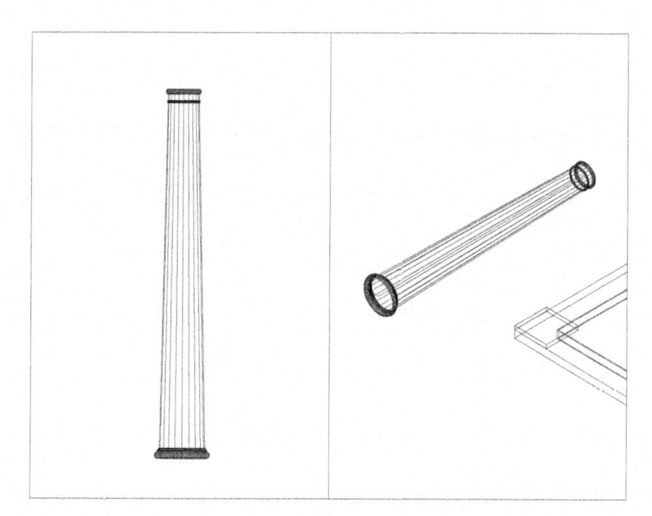

Figure 15-12
Move the UCS to the top lower-left corner of the base

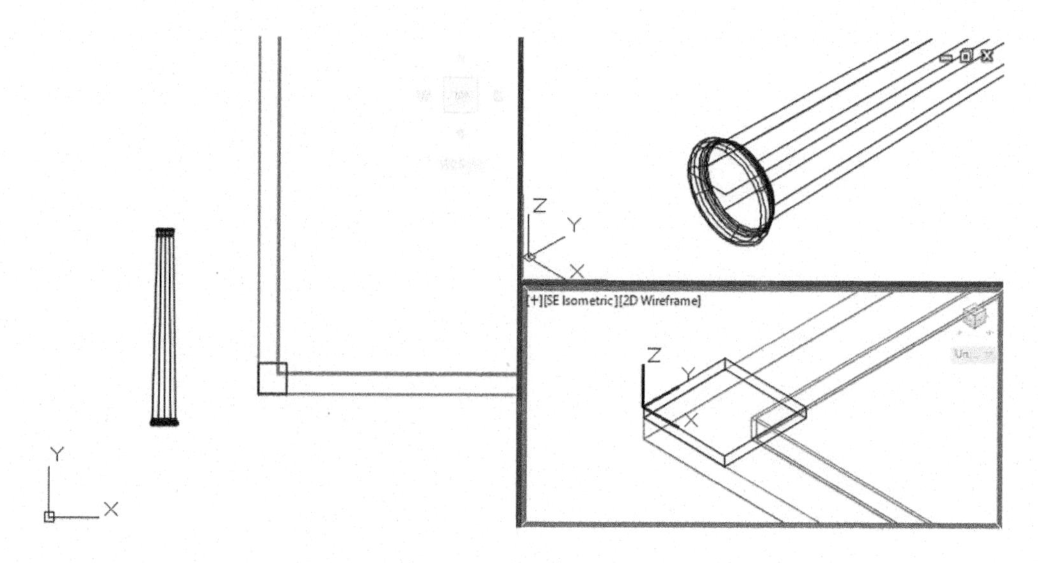

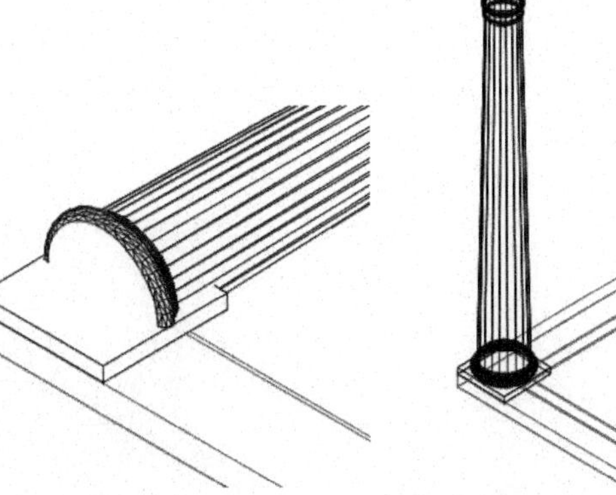

Figure 15-13
Move the column to the center of the base

Figure 15-14
Rotate the column to its upright position

1. Use the dimensions in Figure 15-10 to draw the column in an open area of your drawing. Use the **LINE** and **CIRCLE** commands to draw this figure. After you have drawn the circles and lines at the bottom and top of the column, draw a line from the quadrant of the lower circle on the top to the quadrant of the upper circle on the column bottom. Then, trim the circles to form the arcs.

> **TIP**
>
> Be sure to trim all parts of the circles so there are no double lines.

2. Use **JOIN** to join all the parts of Figure 15-10 into a single polyline.
3. Use the **REVOLVE** command to create the solid column as shown in Figure 15-11. Select both ends of the vertical line using **Osnap-Endpoint** as the axis of revolution.
4. Use the **VPORTS** command to split the right viewport into two horizontal viewports **(three:left)** and zoom in on the bottom of the column and the box you drew as the column base, as shown in Figure 15-12 in both horizontal viewports. (You may need to adjust your view in the left viewport—type **PLAN <Enter>**.)
5. Use the **UCS** command to move your UCS to the lower left corner of the top plane of the base, as shown in Figure 15-12, in both right viewports.
6. Use the **MOVE** command to move the column to the center of the base, as shown in Figure 15-13. Use **Osnap-Center** as the base point and click the extreme bottom circular center of the column in the upper-right viewport. Type **9,9** as the second point of displacement to move the column to the center of the base.
7. Use the **3DROTATE** command to rotate the column **90°** about the x-axis, as shown in Figure 15-14.
8. Use the **VPORTS** command to return the display to two vertical viewports.

Step 5. Add the cornice at the top of the column.

Insert drawing 14-3 (from Exercise 14-1, Figures 14-40 through 14-45) to form the cornice at the top of the column (Figures 15-15 and 15-16).

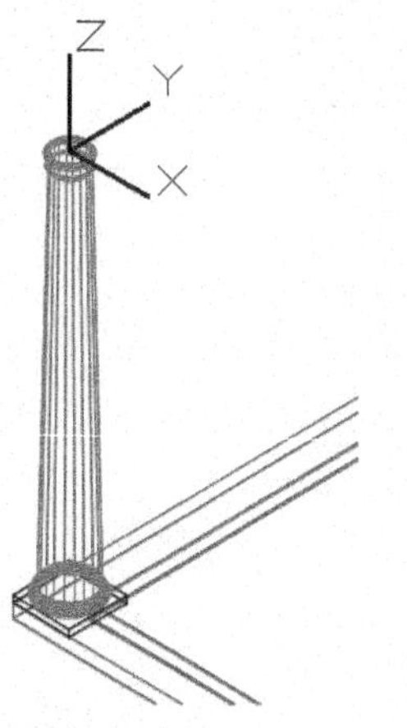

Figure 15-15
Move the UCS to the center of the top of the column

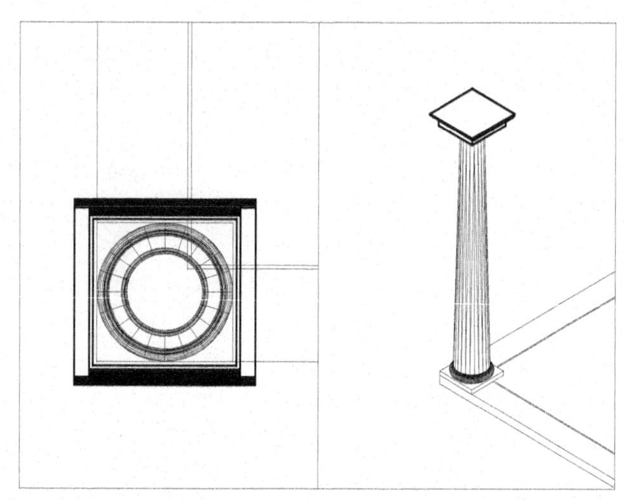

Figure 15-16
Inserting the cornice

1. Set layer **Cornice** current.
2. Use the **Move** option of the **UCS** command to move the UCS to the extreme top of the column as shown in Figure 15-15. Use **Osnap-Center** to locate the UCS at that point.
3. Use the **INSERT** command to insert drawing 14-3 onto the top of the column (Figure 15-16). Use the following:

> **TIP**
>
> Be sure the insertion point is positive **9-1/2**, negative **–9-1/2**. If you did not pick the correct insertion point when you Wblocked drawing 14-3, draw a line from a bottom corner to the diagonally opposite corner. Use the midpoint of that line to move drawing 14-3 to coordinates 0,0.

Insertion point: Type **9-1/2** in the **X:** box and –**9-1/2** in the **Y:** box. (Be sure to include the minus in the Y direction.) Leave **Z:** at 0. (The bottom of the cornice drawing measures 19″. Because you picked the endpoint of the lower corner as the insertion point when you Wblocked the shape, 9-1/2, –9-1/2 will place the center of the shape at the center of the column top. The shape must measure **24″ × 24″** when you insert it. The arithmetic requires you to subtract 5″ from both measurements and divide by 2.)

After you have typed the insertion point in the **X:** and **Y:** boxes of **Insertion point**, type **12** in the **X: Scale** box and select the **Uniform Scale check box.**

(The shape measures 2″ square, so an X scale factor of 12 will make the shape 24″ long.)(The shape must also be 24″ in the Y direction, so **Uniform Scale** must be selected.)

(The height of the original shape was reduced to 1/12 of the 5-1/2″ dimension, so a scale factor of 12 will make it 5-1/2″ in this drawing.)

Leave **Rotation angle: 0**. Click **OK**.

4. Use the **EXPLODE** command to explode the inserted cornice so it can be joined to form longer cornices. *Explode it only once.* If you explode it more than once, you destroy it as a solid. If you are not sure whether you have exploded it, use the **LIST** command to find out. LIST should tell you it is a 3D solid, not a block.

5. Go to **3D Views-Front** (on the **View** menu) or use **ViewCube-Front** occasionally to be sure all parts are in the correct location, and then return to the previous view.

Step 6. Draw the bases, columns, and cornices at the center and one corner of the structure.

Copy the column and cornice to create supports at the center of the structure (Figures 15-17 and 15-18):

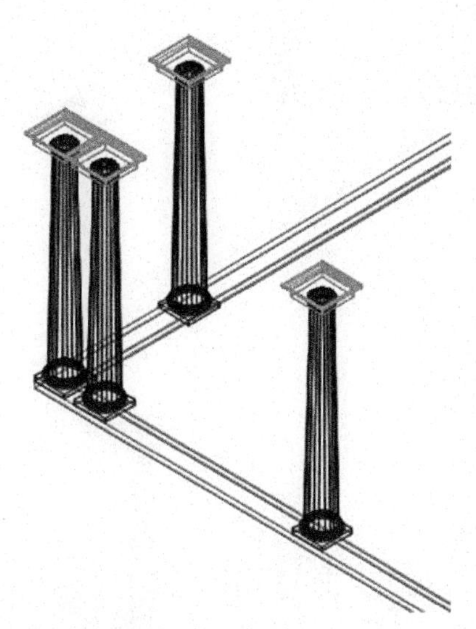

Figure 15-17
Copy the base, column, and cornice twice in the X direction and once in the Y direction

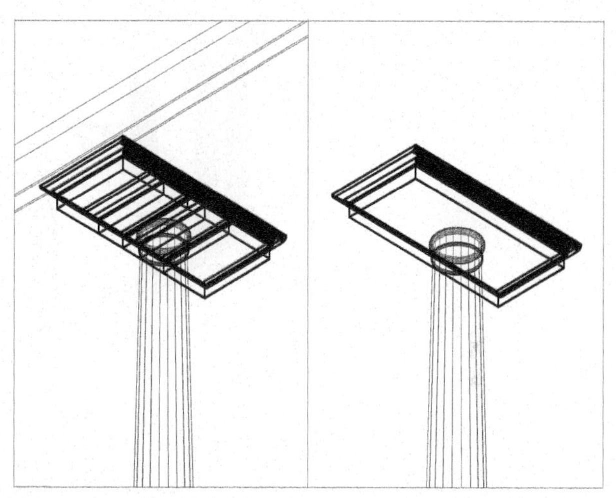

Figure 15-18
Copy the cornice in the positive X direction and the negative X direction and union the three cornice shapes

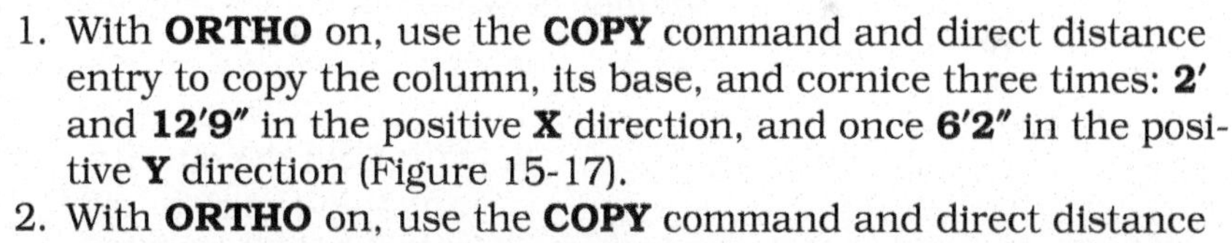

1. With **ORTHO** on, use the **COPY** command and direct distance entry to copy the column, its base, and cornice three times: **2′** and **12′9″** in the positive **X** direction, and once **6′2″** in the positive **Y** direction (Figure 15-17).
2. With **ORTHO** on, use the **COPY** command and direct distance entry to copy the cornice on the column that is to the far right **12″** in the positive **X** direction and **12″** in the negative **X** direction so that the cornice on this column will measure 48″ when the three are joined.
3. Use **UNION** to join the cornice and the two copies to form a single cornice that is 48″ long (Figure 15-18).

Copy the cornice and join all the cornice shapes on the three corner columns to create the L-shaped cornice at the corner of the structure (Figure 15-19).

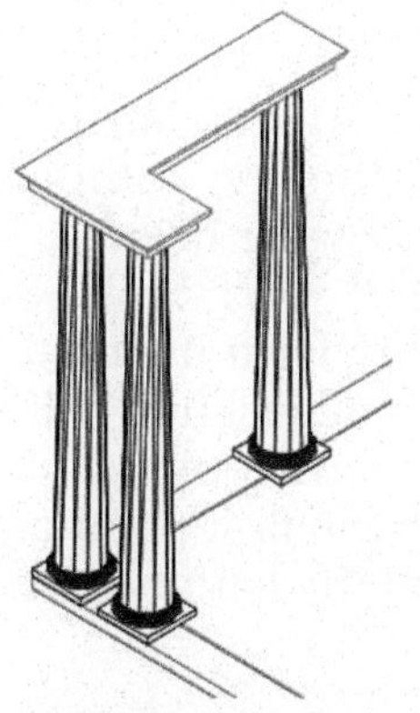

Figure 15-19
The L-shaped cornice after using the **UNION** and **HIDE** commands

1. With **ORTHO** on, use the **COPY** command and direct distance entry to copy the cornice on the corner column six times: **12″** and **24″** in the positive **X** direction and **12″**, **24″**, **36″**, **48″**, **60″**, and **72″** in the positive **Y** direction so that the cornice on the three corner columns will measure 48″ in the X direction and 96″ in the Y direction when all these shapes are joined.
2. Use **UNION** to join all the cornice shapes on the three corner columns to form a single L-shaped cornice (Figure 15-19).

Step 7. Draw all the remaining columns.

Mirror the existing columns twice to form the remaining columns (Figure 15-20).

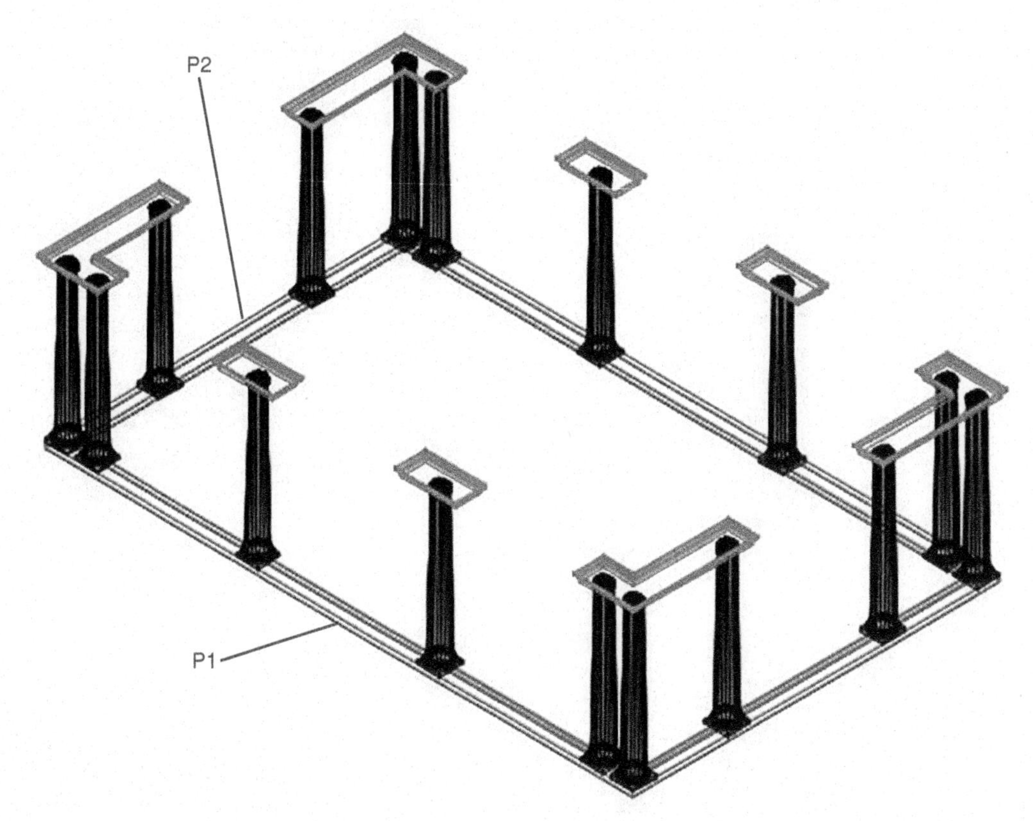

Figure 15-20
Copying the columns using the **MIRROR** command

1. Use the **UCS** command to return to the World UCS.
2. With **ORTHO** on, use the **MIRROR** command to form the columns on the right side of the structure. Select all existing columns, bases, and cornices. Press **<Enter>**, and then using **Osnap-Midpoint**, click **P1→** (Figure 15-20) as the first point of the mirror line, then click any point directly above or below **P1→**. Do not erase source objects.
3. With **ORTHO** on, use the **MIRROR** command to form the columns on the back side of the structure. Select all existing columns, bases, and cornices. Press **<Enter>**, and then using **Osnap-Midpoint**, click **P2→** (Figure 15-20) as the first point of the mirror line, then click any point directly to the left or right of **P2→**. Do not erase source objects.

Step 8. Draw the upper part of the structure.

Draw the front and rear elevations of the upper structure (Figure 15-21).

1. Set layer **Roof** current.
2. Use the **View Control** at the top-left corner of the left viewport to change the view from **Top** to **Front.**
3. Draw the upper part of the structure in an open area. You will move it to its correct location after it is completed.
4. Use the dimensions from Figure 15-21 to draw that shape with the **RECTANGLE**, **CIRCLE**, and **TRIM** commands.

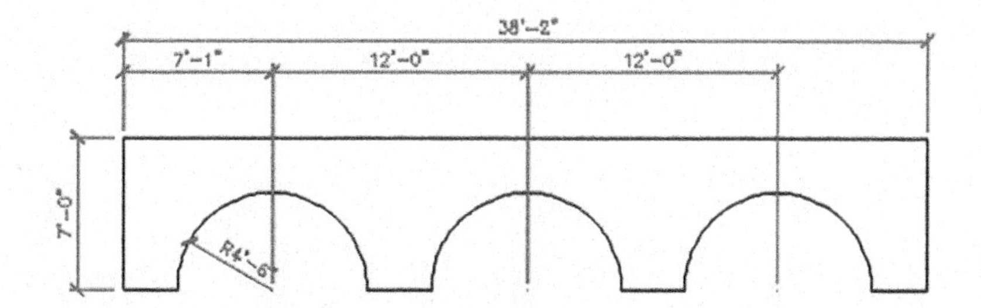

Figure 15-21
Dimensions for the front and rear elevations of the upper structure

5. Use the **PRESSPULL** command to extrude the polyline **8″**. With **PRESSPULL**, having a closed polyline is not necessary. Just click inside the boundary, move your extrusion in the direction you want, and type the distance (**8**).
6. Use the **COPY** command to copy this shape **22′-6″** in the negative **Z** direction (*Base point:* click any point; *Second point of displacement:* type **@0,0,-22′6 <Enter>**).

Draw the left and right elevations of the upper structure (Figures 15-22 and 15-23).

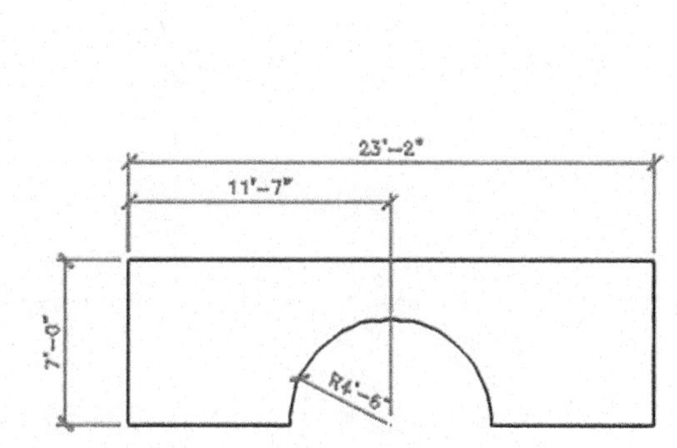

Figure 15-22
Dimensions for the left and right elevations of the upper structure

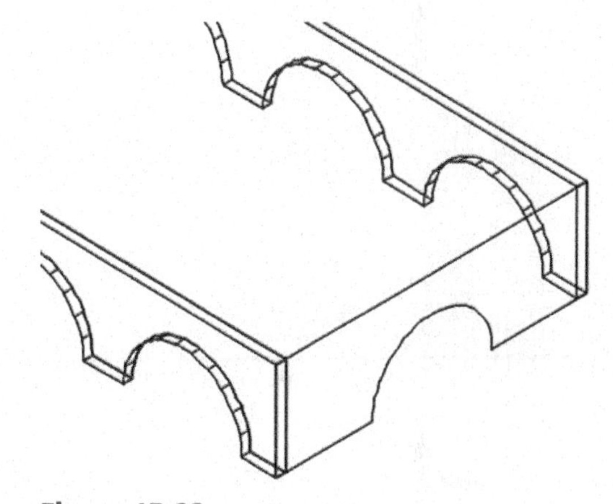

Figure 15-23
Draw the right elevation on the right ends of the front and rear planes

1. Use the **View Control** to change the view to **Right**.
2. Use the dimensions from Figure 15-22 to draw that shape with the **RECTANGLE**, **CIRCLE**, and **TRIM** commands across the ends of the front and rear elevations.
3. Draw the right side of the structure on the right ends of the front and rear planes (Figure 15-23).
4. Use the **PRESSPULL** command to extrude the polyline **8″**.
5. Use the **COPY** command to copy this shape **37′-6″** in the negative **Z** direction (*Base point:* click any point; *Second point of displacement:* type **@0,0,-37′6 <Enter>** or move your mouse in the negative **Z** direction with **ORTHO** on and type **37′6 <Enter>**).

Draw the roof and complete the upper part of the structure (Figures 15-24, 15-25, 15-26, and 15-27).

1. Confirm that the **Roof** layer is current.
2. Use the **UCS** command to return to the World UCS.

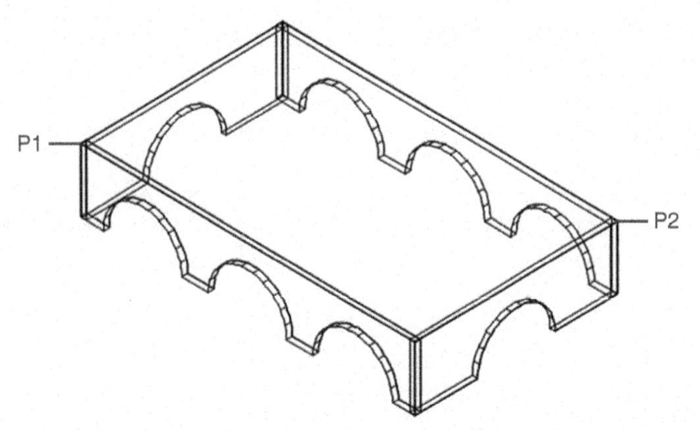

Figure 15-24
Draw a rectangle to form the roof

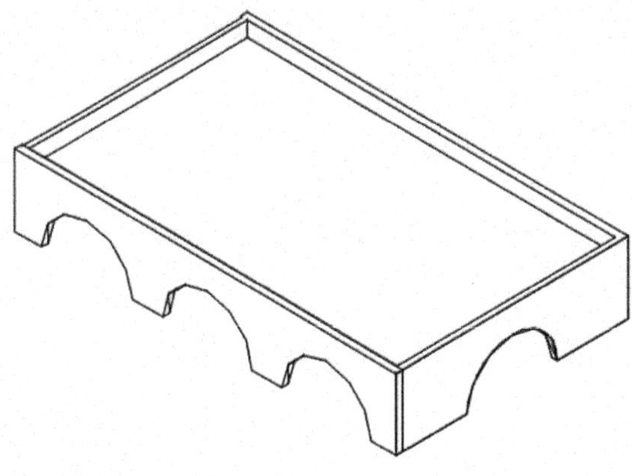

Figure 15-25
The completed upper structure

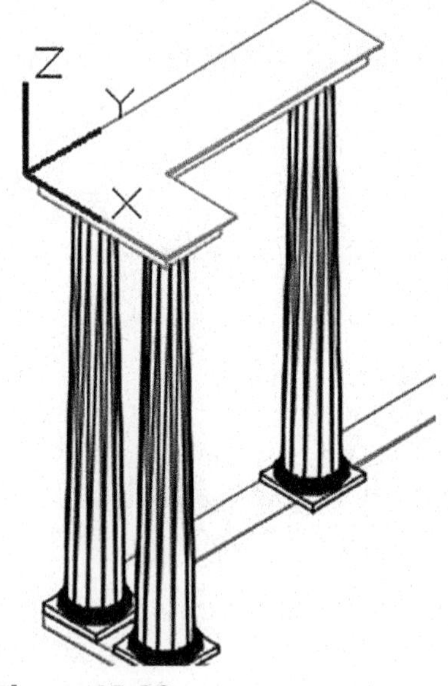

Figure 15-26
Move the UCS to the top of the cornice corner

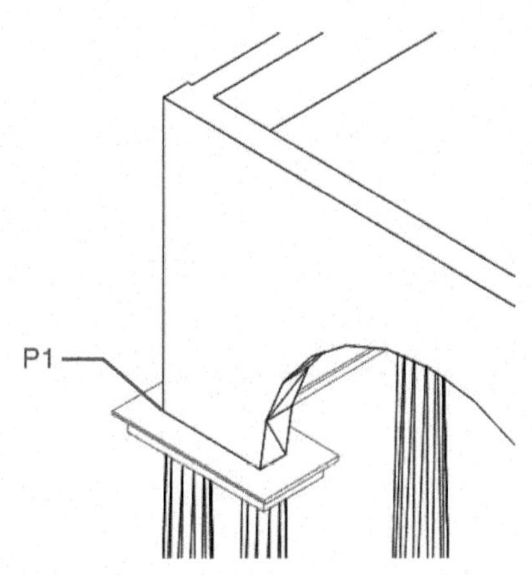

Figure 15-27
Move the upper structure into position

3. Use the **RECTANGLE** command to draw a rectangle to form the flat roof inside the upper part of the structure (Figure 15-24).
   First corner: **P1→**
   Other corner: **P2→**
4. Use the **EXTRUDE** command to extrude the rectangle **8″** in the negative **Z** direction.
5. Use the **MOVE** command to move the extruded rectangle **18″** in the negative **Z** direction (*Second point of displacement:* type **@0,0,-18 <Enter>**).
6. Use the **UNION** command to join all parts of the upper structure into a single unit.
7. Use the **HIDE** command to make sure your model appears as you want it to (Figure 15-25).
8. Use the **UCS** command to move the origin of the UCS to the endpoint of the lower-left cornice (Figure 15-26).
9. Use the **MOVE** command to move the endpoint, **P1→** (Figure 15-27), of the lower-right corner of the upper part of the structure to absolute coordinates **8,8,0**. Be sure you do not put the @ symbol in front of the coordinates.

Step 9. Insert chairs to complete the model.

Insert a chair at the correct elevation, copy it, rotate it, and complete Exercise 15-2 (Figure 15-29).

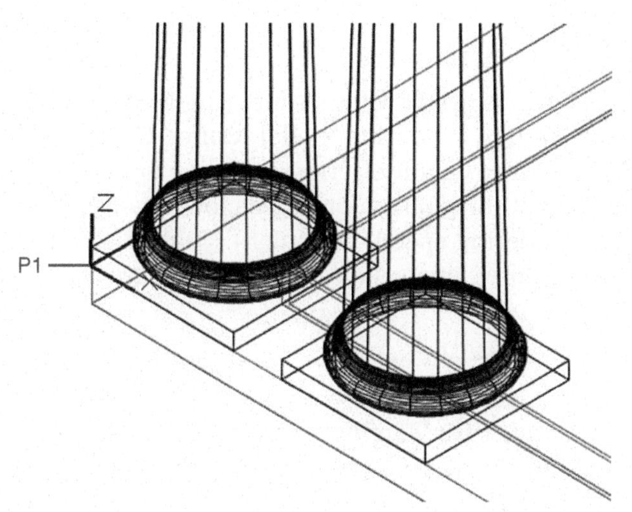

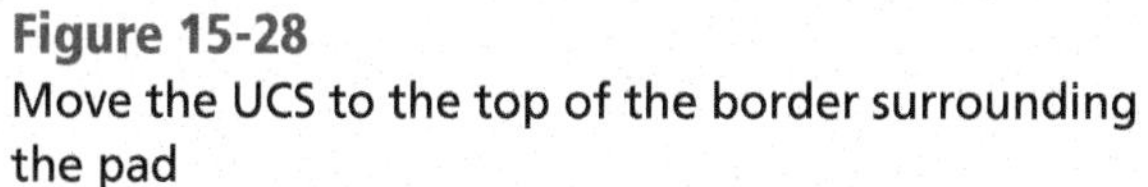

Figure 15-28
Move the UCS to the top of the border surrounding the pad

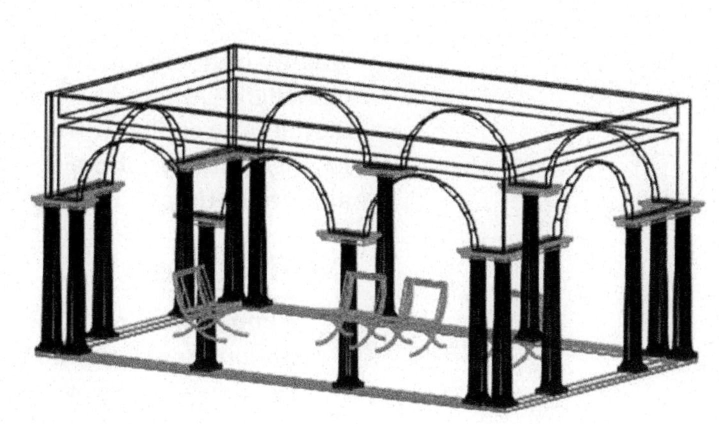

Figure 15-29
Locating the chairs

1. Use the **UCS** command to move the origin of the UCS to the top of the border surrounding the concrete pad, **P1→** (Figure 15-28).
2. Use the **INSERT** command to insert the chair drawing, **CH15-EXERCISE1**, at absolute coordinates **30′,14′,0**.
3. Explode the inserted chair **once**. If you explode it more than once, you will have destroyed it as a solid.
4. With **ORTHO** on, use the **COPY** command to copy the chair three times to the approximate locations shown in Figure 15-29. (Remember that the frame and the cushions are separate solid objects.)
5. Use the **ROTATE** command to rotate the chair on the far left **90°**.
6. Use the **Viewpoint Presets** dialog box to select a viewpoint of **315,10**.
7. With the right viewport active, use the **SIngle** option of the **VPORTS** command to return the display to a single viewport.
8. On the **Navigation Bar**, choose **Orbit-Free Orbit. Use the** right-click menu to set **Perspective** projection and **Visual Styles - Hidden** to obtain a view similar to Figure 15-7.
9. Click **Layout1** and place the viewport boundary on a new layer that is turned off.
10. Use the **Single Line Text** command (type **DT <Enter>**) to place your name in the lower right corner **1/80** high in the simplex font. Your final drawing should appear as shown earlier in Figure 15-7.
11. Use the **Shade plot - As Displayed** option in the **Plot** dialog box to remove hidden lines when you plot.

3D ORBIT	
Ribbon/Panel	View/ Navigate
Navigation Bar:	
3D Navigation Toolbar:	
Menu Bar:	View/Orbit/ Free Orbit
Type a Command:	3DORBIT
Command Alias:	3DO

Step 10. Use the **Save As** command to save your drawing in two places.

Step 11. Plot or print the drawing at a scale of **1 = 1**.

RENDER

Render: A command that uses objects, lighting, and materials to obtain a realistic view of a model.

The ***Render*** command uses objects, lighting, and materials to obtain a realistic view of a model.

Render Quality

The six preset rendering quality options are Low (one rendering level), Medium (five rendering levels), High (ten rendering levels), Coffee-Break Quality (renders for 10 minutes), Lunch Quality (renders for one hour), and Overnight Quality (renders for twelve hours). Low produces low-quality rendering but results in the fastest rendering speed. Overnight Quality is used for high-quality, photo-realistic rendered images and requires the greatest amount of time to render.

Destinations

Render Window: Choosing **Render in: Window** as your render destination means the image will be created in a specified **Render Size** in the Render window when processing is complete.

Viewport: Anything currently displayed in the viewport gets rendered.

Region: Anything inside an area in a viewport that you specify gets rendered.

Render in Cloud: Allows you to render to your Autodesk Rendering Account after you have created the account. You can create high-resolution final images in the cloud.

Save rendering to a file: Allows you to save the rendering to a disk with the file name and location you choose. To render to a file, choose **Render to Size** on the **Visualize** tab's **Render** panel. Then select **More Output Settings...**, select the **Save Image** check box, and click **Save**.

Lights

lights: Objects used in the **RENDER** command to light scenes. In addition to natural light sources—sunlight and moonlight—there are four types of artificial lights that can be used to render a scene: point, distant, spot-, and weblights.

AutoCAD has two broad types of light: natural and artificial. The light you choose will depend on the type of model you are creating. Artificial lights tend to be for indoor objects, and natural light—sunlight or moonlight—are for the out of doors. AutoCAD's lights are photometric, which means they are scientifically designed using light energy values. This part of the book covers light objects that you create and place in your model. There is also a "default" lighting system that you can use to render models with when no lights are placed in your drawing. You must turn off the default system if you want to use natural or artificial lights.

Natural light in AutoCAD can be either sunlight or moonlight.

Four types of artificial light objects are available in AutoCAD:

Point Lights: Point lights shine in all directions much like a common lightbulb. You can set the intensity or color of a point light by selecting the light and opening the **Properties** palette.

Distant Lights: Distant lights shine as a parallel beam in one direction illuminating all objects that the light strikes. You can use this light to simulate the sun or another similar light source. You can use one or more distant lights and vary their intensity to achieve the result you want.

Spotlights: Spotlights shine in one direction in a cone shape. One of the settings for this light is the hotspot, at which the light has the greatest intensity. The other setting is the falloff, at which the light begins to decrease in intensity. You can use spotlights in a manner similar to spotlights in a theater or to light a display.

Weblights: These lights are similar to those bought in a store: fluorescent, low-pressure sodium, incandescent, and high-intensity discharge. Weblights can display a far more precise, manufacturer-based light property than point lights or spotlights.

AutoCAD has two lighting options: international (SI) and American. The default lighting for AutoCAD 2022 is photometric based on American lighting units. This option creates physically correct lighting. American differs from international in that illuminance values are measured in foot-candles rather than lux.

You can change the lighting option by typing **LIGHTINGUNITS <Enter>**, and then changing the number to 1 or 2:

1 Photometric lighting in international SI units
2 Photometric lighting in American units

You can add photometric properties to both artificial lights and natural lights. Natural lights are the sun and the sky.

You can create lights with various distribution and color characteristics or import specific photometric files available from lighting manufacturers. Photometric lights always attenuate using an inverse-square falloff and rely on your scene using realistic units.

Which of these options you use will depend on how your scene is constructed and what your preferences are.

With photometric lights and the sun, you will often need to perform tone mapping. The **RENDEREXPOSURE** command allows you to adjust the tone mapping. Type **RENDEREXPOSURE <Enter>** to display the **Render Environment & Exposure** palette, which provides controls for adjusting the tone mapping.

Materials

materials: Items that can be attached to solid shapes to give those shapes the appearance of metal, wood, brick, granite, textiles, or any one of a number of other materials. Materials are used in the **RENDER** command to make a scene.

AutoCAD has several palettes containing ***materials*** that can be attached to the surfaces of 3D objects in your drawing. You can also create new materials from scratch and modify existing materials and save them with a new name. In this exercise, you will use only existing materials. If you attach a material to an object and decide you do not like its appearance, the **Materials Browser** allows you to detach the material from that object.

Other Commands Available to Render, Animate, Attach Scanned Files, and Shade 3D Models

Orbit: As discussed in previous chapters, the **Orbit** command has several features that you can use to give a 3D model a photo-realistic appearance.

New View/Shot Properties: Allows you to add a solid, a gradient, or an image background to your model.

Point Cloud: The **Point Cloud** feature allows you to convert scanned pictures to a point cloud format that can be inserted into your drawing. The scanned pictures must be in one of these formats: PTG, PTS, PTX, LAS, XYZ, TXT, ASC, XYB, FLS, FWS, CLR, or CL3. The point cloud pictures are three-dimensional and can be placed in a 3D model to make a presentation.

The **Point Cloud Editor** is used to modify the point cloud; use it as a guideline for drawing, change its display, or apply color mapping to distinguish different features.

Render Environment: Allows you to simulate an atmosphere that enhances the illusion of depth. You can change the color of the fog to create different visual effects.

Motion Path Animations...: Moves a camera along a path you choose.

3D Walk: Allows you to walk through your model controlling height and speed.

3D Fly: Allows you to fly through or around the model.

EXERCISE 15-3
Use Render Commands to Make a Photo-Realistic Rendering of the Solid Model in Exercise 15-2

In this exercise you will use the **Materials Browser** to select materials to attach to your model. You will then place lights in a manner that will illuminate your model. Next, you will give the model perspective projection, and finally, you will render the model using the **RENDER** command and the **Visual Styles Manager** (Figure 15-30).

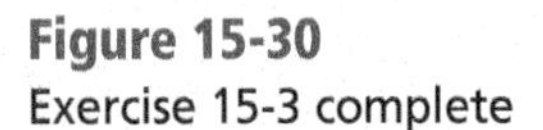

Figure 15-30
Exercise 15-3 complete

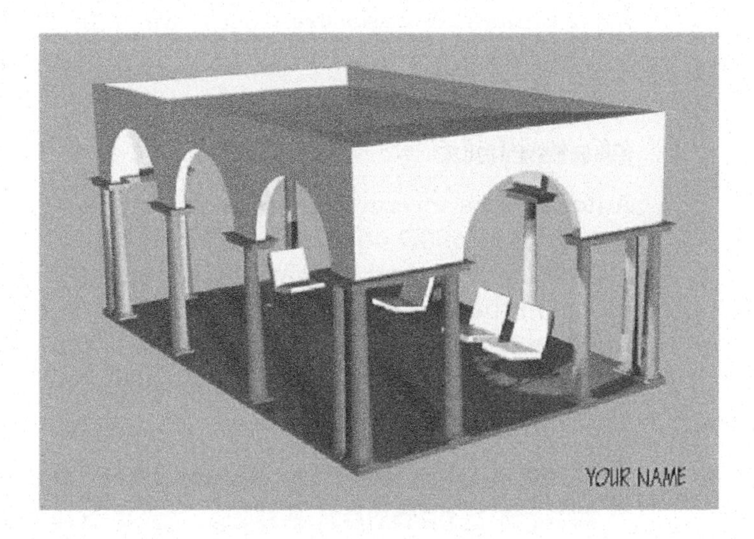

Step 1. Use your **3D** workspace to make the following settings:

1. Open drawing **CH15-EXERCISE2** and save it as **CH15-EXERCISE3**.
2. Click the **MODEL** tab to return to model space.
3. Click in the right viewport to make it active and change the display to a single viewport if it is not already a single viewport.

Step 2. Move one of the chairs out of the patio so you can easily attach materials to its parts.

> **TIP**
>
> If all parts of the chair are a single block, you will have to explode it once—only once, so you can apply material to its individual parts.

Step 3. Select the **White Canvas** material from the **Materials Browser** and place it onto the back and cushion of the chair you just moved, as described next:

Prompt	Response
Type a command:	**Materials Browser** (from the **Visualize** tab's **Materials** panel)

> **NOTE**
>
> The **Visualize** panel is not visible by default. To display it, right-click on any panel label, select **Show Tabs**, and then check **Visualize**.

The **Materials Browser** (Figure 15-31 appears):	Click **Autodesk Library**
The available materials appear:	Click **Fabric, Canvas White**
	Click the cushion and the back of the chair (you must select the object before you apply the material)
	Click **Canvas White** (The cushion and the back of the chair now has the white canvas material.) Be sure to click the **Add material** button to the far right of the material name

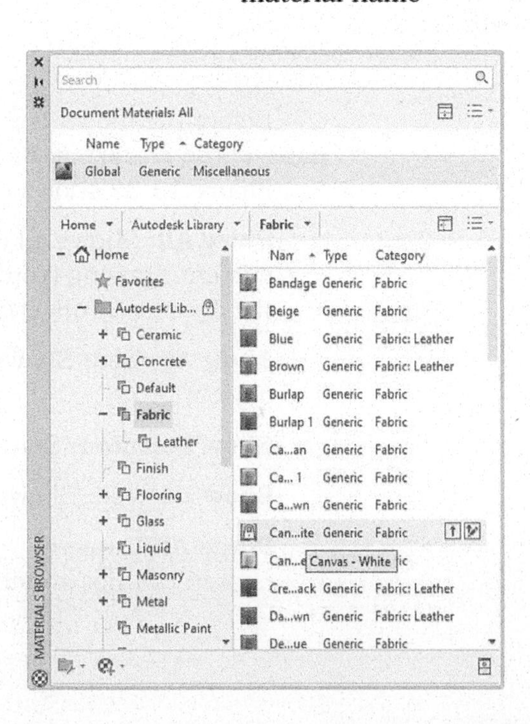

Figure 15-31
The **Materials Browser**

Step 4. Select the **Semi-Polished** material from the **Materials Browser** and place it onto the metal parts of the chair you just moved, as described next:

Prompt	Response
	Click **Metal-Aluminum, Semi-Polished** (**Semi-Polished** is at the end of the list)
	Click the metal parts of the chair
	Click **Aluminum, Semi-Polished**

Step 5. Check to be sure the material has been applied, as described next:

Prompt	Response
Type a command:	Type **RENDER <Enter>**
The chair (and the other parts of the drawing that have not had material applied) is rendered:	Close the **Render** dialog box.

Step 6. Move the chair back to the patio, erase the other chairs, and copy the chair with the material to replace the erased ones.

Step 7. Select the following materials from the **Materials Browser** and place them onto the specified objects. (Remember, you have to select the object before you attach the material.)

Prompt **Response**

1. **Masonry-Brick, Herringbone-Red** for the patio floor pad
2. **Masonry-Brick, Common** for the border around the patio floor pad
3. **Concrete-Cast-In-Place, Exposed-Fine** for the columns and bases
4. **Masonry-CMU, Scored-Running** for the roof
5. **Masonry-CMU, Split Face-Running** for the cornices

Before the model is rendered with materials attached, look at the other parts of the **Materials Browser**.

Figure 15-32 shows the **Document Materials** options:

Show All: Shows all the materials that have been chosen for use in the current drawing (You can drag and drop materials from the list onto the document materials area.)

Show Applied: Shows all the materials that have been attached to objects

Show Selected: Shows all materials that have been selected

Show Unused: Shows all materials that have been chosen but not used

Purge All Unused: Used to purge all unused materials that have been chosen but not attached to objects

Figure 15-33 shows the options that are available when you right-click on a material swatch.

Figure 15-32
Materials Browser - Document Materials

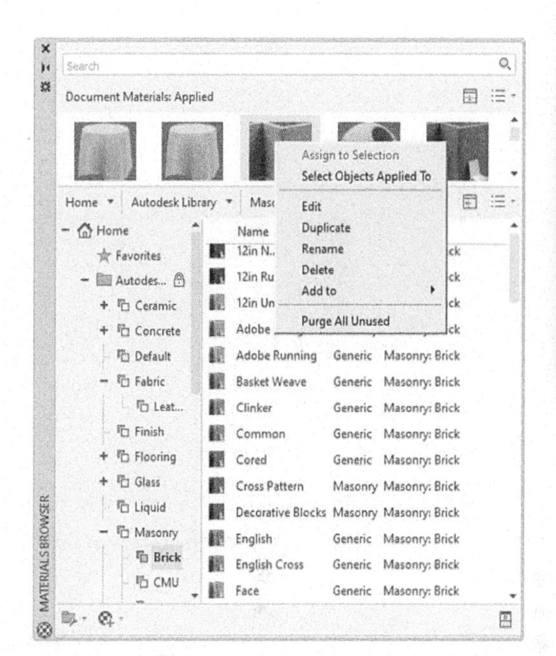

Figure 15-33
Right-click options for each material

Assign to Selection: Allows you to attach the material to an object that is already selected (It is grayed out because no object was selected before the right-click.)

Select Objects Applied to: Selects the objects to which this material has been attached

Edit: Opens the **Material Editor** and allows you to edit the material

Duplicate: Copies the material

Rename: Allows you to rename the material

Delete: Deletes the material from the document materials

Add to: Allows you to add this material to **My materials** or to an active tool palette

Purge All Unused: Deletes any document materials that are unused in the drawing

Figure 15-34 shows the **Libraries** drop-down list. This list allows you to create, open, or edit a user-defined library.

Figure 15-35 shows the drop-down list for how materials are displayed:

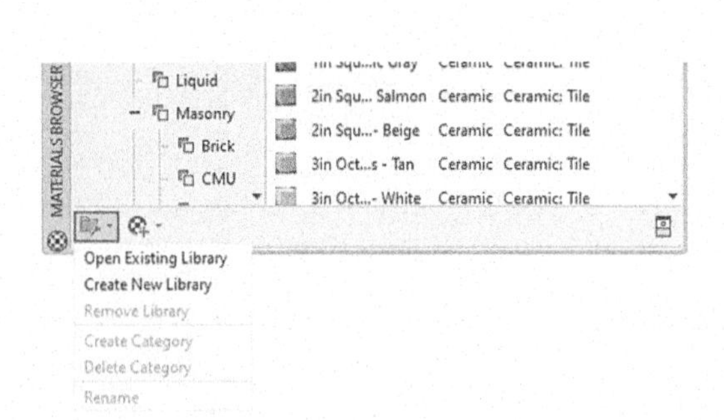

Figure 15-34
The **Libraries** drop-down list

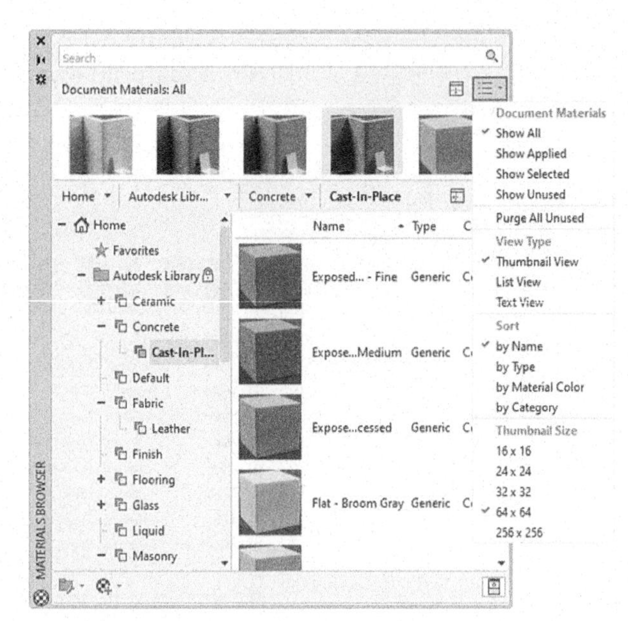

Figure 15-35
The **Libraries** button

Thumbnail View: Shows a swatch of the material with its title beneath

List View: The default, and shows a swatch of the material with its category shown to the right

Text View: Does not show a swatch of the material and lists the material

Figure 15-35 shows the option that allows you to change the size of the swatch. When you click any of the sizes under **Thumbnail Size**, the size of the swatches changes.

The last button on the lower right displays the **Material Editor**. The **Material Editor** lets you modify material properties.

Step 8. Use the **Visual Styles Manager**, Figure 15-36, to render the model with the **Realistic** style.

Prompt	**Response**
Type a command:	**Visual Styles Manager**
	Double-click the **Realistic** style icon

The model is rendered as shown in Figure 15-36.

Now you will add lighting, turn on shadows, select the background, and render the model with the **RENDER** command to produce a realistic image.

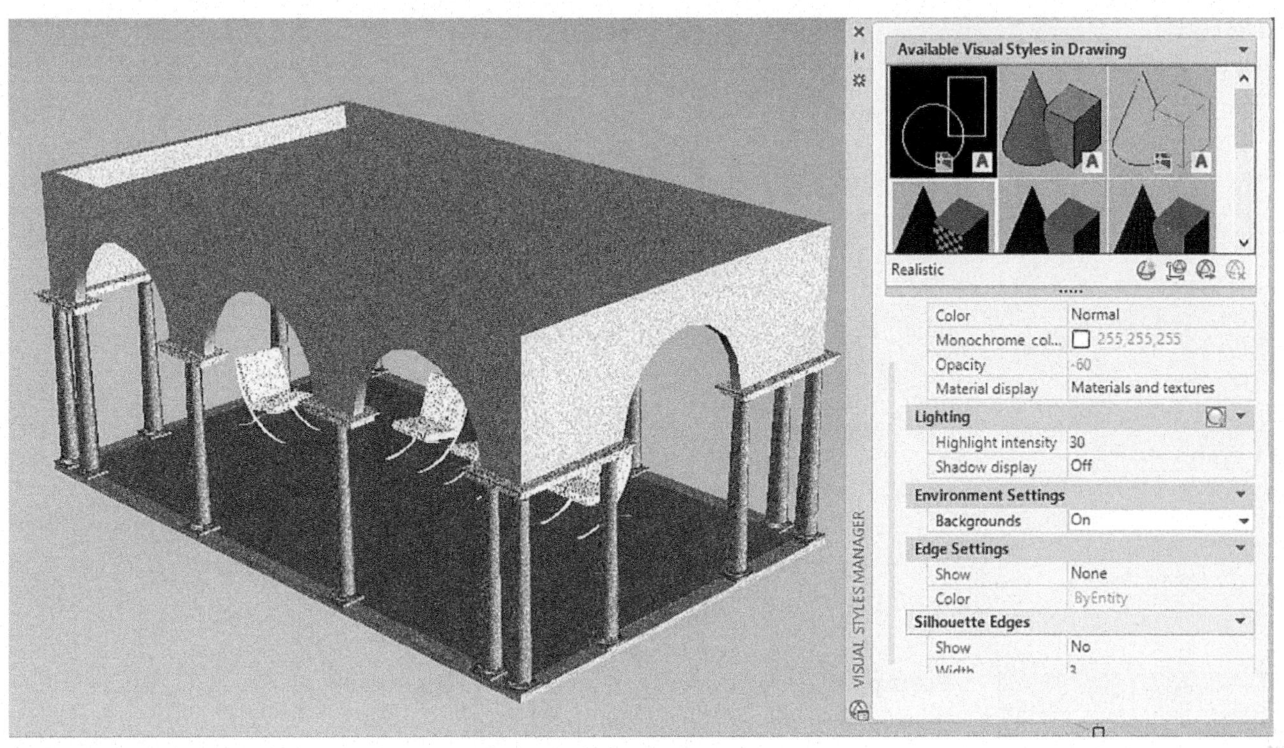

Figure 15-36
Realistic visual style

Step 9. Add distant lights using lines to locate the lights and targets.

1. With **ORTHO** on, use the **LINE** command to draw **30′** lines from the midpoints of the arches on the front and right side of the patio, as shown in Figure 15-37.
2. Draw a line from the midpoint of one side of the roof to the opposite side of the roof, and then draw a **30′** line straight up with **ORTHO** on.

Prompt	Response
Type a command:	Type **LIGHT <Enter>**. (You can also click **Distant Light** on the ribbon **Visualize** tab and skip the next prompt. A warning regarding default lighting may appear. If it does, click **Turn off the default lighting**.)
Enter light type [Point Spot Web Targetpoint Freespot freeweB Distant] <Freespot>:	Type **D <Enter>**
The **Lighting – Photometric Distant Lights** warning appears	Click **Allow Distant Lights**. You cannot see the effect of distant lights otherwise

Figure 15-37
Add lines for distant lights

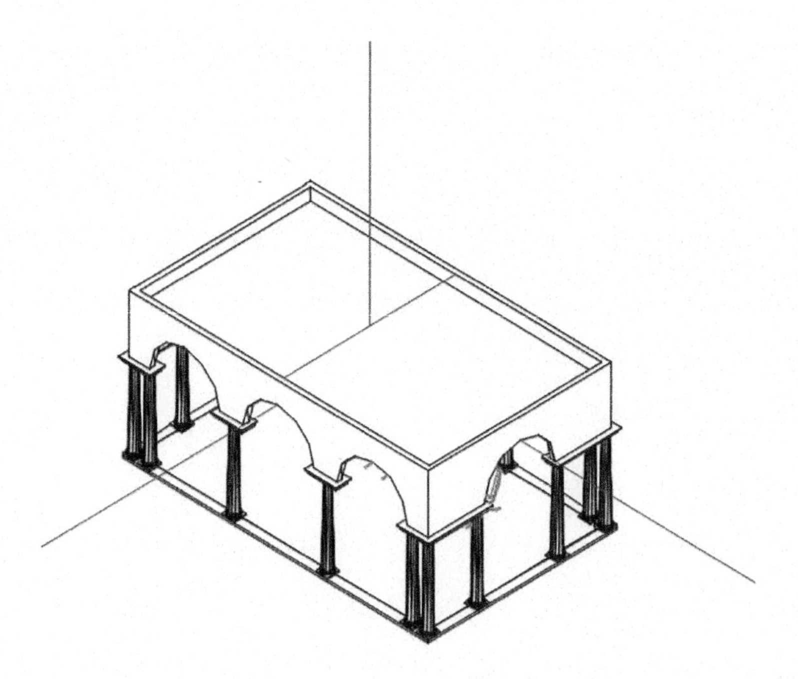

DISTANT LIGHT	
Ribbon/ Panel	Visualize/ Lights
Lights Toolbar:	
Menu Bar:	View/Render/ Light
Type a Command:	LIGHT

Prompt	**Response**
Specify light direction FROM <0,0,0> or [Vector]:	**Osnap-Endpoint**; click the end farthest from the model of one of the 30′ lines
Specify light direction TO <1,1,1>:	**Osnap-Endpoint**; click the other end of the same line
Enter an option to change [Name Intensity Status shadoW Color eXit] <eXit>:	Type **N <Enter>**
Enter light name <Distantlight1>:	**<Enter>** (to accept the name **Distantlight1**)
Enter an option to change [Name Intensity Status shadoW Color eXit] <eXit>:	**<Enter>**

1. Add two more distant lights at the ends of the other two 30′ lines pointed toward the model.
2. Erase the construction lines locating the distant lights.

Distant lights shine uniform parallel light rays in one direction only. The intensity of a distant light does not diminish over distance; it shines as brightly on each surface it strikes no matter how far away the surface is from the light. Distant lights are used to light the model uniformly. You can change the intensity of a distant light if you want all surfaces on that side to be lighter or darker.

Step 10. Add spotlights to shine on the chairs. You may find it easier to locate points if you change the visual style to **Wireframe**.

Prompt	**Response**
Type a command:	**Spot** (or type **SPOTLIGHT <Enter>**)
Specify source location <0,0,0>:	Click the inner endpoint of the long side of the L-shaped cornice on the right side of the model, as shown in Figure 15-38

Prompt	Response
Specify target location <0,0,-10>:	Using **Osnap-Endpoint,** click a point on the two chairs closest together

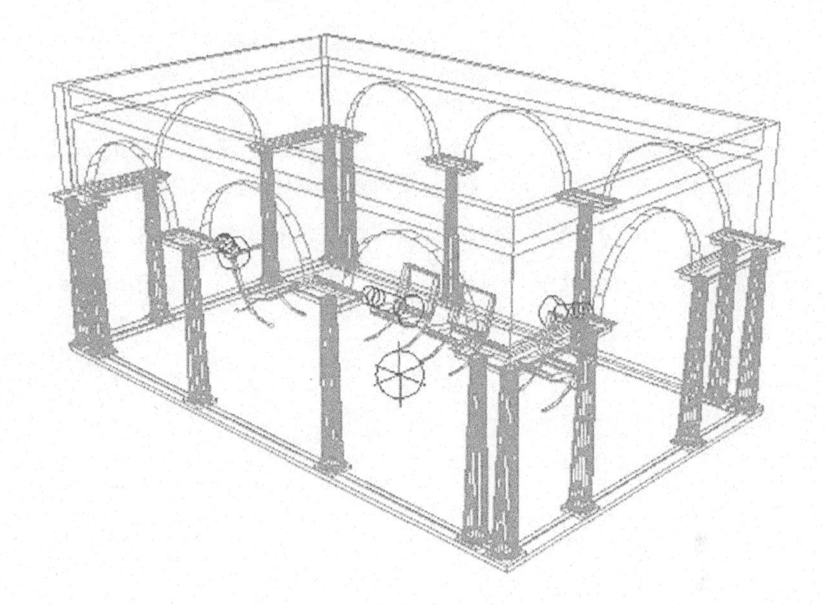

Figure 15-38
Locate spotlights and point lights

SPOTLIGHT	
Ribbon/ Panel	Visualize/ Lights
Lights Toolbar:	
Menu Bar:	View/ Render/Light
Type a Command:	LIGHT

Prompt	Response
Enter an option to change [Name Intensity Status Hotspot Falloff shadoW Attenuation Color eXit] <eXit>:	Type **N <Enter>**
Enter light name <Spotlight4>:	**<Enter>**
Enter an option to change [Name Intensity Status Hotspot Falloff shadoW Attenuation Color eXit] <eXit>:	**<Enter>**

1. Add two more spotlights on the cornices of the two single columns on the front pointing to points on the other two chairs, as shown in Figure 15-38. Name the lights **Spotlight5** and **Spotlight6**.

A spotlight shines light in the shape of a cone. You can control the direction of the spotlight and the size of the cone. The intensity of a spotlight decreases the farther it is from the object. Spotlights are used to light specific areas of the model.

Step 11. Add a point light near the center of the patio.

Prompt	Response
Type a command:	Type: **POINTLIGHT<Enter>**
Specify source location <0,0,0>:	**Osnap-Endpoint**; click a point near the center of the floor of the patio
Enter an option to change [Name Intensity Status shadoW Attenuation Color eXit] <eXit>:	Type **N <Enter>**
Enter light name <Pointlight7>:	**<Enter>**
Enter an option to change [Name Intensity Status shadoW Attenuation Color eXit] <eXit>:	**<Enter>**

A point light shines light in all directions. The intensity of a point light fades the farther the object is from the light unless attenuation is set to **None**. Point lights are used for general lighting.

Step 12. Turn on the **Sun** light and adjust it to a summer month at midday. Click **Sun Status: OFF** to turn it on. If you see an exposure settings warning, choose **Adjust exposure settings (recommended)**.

Step 13. Type **Orbit <Enter>** or click **Orbit** (**View** tab), and then right-click and click **Perspective** to change the view to a perspective view.

Step 14. Make advanced render settings.

SUN PROPERTIES	
Ribbon/ Panel	Visualize/ Sun & Location (slideout)
Lights Toolbar:	
Menu Bar:	View/ Render/Light
Type a Command:	SUN PROPERTIES

Prompt	**Response**
Type a command:	**Advanced Render Settings...** (or type **RPREF <Enter>**) to open the Render Presets Manager palette
The **Render Presets Manager** palette appears:	Set **Render in:** to **Window**. Set **Render Size:** to **800 x 600 px – SVGA.** Set **Current Preset:** to **High** (Figure 15-39) Close this palette Click **Ground shadow** on the **Visual Styles Manager** (on the **View** tab) to turn shadows on; close this palette

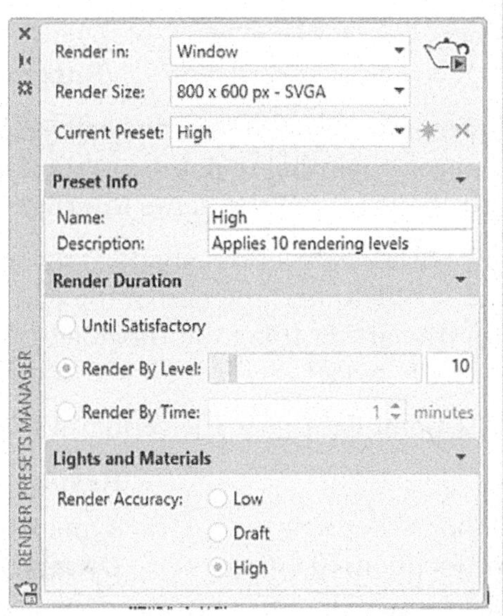

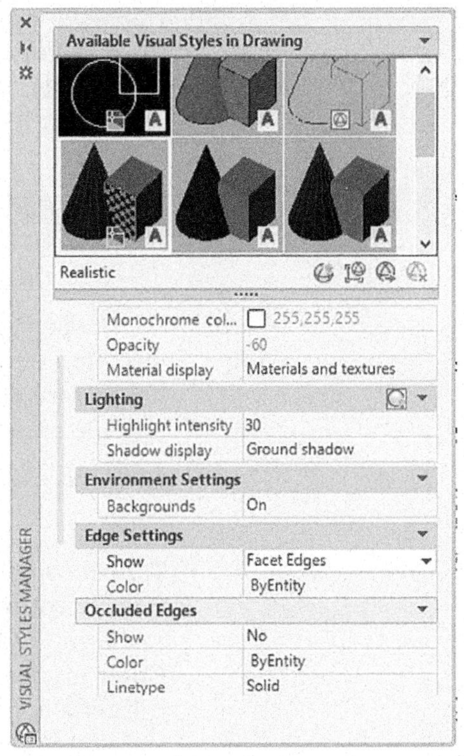

Figure 15-39
Render preset **High**, render to an SVGA window, turn ground shadow on

Step 15. Change the background to a color before rendering.

VIEW	
Ribbon/ Panel	Visualize/ Named Views
View Toolbar:	
Menu Bar:	View/Named Views...
Type a Command:	VIEW
Command Alias:	V

Prompt	Response
Type a command:	**Named Views...** (or type **V <Enter>**)
The **View Manager** appears:	Click **New...**
The **New View/Shot Properties** dialog box appears:	Type **VIEW 1** in the **View name:** input box. Click **OK**
The **View Manager** reappears:	In the **Background** area, click **<None>**, then Click **Gradient**
The **Background** dialog box appears (Figure 15-40):	Under **Gradient options**, click **Top Color**
The **Select Color** dialog box appears:	Click the **True Color** tab and change the **Color model** from **HSL** to **RGB**. In the **RGB Color**: box, type **155,255,255 <Enter>**. Click **OK**
The **Background** dialog box reappears:	Click **Bottom color:** and type **225,255,255 <Enter>**. Click **OK** Click **OK**

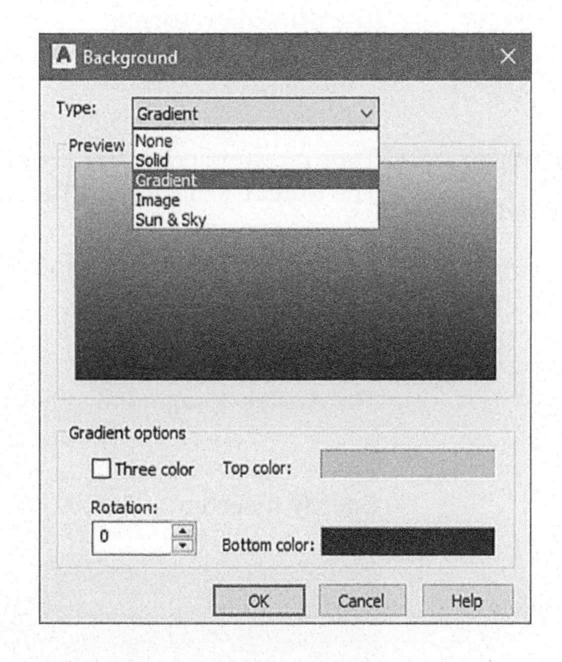

Figure 15-40
Background types

This list allows you to have a single-color solid background, a two- or three-color gradient background, an image file background, or a Sun & Sky background for your rendering.

Prompt	Response
	Close the list with **Solid** selected and click **OK**
The **New View/Shot Properties** dialog box appears:	Click **OK**

Prompt	Response
The **View Manager** appears:	Click **VIEW 1** in the list to the left Click **Set Current** Click **OK**

Step 16. Render the drawing and insert it into a paper space viewport.

Prompt	Response
Type a command:	**Render** (or type **RENDER <Enter>**)
The rendered model appears similar to Figure 15-41.	Click **File-Save...** (if you like what you see; if not, add, erase, or change the intensity of lights, replace materials, and so forth)
The **Render Output File** dialog box appears:	Type **CH15-EXERCISE3** (in the **File Name:** input box) Select **TIF** in the **Files of type** input box Save the file on a disk and make note of the disk and folder
The **TIFF Image Options** dialog box appears:	Click **OK** Close the **Render** window
The drawing returns:	Click **Layout1**
The active model space viewport appears:	Click any point on the viewport border and erase the viewport
Type a command:	**Insert - Raster Image Reference...**
The **Select Reference File** dialog box appears:	Click the file **CH15-EXERCISE3** (on the disk where you saved it); you may need to make **Files of type:** read **All Image files**) Click **Open**
The **Attach Image** dialog box appears:	Select the **Specify on Screen for Scale** check box Click **OK**
Specify insertion point <0,0>:	**<Enter>**

ATTACH RASTER IMAGE	
Ribbon/ Panel	Insert/ Reference
Insert Toolbar:	
Menu Bar:	Insert/Raster Image Reference
Type a Command:	IMAGEATTACH
Command Alias:	IAT

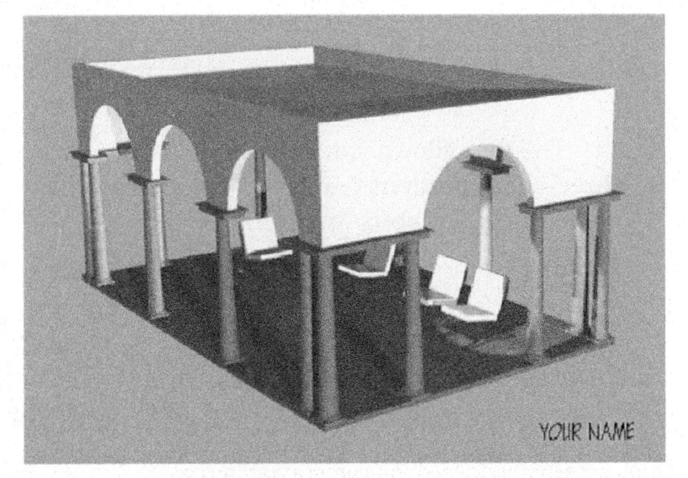

Figure 15-41
Exercise 15-3 complete

Prompt	Response
Specify scale factor or [Unit] <1>:	Drag the upper-right corner of the image to fill the viewport, then click to complete the command

The rendered image fills the viewport.

Step 17. Type your name **3/16″** high in the CityBlueprint font in the lower-right corner of the drawing.

Step 18. Save the drawing in two places.

Step 19. Plot the drawing to fit on an **8-1/2″ × 11″** sheet, landscape.

EXERCISE 15-4
Create a Walk-Through AVI File for the Rendered 3D Patio

CAMERA	
Ribbon/ Panel	Visualize/ Camera
View Toolbar:	
Menu Bar:	View/Create Camera
Type a Command:	CAMERA
Command Alias:	CAM

Step 1. Begin **CH15-EXERCISE4** on the hard drive or network drive by opening the existing drawing **CH15-EXERCISE3** and saving it as **CH15-EXERCISE4**.

Step 2. Make a new layer, name it **Path**, color white, and make the **Path** layer current.

Step 3. Split the screen into two vertical viewports and make the left viewport a plan view of the World UCS. (Type **UCS <Enter>**, press **<Enter>** again to accept **World** as the UCS, type **PLAN <Enter>**, and press **<Enter>** again to get the plan view of the World UCS.)

Step 4. Use the **Polyline** command to draw a path similar to Figure 15-42. The exact size and angle are not important.

Step 5. Make the settings for the camera.

Prompt	Response
Type a command:	**Create Camera** (or type **CAM <Enter>**)
Specify camera location:	Click **Osnap-Endpoint**. Click **P1→**, Figure 15-42

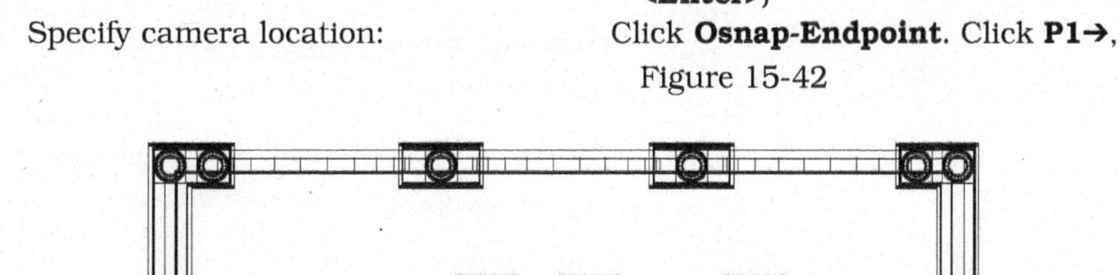

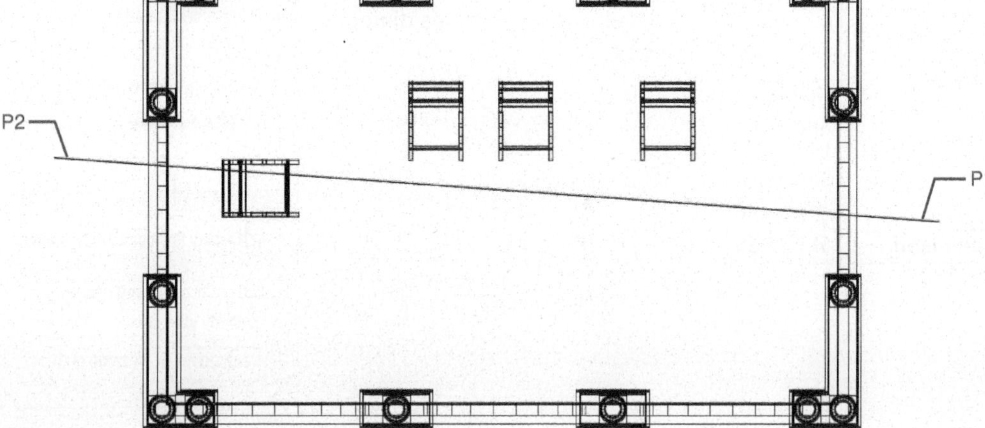

Figure 15-42
Draw a path and locate the camera and target

Prompt	Response
Specify target location:	Click **Osnap-Endpoint**, click **P2→**, (Figure 15-42)
Enter an option [? Name LOcation Height Target LEns Clipping View eXit] <eXit>:	Type **N** **<Enter>**
Enter name for new camera <Camera1>:	**<Enter>**
Enter an option [? Name LOcation Height Target LEns Clipping View eXit] <eXit>:	Type **H** **<Enter>**
Specify camera height <00>:	Type **6′** **<Enter>**
Enter an option [? Name LOcation Height Target LEns Clipping View eXit] <eXit>:	Type **V** **<Enter>**
Switch to camera view? [Yes No] <No>:	Type **Y** **<Enter>**

The camera view should be similar to Figure 15-43.

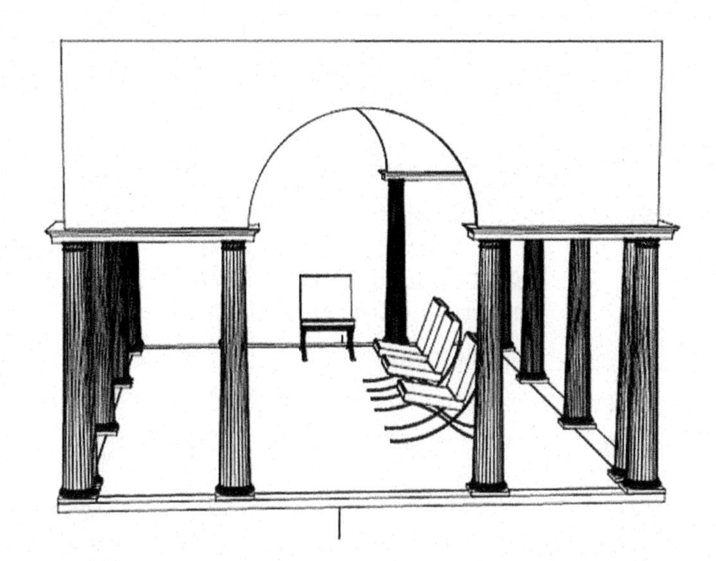

Figure 15-43
Camera view

WALK AND FLY SETTINGS	
Ribbon/Panel	Visualize/ Animations
3D Navigation Toolbar:	
Menu Bar:	View/Walk and Fly/ Walk and Fly Settings...
Type a Command:	WALKFLY-SETTINGS

Step 6. Type **WALK** (or **WALKFLYSETTINGS**) **<Enter>** to display the **Walk and Fly Settings** dialog box. Make the settings shown in Figure 15-44.

Figure 15-44
Walk and Fly Settings dialog box

3D walk: A program that allows you to walk through a model while controlling height and speed.

Step 7. Activate the ***3DWALK*** command and make an animation file.

Prompt	Response
Type a command:	**Walk** (or type **3DWALK <Enter>**)

To move forward, you can press and hold the up arrow or the **W** key. Similarly, use the left arrow or the **A** key to move left, down arrow or **S** to move back, and right arrow or **D** to move right. You can also hold down the left button on your mouse and move the display in the **Position Locator** palette, as shown in Figure 15-45.

Prompt	Response
Press **<Esc>** or **<Enter>** to exit: or right-click to display shortcut menu:	Hold your mouse over the drawing and right-click
The right-click menu appears:	Click **Animation Settings...**
The **Animation Settings** dialog box appears:	Make the settings as shown in Figure 15-46; click **OK**
	Hold your mouse over the drawing and right-click

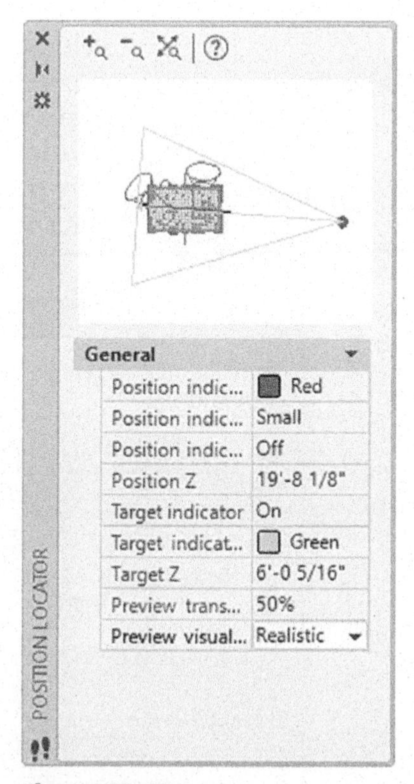

Figure 15-45
Use the mouse to move the camera through the walk

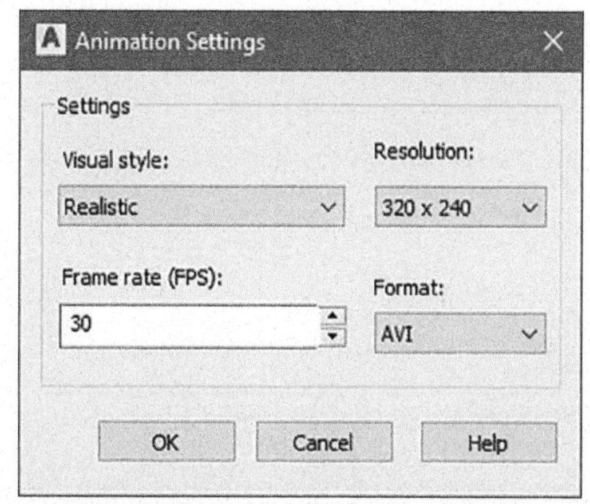

Figure 15-46
Animation Settings dialog box

Prompt	Response
The right-click menu appears:	Make any other necessary changes to your settings—you probably will not have to make any
	Click any point in the drawing to get rid of the right-click menu and right-click on the ribbon with the **Render** tab active to get the **Animations** panel
	Click **Animation Motion Path** on the ribbon
The **Motion Path Animation** dialog box appears:	In the **Camera** area, click **Path**
	Click the selection button and click the polyline path you drew in Step 4
	Click **OK**
The **Path Name** dialog box appears.	In the **Target** area, click **Point**
	Click the selection button, and then click point **P2** at the far end of the path
	Click **OK**
The **Point Name** dialog box appears.	Make the remaining settings in the **Motion Path Animation** dialog box shown in Figure 15-47
	Click **OK**

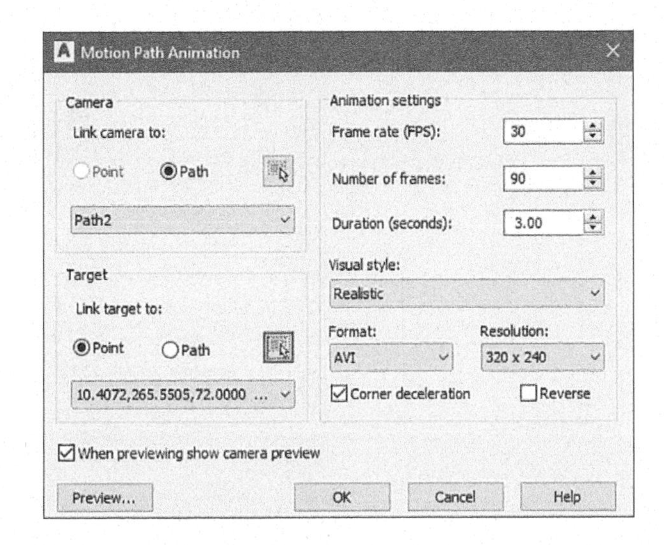

Figure 15-47
Animation Motion Path dialog box

Prompt	Response
The **Save As** dialog box (Figure 15-48) appears:	Type **Walk 1** in the **File name:** box
	Select **AVI Animation (*.avi)** in the **Files of type:** box
	Be sure to save the file on a disk and in a folder where you can find it

Figure 15-48
Save the animation file as an .avi file

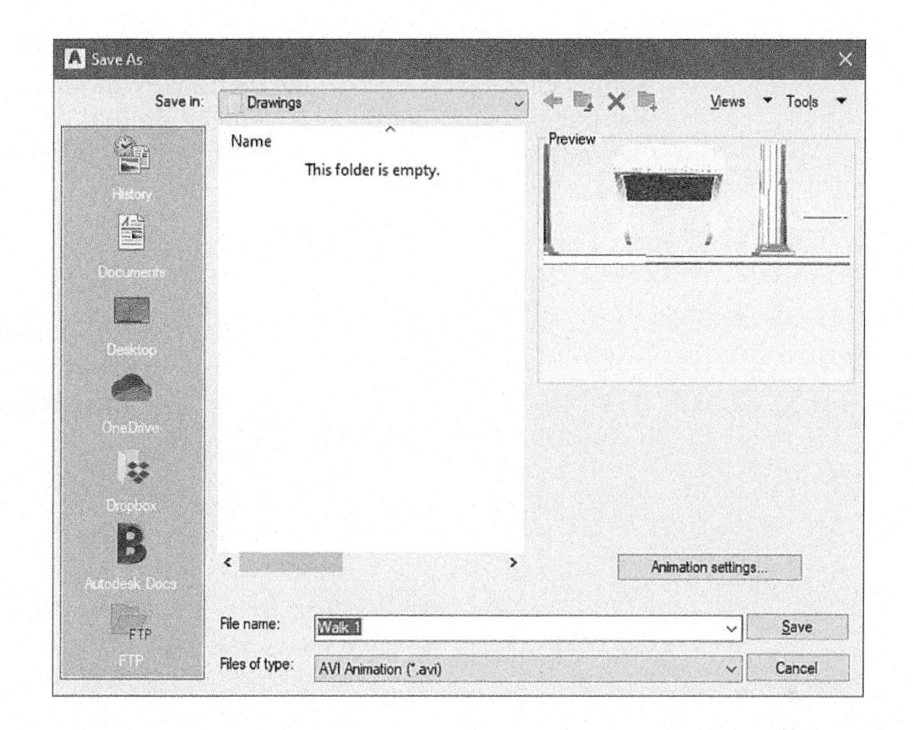

TIP

If the **Animations** panel is not visible, right-click on a blank spot on the ribbon and click **Show Panels - Animations**.

Step 8. Preview the animation file, and then exit the **3DWALK** command. Make changes if needed.

Prompt	**Response**
Press **<Esc>** or **<Enter>** to exit, or right-click to display shortcut menu:	Click **Play Animation**
The **Animation Preview** program appears:	View your animation (Figure 15-49) Close the **Animation Preview** box Press **<Esc>** or **<Enter>** to exit the **3DWALK** command

Figure 15-49
Play animation preview

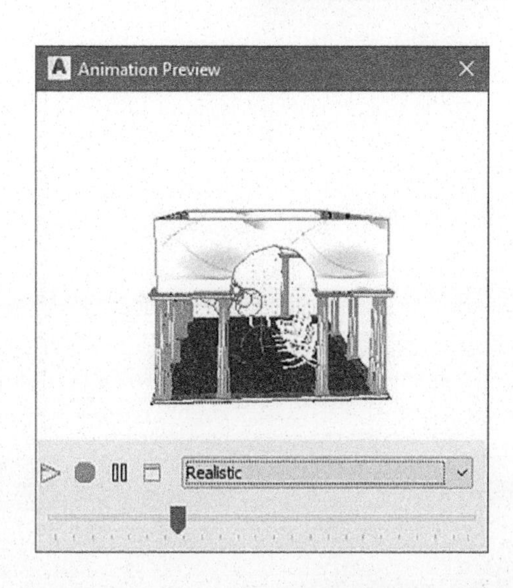

If you like your animation, keep it. You can view it outside of AutoCAD by simply clicking on the .avi file using Windows Explorer. If you want to make lighting or material changes, you can do that easily, and then do another 3D walk and save it with the same name to overwrite the original file.

Chapter Summary

This chapter provided you the information necessary to build solid models of rooms with furniture; attach materials; and light, render, and animate scenes. In addition, you learned to use the materials library, make a background, and build solid models on your own from sketches. Now you have the skills and information necessary to produce complex solid models with materials, render those models, and make animations such as walk-throughs.

Chapter Test Questions

Multiple Choice

Circle the correct answer.

1. Which type of light is used to lighten or darken all the images in the scene by the same amount?
   a. Sun   c. Distant
   b. Point   d. Spotlight
2. Which type of light shines in one direction in a cone shape?
   a. Sun   c. Distant
   b. Point   d. Spotlight
3. Which type of light can be used as an incandescent lightbulb?
   a. Web   c. Distant
   b. Point   d. Spotlight
4. Which type of light shines in a parallel direction?
   a. Sun   c. Distant
   b. Point   d. Spotlight
5. Which of the following lights is *not* on the **Render** tab of the ribbon?
   a. Point   c. Distant
   b. Blue Point   d. Sun
6. When you select a new distant light, which of the following is the first prompt AutoCAD gives you?
   a. Locate distant light
   b. Click: First Point
   c. Specify light direction TO<1,1,1>:
   d. Specify light direction FROM<0,0,0> or [Vector]:
7. Which command is used to obtain a perspective projection of a solid model?
   a. **Shade**   c. **Viewpoint**
   b. **3DOrbit**   d. **Viewport**

8. Which of the following opens the **Render Presets Manager** palette?
   a. **ARS**
   b. **Render**
   c. **Render Pref**
   d. **RPREF**
9. Which of the following is *not* a type of background that can be used in a rendering?
   a. Solid
   b. Image
   c. Gradient
   d. Picture
10. Which of the following is a panel on the **View** tab of the ribbon?
   a. **Model Viewports**
   b. **Viewport Tools**
   c. **Section**
   d. **Camera**

Matching

Write the correct answer on the line.

a. **Materials Browser** ______
b. **VPORTS** ______
c. **_POSITION LOCATOR** ______
d. **RPREF** ______
e. **VIEW** ______

1. A destination for a rendering
2. A palette that allows you to attach materials
3. A command that opens the **Render Presets Manager** palette
4. A command that can be used to make a background
5. A dialog box that allows you to move a camera along a path

True or False

Circle the correct answer.

1. **True or False:** Materials cannot be detached after they are attached to a model.
2. **True or False:** The material preview uses several types of objects so you can see what the material looks like.
3. **True or False:** The size of the material image in the **Materials Browser** cannot be changed.
4. **True or False:** The object must be selected first before the material is applied.
5. **True or False:** The **Animation** panel on the **Render** tab of the ribbon can be turned on or off.

List

1. Five options of the polyline edit (**Pedit**) command.
2. Five options of the **UCS** command.
3. Five prompts when executing the **Box** command.
4. Five aspects of improved rendering due to material selection.

5. Five lighting options in rendering.
6. Five tools under the **Visualize** tab/**Animation** panel.
7. Five tools under the **Mesh** tab/**Mesh** panel.
8. Five materials available in the **Materials Browser**.
9. Five settings from the **Advanced Render Settings** palette.
10. Five steps to get to perspective view through the **Orbit** command.

Questions

1. In what situations would you use rendered solid models?
2. In what situations would you use an animation?
3. Are rendered solid models and surfaces as effective as 2D drawings for construction?
4. When should you use perspective projection versus isometric projection?
5. Where can you get more materials for use on solid models if you need them?

Chapter Projects

Project 15-1: *Make a Solid Model of the Picnic Table Shown in the Sketch. Use Render Commands to Make a Photo-Realistic Rendering of the Solid Model* **[BASIC]**

1. Draw a solid model of the picnic table shown in Figure 15-64.

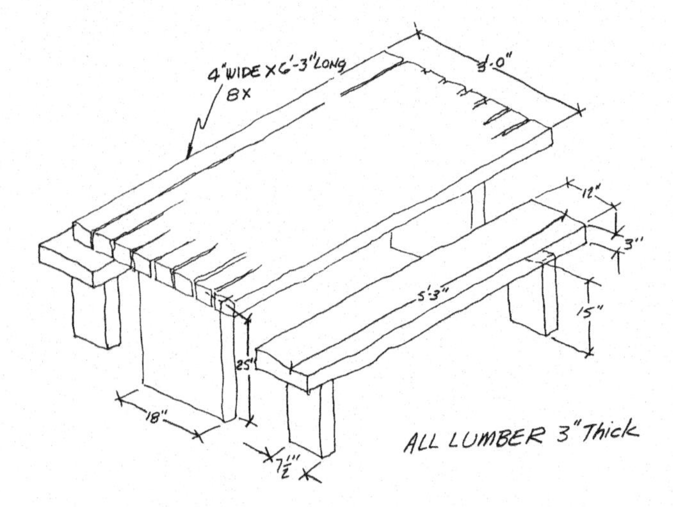

Figure 15-50
Project 15-1: Picnic table

2. Attach the same wooden-appearing material to the entire drawing.
3. Position distant, point, or spotlights to illuminate the picnic table. Adjust the sunlight so the picnic table shows well.
4. Change the view to **Perspective** projection.
5. Use the **RENDER** command to render the scene in a single viewport.
6. Print the rendered drawing centered on an **11″ × 8-1/2″** sheet.

Project 15-2: *Make a Solid Model of the Chair Shown in the Sketch. Use Render Commands to Make a Photo-Realistic Rendering of the Solid Model* **[INTERMEDIATE]**

1. Draw a solid model of the chair shown in Figure 15-65.

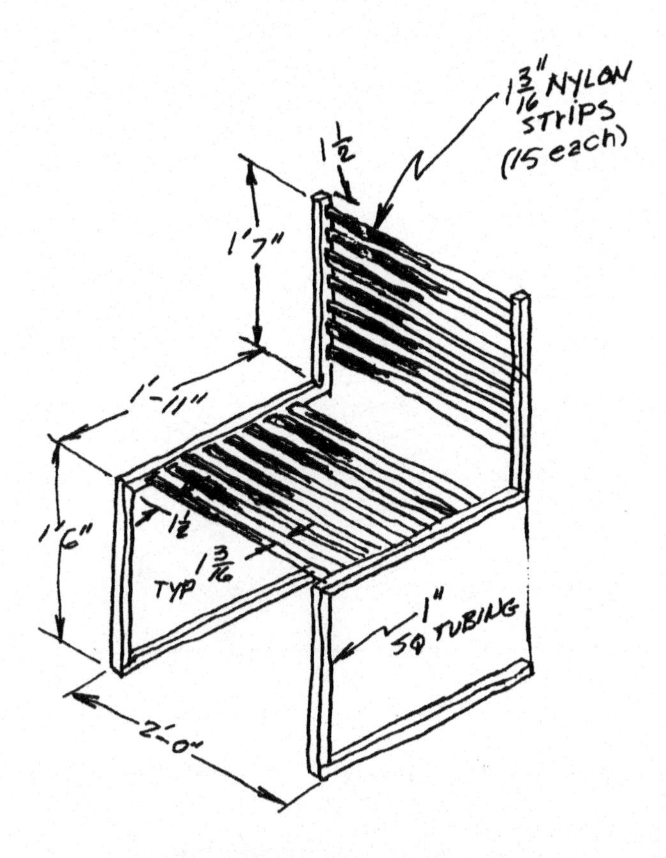

Figure 15-51
Project 15-2: Chair

2. Attach appropriate materials to the legs, back, and seat. Use one material for the legs and another for the back and seat.
3. Position distant, point, or spotlights to illuminate the chair. Adjust the sunlight so the chair shows well.
4. Change the view to **Perspective** projection.
5. Use the **RENDER** command to render the scene in a single viewport.
6. Print the rendered drawing centered on an **11" × 8-1/2"** sheet.

Project 15-3: *Make a Solid Model of the Table Shown in the Sketch. Use Render Commands to Make a Photo-Realistic Rendering of the Solid Model* **[ADVANCED]**

1. Draw a solid model of the table shown in Figure 15-66. Estimate any measurements not shown.

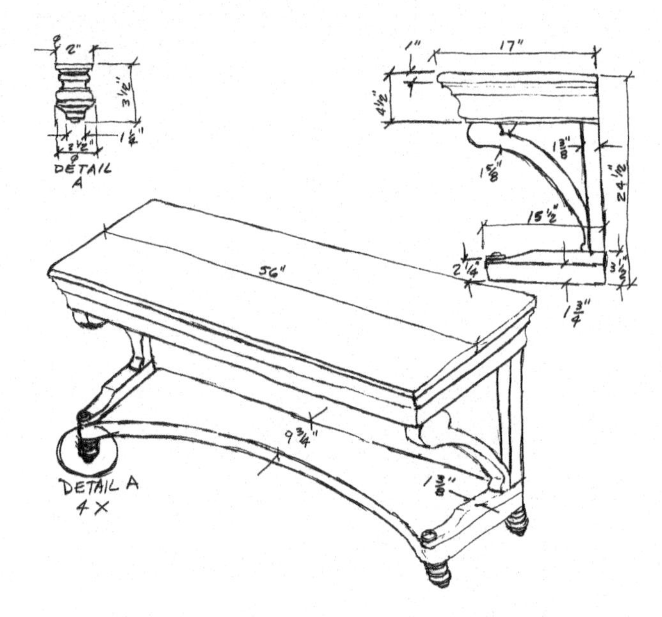

Figure 15-52
Project 15-3: Table

2. Attach the same wooden-appearing material to the entire drawing.
3. Position distant, point, or spotlights to illuminate the table. Adjust the sunlight so the table shows well.
4. Change the view to **Perspective** projection.
5. Use the **RENDER** command to render the scene in a single viewport.
6. Print the rendered drawing centered on an **11″ × 8-1/2″** sheet.

appendix A Keyboard Shortcuts

This appendix contains the AutoCAD command aliases (also called keyboard macros or keyboard shortcuts) that you can type to activate a command. Aliases and commands with a minus sign before the letters do not display a dialog box but instead show prompts at the command line.

To use the short form of a command rather than typing the full command name, use the letters and numbers in the left column to execute the command in the right column.

Command Alias	Command
3A	3DARRAY
3AL	3DALIGN
3DMIRROR	MIRROR3D
3DNavigate	3DWALK
3DO	3DORBIT
3DP	3DPRINT
3DPLOT	3DPRINT
3DW	3DWALK
3F	3DFACE
3M	3DMOVE
3P	3DPOLY
3R	3DROTATE
3S	3DSCALE
A	ARC
AA	AREA
AC	BACTION
ADC	ADCENTER
AECTOACAD	-ExportToAutoCAD

Command Alias	Command
AL	ALIGN
AP	APPLOAD
APLAY	ALLPLAY
AR	ARRAY
-AR	-ARRAY
-ARM	-ACTUSERMESSAGE
ARR	ACTRECORD
ARM	ACTUSERMESSAGE
ARU	ACTUSERINPUT
ARS	ACTSTOP
-ARS	-ACTSTOP
ATE	ATTEDIT
-ATE	-ATTEDIT
ATI	ATTIPEDIT
ATT	ATTDEF
-ATT	-ATTDEF
ATTE	-ATTEDIT
B	BLOCK
-B	-BLOCK
BC	BCLOSE
BE	BEDIT
BH	HATCH
BLENDSRF	SURFBLEND
BO	BOUNDARY
-BO	-BOUNDARY
BR	BREAK
BS	BSAVE
BVS	BVSTATE
C	CIRCLE
CAM	CAMERA
CBAR	CONSTRAINTBAR
CH	PROPERTIES
-CH	CHANGE
CHA	CHAMFER
CHK	CHECKSTANDARDS
CL	CENTERLINE
CLI	COMMANDLINE
CM	CENTERMARK
CMATTACH	COORDINATIONMODELATTACH
-CMATTACH	-COORDINATIONMODELATTACH
CO	COPY
COL	COLOR
COLOUR	COLOR
CONVTOMESH	MESHSMOOTH

Command Alias	Command
CP	COPY
CPARAM	BCPARAMETER
CREASE	MESHCREASE
CREATESOLID	SURFSCULPT
CSETTINGS	CONSTRAINTSETTINGS
CT	CTABLESTYLE
CUBE	NAVVCUBE
CURVATUREANALYSIS	ANALYSISCURVATURE
CYL	CYLINDER
D	DIMSTYLE
DAL	DIMALIGNED
DAN	DIMANGULAR
DAR	DIMARC
DELETE	ERASE
DBA	DIMBASELINE
DBC	DBCONNECT
DC	ADCENTER
DCE	DIMCENTER
DCENTER	ADCENTER
DCO	DIMCONTINUE
DCON	DIMCONSTRAINT
DDA	DIMDISASSOCIATE
DDEDIT	TEXTEDIT
DDI	DIMDIAMETER
DDPTYPE	PTYPE
DDVPOINT	VPOINT
DED	DIMEDIT
DELCON	DELCONSTRAINT
JOG	DIMJOGGED
DI	DIST
DIV	DIVIDE
DJL	DIMJOGLINE
DJO	DIMJOGGED
DL	DATALINK
DLI	DIMLINEAR
DLU	DATALINKUPDATE
DO	DONUT
DOR	DIMORDINATE
DOV	DIMOVERRIDE
DR	DRAWORDER
DRA	DIMRADIUS
DRAFTANGLEANALYSIS	ANALYSISDRAFTANGLE
DRE	DIMREASSOCIATE
DRM	DRAWINGRECOVERY

Command Alias	Command
DS	DSETTINGS
DST	DIMSTYLE
DT	TEXT
DV	DVIEW
DX	DATAEXTRACTION
E	ERASE
ED	TEXTEDIT
EL	ELLIPSE
EPDFSHX	PDFSHX
ER	EXTERNALREFERENCES
ESHOT	EDITSHOT
EX	EXTEND
EXIT	QUIT
EXP	EXPORT
EXT	EXTRUDE
EXTENDSRF	SURFEXTEND
F	FILLET
FI	FILTER
FILLETSRF	SURFFILLET
FREEPOINT	POINTLIGHT
FSHOT	FLATSHOT
G	GROUP
-G	-GROUP
GCON	GEOMCONSTRAINT
GD	GRADIENT
GENERATESECTION	SECTIONPLANETOBLOCK
GEO	GEOGRAPHICLOCATION
GR	DDGRIPS
H	HATCH
-H	-HATCH
HB	HATCHTOBACK
HE	HATCHEDIT
HI	HIDE
I	INSERT
-I	-INSERT
IAD	IMAGEADJUST
IAT	IMAGEATTACH
ICL	IMAGECLIP
IM	IMAGE
-IM	-IMAGE
IMP	IMPORT
IN	INTERSECT
INF	INTERFERE
INSERTCONTROLPOINT	CVADD

Command Alias	Command
QVLC	QVLAYOUTCLOSE
R	REDRAW
RA	REDRAWALL
RAPIDPROTOTYPE	3DPRINT
RC	RENDERCROP
RE	REGEN
REA	REGENALL
REBUILD	CVREBUILD
REC	RECTANG
REFINE	MESHREFINE
REG	REGION
REMOVECONTROLPOINT	CVREMOVE
REN	RENAME
-REN	-RENAME
REV	REVOLVE
RO	ROTATE
RP	RENDERPRESETS
RPR	RPREF
RR	RENDER
RW	RENDERWINDOW
S	STRETCH
SC	SCALE
SCR	SCRIPT
SE	DSETTINGS
SEC	SECTION
SET	SETVAR
SHA	SHADEMODE
SL	SLICE
SMOOTH	MESHSMOOTH
SN	SNAP
SO	SOLID
SP	SPELL
SPE	SPLINEDIT
SPL	SPLINE
SPLANE	SECTIONPLANE
SPLAY	SEQUENCEPLAY
SPLIT	MESHSPLIT
SSM	SHEETSET
ST	STYLE
STA	STANDARDS
SU	SUBTRACT
T	MTEXT
-T	-MTEXT
TA	TEXTALIGN

Command Alias	Command
TB	TABLE
TEDIT	TEXTEDIT
TH	THICKNESS
TI	TILEMODE
TO	TOOLBAR
TOL	TOLERANCE
TOR	TORUS
TP	TOOLPALETTES
TR	TRIM
TS	TABLESTYLE
UC	UCSMAN
UN	UNITS
-UN	-UNITS
UNCREASE	MESHUNCREASE
UNHIDE	UNISOLATEOBJECTS
UNI	UNION
UNISOLATE	UNISOLATEOBJECTS
V	VIEW
-V	-VIEW
VGO	VIEWGO
VP	VPOINT
-VP	-VPOINT
VPLAY	VIEWPLAY
VS	VSCURRENT
VSM	VISUALSTYLES
-VSM	-VISUALSTYLES
W	WBLOCK
-W	-WBLOCK
WE	WEDGE
WHEEL	NAVSWHEEL
X	EXPLODE
XA	XATTACH
XB	XBIND
-XB	-XBIND
XC	XCLIP
XL	XLINE
XR	XREF
-XR	-XREF
Z	ZOOM
ZEBRA	ANALYSISZEBRA

appendix B

Shortcut and Temporary Override Keys

This appendix contains a listing of the combination of keys that you can use to perform the described actions. For example, a shortcut key shown as **<Ctrl>+1** requires you to hold down the **<Ctrl>** key and press the **1** key while you continue to hold down the **<Ctrl>** key. This combination will display the **Properties** palette if it is not displayed or turn off the **Properties** palette if it is displayed.

<F1> through **<F12>** function keys are not used in combination with other keys to perform the stated functions. Just press the key.

<Ctrl>+A	Select all
<Ctrl>+B	Turns **SNAP** on and off
<Ctrl>+C	Copy to the Windows Clipboard
<Ctrl>+D	Turns on and off **Dynamic UCS (DUCS)**
<Ctrl>+E	Cycles through isoplanes in isometric drawing
<Ctrl>+F	Turns **OSNAP** on and off
<Ctrl>+G	Turns **GRID** on and off
<Ctrl>+H	Toggles **PICKSTYLE**
<Ctrl>+I	Turns coordinates on and off
<Ctrl>+J	Repeat the last command
<Ctrl>+K	Insert a hyperlink
<Ctrl>+L	Turns **ORTHO** on and off
<Ctrl>+N	Start a new drawing
<Ctrl>+O	Open an existing drawing
<Ctrl>+P	Plot or print the current drawing
<Ctrl>+Q	Exit the AutoCAD program
<Ctrl>+R	Cycles through the active viewports on the current layout
<Ctrl>+S	Save the current drawing

<Ctrl>+U	Turns **POLAR** on and off
<Ctrl>+V	Paste from the Windows Clipboard
<Ctrl>+X	Cut to the Windows Clipboard
<Ctrl>+Y	Redo last action
<Ctrl>+Z	Undo last action
<Ctrl>+<Shift>+C	Copy with base point (COPYBASE command)
<Ctrl>+<Shift>+I	Toggles **Infer Constraints**
<Ctrl>+<Shift>+P	Turns on and off **Quick Properties**
<Ctrl>+<Shift>+S	**Opens Save As** dialog box
<Ctrl>+<Shift>+<Tab>	Switch to previous drawing
<Ctrl>+<Shift>+V	Paste as block (PASTEBLOCK command)
<Ctrl>+0	Toggles **Clean Screen**
<Ctrl>+1	Displays and closes the **Properties** palette
<Ctrl>+2	Displays and closes the **DesignCenter**
<Ctrl>+3	Displays and closes the **Tool Palettes**
<Ctrl>+4	Displays and closes the **Sheet Set Manager**
<Ctrl>+6	Displays and closes the **dbConnect Manager**
<Ctrl>+7	Displays and closes the **Markup Set Manager**
<Ctrl>+8	Displays **QuickCalculator**
<Ctrl>+9	Displays and closes the command line
<F1>	Displays and closes Help
<F2>	Displays and closes the text window
<F3>	Turns **OSNAP** on and off
<F4>	Turns **3DOSNAP** on and off
<F5>	Cycles through isoplanes in isometric drawing
<F6>	Turns **Dynamic UCS** on and off (**DUCS**)
<F7>	Turns **GRID** on and off
<F8>	Turns **ORTHO** on and off
<F9>	Turns **SNAP** on and off
<F10>	Turns **POLAR** on and off
<F11>	Turns **OTRACK** on and off
<F12>	Turns **Dynamic Input (DYN)** on and off

glossary

3D walk: A command that allows you to walk through a model controlling height and speed.

absolute coordinates: Coordinate values measured from an origin point or 0,0 point in the drawing.

annotation scale: A setting that controls how text and other annotative objects appear on the drawing.

annotative: A property that belongs to objects, such as text, blocks, dimensions, and hatch patterns, that are commonly used to annotate drawings.

annotative text: Text that has a property that allows it to change as the scale of the entire drawing changes.

array: A circular, rectangular, 2D, or 3D path-based pattern of objects.

attribute: A label that attaches data to a block. It consists of a tag and a value.

attribute definition: Text that is included in a block to store data. Attribute definition values can be predefined or specified when the block is inserted. Data from attributes can be extracted from a drawing and inserted into tables or other files.

axonometric: Forms of 2D drawing that represent 3D objects. The three axonometric drawing forms are isometric, dimetric, and trimetric. Isometric projection tools are included in AutoCAD.

block definition: A user-defined collection of drawing objects (and often attributes) that are assigned a base point and a name. A block can be inserted into a drawing multiple times. When a block is updated, all blocks in the drawing with the same name are automatically updated.

Cartesian coordinate system: A coordinate system that has three axes, x, y, and z. The x-axis value is stated first and measures left to right horizontally. The y-axis value is stated second and measures from bottom to top vertically. The z-axis value is stated third and is used in three-dimensional modeling.

chamfer: An angle (usually 45°) formed at a corner.

color-dependent plot style: A plot style that is organized by the AutoCAD Color Index (ACI) number. Color-dependent plot styles are automatically assigned by the color of the AutoCAD object and can be changed to plot any color specified. Color-dependent plot styles are often made to print all colors black.

command line window: The text area above the status bar used for keyboard input and prompts, and where AutoCAD displays messages. Often referred to as the command line or the command prompt.

data extraction: A method of extracting data such as attributes from drawings into a table or other file.

DesignCenter: A palette that allows you to use existing blocks that AutoCAD has provided, or blocks or other named objects that you have created in other drawings. Drag and drop blocks; layers; linetypes; layouts; dimensions; text and multileader styles; and external references from any existing drawing.

dimension variables: A set of numeric values, text strings, and settings that control dimension features.

direct distance entry: The process of specifying a second point by first moving the cursor to indicate direction and then entering a distance.

drawing limits: The user-defined rectangular area of the drawing covered by lines or dots (when specified) when the grid is on.

drawing scale: The scale at which drawings are made.
drawing template: A drawing used to ensure consistency by providing standard styles and settings.
dynamic block: The user-defined collection of drawing objects that can be changed without exploding the block.
external reference (xref): A drawing file that is inserted into another drawing. External references have the advantage that the primary drawing always contains the most recent version of the external reference. External references can also include raster images, PDFs, and Microstation DGN files.
font: A distinctive set of letters, numbers, punctuation marks, and symbols.
From: A command modifier that locates a base point and then allows you to locate an offset point from the base point.
gradient hatch: A method of rendering 2D drawings that is similar to air-brush rendering.
grid: An area consisting of evenly spaced dots or lines to aid drawing. The grid is adjustable. The grid lines or dots do not plot.
grips: Small squares, rectangles, and triangles that appear on objects you select when no command is active. After selecting the grip, you can move, stretch, rotate, scale, copy, add a vertex, convert a line to an arc, convert an arc to a line, or mirror the objects without entering commands.
hatch: The process of filling in a closed area with a pattern. Hatching can consist of solid-filled areas, gradient-filled areas, or areas filled with patterns of lines, dots, or other objects.
helix: An open 2D or 3D spiral.
isometric: A 2D axonometric drawing method that is used to give the appearance of three dimensions.
layer: A group of drawing objects created on transparent "overlays" on a drawing. Layers can be viewed individually or in combination with other layers. Layers can be turned on or off, frozen or thawed, plotted or not plotted, and filtered.
layout: A two-dimensional page setup made in paper space that represents the paper size and what the drawing will look like when it is plotted. Multiple layouts can be created for each drawing.
lights: Objects used in the **RENDER** command to light scenes. Five types of lights can be used to render a scene: sun, point, distant, spot, and photometric, also called *web lights.*
linetype: How a line, arc, polyline, circle, or other item is displayed. For example, a continuous line has a different linetype than a hidden line.
lineweight: A width value that can be assigned to objects such as lines, arcs, polylines, circles, and many other objects that contain features that have width.
loft: A method of making a solid or surface by drawing it through a set of two or more cross-section curves. The cross sections make the profile (shape) of the resulting solid or surface.
materials: Items that can be attached to solid shapes to give those shapes the appearance of metal, wood, brick, granite, textiles, or any one of a number of other materials. Materials are used in the **RENDER** command to make a scene.
menu bar: The bar containing menus displayed when the **Quick Access** toolbar customization button is pressed; contains commonly used commands.
mesh model: A tessellated object type that is defined by faces, edges, and vertices. Mesh models can be smoothed to achieve a more rounded appearance and creased to introduce ridges.
Midpoint: An **Osnap** mode that helps you snap to the midpoint of a line or arc.
model: A two- or three-dimensional object.
model space: One of the two primary spaces in which objects are made.
multileader: A leader created as a single AutoCAD object. Multileaders can be customized to show index numbers inside circles, hexagons, and other polygons.
multiline: A method of drawing as many as 16 lines at the same time with or without end caps.
MVIEW: A command that operates only when **TILEMODE** is set to 0 (OFF) and that is used to make and control viewport displays in model space and paper space.
MVSETUP: A command that allows you to set units, scale, and paper size when **TILEMODE** is on. When **TILEMODE** is off, **MVSETUP** allows you to align, create, and scale viewports and insert title blocks.
named plot style: A plot style that is organized by a user-defined name. Named plot styles can be assigned to AutoCAD layers or to individual drawing objects.
navigation bar: An area in the AutoCAD user interface that contains navigation tools that are common across multiple Autodesk programs. The unified navigation tools include Autodesk ViewCube, SteeringWheels, ShowMotion, and 3Dconnexion.
Node: An **Osnap** mode that helps you snap to a point entity.
object snap tracking: A setting that allows you to specify points by hovering your pointing device over Osnap points.
Orbit: A command that allows you to obtain a three-dimensional view in the active viewport.

Ortho: A setting that limits pointing device input to horizontal or vertical (relative to the current snap angle and the user coordinate system).

Osnap: An abbreviation of *object snap*, which specifies a snap point at an exact location on an object.

page setup: A collection of plot settings that are applied to a drawing layout. Page setups can be used and shared among multiple drawings.

paper space: One of two spaces in which objects are made or documented. Paper space is used for making a finished layout for printing or plotting. Often, drawings are restored in paper space in a drawing title block and border.

Path Array: A command that allows you to make multiple copies along a 2D or 3D path.

PDF (portable document format) files: Files of drawings that are made using the **Plot** dialog box. These files can be opened and read without the use of the AutoCAD program.

plot style: An object property that makes a collection of settings for color, dithering, grayscale, pen assignments, screening, linetype, lineweight, end styles, join styles, and fill styles. Plot styles are used at plot time.

plot style table: A collection of plot styles. Plot styles are made using plot style tables. They apply to objects only when the plot style table is attached to a layout or viewport.

point filters: A method of entering a point by which the X, Y, and Z coordinates are given in separate stages. Any one of the three coordinates can be first, second, or third.

Polar: The option of the **ARRAY** command that allows you to make multiple copies of an object in a circular array.

polar coordinates: Coordinate values that are entered relative to the last point picked. They are typed starting with an @ followed by a distance and angle of direction; the angle is preceded by a < sign.

polar tracking: A means of specifying points (similar to using **ORTHO** to constrain screen pointing motion) using your own increment angle.

POLYGON: Command that draws a polygon with 3 to 1024 sides.

polyline: A continuous line or arc composed of one or more segments, the width of which can be changed.

properties: All the attributes of an object such as color, layer, linetype, linetype scale, lineweight, and thickness.

Quick View: A command allowing you to preview and switch between open drawings and layouts.

raster image: An image consisting of dots that can be inserted into AutoCAD.

Rectangular Array: A command that allows you to make multiple copies in a rectangular pattern.

reflected ceiling plan: A drawing showing all the lighting symbols and other items such as exit signs that attach to the ceiling in their correct locations in the space. The plan also shows all the switching symbols needed to turn the lights on and off.

relative coordinates: Coordinates specified in relation to a previous point picked. Relative coordinates are entered by typing @ followed by the X and Y coordinates. For example, after a point is entered to start a line, typing and entering @1,0 will draw the line 10 in the X direction and 00 in the Y direction.

Render: A program that uses objects, lighting, and materials to obtain a realistic view of a model.

ribbon: The user interface below the **Quick Access** toolbar that comprises tabs and panels with flyouts used to access the commands for both 2D drawing and annotation and 3D modeling, viewing, and rendering.

sans serif: Any text font that does not contain serifs. Serifs are the small features at the ends of letters and numbers.

sheet set: An organized and named collection of sheets made from multiple drawing files.

SOLIDEDIT: A program allowing you to change solid objects by extruding, moving, rotating, offsetting, tapering, copying, coloring, separating, shelling, cleaning, checking, or deleting features such as holes, surfaces, and edges.

SteeringWheels: Icons that are divided into sections. Each section on the SteeringWheel is a tool that allows you to pan, zoom, or show the motion of the current view of the model.

surface model: A 3D model that is a thin shell. Surface models are formed using the commands **Surface Loft**, **Surface Sweep**, **Surface Offset**, **Surface Revolve**, **Surface Fillet**, **Surface Extend**, **Surface Trim** and **Untrim**, and **Surface Sculpt**.

table: A tool to make tables such as door schedules, tables for drawing sets, tabular drawings, window schedules, and similar items. Tables often contain information about the materials needed for the construction of the building. In manufacturing, they are often referred to as bills of materials or parts lists.

TILEMODE: A system variable that controls whether viewports can be made as layout viewports that can be moved or resized or as model viewports that lie side by side and do not overlap. If you are working in the **Model** tab, TILEMODE = 1. If you are working in any layout tab, TILEMODE = 0.

toolbar: A graphical interface containing icons that represent commands.

tracking: A means of reducing if not eliminating the number of construction lines you draw by specifying points.

transparency: A setting that makes an object more or less transparent.

transparent command: A command that can be used while another command is in progress.

units: A setting referring to drawing units. For example, an inch is a drawing unit. Architectural units utilize feet and fractional units. Decimal, fractional, engineering, and scientific units are also available in the **Drawing Units** dialog box.

user coordinate system: A user-defined variation of the world coordinate system. Variations in the coordinate system range from moving the default drawing origin (0,0,0) to another location to changing orientations for the x-, y-, and z-axes. You can rotate the world coordinate system on any axis to make a UCS with a different two-dimensional XY plane.

user coordinate system icon: An icon showing the orientation of the x-, y-, and z-axes of the current coordinate system. In two-dimensional drawings only the x- and y-axes are used. The UCS icon is located at the origin of the current UCS (0,0).

user interface: All the elements such as the AutoCAD screen that make up the interface between the user and the AutoCAD program.

ViewCube: A 3D viewing tool that can be used to switch from one view of a model to another.

viewports: Windows in either model space or paper space. Two types of viewports are available in AutoCAD, tiled and nontiled. Tiled viewports are those that exist in model space with **TILEMODE** on. Nontiled viewports exist in either model space or paper space with **TILEMODE** off.

workspace: A specific arrangement of user interface elements including their contents, properties, display status, and locations. Workspaces allow the user to quickly switch between specific arrangements of menus, toolbars, and dockable windows as well as many other settings previously specified.

zoom: The process of moving around the drawing. Zooming in shows you a close-up view of a drawing area. Zooming out shows you a larger viewing area.

Index

SYMBOLS

@ (at symbol), as second break point, 134

NUMBERS

2 Point option (CIRCLE command), 62
3 Point option (CIRCLE command), 63
3D modeling, types of, 547. *See also* solid modeling
3D Views menu options, 549–551
3D walk, 622
3DORBIT command, 597
3DROTATE command, 565–566
3-point method (drawing arcs), 74

A

absolute coordinates
- defined, 56
- drawing lines with, 56

ADCENTER command, 287, 436
Add option (selecting objects), 71
Add Vertex grip, 149–150
adding leaders to multileaders, 367–368
AIMLEADEREDITADD command, 367
Align Text option (editing dimensions), 322
Aligned option (linear dimensions), 315
aligning
- multileaders, 362
- plans in viewports, 492–494

All option (selecting objects), 71
ANGDIR system variable, 118
Angle option (CHAMFER command), 115
angles
- extruding structural angles, 560–561
- isometric drawing, 521–523

animations, creating, 621–626
annotation scale, 50
- defined, 50
- for linear dimensions, 309–310
- in Plot dialog box, 88
- in Text Style dialog box, 282–284
- tools for, 21

annotative text, 88, 187, 282–284, 310
apertures in Osnap modes, 130
application menu commands, 7–8
ARC command, 74
Arc option (polylines), 145–147
arcs, drawing, 74–77
- 3-point method, 74
- Continue method, 77
- Start, Center, Angle method, 76
- Start, Center, End method, 76
- Start, Center, Length method, 76
- Start, End, Angle method, 77
- Start, End, Direction method, 77
- Start, End, Radius method, 77

AREA command, 326
ARRAY command, 138, 152, 258–260
ARRAYEDIT command, 141
ARRAYPATH command, 141
ARRAYRECT command, 258–260
arrays
- creating, 138–141
- editing, 141
- polar, 152–155

artificial lights, 608–609
associative arrays, 141
associative dimensions, 319–321
at symbol (@), as second break point, 134
attaching external references (xrefs), 456, 457–462
ATTDEF command, 403
ATTDISP command, 422
ATTEDIT command, 420
attributes
- adding to furniture symbols, 403–413
- constant, 408–410
- defined, 403
- editing, 413–414, 418–422
- extracting, 424–429
- inserting with furniture symbols into drawings, 416
- moving, 413
- redefining blocks, 422–424
- saving furniture symbols with, 414
- synchronizing, 423–424
- variable, 410–412
- verify, 412–413
- visibility of, 422

ATTSYNC command, 423
AutoCAD
- calculators, 329–330
- closing, 25
- Help system, 24–25
- user interface. *See* user interface

AutoCAD DesignCenter, 287–290, 436–445
- buttons, 437–438
- defined, 436
- minimizing, 444
- tabs, 436–437

Autodesk Docs, 2
automatic numbering for text, 202
Axis, End method (drawing ellipses), 77
axonometric drawing, 509
- defined, 509
- types of, 509

B

background color in photo-realistic rendering, 619–620
BASE command, 459
Baseline option (linear dimensions), 315–318
basic 3D modeling, 547
BATTMAN command, 423
BEDIT command, 445
beveling corners, 114–116
binding external reference subsets, 457
Block Attribute Manager, 423
BLOCK command, 275
Block Editor, creating dynamic blocks, 445–456
blocks, 273–285
- advantages, 284–285
- creating library of, 276–278
- defining drawings as, 273–276
- dynamic, creating, 445–456
- exploding, 280
- inserting, 278–282, 284
- redefining, 422–424
- scaling, 281–282
- title block in presentations, 487–490, 498–499
- visibility, 452–454

boundaries for hatching
- options, 378, 380
- Pick Points boundary method, 373–376
- preparing, 371–372
- Select Objects boundary method, 372–373

bowls, creating, 575
BOX command, 554
boxes
- chamfering/filleting edges, 566
- drawing, 555

BREAK command, 133, 371
BREAKATPOINT command, 371–372

C

CAL command, 329–330
calculating total square footage, 326–330
calculators in AutoCAD, 329–330
CAMERA command, 621
canceling commands, 37, 56
Cartesian coordinate system, 37–38
Center, Diameter option (CIRCLE command), 62
Center, Radius option (CIRCLE command), 61–62
Center method (drawing ellipses), 79
centering plots, 89
- with four viewports, 246
- with one viewport, 230–232
- with two viewports, 237–239

centerline, isometric ellipses on, 518–520
chairs for advanced modeling, drawing, 594–597
chairs in conference rooms, drawing, 162–164
CHAMFER command, 114
chamfering
- corners, 114–116
- solid edges, 566–568

changing. *See* editing
CIRCLE command, 60
circles
- drawing, 60–63
  - 2 Point option, 62
  - 3 Point option, 63
  - Center, Diameter option, 62
  - Center, Radius option, 61–62
  - solid rings/circles, 79–80
  - TTR option, 63
- as ellipses in isometric drawing, 513–515
- extruding, 558
- with multileaders, 357

Clean Screen tool, 22
Close option (polylines), 147
closing AutoCAD, 25
collecting multileaders, 366
color-dependent plot styles, 226
- creating, 226–228
- defined, 225

colors
- for layers, 223–224
  - assigning, 44
- selecting, 270–271

columns, drawing, 257–260
command history, 82–83
command line window, 8, 11
commands
- for advanced modeling, 609
- on application menu, 7–8
- canceling, 37, 56
- command line window, 11
- for composite solids, 548
- flyouts, 10
- From modifier, 133–168
- previewing, 165–166
- for primitives, 548
- Quick Access toolbar, 11–12
- on ribbon, 8–9
- selecting, 8
- setting dimension variables, 303
- tooltips, 10
- transparent, 66–67
- undoing/redoing, 54–56, 73–74

composite solids
commands for, 548
HIDE command, 571
initial drawings for example, 568–570
intersecting, 577–582
joining with UNION command, 570
lofting, 574–575
Planar Surface command, 575–576
polysolids, 576–577
subtracting, 570–571
sweeping, 571–574
CONE command, 556
cones, drawing, 556
conference rooms, drawing
chairs in, 162–164
chamfer corners, 114–116
copying objects, 117–118
curved conference rooms
Add Vertex grip, 149–150
Convert to Arc grip, 151–152
initial settings, 144–145
polar arrays, 152–155
with polygons, 148–149
with polylines, 145–147
dividing objects, 120–121
drawing template for, 105–107
filleting for chairs, 116–117
furniture in, 164–165
ID points, 109–110
initial settings, 103–105
measuring objects, 121
mirroring objects, 124–127
object snap modes, 117–118, 122–123, 127–130
points, 119–120
with polar tracking, 155–165
with polylines, 107–109
rectangles for doors/furniture, 111–113
rotating objects, 118–119
trimming objects, 111
constant attributes, 408–410
Continue method (drawing arcs), 77
Continue option (linear dimensions), 311–312
continuous lines, drawing, 56
Convert to Arc grip, 151–152
coordinates. *See also* UCS (user coordinate system)
absolute, drawing lines with, 56
Cartesian coordinate system, 37–38
polar, drawing lines with, 58–59
relative, drawing lines with, 57–58
COPY command, 117
copying
objects
multiple copies along path, 138–141, 152–155
with object snap modes, 117–118, 123
in rectangular pattern, 258–260
viewports, 237
corners
beveling, 114–116
filleting, 116–117
rounded with isometric ellipses, 520–521
Create Layout Wizard, 486–487
Crossing Window option (selecting objects), 71
cross-sectional areas, lofting with, 574–575
cubes, isometric, 513–515
current layer, 272
curved conference rooms, drawing
Add Vertex grip, 149–150
Convert to Arc grip, 151–152
initial settings, 144–145
polar arrays, 152–155
with polygons, 148–149
with polylines, 145–147
customizing. *See also* editing
drawing window, 5–7
grid, 38–40
linetypes, 63
lineweights, 46–48
mouse, 51
Quick Access toolbar, 12–13
ribbon, 9
status bar, 60
workspaces, 23–24
CYLINDER command, 557
cylinders
chamfering/filleting edges, 567–568
drawing, 557

D

Data Extraction wizard, 425–429
DATAEXTRACTION command, 425
default drawing template, 184
Defpoints layer, 322–323
deleting layers, 50
deselecting all layers, 491
DesignCenter, 287–290, 436–445
buttons, 437–438
defined, 436
minimizing, 444
tabs, 436–437
Dialog Box Launcher, 9
dialog boxes, opening, 9–10
DIMALIGNED command, 315
DIMASSOC dimension variable, 319–321
DIMBREAK command, 318
DIMCONTINUE command, 312
DIMEDIT/Oblique command, 321
dimension breaks, 318
Dimension Style Manager dialog box, 304–309
dimension variables, 298–301
defined, 298
DIMASSOC, 319–321
setting, 303–309
dimensions
drawing templates with, 310
editing, 319–326
Align Text option, 322
Defpoints layer, 322–323
DIMASSOC dimension variable, 319–321
with grips, 323–324
Match Properties command, 323
Oblique option, 321–322
Override option, 322
Properties palette, 323
revision clouds, 324–326
Update option, 322
in isometric drawing, 532
linear, 301–319
adjusting spacing, 318–319
Aligned option, 315
annotation scale, 309–310
Baseline option, 315–318
Continue option, 311–312
dimension breaks, 318
scaling, 310
setting dimension variables, 303–309
total square footage, calculating, 326–330
types of, 297–298
dimetric drawing, 509
DIMLINEAR command, 311
DIMOVERRIDE command, 322
DIMSPACE command, 318
DIMSTYLE command, 304
DIMSTYLE/Apply command, 322
DIMTEDIT command, 322
direct distance entry
defined, 59
drawing lines with, 59
displaying. *See* viewing
DISTANCE command, 141
distances, measuring, 141–144
distant lights, 615–616
DIVIDE command, 120
dividing objects, 120–121
DONUT command, 79
door schedule tables, 203–214
doors, drawing, 273–285
creating library of blocks, 276–278
defining drawings as blocks, 273–276
inserting blocks, 278–282, 284
Drafting Settings dialog box, 41–42, 511–512
drawing
arcs, 74–77
3-point method, 74
Continue method, 77
Start, Center, Angle method, 76
Start, Center, End method, 76
Start, Center, Length method, 76
Start, End, Angle method, 77
Start, End, Direction method, 77
Start, End, Radius method, 77
circles, 60–63
2 Point option, 62
3 Point option, 63
Center, Diameter option, 62
Center, Radius option, 61–62
TTR option, 63
columns, 257–260
composite solids
HIDE command, 571
initial drawings for example, 568–570
intersecting, 577–582
joining with UNION command, 570
lofting, 574–575
Planar Surface command, 575–576
polysolids, 576–577
subtracting, 570–571
sweeping, 571–574
conference rooms
chairs in, 162–164
chamfer corners, 114–116
copying objects, 117–118
dividing objects, 120–121
drawing template for, 105–107
filleting for chairs, 116–117
furniture in, 164–165
ID points, 109–110
initial settings, 103–105
measuring objects, 121
mirroring objects, 124–127
object snap modes, 117–118, 122–123, 127–130
points, 119–120
with polar tracking, 155–165
with polylines, 107–109
rectangles for doors/furniture, 111–113
rotating objects, 118–119
trimming objects, 111
curved conference rooms
Add Vertex grip, 149–150
Convert to Arc grip, 151–152
initial settings, 144–145
polar arrays, 152–155
with polygons, 148–149
with polylines, 145–147
doors, 273–285
ellipses, 77–79
Axis, End method, 77
Center method, 79
extruded solids
circles, 558
polygons, 558–559
rectangles, 559–560
shapes, 561–562, 578–579
structural angles, 560–561
furniture symbols, 403
helixes, 573
isometric. *See* isometric drawing
lecture rooms
initial settings, 130–145
measuring distances, 141–144
multiple copies of objects, 138–141
solid walls, 132–137
lighting legend symbols, 471

lines
with absolute coordinates, 56
continuous, 56
with direct distance entry, 59
with dynamic input, 59–60
with grid and snap, 53–54
Multiline command, 262–268
Multiline Style dialog box, 260–262
with polar coordinates, 58–59
with polar tracking, 157–158
with relative coordinates, 57–58
for walls, 132
mullions, 257–260
multileaders, 360
with Object Snap Tracking, 389–392
with point filters, 386–389
points, 119–120
polygons, 148–149
polylines, 107–109
exploding, 109
offsetting, 108–109
Undo option, 108
primitives
boxes, 555
cones, 556
cylinders, 557
initial settings, 553–554
spheres, 555
torus, 557
wedges, 556
rectangles, 111–113
revision clouds, 324–326
revolved solids
paper clip holder, 565–566
rectangles, 564
shapes, 562–564
solid chairs/patios, 594–607
solid rings/circles, 79–80
solid walls, 132–137
editing polylines, 134–135
erasing parts of objects, 133–134
hatch patterns, 136–137
with lines, 132
voice/data/power plan symbols, 474
drawing coordinates, toggling, 18
drawing limits, 37–38
drawing orientation in Plot dialog box, 90
drawing scale, 37
drawing templates, 2–4, 31
for conference room drawing, 105–107
default, 184
defined, 105
with dimensions, 310
drawing tools, 18–21
function keys, 19–21
toggling, 18–19
drawing window, 4–7
customizing, 5–7
model space/paper space, 21
drawings
annotation scale, 50
copying objects, 117–118, 123
creating, 31–32
creating library of blocks, 276–278
defining as blocks, 273–276
dividing objects, 120–121
erasing and undoing, 54–56
external references (xrefs)
advantages, 456
attaching, 456, 457–462
binding subsets, 457
features of, 457
XREF command options, 456–457
filetypes, 34–35
floating, 4
highlighting in, 67
ID points, 109–110
inserting blocks, 278–282, 284
inserting furniture symbols with attributes, 416
inserting into drawings, 233–235
inserting text, 82
layers, 42–50
measuring objects, 121
mirroring objects, 124–127
moving objects, 67–69
naming, 34, 35
opening, 4
panning, 66
printing/plotting, 83–91
annotation scale, 88
drawing orientation, 90
to files, 85
page setups, 84
paper size, 86–87
as PDF files, 247–249
plot area, 87
plot devices, 84
plot offset, 89
plot options, 89–90
plot scale, 87–88
plot styles, 85–86, 224–228
preview, 90–91
redrawing, 67
regenerating, 67
returning to, 36–37
rotating objects, 118–119
saving, 32–35, 50–51, 106–107
scaling objects, 80–81
selecting objects, 70–73
Add option, 71
All option, 71
Crossing Window option, 71
Fence option, 71
grips, 72–73
Last option, 71
Previous option, 71
Remove option, 71
Undo option, 72
Window option, 71
switching, 4
tenant space project. *See* tenant space project
text on
automatic numbering, 202
changing text properties, 198–202
initial settings, 183–185
Multiline Text command, 195–198
Single Line Text command, 189–195
spell check, 202
text style settings, 185–189
trimming objects, 111
units, 36
zooming, 64–66
Zoom-All, 41, 65
Zoom-Extents, 66
Zoom-Object, 66
Zoom-Previous, 65–66
Zoom-Realtime, 66
Zoom-Window, 64–65
Dtext. *See* Single Line Text command
DWS filetype, 34
DWT filetype, 34
DXF filetype, 34
dynamic blocks
creating, 445–456
defined, 445
visibility, 452–454
dynamic input, drawing lines with, 59–60
Dynamic UCS, 549
DYNMODE command, 59

E

EATTEDIT command, 418
Edge option (POLYGON command), 148–149
edges, chamfering/filleting, 566–568
Edit Multiline command, 268–269
editing. *See also* customizing
arrays, 141
attributes, 413–414, 418–422
dimensions, 319–326
Align Text option, 322
Defpoints layer, 322–323
DIMASSOC dimension variable, 319–321
with grips, 323–324
Match Properties command, 323
Oblique option, 321–322
Override option, 322
Properties palette, 323
revision clouds, 324–326
Update option, 322
gap tolerance, 372
hatch patterns, 381–384
multilines, 268–269
polylines, 134–135, 159–160
properties, 269–273
solids, 548, 552
Standard multileader style, 357
text properties, 198–202
elevation (tenant space project)
completing drawing, 354–356
drawing lower cabinets, 344–345
drawing upper cabinets, 341–342
initial settings, 337–339
mirroring objects, 342–344
stretching objects, 345–354
UCS (user coordinate system), setting net, 339–340
UCS icon options, 340–341
ELLIPSE command, 77, 386
ellipses
drawing, 77–79
Axis, End method, 77
Center method, 79
isometric drawing, 513–515
on centerline, 518–520
rounded corners with, 520–521
to show thickness, 515–518
ERASE command, 54
Erase option (OFFSET command), 109
erasing
objects, 54–56
parts of objects, 133–134
viewports, 496
expanding panels, 9
EXPLODE command, 109
exploding
blocks, 280
multilines, 269
polylines, 109
EXTEND command, 269
external references (xrefs)
advantages, 456
attaching, 456, 457–462
binding subsets, 457
defined, 456
features of, 457
XREF command options, 456–457
extracting attributes, 424–429
EXTRUDE command, 557
extruded solids, drawing
circles, 558
polygons, 558–559
rectangles, 559–560
shapes, 561–562, 578–579
structural angles, 560–561

F

Fence option (selecting objects), 71
files, plotting to, 85
filetypes for drawings, 34–35
FILLET command, 116
filleting
rectangles, 116–117
solid edges, 566–568
first break point, selecting, 134
Fit option (Single Line Text command), 191
floating drawings, 4
floor plan (hotel room)
DesignCenter, 287–290

initial settings, 285–286
floor plan (tenant space project)
annotative text, 282–284
columns and mullions, 257–260
dimensions
editing, 319–326
linear, 301–319
total square footage, 326–330
doors, 273–285
initial settings, 256–257
walls
changing properties, 269–273
drawing, 260–268
editing, 268–269
lengthening lines, 269
flyouts, 10
font name, 185–186, 188
fonts, 185
freezing
layers, 49
viewport layers, 490–491
From command modifier, 133–168
function keys for drawing tools, 19–21
furniture in conference rooms, drawing, 164–165
furniture installation plan
reception area project, 435–440
tenant space project
adding attributes to furniture symbols, 403–413
drawing furniture symbols, 403
editing attributes, 413–414, 418–422
extracting attributes, 424–429
initial settings, 402–403
inserting furniture symbols with attributes into drawings, 416
redefining blocks with attributes, 422–424
saving furniture symbols with attributes, 414
visibility of attributes, 422
training room project, 440–456
furniture symbols
adding attributes, 403–413
drawing, 403
editing attributes, 413–414, 418–422
inserting into drawings, 416
saving with attributes, 414
visibility of attributes, 422

G

gap tolerance
changing, 372
for hatch patterns, 380
gradient hatch patterns, 532–537
defined, 533
guidelines, 532–533
in isometric drawing, 533–537
graphics cursor, 4–7
resizing, 5–7
grid, 38–41
customizing, 38–40
defined, 38
drawing lines with, 53–54
hiding, 229
snap grid, 40–41
GRID command, 40
GRIDDISPLAY system variable, 38–40
grips, 72–73
Add Vertex, 149–150
Convert to Arc, 151–152
defined, 72
editing dimensions, 323–324

H

Half Width option (polylines), 146
hardware acceleration, toggling, 22
Hatch and Gradient dialog box, 376–381
HATCH command, 136, 258
hatch patterns, 136–137
angle and scale, 377–378
boundaries, 378, 380
editing, 381–384
gap tolerance, 380
gradient hatch, 532–537
inheriting options, 380
Island display, 380
miscellaneous options, 378–379
origin, 378
types of, 376–377
HATCHEDIT command, 381
hatching
defined, 136
door jamb detail (tenant space project), 385–386
Pick Points boundary method, 373–376
preparing hatch boundaries, 371–372
Select Objects boundary method, 372–373
HELIX command, 573
helixes, drawing, 573
Help system, 24–25
hexagons, isometric drawing, 524–525
HIDE command, 571
hiding
grid, 229
with HIDE command, 571
HIGHLIGHT command, 67
highlighting in drawings, 67
hotel room floor plan
DesignCenter, 287–290
initial settings, 285–286
HPGAPTOL system variable, 372

I

ID command, 109
ID points, 109–110
IMAGEATTACH command, 620
Infocenter, 18
INS object snap mode, 279
INSERT command, 233, 414
inserting
blocks, 278–282, 284
drawings into drawings, 233–235
furniture symbols with attributes into drawings, 416
text, 82
title blocks in presentations, 498–499
installation plan. *See* furniture installation plan
INTERSECT command, 579
intersecting composite solids, 577–582
isometric drawing, 509–510
angles, 521–523
defined, 509
dimensioning, 532
Drafting Settings dialog box, 511–512
ellipses, 513–515
on centerline, 518–520
rounded corners with, 520–521
to show thickness, 515–518
gradient hatch patterns, 533–537
hexagons, 524–525
initial settings, 510–512
rectangles, 512–513
switching with standard style, 511
tenant space project, 525
ISOPLANE command, 514
isoplanes, 513

J

joining solid shapes, 570
Justify option (Single Line Text command), 191–192

L

lasso selection method, 166
Last option (selecting objects), 71
LAYER command, 43
layer lists, 44
Layer option (OFFSET command), 109
Layer Properties Manager, 490–491
layers, 42–50
colors, 223–224
assigning, 44
current, 272
defined, 42
Defpoints, 322–323
freezing viewport layers, 490–491
linetypes, 45–46
lineweights, 46–50
managing, 49–50
naming, 223–224
renaming, 49
selecting/deselecting all, 491
viewing names, 257
LAYMCUR command, 272
Layout1 tab, 229
preparing for plotting, 496–498
renaming, 496
restoring viewports into, 244–245
Layout2 tab, 229
preparing for plotting, 496–498
renaming, 496
layouts
defined, 229
plotting
with four viewports, 241–247
with one viewport, 228–233
preparing tabs, 496–498
with two viewports, 233–240
previewing, 500
LAYOUTWIZARD command, 486
leaders. *See* multileaders
learning AutoCAD, resources for, 2–3
lecture rooms, drawing
initial settings, 130–145
measuring distances, 141–144
multiple copies of objects, 138–141
solid walls, 132–137
Length option (polylines), 147
lengthening lines, 269
libraries of blocks, creating, 276–278
LIGHT command, 616
lighting legend (tenant space project)
drawing symbols, 473
initial settings, 471
LIGHTINGUNITS command, 609
lights
defined, 608
in photo-realistic rendering, 615–618
types of, 608–609
LIMITS command, 37
LINE command, 53
Line option (polylines), 145–147
linear dimensions, 301–319
adjusting spacing, 318–319
Aligned option, 315
annotation scale, 309–310
Baseline option, 315–318
Continue option, 311–312
dimension breaks, 318
scaling, 310
setting dimension variables, 303–309
lines. *See also* polylines
drawing
with absolute coordinates, 56
continuous, 56
with direct distance entry, 59
with dynamic input, 59–60
with grid and snap, 53–54
Multiline command, 262–268
Multiline Style dialog box, 260–262
with polar coordinates, 58–59
with polar tracking, 157–158

with relative coordinates, 57–58
for walls, 132
editing multilines, 268–269
lengthening, 269
linetypes
customizing, 63
defined, 46
for layers, assigning, 45
scaling, 127
selecting, 272
types of, 46
Lineweight Settings dialog box, 46–48
lineweights, 46–50, 223–224
customizing, 46–48
defined, 46
selecting, 272
viewing, 48
LIST command, 270
listing properties, 270
living room solid model, 627
locking
layers, 49
toolbars/windows, 22
viewports, 238
LOFT command, 574
lofting composite solids, 574–575
LTSCALE command, 63, 127

M

managing layers, 49–50
markers in Osnap modes, 130
matching properties, 272–273
MATCHPROP command, 272, 323
materials
defined, 609
in photo-realistic rendering, 611–614
types of, 609
Materials Browser, 611–614
MEASURE command, 121
measuring
distances, 141–144
objects, 121
menu bar, 8
mesh modeling, 547
mEthod option (CHAMFER command), 115
minimizing DesignCenter, 444
MIRROR command, 124, 342
mirroring
objects, 124–127, 342–344
text, 343
MLEADER command, 360
MLEADERALIGN command, 362
MLEADERCOLLECT command, 366
MLEADERSTYLE command, 357
MLEDIT command, 268
MLINE command, 262
MLSTYLE command, 260
model space, 21, 83
defined, 21, 229
multiple viewports in, 242–244
UCS icon for, 339
zooming in, 239
Model tab, 229
mouse, customizing, 51
MOVE command, 67
moving
attributes, 413
objects, 67–69
MTEXT command, 196
mullions, drawing, 257–260
multileaders, 357–368
adding leaders to, 367–368
aligning, 362
circles with, 357
collecting, 366
creating new style, 362–366
defined, 357
drawing, 360
editing Standard style, 357
initial settings, 357
Multiline command, 262–268
Multiline Style dialog box, 260–262
Multiline Text command, 195–198
multilines
defined, 262
drawing, 262–268
editing, 268–269
exploding, 269
lengthening, 269
multiple copies along path, 138–141, 152–155
Multiple option (CHAMFER command), 115
MVIEW command, 244, 496
MVSETUP command, 492–494

N

name plot styles, 225
naming
drawings, 34, 35
layers, 223–224
natural lights, 608–609
Navigate panel (View tab), viewing, 64
navigation bar, 17
NEW command, 31
NEWSHEETSET command, 501–503
numbering text automatically, 202

O

object snap modes, 122–123, 127–130
activating, 122–123
copying with, 117–118, 123
defined, 117
list of, 127–129
running, 129
settings, 130
Object Snap Tracking
defined, 386
drawing with, 389–392
Oblique option (editing dimensions), 321–322
OFFSET command, 108
offsetting polylines, 108–109
OOPS command, 54
opening
dialog boxes, 9–10
drawings, 4
palettes, 9–10
OPTIONS command, 4
Orbit command, 551
orientation for plotting, 90
ORTHO command, 52
Ortho mode, 52
defined, 52
overriding, 52
orthographic drawings, creating, 386–392
Osnap (object snap), 122–123, 127–130
activating, 122–123
copying with, 117–118, 123
defined, 117
list of modes, 127–129
running, 129
settings, 130
Osnap-Midpoint mode, 117–118, 123
Osnap-Node mode, 123
Override option (editing dimensions), 322
overriding
dimension styles, 304, 322
Ortho mode, 52

P

Page Setup Manager, plotting layouts
with four viewports, 245–246
with one viewport, 229–230
with two viewports, 236
page setups in Plot dialog box, 84
PAGESETUP command, 229
palettes, opening, 9–10
PAN command, 66
panels, expanding, 9
panning drawings, 66
paper clip holder, revolving, 565–566
paper size in Plot dialog box, 86–87
paper space, 21
defined, 21, 229
multiple viewports in, 242–244
UCS icon for, 339
paragraph text, 195–198
Path option (ARRAY command), 141
patio for advanced modeling, drawing, 597–607
PDF files
defined, 247
printing drawings as, 247–249
PEDIT command, 134
photo-realistic rendering, 610–621
background color, 619–620
lights, 615–618
materials, 611–614
Pick Points boundary method (hatching), 373–376
pickbox, 4–7
resizing, 5–7
for selecting, 70
Planar Surface command, 575–576
PLANESURF command, 575
PLINE command, 107
plot area in Plot dialog box, 87
PLOT command, 83, 233
plot devices in Plot dialog box, 84
plot offset in Plot dialog box, 89
plot options in Plot dialog box, 89–90
plot scale in Plot dialog box, 87–88
plot style tables, 85
plot styles, 50, 85–86
creating color-dependent, 226–228
defined, 224
selecting, 224–226
plotting. *See also* presentations
drawings, 83–91
annotation scale, 88
drawing orientation, 90
to files, 85
page setups, 84
paper size, 86–87
as PDF files, 247–249
plot area, 87
plot devices, 84
plot offset, 89
plot options, 89–90
plot scale, 87–88
plot styles, 85–86, 224–228
preview, 90–91
layouts
with four viewports, 241–247
with one viewport, 228–233
preparing tabs, 496–498
with two viewports, 233–240
POINT command, 119
point filters
defined, 386
drawing with, 386–389
point lights, 617–618
points
drawing, 119–120
ID, 109–110
specifying with tracking, 160–162
polar arrays, 152–155
polar coordinates
defined, 58
drawing lines with, 58–59
in isometric drawing, 512–513
polar tracking
defined, 157
drawing lines with, 157–158
initial settings, 155–157

POLYGON command, 148
polygons
drawing, 148–149
extruding, 558–559
Polyline option (CHAMFER command), 114
polylines, 107–109
defined, 107
editing, 134–135, 159–160
exploding, 109
with lines and arcs, 145–147
offsetting, 108–109
Undo option, 108
POLYSOLID command, 576
polysolids, drawing, 576–577
presentations
aligning plans in viewports, 492–494
completing, 494–495
Create Layout Wizard, 486–487
freezing viewport layers, 490–491
initial settings, 485–486
as sheet set
initial settings, 495–496
inserting title block, 498–499
New Sheet Set command/Sheet Set Manager, 501–503
preparing layout tabs for plotting, 496–498
previewing with Quick View tools, 500
renaming layout tabs, 496
title block, 487–490
PRESSPULL command, 559
previewing
commands, 165–166
layouts, 500
plots, 90–91
Previous option (selecting objects), 71
primitives
commands for, 548
drawing
boxes, 555
cones, 556
cylinders, 557
initial settings, 553–554
spheres, 555
torus, 557
wedges, 556
retaining, 572
printing. *See also* presentations
drawings, 83–91
annotation scale, 88
drawing orientation, 90
to files, 85
page setups, 84
paper size, 86–87
as PDF files, 247–249
plot area, 87
plot devices, 84
plot offset, 89
plot options, 89–90
plot scale, 87–88
plot styles, 85–86, 224–228
preview, 90–91
layouts
with four viewports, 241–247
with one viewport, 228–233
with two viewports, 233–240
properties
changing, 269–273
defined, 269
listing, 270
matching, 272–273
text properties, changing, 198–202
PROPERTIES command, 202, 269–270
Properties palette
attributes, 414
dimensions, 323
PTYPE command, 119

Q

Quick Access toolbar, 11–13
commands, 11–12
customizing, 12–13
Quick Properties palette, 414, 422
Quick View tools, 21, 500
QUICKCALC command, 330

R

R14PENWIZARD command, 226
reception area furniture installation plan, 435–440
RECTANG command, 111, 257
rectangles
chamfer corners, 114–116
drawing, 111–113
extruding, 559–560
filleting, 116–117
isometric drawing, 512–513
revolving, 564
rectangular arrays, 258–260
Rectangular option (ARRAY command), 138
redefining blocks, 422–424
REDO command, 54, 73
redoing commands, 73–74
REDRAW command, 67
redrawing drawings, 67
Reference option
rotating objects, 119
scaling objects, 80–81
reflected ceiling plans
creating, 473–474
defined, 471
initial settings, 471
REGEN command, 67
regenerating drawings, 67
relative coordinates
defined, 57
drawing lines with, 57–58
Remove option (selecting objects), 71
renaming
layers, 49
layout tabs, 496
RENDEREXPOSURE command, 609
rendering
background color, 619–620
defined, 608
lights, 608–609, 615–618
materials, 609, 611–614
photo-realistic, 610–621
render quality options, 608
resizing
graphics cursor, 5–7
pickbox, 5–7
restoring viewports, 496
retaining primitives, 572
REVCLOUD command, 324
revision clouds, drawing, 324–326
REVOLVE command, 563
revolved solids, drawing
paper clip holder, 565–566
rectangles, 564
shapes, 562–564
ribbon
commands, 8–9
customizing, 9
defined, 8
Right-Click Customization dialog box, 51
rings, drawing solid rings/circles, 79–80
ROTATE command, 118
rotating objects, 118–119
rounded corners with isometric ellipses, 520–521
running Osnap modes, 129

S

sans serif, 196
SAVE AS command, 32
SAVE command, 32
saving
drawings, 32–35, 50–51, 106–107
furniture symbols with attributes, 414
workspaces, 23–24
scale. *See* drawing scale
SCALE command, 80
scaling
blocks, 281–282
linear dimensions, 310
linetypes, 127
objects, 80–81
for plotting, 87–88
with four viewports, 246
with one viewport, 230–232
with two viewports, 237–239
viewports, 238
second break point, @ (at symbol) as, 134
sectional view (tenant space project)
editing hatches, 381–384
Hatch and Gradient dialog box, 376–381
initial settings, 368–371
Pick Points boundary method (hatching), 373–376
preparing hatch boundaries, 371–372
Select Objects boundary method (hatching), 372–373
Select Objects boundary method (hatching), 372–373
selecting
all layers, 491
colors, 270–271
commands, 8
first break point, 134
linetypes, 272
lineweights, 272
objects, 70–73
Add option, 71
All option, 71
Crossing Window option, 71
Fence option, 71
grips, 72–73
lasso selection method, 166
Last option, 71
Previous option, 71
Remove option, 71
Undo option, 72
Window option, 71
plot styles, 224–226
shapes
extruding, 561–562, 578–579
joining, 570
revolving, 562–564
subtracting, 570–571
Sheet Set Manager, 501–503
sheet sets
initial settings, 495–496
inserting title block, 498–499
New Sheet Set command/Sheet Set Manager, 501–503
preparing layout tabs for plotting, 496–498
previewing with Quick View tools, 500
renaming layout tabs, 496
SHEETSET command, 503
Single Line Text command, 189–195
Fit option, 191
Justify option, 191–192
special characters, 192–195
Vertical option, 191–192
SNAP command, 40
snap grid, 40–41. *See also* object snap modes
drawing lines with, 53–54

solid modeling
advanced methods
animations, 621–626
chair and patio for exercises, 594–607
commands for, 609
lights, 608–609
living room exercise, 627
materials, 609
photo-realistic rendering, 610–621
rendering, 608–609
chamfering/filleting edges, 566–568
composite solids
commands for, 548
HIDE command, 571
initial drawings for example, 568–570
intersecting, 577–582
joining with UNION command, 570
lofting, 574–575
Planar Surface command, 575–576
polysolids, 576–577
subtracting, 570–571
sweeping, 571–574
editing solids, 548, 552
extruded solids
circles, 558
polygons, 558–559
rectangles, 559–560
shapes, 561–562, 578–579
structural angles, 560–561
primitives
boxes, 555
commands for, 548
cones, 556
cylinders, 557
initial settings, 553–554
retaining, 572
spheres, 555
torus, 557
wedges, 556
revolved solids
paper clip holder, 565–566
rectangles, 564
shapes, 562–564
UCS (user coordinate system) in, 549
viewing solids, 549–552
solid rings/circles, drawing, 79–80
solid walls, drawing, 132–137
editing polylines, 134–135
erasing parts of objects, 133–134
hatch patterns, 136–137
with lines, 132
special characters in text, 192–195
spell check, 202
SPELL command, 202
spheres, drawing, 555
spotlights, 616–617
square footage, calculating, 326–330
Standard multileader style, editing, 357
Standard text style, 185
Start, Center, Angle method (drawing arcs), 76
Start, Center, End method (drawing arcs), 76
Start, Center, Length method (drawing arcs), 76
Start, End, Angle method (drawing arcs), 77
Start, End, Direction method (drawing arcs), 77
Start, End, Radius method (drawing arcs), 77
Start tab, 2
status bar, 18
customizing, 60
STB files, 225
SteeringWheels, 551–552
STRETCH command, 345
stretching objects, 345–354
structural angles, extruding, 560–561
STYLE command, 186
style name, 185
SUBTRACT command, 570
subtracting solid shapes, 570–571
SUNPROPERTIES command, 618
surfaces
lofting, 574–575
Planar Surface command, 575–576
SWEEP command, 571
sweeping composite solids, 571–574
switching
drawings, 4
isometric and standard styles, 511
workspaces, 22, 23
synchronizing attributes, 423–424

T

TABLE command, 204
tables
for door schedules, 203–214
for window schedules, 214
tangents, 63
templates. *See* drawing templates
tenant space project
dimensions
editing, 319–326
linear, 301–319
total square footage, 326–330
door jamb detail with hatching, 385–386
elevation
completing drawing, 354–356
drawing lower cabinets, 344–345
drawing upper cabinets, 341–342
initial settings, 337–339
mirroring objects, 342–344
stretching objects, 345–354
UCS (user coordinate system), setting net, 339–340
UCS icon options, 340–341
floor plan
annotative text, 282–284
changing properties, 269–273
columns and mullions, 257–260
drawing doors, 273–285
drawing walls, 260–268
editing walls, 268–269
initial settings, 256–257
lengthening lines, 269
furniture installation plan
adding attributes to furniture symbols, 403–413
drawing furniture symbols, 403
editing attributes, 413–414, 418–422
extracting attributes, 424–429
initial settings, 402–403
inserting furniture symbols with attributes into drawings, 416
redefining blocks with attributes, 422–424
saving furniture symbols with attributes, 414
visibility of attributes, 422
isometric drawing, 525
lighting legend and reflected ceiling plan
creating reflected ceiling plan, 473–474
drawing symbols, 473
initial settings, 471
orthographic drawing, 386–392
overview, 255
presentation of
aligning plans in viewports, 492–494
completing, 494–495
Create Layout Wizard, 486–487
freezing viewport layers, 490–491
initial settings, 485–486
as sheet set, 495–503
title block, 487–490
sectional view
editing hatches, 381–384
Hatch and Gradient dialog box, 376–381
initial settings, 368–371
Pick Points boundary method (hatching), 373–376
preparing hatch boundaries, 371–372
Select Objects boundary method (hatching), 372–373
voice/data/power plan, 474–477
text
aligning in dimensions, 322
annotative property, 88, 282–284
automatic numbering, 202
initial settings, 183–185
inserting, 82
mirroring, 343
Multiline Text command, 195–198
properties, changing, 198–202
Single Line Text command, 189–195
Fit option, 191
Justify option, 191–192
special characters, 192–195
Vertical option, 191–192
spell check, 202
text styles, 185–189
creating, 186–189
font name, 185–186
style name, 185
TEXT command, 82
Text Style dialog box, annotation scale, 282–284
TEXTEDIT command, 199, 413
thawing layers, 49
THICKEN command, 575
thickness in isometric drawing, 515–518
Through option (OFFSET command), 109
title block in presentations, 487–490, 498–499
toggling
drawing coordinates, 18
drawing tools, 18–19
hardware acceleration, 22
toolbars
defined, 8
locking/unlocking, 22
viewing, 13
tooltips, 10
torus, drawing, 557
TORUS command, 557
total square footage, calculating, 326–330
tracking
defined, 160
specifying points, 160–162
training room furniture installation plan, 440–456
transparency, 49
transparent commands, 66–67
TRIM command, 111
Trim option (CHAMFER command), 115
trimetric drawing, 509
trimming objects, 111
TTR option (CIRCLE command), 63
tutorials, instructions for, 30

U

UCS (user coordinate system), 14
defined, 339
setting new, 339–340
in solid modeling, 549
UCS command, 339
UCSICON command, 341
UNDO command, 54, 73
Undo option
CHAMFER command, 114
drawing polylines, 108
selecting objects, 72
undoing commands, 54–56, 73–74
UNION command, 570
units, 36
defined, 36
setting, 36

UNITS command, 36
unlocking
layers, 49
toolbars/windows, 22
viewports, 238
Update option (editing dimensions), 322
UPSIDE DOWN style (text), 195
user coordinate system icon
defined, 14
model space, 339
options, 340–341
paper space, 339
user coordinate system (UCS), 14
defined, 339
setting new, 339–340
in solid modeling, 549
user interface
annotation scaling tools, 21
application menu, 7–8
Clean Screen tool, 22
command line window, 11
defined, 4
dialog boxes/palettes, 9–10
drawing tools, 18–21
drawing window, 4–7
flyouts, 10
graphics cursor, 4–7
grid, 38–41
Infocenter, 18
locking/unlocking toolbars/windows, 22
model space/paper space, 21
navigation bar, 17
Ortho mode, 52
overview, 2–4
panels, 9
Quick Access toolbar, 11–13
Quick View tools, 21
ribbon, 8–9
status bar, 18
toolbars, 13
tooltips, 10
UCS (user coordinate system), 14
ViewCube, 16
Viewport Label Menus, 14–15
workspaces, 22–24

V

variable attributes, 410–412
verify attributes, 412–413
Vertical option (Single Line Text command), 191–192
VIEW command, 618
ViewCube, 16, 552
viewing
layer names, 257
layers, 49
lineweights, 48
Navigate panel (View tab), 64
properties, 270
solids, 549–552
toolbars, 13
Viewport Label Menus, 14–15
viewports
aligning plans in, 492–494
copying, 237
defined, 486
erasing/restoring, 496
freezing layers, 490–491
locking/unlocking, 238
in model space, 242–244
in paper space, 242–244
plotting layouts
with four viewports, 241–247
with one viewport, 228–233
with two viewports, 233–240
restoring into Layout1 tab, 244–245
scaling, 238
on single sheet, 486–487
visibility
of attributes, 422
of dynamic blocks, 452–454
voice/data/power plans, 474–477
creating, 476–477
defined, 474
VPORTS command, 242

W

WALKFLYSETTINGS command, 622
walk-through AVI files, creating, 621–626
walls. *See also* solid walls
changing properties, 269–273
drawing, 260–268
Multiline command, 262–268
Multiline Style dialog box, 260–262
editing, 268–269
lengthening lines, 269
WBLOCK command, 276, 414, 580–581
WEDGE command, 556
wedges, drawing, 556
Width option (polylines), 146
Window option (selecting objects), 71
window schedule tables, 214
windows, locking/unlocking, 22
workspaces, 22–24
customizing, 23–24
defined, 22
saving, 23–24
switching, 22, 23
types of, 22

X

X scale factor for blocks, 281–282
XATTACH command, 456, 459
XBIND command, 457
XREF command, 456
xrefs (external references)
advantages, 456
attaching, 456, 457–462
binding subsets, 457
defined, 456
features of, 457
XREF command options, 456–457

Y

Y scale factor for blocks, 281–282

Z

ZOOM command, 41
Zoom-All command, 41, 65
Zoom-Extents command, 66
zooming
defined, 41
drawings, 64–66
Zoom-All, 41, 65
Zoom-Extents, 66
Zoom-Object, 66
Zoom-Previous, 65–66
Zoom-Realtime, 66
Zoom-Window, 64–65
in model space, 239
Zoom-Object command, 66
Zoom-Previous command, 65–66
Zoom-Realtime command, 66
Zoom-Window command, 64–65